# FROMMER'S

COMPREHENSIVE TRAVEL GUIDE

# FLORIDA '91

by Marylyn Springer
and Donald Schulz

PRENTICE
HALL
PRESS

NEW YORK • LONDON • TORONTO • SYDNEY • TOKYO • SINGAPORE

**FROMMER BOOKS**

Published by Prentice Hall Press
A division of Simon & Schuster Inc.
15 Columbus Circle
New York, NY 10023

ISBN 0-13-326810-1
ISSN 1044-2391

Manufactured in the United States of America

# CONTENTS

# MAPS

## A Disclaimer

Although every effort was made to ensure the accuracy of the prices and travel information appearing in this book, it should be kept in mind that prices do fluctuate in the course of time, and that information does change under the impact of the varied and volatile factors that affect the travel industry.

Readers should also note that the establishments described under the Readers' Selections or Suggestions have not in many cases been inspected by the authors, and that the opinions expressed there are those of the individual reader(s) only. They do not in any way represent the opinions of the publisher or authors of this guide.

# INTRODUCING FROMMER'S FLORIDA

**A** royal British landlord, so the story goes, owns land under the U.S. Embassy in London that no amount of American entreaty can convince him to sell. Ambassador after ambassador has been dispatched to offer million-dollar deals, but to no avail. Frustrated by that famed British resistance, one U.S. ambassador finally felt compelled to ask the titled gentleman just what on earth he *would* take for the land. He frowned. He pondered. At last he replied—he would consider Florida.

He'll have to get in line.

## 1. The Reason Why

In the drizzling days of spring and the chilly, cheerless nights of February, 42 million people "consider" Florida, and every last one of them sets off by plane, train, bus, or car to get a two-week piece of this sand-trimmed rock on the southernmost tip of the nation.

They arrive tense and racing, jumpy and crisis-weary. Slowly, in long, lazy days on silver beaches and in jasmine-scented velvet nights, Florida works its magic as inexorably as the diamond-tipped tides that lap endlessly over these shores. Warm in body and soothed in spirit, they whiz away, willing victims to the seductive snare of the nation's last resort.

It's a magic place, this Florida, a place that stuns you with the exotic, that sharpens your senses and lulls your fears. It assails you with pastel colors never dimmed by industrial grime, delights you with air clear as a teardrop and waters as infallibly warm in January as they are in June.

Scoff as you will, but you'll waken some miserable March morning when the Christmas snow has become a dirty-gray blanket that dampens your toes and chills your soul, when sleet seems a way of life and spring light-years away. Then *you*, too, will "consider" Florida—and hours later, on sand soft as talcum, in warm opalescent waters, you, too, for all your cosmopolitan sophistication, will find yourself bewitched, dazzled, convinced you've stumbled into some exotic foreign land.

You *have*. This is America's tropics, the southernmost place in the U.S., a state like no other in the continental 48. When you cross the border, you are already 120 miles south of any beach California can boast and more than 1,000 miles south of the fabled French Riviera!

Thanks to the Gulf Stream, you can come here on the coldest days and find the nation's warmest winds, or arrive in summer to find tropical breezes cooling the land.

It is, of course, those incredibly cooperative temperatures that have lured people for thousands of years to this U-shaped limestone peninsula, jettisoned by ancient upheavals and bathed by warm waters. Beneath the sand you stand upon is a land half a billion years old. Over it roamed camels and rhinoceroses, whose bones merged into deep deposits of phosphate, a mineral vital to those who live here now. Beneath your feet, cold springs are rushing through porous limestone to emerge in streams of water that support the 12 million people who inhabit this land.

It's a place like no other, a place where everything is different, unexpected. Strange sweet-scented blossoms, instead of surviving on the land like any normal flower, lure living creatures into their lovely lethal blooms. Weird reptiles with long snouts, short legs, and a hide created by committee lurk in dark ancient waters. Even birds don't come in basic brown but in the exotic colors of sunset, dwelling in deep-green forests like brushstrokes on a pointillist canvas, their spectacular plumage camouflaged by brilliant scarlet hibiscus, flaming poinciana trees, burgundy bougainvillea.

It is a land of contrasts, from a delicate strip of sandy coral islands strung out like a trailing ribbon on a gift package to vast fields of Florida "prairie" grass.

Its climate is strange. No falling leaves, no drifts of snow, and only two temperatures: warm and warmer.

It doesn't even rain the same here. There are no long gloomy days of dreary gray chill. Instead suddenly, in an ear-splitting, cracking thunderclap, lashing torrents pour from a great impenetrable gray curtain hung from scudding black clouds. Rain falls not gently, not softly, but with ripping intensity, with roars and cracks of thunder that send the timid cowering. Then, flash. Gone. Nothing left but trailing white wisps racing across the skies as rays of sun as sharp as rapiers shatter droplets into a cataclysm of rainbows and spread nature's art gallery across the sky.

Weird things grow here: the traveler palm, a jungle St. Bernard whose leaves point north and whose base carries a quart of life-saving water; spiky aloe, whose jellied inner core soothes sunburn; gangly mangroves, whose roots forsake the ground to live on air but dip into water, catching flotsam that will someday become an island.

Its creatures are oddballs: manatees, those round, plump, whiskered throwbacks to antiquity, the cows of the sea; frolicking porpoises, whose squeaks and squeals may someday tell us of underwater mysteries; gray/white cattle with camel humps, floppy ears, and flapping chin wattles; tiny deer no bigger than collie dogs.

Those who live here are as exotic as the land around them. They're isolationists by geographical accident, iconoclasts by choice and experience, neither overcome nor unimpressed by the trappings of success.

Conditioned by generations of alteration, by great tidal sweeps of change across their land, they can take the measure of a man with unerring accuracy. Once strangers themselves in a strange land, they are quick to forgive fear and eccentricity but will never forget a slight to their chosen place in the sun.

For generations "conch" fishermen in the south and whip-snapping "crackers" in the north have fought to tame this unyielding land. They share it now with those who came here only yesterday, searching for the brass ring of prosperity or a peaceful place to wind down their lives. They share it willingly, recognizing that daring and courage similar to their own has helped these newcomers forsake less adventurous but more predictable lives to stake their futures on Florida.

It is perhaps their admiration for the offbeat that makes Floridians the most cussed individualists you'll ever meet. Not one tree changes in Florida without argument: Cut it down, leave it standing, transplant it, or build a treehouse and rent it. They've been at it for generations. In fact, when Massachusetts Revolutionaries harried the British with midnight rides, Floridians hanged Sam Adams and John Hancock in effigy in St. Augustine's public square, then toasted King George III!

## A CAPSULE HISTORY

Two hundred years earlier Ponce de León arrived here on Easter morning in 1513 to name the new land after Spain's *pascua florida* Easter celebration, only to start the state's first argument over who should own this land. Florida's natives had the last word: They shot an arrow into his armor and sent him back to Puerto Rico to die without gold, without his mysterious fountain of youth, and without Florida.

Three other Spaniards didn't do much better. Hernando de Soto marched through Florida with 700 troops, hassled all the way by Florida tribes, and never found the gold he sought before he died on the banks of the Mississippi. Panfilo de Narvaez, who gets credit for discovering Tampa Bay, found a gold piece but no welcome among the Apalachee Indians, who killed most of his men. Up in Pensacola, conquistador Don Tristan de Luna tried futilely to organize a Pensacola colony, but all he did was start a longevity argument with St. Augustine that continues to this day.

Even those 100,000 original Floridians, the tribes who were here when Columbus discovered the New World, were a nonconformist lot. Seven-foot-tall Calusas on the west coast and Tequestas on the southern tip refused to work the land, choosing instead to hunt and fish and fight. Over on Tampa Bay, in the forests of Ocala and up in Tallahassee, the Tocobaga, Timucuan, and Apalachee Indians argued that farming was survival. None lived long enough to win the dispute. By 1765 all were dead, victims of disease, warfare, and enslavement by the Spanish, leaving as a memorial only great mounds of shells and skeletons 6,000 years old.

Their successors, the immigrant Creek, were no conformists either—they split from their tribe in the 1700s and moved to Florida to become, in Spanish, *cimarrones,* wild ones, runaways—Seminoles.

Legion are the characters who have populated this land. Spain's king plucked smuggler Pedro Menéndez de Áviles from a Spanish jail and set him off to start the nation's first colony in St. Augustine in 1545. Stationed here to protect Spanish galleons from treasure-seeking pirates who already called Florida home, Menéndez arrived to find a small French colony of Huguenots huddled in Fort Caroline, 50 miles away. That sparked another of the many Florida arguments over possession. Menéndez attacked the French, finally winning by default when a ship carrying his Huguenot opponents was wrecked on the shores of a bay that was later to be called Matanzas ("slaughter") in memory of Menéndez's hasty dispatch of the wreck's survivors.

The Spanish and English, whose blood runs thick in Floridian veins, never did get along too well, and whatever dispute they were having always seemed to involve Florida. When British seaman Sir Francis Drake did in the Spanish Armada in 1588, Britain acquired high seas sovereignty. As it turned out, England also acquired Florida in a historic swap with Spain, which settled for Cuba, perhaps with relief.

In the Revolutionary War, Florida, untouched by curbs on trade and freedom, bet its future on the British, a bad gamble. When Britain lost the American colonies,

Florida became a military and economic liability to the motherland, which promptly tossed it back to the Spanish.

By now the state reached all the way from the Atlantic to the Mississippi, and was divided into English East and Spanish West Florida. Spain decided not to disturb the status quo and let the ragtag lot left behind by the British stay on in Spanish Florida. That was a mistake.

Before long, typically Floridian machinations hatched every sort of bizarre plot to wrest Florida from Spain, although the plotters were characteristically divided on what to do with the state once it was freed.

Into the fray came Pres. Thomas Jefferson, who wanted to annex Florida (perhaps he needed a vacation), and was forever scheming with Florida adventurers or sending Gen. Andrew Jackson down to harass the Spanish. Spain finally tossed in the towel and sold Florida to the United States for $5 million. But in canny cracker style, the $5 million was never paid: Floridians claimed it all as payment for damages incurred during the Spanish occupation!

Florida, free at last to go its independent way, was by now a land of huge plantations that needed growing space. Fertile farmlands, controlled by the peaceful Seminoles, ranged from Tallahassee to Lake Okeechobee and seemed a good place to start expansion. To get those lands, General Jackson, who caused more trouble in Florida than the British and Spanish put together, moved in to push the tribe southward. He set off a bloody and altogether justifiable Seminole rebellion known as the First Seminole War. In 1823 the Seminoles ended that war by agreeing to settle in Central Florida on a reservation extending from Ocala to Lake Okeechobee. But peace was not to last. Soon someone had dreamed up a "compromise" plan to ship the Indians off to a reservation in Oklahoma, then called the "Indian Territory." That idea was answered by a great debater indeed, the tribal leader and fierce warrior Osceola, whose response was wordless—he just tossed his long knife into the white man's treaty, so the tribe remains today technically at war with the United States.

Blood ran over the land for seven years, beginning with a Christmas Day ambush of Maj. Francis Dade and 100 of his men near Tampa. Plantations burned and guns roared as 1,500 native Americans used guerrilla tactics to hold out against 9,000 soldiers, who won finally, but dishonorably, by capturing Osceola under a flag of truce. Imprisoned in the Castillo de San Marcos in St. Augustine, the Seminole warrior was later shipped off to die in a South Carolina prison. Seminole resistance died with him. Most of the tribe was exiled to Oklahoma with just 300 remaining behind, hiding in the impenetrable Everglades, where their descendants still dwell.

Those bitter clashes behind them, Floridians argued once again, this time over the wisdom of joining the United States. In 1845 they finally agreed to do so, wearily choosing a flag emblazoned: "Let Us Alone."

Florida wasn't exactly booming in those days. Just 60,000 people lived here in 1850, scattered about in small settlements and traveling on river steamers, rough roads, and small railroads. Most were farmers, many earning their cracker appellation using long snapping whips to herd cattle. Stability proved fertile breeding ground for some of that Floridian individualism to surface. Fierce debates arose between small businessmen and plantation owners, first over state economics, then over participation in a great storm brewing a few miles north—the War Between the States. Secession prevailed, but Floridians argued so bitterly over the nature and extent of the state's participation in the Confederacy that at the close of the war the state's harassed governor committed suicide.

What many had warned would happen to plantations without slave labor did happen. After Reconstruction, Florida was, in a word, broke. Its railroads were bankrupt and its land was tied up as security for the railroads. Wily crackers made a deal: To millionaire Hamilton Disston, a Philadelphia manufacturer, went four million acres of land right smack across the state; to Florida went $1 million of Disston's money. Poor Disston should have gotten the better part of the deal, but various reverses and a major national economic slump made him the first of many land developers to bite Florida dust.

Meanwhile, Florida wasn't doing too badly. Henry Flagler, another millionaire, who'd made a fortune helping John D. Rockefeller get Standard Oil on its feet, was searching, they say, for a divorce from a deranged second wife. New York wouldn't change its no-divorce laws so Flagler looked south. With a wisdom both farsighted and myopic, Florida changed its no-divorce law long enough for Henry to take a third bride, then changed it right back again!

Flagler became the pied piper of the peninsula, laying his railroad tracks down the sunny east coast, luring frozen northerners farther and farther south. He spent tens of millions of dollars in the state, climaxing his efforts with the "Railroad That Went to Sea," a $27-million link between Key West and the mainland. On the west coast, still another millionaire, Henry Plant, did likewise and the boom was on. On the heels of Plant and Flagler came a wild-eyed, frenzied gaggle of land developers, their sights firmly fixed on a rainbow that ended in the Sunshine State.

Florida's land boom in the 1920s was a Marx Brothers comedy. Salesmen larded beaches with doubloons and promised instant millionairedom. They stood in the streets of Miami, Palm Beach, and Tampa and sold scraps of paper promises. They collected millions of dollars in down payments, stuffing greenbacks casually into shoes and shoeboxes. They attracted throngs of hopeful, about-to-be-millionaires—one million in one year, two million the next. So helter-skelter and hysterical was the rush to get south that once the trains pulled into the station they couldn't get back out again because so many were backed up behind them! Some developers made a killing in real estate, some just killed themselves when weather once again intervened in the state's history: In 1935 a wicked hurricane finished off what a national depression had started.

In the aftermath of promotion, the state went wild with development. Nothing stood in the way of those who would tear down, but in recent years conservation has once again given Floridians something to argue about, and it's had its successes too: Once-threatened alligators have increased to such numbers they now appear legally on some of the more bizarre menus; manatees hunted out of the big springs of the central peninsula are back again, along with otter, beaver, heron, great white egrets, and roseate spoonbills once nearly decimated for the fancy hat plumes of the early 1900s.

Just as they have for centuries, clear springs bubble in deep-emerald forests. Warm turquoise seas border strips of silver sand. The Garden of Eden's Torreya tree grows here and, mysteriously, nowhere else in the world.

All of that is why so many tourists come to Florida, and why so many never leave.

## THE CLIMATE

If there's one thing that separates Florida from the rest of its continental buddies, it's sunshine: When you need it bad, they've got it good.

### Temperatures

It has that warming sun for reasons of latitude and longitude, Gulf Stream currents, and to hear some people talk, the uplifted voices of hundreds of hoteliers and restaurateurs beseeching Mother Nature not to fail them this season.

Nature rarely does. From December to April you can count on average winter temperatures of at least 60° to 70°, Fahrenheit, south of Orlando, 10° to 15° lower north of that city. Even if, as sometimes happens, there's a freak cold spell (in Florida all cold spells are by definition freaks—ask any chamber of commerce), it's still warmer here than back home in Hoboken—or anyplace else north of the state line.

In summer, temperatures from Orlando south reach into the 80s but rarely

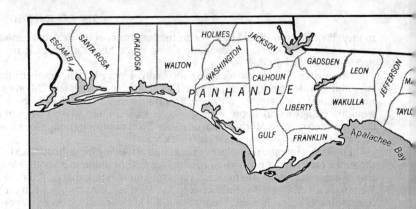

GULF OF MEXICO

N

| 0 | miles | 30 |
| 0 | kms | 50 |

# FLORIDA COUNTIES AND REGIONS

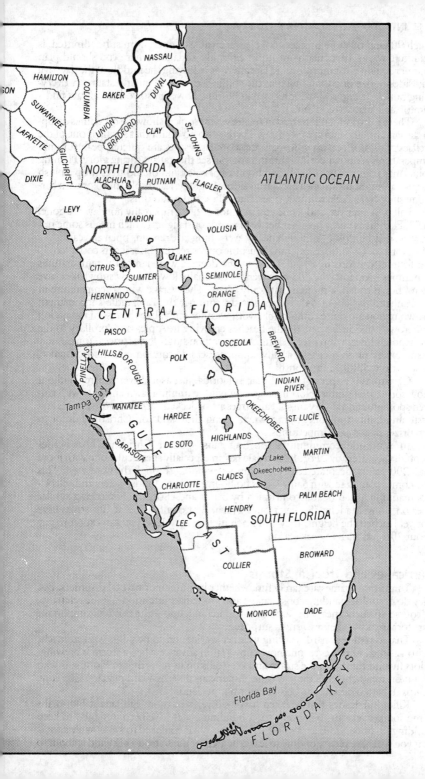

touch 90° and offshore breezes cool coastal areas. Summer, it must be admitted, is definitely warm, particularly inland in cities like Orlando where you should plan summer activities for morning and late afternoon, leaving the middle of the day for a poolside snooze or a long lunch in the confines of a cool, quiet restaurant. Everything but *everything* is air-conditioned in Florida, however, so you can always find a comfortable place to cool off.

There's no doubt it is humid in spring when tropical showers sometimes dampen the land briefly several times a day. There's also no doubt that spring is one of the prettiest times of year to visit the state. Popular resorts are quieter, peak summer temperatures are nowhere in sight, and you can see the state in spring glory. Flaming poincianas turn streets into blazing bonfires of color and orchid trees drop a plush purple carpet. Bougainvillea break into a downright lyrical display of color with harmony sung by azaleas, trumpet vines, tiger lilies, and geraniums.

Fall is quieter yet, and while you may not notice a nip, really hot days are gone. In fall Floridians take a breather between visitor onslaughts, which means some restaurants may be closed, although nearly everything else remains open all year.

North of Orlando, everything's just the opposite. In winter it gets cool ("cold" is a four-letter word in Florida) and in the deepest winter months temperatures sometimes drop into the 50s, only very occasionally lower. A few snowflakes have been known to fall, although that really *is* rare. The average winter temperature in the Panhandle is about 64°, Fahrenheit. In summer the Panhandle and northern Crown region are quite comfortable, with weather much like the rest of the nation and crowds of Southerners on the beaches enjoying it. A pleasant corollary to the Panhandle's lower winter temperatures is correspondingly lower prices. You can stay in some very plush quarters, a fully equipped seaside condominium, for instance, for as little as $300 . . . a month!

Christmas is a special time of year in Florida, just as it is everywhere. Without snow for natural glitter, Floridians go hog wild, trimming lawn and lane with colored spotlights and silvery tinsel. Palm trees are bedecked with flashy ornaments and glistening lights and some homeowners spend thousands on Christmas decor to win prizes in annual competitions.

In waterside communities, boating fans sponsor Christmas boat-a-cades through the waterways. Fort Lauderdale has an especially spectacular one with more than 200 yachts, decorated mast to gunwale, winding through the waterways. This one comes complete with Santa Claus ho-ho-ing through loudspeakers and celebrities manning a lead boat accompanied by bands and choruses. Something similar goes on along Madeira/St. Petersburg Beach. Best of all, prices at Christmas have not yet reached the heights they will reach by February 1, so you can expect to pay about 20% less than in peak season.

## Hurricanes and Tropical Storms

Tumultuous times are rarely fun, whether by human or natural disorders. But they do occur, demanding considerable and immediate attention. We are referring, of course, to hurricanes. They are a little frightening, but—and this is the important part for visitors—they are *never* a surprise.

Thanks to a very hard-working weather service and some pilots with stomachs as iron as their nerve, everyone now knows far in advance when a storm is brewing. Pilots fly into the eye of the storm and keep tabs on it, reporting to Floridians who plot it on weather charts the way other Americans do crossword puzzles. Everyone begins to batten down long before a storm nears land.

Killer hurricanes that wreaked havoc 50 years or more ago taught Floridians some somber lessons. Now very strict building codes have been designed to keep buildings as impervious as possible to a storm. What you need to know as a visitor is that you will have plenty of time to leave the area, or the state, if a big wind is about to blow. But even if you stay, you are likely to weather the storm safely, thanks to emergency crews with lots of practice. Officially, the storm season runs from June to November, but storms in summer are rare—most occur between August and November.

## Suntans and Sunburns

On to something considerably more pleasant: sun. That's what you want, that's what you came here to get, and that's what Florida is going to give you.

What Florida cannot yet give you is a cure for sunburn. Hoteliers and doctors, if need be, will hold your hand, bring you an aspirin, smear some aloe plant on your back, and commiserate, but that's cold comfort when your back is on fire. We know *you* wouldn't do anything silly like staying out in the sun for four hours the first day you arrive, but perhaps you can pass this advice on to someone else:

No matter how innocent those little rays of sunshine look, no matter how many clouds are blocking the sun, no matter how overcast the day, Ole Sol is burning your epidermis. It won't help to hide in the ocean or the pool—that sun will find you wherever you are. Skin that has spent the last few months swaddled in clothes is no match for the Florida sun. Suntan oils can help, but they can also hurt. If you recall what happens when you apply heat to a frying pan full of oil, you'll get some idea how your unsuspecting cells are being sautéed.

Sunscreens are very effective products, and combined with a sensible sunning schedule can give you a nice tan instead of a blotchy mess that flakes off behind you in little trails of peeling skin. As for that tanning schedule, it goes something like this: Stay out of the sun between 11am and 2pm, at least for the first few days. During other hours, get only 10 minutes of sun the first day, 15 the second, then 25, 35, 50, 75, and on the seventh day, 105 minutes.

In a nutshell (which is what you'll look like if you overdo it): Protect your skin with sun-screening products but avoid oils; pack a cover-up to wear over your bathing suit and a hat, and use them when you begin to feel the sun burning; don't fry during the middle of the day; drink lots of fluids; and don't try to become a bronzed god or goddess in eight hours.

---

# 2. Visitor Information

Florida has been opening its hotels, homes, and hearts to new arrivals for generations so it's had plenty of time to compile answers to your many questions and find ways to make your visit a happy and carefree trip.

## TOURIST INFORMATION

If you drop a line to the **Florida Department of Commerce, Tourism Division,** Visitor Inquiry Section, 126 Van Buren St., Tallahassee, FL 32399–2000 (tel. 904/487-1462), explain just what cities you're interested in visiting, and mention any specific interests you might have, they'll respond with all you ever wanted to know, and more. Ask for the state's fine free publication *Florida Vacation Guide;* it's crammed with information on Florida and its facilities.

If you're an outdoor type, the **Florida Department of Natural Resources,** Division of Recreation and Parks, Room 613, 3900 Commonwealth Blvd., Tallahassee, FL 32399 (tel. 904/488-7326), has a wealth of information on saltwater fishing and on state parks and what they have to offer. Ask for the "Florida State Parks Guide" brochure and the one titled "Enjoy Florida Sport Fishing."

Florida's **Game and Freshwater Fish Commission,** Bryant Building, 620 S. Meridian St., Tallahassee, FL 32399–1600 (tel. 904/488-4066), can tell you where to seek the big fish and all the details you need to know about freshwater fishing, stopping just short of guaranteeing you a fish dinner. Many of Florida's freshwater lakes are in Lake County, so you can be sure that the **Eustis Chamber of Commerce,** 1 W. Orange Ave., Eustis, FL 32726 (tel. 904/357-3434), can give you the low-down on fish camps and guides. If hunting is your game, you can call a toll-free number to find out what season is when: 800/282-8002 (also for fishing information).

If you'd like to camp out in this sunny state, the **Florida Campground Association,** 1638 N. Plaza Dr., Tallahassee, FL 32308 (tel. 904/656-8878), has a long list of commercial campgrounds in Florida and descriptions of camp facilities available free. Another camping and parks information resource is the **National Parks Service,** U.S. Department of the Interior, Washington, DC 20025, which can supply you with general information on national parks in the state.

Hikers can find out what trails to hike through Florida from the **Florida Trail Association,** P.O. Box 13708, Gainesville, FL 32604 (tel. 904/378-8823).

**Official Airline Guides** (OAG) publishes a wealth of information on hotels and airlines that is distributed to travel agents, who will be happy, by the way, to help you plan a trip *to* the Sunshine State or *from* it on cruises or Caribbean sojourns. If you're a frequent traveler, you can subscribe to the OAG's *Pocket Flight Guide,* which tells you what planes fly into and around the state. Contact them at 888 Seventh Ave., New York, NY 10019 (tel. 212/977-8300, or toll free 800/323-3537).

Costs of **automobile travel** have not changed radically in recent years. The American Automobile Association, which keeps records of such costs, figures estimated daily driving costs in 1990 at about $173 daily for a couple traveling 500 miles a day. That includes $93 for meals and $80 a night for lodging; car expenses are about $8.40 per 100 miles. Add about $5 a day for each child traveling with you and be prepared to adjust these estimates up or down 25% to 75% depending on the popularity of the region in which you are driving, the association says.

Our next suggestion is more along the lines of bargain-seeking than information-gathering. A publication called *Florida Traveler Discount Guide* is being distributed at many hotels, motels, and restaurants along the Florida border and elsewhere in the state. It contains quite a number of maps showing various exits from major highways in the state, and where you'll end up if you take those exits. Included in the booklet are dozens of coupons offering over $5,000 in discount coupons on everything from ice-cream cones to hotel rooms and dinners—even free orange juice. Send $1 to cover postage and handling to **Exit Information Guide Inc.,** 3014 NE 21st Way, Gainesville, FL 32609 (tel. 904/371-EXIT).

Many Florida cities and regions have recently supplemented their chambers of commerce with tourist development councils and commissions. To get a complete list of those organizations, write **TDC Listing, Florida Department of Commerce,** Visitor Inquiry, 126 Van Buren St., Tallahassee, FL 32399 (tel. 904/487-1462).

Finally, and certainly not least, every town (and we do mean *every*) has a **chamber of commerce** and/or a **visitor information bureau** waiting to answer your questions. Some of the state's most dedicated boosters work for the chambers of commerce, and they are wonderful people to know when you need help with anything. If you're looking for a room, write to any chamber of commerce and ask to have your name circulated among members. You'll soon hear from everyone in town.

Wherever you go in Florida, if you need help with anything, from a city map to a dentist, go to the chamber of commerce. Helpful, friendly, knowledgeable people will help you out of a jam—and sometimes even take you home with them. They're wonderful and can't be praised highly enough for the long hours they give to the state and its visitors.

To get all the telephone numbers and addresses of every chamber of commerce in the state, write to the **Florida Chamber of Commerce,** 136 S. Bronough St. (P.O. Box 11309), Tallahassee, FL 32303 (tel. 904/222-2831). Ask for *People Under the Sun,* which costs $8.75. The chamber's newest series of books provides information, facts, and figures on retirement, family, and business opportunities. Call or write them, stating your interest. Ask for the "Sunshine Series"; the books are $10.35 each.

## BOOKS TO READ

Florida has proven itself many things to many people, some of whom have recorded their admiration in fascinating volumes about the state. We're not offering any comprehensive bibliography here, just some of our favorites—books we think will give you an intriguing look at Florida to help you see behind the surface and into the heart of this lovely land.

If you ever pick up just one shell, Anne Morrow Lindbergh's *Gift from the Sea* will enchant you. Ms. Lindbergh and her aviator husband were Sanibel vacationers, and it was there she was inspired to pen some touching observations on the ties that bind us to the sea and to each other.

Robert Wilder left behind a New York advertising career to take a shot at novels. He managed to turn the story of early Tory immigration to the Bahamas, much of it from Florida, into a beautiful saga of life in the islands, *Wind from the Carolinas.* He wrote a similar re-creation of life in early Florida called *Bright Feather,* a touching story of Osceola's hopeless struggle to save himself and his people from destruction by the same inexorable forces that were at work on other native tribes around the nation. Wilder's masterful work offers a fascinating look at the St. Augustine and Apalachicola River Valley in the early 1800s, and is a gripping novel besides.

Florida's favorite daughter is Marjorie Kinnan Rawlings, and she's most deserving of the honor. Not only did she write a Pulitzer Prize–winning novel, *The Yearling,* about country life in Florida, but she wrote *Cross Creek,* a haunting story about her part in that life. *Cross Creek* didn't please everyone in the tiny enclave she inhabited, but it has been enchanting readers outside that community for decades. She added to that autobiographical novel with a *Cross Creek Cookbook,* containing recipes still used today by a nearby restaurant.

No one has written more beautifully about the canny, charming, and sometimes cantankerous inhabitants of northern Florida than Gloria Jahoda, in a book called *The Other Florida.* Ms. Jahoda moved to Tallahassee from New York, much to the dismay of her friends who were convinced she was dropping off the face of the earth. In *The Other Florida* Jahoda shows them that heart is where the home is.

Among recent novels, *A Land Remembered* by Patrick Smith (Pineapple Press), who lives here now, received the Florida Historical Society's Tebeau Prize as the most outstanding Florida historical novel of 1986. It is notable as the first novel to cover 110 years of the development of the state and follows the lives of three generations of a fictional pioneer family.

Another fairly new novel tells the story of Henry Morrison Flagler's railroad to the Florida Keys, a railroad that cost huge amounts of money and the lives of many workers killed by a hurricane that finally destroyed the tracks. That railroad also altered the lives of the islanders and changed the future of these islands. F. W. Belland's novel *The True Sea* (Holt, Rinehart & Winston) details some of those massive changes.

If you like mysteries, John MacDonald's novels are a look at the Gold Coast through the eyes of yacht-dwelling detective Travis McGee, who lives in Fort Lauderdale's Bahia Mar yacht basin aboard a boat invariably draped with long-legged women with problems. Naturally, McGee helps.

Ralph Waldo Emerson came to St. Augustine in 1827 to recuperate from a lung condition. He didn't much like what he found, according to one biographer who

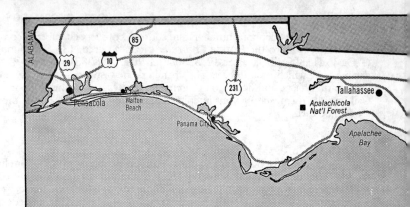

GULF OF MEXICO

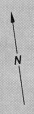

N

```
0    miles   30
├───────────┤
0    kms     50
```

**FLORIDA**

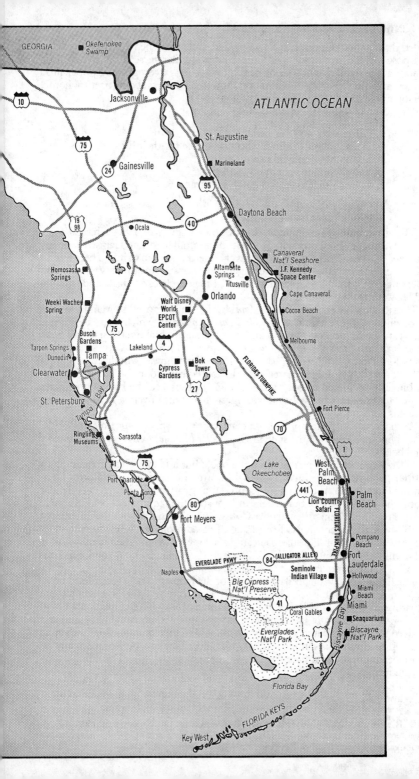

claimed that "at first [Emerson's] New England soul, nourished firmly on the belief in Purpose and the preciousness of Time, contracted like the sepals of a Calvinistic anemone at the sight of Southern laziness and slackness, accompanied by not a little dinginess and dirt." Florida won him over, however as he was about to return home, Emerson wrote of St. Augustine:

> Farewell: and fair befall thee, gentle town.
> The prayer of those who thank thee for their life
> The benison of those thy fragrant airs,
> And simple hospitality hath blest,
> Be to thee ever as the rich perfume
> Of a good name, and pleasant memory!

That inveterate traveler Henry James headed south in 1904 after 30 years abroad. He spent just a week in Florida, long enough to rail against the many "boarders" he found there but he, too, was charmed enough to write: "There was no doubt . . . that Florida still had, in her ingenuous, not at all insidious way, the secret of pleasing. . . . I found the plea, for myself, I may declare, exquisite and irresistible." He was not alone.

Harriet Beecher Stowe, of *Uncle Tom's Cabin* fame, moved to Mandarin near Jacksonville and wrote a little tome called *Palmetto Leaves,* which offers an intriguing look at Florida life. Poet Sidney Lanier wrote beautifully about the state in a book called *Florida, Its Scenery, Climate and History.*

As Key West legend would have it, Ernest Hemingway, who lived here for a number of years, often disappeared into the locked back room of Sloppy Joe's for long binges punctuated by Joe's stories. Many of those, so the legend goes, later became Hemingway's bestsellers. Hemingway based his novel *To Have and Have Not* on his home in Key West.

Authors McKinley Kantor and Stephen Crane both spent some time in Florida, so you'll find reflections of the state in Crane's *Red Badge of Courage* and Kantor's several books.

What we're about to mention is not a book, but it is something to read. It's a **calendar** published by the Environmental Information Center of the Florida Conservation Foundation. You'll find some entertaining cartoons in it (a recent calendar cartoon showed a group of bulldozers and construction equipment behind a huge billboard reading "Scenic View Under Construction"). In line with the interests of its publishers, the calendar also features an often-amusing record of the history of environmental issues in Florida. You can get a copy by writing the organization at 1251B Miller Ave., Winter Park, FL 32789 (tel. 407/644-5377). A "minimum donation" of $7.50 is requested for each calendar.

Finally, in 1791 William Bartram, son of the internationally recognized botanist, John Bartram, published a book about travels with his father, including some fascinating experiences in Florida. It's called *Travels Through North and South Carolina, Georgia, and East and West Florida.* His book met with acclaim in England and was given to Samuel Taylor Coleridge, who is said to have been reading it when he fell asleep to dream his famous tale of "Xanadu . . . where blossomed many an incense-bearing tree/And here were forests ancient as the hills/Enfolding sunny spots of greenery . . ."

Florida?

Why not?

**READER'S RECOMMENDATION:** "**Betty Brothers,** a real estate agent in the Florida Keys, has written several books, among them *Trigger Fish: Tales of the Florida Keys,* which is geared to the younger set" (Linda Sambel, Pittsfield, Mass.).

# 3. Tips on Food and Lodging

## HOTELS AND MOTELS

We cannot stress too often that in and around peak seasons (December to May in central and southern Florida; May to September in the Panhandle), it is just short of insanity to travel to Florida without a reservation. Many are the tales of woe from visitors who spent all those beautiful beach hours (sometimes days!) pounding the pavement in search of a room. It isn't worth it—and it isn't necessary. A telephone call or a note can save you much grief, and perhaps even a miserable night in the car.

If you persist in unplanned forays and can stand the suspense, here's a searcher's tip: You'll often have most success from 4 to 6pm when reservations that haven't been claimed are cancelled and given away on a first-come basis.

In Florida you need never fear being stranded so far out in the boondocks that you can't find a hotel. In the backwoods you may be, but without a hotel or motel somewhere near? Never. Moderately priced chain motels like Howard Johnson, Holiday Inn, Days Inn, and Motel 6 (a really low-budget stop) have representatives everywhere in Florida. When one of those operations was something extra-special, we've noted that for you. Otherwise, here's a list of toll-free numbers for the major chain operations in moderate price brackets. (Note: **Motel 6** has no toll-free numbers.)

**Best Western** (tel. 800/528-1234); **Days Inn** (tel. 800/325-2525); **Econo Lodges** (tel. 800/446-6900); **Holiday Inns** (tel. 800/465-4329); **Howard Johnson** (tel. 800/654-2000); **Quality Inns** (tel. 800/221-2222); **Ramada Inns** (tel. 800/228-2828); **Red Carpet Inns** (tel. 800/251-1962); **Rodeway Inns** (tel. 800/228-2000); **Scottish Inns** (tel. 800/251-1962); **TraveLodge** and **Viscount,** now **Trusthouse Forte** chain members (tel. 800/255-3050).

Now, some final words about saving money on Florida hotel rooms: Small motels a block or two from the sand are cheaper, sometimes 50% cheaper, than larger oceanside resorts; in beachfront hotels, rooms not facing the ocean are often cheaper than those overlooking the water; the fewer a resort's amenities—like telephones, restaurants, lobbies, etc.—the lower the price; and, of course, the less popular the season and the farther outside large resort cities you go, the less you'll pay, although massive sports resorts are exceptions to that.

Miami is the most expensive city in the state, though much more moderately priced than many American and European cities of a similar size, so prices go down as you radiate outward. Orlando, thanks to the popularity of Walt Disney World, is something of an aberration as prices there tend to stay about the same year round and are on the high side of moderate, offset a bit by many moderately priced restaurants. You'll find the cheapest beach vacations in Florida north of a line that runs from about Daytona on the east coast to Tampa on the west. When you get a bill in the Panhandle, you're likely to think they've made a mistake—in your favor!

As for that little matter of price. All the prices we've mentioned here, except in one or two cases specifically noted, are for a *room for two.* When you inquire about prices in Florida, you will always be given the price of a double room. "Always" is, of course, a big promise, so let us add that occasionally some hotels do advertise a price per person, but in general you need not fear that a quoted price is per person. Prices hop around like a Mexican jumping bean in Florida, so be prepared for a few dollars higher than what we've quoted and do expect higher prices during any special event like football games, Speed Weeks in Daytona, etc.

Prices for a third or fourth person sharing a room are usually very low, perhaps

$5 to $10 or less, and children sharing a room with their parents are free in most large motels and many smaller ones too.

Florida even has its own language: hotel-speak. When you ask a hotel for its rate, they'll start reeling off words like efficiencies, hotel rooms, villas, apartments, and Bahama beds. Here's what they mean:

**Hotel rooms**—the typical room with one or two beds, sometimes king- or queen-size beds.

**Twins**—two single beds in the room.

**A double**—one double bed in the room in small hotels, usually two double beds in large hotels.

**An efficiency**—an especially large room with an area set aside for cooking and usually equipped with stove, oven, small refrigerator, dishes, pots, etc.

**One-bedroom apartments**—Usually two rooms, but sometimes three, one for sleeping plus a kitchen and sometimes a small living room.

**Bahama or Hollywood beds**—Usually found in an efficiency, Bahama beds are twin beds, usually with back bolster cushions and no headboard. Covers go on the beds during the day so they look just like couches. Hollywood beds are just another word for the same thing. Both are also sometimes called studio beds or couches, but they differ from a "roll-out" or convertible couch in that they have box springs as well as mattresses and are generally more comfortable than convertible couches.

**Condominium resort**—Somewhere along the way someone decided a good way to sell condominium apartments was to operate a number of the apartments as a hotel, thus making them a dandy write-off and an income-provider for owners. As people began to demand better and fancier accommodations with golf courses, restaurants, pools, and entertainment, condominiums became the perfect solution to both the needs of the owner and the needs of the traveler.

**Villas**—A term often encountered at condominium resorts and usually referring to a complete apartment with one or two separate bedrooms, large living room, kitchen. The term also is now sometimes used by large hotels to indicate an especially plush room, a large suite, or perhaps a cottage set off by itself.

## CONDOMINIUMS

If you're staying a while, you might like a real home away from home in a condominium apartment. Thousands of condo owners in Florida rent their apartments seasonally, and sometimes by the week during slow seasons. Condominiums are a bargain since you have all the amenities of a hotel (except perhaps restaurants, and sometimes even those) and a great deal more space for the dollar. A note to the chamber of commerce in any city will elicit response from condominium owners. If you want still more choice, here's a list of a few—by no means all—condominium rental agents in some of the popular condo areas:

### Fort Lauderdale Area
**Cleo de Mott Associates,** 3360 NE 34th St., Fort Lauderdale, FL 33308 (tel. 305/563-9337).

### The Keys
**Wilbur Mead,** 82685 US 1, Mile Marker 82, Islamorada, FL 33036 (tel. 305/664-4446); **Marathon Realty,** 10800 Overseas Hwy., Marathon, FL 33050 (tel. 305/743-4500); **Casa Solana,** 3312 Northside Dr., Key West, FL 33040 (tel. 305/294-2455).

### Palm Beach
**Carter Realty,** 449 Blue Heron Blvd., Riviera Beach, FL 33404 (tel. 407/793-3993).

## The Panhandle
**Merica Metro Realty,** 221 S. Baylen St., Pensacola, FL 32501 (tel. 904/432-9944); **John W. Brooks Realty, Inc.,** 43 Miracle Strip Pkwy., Fort Walton Beach, FL 32548 (tel. 904/244-2121).

## Miami/Miami Beach
**Century 21,** 3100 NW 77th Court, Miami, FL 33122 (tel. 305/591-3521); **Condo Resales & Rental,** 1801 S. Ocean Dr., Hollywood, FL 33020 (tel. 305/456-2410 or 945-6579); **Keyes,** 100 N. Biscayne Blvd., Miami, FL 33152 (tel. 305/371-3592).

## Sanibel/Captiva Islands
**Priscilla Murphy Realty,** 1177 Causeway Rd., Sanibel, FL 33957 (tel. 813/472-4121).

## TIME-SHARING
Interval ownership, also called time-sharing, went slightly crazy in Florida for a while, with even the tiniest motels offering the vacationer the chance to "buy" ownership of accommodations for several thousand dollars—although you do not *own* the property. Since the time-sharing dust has not yet settled, we have generally avoided properties that are converting to time-sharing operations or are already heavily involved. There are two major reasons for that: (1) a resort's prices seem not to be stable during a conversion, and (2) if they're running a boiler-room operation, as some most definitely are, you're likely to be subjected to a sales pitch, like it or not, a practice we find abhorrent at best. If you want to know more about time-sharing, you won't have any difficulty finding out: Newspapers will tell you who's selling and sellers will offer you everything from silver dollars to instant cameras to listen to their sales spiels.

## RESTAURANTS
Nothing changes faster in Florida than restaurants, and the bigger the city, the faster the change. We've tried to stick to restaurants that have emerged victors in the war of the whisks, but we're offering no guarantees on either continued existence or price. As for those prices, we've tried to indicate about what we think you'll pay for a *basic* meal. If you love soups before, desserts after, and a bottle of wine or a martini or two in between, your bill will rise accordingly and rapidly. In general, dinner entrée prices in Florida include salad, vegetable, meat, bread, butter, and often coffee.

Florida restaurants are much more casual than their counterparts in other sections of the nation. For men, a jacket in hand (not necessarily on shoulders) will do just fine, even in peak winter season in southern Florida when things are at their most formal. Palm Beach and Miami Beach are perhaps the most formal cities in Florida, so at top restaurants and hotels there the absence of a tie and jacket may be at best frowned upon, at worst cause for dismissal.

Elsewhere, and in all moderately priced restaurants, you won't feel out of place without a tie in winter, and certainly not in summer, when Miami and every other city in Florida slips into as little as possible.

For women, dresses or attractive pants outfits go anywhere; designer jeans, almost anywhere. At beachside restaurants and some of the more rustic seafood spots, shorts and shirts are acceptable; bathing suits, only if covered. Must you wear shoes? Yes.

## Local Foods
Even food is different in Florida. Next to their Persian lime brothers, for instance, key limes look like little yellow jokes, but the pie that comes from them—it must be yellow to be authentic—is a symphony of graham cracker crust and

whipped cream or meringue. You can only get the authentic version of this creation in Florida.

Lest you still think Florida purveys only sunshine, listen to these statistics. Florida produces more than $12 billion in agricultural products each year, including more than 50% of the world's grapefruit, 25% of the world's oranges, and 90% of the nation's limes. It is the world's largest citrus-producing region.

Tomatoes you buy in the dead of winter have probably come from Florida— they are the state's largest winter crop, much of it grown south of Miami in Homestead, a major tomato-farming community in the state. Up in Zellwood in central Florida and around Belle Glade, the rich mucklands produce peppers, eggplants, sugarcane, pecans, kumquats, and some strange tropical fruits called carambola, mangoes, and papayas.

As you drive through the state you'll also see hundreds of little rectangular boxes sitting in the fields. These are occupied by thousands of bees, which produce more honey each year than is produced in any other state in the nation.

Chicago may be the world's butcher but Florida ranks second in the nation in beef production, right after Texas. Cowboys still ride the range here. In fact, there are more cows in Florida than in any other state east of the Mississippi. Florida has more than 21,000 cattle ranches! You'll see many of these vast ranches in central Florida, and you can even attend a cattle auction in Kissimmee, near Orlando. Florida cattle farms are now experimenting with a new cattle breed said to produce meat with fewer calories and less cholesterol.

Finally, Florida is one of the nation's most prolific producers of seafood. Fishermen here pull more than a billion pounds of fin and claw from the sea each year.

Stone crabs are a special Florida treat, and it's nice to know no one has to kill anything to get them. Stone crab fishermen near Naples, on the west coast of the state, capture the crabs, break off one large claw, then throw the crabs back into the deep, where they grow another claw to replace the missing one. Stone crabs are best during their harvest season, from mid-October to mid-May. Many restaurants can produce them later in the year, but they'll probably have been frozen.

So much seafood comes from these waters it's hard to know where to start, so we'll just mention some you may not be familiar with. Pompano is a very light and delicate fish much loved by gourmets. Scamp is not misspelled scampi, but a flaky white fish found on the state's west coast and in Florida's Panhandle. It's rarely seen on menus since fishermen usually keep it for themselves! North Florida's mullet lives in clear, sandy water, and has a light, much-loved flavor different from and better than mullet found elsewhere in the nation.

Florida lobsters aren't like Maine lobsters. They're much smaller and usually much cheaper. Apalachicola oysters are a Florida specialty, and are as different from their Bon Secour Alabama brothers as they are from any other oysters. Rock shrimp, sometimes called *langostinos*, are something like shrimp-size lobsters. Clams and scallops are abundant here. You'll find two kinds of scallops, bay and deep sea, the former much tinier and sweeter.

Fresh hearts of palm (try Cap's Place, in Lighthouse Point near Fort Lauderdale) are a delicacy far superior to the canned variety. They're cut from the heart of the cabbage palm with a technique learned from the Seminoles. Once you try them, you'll be forever spoiled for the canned version.

From the many nationalities that have merged on this land—Bahamians, Cubans, Indians, Spanish, English, French—Floridians have acquired a taste for crusty Cuban bread and steaming thick black coffee in thimble-size cups; for conch chowder made from ground conch (pronounced "konk," it's the creature that lives inside the pink shells you "listen" to), tomatoes, and plenty of hot spices, topped by a dollop of sherry; for spicy conch salad marinated in fermented lime juice; for paella, a rice and seafood and vegetable combination; for piccadillo, a mix of ground meat, olives, and raisins in a spicy sauce; for pilau, a spicy stew found in the St. Augustine area; for creole foods like muffaletta sandwiches and gumbo served in the Panhandle.

## Citrus

Breathtakingly beautiful citrus groves cover the rolling hills of central Florida from horizon to horizon. In cold snaps those old tires you'll see piled in fields are burned to heat the air and keep frost from nipping tender trees. At groves throughout Florida you can pick your own oranges, send oranges to friends here or abroad, ship fruit home, and sometimes get all the just-squeezed orange juice you can drink free! If you're taking some citrus home on a plane, be sure to put your name or some identifying ribbon on it since everyone else on the plane is likely to have some too. If you'd like to see frozen orange juice in the making, visit the Citrus World plant at Lake Wales on US 27 (tel. 813/676-1411) for free films and tastings.

Here's a look at some of the citrus you'll find here:

**Navel oranges**—best from November to January and recognizable from tiny "navels" and smooth skin, usually almost seedless and easily peeled.

**Valencia oranges**—March to July, juicy and aromatic.

**Temple oranges**—January to March, a favorite eating orange with a lightly pitted skin.

**Murcott oranges**—February to April, and almost red inside.

**Hamlin oranges**—October to December, seedless, thin-skinned, a juice orange.

**Pineapple oranges**—December to February, very juicy and very sweet.

**Tangelos**—December to March, a cross between tangerines and oranges, with an easy-peel skin.

**Tangerines**—December to February, the zipper-skin fruit.

**Duncan grapefruit**—October to May, a thin, pale-yellow skin, very juicy and seedy.

**Seedless grapefruit**—November to June, smooth yellow skin, few seeds.

**Pink seedless**—October to May, rose-colored interior.

Other interesting ones are tiny pucker-maker **kumquats** often used in jellies, Persian **limes** (the big green ones), and Ponderosa **lemons,** often nearly as big as a large orange.

Many of the **exotic fruits** of the tropics grow here: mangoes, papayas, star-shaped carambolas, Surinam cherries, and dozens more. You can learn about them at Redlands Fruit and Spice Park or Fairchild Gardens in Miami.

You can even try citrus wine! It's made at Florida Vineyard and Fruit Gardens in Orange Lake between Gainesville and Ocala, and sold in most liquor and some grocery stores, and at roadside Stuckey's stores along the Florida Turnpike.

Citrus candies and jellies, goat's milk fudge, and coconut patties are favorites in Florida too. You can buy coconuts, which are brown and slosh when you shake them if they're ripe, already hulled in grocery stores.

Food festivals are favorite entertainment in Florida. Among the most popular are the corn festival in Zellwood (near Orlando) each May, the Strawberry Festival in Plant City in February, and the Watermelon Festival each June in Monticello. There are dozens of seafood festivals too.

# 4. Final Thoughts

## ABOUT THIS BOOK

No restaurant, hotel, or other establishment has paid to be included in this book. What you read are personal recommendations, carefully checked out and judged by the strict yardstick of value. If they measured up—gave good value for your money—they were included, regardless of price range.

Because, however, most of today's travelers are in the medium-income group, you'll find that the majority of listings are geared to neither the super-rich nor the best-things-in-life-are-free contingent. Rather, the book is aimed at the dollarwise, middle-income traveler who wants occasionally to splurge and occasionally to save, but always to get maximum value for his or her dollar. The evaluations in this book were made with an eye on cost, but primarily with an eye on quality.

## A WORD ABOUT PRICES QUOTED

Inflation, it seems, is here to stay as a part of the American scene. Thus the prices shown here are *only those in effect at the time of writing*. Even if there is a variation in price by the time you reach a particular destination, however, the price *range* is likely to be the same—that is, a medium-range hotel today will probably still be medium-priced for the area even with a hike in charges, although "medium" may be somewhat higher than at the time of this writing. In this sense, this is a *guide* as the name says, to finding low-, medium-, and top-priced facilities.

## A NOTE ABOUT CRIME

Whenever you're traveling in an unfamiliar city or area, stay alert. Be aware of your immediate surroundings. Wear a moneybelt and don't sling your camera or purse over your sholder; wear the strap diagonally across your body. This will minimize the possibility of your becoming a victim of crime. Every society has its criminals. It's your responsibility to be aware and be alert even in the most heavily touristed areas.

## AN INVITATION TO READERS

Like all Frommer Guides, *Frommer's Florida* is our best effort to clue you in on how to get the most for your money. If, as a traveler, you find we've missed an establishment that you find to be a particularly good value (or even one that's just fun and other readers ought to know about), we'd like to hear about it. We invite you to write so it may be included in the next edition of this book. If, on the other hand, by the time you get to a particular destination you find a restaurant or hotel is *not* up to our description (chefs *do* change and hotels *do* deteriorate!), please write us about that as well—the last thing we want in this book is misleading or untimely information. Any additional travel tips you may come up with (off days to visit attractions when they're less crowded, etc.) will also be appreciated. And, yes, if you find this guide to be especially helpful, do drop us a line about *that*. You have our word that each and every letter will be read by us, although we find it well-nigh impossible to *answer* each and every one. Be assured, however: We're listening. Send whatever you have to say to Marylyn Springer and Donald Schultz, Prentice Hall Press, 15 Columbus Circle, New York, NY 10023.

---

# 5. Frommer's Dollarwise Travel Club—How To Save Money On All Your Travels

---

In this book we'll be looking at how to get your money's worth in Florida, but there is a "device" for saving money and determining value on *all* your trips. It's the popular, international Frommer's Dollarwise Travel Club, now in its 31st successful year of operation. For information about the Club and order forms listing all Prentice Hall travel guides, turn to the last four pages of this book.

# 213 REASONS TO GO TO FLORIDA

It won't take many Florida billboards heralding the world's largest . . . the world's biggest . . . the world's loveliest . . . the world's only . . . for you to realize that Florida was born with a silver superlative in its mouth.

But unlike Texas, Florida doesn't seek to be the biggest at everything—it just wants to be the first at the party.

So long has this sunny state been doggedly pursuing the world's sun-and-fun seekers that Floridians may know more than anyone in the world about how to appeal to cold and tired masses yearning to get hot.

In a word, Florida is *savvy*. Whatever the trend, you'll find it happening here, interpreted with cachet or with cacophony, whatever it takes.

That means, of course, that when you come to Florida, you face such a multitude of things to see and do that you can end up racing around in circles to fulfill fantasies and end up just filling the gas tank.

Now, much as we would like to think of you lying in bed, reading this book cover to cover, we are regrettably forced to consider the possibility that you may skip a word or two. To do that, however, leaves you wide open to the possibility that when you get home, loose and laid-back after a couple of blissful weeks in sun and sea, some snide soul will say "But surely you saw Blippity Beach, the most beautiful beach in Florida? No? What a shame!" So that you should not have to suffer such an indignity—or at least so you should be able to deliver your own "onesnubs-manship" in return—we have devised this chapter. In it we've rounded up lists of temptations in Florida that are going to drive you wild with desire to get down there and see it, do it, and—later—talk about it.

So here it is, folks, our absolutely biased, not even remotely objective statewide choice of things and places we think you'd like to know before you go or soon after you get there. In most cases we haven't gone into a lot of detail here since this chapter is designed to provide a quick look at the possibilities. If you want to know more, you'll find details in the chapters relating to the region mentioned.

Go on, get out there and do something!

## 1. Take It Off, Take It All Off

Lives there a soul so dead who never has muttered: "Gawd, I've got to do something about this body."

Florida is standing right at your side the moment those words are uttered. Floridians have known about this fitness-freak thing for about two decades longer than it's been a fad—and now that fitness is in fashion the state's longtime spas have come out of the closet to be joined by many new competitors.

Don't think for a minute that we're going to explain any of this stuff they're offering—seaweed is still seaweed to us, no matter where you put it. Here's a list of some of the state's spas, new and old, in no particular order. Prices vary widely depending on the number, length, and kind of treatment you elect, but we've included a few indicative fares.

### WEST FLORIDA

The **Belleview Biltmore**, 25 Belleview Blvd., Belleair-Clearwater, FL 34616 (tel. 813/442-6171, or toll free 800/237-8947, 800/282-8072 in Florida). Enter the world of Roman baths à la Victoriana at this $2-million spa that bills itself as an "intimate smaller spa for 50 to 70 guests, not a factory." There's a warm pool, extra-big whirlpool, individual whirlpools, Swedish showers, skylights that roll back, Paramount weights, aerobics and traditional cardiovascular exercise areas, separate mens' and womens' massage areas, cosmetology, herbal wraps, mud packs, aromatherapy, a 14-day-cycle spa menu, and dieticians here. A one-day plan is $99 per person.

**Safety Harbor Spa and Fitness Center**, 105 N. Bayshore Dr., Safety Harbor, FL 34695 (tel. 813/726-1161, or toll free 800/237-0155). One of Florida's oldest spas, this one has been around for decades. Two Jacuzzis are filled by mineral springs as are two exercise pools. Some programs concentrate on "make-over weight-loss plan," others on a "cardiovascular risk-reduction plan." There are weekend programs and week-long programs, unlimited exercise classes, beauty services, medical aid, fitness programs, a Lancôme salon, indoor and outdoor lap pools, bicycles, saunas, steamrooms and a whirlpool, tennis, and golf. An eight-night weight-loss and spa program begins at $1843 per person double in winter, about $400 more single, both plus 27% service fee.

**Sonesta Sanibel Harbour Resort**, 17260 Harbour Pointe Dr., Fort Myers, FL

33908 (tel. 813/466-4000, or toll free 800/343-7170). This comparatively new hotel saw the fitness handwriting on the wall and built a spa right into its operation. Quite a natural, actually, since this hotel also is a major tennis center. Admission for hotel guests is $5 a day, and features include body and beauty treatments, strength-training equipment, an indoor pool, aerobics, a whirlpool, steamroom, sauna, Swiss shower, and racquetball.

## SOUTH FLORIDA

The **Fontainebleau Hilton Resort and Spa,** 4441 Collins Ave., Miami Beach, FL 33140 (tel. 305/538-2000, or toll free 800/932-3322). It's still the same venerable Fontainebleau but now it includes a multi-million-dollar spa, complete with everything from herbal wraps to individual mineral baths, an Adrien Arpel Skin Care Salon, massages, Nautilus equipment, aerobics, and beachfront jogging. Hotel guests pay $8 a day, others $50 a week.

**Palm-Aire Resort and Spa,** 2501 Palm-Aire Dr. North, Pompano Beach, FL 33069 (tel. 305/972-3300, or toll free 800/327-4960). Liz Taylor is one of many celebs who have dined on special diets, trimmed in the spa's total fitness program, golfed, sniffed in the eucalyptus steamroom, swirled in the whirlpool, or paddled it off in the elegant swimming pool. Palm-Aire has exercise programs, herbal wraps, beauty care, loofah treatments, lectures on stress management and other similarly stressful topics, and sends you home with a take-out fitness plan. A three-night mini-spa is $1,336 in winter single.

**Sheraton Bonaventure Resort and Spa,** 2501 Racquet Club Rd., Fort Lauderdale, FL 33326 (tel. 305/389-3300, or toll free 800/327-8090). This one burst on the spa scene with the most elaborate of equipment and programs and is now mentioned among the top 10 spas in the nation. Medical screening, unlimited fitness classes, all kinds of beauty and body treatments, aromatherapy, Paramount equipment, Swiss showers, a spa menu, and package plans are its lures. A seven-night winter spa stay, per person double, is $1,920.

**Doral/Saturnia International Spa Resort,** 8755 NW 36th St., Miami, FL 33178 (tel. 305/593-6030, or toll free 800/327-6334). Famous for its monstrously challenging golf courses, Doral is now working on becoming famous for its spa and has opened a 148,000-square-foot complex offering hydrotherapy using reconstituted mineral salt, mud, and plankton extracts from Italy's Terme di Saturnia. Add to that American fitness, stress-management and nutrition, David equipment, three exercise studios, pools, indoor and outdoor tracks, organized sports, exercise classes including low-impact aerobics and beauty services, hydromassage, and mud packs. A one-day plan is $177 for hotel guests with longer plans available.

**Spa at Turnberry,** 19755 Turnberry Way, N. Miami Beach, FL 33180 (tel. 305/932-6200, or toll free 800/327-7028). An important part of Turnberry Isle Yacht and Country Club, this spa includes exercise classes, Nautilus equipment, herbal wraps, Swiss showers, Vitabath treatments, a medical exam, nutritional consultations, and massages. A seven-night program is $1,510 single in winter.

**Russell House,** 611 Truman Ave., Key West, FL 33040 (tel. 305/294-8787). You can get someone to help you stop smoking here, lose weight, or just get healthier. Coed one-week plans are a mainstay of this spa, which also will help you fast, or get you into its outdoor Roman tub and onto its exercise deck. Massage and herbal steam is part of the program, as are beauty and body treatments. Week-long programs begin at $750 rising for more elaborate rooms.

---

# 2. Food and Water, South Florida Style

---

There's quite a lot of water in South Florida so you aren't going to find every South Florida waterside restaurant listed here. There are spots we think are good, atmospheric, romantic, lively, all of the above, or something else. Prices are low to moderate ($10 to $17 for entrées) unless otherwise noted (then expect $15 to $20 for entrées alone). These choices are listed from south to north. We welcome additions.

## MIAMI

**Crawdaddy's,** 1 Washington Ave. (tel. 673-1708). A new entry into the waterside arena, this one is located right at the tip of South Miami Beach. Fun and lively, it specializes in well-prepared seafood but has other options as well as a view of the bay.

**Sand Bar Restaurant and Lounge,** 301 Ocean Dr., Key Biscayne (tel. 361-5441). Beloved by locals who nip in here to avoid the Crandon Park crowds, the Sand Bar is just about what its name suggests. Great spot to see what's at sea while you sip.

**Mike Gordon's Seafood Restaurant,** 1201 NE 79th St. (tel. 751-4429). Certainly one of the most popular seafood restaurants in Miami, Mike Gordon's is packed, packed, and packed all the time. But what else would you expect from a spot specializing in fresh seafood and great water views.

## KEY WEST

**Half Shell Raw Bar,** 1 Land's End Village (tel. 294-7496) is hard by the shrimp docks. You dine, so to speak, at one long, banged-up bar we shall dub rustic or on an outdoor patio. Tales of "Cincinnati Patti" are the entertainment here, as are the old salts who frequent this unusual hangout.

## HOLLYWOOD

**Martha's,** 6024 N. Ocean Dr. (tel. 923-5444). This snazzy spot has a raw bar upstairs, a spiffily elegant restaurant downstairs.

**Hunky Dory's Raw Bar Seafood,** 1318 N. Ocean Dr. (tel. 925-1011). A snacky, inexpensive spot, there are wood benches and views over the Intracoastal Waterway.

**Le Tub,** 1100 Ocean Dr. (tel. 921-9425). Tubs and other "facilities" provide amusing decor at this popular outdoor hangout.

**Dockside Raw Bar and Restaurant,** 908 N. Ocean Dr. (tel. 922-2265). There's shrimp and stuff at this Intracoastal spot that's right in a row with Le Tub and Hunky Dory's so you can graze your way down the street.

## DANIA

**Tugboat Annie's,** 1000 NE 3rd St. (tel. 925-5400). Packed nearly every night and always on Sunday, Tugboat Annie's feeds but mostly waters. Reggae and calypso are weekend foci. Dining is under the trees or along the water of Dania's Whiskey Creek.

**Sea Fair,** 101 N. Beach Rd. (tel. 922-5600). This imbibing spot is plunked right down on the beach in a Victorian-façaded development.

**Rustic Inn Crabhouse,** 4331 Ravenswood Rd. (tel. 584-1637). All the garlicky, soft-shell crabs you can cram are the lure here at a very rustic spot indeed — busy, bustling, and jammed.

## FORT LAUDERDALE

**Burt and Jack's,** 2100 Eller Dr. in Port Everglades (tel. 522-5225). Owned by Burt Reynolds and friend, this handsome restaurant is expensive but worth it for the views of cruise ships that pass right by the windows here.

**15th Street Fisheries,** 1900 SE 15th St. (tel. 763-2777). Trimmed with tiny white lights, this spot at Fort Lauderdale's major ocean outlet has great yacht views. There's an inexpensive raw bar downstairs, more expensive but quite innovative fare upstairs.

**Shirttail Charlie's,** 400 SW Third Ave. (tel. 463-3474). This is one of the most

"Florida" spots you'll ever find and the city's top "in" spot on Friday and Sunday. Dine outside on the dock on a limited menu or upstairs in the cool with views over New River.

**Chart House Restaurant at Historic Bryan Homes,** 301 SW Third Ave. (tel. 523-0177). This beautiful, upscale restaurant was formed from two of the city's oldest homes. Lawns stretch right down to the river where a ferry once transported travelers on their way to Miami. Moderate to expensive but very scenic inside and out.

**Casa Vecchia,** 209 Birch Rd. (tel. 463-7575). A beautiful old home-turned-restaurant, this one is quite expensive but delivers for all its worth both in view of the Intracoastal Waterway and in interior decor and fine northern Italian cuisine.

**Down Under,** 3000 E. Oakland Park Blvd. (tel. 563-4123). Woodsy, plantsy, filled with antiques and interesting *objets,* Down Under is pricey but tops for award-winning cuisine and good views of the Intracoastal Waterway.

**Yesterday's,** 3001 E. Oakland Park Blvd. (tel. 561-4400). A lounge and two restaurants are here, one expensively gourmet, the other slightly lower priced with a wide variety of selections. Yesterday's also has a popular lounge. Again, there are Intracoastal views.

**Charlie's Crab,** 3000 NE 32nd Ave. (tel. 561-4800). There's an innovative seafood menu here and both indoor and outdoor dining.

**Bootleggers,** 3003 NE 32nd Ave. (tel. 563-4337). Throngs gather here to see, be seen, and dine outdoors on snack-food, raw-bar stuff. Many stroll between this one and Shooter's.

**Shooter's,** 3033 NW 32nd Ave. (tel. 566-2855). This one lures the upscale crowd to grazing and sipping in chic and trendy, brass-railed, blue-canopied surroundings.

**Stan's,** 3300 E. Commercial Blvd. (tel. 772-3700). Stan's draws the up-and-hoping crowd and the already-got-there group to indoor and outdoor dining overlooking the Intracoastal Waterway.

**Benihana of Tokyo,** 4343 W. Tradewinds Ave., Lauderdale-by-the-Sea (tel. 776-0111). This spot concentrates more on the inside showmanship of its knife-wielding Japanese chefs but water views are available in this very popular restaurant.

**Bahia Cabana Dockside Bar,** 3001 Harbor Dr. (tel. 524-1555) was once billed by a boating magazine as the best dockside patio bar in the world. Good view, pleasant casual atmosphere.

## POMPANO BEACH

**Sea Watch,** 6002 N. Ocean Blvd. (tel. 781-2200). Always packed, this oceanfront restaurant is one of the very few restaurants in the area to offer a view of the sea. Handsome decor here.

**Fishtales,** at Sands Harbor Hotel and Marina, 125 N. Riverside Dr. (tel. 942-9100). This tranquil spot offers all three meals so you can breakfast with a water view.

## LIGHTHOUSE POINT

**Cap's Place Island Restaurant,** 2765 NE 28th Court (tel. 941-0418). This is the most interesting waterside dining spot of them all in quite an old and Hemingway-esque building on an island you sail to on a boat they send over for you. A rarity available here: fresh hearts of palm.

## DEERFIELD BEACH

**The Cove,** 1755 SE Third Court (tel. 421-9272). Sunday is calypso music day, but any day's a good day to sit on the porch here and imbibe. Views and potables make for a lulling atmosphere.

**Pal's Captain's Table,** 1755 SE Third Court (tel. 427-4000). Pal's is a mainstay of this coastline with great views over the water and food to match.

**Riverview Restaurant and Seafood Bar,** 1741 Riverview Rd. (tel. 428-3463). A former gambling den, this restaurant has been around for a long time in one form or another. Now it offers good seafood and stunning vistas of the sparkling Intracoastal Waterway and the activity thereupon.

**Banana Boat,** 739 E. Ocean Ave. (tel. 732-9400). Here's a lively, laugh-it-up spot where anything goes, including tons of fresh seafood and plenty of steaks.

---

## 3. Florida's Most Glamorous Hotels and Resorts

---

There are many outstanding hotels in Florida but there are some that are top of the top. They're all famous but none of them is a budget stop, although many may have some very good deals available during the off-season. These are just our purely subjective choices, places we think you should consider if you're looking for the cream. We've listed them by region so you can look them up easily in other chapters.

### NORTH FLORIDA
**Amelia Island Plantation,** Amelia Island, near Jacksonville; **Marriott at Sawgrass,** Ponte Vedra; **Marriott's Bay Point Resort,** Panama City Beach.

### CENTRAL FLORIDA
**Hyatt Regency Grand Cypress,** Lake Buena Vista; **Grand Floridian Hotel,** Walt Disney World; **Buena Vista Palace Hotel,** Lake Buena Vista; **Marriott's Orlando World Center,** Lake Buena Vista; **Stouffer's Sea World Hotel,** Orlando.

### WEST FLORIDA
**Naples Ritz Carlton,** Naples; **Don CeSar Beach Resort,** St. Petersburg Beach; **Belleview Biltmore,** Belleair; **South Seas Plantation and Yacht Harbor,** Captiva Island; **Innisbrook Resort,** Tarpon Springs; **Saddlebrook,** Wesley Chapel.

### SOUTH FLORIDA
**Biltmore,** Coral Gables; **Doral Hotel and Country Club,** Miami; **Grand Bay,** Coconut Grove; **Doral Beach Resort,** Miami Beach; **Fontainebleau Hilton Resort and Spa,** Miami Beach; **The Alexander Hotel,** Miami Beach; **Marriott's Casa Marina Resort,** Key West; **Pier Sixty-six Resort and Marina,** Fort Lauderdale; **Marriott Harbour Beach,** Fort Lauderdale; **Sheraton Bonaventure Hotel and Spa,** Fort Lauderdale; **The Breakers,** Palm Beach; **Boca Raton Hotel and Club,** Boca Raton.

---

## 4. Knocking It Outta da Park

---

There are those among us whose candidate for All-American beauty is a little white orb flying over a fence. If you're one of those, you will of course plan a vacation in Florida, where you can get your baseball cards signed by the greats, all of whom will be here for spring practice sessions. So that you'll know where to go to keep your eye on the ball, here's a list of spring training grounds and the teams that play on them.

### SOUTH FLORIDA
**Atlanta Braves,** West Palm Beach Municipal Stadium, 715 Hank Aaron Dr., West Palm Beach, FL 33402 (tel. 407/683-6100).

**Baltimore Orioles,** Miami Stadium, 2301 NW 10th Ave., Miami, FL 33127 (tel. 305/633-9857).

**Montreal Expos,** West Palm Beach Municipal Stadium, 715 Hank Aaron Dr., West Palm Beach, FL 33401 (tel. 407/684-6801).

**New York Yankees,** Fort Lauderdale Yankee Stadium, 5301 NW 12th Ave., Fort Lauderdale, FL 33309 (tel. 305/776-1921).

**New York Mets,** St. Lucie County Sports Complex, 525 NW Peacock Blvd. at University Blvd., Port St. Lucie, FL 34986 (tel. 407/871-2100).

## CENTRAL FLORIDA

**Boston Red Sox,** Chain O'Lakes Park, Winter Haven, FL 33801 (tel. 813/293-3900).

**Detroit Tigers,** Marchant Stadium, 2301 Lakeland Hills Blvd., Lakeland, FL 33805 (tel. 813/682-1401).

**Houston Astros,** Osceola Stadium, 1000 Osceola Blvd., Kissimmee, FL 32741 (tel. 407/933-5500).

**Kansas City Royals,** Boardwalk and Baseball, I-4 and US 27 (P.O. Box 68000), Haines City, FL 33844 (tel. 813/424-2424).

**Los Angeles Dodgers,** Holman Stadium, Vero Beach, FL 32961 (tel. 407/569-4900).

**Minnesota Twins,** Tinker Field, 287 S. Tampa Ave., Orlando, FL 32805 (tel. 407/849-6346).

## WEST COAST

**Chicago White Sox,** Ed Smith Stadium, 2700 12th St. (P.O. Box 1702), Sarasota, FL 34230 (tel. 813/953-3388).

**Cincinnati Reds,** 1900 S. Park, Plant City, FL 33556 (tel. 813/752-1878).

**Philadelphia Phillies,** Jack Russell Stadium, 800 Phillies Dr., Clearwater, FL 33515 (tel. 813/442-8496).

**Pittsburgh Pirates,** Pirate City, 1701 27th St. East, Bradenton, FL 33508 (tel. 813/747-3031).

**St. Louis Cardinals,** Al Lang Field, 302 2nd St. South, St. Petersburg, FL 33701 (tel. 813/893-7490).

**Texas Rangers,** Charlotte County Stadium, 2300 El Jobean Rd., Port Charlotte, FL 33948 (tel. 813/625-9500).

**Toronto Blue Jays,** Grant Field, 373 Douglas Ave., Dunedin, FL 33528 (tel. 813/733-0429).

# 5. A Fin on the Nose

Gamblers are a weird lot: they can tote odds faster than a computer but can't keep a checkbook straight. They can remember the results of the last three races run by every horse on today's card at Hialeah but can't quite recall their wedding anniversary. (Please don't ask how we know this.)

If you're one of those, here's the only list *you're* going to care anything about. We can't give you specific racing dates because dates change annually according to the whim of the state racing commission.

## THOROUGHBRED, QUARTER HORSE, AND HARNESS RACING

**SOUTH FLORIDA Calder Race Course,** Tropical Park, 21001 NW 27 Ave., Miami, FL 33056 (tel. 305/625-1311). Racing dates are announced annually but are usually from May to November.

**Gulfstream Park,** 901 S. Federal Hwy. (US 1), Hallandale, FL 33009 (tel. 305/944-1242 or 454-7000). Racing dates run from November to May with exact dates announced annually and usually alternating annually with Hialeah Park.

**Hialeah Park,** 2200 E. Fourth Ave. (park stretches from NW 21st Street to NW 32nd Street), Hialeah, FL 33013 (tel. 305/885-8000). Racing is from November to May with exact dates announced annually and usually alternating with Gulfstream Park.

**Pompano Harness Track,** 1800 SW 3rd St., Pompano, FL 33069 (tel. 305/972-2000 or toll free 800/561-7223). Quarter horse racing dates run from mid-May to early August, harness racing dates from October to May.

WEST FLORIDA  **Tampa Bay Downs,** Racetrack Road (P.O. Box E), Oldsmar, FL 33557 (tel. 813/441-9701). Racing is from December to April.

## GREYHOUND RACING

NORTH FLORIDA  **Ebro Greyhound Track,** Fla. 79 (Box 111), Ebro, FL 32437 (tel. 904/535-4048). Racing is from late March to late September.

**Jacksonville Kennel Club,** 1440 N. McDuff Ave., Jacksonville, FL 32205 (tel. 904/646-0001). The Jacksonville track shares year-round racing dates with the Orange Park Kennel Club and Bayard Raceway.

**Orange Park Kennel Club,** 455 Park Ave. (US 17 at I-295), Orange Park, FL 32073 (tel. 904/264-9575 or 388-2623). Shares year-round racing dates with the Jacksonville Kennel Club and Bayard Raceway.

**Bayard Raceway,** 24901 Phillips Hwy. (US 1), Bayard, FL 32224 (tel. 904/268-5555). It also shares year-round racing dates with the Orange Park Kennel Club and the Jacksonville Kennel Club.

**Jefferson County Kennel Club,** US 19 N (P.O. Box 400), Monticello, FL 32344 (tel. 904/997-2561). Racing is from March to October 7.

**Pensacola Greyhound Park,** 951 Dog Track Rd., Pensacola, FL 32506 (tel. 904/455-8595). The park is open year round.

WEST FLORIDA  **Naples-Fort Myers Kennel Club,** 10601 Bonita Beach Rd. (P.O. Box 2567), Bonita Springs, FL 33923 (tel. 813/992-2411). Racing is year round.

**Derby Lane Greyhound Track,** 10490 Gandy Blvd., St. Petersburg, FL 33702 (tel. 813/576-1361). Racing is generally from January to May.

**Sarasota Kennel Club,** 5400 Bradenton Rd., Sarasota, FL 33580 (tel. 813/355-7744). Racing dates are May 8 to September 5.

**Tampa Greyhound Track,** 8300 N. Nebraska Ave. (P.O. Box 8096), Tampa, FL 33604 (tel. 813/932-4313). Racing is from September to early January.

CENTRAL FLORIDA  **Seminole Greyhound Park,** 2000 Seminole Blvd., Casselberry, FL 32707 (tel. 407/699-4510). Racing is from May to September.

**Sanford-Orlando Kennel Club,** 301 Dog Track Rd. (P.O. Box K), Longwood, FL 32750 (tel. 407/831-1600). Racing is from December through April.

**Daytona Beach Kennel Club,** 2201 Volusia Ave. (P.O. Box 2360), Daytona Beach, FL 32014 (tel. 904/252-6484). Open May to October.

SOUTH FLORIDA  **Palm Beach Kennel Club,** 1111 N. Congress Ave., Palm Beach, FL 33409 (tel. 305/683-2222). Racing is from October through April.

**Hollywood Greyhound Track,** 831 N. Federal Hwy., Hollywood, FL 33009 (tel. 305/454-9400 or 758-3647). Racing is from late December through April.

**Biscayne Kennel Club,** 320 NW 115 St., Miami Shores, FL 33168 (tel. 305/754-3484), open late April to July, September to November, exchanging dates with Flagler.

**Flagler Kennel Club,** 401 NW 38th Court (P.O. Box 35-460), Miami, FL 33126 (tel. 305/649-3000). Open July to September and October to December 25, exchanging dates with Biscayne.

**Berensons' Key West Kennel Club,** 350 Fifth Ave. (P.O. Box 2451), Key West, FL 33040 (tel. 305/294-9517). Racing is from November to April.

## JAI-ALAI

**NORTH FLORIDA** **Big Bend Jai Alai Fronton,** Fla. 278 (mailing address: Route 1, Box 1251), Chatahoochee, FL 32324 (tel. 904/442-4111). Games from October to April or May.

**WEST FLORIDA** **Tampa Jai Alai Fronton,** 5125 S. Dale Mabry Hwy., Tampa, FL 33611 (tel. 813/837-2441). Games from January to June.

**CENTRAL FLORIDA** **Florida Jai Alai Fronton,** 211 S. US 17/92, Fern Park, FL 33801 (tel. 407/331-9191). Games from October through February.
**Ocala Jai Alai,** Fla. 318 (P.O. Box 548), Orange Lake, FL 32681 (tel. 904/591-2345). Games from June to November.
**Daytona Beach Jai Alai,** 1900 Volusia Ave. (P.O. Box 2630), Daytona Beach, FL 32015 (tel. 904/255-0222). Games from February to August.
**Fort Pierce Jai Alai,** 1750 S. Kings Hwy., Fort Pierce, FL 33451 (tel. 407/464-7500). Games from January through July.

**SOUTH FLORIDA** **West Palm Beach Jai Alai Fronton,** 1415 W. 45th St., West Palm Beach, FL 33407 (tel. 407/844-2444). Games from September to July.
**Dania Jai Alai,** 301 E. Dania Beach Blvd., Dania, FL 33004 (tel. 305/945-4345). Games from May to mid-April except October.
**Miami Jai Alai,** 3500 NW 37th Ave., Miami, FL 33142 (tel. 305/633-9661). Games from May to mid-September and December through April.

---

# 6. Florida's 13 Best Beaches

We can't wait to hear the screaming from this one, but we can take it. Best, of course, is in the eye of the beach-ite, so if you think you've found a great one, let us know. We'll even read letters from chambers of commerce—which is not to say we'll change our minds. Why did we pick 13? Because.

**North Florida:** Fernandina Beach, Amelia Island; Flagler Beach, between Daytona and St. Augustine; Navarre Beach, east of Pensacola; St. Andrews Recreation Area, Panama City Beach; Seaside Beach, Seaside.

**West Florida:** Caladesi Island, Dunedin; Captiva Island; Anna Maria Island, Sarasota/Bradenton.

**South Florida:** Matheson Hammock, Coral Gables; John Lloyd Park Beach, Dania; Delray Beach Municipal Beach, Delray Beach; South Inlet Park, Boca Raton; Vero Beach, at Fla. 60 and the ocean.

---

# 7. Scenic Drives in Florida

If you want to get there fast, you'll just get on I-95, I-75, I-10, the Florida Turnpike, or I-4 and race around from place to place. But if you want to see what brings 7,000 people a week to new homes in Florida, then get off those dullsville Interstates and turnpikes and see something besides 500 miles of macadam. Here are our nominations for the most scenic drives in the state. We welcome suggestions (related to scenic drives, we hasten to add).

## NORTH FLORIDA

**Fla. 30A from Santa Rosa Beach to US 98 near Sunnyside.** You'll have to look sharp to find this one, which takes off to the east 17 miles east of Destin. A major development along the way at Sea Grove Beach is changing the face of the landscape here with Victorian-style cottages and beach houses. You'll get a look at some lovely Gulf Coast views and a couple of rustic old Florida villages along the way.

**Fla. A1A from Daytona to Jacksonville.** Take this for fabulous looks at mile after mile of sand and sea undisturbed by high-rises and other architectural lows.

## CENTRAL FLORIDA

**US 441 from Orlando to Mount Dora.** Rolling through the citrus groves of central Florida, this wide, easily traversed highway is a particularly pretty drive when the citrus is ripening in winter. Don't miss a stop at lakeside Mount Dora, one of the loveliest of Florida's villages.

**US 27 from South Bay to Moorehaven, then Fla. 78 around the lake to Okeechobee.** If you branch off this one at County Road 721 you'll drive through the center of the Brighton Seminole Indian Reservation. For more details on a circle-lake tour, see Fort Lauderdale side trips in Chapter VI.

**US 17A and US 17 from Avon Park to Sebring.** Winding through acres of orange and grapefruit groves, this intriguing back road dips and meanders past lakes and handsome old homes. This is Florida as it used to be—and fortunately still is, here. You can continue on US 17 through more of the same backcountry scenery to its junction with US 27 near Lake Placid.

## WEST FLORIDA

**Alternate US 19 from Clearwater to Tarpon Springs.** Running alongside the ocean, this scenic drive offers glittering ocean views on one side, wide lawns and attractive old homes on the other. Tarpon Springs is an interesting Greek colony. For more on that, see Tampa Bay side trips in Chapter XII.

## SOUTH FLORIDA

**Fla. A1A from just south of Titusville through Melbourne to just south of Fort Pierce.** Take this drive for an interesting look at a part of Florida that has changed little in a century or so.

**A local road through Palm Beach Shores.** You can find this one north of Palm Beach by taking US 1 to Blue Heron Boulevard; then turn east on Lake Drive to Ocean Avenue and turn north on the local road that has no route number. Winding through a heavily wooded section, this local road follows the ocean north through Palm Beach Shores past beautiful homes, finally returning to US 1.

**County Road 707 from the Jupiter Lighthouse to Port Salerno.** A scenic waterside road, County Road 707 winds through huge old banyan trees past imposing oceanfront manses.

**The Overseas Highway.** This is Fla. A1A from Miami to Key West, which zips past rustic fishing villages and miles of glittering water. Seven Mile Bridge is a don't-miss.

**From the entrance to Everglades National Park to Flamingo.** While this road through the park is occasionally a yawner, the vastness of the Indians' River of Grass stretching out on all sides and teeming with exotic life is a stirring sight indeed. Around and above you are wild orchids and plants that live in the air with no soil to nurture them, bony birds called anhingas that drape themselves awkwardly around reeds, pop-eyed alligators still as stones. With occasional stops at nature trails, this 50-mile drive can while away a day but it will be a memorable one.

**Fla. A1A from Hillsborough Beach to Palm Beach.** This is the Mansions Highway, a diverse strip of macadam that drifts first past huge sandside Hillsborough homes set in tropical jungle so thick you get only a glimpse of them. Through Boca elegant condominiums and stretches of seagrape-shaded beaches vie for attention and in Palm Beach there's ocean on one side and massive, eyepopping multijillion-dollar mansions on the other.

## 8. Freebies in Florida

Is there a lovelier word in the English language than "free"? Doubtful. If you find the thought of something for nothing appealing, tune in here to a list of free tours and free things you can do in the Sunshine State.

We have this mile-long list and we haven't even included state parks, many of which are free or charge less than a dollar admission. Nor have we included museums, many of which are free in Florida, or art galleries, most of which are free. Special events often have free parades, arts-and-crafts shows, and lots of fun events, all for free. Every chapter of *Frommer's Florida* now has a list of the best special events in that area.

Free things are everywhere just waiting to be taken advantage of—and that's certainly more than you can say of most things. If you have found some interesting ones, let's hear 'em.

### NORTH FLORIDA

**Anheuser-Busch Brewery.** You can have a brew and see it brew at this brewery, 111 Busch Blvd. (P.O. Box 1807), Jacksonville, FL 32229 (tel. 904/751-0700).

**Ormond Rockefeller Memorial Gardens and Art Museum.** Whatever the Rockefellers do is done with panache as you'll see at these restored formal and informal gardens at 78 Granada Blvd., Ormond Beach, FL 32074 (tel. 904/677-1857). Florida artists working in various media are showcased in monthly shows at the museum, while botanical gardens and ponds around the museum invite contemplation every day from dawn to dusk. The museum opens at noon daily except Monday and closes at 5pm.

**John D. Rockefeller's home.** Called the Casements, this small but architecturally intriguing home at 25 Riverside Dr., Ormond Beach, FL 32074 (tel. 904/673-4701), can be toured for free from 10am to 5:30pm Monday through Friday and open from 8:30am to 12:30pm on Saturday (often shorter hours in summer months, so call to be sure); closed Sunday.

**Mayport Naval Station.** Tours of the Sixth Fleet's aircraft carriers and other vessels are conducted on weekends when ships are in port. Hours for tours are generally 10am to 4pm on Saturday and 1 to 4pm on Sunday. Contact the Mayport Naval Station Public Affairs Office, P.O. Box 205, Mayport, FL 32228 (tel. 904/246-5226), to find out what's in port and when.

**Self-Guided City Tours.** Amelia Island nas a 30-block restoration district and the chamber of commerce there can provide you with a self-guided tour map. The same is true of Pensacola, which has maps of its two restoration areas, Seville Square and North Hill Preservation District's Victorian homes. St. Augustine, wall-to-wall history, also has a self-guided tour map available at the visitor center.

**Naval Aviation Museum.** Tours of an aircraft carrier, the U.S.S. *Lexington*, are conducted from 9am to 5pm on weekends. You can also visit the Naval Aviation Museum where an amazing array of vintage and modern aircraft is on display. Get in touch with the Naval Aviation Museum, U.S. Naval Air Station, Pensacola, FL 32508 (tel. 904/452-3604). Hours at the museum are 9am to 5pm daily.

### CENTRAL FLORIDA

**Ocala Thoroughbred Racehorse Farms.** The Ocala/Marion County Chamber of Commerce has a 16-page directory of farms that can be toured free. At some you need to call in advance so they can find someone to show you around. Contact the chamber at P.O. Box 1210, Ocala, FL 32678 (tel. 904/629-8051), or stop in to see them at 110 E. Silver Springs Blvd.

**Frank Lloyd Wright Architecture.** You can take a self-guided tour of the nation's largest collection of Frank Lloyd Wright–designed buildings at Florida Southern College. For a map and tour, write or stop in at the Administrative Building, 111 Lake Hollingsworth Dr., Lakeland, FL 33801 (tel. 813/680-4116).

**Mead Gardens.** Acres and acres of floral tributes, many of them rare tropical blooming things, are on display at these gardens located three blocks south of Orange Avenue on South Denning Avenue, Winter Park, FL 32879 (tel. 305/644-9860).

**Citrus World.** You can see how oranges get from tree to can in a 15-minute film shown at this orange-juice-canning factory, and sample their product too. You can sniff your way to it, but you'll find it on US 27 near the intersection with Fla. 60; look for Donald Duck on the water tower. By mail you can reach them at P.O. Box 1111, Lake Wales, FL 33853 (tel. 813/676-1411); films are shown from 9:15am to 3:45pm Monday through Friday.

**Slocum Water Gardens.** Acres of water lilies wave graceful petals here at this extensive display of water plants. You'll find them at 1101 Cypress Gardens Dr., Winter Haven, FL 33880 (tel. 813/293-7151).

**Tupperware International Headquarters.** Perhaps you've wondered what cavemen and women did before Tupperware was invented. Perhaps you haven't but we've got you thinking. Well, step right up to the Tupperware International Headquarters, Fla. 441 and US 17/92 in Orlando (tel. 305/847-3111), where you can see a display of containers dating back to 4000 B.C. It's open Monday through Friday from 9am to 4pm.

**Florida Cactus, Inc.** If you know someone with a prickly personality, we recommend that they stop here where they can fit right in with thousands of their fellow prickles. Self-guided tours (every day but Sunday) take you through five acres of cacti interestingly displayed: There's a clock and a map of the U.S. made from cactus. Don't say we don't find unusual things for you to do! You'll find this stickery spot on Peterson Road in the tiny town of Plymouth, but their mailing address is P.O. Box 2900, Apopka, FL 32704 (tel. 407/886-1833). Plymouth is on US 441 and once there you can just follow the signs. Florida Cactus is open Monday through Friday from 7am to 5pm, on Saturday to 11:30am.

**Kissimmee Cattle Auction.** Get a look at steak on the hoof at 1pm every Wednesday at this cattle auction, one of the major auctions in the state. You'll find cattle barons and lots of bull at this countrified event, which takes place at the Kissimmee Livestock Market, 1805 E. Donegan Ave. (tel. 305/847-3521), just north of US 17/92 and Fla. 441.

**Self-Guided City Tour.** Winter Park, an elegant enclave near Orlando and home to the world's largest collection of Tiffany stained glass, has a tour map that will help you find your way through the shady lanes of this beautiful village.

## WEST FLORIDA

**Honey Bee Observatory.** Everybody's busy as a bee at this honey factory where you can get a close look at how honey makers do what they do. You can also sample 10 kinds of honey, see a film on the creation of this sweet stuff, and visit a gift shop. Honey Bee is on Fla. 13 (P.O. Box 690), Fort Myers, FL 23401 (tel. 813/394-5592).

**Shell Factory.** Learn the difference between a cat's paw and an angel wing at this display where thousands of shells from all over the world are cleaned, polished, sorted, and turned into shell creations of all kinds. You'll find it at 2787 N. Tamiami Trail, Fort Myers (tel. 813/995-2141). Open from 9am to 6pm daily.

**Davidson of Dundee.** Citrus goes in orange and grapefruit and comes out candy at this citrus candy factory. You can see how it's done and sample the product at this factory at 205 US 27N, Dundee (tel. 813/439-2284). Open Monday through Friday.

**Stroh Brewery Company.** Hops and malt join hands at 11111 N. 30th St., Tampa (tel. 813/972-8528), to create this popular beer. Thirty-minute tours of the brewery (from 10am to 3pm Monday through Friday) are followed by a free tasting of the spirited product.

**Self-Guided City Tours.** Tarpon Springs and Ybor City are two unusual and historic towns near Tampa. The chambers of commerce there can supply you with self-guided tour maps. Ybor City's chamber is at 1513 Eighth Ave., Tampa, FL 33605 (tel. 813/782-1913); Tarpon Spring's chamber is at 210 S. Pinellas Ave., #120, Tarpon Springs, FL 34689 (tel. 813/937-6109).

## SOUTH FLORIDA

**Key West Fragrance and Aloe Cosmetics.** Sniff the air and you may be able to find your way to this perfumed spot. Tours of the factory, which creates fragrances from unusual tropical blooms like jasmine and ginger, are available from 9am to 5pm Monday through Friday. You'll find the factory at 540 Green St., Key West (tel. 305/294-5592).

**Redlands Fruit and Spice Park.** Exotica is common in Florida, both in flora and in fauna. You can get a look at the floral oddities that grow in tropical climes at this park at 24801 SW 187th Ave., Homestead, FL 33031 (tel. 305/247-5727). It's open from 10am to 5pm daily.

**Miami Beach Garden and Conservatory.** A dome soars overhead, filtering soft light onto a wonderland of blooming things, some exotic, others just conventionally gorgeous. You'll find the conservatory at 2000 Convention Center Dr., Miami Beach, FL 33139 (tel. 305/673-7720), and it's open daily from 10am to 3:30pm.

**Jupiter Lighthouse Museum.** If you always wanted to see how one of those things works, contact the Loxahatchee Historical Society, P.O. Box 1506, Jupiter, FL 33458 (tel. 407/746-5257 or 747-6639), for a self-guided tour of the museum at Jupiter Inlet. It was built in 1858 and is open on Sunday for tours from noon to 2:30pm.

**Art Deco District Self-Guided Tour.** A map that will guide you through the 10 blocks of this historic district, which contains the largest single concentration of art deco structures, is available from the Miami Design Preservation League, P.O. Box Bin L, Miami, FL 33119 (tel. 305/672-2014).

**Cauley Square.** Little houses built by Dade County pioneers have been restored here into a labyrinth of antique and boutique shops. There's an art gallery, craftspeople at work, and a garden for meditating over it all. You'll find Cauley Square north of Miami at 22400 Old Dixie Hwy., Goulds, FL 33170 (tel. 305/258-3543).

**Audubon House.** Built in 1931, which is old for South Florida, this Spanish-style house was constructed of yellow oak with some rooms done in Dade County pine, a wood that becomes so hard with age that termites can't eat it and a nail won't go in it. Now home of the county's branch of the Audubon Society, the house is open from 9:30am to 1:30pm Monday through Thursday but closing at 4:30pm on Wednesday. Call to be sure, however. Audubon House is at 5530 Sunset Dr., South Miami, FL 33143 (tel. 305/666-5111).

**Dubois Home Museum.** A handsome old residence is the home of the Loxahatchee Historical Society, which maintains a museum of local history in it. The Dubois Home Museum can be toured from 1 to 3:30pm on Sunday and at other times by appointment. You'll find the house at Dubois Park, just off US A1A (P.O. Box 1506), Jupiter, FL 33486 (tel. 407/747-6639).

**Morikami Museum.** This museum records the history of Japanese pineapple farmers who settled here in the early part of the century. Their industry failed, but this museum lives on with bonsai displays and Japanese festivals. You'll find it at 4000 Morikami Park Rd., Delray Beach, FL 33446 (tel. 305/499-0631).

**Self-Guided City Tours.** Coral Gables and Key West, both of which have interesting historical backgrounds and much unusual architecture, have city tour maps available from the chambers of commerce in those cities.

---

# 9. Florida's Most Interesting Museums

Wait, don't tune out! We are well aware that the very word "museum" threatens the onset of terminal boredom to some, but in Florida many museums these days are quite contemporary hands-on spots with buttons to push, flashing lights, dinosaurs, and fun stuff. We've got favorites and here they are.

## NORTH FLORIDA

**Museum of Florida History.** Climb aboard a steamboat, wander through a pioneer home, thump a Spanish conquistador's metal armor, and get into things at this hands-on museum that traces Florida's history with real samples of it. Located at the R. A. Gray Building, 500 S. Bronough St., Tallahassee, FL 32399 (tel. 904/488-1484), the museum is open from 9am to 4:30pm Monday through Friday, opening at 10am on Saturday and at noon on Sunday.

**Historic Pensacola Village.** Here you can roam through 10 historic buildings from a Greek Revival house to an old warehouse and the cottage home of the state's first free black woman. A treasure trove of early Florida history, this cluster of museum buildings centered at 205 E. Zaragoza St., Pensacola, FL 32501 (tel. 904/444-8905), leads you through many generations of life in this old Florida city.

**Naval Aviation Museum.** A must for aviation buffs, this museum houses 40 aircraft from antique to space shuttles. It's at the U.S. Naval Air Station, Pensacola, FL 32508 (tel. 904/452-3604), and is open from 9am to 5pm daily.

## CENTRAL FLORIDA

The **Florida Museum of Natural History.** At this intriguing museum on Museum Drive on the University of Florida campus, Gainesville, FL 32611 (tel. 904/392-1721), you can explore a Mayan temple, crawl into a Florida cave, prowl through a forest, and get a look at the bones of a prehistoric camel that once roamed these sands! A favorite of the 200,000 visitors who come here each year is the Object Gallery, where you can explore through drawers of things the museum has collected, from hashish pipes to rocks, minerals, and bat skeletons. Hours are 9am to 5pm Monday through Saturday, opening at 1pm on Sunday.

**Gillespie Museum of Minerals.** More than 25,000 glittering minerals, 1,000 of them glowing with fluorescence, are on display at this museum on the campus of Stetson University, Michigan and Amelia avenues, Deland, FL 32720 (tel. 904/734-4121). There's even a meteorite here amid the emeralds and aquamarines, on display from 9am to 4pm daily except Sunday (closed Saturday in the summer months).

**Morse Gallery of Art.** Although technically not a museum, this gallery has more than 4,000 examples of stained-glass work by famed Louis Comfort Tiffany. Leaded windows, blown glass, lamps, paintings, pottery, metal work, and furniture designed by the master are on exhibit. Gallery owner Hugh McKean was Tiffany's biographer. Admission is $2.50 for adults, $1 for children under 12. Hours are 9:30am to 4pm Tuesday through Saturday and 1 to 4pm on Sunday. You'll find the gallery at 151 E. Welborn Ave., Winter Park (tel. 305/644-3686).

## WEST FLORIDA

**John and Mabel Ringling Museum of Art.** Said to be among the most beautiful museums in the world, this colonnaded Sarasota beauty is testimony to the good taste and/or shrewd buying of circus kingpin John Ringling. Sporting columns and formal gardens, the art museum has one of the world's finest baroque collections, including a group of works by Rubens. You'll find the museum at 5401 Bay Shore Rd., Sarasota, FL 33577 (tel. 813/355-5101), and open from 10am to 6pm daily, closing at 10pm on Thursday.

**Salvador Dali Museum.** Weird and weirder, this surrealist mecca is the nation's largest collection of Dali's works, more than 1,300 of them rotated frequently. Whimsical and humorous, this salute to surrealism is not to be missed for shock value alone. It's at 1000 3rd St. S., St. Petersburg (tel. 813/823-3767).

## SOUTH FLORIDA

**Historical Museum of Southern Florida.** The telephone number here is 1492, which gives you a clue to the clever ideas at work here. As you wander this museum, you are encouraged to push buttons, listen to talking displays, and light lights as you wander past a Spanish fort, crawl into a Seminole dwelling, and clang away on an antique trolley. Open from 10am to 5pm Monday through Saturday (to 9pm on Thursday) and from noon to 5pm on Sunday, the museum is part of the city's Cultural Center at 101 W. Flagler St., Miami, FL 33130 (tel. 305/375-1700 or 375-1492).

---

# 10. Florida's Magnificent Mansions and Other Hallowed Halls

---

Some very rich fellows turned Florida's scrubby sands into pleasure playgrounds and built some pleasure palaces for themselves in the process. In these huge mansions and hotels you can get a glimpse of the way we were—and the way we'd all like to be!

## NORTH FLORIDA

**Zephaniah Kingsley Plantation.** Oldest plantation house in the state, this manse was built in 1817 by Kingsley, who was king of the slave traders and married a princess of an African tribe. The plantation is on Fort George Island at Heckscher Drive (tel. 904/251-3122) and is open from 8am to 5pm daily. Tours Monday through Thursday.

**Eden State Plantation and Ornamental Gardens.** Off all by itself in the village of Point Washington near Destin, Eden is an Eden, a tranquilly beautiful antebellum-style house filled with period antiques. Tours are given from 9am to 4pm daily, May through September; closed Wednesday and Thursday in other months. You'll find it on US 98E at Point Washington, Seagrove Beach (tel. 904/231-4214).

## CENTRAL FLORIDA

**DeBary Hall.** Considered one of Florida's five most important historic structures, this huge hall has central hallways running the entire length of both floors of the house. Every room opens onto a hallway, onto the next room, and onto the porch. A very welcoming Martha Hummiston is there Monday through Friday from 9am to 1pm and will be happy to show you through this enormous home made of cypress wood shipped here from Georgia. There is no admission charge but reservations are required. You'll find the house at 210 Sunrise Blvd., DeBary (tel. 305/668-5286).

**John Ringling's Ca' d'Zan.** Circus king John Ringling of Ringling Brothers fame made scads of money and spent plenty of it on his 30-room Venetian Gothic palazzo in Sarasota. One of the richest men in the nation, Ringling gilded everything, including the bathroom fixtures. It's a sight and is open from 10am to 6pm daily at 5401 Bay Shore Rd., Sarasota (tel. 813/355-5101).

## WEST COAST

**Don CeSar Hotel.** F. Scott Fitzgerald was a habitué of this bubble-gum-pink hotel that just missed the wrecking ball and is once again the playground of celebrities. It's at 3400 Gulf Blvd., St. Petersburg Beach, FL 33706 (tel. 813/360-1881).

**Belleview Biltmore.** Said to be the world's largest frame structure, this sprawling hotel sports 2½ *acres* of roof! Built in 1897, the hotel has been restored to massive elegance. It's at 25 Belleview Blvd., Belleair, Clearwater, FL 34616 (tel. 813/442-6171).

**University of Tampa.** Built by railroad kingpin Henry Plant, this bizarre onion-domed hotel sports hallways so wide guests were once transported down them in rickshaws! You can get a look at them at 401 W. Kennedy Blvd., Tampa, FL 33606 (tel. 813/253-8862 or 253-3333). Tours are at 1:30pm on Tuesday and Thursday.

**The Casements.** Built by John D. Rockefeller when he discovered his hotel was overcharging him—"because we thought you could afford it"—The Casements is a very big house, restored and in use as a community center. You can get a look at it—and at the massive Ormond Beach Hotel he taught a lesson (it's just across the street, to add insult to injury)—at 25 Riverside Dr., Ormond Beach, FL 32074 (tel. 904/673-4701). It can be toured for free from 10am to 5:30pm Monday through Friday and open from 8:30am to 12:30pm on Saturday, often shorter hours in summer months, so call to be sure; closed Sunday.

## SOUTH FLORIDA

**Henry Flagler's Whitehall.** One of many Palm Beach mansions, but the only one you're likely to be invited to tour, railroad magnate Henry Flagler's huge house is a gilded lily lined in acres of marble. Outside is his elaborately decorated private railroad car. Whitehall is on Coconut Row in Palm Beach (tel. 305/655-2833), and is open daily except Monday from 9am to 5pm, opening at noon on Sunday; last tours at 4pm daily.

**Vizcaya.** Built by International Harvester heir James Deering at a cost of $15 million—in those days!—this palatial mansion took 1,000 craftsmen five years to complete and was worth every penny and every minute of it. You'll find it at 3150 S. Miami Ave. (tel. 305/579-2708).

**Boca Raton Resort and Club.** As the best example of architect Addison Mizner's damn-the-bankbook style, this hotel gives you a peek into the extravagance of the '20s boom in Florida. It remains chicly tranquil. You can see it at 1 Camino Real, Boca Raton, FL 33432 (tel. 407/395-3000 or toll free 800/327-0101).

**Breakers.** The Breakers *is* Palm Beach, and vice versa. An address of elegance for generations of the upper crust, the Breakers is something! You can see its painted ceilings and gilded magnificence at 1 S. County Rd., Palm Beach, FL 33480 (tel. 407/665-6611).

---

# 11. Have a Grape Day

---

Grapes are a hardy lot that seem to grow anywhere, much to the gratitude of wine lovers. You'll even find grapes in, of all places, hot, sunny Florida, a long way from the cool rolling hills of France. Florida's wines aren't quite ready to give France a run for the money yet, but they're interesting. You can taste them and see for yourself at three wineries in the state.

**Lafayette Vineyards and Winery.** This vineyard is a salute to the memory of the Marquis de Lafayette, who aided the American cause in the Revolutionary War and was given 36 miles of territory in northern Florida in gratitude. French to the core, he naturally planted vineyards. They're carrying on his tradition at 6505 Mahan Dr., (just off I-10 Exit 31A) Tallahassee, FL 32308 (tel. 904/878-9041 or toll free 800/768-WINE), where tasting hours and days are 10am to 6pm daily, from noon Sunday.

**Lakeridge Winery & Vineyards.** This recent addition to the Florida vineyard scene, located at 19239 US 27 North, Clermont, FL 32711 (tel. 904/394-8627 or toll free 800/476-VINE), opened in 1988 with 25 acres of vines producing Blanc, Du Bois, Suwannee, and Stover grapes. Each year they're adding acreage to this vineyard, intent on covering 125 acres with grapes. You can see what's going on here from 10am to 6pm daily, from noon to 6pm Sunday. There's no charge for the tour, which ends with the best part, a tasting of the product.

**San Carlos Winery.** Learn how grapes get into a bottle at this new winery at 112 South 3rd St. in Fernandina Beach, FL 32034 (tel. 904/277-3236) on Amelia Island near Jacksonville.

**Eden Vineyards,** 19850 St. Rd. 80, Alva, FL 33920 (tel. 813/728-9463) has quite an interesting operation complete with tram tours to the winery, tastings of four wines, a nature walk, picnic area, and deli. This vineyard produces six wines including a Lake Emerald white, a rouge and a sangría-like Eden Spice wine, the favorite of most visitors. Hours are 10am to 6pm daily with tours from 11am to 4:30pm. You'll find it 10.2 miles from I-75, Exit 25 East.

**Chatauqua Vineyards,** Box 1308, 1330 Freeport Rd., De Funiak Springs, FL 32443 (tel. 904/892-5887) has tastings and tours of the winery and, of course, sells its product. This winery and 100-acre vineyard specializes in muscadine grapes and makes a variety of wines from them, including a sweet, semisweet, dry, and champagne. You'll find it off I-10 at Exit 14 and it's open daily from 10am to 4pm and Sunday from 1pm.

---

## 12. Tubing and Tripping on Florida's Springs

---

Sparkling sapphire in the sun and pouring out crystal water by the billions of gallons, Florida's springs are one of the lesser-known delights of this state.

Delights they are: You can swim in them, tip a canoe in them, go tubing on them, scuba dive and snorkel in them, go cave diving in them, even feed the fish and visit mermaids in them.

Real enthusiasts can get a list of Florida's 25 springs from the state **Department of Natural Resources,** Marjory Stoneman Douglas Bldg., 3900 Commonwealth Blvd., Tallahassee, FL 32399. No one should leave the state without a look at these natural wonders.

Besides, there is no finer place on a hot summer day than the center of a fat innertube lazing its way down the gurgling waters of a spring. Here are some of the prettiest springs.

### NORTH FLORIDA

**Wakulla Springs.** A tranquilly beautiful spot that's home to a famous old lodge-hotel, Wakulla Springs is 14 miles south of Tallahassee off Fla. 61 (tel. 904/224-5950). Divers who have paddled down 250 feet say there was no bottom in sight when they got there. Mastodon bones have been found in this spring, believed to be the deepest in Florida. You'll find more details on it under side trips from Tallahassee in Chapter XI.

**Natural Bridge Springs.** Located in Oleno State Park near the site of a major Civil War battle in Florida, this spring is south of Tallahassee six miles east of Woodville off County Road 354 (tel. 904/454-1853). Snorkeling, scuba diving, and fishing are popular here, and each year the Battle of Natural Bridge, fought by men and young boys who had been too young or unable to join the regular force, is reenacted here.

**Ichetucknee Springs.** Rising northwest of Gainesville and north of US 27 near Fort White, these springs (pronounced "itch-eh-tuck-knee," a native American word for pond with beavers) are owned and operated by the state park system. Long a favorite playground for tubing enthusiasts and canoeers, the springs in summer are a busy place, loved by funseekers who come here to roll merrily along the cool waters. You can contact the spring, which charges $2 for the driver and $1 for each passenger, at Route 2, Box 108, Fort White, FL 32308 (tel. 904/497-2511).

## WEST FLORIDA

**Weeki Wachee Springs.** Mermaids swim these waters, playing with the fish and entertaining throngs of visitors, many of whom make a day of it here, picnicking and playing in the tempting waters. You'll find them 12 miles south of Brooksville off US 19 (tel. 904/596-2062). More details are under "Side Trips from Tampa Bay" in Chapter XII.

**Homosassa Springs.** Known also as the Spring of Ten Thousand Fish, these waters are home to alligators, gentle manatees, and even hippos. You can see them all aboard glass-bottom boats that roam the springs. These springs, on US 19 about 75 miles north of Tampa/St. Petersburg (tel. 904/628-7311), also are detailed under "Side Trips from Tampa Bay" in Chapter XII.

**Manatee Springs.** A state park, these springs are far to the north of Tampa and just to the north of the turnoff to Cedar Key, six miles west of Chiefland (tel. 904/493-4288). They remain much the same today as they were when Native Americans camped around their banks centuries ago. You can see the waters boiling up from an opening under a ledge near the center of the spring pool here. Extensive underwater caves make this a popular spot for snorkeling.

## CENTRAL FLORIDA

**Silver Springs.** Best known of all the springs, these waters have been a tourist attraction for generations. Silver Springs charges admission and is open from 9am to 5pm daily for glass-bottom-boat looks down into the depths. It flows from a site one mile east of Ocala on US 40 (tel. 904/236-2121). More on this spring under "Side Trips Around Central Florida" in Chapter VIII.

**Blue Springs.** The focal point of Blue Springs State Park, these springs are located in central Florida north of Orlando, two miles west of Orange City. They are home to endangered manatees, which congregate here November through spring, providing entertainment for those who walk the footpaths in the palm and hardwood forest here. There's no swimming when the manatees are in residence, but you can paddle about at other times of the year. Hiking, picnicking, and camping are popular here. Contact the park at 904/775-3663.

---

# 13. Everyone Needs a Porpoise in Life

---

What Scrooge among us hasn't envied Cinderella, as she enlisted creatures of the forest in her quest for a new dress? And who hasn't swallowed hard as Dr. Dolittle, Snow White, and the Hobbits befriended animals, only to reap far more than they sowed in kindness. Creatures of the deep seas have not fared so well in the anthropomorphizing department, however. Few of us go all teary-eyed over a gold-fish and many a terror film has starred a toothy creature from the sea.

Dolphins, however, have for centuries gotten some very good press for their apparent interest in helping humans out of water jams. So positive is the attitude toward dolphins, in fact, that they've even taken on amulet qualities and in many quarters are considered good-luck symbols.

Here in Florida you can see for yourself why these gentle mammals of the sea have gotten such a good reputation—and now you can even join them right there in their own world.

*Yes, you can swim with a dolphin.*

Here's how this opportunity arose. Dolphins, which end up entertaining visitors to Sea World in Orlando, Ocean World in Fort Lauderdale, and the Seaquarium in Miami, don't just come by all those cute tricks naturally. Yes, of course they leap and frolic naturally, but someone has to teach them how to make their leaping productive—through a hoop or over a rope. From that need and others, including a desire to see if man can learn to speak dolphin, arose research and training programs.

It wasn't long before Florida researchers discovered that when the dolphins' practice sessions were over and human instructors were exhausted, the dolphins were still going strong—and looking for another playmate. One sure way to keep dolphins entertained is to send in some landlubbing human for them to play with, a realization that led quickly to the idea of keeping the dolphins entertained by inviting adventuresome folks to jump in for a swim.

Voilà, a swim-with-the-dolphins program was born.

If you think you'd like to get in there and slash through the water like Neptune on horseback, there are now two training centers that will welcome you for a 15-minute swim with these playful creatures.

They'll be quick to warn you that the tanks you'll be swimming in are the dolphins' own territory and you are just a visitor there. While dolphins have never been known to hurt anyone, their curiosity leads to many nudgings and nuzzlings from creatures who don't know how embarrassingly easily we humans bruise. You'll be asked to sign a liability waiver too.

Now that we've gotten past the warnings, here comes the fun. Jump in and for 15 minutes or so you splash around with Flipper and folk while you all get to know each other. Then the dolphin's number-one friend brings out a barrelful of tasty fish and the dolphins know just what that means—lunch! That kettle of fish is your key to hie down to the end of the pool and get ready. You may get quite a lot of encouragement from your newfound—and hungry—finny friends.

Then here they come, nudging you into position and squeaking merrily to encourage you to hurry up and grab onto a fin. Once you've taken hold, off they go, tearing like tornadoes across the pool, giving you the ride of a lifetime!

Here's where to go to walk, talk—and swim—with the animals.

**Dolphin Research Center,** Mile Marker 59, Overseas Hwy. (P.O. Box Dolphin), Marathon Shores, FL 33050 (tel. 305/289-1121). Hours are 9:30am and 1:30pm and the price is $65; closed Monday and Tuesday.

**Theater of the Sea,** Mile Marker 84.5, Islamorada, FL 33060 (mailing address: P.O. Box 407; tel. 305/664-2431), brings its dolphins out to play with you every day except Friday from 9am to 4pm, but you must make a reservation for the swim. Admission to the show is $10.25 for adults; $5.50 for children 4 to 12. Admission to the dolphin swim program is $50; minimum age is 13.

## 14. Home Is Where the Boat Is

Will the adventurers among us please stand up? Okay, now that we know who you are, we're here to tell you that you don't have to settle for just another lazy vacation on the beach even if you're traveling with someone to whom a lazy vacation on the beach has paradisical overtones.

How to reconcile these basic human differences? Simple. Have them both via a houseboating vacation. What you do is call one of these companies, rent a houseboat, and chug off into the sunset surrounded by your floating motel.

Houseboating has become such a popular getaway with Floridians, who often eschew vacations elsewhere to pursue the pleasures right here in their own backyards, that there are now houseboat-rental operations all over the state. That means that you can explore the historic and tranquilly scenic sights along the north-flowing St. Johns River, the fascinating beachy wonderland of the Keys, the sapphire glitter of the Indian River, the murky, mysterious Everglades, and the musically legendary waters of the Suwannee River.

As you're sailing along on moonlight bay, you'll be in infamous, if not good, company: Pirates once plied all these waters, along with early explorers, steamships carrying wealthy turn-of-the-century vacationers, and fleets of fishing boats still to be found here.

Here's where to get houseboating. Rates vary by season and size of boat, but you can figure on paying $500 to $1,000 for three-day voyages, $1,000 to $1,700 for a week's rental.

### NORTH FLORIDA
**Miller's Suwannee Houseboating,** Suwannee River (P.O. Box 280), Suwannee, FL 32962 (tel. 904/542-7349).

**Holiday Boat Rentals,** at the Holiday Lodge Marina, 6400 W. US 98 (write to 321 Greenwood Dr.), Panama City Beach, FL 32407 (tel. 904/234-0609).

### CENTRAL FLORIDA
**Sanford Boat Rentals,** 4350 Orange Blvd., Sanford, FL 32771 (tel. 407/321-5906).

**Go Vacations Houseboat Vacations,** 2280 Hontoon Rd., Deland, FL 32730 (tel. 904/736-9422).

### SOUTH FLORIDA
**Florida Keys Sailing School,** Mile Marker 85.9, Overseas Hwy. (P.O. Box 1202), Islamorada, FL 33036 (tel. 305/664-4009).

**Flamingo Lodge and Outpost Resort,** Everglades National Park, P.O. Box 428, Flamingo, FL 33030 (tel. 305/253-2241).

## 15. A Bloomin' Good Time

If *you* like a little sunshine now and then, think how a plant feels!

Here in the Sunshine State, where temperatures only vary from warm to warmer, no one has to ask "How does your garden grow?" It grows and grows and grows. Which is why some of the state's oldest and best-known attractions are fabulous gardens where orchids cascade off branches in a waterfall of color and strange tropical plants snap at flies.

Here are our choices for the state's most gorgeous gardens.

### NORTH FLORIDA
**Alfred B. Maclay Gardens.** These gorgeous gardens are Disneyland for azaleas. You'll find them spread across 308 acres, 28 of them devoted to a magnificent collection of azaleas and camellias, at 3450 Thomasville Rd., Tallahassee (tel. 904/487-4556). The Maclay Gardens are open from 9am to 5pm daily year round.

**Ravine Gardens.** Deep in natural ravines grow 1,000,000 varieties of azaleas and other flowering beauties living in a dramatic setting well worth a detour. You'll find the gardens at Twigg Street and Moseley Avenue in Palatka (tel. 904/329-3721).

## CENTRAL FLORIDA

**Cypress Gardens.** Grandaddy of all the gardens, this central Florida attraction has been around for more than half a century and is more interesting now than ever. In fall it's a study in chrysanthemums; in spring, a glory of roses—and there's always a blooming clock that's a real stunner. Daredevil waterskiers and other diversions add to the lure here. They're at Cypress Gardens Boulevard in Winter Haven (tel. 813/324-2111). Admission is $18.50 for adults, $12 for children.

## SOUTH FLORIDA

**Vizcaya Estate and Gardens.** As beautiful for its formal gardens as for its magnificent estate, Vizcaya is the prettiest place in Miami. In spring there's a Renaissance fair and a Shakespeare festival in the gardens. You'll find them at 3251 S. Miami Ave., Miami (tel. 305/579-2813). It's open daily except December 25 from 9:30am to 4:30pm and admission is $8 for adults, $4 for persons 6 to 18.

**Fairchild Tropical Garden.** You can ride a tram through a rain forest, visit some of the world's rarest plants, and sink into a sunken garden. Fairchild's spring plant sale, the Fairchild Ramble, is a big event hereabouts too. These gardens are at 10910 Old Cutler Rd., Miami (tel. 305/667-1651), and are open from 9:30am to 4:30pm. Admission is $4 for adults, free to children under 13.

---

# 16. Good Grief! What's That?

---

It certainly will come as no surprise to Florida habitués that this state is blessed, we guess you could say, with more than its fair share of creativity. Where else would you have Cinderella's Castle just a wand wave away from a giant geodesic golf ball?

Knowing you are holding your breath to see where we are going with this, let us just say that herewith we present some sights you should see, if you're anywhere near them, just because they're big, or strange or impressive or long or tall or short or all of the above.

A Colossus of Rhodes these are not, but we defy you to come up with stranger and more E.T.-please-call-home structures than some of these wonders of the Florida world. Here are our candidates for don't-miss:

**1. Vehicle Assembly Building at Kennedy Space Center.** Although Marylyn has now slept through seven bus tours at the Space Center, she always wakes up in time to gawk with the rest of the bus passengers at this steel spider web in which space shuttles are assembled. Later, she tells everyone she never slept a wink and spouts these figures to prove it: It's 525 feet tall, the world's second-largest building by volume after Seattle's Boeing plant. It consumed 98,000 *tons* of steel and it took 37 months to tuck it under an eight-acre roof and over a concrete floor eight feet thick. Each of 125 ventilators on the roof is bigger than a basketball court. You can't miss it—there's a giant flag painted down the side of the building.

**2. Bok Tower.** You can't miss this one either since it dominates one of Florida's few hills, this one in Lake Wales. Ethereally lovely, this 205-foot Gothic delight in pink and gray marble seems to float in above surrounding gardens and over the lake 295 feet below. When the carillonneur strikes up the 57 bronze bells weighing in at 17 pounds to 12 tons, the world goes misty-magic.

**3. Miami Beach's Art Deco District.** You step into a rainbow here and are served a platter of pastel petits fours. This collection of more than 600 weirdly frothy edifices would put even a jumbo box of Crayolas to shame and will put you into a trance. Porthole windows, eyebrows over doors, neon lights, etched glass, relief sculpture, glass bricks, rounded corners, and up-thrusting, needle-nosed towers that threaten to tear a hole in the sky add to the Disneyish fantasy of this neighborhood. Boundaries are Fifth Street on the south, 22nd Street on the north, Ocean Drive and Alton Road on east and west.

**4. Lightner Museum and the Ponce de Leon Hotel.** Flagler knew panache when he saw it and he saw it on every architectural drawing he approved. Witness these masses of masonry in St. Augustine where the railroad king built them to house his friends and provide a backdrop for his equally impressive parties.

**5. Skyway Bridge.** This 4.1-mile span linking St. Petersburg with Sarasota over Tampa Bay has had its triumphs and tragedies but is more impressive than ever now. Equipped with warning lights for motorists and barriers for off-course ships, it is never likely to experience another shipwreck disaster like the one that sent 35 motorists to their deaths some years ago. It can withstand winds of 290 m.p.h. now, cost $244 million and took five years to reconstruct after the disaster.

**6. Disney World's Cinderella Castle and EPCOT Earth Station.** Fantasy all the way from flying flags to golf ball dimples and very little more needs to be said.

**7. Breakers, Belleview Biltmore and Fontainebleau hotels.** Massive, showy, flashy, historic, posh, and a wonderment of weird facts—Fontainebleau fans in years gone by lifted stationery at such a pace the hotel reckoned each guest could have written 35 letters every day; the Belleview Biltmore is the world's largest occupied frame structure with 2.5 acres of roof; and the Breakers has so much history to tell it has its own in-house historiam.

**8. Henry Plant's Tampa Bay Hotel (now the University of Tampa).** Florida's Taj Mahal, this onion-domed oddity is Disney West. Its halls are so wide guests once rode down them in rickshaws!

## 17. Things You Always Wanted to Know About Florida but Were Afraid to Ask

**Florida's Nickname:** The Sunshine State.

**Florida's State Bird:** Mockingbird—considering the state's nickname, makes sense.

**Florida's Official Freshwater Fish:** Florida largemouth bass—all things considered, no comment.

**Florida's Official Saltwater Fish:** Atlantic sailfish.

**Florida's Official Mammal:** Manatee.

**Florida's Official State Song:** Stephen Foster's *"Old Folks at Home."*

**Florida's State Tree:** Sabal Palm.

**Florida's Official Beverage:** Orange juice.

**Florida's State Gem:** Moonstone.

**Florida's Official Stone:** Agatized coral.

**Florida's State Shell:** Horse conch.

**Soon to be Florida's Official State Pie:** Key lime pie.

**Soon to be Florida's Official State Soil:** Myakka sand—what else?

**Florida's State Flower:** Orange Blossom—surprise, surprise.

**Florida's Motto:** "In God We Trust."

# GETTING TO AND AROUND FLORIDA

## 1. GETTING THERE
## 2. GETTING AROUND

**N**ot long ago we visited a fabled group of islands across the Atlantic, finally setting trembling foot ashore after a long, wet, bouncing journey across an open sea, a crashing arrival at a clump of limestone rock, and a terrifying leap from heaving craft to slippery pitted rock.

It is our very great pleasure to tell you that getting to Florida is fraught with none of those terrors. Getting there, in fact, could hardly be easier—and in these days of rip-roaring airline competition, could hardly be cheaper.

This sunny peninsula is prime time in the travel business, a place so many people want to visit that airlines, trains, buses, and car-rental companies are locked in cut-throat competition for a place in the sun. Fortune thus smiles upon the southbound traveler: Competition translates to low prices and to so many money-saving deals that it hardly pays to stay home.

Finding your way to those deals through the maze of fares, tours, packages, and optional extras, however, is like touring the Everglades without a compass: You may succeed, but you'll spend weeks wandering in the wilderness.

There is an easy way: Visit a travel agent. It won't cost you a cent to pick the willing brains of these walking computers who spend all their time studying tariffs, hotels, and tour packages. A travel agent's only business is travel, and survival in that business depends on knowing how to satisfy travelers on every economic level. Agents' help is free since their income comes solely from commissions paid by travel entities like airlines, car-rental companies, and hotels. You'll still have to make the big decisions on how much time and money you want to spend in the Sunshine State, but with an agent's help the planning can be easy.

## 1. Getting There

To give you an idea how you can escape to the tropics—and how much that escape will cost—here's a look at air, train, and bus fares, and even a glance at what you can expect to spend traveling by automobile. Now here comes the disclaimer: We wouldn't guarantee the cost of toothpaste tomorrow much less air fares a month or two from now, so please don't blame me if the prices you're quoted on transportation costs differ from what you read here. If there's one thing we *can* guarantee it's that those prices will be different—but, glorious day, they may even be *lower!*

## BY AIR

You can slosh through the slush of Manhattan or Düsseldorf, St. Louis or London, some March morning, then enter the miraculous silver bird and emerge a few hours later to dip a very grateful toe into Florida's warm turquoise waters. Such is the glory of the Wright brothers' invention.

Such is the glory of airline competition that airfares may be one of the few things left in the world whose cost actually goes down! In the wake of deregulation, competition has led to so many different kinds of fares—APEX, Super-APEX, chicken-feed, peanut, no-frills, excursion, half fares, discounted fares—that we're fully expecting to see a no-fare fare any day now.

While we're all waiting for that glorious moment, you should be aware that (1) the farther ahead you can plan your trip, the more airfare money you're likely to save; (2) the more unpopular the hour and day you travel (like wee hours and nonweekend or holiday days), the better deal you'll find; and (3) the more you tell airline reservationists or travel agents about your age, your travel companions, your destination, and/or your budget, the better equipped they are to find you a bargain.

Every airline serving the state has at least one (and usually many) package plans that help you save money on rental cars and hotel rooms in the state, and often throw in a number of attraction admissions and discounts as well. Any airline or travel agent will be happy to tell you about these budget-wise Florida travel packages.

Many small airlines have joined the crowded skies in recent years. They remain in business by offering inexpensive flights they hope will make up in volume what they lose in markup. Often you can save a bundle by flying one of these carriers, although you do have to consider the cost of transportation to departure and arrival points like Buffalo, Sarasota, or West Palm Beach.

## BY TRAIN

As train lovers, we couldn't be happier about what's happening to the silver streakers on the Florida run. A few years ago trains were costing about as much as planes and sometimes more, and they weren't getting much good press on the quality of their service.

Those things, happily, are changing now: Amtrak's prices are quite competitive, its service has improved both in quality and quantity, and there are new or refurbished cars on the route. All these things are making it more comfortable than ever to travel by train.

If you have the time to spend, trains offer a lovely, leisurely way to see the beauties of this sunny peninsula.

At the moment two trains travel to Florida along the northeast coastal corridor from New York to Miami and Tampa/St. Petersburg. The *Silver Meteor* is the more direct of the two, leaving New York's Penn Station about 4:30pm and arriving in Miami about 6:30pm the following day. The *Silver Star* leaves the same station at 9:15am and arrives in Miami about 11:15am the following day.

At Jacksonville the trains split, so part of the train can travel to Tampa, part to Miami, so it's wise to note carefully which cars are going where. Major stops on the New York–Miami run include Newark, Trenton, Philadelphia, Wilmington, Baltimore, Washington, Richmond, Raleigh, Columbia, Charleston, Savannah, and Jacksonville. From Winter Haven and Tampa, Amtrak offers what it calls "dedicated" bus service. That translates roughly to bus service from Winter Haven to Walt Disney World and Orlando hotels; and from Tampa to St. Petersburg and Clearwater areas. Very convenient.

To get to the state by train from the Midwest, you ride through Philadelphia or Washington, D.C. To get to Florida by train from the western reaches of the U.S.

you must trek to New Orleans or Atlanta, where you can catch a bus to Jacksonville and reboard the train for the rest of the journey.

In 1987 Amtrak first introduced **All Aboard America fares** that offered bargain prices on unlimited travel within three geographic areas, roughly divided into eastern, central, and western U.S. All Aboard America fares permit travel within a 180-day period with three stops. You can also pay varying additional fares to book sleeping accommodations on the train. All Aboard America fares are $189 for travel within one geographic region, $269 in two, and $309 in three (the whole country).

Since the journey will take 24 hours or more, you might consider a **slumber coach,** which is the railroad's economy sleeper for one or two and includes private toilet facilities. Amtrak's single **roomettes** are a cut above the slumber coach and offer slightly classier and roomier travel. As this guide went to press, Amtrak sleeping accommodations cost $50 to $700 per person, one way, additional, depending on the level of facilities and how far you're traveling in them. Roomettes and bedroom facilities include meals too.

**Food service** on trains has changed from the old cooked-aboard style to something approximating airline food service to the current system somewhere between the two. Many meals are prepackaged and heated on the trains, but some are now cooked aboard—including a steak with all the trimmings! While it may not be the finest of gourmet fare, train chow is easily as good as what you'll eat on an airplane and very reasonably priced in the $8 to $10 range for dinner.

Amtrak has also revived the flagging fortunes of the **Florida Auto Train,** which carries passengers and their cars from Lorton, Virginia (just south of Washington, D.C.), to Sanford, Florida, near Orlando. The Auto Train has domed cars for a good view of passing scenery, and includes a buffet dinner and breakfast in the ticket price. Movies are shown after dinner. Sounds to us like the perfect way to "drive" to Florida. Fares are $70 to $120 for adults, $35 to $60 for children 2 to 12, and $115 to $207 for your car. Special incentive fares discounted as much as 50% are often available when the predominant traffic is southbound, and vice versa. Be sure to ask, particularly if your plans are flexible. Sleeping accommodations—recommended —in either direction are $149 to $285 for a bedroom and $85 to $145 for a roomette.

If you're coming to Florida from Europe, you can buy a **USA Railpass** (available only to overseas visitors) for $299 for 45 days of unlimited train travel. Top travel agents like Thomas Cook in England and Kuoni on the continent, plus some airlines, sell the passes, which are also available at Amtrak offices in gateway cities including Seattle, San Francisco, Los Angeles, Chicago, New York, Miami, Boston, and Washington, D.C.

For information on tour packages and timetables, write to Amtrak Distribution Center, P.O. Box 7700, 1549 W. Glen Lake Ave., Itasca, IL 60143, or call the railroad toll free in any of the continental states (tel. toll free 800/USA-RAIL). You can also get an Amtrak timetable by contacting them at 400 N. Capitol St. NW, Washington, DC 20001.

## BY BUS

If you like the idea of leaving the driving to them, you might consider traveling to Florida by bus. **Greyhound/Trailways** can bring you here from anywhere. What's more, with their Ameripass, you can travel anywhere for a flat fee of about $189 for 7 days, $249 for 15 days, and $349 for 30 days, with extensions available for about $10 a day. Children 5 to 11 pay half fare; one child 4 or under free per adult.

A new Moneysaver program offered by Greyhound offers round-trip fares between any two cities serviced in the U.S. for $68 each way, $118 round trip (leaving and returning Monday through Thursday); tickets must be purchased 30 days in advance and travel must be completed within 30 days after departure. For further information, call toll free 800/237-8211.

Express buses have cut the time you'll spend getting here, but you still should plan at least 36 hours from Chicago to Miami, about 28 hours from New York, 24 hours from Washington, D.C., and about three days from Los Angeles.

Buses offer quite good prices on round-trip excursion tickets.

## BY CAR

Hundreds of thousands of Florida travelers get to the Sunshine State by car, arriving after two or three days of leisurely travel through the deep pine forests of Georgia, the tobacco fields of Virginia, the breathtaking mountain vistas of Appalachia, or the serene coastal highways of the Deep South.

Those blessed with stamina, determination, hampers full of road food, and a compulsion not to miss a minute of sunshine, sometimes alternate drivers to arrive from the Northeast or Midwest in 24 to 26 hours. Good roads and plenty of rapid expressways make that possible. Certainly it is less expensive to travel by car despite increasing fuel prices. According to recent figures compiled by the American Automobile Association, you can figure on paying about $173 a couple a day for food, lodging, plus $8.40 per 100 miles for car expenses.

If you do drive to Florida, you'll be welcomed with plenty of sunny smiles at the state's **Welcome Centers,** on major arterial roads along Florida's borders. Stations are at major state-line crossing points, including Yulee (I-95), Hillyard (US 1 and US 301), Campbellton (US 231), Jennings (I-75), Pensacola (I-10), and in Tallahassee in the new Capitol Building.

---

# 2. Getting Around

---

## BY AIR

Right in there pitching for business in Florida are **American, Eastern, Delta, Pan Am,** and **USAir.**

Here's a look at what airlines were charging for intrastate one-way economy fare travel when this guide went to press: Miami–Jacksonville, $98; Miami–Tampa, $54; Miami–Orlando, $54; Miami–Tallahassee, $95; Orlando–Tallahassee, $104.

## BY TRAIN

**Amtrak** (tel. toll free 800/USA-RAIL) trains serve 22 cities in the state with the *Silver Meteor* traveling from Jacksonville to Tampa/St. Petersburg via Palatka, Deland (for Daytona), Sanford, Winter Park, Orlando, Kissimmee, Lakeland, Tampa, and Clearwater. Meanwhile, the *Silver Star* travels from Jacksonville to Miami with stops at Waldo (for Gainesville), Ocala, Wildwood, Winter Haven, Sebring, West Palm Beach, Delray Beach, Deerfield Beach, Fort Lauderdale, and Hollywood.

Some sample one-way fares are: Jacksonville–St. Petersburg, $43; Jacksonville–Miami, $68; Jacksonville–Orlando, $26; Orlando (Kissimmee)–Miami, $46; Miami–West Palm Beach, $12; and Jacksonville–West Palm Beach, $54. Round-trip bookings save money.

## BY BUS

**Greyhound/Trailways,** and local bus lines are listed in each chapter. They make it comparatively easy to get around, particularly in the larger cities, although you will not find in Florida any mass transportation system approximating those in the large cities of the Midwest, Northeast, or Europe.

One-way intrastate fares run from about $5 to about $60, depending on how far you're traveling.

Greyhound/Trailways offers you a big, free map of its route system in the U.S. too. It's got lots of bus-trip-planning tips and is a great way for the kids to learn geography. You can get one by writing the company at 901 Main St., 25th Fl., Dallas, TX 75202. The company also has several package tours from Miami to Orlando and to various tourist attractions in Orlando; call 214/655-7000 for further details.

## BY CAR

Florida's emphasis on its two shining lights, the Gold Coast and Orlando's Walt Disney World, has left much of the rest of the state in shadow. If there's one single misconception about the Sunshine State, it is distance.

### Distance

You cannot bunk down in Miami Beach, run up to Walt Disney World for the afternoon, and be back in time for the 11pm news. From the southern tip of Florida to the northern border is 500 miles. You'll drive 400 miles to get from Jacksonville on the east coast to Pensacola at the Alabama border, while the rest of this waterfringed peninsula is 100 to 200 miles across.

Florida stretches across two time zones, Eastern in most of the state, Central in much of the Panhandle. On its limestone surface are 10,000 lakes, more than 166 rivers, and dozens of springs, one so deep nobody has yet found the bottom. Florida is huge and it's . . . flat. Up in the Panhandle near the Georgia border you'll find the state's highest point, all of 345 feet above sea level!

Because it's so flat and so large, Florida has become a driver's state. Miami workers think nothing of driving 25 to 50 miles home each night, and on the state's west coast it can take nearly an hour to get from a hotel on the beach to dinner on the mainland.

### Major Routes and Rules

As a state that grew up in the era of the auto, Florida has spent much more money on highways than on mass transportation, so you'll find many fine and rapid roadways throughout the state. Fast as you *could* go on many of them, may we just add that the state's highway patrol seems quite serious about enforcing Florida's 55- and 60-m.p.h. speed limits.

Major expressways in the state include **I-95,** which runs from the Georgia state line to Miami via the east coast; **I-75,** which goes from the Georgia state line to Tampa/St. Petersburg, and soon to Fort Lauderdale; **I-10,** which travels from the Alabama state line to Jacksonville; **I-4,** which links Tampa and Daytona Beach through Orlando; and the **Florida Turnpike,** a toll road varying in price to about $7, which runs from Wildwood in central Florida to south of Miami.

Other major arteries include **US 1,** from Georgia to Key West via the east coast, **Fla. A1A,** from Fernandina Beach north of Jacksonville to Miami; **US 98,** which links Pensacola, on the western border of the state, and Tallahassee; **US 41,** also called the **Tamiami Trail,** from Tampa to Miami; and a similar east-west artery, **Fla. 84,** known as **Alligator Alley** from just west of Fort Lauderdale to Naples.

Road rules are about what you'd find anywhere in the nation with these possible exceptions: You can turn right on red lights in Florida except where posted to the contrary; you are required to stop for school buses no matter which direction you or they are going (unless the bus is on the opposite side of a divided highway that has an unpaved space of more than five feet or a physical barrier); and headlights must be used between sunset and sunrise, low beams in other hours if vision is reduced by rain, smoke, or fog. Seat belts are mandatory.

### Rental Cars

Renting a car is cheaper in Florida than anywhere else in the nation, and every major rental-car company—and hundreds of minor ones—operates here. Alamo, one of the budget leaders, in 1990 charged just $79 a week for a subcompact

Chevrolet. Be sure to check with your airline to see if they offer any special deals with car-rental companies.

Here are the toll-free numbers of some of the rental-car companies: **Alamo** (tel. 800/327-9633); **Avis** (tel. 800/331-1212); **Budget** (tel. 800/527-0700); **Hertz** (tel. 800/654-3131); **National** (tel. 800/328-4567); **Dollar** (tel. 800/421-6868).

You should know, however, that companies offering very low rates often recoup a little with insurance, for which you will pay $9 to $11 a day or more. You can sometimes forgo that insurance if you're willing to leave a cash deposit and/or agree to be responsible for all or some of the damage to the car. It would be wise to check with your insurer or your credit card companies to see if you are already covered in a rental car. If you are, you may be able to save a lot of money by waiving insurance coverage.

In Florida, by the way, most rental-car companies set the minimum rental age at 21 for men, 18 for women, when reserving through an airline or travel agent, 25 years old when booking directly. A few have even set a maximum age.

Some of the accoutrements of car touring that make life on the road easier are maps with city insets (and/or city maps purchased as soon as you roll into town), a Styrofoam cooler with ice and some sustenance (in case your hunger and a good restaurant don't occur simultaneously), a plug-in hot pot (or one of those coils that boil water), and instant tea or coffee for morning gratification. (Don't forget that many Florida hotels and motels offer free Continental breakfasts that are real time- and money-savers when you're traveling.) Finally, zip-lock plastic bags are worth their weight as litter bags, wet laundry holders, and heaven knows how many other uses; foil-wrapped towelettes are great for everything from cleaning windows to cooling a sun-warmed brow.

# GETTING AROUND FLORIDA
## (Driving Times and Distances)

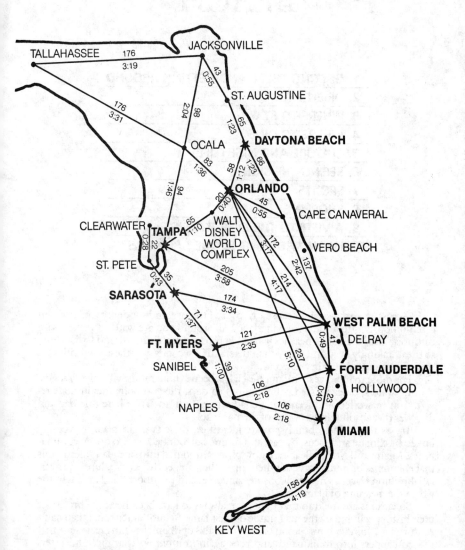

Map courtesy of Alamo Rent A Car

# MIAMI AND MIAMI BEACH

Across an arrow-straight causeway, over a little rise, and suddenly you drop unceremoniously into a watery wonderland. All around you are waters streaked with turquoise and jade, sandy beaches fringed in palms, a pastel fantasyland so dazzling, so breathtakingly beautiful that you understand in seconds why these twin cities are the most famous resort in the world.

For more than 50 years Miami Beach has been synonymous with silvery sands, shining waters, breeze-kissed palms, sun-filled days, the good life, the ultimate resort. You've scoffed and jeered at the adjectives only to arrive here one day and discover that absolutely every one of them is true!

Try as they will to build separate identities, these two cities are irrevocably linked by climate and focus, by past and future. Surrounded by two dozen communities, Miami and Miami Beach are now physically joined into one giant metropolis that encompasses much of the southern tip of the state. Each year they lure here nearly 14 million travelers in search of sun, sand, sea, and the resort life that taught the world the meaning of glamorous.

So famous are the duo that they seem always to have been here, the brevity of their history eclipsed by the magnitude of their fame. Yet not much more than half a century ago, "binder boys" stood on the sidewalks of Miami hawking real estate that turned paupers into millionaires and back again in months. That those hucksters were able to sell a piece of mangrove swamp and mosquito-infested jungle is thanks, they say, to a miracle wrought by one Julia Tuttle, a shrewd and feisty lady who knew how to say plenty without talking much. If the legends are true, Ms. Tuttle very much wanted railroad magnate Henry Flagler to toot his little train to Miami. Flagler didn't think much of the idea and made no move southward until the day a freak freeze created frozen orange juice as far south as Palm Beach. When Julia heard about the citrus damage, she sent Flagler a blooming branch of orange blossoms from toasty Miami. He got the message, extended his railroad and the boom was on.

Ten years earlier a wooden bridge was all that connected Miami to Miami Beach. Avocado farmer John Collins, whose name now graces the main boulevard of Miami Beach, used it to get his crop to market until he dumped that career and sold 1,600 acres of unprofitable avocado farm to Carl Fisher. Fisher, who had made a fortune in automobile headlights and built the Indianapolis Speedway, could afford the gamble. His money and a pump soon dredged sand from the bay bottom and wrought an artificial island called Miami Beach. Miracle that it was, Fisher's efforts were not heard round the world. At one point the despairing millionaire offered to *give* a solid block of oceanfront land to anyone who would build a hotel on it. Alas, there were no takers. When Florida's real estate boom swung into high gear in the 1920s, Fisher was said to have acquired a worth of $100 million. When everything bottomed in 1929, he lost almost as much.

But in the years that followed, Miami Beach, the starlet, got itself discovered. Up went hotel after endless hotel, each more amazing than the last, each trying to grab the traveler's attention with facades that have to be seen to be believed. On one, a giant sea maiden, plaster hair streaming out over the driveway, holds aloft what is either a trident or the biggest rat-tailed comb in town. Collins Avenue's hotel row is a sight like no other in the world, one no Florida traveler should miss. It's a drive that will amaze you and amuse you, and, finally, help you to understand this bizarre and sometimes slightly berserk city that's the epitome of blatant, blaring resortomania, an island at once garish and childishly touching, sophisticated and naïve, the never-say-die grande dame of resorts.

Now once again the starlet has won a major part, this time with cameo appearances in a prize-winning television series that spotlights the region's flamboyant tropical colors, its glitzy, cosmopolitan life-style, and its casual, unflappable approach to most anything that comes its way. That show is of course "Miami Vice," a southern western that has broadcast the scenic allure of southern Florida across the nation and the world.

Much of the credit for the renaissance of Miami Beach goes to that shoot-'em-up show, in fact. Although its portrayal of big-city street violence has blanched many a countenance in these parts, few would deny that the major thrust of regional renaissance went into high gear when the nation tuned in for a look. Little by little the fascinating neighborhoods of Miami Beach's long-neglected South Beach are coming to life again, painted and primped into a pastel wonderland.

Meanwhile, over on the other side of the causeway, miles from the island of Miami Beach, an already-big city is bursting at the seams and looking better than ever. Roll over one of the causeways from the beach to downtown Miami some night and you'll be treated to a wonderland of lights that have sizzled Miami's ever-rising skyline into a fantasyland of twinkle.

Ice-blue and red-hot neon tubes streak into the sky racing up the sides of artfully lighted architecture on Brickell Avenue. As the city's new elevated MetroRail skyway transport zips through the city, it passes over a neon rainbow strung high over the Miami River. A bank's skyscraping curves are awash in colored light and atop Museum Tower flies a funky roofline.

This downtown fandango of belighted oneupsmanship has zapped the city with a whimsical carousel of color that glows by night and by day. One stand-out condominium on posh Brickell Avenue sports a hole right through its middle, and in it is a curving staircase to nowhere that shelters a high-in-the-sky palm tree, swaying umpteen floors up. To keep up with the colorful Joneses, a neighboring high-rise turned itself into a vertical rainbow by painting each floor, every balcony, indeed every visible surface, a different color. Add to that Miami's new bayfront development, a study in peach pastels adorned with glittering lights mirrored by the deep-blue waters of the bay, yet another touch of fun and funk to a city that is on the grow again.

In five years here, marble-clad hotels have risen along the bay, cruise ships have flocked into the city's handsome port, and graceful old neighborhoods have come back to life, renewed by the unquenchable spirit that lives here.

Miami is now an undisputed international banking center and home to so many nationalities that most of the city's population can manage an occasional *gracias, merci, danke, grazie,* or the equivalent in Chinese, Vietnamese, Indian, Creole . . . *sayonara.*

Here in these twin metropolises you can revel in posh and plush hotels with all the facilities of a small city. Or you can sneak off to shady, secluded, hideaway suburbs like Coral Gables, Key Biscayne, and Coconut Grove. You can drink thick black coffee amid the chatter of Little Havana or explore secret beaches and chic neighborhoods. You can see the way we were on Miami Beach, then cross a causeway to Miami to get a look at Today, capital T.

You can be entertained in glitzy showrooms by bespangled showgirls and dine in some of the nation's best restaurants. You can dance until you drop in flashing, smashing ear-splitting blitz havens or amble along a lazy lagoon where only the silence is loud.

You can chortle at the antics of parrots or porpoises, visit a zoo without cages, see a Broadway musical, or make your own music in a resort that's making history even as you watch.

# 1. Getting There and Getting Around

## GETTING THERE

More than 80 airlines fly into **Miami International Airport,** so you shouldn't have any trouble getting here. Domestic carriers include American, Continental, Delta, Eastern, Midway, Northwest, Pan Am, TWA, USAir, and United. Air Canada brings thousands of Canadians south, Lufthansa comes in from Germany, Air France from Paris, KLM and Martinair Holland from Amsterdam, and British Airways flies directly here from the British Isles. British Airways goes one better than that in fact: The airline that claims to fly to more places than any other airline in the world now flies its needle-nosed supersonic Concorde here to Miami from London via a stop in Washington, D.C., champagne and caviar all the way.

On the other end of the spectrum, Virgin Atlantic Airlines flies budgeteers and business travelers here from London. Every South and Latin American nation and every Caribbean country with a flag carrier flies into the city, making this the busiest airport in the state and one of the biggest in the nation. The few European flag carriers that do not fly directly here have connections from other cities.

You'll land in the western section of the city at Lejeune Road and NW 36th Street. Miami's International Airport has in recent years become a thoroughly modern MIA. International travelers zip out to awaiting aircraft on a whooshing monorail. Concourses are lined with smart and fascinating boutiques featuring an array of products as international as the passengers who arrive here. So sophisticated has this airport become, in fact, that you can do your banking here, exchange currency, buy Native American—or Asian Indian—creations, seek information in several languages (most prominent of which is Spanish), even play electronic games!

Miami's sleek airport now also features a $24-million Skyride, an elevated moving sidewalk to transport you from terminal to parking areas. Planned expansion of that system will include moving sidewalks that skim you all around this huge airport.

If you want to do some shopping while you wait for a plane, stow your gear in a locker and go. Lockers are located near exit doors and baggage-storage facilities that will take care of your treasures for days are located at Concourse B on the upper level, Concourse F on the lower level. Lockers are available for 24 hours; storage is several dollars a day depending on how much you're storing.

If you need help with anything ranging from directions to a hotel room, a multilingual staff is on duty in person from 7am to 11pm. At other hours you can still get your questions answered: A telephone at the Information Desk (tel. 871-7515) is manned around the clock. In peak season—winter, of course—the Information Desk staff has an up-to-date list of hotel vacancies to help you find a room. At any time of year the staff can supply you with a list of area hotels arranged by price. The desk is on the second level of the airport at Concourse E. Paging is also done from this desk.

The airport has a raft of fast-food eateries and a quite elegant dining room, Top of the Port Restaurant (tel. 526-6473), that's a popular—and viewful—spot. Prices are on the high side of moderate, but this restaurant is definitely the most tranquil spot in the airport.

Dade County's Metropolitan Transit Authority has four **bus** routes that pass through the airport. Contact 638-6700 for details.

Super Shuttle (tel. 871-2000) will take you to downtown and Miami Beach hotels for about $8 to $12, and also go to cities along the Gold Coast as far north as Fort Lauderdale. The fare is about $13 to $25 per person to Fort Lauderdale.

Like many big cities, Miami got many complaints about rude cabbies who loathed the idea of losing their place in the airport taxi line-up to take some unsuspecting arrival on a short hop to local airport-area hotels. Miami solved that problem by creating a fleet of "blue cabs" (they're all painted a bright blue) officially known as **Airport Area Taxi Service.** So if you're staying in a hotel near the airport, save yourself a lot of grief by looking for the blue cabs. Rates are the same.

Be warned, too, that some less-than-scrupulous folks who happen to own big black limousines often pull up at arrival gates and offer to drive you to hotels. If you've got a big family or are traveling with several other people, you may be able to strike a good deal. Otherwise, forget it and stick with the taxis and the shuttle service, which uses medium-size white vans.

If you're renting a car, don't forget that rental-car companies provide free transportation to their airport-area rental offices.

And remember that many large hotels near the airport and even downtown may provide free transportation.

Miami's airport, by the way, is just eight miles from downtown, about $12 to $15 by **cab.**

**Amtrak trains** roll in here too, twice a day, making their most southerly stop at 8303 NW 37th Ave. (tel. toll free 800/872-7245, or 835-1200).

**Greyhound/Trailways** buses come from all over the nation and the state to terminals in the Miami area. Terminals are located at 99 NE 4th St. (tel. 374-7222) and 4111 NW 27th St. (tel. 871-1810), at 2300 Salzedo St. in Coral Gables (tel. 443-1664), at 16250 Biscayne Blvd., North Miami Beach (tel. 945-0801), and there is a station located in Miami Beach at 7101 Harding (tel. 538-0381), and one at 99 NE 4th St. (tel. 374-7222).

## GETTING AROUND

Dozens of **rental-car companies** operate in the city at rates that change frequently but average about $80 to $100 a week. **Alamo,** at 3325 NW 22nd St. (tel. 633-4132), is a strong budget contender and can always be counted on for competitive rates. All except the smallest local companies (and even many of those) will pick you up at the airport, take you to your car, then deliver you when you leave town, all at no charge. **Avis,** 255 NE 1st St. (tel. 377-2531), **Hertz,** 666 Biscayne Blvd. (tel. 377-4601), and **National** (tel. 526-5200) all have in-airport rental desks at Miami International.

**Yellow Cab,** 3775 NW 36th St. (tel. 444-4444), operates many, many taxis in town. That cab company, and all others, charge $1.10 at the drop, $1.20 a mile. **Metro Taxi** (tel. 888-8888) is another large city cab company.

**MetroBus** is operated by the Metropolitan Dade County Transit Authority, 3300 NW 32nd St. (tel. 638-6700), and can take you anywhere in the county for $1. Workers will be happy to give you information on routes. The service operates from about dawn to dusk.

Miami's proudest new acquisition is its sleek **MetroRail,** a whizzing above-ground rapid-transit system that at the moment transports passengers between downtown Miami and South Miami. Soon the line will extend north to Hialeah and west to Miami International Airport. Rides are $1. You can find out the exact schedule for the train by calling 638-6700.

From south to north, the stations by name and address are: Dadeland South (9150 Dadeland Blvd.), Dadeland North (8300 S. Dixie Hwy.), South Miami (5949 Sunset Dr. at SW 7th Street), University (5500 Ponce de Leon Blvd.), Douglas Road (3100 SW 37th Ave. at Douglas Road), Coconut Grove (2780 SW 27th Ave.), Vizcaya (3201 SW First Ave.), Brickell (101 SW First Ave.), Government Center (101 NW 1st St.), Overtown (100 NW 6th St.), Culmer (701 NW 11th St.), Civic Center (1501 NW 12th Ave.), Santa Clara (2050 NW 12th Ave.), Allapattah (3501 NW 12th Ave.), Earlington Heights (2100 NW 41st St.), Brownsville (5200 NW 27th Ave.), Martin Luther King, Jr. (6205 NW 27th Ave.), Northside (3150 NW 79th St.), Hialeah (115 E. 21st St.), and Okeechobee (205 W. Okeechobee Rd.).

MetroRail now conveniently connects to **MetroMover,** an elevated monorail that circles 1.9 miles of downtown Miami. Stops are at the Metro-Dade Cultural Center at 101 Flagler St., the Government Center at NW 1st Street and NW First Avenue, Fort Dallas Park at NE 3rd Street and Miami Avenue, the World Trade Center at SE 3rd Street between SE First Avenue and SE Second Avenue, Bayfront Park on NE 1st Street, Edcom on NE First Avenue and NE 5th Street, and at State Plaza at NW First Avenue and NW 5th St.

MetroMover, like MetroRail, operates from about 6am to midnight, although hours are occasionally changed. Best to give them a call if you're hoping to use the system in the wee hours.

A MetroMover car arrives at any given stop every 90 seconds during rush hours, every 2½ minutes in less busy times, and every 10 minutes at its slowest. A circle ride takes 10 minutes. MetroMover fare is 25¢, but the ride is free if you're connecting to the MetroMover from MetroRail. If you pay your quarter on MetroMover and then board MetroRail, the MetroRail fare is 75¢ instead of the usual $1.

If you can work your life into *its* schedule, a new commuter train can get you from Miami to Palm Beach with intermediate stops in Fort Lauderdale, Hollywood, and a number of other smaller municipalities. Serving three counties—Palm Beach, Broward, and Dade—the 67-mile **Tri-Rail** train (305 S. Andrews Ave., #200, Fort Lauderdale) runs from about 5 to 8am and from 3:30 to 7:30pm Monday through Friday with a trip at noon, same hours southbound. Fares are $3 one way. This is quite a new service and is changing rapidly so it would be wise to check with them for exact schedules (tel. 800/874-7245 in Florida). In Miami the Tri-Rail service links with MetroRail at the 79th Street station in Hialeah.

**Old Town Trolley,** 650 NW 8th St., Bayside Marketplace Information Booth in downtown Miami (tel. 374-8687), operates open-air trolley cars around the downtown area. Fares are $1 for trips to Port of Miami, Omni International shopping mall, and many downtown hotels and landmarks. Trips begin 9:15am to 5:15pm daily.

We wouldn't recommend **bicycles** for much downtown travel, but if you're staying in the suburbs or over on Miami Beach, and keep a sharp eye out for gawking drivers, you can enjoy a bicycle here. That's particularly true in Coral Gables and Coconut Grove, where you'll find bicycle trails. The Greater Miami Convention and Visitor's Bureau, 4770 Biscayne Blvd., Penthouse G, (tel. 305/539-3000) can supply you with a brochure, *Miami on Two Wheels,* which maps out some pretty trips around town. On Miami Beach, try the **Miami Beach Bicycle Center,** 923 W. 39th St. (tel. 531-4161), and in Coconut Grove, **Dade Cycle Shops,** 3216 Grand Ave. (tel. 443-6075). Key Biscayne is a bicyclist's heaven—**Key Biscayne Bicycle Rentals** at 200 Crandon Blvd. (tel. 361-5555) can supply you with two wheels. Rates are $8 to $12 a day.

---

# 2. Orientation

---

Despite their best efforts to build separate identities, Miami and Miami Beach are to most people the same place, with surrounding communities tossed casually into the amalgam. Boundary lines in this huge metropolis have long been fuzzed by border-to-border expansion, but part of the fun of visiting the area is discovering these cities within cities. Here's a look at some of them.

## MIAMI BEACH

In the 1930s the southern tip of the beach, now known as **South Beach,** *was* Miami Beach. With the current revival of interest in the 1930s and in art deco, this end of the beach is getting more attention than ever. It is now listed on the National Register of Historic Places for its more than 100 unique art deco buildings. Two amazing renovations here, the Victor and Cardozo hotels, are so beautifully done that you'll step right into a time machine and back to the days of F. Scott Fitzgerald.

Speaking of the old, that's something you see a lot of on South Beach in winter, for this is the gathering place of elderly visitors who have been coming for decades to the same room in the same hotel to sit in the same porch chair and talk to the same friends. It's a sociological study that's excited many a budding anthropologist and is indeed something to see: mah-jongg on the sand, day-long gossips, and impromptu vaudeville performances by talent that is rusty but lusty.

In the middle of the beach is Hotel Row, and in the middle of that is the only hotel in the world that's always been a tourist attraction, the fabled Fontainebleau. Thousands stream, gawking, through this hotel each year, and enough hotel stationery disappears for each guest to write 35 letters!

A little farther north are the handsome cities of **Surfside** and **Bal Harbour,** the latter the site of posh Bal Harbour Shops where at Gucci's enclave a dignified gentleman at the door ushers you into hushed recesses.

These days Miami Beach is crowing over its "new" beach, a $65-million strip of silica widened by a dredging operation that pumped enough offshore sand onto the beach to create a 300-foot-wide strip. There's a delightful mile-long beach boardwalk too.

## MIAMI

**Coral Gables,** just south of Miami, was the creation of a dreamer named George Merrick, who in the early 1900s built a charming city of stone archways, an imposing city hall, and a swimming pool that's often called one of the world's most beautiful swimming holes. The Biltmore Hotel, a city landmark and a lovely old-world creation with frescoed ceilings, is open again. In Coral Gables is the University of Miami's 260-acre campus and 20,000 students.

**Coconut Grove** is past and present linked. In its shady streets "old" Miami lives on, attracting artists, crafts workers, wealthy escapists, international boutiques. Bohemians and billionaires mix with ease here, and once a year at the February Art Festival all the rest of the city drops in to stir the batter. Antique Coconut Grove Theater presents outstanding plays and Dinner Key Marina is stem to stern in sailing craft. Coconut Grove has the oldest streets in the county and more 19th-century buildings than any other area of South Florida.

**Key Biscayne** is "the beach" to much of Miami, so on weekends a nightmarish line of traffic forms at the causeway entrance to the key. Once past the $1 tollbooth, you'll discover why everyone streams here for sunshine. Beautiful strips of sand line both sides of the causeway and shallow waters lap at the shore. On the key, jungly Crandon Park offers more than two miles of sand.

In downtown Miami on SW 8th Street you'll find Miami's **Little Havana,** an area revitalized by Castro-fleeing Cubans in the early 1960s. Today it's a lilting, laughing mélange of Latin nightclubs, inexpensive restaurants, strolling *tunas* singers, a touch of Old Spain.

Downtown along Biscayne Boulevard is Bayfront Park, 62 acres of tropical blooms, pools, shady walkways, with a bandshell where open-air concerts are performed free and the Torch of Friendship burns, honoring Miami's ties with Latin American neighbors. A few blocks north, massive cruise ships line up at **Dodge Island** like fat ducks as they drop off and pick up passengers headed for Caribbean isles and ports around the globe. It's now the busiest cruise port in the world, with more than a million passengers each year.

## A LITTLE GEOGRAPHY

Getting around these cities can be an exasperating business if you try to travel during the rush hours (from 7 to 9am and from 4 to 6pm) and if you don't buy a map and get your bearings. Here's a cartographer's look at what you'll find here.

Miami is divided into quadrants by **Flagler Street** and **Miami Avenue.** Courts, avenues, and places run north-south, streets and terraces go east-west, with numbers starting downtown and going up in outlying areas. Make careful note of the NW, SW, etc, in adresses or you're lost. **Biscayne Boulevard** is also US 1, and runs north-south through downtown.

On Miami Beach, **Collins Avenue** is the number one thoroughfare, running north-south all the way up the seven-mile island. East-west streets are numbered from one on the south. Six **causeways** link Miami and Miami Beach. From south to north they are at 5th Street (MacArthur Causeway); just north of 17th Street at Dade Boulevard (Venetian Causeway), connecting to downtown Miami; at 41st Street (Julia Tuttle Causeway), connecting to the airport; at 71st Street (North Bay Causeway); at 96th Street (Broad Causeway), for Miami addresses above 79th Street; and at 163rd Street on Miami Beach connecting to 167th Street on the mainland (163rd Street or Sunny Isles Causeway).

**I-95** is the quick route north from Miami, and is also the closest expressway to downtown Miami and the beaches. Farther west, the **Palmetto Expressway** and the **Florida Turnpike** both head north and south.

Traffic is hideous at rush hours and parking is a real problem. Garages and parking lots downtown and on Miami Beach will save your nerves even if they do cost a few dollars.

To get to the **suburbs** from downtown Miami, first take US 1 south. Then turn left at Rickenbacker Causeway for Key Biscayne. At the next traffic light on US 1 (South Bayshore Drive), bear left for Coconut Grove. Turn right off US 1 at Coral Way (SW 22nd Avenue) to get to Coral Gables.

## USEFUL INFORMATION

For **police or medical emergency,** call 911 anywhere in the county . . . For **doctor or dental referrals,** call the Dade County Medical or American Dental Association (tel. 324-8717 for a doctor, 944-5668 for a dentist) . . . For quick cleaning, call **Bernie's Crest Cleaners** (tel. 238-7532) . . . **Eckerd Drugs** at 1825 NE Miami Gardens Dr. (tel. 932-5740) and several other locations can fill prescriptions 24 hours a day . . . **Circle K** grocery stores are all over the county and open around the clock . . . Weather info at 661-5065.

## TOURIST INFORMATION

The **Greater Miami Visitor's and Convention Bureau,** 4770 Biscayne Blvd., Penthouse G, Miami, FL 33137 (tel. 305/539-3000), has lots of brochures and information on current and future events, and employees who keep up with *every* detail . . . The **Miami Beach Chamber of Commerce,** 1920 Meridian Ave., Miami Beach, FL 33139 (tel. 305/672-1270), will be happy to help you too . . . The **Southern Florida Resort Hotel Association,** 6701 Collins Ave., Miami Beach, FL 33139 (tel. 305/861-3567, or toll free 800/531-3553), will ask its members to send you hotel information. The friendly folks at the **Coral Gables Chamber of Commerce** will see that you get a self-guided tour map so you can investigate this lovely city. They're at 50 Aragon Ave., Coral Gables, FL 33134 (tel. 305/446-1657) . . . The **Coconut Grove Chamber of Commerce** has all the answers about its arty community and will help you if you'll stop by 2820 McFarlane Rd., Coconut Grove, FL 33133 or call them at 305/444-7270. . . . The same applies to the **Key Biscayne Chamber of Commerce,** at 95 W. McIntire St., Key Biscayne, FL 33149 (tel. 305/361-5207), and the **Monroe County (Florida Keys) Tourist Development Council,** 416 Fleming St., Key West, FL 33040 (tel. 800/648-5510).

---

# 3. Where to Stay

---

How much you pay for a hotel room hereabouts depends on where it is, when it is, and how much ocean you can see from the window.

On Miami Beach, the luxury strip known as Hotel Row extends from Lincoln Road to Surfside and Bal Harbour, where it gives way to more moderately priced accommodations on Motel Row. On South Beach—with two notable exceptions—hotels are old and look it, frequently offering very basic accommodations that are little more than roof and bed. Prices are lower, but we don't think they're low enough to compensate.

*When* you go can make as much as a 50% difference in the bottom line of your motel bill. Traditionally, rates drop just after Easter and stay very low until about Thanksgiving, although these days international summer travelers are blurring those traditional seasonal dips a bit. On the other side of the coin, you can now find more services and entertainment in summer as the area reaches for year-round-destination status.

In downtown Miami prices are high all the time (as they are in most cities), but you'll find some very luxurious hotels for your money.

Miami and Miami Beach have been resorts for a long, long time, so you can be sure all but the very smallest motels have color televisions, phones, and swimming pool (although sometimes they're saltwater), so except where those things are missing we haven't mentioned what most travelers take for granted these days. We've also divided hotels first by location and then in descending order by price.

## BED-AND-BREAKFAST

An interesting way to see it like a native in Miami is via the B&B home-away-from-home. Here the **Bed & Breakfast Accommodations** is headed by Marcella Schaible, P.O. Box 262, South Miami, FL 33243 (tel. 305/661-3270).

## HOTELS IN MIAMI BEACH

Hotels on the beach are naturally more expensive, but when they're beautiful, they're *very* beautiful. Prices change rapidly and seasonally here too, so anticipate slightly higher figures to give your budget some breathing space. You'll always save money by forgoing oceanfront or ocean-view rooms, which can be 50% higher than less desirable views.

## The Luxury Leaders

The flagship, landmark, and number one pride and joy of Miami Beach is the **Fontainebleau Hilton Resort and Spa,** 4441 Collins Ave., Miami Beach, FL 33140 (tel. 305/538-2000, or toll free 800/HILTONS, in Florida 800/548-8886), a 14-story towering mass of concrete that curves its elegant way around nearly half a mile of oceanfront. So famous was this strip of real estate that until Hilton moved in a few years back, the hotel felt it unnecessary to put its name out front—if you didn't know this was the Fontainebleau you didn't deserve to know!

Owner Stephen Muss put $60 million into a massive renovation of the Fontainebleau Hilton's fading elegance and began with a quite incredible rock grotto swimming pool. In the middle of this 140-by-140-foot creation, water cascades down a five-story half-acre artificial mountain containing a Lagoon Saloon. Around the pool are three whirlpools, a beachfront bar, and masses of tropical foliage that creates a jungly waterside hideaway between hotel and beach. On the walkway to the pool is an open-air café under the trees, where a calypso band plays. Inside the sweeping lobby, a tall ficus tree reaches up from the center of a huge round bar to an overhead skylight. Nothing is small here. You can get lost in the lobby. You will certainly get scrambled in the maze of corridors and shops.

When Hilton renovated "the Font," all the furniture was refinished and double and king-size beds were built especially for the hotel. Color schemes differ—peach, lime green, sky blue, golden yellow—so at least you have a chance of finding the right room! All of them have big closets and separate dressing rooms, loads and loads of room to walk around in, and balconies if you want one.

On 16 acres here you'll find 1,206 rooms, including 60 suites, two outdoor pools, 30 cabañas, windsurfing and other water sports, a two-level tennis complex, shuttle service to a nearby golf course, 11 different spots for dining and drinking, including the sophisticated Poodle Lounge and Steak House with black walls, shining crystal, mirrors, art deco decor, and an eye-popping black lounge with dramatic lighting focusing on pale-pink female mannequins surrounded by huge transparent bubbles. The Dining Galleries are a cluster of restaurants filled with antiques and art treasures, and feature four different dazzlingly contemporary dining spots. The service is wonderful.

To read the figures on numbers of employees here (144 maids, 275 food workers) or the quantities consumed (4,000 fresh oranges squeezed every day) is to gain just the slightest idea how huge, how slick this great hotel is. One owner humbly termed it the "eighth wonder of the world."

You can now get sleek at the hotel's fancy spa, which offers such pampering as salt-glow loofah, sauna, steam and whirlpool, individual mineral baths, a solarium, herbal wraps, an indoor/outdoor massage center, and a staff of fitness counselors prepared to tell you, by computer, just what it will take to get this blob back in shape. All kinds of equipment from rowing machines to treadmills and bicycles help you get it going. You can escape from them in an outdoor pool where aqua-aerobic classes will get you right back in the stretch of things.

Finally, the Adrien Arpel Skin Care Center will get your skin in shape to match your body with treatments and makeup. There's a shop to get outfitted for this torture and a natural-foods restaurant so you don't slip back into those old pound-of-pasta ways.

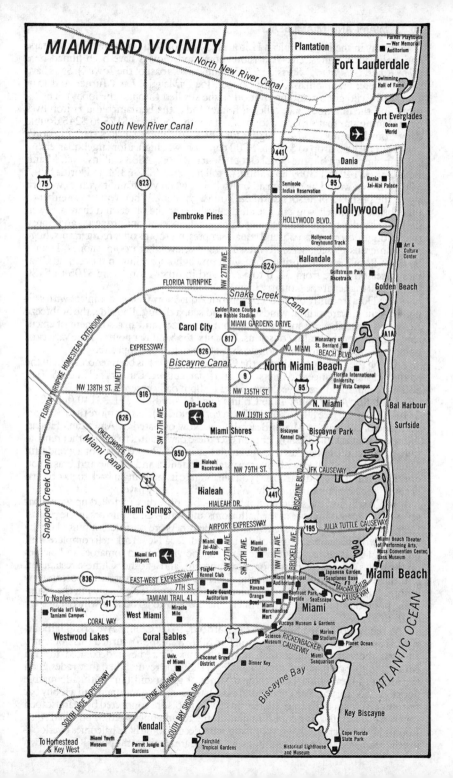

To stay in the Fontainebleau Hilton is to hobnob with moviemakers and stars, national leaders, kings, etc. Television shows and movies have been filmed here *(Tony Rome, Goldfinger,* "Surfside 6," Ed Sullivan's "Toast of the Town"). Stars have stopped here: Frank Sinatra, Gary Cooper, Joe DiMaggio, Lana Turner, and Joan Crawford (who got a standing ovation as she strolled through the lobby). The famous and the infamous have called it home. Today the Fontainebleau Hilton lives on, a shining star that's found a fountain of youth. You'll pay $175 to $245 double daily from December to May, higher for suites. In summer, prices certainly don't crash, but they do drop to $135 to $200 daily for two, higher for larger quarters.

Up the street a bit, the **Doral Ocean Beach Resort,** 4833 Collins Ave., Miami Beach, FL 33140 (tel. 305/532-3600, or toll free 800/327-6334, in Florida 800/FORA-TAN), would be enough all by itself, but when you team it with its western sister, the posh **Doral Resort and Spa,** you've got it all. When you stay at either of these beautiful hotels you can use all the facilities at the other, and there are even daytime shuttles to get you back and forth. At the oceanfront property, an impressive baroque decor greets you, and equally impressive rooms offer refrigerators, huge and numerous closets, separate dressing rooms, even bathroom phones. Doral's Starlight Roof is an enchanting place, with tiny lights sparkling in the ceiling. Doubles in season range from $170 to $270, and in other months are $105 to $180 (about $50 higher at the Country Club).

The Doral recently opened a beachfront AquaSport Center complete with sailing, jet-skiing, waterskiing, windsurfing, and scuba diving. Poolside, the Seabreeze Restaurant specializes in stir-fry treats, gourmet pizzas, and an assortment of epicurean delights for the health-conscious. Upstairs, the Sand Bar pours a wide variety of potables from fruit juices and nonalcoholic beer to just the opposite.

Up on the 18th floor, Alfredo the Original of Rome has been redecorated in the spirit of casual elegance and offers Roman Italian cuisine. Dinners fall in the $20 to $30 price range and are served from 6 to 11:30pm daily except Monday.

**Eden Roc Americana,** 4525 Collins Ave., Miami Beach, FL 33140 (tel. 305/531-0000, or toll free 800/327-8337, except in Florida), has for more than 30 years been one of the stars of Miami Beach hotels. Now operated by Americana Hotels, this show spot is looking showier than ever these days thanks to yet another renovation, a project the hotel likes to call a rehabilitation. "When you've got a wonderful hotel like this one filled with huge crystal chandeliers and marble and brass, you don't just tear it out and start over, you rehabilitate it and bring it back to its original beauty," the hotel reports proudly. Well, rehabilitate they have.

You'll still find the same spacious rooms, but now they're dolled up with what seems to be acres of marble in the bathrooms and walls-full of mirrors in the rooms. Deep jewel tones appear in some rooms while others are outfitted in muted earthy shades. Two fascinating fixtures of the hotel: Sadie's, a New York deli complete with bunches of sausages hanging on the walls, big bowls of green tomatoes and pickles on the tables, and Israeli music for entertainment, and a kosher Chinese restaurant. Still there but prettier than ever is the resort's Porch Restaurant and its ocean-view lounge, which also offers you an underwater look at what's going on in the swimming pool. Summer rates at the Americana are $90 to $150 and winter rates are $110 to $175.

A renovation at the **Sheraton Bal Harbour,** 9701 Collins Ave., Bal Harbour, FL 33154 (tel. 305/865-7511, or toll free 800/325-3535), turned this hotel into an even showier showplace than it already was. First they redecorated the Bal Masque supper club, famed for its Las Vegas showgirl revues; then they redesigned the lobby to create Caribbean color schemes of green and blue with jade marble floors. A two-story atrium enclosed in glass has a cascading fountain and a lobby bar features exotic seashells encased in resins. Twin pools are connected by a landscaped waterway, and "20's" is a coral-and-gray dining room punctuated by polished steel. Rooms here are very large with contemporary decor. Some have balconies overlooking the sea, some are penthouse suites, and some are lanais by the pool. Rates for two are $205 to $285 in peak season, $140 to $225 in other months (oceanfront terrace suites and lanais are higher). Children under 18 are free in their parents' room.

**Castle Resort,** 5445 Collins Ave., Miami Beach, FL 33140 (tel. 305/865-1500, or toll free 800/327-0535), used to be a Playboy hotel and still has that plush dramatic look you find at such operations: sweeps of thick carpets, vivid colors, attractive paintings, contemporary decor, even a black-glass facade that once sported the rabbit. Now it's a newly refurbished property with entertainment, a big swimming pool and wading pool, sauna, exercise rooms and solarium, a lounge with dance music, a coffee shop, and a handsome dining room. Nicest of all is a hardworking staff that really seems to go out of its way to make you happy. Two people pay $175 to $195 in winter, $90 to $125 in other seasons.

The **Deauville Hotel** lobby is a knockout and the rest of this stunning 550-room hotel matches. Right on the ocean at 6701 Collins Ave., Miami Beach, FL 33141 (tel. 305/865-8511, or toll free 800/327-6656), the Deauville glitters with chandeliers and glows with contemporary furniture scattered about a massive lobby where the sun gleams through two-story windows. Upstairs in your room you'll find oversize beds, walk-in closets, mirrored walls, and lovely ocean views through a wall of glass. Outside is all that beach, plus three tennis courts, a glamorous saltwater swimming pool surrounded by lounge chairs for sunning, a whirlpool, sauna, and an exercise room. Inside are a dramatic black lounge with a piano bar, a top nightclub, and an elegant candlelit dining room where chefs present outstanding cuisine amid glittering crystal chandeliers, silver, and fresh flowers. From mid-December to May, two people pay $99 to $139, $66 to $99 in other months.

**Harbour House,** 102nd Street at the ocean, 10275 Collins Ave., Miami Beach, FL 33154 (tel. 305/864-2251), has thought of everything: Not only does every one of the attractive rooms have a kitchen, but there's even a gourmet grocery in the building. You're greeted by an elegant marble lobby and treated to a formal dining room, an inviting lounge, tennis, a putting green, a full mile of beach, a solarium, and two swimming pools. The spacious rooms have pretty touches like Victorian wicker chairs, bright floral prints, a couch for lazy-day reclining, and dazzling views of the ocean from private balconies. Outside, the beautifully landscaped grounds are a tranquil spot to stroll past bubbling fountains and swaying palms. Harbour House rises 14 stories into the sky, and goes on and on with extras: art galleries and classes, beauty and barber shops, boutiques, even a doctor and dentist in the building. A very big and lovely spot, in summer Harbour House charges $65 to $95, depending on the view, and $100 to $165 in winter.

There's an air of subdued elegance at the **Sea View Hotel,** 9909 Collins Ave., Bal Harbour, FL 33154 (tel. 305/866-4441, or toll free 800/447-1010), where you'll find tasteful furnishings in jewel-like colors. The renovated lobby, terrace room, and a cocktail lounge lend a European elegance. Rooms here are large, with lots of closet space and attractive light wood furniture, arched headboards, and contemporary touches. Refrigerators are available if you ask. Outside this posh and pleasant address is a full mile of private sand, a huge pool, cabañas, shuffleboard courts, a solarium. They're happy to point out that servants' and chauffeurs' quarters are also available. Poolside, there's a snack counter and bar, and for other meals there's a formal Gatti's Italian dining room with occasional dinner dances and a very handsome paneled lounge for sundown celebrating. For a quiet and elegant stay here you'll pay $104 to $173 from mid-December to mid-April, $55 to $85 in other months.

## First-Class Hotels

A clever designer at **Palms on the Ocean,** 9449 Collins Ave., Surfside, FL 33154 (tel. 305/865-3551, or toll free 800/327-6644), made a couch out of a bed and created a room divider at the same time, so rooms here are now larger than ever. A renovation program equipped rooms with new carpets offset by bedspreads in bright contemporary tones. A new, airy look has swept through this good-looking hotel, which now also sports lush new landscaping and marble floors that make it one of the spiffiest properties along this section of the beach. Winter rates, from December through April, are $85 to $105 double. In other months, rates drop to $60 to $75 for two, higher for suites.

We could sit forever on a balcony at the **Thunderbird,** 18401 Collins Ave., Miami Beach, FL 33160 (tel. 305/931-7700, or toll free 800/327-2044), and when you see what a tranquil spot this is, you may do likewise. You'll get into the tropical ambience when you step into the lobby where palms grow up to the ceiling in a lush garden. You'll really ease into things when you see big bright rooms with two double beds (or a king-size bed) in a trim contemporary setting with white furniture. You'll be immersed when you see the view over the pool and ocean from your balcony or terrace. The Thunderbird is home to Christine Lee's Gaslight Restaurant, one of the city's best-loved Chinese restaurants. If you're a tennis player, you can lob free here, and if you'd like to learn to waterski, they'll give you a lesson free. Windsurfing's a new sport here too. In winter season, two people pay $77 to $110, and in summer, $48 to $68, with higher prices for an oceanfront or poolside lanai. Ninety of the 177 units have kitchens; add $10 to the rates.

**Beacharbour Resort,** 18925 Collins Avenue, Sunny Isles, FL 33160 (tel. 305/931-8900, or toll free 800/327-2042, except in Florida), is a slick harbor for visitors to drop anchor. Big, big picture windows overlook manicured grounds; carpeted terraces view sweeping vistas of white sands and blue Atlantic. You can watch the waves from the hotel's dining room too, or sneak off to a patio bar to listen to musical entertainment. Lots of entertainment here from a nifty revue to a piano lounge and poolside warblers. In-room movies are a special feature, and all rooms have refrigerators to store your afternoon snacks. There's a private beach, Olympic-size pool, another heated pool, and a kiddie splasher. A double room costs $70 to $95 (view is everything) from mid-December to May, $45 to $65 in other months; add $10 for kitchen facilities.

If you like apartment living, **Beekman Towers,** 9499 Collins Ave., Miami Beach, FL 33154 (tel. 305/861-5313), is a plush central address featuring luxurious one- or two-bedroom apartments with all the conveniences of home (maybe more). You'll have lots and lots of space here, where living rooms are 15 by 29 ft for instance, and open onto private terraces overlooking lovely sea or city views. Some smaller studio apartments are tucked away too, and also have pretty private terraces. Walk-in closets are a welcome extra if you're staying, and lively citrus colors add a welcome tropical air. In peak season, you'll pay $90 a day for studio apartments, $155 for larger quarters accommodating four. In other months, prices drop about $30. Ask about money-saving weekly and monthly rates. Beekman Towers is quite a quiet place; it has a pool, patio, and pretty beach, and is near shopping and restaurants.

Step out onto a terrace overlooking ocean liners cruising past the golden sands of Miami Beach at the **Singapore Resort Motel,** 9601 Collins Ave., Bal Harbour, FL 33154 (tel. 305/865-9931, or toll free 800/327-4911, 800/432-4052 in Florida). A block-long hotel stretching out alongside those famous sands, the Singapore tries to think of everything: There's even a 20-station physical-fitness course right on the sand. A little city of its own, the Singapore has two pools and a patio bar, sundeck, private beach, coffee shop, and dining room, free tennis nearby, a beauty salon, boutiques, free parking, a lounge that rocks to the wee hours, plus attractive rooms with two double beds and bright tropical colors. Some rooms have kitchenettes, and two-room suites are available. Two people pay $75 to $95 in winter, $48 to $62 in summer and fall.

**Marco Polo Resort,** 19200 Collins Ave., Miami Beach, FL 33160 (tel. 305/932-2233, or toll free 800/327-6363), is a fanciful place with faintly Moorish touches and lots of bright colors. These days, the hotel is often home to standing-room-only musical shows, and at any time this resort is a swinging place much loved by the younger set who frequent its lively lounges. Vivid colors are a highlight of the rooms, many of which have balconies overlooking the city and the ocean. There's lots and lots of space in quarters here, with his-and-hers walk-in closets, separate dressing rooms with two vanities, even refrigerators. Other goodies include a pool, shopping arcade, bars that rock until 5am, a rib room and Polynesian restaurant, tennis, games, and an outdoor bar. A very lively place, the Marco Polo charges $80 to $120 double for a room or efficiency until May, when prices drop to $46 to $70.

Nights are active at the **Holiday Inn Newport Pier Resort,** 16701 Collins Ave., Miami Beach, FL 33160 (tel. 305/949-1300, or toll free 800/HOLIDAY), where one of the city's most popular nightclubs holds forth in rocking splendor with SRO crowds until 5am. A massive hotel (513 rooms) stretching out along two full blocks of sand, the Newport is strong on bright, bright colors, and features lots of lively colors in the rooms as well. Extra-length beds are a special feature, and big walls of glass open onto wide balconies with spectacular ocean views. The Newport is very close to a big shopping center and there are lots of restaurants nearby, although the restaurant here does wonders with thick steaks. If you want rip-roaring action and very good shows, make a beeline to the Seven Seas Lounge, where things don't quiet down until the sun rises. You'll pay $99 to $129 in summer and fall, prices are $115 to $140 in winter.

Finally, here's a real charmer—**Bay Harbor Inn,** 9660 E. Bay Harbor Dr., Bay Harbor Islands, FL 33154 (tel. 305/868-4141). Billed as Miami's only waterfront inn, this small but significant hostelry is tucked away just a bit off the beaten Collins Avenue track alongside one of the region's many Venice-like waterways. Outside a circular pool sparkles beneath rustling palms, while inside the resort sports a split personality—half antique, half contemporary.

Barely a shopping-mall-length walk from posh Bal Harbour Shops, the inn's lobby is togged out in turn-of-the-century antiques. Polished wood floors glow, Victorian-era rockers sway, and paddle fans whir. In each of the two-room suites in the Townside section of the inn, that same inviting antiquity reigns with tall poster beds flanked by charming antique lamps and a sitting room furnished in curvy Victorian couches upholstered in soft, soothing shades. On the opposite side of the street and the opposite side of the antiquity coin, Creekside accommodations feature sleek contemporary decor and pastel prints. Some rooms have broad glass doors opening onto a terrace.

Unusual for such a small hotel, the inn has two restaurants: the intimate New York Palm, sister to New York restaurant of the same name established in 1927 and specializing—as does its namesake—in steaks and Maine lobsters; and the more casual Seafood Garden, where you can dine indoors or out overlooking the water on intriguingly innovative seafood options in the $15-to-$20 range. Antiques from London's Vanderbilt mansion grace the piano bar, where guests gather for specialty coffees and desserts.

Rife with French doors, arching architecture, impeccably polished woods, and pleasantly fluffy touches, the inn has yet more very thoughtful touches: valet parking, morning newspapers, movie and sports channels, Continental breakfast on a yacht, and high tea complete with champagne and cucumber sandwiches—and they're all free.

Reconstructed with consummate skill from part of what was once called the Albert Pick Hotels, this inn is a most welcome newcomer to Miami's beach resorts. Winter rates are $75 to $110, depending on view and size of room; in summer those drop to $60 to $80, a bargain in Miami, where price and value do not always match as well as they do here.

## Moderately Priced Hotels

**Hawaiian Isle Beach Resort,** 17601 Collins Ave., Sunny Isles, FL 33160 (tel. 305/932-2121, or toll free 800/327-5275), brings a touch of the exotic to Miami Beach. Bamboo and straw matting decorate a dining room and bar; there's an Outrigger oceanfront lounge, and bright tropical colors in average-size rooms with refrigerators. Beach umbrellas line 400 feet of private sand and you can roam about on five acres of grounds. For entertainment there are poolside songsters, water sports, bingo, Ping-Pong, volleyball, tennis, and basketball. You can join in lots of planned activities from egg-tossing contests to Everglades trips, and fraternize at complimentary cocktail parties. A lively disco rocks until the wee hours, and there's plenty to keep the children busy. In winter, you'll pay $56 to $82 for rooms or kitchenette units; in summer, $38 to $48.

Another attractive, moderately priced Miami Beach motel is the **Dunes,** 7001 Collins Ave., Miami Beach, FL 33160 (tel. 305/947-7511). A tropical atmosphere prevails in rooms where big picture windows offer pretty views and shed a bright glow over orange or blue and green decor. The Dunes is close to shopping and restaurants, but we don't know when you'll find time to leave this resort's bar, restaurant, beach, pool, or sport and game tournaments. The Dunes is a nice casual spot where people mingle at the patio bar and joke with friendly, efficient workers. You'll pay $70 to $95 for a double room here in peak season, $35 to $65 in summer.

You can have a room with a balcony overlooking pretty lawns and bright blossoms at **Château-by-the-Sea,** 19115 Collins Ave., Miami Beach, FL 33160 (tel. 305/931-8800, or toll free 800/327-0697, except Florida). A rustic exterior prevails here, but inside there's a very contemporary look, from the glittering lounge (where there's nightly entertainment in season) to cheery rooms sparked with lively colors. All the resort amenities are here, from a good restaurant specializing in seafood and steaks to a big swimming pool, shuffleboard, shops, and a patio bar. You can have a refrigerator in your room if you ask, too. Room rates in winter are $59 to $76 (location is everything), dropping in summer to $39 to $55. Two children under 12 can bunk in with you at no extra charge.

A small and simple spot in the middle of quiet Bal Harbour is the **Coronado Motel,** 9501 Collins Ave., Miami Beach, FL 33154 (tel. 305/866-1625). The friendly staff prides itself on cleanliness, so you'll find everything spick and span. The pretty lobby is crowned by a dazzling crystal chandelier, and is a nice place to meet for shopping expeditions to nearby Bal Harbour Shopping Center. You could easily do without a car here since so many restaurants are right nearby, and the beach is just outside your private balcony. Nice-size rooms are decorated in bright colors and have refrigerators, and for an extra $1 a day, hotplates. Mornings, wander out for a swim in the heated pool or a sunning session on the beach. In this location you can hardly beat the prices: $59 to $80 in peak season through mid-March, $39 to $59 in summer, $4 more for efficiencies.

**Waikiki,** 18801 Collins Ave., Miami Beach, FL 33160 (tel. 305/931-8600, or toll free 800/327-6363), is under the same management as the Marco Polo Hotel, a few blocks up the road. There are 350 rooms here, with two double beds in each, and all are decorated in lively tropical colors. Three swimming pools are scattered about the grounds, and there's a cocktail lounge and restaurant. They show movies or have bingo games every night. Two people pay $44 to $70 for hotel rooms, $5 more with kitchenettes. Children stay in their parents' room for free, except during holidays and February, when there's a $5-per-person charge. In summer, rates drop to $40 to $60.

The **Radisson Pan American Ocean Hotel,** 17875 Collins Ave., Miami Beach, FL 33160 (tel. 305/932-1100 or toll free 800/333-3333), is a quietly elegant spot along the ocean in Sunny Isles with a putting green to play on and a pool to swim in, plus an attractive beamed dining room and lounge, a pretty patio dining area, a poolside bar, coffee shop, and beauty and barber shops. There are refrigerators in the comfortable rooms, and balconies with beautiful views of the sea. The Pan American is spiffy, with a bright up-to-date decor, and the pool bar's a lively spot to while away an afternoon. Rooms here go for $125 to $155 January through March, $79 to $110 in other months.

Lobbies are important things on Miami Beach, and at the **Desert Inn,** 17201 Collins Ave., Miami Beach, FL 33160 (tel. 305/947-0621, or toll free 800/327-

6362), the lobby is cavernous. You shouldn't have any trouble finding this desert-theme resort—just look for the covered wagon and horses outside the entrance. Spread out over two blocks, the Desert Inn has handsome paneled rooms with big picture windows and bright floral prints, and all have refrigerators too. A Laundromat on the grounds is helpful, and while that's whirring you can spend your time on the tennis court or in the pool. There's dining inside or out, dancing every night in the lounge, and a steady round of entertainment for both adults and children. Prices in winter range from $59 to $84, in summer from $40 to $64 ($7 a day more for efficiencies). Meal plans can save you money here, too.

## Very Special Hotels

Art deco architecture reached its zenith in Miami, and Miami Beach has retained more art deco structures than any other city in the country. Now you can see what life was like in the 1920s when this art style was born via a visit to one of several "new" art deco hotels. A large hotel development company bought six of the hotels and is hard at work to bring them back to their former glory.

A number of hotels in Miami Beach, particularly in the art deco district, have been restored and/or renovated in recent years and one of the best of those is the **Broadmoor on the Beach,** 750 Ocean Terrace, Miami Beach, FL 33141 (tel. 305/886-1631, or toll free 800/PLAYINN). Built in 1941, which really were the waning days of the art deco period, the hotel nevertheless sports many deco touches. Witness the fancifully painted fireplace and the now bright blue curved ceiling moldings. Recently renewed top to bottom, the Broadmoor outside is a striking combo of pink and turquoise and inside a pastel wonderland with jade accents and a marble-patterned front desk. Whimsical artwork is a highlight of this 100-room hostelry, which, while not a luxury hotel, is a spiffy, moderately priced place to play. An oceanfront terrace is a gathering spot for water enthusiasts who come here to watch the waves crash and bubble. Taking advantage of the view are the hotel's restaurant and lounge. There's also the requisite swimming pool, and room amenities include bright bedspreads, blond furnishings and refrigerators. Rates are $70 to $90 in winter, $35 to $45 in summer, higher for suites.

Another renovated property is **Essex House,** 1001 Collins Ave., Miami Beach, FL 33139 (tel. 305/534-2700, or toll free 800/645-5687), which now bills itself as "A Romantic Inn." We wouldn't quarrel with that description of this 50-plus hostelry that's a shining example of a style known as "streamline moderne." Now listed in the National Register as an historic landmark, the hotel was painstakingly restored by inn historian Patricia Murphy. Designer linens; original art deco furnishings; mints on your pillow; pastel pinks, seafoam greens, pale yellows, oak hand-finished to a driftwood tone; ziggurat headboards, feather/down pillows (six of them on some beds), dust ruffles; polished terrazzo floors, louvered doors; ocean views; ceiling fans. Add to the antiques all the modern conveniences from push-button telephones to plush carpeting and room security. The lobby features a massive mural painted in 1938 and restored by the original artist 51 years later! One of the beach's most notable restorations, Essex House charges $85 to $295 per night. A couple of items you should know before making reservations: Smoking is permitted only in the lobby/lounge area and children aren't on the program here.

Things began at the **Cardozo Hotel,** 1144 Ocean Dr., Miami Beach, FL 33139 (tel. 305/534-2135). If you think things were beautiful in art deco days, you'll adore the Cardozo, which, with its sister hotel, the Victor, is the shining star of Miami Beach's art deco renovation. What they've done with this old beauty is nothing short of a miracle. All the modern comforts have been added without destroying the classic old 1930s architectural furbelows like pale pastels, puffy furniture, round mirrors, and oval shapes. One pretty corner room overlooking the beach curves at the edges to follow the building's lines, and has been carpeted in pale aqua accented by a peach bedspread and drapes that tie the two colors together. Painted furniture that could easily sell for thousands in a New York antique store was left in the hotel and it was refurbished and covered in the pastels so popular in that period. Downstairs in the lobby are puffy art deco couches, a multicolored terrazzo floor in an intricate design, a reception desk made of pink marble dust, an etched-glass elevator door, a fireplace trimmed with mirrors. You can have one of the Cardozo's rooms for $80 to $145 in high season, $70 to $135 in summer. (Ask for one of the renovated rooms since not all rooms are quite so glamorous.) Those prices, on Miami Beach just across from a long, long strip of public sand, are a bargain indeed.

Included among the deco hotels being restored are the **Leslie, Cavalier, Carlyle,** and **Victor.** For the moment all are listed at 1244 Ocean Dr., Miami Beach, FL 33139 (tel. 305/534-2135, or toll free 800/327-6306), and all are located on the south end of Miami in about the 1000 to 1200 block of Collins Avenue, which some claim is the loveliest strip of beach on Miami Beach. What's more, many rooms face right onto the beach across the street. Rates are in the $70 to $165 bracket year round at these hotels, which provide a fascinating journey back in time to days of F. Scott Fitzgerald and his cronies.

## Budget Hotels

Rooms are not gilt trimmed at the **Waterside Inn,** 2360 Collins Ave., Miami Beach, FL 33139 (tel. 305/538-1951), but then neither are the prices. You'll pay just $60 to $65 for an average-size hotel room, a little more for a spacious efficiency in high season (still in the budget range). In other months prices drop to $50 to $65, and anytime you'll find bright colors here, a nice pool, and lots of beach to play on.

A likely budget selection is the **Beach Motel,** 8601 Harding Ave., Miami Beach, FL 33141 (tel. 305/861-2001 or 866-1180), which isn't right on the sand but isn't far away either. All rooms have kitchenettes and showers, and there's a heated pool in the center of the grounds. In winter, rates range from $45 a day for an efficiency. In summer, prices drop to $25 to $30 a day, and there are money-saving weekly and monthly rates.

**Ocean Roc,** 19505 Collins Ave., Miami Beach, FL 33160 (tel. 305/931-7600, or toll free 800/327-0553), used to be a Holiday Inn so the rooms are especially spacious and decorated in lively colors. Two double beds don't begin to fill up the space, and big private balconies give you even more breathing room. Tennis is free, plus there's a little pool for children, a big one for adults, an oceanfront restaurant, and an attractive bar. The Ocean Roc is one of the northernmost of the motel row resorts, so it's quite a relaxing location that seems far from everything—but isn't. Winter rates are just $48 to $68, dropping in summer to $34 to $44 (lower for long stays).

**Adrian Hotel** is a pleasant South Beach option, deep in the heart of the art deco district. A historic structure that has been restored and is now all decked out in peach and cream, Adrian is a compilation of three buildings at 1060 Ocean Dr., Miami Beach, FL 33139 (tel. 305/538-0007 or toll free 800/DECOTEL). Its ornate twisting columns, arches, and barrel-tile roof echo the Mediterranean style once so popular in South Florida, while inside are comfortable rooms with simple but serviceable furnishings.

All in all, this makes for a cozy spot to experience the '20s atmosphere of this eclectic collection of rainbow-hued architecture. All rooms have air conditioning, telephones, color television, refrigerators, and some have small kitchens and riveting ocean views. Porthole windows are a particular trademark of this hotel, which charges $35 to $55 double from April to mid-November, $50 to $70 in peak winter months.

In the rock-bottom price bracket in Miami Beach hostelries is the **Miami Beach Youth Hostel,** 1438 Washington Ave., Miami Beach, FL 33139 (tel. 305/534-2988), which charges $10 to $12 to members of the American Youth Hostel organization. Membership in that group can be arranged by writing American Youth Hostels, National Offices, P.O. Box 37613, Washington, DC 20013 (tel. 202/783-

6161). This hostel has 80 beds and kitchen facilities and is located in the historic art deco section of South Beach.

## HOTELS IN MIAMI

You'll find most of Miami's hotels downtown, at the airport, in Coral Gables, or in Coconut Grove, so we've picked out a few of the best representatives in those neighborhoods.

### Downtown

As in any big city, Miami's downtown hotels are expensive, but quality is high. Poshest of the downtown hotels is the magnificent **Omni International,** at 1601 Biscayne Blvd., Miami, FL 33132 (tel. 305/374-0000, or toll free 800/228-2121), a spectacularly contemporary spot with waterfalls gurgling from level to level in a dramatic lobby lounge. The casually elegant restaurant serves seafood in the $16 to $26 range. You can zip right from your spacious ultramodern room, decorated with lots of shiny glass, chrome, and soft contemporary hues, to the massive Omni shopping center, where 165 of the city's most elegant boutiques and department stores offer up treasures from many lands. One of the city's most elegant hostelries, the Omni charges $135 to $160 double year round for its 535 rooms.

The **Hotel at Plaza Venetia,** 555 NE 15th St., Miami, FL 33100 (tel. 305/374-2900), is a comparatively new hotel occupying three floors of a 25-story apartment tower on Biscayne Bay. Right next door to the Omni, the Hotel at Plaza Venetia has 50 handsomely decorated rooms with very contemporary decor, and balconies overlooking the marina and bay. There are plush suites, a health spa, two dining rooms, tennis courts, racquetball courts, and a pool. Rates for two are $85 to $125 in winter, $65 to $100 in summer.

Near Plaza Venetia and connected to it by a bayside walkway is a new Miami Hotel, the **Grand Prix,** 1717 N. Bayshore Dr., Miami, FL 33132 (tel. 305/372-0313, or toll free 800/872-PRIX). Connected to Omni Mall by a skywalk, the hotel is a top-flight location for downtown expeditions on business or pleasure.

All of the 152 rooms have views of Biscayne Bay and are equipped with two double beds or king-sized sleepers, and lots of special amenities like bathrobes and hair dryers. There's a business center for executive use, concierge service for the ultimate in pampering, and a private bar on the corporate floor. Outside there's a yacht basin and marina, tennis and racquetball courts and convenience store, all shared with Plaza Venetia.

Sunners gather beside a large swimming pool and, on the 10th floor, hedonists can soak in a whirlpool shaped like a four-leafed clover while enjoying a view of both the glitter of Biscayne Bay and the elaborate architectural lighting that now characterizes downtown Miami. For dining, the hotel has a handsome restaurant called Windows of Venetia, as well as a seafood and pasta eatery. A real find, little known even in Miami, the Grand Prix charges $120 to $275 for rooms and suites from January to May and $95 to $220 in other months.

A $12-million renovation metamorphosed the **Everglades Hotel,** 244 Biscayne Blvd., Miami, FL 33132 (tel. 305/379-5461, or toll free 800/327-5700), into a shining contemporary hostelry. Deep carpets in glowing colors set the tone for sparklingly contemporary rooms in earth tones. The lobby is lovely again, and the Brasserie restaurant, decorated in rosewood and brass, has taken the city by storm, thanks to a talented French chef who's producing outstanding cuisine at quite reasonable prices (in the $10 to $15 range). Year round a double room here is $79 to $100.

Another beautifully revamped downtown hotel is the **Best Western PLM Marina Park,** 340 Biscayne Blvd., Miami, FL 33132 (tel. 305/371-4400), which bears no resemblance whatsoever to the old hotel that once inhabited this spot. Now there are plush rooms decorated in airy wicker or rattan, with fascinating ornate headboards and colors that shine like jewels. From many windows there's a serene view of the city and the marina across the street. Downstairs is a riveting lounge with brick walls and a huge tented ceiling. The hotel's quite convenient to the port if you're off on a cruise. The Best Western PLM Marina Park has an appealing European inn coziness about it, and when its long-range plans are complete, it will have a raft of interesting boutiques too. Two people pay $78 to $92 in season and $73 to $89 in other months, with higher prices for suites.

A showy recent addition to Miami is the **Hotel Inter-Continental,** 100 Chopin Plaza, Miami, FL 33131 (tel. 305/577-1000), a study in beige travertine marble outside, acres of other marbles inside. Quite a showplace, the 34-story, 645-room Inter-Continental has cut a wide swath through Miami's roster of downtown hotels. Outside, lights glitter and a uniformed doorman welcomes you to a marble-lined lobby dominated by a massive marble sculpture. Rooms are spacious, cooly decorated in sophisticated hues, and as elegantly appointed as every other part of this bayfront dazzler. Don't panic, however, if you can't find the shower: It's hidden behind a door. Keep looking.

Convenient to the city's new Bayside waterfront marketplace and the improvements that are taking place at Bayfront Park next door, this elegant downtown hotel has quickly become An Address for those who want the convenience of a downtown location and all the amenities up to and including a health club. The Inter-Continental's Pavillon Grill is a showstopper with imaginative, award-winning cuisine that costs plenty (figure $40 or $50 or more per person for dinner) but is worth it for a truly memorable meal (see our restaurant recommendations). Double rates here are $160 to $180 year round, but you can cut the price in half with weekend packages that may also include an upgrade to a suite and a drink or two in one of the hotel's five restaurants and lounges.

## Key Biscayne

Far from the crowds of bustling Miami—but not very far—and close to the sea are several resorts popular all year with visitors in winter and with Miamians escaping to the beach in summer.

Top of the pack is the **Sonesta Beach Hotel and Tennis Club,** 350 Ocean Dr., Key Biscayne, FL 33149 (tel. 305/361-2021, or toll free 800/343-7170), a massive hotel with every possible sport from swimming to tennis, sailing, and golf. For dining there are five restaurants, including the Rib Room and the outstanding Japanese-Chinese Two Dragons restaurant. For entertainment, will four lounges do? On a street behind the hotel, the Sonesta has bought up every house that came on the market, redecorated them, and now rents them as luxurious villas. Some have as many as five bedrooms! All the 292 rooms here have private balconies, two double or king-size beds, and contemporary furnishings. It's a lovely waterside hideaway that has "Just Us Kids" programs that are so jam-packed with activities it's a wonder adults don't picket to join them. You'll pay $230 to $265 in winter months, $145 to $225 in summer, for two. The villas range from $475 to $875 in peak season, about 25% less in summer; three-day minimum at all times.

**Sheraton Royal Biscayne Beach Resort & Racquet Club,** 555 Ocean Dr., Key Biscayne, FL 33149 (tel. 305/361-5775, or toll free 800/325-3535), is a serene hideaway with a 1,200-foot strip of sand, two pools, sailing, fishing, tennis courts, golf nearby, and spacious, pretty rooms decorated in tropical colors. You can sit on your screened porch and listen to the sound of the waves breaking over the sand in the evening. Royal Biscayne likes to call itself a Caribbean island in Florida, and with its sleepy serenity and all that beach we think they're pretty close to right. In winter, rates are $135 (for a standard room) to $375 (for a suite); in summer and fall, prices range from $85 to $330.

Even a small motel can command top prices on Key Biscayne, and that's why the **Silver Sands Oceanfront Motel,** 301 Ocean Dr., Key Biscayne, FL 33149 (tel. 305/361-5441), can price its efficiency apartments at $105 to $190 for two in winter months, $74 to $139 in summer. One of the most popular spots in town is the motel's Sand Bar, where you can while away an afternoon staring out across the sea through walls of glass. Outside on the wooded grounds there's always a laughing crowd at the pool. Inside, there's a comfortable restaurant serving good beef and seafood at moderate prices. Oceanfront patio apartments at Silver Sands are $115 to $139 in winter, $79 to $89 in summer.

## At the Airport

Not far from the airport is the very plush and comfortable **Doral Resort & Country Club,** 4400 NW 87th Ave., Miami, FL 33178 (tel. 305/592-2000, or toll free 800/FORA-TAN), sister to the Doral Ocean Beach Resort. Set down in the middle of one of the nation's most famous golf complexes and home of the Doral Ryder Open, the resort has regular shuttle transportation to the beach so you won't feel deprived of sand. How you could feel deprived of anything here we can't imagine, since there are lovely spacious rooms decorated in lively colors, 15 tennis courts, *five* golf courses, lakes, bicycles, a spa, pool, clubhouse, restaurants, and lounges. There's a serene air about the place too, that may, now that we think of it, be the result of many a subdued golfer's umpteen-over-par score on the "Monster" course. Two people pay $155 to $215 in summer, $230 to $300 in peak season.

A recent addition to this very sleek hotel is a $28-million spa called Doral/Saturnia International Spa Resort. Adjacent to the country club, the 48-suite, four-story complex features a program of nutrition, fitness, stress management, and, we swear, "image-making." Here you can firm it up in aerobics classes, a steamroom, sauna, and hot tubs, and on Nautilus equipment, all to the accompaniment of applause from an instructor. At the new Garden Terrace Restaurant you can watch duffers rolling around the Monster course while you dine on cuisine that's distinctly American in flavor. One more new thing at this resort: A 24-stable Doral Equestrian Center where you can learn how good riders make it look so easy.

The **Marriott Miami Airport Hotel** is an attractive 782-room hotel quite near the airport at 1201 NW LeJeune Rd., Miami, FL 33126 (tel. 305/649-5000, or toll free 800/228-9290), where you can look out over the lights of Miami and a nearby lake through big picture windows. Nice extra touches are electric alarm clocks, in-room movies, and automated wake-up service. You'll find lots of tennis courts and a full program of instruction and clinics. The newly renovated Porter's restaurant has a spectacular view over the city, and two lounges offer spirited entertainment. Rooms for two are $139 to $158; special deals on weekends.

**Radisson Mart Plaza,** 711 NW 72nd Ave., Miami, FL 33126 (tel. 305/261-3800, or toll free 800/228-9822), is another of Miami's newer arrivals. Opened in 1984, the hotel offers 334 quite luxurious rooms, all with plenty of extra amenities like special soaps and shampoos. Health fans can work up a sweat at the fitness center, on the racquetball or tennis courts, or in the resort's pool, sauna, and whirlpool, then destroy their efforts in the plush continental dining room here. Located five minutes from the airport, the hotel is a favorite stopping spot for those attending trade shows and meetings at nearby Miami International Merchandise Mart and Expo Center. The highest prices are paid for rooms on a special floor called the Plaza Club, which offers complimentary breakfast in the morning and an open bar each evening. Double rates are $110 to $120 for regular rooms, $125 to $135 for Plaza Club rooms.

The **Sheraton River House,** 3900 NW 21st St., Miami, FL 33142 (tel. 305/871-3800, or toll free 800/325-3535), has 408 spacious, comfortable rooms with sweeping wicker headboards, airy tropical furniture and colors, and big picture windows overlooking the tranquil Miami River. There are tennis courts, a pool, a sauna. If you want to go really first class, the Sheraton has rooms in the Continental Tower with brass beds, vivid colors, plush carpets, phones at bed and bath, chocolates on your pillow, and a newspaper at your door. The Sheraton is home to Daphne's, the hotel's sophisticated restaurant where waitresses wear chic outfits and smart hats, and are sometimes difficult to distinguish from diners in same. Thick steaks, hefty slabs of prime rib, interesting salads, and a devastating chocolate mousse pie are on the menu here, where you dine for $15 to $25 amid stained glass, leather chairs, and original artwork. A lively disco makes this a very popular Miami gathering spot too. Rooms run $110 to $120 double year round.

**Viscount Hotel,** 5301 NW 36th St., Miami Springs, FL 33166 (tel. 305/871-6000, or toll free 800/255-3050), stands tall among its lower-rise neighbors, offering a clear view of aircraft soaring across Miami skies. Nestled alongside the perimeter of the airport, the Viscount is a convenient stop for those who need quick and easy access to the airport area. Once known as Miami Springs Kings Inn, this 300-room hotel is now part of the TraveLodge/Trusthouse Forte chain and comes complete with a few amenities unusual to airport hotels—a pool, tennis and racquetball courts, and access to an 18-hole golf course virtually next door. Soundproofed and simply furnished, the hotel offers rates of $68 single, $78 double year round. On an upper floor, where rates are $78 single and $88 double, rooms are more attractively furnished and amenities include a complimentary Continental breakfast and an afternoon wine and cheese break. There's a restaurant here, too.

If you're flying in and right back out again, the **Airport International Hotel,** in the terminal (P.O. Box 5920), Miami, FL 33159 (tel. 305/871-4100, or toll free 800/327-1276), has double soundproofing to silence jet roar and comfortable, colorful rooms with king-size or extra-long double beds. They're used to harried travelers here, so check-in and check-out is fast, and there's a multilingual staff and 24-hour wake-up service. They'll arrange baby-sitters and welcome your pet, then send you up to a handsome rooftop restaurant and cocktail lounge where you can watch those mechanized birds zoom off into the sunset. Double rates are $109 to $119, and the friendly management will give you half-price rates if you need the room just during the day.

Restaurant chains dreamed up cafeterias so there doesn't seem to be any reason why **Serv-Ur-Self Miami Airways Motor Lodge,** 5001 NW 36th St., Miami Springs, FL 33166 (tel. 305/883-4700), shouldn't run a cafeteria-like motel. Here you get your towels, soap, and glasses when you arrive and return them when you leave (exchanging them in between for new ones), thus eliminating the cost of a maid. Rooms are rock-bottom, budget-basic, but there's a pretty pool outside and family suites are available. The rates are the best part of this operation: $37—plus discounts of 3% to 12% for stays of 2 to 9 days. Self Service Inns also operates the **Airliner Hotel,** 4155 NW 24th St., Miami, FL 33148 (tel. 305/871-2611). Rates are $59 double.

**READER'S TIP:** "You should mention that readers planning on staying at the **Doral Resort & Country Club** should have a car. The shuttle from the Doral Resort & Country Club to Doral Ocean Beach Resort operates daytime only. In the evening if you want to return to the country club, you must spend at least $15 in taxi fares" (Diane Miyazaki, New York, N.Y.).

## Coral Gables

Miracles will happen, even in a big city certainly not known in recent years for the production of miracles. However, this miracle actually occurred in the lovely suburb of Coral Gables where the main street is called Miracle Mile, so perhaps that explains it.

All this is by way of introduction to the glamorous **Biltmore Hotel,** 1200 Anastasia Ave., Coral Gables, FL 33134 (tel. 305/445-1926, or toll free 800/223-6620), a 1926 society queen who has regained her rightful place in the hotel pecking order. Back in those days they did things with panache, as you will discover on a visit to this awesomely huge and unutterably magnificent hotel.

Restored and reopened in 1986, the Biltmore easily absorbed $40 million in its return to glory. Used for many years as quite a showy veterans' hospital (of all things), the Biltmore had fallen on dark days and seemed about to fall to the wrecker's ball. Determined preservationists kept it alive, however, first as an art museum and now as an imposing hotel. Here you stroll under 25-foot-high vaulted ceilings adorned with frescoes, an oak reception area, beneath ornate iron chandeliers, past casement windows, carved masonry, and a fireplace big enough to roast an ox.

In the hotel's early days Ginger Rogers, Rudy Vallee, and Bing Crosby wandered along these massive hallways and Sally Rand's feathers flustered the company. Johnny Weissmuller gave swimming lessons in a pool in which nearly 50 large waterskiing shows took place! Then came the dark days: In World War II the Biltmore became a hospital and remained one—complete with delicately detailed ceiling paintings in a two-story rotunda—until its closing in 1968.

Now a national historic monument, the 270-room hotel features hand-carved headboards created in Europe, antique double-doored armoires hiding television sets, two bars, a Biltmore Grill, a golf course on call, a tennis center with 10 lighted courts, a spa, and a pool. Done up in sunset peach, thought to be the original color of the building, this towering hotel was restored by a talented designer who strove to retain authenticity while updating the hotel to modern standards of comfort. He has succeeded and then some. Elegantly restored and waiting to enchant you, the Biltmore remains one of those eye-popping historic settings that only Florida seems able to carry off with so much chutzpah. Whether or not you stay here—and certainly every romanticist ought to give this a go—stop by and take a look at it. Behemoths like this are a rare breed indeed, which makes them all the more enticing. Rates at the Biltmore are $135 to $185 year round, but there are a number of special packages and money-saving deals, particularly in summer when this hotel would certainly rank among the region's most ideal romantic getaway spots. Suites are also available, as are rooms on the deluxe Concierge level called the Premier Club.

A smaller but equally impressive miracle has occurred here at **Hotel Place St Michel,** 162 Alcazar Ave., Coral Gables, FL 33134 (tel. 305/444-1666). Built in 1926 by the Puerto Rican family that created Don Q rum, this three-story, 28-room beauty of stone, stucco, miradors, balconies, and Spanish tile was for years mired beneath a mishmash of 1950s "improvements" and had degenerated to a . . . well, let's not talk about it. Suffice to say it was no one's pride until a few years ago when a couple of clever fellows peeked beneath the fluorescent lights and grim paneling to discover elegant stuccoed walls, good-looking terrazzo floors, vaulting arches, high ceilings, and fancy tile. To that very good foundation they added brass and glass, fresh flowers, handsome antiques, and pretty furbelows to create a delightfully cozy small hotel. Charmingly done up now in laces, prints, gilded mirrors, and a ton or two of atmosphere, the hotel is once again small but significant. A restaurant here is a very, very popular place too. Rates at the Hotel Place St Michel are $105 in winter, $85 in summer, with suites beginning at $125 in winter.

This lush old Spanish city that's home to the University of Miami also has a few small motels along US 1 near the campus, and one large hotel downtown.

Poshest and plushest of the lot is the **David William Hotel,** 700 Biltmore Way, Coral Gables, FL 33134 (tel. 305/445-7821, or toll free 800/327-8770). It's the city's number one hostelry address, and here you'll find everything from a marble and crystal lobby to a rooftop half-acre pool, gymnasium, sauna, masseurs, and attractive, spacious rooms and efficiencies, some with private terraces. Perhaps more famous than the hotel itself is its Chez Vendôme restaurant, where you dine in a recently refurbished fin-de-siècle setting on some of the city's most outstanding cooking, much of it flambé tableside preparations. Prices are in the $25 range. Rates at the hotel are $120 double year round.

**Gables Waterway Executive Apartments,** 1390 S. Dixie Hwy., Coral Gables, FL 33146 (tel. 305/663-3507), is the closest you can come now to staying in the long-revered University Inn near the University of Miami. Now an office complex, University Inn is no more, but part of its attractive site has been converted into this interesting cluster of 20 one-bedroom and efficiency apartments. Six efficiencies are a living room/bedroom combination with dressing area, balcony, and bath, while the remaining 14 units are one-bedroom apartments with living room, bedroom, two baths, and a balcony. All have color cable TV, completely equipped kitchens, local phone calls, maid service, and the usual amenities. Designed for visitors who are staying a week or more, the apartments are rented only by the week or month. Year-round rates are $325 a week for efficiencies, $385 a week for one-bedroom apartments, a bit cheaper by the month.

Coral Gables has added several handsome new hotels in recent years. One of those is the **Colonnade Hotel,** 180 Aragon Ave., Coral Gables, FL 33134 (tel. 305/441-2600, or toll free 800/533-1337), a five-story hotel that occupies part of a large historic building that is now used as an office-hotel complex. Part of the lovely old Colonnade building built in 1926 by Coral Gables developer George Merrick, the Colonnade Hotel is on the penthouse level of the complex, the focal point of which is a massive 75-foot-high marble rotunda. There are now 157 devastatingly handsome rooms with mahogany furniture and armoires, brass lamps, and black marble-topped sink and bars. An impressive lobby with elaborate millwork, imported marble floors, Oriental rugs, and crystal chandeliers is a showstopper. In the building is a rooftop health club, and an eye-popping colonnaded pool, snackbar, whirlpool, and two chic restaurants (see restaurant recommendations). Rates from October to May are $170 to $230 double; in other months, $130 to $190, higher for suites.

## Coconut Grove

In such a lovely community you'd expect to find a lovely hotel or two, and you will.

When the **Grand Bay Hotel,** 2669 S. Bayshore Dr., Coconut Grove, FL 33133 (tel. 305/858-9600, or toll free 800/327-2788), opened in late 1983, invitations to the opening of this posh new hotel were such hot items one expected scalpers to be standing at the entrance. With French nightclub entrepreneur Régine in attendance at her plush top-floor nightspot and every socialite in town glittering, this hotel was the place to be seen. It still is.

A very beautiful hotel indeed, Grand Bay has something more important than mere physical beauty—panache. Here you sip tea from silver pots each afternoon, dine in an elegant French nouveau atmosphere, and sleep in rooms of subtle elegance.

No check-in counter here. Instead you're greeted by a concierge at a goldleaf-trimmed antique desk. Huge bowls of fresh flowers (often orchids) are carefully placed to attract, without overwhelming, the eye. A comfortable lobby is skillfully divided to offer intimate little groupings of handsome furnishings, cozy retreats in which a quiet conversation with friends is possible.

Outside, a towering red metal sculpture is a fitting frontal piece for the unusual stepped architecture of this hotel. Beautiful landscaping at the pool and on every level of the hotel just adds one more touch to the elegance of the place. Rates at the 181-room Grand Bay are $225 to $255 double from mid-December through mid-May, and suites run $290 to $800; in summer, double rates are $200 to $225 for rooms. Grand Bay is operated by the posh CIGA Hotels chain of Italy.

Over at the **Doubletree at Coconut Grove,** 2649 S. Bayshore Dr., Coconut Grove, FL 33133 (tel. 305/858-2500, or toll free 800/528-0444), art deco reigns in the handsome decor that is a trademark of this chain. Attractive suites with living rooms are available and the Club Casablanca, high atop the hotel, is a viewful dining spot. The hotel has use of Grand Bay's gym and sauna, its own swimming pool, and water sports. Rooms are $115 to $130 double, year round.

**Grove Isle,** 4 Grove Isle Dr., Coconut Grove, FL 33133 (tel. 305/858-8300), is one of Miami's newest and poshest hotels, an enclave that shares an island with a private club of the same name. It is elegant, it is expensive, and it is exclusive. Contemporary sculpture by some of the world's finest modern sculptors—Lieberman, Calder, Miró, Dubuffet—greet arrivals, dot the lobby, and rise beside the swimming pool. Formal sculpture gardens make for a fascinating stroll. Now a decade old, the hotel has just four floors and 49 rooms, each with a tasteful tropical theme.

For playtime, there's a large swimming pool, 12 lighted tennis courts, bike and jogging paths, and whirlpool baths. In the dining room, haute cuisine is matched by haute couture and à la carte prices. Rates at Grove Isle are $185 to $225 from mid-December to mid-April, a bit lower in summer.

---

# 4. Where to Dine

---

Miamians work, but only between meals. Business starts over breakfast, moves on to lunch, and gets really serious over five-course dinners. While Miami is a city bustling with international commerce and some very high finance, it differs greatly in pace from its big-city counterparts, thanks to a liberal sprinkling of Latin Americans and Europeans to whom a two-hour lunch falls about an hour short of civilized.

In southern Florida you'll find restaurants at practically every corner, in every office building, every hotel, and many a condominium. You'll find every price bracket, every theme, every culinary specialty from haute to Hungarian, gefilte fish to gnocchi. Reading the Yellow Pages restaurant listings here is like circling the globe: You'll find Cuban, Italian, Chinese, French, Japanese, Mexican, Thai, Spanish, Greek, Colombian, Argentinian, West Indian, Middle Eastern, Nicaraguan, Indian, German, Jamaican, Korean, Hungarian, Puerto Rican, kosher, Haitian, Danish, Vietnamese, Brazilian, Mediterranean, Bavarian, Basque, Swiss—whew!

In fact, locating "this great little restaurant just in back of the . . ." is half the fun of a Miami vacation. To get you started on your search, we've divided the area up by cities and by types of cuisine offered. Prices we've cited are for entrées, although that usually includes salad, one or two vegetables, and often coffee as well.

## RESTAURANTS IN MIAMI BEACH

Many many hotels on Miami Beach have fine restaurants, and you'll find a wide range of cuisine and prices.

### American/Continental

**The Dining Galleries,** at the Fontainebleau Hilton, 4441 Collins Ave. (tel. 538-2000), are simply gorgeous—chic, elegant, très posh. You can dine here on things like terrine de foie gras Strasbourg and pompano with crab Savarin for $35 to $50 a person from 6pm to midnight daily. Sunday brunch, served from 10am to 3pm, costs $22.50 per person.

Baroque decor (Miami Beach interpretation), opulence, drama, stained-glass skylights, Viennese crystal chandeliers, art nouveau touches, antiques from every era—that's **The Forge,** 432 Arthur Godfrey Rd. (tel. 538-8533). In a huge wine cellar lie treasures of the collector's world, from rare classical wines to something one dares to drink. From the kitchen come award-winning preparations of steaks, chops, prime rib, seafood, and nouvelle cuisine specialties. Try the cream of escargots soup. The Forge is open from 6pm to 1am daily, with an adjoining lounge open until 5am. Reservations are suggested, especially in winter. Prices are likely to reach above $25 per person.

**Dominique's,** in the Alexander Hotel, 5225 Collins Ave. (tel. 865-6500), rose to fame in Washington, D.C., where it is the place to be seen now as always. Miamians were, of course, thrilled when chef Dominique D'Ermo was lured to Miami, specifically to very posh quarters in a very posh hotel called the Alexander. Dominique's has not failed Miami. While the hype surrounding the restaurant's opening was so great as to make you wonder if they were trying to cover minimum with maximum, Dominique's has turned out to be one of the city's finest.

You will be impressed by the setting: You enter by glass-enclosed walkways bounded by gardens and dine amid the poshest of accoutrements, from Oriental rugs to glowing antique French furnishings, in a delicate pink-and-green color scheme. Service is positively impeccable, yet not stuffy or overbearing, and the food is wonderful, laden with classically rich sauces, delicately applied herbs, and the best of meats and seafood. You may let your taste buds roam through such treats as pasta stuffed with salmon and topped with lobster sauce, veal scallops daubed with goose liver and served atop fettuccine in a cream-and-peppercorn sauce, or quail with tiny fried quail eggs with a raspberry-vinegar and honey sauce. Prices are high but entrées are accompanied by five vegetables that create a colorful display. Top it all with huge and sinfully rich desserts, dark chocolate truffles perhaps. Entrées fall in the $30 price range, appetizers in the $12 bracket, and desserts run $4 to $6, so figure $40 to $50 a person for dinner, more with wine. Hours are 7:30am to 2:30pm for breakfast and lunch, and 6 to 11:30pm for dinner.

Sunday brunch could hardly be more beguiling than the array of treats served under perky umbrellas and swaying palms at **Fairmont Gardens Bar & Grille,** 1000 Collins Ave., (tel. 531-8877), one of the handful of new restaurants that have opened recently in the South Miami Beach Art Deco district. Fresh smoked salmon, omelets, pancakes, eggs Benedict, fresh breads, cakes, and plenty of fresh fruit are dispensed here each Sunday in the courtyard of a hotel lauded recently for the excellence of its renovation. At dinner such stand-by treats as oysters Rockefeller, coquilles St-Jacques, shrimp scampi, and tournedos of beef fill the menu. Lunch is also available and at attitude-adjustment hour a light menu called Papa's Tapas is served. Prices here fall in the $15 to $20 range for dinner entrees, $13 for Sunday brunch. Hours are 11:30am to 1am daily, with live entertainment every night.

Oops, is that a Rolls-Royce bumper over there? Nope, just a ghost of past days here at **Scratch,** which is housed in what was, back in the 1920s, a Rolls-Royce repair garage on South Beach. Now a restaurant at 427 Jefferson Ave. (tel. 532-8315), Scratch rolls out New American cuisine and an interesting blend of Floridian and Caribbean flavors. Dining is indoors or out at this unusual spot that offers dinner prices in the $10 to $15 range. Scratch is open from 5pm to 2am daily.

## Steaks

A favorite steakhouse on Miami Beach is **Place for Steak,** 1335 79th St. Causeway (tel. 758-5581). Long a beach landmark, Place for Steak has good continental cuisine and excellent steaks in the $15 to $25 bracket; hot and cold buffets daily. Hours are 4:30 to 11pm, with light suppers served after 11pm and entertainment to the wee hours.

## Danish

For years **Prince Hamlet** was one of the most famous restaurants in Miami and one of the best loved of the city's dining spots. Then the neighborhood in which the restaurant was located suffered some setbacks and to everyone's amazement Prince Hamlet closed its doors. In 1984, to the good wishes of herring-starved Miami diners, Prince Hamlet's Danish founder got it all going again and reopened his landmark restaurant at a new location—on the north end of Miami Beach at 19115 Collins Ave. (tel. 932-8488), in a section known as Sunny Isles.

Much to everyone's relief, Prince Hamlet still features a groaning Danish cold table, but now it's even larger than it used to be, laden with all kinds of seafood, fresh vegetables, cheese, salads, and cold pasta creations. A wondrous spot for the true trencherman, Prince Hamlet offers 22 entrées ranging from rack of lamb to roast duck, chicken, snapper, salmon, scampi, and steaks, all of them including a visit to that cold table. Prices are quite reasonable too, considering that you could live for a week on what you can consume here: The range is $14 to $24 for dinner, which is served daily from 5 to 10pm. On Sunday the Prince opens at 4:30pm.

## French

A number of years ago, talented restaurateur Roger Chauveron moved to Miami but fortunately he didn't retire, just brought his successful **Café Chauveron,** 9561 E. Bay Harbour Dr. (tel. 866-8779), with him and created a legendary restaurant that's been winning top culinary awards since the day it opened. Subtle decor, a tranquil waterside setting, and talented, subtle service are all guaranteed at Café Chauveron, as is some of the most exquisitely prepared food outside Paris. Try salmon mousse with lobster sauce, chateaubriand bouquetière, a Grand Marnier soufflé, or chocolate mousse for which any gourmand would sacrifice his Dieter's Anonymous membership. At least five specialties are prepared daily, so be sure to ask what's cooking. Our life's goal is to savor our way through each item on the menu (we're a long way from completing that task). You can't go wrong, but you could perhaps go broke. Entrées on this à la carte menu run $21 to $35, but it's a memorable experience. The café's open from 6 to 11pm daily (closed August to October).

**Café des Arts,** 918 Ocean Dr. (tel. 534-6267), even *looks* arty, nestled as it is in one of the oldest Mediterranean buildings in the art deco district. Quite an attractive restaurant inside and out, Café des Arts attracts an arty crowd as well, so half the fun of going here is seeing who else is going here. As for the other half, that's about evenly divided between the art gallery here and the indoor/outdoor dining on European and Mediterranean specialties based on beef and seafood. There's often musical accompaniment to your art appreciation course. You'll pay $15 to $20 for dinner, more if the artful menu tempts you mightily. Café des Arts is open from 6:30 to 11:30pm daily except Monday, later on weekends.

**Chez Philippe,** 13505 Biscayne Blvd., North Miami Beach (tel. 945-5807), moved into the north end of Miami Beach and fast became close *amis* with French-cooking fans. Classic French cuisine is the focus at this excellent restaurant that sports an unusual combination: very good French food and reasonable prices. You'll pay $12 to $20 for dinners that include salad, two carefully cooked vegetables, and potato. You dine in a friendly, cozy atmosphere engendered by a small restaurant and restaurateurs that are both charming and talented. Chez Philippe is open from 5:30 to 10:30pm daily, 11:30am to 2:30pm weekdays for lunch.

## Italian

**Gatti,** 9909 Collins Ave., in the Sea View Hotel (tel. 865-1106), serves topnotch northern Italian cuisine in a formal ristorante that's been a culinary landmark for more than 60 years. Pastas made right here are so light you should keep a fork on them to hold them down, and seafood gets very special treatment at Gatti. Fresh vegetables and bread baked in their own kitchens are two of the treats in store, but for quality like this you pay $30 or more for a complete dinner. Gatti is open from 6 to 10pm daily. Jackets required.

**Ristorante Tiberio,** 9700 Collins Ave. (tel. 861-6161; outside Florida, toll free 800/TIBERIO), is as fashionable and chic as the buyers who waft around the Bal Harbour Shopping Mall, home to this elegant and expensive dining spot. Waiters are formally attired and efficient, the pastas memorable and light. Try veal Amerigo Vespucci (topped with mushrooms and truffles in brandy cream) or sole in a wine-laced sauce. Expect to pay $40 to $60 each for dinner. Tiberio is open from noon to 3pm and 6 to 11pm weekdays, later on weekends.

On Miami Beach, the things that go bump at mezzanotte are just the crowds flocking into **Mezzanotte,** 1200 Washington Ave. (tel. 673-4343). A very contemporary spot that has become one of the biggest hits in the South Beach Art Deco

District, Mezzanotte is a happy, bouncy spot that purveys plenty of fun along with the food. As for the food, it is, in a word, outstanding. In two words, it's innovative and outstanding. A house antipasto focuses on melted mozzarella topped with a sprinkling of sautéed artichokes, chopped tomatoes, herbs and olives, and is served with a basket of breads baked on premises. Creativity is a byword: Vermicelli is topped with black olives, capers, and an herby tomato sauce; shrimp is christened with garlic and topped with tomato, arugula, olives, capers, and sparked with the flavors of wine and lemon. You'll pay prices in the $10-to-$17 bracket for most selections, and hours are 6pm to—what else?—midnight daily, to 2am Friday and Saturday.

Before or after a performance at the nearby Jackie Gleason Theater of the Performing Arts or during a convention in the newly expanded Miami Beach Convention Center, the hands-down choice is **Osteria del Teatro,** 1443 Washington Ave. (tel. 538-7850). Another welcome addition to the long-time-dormant South Beach area, this sleek restaurant is a welcoming spot that greets you with fresh flowers at the entrance and wishes you *ciao* after a memorable repast. Some very creative cooking is going on here; witness the marinated chicken breast nestled in lightly sautéed radicchio and green beans sprinkled with red cabbage and accompanied by a hillock of puréed vegetables, or the crêpes stuffed with ricotta and spinach and topped with cream and cheese. One could go temptingly on, but there really are things you should do for yourself. As in get on over here. Prices for entrées range from $12 to $17, and hours are 6 to 11pm daily except Tuesday, closing at midnight on Friday and Saturday.

## Caribbean

Despite its close ties with the Caribbean, Miami has few restaurants specializing in the tantalizing tastes of the islands. One of those is the **Palm Café,** 7118 Collins Ave. (tel. 868-1000). A cheery spot decked out in pink tile with waiters in colorful island prints, Palm Café includes the ubiquitous black beans and rice with every entrée, but the house salad topped with a cumin-kissed avocado purée is worth the price of dinner all by itself. If you've never tried Jamaican jerk chicken or pork, now is the time for an introduction to this spicy (but here not super-spicy) barbecue. Try a fresh fruit shake or fish topped with an alluring combination of ginger and scallions. You'll pay $10 to $15 for most entrées. Palm Café is open 5:30 to 10:30pm daily, closing a bit later on weekends.

## Asian

Release from your mind any thoughts of red paper lanterns and fire-breathing dragons. Replace all Oriental clichés with stately flower arrangements, glittering ebony and gold, furnishings inlaid with mother-of-pearl scenes, rich upholstery, fine china service, and you've got **Taste of Szechuan,** 1207 71st St. (tel. 868-8886). Those surroundings alone ought to be enough to bring even the most recalcitrant no-Chinese-food diner here, but there's more: an ethereal appetizer platter that gives you, as promised, a taste of Szechuan; shrimp Szechuan combined with dried chilies, peanuts, hot red-pepper squares, and fresh Oriental mushrooms; beef kissed with a hint of orange; crispy duck; a flaming fruit-combo dessert. A la carte entrée prices are in the $13 to $20 range and tasting occurs here from noon to 2:30pm weekdays and 4pm to midnight daily.

A highlight of an evening at **Christine Lee's Gaslight,** 18406 Collins Ave., in the Thunderbird Motel (tel. 931-7700), is a tableside visit with the elegant Ms. Lee herself, who strolls around her tasteful Asian empire to be sure all is going well. The decor is as chic as the owner, and the cuisine is Cantonese, Mandarin, and Szechuan, things like coconut shrimp or braised duckling fried golden and sprinkled with toasted almonds and nesting on a bed of bean sprouts. If there are four or more of you, try a Mandarin or Szechuan feast. Entrées are in the $12 to $20 range. The restaurant's open from 5pm to 1am daily. There's lots of entertainment in the adjacent bar too.

## Natural Foods

Wait, wait, don't tune out. Despite the grief you may have suffered at natural-food and vegetarian restaurants, you will rejoice over **Pineapples,** 530 Arthur Godfrey Rd. (tel. 532-9731). While they try to keep things whole grain and healthy here, they don't carry it to tofu extremes. There are interesting choices—many of them—each tastefully prepared: grilled dolphin with ginger and scallions; perfectly cooked shrimp served with carefully, crisply cooked vegetables with a touch of soy sauce; a whole-wheat pizza with pesto and sun-dried tomato topping or piled with crisp vegetables and lots of mozzarella cheese. Salads are as fresh as tomorrow, chicken selections are numerous and interesting, and daily specials are temptingly fresh and intriguingly prepared—spinach fettuccine with walnuts, spinach and feta cheese, for instance. Try an eggroll—huge and wonderful. Dinner prices are in the $8 to $14 range for dinner. Pineapples is open from 11am to 10pm daily.

## Seafood

**Joe's Stone Crabs,** 227 Biscayne St. (tel. 673-0365), is down on the very tip of South Beach still dispensing heaping platters of stone crabs as it has for more than 70 years. The atmosphere is basic subdued nautical with cypress walls and nothing much you can damage as you dig through those succulent claws. There's lots of other good seafood on the menu, but stone crabs are wonderful, so don't miss this grown-in-Florida treat. For these treasures from the sea you'll pay about $20 to $25 a person. The restaurant is open from 11:30am to 2pm Tuesday through Saturday for lunch and from 5 to 10pm daily for dinner (closed mid-May to October), but get there early or be prepared for a long, long wait. Don't bother to bribe—it won't help.

Just down the way, one of Miami Beach's newest, and one of its few waterside dining spots, **Crawdaddy's,** 1 Washington Ave. (tel. 673-1708), is plunked down on the beach's newest park, South Pointe Park. Crawdaddy's is part of a chain of theme restaurants that includes the Rusty Pelican on Virginia Key and 94th Aero Squadron at Miami International Airport. Crawdaddy's is fun: overstuffed chairs, Victorian frosted glass, bloomers hanging from laundry lines, quite eclectic decor focusing, if that could be said, on steamships. There's good reason for that focus at this rustic, woodsy spot—it's right alongside a major Miami inlet waterway so the floor show is provided by massive cruise ships steaming out to sea with a backdrop provided by the glitter of Miami's high-rises across Biscayne Bay. Developers of this 500-seat spot spent more than $2 million on it, and it's quite a sight. When you've consumed the view, you can move on to something more nourishing. On the menu is a wide range of steak, lobsters, local seafood, even Everglades frogs' legs. Prices are in the $13 to $17 range for entrées, and Crawdaddy's is open from 11am to 3pm daily, and 4:30 to 11pm weeknights, closing at midnight on weekends. You can't miss it—just look for a wooden wagon out front.

**The Strand,** 671 Washington Ave. (tel. 532-2340), has become the place to see and be seen in Miami Beach. "It's amazing on weekends," reports one employee. "There are people running all over the place, table-hopping and saying things like 'Oh, I didn't know *you* were in town.'" Occupying quarters once home to a famous beach restaurant fittingly called The Famous, the Strand plays up its art deco atmosphere, plays down its prices, and just lets the crowds roll in—as they do, to the tune of SRO-only on weekends, often with lines even in the wee hours of the morning after a popular production at the Miami Beach Theater of the Performing Arts, just up the road. Amid black and white checks and deco design, you dine on lots of grilled seafood, saffron pasta with crayfish, pheasant, wild boar sausage, or steak if you like. Lots of oysters and clams pour from the kitchen, which is open from 6pm to 3am daily. Prices begin at $4 but fall generally in the $10 to $20 range for dinner.

## Budget Stops

To pass by **Pumpernik's,** which moved north to Hallandale (tel. 944-6663), is to miss seeing the great mainstream of Miami Beach life streaming through these portals for a go at bowls of kosher dills and coleslaw, pickled tomatoes, matzoh-ball soup, enormous sandwiches, and dinners for one that could feed three or four. Low prices in the $10-or-less range for dinner, $3 to $5 for lunch, make this a belt-bustin', budget-wise stop. The colorful crowd that pops in here makes meals a sociological study as well. Open from 7am to 1am daily, later on Saturday, at 917 E. Hallandale Beach Blvd.

**Wolfie Cohen's Rascal House,** 17190 Collins Ave. (tel. 947-4581), is carved from the same inimitable mold as Pumpernik's and has long lines from about 6pm every night, so go early. Copious quantities make this a mecca for stuffees and for anyone who likes good cooking, potato pancakes with sour cream, sensational onion rolls, mile-high sandwiches. Prices from $5 to $15. Open from 7am to 1:30am daily.

After a long, hard day with Gucci and Neiman-Marcus, slip off to the cool confines of **Miss Grimble's,** 9700 Collins Ave., in the Bal Harbour Shopping Mall (tel. 861-4544). Sit out at tiny tables under the trees or inside in a little café/teashop where you can rest your eyes on fluffy quiches, fresh spinach salads, croissants, light dinners and pastries that may change what you say when the next boutique asks you your size. It's open from 10:30am to 10pm daily. Prices are in the $8 to $13 range.

Miss Grimble has prospered over the years, as is the American way for those who work hard and long. In salute to that success there is now a second Miss Grimble-creation in the same shopping center, and it's called, what else, the **American Way Café and Patio Bar,** Bal Harbour Mall, 9700 Collins Ave. (tel. 866-0101). Located on the upper level of this posh shopping enclave, the American Way offers a prix-fixe dinner for $10 to $15 including soup or salad, an entrée, a basket of beignets, and coffee or tea. Among those entrées are pastas, stir-fried cashew chicken, fish with pecan butter, and steak. Those in search of lighter dining will find the usual array of soups, salads, burgers, sandwiches, those beignets served with minted chocolate and brandied apricot sauce, and a dessert called chocolate suicide. Warning: Do your trying-on *before* you come here. Hours are 11am to 9pm daily, to 5pm Saturday and Sunday. Entrée prices are in the $10 to $14 range, about half that for salads and sandwiches.

Mexico is ever with us these days and here on Miami Beach it's with us at **Tijuana Joe's,** 1580 Washington Ave. (tel. 531-9082). Everything has volume here from the music to the portions, but it all adds up to a pleasant casual spot to imbibe some south-of-the-border calories. Fajitas have won acclaim here, as has the ceviche marinated with cilantro. Elsewhere on the menu you'll find quesadillas stuffed with cheese, beef sausage and mushrooms, enchiladas, chimichangas, tacos, and the like. Prices fall easily under $10 at this colorful spot that is open from noon to 11pm daily, closing an hour later on weekends.

**Villa Deli,** 1608 Alton Rd. (tel. 538-4552), has been stuffing Miami Beach for ages now, and although it's recently blushed a quite surprising shade of pink, it's still the same stand-by it has always been. Massive beef, brisket, and corned beef sandwiches, free whole garlicky pickles, stuffed cabbage, boiled chicken—large portions, small prices, that's Villa verity. You're unlikely to pay more than $10 for dinner here, and you can certainly do it up for half that. Hours are 6am to 8pm daily, with dinner service beginning at 4pm, opening at 7am on Sunday.

In Miami Beach or anywhere else in South Florida, a restaurant that has been around for more than 50 years is a place to see for rarity value alone. Just such a spot is **Curry's,** 7433 Collins Ave. (tel. 866-1571), a mid-beach hanger-on that just won't let go. Many are those who are thrilled about that and throng in here every night for clam chowder, chopped liver, and a $7 to $9 choice from a list of more than 40 entrées ranging from sizzling steaks to calves' liver, baked ham, broiled pork chops, barbecued spareribs, and filet mignon. Service is deli-brusque in a South Seas atmosphere with linen cloths and a palm tree strung with tiny lights. But who cares when you're paying bargain prices for well-prepared food? Curry's is open from 4:30 to 9pm daily, opening at 4pm on Sunday.

## RESTAURANTS IN MIAMI

Miami has a raft of award-winning restaurants, and more are opening every day.

### American/Continental

**Reflections on the Bay,** Bayside, 401 Biscayne Blvd. (tel. 371-6433), occupies quarters high up on the second level of a building at Miami's downtown yacht marina. From that lofty perch you can get a look at some spectacular sunsets followed by lots of glitter as the lights of this growing city brighten up the night. A posh spot, Reflections is a popular place for after-work sipping that often moves right on into dinner. You dine on delicacies like lobster mousse, gingered clams, and pompano, served in this glass-enclosed salon overlooking sleek sailing craft. You also pay for the privilege, to the tune of about $20 to $30 for dinner, served from 6pm to midnight daily; Sunday brunch from 11:30am to 3pm.

**Chef Allen's,** 19088 NE 29th Ave., Aventura (tel. 935-2900), is a handsomely contemporary dining room with art deco overtones. Here a most talented chef is creating equally contemporary American culinary triumphs, teaming pastas, seafood, beef, and veal with unexpected herbs and vegetables. Chef Allen's rose rapidly in importance here and is now one of the leading lights of Miami's fine restaurants. Deservedly so, for Chef Allen's is elegant, innovative, and a top-notch dining room in every way. For this kind of quality, prices are naturally top-notch as well, but this establishment is more than worth it. Entrées fall in the $14 to $21 bracket, but à la carte selections will increase the total rapidly, so expect to pay $30 to $40 apiece for a repast that will be memorable.

You can absorb a little Miami history while you dine at **Firehouse Four,** 1000 S. Miami Ave. (tel. 379-1923). A 1923 fire station-turned-restaurant, the Firehouse Four was renovated recently and now produces grilled veal, chicken, salads, and the like at both indoor and outdoor tables. Prices fall in the $2 to $8 bracket downstairs, $10 to $15 for dinner upstairs. The Firehouse blazes from noon to 3pm and 5 to 11pm or midnight daily, closed on Sunday.

Dramatic presentations, unusual mergers, sweetly simple backdrops, that is the stuff of top-quality dining and is also the stuff of **Max's Place,** 2286 NE 123rd St., North Miami (tel. 893-6888). What you will dine on here depends on what top-flight chef Mark Militello is dreaming up that night, but you can be sure it will be the *haute-est* in *haute cuisine.* Perhaps a blue-corn pasta topped with squab in a roast corn sauce or yellowtail crunchy with pistachios, duck blended with ginger and soy. Whatever it is, you will be transported by it and by the handsome soft pastel setting in which it is served. Elegant and serene, Max's Place will set you back a bit, say $17 to $28 for à la carte entrées alone, $10 to $20 more to add appetizers, desserts, wine, salads, and the like. Hours are noon to 2:30pm weekdays, to 10:30pm daily, 6 to 11pm on weekends, and closing at 10pm Sunday.

**Pavillon Grill,** Inter-Continental Hotel, 100 Chopin Plaza (tel. 577-1000), has swept through Miami dining circles with hurricane force. In an elegant setting a harpist plunks background music for a symphony of innovative culinary creations that range from potato and apple tartin to black and gold fettucine with Florida lobster and curry smoked lamb chops. Unusual, yes; melt-in-your-mouth delicious, yes; frighteningly avant garde, only for a minute. Prices for this culinary concert are high

—figure at least $40 to $50 per person for dinner—but some memories are worth it. Pavillon Grill is open from 6pm to 11pm Monday through Saturday.

**Oak Room,** Inter-Continental Hotel, 100 Chopin Plaza (tel. 577-1000), holds court for the impeccably suited at lunch each day, so if you're intent on power lunching or launching this is the spot. A paneled sanctum for Miami's corporate power brokers, the Oak Room keeps them fed with a legendary buffet and happy with a wide variety of drafts and spirited potables. A daily theme buffet lures the same crowd back for more of the same at attitude-adjustment hour. Open daily from 11:30am to 2:30pm, with lunch prices in the $10-to-$15 range.

**Esplanade,** in the Hyatt Regency City Center Hotel, 400 SE 2nd Ave. (tel. 358-1234), is another Miami restaurant experimenting in a mélange of unexpected flavors. A handsome spot with burled wood paneling, lots of etched glass, and a jungle of greenery, Esplanade is both elegant and comfortable and a great place to while away a few afternoon or evening hours in soothing surroundings. On the menu here are such unusual offerings as seafood sausage with shiitake mushrooms, saffron linguine with grilled prawns and black-bean tomato sauce, grilled lamb loin on a mound of couscous, and Cuban espresso cheesecake with raspberry sauce. Innovations like those do not come cheap: Lunch is likely to fall in the $10-to-$15 bracket, dinner from $20 to $30 per person. On weekends, a jazz trio plays in the lounge from 7 to 10pm. Restaurant hours are 11:30am to 2pm weekdays, 6 to 11pm daily except Sunday.

## Italian

**Il Tulipano,** 11052 Biscayne Blvd. (tel. 893-4811), has been lauded by some as the finest Italian restaurant in Miami. Certainly it's easily up there among the tops in innovative and downright wonderful Italian cuisine. You'll dine in a country-chic atmosphere that's cozy and pleasant. Agnolotti here is to die for, unless you want to live on to try the veal chop Valdostana. Dinner prices fall in the $15 to $30 range à la carte. Il Tulipano is open for dinner only from 6 to 11pm daily except Tuesday, closing an hour later on Friday and Saturday nights.

## Seafood

You'll probably have to wait at **Mike Gordon's,** 1201 NE 79th St. (tel. 751-4429), but since 1946 legions of Miamians have considered any wait worthwhile. You can watch the yachts buzz by while they're finding you a place. Once you've got one, you'll dine on extraordinarily good cooking—red snapper chowder or black grouper, for instance, plus oysters and clams shucked before your eyes. It's open from noon to 10pm. Tuesday through Sunday, with prices in the $15 to $20 range.

**Joe's Seafood Market and Restaurant,** 400 NW North River Dr. (tel. 374-5637), is one of those places you thought you could never find in a big, bustling city like Miami. It's rustic, simple, right on a wharf overlooking the Miami River, and reasonably priced. Expect nothing fancy, no toney sauces or fine china—just very fresh seafood served by people who know what fresh seafood should be (the place began as a seafood-processing plant). Little by little Joe's responded to demand and now features snapper filets, black grouper steaks, sea trout, fried shrimp, deviled crab, squid, and conch for prices that hover between $6 and $8. You can spend more if you're after swordfish, shrimp in a green sauce, Florida lobster, or stone crabs (say, $10 to $15), but you don't have to—and that's a miracle in Miami. You can dine indoors in air conditioning or outdoors watching yachts pass by. Hours are 11am to 9pm daily, closing an hour later on Friday and Saturday.

There are often trade-offs in life and the trade-off at **The Fish Peddler,** 8699 Biscayne Blvd. (tel. 757-0648), is crowds. At peak dining times on almost any evening here you'll have to join the flocks who throng here to chow down on fresh, and refreshingly prepared, seafood at quite reasonable prices. Despite its lack of pretentious decor, the Fish Peddler lures quite a chic crowd, Miamians who know value and know they'll get it here. When we say unpretentious, we mean it: checked tableclothes, uninspired china, dark-wood walls, a counter around the cooking area, a couple of stuffed sea creatures as wall decor, noise. But while it may not be the spot for an assignation, it's definitely the spot for stone crabs at a reasonable price (about $16 last time we heard), black grouper filet, pan-fried yellowtail, broiled mackerel or cod in Creole sauce, shrimp steamed in beer or presented in garlic sauce, Maryland oysters, fried clams, cherrystone clams, mussels in garlic sauce, Ipswich steamed clams, oyster stew—have we gotten your attention? Nearly everything on the menu falls in the under $12 range and for seafood in South Florida, that is value. The Fish Peddler is open from noon to 9:30pm daily except Monday. Closed the last two weeks in May.

## German

You won't find any frivolous little finger foods at **Zum Alten Fritz,** 1840 NE 4th Ave. (tel. 374-7610). Here they believe in serious dining and turn out platters of wienerschnitzel, spaetzle dumplings, gravy, red cabbage, and all the rib-sticking fare for which German cooks have become famous. A mini-band with accordion and drums beats out an oom-pah-pah or two in the Biergarten and Brew Pub and everyone seems to have a good time at this informal downtown restaurant that brews its own beer. As important as beer is to a German, you can be sure you'll find an extensive list of other brews as well. Dinner prices fall in the $10 to $15 range, and hours are 11am to 3:30pm weekdays, 5 to 10pm daily except Sunday, later on weekends and in the pub.

## Budget Bets

Once upon a time a famed Havana bartender named Constante created a drink that was to become an international favorite, the frozen daiquiri. That drink drew droves (including Hemingway) to a restaurant called **El Floridita** that has now been cloned in downtown Miami at 145 E. Flagler St. (tel. 358-1556). Cuban daiquiri connoisseurs assure me that Miami's Floridita comes very close in excellence to the Havana creation. Even if you don't want a daiquiri you'll like the romantic setting, down in what comes as close as Miami can come to a basement. You won't pay more than $10 to $15 for good seafood and Cuban fare, and there's entertainment, too. Open from 11am to 7pm daily, to 9pm Friday and Saturday.

Seafood comes right out of the depths of fishing boats that dock at **East Coast Fisheries,** 360 W. Flagler St. (tel. 373-5516), which is first a wholesale fish house and second a wonderful, trendy-rustic restaurant. The setting couldn't be less pretentious, but the seafood couldn't be fresher either. Everything's sea-fresh, simply cooked and simply sensational. The chowder is made from grouper here, the shrimp and stone crabs are to die for, and prices are in the $10 to $15 (or less) range. Open from 11am to 10pm daily. A don't-miss.

**Hy-Vong Vietnamese Cuisine,** 3458 SW 8th St. (tel. 446-3674), is one of the few Vietnamese restaurants in Miami, and one of the few not only to survive but to prosper here. Flocks of the hungry fill the place to SRO on weekends and keep it very busy on other days as well. A tiny storefront restaurant nearly hidden by the neon jungle of its 8th Street neighbors, Hy-Vong cooks well, presents dishes with élan and ties up a very alluring culinary package with efficient service. Try this on for taste: spring rolls filled with chopped black mushrooms and bean threads, served with a leaf of buttery Boston lettuce you wrap around the eggroll before dipping it in a light garlic sauce. Or this: a winter-squash soup with coconut milk, lime juice, and scallions. Daily specials feature whatever looks good in the market, and there are always a wide variety of chicken, seafood, beef, and duck entrées available. Don't let it worry you that you don't know anything about Vietnamese food: Friendly workers will lead you to the best of fiery or cool selections, many of them garnished with exotic fruit, nuts, lightly cooked vegetables. Outstanding curries, stir-fries, and our favorite, a fiery-flavored chicken with lemon grass, make this one of the city's most highly rated restaurants. What's more, the price is right: Dinner entrées range in price from $5 to $10. Hy-Vong is open from 5:30 to 10:30pm; closed Monday.

Tops for real budget seekers is **S&S Restaurant,** 1757 NE Second Ave. (tel. 373-4291), a place almost never visited by tourists but packed with Miamians at lunch, and even at breakfast, when there's often a line out front waiting for the doors to open. We've spent many an hour here, enjoying cheap, earthy home cooking—all the stuff your mother used to make. Don't expect atmosphere, just a U-shaped counter with stools and three waitresses who have been here since the Renaissance and sling hash with delightful aplomb. Do expect the house specialty: *real* mashed potatoes. Don't even think about trying to get in when they're serving turkey. Instead, spend that day dreaming of strawberry pie with whipped cream, ham steak, creamed carrots, Salisbury steak, eggs with catsup, sandwiches with real mayo. Prices are in the $5 to $7 range, sometimes less, and hours are 6:30am to 8pm weekdays, closing at 2:30pm on Saturday. Closed all day Sunday. Very crowded at peak lunch hour, worse now that the restaurant has been listed in the National Register of Historic Places in tribute to its unsullied art deco design.

It would seem at first glance that **Big Fish,** 55 SW Miami Ave. (tel. 372-3725), has a couple of negatives: Finding it nearly requires a compass, and when it rains the dining rooms, both of them, get soaked. This has not stopped this establishment from becoming very popular indeed. That popularity owes much to tangibles like fish sandwiches so fresh they almost swim to the table, and intangibles like the old-shoe comfort of the place and its chatty, indefatigable, unflappable owner. Tables here are just wood disks bolted to gallon drums bolted to floors made of scrap wood mounted on construction pallets. Overhead is a corrugated aluminum roof. Proprietor T. O. Sykes calls the decor "early scrounge," but he plays classical music for background, a typical anomaly. Fish sandwiches, far and away the house speciality, cost $5; other seafood selections, when they have any, range from $2 to $10. To get here take the Miami Avenue Bridge south and make the first right after crossing the river, or take Brickell Avenue to SE 5th Street and go west past the Miami Avenue Bridge. Open Monday through Saturday from 11am to 3pm.

Pan Am flew its first commercial flight from right here in Miami at Dinner Key, a site now known for its big convention center and Miami City Hall. A new restaurant, **Havana Clipper,** 3360 Pan American Dr. (tel. 859-2100), salutes that historic flight with photos and memorabilia of the Thirties and Forties, when those flights began. A second-floor spot with lovely views across the waters here, Havana Clipper salutes Cuban cuisine. It features all the traditional Cuban favorites, from fruit-flavored milkshakes, called *batidos,* to *lechón asado a la criolla* and *boliche.* Prices fall in the $5 or less range for *media noche* sandwiches of grilled ham and cheese, higher for full dinners. Havana Clipper's hours are typically Cuban—11am to 2am, later on weekends.

**Tony Roma's,** 15700 Biscayne Blvd. (tel. 949-2214), is a clone of the phenomenally successful Fort Lauderdale operation with those same spicy, crunchy barbecued ribs and loaves of crispy onion rings for prices that hover at $12 or less. There's another Tony's at 6601 S. Dixie Hwy. (tel. 667-4806), and they're both open from 11am to the wee hours—like 5am—Monday through Saturday, from noon on Sunday.

We couldn't decide where to list **Lila's** (pronounced *Lee*-la), and finally decided that prices like these just had to be front and center. At Lila's, 8518 SW 24th St. (tel. 553-6061), you can stock up on steaks that lop over the plate and are buried under a mountain of french fries for, get this, $5.50. Lila's done so well with her Cuban steaks and fries (the steaks are the thin ones popular in Cuban restaurants) that she's now opened another restaurant in Westchester Mall on Coral Way. You can't beat these eateries for local color or for culinary outpourings. Open from 11am to 11pm daily.

## Vegetarian

**Granny Feelgood's Restaurant,** 190 SE First Ave. (tel. 358-6233), is a wealth of natural foods: tofu, soy pancakes, omelets, carrot juice, vegetarian cheeseburgers, and the like. If you're not quite ready to go, um, cold-turkey vegetarian, you can ease into this with lobster salad platters, pasta, eggs, or chicken parmesan. Granny produces quite an extensive menu, ranging from a platter of fresh fruit to stir-fried chicken, nachos, and guacamole. Prices are right too—well under $10 for most selections. Granny cooks from 7:30am to 6pm daily except Sunday, 11am to 3pm Saturday. A second location, albeit a very crowded one at lunch hour, is at 111 NW First St. and is open 7am to 5pm weekdays, serving fast-food style.

## RESTAURANTS IN LITTLE HAVANA

For my money there are no better or tastier bargains in Miami than Little Havana's raft of inexpensive and colorful restaurants. You can eat like the proverbial king (or a Hawaiian queen) here for much more reasonable prices than you'll find in many area restaurants—and feel as if you've just landed in Cuba at the same time. Fun and food are an unbeatable combination, and you'll find them in Little Havana, which is Miami's SW 8th Street.

## The Food

Menus in Little Havana explain things in English to accommodate hordes of Norteamericano diners who have come to know and love Cuban food. But just to be sure you understand, here's a list and a brief explanation of some of the most popular Cuban dishes:

**Arroz con pollo** (pronounced "ah-*rose* cone poyo") is roast chicken and yellow rice dotted with red pimiento.

**Picadillo** (pronounced "peek-ah-*dee*-yo"), one of our favorites, is a combination of ground meat, a rich brown gravy, peas, pimiento, olives, and raisins.

**Plátanos** (pronounced "*plot*-a-nose") or **plantains,** a mildly flavored fruit used to make **tostones** (pronounced "toast-*tone*-ace"), which are round slices of fried green plantains, or to create plátanos, which are ripe fried plantains. Tostones are crunchy, very bland, and usually have a slightly salty flavor, while plátanos are sweet and soft.

**Pan Cubano** (pronounced "pahn *Kew*-bawn-oh") is a long white loaf of bread with a crumbly, crusty exterior.

**Ropa vieja** (pronounced "rope-ah vee-*ay*-ha") literally means old clothes, named for its stringy resemblance to rags, but it is a rich beef stew.

**Cafe Cubano** (pronounced "cah-*fay Kew*-bahn-oh") is very strong, black coffee thickened with lots of sugar and served in tiny cups holding only a couple of tablespoons, just enough to open your eyes for a week. If you want the kind of coffee you usually drink, ask for **cafe regular** (pronounced "cah-*fay* ray-goo-*lar*").

**Palomilla** (pronounced "paul-oh-*me*-ya") is a thin sliced steak, similar to what English speakers call minute steak, usually served with onions, parsley, and a towering pile of thick french fries.

**Camarones** (pronounced "cah-mar-*own*-ace") is shrimp.

**Paella** (pronounced "pah-*eh*-ya") is a combination of chicken and often Spanish sausage, seafood, and pork, mixed with yellow rice and peas.

**Fabada Asturiana** and **caldo gallego** (pronounced "fah-*bah*-dah Astew-ree-*awna*" and "call-dough gall-*yeggo*") are thick Basque soups made with beans and sausage.

**Tapas** (pronounced "*top*-ahs") are Spanish hors d'oeuvres, little mouthfuls you pick out of many displayed. Although they usually are consumed with pre-dinner cocktails, they are not free happy hour goodies: You pay a small price for each selection you make.

**Fritas** (pronounced *free*-taws) are to Cubans what hamburgers are to Americans, just more interesting. These are tiny hamburgers, two to three ounces of ground beef and pork, seasoned with smoked Spanish paprika, slipped into a bun and topped with chopped sautéed onions and tiny matchstick-thin french fries.

## Tapas Bars

Although Americans don't understand the tradition too well yet, in Miami the tapas bar, laden with lots of bowls and platters of things to munch on before dinner, is catching on here. If tapas are not displayed at the restaurants we name here, you can ask them to make up a platter of tapas for you. That will often include olives, bits of cheese, perhaps a ham called jamón Serrano, or boquerones, spicy sardine filets. Tapas bars in Miami include:

**Casa Juancho,** 2436 SW 8th St. (tel. 642-2452), has 40 different tapas available, from cheese to chorizo sausage, omelets, shrimp in green sauce, and thin strips of broiled sirloin marinated in garlic and onions.

**Centro Vasco,** 2235 SW 8th St. (tel. 643-9606), is where you can try croquetas, the Cuban version of croquettes, along with other choices.

**Madrid,** 2475 Douglas Rd. (tel. 446-2250), also features fried squid and shrimp in garlic sauce.

At **Malaga,** 740 SW 8th St. (tel. 858-4224), barbecued pork, grilled chorizo, and baby eels are added to a lengthy list of tapas.

**El Bodegon Castilla,** 2499 SW 8th St. (tel. 649-0863), has a variety of tapas for the asking.

**El Cid,** 117 NW Le Jeune Rd. (tel. 642-3144), has all the usual and specializes in shrimp in garlic sauce.

**Alcazar,** 7711 SW Bird Rd. (tel. 261-7249), has empañadas, mushrooms in garlic sauce, fried chicken, and a cold potato-and-onion omelet in addition to the usual tapas selections.

## The Restaurants

A note here on dining at Cuban restaurants: Cubans rarely begin even *thinking* of dinner before 8 or 9pm. So if you find a dining room practically empty at normal American dining hours from 6 to 8pm, don't assume the place isn't popular. Stay, and you'll discover that about the time you are finishing dinner at 10 or 11pm the crowds are just arriving!

**Juanito's Centro Vasco,** 2235 SW 8th St. (tel. 643-9606), is the epitome of Miami's Cuban restaurants, the one almost everyone will send you to and one of the forerunners of dozens of successful Cuban restaurants. Juanito's was a popular place in Havana; it's every bit as popular here, and has been since 1965 when Juanito Saizarbitoria opened this emporium. Try some unusual specialties like oxtail or just stick to more familiar fare like snapper fingers in a delicate wine sauce, steaks with interesting Spanish touches, fried garbanzos, gazpacho, sangría. You'll pay about $11 to $15 for dinner. Centro Vasco is open, with entertainment and a lounge, from noon to midnight daily.

Budgeteers should head for **La Tasca,** 2741 W. Flagler St. (tel. 642-3762), where you can eat enough for an army and still spend less than $10. Arroz con pollo, paella, ropa vieja, pork, chicken, seafood, and a long list of inexpensive items make this a money-saving choice. Open from 11am to 11pm daily, La Tasca is quite close to the Dade County Auditorium if you're planning an evening of the opera, concerts, or dance programs there.

Everyone who's anyone in Little Havana passes through the doors of **Versailles,** 3555 SW 8th St. (tel. 445-7614), a pretty little place lined with mirrors in the back room and with a lunch counter in front. Order your coffee Americano here or you'll get the super-thick teensy little cups of rich Cuban coffee (which, by the way, is wonderful). Politicians flock here in campaign times and even Florida's governor worked a day here once when he was campaigning. Good media noche sandwiches (grilled ham and cheese) and all the usual Cuban flavors are here, from yellow rice to batida milkshakes in exotic flavors like mango. Prices are very low, in the $5 range or less for many things. Versailles is open from 8am to 2am weekdays, later on Friday and Saturday, and from 8am on Sunday.

**La Carretera,** 3632 SW 8th St. (tel. 444-7501), shows nostalgic slides of Old Havana during dinner while preparing excellent seafood and beef at prices in the $8 to $16 range, a full lunch for $5 (and in Little Havana, that's *really* full). It's open 24 hours daily.

**La Esquina de Teja,** 101 SW 12th Ave. (tel. 545-5341), is named after a famous corner in Havana and produces typical Cuban fare for prices well under $10. It's open daily from 7am to 11:30pm. Even Ronald Reagan has dined here!

**El Meson Castellano,** 2395 NW 7th St. (tel. 642-4087), serves one of the traditional appetizers of Cuba—a fruit cocktail of apple, papaya, mango, orange, melon, and whatever else they can find in the market sweetened by a light honey sauce. Specialties include chicken broiled with a crispy skin, cocido madrileño (a soup of chick peas, Spanish sausage, ham, chicken, beef, and cabbage), lamb roast in the Galician style, and white beans refried with pieces of Spanish sausage. Your finale should be brazo gitano, a cake stuffed with egg custard. You won't pay more than $6 or $8 for dinner entrées at this lively restaurant open from 11:30am to 10pm. Closed Monday.

**Málaga,** 740 SW 8th St. (tel. 858-4224), has as many—maybe more—American customers as it does Hispanic diners. Hundreds of pounds of arroz con pollo a la chorrera (chicken and rice) are created in this kitchen, along with an excellent paella laden with pork, fish, and chicken, as well as seafood and rice; pork chops; boliche mechadeo, created from eye of the round roast stuffed with rice and beans; and fabada Asturiana, a Basque soup of white beans with sausage. If you like fish, waiters will bring out trays of red snapper so you can see how fresh and how big they are. Prices here are in the $7 to $15 range for sumptuous dinners, and hours are 11am to 11:30pm daily.

**Villa Habaña,** 3398 Coral Way (tel. 446-7427), seems to do everything just right from the caldo gallego (Spanish bean soup) to the deliciously garlicky sauce ladled over fat shrimp to Cuba-style sandwiches made right in front of your eyes. Caramelized plantains, rice, and black beans come with everything, and even they are prepared with care. Other choices are pork or ham tamales, grilled pork steak, flank steak, grilled snapper, and a seafood casserole. Bread is fresh and crispy, service is prompt and capable, and decor is basic but comfortable, as are the prices: Dinner tops out at about $10; other meals, $3 to $5. Villa Habaña, a very good and very Cuban restaurant, is open from 7:30am to 11:30pm daily.

**Fritas Domino,** 936 SW 67th Ave., in the Trail Shopping Center (tel. 266-8477), has become Mecca for Cubans homesick for a taste of the old island—or the now second- and third-generation Cubans hungry for a taste of what they heard about from their parents. Tucked in between two American fast-food spots, this very Cubano restaurant is operated by the second generation of the family that once ran three such establishments in Miami. Tiny, tiny hamburgers spiced with exotic smoked Spanish paprika are flipped into a bun, topped with chopped, sautéed onions and served up with a heaping mound of french fries crisp as breadcrust and thin as matchsticks. A frita costs $1.25 and you can enjoy one any time from 11am to 10pm daily, from noon on Saturday and Sunday.

## RESTAURANTS IN CORAL GABLES/SOUTH MIAMI

Coral Gables has become the gastronomic capital of this section of Florida, so you'll find many of the city's top-rated dining spots lining the streets of this old and prosperous community, inhabited by some of the region's wealthiest citizens. Restaurants here, and in yuppie-haven South Miami, fall in all price categories, however, and are often tucked away in romantic settings.

## American/Continental

Technically, **Savannah Moon,** 13505 S. Dixie Hwy. (US1) (tel. 238-8868), is not in Coral Gables but in South Miami, but it's worth the trek southward to sample their cuisine. Specializing, naturally enough, in the flavors of Dixie, Savannah Moon whips up Charleston crab cakes, Carolina turnovers, Georgian roast duck, steak flavored with honey butter, bayou barbecued shrimp, red snapper topped with pecans. A dessert cart makes you wonder how Southern belles maintained those handspan waists. The Decor is attractively contemporary, but there remains an oh-dahlin'-ah've-dropped-mah-little-white-glove air about the place. When dinner's over, Old South gives way to New South as the lounge goes on into the wee hours as swing or jazz bands play for listening and dancing or vocalists warble. Dining hours here are 11:30am to 2:30pm weekdays and 5:30 to 11pm daily, closing an hour later on weekends. The bar (with entertainment) usually swings nightly except Monday, closing weeknights at 2am, Friday and Saturday at 3am.

**Two Sisters Restaurant,** 50 Alhambra Plaza (tel. 441-1234), is tucked away in another of Coral Gables plush new hotels, the Hyatt Regency Coral Gables, where you're greeted by doormen in medieval costume. As elegant as the hotel that surrounds it, Two Sisters does things right: hand-painted china, real silver, and glittering lead-crystal stemware. Culinary efforts lean toward the Mediterranean, so you can feast on elegantly seductive platters of tapas at cocktail hour, then move on to what we'd call nouvelle Spanish/American—filleted red snapper topped with tomatoes and basil; roasted chicken rubbed with olive oil and herbs; monkfish topped with toasted black walnuts and orange wedges garnished with porcini strips and miniature vegetables; lightly smoked duck breast with blanched and oiled greens and warmed white bean salad; medallions of beef with roasted pearl onions. For a finale, the chocolate walnut terrine with mint sauce makes memories. A very showy spot, Two Sisters is open for all three meals from 7am, with lunch served from 11am to 3pm and dinner from 6 to 11pm daily, closing an hour later on weekends. A walk-away-groaning Sunday brunch is offered from 10am to 2pm. You'll pay $10 to $15 for lunch, $15 to $25 for dinner.

**Aragon Café,** in the Colonnade Hotel, 180 Aragon Ave., at Miracle Mile and Ponce de Leon Boulevard (tel. 441-2600) features what this and a number of other South Florida chefs like to call "New World cuisine." That translates to an unusual melting pot of flavors, drawing inspiration from the herbs and culinary skills of the Hispanic community, Native American dishes, and the exotic flavors of the Caribbean. You'll find such delicacies as turkey in coriander and dill served with pear and avocado on a bed of sweet potato strings and smoked salmon bavaroise with gazpacho sauce and a marinated garnish. Add to that grilled pompano brioche with saffron-flavored orange butter, Florida lobster wrapped in radicchio surrounded by a velvety vermouth sauce, or lamb roasted with garlic cloves and herbs and served with an eggplant custard. For such innovations served in a handsome old-world atmosphere of marble, mahogany, and glowing jewel tones, you'll pay $20 to $25 for entrées. Lunch is served from 11:30am to 3pm weekdays, dinner from 6 to 11pm daily except Sunday.

Some quite diverting hours were once spent with some convivial companions —quickly made more convivial here—at **Doc Dammer's Saloon,** also in the Colonnade Hotel, 180 Aragon Ave. (tel. 441-2600). Despite that saloon reference, Doc Dammer's is more than just a local watering hole, although it has garnered considerable attention down this way for its skills in that direction, too. Named after Coral Gables' first mayor, Doc Dammer's carries out its historic ties with an entertaining array of early city photographs, some of them from the collection amassed by Coral Gables founder George Merrick. Designed to resemble a 1920s bar and grill, this diverting establishment features those high ceilings of yore, sparked by white marble floors, some mahogany here and there, and a casual, lively ambience that draws crowds. Folks come here also to feast on some unusual grazing foods ranging from Peruvian ceviche of scallops, shrimp, and grouper marinated in lime juice and cilantro to duck empanadas, grilled mussels, lamb ribs, and seven onion and black bean soup. That's abetted by a wide variety of salads—including a couscous seafood salad, sandwiches, pizzas, the ubiquitous burger topped with everything from bacon to boursin, and such rib-stickers as good old-fashioned meatloaf, skirt steak, and chicken pot pie. Most nibbles range from $3 to $7, with a few more elaborate entrées in the $10 to $15 range. Doc Dammer's is open 7 days—Monday through Thursday and Sunday from 7pm till midnight, Friday and Saturday till 2am.

There's a pillow for the dainty feet of mademoiselle and a rose for her delicate hand at **Vinton's,** 116 Alhambra Circle in La Palma Hotel (tel. 445-2511). There's a very special atmosphere here. You can sit out under the stars in a pretty courtyard or inside in eclectic but charmingly romantic surroundings. On Monday there are fixed-price dinners with many a gourmet touch; other nights there is a list of French-inspired creations that will send you away richer in spirit and calories. Vinton's is open from 11:30am to 2:30pm weekdays and 6:30 to 11pm daily, except Sunday. Average entrée prices are about $15 to $25. Pre-theater dinners from 6:30pm, too.

## French

A charming decor of etched glass and mirrors makes the **French Connection,** 2626 Ponce de Leon Blvd. (tel. 442-8587), a pretty place to sample delicious creamy concoctions en croûte, escargots au roquefort, and there's even an ice cream en croûte. You'll pay $12 to $24 for a full dinner here. Make your own French connection for lunch from noon to 3pm weekdays and Saturday, for dinner from 6 to 11:30pm every day but Monday.

In the David William Hotel, 700 Biltmore Way (tel. 445-7821), is an uppercrust and upper-price spot, **Chez Vendôme,** a *très élégante,* formal dining room with many continental selections and dinner prices in the $20 to $25 range. Hours are 11:30am to 3pm daily for lunch and 5:30 to 10pm for dinner.

Mustachioed Maurice charms you with his bubbling personality, then bewitches you with his pâtés and seafood, his veal and calvados chicken, his vacherin and puffy pastries at **Chez Maurice,** 382 Miracle Mile (tel. 448-8984). So dazzled are you in this cozy atmosphere of wood beams and half-timbered walls that you don't even mind the check, which is likely to fall in the $11 to $20 range for entrées. Lunch is served from 11:30am to 2:30pm Monday through Friday, dinner from 6 to 11pm every day but Sunday.

**Charade,** at 2900 Ponce de Leon Blvd. (tel. 448-6077), is tucked away on this busy boulevard in one of the loveliest buildings in this lovely town. In the center of things outside is a charming Spanish-inspired courtyard, but the focus inside is on outstanding Swiss/French cooking that has inspired such delicacies as veal geschnetzeltes (veal and mushrooms bathed in a wine and cream sauce), pan-fried rainbow trout stuffed with prosciutto, bouillabaisse, and shrimp sautéed with onions and spiced with curry and brandy. Prices are in the $12 to $18 range, and the restaurant's open for lunch from 11:30am to 3pm weekdays and for dinner from 6 to 11pm every day (closes earlier on Sunday). There is a prix-fixe Sunday brunch ($13.95) served also. Reservations are wise.

Good value and good food are the trademarks of **Madrid,** 2475 Douglas Rd. (tel. 446-2250), which has been a landmark in Miami since the 1950s. To really keep the check down, try their gazpacho-to-flan nightly specials. Lobster, roast suckling pig, white- or black-bean soup, pork chops fried in garlic sauce, snapper in green sauce, *tapas* (hors d'oeuvres) and paella are all on the menu here, where you'll pay $12 to $18 for dinner. It's open from 11:30am to 11pm daily, later on weekends and in the remodeled lounge (closed Sunday).

**The Bistro,** 2611 Ponce de Leon Blvd. (tel. 442-9671), is a popular spot in this town so you can always be sure to find the hungry gathered here. What they're gathered in this pleasant setting for is a wide variety of seafood, steaks, veal, and chicken, much of it featuring a French touch, although the restaurant likes to call its cooking Continental. Whatever you call it, many call it tops. Hours here are 6 to 10:30pm weekdays, closing at 11pm on weekends. Entrées fall in the $15 to $20 price range, including salad and vegetable.

To see the chocolatey glory of the chocolate soufflé topped with sabayon at **Le Festival,** 2120 Salzedo St. (tel. 442-8545), is to abandon without regret those New Year's resolutions. After you've dined on chicken doused with brandy-cream sauce, tournedos, crêpes, or delicate pâtés, what difference can a little chocolate soufflé make? You'll pay $12 to $18 at least for this temporary breakdown, and it's worth every calorie. Newly redecorated Le Festival is open for lunch from 11:45am to 2:30pm on weekdays, for dinner from 6 to 10pm every day but Sunday. On winter weekends there are seatings at 7 and 9:15pm only, and reservations are mandatory.

Try papery crêpes, hearty onion soup and lobster bisque, quiches, and croque monsieur for openers at **Place St Michel,** 162 Alcazar Ave., in the Hotel Place St Michel (tel. 446-6572). Then they toss in art deco chandeliers rescued from the old Mayfair Theater, background music from the 1930s, and a cozy, friendly ambience. Finis, monsieur—we give up. It's open from 11am to 3pm and 6am to 10:30pm weeknights and stays open later on weekends. You'll pay $12 to $17 for most dinners.

## Indian/Thai

Indian food may *sound* strange, but once you try these exotic flavors, you'll be hooked forever. You might as well begin trying them at **House of India,** 22 Merrick Way (tel. 444-2348), which has been holding forth since 1975 and now welcomes a loyal crowd of devotees who flock here to try flaky pastry vegetable samosas, fiery curries, mild and intriguingly spiced chicken tandoori. They stop here to take advantage of very reasonable prices too: The luncheon buffet, weekdays and Saturday from 11:30am to 3pm is just $5 to $6; dinner, daily from 5 to 10pm (an hour later on weekends), is likely to be less than $10.

**Lotus Gardens,** 380 Andalusia Ave. (tel. 446-2360), ranks among the best of the many Thai restaurants that have been opening in South Florida in recent years. The atmosphere is simple and straightforward here, but the food is quite good and quite inexpensive. If you've never sampled Thai food, this may be the time to Thai on some tom yum goong, a light broth tangy with lime juice and lemon grass, a touch of hot pepper, a float of scallions, and shrimp. Fire-lovers should adore jumping shrimp, charcoal-grilled then blended with lemon grass and chili peppers. Samplers will delight in more than 60 entrée items, and whoever is paying the bill will delight in a check that is unlikely to top $12 to $15 *for two.* Hours here are 11:30am to 10:30pm Monday through Saturday, 5 to 10:30pm on Sunday.

## Italian

Hum an aria or two as you find your way to **Ristorante Rigoletto,** 65 Merrick Way (tel. 445-1200 or 445-5544), where bravos go to the kitchen for Italian preparations that are both innovative and comfortingly familiar. Here you can stick to basics like vitello marsala or branch out into tortellini alla capricciosa, that stuffed pasta topped with cream, prosciutto, and green peas, or try paglia e feino con salsa rosa, in which both green and white pastas are teamed and topped with a pink sauce, shades of the Italian flag. Angel hair pasta, a comparative newcomer to the pasta platter, is here joined by rigatoni, ziti, linguine, fettuccine, and all the other traditional favorites. Seafood, chicken, veal, and beef fill out the offerings at this handsome dining room where prices fall in the $11 to $17 range for most entrées. Rigoletto's sings its siren's song from noon to 3pm and 6 to 11pm daily except Sunday.

Venice's opera house, La Fenice, glitters but not much more brightly than **La Fenice,** 2728 Ponce de Leon Blvd. (tel. 445-6603). A most elegant dining hall, La

Fenice is a study in cascading fountains, stained-glass windows, glittering crystal chandeliers, skylights, and chic Italian furnishings. There are three dining rooms in this posh spot and a wide variety of Italian and American specialties. Dinner will cost $15 to $25 or more, but you'll have dined in splendor. Hours are 11:30am to 2:30pm weekdays and 6 to 10:30pm except Monday, closing at 11:30pm on weekends.

Yet another elegant Italian dining spot is the **Italian Pavilion** at the beautifully restored Biltmore Hotel, 1200 Anastasia Ave. (tel. 445-1926). An extensive array of traditional American choices from steaks to rack of lamb supplement an equally wide choice of Northern Italian selections. A pianist and guitarist entertain and you can dine both indoors and out here at this chic spot. Prices fall in the $25 to $30 bracket for dinner, and hours are 6 to 11pm daily; brunch from 11am to 2:30pm Sunday.

**Caffè Bacci,** 2522 Ponce de Leon Blvd., Coral Gables (tel. 442-0600), kissed its way right to the top among area Italian restaurants and now seems to have a firm liphold on the upper ranks. That is likely due to the enthusiastic huzzahs accorded the artistic marriage of nouveau styles with antiquo recipes. Fettuccine may be teamed with porcini mushrooms, and gnocchi with a gorgonzola and cream sauce lightly caressed with the tomatoes. Colors and flavors are melded and presented with such skill and flair for the dramatic that you will find yourself lured into concoctions you'd never otherwise dream of trying. That's the joy a fine chef can create and that's the joy that is created here for dinner prices that fall in the $25 to $35 range. Bacci is open from 11:30am to 2pm weekdays and from 6 to 11pm daily.

So good was Nino Pernetti at "kisses" (Caffè Bacci's logo is a pair of bright red lips) that he shortly threw himself into "hugs" as well, creating **Caffè Abbracci,** 318-320 Aragon Ave. (tel. 441-0700). A much larger and more elegant endeavor, Abbracci has met with equal success deservedly. It is a very handsome spot trimmed with two-tone wood, dark green marble and mirrors. Abbracci is the first sit-down restaurant bar in Coral Gables, and it is a chic spot indeed. Similarly new-wave Italian in culinary style, Abbracci features such options as seashell pasta with zucchini and fresh basil and mint, lamb and veal chops, plus lots of innovative medleys. Hours are 5 to 11pm daily, and prices are in the $25 to $35 range.

**Café Marquesa,** 600 Fleming St. (tel. 292-1244), which took over where the former Mira left off in the beautifully restored Marquesa Hotel, is now featuring a blend of—are you ready?—basic American cuisine teamed with South American, African, and Californian touches. That translates into lamb chops the restaurant calls "African style," and such unusual offerings as lobster raviolini, shrimp teamed with corn or topped with a spicy piripiri sauce, a variety of unusual soups, a Delmonico steak with spicy Peruvian chimichuri sauce. Entrées fall into the $12 to $22 price range. Café Marquesa is open from 6 to 11pm daily.

## Budget

Easily the city's best candidate for budget dining in the seafood category is **Shells,** 1813 NE 163rd St., North Miami Beach (tel. 274-5552). A chain restaurant that hit the Florida beaches like a hurricane, Shells has had a real windfall from its presentation of inexpensive seafood in a simple, to say the most, atmosphere. Sooner or later you will see 'most everyone sneaking in here for a dozen oysters at less than $2, a lobster for less than $10, some rib-sticking seafood-topped pasta selections for well under $10. When it's all said and done, Shells is sensational. This shell opens at 5pm daily, closing at 10 weekdays, at 11pm weekends.

**Tiger Tiger Teahouse,** 5785 Sunset Dr. in South Miami (tel. 665-5660), has been around Miami in one place or another for many a moon. A specialist in gourmet Chinese cooking, Tiger Tiger features a Mandarin buffet, then really winds it up to create Peking duck. It's all served in a pleasantly contemporary atmosphere that extends from indoors to out. You're not likely to pay more than $10 to $15 for dinner at Tiger Tiger, which roars from 11:30am to 11pm weekdays, 5:30 to 10pm Saturday and Sunday.

In days gone by Marylyn spent many a joyous gorged-out hour at **Shorty's Barbecue,** 9200 S. Dixie Hwy., South Miami (tel. 665-5732), which had all the prerequisites required in cash-shortfall college days: cheap, hearty food, and lots of it. Shorty's burned down once in the interim, but the charcoal pits have been fired up again with hickory wood and are still going strong, producing memorably great barbecued ribs and chicken. The coleslaw here is the best anywhere in the world and not at all like that ordinary grated stuff—it's little squares of cabbage and lots of celery seed with mystery ingredients. Finish it all off with corn on the cob and something bubbly and you'll see why many an hour's help with term papers was traded for a ride to Shorty's. Prices still are less than $7 for a platter of ribs. Shorty's is open from 11am to 10pm weekdays, opening half an hour later on weekends. There's always a crowd at the dinner hour, but it's worth the wait.

## RESTAURANTS IN COCONUT GROVE

Just locating restaurants in Coconut Grove can be a challenge. Many are tucked away on tiny streets, but all of them are as pretty as the small community around them.

### Continental

Hotel restaurants are all too often as overpriced as they are undertalented in the kitchen. Not so with the **Grand Bay Hotel,** 2669 S. Bayshore Dr. (tel. 858-9600), which welcomes you to a tasteful French nouveau dining room that's a study in mauve, pink, fabulous floral creations, and candlelight glittering on brass and crystal. Lovely as it is, Grand Bay's dining room is not outrageously expensive—unless you cannot live without beluga caviar or the rarest of champagnes. Start, perhaps, with an appetizer of lobster ravioli or grilled shrimp, scallops and mushrooms in a tomato-garlic sauce graced with jalapeño and cayenne peppers. Move on to a salad of duckling breast with a walnut-oil vinaigrette or tortellini soup with truffles and morels. Keep going past black linguine with squid in lime-and-butter sauce, poached salmon in ginger-leek sauce, lobster, sea scallops, to the flaky, fluffy desserts. A grand café, this one's open daily from 7am to 3pm for breakfast and lunch and from 6 to 11pm for dinner daily. You'll pay $17 to $25 for dinner entrées, but the bill will rise rapidly with the addition of other irresistibles.

You'll see the real thing, that moon over Miami, at the **Club Casablanca,** 2649 S. Bayshore Dr. (tel. 858-5005), high atop the Doubletree at Coconut Grove. It changes its menu every few months, but can always be counted on to provide innovative seafood choices and desserts that are sugary hallucinations. Entrée prices are in the $15 to $25 bracket, and the dining room opens at 6pm every day but Sunday.

**Café Europa,** 3159 Commodore Plaza (tel. 448-5723), is an elegant café with indoor or outdoor dining in the $12 to $20 range for dinner. So popular has the salad dressing proven that it's now bottled and sold to diners, who also seek the chef's recipes for escargots au roquefort or artichoke hearts mornay. Open from 5pm to midnight daily, noon to midnight on weekends.

Restaurateur Monty Trainor went head-to-head with Miami's SRO Joe's Stone Crabs Restaurant when he opened **Monty's Stone Crabs** at 3390 Mary St. (tel. 448-9919) in Coconut Grove. Monty's also features those delectable South Florida crab claws at this good-looking dining spot replete with lots of oak, marble, and brass. Stone crabs are the star, but other seafood selections play very good supporting roles at this new Grove dining spot, which features entrée prices in the $15 to $25 range. Hours are 11:30am to 11:30pm daily.

**Kaleidoscope,** 3312 Commodore Plaza (tel. 446-5010), is jammed at lunch when the multitudes flock here for crêpes, eggs Benedict, or unusual salads and sandwiches. It's not much less crowded at dinner when intriguing seafood, beef, pork, and duck dishes are on the menu. They know what people want at Kaleidoscope, and deliver it to them with a friendly dispatch that's made this a favorite gathering spot in Coconut Grove. You can dine outside on a terrace or balcony, or inside in a bistro for prices in the $10 to $20 range. You'd be wise to have reservations. It's open from 11:30am to 3pm and 6 to 11pm daily, later on Friday and Saturday, entertainment nightly except Friday and Saturday.

## Seafood

Conch is king at **Monty Trainor's Bayshore Restaurant,** 2560 S. Bayshore Dr. (tel. 858-1431). You can have some of that elusive creature that hides inside those big pink-eared shells for prices in the $12 to $17 range, or feast on spicy-hot chowders, fritters, shrimp, oysters, perhaps even a grouper or snapper sandwich. Thatched huts are the dining rooms here. It's open from 11am to midnight daily. A lounge, open to 3am, booms out jazz or Top-40s music every night.

**Chart House,** 51 Chart House Dr. (tel. 856-9741), occupies a bayfront location just off Bayshore Drive south of 27th Avenue so you're treated here to a fabulous view of sailboats zipping across the bay. Inside, the view is quite handsome too: lots of wood and plants growing lustily in sunlight that streams down from a skylight. Steaks, chops, prime rib, and a variety of Florida seafood appear on the menu here. A Sunday brunch here is fine fare, including as it does a cold salad and fruit buffet, banana and pumpkin muffins, as well as such selections as a crab omelet and eggs Oscar featuring crab and artichoke hearts served in a puff pastry case. Dinner entrée prices are in the $12 to $20 range and hours are 5 to 11pm daily.

## Light Dining

Coconut Grove remains a village in the midst of a city so it's fitting that many sing the praises of the **Village Inn,** 3131 Commodore Plaza (tel. 445-8721). Popular with shoppers roaming the Grove's shady streets, this dining spot carries that popularity over into the wee hours when there's a band every night of the week. You can nosh on hamburgers here or go the route with a full dinner of pasta, seafood, steaks, or poultry in the $10 to $15 bracket. She-crab soup is an unusual selection here, and the key lime pie has devotees all the way to the Keys. You can see how the village lives from 11am to 3am daily.

## Italian

**Café Sci-Sci** (pronounced "shee-shee"), 3043 Grand Ave. (tel. 446-5104), fits its name quite well, catering to tired masses, exhausted from breathing the rarified air of Mayfair in the Grove shops. Here you dine al fresco beneath pink-and-white umbrellas on Grand Avenue or inside in a chic dining room on 13 varieties of pasta, plenty of seafood selections, veals, chicken—try the pappardella rustica, noodles with shrimp, asparagus, peas, cream, and saffron. Everything's top rate here from zucchini fritti starters to a gelato finale. Things are all Sci-Sci here for lunch and dinner daily (no lunches on Monday) from noon to 12:30am, closing later on weekends. You'll pay prices in the $11 to $21 range for à la carte dining.

## Mexican

Ribit, ribit—what's this huge green lily pad doing here in Coconut Grove? Why, it's the home of Señor Frog, what else? Funky, frog-green, and fun just begin to describe a zany spot called **Señor Frog's,** 3008 Grand Ave., Coconut Grove (tel. 448-0999). Sepia-tone photos of Mexican revolutionary heroes adorn the walls, and outdoors there's a shady patio where you can imbibe a couple of Dos Equis beers and munch on baskets of tortilla chips with zippy tomato-jalapeño sauce. Later you can chow down on Talk-to-Me-Sideways brochette, moo flute or peep flutes, which translate to beef or chicken flautas, or yummy enchiladas in a green sauce. Despite the sound of it, this is no fast-food taco joint. Mr. Frog tries to keep dining as authentically Mexican as he can, serving up tortilla soup, tostadas Xochimilco with chipotle, and a favorite, pollo Plaza with chicken in a *mole verde* sauce. If you haven't the vaguest idea what any of that is, never fear, gringo, someone will help you over the Spanish barrier. Prices are moderate—you'll pay tariffs in the $5 to $12 bracket for anything on the menu here. Señor Frog welcomes you to his pad from 5pm to 2am weekdays, 2pm to 2am on Saturday and Sunday.

## RESTAURANTS IN KEY BISCAYNE

This sandy island isn't big enough to have many restaurants, but those it does have are popular with islanders and with those they call "off islanders" (everyone else).

**Stefano's,** at 24 Crandon Blvd. (tel. 361-7007), is a welcome newcomer that's been getting lots of attention—and with good reason. You can find excellent pastas here, and dine on steaks, veal, chicken, and seafood treats with Italian touches. Stefano's is open from 6pm to 1am daily for dinner; the lounge is open and has entertainment to 5am. Entrée prices are in the $12 to $20 range.

The Sonesta Beach Hotel, at 6350 Ocean Dr. on Key Biscayne, has two Asian restaurants, one Chinese, one Japanese, and both dwell together in a restaurant called the **Two Dragons** (tel. 361-2020). There's a pretty view of garden greenery in the Chinese room's pagodas. Some top creations here are steamed wonton dumplings, roast duck Kowloon, and an intriguing number called Eight Immortals. There's a complete Japanese menu as well. Try a Japanese beer, Kirin, while you're here. Dinner's from 6 to 11pm daily, and entrée prices are in the $15 to $21 range. Two Dragons is also open for Sunday brunch from 10:30am to 2:30pm (prix-fixe $20).

A former Key Biscayne landmark called the Jamaica Inn has been transformed into the **English Pub,** 320 Crandon Blvd. (tel. 361-5481), specializing in beef and seafood creations. Dinner prices are in the $10 to $15 range or less, and there's often entertainment here too. Hours are 11:30am to 3pm weekdays and 6 to 11pm daily, closing an hour later on weekends.

Among the island's newest dining diversons is a Nicaraguan restaurant called **La Choza,** 973 Crandon Blvd. (tel. 361-0113). Beef is a mainstay here, so you'll find tenderloin—called churrasco—perfectly grilled and served, if you like, with a jalapeño sauce or grilled onions. A Nicaraguan version of teriyaki appears on the menu too. This is a great place to introduce yourself to a new Hispanic cuisine that is just beginning to make inroads in the area. Dinner prices are in the $15 to $20 range. Hours are noon to 3pm weekdays for lunch, 6 to 11pm daily for dinner.

---

# 5. Culture and Nightlife

Nightlife on Miami Beach and in Miami can be as quiet or as lively as you want it to be. Sparkling sequined beauties strut through Vegas-style dance routines; supper clubs have entertainment and dancing. There's music from jazz band to jukebox, and performers from comedians to dancers, including some of the nation's most famous entertainers.

You can fly to Freeport, the Bahamas (for very low rates and sometimes even for free), if you're willing to stake a few dollars at the gaming tables there.

Here in Miami, as everywhere, lavish entertainment isn't cheap, so be prepared to fork over $100 or more for a night of dancing, dining, and entertainment, depending on your proclivity for posh. Drinks are comparatively expensive in top clubs too. Although most smaller lounges don't have cover charges, they frown on one who nurses a solitary drink all evening.

Superstars come to Miami Beach in December and stay through the winter season to provide a continuing round of glittering name entertainment through April. To see the very top stars perform will definitely be expensive—one New Year's Eve recently a top star was pulling $200 a person! You can find out who's where and when in several free magazines distributed in motel and hotel lobbies—*See, Where,* and *This Week in Miami.*

Latin nightclubs are some of the most popular places in town, and not only with the city's large and lively Latin population. Shows at these clubs are every bit the extravaganza you'd see in Vegas, with lots of glitter and excitement. It's just the prices that aren't quite so flashy.

If you'd like to see a show or two and leave the driving to them, call **American Sightseeing Tours** at 688-7700. They'll pick you up at your hotel, give you a choice of nightclubs, and toss in dinner, tips, and transportation. Tours are $40 per person.

First we'll take a look at special events and the culture scene, and then look at Miami and Miami Beach after dark. Also, reread our hotel and restaurant recommendations for additional nightspots and details.

## SPECIAL EVENTS

Miami loves a party. At no time of year is that more evident than on New Year's Eve, when the city turns out for its annual **Orange Bowl Parade.** A nationally televised event, the parade features marching bands and floats, high-stepping majorettes, and an Orange Bowl Queen surrounded by her glittering princesses. The parade is the culmination of several weeks of parties, tournaments, and shows of all kinds.

Later in January, the city's Hispanic community celebrates Christmas on Cuban time—three weeks or so after the event! Called the **Festival de los Tres Reyes,** this mid-January celebration honors the Three Kings of biblical fame with a parade and plenty of feasting.

In February the activity moves to Coconut Grove, when artists, sculptors, billionaires, and bohemians gather for the annual **Coconut Grove Art Festival.**

As Miami's Cuban connection has become more familiar to the city's American population, Miamians have begun to capitalize on their city's lusty Latin flavor. Some years ago festival-loving Cubans began a small annual party called **Carnaval Miami.** At first Carnaval looked a little like a party to which no one came, but over the years this fiesta has grown like the proverbial Topsy until today it's a huge 10 day event that lures hundreds of thousands to the merriment, music, and maracas of SW 8th Street. If you're here for this potpourri of Latin music, food, dances, and a wildly colorful parade, you will learn a great deal about the "new" Miami—and perhaps also learn to salsa, drink a coco frio, and pound out a mean beat on the maracas as you dance in the streets. One thing is certain: You won't be bored. Carnaval occurs each March and gets lots of publicity in local newspapers. The **Miami Latin Chamber of Commerce,** 1417 W. Flagler St. (tel. 642-3870), also can fill you in on details of this fun-and-frolic fiesta.

## THE CULTURE SCENE

Over the years Miami has taken a lot of flak for its lack of cultural pursuits. That criticism is not really fair, at least not anymore.

The newest star in Miami's cultural life is the **Metro-Dade Cultural Center,** 101 W. Flagler St., which is home to both the Center for the Fine Arts and the Historical Museum of Southern Florida.

Miami's quite proud—and justly so—of its new **Center for the Fine Arts** (tel. 375-1700), which was designed by famed architect Philip Johnson. Top traveling exhibitions are backed by a permanent collection housed in a quite contemporary two-story building. Hours at the downtown museum are 10am to 5pm Tuesday to Saturday (closing at 9pm on Thursday), and noon to 5pm on Sunday. Admission is $3 for adults, $2 for children.

At the **Historical Museum of Southern Florida** (tel. 375-1492) exhibits chronicle more than 10,000 years of habitation on these sunny shores. Quite an innovative hands-on spot, the museum features a Spanish fort, two Seminole chickees, a sailing ship, a restored trolley car that once clanged its way around the city. Hours and admission fee are the same as the Center for the Fine Arts.

The **Greater Miami Opera Association** (tel. 854-1643) presents grand and light opera in the winter months at the Dade County Auditorium, at 2901 W. Flagler St., Miami, and the **International Cultural Exchange** brings talented international singers, dancers, and musicians to the auditorium all year long.

Producer Zev Bufman must get much of the credit for putting Miami on the theater map. Top stars now appear here in a winter-long series of Broadway plays at the **Theater of the Performing Arts** (TOPA), 1700 Washington Ave., Miami Beach (tel. 673-8300). *A Chorus Line, Annie, Les Miserables,* and *Cats* were a few of the many recent shows, and Elizabeth Taylor debuted her popular *Little Foxes* here. Tickets generally cost $25 to $40. The **Miami Beach Symphony** also plays at TOPA, which has recently been renovated, making it better than ever.

In Coconut Grove, the lovely old **Coconut Grove Playhouse,** 3500 Main Hwy. (tel. 442-4000) has world premiere and classic plays (and sometimes pre-Broadway runs) for $10 to $35.

Miami's **Gusman Center for the Performing Arts,** 174 E. Flagler St. (tel. 358-3388), is an attraction in itself, never mind what's going on there. Interiors dating back several decades are studded with Spanish turrets and stars twinkle on the ceiling. There's an antique Wurlitzer pipe organ and an ornate, velvet-curtained ticket office. Many different kinds of acts and concerts make an appearance here. Local newspapers, the *Miami Herald* and *Miami News* will tell you what's going on. Ticket prices vary, of course, according to the fame of the performers.

Young actors get their start at the **University of Miami's Ring Theater,** one of the nation's outstanding university theaters. Plays, many of them avant-garde productions, are performed here regularly in both winter and summer seasons. Tickets are $5 to $17 for most presentations, but times and dates vary so give them a call at 284-3355. You'll find the theater on the campus at 1380 Miller Dr., entrance #6, in Coral Gables.

## MIAMI BEACH

**Sheraton Bal Harbour Hotel,** 9701 Collins Ave. (tel. 865-7511), has won critics' awards for its lavish, sparkling Las Vegas–revue show featuring huge casts of showgirls, spangled and fandangled sets, and costumes glittering with sequins and rhinestones. It's top entertainment, and shows are at 9 and 11pm (it would be wise to check, as times do change). You can have dinner here too. Reserve and bring money.

The **Fontainebleau Hilton Resort and Spa,** 4441 Collins Ave. (tel. 538-2000), has not remained one of Miami Beach's flagship hotels all these years by sleeping on the job. They flow with the tides here as you'll see if you stop by the hotel's Poodle Lounge, where something is always happening. Tropigala is a spangled, high-stepping, high-energy revue here for $13.50 plus two drinks.

Beach hotels (the Castle Resort, Deauville, Eden Roc, Fontainebleau Hilton, and the Diplomat in nearby Hallandale, to name a few) bring **top-name talent** here during the winter season. It can cost quite a bit to see them, and naturally the bigger the name the bigger the price. Frank Sinatra, Liza Minnelli, and the late Sammy Davis, Jr., have all appeared here and filled huge rooms at prices of $100 a person or more.

There is no better way to immerse yourself in the city's art deco past while remaining firmly in its deco-rous present than to join the throngs who pack themselves bicep-to-proboscis into **Deco's,** 1235 Washington Ave., Miami Beach (tel. 531-1235). This hysterically popular nightspot began life in 1938 when it was the French Casino, built at a cost of $5 million as sister to a similar showplace of the same name in New York. Over the years it also served as the city's cinema theater and as a vaudeville house.

In 1984 after a $5-million renovation, the building was restored to its former art deco glory. Here you'll find a long, curving bar made of iridescent mother-of-pearl, recessed neon lighting bordered in etched-glass mirrors, chrome-and-glass lighting fixtures rimming a sweeping staircase that rises to a balcony lounge, and spectacular art deco murals. More than 2,000 people can see and be seen in here at one time, and on some evenings the place seems stuffed to the max. The cover charge varies according to what's going on, but you can figure to pay $10 to $15 to get in, about $3 for drinks. Deco's is open on Thursday, Friday and Saturday, and once a month on Sunday from 10pm to 5am.

**Place for Steak,** 1335 79th St. Causeway, North Bay Village (tel. 758-5581), features a variety of musical options from pianist to trios every night from 8pm to 2am. No cover charge.

Once again, for the most up-to-date information on what's happening each weekend, check the *Miami Herald* or *Miami News* entertainment pages each Friday.

A popular Miami Beach amusement is called **Friday Night Live** and occurs—guess when?—at South Pointe Park, 1 Washington Ave. (tel. 673-7730). Here you sit outside in a park by the sea while performers entertain you with everything from blue grass to an Elvis Presley Revue. Shows differ, but occur every week from June to October and they're free. Bring a beach chair or blanket; there are no seats.

Pink neon poodles prance at the **Poodle Lounge** in the Fontainebleau Hilton Resort, but that is not all that prances here. A lively spot with live entertainment, the Poodle is informal but not casual; it's up to you to decipher the difference. Hours are 6pm to the wee moments daily in winter; closed Monday in summer. There's no cover charge.

Those in the know in Miami Beach hie on over to the poolside bar at the **Clevelander,** 1020 Ocean Dr. (tel. 531-3485). In the heart of Miami Beach's art deco district, the Clevelander serves up exotic tropical concoctions, usually some entertainment and grazing food from noon to 4am daily. There's no cover charge.

**Island Club,** 701 Washington Ave. (tel. 538-1213), keeps some very late hours, late enough at least to satisfy the trendy crowd that now populates South Beach wee-hour spots. A very casual spot, the Island Club has a compact disc jukebox, a Ping-Pong table and a *Why Not* art gallery showing the work of two local folk artists. A hanging-around haven in the deco district, Island Club is open from 5pm to 5am daily except Sunday, and there's no cover charge.

Marco Polo Resort's **Club Bennett's,** 19201 Collins Ave., Sunny Isles (tel. 932-2233) has had many incarnations over the years but at the moment it's featuring music of the '50s, '60s, and '70s played on a fancy sound system hosted by a disc jockey. A casual club, it's open from 5pm to 3am daily and there's a cover charge only on special occasions.

Winter season always finds something rocking at Marco Polo, which has had a legendary lounge show of one kind or another for decades. A recent offering here was the Miami Ice Follies, a showy show-girl revue à la Las Vegas, so expect something similar. Shows are usually at 8pm Wednesday through Sunday, with a Sunday matinee at 2pm and an admission charge of $15 or so.

One of the biggies on the Beach is **Club Nu,** 245 22nd St. (tel. 672-0068). Nothing is ever the same here from night to night and that includes the decor and the nightly entertainment, not even to mention the crowd. Perhaps the trendiest of trendy spots, Club Nu often has a $10 to $15 cover charge on weekends and is open from 9pm to 7, 8 or 9am; closed Sunday and Monday.

**New Chevy's on the Beach,** in the Quality Inn–Surfside, 8701 Collins Ave.,

Surfside (tel. 868-1950 or 865-6661), is new in name only. Here the past reigns supreme from the classic car at the entrance to the '50s and '60s music and the matching-era neon. Jukebox music, disc jockettes, weird contests, and special events are what goes on in the back seat of this Chevy from 9pm to 2 or 3am Thursday, Friday, and Saturday. There's sometimes a $5 cover charge for big events, and although the atmosphere is casual, that doesn't include T-shirts, shorts, or cutoff jeans.

Whatever formula lounge entrepreneur Jack Penrod uses to ensure the success of a new nightspot is the right one. Wherever a Penrod's pops up, the crowds follow. That's what has happened here at **Penrod's on the Beach,** First Street and Ocean Drive (tel. 538-1111), where the crowds stream in from noon to the never-never hour. Quite an interesting spot it is too, complete with immense strip of beach in front, swimming pool in the middle, and nubile bodies everywhere. What can be seen here is plenty, both in quantity of skin and in general people-watching. Perhaps you should be seen here too, one way or the other. Penrod's has live music every night and a cover charge of $5 for those over 21, $10 for younger attendees. Hours are from 11pm to 2am weekdays, until 5am Friday and Saturday.

**Fifth Street,** 429 Lenox Ave. (tel. 531-1910), features a live rhythm and blues jazz band every Friday, recorded music the rest of the week, but draws crowds every day until the wee hours. A dining room called **Natalie's** (tel. 672-9774) shares the action here, serving what they like to call New American cuisine, such as filet mignon and seafood, crêpes, and the like, often with unusual combinations of flavors. Dinner prices are in the $10 to $17 range for entrées. The restaurant serves dinner from 6pm to 2am Wednesday through Sunday, but it's the music that draws the crowds here—and that goes on from 10pm to 4am daily, from 5pm on Friday.

There's lots to see and do at **Scratch,** 427 Jefferson Ave. (tel. 674-1831), which won popularity as a casual restaurant serving all the American favorites from pasta to beef and fish dishes. Add to that a dance club with recorded disco music on Saturday nights and a small theater out back that often presents one-act *avant garde* plays. You can Scratch from 5pm to midnight daily except Monday.

Just at the edge of the Art Deco district you'll find the Hotel Esplanade and in it a wildly popular spot called the **Kitchen Club,** with an adjoining and equally popular and populated place called **Beirut,** both at 100 21st St. (tel. 538-6631). At the Kitchen Club they stir up progressive sounds from Thursday to Sunday (ladies' night on Friday) from 10pm to 5am, and in Beirut, rock 'n' roll joins Mid East and Midwest and all points between. The cover charge at either is $5.

**News Café,** 800 Ocean Dr. (tel. 538-6397 or 531-0392), and the adjoining **Music Room,** aren't really nightspots, but if you're touring Miami Beach's after-dark action—as most everybody in South Florida seems to be these nights—they make a great stopping spot for late-night light bites and libations. Fare leans toward quiches, huge sandwiches, fruit, homemade breads, and bistro basics at the News Café, and to desserts and drinks in the Music Room, where '20's decor and swing sounds bring the deco era to 1990's life. Prices are in the $5 to $7 range and hours are 8pm to 2am.

To find out what's rocking in town, look for a copy of a local nightspot-newspaper called *New Times* on sale at record shops like Spec's and on newsstands

## MIAMI

Miami's jazziest nightclubs are Latin operated, which is not surprising considering the raves one hears about Old Havana's nightclubs. Top spot is **Les Violins,** 1751 Biscayne Blvd. (tel. 371-9910), which produces spectacular shows filled with dancing, singing, strutting showgirls dressed in flashy costumes performing on sets that rise, fall, open up, and practically perform their own show. Shows are usually at 9 and 11pm, and there's very good Spanish cuisine here in the $10 to $20 range.

Running a close second is **Malaga,** 740 SW 8th St. (tel. 858-4224), which has flamenco dancers, guitarists, singers, and dinners in the same general price range as

Les Violins. There are two, sometimes three, shows nightly and a two-drink minimum some evenings. In true Latin style, nothing starts popping here before 9pm but really warms up about midnight. Shows are so good you'll feel transported from Miami straight to the Costa del Sol.

Many of Coconut Grove's restaurants have good evening entertainment (see our restaurant recommendations), and you'll spend an amusing evening at **Coco Loco,** 495 Brickell Ave. in Sheraton Brickell Point Hotel (tel. 373-6000), and hear some good jazz or reggae at **Monty's.**

In July and August stars like Andy Williams, Ray Charles, and Dionne Warwick join the Florida Philharmonic for a series of concerts at **Key Biscayne's Marine Stadium** (tel. 361-6730), an outdoor stadium under the stars on Biscayne Bay. Boaters attend too, with front-row seats right out on the water. You can sometimes buy tickets that include dinner at restaurants on the island, and the show, for $25 to $35. Tickets are available through island hotels; the concerts alone cost $5 to $12.

Latin restaurants like **El Floridita, Bilbao, El Baturro,** and **El Cid** in Little Havana have music for dancing and flamenco dancers, guitarists, strolling singers, and lots of fun for nothing more than the price of a drink or two, and those are only $2 to $3.

All over the county **Big Daddy's** operates lounges popular with the young set who take advantage of drink bargains and lively entertainment.

Looking for something to do before the 4am plane? Out near the airport, **Daphne's** in the Sheraton River House is one of the city's hot spots and goes on to the wees as does **Gambits** in the Marriott and **Scandals** at Ramada.

Jazz/blues spots: **Suzanne's in the Grove,** 2843 S. Bayshore Dr., Coconut Grove (tel. 441-1500), open from 4pm to 5am daily except Monday; **Tobacco Road,** 626 S. Miami Ave. (tel. 374-1198), is a rustic, historic spot with both upstairs and downstairs rooms, open from 9pm to 5am with a $5 cover charge.

**Monty Trainor's Bayshore Inn,** 2560 S. Bayshore Dr., Coconut Grove (tel. 858-1431), is another favored hangout, with a band on weekends.

A number of top-name performers warm up in winter with performances in Miami. Many of those performances are at **Gusman Center,** 174 E. Flagler St. in the heart of downtown Miami (tel. 374-2444), or at the **James L. Knight Center,** next door to the Hyatt Hotel at 400 SE 2nd St. (tel. 372-0929). Tickets vary in price.

**Copacabana Supper Club,** 3600 SW 8th St. (tel. 443-3801), is another Latin spot that has become very popular. It offers good shows with singers, dancers, and an orchestra, and is open from 8pm to 3am daily except Monday. There's a two-drink minimum and sometimes a small cover charge.

If you're a jazz music fan, you can call a **Jazz Hot Line** (tel. 382-3938) to see what's playing. Blues fans can do the same with the **Blues Hot Line** (tel. 666-6656).

Oh dear, what have we here? **Fire and Ice,** 3841 NE Second Ave. (tel. 573-3473), certainly will strike you hot or leave you cold, depending entirely on what you bring here—and we don't mean your companion. Friday is a particularly unusual night, a night when this disco sponsors something called Artifacts. Art is feted at this event, and area artists are invited to do their damnedest to turn the evening into an Event that falls somewhere between a happening and a what-happened. Among the memorable Artifacts moments have been the creation of a New York City streetscape, a Dadaist fantasy featuring a Citroën and a coffin filled with colorful bowling pins, and a Suburban Nightmare starring giant boxes of Tide and Kellogg's Corn Flakes. According to reports, a couple of creative types once turned up dressed as a nuclear-powered aircraft intent on getting destroyed here. On really good evenings you may become part of the painting, a little splash here, a couple of daubs there. Fire and Ice flames hot and cold Thursday, Friday, and Saturday from 8pm to some early a.m. witching hour. After 11pm, cover is $5.

Up on the north end of the beach, the **Marco Polo Resort** rocks to the wee hours, as does the **Holiday Inn Newport Pier Resort.** Both draw crowds of young people.

On Key Biscayne, the **Sonesta Beach Hotel** always has something going in its lounges, as does the **Royal Biscayne Hotel.**

**Tobacco Road,** 626 S. Miami Ave. (tel. 374-1198), possesses Liquor License No. 001 in Miami, which speaks tomes about its longevity in this chameleon city. Still going strong after 75 years, Tobacco Road was once a Prohibition speakeasy, later a gangster den, then a gambling parlor, then a jazz club. It still looks about like any other bar but there's a ghostly ambience here and a secret staircase that continues to lure funseekers in search of a lively evening. Open every night to 3am. Tobacco Road begins smoking about 10pm when the night's entertainment begins. There's a $5 cover charge on weekends and for special events.

**Uncle Funny's Comedy Club,** in Holiday Inn–Calder Hotel, 21465 NW 27th Ave., Carol City (tel. 624-7266), features stand-up comedy with some top comedians in a new show every week. Cover charge is $5 or $6 and there's a two-drink minimum. You find everyone feeling funny here at 9pm Thursday through Saturday with a second show at 11pm Friday and Saturday.

On Key Biscayne, **Desire,** in the Sonesta Beach Hotel, 350 Ocean Dr. (tel. 361-2021), is a lively spot with chic decor and a trendy crowd that stops by to dance away the hours. A little romantic, a little trendy, a lot lively, Desire serves up exotic sipping and continuous music from 8pm to 2am Thursday through Saturday and to midnight Sunday through Wednesday.

Façade is what it's all about at **Façade Nightclub,** 3509 NE 163rd St., North Miami Beach (tel. 948-6868). A two-story hi-tech showplace, Façade's takes a look at your facade while you're taking a look at its. Whatever yours may look like, Façade's facade includes a multimillion-dollar light-and-sound show, a huge sunken dance floor, six bars and two champagne rooms, whew! There's a varying cover charge usually $10 to $15, often free for women, at this biggie, which is open from 9pm to 6am Tuesday through Sunday and frowns on super-casual dress defined as sneakers and T-shirts.

The Grand Bay Hotel's **Ciga Lounge,** 2669 S. Bayshore Dr. in Coconut Grove (tel. 858-9600), has a duo nightly except Friday and Sunday.

Rock, pop, and reggae can be found at **Churchill's Hideaway,** 5501 NE Second Ave. (tel. 757-1087), which often showcases new bands.

Two upscale, once private clubs are now open to all and sundry and lure some of Miami's chicest visitors and residents.

One of those is **Stringfellows,** 3390 Mary St., Coconut Grove (tel. 446-7555). Now calling itself a semiprivate club, this handsome nightspot still has an impressive membership list but will add your name to the nightly visitors roster for a $15 cover charge for gentlemen, $10 for ladies. Open Tuesday through Saturday, Stringfellows strings out the early evening with jazz sounds from 8 to 11pm, then gets fellows and gals jumping from 11pm to 5am with a live band or deejay heating up the disco night.

Those with a penchant for discipline but no desire to go too far with it can consign themselves to the unit headed by **Ensign Bitters,** in the Mayfair House, 3000 Florida Ave., Coconut Grove (tel. 441-0000). You probably won't find any ensigns here but you will find the chic and trendy saluting each other at the occasional lambada night or just dancing up a basic dance storm at the deejay-led disco. Ensign Bitters stands at attention Tuesday through Thursday from 5pm to 2am, and on Friday and Saturday from 7am to 5am. Cover is $15 for gentlemen, free to ladies.

**Peacock's Café,** 9477 McFarland Rd., Coconut Grove (tel. 442-8877), starts its happy hour buffet at 5pm daily except Monday and keeps it going until 2am. On weekends the Peacock crows upstairs with a deejay and disco sounds. No cover charge.

In a town made famous by a "moon Over Miami" melody, one hesitates to mention **Savannah Moon,** 13505 S. Dixie Hwy. (US1), South Miami (tel. 238-8868). Fortunately the moon also shines on this Savannah, where music lovers gather for dining, then move on to the lounge for listening and dancing to the sounds of big band and jazz music from 10pm to 2am, an hour later on weekends. There's no cover charge.

**Currents Lounge,** in the Hyatt Regency City Center, 400 SE 2nd Ave. (tel. 358-1234), flows with the tidal wave of tourists and residents who meander through this big downtown hotel adjacent to the Knight Center where many top-name acts appear. A band is on hand with Top Forties music from 9pm to 1am or later Wednesday through Saturday. There's no cover charge.

**Tavern in the Grove,** 3416 Main Hwy., Coconut Grove (tel. 447-3884), is packed nearly every evening with Groveites and visitors reveling in the "it's my locale" feel of this casual lounge purveying beer and wine and conviviality. Hours are 3pm to 3am weekdays and 1pm to 3am on weekends, when ladies' drinks are free.

To find out what's on this week, check the *Miami Herald*'s Showtime section published each Friday.

---

# 6. Seeing the Sights

From the oldest building in the hemisphere to a simulated hurricane, Miami and Miami Beach run the gamut in attractions. Calle Ocho's (Little Havana's 8th Street) infectious gaiety is waiting to entertain you and a performing dolphin would like a moment of your time. Miami beats Miami Beach in attractions, so let's take a look at what to see and do in that city first.

## THE SIGHTS OF MIAMI

At the top of our list of things to see in Miami is **Vizcaya,** at 3251 S. Miami Ave. (tel. 579-2813), an enchanting private villa built by James Deering, the International Harvester millionaire, who for $15 million constructed a Renaissance palace and filled it with a fortune in art and treasures he'd collected for more than 20 years. You can tour 34 of the villa's 70 rooms and roam the serene formal gardens put together by 1,000 craftspeople who worked on this creation for five years. Those gardens wind around fountains, statuary, and reflecting pools, and range over 10 acres of ground, some of it untouched jungle. Inside are frescoed ceilings, tapestries, and priceless paintings. Outside, wide steps lead to the sea, where across the water is "moored" a stone barge that serves as a breakwater for the mansion. (You can even get married in the romantic stone courtyard—we should know.) Vizcaya is open every day except Christmas from 9:30am to 4:30pm. Admission is $8 for adults, $4 for children 6 to 18.

Not far away, Charles Deering, once board chairman of International Harvester, bought 360 acres in 1914 and moved into a frame structure that had been a hotel. Next door he built a fireproof stone house for himself and his art treasures with walls ten inches thick, no kitchen, and no direct lighting that could cause fires. Although that stone house, which is now owned by the city of Miami and called the **Deering Estate,** was opulent for its day, it does not compare in grandeur with Vizcaya. Both are being restored.

Acquisition of the estate's grounds, acres and acres of barely touched natural forest, are a major coup for a county that has been so developed there are few areas of natural beauty left. Here, however, you can roam through 100 acres of mangroves, 100 acres of pineland, and a towering stand of royal palms to get a look at what a natural wonder this part of the state must once have been—and here still is. Plans are afoot to turn the houses into bed-and-breakfast inns and add an interpretive nature museum. Meanwhile you can visit the Deering Estate on weekends from 9am to 5pm. Admission is $4 for adults, $2 for children under 12. You'll find the estate at 16701 SW 72nd Ave. (tel. 235-1668), not far from the intersection of Old Cutler and Ludlum roads.

Near Vizcaya is the **Museum of Science and Space Planetarium,** 3280 S. Miami Ave. (tel. 854-4247), a place often billed as a retreat for children. Let me tell you, however, that we once spent part of a delightful day here making huge soap bubbles, watching our hair stand on end at the electricity maker, talking over the parabola thing, and just generally poking around the fascinating hands-on exhibits. Here are all the concepts you once learned in science class but have long since forgotten, are brought to life with wood blocks, pendulums, and things that whir and twirl. When you finish playing, you can browse through the Natural History Collection Gallery, where weird and/or wondrous things are displayed in pull-out drawers and wall exhibits. At the Wildlife Center there are more than 180 live creatures. This offers you the opportunity to touch a tarantula, stroke a snake, or pet a turtle, if you're inclined toward that sort of amusement. There's no doubt about it, children will love this place, but you're likely to be elbowing them aside so you can play too. Figure about three or four hours playtime here, and don't miss the gift shop where some unusual educational toys are on sale. At the Planetarium you can stargaze with people who know what's up. The museum is open from 10am to 6pm daily, and admission is $5 for adults and $3.50 for children 3 to 12. For planetarium star, multimedia, and laser showtimes and prices, call 854-2222.

**Miami Youth Museum,** 5701 Sunset Dr., in the Bakery Centre, South Miami (tel. 661-ARTS), is larger than ever now and is still a charming spot for children to dress up in a suit of armor, weave baskets, and crawl into a cave set with caveman utensils. Open from 10am to 5pm Monday through Friday and from noon to 5pm on Saturday and Sunday, the hands-on Youth Museum charges $3 admission.

Here is one who knows plenty about oceans: Flipper the performing dolphin at **Miami Seaquarium,** Rickenbacker Causeway, Virginia Key (tel. 361-5703). He (or is it she?) and friends do high jumps while laughable sea lions and seals flipper and flutter about. You can see the whole 60 acres on a monorail trip, then visit habitats of sea mammals, birds, and turtles, and sea lion magicians every day from 9:30am to 6:30pm with continuous shows. Admission is $13.95 for adults, $9.95 for children 3 to 12.

Finally on Key Biscayne is **Bill Baggs State Park,** which isn't exactly an attraction but it's awfully attractive. During some bad days with the Seminoles in Miami, the lighthouse keeper here was nearly burned out of his aerie, but he tossed down a keg of gunpowder. It frightened away the survivors and signaled a ship at sea, which came to his rescue. Today the park's a beachy sylvan retreat.

If you fondly remember that orchid you wore to the prom or got or gave for Mother's Day, you'll adore **Orchid Jungle,** 26715 SW 157th Ave. (tel. 247-4824). It's the world's largest outdoor orchid garden, and has blooms in every color of the rainbow. Admission is $5 for adults, $1.50 for ages 6 to 13, $4 for ages 13 to 17. Hours are 8:30am to 5:30pm daily.

Miami's **Bayside Marketplace** shopping center isn't really a "sight" in the strictest sense of the word, but as cornerstone to a massive development at the city's smashingly beautiful bayfront, it's worth a look. An enclave of nearly 200 trendy restaurants and chic boutiques, this stroll-around indoor-outdoor waterfront spender-haven makes an interesting spot to get that Florida feeling everyone's always talking about. Bayfront is at its best at night when its artful lighting creates a romantic seaside setting here. You'll find it at 401 Biscayne Blvd., right at the entrance to the Port of Miami.

**MGM's _Bounty_** is another new sight in Miami, and quite a sight it is too, its bright flags flapping merrily and its massive decks gleaming. It's not at all difficult to imagine the epic contest between Captain Bligh and Mr. Christian when you're aboard hearing narration by Charles Laughton and Clark Gable! This _Bounty_ is a replica of the ship used to film _Mutiny on the Bounty,_ and after spending many years in St. Petersburg is now here in Miami at a dock tucked out in front of Bayside's waterfront boutiques, 401 Biscayne Blvd., and is open from 9am to 5pm daily. Admission and tour is $3.50 for adults, $1.50 for children 4 to 12. You can reach the ship at 375-0486.

Another sailing ship recently joined the entertainment ranks in Miami. This one is called **Harrah's Belle** and it's an 80-foot replica of the paddlewheel riverboats that spawned natty riverboat gamblers and handsomely gowned belles. *Harrah's Belle* sails Indian Creek and the Intracoastal Waterway on a variety of cruises ranging from brunch to buffet lunch, dinner, and starlight cruises. Prices range from $10 to $35 per person, $3 to $5 less for children. *Harrah's Belle* is docked at the Eden Roc Yacht and Charter Club, 4525 Collins Ave., Miami Beach, from mid-November to May (tel. 672-5911 in those months, or 201/528-6620 in other months).

We are all well aware that it is a jungle out there, but two other Miami "jungles" make the jungle look fun.

At **Parrot Jungle and Gardens,** 11000 SW 57th Ave. (tel. 666-7834), more than 1,000 rainbow-hued parrots, macaws, toucans, and the like fly free, ham it up for photographers, ride bicycles, and perform in a variety of entertaining shows at this 30-acre tropical park and wildlife habitat. Bird shows, a children's playground, and a petting zoo await from 9:30am to 6pm daily. You can even dine among the squawkers at the Parrot Café, which serves from 8am to 5pm. Admission to Parrot Jungle and Gardens is $10.50 for adults; $5.25 for children 3 to 12; those aged 2 and under are free.

At **Monkey Jungle,** 14805 SW 216th St. (tel. 235-1611), people are caged and monkeys roam free—which may be the way it was meant to be. Hours at this always-entertaining kingdom of the monkeys are 9:30am to 5pm daily. Admission is $8.25 for adults, $4.50 for children 4 to 12.

Miami has a fascinating new zoo, called **Metrozoo,** where the animals roam free on 290 acres, separated from visitors by moats and natural barriers. You can get a look at the zoo from 9:30am to 5:30pm daily (last entry at 4pm) at $8 for adults, $4 for children 3 to 12. Don't miss the cuddly koalas or big cats—gorgeous white tigers—slinking around an Angor Wat temple look-alike. The zoo's at 12400 SW 152nd St. (tel. 251-0400), near the Florida Turnpike.

You can spend hours here roaming among the "islands" where gorilla moms and pops romp with their children, tweeting with the birds in a giant "Wings of Asia" aviary exhibit, and visiting the Eurasian steppes, a European forest, and the African veldt. Try an elephant ride for big laughs. You get around it all on a monorail which you can ride all day from one section of this massive zoo to another. There are restaurants and gift shops here, animal feedings and shows, and you can even ride an elephant.

A vintage steam engine pulling antique railroad cars now chugs along beside Metrozoo. Called the **Gold Coast Railroad Museum** (tel. 253-0063), the historic railroad cars were once stationed at Fort Lauderdale's airport but were moved here in 1985 to make way for airport expansion. You can ride the cars, which include a 1913 steam locomotive, a Silver Crescent car with observation dome, something called a Ferdinand Magellan, and lots of others, at $5 for adults, $2 to $3 for children 3 to 12. Trains toot off from 10am to 3pm weekdays, to 5pm on Saturday and Sunday. To get to the railroad, use the Metrozoo access road at 12400 SW 152nd St., but turn right at the bridge to 12450 SW 152nd St.

One way to see many of Miami's sights is aboard the **Old Town Trolley of Miami,** 650 NW Eighth St., Miami (tel. 374-TOUR). A snappy trolley whizzes you around the city from downtown Miami along shady Brickell Avenue and Bayshore Drive and through Coconut Grove. Stops include several large hotels, the Bayside Marketplace, Miami Seaquarium, Vizcaya, Mayfair, the elegantly restored Biltmore Hotel, Venetian Pool, and Calle Ocho, the city's Little Havana Cuban center.

A narrated journey, the tour will fill you in on Miami's fascinating and character-filled history. You can get on and off whenever you like as the tours run the same route all day from 9am to about 4pm. Fares are $12 for adults, $4 for children 4 to 12.

A tall ship called **Heritage of Miami II** sailed into town in 1988 and is now moored at Bayside Marketplace, adding a touch of old world glamour to that very contemporary spot. A topsail schooner, *Heritage* has old lines but is a new craft with a design based on turn-of-the-century vessels that plied these waters with cargo and passengers headed into the tradewinds. Painted a lively Kelly green, the 83-foot-long vessel has more than 5,000 square feet of topsails, squaresails, and headsails. Teak decks and brass fittings glow and there's seating for 49 passengers. *Heritage* sails on two-hour Biscayne Bay cruises that depart at 1:30, 4, 6:30 and 9pm. The hours may differ occasionally, so it's wise to give them a call. You'll find the ship docked at the stage at Bayside, 401 Biscayne Blvd. (tel. 442-9697). Cruise prices are $10 for adults, $5 for children under 12. Mailing address: 3145 Virginia St.

In Coconut Grove, the home of Commodore Ralph Munroe, one of the first Coconut Grove residents, was built at the turn of the century and has been beautifully restored and maintained. Now the **Barnacle State Historic Site,** the home is at 3485 Main Hwy. (tel. 448-9445), and is open from 9am to 4pm, with tours at 10am and 1 and 2:30pm Thursday through Monday. Admission is $1; children under 12 pay 50¢.

Publisher William Randolph Hearst dismantled and shipped to Miami the complete Spanish **Monastery of St. Bernard,** built in 1141, the oldest building in this hemisphere. It was to go in his home at San Simeon, but Customs officers, fearing hoof-and-mouth bacteria, asked that all packing straw in the crates be burned. Years later it was discovered that the stones were not returned to their original crates —what a jigsaw puzzle! It took five years to solve it, but you can now see the monastery and a collection of priceless medieval art, at 16711 W. Dixie Hwy. (tel. 945-1461). Hours are 10am to 5pm daily (opening at noon on Sunday); the donation is $4 for adults, $1 for children 6 to 12.

A weird sight you might have seen on television's "That's Incredible" is **Coral Castle,** 28655 S. Federal Hwy., Homestead (tel. 248-6344), built by a Latvian immigrant who hoisted coral rocks weighing as much as 30 tons into place with no modern tools or machinery. No one knows yet quite how he did it, but the woman whose love he sought never saw it—she jilted him on the eve of their wedding. You can see it though, and rock in a stone rocking chair balanced atop a wall or move a three-ton gate with one finger. It's weird and wonderful, this rock castle, and it's open from 9am to 9pm daily at $7.35 for adults, $4.50 for children 6 to 12, but two children are admitted for the price of one.

If you're fascinated by exotic tropical plants, you can find out all about them and see 83 acres of tropical greenery at **Fairchild Tropical Garden,** 10901 Old Cutler Rd. (tel. 667-1651). There's a rain forest here, a rare plant house, a sunken garden, and lakes. Motorized tours are available if you don't feel up to 84 acres of hiking. Fairchild is open from 9:30am to 4:30pm daily, and admission is $4 for adults, free for children under 13. Tram rides cost adults $1; children 50¢.

**Redland Fruit and Spice Park,** at 24801 SW 187th Avenue (tel. 247-5727), has more of the same plus some quite unusual tropical fruits like the star-shaped carambola and Surinam cherry plants. It's free and open from 10am to 5pm daily. Guided tours are conducted at 1 and 3pm on Saturday and Sunday: $1 for adults, 50¢ for children.

## MIAMI BEACH

Miami Beach has the nation's largest collection of art deco architecture now on the National Register of Historic Places. It's a wonderful place to tour, ogling the soaring lines and funny furbelows of the 1930s. You can get a walking-tour map from the **Miami Design Preservation League** office at 661 Washington Ave. (tel. 672-2014). Ninety-minute walking tours of the city's now-famous art deco district begin at 10:30am every Saturday at the same office and cost $5 a person.

Just strolling the boulevards hereabouts is both an eye-popping event and a fascinating sociological study. On Ocean Drive, the pastel colors and tropical ambience that once put Miami Beach on world maps is now all primped and prettied for gawkers. How painters managed to get so many pastel colors in each building all at one time and maintain cohesion defies comprehension. Along the way you're likely to spot some of the ethnic diversity of South Beach, everything from black top hats and long beards to mah-jongg games and street stickball contests.

Don't miss a stroll down Española Way, a six-block lane running from Collins to Jefferson avenues just south of 15th Street. Here you enter another world, a world of Soho ambience, narrow sidewalks, old-world flavor, Spanish facades. Hollywood set-like in its funkiness, Española has appeared many times on "Miami Vice" and is slowly but surely becoming an enclave of artists and boulevardiers.

# 7. Sports

There's practically no end to the sports facilities in Miami, whether you're a participant or a beach warmer.

## GOLF

This section could go on forever—there are 42 courses in a 35-mile radius of downtown. There are 34 open to the public, ranging from the city of Miami's **Mel Reese Municipal Course,** at 1802 NW 37th Ave. (tel. 635-6770), to the famous 7,000-yard **Blue Course,** nicknamed the "Monster," one of five courses at the Doral Hotel and Country Club (tel. 592-2000), home of the annual Doral Open. Fees vary from the $14 to $26 charged at Mel Reese to the $70 to $110 charged for winter play at the Doral, including cart.

A sampling of other courses in the area includes the **Key Biscayne Golf Course** on Crandon Boulevard (tel. 361-9129), which charges $52 in winter, $26 in summer, and $25 for carts year round; the **Diplomat,** in Broward County just north of Miami Beach (tel. 949-2101), which charges nonguests $32 in winter and gives preference to the hotel's guests; and **Normandy Shores,** an 18-hole municipal course at 2401 Biarritz Dr. on Miami Beach (tel. 673-7775), which charges $25 to $35 in winter including cart. At **Bayshore,** 2301 Alton Rd., Miami Beach (tel. 673-7707), and in Coral Gables at the **Biltmore,** 1201 Anastasia Ave. (tel. 442-6485), fees are $15 to $20 plus carts.

Many hotels and motels can arrange money-saving guest privileges, so be sure to check first with your front desk.

## TENNIS

On Miami Beach, **Flamingo Park,** at Michigan Avenue and 12th Street (tel. 673-7761), has 17 public courts, some lighted, and is open from 9am to 9pm with a fee of about $2 per person an hour. The same price prevails at **North Shore Park,** 350 73rd St. (tel. 993-2022), which has 13 courts, and at **Haulover Beach Park,** 10800 Collins Ave. (tel. 940-6719).

On Key Biscayne, **Calusa Park,** on Crandon Boulevard (tel. 361-2215), has four public courts.

**City recreation departments** in Miami Beach (tel. 673-7700), Miami (tel. 579-6916), and the smaller communities will be happy to tell you where courts near you are located.

## BEACHES

Beaches are practically everywhere you look in Miami and Miami Beach, but naturally there are a few really pretty ones you'll want to explore. Our choice of all of them is Key Biscayne's **Crandon Park Beach,** 4000 Crandon Blvd. (tel. 361-1161). First, there are four miles of it, lined with palms and sea grapes so you can always find a shady spot. And there are lots of other diversions—windsurfing, picnic tables, beach cabañas ($12.50 a day), and lots of parking. **Bill Baggs State Park** at the tip of the island is pretty too (it's named after a crusading *Miami News* editor), and has lots of shallow water. You can tour the park and historic lighthouse for $2 for the driver, $1 each passenger.

On Miami Beach, there are nice strips of silica at **Pier Park** (55 Ocean Dr.), where surfers search for waves; at **Lummus Park** (from 6th to 14th Streets); at 21st Street, where young people gather; at 35th Street (for shells). At 46th Street there are rental boats at nearby hotels. Go to 53rd and 64th Streets to avoid crowds, and 74th Street to join crowds. **North Shore Open Space Park,** 79th to 87th Streets, is lined with sea grapes and wooden boardwalks; **Surfside Beach,** at 93rd Street, has pretty white sand, and **Bal Harbour** has an exercise course.

Last, and perhaps best, is **Haulover Beach Park,** which begins at Bal Harbour and continues nearly to 163rd Street. Once a narrow strip of land where boats were "hauled over" to the ocean, Haulover offers a mile and a half of sand and sea where you can surf, toss a Frisbee or a fishing line, picnic, barbecue, launch a boat, or roam a paved walkway along the sand.

## WATER SPORTS

Water is everywhere, so naturally water sports are not far behind. For instance: **American Sport Diving Schools** (tel. 253-5353) offers private lessons, equipment, and diving trips with Diver One (tel. 544-2605). The best diving area is around Fowey Rocks Light just south of Key Biscayne, good for underwater photography (but you must have a diving flag).

You can rent **Hobie Cat sailboats** at the **Eden Roc Americana** (tel. 531-0000), the **Fontainebleau Hilton** (tel. 538-2000), and in Coconut Grove at **Adventurers Yacht and Sailing Club,** 2480 S. Bayshore Dr. (tel. 854-3330), for about $100 to $125 a day. **Windsurfing** boards (tel. 361-SAIL) go for $15 an hour at Sailboards Miami on Virginia Key.

Adventurers Yacht also rents other kinds of larger day-sailer sailboats, as does **Castle Harbor Sailboats** at Dinner Key Marina in Coconut Grove (tel. 858-3212).

**Surfers** shouldn't expect too much (Miami doesn't have really good surfing waves unless there's a storm), but some days the surf is up. When that happens, head to **Haulover Beach Park** or **Pier Park** at South Beach where you'll find areas reserved for surfing.

**Coral Gables Venetian Pool,** 2701 De Soto Blvd., Coral Gables (tel. 442-6483), is such a treasure you really ough to go over just for a look at this grotto-like creation. It's a wonder of lagoons, porches, and towers of coral rock, open 11am to 4pm daily except Monday. Admission is $4 for adults, $1.50 to $3.50 for children.

**Glass-bottom-boat rides** are available at Biscayne National Park, on Canal Drive in Homestead (tel. 305/247-2400). To find the park, take US 1 south to Tallahassee Road and follow that to Canal Drive (SW 328th Street); the park's at the end of Canal Drive. Three- and four-hour trips are $15.50 for adults, $8 for children under 12, as are picnicking trips that visit lonely Elliott Key. Scuba and snorkeling trips also are available at prices that begin at $19.50 for snorkeling expeditions. Biscayne Park's tour boat office is open from 8am to 6pm daily, but the park itself is open from 8am to sunset daily.

## RUNNING, ROLLING, RIDING, AND ROMPING

For **joggers,** there's a Vita course in Coconut Grove's **David Kennedy Park,** and for **bicyclers,** 138 miles of bike paths.

South Miami is the center of Miami's equestrian world. Among the ranches offering trail rides, hayrides, and instruction are **Country Gentleman Stables,** 15500 SW 200th St. (tel. 252-9617); **Golden Eagle Ranch,** 41 SW 122nd Ave. (tel. 221-4312); and **Hunting Horn Stable,** 6155 SW 123rd Ave. (tel. 274-3133). On the north side of town, **Rockin' N Ranch,** 13501 NE 16th Ave., North Miami (tel. 891-9512 or 891-7107), has a pony ring for the youngsters. You'll pay about $10 to $15 a person for an hour's ride.

You can go gliding in Miami too, on thermal drafts that carry you silently atop the world. **Kendall Glider Port,** 17225 SW 122nd Ave. (tel. 253-3290), is home base for gliders, which cost $69 for 20 to 30 minutes. Phone ahead.

## FISHING

No matter how you like your fish—baked, broiled, or mounted—you can catch one in Miami. **Fish free from bridges** at MacArthur and Rickenbacker causeways. For **pier fishing,** head for Haulover Park, Pier Park on South Beach, Sunny Isles, 167th Street and Collins Avenue, or Dinner Key in Coconut Grove.

If you'd like to go after the devils of the deep in the Gulf Stream, seek out a **charter boat** at Dinner Key Marina in Coconut Grove, Haulover Park, Crandon Park Marina on Key Biscayne, Bayfront Miamarina in downtown Miami, or the docks at the Castaways. You'll pay $300 to $500 for six people for a day of fishing.

If you don't think a snapper dinner's worth quite that much, angle aboard a **party boat** that takes out several dozen people. They leave from the same marinas and cost about $20 a person.

## PROFESSIONAL SPORTS

Miami is the home of the **Orange Bowl** game, so from August to January you can see plenty of football here. Ticket prices vary. Don't forget the Orange Bowl parade, the one you see on television every year, which takes off down Biscayne Boulevard on New Year's Eve (tel. 620-5000).

At Miami Marine Stadium on Key Biscayne (tel. 361-6730) you can see a nine-hour endurance **speedboat race** in January and top speedboat races all year long. Tickets are about $13.

Miami is the spring training camp for the **Baltimore Orioles,** who practice at Miami Stadium, 2301 NW 10th Ave. (tel. 635-5395), from about mid-February.

Super Bowl–winning **Miami Dolphins** can now be spotted in the $100-million, 73,000-seat Miami **Joe Robbie Dolphin Stadium,** opened in 1987. Located in the far northern reaches of the county almost at the Broward County line, the new stadium is at 2269 NW 199th St. (tel. 576-1000). It was the site of the 1989 Super Bowl.

In 1987 Miami caught basketball fever. A National Basketball Association franchise for the city seemed iffy until Miami turned on the heat—provided by the considerable clout of play producer Zev Bufman and local cruise-ship millionaire Ted Arison. Thus was born the Miami Heat. Now you can see them play at Miami's new downtown **Miami Stadium,** four blocks south of Bayside Marketplace at North Miami Avenue between NW 6th and 8th streets. Tickets, priced from $6, are available at 633-2277.

## HORSE RACING

One of the world's most beautiful tracks, and now a National Historic Place, is the **Hialeah Race Course,** East Fourth Avenue between 21st and 32nd Streets (tel. 885-8000). Racing fan or not, you shouldn't miss this spectacular track. The grounds ramble on through acres and acres of formal gardens, tropical jungles, and royal palms. The clubhouse and grandstand are in elegant French Mediterranean style with ivy-covered walls and sweeping stone staircases. In the center of it all is a colony of flamingos that lives on an island in the middle of the track oval. After the seventh race, they fly a circuit around the course in a spectacular display of black-tipped pink plumage.

There's a French walking ring, and a display of racing skills in the elegant clubhouse. It's open to the public all year long, except the two weeks prior to the racing season, and you can tour it by train. Admission is $2 to the grandstand; $4 to the clubhouse.

Some of the nation's finest horses train and run here. Winter racing dates will overlap with **Gulfstream Park Race Track,** on US1, Hallandale (tel. 944-1242).

Hialeah's dates are January to March; Gulfstream's dates are mid-January to the end of May. Grandstand admission is $2; clubhouse, $4. Gulfstream is also a very pretty track, with a long entrance lined with royal palms. On Florida Derby Day, near the end of the season, the track sponsors some amusing races in which jockeys ride all sorts of strange mounts (ostriches, for instance). In 1990, Gulfstream hosted to the Breeder's Cup races, the richest and most prestigious thoroughbred races.

**Calder Race Course,** NW 210th Street and NW 27th Avenue (tel. 625-1311), has summer and fall racing dates from early May to mid-January. It's up at the north-west corner of the county and has an attractive Turf Club dining room overlooking the track. Grandstand admission is $2; clubhouse, $4; plus a small additional charge for reserved seats.

**Metro Transit Authority** (tel. 638-6117) runs special buses to the tracks, as does **A-1 Gray Line** (tel. 325-1000). Fares are about $9.

## GREYHOUND RACING

Put a dollar or two on the doggies at the **Biscayne Dog Track,** I-95 at NW 115th Street, Miami (tel. 754-3484), or the **Flagler Dog Track,** 300 NW 37th Ave. (tel. 649-3000). Races are at 7pm daily (except Sunday), with matinees on Tuesday, Thursday, and Saturday at 12:30pm. General admission is $1; to the clubhouse, $2.

## JAI-ALAI

Basques first began this fast handball game in the 1600s and brought it here from Spain. Players wrap a long curved basket (*cesta*) around their wrists and catch a speeding ball (*pelota*) in it, then toss the ball back against a wall for the other player to catch. You bet on individual players, who are as respected in these environs as jockeys are at the racetrack. The ball travels as fast as 100 m.p.h., so the game is dangerous as well as exciting. Miami's **Jai-Alai Fronton** is at NW 36th Street at 37th Avenue (tel. 633-9661), and games start at 7:15pm daily except Tuesday and Sunday (matinees on Monday and Saturday and sometimes on Wednesday at noon). The fronton is open from November through late April and from May to September. Admission is $1.

You can learn to play jai-alai if your eye and nerves are good. The nation's only amateur jai-alai fronton is **Miami Amateur Jai-Alai Fronton,** 1935 NE 150th St. (tel. 944-8217), which charges $3 to $4 an hour. A school operates year round. Open from 10am to midnight daily.

---

# 8. Shopping

---

Sometimes Miami seems to be one big shopping center. You can buy every-thing here from Spanish piñatas to $1,000 designer gowns. Wherever you are, you won't be far from a shop. Here are a few places to get you started buying:

Tops among the city's shopping spots now is peachy new **Bayside Market-place,** a sunset-pink enclave of nearly 200 shops and dining emporiums stretching artfully out alongside the waters of Biscayne Bay. Located in downtown Miami at 401 Biscayne Blvd. (tel. 577-3344), at the corner of Biscayne Boulevard and the en-trance to the Port of Miami, the comparatively new waterfront buying spot is the talk of this town's shoppers and diners. You'll find snack emporiums, chic restau-rants, and boutiques luring you into their cool recesses overflowing with jewels and silks, art and craft, fun and frolic.

**Bal Harbour Shops,** at Collins Avenue and 97th Street, harbors some very ex-clusive shops (Gucci, Lapidus, Saks, Neiman-Marcus, for openers) in a beautiful mall filled with flowering orange trees and splashing fountains. Prices are awesome, but so is the style.

**Lincoln Road Mall** is struggling to rise again as eight blocks of artists and shops closed to traffic. It runs east and west between Collins Avenue and West Avenue at 17th Street. There's a tram that scoots around from one end of the mall to the other, and you're always close to shady benches, fountains, and flowers. It's a nice place for a stroll even when the shops are closed.

In Miami, **Omni,** Biscayne Boulevard at 16th Street, is the crown prince of Miami shopping plazas. It's a two-level creation filled with 21 restaurants, six movie theaters, shops in every price range, even an Italian carousel. Jordan Marsh department store and a cluster of carpeted, subtly lit, hushed boutiques with names like Bally, Cardin, and Gucci occupy one end of the mall, J.C. Penney the other.

House-proud visitors to Miami might want to have a look in the shops on **Decorator's Row,** at NE 40th Street between North Miami Avenue and NE Second Avenue. All kinds of furniture and accessories for the home are sold here, although if you find something you want to buy, you'll probably have to contact an interior decorator as most of these shops sell to the trade only.

On the north end of town is the Mall at 163rd Street, which hypists are now calling **"The Miracle at 163rd Street"**—get it, get it? What they're really talking about is the roofing-over of this mall, which was once a bit seedy but was much improved by the addition of a fiberglass roof. At the 163rd Street Mall you'll find both Burdine's and Jordan Marsh department stores, movie theaters, and quite a number of small shops. It's in North Miami Beach at NE 163rd Street between Biscayne Boulevard and the Golden Glades Interchange on I-95. It's open daily from 10am to 9:30pm (noon to 5:30pm on Sunday).

A new shopping area on the north end of town is called **Loehmann's Plaza** in honor of the store that is most important here—at least to local socialities, who sneak off, suitably disguised, for a visit to Loehmann's, which sells overruns and extras of designer clothing (labels removed) at discount prices. If you want to know who designed that outfit you can't resist, don't despair. By now everyone has figured out how to read the codes on the price tags, so just ask somebody to decode for you. You'll find Loehmann's and several other discount shops in Marina del Rey at Biscayne Boulevard at 187th Street. Loehmann's is open to 9:30pm Wednesday, normal hours every other day, and noon to 5pm on Sunday.

**Aventura Mall,** 19501 Biscayne Blvd., has four major department stores including Lord & Taylor's, Penney, Sears, and—blare of trumpets—Florida's very first Macy's. More than 200 stores are here selling everything from heels to meals. Open Monday through Saturday from 10am to 9pm, and on Sunday from noon to 5pm.

At the south end of the county, **Dadeland Mall,** 7535 N. Kendall Dr., is one of the largest malls in the nation, with five carpeted arcades, fountains, foliage, and dozens of restaurants and shops including representatives of the largest department stores operating in Florida—Burdine's, Jordan Marsh, Sears, Saks, and Lord & Taylor.

In the middle (in location only, we hasten to add) is Coconut Grove's posh **Mayfair in the Grove,** at 3390 Mary St., where you should bring money not in a wallet but in a shopping bag. Valentino, Ralph Lauren, Pierre Balmain—all the "names" are here.

In Coral Gables, **Miracle Mile** is a four-block-long strip between Douglas and LeJeune roads filled with shops, restaurants, theaters, and plenty of exclusive names on the front windows.

If you'd like a handcrafted guitar, one of those piñatas for the kids to break open blindfolded on birthdays, bullfight posters, mantillas, oil paintings, furniture, handrolled Cuban cigars, Cuban coffee, or rum-soaked pastries that will knock your socks off, the place to go is **Little Havana,** Miami's SW 8th Street. Prices are lower here than anywhere else in town, and you can have a wonderful time even if you don't buy anything. Padron cigars are famous here.

Real bargain hunters will want to look at the **Miami Fashion District,** the third-largest garment district in the nation. It's been here, between NW Fifth Avenue and

22nd to 29th Streets, since the early 1930s. You'll find 225 businesses purveying everything from handbags to shoes, home accessories, sporting goods, and electronics. Most of the stores lack fancy fitting rooms and don't offer refunds, but you can find some excellent bargains with a little searching.

Another spot to see a lot in a little space is the **Seybold Building,** at 36 NE 1st St. Hong Kong–miniaturized with 10 floors of jewelers and enough jewelry to keep even Imelda Marcos bedecked, the Seybold has been harboring the city's jewelers for more than two decades. People tell us the discounts are worth the trip here, but you'll have to make that decision for yourself.

A handsome shopping center in Miami is **The Falls,** just off US 1 and SW 136th Street. Stroll here amid rain-forest lagoons, waterfalls, cedar- and glass-trimmed waterside gazebos, and try to remember you're here to look at the stores. The biggest news here is a branch of New York's Bloomingdale's.

---

# 9. A Visit to the Everglades

Just a few miles south of Miami on the way to the Florida Keys is a vast primeval prairie that sweeps across 2,000 square miles and 1½ million acres of wilderness. Much of this ancient swampland is rarely if ever seen. It harbors a complex biological life chain topped by humans who have sheltered this mysterious swamp from the creeping tide of Florida's commercial development and guarded its fragile population of near-extinct creatures.

Limestone rock underlying the Everglades and, farther north, Big Cypress Swamp, is six million years old. Over it flows fresh water that supports a bustling community of creatures from microscopic algae to the king of Everglades beasts, the alligator.

As you drive through this vast subtropical jungle, you'll see why the Native Americans who lived in these glades called the waters here Pahayokee (pronounced "Pay-*high*-oh-key"), the River of Grass. That's all you'll see as you drive into the heart of the Everglades at Flamingo Park, vast sweeps of marshland covered with golden grasses and dotted by islands of trees. These islands, called hammocks (from a Native American word for garden place), shelter live oaks, mahogany, gumbo limbo trees, and a world of creatures from the red-shouldered hawk to tiny tree frogs, nocturnal opossums, great white herons, crocodiles, sea cows, and the nearly extinct Florida panther. All roam these swamps and settle on these islands built up around odd trees called mangroves, which are supported by dense networks of roots reaching into the water. Decaying vegetation that collects around the roots eventually forms islands where wild orchids bloom in desolate stands of gray trees. Spiky-leafed air plants feed on tiny particles of airborne fertilizers. Exotic bromeliads grow here and strangler figs twine around trees finally killing them, then taking their place in the ever-changing forest.

To get there, follow US 1 south through several suburbs of Miami. Just south of Homestead, you'll see a sign directing you to the park entrance and visitor center. At the center (tel. 247-6211), you'll find exhibits, orientation programs, and detail maps of the area. Admission to the park is $5 a car.

## FLAMINGO

As you drive the 50 miles to Flamingo, you'll see clearly marked trails and raised boardwalks leading into the swamp. The **Royal Palm Visitor Center** has two very interesting trails, Anhinga (named after a bird that looks unhinged) and the Gumbo Limbo Trail, where the foliage is so thick you can see only a few feet in front of you. At Shark River Basin you can overlook the swamp from an elevated trail, and at Taylor Slough you can spot alligators, water birds, perhaps even otter, deer, black bear, or a bobcat.

Flamingo is a serene little village on Florida Bay where there's an attractive, spacious motel called the **Flamingo Lodge,** P.O. Box 428, Flamingo, FL 33030 (tel. 305/253-2241 or 813/695-3101). Rates are $46 to $80 double in summer and $74 to $112 in winter for rooms, cottages, and suites.

Flamingo has a popular campground operated by the National Park Service, although the mosquitoes are a little rough in summer. There are no water or electricity hookups, however, just cold showers and space to park your recreation vehicle or pitch a tent. Rates are $4 to $7.

There is a bit of a village here, a very small one, but with most of the things you'll need, from groceries to bait and souvenirs.

If you're just driving down for the day, stop in for lunch or dinner at the second-story restaurant (closed May to November) where you can dine on excellent fresh seafood and steaks (they'll even cook *your* catch) for $7 to $15 and watch spectacular sunsets through a wall of windows.

If you're looking for something to do here, sail away on three-hour **Backcountry Cruises** ($9 for adults, $4.50 for children 6 to 12) that explore deep into the back waters of the Everglades, near the southernmost point in the continental United States. A special sunset cruise on Florida Bay is a blazing spectacular—it's $6.75 for adults, $3.50 for children. Or ride a **Wilderness Tram** (open from November to April; admission is $7 for adults, $3.50 for children) for a closeup look at the wilderness. You can rent canoes, big houseboats, or outboard motorboats, and take off for a day out on your own in this mysterious land. There are marked boat trails so you won't become the Lewis and Clark of the Everglades.

If you'd like to hook your own dinner from the deep, there are charter boats with captains who know where those elusive creatures hide. Make fishing arrangements when you reserve space at the Flamingo Lodge or the National Park Service campground since the park is often filled with anglers with similar intentions.

There's a National Park Service Visitor Center and a museum staffed by a naturalist.

Now, there are no guarantees that you're going to see a wild animal, an alligator, or even a bird while you're out here exploring the Everglades. However, there is a place where we can guarantee you a look at some of those shy fellows who inhabit the Glades. It is called, fittingly enough, Eden of the Everglades.

Some people are just meant to spend their days in the wilderness, and a fellow named Ervin Stokes is one of those. He worked for it, he earned it, and now he's got it—a little piece of peace he calls **Eden of the Everglades,** Dupont Road, Everglades City (tel. 813/695-2800). Eight acres of swampland along Panther Creek, this Eden offers you a chance to walk on a cypress boardwalk winding through a mangrove forest manned by rainbow-hued macaws, cockatiels, cockatoos, parakeets, lovebirds, toucans, some alligators, tortoises, even a pair of bobcats. Who says this isn't Eden? Eden of the Everglades is on Fla. 29 about three miles south of US 41 near Everglades City. Admission is $12 for adults, including a boat ride into the backcountry of the Everglades, $8 for children 3 to 10. It's open daily from 10am to 5pm.

## EVERGLADES CITY

If you're headed to Florida's west coast, you can visit the park from Miami by taking the Tamiami Trail (US 41) west 80 miles to a second park entrance at Everglades City. Along the way you can visit a **Miccosukee Indian Village** on US 41 (look for the signs). The Miccosukees are a branch of the Seminole tribe that settled here 150 years ago, and a few still live in the traditional thatch-roofed huts called chickees, open sided to catch the breeze. At the village you'll see a typical camp with the traditional star-shaped fire, and separate sleeping, working, and cooking quarters. After the tribe moved to the Everglades following the Seminole Wars, they traded animal skins for brightly colored cloth and sewing machines, which they still use to create intricate bright patterns from tiny scraps of cloth. Fashioned into dresses, jackets, blouses, and vests, these are colorful souvenirs of the Everglades and a product unique to this tribe. Miccosukees, by the way, may have had the first mother-in-law jokes: Their tribes are ruled by women, and grooms have to move into the camp of the bride's mother.

Near the Indian Village is **Shark Valley,** where automobiles are forbidden but you can take rubber-tired trams on two-hour journeys into the park to the Shark Valley observation tower. A guide describes the natural history of the area. Trams operate at one-hour intervals from 9am to 4pm in winter season and at two-hour intervals in other months. The gates are open from 8:30am to 6pm. The cost of the tour is $6; the park fee is $3 a car.

If you need help with specific details of a visit to the Everglades, write Everglades National Park, P.O. Box 279, Homestead, FL 33030.

**READER'S RECOMMENDATION:** "My wife and I . . . dropped by Key Largo Chamber of Commerce [and found **Everglades Air Boat Tours**]. Of all the air boat rides, this was far the best. This man [Capt. Ray Kramer] has been in these swamps all his life . . . and is the third generation there of his family. He charges $45 per person for two hours, but actually we spent the whole afternoon from 1pm and got back in the evening. He has a very [complete] knowledge of the Everglades from . . . his past, his oneness with the swamps" Richard Druery, Plattsmouth, Neb. [*Authors' Note:* Capt. Kramer can be contacted at 1307 Almay St., Key Largo (tel. 852-5339), or at Gilberts, Mile Marker 107.5, and we hear he does indeed know the Everglades well. He can show you alligator nests and raccoons washing their lunch and will lead you through a remote ecological world that is a wonder to behold. His trips are by prearrangement only and rates are $45 per person for a two-hour ride. Longer tours also are available.]

While you're here, Everglades City is an interesting spot that's plunked down at the entrance to Florida's Ten Thousand Islands. Land on which the "city" (it's a very tiny settlement) now stands was acquired in the 1920s by advertising executive Barron Collier, who meant to build a metropolis here, and almost succeeded. Between the Depression and a population move northward, Everglades City never quite made it to fame, but fortunately the **Everglades Rod and Gun Lodge,** Everglades City, FL 33929 (tel. 813/695-2101), was built. For 100 years this lodge has been an exclusive sportsman's hideaway; four presidents (including Truman, Eisenhower, and Nixon), plus former Supreme Court Chief Justice Warren Burger and actors Burt Reynolds and David Carradine, have visited here. A huge old banyan tree 15 feet around has stood sentinel over this rambling wood structure for all its years of welcoming fishermen and hunters. Inside the lodge, all that masculine comfort lives on in a high-ceilinged, wood-beamed clubby lobby, plump wing chairs, deep-cushioned couches, a massive hooded fireplace, pool table, and on the wall an eight-foot alligator with an electric plug in its mouth! That same atmosphere flows right into the dining room where immense brass chandeliers cast a soft glow over the formal setting, the walls and ceiling paneled in pecky cypress that's now a high-priced rarity (but was once an inexpensive wood). Sea trophies are the only adornment here, and the friendly smiling help will even cook your catch for you. If you somehow are not lucky on the fishing grounds, you can choose from a limited but excellent menu of scallops, stone crabs from fishermen whose traps you'll see nearby, grouper, or any of the 50 varieties of fish that swim in waters a 15-minute boat ride away. Dinner prices are in the $10 range. Everglades Lodge is open all year but is at its best in winter when it lures the famous and fishing fanatics. The Rod and Gun Lodge has 25 rooms, all of them clean and decorated in deep jewel-like colors. Rates are $49.82 double year round.

You'll also find a very nice resort called the **Captain's Table Resort,** 102 Broadway St., Everglades City, FL 33929 (tel. 813/695-4211), with small but very clean and nicely decorated rooms in a two-story building as well as a wide range of other accommodations including villas on stilts and rooms with screened porches. Two people will pay $48 to $100 in the winter season. Next door is the Captain's Table restaurant, a charming place way out here in the wilds with wide glass windows so you can watch the changing moods of the Everglades. Prices are in the $10 to $12 range. It's open for breakfast, lunch, and dinner in winter, less frequently in summer.

**Outdoor Resort and Marina,** Chokoloskee Island, FL 33929 (tel. 813/695-2881), is a nice place, neat and clean with carefully tended lawns and a trim look from fin to fin. There's nothing pretentious about this simple single-story hideaway, but there's nothing pretentious about the price either: $50 to $60 for a kitchenette for four, year round. Motorhome parking is $25 to $35.

If you'd like to tour the park by boat, a park ranger operates a **sightseeing boat** (tel. 813/695-2591) in the winter months at $9 for adults, $4.50 for children 6 to 12.

Two of the weirdest ways to get around in Florida are contraptions called swamp buggies and airboats. You can ride either or both of them at **Wooten's Air Boat Ride,** Star Route 121, Ochopee, FL 33943 (tel. 813/695-2781), just east of the entrance to Everglades City on US41. Swamp buggies are Jeep bodies atop heavy-treaded tractor tires, and they plow through the shallow waters of the swamp for $10 per person. And if you think swamp buggies are a Rube Goldberg creation, wait till you see an airboat! These are flat-bottomed skiffs with airplane propellers, powered by car engines mounted at the rear. They skim across the surface of the swamp. You can ride on one of the noisy but exciting weirdies for $10, well worth the experience.

If you'd like to stay in a very plush resort that is indeed far from the madding crowd, **Port of the Islands,** US 41E, Marco, FL 33937 (tel. 813/394-3101), is about 80 miles west of Miami and 20 miles east of Naples. This is one gorgeous 200-room place: six tennis courts, a beige stucco building with Mediterranean tiled roofs, arched windows and entrances, double doors with tiny glass panes opening onto balconies, rental boats, trap and skeet shooting, pool, and a private landing strip. One step into the soaring tiled lobby and you know you're somewhere very special. Two stories above you, huge wooden beams stretch across an immense reception area and higher yet is a skylight. Wood-railed loggia hallways rim the second level, and off the halls are elaborately decorated suites and rooms. The focal point of the reception area is a massive fireplace crowned by a starkly dramatic painting of a stately white heron. Beautiful puffy contemporary furniture is everywhere, and there's a pale-peach restaurant and Charley's Bar, a forest-green lounge.

New at this resort is a thatched-roof chickee-hut waterfront bar overlooking the county's only official manatee sanctuary; a two-hour narrated Island Nature Cruise through the 10,000 islands on a 49-passenger boat; a health spa/fitness center with all the requisite steaming and straining facilities; and a pleasantly intimate library and reading room.

Clustered around the pool are rooms in single-story buildings. They have beamed ceilings, contemporary muted tones, and arched rattan headboards. In winter months, rates are $80 to $90 for most rooms, to $115 for suites. In other months, rates drop to $55 to $100 and children under 15 are free. The resort was recently listed in the top 20 hunting and fishing lodges in North America.

## 10. Island Hopping to the Bahamas

Miami is so near the Bahamas that some people have considered swimming it, but if you'd like a little more traditional way to go, try **Bahamasair,** which is that nation's national carrier. For quick trips to the beautiful out island of Eleuthera, also seek out Bahamasair, which flies there and to other Bahamian islands. Both Freeport (on Grand Bahama Island) and Nassau (on New Providence Island) have gambling, and in winter season there are a number of quite inexpensive gambling junkets that go over and return the same day. The price is low, frankly, because the odds favor the house as they do in all casinos, but at any time you can fly to the islands and back for $100 or less. Some junkets may even be free, but require a bankroll and gambling commitment.

To see things the leisurely way, hop aboard any of the **cruise ships** at Miami's Dodge Island port or Fort Lauderdale's Port Everglades. There are trips of all durations, from a four-day weekend to three months aboard the *Queen Elizabeth II*. To get a peek at the cruise ships, visit the Port of Miami on Dodge Island, where the big white bruisers are lined up like sentinels on weekends.

The **Port of Miami** is now the busiest port in the world, welcoming more than two million passengers every year. And many of those decide that a week-long cruise, begun and followed by a few days of Miami or Fort Lauderdale sunshine, is a very tempting idea.

If you're interested in a cruise or would just like to hear what cruises are all about, we'd (modestly, of course) like to recommend another Prentice Hall book, **Frommer's Cruises,** co-authored by (guess who?) Marylyn Springer and Donald Schultz. In this book you'll find detailed descriptions of all the ships that sail off into the sunset from Miami and from many other ports, including Miami's northern neighbor, Fort Lauderdale.

If you'd like to take a look at a cruise ship, find your way to the MacArthur Causeway, which runs along the north side of the port. By the side of the causeway you'll see some trees and some public parking areas where you can stop the car and gaze in awe at these huge ocean ships towering over you like so many fat ducklings in a row.

Most ships depart from the Port of Miami on Saturday in the late afternoon, say, 4 to 5pm, so if you stop by on that day, you'll see quite a line of them—and thrill to their booming horns as they announce their departure!

If you'd like to get an even closer look at a ship and what it has to offer, don't hesitate to call any of the cruise lines we're about to name and ask them for a guest pass. They're anxious to have you for a passenger, so they'll be happy to oblige. Then get on over there and prowl around the ship all you like. You're welcome to have a drink in the open bars and listen to the calypso bands—just be sure to get off when the "all ashore that's going ashore" is sounded.

Among the cruise companies operating year round from the Port of Miami are Admiral, Carnival, Commodore, Dolphin, Chandris, Norwegian Caribbean Lines, Royal Caribbean Cruise Lines, and SeaEscape Cruises (which operates one-day, no-overnight cruises).

In the winter months you may also see ships operated by Costa Cruise Line and Royal Cruises.

# V

# THE FLORIDA KEYS

## 1. UPPER AND LOWER KEYS
## 2. KEY WEST

**A** silver ribbon of highway streaks southward across the merging waters of two great seas. On and on it goes, 113 miles of it slicing through silvery coral islets where palms rustle and sway in unceasing sea breezes. Leap-frogging across 41 bridges, it passes sleepy fishing villages and dazzling strips of sand baking under a relentless tropical sun until at last it reaches bridge 42. Here it flies over seven glorious, spine-tingling miles of diamond-tipped waves and foaming white water lapping gently over bars of golden sand.

It's an incredible feat of engineering, this strip of macadam known as the **Overseas Highway,** a feat begun by none other than that dreamer and empire builder, railroad tycoon and hotelier Henry Flagler. In 1912 aboard his luxurious private car called Rambler, an elderly and nearly blind Flagler rode triumphantly into Key West, $27 million poorer but the proud creator of Flagler's Folly, the "Railroad That Went to Sea" across 29 islands. Time was to prove that Flagler's railroad was more foresight than folly, but his dream died when a vicious hurricane swept across these keys, killing hundreds of people and turning his dream railroad into a mass of twisted metal. Years later Flagler's "folly" formed the bed of the Overseas Highway, which today brings a million sun-struck tourists to these sleepy strips of limestone and coral.

First you'll pass through **Key Largo** (shades of that Bogart-Bacall movie). Today the island's fame is the John Pennekamp Coral Reef State Park, a watery wonderland where you can watch rainbow-hued tropical fish darting about as you swim among them or peer through the hull of a glass-bottom boat.

Next is **Upper and Lower Matecumbe Keys,** named for the Spanish words *matar* (to kill) and *hombre* (a man), a reference to shipwrecked sailors killed or enslaved by tribes here. Islamorada is the focus here, a purple island named for the color early Spanish explorers saw from the sea. That color was created by purple snail shells covering the beaches.

Then comes **Marathon,** on Vaca Key. Halfway between the mainland and Key West, Marathon was once the site of the supply store for the 3,000 railroad workers who said that by the time the tracks reached here, the job had become a marathon, an endurance test.

**Bahia Honda** (Spanish for "deep bay") is the geological transition from Upper to Lower Keys, and is a sandy state park where botanists study rare plants like West Indies satinwood, Jamaica morning glory, and the wild dilly. Here, too, historians can see the remains of Flagler's railroad.

**Big Pine Key** is a haven for tiny Key deer, some no bigger than collie dogs. Herds of the deer had once dwindled to only a few dozen, but now are protected in a refuge and number about 500, ranging over 18 keys.

Then there's **Sugarloaf Key,** where you'll see one of the weirder sights of these quiet islands—a 30-foot $10,000 bat tower, complete with bat rat protector and bat graveyard, designed to attract migrating bats that scientists hoped would settle in and rid the island of mosquitoes. The project failed—the bats never showed up. There are even some wags who say the mosquitoes ate the bats, but these days islanders have solved the problem with sprays.

Snuggled in between these larger keys are spots with intriguing names like Cudjoe Key (said to be named after someone's Cousin Joe), Lignum Vitae (named for the ironwood trees that grow there), and Duck Key. They're sandy without having many really good beaches; they're neither elegant nor lined with attractions, but they're as hypnotizing as sun and sea can make them, as intriguing today as they were to long-gone pirates.

They're Florida's "out islands," entrancing strips of sand on which you'll discover some of the swashbuckling, rough-and-tumble history of this state, and meet outgoing, eccentric, rock-strong, hospitable, and ever-cheerful islanders who move at a slow pace and can teach you to do likewise.

## GETTING THERE

American, Delta, Eastern, USAir, and Airways International fly into Key West and Marathon regularly from Miami and connect to other Florida cities. **Greyhound** buses (tel. toll free 800/237-8211) also travel through all the keys from Miami.

## GETTING AROUND

You can rent a bike from **Key Colony Bike Shop,** 11518 Overseas Hwy. at Mile Marker 53, Marathon (tel. 289-1670). Bikes are $8 a day, $45 a week.

Since most people drive here from Miami, rental-car facilities are limited, but **Alamo** has an outlet in Key West (tel. 294-6675).

**Taxi** services operate on all the Keys.

---

# 1. Upper and Lower Keys

---

Here on this string of islands people like to divide the Keys into three sections: upper, middle, and lower. The Upper Keys begin at Key Largo and stretch south through Upper and Lower Matecumbe (Islamorada). The Middle Keys run through Marathon, and the Lower Keys are what's left over, including Key West.

Scattered about, and accessible only by boat, are dozens of other keys with fascinating names, my favorite of which is a true conchism: No Name Key.

As you drive through the Keys, you'll see numbered markers along the righthand side of the road known as **Mile Markers.** They indicate the distance from Key West and are about the only addresses you'll find in the Keys. The numbers go down as you go south, up as you go north.

**READER'S WILDLIFE-VIEWING TIPS:** "Travelers are invited at no charge to Betty Brothers Real Estate at the bridge in **Little Torch Key.** Her two pet dolphins are fed and do tricks for anyone who drops by at 10am and 5pm every day. The dolphins are free to come and go as they please to the open ocean, but always come back every day. On Key Deer Boulevard (1¼ miles north of the Watson Road intersection) is what is known as the **Blue Hole.** This is an old rock quarry filled with fresh water. Several alligators make their home there, as well as other wildlife. Also, drive out onto **No Name Key** after dark, coast slowly down the main road (a dead end), and keep looking into the woods. Your car should soon be surrounded by raccoons begging for food. They eat anything, but Saltines seem to be one of their favorites" (Linda Sambel, Pittsfield, Mass.).

## WHERE TO STAY

Let's take a look at the islands from north to south, starting with Key Largo, where you'll find both a **Holiday Inn,** 99701 Overseas Hwy., Mile Marker 100 (P.O. Box 708), Key Largo, FL 33037 (tel. 305/451-2121, or toll free 800/THEKEYS), and a **Howard Johnson's Resort,** US 1, Key Largo, FL 33037 (tel. 305/451-1400, or toll free 800/654-2000). Both are spiffy motor lodges that between them can provide tennis courts, swimming pools, glass-bottom-boat tours, fishing, diving, and snorkeling, and rates that range from $88 to $150 in peak season, $88 to $120 in summer.

If you'd rather fish than anything, **Gilbert's Motel,** 107900 Overseas Hwy., Mile Marker 107.5, US 1 at Jewfish Creek, Key Largo, FL 33037 (tel. 305/451-1133), is right smack on the key, and has radios, TVs, and phones in the motel rooms, and in the few efficiencies. There's a pool, a ramp for your boat, and a marina, plus a small restaurant that's open from 8am to 10pm (prices in the $4 to $16 range) and a lounge. Winter room rates are $75 to $85; in summer, $65 to $75.

At Mile Marker 87, you'll find **Plantation Yacht Harbor Resort,** 87000 Overseas Hwy., Mile Marker 87, Islamorada, FL 33036 (tel. 305/852-2381, or in Miami 305/248-6807, or toll free 800/356-3215, in Florida 800/432-3454), a bright white resort set on acres and acres of grass overlooking the multicolored waters of a yacht harbor. Owned by a company that sends its executives here to rest, the resort's an eye-catcher with contemporary colors and decor that differs from room to room but can include sunken sitting rooms, color TVs, phones, and private porches.

Outside, the grounds seem to go on forever, with a pool, tennis courts, private beach, barbecue grills, jet-skis, shuffleboard, dive shop, and basketball. El Capitan and Commodore dining room, at water's edge, is a lovely place to end the day with some delicacies like cioppino, seafarer's pie, conch fritters, or a steak for prices in the $11 to $20 range. It's open from 7am to 1am, and the lounge, where you'll find lively entertainment, is open to the wee hours. Rates are $65 to $85 year round.

**Pelican Cove Resort,** 84457 Old Overseas Hwy., Mile Marker 84.5 (mailing address: P.O. Box 633), Islamorada, FL 33036 (tel. 305/664-4435, or toll free 800/445-4690), sports such Keys-ian architecture, it seems to grow here by the sea. A very attractive new getaway spot in the Keys, this four-story hideaway nestles up to its own beach and provides such accoutrements as an oceanside whirlpool, freshwater pool, poolside sipping spot, and multitudes of water sports. You can settle into a handsomely decorated balconied room, efficiency, or Jacuzzi-equipped suite here, play on a tennis court, sail, windsurf, snorkel, scuba, fish—well, you get the picture. Rates range from $115 to $150 in summer and fall, and from $145 to $175 from mid-December to April, higher for suites.

**Cheeca Lodge,** at Mile Marker 82.5 on Upper Matecumbe Key (P.O. Box 527), Islamorada, FL 33036 (tel. 305/664-4651, 305/245-3755 in Miami, or toll free 800/327-2888), is expensive, but it's worth the money if you're in the mood for a big splurge. Once an exclusive fishing club, the lodge is now open to the public and continues to offer a warm welcome, outstanding service, fine food, and a relaxing hideaway where you can let tomorrow take care of itself.

There's a golf course here (executive, with no hole more than 115 yards), built by the company that puts Jack Nicklaus's courses together, and Nicklaus himself is a frequent guest here, as is Pres. George Bush. You can play tennis too, swim in a large freshwater pool or saltwater lagoon, fish from a pier, and take your catch inside where an excellent restaurant will apply to it the skills they use on menu items. Spacious newly redecorated rooms—they spent $40 million on the revamp—are set high over the sea and sport beautiful views of the Atlantic just outside the door. They're tastefully decorated in subtle shades that echo the tones of beach, sky, and

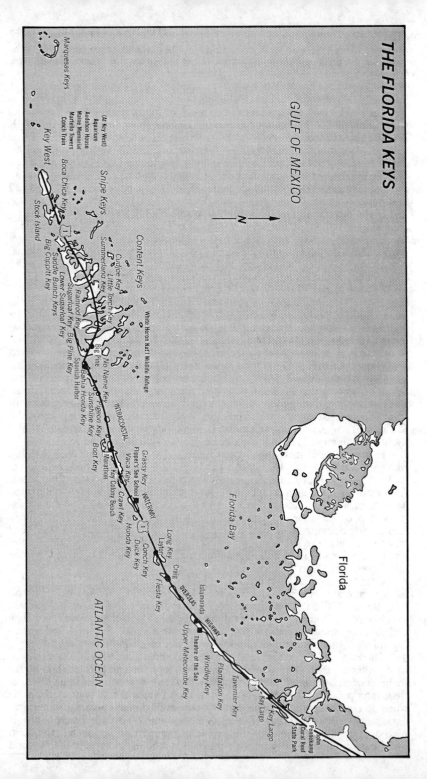

THE FLORIDA KEYS

GULF OF MEXICO

N

Florida

Florida Bay

ATLANTIC OCEAN

Marquesas Keys

(At Key West)
Aquarium
Audubon House
Martello Towers
Conch Train

Key West
Boca Chica Keys
Stock Island

Snipe Keys
Summerland Key
Cudjoe Key
Little Torch Key
Ramrod Key
Sugarloaf Key, Big Pine Key
Lower Sugarloaf Key
Big Saddle Bunch Keys
Big Coppitt Key

Content Keys

White Heron Nat'l Wildlife Refuge

No Name Key
Big Pine
Spanish Harbor
Bahia Honda Key
Sunshine Key
Pigeon Key
Boot Key

INTRACOASTAL

Marathon
Key Colony Beach
Flipper's Sea School
Grassy Key
Vaca Key
Craw! Key

WATERWAY

Honda Key
Duck Key
Conch Key
Fiesta Key

Long Key
Layton
Craig

OVERSEAS HIGHWAY

Islamorada
Theatre of the Sea
Windley Key
Upper Matecumbe Key
Plantation Key
Tavernier Key
Key Largo

Pennekamp
Coral Reef
State Park

sunset outside. Two people pay $195 to $325 a night in winter months, $140 to $230 in other seasons.

**Kingsail Resort Motel,** 7050 Overseas Hwy. (P.O. Box 986), Marathon, FL 33050 (tel. 305/743-5246, or toll free 800/423-7474), is a pleasant small motel in the Middle Keys. You'll find just 40 rooms here, most of them one-bedroom efficiency units or smaller units with kitchens kept neat, clean, and attractively, if simply, decorated. Guests gather around the swimming pool and in an open-air Tiki hut overlooking the docks where fancy fishing boats bob. There's a small grocery store, dive shop, fishing and diving charter operations and equipment, laundry, grill, boat ramp, trailer parking, and boat docks. Could you need more in the Keys? Rates are $42 to $104 in summer, depending on location and size of accommodations, $59 to $134 in winter, slightly higher on holidays and during special events like the opening of lobster season.

Islamorada's a favorite getaway spot for many Miamians who troop off to **Holiday Isle Resort,** US 1 at Mile Marker 84.5 (P.O. Box 588), Islamorada, FL 33036 (tel. 305/664-2321), as much to sit in the cool comfortable depths of the Tiki Bar and Restaurant as for the resort's other offerings. There are lots of Polynesian touches here in a maze of beachy-looking apartments, motel rooms, and efficiencies circling a heated pool. There's a strip of beach, a marina and ramp for boaters, and, naturally, fishing. In the Tiki Restaurant you can feast on mango cake, thick and crusty Bimini bread, and fresh seafood for prices in the $14 to $19 range. Evenings, there's entertainment in the lounge. You'll pay $100 to $325 in summer, $115 to $350 in winter.

Just 20 minutes off the shore from **Harbor Lights Resort,** 84951 Overseas Hwy., Islamorada, FL 33036 (tel. 305/664-3611), you can dive among coral gardens and sunken Spanish galleons. In between dives, rest up in this three-story motel where some of the simply decorated rooms have screened porches. Coconut palms shade the pool, and there are various games scattered about the resort's grounds. You'll find an inexpensive harbor here for $50 to $70 in winter, $55 to $80 in summer, less in fall.

**Hawk's Cay Resort and Marina,** Duck Key, Mile Marker 61 on the Overseas Highway, Marathon, FL 33050 (tel. 305/743-7000, or toll free 800/327-7775, in Florida 800/432-2242), used to be called Indies Resort and Marina, but the name is just one of hundreds of things that have changed at this casual and now very comfortable resort on Duck Key. In 1984 the new owners spent $10 million on a top-to-toe revamp of this long-popular getaway, and they have much to show for their money.

A rambling West Indies–style resort on a 60-acre island, Hawk's Cay is now as contemporary as a Canaveral launch, decked out in dusky pinks, greens, and turquoises that somehow seem to reflect these very tropical surroundings. Wicker furnishings are offset by tile floors in those same muted shades, and overhead paddle fans whir. Here, too, you'll find a lovely sand-ringed saltwater lagoon, freshwater pool, tennis courts, two whirlpool spas, fishing and sailboats, diving and snorkeling equipment, windsurfing boards, bicycles, a fitness trail, and an adult game center with billiards, darts, and bumper pool.

Dining at Hawk's Cay ranges from the poolside Cantina, specializing in piña coladas and conch chowder, to the formal Caribbean Room, where continental cooking is favored, and the dockside Ship's Galley overlooking the marina. Each morning guests are treated to a sumptuous complimentary breakfast buffet in the Palm Terrace dining room.

Rooms are just as lovely as every other part of this spiffy new complex. Large, airy, and tropical, they feature balconies or terraces with wide expanses of glass, walk-in closets, dressing areas, color TV, and telephones. Rates range from $190 to $300 double from January 1 to mid-April, $125 to $190 in other months. Suites also are available at higher rates.

At Key Vaca (Mile Marker 49) you'll find **Buccaneer Lodge,** 2600 Overseas

Hwy., Marathon, FL 33050 (tel. 305/743-9071, or toll free 800/237-3329, in Florida 800/843-1799), a sprawling 10-acre resort spread out across sandy water-side acreage said still to be haunted by pirates. We didn't see any—just lots of people laughing by the pool, zipping around on jet-skis, and splashing on the inn's sandy beach. There's quite a good dining room, with lots of seafood on the menu for about $10 to $13, and a lounge to while away some cool hours. Summer rates are $49 (for room) to $200 (for kitchen units); in peak season, from December on $65 to $225.

Few if any of the resorts in Florida can offer you a performing dolphin for enter-tainment. But Sugar is the star at the **Sugar Loaf Lodge,** Mile Marker 17 on US 1 (P.O. Box 148), Sugar Loaf Key, FL 33044 (tel. 305/745-3211), and performs happily for gawking guests. Paneled rooms are tucked away in one- and two-story buildings overlooking the waters of Sugar Loaf Sound, with bright colors that echo the blue of the waters outside your balcony. There are tennis courts, miniature golf, and a pretty glass-walled restaurant overlooking the water (prices, $10 to $15) so you can watch Sugar. For rooms you'll pay $90 to $100 in peak season (and during late-July lobster-fishing days), $75 to $85 in other months. Children under 12 are free; others are charged $10.

## A Motel Beneath the Sea

You can sleep in many different kinds of settings in Florida including—are you ready—underwater. No, we are not making this up. You can indeed sleep down there in the briny blue at a weird but quite diverting resort called **Jules Undersea Lodge.** Once used as an underwater research center called Sealab, this 50-foot long steel lodge was moved to Key Largo some years back to become this motel beneath the sea. There are two 8-by-10-foot bedroom suites on one side and an 8-by-20-foot suite that serves as living room, entertainment center, and kitchen on the other. Be-tween the two is a bathroom. Suites are carpeted, have a stocked refrigerator and sink.

Nondivers must take a resort diving course ($75) and are then shown to their rooms by divers called "mer-persons." Guests are connected to the outside world by an intercom, telephone, and marine radio, and there's always someone on duty to answer a room service call. Meals are provided and there's a microwave for warming and cooking.

For diversion there are a videocassette recorder and stereo with a library of films, but the best entertainment comes from outside the big portholes where wildly colorful fish and perhaps a lobster or two peer curiously into the home of their new neighbors.

Naturally, this is an expedition that appeals most to divers, but anyone can be part of this underwater adventure, which takes place at Bora Bora Lagoon at Key Holiday Inn, 51 Shoreland Dr., Mile Marker 103.2, off Transylvania Avenue in Key Largo (mailing address: P.O. Box 3330, Key Largo, 33037) (tel. 305/451-2353). Rates are $195 to $295 per person, including dinner and breakfast.

## Take Me Away From All This

Some miserable day when the rain and sleet are pelting down and there are more hassles than hope in the office, when you're feeling downright miserable, when your thoughts turn to a hot, sunny island with no telephones, well, you are thinking of **Little Palm Island,** Route 4, Box 1036, Little Torch Key, FL 33042 (tel. 305/872-2524, or toll free 800/3-GET-LOST).

If you can live without—indeed *want* to live without—the joys of telephone and television while luxuriating in quite a number of other joys, this island in the Florida Keys is for you. Here a couple of enlightened developers, convinced they see the way of the future, spent a bundle to build a resort you can only get to by boat and that has no telephones or televisions to bring the horrors of the outside world into paradise. Nothing else is missing, however. You dwell in one of 30 quite luxuriously appointed thatch-roofed suites that come complete with whirlpool bath and wet bar.

Outside is a lagoon swimming pool with a waterfall, a Tiki bar, a sauna, and plenty of sailboats and water-sports diversions.

You arrive by private launch and there's a serene restaurant here to see to your hunger pangs. Hedonism does not come cheap, so be prepared to pay $500 a couple nightly including all meals from December through April, $410 to $460 per couple in other months. Little Palm Island is just offshore from Little Torch Key, about 30 miles north of Key West.

## Camping

**Royal Palm Recreational Vehicle Park,** US 1 (P.O. Box 520), Big Pine Key, FL 33043 (tel. 305/872-9856), at Mile Marker 31.5, has 37 sites; and **Sunshine Key Camping Resort,** US 1 (P.O. Box 790), Sunshine Key, FL 33043 (tel. 305/872-2217), has 386 sites on a 73-acre island complete with recreational facilities. Rates are $31 to $38 a day, less by the week.

**Outdoor Resort of America** at Long Key, FL 33001 (tel. 305/664-4860), on Islamorada, at Mile Marker 66, has all kinds of amenities: tennis, pool, miniature golf, health club, and sauna. Rates are $36 to $44 for two, $6 per extra person.

State parks in the Upper Keys include **John Pennekamp, Bahia Honda,** and **Long Key.** Camping is $28 to $34 a night, but there is a 14-day minimum stay and the parks are often very crowded (especially Pennekamp) so it's wise to reserve ahead. Call Pennekamp at 305/451-1202 for reservations.

## WHERE TO EAT

Again moving from north to south, let's start with Mile Marker 100 on Key Largo where you'll find **Ganim's, A Family Restaurant,** 99696 Overseas Hwy. (tel. 451-2895). You can feed a passel of hungry mouths cheap on huge submarines, inexpensive luncheon specials, and family-priced home-style cooking, like breakfast for $2. Fresh biscuits, pies, and pastries are made daily. Open from 6am to 2pm daily.

Islamorada is the culinary capital of the Keys and many a Miamian—and even one Fort Lauderdale restaurateur we know—slips off to get in on the goodies. Here you'll find **Ziggie's Conch Restaurant,** at Mile Marker 83 on US 1 (tel. 664-3391), and it's not to be missed. In this unprepossessing little spot, where the decor runs to mounted fish, you'll find simply the best food for many a mile. Most of it's not on the menu though, so be sure to ask what other delectables are being cooked up in the kitchen—fluffy conch fritters, lobster de jonge, oysters Rockefeller, wonderful pastas with unusual sauces. It's sensational. Prices are in the $10 to $20 range, and Ziggie's is open from 5 to 10pm, except Thursday (closed from Labor Day to mid-October).

**Sid and Roxie's Green Turtle Inn** (tel. 664-9031) has been a fixture in the Keys since 1947. From their kitchens at Mile Marker 81.5, Islamorada, come turtle soup and conch chowder so good it's canned and sold through gourmet outlets, and there's plenty of good seafood and steaks in a roadside-tavern atmosphere. Decor in this casual spot is hundreds of business cards stuffed in every empty space. It's open from noon to 10pm daily, except Monday, and prices are $10 to $20. You can buy the soups in a six-pack for $10.

A Keys newcomer destined for the heights is Erik Jorgensen, once chef at Miami's posh Chez Vendôme. Now he's bought a houseboat and clipped miles of red tape to install it as **Erik's Floating Restaurant** at Mile Marker 85.5 on Windley Key (tel. 664-9141), quite close to Islamorada. Once again he's producing cuisine that draws crowds to his beneath-the-bridge hideaway. Erik is a Viking charmer, and the houseboat is a study in beautiful views inside and out, with lots of crystal, linens, a fireplace, Peruvian llama rugs on the walls, and silk rosebuds on the tables. There's a skylight above and a tiny wine "cellar" with leather high-backed hand-carved chairs and Copenhagen china, silver, and goblets. For the Keys, this is spectacular. For anywhere, this is spectacular! Prices are in the $12 to $17 range, and Erik's labor of love is open from 6 to 11pm Wednesday through Monday, probably also for lunch in winter. Call for reservations.

At Mile Marker 83.5 at the Whale Harbor Docks in Islamorada, you won't have any trouble finding the **Whale Harbor Inn** (tel. 664-4159)—just look for the lighthouse. That lighthouse was high ground during a hurricane that the owners rode out right here, while their chairs floated around in the dining room below. You can see photos of the storm damage at the entrance, and then treat yourself to lunch or dinner inside overlooking a fleet of charter boats. There's a second-story gathering spot called Rott'n Ralph's that probably shouldn't be missed. Downstairs, you dine on lots of fresh seafood in a comfortable casual atmosphere. Prices average $10 to $15, and the restaurant's open from 4 to 9pm daily, the lounge to the early a.m., noon to 9pm on Sunday.

If you like quantity as much as quality, don't miss the **Coral Grill** at Mile Marker 83.5, Islamorada (tel. 664-4803), where you can stoke up for a long winter at a belt-busting table guaranteed to send you away in overstuffed joy. More than 40 appetizers, entrées, salads, and desserts, ranging from prime rib to fried shrimp and flaky pies, are featured in the buffet. Meanwhile a downstairs dining room offers menu service that includes a soup and salad bar. Buffet price is $13; downstairs dining falls in the $10 to $17 range for dinner. Hours are 4:30 to 9:30pm Tuesday through Saturday, noon to 9pm on Sunday; closed Monday.

You shouldn't have much trouble finding **Marker 88** in Islamorada (tel. 852-9315) since its name is also its location. A bilevel waterfront restaurant with terrific views out over Florida Bay at sunset, Marker 88 is a cheerfully handsome restaurant that is very, very popular hereabouts. Reservations are most wise. Marker 88 deserves its popularity too, for the restaurant serves top-quality food prepared under the supervision of chef/owner André Mueller, who whips up such specialties as baby snapper Rangoon topped with mangoes, papayas, pineapples, and bananas in a lemon-parsley butter; shrimp curry with mango chutney; Florida lobster stuffed with crabmeat; and rack of lamb provençal. Try the lobster bisque and consider one of the restaurant's Caesar, Greek, or German wilted-leaf-lettuce concoctions. Personally we'd never think of resisting the oysters Bienville. The menu is à la carte, and thus can climb pretty high for gorgers like us. Entrées alone are $14 to $25. Despite the fancy food, dress is Keys-casual. Hours are 5 to 11pm daily except Monday.

**READERS' RESTAURANT SELECTIONS:** "On Sugarloaf Key at Mile Marker 20 is a restaurant called **Mangrove Mama's** (closed all day Tuesday and the month of September; tel. 745-3030). They create with local seafood, and serve meals, which include home-baked bread, in an oldtime Keys atmosphere. That's a bit different in the Keys. Fish tempura is a standout here, where prices are about $10 to $14. Hours are 11am to 3pm and 5 to 10pm daily except Tuesday, with reggae music in winter. Also on Big Pine Key, near Mile Marker 30, is **Serendipity** (tel. 367-3493). They have great deli sandwiches, grinders (a meal in themselves), and ice-cream sundaes. It's scrupulously clean and the service is excellent" (Linda Sambel, Pittsfield, Mass.).

"We recently returned from a trip through the Florida Keys—a fantastic experience I'd recommend to anyone! I thought I'd share a wonderful restaurant in Key Largo called **Sundowners,** Mile Marker 104 (tel. 451-4502). Every seat in this open-air establishment has a view of a truly spectacular sunset over the ocean—even better than the view at Key West! Prices are reasonable, dinner entrées in the $12 to $18 range, and they make a great cracked conch" (Janet and David Scire, West Haven, Conn.).

## THE SIGHTS

**John Pennekamp Coral Reef State Park,** Mile Marker 102, Islamorada (tel. 451-1202, or toll free 800/432-2871 in Florida), is an underwater garden 21 miles long and 4 miles wide, an undersea fairyland of more than 40 species of coral and 650 kinds of colorful tropical fish. Molasses Reef is the focal point of the park, a panorama of unsurpassed beauty in water 25 to 40 feet deep. All kinds and colors of coral and an explosion of fish greet divers, and there's even an underwater statue, *Christ of the Deep*. There's no charge for admission to the visitor center, open from 8am to sundown, but admission to the park (open sunrise to sunset) is $1.50 to $2 a person.

Discovery Undersea glass-bottom-boat tours leave at 9am, noon, and 3pm daily, and cost $10 to $11 for adults, $6 for children under 12. Scuba expeditions are $30 for a two-tank dive. Snorkeling trips (at 9:30am and 1:30pm) are $17 to $19 per person. If you throw sailing in with the snorkeling, trips are $50.

**Diver's World,** at Mile Marker 99.5 (tel. 451-3200), has daily Pennekamp reef and wreck adventures and all the equipment you'll need for $35 for a four-hour trip. Three- and five-day trips, too.

You've seen them at the Seaquarium or Ocean World or Sea World, or even out in the wild, but have you ever ridden a dolphin? Well, here's your chance, at **Dolphins Research Center,** Mile Marker 59, (P.O. Box 2875) in Marathon Shores, FL 33052 (tel. 289-1121 or 289-0002). Dolphins raised since birth by humans await whatever humans are game to enter their playground. Tame as they are, these are still creatures of the wild, so you sign a waiver of liability if you want to get in there and swim with them at this Dolphin Encounter. Once in, you'll find them playful, curious—and very, very big. After you've splashed around together a while, the dolphins' trainers will bring out a fishy reward—for the dolphins. They know what that means and they know just what to do to get their treats: Race down to the end of the tank where you're waiting, nuzzle you impatiently to remind you to grab onto their fins, then race with you in tow down to the other end of the tank where they are paid off in dolphin currency. It's quite a thrilling event, so we hear, although some bathing suits come right off during the streaking ride across the pool, and some nerve gets lost at the first look at these big puppies of the sea waiting to show you whatever they want to show you. You pay $65 for 15 minutes of frolic at 8:30am and 1:30pm Wednesday through Sunday.

**Theater of the Sea,** Mile Marker 84.5 (P.O. Box 407), Islamorada, FL 33036 (tel. 664-2431), was featured on NBC's "Today" show and has continuous dolphin and sea lion shows from 9:30am to 4pm daily. You'll see tarpons, bonefish, porcupine fish, colorful parrot fish, angel fish, rays, and trained dolphins, not to mention some not-very-fun-loving sharks. Admission is $10.25 for adults, $5.50 for children 4 to 12 (under 4, free) and you can swim with a dolphin for $50.

If you're wondering about that enormous bubble you see floating in the air around the Seven Mile Bridge, that's **Fat Albert,** a U.S. Air Force thing—but they're not saying just what. Rest secure in the knowledge that Uncle is watching over you aboard this fat little sausage with fins.

Local festivals, art shows, fish fries, and the like are detailed in the **newspaper** of the Upper Keys, *The Keynoter,* published in Marathon.

Another publication, *Florida Keys* magazine, 2111 Overseas Hwy., Marathon, FL 33050 (tel. 305/451-4429), chronicles some fascinating details of life in the Keys. Stories in the magazine have offered a profile of Mel Fisher, the lowdown on high-flying Fat Albert, an interesting look at Keys birds, the story of Zane Grey's visit to the islands, and a look at an early pioneer woman's struggles as a lime farmer. Lots of news on upcoming activities too.

## NIGHTLIFE

Things are pretty quiet evenings in the Upper Keys, but here's a look at a few things you'll find moving after dark. Many of the hotels listed back a few pages have entertainment too.

### Key Largo

**Gilbert's Motel and Marina** (tel. 451-1133) has a trio for listening and dancing on Friday and Saturday nights, and lounges at the **Holiday Inn** (tel. 451-2121) and **Howard Johnson's** (tel. 451-1400) usually have some kind of entertainment most nights.

## Plantation Key/Tavernier

**Plantation Yacht Harbor** (tel. 852-2381) is the big action in these parts, with dining and dancing and live entertainment nightly, and piano entertainment Thursday through Monday.

## Islamorada

Holiday Isle's **Horizon Lounge,** at Mile Marker 84.5 (tel. 664-2321), has entertainment from 9:30pm to midnight daily. **Whale Harbor** (tel. 664-4159) has lounge entertainment every day but Tuesday.

Something's always jumping at **Cheeca Lodge** (tel. 664-4651), where there's entertainment nightly except Sunday from 7pm.

## Marathon

**Brass Monkey Liquor Store and Lounge,** at Mile Marker 50, in the K-Mart Plaza (tel. 743-5737), provides local night action. Other live spots in Marathon: **Side Door Lounge,** 5101 Overseas Hwy. (tel. 743-4622), and **Hurricane Restaurant and Lounge,** 4650 Overseas Hwy. (tel. 743-5755).

## SPORTS

Naturally, fishing and water sports are the big, big thing in the Keys, so you won't have any trouble at all arranging a fishing or diving expedition. Dive shops, charter boats, party boats, boats of all kinds, are scattered everywhere in the Keys. They are especially plentiful at **Gilbert's** on Key Largo and at **Whale Harbor** on Islamorada. You can rent a sailboat or a windsurfer at **Buccaneer Lodge Beach,** at Mile Marker 49 (tel. 743-9071), for prices in the $18 to $30 range.

Travel with **Stan Becker** (tel. 872-2620) through the beautiful Key Deer Refuge on Big Pine Key on a seven-hour natural-history excursion including canoes, lunch, and this naturalist's wisdom. The cost is $60 per person, reservations required.

**Key Colony Beach Golf Course,** at Mile Marker 53.5 in Marathon (tel. 289-1533), is a par-three course open from 7:30am to 5pm, at $5 for nine holes. In Marathon, **Sombrero Country Club,** at Mile Marker 50 (tel. 743-2551), has 18 holes and greens fees of $35; carts cost $24 for two.

---

# 2. Key West

---

It's elegant and antique, contemporary and a little crazy, a world of its own 100 miles—and light-years—away from Miami. It's the farthest you can get from the madding crowd and is, as a matter of fact, as far as you can get in the United States from anywhere.

As the southernmost city in the nation, Key West has the dubious distinction of being the starting point (or the end) of the Maine-to-Florida seaboard highway known as US 1.

In this tiny town people are short on the frenetic, long on tolerance, and dedicated to the pursuit of self-indulgence, an activity that enjoys a wide variety of interpretations on the island.

People-watchers are likely to suffer from exhaustion quickly here: Key West is home to author Philip Caputo, and has welcomed Gay Talese, Kurt Vonnegut, Jr., Vincent Price, Robert Frost, John Dos Passos, designer Calvin Klein, actor Dustin Hoffman, and was the starting place for folk singer Jimmy Buffett. It also was home to playwright Tennessee Williams, and of course writer Ernest "Papa" Hemingway.

What draws the famous, the infamous, and the thousands of the rest of us who are not yet either is a strange, inexplicable magic. You'll feel it as you settle in here and begin to roam among rambling pastel wooden houses that have sheltered generations of lawbreakers and lawmakers. You'll feel it as you stroll beneath huge trees shading sidewalks trod for centuries and peek around corners of towering conch houses, their sprawling verandas trimmed in gingerbread wood cutouts, their etched glass sparkling, and mahogany glowing.

Just five miles long and three miles wide, the island of Key West was discovered in the 1500s by Spanish explorers who named it Cayo Hueso, "bone island," for the bones of slain settlers they found there. Not much of a start for this island, but a herald of things to come. As Spain took to looting the New World, the Florida Keys became a storm-wracked, nightmare gauntlet for treasure-laden ships to run on their return to Spain. One Friday the 13th in 1733 a fleet of Spanish merchant ships left Cuba bound for Europe carrying what was said to be $68 million in gold and silver. A gale struck off Plantation Key and the fleet floundered. That treasure is still the life's dream of many a diver here.

So shallow are these waters that, without lights or maps for guidance, early sailors frequently ran aground. By doing so they created a trade known as wrecking, which involved retrieving valuables from shipwrecks—occasionally even ensuring there would be a shipwreck. At one time nearly everyone in Key West was a wrecker or involved in wrecking operations. A Bahamian named William Curry is said to have built such a financially rewarding career supplying wreckers that he became the first Florida millionaire, wealthy enough to buy a gold Tiffany table service for $100,000.

Wrecking has given rise to many a rollicking tale. Here's one: Since the first wrecker to reach the wreck was dubbed "wrecking master" and entitled to a major share of the loot, the race was on. One wrecker, who worked in his spare time as community pastor, was delivering a solemn sermon when he looked out the church windows and saw a ship foundering on the rocks. With true Keys ingenuity, he launched into a dramatic presentation so gripping that the audience sat riveted as he moved slowly toward the exit. When he knew he was close enough to the door to lead the racing pack, he called out "Wreck ashore!" and tore out the door—first, of course!

They're like that, these people who call themselves "conchs." They're canny, and a little crazy, spirited and loyal, hospitable and happy-go-lucky, sometimes eccentric, always individualistic, rarely surprised, and almost never shocked by the fascinating mélange of life-styles that ebbs and flows across these islands with tidal inevitability. And in addition to its writers, artists, and other "bohemian" types, Key West has joined the ranks of Fire Island, N.Y., and Provincetown, Mass., as a sun-and-fun destination for many gay tourists.

Only the island-born, by the way, can call themselves "conchs" (pronounced "konks"), but if you manage to stay around seven years you may refer to yourself in polite circles as a "freshwater conch." Tourists, however, must remain tourists until they've visited often or long enough to assume the exalted rank of "Visitor." What better reason to sink in here for a few weeks?

It is perhaps not what these islanders are but what they aren't that makes this place a refuge for the weak and weary, the strong and ambitious, the leftover pieces from the puzzle of life. Forgiving of frailties and immune to differences, Key West manages to contain some of the world's more unusual occupants and suffers little from slavish adoration of tradition. There is, however, one inviolate tradition here, a moment of unspoken homage to nature that unites even this most heterogenous population.

This exercise in Central Park South is known as **Mallory Dock at Sunset,** and consists mainly of showing up on the dock at sunset as the town's *rarae aves* congregate to observe the setting sun and each other. Here you'll find jugglers, mimes, blue-grass singers, unskilled-but-willing magicians, anachronistic remnants of the counterculture enveloped in some sweet smoke, the Iguana Man whose best friend is on his shoulder, some socialites, some politicians, who knows? You'll also see a setting sun. That may not sound like much, but way down here in the tropics, Old Sol really does do a rather spectacular job, turning the sky and ocean to molten gold and scarlet before dropping suddenly below the sea in a haze of royal blue.

It's quite a sight, as is most everything in this city that has for three centuries or more rolled with the punches, accepted the inevitability of its invaders, and lured into its seductive web visitors from pirates to Pittsburghers.

## ORIENTATION

In Key West, Duval Street is the main drag, running through the middle of town to the edge of Mallory Dock and the Pier House Hotel. US 1 becomes South Roosevelt Boulevard, running past the airport on the Atlantic side of the island, and North Roosevelt Boulevard on the north side of the island. North Roosevelt runs into Truman Avenue (the president once made this city the winter White House), which crosses Duval in the middle of downtown Key West.

## GETTING TO AND AROUND THE KEY

You can fly in on **USAir** or **Delta** Airlines, or bus in by **Greyhound,** which has service from Miami and even has a bus directly from Miami International Airport to Key West and back. For schedules, call the company in Miami (tel. 305/374-7222).

Once here, you can rent cars from **Hertz** (tel. 294-1039), **Avis** (tel. 296-8744), or **Dollar** (tel. 294-6675).

For less expensive transportation that's easier to park, rent a moped from **Moped Hospital,** 601 Truman Ave. (tel. 296-3344), for $8 for two hours, then $1 an hour. **Lang's** (tel. 296-3287), with two locations on the island, rents bikes and snorkeling gear too. You can also rent a bike for $5 a day, $25 a week, at the **Bike Shop,** 1110 Truman St. (tel. 294-1073).

A taxi company called **Five Six Cab Co.** (tel. 296-6666) operates here for $1.40 a mile plus $2.45 for the first mile.

## VISITOR INFORMATION

They can tell you anything you need to know about this island at the **Greater Key West Chamber of Commerce,** 402 Wall St., Key West, FL 33040 (tel. 305/294-2587). The **Florida Keys Visitors Bureau,** 416 Fleming St., Key West, FL 33040 (tel. toll free 800/FLA-KEYS), covers accommodations options in all the Keys.

Keys dwellers have long been famed for unusual ideas so it comes as no surprise to us that Keysian Susan Kieffer has come up with a novel idea called **Island Club International.** Anyone can join this club by paying $48 for the first year, $24 thereafter, or $9 for a limited-time visitor membership for two. What you get for your money is a list of dozens of different kinds of businesses that offer special bargain prices and discounts to club members. A list of those wheeling-dealing businesses now fills a 26-page brochure that surely must include nearly every business in the Keys! Cardholders receive everything from half-price dinners or drinks at Keys restaurants and lounges to a discount on jewelry, art, boating, fishing, windsurfing, hotels, rental cars, airline fares, even automotive parts! To make it all even more interesting, this "club" meets once a month for a lively party at which dozens of gifts donated by area businesses are raffled. For the full story, contact Ms. Kieffer at Island Club International, P.O. Box 930, Summerland Key, FL 33042 (tel. 201/661-6408).

Because the island has become popular with gay travelers, there are now some hostelries that cater only to gay men or women or both. Most are quite frank about their target market, however, so don't be shy about asking if you want to find—or avoid—an establishment with such a dedication.

You can also obtain from the Greater Key West Chamber of Commerce an **accommodations guide** that lists all the hotels, motels, and guesthouses in the city.

## WHERE TO STAY

Key West's hostelries are scattered around a bit, but no matter where you stay you're just a few minutes' drive from those charming old downtown streets you'll want to explore. And when we say downtown, think mite-sized, not Manhattan.

### The Luxury Leaders

The **Pier House,** 1 Duval St., Key West, FL 33040 (tel. 305/294-9541, or toll free 800/327-8340), is one of Key West's grandest hotels, refurbished with millions of dollars and such skill you'd like to keep its decorator on retainer. In Key West you translate "grand" not as multi-storied, but as tasteful, pretty, quiet, and fun. At Pier House you'll find a rambling wood-sided oceanfront structure that's long been one of Key West's favorite meeting spots. Rambling over acres of ground and a dazzling strip of private beach, the resort is thoroughly modern from subtle earth colors to wicker furnishings, bold jewel colors, and whirring paddle fans. It has striking geometric lines and 101 rooms, no two alike, tucked into just about every available space.

Worries slip away here as they do everywhere in Key West as you sip a frosty problem-solver at Old Havana Docks lounge, where a parrot perches atop a shoulder and demands to know what you'll have. In the Roof Top bar, where musician Jimmy Buffett began his career, you can watch the sunset and rituals at Mallory Dock through panoramic windows. In the Pier House Restaurant, built out over the sea, you can feast on a gigantic Sunday brunch or an excellent dinner in a greenery-filled, multilevel dining room (prices, $14 to $24) where Tennessee Williams was a frequent guest. In the Wine Galley Bar you can sip more than 250 wines—not all at one sitting, we hope. If it's al fresco dining you have in mind, head for the outdoor Harbour View Café, which offers what its name suggests.

The spacious rooms are comfortable and modern, filled with bright colors. You can have one overlooking the ocean or the plant-bedecked pool area for $185 to $325 in peak season, or a suite for $650. In other months, rates range from $135 to $215 for rooms.

**Marriott's Casa Marina Resort,** 1500 Reynolds St., Key West, FL 33040 (tel. 305/296-3535, or toll free 800/235-4837), at the foot of Reynolds Street, is as much a landmark on this island as the Hemingway or Audubon houses, and is just as historic: It was originally built in 1921 by powerhouse Henry Flagler as the pot of gold at the end of his Overseas Railroad rainbow. A Spanish Renaissance-style hotel on 1,100 feet of beachfront, Casa Marina was the playground for the likes of the Astors, Robert Frost, Gregory Peck, Guy Lombardo. When a hurricane ruined the railroad, Casa Marina began a downhill slide that lasted until 1978 (for years the hotel was shuttered) when Marriott poured $10 million into restoration of this magnificent memorial to those classically elegant days.

Today you're greeted by attendants in safari suits and shown to a reception area that's the hotel's showplace. A restored version of Flagler's magnificent entryway, it has a massive fireplace reaching to a beamed ceiling, tall columns, French doors, and serene little groupings of wicker furniture cushioned in deep burgundy tones. Outside on the veranda overlooking the sea, paddle fans whir and high-backed wicker chairs are inviting. On a lower level, the resort's pool glitters and a 20-foot Jacuzzi whirlpool bubbles and swirls. A long strip of beach is lapped by gentle waves and lined with attractive chaises.

Very large rooms—314 of them, some in a new wing, some in the original hotel—have all the extras you'd expect in a fine hotel: large mirrored dressing areas, attractive tiled bath/shower combinations, two double beds, a glass wall leading to a private balcony. To keep you busy there are tennis courts, a fishing and boating pier, rental sailboats, a game room, exercise room, boutiques, and on Sunday you can lose a whole day at Henry's Restaurant when the hotel presents its massive brunch that includes, among other things, two steamship rounds of beef, each 70 to 80 pounds, veal, turkey, pork, mutton, grouper, etc. Rates in winter range from $195 to $315; in summer, they're $130 to $195.

Hyatt hotels can be counted on for top-quality lodgings and that is what you will find here in Key West. Opened in 1988, the **Hyatt Key West,** 601 Front St. (tel. 305/296-9900), formerly the Front Street Hotel & Marina, is something of a new concept in Hyatts. They're calling it a "boutique resort" to distinguish it from most Hyatt hotels, which are much larger. You'll find just 120 handsomely appointed rooms here in this attractive property, all of them furnished in soft tropical shades that evoke the sands and ocean just outside the door. When hunger strikes, you can join the crowds at the outdoor raw bar or settle into a viewful seat in the upstairs grill and lounge or in the resort's prime-time restaurant. For amusement, there's a swimming pool and Jacuzzi and an exercise room with a trainer to tell you how to get more from all that exercise than tired. You'll pay $105 to $210 for a room here during the summer months, $185 to $285 in peak winter season from late December to mid-April. An additional diversion here is a sailboat that sails you off into the sunset or on afternoon cruises into the tear-clear waters here.

**Best Western Key Ambassador,** next door at 3755 S. Roosevelt Blvd., Key West, FL 33040 (tel. 305/296-3500, or toll free 800/528-1234), offers a sumptuous Continental breakfast free to guests each morning in a small breakfast room where attendants whip up raisin toast, assorted breads, English muffins, and lots of coffee, tea, and orange juice. In the center of this sprawling resort is a sparkling pool shaded by huge trees that tower over the manicured grounds and multilevel sundeck. Spacious hotel rooms and studios here have sliding glass doors opening onto balconies from which you'll have a view of the pool or ocean. In winter, you'll pay $140 to $173; in summer, $75 to $95—depending on your view.

## What Doesn't Fit Gets You Fit

Now, this next hotel defies categorization under anything as simple as luxury, moderate, and budget properties. That's why it doesn't fit. Here's how it gets you fit: **Russell House,** 611 Truman Ave., Key West, FL 33040 (tel. 305/294-8787), bills itself as a European-style health resort specializing in holistic mergings of body, mind, and spirit. All this merging takes place in a cluster of rooms circling a courtyard where a Roman tub and swimming pool are focal points. A patio dining room is tucked into a leafy corner, and near the pool is an iced-tea bar. There is an exercise deck, a spa, sauna, showers, steam cabinet, massage room, and a spot for herbal wraps and beauty treatments.

What they hope to do for you here is "eliminate the cause of stress and disease"; provide an environment that lends itself to total relaxation, weight loss, "elimination of destructive habits"; and to cleanse and detoxify the body, improve skin and body tone, teach self-awareness, and send you home "feeling better and healthier than ever before." Rather a tall order, but they're determined—and if you are too, this may be just the place to give it all a try. Yoga and juice fasts can be on the menu for you, along with seminars that help you give up smoking. Your daily schedule is likely to begin at 7am, include plenty of walks, exercise, and the occasional potassium cocktail before it's lights out at 11pm—listen, do you want to improve yourself or not? Check-ins and check-outs are on Sunday and rates range from $750 a week for a dorm room (which may be private but would share a bath with four or more others) to $1,635 a week for a Celebrity House private top-of-the-line room and bath. Mid-priced quarters in the spa's Clubhouse are private room and bath for $950 to $1,200 a week. Prices include food, exercise, use of equipment, lectures— everything but facials, herbal wraps, massages, and other spa treatments. All rooms have television, air conditioning, and maid service. Russell House also has a skin-care program with a variety of treatments from eyelash tinting to facial waxing and eyebrow arching. All are priced separately. Double rates bring the per-person prices down a bit. Russell House is open year round.

## Moderately Priced Hotels

Orange and green trim highlights the **Santa Maria,** 1401 Simonton St., Key West, FL 33040 (tel. 305/296-5678), where rooms surround a central courtyard. At the bottom of the pool you'll get another look at Key West's pirate heritage: There's a galleon down there! Balconies overlook the pool, and the medium-size rooms are decorated in more bright shades. Off the eclectically decorated lobby is a small dining room. Rates here are $120 to $250 from December to May 1, $64 to $100 in other months.

Naturally, in this southernmost city there are a number of things that can legitimately call themselves "the southernmost." The **Southernmost Motel,** 1319 Duval St., Key West, FL 33040 (tel. 305/296-6577), at South Street, is one of them. A pretty little place just across the street from the huge and colorful "Southernmost House," the motel has a pool lined with yellow polka-dot patio umbrellas. There are lots of colorful blossoms here in shades of pink and yellow, and you'll see those same tropical shades in the rooms, many of which have two double beds and forest-green carpeting set off by yellow accents, plus color TVs and phones. There's a rooftop solarium, and the motel's within walking distance of most of Key West. From mid-December to April, rates are $95 to $155, dropping in other months to $65 to $105.

The **South Beach Oceanfront Motel,** 508 South St., Key West, FL 33040 (tel. 305/296-5611), runs from the street to a small fishing pier where a light pole announces "You have now reached the South Pole." There's no refuting that logic, which is indicative of the kind of easy humor you'll find in this small motel that's just across a bay from the Southernmost House. Here you can watch those flaming Keys sunsets in quiet isolation without fighting the traffic at Mallory Dock. A teensy vest-pocket beach dotted with Tiki huts is just next door (it's so small and cute you want to wrap it up and take it home). Rooms are simply furnished but have a nice uncluttered beachside look, and there's a pool where plaster dolphins create mini-waterfalls. An antique Victorian house next door has been restored by the friendly folks who run the South Beach, and is open to guests. Rates are $125 to $195 for two in peak season, $85 to $135 in the summer months.

A sparkling tiled pool surrounded by a jungle of tropical plants is a lovely feature of **Key Lodge,** at Truman Avenue and Duval Street, Key West, FL 33040 (tel. 305/296-9915 or 296-9750). A tiny motel with just 22 rooms, Key Lodge has a winding driveway out front with the owner's zippy antique convertible parked in it. Inside, you'll find interestingly eclectic rooms (one apartment has a whole wall covered with an antique map); all have paddle fans. They're neat and clean, if a bit on the small side, and rates range from $95 to $111 for motel rooms, efficiencies, and apartments. In other months, prices drop to $52 to $94.

Key Lodge's owners operate two other motels within three blocks of Key Lodge—**Halfred Motel,** 512 Truman Ave. (tel. 305/296-5415), where prices are about $5 less than those at Key Lodge; and **Red Rooster Inn** (tel. 305/296-6558), 709 Truman Ave., where prices are about $10 less than Key Lodge rates. Neither has a pool or room telephones.

**READER'S RECOMMENDATION:** Susan Kieffer, who runs a travel-consumer club in the Keys (see Visitor Information for more on that) writes that in addition to *her* budget-saving deals ". . . for the budget minded, there's something really good and almost totally unknown. If someone is willing to stay a bit outside of Key West and has a car . . . on Cudjoe Key about 23 minutes' drive from Key West, there's a firm that rents separate patio condo units for $300 to $500 a week! These units, sleeping four to six, fall under an old Housing and Urban Development proviso allowing a so-called RV resort condominium park. While these units aren't condo apartments, they are also not what HUD thought would be there, which was an RV trailer towed behind a vehicle. Instead, and legally, they usually are so-called park model units . . . about 800 very comfortable square feet [that sell at high prices]. These units are on a 69-acre *immaculate* five-star condominium park resort, oceanfront, with canals, security, Olympic pool, Jacuzzi, marina, boat ramp, tennis, basketball, horseshoes, waterfront barbecue Tiki hut, convenience store, post office . . . really nice, and fantastic for the money. Each unit has a kitchen and comes fully furnished. We really think for the price this is a dollarwise bargain. For information, readers should contact **Hartline Real Estate** (they are the exclusive agents for the resort and have vacation house rentals as well), Vacation Rental Department, P.O. Box 515, Summerland Key, FL 33042 (tel. 305/745-1590)" (Susan Kieffer, Summerland Key, Fla.).

## Guesthouses and/or Budget Accommodations

Key West now has more than 40 guesthouses, some catering to gay tourists or other guests with very specific interests. Down this way, folks are pretty frank about their diversions and life-styles, so if you find, or hear about, a guesthouse that interests you, give them a call and ask your questions frankly. You can be sure you will get a direct answer. Although guesthouses are among the coziest and loveliest of Key West accommodations, unless you're as open-minded as the locals or know the city well enough to choose the guesthouse that will best suit you, you might be wise to stick to our recommendations or to hotels and motor inns on the island.

Many of the city's guesthouses are downright gorgeous places, occupying lovely old homes that have consumed many thousands of renovation dollars. Settling into one is like becoming a Conch (that's what native Key Westers or those who have been here many years like to call themselves) in very comfortable style. Room rates run from moderate to very expensive.

Among the newest is the exquisitely renovated **Marquesa Hotel,** 600 Fleming St., Key West, FL 33040 (tel. 305/292-1919). A jewelbox hotel, this guesthouse has just 15 rooms togged out in an eclectic but charming mélange of antique and contemporary furnishings. Soft tropical colors predominate, and outside is a pool and inside a top-flight restaurant, the Mira, that has become one of the island's best dining spots. Rates are $165 to $260 from December through April and from $105 to $175 in other months.

Another new and very beautiful addition to the guesthouse roster here is **La Mer,** 506 South St., Key West, FL 33040 (tel. 305/296-5611). La Mer overlooks the ocean and is a delightful place to settle back in one of the porch rockers and just let the world do whatever it's doing. There are just 11 units here, 6 with kitchens, each attractively furnished, and the house itself is a lovely old Conch creation. Rates are $142 to $199 from December to April, $125 to $189 in other months.

**Island City House,** 411 William St., Key West, FL 33040 (tel. 305/294-5702), is a study in lacy Victorian furbelows. Wraparound white verandas, brick walkways, and a jungle of plants make this a beguiling spot to escape reality. One- and two-bedroom apartments here are decorated in lovely Victorian-era prints and each has a complete kitchen. Outside, there's a heated pool, Jacuzzi, and rental bicycles. This inn, like many others in Key West and elsewhere, has no telephones in the rooms, but a pay phone is available and the staff will help you make dining reservations. Rates are $75 to $125 from April to December and $120 to $200 in peak winter months.

A most intriguing alternative to the island's large hotels is a room next door— and part of—an island showplace called **The Curry Mansion,** 511A Caroline St., Key West, FL 33040 (tel. 305/294-5349). Opened in late 1988 by the mansion's personable owners, Al and Edith Amsterdam, the inn is not actually in the house, since most of that is now open to the public, but is in an equally charming building alongside the 1899 house.

Togged out in charming dramatic wicker furnishings including fancy, lace-trimmed four-posters, the inn has just 15 rooms filled with antiques, pretty pastel quilts, plants, and all the little extras that make inns inn-teresting. Airport pickup, homemade Continental breakfasts, daily complimentary cocktails, invitations to the

Amsterdams' frequent cocktail parties, access to the 22-room Curry Mansion, which was the home of Florida's first millionaire, and privileges at the Pier House Beach Club just a block away are all part of the deal. Many rooms have balconies, all have air conditioning, and there's an inviting circular pool for sunseekers. In winter from December to mid-April, rates are $150 to $175 for rooms; in summer, $90 to $130; higher for a suite.

A new economy retreat here is called the **Inn at the Wharf**, 2400 N. Roosevelt Blvd., Key West, FL 33040 (tel. 305/296-5700, or toll free 800/225-6178, 800/843-5888 in Florida). Located a bit out of, but just a five-minute drive from, the center of things, the new inn is right next door to another new development. An enclave of shops, restaurants, and galleries, complete with a daily dolphin and sea show, the new diversion is called The Wharf. Meanwhile, the hotel offers a pool with outdoor bar and 100 rooms decorated in bright colors and simple contemporary furnishings. Double rates are $69 to $89 in summer; $139 to $149 in winter, higher for suites.

We're going to say right up front here that the **Southern Cross Hotel**, 326 Duval St., Key West, FL 33040 (tel. 305/294-3200), is not for everyone. In fact it seems safe to say that it's only for those few people willing to sacrifice all fancy amenities for location and an unmistakable, if indescribable, ambience. A paint job a couple of years ago has given this old hotel a much-needed facelift, but it remains kind of cozily shabby, to put the best face on it. Rates are bargain basement in this now-pricey village: $79.50 to $99.50 a night in winter, which buys you clean beds, bathroom, enchantingly high-ceilinged rooms, a new sun deck, and a location smack in the middle of town, smack in the middle of Key West's main street. From an advantageous second-floor balcony here you can look down on the many moods of Duval as it changes from early-morning bustle to afternoon tourist haven to its best face of all in the quiet of early evening. It's a great place in its way, but no Hilton. Summer rates are $20 lower.

**READER'S GUESTHOUSE SELECTION:** "I moved into this wonderful guesthouse, **Wicker Guesthouse**, 913 Duval St., Key West, FL 33040 (tel. 305/296-4275). The owners are very friendly, the complimentary breakfast was plentiful and delightful, and I was able to chat with other vacationers. I strongly recommend it" (Mariette Givoiset, Villeneuve la Garenne, France). [*Authors' Note:* Today Wicker Guesthouse occupies two large houses and a third smaller building, together offering a total of 16 guest rooms and an efficiency apartment. One of the houses is a restored Conch two-story house rimmed with porches on both floors. Wicker has a whirlpool and two large sundecks. Double-occupancy rates from May 1 to December 15 range from $50 to $75. Winter-season visitors will pay $68 to $85, inclusive of Continental breakfast. All but the most expensive rooms share a bath. The guesthouse also takes guests on boating trips to a barrier reef nearby.]

## WHERE TO EAT

Restaurants open and close or are somewhere between the two events with such frequency here that an *old* restaurant is one that's been around more than a year. Casual is the mode here, so for any except the most upper-crust spots you won't need to dress up, particularly in summer when pants longer than your knees are considered formal. In winter things are a bit dressier, but just a bit. This is, after all, the last resort. Remember that the prices we've cited are for entrées, but that these usually include one or two vegetables, salad, and perhaps coffee.

### Top of the Line

If you share with us a fascination for old houses, book a table at **Pigeon House Patio**, 301-303 Whitehead St. (tel. 296-9600), a rambling old home built by ships' carpenters in 1886 and moved here during World War I. Pigeon House got its unusual name when an airline without radios used carrier pigeons as messengers and kept the birds here. You can sit outside on a garden patio or inside under a whirring paddle fan to dine on fresh local seafood and Continental and American specialties.

Prices start at $3.50 for lunch and $10 for dinner. The restaurant's open from noon to 2am daily.

**The Buttery,** 1208 Simonton St. (tel. 294-0717), is tucked away in a small shopping area, but once you've discovered this sterling spot you'll find your way back again and again to dine in four candlelit, plant-bedecked rooms, the newest of which is an enclosed garden room. Continental cuisine with French touches and lots of delectable Key West seafood is the fare here, where you'll pay $12 to $24 for dinner. It's open nightly from 6 to 11pm, 7 to 10:30pm in summer.

**Bagatelle's,** at 115 Duval St. (tel. 296-6609), is a shining star in the firmament of restaurants in Key West. Caribbean specials like escargots Martinique and Bahamian cracked conch are the focus here. You dine in the antique atmosphere of an old conch house, upstairs or down on a veranda overlooking Duval Street. You'll pay about $15 to $25 for a full dinner, and the restaurant's open from 11:30am to 11pm daily.

**La Terrazza de la Marti,** 1125 Duval St. (tel. 294-8435), is known around town as La-Ti-Da and as one of the loveliest spots in the city. La-Ti-Da is indeed a very pretty place, with a double-decker porch overlooking a pool. The decor is so perfect that you can hardly find a glass that isn't beautiful. Brunch here ($4 to $13) is a favorite with islanders, who dine on things like brioche stuffed with ham and sausage, and garnished with fruit and vegetables. At 6pm the upstairs bar produces Szechuan specialties in the $11 to $17 range until 3am. Fixed-price dinners downstairs (7 to 11pm, with seating on the half hour) are four courses that change each evening, including shrimp or scallops Thermidor, for $30. The restaurant's open from 9am to 1:30am daily.

**Louie's Backyard,** 700 Waddell Ave. (tel. 294-1061), isn't really Louie's backyard or anyone else's. It's a handsome old two-story home converted into a chic dining spot. On warm and wonderful days, of which there are many here in the nation's last resort, you dine outside in the backyard under giant seagrape trees by the water's edge with a pale moon floating conveniently overhead. On those rare "other" days you settle into this elegant old house togged out in period furnishings. Upstairs the fare is nouveau Cuban with the traditional Cubano favorites lightened and freshened with inventive fillips. Throughout the menu, there's a Caribbean influence that reflects this island's heritage and the kitchen's skill. Prices are in the $15 to $20 and up range for dinner entrees, $6 to $10 for lunch. Louie rolls out the backyard from 11:30am to 3pm daily for lunch, 7 to 11pm daily for dinner.

## Budget Spots

**La Crêperie,** 124 Duval St. (tel. 294-7677), is the spot for light lunches or late snacks of quiche, wonderful crêpes, escargots, onion soup, and salads. If you're really starving they can provide steaks, seafood brochet, grouper filet, or bouillabaisse for prices ranging from $10 to $15. You can dine inside or al fresco on the patio from 11am to 2:30pm and 6:30 to 10pm daily.

Longtime favorite in the city is the **A & B Lobster House,** 700 Front St. (tel. 294-2536). Atmosphere there isn't—just wood floors, a second-story view over the docks, and basic nautical decor. But great seafood there is: brimming seafood platters plucked right out of the sea and plunked onto your plate with a little talented cookery in between. There are landlubber selections as well, plus a raw bar. A & B has been at this game for decades so it's safe to assume they're doing something right. This is a jeans and T-shirt place, open from 11am to 9pm (10am to 10pm in the raw bar) daily, except Sunday and the month of September. Dinner prices average about $10 to $15, some entrées higher.

**El Cacique,** 125 Duval St. (tel. 294-4000), is an insignificant little storefront place that turns out some of the best black-bean soup and media noche sandwiches, batidas, and Cuban coffee this side of Miami for ridiculously low prices. You can gorge here on all kinds of Cuban treats for $5 or less. El Cacique is open from 8am, closing at 10pm every day.

**Captain Bob's,** 908 Caroline St. (tel. 294-9005), is much loved by honeybun fans. Those sweet pastries are the house specialties, but so is seafood straight from the sea. Prices are in the $10 to $15 range for dinner and hours are 7am to 10pm daily.

**READERS' RECOMMENDATIONS:** "In Key West we found that **Café Exile,** 700 Duval St. at Angela Street (tel. 296-0991), became a favorite place for breakfast or lunch. Seating is outside on a shady patio, so you can eat in comfort and still take in the sights—including two huge multicolored parrots that perch on a stand just outside the patio's perimeter. Food was plentiful and good, [dinner prices $10 to $15], and the trolley stop is just across the street. We've enjoyed your books. They add a special dimension to vacations that's like having a friend who's a native and can tell you all the good spots" (Joan and David Scire, West Haven, Conn.). [*Authors' Note:* Our thanks to the Scires for several good suggestions—and for their praise. Hours are 8am to 3pm daily.]. . . "We discovered a wonderful Spanish restaurant [where] the owner talked with us at length about Spain. It was **El Meson de Pepe Spanish-American Restaurant,** 1215 Duval St. (tel. 296-6922), and the owner is José M. Diaz. We ordered Cuban food . . . complete dinners [with] generous portions of roast pork with side dishes of beans, rice, potatoes, salad or yucca . . . our bill for four was $24! All the meals were outstanding and we wanted to pass the name of the restaurant on so others will also find it . . . a delightful little taste of Spain in Key West (Margie Renazco, Houston, Tex). [*Authors' Note:* Hours are 11am to 10pm at El Meson.]

## SEEING THE SIGHTS

There's lots to see and do in Key West, from island tours to Hemingway haunts.

### Touring the Island

The quickest way to see all of Key West and get your bearings at the same time is to hop aboard the **Conch Tour Train** (tel. 294-5228), which takes you on a 1½-hour narrated tour of the island and tells you some of the greatest anecdotes you'll hear anywhere. You'll even learn the four *natural* ways Key Westers air-conditioned their houses (and we think we've progressed!) and get a good look at the cisterns that were so vital to survival until the water pipe was laid from the mainland and desalinization techniques discovered. More than 60 of this enchanting island's beautiful old conch homes and historical sites are pointed out on this don't-miss tour, which tells you in a nutshell the weird and wonderful history of Key West. Tours leave daily from 9am to 4pm from depots at 501 Front St., Mallory Square, and 3850 N. Roosevelt Blvd. Fare is $10 for adults, $4 for children 4 to 12. Just show up and hop aboard.

You ride comfortably, if not quite as adventurously, aboard **Old Town Trolley Tours,** 1910 N. Roosevelt Blvd. at Mallory Square (tel. 296-6688). You can board a trolley at Mallory Square (free parking provided) or at most major motels in Key West, disembark anywhere you like to shop or look around, then get back on later. Trolleys leave Mallory Square every 30 minutes and give you quite a complete tour of the island with detailed accounts of its wrecking, rollicking history. Tickets are $11 for adults, $5 for children 5 to 12.

*Miss Key West,* at the foot of Duval Street (tel. 296-8865), shows you a sunken Spanish galleon and other sunken craft, a naval base, and 45 other sights. There's also a sunset cruise with island music. The fare is $8 for adults, free for children under 13. Sailing schedules vary from season to season.

### Special Events

Key West has become very event-conscious in recent years, partly because there are so many free spirits around ready and willing to throw themselves into any excuse for a party and partly because these conchs are canny enough to know the value of an "Event" in luring visitors.

So you will now find the city celebrating **Hemingway Days,** a week or so of craziness culminating on Papa's birthday, July 21. Events include arm wrestling, beer chugging, a billfish tournament, and short-story competitions, all events in which the master himself is said to have excelled. Most fun of all is a Hemingway look-alike contest.

From mid-January to March the city celebrates **Old Island Days,** a celebration designed to honor the conchs' cantankerous forefathers, many of whom were Loyalists, remaining perversely loyal to the King of England when the other American colonists were throwing a tea party. Most interesting of the events that occur during these days are the conchshell-blowing contest and tours of old island homes, most of them private dwellings opened to visitors only for these tours. Other diversions: a wrecker's auction.

**Fantasy Fest** turns the city into a weird and wild place each October—and significantly enhances what would otherwise be a pretty slim tourist month. Fantasy Fest occurs on the weekend closest to Halloween and comes complete with concerts, street dancing, arts-and-crafts exhibitions, and lots of other exhibitions without inhibitions, including some of the weirdest costumes this side of Fire Island. All we can tell you about this event is that our hairdresser sprayed glow-in-the-dark paint on his hair and perhaps sundry other parts for a recent appearance—and his was among the more conservative costumes. Definitely a PG rating if not an X.

## The Sights

The best-known treasure seeker in Florida, maybe the world, is a fellow named Mel Fisher who successfully sought and found a number of sunken Spanish galleons including the famed *Nuestra Señora de Atocha* and the *Santa Margarita,* both of which went aground on reefs about 40 miles offshore in 1622. To get a look at the treasures he's dug up from the briny deep—$60 million worth, they say—hie on over to Mel Fisher's **Treasure Exhibit,** 200 Greene St. (tel. 294-2633). You'll get a closeup look at gorgeous gold and silver jewelry, some precious stones, and lots of coins and artifacts from those galleons. Admission of $5 for adults and $1 for children 6 to 12 includes a look at a National Geographic film on the business of treasure-seeking. Hours are 10am to 5pm daily. Skilled divers can now dive at the Atocha site. Information on how to arrange such an expedition is available at the museum.

Key West's, in fact South Florida's, oldest house is now a museum. Called the **Wrecker's Museum,** this 1829 structure is at 322 Duval St. (tel. 294-9502) and was the home of wrecker Capt. Francis B. Watlinton. Here you can learn all about the wrecking game—including the rules! Admission is $2 for adults and 50¢ for children under 12; the house is open daily from 10am to 4pm.

**Audubon House,** 205 Whitehead St., at Greene (tel. 294-2116), is named after the famous naturalist and artist who visited here in 1852. It's one of the island's historic houses, restored and open to the public from 9:30am to 5pm daily at $5 for adults, $1 for children 6 to 12. Audubon's original life-size etchings of birds and the period furnishings make Key West's past come alive.

**The Ernest Hemingway Home and Museum,** 907 Whitehead St. (tel. 294-1575), is home to more cats than people, just as it was when Hemingway lived here. A Spanish colonial house of 1851 vintage, it was the author's residence from 1931 to 1961, some of his most productive years. Descendants of his six-toed cats still ramble gracefully about, and there's even a special fountain for them created by the author from a Spanish olive jar and plumbing fixtures he lifted from Sloppy Joe's Bar. A pool in the courtyard has a penny imbedded in it—Hemingway said it took his last penny to install the pool! Admission is $5 for adults, $1 for children 5 to 12, and the house is open daily from 9am to 5pm.

**East Martello Art Gallery and Museum** was once part of the fortifications of Key West, and today has displays of the city's successful cigar-making, sponging, and railroad industries. Admission is $3, $1 for children 7 to 15. It's open 9:30am to 5pm. A short distance away, the **West Martello Tower** is now occupied by the Key West Garden Club, which has a lovely display of tropical plants in a garden that's open daily. It's free and both are located on South Roosevelt Boulevard (tel. 296-3913).

At the **Turtle Kraals,** 2 Lands End Village (tel. 294-2640), there's a holding pen full of turtles, sharks, rays, and tropical fish. The Kraals are open from noon to 6pm, and there's no admission charge.

A historic lighthouse—98 steps up—has been made into the **Lighthouse Museum,** 938 Whitehead St. (tel. 294-0012), where you can see battleship *Maine* and lighthouse artifacts. Hours are 9:30am to 5pm. Admission is $3 for adults, $1 for children 7 to 12.

## NIGHTLIFE

Going to Key West without hitting a few of this city's famous, and perhaps infamous, bars is like going to Florida to sit in the shade. You can meet all kinds of people at these lively, informal, and highly individualistic spots that open about dawn and may never close, for all we know. Things really heat up about cocktail hour, and are in full, high-decibel stride about 10pm.

The numero uno don't miss, go-even-if-you-hate-bars, superstar spot is **Sloppy Joe's,** 201 Duval St. It is, of course, true that Hemingway took to Sloppy Joe like a fish to a hook, and it is said that Papa and Sloppy Joe retired on frequent occasions to a locked back room armed with a case of whisky, which they put to good use while Joe told his wildest and woolliest sea stories. Hemingway absorbed those tales, so the story goes, and from them created some of the literary masterpieces he produced while living here. It's even said he did some of his writing in the bar, his manuscript held securely by a beer mug (now that's the way to write a book!). On the wall is a sailfish he's supposed to have caught, and parachute silks adorn the ceiling. It has, shall we say, character—and characters.

Hemingway adored the rustic watering spots of Key West, so it's easy to believe that **Capt. Tony's Saloon,** 428 Greene St., is the *real* Sloppy Joe's. That's what they say (whoever "they" are), and it certainly looks plenty like a Sloppy Joe's. There's a fascinating casual-going-on-seedy air about the place that's well nigh irresistible, and besides, everyone in town roams through here at least once an evening. So if you stay put, you'll see most of Key West. Captain Tony himself is a colorful character who's been around Key West a long time, and for what it's worth his bar was *Esquire*-rated as one of the top 10 in the country.

More whoop-de-doo at **The Copa,** at 623 Duval St. (tel. 296-8521) and **Follies** at 218 Duval St. (tel. 294-4383).

**Café Exile,** 700 Duval St. (tel. 296-0991), closes for just three hours every day. All the rest of the time there's food or drink or entertainment—or all three—at this jumpin' spot in the middle of downtown Key West. Open daily, the restaurant and lounge keeps 'em stompin' in the inside disco, while mellower jazz sounds fill the night air outside the Exile, which is open from 8am to 5am daily. There's no cover charge.

There is entertainment of somewhat more subdued nature at **Pier House** and **Marriott's Casa Marina.** (See the accommodations listings for details.)

**Turtle Kraals,** 2 Lands End Village, at the foot of Margaret St. (tel. 294-2640), is now a cross between an attraction and a lounge/restaurant! There is no admission fee to see the turtle cannery museum and holding tanks full of live sea turtles, sharks, and tropical fish. While you're here, try grouper chowder in the Turtle Kraals Restaurant and sample one of 32 imported beers, a thick piña colada, or a fancy, flavored coffee. Food and drink prices are under $5 and the place is open from noon to 1am with entertainment.

Finally, for nighttime activity of a more subdued nature, the **Tennessee Williams Fine Arts Center,** Florida Key Community College in Key West (tel. 294-6232), presents musicals, plays, and dance performances throughout the year.

Jan McArt, who first acquired Florida fame when she opened a Boca Raton theater, now operates here as **Jan McArt's Cabaret Theatre** at Mallory Square (tel. 296-2120, or toll free 800/346-3240). Called cabaret in salute to the tables-for-four seating arrangements, the theater features musicals with performances at 8pm nightly except Monday. Prices are $18 to $20.

## SPORTS

With all that water around, most sports naturally involve the ocean—so you won't find the hordes of tennis courts and golf courses here that you find elsewhere in the state. (Besides, there's no place to put them on these small islands.)

### Golfing

**Key West Club,** on Stock Island (tel. 294-5232), has an 18-hole, par-72 course open daily. Greens fees are $30 to $32 including cart.

### Diving and Sailing

If you want to see what lives down under the waves, try **Reef Raiders Dive Shop,** on US 1 at Mile Marker 4.5 on Stock Island (tel. 294-0660), which takes groups on diving trips and can set you snorkeling or teach you how to use deep-water diving equipment.

### Fishing-Exploring

*Yankee Captain* and *Yankee Freedom,* 31 Boundary Lane (tel. 294-7009, or toll free 800/634-0939), two 100-foot aluminum craft, are docked at Lands End Marina on Carolina Street, and sail to the Dry Tortugas at varying times on two-night exploration adventure trips and on one-night fishing trips, from December to May for $150 or $90, respectively.

To find plenty of charter boats, go to **Garrison Bight Marina,** about halfway up the north shore on US 1 at 711 Eisenhower Dr. (tel. 294-3093), where you'll find the city's charter-boat docks. Bay and deep-sea boats are for hire with or without a guide. Drop by about 4pm even if you're not going fishing and pick up some fresh fish for dinner. Charter rates are about $350 to $500 a day.

## TO SEA TO SEE A WEIRD NATIONAL MONUMENT

The nation's most inaccessible national monument is **Fort Jefferson,** but it's one that's exciting to visit by boat or plane. You can get there for $99 a half day, $175 a full day, per person round trip aboard **Key West Seaplane,** which flies from Murray's Marina, 5603 Junior College Rd. on Stock Island (tel. 294-6978), twice a day.

On Dry Tortugas (named by Ponce de León for the hundreds of sea turtles he saw sunning there; dry because it has no water) is a massive circular fortress, the largest 19th-century coastal fort built in the United States, with walls 50 feet high and 8 feet thick. Work on this massive crumbling structure took 30 years to complete and cost $3.5 million. Although the fort had 140 guns ready and waiting, it never saw a day of battle. Its most noteworthy moment came when it held Dr. Samuel Mudd, who was imprisoned here after he set the broken leg of Abraham Lincoln's assassin, John Wilkes Booth, giving rise to the your-name-is-mud expression. Mudd spent two years on this desolate island before he was pardoned for his help in a yellow fever epidemic. It's a lovely flight over and you'll pass several sunken ships. Once you get there, a ranger with a very lonely job will be happy to show you around.

## SHOPPING

Mallory Square is an enclave of smart shops, and at **Key West Handprint Fabrics,** you'll find wildly colorful prints used by dress designer Lilly Pulitzer, who created a "look" with them. There's a retail shop with clothing for both men and women.

**Key West Fragrances,** 524 Front St. (tel. 294-5592), has unusual scents like white ginger and frangipani that make intriguing gifts.

In Pirates Alley, across from Mallory Square, is a little brick courtyard where you can see cigars being rolled by hand, the last example here of that once-vital industry.

Key West's department store has a quite unforgettable name: **Fast Buck Freddie's** (tel. 294-2007). It's at 500 Duval St. Next door is singer Jimmy Buffett's store.

At the southernmost point of the island (you can't miss it) and at several other places around the island, boys dive for **conch** and sell the shells for $2 to $5, sometimes more for the very biggest ones. You can even find one yourself out there in the sea. Just poke an unsuspecting toe around in the sand.

# VI

# THE GOLD COAST

## 1. PALM BEACH AND BOCA RATON
## 2. FORT LAUDERDALE

Florida's Gold Coast is proof that alchemy exists. Sixty years ago much of what is now glowing beaches, glittering hotels, and condominiums was palmetto scrub and swampland. More mosquitoes lived here than people, and only a barefoot mailman strode the sands between Miami and Palm Beach.

Long, long ago, the Abaniki tribe lived here beside the sea. Then came pirates, who lay in wait to scuttle gold-laden Spanish galleons heading home from Central America. What few shoreside pioneers there were in those days picked up some nasty pirate habits and were soon participating in a career known as "wrecking." Adventurers who lived along these sand-trimmed shores didn't shrink at creating their own wrecks, although they rarely had to, since nature usually did it for them. Storms and inadequate navigational aids sent so many ships onto the rocks here that shoreside dwellers held regular meetings to pray for *specific* booty. Divinity answered in considerable style: A great party went on for days in Boca Raton one year in the wake of a wrecked Spanish ship carrying hundreds of barrels of sherry. So well rewarded were wreckers for their unusual trade that by the late 1800s they were complaining about the quality of the products washed ashore and accusing shipowners of scuttling worthless cargoes to turn a profit on insurance money.

Gall like that has long been the byword of this coastline where some flamboyant characters have made miracles and millions turning these sands into a tropical paradise. Perhaps the liveliest of them all was architect Addison Mizner, who came here to die but gave up that dismal project in favor of making himself a millionaire and this bit of Florida the stuff of every northern dream.

As usual, the first empire builder to trek southward was Florida's godfather, Henry Flagler, who brought his railroad tracks to Palm Beach. Mizner rode those tracks for a swim in Florida sunshine, but when he saw these beaches what swam before his eyes were dollar signs.

He started with Palm Beach, whose architecture he considered so unimaginative he is said to have remarked that if he could change the city, he'd build something that wasn't made of wood and paint it some color besides yellow. He shortly began to do just that, building first the Everglades Club, an imposing oceanfront stucco edifice that's about the first thing you'll see as you drive northward along the Gold Coast to Palm Beach. With that and subsequent creations, Mizner founded an architectural vogue sometimes known as "Bastard–Spanish–Moorish–Romanesque–Gothic–Renaissance–Bull-Market–Damn-the-Expense" style.

His ultimate sights were set, however, on a nearby strip of sand called Boca Raton. Before long Boca Raton had its first and still most impressive hotel, the

Cloister Inn, a $1.25-million creation said to be the most expensive 100-room hotel ever built. Mizner's grand design for an unsurpassed resort (lined with waterways plied by gondolas) centered on the Cloister Inn, but in the land around it was the fortune he sought.

To help sell that land he lured such famous names as Harold Vanderbilt, Marie Dressler, and Irving Berlin to the hotel in a characteristically shrewd bid for attention: "Get the big snobs," Mizner is supposed to have said, "and the little ones will follow." To give that surge of sun-seekers a little impetus, he introduced an advertising campaign that epitomized the style of 1920s Gold Coast land boom: "I Am the Greatest Resort in the World," the ads proclaimed, adding gently in smaller print below, "a few years hence." It worked. Sales at Mizner's development company, which also owned a mile of nearby Boynton Beach, averaged $2 million—a week!

Meanwhile, up in Palm Beach, Flagler had already created his Breakers Hotel, a massive wooden edifice that was winter home to an awesome list of monied guests including the Wideners, Wanamakers, and Stotesburys. Nearby, Paris Singer of sewing machine fame was hard at work creating the Addison-designed Singer Island, a resort bent on making "Palm Beach look like a slum."

Little by little the boom spread southward as canny characters up and down the Gold Coast set out to try a little alchemy of their own, turning land into gold. Nothing fazed these slicksters, who didn't blanch at salting beaches with "pirate gold" to stir the pot of already-frenzied buyers. So down and dirty did sales pitches get that at the summit of the plummet Boca Raton was known as Beaucoup Rotten!

Meanwhile, down in Fort Lauderdale, general store and ferryboat owner Frank Stranahan was taking in land-buying boarders, and on the streets of Miami binder boys were getting names on the dotted lines of land-sales contracts faster than you can say "Boom".

The national economic depression broke the Gold Coast bubble but Mizner went down in characteristic style. When he was sued by a man who claimed he'd been sold his barren plot with false promises, Mizner was asked in court if he really had promised the man he would grow nuts on the land. "Oh, no," Mizner replied, "I said he could *go* nuts on the land."

Some may have gone nuts, and certainly many went broke, but as the years passed the Gold Coast recovered. In succeeding decades a somewhat less spectacular spiral began, including the purchase of Mizner's Cloister Inn by Arthur Vining Davis for $22.5 million, the largest real estate swap in Florida history—and $17 million more than the United States had paid to buy the entire state!

From that boom spiral emerged a golden coastline that has worked its way through gold plate, 18-karat gold, solid gold—and fool's gold—to emerge as a beach-lover's vacation paradise, where gold comes not from nuggets but from nature.

## GETTING THERE

**Fort Lauderdale/Hollywood International Airport** has the most service to the area, but you can also fly into Palm Beach International. Fort Lauderdale's airport, which has recently tripled in size, is about 15 minutes from beach hotels. Airlines flying to these cities include American, Chalk's, Continental, Delta, Eastern, Midway, Nordair, Northwest, Pan Am, TWA, United, WardAir, and USAir.

You can get to **Palm Beach International Airport** on Delta, Pan Am, United, USAir, and TWA.

**Amtrak** stops twice a day at Fort Lauderdale, arriving at the station near Broward Boulevard at 200 SW 21st Terrace (tel. 463-8251), just west of the downtown area. **Greyhound/Trailways** buses connect the city to the state and nation, and have downtown terminals at 515 NE 3rd St. (tel. 764-6551).

You can also get to Palm Beach by train, arriving at the Amtrak station, 201 S. Tamarind Ave. (tel. 832-6169). Greyhound/Trailways has service to the city. The terminal is at 100 1st St. (tel. 833-0825).

## GETTING AROUND

Every national **car-rental company** operates in the two cities. Alamo leads the low-price competitors, but Avis, Hertz, National, Budget, Dollar, General, and Econo-Car are among many others competing hard for customers.

From Fort Lauderdale International Airport, **Airport Express,** 599 N. Federal Hwy. (tel. 527-8690), will take you to beach hotels in Fort Lauderdale and environs for $6 to $8. If you're going farther up the line to Pompano or Boca Raton, the fare rises to $10 to $13. **Super Shuttle** (tel. 764-1700) will take you to Miami International Airport from Fort Lauderdale hotels for $18.

Broward County, in which Fort Lauderdale is located, has a new fleet of sleek orange-striped white **buses** that zip around the county from dawn to about 9pm daily for 75¢. Friendly folks at the **Broward County Transit Division** (tel. 357-8400) can help you with route information and sell you a discounted weekly pass. There's also a bus called the **Dune Buggy,** which for the same price travels from near the county line on the south of Hallandale through Fort Lauderdale and Hollywood to Pompano. During racing seasons and in winter and spring there are usually special racetrack buses that stop at major beachfront hotels and can be flagged down at any corner along Fla. A1A from Pompano to US 1 in Fort Lauderdale. Tickets are $3 to $5 round trip.

In Palm Beach, the **Palm Beach County Transit system** (Cotran) has service throughout the county, but is not the best way to sightsee since buses are not allowed on the city's main shopping street, Worth Avenue, or on Fla. A1A, where just about everything else you'll want to see is located. You can call them for route information at 686-4555.

**Taxis** are, as always, a somewhat expensive way to get around, more so in Fort Lauderdale, where things are a bit more spread out than they are on the compact island of Palm Beach. In Broward County, taxi fares are $2.20 for the first mile, $1.50 for each additional mile. Try **Yellow Cab** (tel. 565-5400) or **Broward Checker** (tel. 485-3000).

In Palm Beach, taxis cost $1.25 for the first mile and $1.50 for each additional mile; **Yellow Cab** operates there (tel. 689-2222).

## A LOOK AT GOLD COAST CITIES

If you're driving, it's interesting to ride north from Miami Beach following Fla. A1A (or south from any of the northern Gold Coast cities), which runs between the ocean and the Intracoastal Waterway most of the way. To give you an idea of what you'll see, here's a look at the Gold Coast, starting at the Dade County border (Golden Beach) and heading north.

First city north of Dade County is **Hallandale,** a strip of sand crowned by dozens of condominiums built along the beaches. If you were here 15 years ago, you'll think you're lost now: Many of these towering apartment complexes have risen in the past 10 to 15 years. Flagship of Hallandale is the Diplomat Hotel, and the city is also home to showy Gulfstream Park Race Track.

Hallandale blends right into **Hollywood,** where you'll see a few clusters of very small resorts. A boardwalk along the sand is lined with bars, hot-dog stands, and usually lots of young people out for a day at the beach. If you're a greyhound-racing fan, Hollywood has a dog track open much of the year. Hollywood's a favorite destination for Québec visitors.

Tucked between Hollywood and Fort Lauderdale is the tiny town of **Dania,** once home to many tomato farmers. Today most of the action here is at the Dania Jai-Alai Fronton or huge John Lloyd State Park, where you'll find a lovely wooded strip of beach and plenty of places to picnic on sand less crowded than beaches in neighboring communities. A new beachside complex called Seafare is an interesting array of shops and restaurants.

In Dania, Fla. A1A turns westward to join US 1, but you can get back on the beach highway again at SW 17th Street in **Fort Lauderdale,** where you cross the Intracoastal Waterway and pass the city's cruise-ship port, Port Everglades. A mile farther north you'll see the city's magnificent beach stretched out in front of you. You can drive right beside it for much of the next three miles to small **Lauderdale-by-the-Sea,** and into **Pompano,** where the beach is hidden behind a few resorts and many condominiums. Ocean waters sneak back into view at the city's big fishing pier just north of Atlantic Boulevard.

Next comes **Hillsboro Beach,** one of the most beautiful drives in the area. Here Fla. A1A scoots between the Intracoastal Waterway and some massive estates built right on the sand. **Hillsboro Inlet** is home to a fishing fleet, and you can always count on finding a fishing trip there, or some fresh fish from someone who's just been lucky at sea.

Continuing northward, you cross the small community of **Deerfield Beach,** where a few small resorts are clustered around the highway, and finally you'll see **Boca Raton,** where the Boca Raton Hotel and Club occupies most of the city's south side.

**Delray Beach** is home to the horsey set these days, and there's a large breeding farm west of town. Here and in Boca Raton the beach becomes visible again. It's just a few feet from the right side of your car as you drive north along a ridge that runs high above the edge of the sand, so there are some smashing views of turquoise waters that darken as the water deepens. That very dark blue is the Gulf Stream. If you're a diver, you'll find good diving territory off the coast of Boca Raton and Delray. Delray is home to several excellent restaurants and has a sleepy old-town air with many Spanish-style homes lining the streets.

Don't miss the village of **Gulfstream,** which is so tiny you may almost miss it—but many *Fortune* 500 types didn't: It's one of the wealthiest villages on the Gold Coast (and the quietest about its net worth).

Farther north on this sand-and-sea boulevard you'll pass **Briny Breezes** (isn't that poetic?), then **Boynton Beach,** which has a very attractive beach high on a dune —it will cost you $10 to sit on it (one of the very few Gold Coast beaches that isn't free).

Drive through **Ocean Ridge, Manalapan, Lake Worth,** and finally you're in **Palm Beach,** where Fla. A1A takes you right past Mar al Lago, Marjorie Merriweather Post's pink palace, and straight through Palm Beach past the Breakers, to a point about three miles from the tip of the island, where you cross the Flagler Bridge to return to US 1 for a few miles. You can pick up Fla. A1A again at **Singer Island** (you'll see a sign pointing the way) and follow it north to about **Jupiter,** where it again joins US 1.

## 1. Palm Beach and Boca Raton

*Town and Country* magazine, and news magazine of the very rich, once assessed Florida's Gold Coast by karat. Towns like Fort Lauderdale and Manalapan, John's Island in Vero Beach, and Boca Raton were accorded 18 to 19 karats; Delray Beach, Coral Gables, Coconut Grove, and the village of Gulfstream near Palm Beach, 20 to 23 karats. Palm Beach? Why, you should know without asking. Solid gold, of course.

That's Palm Beach, bastion of those who have no need of upward mobility since there's nowhere higher up. Winter playground of the Rolls-Royce-raffle set, Palm Beach is a place where "divine" has nothing to do with divinity and shopkeepers pay more for a tiny square of Worth Avenue storefront than the average American makes in three years.

Henry Flagler was the man who started all this, and today the wide straight boulevards he created are lined with towering royal palms and gardens perfect to the last petal. Should a blade of grass be out of place, it will, we assure you, be controlled.

Control, after all, is what created Palm Beach—and those who escape here. It's also what put on the books laws (*laws*, mind you) prohibiting car washes and jogging without a shirt.

Names on guest lists here read like a Guinness Book of Zillionaires—or Ripley's Believe It or Not! Widener, Wanamaker, Vanderbilt, Stotesbury, Dodge, Sanford, Kennedy, Post, Arthur Vining Davis.

If all this sounds a bit intimidating, fear not, for the rich are just like you and us except they drive Rolls-Royces down Worth Avenue and spend the winter in Palm Beach. But even the vanguard of this old guard has loosened up some with the arrival of "new" money and contemporary lifestyles. We won't include Palm Beach's most famous recent visitors, Prince Charles and Diana in those ranks, but a New York developer recently bought a $10-million piece of property here and an heir to some or other empire bought a home for a price closing rapidly in on $3 million.

In Palm Beach you can move among the royal and the regal, strut your stuff in Gucci and Courrèges, prowl the corridors of the Breakers, and hob with nobs whose average income is precisely twice that of the rest of the nation. It's fun as well as fantasy to roam through streets kept spotless by an army of sanitation workers, past homes so huge an army could perhaps be lost in them, and into stores offering the world's most tempting treasures and highest prices.

To drive through this lovely old town is an adventure all its own, and finding a parking space is even more of an adventure. Surrounding towns are quiet, genteel, antique-lovely, where determined residents have successfully warded off the more plastic aspects of modern life.

Boca Raton, whose euphonious name translates somewhat less pleasantly to Rat Bay (a reference, it is said, to sharp rocks at the bay entrance), is lady-in-waiting to Palm Beach. It would have been queen had it not suffered a setback after the scandals of the property boom (during which it was known as Beaucoup Rotten) and burst with the bubble of the nation's economy in the 1920s. It recovered with alacrity and style, however, and is now said to be the wealthiest community in the nation. Small neighbor Delray Beach was once the toast of the town too, but now is Melba toast, still in the running but not quite the real thing.

North of Palm Beach, the communities of Stuart, Hobe Sound, Jupiter, Juno and Hutchinson Island are about equally divided between upper crust and below the salt.

It's fun discovering it all, and while you're at it, you'll see some of Florida's (perhaps the nation's) most beautiful communities and shops. Could you ask for more?

## USEFUL INFORMATION

For **Police or medical emergencies,** call 911 . . . If you need a **dentist,** the county's dental association can help; call 775-0268 . . . For **non-emergency medical help,** call the county medical society at 433-3940 . . . There's a **24-hour drugstore,** Eckerd's, at 3343 N. Congress (tel. 965-3367) . . . If you bring your dry cleaning in by 9am, **Coconut Palm Cleaners,** 159 Chilean Ave. (tel. 659-7080), can have it back by 4pm that day . . . For a **24-hour restaurant,** try Clock, at 1420 Broadway in Riviera Beach (tel. 965-4400) . . . area code is 407.

## TOURIST INFORMATION

You can find brochures and information about what to see and do in the city at the **Palm Beach Chamber of Commerce,** 45 Coconut Row, Palm Beach, FL 33480 (tel. 407/655-3282). The **Chamber of Commerce of the Palm Beaches** is at 401

N. Flagler Dr., West Palm Beach, FL 33401 (tel. 407/833-3711) and promotes West Palm Beach. The **Palm Beach County Convention and Visitors Bureau,** 1555 Palm Beach Lakes Blvd., West Palm Beach, FL 33401 (tel. 407/471-3995), can send you a helpful *Palm Beach County Attractions Guide* detailing beaches and parks along the county's 47 miles of shoreline, water sports, golf, tennis, polo, greyhound racing, horseback riding, skating, shooting, biking, baseball spring training, zoos, shopping spots, and cultural facilities.

## ORIENTATION

Fla. A1A wends through the city skirting along the ocean most of the time, and is called North or South County Boulevard as it goes through town. At the north end of town it turns west to join US 1 for a short distance; you can return to it again at Singer Island.

Three bridges link the island of Palm Beach with the mainland of West Palm Beach (when Palm Beachites cross the bridges, they say they're going "to Florida"). On the south end of the island, the Southern Boulevard bridge crosses Lake Worth and goes past the city's international airport. A few miles farther north, the Royal Palm Way crosses the water to become Okeechobee Boulevard. Still farther north, your last chance to cross the lake is at Flagler Memorial Bridge on Royal Poinciana Way, which goes to West Palm Beach crossing Olive Street and South Dixie Highway, which is US 1.

## HOTELS

In posh Palm Beach your quarters are superstar or they are co-star, but they are not road show. Strictly prime time, this upper-crust resort accords high status to only one hotel, although it will occasionally unbend enough to accept two or three other jet-set stops. Those of us who have not yet acquired keys to a Lear must stick to the fringes or sneak off to some very nice and moderately priced resorts nearby (just tell everyone you're staying with friends—and you will be).

We've grouped hotels by location, including Singer Island, downtown, a beach strip just south of the city, and West Palm Beach, then tossed in a posh cluster of hotels in Boca Raton, and some moderately priced selections in Delray Beach for good measure.

### Downtown

Queen of the island, world-famous superstar, glamour girl, and landmark of Palm Beach is **The Breakers.** 1 S. County Road, Palm Beach, FL 33480 (tel. 407/655-6611, or toll free 800/833-3141), a place so fabulously beautiful and carefully crafted that even the doorlocks are tiny brass lion's heads. Only Don Rickles could find fault with the Breakers, which you ought to visit even if you don't stay here. It's quite a place—make that palace—a throwback to days when nearly everything was palatial and perfect. It is a wonder indeed, this barrel tile-roofed seaside behemoth. A walk through the Breakers is like strolling through a miniature Versailles. Every one of its public rooms is a glorious anachronistic study in huge glittering crystal chandeliers, tapestries, magnificent ceiling paintings, gilt, massive fireplaces, frescoes, and furbelows. Originally built by railroad magnate Henry Flagler, the Breakers was in those days a vast wooden structure that became winter home to such high-livers as the Rockefellers, John Jacob Astor, J.P. Morgan, William Randolph Hearst, Andrew Carnegie, the Duchess of Marlborough, and Pres. Warren Harding. Guests in those days arrived in private railroad cars with servants, and stayed the winter, of course. Their snowbird sojourn culminated in a grand finale, Washington's Birthday Ball: While guests danced, luggage was transported to railroad cars, and after the last waltz they departed, still in their finery, to whiz off homeward by track. Twice razed by fire, the hotel's present glamour was created in 1925 by Flagler's heirs, who fashioned the Breakers after the most outstanding villas of Italy. Some 75 artisans from Europe created the magnificent ceiling paintings. One year and $6 million later, the huge hotel was again open for business.

Today you'll see belvedere towers and arches inspired by Rome's Villa Medici and a Florentine fountain at the entrance just like one in Florence's Boboli Gardens. A secluded central courtyard is bordered by loggias streaking east to the ocean. There's a Mediterranean Ballroom inspired by the Palazzo degli Imperiale at Genoa, a ceiling in the Gold Room copied from Venice's Doges' Palace with portraits of those who participated in the discovery of the New World. In the Florentine Dining Room the beamed ceiling is painted much like the ceiling of Florence's Palazzo Davanzati, and in the Circle Dining Room scenes of Italian cities are lighted by a huge Venetian chandelier of bronze, mirrors, and crystals hanging from a circular skylight. In both, chefs do justice to the surroundings with outstanding cuisine ($20 to $40 for dinner). Mirrors everywhere reflect solid marble floors and more gold than a spanish galleon could boast.

In recent years the hotel completed an $11 million renovation, added a beach club with an Olympic-size outdoor pool. A palm-lined Ocean Golf Course is now supplemented by Breakers West, which has another course and tennis courts. There's a masseuse and masseur, biking, shuffleboard, snorkeling and scuba, croquet (!), a private (naturally) beach, dancing and entertainment in ornate and plushly comfortable lounges.

If you stay here, you'll find big, big rooms (567 of them), many with private balconies overlooking the sea and all with deep wall-to-wall carpeting, vivid colors, big closets and baths, and all the comforts and services that have made this palatial hotel one of Florida's premier resorts. In winter, the resort charges $260 to $400 double. In other months, prices range from $125 to $220 without meals. Suites are available at higher rates.

Tall white pillars trim the lemony-yellow exterior of Palm Beach's elegant **Colony Hotel,** 155 Hammon Ave., Palm Beach, FL 33480 (tel. 407/655–5430), a *very* good address in Palm Beach. Swim in the Colony's long swimming pool shaded by swaying palms, then slip under a poolside umbrella and sip something cool. Retire later to beautifully decorated rooms or suites lined with deep carpets and furnished with light wicker furniture accented by sunny yellow or cool green. Just a block away are the fabulous shops of Worth Avenue. For evening entertainment there's dancing and music every night at the Colony, plus dining in the glow of candlelight at one of the city's most popular gathering spots. "Genteel" is the best word for the Colony, which charges $180 to $240 daily in winter, $80 to $140 in summer.

Discretion, understatement, and elegance are as foreign to most hotels as frump is to Palm Beach society. It's a heady world here in the *haute* of *hautes,* but it's a fascinating one that can, if you're alert, teach you the value of such things as discretion, understatement, and elegance. You could find no better place to research those concepts than **Brazilian Court Hotel,** 301 Australian Ave. at Brazilian Avenue, Palm Beach, FL 33480 (tel. 407/655–7740, or toll free 800/351–5656).

Called a hotel because no one could—or can yet—quite find the appropriate term to describe it, this discreetly elegant hideaway is tucked so neatly into Palm Beach that most visitors do not even know it is here. Those who do know, however, are those who are *known.* Among the notables who have placed revered heads on pillows here in the nearly seven decades since this hotel was built in 1925 are Errol Flynn, Cary Grant, Carol Channing, Gary Cooper, Alistair Cooke, Christopher Plummer, and James Michener.

They came here because this small hideaway, just a diamond's toss from Worth Avenue, knows quite well the meaning of discretion, and in recent years management has completed a multimillion-dollar renovation that easily added elegance and understatement to the lexicon.

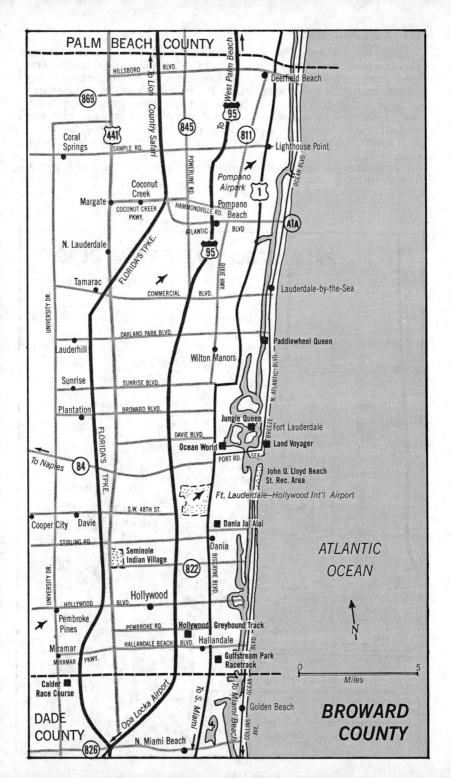

Now you pass through the antique flower-bedecked archway that frames a burbling courtyard fountain and enter a world that is both today and yesterday. All the touches that made 1920s Mediterranean architecture so endearing remain and are now abetted by the comfort and style of modernity. English floral prints in soft lemon yellow and sea blue shades turn hotel rooms into airy charmers that teach you what tropical means—or should mean. Brass lamps, bleached wood floors, silver tea services, ornately twisted columns, feathery palms, glittering crystal chandeliers, fresh flowers, canopied beds, French provincial styles all mesh into a haze of cool, understated comfort.

A cluster of one- and two-story buildings, Brazilian Court has just 134 rooms,

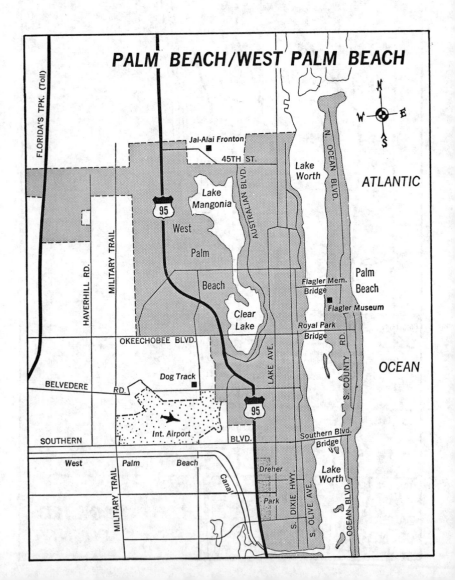

each designed to conjure up a private-villa ambience. Outside, the hotel's pool and two patios are located in such a way as to provide guests with the option of fraternizing with other guests near a picturesque fountain or sneaking off for a private introspective moment. Evenings, the simply named The Dining Room turns on a charm so lethal it has delighted even the most jaded of area restaurant reviewers. Later yet, the action moves to a small lounge where entertainment is provided by musicians who made their fame at Palm Beach's long-loved Ta-Boo restaurant.

Let us just add this comforting parting thought: Do not fear that all this emphasis on discretion and elegance translates to stuffy and boring. Quite the reverse, in fact, since it is well to remember that there could be no discretion without indiscretion, and that, dahlings, is something Palm Beach knows much about—and tells. Here room rates are $210 to $475 in winter, $85 to $185 in summer. Suites sport higher tabs. Children under 12 free.

A jungle of greenery surrounds the glittering swimming pool at **Heart of Palm Beach Motor Hotel,** 160 Royal Palm Way, Palm Beach, FL 33480 (tel. 407/655–5600), a conveniently located, moderately priced 88-room hotel in downtown Palm Beach. Settle into attractive paneled rooms here, with big picture windows or sliding glass doors leading to private balconies overlooking this serene city. Bright colors glow against dark wood, and comfortable chairs are a nice place to relax after a long day at the pool. Heart of Palm Beach has some larger accommodations too, if you'd like more space, and the resort's Bird-in-Hand Pub is a cheery place to seek something tall and cool, or to lunch inside, or on the poolside patio. Double rates here are $65 to $80 in summer, rising to $125 to $145 in peak season. Suites are priced higher.

## South of Downtown on Fla. A1A

There are some lovely resorts just south of the city and less than a 15-minute drive from Worth Avenue. One of them is the **Palm Beach Hawaiian Inn,** 3550 S. Ocean Blvd., Palm Beach, FL 33480 (tel. 407/582–5631), about eight miles south of town on Fla. A1A, where it occupies a lovely uncrowded strip of ocean front sand. The large rooms are nicely decorated in lively colors, and there's a pool and coffee shop, sundeck and beach cabañas, an oceanfront dining room and patio bar. You can bring your pets along here, and choose your accommodations from a list that includes rooms, efficiencies, one-bedroom apartments, and two-bedroom quarters for four. From mid-January to May two people pay $95 to $150, and about $67 to $124 in summer.

Another star in the galaxy of Palm Beach resorts is the **Palm Beach Hilton,** 2842 S. Ocean Blvd., Palm Beach, FL 33480 (tel. 407/586–6542, or toll free 800/HILTONS in Florida, or 800/433–1718 elsewhere). Right on the ocean, about 10 minutes from Worth Avenue, the Hilton has 134 beautifully decorated rooms with lots of special touches. Of course, there are all the other resort amenities like a big swimming pool, a long strip of private sand, a beauty salon, free valet parking, a cocktail lounge where you can watch the surf rolling in, and a lovely dining room with continental cuisine, entertainment, and dancing every night. There are tennis courts to play on, water sports of all kinds, and beautiful balconies where you can look down on people doing all those things. In winter season, from mid-December to May, rates are $175 to $250 double, dropping in the summer months to $95 to $155.

In 1990 Palm Beach welcomed the first new oceanfront hotel to be built in many years, the **Ocean Grand,** 2800 S. Ocean Blvd. (P.O. Box 711), Palm Beach, FL 33480 (tel. 407/582-2800). Here you're greeted at an impressive triple-arched entranceway that plays backdrop to a frothing fountain and waterfall. Glamour continues inside, where handsome tropical furnishings in soft pastels are an introduction to rooms similarly soothing. Spacious, colorful, and comfortable, this new 169-room resort is spread across three buildings. Tucked in among them are a spa and aerobic gym with massage rooms, whirlpools, saunas and steamrooms, tennis courts, and a pool. Out front, or out back, is the Atlantic and a wide strip of beach on which the hotel's windsurfers and Hobie Cat sailboats await. Rooms have two queen-size beds or king-size sleepers and a wide variety of amenities from digital safes to electronic minibars, hair dryers and bathrobes in the marble bathrooms, remote-control televisions and videocassette recorders. Pretty Grand indeed. Rates are $100 to $305 in winter months, dropping to about $125 to $150 in summer.

## On Singer Island

Singer Island is a small key just north of the city where there are several large resorts and some small family operations. One of the larger hotels is the **Howard Johnson,** 3800 N. Ocean Dr., Riviera Beach, FL 33404 (tel. 407/848-5502, or toll-free 800/654-2000), which sprawls along a long section of oceanfront sand on Singer Island. Unusual half-circle balconies offer you an ever-changing view of the ocean, and some of the spacious, brightly decorated rooms open right onto the pool, so it's only a few steps between dreams and reality. Bring your tennis racquet and lob a few over the net at the tennis court, night or day, or invest in a snorkel so you can prowl the deep. Some efficiencies are available, and there are suites if you like lots of space. Double rates, determined by floor and view, in winter are $94 to $174; in summer, $74 to $134.

**Best Western SeaSpray Inn,** 123 Ocean Ave., Palm Beach Shores, FL 33404 (tel. 407/844-0233), is a pretty place where you begin to sink into the tropics the moment you enter the attractive reception area. You know you've arrived as you gaze out over the ocean from your private balcony or sink into the comfort of the SeaSpray's newly redecorated quarters. An unusually shaped motel with lots of jutting angles, the SeaSpray has some rooms that fit into those angles, creating interesting corners and odd nooks. A plant-bedecked rooftop restaurant and cozy lounge with entertainment, plus tropical furniture and vivid colors, get you into the spirit of this southern resort. There's a pool and sundeck too, and just over there, the golden sands and blue, blue ocean. In peak season, two people pay $79 to $109; in summer, $43 to $85—with ocean views determining prices.

You can go after those really big denizens of the deep—sailfish—at the **Sailfish Marina,** 98 Lake Dr., Palm Beach Shores, FL 33404 (tel. 407/844-1724), where there's a fleet of charter fishing boats right at your door. Just sit by the sparkling aquamarine pool and do nothing at all. Or take a short walk to explore the miles and miles of sand. And inside your room are beamed ceilings, wood paneling, simple contemporary furniture, and bright colors. It's a pretty place for anyone, but nirvana for fishing fans. Rates in summer are $50 to $77 double (for an efficiency for four), $80 to $115 in winter.

## West Palm Beach

Flagler built West Palm Beach as a dwelling place for Palm Beach workers, but today it has acquired a personality of its own far removed from the lofty life of Palm Beach. There's no ocean here, but there are some nice resorts convenient to I-95 and one very posh enclave where Prince Charles stayed when he came here for a polo game. When they heard he was coming, the resort spent $80,000 to redecorate his quarters.

One of the most attractive properties in the **Holiday Inn** chain is at 4431 PGA Blvd., Palm Beach, FL 33401 (tel. 407/622-2260, or toll free 800/HOLIDAY), just west of I-95. Set under some tall pines, the resort has won awards for the quality of its 282 spacious, paneled rooms and crisply contemporary decor complete with double or king-size beds and balconies. It could also be cited for its large tiled lobby and handsome candlelit restaurant, its alluring lounge with two-story-tall windows, and its overall efforts to make your stay a pleasant one. If you're a golfer, it's just a few minutes' drive to the PGA championship course. Double rates are $40 to $55 in summer and $100 to $120 in winter.

If you are (or think you'd like to be) a polo groupie, canter on out to **Palm Beach Polo and Country Club,** 13198 Forest Hill Blvd., West Palm Beach, FL 33411 (tel. 407/793-1113, or toll free 800/327-4204, or 800/432-4151 in Florida). You can ride at an equestrian center; play tennis on 24 courts, racquet-ball, croquet, or golf; swim; perhaps even chukker about a bit on these world-famous polo grounds where a frequent player is Charles, Prince of Wales, future king of England. The club's a collection of villages each with its own pool, and each cluster is located next door to the sport it's named after. There's a dining room and lounge too. Villas (or lodges as they call them here) are privately owned, but are available for rental at winter prices beginning at $175 to $465, $85 to $275 in summer. You'll need a car here, absolutely. Weekly rates save you one day's rent.

## Boca Raton

**Boca Raton Resort and Club,** on Camino Real, Boca Raton, FL 33432 (tel. 407/395-3000, or toll free 800/327-0101), is not just a hotel, it's a way of life that proves once and for all what can be done—and had—for money. Flamboyant architect Addison Mizner certainly didn't pinch any pennies back in 1925 when he built this pink palace he called the Cloister for $1.25 million, pouring into it more money than anyone had ever spent on a 100-room hostelry. It was the pivotal point (and still is) of a booming resort city that was humbly to announce in its advertising "I am the greatest resort in the world." It is filled with Mizner's collection of treasures, including so many roof tiles from Spanish churches some feared every worshipper in Spain would be soaked.

You can get a look at the essence of 1920s boomtown Florida at the Boca Raton Resort and Club, and get a pretty good look at boomtown 1980s Boca as well: Marble pillars soar to high, high ceilings, a little statue of Pan pipes merrily away at the entrance gate, water pours from the mouth of a fanciful dolphin into trilevel pools lined with ornate ceramic tiles, candles glow and chandeliers glitter, everything seems touched with gilt, *nothing* has been overlooked—a water fountain here is no basic-gray metal stand but a stream flowing from the mouth of a somewhat perplexed brass lion.

Long hallways wide enough for a marching band are dotted with intimate little groupings of plump couches and comfortable chairs. Massive Spanish tables glow with decades of wax and daily polishing. Brass gleams, crystal glitters, candles flicker, and an ethereal golden glow filters through arched windows. You're transported into a world that doesn't concern itself much with the passage of time, enveloped in an old-world cocoon light-years from the bustle out there in the real, and oh-so-crass, world.

Mizner loved those touches of Old Spain (he's even said to have run up and down stairs in hobnailed boots to "age" them) so you'll see Spain in these beautiful big rooms too. You'll also see all the contemporary comforts from deep chairs to modern tiled baths, big fluffy towels, and all the efficient, friendly service you'd expect at one of the nation's top resorts.

As for dining, an evening in the Cathedral is a little like dining in a ducal palace. Candles shed a delicate golden glimmer over soaring pillars and alabaster arches. Waiters in formal wear hover discreetly, buffets approach gastronomic decadence, and if you're ever looking for an exceedingly romantic spot in which to make a proposal (any proposal), this is it.

That doesn't begin to be all, of course. This dowager duchess of genteel old-world resorts gave birth to a bouncing $20-million baby, the **Boca Beach Club,** which is everything to the late 20th century that the Cloister was to the early years. Built on its own island connected to "mother" by highway and private launch, the seven-story beach club is a study in modern magnificence: Courtyards are scented by the exotic perfumes of tropical blooms and there's a quarter mile of silver sands. Spacious rooms have deep plush carpets and pale-peach decor, high-backed wicker chairs, oak doors, and even Gucci soap and guest packs designed especially for the hotel. You're treated to fluffy terry-cloth robes, stocked mini-bars, *USA Today* at your door each morning, chocolates on your pillow, glass elevators, nighttime shoe-shines, private balconies, skylighted dining rooms filled with greenery. You don't even have to go through all that mundane front desk routine: You're greeted by name at the desk (clue: The doorman phoned up), seated, and treated to an orange juice and champagne cocktail.

At Boca Raton Resort you'll find yet a third hotel, the **Tower,** 27 stories of pink stucco with spacious and dramatic rooms plus an elegant rooftop dining room over-looking Lake Boca Raton. Finally, west of town is yet a fourth in the clan, **Boca Golf & Tennis Club,** a resort haven surrounded by cool clear lakes, seven clay tennis courts, and another championship golf course. As a guest of the Boca Raton Hotel and Club you can use all the facilities—which total two golf courses, 27 tennis courts, every conceivable water sport, four swimming pools, a cabaña club at the beach, health club, bicycles, and jogging track.

At the Boca Raton Resort, rates in high season from January to May are $230 to $360. In other seasons, rates are $95 to $215. Special money-saving packages are available. Suites are priced higher. Dinners at any of the resort's beautiful dining rooms are $25 to $35 or more per person.

## Delray Beach

High on a dune you'll find **Côte d'Azure,** 2325 S. Ocean Blvd., Delray Beach, FL 33444 (tel. 407/278-2646), an attractive small motel with a variety of accom-modations ranging from hotel rooms to two-bedroom oceanfront villas. The Côte d'Azure streaks back in one long wing from Fla. A1A to the beach, and has a pretty pool and thatched Tiki huts for shelter from the sun. Just at the end of the building is the beach, where you can walk or swim for miles along the oceanfront. Small rooms here are decorated in bright colors, and efficiencies have electric kitchens and tile baths. There are TVs and phones in the apartments too. Rates from February through mid-April range from $85 for hotel rooms, oceanfront or poolside (al-though there aren't many oceanfront rooms), to $140 for one-bedroom apartments. In other months, prices drop as low as $40 to $58.

Arches, arches, and more arches set the tone at **Spanish River Resort,** 1111 E. Atlantic Ave., Delray Beach, FL 33444 (tel. 407/276-7441, or toll free 800/543-SWIM), where semicircular balconies are reached through arched glass doors. Across the street from the ocean, Spanish River Inn soars 11 stories and has 72 very spacious apartments decorated in tropical colors with king-size or double beds, plenty of closet space, queen-size sleeper sofas, and balconies in every apartment—three balconies in two-bedroom apartments! On the palm-strewn grounds are two pools, tennis courts, saunas, and a game room on an activities deck. Double rates are $115 for a studio, rising to $260 for a two-bedroom executive suite in peak season, $70 to $165 a day in summer. All the beach is public in Delray, so you have miles of sand just across the street.

## Camping

You can camp inexpensively in **Jonathan Dickinson State Park** (tel. 407/546-2772), and here in Palm Beach, the **Vacation Inn Trav-L-Park,** at 6566 N. Military Trail, West Palm Beach, FL 33407 (tel. 407/848-6166), has an attractive country campground with a well-equipped recreation room, bike trails, snackbar and grocery store, two large pools (one with a slide and a wading pool), lagoon, and barbecue area. Full hookups are $30 to $35 for two people.

## PALM BEACH RESTAURANTS

Naturally Palm Beachites demand the best, and naturally they get it, at some of the state's better restaurants. They pay for it too, at prices that are on the steep side by Floridian standards but moderate if you're just in from Manhattan. By that we mean a few restaurants will probably present you with a bill for two in the $50 to $75 range, but you can also find a number of moderately priced restaurants as well. Here are some of Palm Beach's best, grouped by their specialties, followed by recommendations in surrounding communities.

## Continental/American

Reverse chic is always in in Palm Beach, so it should come as no surprise to any of us that **Chuck & Harold's,** 207 Royal Poinciana Way, Palm Beach (tel. 659-1440), is the rage these days. You can expect to wait for a table here, for the place is almost always packed. A handsome atmosphere of Mexican tiles and beamed ceilings of hand-painted pecky cypress accounts for some of the C & H popularity, but the main attraction is homemade pizza-dough bread sprinkled with poppy seeds. Other favorites are seafood pasta Pagliara and smoked salmon on fettuccine. Mussels, oysters, Bahamian conch chowder, burgers, steaks, and seafood are all on the varied menu here. Entrées average $12 to $20 for dinner. Try the shrimp and artichoke linguine—hearty and cheerfully unpretentious. Hours are 7:30am to midnight daily, later on weekends.

Take an old English pub atmosphere, throw in a little gilt and grandeur, and you've got **Doherty's,** 288 S. County Rd. (tel. 655-6200), an uncomplicated and casual restaurant where the accent's on well-prepared food at prices that are, for Palm Beach, reasonable. Dine on steaks and prime rib, bay scallops, stone crab, Maine lobster, cold crisp salads, or hearty bacon-topped hamburgers rapidly produced in an always-busy setting full of people having a good time. Entrée prices are in the $10 to $18 range. Doherty's is open from 11:30am to 2:30pm for lunch and from 5:30 to 11pm for dinner daily. Sunday brunch is served from 9am until 3pm.

Addison Mizner has won fame far and wide for his architectural creations, while his brother, Wilson, won local reknown as a dashing bon vivant. At last, Wilson is acquiring some contemporary luster, thanks to a new restaurant called Wilson's, in salute to the "other" Mizner brother. **Wilson's,** at 237½ Worth Ave. (tel. 832-7770), occupies a most prestigious address. Indeed it is in a building designed for Wilson by his architect brother. Inside you will see some of the trademarks of Mizner design—a heavy beamed ceiling of pecky cypress, Spanish tile floors, and a stone-framed working fireplace where a fire often blazes. On the menu here are some unusual creations, dishes like a chile lime crêpe with cilantro-tinged sour cream, poached Norwegian salmon with star anise, ginger-spiced julienned vegetables, yellowtail snapper with warm lemon pecan vinaigrette, and a veal chop with parsnip pancake and ratatouille in zinfandel sauce. Desserts are terrifyingly tantalizing. Quite an impressive new spot, Wilson's has impressive prices as well, falling in the $17 to $25 bracket for entrées on an à la carte menu, and a bill that rises rapidly with the addition of other temptations. Hours are 11:30am to 3pm and 6 to 11pm daily except Sunday.

**Butlers,** 363 Cocoanut Row (tel. 659-5800), a new restaurant in the Chesterfield Hotel, which is itself a newcomer to the Palm Beach hotel roster, has been garnering rave reviews for its straightforward but showy presentation of seafood, pastas, veal and beef, the latter rolled up to your table on a copper trolley and carved at tableside. Pastries are an *après dîner* lure at this attractive restaurant where entrées are priced at $15 to $22. Butlers serves from 5:30 to 11pm daily.

## French

East coast Floridians welcomed **Café L'Europe,** 150 Worth Ave. (tel. 655-4020), in the Esplanade shopping plaza, with the same enthusiasm the restaurant received on the west coast where it holds forth elegantly in Sarasota. They've done it again here: beautiful decor, efficient service, upper-crust atmosphere, shining crystal, and outstanding cuisine with the usual French talent for blending and surprising. After a dinner here, the bottom line on the check could hover in the $25 to $30-a-person range, more if you indulge in the full line of temptations. It's open from 11:30am to 3pm and 6 to 10pm daily except Sunday.

Café L'Europe also operates a tiny, casual spot called **L'Express,** in the Esplanade shopping plaza (tel. 833-2117). Open for breakfast, lunch, and dinner from 7:30am to 9:30pm daily except Sunday, this small spot has a few tables, a counter, a new liquor license, and take-out service, all of it kept very busy by the hungry in search of a casual-dress enclave. Fresh bread is sold here, along with deli goodies, sandwiches, intriguing pastas, gorgeously sinful pastries, and a chocolate freak-out called the Black Feast. Prices for any meal can easily fall under $10, perhaps a bit higher for dinner.

A Monaco native created **Le Monegasque,** 2505 S. Ocean Blvd. (tel. 585-0071), nestled away in the corner of the Palm Beach President condominium. That native is Aldo Rinero, who has a long and impressive career behind him (Forum of the Twelve Caesars, Delmonico's, Toque Blanche) and knows exactly what he's about in his tiny world. You'll find treats like filet of pompano, chateaubriand, foie de veau Grande Bretagne, delicate veal dishes, accompanied by vegetables cooked to a T and desserts that are, well, you decide how rapturous the description. You'll pay about $20 to $30, depending on your indulgence, and the restaurant is open from 6 to 10pm Tuesday through Sunday (closed September).

**L'Anjou,** 717 Lake Ave., Lake Worth (tel. 582-7666), is another very popular French restaurant in Palm Beach County. Prices are quite reasonable here with complete dinners beginning at $14, top price about $17. Service is pleasant and charmingly French in accent and demeanor. This, too, is a popular restaurant and reservations are very wise, particularly in winter months. L'Anjou is open from 5 to 9:30pm daily.

A top-notch French restaurant in the Palm Beach area is **Café du Parc,** 612 Federal Hwy., Lake Park (tel. 845-0529). It's located opposite Kelsey Park at Park Avenue and is run by a husband and wife from the Lot Valley in southwestern France, an area known for its three-star Michelin-rated hotels and restaurants. Café du Parc is in an old wooden frame house, pleasantly furnished and with a cozy atmosphere that attracts faithful followers. Madame greets many arrivals by name and in various languages too. Café du Parc is a lovely spot much revered by the Palm Beach set. Classical French cooking at its best is available here from 5:30 to 10pm daily in winter, closed Sunday and Monday from early May to November. Entrée prices are in the $17 to $25 range.

## Italian

A charming little garden patio and one of the few sidewalk cafés on this coastline would be reason enough to head for **Testa's,** at 221 Royal Poinciana Way (tel. 832-0992), but wonderful pasta and Italian concoctions and excellent steaks and seafood clinch matters. The same family has kept this pretty little place running for more than 60 years now, and is thoughtful enough to provide a children's menu so you can take the young ones along without breaking the bank. Dinners average about $12 to $20. In summer the family takes off to a northern restaurant operation, closing this Testa's from May to the first week in December. It's open daily from 7am to 1am.

Fettuccine Alfredo, softshell crabs, saltimbocca alla romana, scampi—what more could there be in life? Whatever more there is, you'll find at **Nando's,** 221 Royal Palm Way (tel. 655-3031), where you dine on fine Italian creations in a brick-lined gardeny atmosphere trimmed with ornate ironwork. You're entertained in winter by strolling musicians, and anytime by soft music from the piano in the intimate candlelit lounge. Entrées here average $12 to $21, and Nando's is open from 5:30 to 11pm daily.

A spot with the unlikely—but very well-known hereabouts—name of **This Is It Pub,** 424 24th St., West Palm Beach (tel. 833-4997), draws crowds to lunch and dinner. It has been doing so for almost 30 years now, and there seems no end in sight to the popularity of this place that relies entirely on word of mouth to spread its reputation for good steaks and seafood, rack of lamb, and bouillabaisse. Northern

Italian cooking is featured here, so you'll always find some delectable veal dishes among the offerings. This Is It is open from 11:30am to 10pm daily (no lunch Saturday), closed Sunday, and prices are in the $15 to $25 range for dinner.

## Seafood

Palm Beach's **Charley's Crab,** 456 S. Ocean Blvd. (tel. 659-1500), brother to the Sarasota operation that lures throngs of hungry seafood lovers. Naturally, the accent is on fresh-from-the-sea creatures, so each night there are specials, depending on what's just off the boat that day. Sashay up to the raw bar for iced oysters and cherrystone clams, and try the mussels or linguine with red clam sauce. There's an intimate, pubby atmosphere in this restaurant just across the street from the ocean, and dinner prices are in the $20 to $30 range. Charley's is open from 11:30am to 10pm daily, later on weekends, and from 10am to 2:30pm for Sunday brunch ($16.95).

## Budget Stops

Millionaires and would-be tycoons alike whip into **Hamburger Heaven,** 314 S. County Rd. (tel. 655-5277), to dine or chow down on some of the best hamburgers in town. That's the specialty here (they grind their own beef daily), but there are plenty of other sandwich and salad choices at prices everybody likes: under $5. Open from 7:30am to 9pm daily.

**Tony Roma's,** at 2215 Palm Beach Lakes Blvd., West Palm Beach (tel. 689-1703), produces barbecued ribs with a spicy sauce so excellent he's cloned his restaurant many times now to provide for throngs of hungry diners. You'll also find hamburgers on the menu, along with inexpensive steak (about $11), very inexpensive London broil (about $5), and a loaf of onion rings the likes of which you'll find only at Tony Roma's. Nothing on the menu is more than $13, and the restaurant's open from 2 to 11pm daily, until midnight on Friday and Saturday.

## DINING IN THE SUBURBS

All the communities surrounding Palm Beach are also well supplied with fine restaurants.

## Boynton Beach/Lantana

On Friday night you'd think everyone in three counties was packed into the **Banana Boat,** 739 E. Ocean Ave., Boynton Beach (tel. 732-9400). There's always a crowd chattering away at the tables outside on the porch overlooking a marina or inside where low lighting glows on flocks of hungry seafood fans. Sea creatures are the specialty here, although you can find enough other selections to please everyone. The Boat's a favorite local spot for younger diners, who stay on for entertainment that lasts well into the wee hours. Prices are in the $5 to $15 range, and the Banana Boat is open at 11am daily.

**Two Georges Marina** in Boynton Beach hides a place well loved by boaters who nip in here to while away an afternoon or evening chowing down on jumbo shrimp, conch fritters, fresh filets of whatever's been caught today, even fresh-water catfish. Most people only know it as Two Georges Marina, but it really is the **Harbour Hut Restaurant & Raw Bar** (tel. 736-2717), and is open from 7am to 10pm daily. Prices range from $7 to $15.

**Anchor Inn,** 2810 Hypoluxo Rd., Lantana (tel. 965-4794), sticks to seafood but does a very good job of it, so good that you often find local restaurant owners dining here! There are always buckets and buckets of oysters being shucked for presentation on the half shell, as oysters casino, or in a special house preparation called oysters Anchor. Options for landsmen include thick broiled-to-order steaks and chicken. Fish is simply prepared here, but is always fresh from the sea and reasonably priced—most dinners in the $13 to $22 range. Hours at Anchor Inn are 5 to 10pm daily, and you'll find the restaurant a half mile west of I-95 at Exit 45.

## Delray Beach

When we peeked in a window of **The New Bridge,** 840 E. Atlantic Ave. (tel. 278-7816), one day and spotted an atmosphere straight out of Manhattan, we returned to try it out—and returned and returned and returned. A charming and savvy New Yorker opened this spot years ago in a tiny but very sophisticated dining room that could seat perhaps a dozen. Big picture windows overlooked the waterway and the decor ran to dark walls, elegantly framed French posters, and giant ferns. These days the Bridge is chic-er than ever in both decor and clientele, but has kept the same excellent menu that changes regularly as the restaurant finds seasonal goodies to place before you, contemporary, cosmopolitan, and gorgeous. You'll pay about $20 to $25 for a memorable dinner here. The New Bridge is open from 11:30am to 3pm and 6 to 10pm daily.

There's something about this north Gold Coast area that draws Italians, and they come armed with whisks and award-winning cuisine that keeps them in business long after others have come and gone. **Vittorio's,** 25 S. US Hwy. 1 (tel. 278-5525), is one of those that's succeeded in creating a pleasant atmosphere in which the kitchen can display its many and varied culinary talents. The accent here is on northern Italian cuisine, with lots of light creamy sauces and melt-in-your-mouth pastas served in an atmosphere heavy on candlelight, antiques, and greenery. For the excellent food and matching surroundings you'll pay $12 to $20 for entrées. Vittorio's is open from 5:30 to 10pm daily. Jackets are required for gentlemen.

**Paoletti's,** at 815 N. Federal Hwy. (tel. 272-2988), began with an enchanting restaurant in Coral Gables years ago before it moved northward to bring its award-winning Italian cuisine to Delray—to a nice little dining room, complete with intimate, low lighting and romantic, comfortable booths. Here's also that outstanding cuisine for which the restaurant was so justly famous. Fresh seafood, pasta, veal—it's all there at Paoletti's, at prices in the $13 to $24 vicinity. Hours are 6 to 10pm daily. Often closed May through October.

Just the thought of lobster Savannah, swimming in a creamy mornay sauce and accented with delicate spices, can send us racing off for another visit to **Busch's,** 5855 N. Ocean Blvd., in the village of Ocean Ridge (tel. 732-8470). Lace curtains on the windows, a shady lounge with quiet background notes from the piano, plus the cozy look of an old house (which it is) combine to make an evening at Busch's not only gastronomically divine but atmospherically heavenly as well. After dining on the likes of she-crab soup (Thursday), broiled pompano, or red snapper fresh from the sea, you'll leave with a check in the $14 to $20 range for entrées. Hours are 5 to 10pm daily except Monday. A clambake dinner for two is a gourmand's delight for about $40.

You have to give **Arcade Tap Room,** 411 E. Atlantic Ave., Delray Beach (tel. 276-7200), credit for longevity in a state in which restaurant longevity is the exception rather than the rule. Operating here now for half a century (!), the Tap Room is the kind of place in which you will eventually see everybody in town if you wait long enough. A popular meeting spot for Palm Beach County dwellers and visitors, the Tap Room features basic American cooking—prime rib, steaks, seafood (accent on seafood)—for prices in the $15 to $25 range. No doubt about it, this is an institution on the Gold Coast, and worth a look just to see who else is looking. Hours are 11am to 10pm daily.

## Boca Raton

Addison Mizner, who created the glamorous Boca Raton Hotel and many elegant homes in this city, was the inspiration behind a pretty little house two top restaurateurs have turned into **La Vieille Maison,** at 770 E. Palmetto Park Rd. (tel. 391-6701). That means "the old house," but doesn't do this old house justice. Surely they should have added "belle" or "magnifique" to the name, for this 50-year-old beauty is all of that. Each of several dining rooms is decorated differently, one with a country look, another with formal high-backed chairs. Tiny tables are tucked around the tiny patio where a tree grows right through the roof, and there's a wine cellar lined with bottles. Fountains bubble, Cuban tiles add splashes of color, and flowers, flowers, and more flowers trim every flat surface. Everything's exquisite, from the crystal and fine china, to the award-winning cuisine that moves effortlessly from a pastry-trimmed pâté to escargots, pan-roasted quail in cognac, ending finally with crisp tart salads, a packed tray of cheeses and fresh fruit, double chocolate mousse, or a lemon crêpe soufflé. Prix-fixe prices here are $44 for a complete six-course dinner, $17 to $30 à la carte. On busy nights, seatings are on the half hour from 6:30 to 9:30pm, otherwise anytime by reservation. Jackets for men are required in season.

**Arturo's Ristorante,** 6750 N. Federal Hwy. (tel. 997-7373), is something of a newcomer to the area but has cut a rather wide swath here since it opened. A large and lovely restaurant with tall French windows, Arturo's specializes in Italian flavors and makes all its pasta right here. One of the specialties, spaghetti Gismondi, combines bacon drippings, Nova Scotia salmon, tomato and cream sauce with thin, thin pasta. Angel-hair pasta turns up al pesto, flavored with basil and parmesan. Mostaccioli is teamed with cognac, fettuccine with fresh tomatoes, and linguine with clam sauce. Prices are in the $14 to $27 range and hours are 11:30am to 3pm weekdays, 6 to 10pm daily. Closed July.

**Joe Muer's,** 6450 N. Federal Hwy. (tel. 997-6688), is the Florida branch of a Detroit restaurant that settled in here about a decade ago. Muer's concentrates on seafood and does quite a creditable job, offering a wide range of seafood specialties, as well as steaks for landlubbers. This is a good place to go to try some of the more unusual Florida seafood—pompano, for instance. You'll pay $16 to $23 for entrées at Muer's, which is open for dinner from 4:30 to 10pm daily. Also open for lunch from 11:30am to 2:30pm daily.

**Raffaello's Restaurant,** 725 Palmetto Park Rd. East, Boca Raton (tel. 392-4855), is a pleasant spot up this way. Italian flavors are favored at this colorful spot outfitted in shades of salmon and green. A small cocktail lounge presides over the entrance to this comfortable but rather formal restaurant (jackets are required for gentlemen). Out in the kitchen, talented chefs are whipping up such unusual dishes as tortellini with cauliflower and asparagus tips, a creamy-rich Italian cheese pie, eggplant rollatine stuffed with ricotta cheese and topped with a rich and spicy tomato sauce. Prices are in the $16 to $26 range for entrées, and there's a creditable wine list. Hours are 11:30am to 2:30pm weekdays, 6 to 10:30pm daily. Check for summer hours, which sometimes vary.

**READERS' RESTAURANT SUGGESTIONS:** "I'd recommend **The Ark II** at 2600 Lantana Rd. in West Palm Beach (tel. 968-8550) for inexpensive meals, a great salad bar, and complimentary hors d'oeuvres. Prices are in the $10 to $15 range. [*Authors' Note:* The Ark is open from 5 to 10pm for dinner daily, later on weekends. The lounge is open to 5am most nights.] **The Firehouse** at 6751 N. Federal Hwy., Boca Raton (tel. 997-6006), is also a good restaurant in this area. Prices are $12 to $17 for dinner. Open from 5 to 10:30pm daily" (Jerry Schultz, Boynton Beach, Fla.).

"Tell your readers about **The Seafood Connection** at 6998 N. Federal Hwy., Boca Raton (tel. 997-5562). It's got good and moderately priced seafood ($5 to $20) and is always jammed because good seafood is hard to find around here. It's open from 11:30am to 10pm daily" (Roy Nickels, Delray Beach, Fla.).

## SEEING THE SIGHTS

To tour Palm Beach in true Palm Beach style, you'd need a chauffeured Rolls-Royce or a Bentley! But never mind. Hitch up the Toyota and roam about for a look at these towering man$ion$ and notable homes that range from the massive Flagler

House Museum to the home of a one-time secretary who's now a millionaire—her boss started the McDonald's hamburger chain, and in the early days didn't have enough money to pay her salary so he gave her stock instead!

## The Mansions

The palatial mansions of the rich and super-rich are Palm Beach's major sight-seeing attraction. If you're touring on your own, the best way to see them is on a drive along South Ocean Boulevard, where you'll ooh and aah at the towering edifices that line the sides of this millionaire's boulevard. Don't miss 1100 S. Ocean Blvd., where you'll find a tiny brass plaque announcing the presence of **Mar al Lago,** once the home of cereal heiress Marjorie Merriweather Post, who was the mother of actress Dina Merrill. Mrs. Post was for decades a (if not the) grande dame of Palm Beach society, and gave her home to the nation in her will. A budget-pinched government, however, decided to return it rather than fork over the $1 million a year it takes to maintain this palace that stretches from *mar* (Atlantic Ocean) to *lago* (Lake Worth). It's now owned by New York City developer Donald Trump.

Farther up the boulevard behind a high wall on North County Road is the seaside villa of the Kennedy clan, where the slain president spent the last week of his life.

And of course don't pass up a visit to **The Breakers,** 1 County Rd., Palm Beach. In few other places in the nation, if any, is there a hotel as legendary or as spectacular in its sheer opulence as the Breakers, a behemoth that's long been dear to the hearts of those who call Palm Beach home.

If you'd like to see more of these palatial estates, stay on North County Road and continue past the sign that announces "This road terminates in 3½ miles." It does, but in those 3½ miles you'll see some of the world's richest real estate, one gasp after another. If you'd like to buy a house here, bring cash, at least $1 to $2 million—and that's just a down payment!

Henry Flagler's magnificent mansion on Whitehall Way (tel. 655-2833), is a study in the flamboyance of those *fin-de-siècle* days. You can tour both it and the railroad magnate's elegant private railroad car, each of which holds a fortune in antiques, an awesome sight in these starkly simple days. Built in 1901 for $4 million, the marble palace has a 110-by-40-foot marble-columned entrance that's a knock-out, and rooms full of painted ceilings, gilt furniture, and period decor that reflect the lavish life-style Flagler and his wife adored. There's a special collection of porcelain dolls, paintings, and family treasures as well. It's open Tuesday through Saturday from 10am to 5pm, on Sunday from noon to 5pm, closed Monday. Admission is $3.50 for adults, $1.25 for children ages 6 to 12.

## Other Sights

**Bethesda-by-the-Sea Church,** on South County Road just south of the Breakers, is an enchanting example of 13th-century Gothic design. Next door are the attractive formally landscaped **Cluett Memorial Gardens** (open daily from 8am to 5pm).

The **Society of the Four Arts,** at Four Arts Plaza just off Royal Palm Way, has a library, art museum, gardens, and an auditorium where some excellent musical and dance performances are staged. It's open from 10am to 5pm daily (from 2pm on Sunday) December to April, on weekdays only the rest of the year. There's no admission charge.

See the waterside face of the city (and in Florida that's *always* lovelier than the front door) on an **Intracoastal Waterway Cruise** aboard the *Empress* Dining Cruises, a Mississippi paddlewheeler docked at Phil Foster Park on Singer Island, next to Blue Heron Bridge, 900 E. Blue Heron Blvd., Singer Island (tel. 842-0882). Cruises depart daily from 11am to 7pm and cost $10 adults, $5 for children 5 to 12. Meals are $5 to $18.

The **Norton Gallery of Art,** 1451 S. Olive Ave. (tel. 832-5194), houses an outstanding collection of 19th- and 20th-century American and European art, and a distinguished Chinese art collection. It's open from 10am to 5pm Tuesday through Saturday, from 1 to 5pm on Sunday, and there's no admission charge.

If you'd like to see the stars closer than you can on a beach stroll, the **Science Museum and Planetarium,** 4801 Dreher Trail (tel. 832-1348), has planetarium productions, a computer center, a marine aquarium, an observatory, and a discovery room. It's open from 10am to 5pm daily and Friday nights from 6:30 to 10pm. Adults pay $3; children 4 to 12 pay $1.

For **Lion Country Safari,** take the Southern Boulevard exit off I-95, or Exit 99 or 93 from the turnpike (tel. 793-1084). You can talk with the animals—just stay in your car! Bison, lions, chimps, ostriches, antelopes, and elephants roam around in their natural habitat while you drive through the park (no convertibles). Lion Country is open from 9:30am to 5:30pm daily; admission is $11.95 for adults, $10 for children 3 to 16 (under 3 years, free), and it's 15 miles west of West Palm Beach. You can rent a car to tour the park for $5 an hour, and you can drop Fido at a clean and free kennel while you're going through the grounds. Admission includes a boat cruise inside the park. But don't go on any safari here—stay in the car and drive.

For a look at the **Everglades,** drive out to **Loxahatchee Recreation Area,** Rte. 1, Box 6425, Pompano Beach (tel. 426-2474), at the Palm Beach entrance to the Everglades. (Get there by taking I-95 to Hillsboro Boulevard West to Fla. 441, turn right and then your first left on to Lox Road and drive on for six miles.) You can take airboat rides ($7.50 for adults, $4 for children 4 to 11), through the swamp accompanied by a ranger who'll explain the flora and fauna, or rent boats ($27.50 for five hours in a three-seater motorboat), and venture off on your own—bring a compass.

In Delray is an unusual Florida sight, the **Morikami Museum,** at 4000 Morikami Park Rd. (tel. 499-0631), depicting Japanese culture, arts, and horticulture in honor of early settlers in the area, the Yamato colony of Japanese pineapple farmers. Open daily except Monday 10am to 5pm.

## SPECIAL EVENTS

Palm Beach has discovered tourism in recent years, so to keep the thundering herds thundering, particularly in a slow season, **Sunfest** was born. A four-day festival on the first weekend in May, Sunfest includes a lakeside jazz concert, juried art show, and lots of food.

One could hardly think of a less likely setting than Palm Beach for a blue-ribbon hog, but then one has to do *something* to keep the locals occupied, we suppose. A ten-day **county fair** celebration of creatures that Palm Beach's finest may recognize but do not claim occurs at the end of January at South Florida Fairgrounds, 9067 Southern Blvd., West Palm Beach (tel. 793-0333), when agricultural triumphs are feted.

## SPORTS

If you've never been to a polo match, now is the time to get out there and watch them chukker. Polo's an old and exciting sport with players chasing around on horseback wielding long mallets at a tiny ball. Naturally, in this sunny city you can also find lots of golf and tennis, even some gambling sports.

### Croquet

Croquet? *Croquet?* Of course! In this rarified atmosphere one's sports are rarified. On the lawns of the Breakers you will hear the thunk of mallets, the thud of the ball, and never, never the roar of the greasepaint and the smell of the crowd. Head-to-foot white outfits gleam in the shade as some of the world's champion croqueters take to the lawns in world-class games. Game dates vary, so if you want to watch—quietly, please—a call to the hotel (tel. 655-6611) should put you in the know.

## Baseball

On what definitely could be said to be the opposite end of the sports spectrum from croquet is baseball. Here you can slouch around in any color while you watch the **Atlanta Braves** and the **Montreal Expos**, both of whom do spring training here at the West Palm Beach Municipal Stadium, 715 Hank Aaron Dr. (tel. 471-5362).

## Golf

Five courses at **PGA's National Golf Club**, at 1000 Avenue of the Champions in Palm Beach Gardens, are home to major golfing tournaments each year. You can play where the top names in golf curse and cheer for $30 to $50 in summer or fall, $50 to $100 in winter. Carts are additional $28. Call 627-1804 for tee times.

Other public courses include **North Palm Beach Country Club**, 901 US 1 in North Palm Beach (tel. 626-4343), and the **West Palm Beach Country Club**, 7001 Parker Ave. at Forest Hill Boulevard (tel. 582-2019), where greens fees vary from $20 to $35 year round.

## Tennis

**Lake Worth Racquet and Swim Club**, 4090 Coconut Rd., Lake Worth (tel. 967-3900), has 15 lighted courts for $10 an hour per person, and there are six free public courts at **John Prince Park**, on Lake Worth Road just east of Converse Avenue. The **Palm Beach Recreation Department** can also guide you to other public courts near you. Call them at their leisure line (tel. 967-0109).

## Fishing

**Blue Heron Fishing Fleet** (tel. 844-3573) will take you on fishing expeditions at 8:30am and 1:30pm daily for $18 a person with reel and bait. They're docked at the Blue Heron Bridge near Singer Island.

A number of charter boats also operate in the area, many of them docked at Blue Heron Bridge. Rates vary widely by season, but range from $350 to $450 a day.

## Sailing

Look under the Singer Causeway for **Singer Island Sail-boat Rental**, Phil Foster Park, Blue Heron Boulevard (tel. 848-BOAT), where you can rent boats and windsurfers for $15 to $30 an hour and learn how to sail them too. Charter boats are also available.

## Polo

Polo is the rage in Palm Beach and there are now three polo grounds just short drives from the island. Championship teams play here in winter—England's Prince Charles caused quite a stir when he showed up for a match—to win money and fame in this fast-paced horseback sport.

You can see the players in action at **Gulfstream Polo Field**, off the Sunshine State Parkway on Lake Worth Road (tel. 965-2057), **Palm Beach Polo and Country Club**, 13198 Forest Hill Blvd. (tel. 793-1113), and **Royal Palm Polo Club**, 6300 Clint Moore Rd., Boca Raton Beach (tel. 994-1876). Admission is $10 to $25 at any of the grounds. So posh are the crowds at this rich man's sport—it takes quite a few dollars to keep a string of polo ponies in oats—that vendors here don't hawk soft drinks, they sell champagne!

## Pari-mutuel Sports

Greyhounds streak off after the rabbit at the **Palm Beach Kennel Club,** at Belvedere and Congress roads (tel. 683-2222), from late October to nearly May with races nightly, except Wednesday and Sunday, at 8pm and matinees at 12:30 pm on Monday, Thursday, and Saturday. Admission is $1 to $2.

You can *try* to watch the speeding bouncing ball at the **Palm Beach Jai-Alai Fronton,** 1415 W. 45th St. (tel. 844-2444), from early November through early April. Games are at 7:30pm Tuesday through Saturday. There are matinees Wednesday and Saturday until late February, and on Wednesday, Friday, and Saturday thereafter. Admission begins at $1 and ranges to about $5.

## SHOPPING

In Palm Beach shopping is not just a frivolous pursuit, it's serious business, and for some a full-time job. **Worth Avenue** is the city's famed shopping street, a boulevard on which you'll find Rolls-Royces (chauffeured, of course), diamonds, fine leathers, rare blooms, and tall chocolate letters that spell out "Happy Birthday" if you can afford that many letters (perhaps "happy" will say enough).

**Gucci** and **Cartier** are here. **Saks** is here, **Courrèges** is here, and **Godiva** (we mean the chocolates, although anything is possible in Palm Beach) is here. Fabulous —and fabulously expensive—little shops are tucked away in entrancing alleys and down little "vias" where bougainvillea blooms in a riot of color and vines twine around wrought-iron balconies.

Worth Avenue isn't just a street, you see, it's an experience. And what you can't find here may not be worth having.

A new section of the avenue called the **Esplanade** is part of this posh circus of salesmanship, and **Palm Beach Mall,** at Palm Beach Lakes Boulevard and I-95, is the site of **Lord & Taylor's** and a host of other intriguing shops.

## NIGHTLIFE

**Cocktail rooms** of the bigger hotels like the Colony and the Breakers are where you'll see most people hobbing and nobbing. Before or after dinner (or *for* dinner— it has quite good Continental cuisine) almost everyone drops into the **Ta-Boo,** 221 Worth Ave. (tel. 775-0600), to see who's in town and to dance to nightly trio music.

**Royal Poinciana Playhouse,** at 70 Royal Poinciana Plaza (tel. 659-3310), presents top-quality Broadway musicals and dramas in the winter season. Ticket prices vary, but you can buy a six-performance season ticket for about $200.

Actress Jan McArt's **Royal Palm Dinner Theater,** 303 Golfview Dr., Boca Raton (tel. 392-3755), is an Equity theater specializing in musical comedies presented year round. Ticket prices are $34 to $35.

If you join the **Palm Beach Round Table,** 319 Clematis St., West Palm Beach (memberships begin at $75; tel. 655-5266), you can attend dinner lectures by some of the history makers of our day (Nixon, for instance, was a speaker). Programs run January through April, and tickets are usually available for about $12 to $15.

**Buccaneer Yacht Club** on Singer Island has listening and dancing music from 7pm to midnight every day but Monday.

A spot that's getting rave reviews as much for its beautiful interior design and lovely waterside setting as for its menu is **Wildflower,** 551 E. Palmetto Park Rd., Boca Raton, at the Intracoastal Waterway (tel. 391-0000). There's certainly no denying that this is an enchanting hideaway snuggled into an Intracoastal Waterway nest with decor that will knock your eyes out. A favorite gathering place for happy hour and Sunday crowds, the Wildflower serves salads, steaks, seafood. It's open from 11:30am to 2am daily, with prices about $9 to $12 for dinner, $4 to $6 for lunch. A disk jockey plays dance music nightly.

**Club Boca,** 7000 W. Palmetto Park Rd. at Powerline Road in Boca Bank Corporate Center (tel. 368-3333) is a weirdly whimsical spot inhabited by Boca's beautiful people, who seemingly revel in this nightclub's fluted columns, marble, etched glass, cave drawings of Neanderthals in bikinis, confetti, and metallic gooney birds. Recently rehabbed from stem to sometimes-strange stern by a Boston restaurant entrepreneur who operated a top-rated club in that city, Club Boca is simply the only place to go these days. Eclectic panache sort of sums it up for this handsome dance spot that features live entertainment three or more times a week and keeps the music moving from reggae to 60's and 70's classics to progressive and jazz gigs. Hours are 8pm to 4am daily, opening at 6pm Saturday and closed most Sundays, with occasional Sunday jazz brunches at which the underaged may be in attendance. There's a $3 to $5 cover most nights and occasional freebies for ladies.

**Respectable Street Café,** 518 Clematis St., West Palm Beach (tel. 832-9999 or 832-0706), is in an old Salvation Army building outfitted in art deco furnishings. Under a very high ceiling the decibels keep toes tapping on a huge dance floor and around a glass bar. There's a band most nights and top-notch concerts many nights, often on Wednesdays. Respectable Street is not on the world's most respectable street, but there's good security and valet parking—a wise idea. Throngs of new wave, reggae and blues, and just plain music fans struggle to get in the door each night at this very popular club, which has a $3 to $5 cover charge most evenings, rarely more than a $15 cover for concerts. It's open every night from 7pm to 3am, to 4am on weekends.

Mellow sounds lure an older crowd to **Chuck & Harold's,** 207 Royal Poinciana Way, Palm Beach (tel. 659-1440), although you'll see plenty of young faces out for a quiet dancing evening. Music is provided by a pianist or combos that appear in the lounge from 7am to midnight every night. There's no cover charge at this spot, which also is one of the city's top restaurants.

**Top O'Spray** at the SeaSpray Inn on Singer Island has regular entertainment, as does the **Ramada Inn** (Palm Lakes Boulevard at I-95), and the **Howard Johnson** on Singer Island.

## 2. Fort Lauderdale

Seven miles of dazzling, glittering, golden sand fringed by swaying palms and azure ocean—this sweep of silica is Fort Lauderdale's beach, the city's pride, glory, lure, and landmark.

Certainly this sparkling strip of sand is not all there is to this sunny city by the sea, but it's what matters most to most people, and it's likely to be all the dedicated sun-seeker will see of this one-time Indian trading post, aspirant to the title "Venice of America."

While that Venice tag has perhaps just a whisper of Madison Avenue, Fort Lauderdale does indeed outpace its Italian sister in watery thoroughfares: There are now 165 miles of navigable water here. That's 10 times as many canals as Venice can claim, and the number grows daily as developers dig into Florida's watery land mass, creating foundation and waterfront address in one fell swoop.

Any resemblance to Venice ends at the high-water mark, however, for Fort Lauderdale is no crumbling mass of water-stained masonry, no bastion of history. Even the fort that gave the city its name in 1838 has long since disappeared, victim to waves of sun-seekers who began their inexorable march over this land a century ago. Here and there you can still ferret out a touch of the city's past, but this is a town that lives strictly for today with rarely a backward glance, a place where about the only thing that's permanent is change.

In 1981 Fort Lauderdale was the nation's fastest-growing city, luring the world's sun-seekers with 3,000 sunny hours a year, one of the most accessible strips of sand in the state, temperatures that rarely drop below 70° Fahrenheit, and a freewheeling, unflappable acceptance of traveler's eccentricities.

No longer small, but still retaining a firm grip on its cozy village atmosphere, Fort Lauderdale has neither the cosmopolite glitz of Miami Beach nor the wealthier-than-thou sniffism of its blueblood neighbor, Palm Beach. Green enough in wallet but not blue enough in blood, this city clings voraciously to a middle ground geographically, demographically, atmospherically, and spiritually. Indeed, people here have their own brand of snobbism: They look sneeringly over the wire rims of their sunglasses to dub the neon canyons of Miami Beach as *bas,* Palm Beach too *haute* to be a hot destination.

Millions of the bent-on-bronze seem to agree. They prove it by trekking here year after year for two weeks of suntan lotion and peeling noses, returning again and again to repeat as closely as possible last year's experience. Once upon a memorable time, the most loyal of these were college students, who appeared with lemming-like regularity in hordes, gaggles, and prides, arriving by car, thumb, Jeep, and Learjet. They descended as the last March snow flurries turn to slush on northern campuses. They fried unprepared epidermis to beautiful boiled pink. They consumed, in one bar in one month, 75,000 bottles of brew, and then disappeared after Easter—having proven beyond question Fort Lauderdale's right to its most common sobriquet, Fort Liquordale.

Then, as suddenly as the sun breaks through a tropical storm, the annual barrage of students was gone, storming off to Daytona Beach to turn that city into seven weeks of sun and sudsy swilling. It could have meant disaster, but in what seems record time, Fort Lauderdale has rebounded, found new, more tranquil audiences at whom to aim its undeniable appeal, and welcomed those who had fled spring's invasion for more subdued sun spots.

Now once again the beaches are filled each spring, but the look is different: Collegiate faces have given way to the visages of young up-and-comers who admit, somewhat abashedly now, that they first found this sunshine-mecca on a spring-break visit. They are joined by couples and families, by traveling Europeans lured by favorable exchange rates, by retirees returning to a long-loved haven, and by newcomers discovering this softly seductive city in which mañana often seems entirely too much pressure.

Which brings us full circle in the city's history. It was sun that brought pioneers here at the turn of the century, but it was sin that kept them in the gray days of the Depression and Prohibition. Gambling, scarlet women, and booze boated in from the Bahamas by racy rumrunners first gave the city its Liquordale monicker, then kept it afloat as the nation drowned in red ink.

Pendulums will swing, however, and Fort Lauderdale left swashbuckle behind to return to a more prosaic, more predictable, central spot. Here it remains, peopled by a hardy breed, pioneers whose staunch support of capitalism is exceeded only by their successful manipulation of it.

This is the face Fort Lauderdale presents to you, a sunny, welcoming face, the cheerful countenance of a city waiting to grant you what you seek—and perhaps help you discover what that is.

## USEFUL INFORMATION

For **medical emergencies,** call the Broward County Medical Association (tel. 739-2305). . . . **Dental emergency** information is available from the Broward County Dental Association (tel. 772-5461). . . . Call 765-8950 for **legal aid** . . . **Post office branches** are listed under U.S. Government Postal Service. . . . For fast **police and ambulance assistance,** dial 911. . . . **Foreign-currency exchange** and credit-card services are available at Landmark First National Bank, 1 Financial Plaza (tel. 765-2373). . . . **Western Union** is at 513 NE Third St. (tel. 462-2852, or toll free 800/325-6000). . . . A **24-hour gas station?** Try Euro American Motors, 5751 N. Federal Hwy. (tel. 491-1713). . . . You can get one-hour and one-day cleaning at **Look-on-the-Beach Cleaners,** 3341 E. Oakland Park Blvd. (tel. 561-8412). . . . You'll find **groceries, pharmaceutical needs,** and much more 24 hours a day at Albertson's, 950 E. Commercial Blvd. (tel. 491-0551), and at Cunningham's, 3101 N. Ocean Dr. (tel. 564-8424) . . . **weather info** at 463-2402.

## TOURIST INFORMATION

Friendly folks at the **Greater Fort Lauderdale Chamber of Commerce,** 208 SE Third Ave. (P. O. Box 14516), Fort Lauderdale, FL 33301 (tel. 305/462-6000), will fill your pockets with brochures on the city and its attractions. If you write in advance—and if you're coming here anytime between December and April you'd *better* write in advance—they'll circulate your name to area hotels and motels that will send you information on their properties.

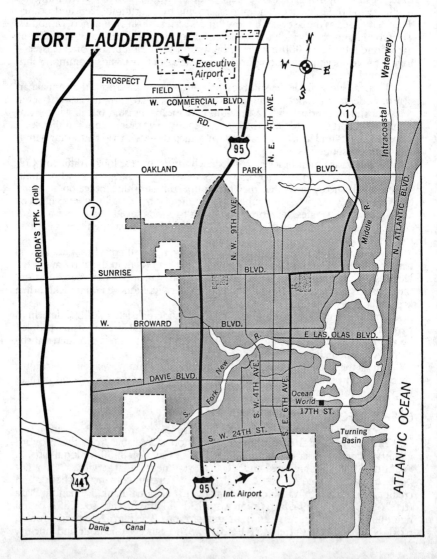

A comparative newcomer to the region's promotional efforts is the **Broward County Visitor and Convention Bureau,** 500 E. Broward Blvd., Fort Lauderdale, FL 33394 (tel. 305/765-4466), where personable Dick Weaver and his staff can provide you with information on hotels and diversions in the region.

Anytime, and particularly during the room crush from February 15 to April 15, the **Broward County Hotel and Motel Assocation,** 1212 NE Fourth Ave. (tel. 305/462-0409), can help you find rooms in member hotels. A tourist directory is free.

Information on local attractions and changing exhibits is listed in the *Fort Lauderdale News/Sun Sentinel,* and the *Miami Herald,* both of which have special what's-up-this-weekend sections.

Still more information on local attractions is in free magazines, *See, Key,* or *Where,* which are available at most hotels and motels.

## ORIENTATION

Fort Lauderdale's streets are laid out on a grid pattern with **Broward Boulevard** dividing the city into north and south sectors, **Andrews Avenue** sectioning it into east and west quadrants. Major east-west arteries are (from south to north): SE 17th Street Causeway, Broward, Las Olas, Sunrise, Oakland Park, and Commercial boulevards. Bridges on each of those arteries (except Broward Boulevard) connect the mainland to the beach.

Fla. A1A runs north and south and is also called 17th Street Causeway, North Atlantic Boulevard, and Ocean Boulevard. With one or two exceptions, which will be noted, all recommended hotels are in the beach area, or near or on Fla. A1A.

Las Olas Boulevard is the city's elegant shopping street. Sunrise Boulevard has a sprawling shopping center near the beach and dozens of boutiques.

## GETTING AROUND FORT LAUDERDALE–STYLE

Just hold up your hand and hail a water taxi! That's simplifying it a bit but you can indeed travel the city in cute little green and yellow boats operated by **Water Taxi of Fort Lauderdale** (tel. 565-5507). Prowling the waterways from 17th Street on the south to Commercial Boulevard on the north and from New River to the 7th Avenue Bridge, these small waterborne hacks will stop anywhere they can find a place to dump you onto dry land. To most people that means the docks outside waterside restaurants or at marinas dotted all over the area.

Rides are $3.50 one way and you can arrange for the taxi to pick you up at the waterway nearest you, take you to a waterside lounge or restaurant, pour you back on much later, and get you, if not right to your door, at least within crawling distance. You can even buy an all-day pass and spend a day on the water for $10. A great way to see the Venice of America's canals on the way to your next appointment.

Landlubbers can try this little diversion: a carriage ride through the city in a snappy white carriage with a top-hatted, tuxedoed driver. You can tune into the clopclop of little hooves on Las Olas Boulevard every evening and catch a carriage for a romantic trot down the city's most famous boulevard by hailing one of the carriages or calling **Van Fleet's Horse and Carriage** (tel. 763-7393) in advance. Rides are $8 to $15 per person.

## FORT LAUDERDALE'S HOTELS

Geographically Fort Lauderdale may be close to Miami, but atmospherically it's as far from it as sunshine from snow. While Miami Beach trades on glitter, Fort Lauderdale sells serenity. To this city over the years have come the rich and the famous in search of quiet elegance, young families seeking a vacation as peaceful and predictable as life back in Hometown, U.S.A., and senior citizens focusing attention on pensions.

This appeal to the less flamboyant traveler has led to a proliferation of small—

sometimes downright tiny—family-run hostelries where you certainly won't be a number and can easily achieve a first-name relationship. So loyal are this city's winter visitors that many small resorts have been welcoming the same guests annually for 20 years or more. In February and March, as one hotelier puts it, "It looks a little like a family reunion around here—Bob and Rose from Ohio, the girls from Detroit, a couple from Kentucky, Ted and Rita—they've all been coming here for years."

There are, of course, a number of large hotels in the city, and several new ones on the planning boards, all of which means that despite the presence of 21,000 hotel rooms hereabouts, you can be sure nearly every one of them is filled on February 15 at the height of the winter season.

The moral of these stories is that you must—*must*—reserve early for the peak winter season (October is not too early). We won't depress you with stories of weary travelers in search of sun and fun who instead found doom and gloom because they failed to reserve a room. But it has happened.

If you want to spend time on the beach without spending half your time getting to it, location is everything. Hotels listed here were chosen for easy beach access and because they share hospitality, cleanliness, and a warm welcome for weary travelers. We've grouped them roughly by price categories, from luxury to budget hotels, based on their highest rates—which occur from mid-December to just after Easter.

## The Luxury Leaders

Amid much fanfare, Marriott Corporation opened its second Fort Lauderdale hotel in 1985, a plush and lovely oceanside resort called **Marriott's Harbor Beach,** 3030 Holiday Dr., Fort Lauderdale, FL 33316 (tel. 305/525-4000, or toll free 800/228-6543). As the name suggests, this hotel is right on the sand, indeed is one of the few hotels in the city at which you can step right outside the door and onto the silica.

You're greeted here by a glittering entrance, safari-outfitted doormen who reign over a huge multilevel lobby decked out in soft contemporary shades. Sleek and lovely silk flower arrangements are everywhere, and even the house phones speak of posh: They're fancy French telephones. Off to one side of the hotel is a cocktail lounge and dancing spot done up in burgundy with a lovely view out over the sand. In the other direction (but still within view of the ocean) is a tropically decorated raw bar and an intimate, candlelit formal dining room festooned with crystal chandeliers (à la carte prices in the $17 to $25 range for entrées).

Outside, a very large pool—one of the largest in the city, in fact—welcomes splashers and lap swimmers while beach cabañas lure those in search of a shady retreat from the sun.

Rooms are quite spacious here and are decorated in soft pastel shades. Many have a view of the ocean and all have loads of little extras ranging from special shampoos to bubble bath. Rates at Marriott's Harbor Beach are $215 to $300 double in the prime winter months from December through April, $120 to $190 in summer.

**Marriott Fort Lauderdale Hotel and Marina,** 1881 17th St. Causeway, Fort Lauderdale, FL 33316 (tel. 305/463-4000, or toll free 800/228-6543, in Florida 800/433-2254), is a tropical waterside (but not oceanside) hotel. With 583 rooms, three restaurants, some of the spiffiest suites you'll see anywhere, it's now also one of the city's largest and one of its showiest resorts. To get a room without a view here you'd have to request a broom closet. Nestled alongside the Intracoastal Waterway with sprawling Port Everglades just across the highway, the Marriott seems to have water everywhere. Rooms on the west side overlook the Intracoastal, where sleek yachts purr in for fuel. From rooms on the east side you can watch the *Queen Elizabeth II* sweep majestically into port. From still other rooms you gaze down on a free-form swimming pool where waterfalls burble into tinkling streams shaded by palms. Outside, wood decking forms a long wide porch overlooking a canal that wends its way along the edge of the hotel's central grounds where fountains flow and small waterfalls rush over rocks.

Choose from rooms in Marriott's central 12-story tower or in two three-story canalside wings, all decorated with plush carpets, dark-wood furniture, and lots of little touches ranging from king-and queen-size beds to stereo radios, alarm clocks, in-house movies, Neutrogena soap, and little bottles of shampoo and bath beads. Rates are $135 to $199, single or double, in season, $115 to $175 double off-season.

While you're probably not likely to opt for the $350-a-day suite, it gives you an idea how plushly this hotel is decorated: Start with velvety-gray carpeting, delicate puffy couches, a dramatic glass-topped Lucite dining table, pale-peach decor in a bedroom loft, bar, even a television in the bathroom! VIP suites have bars and fireplaces too.

There's a complimentary shuttle to the beach (about five minutes away), and golf can be arranged at a local course. There are four tennis courts. There's even a 96-foot yacht available to take you and 100 or so of your closest friends on chartered outings.

Nose to nose across the waterway is Marriott's closest competition, lush **Pier Sixty-Six Hotel & Marina,** 2301 SE 17th St. Causeway, Fort Lauderdale, FL 33316 (tel. 305/525-6666, or toll free 800/327-3796 except in Florida, 800/432-1956 in Florida). The twinkling lights of the Pier's central hotel tower have been a landmark in Lauderdale for years and mark one of the town's top gathering spots. To leave Fort Lauderdale without a sundown trip up the glass elevator to the 17th-floor glass-enclosed revolving lounge is sacrilege. Plunk yourself down in a plump swivel armchair or a long low couch in the Pier Top lounge, lean back, heave a deep sigh, and relax while a 2-h.p. motor slowly revolves the floor in a circumgyration that takes an hour to complete. Gaze blissfully out over bustling Port Everglades, elegant pastel estates, sleek yachts, golden sand, azure ocean, and some of the richest real estate you'll see anywhere in the world. Music for dancing begins at 9pm, but the lounge opens at noon daily for lunch, with minors accompanied by adults welcome from noon to 4pm daily.

Pier Sixty-Six, which poured $27 million into a recent renovation project, likes to call itself "grand but not grandiose," a fine line indeed at a 22-acre hotel sporting 388 rooms, two pools, tennis courts, and two restaurants, all sidled up to canals that rim three sides of the property and provide dock space for some enormous vessels.

In the central tower there are suites on each end of the corridors with rooms between decorated in soft pastel shades and featuring glass sliding doors leading to private balconies. Lanais are a private place to seek the better-than-average tan. On the Tower's ground floor is Windows on the Green, open Tuesday through Sunday from 7 to 10pm, and the Terrace Garden, open daily from 7am to 11pm for casual dining with prices in the $15 to $20 range for dinner.

Rates at Pier 66 are $180 to $260 double in winter, dropping to $105 to $175 in summer. Higher rates for suites. There's no charge for children under 17 staying in their parents' room.

Right in the center of the beach is the **Sheraton Yankee Trader Beach Resort,** at 321 N. Atlantic Blvd., Fort Lauderdale, FL 33304 (tel. 305/467-1111, or toll free 800/325-3535). Now about twice its former size following the addition of an enclosed passageway connecting the original hotel to a new group of 223 rooms, the Sheraton has a total of 441 rooms, all right across Fla. A1A from the beach. (Sheraton's sister property, the Sheraton Yankee Clipper, is also on the beach, one-half mile south.)

At the Sheraton Yankee Trader you're greeted by a lobby filled with contemporary basketweave wicker furniture, lots of glass and chrome, and subtle lighting. From a comfortable seat on a chaise longue at poolside you can gaze out over the splashers to the beach and ocean beyond. The Trader's recently completed 11-story tower is connected to its original building by a street-spanning glass walkway. In winter the hotel's Showplace lounge is jam-packed, but anytime you'll find lots of congenial types seeking the sun.

All the modernity extends to the hotel's rooms, which are decorated in crisp geometric prints, and have wide glass windows from which you can watch the Atlantic lapping gently on miles of sand. There are two restaurants, four lounges, two pools, and tennis courts too. You'll pay $110 to $140 double daily from mid-December to May, $65 to $80 in other months.

Smack in the middle of the city's 40-acre yacht basin is the **Quality Inn Bahia Mar Resort,** 801 Seabreeze Blvd., at Bahia Mar, Fort Lauderdale, FL 33316 (tel. 305/764-2233, or toll free 800/327-8154). Twenty of the 40 acres are underwater, which makes for some impressive yacht-watching but still leaves plenty of space for the hotel, part of which dates to the early 1960s boom days. Surrounding the spacious grounds are docks made famous by author John MacDonald's detective hero, Travis McGree, whose adventures always started on the stern of his boat as he welcomed the sunset with a cocktail. Travis may have been imaginary, but with a little judicious yacht-hopping you can spot some very good imitations around the docks here—and ogle yachts with accoutrements like helicopters and swimming pools.

A most notable feature at Bahia Mar is a long passageway that soars above Fla. A1A so you can walk from the beach to the hotel's second-story pool. The recently renovated accommodations are spacious, and many offer balcony views of marina or ocean. Rates are $95 to $145 in season, $75 to $125 off-season.

**Sheraton Bonaventure Resort and Spa,** 250 Racquet Club Rd., Fort Lauderdale, FL 33326 (tel. 305/389-3300, or toll free 800/327-8090, 800/432-3063 in Florida), is by no means a beachfront hotel, but with all they have going here you may decide you don't need the beach. A sprawling resort, Bonaventure has made quite a name for itself among spa fanciers with a very large and elaborate spa with separate facilities for women and men, each including outdoor exercise swimming pools and sundecks, gyms, saunas, steamrooms, whirlpools, hot and cold plunge pools, Swiss needle showers, herbal wraps, facials, beauty and barber shops, and a large staff of doctors, nurses, and sundry assistants. You can go on a special diet here, then work off even more on the hotel's two golf courses and many tennis courts.

Accommodations at the Bonaventure, which is popular as a convention center too, are very handsome, all decked out in the most contemporary colors and furnishings. A huge resort, the hotel (with 504 rooms, 108 suites) is the center of a very large development and has, simply, everything you need to settle in here and never leave for anything. Its restaurants overlook scenic views of the golf course and have won awards; the resort itself is a top-rated, luxury hotel with everything including riding stables; and the spa is considered one of the top 10 in the nation by some raters.

You'll pay $175 to $250 for rooms from December to May, $85 to $160 double in other months; higher for one- or two-bedroom suites.

A block farther north on Fla. A1A is the **Days Inn Lauderdale Surf Hotel,** at 440 Seabreeze Ave., Fort Lauderdale, FL 33316 (tel. 305/462-5555, or toll free 800/325-2525), a recent addition to Days Inn chain of hotels. Days Inn operates other area hotels but this beachfront acquisition is their showpiece. Rates are $99 to $119 in winter, $69 to $89 in summer; higher for suites.

## The Upper Bracket

One of the city's least heralded hotels occupies one of the more interesting beach locations, hidden away in a posh residential district and fringed by a lagoon on one side, the Atlantic on the other. **Lago-Mar Hotel,** 1700 S. Ocean Lane, Fort Lauderdale, FL 33316 (tel. 305/523-6511, or toll free 800/255-5246), is right smack on the sand, one of only two hotels on the south end of the beach with an on-sand location. Built in 1952, this hideaway is now dwarfed by some of the city's most exclusive high-rise residences and surrounded by homes bearing Fort Lauderdale's most prestigious address, Harbor Beach. On a wall near the hotel's patio dining room, newsletters dating back ten years or more chronicle patrons from *Fortune* 500 board chairmen to a diverse collection of celluloid heroes including Eva Maria Saint, Hugh O'Brien, TV star Johnny Carson, and his sidekick Ed McMahon.

Still, you don't feel overpowered here—just gloriously uncrowded, for this is a remote area of the beach most people never see. Sit at poolside or on the long wide strip of sand and watch cruise ships steam by almost close enough to touch as they head for port just around the bend. Especially appealing to families, the resort has a playground and two pools (one just for the youngsters), four tennis courts and a practice area, a putting green and rental sailboats, a masseur, beauty salon, and boutiques. There's a patio dining room for al fresco nibbling, and outdoor snack and patio bars. Once a week there's a cocktail party and cookout.

Rooms come in several different configurations, ranging from hotel rooms to one-bedroom apartments with separate bedrooms to accommodate four. They're all spacious and nicely decorated, with comfortable furniture and fully equipped kitchens. Rates range from $125 to $245. In the summer months, rates drop to $70 to $115.

On the north end of the beach is a strip of sand known as Galt Ocean Mile, reputedly the most expensive mile of land in the world, a piece of silica that changed hands 30 years ago for $29 million—which wouldn't buy one building there today. Now this multi-billion-dollar mile of beach is hidden from view behind a mile of towering condominiums, but you can see the sand from the **Fort Lauderdale Royce Resort,** 4060 Galt Ocean Dr., Fort Lauderdale, FL 33316 (tel. 305/565-6611, or toll free 800/23-ROYCE).

Remodeled regularly, the Royce has 220 rooms, all with balconies overlooking the ocean or city, and all decorated in contemporary muted buff tones. There are lots of little touches here, from valances with matching spreads to a rug in the lobby custom-designed to repeat the tropical print of plush couches. The Royce has a newly remodeled lounge, and an oceanfront restaurant where prices are in the $11 to $18 range for dinners.

Rates are $125 to $140 double in season, and $75 to $120 double in summer.

On the north end of the beach, North Atlantic Boulevard branches off to the right, continuing to run alongside the ocean while Fla. A1A becomes Ocean Boulevard. It sounds complicated, but what you really need to know is that at 2220 N. Atlantic Blvd., Fort Lauderdale, FL 33316 (tel. 305/565-6661, or toll free 800/327-4460 or 800/423-4359 in Florida), is **Ireland's Inn,** one of the city's venerable old properties and possessor of a dining room so popular you'd better be prepared to wait a little even with a reservation.

Over the years, Ireland's has absorbed several smaller hotels in the area and now has a warren of annexes. The basic structure is a seven-story tower plunked right down on the sand. Ireland's has recently refurbished most of its rooms, so this hotel, which was showing its age in places, these days is looking better than ever. While plenty of things were thrown out in the renovation, what Ireland's kept was cleanliness and a special welcoming friendliness that has for years been luring back crowds of faithful followers, many of whom are now known by name from front door to back hall. Ireland's also has two annexes, one on the oceanfront across the street and the other directly on the beach.

In the main inn you can choose between hotel rooms (featuring two extra-long double beds and spreading picture windows), studio apartments (with kitchens), small suites (with sitting room, bedroom, and kitchen), or penthouse suites. Winter rates are $130 to $195 for two, prices drop by about half in summer to $75 to $99. There's also a three-story east lodge with balconied poolside rooms, and a garden lodge on the west side of the street. Rates there range from $65 to $85. Extra persons are charged $12. Rates drop about 50% on May 1.

Far and away Ireland's best-known facility is its oceanfront dining room. Sparked by bright-rust linens, and cane and rattan chairs, the Ocean Room offers a variety of seafood from bay scallops to red snapper, shrimp, and rock lobster tails. The house specialty is country pan-fried chicken (just like mother used to make), with whipped potatoes, gravy, noodles, hot biscuits, and honey, served family style. There are veal preparations, tournedos périgourdine in madeira sauce, plus a coupe Ireland with fresh tangerines and Mandarine Napoleon liqueur. Prices average $11 to $20 for entrées.

**Embassy Suites,** 1100 SE 17th St. Causeway, Fort Lauderdale, FL 33305 (tel. 305/527-2700, or toll free 800/EMBASSY), has whizzed onto the hotel scene to loud huzzahs. Those who adore this chain are those who want all the comforts of a suite at a (this next pun is irresistible) sweet price, with one or two other goodies tossed in for good measure. You get all of that at this new sunset-pink Fort Lauderdale hotel that towers over 17th Street in furbelowed glory. Enter the lobby and you'll find yourself strolling past huge pastel paintings of Everglades flora, flamingoes, and fauna into a massive enclosed courtyard where fountains burble, ducks paddle about scenic streams, and bridges arch over waterfalls. All that water divides this 12-story glass-topped atrium into dozens of cozy nooks, many of them connected to Saluti, the hotel's tempting Italian restaurant, or to a lively adjoining lounge.

There's lots of good news here. Tops among it is free breakfasts—full buffet breakfasts from eggs-any-way to fruit, muffins, danish, juices, pancakes, french toast, you name it. Add to that free cocktails every night. And add to all that, rooms that are not *just* rooms but two-room suites: separate bedroom decorated in pale-wood furnishings and handsome contemporary prints and a matching living room. Tucked into a hallway between the two of them is a complete kitchen with microwave, sink, refrigerator, coffee maker, the works. You'll find televisions in both the bedroom and living room, very handsome decor, and views from your front window out over the tropical splendor of the atrium.

Saluti's, the hotel's restaurant, has its own brick pizza oven and a delectable display of unusual antipasti. Main courses are in the $12 to $18 range for dinner, and feature some unusual preparations like chicken breast stuffed with ricotta and herbs and served with roasted peppers or linguine topped with a sauce of sun-dried tomato, basil-roasted pine nuts, and parmesan.

Quite a handsome new addition to this town, Embassy Suites charges $120 to $190 in winter, $79 to $114 in summer. This chain has also recently opened a similar property on the western side of town at 555 NW 62nd St., Fort Lauderdale, FL 33362 (tel. 305/772-5400). Rates, too, are similar.

## The Moderate Range

Fort Lauderdale owes its popularity not only to sun and sea but also to its long-time reputation as a family resort where dozens of accommodations are priced well below those of similar quality and location in other areas of the state. This city is, in two words, a Scotsman's dream.

By far the highest quality and the largest number of these moderately priced hotels and motels are located in what has become known as "The Strip," that section of sand running from posh Las Olas Boulevard on the south to Sunrise Boulevard on the north. In that mile or so of land bounded by the Intracoastal Waterway on the west and the Atlantic Ocean on the east, there are hundreds of hotel rooms that vary in quality but share one trait dear to the heart of wallet-watchers: reasonable prices.

While beachfront hotels in this area have rates in the $100 to $300 bracket, smaller properties without restaurants or bars, and located a block or two back from the ocean, are as much as 60% cheaper all year, with summer-season rates well inside the $30 to $50 moderate category.

One of the city's best-kept hotel secrets is **Riverside Hotel,** 620 E. Las Olas Blvd., Fort Lauderdale, FL 33301 (tel. 305/467-0671, or toll free 800/325-3280, in Florida 800/421-7666). Restored with considerable style a few years ago, this 50-year-old hotel now sports a European look—lots of dark woods, French prints, and a few antique pieces—blended with an alluring tropical ambience—wicker furnishings in the plant-bedecked lobby, tile floors, soft pastels. Built when travelers demanded space, Riverside continues to provide large rooms, some of them suites, and has a downright devastatingly beautiful cabaña and pool area right at the edge of scenic New River, just a few doors from historic Stranahan House. Many of the faithful have been coming here for ages and have staked out particular rooms and dining room tables—it's that kind of place. There's a working fireplace in the lounge, one of the few in the city, and the dining room is especially popular on Sunday and during art shows and other street events. Small and select, there is rarely room at this inn but you can try. Rates are $90 single or double in winter, $75 in summer.

In our book (now there's a pun!), **Bayshore Waterfront Apartments,** at 341 N. Birch Rd., Fort Lauderdale, FL 33304 (tel. 305/463-2821), is as lovely and tranquil a spot as you'll find anywhere in town. Nestled along the Intracoastal, the small hotel has a private, clubby look with a long dock stretching behind the property. Step through the front doorway and you're in the middle of an airy foyer leading into a tiny path that wends its way through the garden. Beyond gleams the Intracoastal, sapphire in the afternoon sun. Neatly trimmed hedges are shadowed by tall palms, there's a pool and patio overlooking the water.

Rooms are spacious and beautifully decorated, many of them in Italian provincial furniture with plush wall-to-wall carpeting and floor-to-ceiling drapes in soft shades of green or gold. Small kitchens in one-bedroom apartments are completely equipped right down to wine glasses.

The Bayshore offers hotel rooms, efficiencies, and one- and two-bedroom apartments, some with balconies overlooking the Intracoastal. Winter rates range from $60 to $109.

As the waterway jogs one block farther from the beach, at 435 Bayshore Dr., Fort Lauderdale, FL 33304 (tel. 305/564-3261), you'll find **Casa Glamaretta,** an imposing three-story, tropical-pink building. Mediterranean influences begin at its red Spanish tile roof and continue through a wide arched entrance that opens onto an airy roofed foyer. Step inside and framed before you like a postcard is a sparkling fountain spilling into a hexagonal pool bordered in tiny stalks of bamboo. Beyond is the wide expanse of blue waterway.

Running along one side of the building is a swimming pool shaded by palms, and shuffleboard court, and lounge chairs lined up along the Casa's 80-foot docks. Inside, the decor is simple but comfortable, with rooms done in soft pastels. Rates range from $95 to $125 in winter. In summer, rates drop to $45 to $85.

The **Worthington,** 543 N. Birch Rd., Fort Lauderdale, FL 33304 (tel. 305/563-6819), is a small motel with several nice apartments, large enough for a family, plus some efficiencies and motel rooms. A pretty pool is the focus here, and you don't have to go far from it to pop a top: There's a big refrigerator outside for guests to keep their goodies cold. Rooms are furnished in bright colors, and have color TVs, refrigerators and direct-dial phones. Winter rates are $50 to $70; in summer $35 to $45.

Next door, on the corner of Terramar Street and Birch Road, the **Sea Château,** at 555 N. Birch Rd., Fort Lauderdale, FL 33304 (tel. 305/566-8331), is a two-story manse that's added some nifty inn-y touches. Now you'll find puffy comforters, ruffled pillow shams, jewel-tone carpets, lots of ruffles and ribbons, even tea services in every room à la British B&Bs. That's a radical departure from most Fort Lauderdale motels, which tend to be more serviceable than ornamented. Burgundy trim outside is reflected in a marble-floored lobby where guests settle into high-backed wicker chairs and chatter away during the free danish-and-coffee break that's a popular feature each winter morning. Five spacious efficiency apartments occupy the building's corners with 14 hotel rooms tucked in between. Floor-to-ceiling windows overlook a swimming pool and flower-bedecked central courtyard. Rooms have walk-in closets and marble bathroom floors and windowsills; extra-large efficiencies have Bahama beds (so the rooms are living rooms during the day) and compact, fully equipped kitchens. A tiny fountain tinkles in the corner of the patio and the resort's artful lighting once won it a magazine award. Rates in winter season are $45 to $70, dropping in summer to $30 to $35.

Those prepared to do their own laundry and maid work can save money at the **Five Coins Inn,** 4051 N. Ocean Blvd., Fort Lauderdale, FL 33308 (tel. 305/565-0541). Spacious and simply but nicely decorated rooms here are $50 to $70 in winter season. There are coin laundry machines in the motel, plenty of free parking under the building, a pool and spacious lobby full of plump couches and comfortable chairs, and a free coffee machine available morning to night.

Rooms with two double beds have paneled walls and there are efficiencies and studio apartments with compact kitchens. In summer, rates drop to $150 to $175 a week for hotel rooms.

## A YOUTH HOSTEL

A small Fort Lauderdale hotel near the beach is now a member of the American Youth Hostel program and offers rooms for $12 per person per night. It's the **Sol y Mar,** 2939 Vistamar St., Fort Lauderdale, FL 33304 (tel. 305/566-1023). This 36-bed property garnered the AYH's highest rating and has a pool.

## HOTELS IN SURROUNDING COMMUNITIES

Fort Lauderdale has been around a little longer than its neighbors and has built up the largest following of loyal return visitors, but several smaller towns in the area have some attractive hotels and motels in all price ranges. We've picked out a few in each city.

### Pompano Beach

**Sun Castle,** at 1380 S. Ocean Blvd., Pompano Beach, FL 33062 (tel. 305/941-7700, or toll free 800/228-7105), is a favorite family resort clustered around a sparkling free-form pool and wide lawns dotted with palms. The spacious rooms are decorated in lively tropical colors and have wide windows overlooking the grounds. The Sun Castle's restaurant has long been an area favorite, and has a lounge with regular entertainment. On five beautiful acres are tennis courts, dock, and a putting green. From February to April rates range from $71 to $88 double for hotel rooms, $76 to $100 for efficiency apartments. In other months, rates drop about 50%.

Sun Castle Resort also operates the **Ocean Ranch Hotel,** 1110 S. Ocean Blvd., Pompano Beach, FL 33062 (tel. 305/941-7100, or toll free 800/843-5526). Ocean Ranch has a variety of accommodations, many with balconies facing the resort's strip of beach. There's a pool for splashing, a hot tub and whirlpool, exercise room, sauna, putting green, volleyball court, and game room. When hunger strikes, there's a restaurant, lounge, and beachfront patio bar. If you're in search of golf or tennis games, the hotel can arrange those for you at nearby facilities. Rates in peak winter season are $66 to $82 for hotel rooms or efficiencies, dropping in summer to $41 and up.

**Sea Garden Beach and Tennis Resort,** 615 N. Ocean Blvd., Pompano Beach, FL 33062 (tel. 305/943-6200, or toll free 800/327-8920 except in Florida), is a lovely waterfront resort with a very popular restaurant and lounge. Many of the attractive rooms have refrigerators, and there are efficiencies and one- or two-bedroom apartments. Out in front (across Fla. A1A) the ocean laps at a 250-foot strip of private beach, and scattered about under the palms on six acres of manicured lawns are two pools, a putting green, and seven tennis courts. The Sea Garden's pretty dining room has tiny twinkling lights and glowing candles, lots of windows for an ocean view, and features fine home-cooking with dinners in the $10 to $15 range. The resort charges $80 to $120 from mid-December to mid-April, $45 to $165 in other months. Suites are priced higher.

Howard Johnson's and Holiday Inn both have large hotels in the area. The **Holiday Inn** is at 1350 S. Ocean Blvd., Pompano Beach, FL 33062 (tel. 305/941-7300, or toll free 800/465-4329), with grounds extending from the ocean across Fla. A1A to the Spanish River, and accommodations in rooms, efficiencies, and one-bedroom apartments, all beautifully redecorated. There are three tennis courts with teaching pro on-site, two heated pools, and a putting green, plus a boat dock on the Spanish River. Rates are $110 to $155 from mid-December to April 16, $74 to $96 in other months. Kitchen units and cottages are priced higher.

**Howard Johnson's Motor Lodge** is opposite the beach at 9 N. Pompano Beach Blvd., Pompano Beach, FL 33062 (tel. 305/781-1300, or toll free 800/654-2000). It offers 104 large rooms (a few with kitchens) and a pool. Rates are $98 to $140 from February to mid-April, $46 to $92 in other months.

**Lighthouse Cove Resort,** 1406 N. Ocean Blvd., Pompano Beach, FL 33062 (tel. 305/941-3410), is an oceanfront high-rise with rooms, studio efficiencies, and one-bedroom apartments, many of them overlooking the sea. There are two pools, a patio bar, and tennis courts. Two people pay rates of $145 to $195 double in high season (from February to mid-April), from $80 to $150 in most other months.

A spa? Certainly. **Palm-Aire Resort and Spa** at 2501 Palm-Aire Dr. N., Pompano Beach, FL 33069 (tel. 305/972-3300, or toll free 800/307-4960), will house you in luxury, pummel you, cover you with avocado masks, pamper you with facials, and diet off whatever flab remains with minimally caloric dinners that actually taste good! One of the world's best-known spas, Palm-Aire is frequented by stars, politicians, and many of the world's most famous faces (including Elizabeth Taylor). It's the focal point of a massive development that includes a gorgeous swimming pool and all kinds of sports; they'll even see to it that you get to the beach, which is only a few miles away. Rates are $115 to $200 in summer, $218 to $239 in winter. A year-round spa program is available, and spa suites are priced higher.

## Deerfield Beach

Private balconies are a special feature of some rooms at **Deerpath Apartment Motel,** 714 SE 20th Ave. (which is Fla. A1A), Deerfield Beach, FL 33441 (tel. 305/427-9223), an attractive resort just a few yards from the ocean. There's a soothing view out over the pool and prettily manicured lawns and grounds. Hotel rooms, efficiencies, and one-bedroom apartments, all large and cheerfully decorated in bright colors, are available at rates ranging from $375 to $410 a week in winter season, about $220 to $250 in summer months.

**Berkshire Beach Club,** 500 N. Ocean Blvd., Deerfield Beach, FL 33441 (tel. 305/428-1000), was once known as St. Tropez but changed its name when it became a time-sharing establishment. There are definite elements of St. Tropez here anyway, from the shining white building to the beach just steps away from your door. A tiny place cooled by sea breezes, Berkshire Beach Club has one- and two-bedroom apartments with tiny kitchens tucked away in corners. Since its conversion, the resort has been renovated and now features quite contemporary accommodations that are kept neat and clean. There's also a heated pool, hot tub, barbecue grill, and shuffleboard. Berkshire Beach Club charges range from $70 to $100 for a one-bedroom apartment in the spring, summer, and fall months, $110 to $150 from mid-December through Easter.

## Hallandale/Hollywood

The king of Hallandale and Hollywood Beach is the **Diplomat Resort and Country Club,** at 3515 S. Ocean Dr., Hollywood Beach, FL 33022 (tel. 305/457-8111, or toll free 800/327-1212). The largest hotel in the area (1,009 units), the massive Diplomat towers over its beach-strip neighbors, and for entertainment towers over many a Miami Beach hotel as well. Everybody who is anybody, now or ever, probably has appeared at the Diplomat, which has hosted a dizzying array of the nation's most famous stars. The hotel's elegant Celebrity Room is one of the top French dining rooms in the county (prices, $18 to $35 and up), and in the Tack Room and in Café Cristal you'll see the superstars.

Everything's very contemporary at the Diplomat, even more so now after a top-to-toe revamp in late 1988. Now the most advanced fire-detection equipment in the nation is in place at this hotel, which has updated all its rooms and public areas. Outside, a smashingly beautiful swimming pool, complete with waterfalls, swim-up bar, and towering artificial rocks makes the beach beyond pale in significance. Across the road on Diplomat Parkway is the Diplomat Country Club golf course and still more hotel rooms.

Winter rates are $145 to $200. In summer, the rates drop to $45 to $90.

**Howard Johnson Hollywood Beach Resort Inn,** 2501 N. Ocean Dr., Hollywood Beach, FL 33019 (tel. 305/925-1411, or toll free 800/654-2000), has a 242-room recently renovated hotel on the ocean at Taft Street that occupies a block of ocean frontage. An 11-story beauty, the hotel has all the usual comforts of this chain, plus free parking, a pool, free beach lounges, and satellite television programs free. Rates are $105 to $135 in winter and $55 to $80 in summer.

The **Enchanted Isle Resort,** 1691 Surf Rd., Hollywood Beach, FL 33022 (tel. 305/922-1508), has apartments both on and across from the ocean. You'll find refrigerators and complete kitchens in the studios and apartments. There's a heated pool too. From mid-December to April, rates are $113 to $157, dropping in the summer season to $74 to $90.

## FORT LAUDERDALE'S RESTAURANTS

Fort Lauderdale is said to have more restaurants per capita than any other city in the country. Certainly there's no doubt you can munch yourself into a catatonic state here in short order. So dedicated is Fort Lauderdale to elevating dining to an art form that the opening of a new restaurant here is tantamount to a presidential visit. At last count there were no fewer than six restaurant critics in this small town. In Fort Lauderdale, recommending a good dining spot isn't difficult, but narrowing the choices down to something short of a doctoral dissertation is. Here goes.

### Continental/American

A beautiful new, but old, addition to Fort Lauderdale's roster of dining rooms is now called **Chart House,** 301 SW Third Ave. (tel. 523-0177). When we saw two old stone houses moldering away alongside New River years ago, we hoped someone would work a miracle on them. Someone did—Anthony Gillette by name, a talented and creative man, joined the two small two-story homes and outfitted them in antiques, plants, brass, and etched glass to create this truly beautiful restaurant that's now part of the Chart House chain. If you have a friend with a boat or have an inclination to rent one, the most spectacular way to arrive is by water, up the river. That way the two homes, their surrounding palm trees, and dramatically lighted front lawn loom up out of the blackness like Victorian mirages. Chart House has been put together by a master hand that spent quite a lot of money on both the interior and exterior of these homes that date back to the earliest days of Fort Lauderdale.

Even better, the food is top-quality. Top-price, but top-quality. You dine on very good preparations focusing on seafood, but prime rib, steaks, lobster, shrimp teriyaki and the like are on the menu here. Vegetables are fresh from the produce counter and lightly cooked, sauces are creamy delights, wines are top-quality, the views are beautiful, and the service quite professional. For that you will pay $13 to $22 for à la carte dinner entrées, which are likely to ring out at $35 to $40 a person. Dinner hours are 5:30 to 10pm daily, closing an hour later on weekends.

When Pier Sixty-Six spends money, it spends money beautifully, as you will see when you take a look at this handsomely redecorated hotel's star, **Windows on the Green,** 2301 SE 17th St. Causeway (tel. 525-6666), now Fort Lauderdale's most talked-about restaurant. A strolling violinist entertains in this understated, bilevel restaurant as you dine on beautifully presented nouvelle cuisine—perhaps cold almond soup topped with toasted almonds and threads of saffron, mushrooms in puff pastry, lobster, caviar and cream atop pasta, sea scallops à l'orange, and a finale of chocolate truffles. Elegant, definitely. Expensive? Very. At least $50 a person, and very likely more. You do pay for pleasure these days but it's often worth it. Windows on the Green, which gets its name from a huge, two-story-tall bank of tinted windows overlooking the hotel's tropical greenery, is open from 6:30 to 10pm daily except Monday.

**Le Dome of the Four Seasons** occupies a 12th-floor penthouse aerie atop the Four Seasons Condominium just off Las Olas Boulevard at 333 Sunset Dr. (tel. 463-3303, or toll free 800/330-1721). Flickering candles and subtle piano music set the stage inside while you gaze out over the lights of Fort Lauderdale twinkling far below. Service is dignified and exceptionally efficient, with waiters in formal attire moving effortlessly through the intricacies of service and tableside preparation.

The main dining area is a large room sparkling with pink linens, fresh flowers, and French provincial furniture; two others are somewhat smaller and more intimate, with high-backed chairs and small cozy alcoves. Tables by tall windows are coveted, so reservations here, as in most restaurants in the winter season, are vital.

Raves hereabouts go to the restaurant's crusty bread, which arrives hot and home-baked from the oven, and two house specialties, vichyssoise and steak Diane. Dinner entrée prices average $16 to $20. Hours are 5 to 10pm daily, 11:30am to 2pm weekdays for lunch.

**The Down Under,** 3000 E. Oakland Park Blvd. (tel. 563-4123), the first of three area restaurants owned and operated by Leonce Picot and Al Kocab, has won *Travel/Holiday* awards and a four-star rating consistently for years. To say the decor is eclectic is certainly to understate, but what other way is there to describe a mélange of antiques, open wood beams, wood floors, and a proliferation of plants in a prime-time setting alongside the Intracoastal Waterway?

At last count there were 63 items on the menu, but there may be more even as you read. In any case, you can spend ages just savoring the selections, ranging from oysters Muscovite topped with fresh Sevruga caviar, duck confit, Florida crab cakes, stone crabs, a carpetbag steak stuffed with herb-marinated oysters and sauce diablo, beef Wellington, even Idaho trout. Open for lunch from 11:30am to 2pm weekdays, for dinner from 6 to 11pm daily, Down Under is likely to ring up a bill in the $60 to $70 range for two.

**Ireland's Inn,** 2220 N. Atlantic Blvd. (tel. 564-2331), has been around for ages. Our friend Merry is something of a gourmet cook and, thanks to her well-traveled and well-fed husband, Bob, she's also frequently a gourmet diner reputed to have dined in 25 of the nation's 26 greatest restaurants. Nevertheless, she clucks happily at the mere thought of Ireland's country-fried chicken, a gravy-and-biscuits house specialty served family style to tables-full of equally happily clucking diners.

Ireland's cookery leans toward that kind of down-home simplicity spiced with the occasional touch of something Floridian-ly exotic like conch chowder or Florida pompano. Lamb or pork chops are on the menu, along with Virginia ham steak and veal topped with artichoke and crab. There's entertainment for dancing until the wee hours at the adjoining Edgewater Lounge (which adequately describes its view too). Entrée prices, which include homemade bread, salad, potato, and entrée, fall in the $10 to $15 range, with some of the more exotic specialties rising to $18 or so.

A long, long all-you-can-glurp raw bar is a favorite focus at the **Golden Spike,** 6000 N. Federal Hwy. (tel. 491-6000). Upstairs is plush, downstairs is themey, and there's a huge salad bar and matching dessert selection. In between, there are good beef and seafood dishes for prices in the $12 to $19 range. It's open from 5 to 10pm daily, plus 11:30am to 2pm for Sunday brunch.

**Yesterday's,** 3001 E. Oakland Park Blvd. (tel. 561-4400), offers pleasant dining overlooking the Intracoastal Waterway for prices in the $15 to $28 range for semi à la carte dinners. Try beef Oscar, lamb chops, or the coquilles St-Jacques. In summer there's an inexpensive prix-fixe sunset dinner, and the restaurant has menus in several languages—even braille. It's open 5 to 11pm daily for dinner, later on weekends.

Someone with more than a little imagination has capitalized on the location of **Runway 84,** 332 Fla. 84 (tel. 467-8484), a mile or so from the Fort Lauderdale/Hollywood International Airport. Tiny runway-ish lights glitter at the entrance. A huge red-and-silver re-creation of an airliner cabin forms a cocktail lounge rimmed in tiny rectangular windows through which you can gaze down on the lights of New York, et al. Waiters are decked out in white shirts with epaulets bearing the three gold stripes of a first officer, no less.

Plenty of seafood options are available here, including several different preparations of shrimp, plus scallops, lemon sole, a combination of scungilli diavolo and fried calamari, seafood platters, and Boston scrod. All the usual beef specialties from New York sirloin to prime rib and filet mignon are available. An Italian orientation is evident as veal and pastas occupy a prominent place on the list. Dinner prices, which range from $12 to $23, are quite reasonable when you consider that they include a substantial antipasto, a platter of steamed mussels in a red sauce, salad, spaghetti or potato, dessert, and several different kinds of breads, including an unusual marbelized brown-and-white creation. Hours are 4:30 to 10pm Tuesday through Thursday, an hour later Friday through Sunday; lunch Tuesday through Friday 12 to 3pm; the lounge is open to 2am.

Theme restaurants can be fun, and certainly **95th Bomb Group,** at 2500 NW 62nd St. (tel. 491-4595), is a laugh. Here you dine on steaks or seafood in an aeronautical atmosphere sparked by the small private airfield just beyond the windows of this trendy restaurant. Inside, the exploits of the 95th are detailed along with lots of other aeronautical memorabilia. Prices are in the $10 to $30 range for dinner and the restaurant is open from 4:30 to 10pm daily and for Sunday brunch from 11am to 3pm.

**Charlie's Crab,** 3000 NE 32nd Ave. (tel. 561-4800), kin to the Palm Beach eatery of the same name, is tucked in alongside the Intracoastal Waterway just south of the Oakland Park Bridge. A very popular place, Charlie's Crab specializes in seafood and continental cooking with lots of innovative options, at dinner prices in the $17 to $25 range. You can sit inside in attractive, intimate surroundings or outside on an open, roofed patio alongside the water. There may be entertainment in the lounge, but the best-loved entertainment here comes from the huge yachts that cruise past on the Intracoastal or pull up at the dock to disgorge hungry boaters. Charlie's Crab is open for lunch from 11:30am to 2:30pm and for dinner from 5 to 10pm daily, later on weekends. Charlie's waterside location makes it a popular place, so reservations are wise.

To our way of thinking, there is almost nothing Burt Reynolds could do wrong. His newest venture, **Burt & Jack's,** Berth 23 in Port Everglades, Fort Lauderdale (tel. 522-5225), confirms our suspicion. It's the occupant of a quite handsomely designed building that is a study in Mediterranean architecture: a roaring fire in several fireplaces, fringed hanging lamps, tiny shutters, a pianist playing softly, tiled floors, arches, candlelight, tables outside in an artfully lighted patio.

Burt's menu is small but significant. He's not attempting to mingle strange flavors or create bizarre combinations, but has opted instead for straightforward preparation of straightforward dishes. So you'll find double-cut prime rib of beef that nearly fills the plate, an equally thick baked veal chop topped with a creamy sauce, and for really big spenders, a $27 order of stone crab claws or a whole three-pound Maine lobster. Accompanying dinner is a large baked potato or a house specialty of hash browns for two or an order of large and very skillfully prepared fried onion rings.

Burt & Jack's does not make for a bargain-basement evening—entrées are $13 to $25 à la carte, but figure about $30 to $40 a person for dinner and drinks—but it does make for a very pleasant one in a beautiful atmosphere that could only be improved by the presence of BR himself. Hours are 5 to 10pm daily, closing an hour later on weekends.

**Frankie's,** on the Intracoastal, 3333 NE 32nd Ave. (tel. 566-7853), occupies prime real estate alongside the Intracoastal Waterway just north of the Oakland Park Boulevard bridge. You may have to search a little to find Frankie's, but you won't be alone in your search. This handsomely decorated restaurant has been a favorite in Fort Lauderdale for quite a number of years now, and has a regular following of patrons who swear by the pastas, steaks, seafood, and fine continental preparations featured here. Plants, low lighting, and formal service prevail at Frankie's, which also provides a stunning view of yachts chugging by on the Intracoastal. You'll pay about $15 to $25 for entrées, and the restaurant is open from 5:30 to 11pm daily. In the summer months Frankie's doesn't serve lunch and is usually closed on Sunday, but those dates vary, so if you're here in summer, give them a call.

## French/Swiss

The look of **La Ferme,** 1601 E. Sunrise Blvd. (tel. 764-0987), is a long way from a farm, with imported porcelain chandeliers, mirrors, lace tablecloths. Except for its farm-fresh ingredients, La Ferme's connection to anything back-woodsy is minimal. Sophisticated cuisine and a clientele to match are the bywords of this small and simple restaurant on busy Federal Highway. Braised sweetbreads in a madeira sauce, delicate veal preparations, intriguing pâtés, feuilleté of Dover sole with tarragon sauce, and a distressingly tempting pastry cart are just some of the carefully concocted offerings whipped up by La Ferme's master chef Henri Terrier, whose wife you'll meet at the front door. Everything works here including the efficient staff, so you're likely to remain happy even after you've paid the bill, which will probably run about $14 to $25 per person. La Ferme is open from 5:30 to 10pm Tuesday through Sunday (closed August).

Jean-Pierre, owner, operator, chef, and dynamo of **The Left Bank,** 214 SE Sixth Ave. (tel. 462-5376), has more energy than anyone should, and uses it to produce culinary treats that have made this one of the city's favorite restaurants. Jean-Pierre moves at 78 r.p.m. yet never seems to be rushing as he whips up delectable flaming tableside creations ranging from duckling with an amaretto apricot sauce to steak aux trois poivres with black, white, and green peppercorns and lots of cream and brandy. You can meet personable Jean-Pierre at his restaurant any evening from 6 to 11pm, to midnight on weekends. Entrée prices at the Left Bank, a very cozy restaurant, which is indeed on the left bank of New River, are in the $14 to $20 range.

If you look closely at the last postcard you got from Switzerland, you'll see a replica of **Café de Genève,** 1519 S. Andrews Ave. (tel. 522-8928), on it somewhere. Or is Café de Genève a replica of those homey little Swiss cafés? You can't be sure because this cuddly little spot with red-checked curtains and pictures of the snowy alpine slopes is as close as you'll get to those cool climes in flatland Florida. There's taste of the cantons here too, from the cheese fondues to creamy minced veal and mushrooms, home-brewed bean and pea soups, the Fendant or Neuchâtel wine, the fresh-from-the-oven pastries, and the congenial good humor of a pleasant Swiss-efficient staff. Most prices fall in the $10 to $15 range. It's open from 11:30am to 2:30pm on weekdays and from 5:30 to 10pm daily.

**Le Café de Paris,** 715 E. Las Olas Blvd. (tel. 467-2900), has been a favorite in Fort Lauderdale for many years, thanks to Swiss owner Louis Fermati's deft hand in the kitchen and shrewd assessment of popular taste. There's a cheery, crowded bistro atmosphere, lots of Paris posters, red and blue awnings, dining on two floors, and a generally lusty good humor that somehow keeps you going back even when you know the Gallic confusion means you'll have to wait, reservation or not. There's a long selection of entrées with all those favorites that keep Americans devoted to French preparations: steak au poivre, veal Cordon Bleu, onion soup, great luncheon omelets, tournedos béarnaise. A money-saving tip: Check the left corner of the menu where there's a tiny list of popular full-course dinners several dollars cheaper than you'd pay à la carte. The café is open daily from 11:30am to 2:30pm for lunch, except Sunday when the restaurant is open from 5:30 to 10pm, the same dinner hours it maintains daily. Expect a bill of $35 to $40 for two.

**La Bonne Crêpe,** 815 E. Las Olas Blvd. (tel. 761-1515), may be tiny but its menu is awash with crispy crêpes of all variety—41 of them, in fact. A delightful way to break the burger habit, La Bonne Crêpe is a good choice for lunch for two reasons: First, crêpes don't make you feel like Two-Ton Tessie all the rest of the day, and second, La Bonne Crêpe is only open for dinner on Friday and Saturday evenings. These crêpes, understand, are not the rolled-up sausages some restaurants try to foist off on you. These are wide and high, towering regally over fillings that range from entree crêpes of, say, chicken and mushrooms in a creamy béchamel sauce to dessert crêpes wrapped around fresh strawberries in whipped cream or bananas, ice cream, and chocolate sauce. Prices fall in the $5 to $10 range for crêpes and several other selections, sans crêpes, are also available. La Bonne Crêpe is open from 11am to 4pm Monday through Saturday, from 6 to 10pm on Friday and Saturday only; closed Sunday.

**Newman's La Bonne Auberge,** 4300 N. Federal Hwy. (tel. 491-5522), has stayed around long enough to survive the fierce competition in this city, testimony to its carefully prepared French food. Holding down the corner of a strip shopping center, La Bonne Auberge's look doesn't seem quite to fit the description implied by its name, but inside a cozy intimate atmosphere prevails. On the menu you'll find an interesting blend of Italian and French specialties ranging from pasta primavera and fettuccine with smoked salmon to seafood roulade and chicken and broccoli crêpes. Dinner prices fall in the $15 to $25 range for entrées. Friendly owners will welcome you to their bonne auberge from 11:30am to 2:30pm weekdays, and from 5:30 to 10:30pm daily for dinner.

## Italian

Sooner or later you'll see everyone in town at **Paesano,** 1301 E. Las Olas Blvd. (tel. 467-3266), a cheery informal spot where owner Mario Spinaci will as likely as not break into a quick aria and where you'll feel equally comfortable in jeans or evening dress. A handsome, charming devil from Rimini, Mario delights in basic tasty foods and hearty wines, loves what he does, and infects his staff of countrymen with his own incredibly consistent good humor. The look here runs to casual chic with lots of candles, crystal chandeliers, wine stashed in every nook and cranny. Come here for the comfortably elegant atmosphere and great rib-sticking pasta in the $11 to $22 range, and some well-prepared specialties like veal Sinatra (a mélange of spinach, prosciutto, and veal), tortellini in red or white sauce, mussels marinara, or wonderful (!) swordfish. Open with southern Florida's best fried mozzarella, baked clams, or spaghetti primavera, and be sure to ask Mario what's cooking today that's not on the menu. For that matter, ask Mario anything. Ask him to sing. Paesano's is open from 11:30am to 2:30pm weekdays and 5:30 to 10:30pm daily. There's now a second Paesano of striking architectural design at 3850 N. Federal Hwy., Lighthouse Point (tel. 942-0006), with the same dinner hours; no lunch.

Just down the street at 609 E. Las Olas Blvd. is **Il Giardino** (tel. 763-3733), a study in contemporary decor creating an elegant garden atmosphere, a burbling fountain, tall plants sparkling with tiny Italian lights, candles, and crisp pink linens. Very elegant.

We admit to an addiction to the restaurant's frutta di mare, but there are seafood and angel-hair pasta, plus a raft of delicately prepared veal, chicken, and seafood dishes for your perusal. Prices are in the $12 to $17 range. Lunch hours are 11:30am to 2:30pm Monday to Friday, and 6 to 10:30pm daily for dinner.

It's always heartening to see someone work very hard to learn the restaurant business, then go off to create his own very successful dining spot. That's just what happened at **Primavera,** 840 E. Oakland Park Blvd. (tel. 564-6363), opened by Paolo Peretti, formerly a charming mainstay of Paesano's restaurant. After many years there, Paolo took the plunge and joined partner Carlo Dellapiane to create a sleekly handsome restaurant that has been SRO nearly from the day it opened and won some statewide recognition in its first year of operation.

Decked out in formal wear, Paolo now presides over a tranquilly contemporary setting of soft sea green and creamy beiges, glittering glass, and sophisticated subtlety. A few of each evening's tempting specialties are tantalizingly displayed near the entrance to give you an idea what super-chef Aldo Rabottini has in store for you. A recent crowd-pleaser was grilled shrimp stuffed with crab and topped with a cloud-white cream sauce. So creative is this chef that you'll find some elegant new creation on the menu every month, while all the old favorites, like mouthwatering pastas and marvelously inventive veal and seafood creations, remain there to tempt you still further. Prices fall in a reasonable $13 to $30 range for dinner entrees served from 5:30 to 10pm daily except Monday.

Right up there at the top of the list in both prestige and price is **Casa Vecchia,** 209 N. Birch Rd. (tel. 463-7575), one of the trio of area restaurants owned by *Travel/Holiday* award winners Leonce Picot and Al Kocab. Newest of the duo's stable, Casa Vecchia is a beautiful old home (that's what Casa Vecchia means, by the way) once owned by a member of the Ponds Cold Cream family.

Painted a dusty rose, the rambling old house has been altered as little as possible, so you can still revel in tile floors, a sweeping view of the Intracoastal Waterway, and elaborate formal gardens from whence the chef plucks herbs. Inside, you can dine in rooms holding a single table for four or six or in various larger rooms scattered around the house. Every one of them is different and somehow Picot and partner have managed to take improbably eclectic elements (like a grape cluster lamp) and turn them into an integrated whole considerably greater than its parts. There are plants everywhere—one room is practically a greenhouse—and the food is northern Italian, a creamy cuisine considerably more delicate than the tomato-based offerings hailing from elsewhere in Italy.

The menu is à la carte and the food is superb and expensive. You might begin with carpaccio (paper-thin slices of raw beef with piquant mayonnaise) or breaded oysters wrapped in bacon and sautéed with chives. Move on to homemade cappelli d'angelo, feather-light angel's hair pasta with a light tomato cream sauce, peas, and prosciutto. Or try Idaho trout sautéed with pignoli.

Open daily from 6 to 10:30pm, Casa Vecchia is likely to present you with a bill in the $50 to $70 range for two, more if you select some of the restaurant's more exotic wine selections.

**La Perla,** 1818 E. Sunrise Blvd. (tel. 765-1950), is quite a diminutive restaurant, but one that has a reputation as large as its quarters are small. Pastas are made right here and the cloud-like gnocchi in gorgonzola sauce is to die for. Spinach ziti with cream, sweet peas, mushrooms, and prosciutto is another winner here. Prices are in the $12 to $17 range for dinner, and hours are 5 to 10:30pm daily, later on weekends.

**Ponte Vecchio,** 2500 E. Commercial Blvd. (tel. 772-4138), has won praise around town for its top-quality Italian cooking. Gnocchi al Napolitana wins special kudos for authenticity and downright scrumptiousness and pollo al scarpariello is equally ethereal. A simple but cozy dining room, Ponte Vecchio bridges the hunger gap from 5 to 11pm daily with entrées priced in the $10 to $15 range.

## Cajun

A newcomer to Fort Lauderdale arrived a couple of years ago and has managed to keep 'em pouring in for long enough to be considered a serious contender in the ever-changing sweepstakes of Fort Lauderdale restaurants. That newcomer is **Lagniappe Cajun House,** 200 W. Broward Blvd. (tel. 467-7500), the first Cajun cookery in the city. Lagniappe (pronounced "lan-yap" and meaning "a little something extra") is quite an attractive restaurant in an Orleans-style development and has made clever use of a high ceiling by rimming it with a balcony reminiscent of the famed balconies of New Orleans.

Under that balcony, whirling paddle fans, and lots of plants, you dine on such Cajun specialties as crayfish étouffée, blackened redfish, twice-cooked duck, seafood gumbo, jambalaya. Lively spicy flavors characterize evening meals and lunches, while Saturday-morning breakfast features beignets and New Orleans chickory coffee. There's often Dixieland jazz bands or a blues singer for entertainment. Prices are in the $13 to $18 range for dinner entrées, and hours are 11:30am to 3pm for lunch weekdays and 6 to 11pm daily for dinner.

## Seafood

**Rustic Inn,** 4331 Ravenswood Rd. (tel. 584-1637), is on a back road that at the restaurant's entrance becomes a dirt road. This sort of introduces this rustic spot that looks as if it might collapse in a muddle of weathered wood and nautical junque but hasn't done so for the 20 years or more it's been holding together here beside an ocean-bound canal.

This is the place to head when you have no intention of donning anything more formal than reasonably clean jeans and a pair of sandals, which comes close to being overdressed here. That's as it should be too, for the house specialty is a big, brimming bowl of garlic-tinged steamed blue crabs, presented with a mallet, bib, and yesterday's newspaper. They are messy but worth the pounding and digging. If you don't want to bother, you'll find oysters, shrimp, scallops, lobster, stone crab, fish filets, linguine with red seafood sauce, and many other seafood treats on the menu. The finale should be a piece of the restaurant's authentic key lime pie. You'll pay $12 to $17 for most dinners, which include salad and potato, too. Hours are 11:30am to 3pm Tuesday through Friday and 5 to 11pm daily, opening and closing a bit earlier on Sunday.

Perhaps the only thing better than good seafood is good and *cheap* seafood. That is what has been created by Shells, a newcomer chain of restaurants that has taken Florida by storm. Here in Fort Lauderdale, **Shells** occupies an under-the-pines setting in an otherwise nondescript strip of shops at 1630 Oakland Park Blvd. (tel. 565-0425). Do not come here for tony atmosphere, for you will find nothing fancier than a couple of nets and some boxes piled high to create room dividers. Paper plates, plastic cutlery, that's the look of it, but who cares when you can down a dozen oysters for less than $2, lobster and stone crabs for $10, and some excellent seafood-and-pasta combinations for about $8. Seafood is simply but well prepared here and often served with jacketed new potatoes and a simple salad. Beer by the pitcher, wine by the glass, and customers by the jillion. Shells is open from 5 to 10pm daily, to 11pm Friday and Saturday.

There's always a wait at **Sea Watch,** 6002 N. Ocean Blvd. (tel. 781-2200), but who cares in this rustic oceanside setting filled with plants, wicker peacock chairs, nautical memorabilia, and brass? An hour or so in the upstairs bar under the paddle fans, or outside listening to the waves roar, is super even if you *never* get to dinner downstairs. Bouillabaisse is the best thing on the menu, but the rest of the seafood fare runs a close second and the atmosphere's somehow both boisterous and subdued. It's pretty, good, and fun, the pumpernickel bread is sensational, and the prices are moderate— $10 to $25 for dinner. It's open from 11:30am to 3:30pm for lunch, and 5 to 10pm for dinner.

**Fisherman Restaurant,** 3880 N. Federal Hwy. (tel. 566-2002), is a pretty place on which the owners have spent quite a lot of money over the years. Seafood is now grilled over mesquite, the new fad in open-fire cooking, and the menu has branched out to include a large number of nonseafood items from pork chops with apples and prunes to veal in a roquefort sauce.

You dine in a comfortable and attractive dining room with banquettes lining the walls and the nautical memorabilia kept to reasonable limits. There's always a crowd here, which usually means a comparatively long wait for dinner. On the menu are such treats as snapper Pontchartrain topped with crabmeat, bouillabaisse, pompano, and grilled swordfish, all accompanied by salad and new potatoes. Your check is likely to be in the $12 to $20 range for dinner entrées. Fisherman is open from 4:30 to 10:30pm daily, to 11:30pm on Saturday.

By the time you've found your way to **15th Street Fisheries and Boathouse,** 1900 SE 15th St. (tel. 763-2777), you've earned the good dinner you'll find. On the Intracoastal, across the waterway from Pier Sixty-Six, 15th Street Fisheries has a woodsy upstairs-downstairs dining room filled with plants, brass, and a faintly nautical look. Seafood is best here, and the beef comes in second. The desserts and ambience are top-notch, with prices about $15 to $28 for dinner, including appetizer, salad, Perrier, and dessert. To get to this pretty place, turn north off 17th Street Causeway at Cordova Road and right (toward the Intracoastal) at the first street on the right (15th). It's open from 4:30 to 10:30pm daily for dinner upstairs, from 11:30am in the less expensive raw bar downstairs. The waterway view is terrific here.

## Steaks

One of the best-loved—and best-attended—steak houses in Fort Lauderdale is **Raindancer,** 3031 E. Commercial Blvd. (tel. 772-0337). Such crowds are rarely wrong, and they are quite right to favor the Raindancer, which features good steaks, chops, a really super shish kebab, and top seafood simply prepared. A maze of dining rooms upstairs and down, Raindancer also offers one of the city's most attractive lounges, a second-floor aerie outfitted in antiques, couches, even a roaring fire in the fireplace! There are special dining rooms for those who do not smoke, but we think the best seats are toward the back of this plant-bedecked dining spot where the atmosphere is coziest. In addition to all its other pluses, the Raindancer also has the very best salad bar in town, fresh pumpernickel bread, and skilled service that works like the proverbial well-oiled clock. You'll pay $10 to $18 for dinners, which include that salad bar and good baked potatoes. Raindancer is open daily from 5 to 11pm, closing an hour later on weekends.

**Ruth's Chris Steak House,** 2525 N. Federal Hwy. (tel. 565-2338), is generally considered one of the city's best steak houses and serves its specialty in handsome surroundings. It is unabashedly expensive, however, with the small steak ringing in at about $17.50, others trooping easily up to $25 or more, and all of them à la carte so anything else you order is a separate price. Figure to spend at least $40 a person here on outstanding steaks. For those who are not beef fans, the restaurant offers a variety of selections including swordfish, barbecued shrimp, blackened tuna, and veal, lamb, and pork chops. Hours are 5 to 11pm daily, closing an hour earlier on Sunday.

**Chuck's Steak House,** 1207 SE 17th Street Causeway (tel. 764-3333), has been a mainstay of this neighborhood for umpteen years—and no wonder. For lack of any more fitting cliché: They have it together here. As you can see from the name, this is a steak house and makes no bones about it. They're not messing with sauces, offering a hundred other nonbeef choices, or playing fast and cutesy with garnishes and side dishes. If you want plain, unadorned, good steak, you come here.

Chuck's is popular for reasons other than excellent steaks at reasonable prices: It's dark, intimate, and attractive with woodsy paneled walls, some hanging plants, and simple but crisply tailored wood furnishings. An adjoining bar is a quite popular place too. Prices, which fall easily in the $12 to $18 range, include a big salad bar and baked potato or rice pilaf. Part of a chain that got its start in Connecticut and now has several restaurants in Florida, Chuck's is open daily from 11:30am to midnight, from 5pm weekends.

## Eclectic

One learns fascinating things by word of mouth, and not the least fascinating of those is a restaurant called just that: **By Word of Mouth,** 3200 NE 12th Ave. (tel. 564-3663). Here in this forest-green enclave talented cooks are doing some downright scrumptious cooking. Imagine a tortellini salad with pink-and-white pasta tossed with herbs and a marinade. Or fat chicken breasts topped with a fluffy broccoli soufflé. Or even a lowly meatloaf lifted from obscurity with the addition of a creamy layer of white cheeses. Can we get your attention with the nutty flavor of dried tomatoes in vinaigrette, minty tabbouleh salad, chicken and tomatoes blended with capers and spices? Or lobster lasagne, ziti with prosciutto and ham, pasta bows primavera, beef tenderloin, scallops and shrimp in a sauce of tomato and fresh basil, a sausage ratatouille, an apricot-topped chicken, calamari with percatelli, a peanut-flavored Indonesian chicken? Seafood turns up seasoned with ginger or grilled with mustard sauce; ham, pork, and lamb are teamed with fruit. Add to that a couple of dozen dream desserts that ought to be classified as illegal substances—a wildly destructive chocolate truffle loaf or blackout chocolate cake, for instance.

Begun as a catering operation, the restaurant was a little like some new babies: No one expected it but no one's complaining. Suffice to say, there seems to be simply no way you could be disappointed at this marvelously creative restaurant whose fame is spreading rapidly . . . by word of mouth. Entrées range in price from $14 to $21, but you'll probably spend a bit more with all these temptations. Hours are Monday through Friday from 11am to 3pm for lunch, Wednesday through Saturday from 5 to 10pm for dinner. To get there, turn north on the east side of the railroad tracks at Dixie Highway and Oakland Park Boulevard.

## Budget Selections

Eating on the cheap in Fort Lauderdale is simple and super these days, no small thanks to two restaurants so popular and jam-packed that you'd better get there before 6:30pm or be prepared to while away 30 to 60 minutes waiting for a table.

The first of these is **Carlos and Pepe's 17th Street Cantina**, 1302 SE 17th St. (tel. 467-7192), a spot where by 8pm the crowd is belly to belly in the foyer and bar. All those people have discovered that C&P's Tex-Mex chow is worth waiting for, and the waiting is relatively painless in these serene surroundings of wood paneling, greenery, hand-woven Mexican wall hangings, and fat comfortable Spanish furniture. Tuck into one of Carlos and Pepe's giant, two-fisted margaritas, delivered with basket after basket of hot taco chips and fiery sauce, and *olé!* Before you know it, it's your turn at the tortillas.

C&P's takes informality to new heights, offering you the chance to munch and crunch in jeans or vested suit. Once you've managed to claim a seat here, try our favorite, Carlos's wild tostada, a crispy, high-backed, beef-filled mélange that arrives bearing every resemblance to a Viking ship in full sail. Chili Colorado is a tasty sauced-beef-chunks concoction, and the super-crisp Mexican pizza—a crunchy flour taco topped with meat, mushrooms, tomatoes, olives, and sauce—may ruin you forever for the mundane Italian variety. Probably the very best part of Carlos and Pepe's is the check: Figure $8 to $10 for two for dinner; giant margaritas are $3.25. *Caramba!*

Another entrant in the Tex-Mex sweepstakes here is **Who-Song & Larry's**, 3100 N. Federal Hwy. (tel. 566-9771), where you'll get some crayons and a white paper tablecloth to entertain yourself while you wait for dinner to arrive. All the usual south-of-the-border concoctions from tacos to enchiladas, nachos, tortillas, and chimichangas pour from the kitchen here, some of them served in the sizzling iron pans in which they were cooked. Prices fall easily in the under-$10 range for dinner. Who-Song's opens at 11am and closes at 11pm weekdays, later on weekends.

One of the top budget spots in town is **Bobby Rubino's Place for Ribs**, 4100 N. Federal Hwy. (tel. 561-5305), which has been drawing crowds since opening day, and has become so instantly popular it's now been cloned seven times locally and five times in Canada. This spot is nirvana for barbecued ribs fans. Rubino's serves 'em up with indelicate abandon, accompanied by a loaf—yes, a loaf—of onion rings. It also turns out barbecued chicken in a peppery hot sauce, and a bargain London broil for $7. The atmosphere is dark and lounge-like, and there are attractive wood-trimmed walls, a central U-shaped lounge flanked by comfortable booths, and an upstairs lounge with plump swiveling armchairs.

Ribs are now $13, chicken and ribs combo a bit less, and other items progressively less, so you can figure your bill for two in the $30 bracket or less. Wear your urban cowboy gear. It's open from 11am to 11pm daily, on Sunday from 1pm, Saturday from 4pm.

**Southport Raw Bar and Seafood Restaurant,** 1536 Cordova Rd., just off 17th Street Causeway (tel. 525-2526), has been the cult hangout of yachting enthusiasts and sundry other types for ages. It's not difficult to understand why. Life at Southport is as informal and comfortable as an old pair of jeans, which, incidentally, would be formal wear here. This is your basic get-down, funky spot. Their bumper sticker appears on many a car in town and reads: "Eat fish—live longer, eat oysters —love longer, eat clams—last longer."

Not for fancy-schmancy do you go here, but for good simply prepared seafood and decent raw bar goodies—fat oysters carried through the restaurant in huge plastic buckets and pried apart behind one of the two big bars, cherrystone clams, spiced shrimp, conch or New England clam chowder, clam fritters. Presentation is important in some restaurants, but here refers only to slapping it on a paper plate and schlepping it down in front of you, accompanied by plastic forks, little paper cups of cocktail or tartar sauce or melted butter, a small lidded paper cup of coleslaw.

Certainly it's casual, with music blaring, beer foaming into chilled glasses, but in its own carousel style, it's fun and it's very cheap. You can have dinner and a couple of beers here for less than $15 a couple! Oysters and steamed clams are less than $6 a dozen.

Southport is nothing much to look at either: one big room with a couple of waist-high dividers down the middle, a television in one corner, one of those moving-light advertising gizmos on one wall, some nets and nautical junque scattered about, a bulletin board plastered with business cards no one will ever read. An experience, daily from 11am to 2am.

Two restaurants specializing in curry offer you a choice between a tiny unimposing six-table bistro featuring Thai cuisine and a larger, more elaborate spot specializing in things Indian from vindaloo to belly dancers.

**Siam Curry House** is tucked away at 2010 Wilton Dr., also called NE Fourth Avenue (tel. 564-3411). Cheerful helpers here will work and work until they elicit the smile that means your dinner is just the degree of spiciness that suits your taste. Their curries are based on rich coconut milk and can be ordered from mild to superhot. There are beef, chicken, pork, lamb, shrimp, scallop, and vegetable curries to choose from, plus such fascinating items as floating market soup with transparent noodles, or kaitumkar soup with chicken, spices, lemon grass, and coconut milk.

They make steamed dumplings, and our favorite, Ramwong chicken cooked with vegetables, spices, and peanuts. If you'd like to sample a bit of almost everything here, try the Bangkok Tonight dinner, the Royal Banquet, or the Siamese Fisherman Feast. Curries are in the $5 to $6 range, with the special dinners about $8 to $14, so your bill for two isn't likely to top $20 to $25. Siam Curry House is open weekdays from 11:30am to 2:30pm, and daily 5 to midnight for dinner.

At **Punjab,** an Indian restaurant in a fancy new setting at 5975 N. Federal Hwy. (tel. 491-6710), curries come in mild, medium, hot, and extra-hot. Among the dozens of items on the menu are chicken, beef, or lamb vindaloo, chicken tandoori, and homemade Indian breads from chapati to puri and paratha. Open daily from 11am (from 5pm on Sunday) to 11pm (one hour later on Friday and Saturday), Punjab offers dinner for $8 to $12 per person, served among marble, romantic curtained booths, and burbling fountains.

So, honey. Whaddya want? Your gum-chewing, little-paper-cap-wearing waitress slides into your booth and laboriously scribbles your order down on her little paper pad. What's going on here? Just fun à la '50s at **Joe Bel Air's,** 1717 Eisenhower Blvd. (tel. 463-5637), a good-for-a-laugh spot designed to return us all to days of tailfins a shark would adore, Eiffel-Tower chocolate sodas, banana splits, egg creams, phosphates, Bill Haley and the Comets—well, you get the picture, the *good* old days. Neon trim and a comforting diner atmosphere prevail at this spot, which comes up with full dinners, an ice-cream scoop of potatoes with gravy lathered on, a slab of meat, "eat your vegetables" advice, burgers, sandwiches, and some very good ice-cream concoctions to top it all. Bel Air's is cheap—you'll never pay more than $6 or $7 for dinner here—Bel Air's is fun, and Bel Air's is a trip down a weird memory lane. Where is Dick Clark when we need him? Hours are 6:30am to midnight daily.

Finally, if you scream for ice cream now and then, you mustn't miss **Swensen's,** 2477 E. Sunrise Blvd. (tel. 566-1847), a nifty little Victorian spot with etched glass and enough ice cream to freeze the North Pole. Heaven knows how many flavors they have here, but you can count on pumpkin and watermelon, and at least four varieties of chocolate. (Are you up to bubble gum ice cream?) Full-fledged sundae and soda concoctions are razzle-dazzle items of such dimensions a gasp is always audible here. To go into suitably euphoric descriptions of things like the Black Bart or the Earthquake (that registers a five on the Richter scale) would keep you riveted to this page, thus losing you for the rest of the book. They're your calories—get in there and spend them. Figure $3 to $7 for one of the major concoctions, $1 for fat and sassy cones. They serve sandwiches too, and are open daily from 11am to 11pm, an hour later on Friday and Saturday.

Drugstores aren't usually on our list of top spots, but the **Chemist Shop,** 817 E. Las Olas Blvd. (tel. 462-6587), is. Nothing fancy here except the passing parade of boulevardiers in safari suits, but the sandwiches are huge, the salads fresh, the chili a knock-out, and their sodas and sundaes worth their weight. Open from 7am to 5:30pm Monday through Saturday.

Whatever adjective goes just beyond eclectic must be the perfect description for the odd lot that frequents **Ernie's Bar-B-Q,** at 1843 S. Federal Hwy. (tel. 523-8636). You not only can see *everything* here, you may very well see it all in one evening. Ernie himself has moved along to new challenges, but before he went he covered the walls with his own proverbial thoughts—which are about as unusual as his customers. It doesn't matter really, because what you do here is ignore it all and just pay attention to the best conch chowder in southern Florida, thick luscious Bimini bread, great barbecued pork and beef, nippy conch salads. Once a major corporation even shipped thousands of gallons of Ernie's conch chowder out to California to a giant party, and *that* is testimony! There's a raw bar upstairs and a crowd always. Prices range from about $5 to $8. Ernie's is open from 11am to 11pm daily.

Pizza? Best of the rest is **Two Guys,** 701 S. Federal Hwy. (tel. 462-7140), which serves up thin crusts in its tiny enclave on South Federal Highway or delivers to you for a few dollars more. Pizzas start at $6 or so, and range upward as you add on all the goop. Open from 11am to midnight daily (to 1am Friday and Saturday). Two Guys also has a wide range of sandwiches, salads, and Italian dinners under $10.

## DINING CHOICES IN NEARBY CITIES

Good restaurants are scattered all over the Gold Coast (chefs like warm weather too, you know!). Here are a few of the best in neighboring towns north and south.

### Pompano and Deerfield

Tucked away in an unlikely spot on busy McNab Road is the **French Place,** 360 E. McNab Rd., Pompano (tel. 785-1920), where talented Jean-Pierre Bolline whips up sole meunière, boeuf bourguignon, crusty French bread, poached salmon, and mile-high pastries. He serves them up in a tiny bistro as simply decorated as any you'd see in France, and charms your socks off while he's at it. You'll be happy with the prices too, which won't top $12 to $17 for entrées. Open from 11:30am to 2:30pm for lunch weekdays, 5 to 10pm daily for dinner.

**Café Max,** 2601 E. Atlantic Blvd., Pompano (tel. 782-0606), hit the Gold Coast with a culinary wallop. Popular almost from the day the doors opened, this sleek new café-society hangout is doing everything right, particularly cooking. Some have dubbed what they're doing here *nouvelle Américain* cooking but their edifying use of Florida products perhaps also qualifies them for *nouvelle Floride* plaudits. In any case, you can get mesquite-grilled local fish on the menu here, along with ravioli stuffed with herbed shrimp, creamy soups flavored with oranges and garnished with avocado or mango. A good-looking restaurant and one that disperses memory-making cuisine in the $15 to $25 range, Café Max is open from 6 to 10pm daily.

**Harris' Imperial House,** 50 N. Ocean Blvd., Pompano (tel. 941-2200), looks nothing at all like a Chinese restaurant, which may be why so many conservative diners have taken to this place over the years. The Cantonese food here is quite good, and there's a huge $14 Chinese buffet guaranteed to fill. Prices are in the $10 to $16 range. Open for American Sunday buffet brunch for $13 in the winter season from 10am to 2pm, and from 5 to 10:30pm daily all year.

They come by land and sea to dine at **Pal's Captain's Table,** at the Cove Yacht Basin, Deerfield Beach (tel. 427-4000). Watching the sea arrivals is part of the fun at this waterside restaurant plunked down beside the Intracoastal. At a table overlooking the water, you can watch huge yachts chug slowly by as you dine on sea-fresh seafood and steaks, dark onion rolls and date-nut bread, a relish tray, and perhaps key lime pie for dessert. A low-light nautical bar in front has been the scene of many a discussion, frivolous and not, for the many years Pal's has been operating here. Prices are in the $13 to $25 range, and the restaurant's open for lunch from 11:30am to 3:30pm weekdays, and for dinner from 5 to 10pm daily, later on weekends.

On the walls of the **Riverview,** 1741 E. Riverview Rd., Deerfield Beach, at the Intracoastal Waterway (tel. 428-3463), you'll see remnants of the days when this favorite waterside eatery was a gambling house. Before that it served this fishing community as a packing house, and over the years has been the site of many a frolicking evening. Things are a bit quieter at the Riverview these days, but there's still a nice hideaway atmosphere about the place, and a long menu filled with outstanding seafood and steaks. Stuffed Florida lobster and yellowtail are top of the line, and the clam chowder's a much-sold item, as are the thick cuts of prime rib and sirloin. You'll pay $11 to $24 for dinner. The Riverview is open 11:30am to 3pm daily except Monday, from 6 to 10pm daily for dinner. To find the Riverview, look under the northwest side of the Intracoastal Bridge.

**Cap's Place,** 2765 NE 28th Court, Lighthouse Point, at the Yacht Basin in Lighthouse Point (tel. 941-0418), is the only restaurant we know where getting there is half the fun. Here's how you do that: Head up US 1 to NE 24th Street in Lighthouse Point, where you'll see a sign directing you to the Yacht Club and to Cap's. Wind around some side streets and pull up where you see Cap's sign. If there's no *African Queen* to take you across the water to Cap's, blink your headlights and shortly there will be. You chug across the waters of the Intracoastal, and there, in the middle of the waterway, is a heap of lumber—you've arrived!

Sixty years ago Cap Knight, who occasionally ran some rum into Prohibition-dry Florida, beached himself and a few barges on this islet in the stream. He tossed in a little gambling, probably a lot of proof products, and a little food, and called it Club Unique. That it is, and that it was to the likes of Winston Churchill, Jack Dempsey, Kate Smith, FDR, all of whom dropped by. Their presence still haunts these aging boards and their pictures are what little decor there is in this very rustic heap straight out of a Bogart movie. We can't think of any way they could make this place more atmospheric.

It's worth it to whip up to Cap's, which recently won Historic Register status, just for the fresh hearts of palm salad, one of the few places in the nation you can get the fresh (definitely *not* canned) variety. Besides that rare delicacy, nothing else here has fancy overtones. Just steaming spuds and a list of straight-from-the-sea foods from dolphin to sea trout, bluefish, mackerel, kingfish, sea bass, pompano, crab, shrimp, scallops, and oysters. With every dinner you get a shrimp cocktail too, and fresh bread baked right out back. Best of all. many of the prices are under $10. Don't miss the bar—if ever Bogart decides to haunt a place, this is a place he'd choose! Cap's is open from 5:30 to 10pm daily (to 11pm on Friday and Saturday). You'll find a map showing the restaurant's location in the Pompano Beach *Yellow Pages*.

**The Cove,** 1755 SE 3rd St., Deerfield Beach (tel. 421-9272), is a spot that manages to combine both lively and quiet, retaining the best of both. Loads of plants, cool breezes from the Intracoastal Waterway, lively entertainment, an outdoor wooden deck, candlelight, and inexpensive meals all add up to one beautifully tropical way to spend an afternoon or evening. Outside, halyards clank against masts of sleek sailboats, and inside, a little calypso music finishes your total immersion into Florida Tropical at its best. Menu prices top out at $20 for filet mignon, but there are plenty of choices in the $10 bracket. An especially good place to imbibe some kind of fruity tropical drink you'd never touch anywhere else, the Cove is open from 11am to 1:30am weekdays and from 8am to 2am weekends. Steel band entertainment from 4 to 11pm on Sunday.

## Hollywood/Dania/Hallandale

Right up there at the top of Hollywood restaurants is the **Celebrity Room** at the Diplomat Resort and Country Club, 3515 S. Ocean Dr. (tel. 457-8111). White-gloved, absolutely flawless service, top-quality cooking, a beautiful, elegant dining room, and excellent wines combine to make this restaurant simply superb. Continental cooking is the order of the day here, with excellent steaks, lots of herbs, and creamy sauces. Naturally you must be prepared to pay for perfection, so plan on a check of at least $50 a person. Dance music plays each evening and jackets are required. The Celebrity Room is open from 6 to 11pm every night but Tuesday.

A windowside table overlooking most everything in Hollywood is the chief allure at **Top of the Home,** 1720 Harrison St. atop the Federal Bank Building (tel. 927-1707). Continental cuisine is the fare here, with plenty of seafood and beef dishes to choose from, plus rack of lamb, stone crabs, and an intriguing cappuccino ice cream pie. Jackets are recommended. There is dancing nightly, and the restaurant, which has entrées in the $15 to $25 range, is open from 5pm for cocktails, from 6 to 2am for dinner Tuesday through Sunday.

**Hemmingway,** at 219 N. 21st Ave. (Dixie Hwy.), Hollywood Beach (tel. 923-0500). This popular night-and-day emporium is in Hollywood's old city hall building. It was built in the 1920s so a good-old-days atmosphere prevails: etched glass, eclectic collections of memorabilia, a tinkling piano, and later a big-band sound, plus a long, long menu of crêpes and steaks, salads and soups, burgers and barbecue, all accompanied by fresh fruit. Prices range from $9 to $20. It's open from 11am to 4am weekdays, from 4pm on Saturday and Sunday.

You'll have to drive out to the western reaches of the county to get to this little place, but when you finally arrive, you'll join dozens and dozens of others who have just accomplished the same run. Go early or be prepared to beer-and-wine-it a while in the parking lot outside the **Sea Shanty,** 3841 Griffin Rd., Fort Lauderdale (tel. 962-1921). This place is so popular that when we first drove by, we thought the crowd outside was a wedding! Fresh, fresh seafood is what lures the masses here, and keeps them coming back despite the absolutely-no-atmosphere atmosphere. You can have snapper, yellowtail, shrimp, kingfish, and a grouper parmesan that is to faint for, plus simple breads, salads, and potatoes, with prices about $10 to $20 and service in the genre of New York deli: efficient, period. You'll love it—everybody does. Open from 4:30 to 10pm daily (go very early or very late).

**Never on Sunday,** 129 N. Federal Hwy., Dania (tel. 921-5557), is the new name on an old house owned by experienced Broward County restaurateurs, the D'Arcys. Once the proprietors of Chez Tonton, the couple is now holding forth in Dania, serving up their rich onion soup, quiches, beef Wellington, rack of lamb, and the like for à la carte entrée prices running about $15 to $25—well worth it for the smiling welcome, the interesting location, and the outstanding cuisine. Their hours are from 5 to 10pm daily, except never on Monday!

For pure Spanish cooking—which means light sauces and unusual preparations of beef and seafood (with the accent on seafood)—head for **Old Spain,** at 2333 Hollywood Blvd., Hollywood (tel. 921-8485, or 944-2298 in Miami). Juan Abella is a genial host who sometimes trots through the dining room with a Spanish wine bag he squirts into your mouth, compliments of the house. When you don't see him, rest assured he's out in the kitchen creating paella valenciana, white-bean soup, or that masterful seafood mélange of Spain, zarzuela, as he has been for 14 years. Try a gypsy's arm for dessert or crêpes with vanilla sauce. You'll pay about $20 or so for dinner here. Old Spain is open from noon to 2:30pm for lunch Monday through Friday, and from 6 to 10:30pm for dinner every day but Sunday.

**Manero's,** 2600 E. Hallandale Beach Blvd., Hallandale (tel. 456-1000), has been flipping out those steaks and gorgonzola-topped salads for so long it's possible they may do this blindfolded. More than 25 years in this spot has earned the restaurant a fond place in the hearts of area beef eaters. Prices are reasonable too, with dinner in the $12 to $20 range. Manero's is open daily from 11:30am to 11pm, from 4 to 9:30pm Sunday.

**Martha's,** 6024 N. Ocean Dr., Hollywood (tel. 923-5444), is as intriguing as a $1,000 bill. Tiny lights glitter in the ceiling. Pale-peach and gray tones play counterpoint to polished brass accents, glowing candles, fresh flowers. Off in a corner a handsome circular bar is draped with a trendy crowd of suburbanites, while outside, a second bar and a less formal dining area lure boaters and casual diners. Ms. Martha, who rose to fame with a similar establishment in Key West, and who is anticipating a fair rate of return on her very impressive investment, has not produced a bargain basement here, but neither is it any more expensive than most area restaurants of similarly elaborate design and decor. You'll pay $14 to $25 for entrées, which are accompanied by an attractive crystal bowl of iced crudités and potatoes or vegetables. All else is à la carte, with the tab rising along with your greed.

Unusual treats here include oysters topped with horseradish sauce and baked with three cheeses, a cold mussel soup selection called Billi-bi, and a marvelously spicy seafood gumbo not to be missed. A great bouillabaisse is flavored with saffron. Beef selections include prime rib with Yorkshire pudding and steaks. An ice-cream pie called Pontchartrain pie features sherbet and ice-cream layers topped with a chocolate sauce of such rich bittersweet goodness that a chocolate-hooked companion claimed he was going back for an order of Pontchartrain, hold the ice cream.

If you'd like to try Martha's on the cheap, trot up to the second-floor raw bar, where a selection of stone crabs, clams, oysters, and shrimp are temptingly displayed on cracked ice. Here the atmosphere is more casual: royal-blue fiberglass tabletops trimmed in wood, nauti-facts scattered artfully about, a sensational view of the waterway through a wall of windows. Some of the downstairs menu is available here too, along with steamed clams and mussels, smoked fish and oysters, peel-and-eat shrimp, and a seafood cioppino, all $7 to $20. Hours are 11:30am to 2am daily.

If you think dim sum is a stupid accountant, get right over to **August Moon,** 1301 N. Federal Hwy., Hollywood (tel. 923-4233). There they will show you that dim sum is an ethereal delight of mini-dishes—delicately steamed dumplings, meatballs, stuffed buns. A house specialty is steamed shrimp dumplings created from crescents of papery pastry wrapped around plump shrimp. No. 4 dumplings are filled with an intriguing mix of beef and water chestnuts. Another option features dumplings stuffed with scallion-flavored pork balls. This goes on and on, with the mysterious menu descriptions a challenge to go right on and sample till you drop. There's a regular menu with some pretty standard Chinese fare. Who cares? You come here for dim sum. What else matters? August Moon, a charmer for many a moon here in Hollywood, is open from 11am to 10pm daily, and dinner prices are in the $5 to $8 bracket.

**Spiced Apple,** 3281 Griffin Rd., Fort Lauderdale (tel. 962-0772), is a cute little country place that really is out in what passes for country in this urban area. Here you dine on slabs of country ham, peach cobbler, corn fritters, fried chicken, and the like. Prices are quite reasonable, easily falling into the $10 to $20 range for complete dinners. Hours are 11:30am to 4pm for lunch and weekend brunch, and 4 to 10pm for dinner Monday through Thursday, later on weekends. On Sunday hours are 11:30am to 9:30pm.

**Napoli's,** 1800 N. Federal Hwy., Hollywood (tel. 923-7250), is one of those places that are a joy to try, a tiny pack-'em-in trattoria that's filled with families and big happy groups celebrating with all the gesticulating gusto you find in Italy's best-loved neighborhood restaurants. Toddlers are cuddled by the staff, tables are forever being shoved together to accommodate big family parties, and everybody's smiling.

All the best-loved pasta-with-sauce selections are available for prices in the $5 to $7 range. They serve pizza here too, with an unusual touch that's just what you would expect of this family restaurant: family pizza dinners, which include a basic tomato and cheese pizza with spaghetti, soup, and bread. Everything comes with the usual accoutrements: soup, crusty, hot garlic rolls, and salad or spaghetti. You will also find veal, chicken, shrimp, calamari, lobster, and eggplant in all the usual styles, plus spaghetti carbonara, gnocchi, rigatoni bolognese, zuppa di pesce alla Napoli.

The atmosphere is simple: a tiny foyer jammed with snapshots of family and friends, some oil paintings of Italian architectural landmarks. A boisterous, bouncing, lively spot that's as much fun as it is fulfilling. Napoli's prices are generally under $12 and it's open every day from 4 to 10pm.

If you love that rib-sticking German fare, nothing could be würst than missing **Zinkler's Bavarian Village,** 1401 N. Federal Hwy., Hollywood (tel. 922-7321), where you can gorge on schnitzel, spaetzle, sauerkraut, strolling oom-pah-pah accordion music, and German wines. You may have to buy your liederhosen a size larger! You'll pay $10 to $18 for dinner, and the yodeling begins at 11:30am for lunch (closing at 3pm), and continues from 4 to 11pm for dinner daily (from noon on Sunday).

## SEEING THE SIGHTS

With 165 miles of canals and infinite quantities of ocean, Fort Lauderdale has water sports galore, as do all the cities up and down the coastline. You'll usually find sailboat rentals right on the beach, and in larger towns like Hollywood and Fort Lauderdale shops in the beach area have all the sand requirements from suntan lotion to surfboards.

### Beaches

So popular are Fort Lauderdale's beaches that they have actually been subdivided—quite informally, let me assure you. Certain people go to certain beaches, and after a few days in town you'll know exactly where to find your friends or those who may become your friends. To help you in your search, let it be known that the beach across from the Elbo Room is a collegiate hangout in March. The beach across from the Marlin Beach Hotel is popular with gay sun-seekers. The beach across from the Horizon and Jolly Roger Hotels is quieter, popular with young professionals and those seeking a less raucous atmosphere; and the beach at Sunrise Boulevard is another young professionals hangout most of the year, collegiate grounds in March. Families lean toward the beach from Sunrise north along the edges of Birch State Park.

If Fort Lauderdale's seven miles of sand are not enough for you, don't despair. There are a jillion or so other acres of silica ready and waiting for you to leave a footprint in them. Among those other beaches are:

**Hallandale Beach,** a condo-lined strip of sand at Hallandale Beach Boulevard.

**Hollywood Beach,** which runs roughly from Hollywood Beach Boulevard north to Sheridan Street. Much of the way, the sand is trimmed with a boardwalk, here called the Broadwalk, which is in turn lined by small shops and fast-food eateries.

**Dania Beach,** one of the region's most attractive, thanks to the absence of buildings on most of it. A new addition to the most deserted part of the beach is a long, two-story, cupola-topped, pastel building called Sea Fair that houses some attractive boutiques, a lounge, and quite an attractive restaurant called Whiskey Creek. Clambake fans can get a permit for evening clambakes on the beach, so they tell me. You'll find the beach stretching north from about Sheridan Street to Port Everglades.

**John U. Lloyd State Park,** a very large and jungly park with beautiful beaches, has 245 acres of parkgrounds right on the ocean, picnic tables, and a 50¢ admission charge. It's officially at 6503 N. Ocean Dr., but you'll find it by taking Dania Beach Boulevard to the ocean and taking a right turn at the stop sign there.

**Lauderdale-by-the-Sea,** which stretches roughly from about Commercial Boulevard south to Oakland Park Boulevard along Ocean Drive, features a fishing pier.

**Pompano Beach,** extending along the ocean from Atlantic Boulevard to North Ocean Boulevard, with public beaches at the end of intersecting streets. Much of Pompano Beach is hidden behind condominium buildings, which makes it comparatively deserted most of the time—good for getaway afternoons.

**Deerfield Beach** and **Boca Raton Beach** stretch north from the northern boundary of Pompano Beach and are favored by snorkelers and scuba fans. Many are backed by shady jungle growth.

## Sight-Sailing the Venice of America

Water is so important in this city that two of the most popular ways to tour it are by boat. Fort Lauderdale's primary attractions are its two paddlewheelers, the *Jungle Queen* and the *Paddlewheel Queen.*

Board one of these sparkling white antique craft and you're off down the Intracoastal Waterway for hours of oohing and ahhing at the Gold Coast's downright gorgeous canalside real estate. Waterfront dwellers here consider the water their *front* door, so the view you get of this side of these sprawling mansions is impressive indeed. Rolling lawns so perfectly manicured you could (and some residents do) golf on them, pastel mansions with ornate wide verandas soaring over pools adorned by Roman columns and statuary. One manse even has a plot of, and a lot of, land shaped like the state of Florida! Residents get right into this thing, flicking their porch lights off and on as the boat toots by, and waving merrily as you chug along in antiquated splendor.

In winter you *must* (and in summer you should) reserve a seat on evening cruises well in advance, although you can sometimes luck into a last-minute cancellation if you're on hand about 6:30pm. The *Jungle Queen* departs from **Bahia Mar Yacht Basin,** Fla. A1A, Fort Lauderdale (Mail to: 801 Seabreeze Ave.) (tel. 462-5596), on two daylight tours at 10am and 2pm, and a four-hour dinner cruise at 7pm. You get the grand tour on the way to dinner, stop at an exotic island for family-style, all-you-can-eat shrimp and chicken, then return with vaudeville entertainment. The price is $20 for adults or children for the evening cruise, and $7 for adults and $5 for children 2 to 12 on day cruises.

Meanwhile, if you'd like a little more formal cruise evening, board the *Paddlewheel Queen* 2950 NE 32nd Ave., one block south of Oakland Park Boulevard just west of Fla. A1A (tel. 564-7659), and sail off for a steak dinner and dancing under the stars. There are also day tours at 1pm daily at $7 for adults, $4 for children. Evening cruises Wednesday through Saturday cost adults $27; children, $16 for ages 3 to 12.

To see the land side of the city, book a seat on the **Voyager Train,** 600 S. Seabreeze Ave. (tel. 463-0401). This group of open tram cars (they're covered if it rains) is pulled around town at 10am, noon, and 2 and 4pm daily by small white Jeeps. You'll see homes of the famous and infamous, the city's palm-lined, gaslit Las Olas Boulevard, bustling Port Everglades, and prices are $6.50 for adults, $3 for children 3 to 12.

## Airboat Rides

If you'd like to see some of the mysterious Everglades swampland without driving all the way to the park in Miami, take a trip to the edge of the Glades to an area called Everglades Holiday Park. Here a guide will tuck you into a Rube Goldberg creation called an airboat and whiz you off into the swamp for a look at alligator shoes still on the hoof.

Airboats are flat-bottomed craft designed to skim over the shallow swampland with the aid of an aircraft propeller and some massive roaring engines. Certainly you'll never see one of these in Cincinnati. Besides, roaring around in one for a look at Florida's flora and fauna is just plain fun. You can also rent boats here and whiz off on your own.

Located 30 minutes west of the city at the junction of US 27 and Griffin Road (tel. 434-8111), **Everglades Holiday Park** 21940 Griffin Rd., charges $12 for adults and $6 for children under 12 for this look at the one-of-a-kind swamp. Rides leave every 30 minutes from 9am to 5pm and include an alligator-wrestling show and a narrated 45-minute airboat tour, which also takes you to a Native American Village in the glades.

## Historic Sites

In the secluded area at 231 SW 2nd Street (tel. 462-4115) are the only architectural remnants of the city's past: the small but elegant old New River Inn, a verandaed hotel that's now a **Discovery Center** hands-on museum and historical center, and the King-Cromartie House, which belonged to two of the city's pioneer families.

Plunk down in a porch rocking chair at 75-year-old New River Inn, gaze out over the tranquil New River (said by the Seminoles to have sprung up overnight), listen to the breeze shush through the palms, and you are transported to long-gone days when a tourist in town was big news. Discovery Center is a child-oriented set of nature exhibits with frequent craft classes. It's open noon to 5pm. Sunday and Tuesday through Friday, from 10am on Sunday and Saturday, closed Monday. Admission to the museum is $3.

Next door is another part of the museum, the **King-Cromartie House** (tel. 462-4116), saved from destruction by a local social group and outfitted in furnishings of the period, right down to antique shoes and dresses in the closets and a tiny furnished dollhouse. It's open Sunday and Tuesday through Friday from noon to 5pm, on Saturday from 10am to 5pm. Guided tours, lasting 45 minutes and led by docents in period costumes, explain some of the unusual items collected there. Take a look at the flour sifter in the kitchen—who says we've progressed? At Christmas the house is a fairyland with twinkling lights and tiny wreaths hung in every window.

Back in the early 1900s the small two-story, veranda-trimmed house at 333 S. Federal Hwy. was Fort Lauderdale's trading post, the place Seminoles and pioneer Fort Lauderdale residents came to buy, sell, bargain, and trade. Evenings, trader Frank Stranahan and his new schoolmarm bride, Ivy Julia Cromartie, turned the house into the village's social center, complete with accordion music and lots of laughter. Together, Miss Ivy and Frank had cut the rock-hard wood called Dade County pine into lumber they used to build the simple but elegant home that was to become known as **Stranahan House,** the oldest remaining structure in this city.

Built in 1902, the house was a happy place but had its sorrows too: Frank lost everything in the Great Crash and committed suicide. His wife lived on for 40 years, occupying an attic room at the top of the home until she died in 1971. By that time a restaurant had been opened here, but eventually even that enterprise folded and the city's most historic building lay moldering, its hand-hewn beams slowly pulling apart, its joints loosening.

Then the Fort Lauderdale Historical Society bought the house the Stranahans had worked so hard to build and raised more than $250,000 to hire archeologists, historians, and builders to put it all back together again. When peeling paint had been scraped, brown hues sanded off a fireplace's red and white bricks, staircases replaced, and the pretty porches restored, Stranahan House was reopened.

Now it has again become one of the town's most delightful social centers, often used by local organizations for fund-raising events. Stranahan House is also a museum (tel. 524-4736 or 463-4374), open to the public daily except Sunday from 10am to 4pm. Admission, including a tour, is $3 per person, $2 children under 12.

Romantics might wait until Friday to visit: On that night the city's Historical Society sponsors a Friday-night social, when you can sip a glass of wine, nibble on hors d'oeuvres, and pretend nothing has changed in eight decades. Hours for the Friday-night social are 6 to 8:30pm, and admission, including the tour, is $5. To find the house, take Las Olas Boulevard to the Pantry Pride store at the intersection of US 1 and turn south. You'll find the house just off a tiny circular plaza there.

If you've ever wanted to see how Old Money lived in the Old Days when moola headed south for several months of sunshine each winter, the place to see is **Bonnet House**, 900 N. Birch Rd. (tel. 563-5393). We are, perhaps, being too flippant here, for this lovely house is not pretentious and, indeed, is quite a touching testimony to the love two people had for each other and for their handsome Florida home.

Nestled in a wilderness never seen by the beachgoers who throng to public beaches just opposite this sprawling acreage, Bonnet House is still owned by Evelyn Bartlett, who spends her winters here—she was 101 years old in 1989. She has, however, given the house to a public trust for its use when she is not in residence every winter. Mrs. Bartlett is the widow of Frederick Clay Bartlett, who was given the house and 35 priceless oceanfront acres by his former father-in-law, Hugh Taylor Birch, who also gave the city a huge tract of land now called Hugh Taylor Birch State Recreation Area.

Named for the bonnet lilies that once covered the lovely little pond that rims this house, Bonnet House is a one- and two-story plantation-style manse with 30 lovely airy rooms filled with everything from a shell collection to antique carousel animals. Swans still swim in the pond where black swans once paddled and monkeys still swing through the jungle that surrounds the house, chattering and chortling. It would take several pages to detail all the rooms here, but suffice to say that there is no more serene retreat in all of Fort Lauderdale, perhaps in all of Florida.

Since Mrs. Bartlett, who spends the summer in Beverly, Massachusetts, placed the $35 million property in a public trust and donated $3 million for its upkeep, preservationists have added horse and carriage rides and house tours from April to November at 10am and 1:30pm Tuesday and Thursday and at 1:30pm Sunday. Admission is $7.50 for adults, free to children under 5. A 20-minute surrey ride through the grounds costs $20 for three people. You'll find signs guiding you to the house just off Sunrise Boulevard, about two blocks west of the ocean.

Fort Lauderdale's Historical Society has put together a charming small **museum of local history.** It's just a few steps away from the Discovery Center and the King-Cromartie House at 219 SW Second Ave. (tel. 463-4431). Here you find Fort Lauderdale's history carefully sorted into several time spans and brought to life with letters and pictures of people who lived here way back when. Often quite touching displays of Seminole and pioneer clothing and housewares give you an idea how primitive but tranquil life in this now-bustling city must once have been. There is no admission charge but the society, which raises money with an annual April seafood festival here, would be happy to get a small donation to help them carry on their work. Hours: 10am to 4pm daily except Monday.

If you like your history to stretch back farther than a century or so, stop in at the **Museum of Archeology,** 203 SW First Ave. (tel. 525-8778), where fossils, a diorama of Native American life, tools, and the 2,000-year-old skeleton of a Tequesta girl take you back many generations to the first visitors here. Open 10am to 4pm daily, 1 to 4pm Sunday, closed Monday. Admission is $1 adults, 50¢ for children 5 to 12.

## Sailing Off into the Sunset

It only stands to reason that a city as serenely lovely as Fort Lauderdale (well, most of the time) should have a serenely lovely port. It does! So pretty is it, in fact, that it's worth your time to take a little reconnoiter down there. Actually, you can hardly help doing so—to get to the beach from the airport you'll pass right by the port and see some of the sleek cruise ships that anchor there.

Called **Port Everglades,** Fort Lauderdale's port features several Mediterranean-style buildings painted a pale peach. As you drive along SE 17th Street Causeway and see them on the south side of the road, you'll think you see their pretty windows, balconies, and French doors, but what you're really seeing is a trompe-l'oeil painting, a fool-the-eye facade on what was once just a rather plain old ordinary warehouse!

Port Everglades likes to call itself the "Five-Star Port," a reference to the posh ships that dock here, all of them top-quality, very plush sailing craft indeed. What do we mean? Well, for openers the *QE II* docks here frequently in winter, along with her Cunard/Norwegian American Cruises sister ships, the sleek and lovely *Vistafjord* and *Sagafjord.* Princess Cruises sails several ships from Port Everglades year round on exciting trips through the Panama Canal and to a bevy of tropical Caribbean islands. Costa Lines' *Costa Riviera* and Sun Line's navy blue *Stella Solaris* drop in on their way to South America.

P & O Lines, owners of the "Love Boat" of Princess Lines, sails from here on sun-seeking winter cruises. Royal Viking Lines, which operates lovely spick-and-span Scandinavian-staffed ships, also frequently brings its *Sky* or *Sea* in here to board passengers. Clipper Cruises, which has a lovely small intracoastal cruise ship, occasionally pops in here too.

If you'd like to take a close look at the ships, you can drive into the port and watch them sail off into the sunset. If you want to get even closer, you can call any of the lines and ask if they will arrange a guest pass for you to visit the ship when it's in port. They'll be happy to do that for you.

To read more about these and all the cruise ships operating from here, and from other parts of the U.S., we'd humbly (well, not too humbly) recommend a copy of *Frommer's Cruises,* co-authored by—guesss who!—Marylyn Springer and Donald Schultz.

A **wildlife** freebie here: In Port Everglades you can get a close look at fat manatees, brilliantly colored parrot fish, and other rainbow-hued creatures of the deep. They congregate in a small canal where the water is warmed by heat from a nearby electricity-generating plant. To see them, enter the port at its only entrance on Eller Drive (Fla. 84 just south of NE 17th Street) and follow the road turning to the right at the stop sign. A short way along you'll see a fence into which viewing windows have been cut. It's an informal spot, no admission, no hours except the ones the fish keep.

## The Animal Kingdom

You can pet hijinking bottlenose "Flipper" dolphins at **Ocean World** on the 17th Street Causeway (tel. 525-6611), gaze in wonder at the sharks as they're fed by an intrepid soul, take a boat tour, and watch fish minding their own business in a three-story-high-aquarium. Hours are 10am to 6pm daily (last show is at 4:15pm). Admission is $10 for adults, $8 for children 4 to 12.

**Flamingo Gardens,** 3750 Flamingo Rd., Davie (tel. 473-0010), spreads 60 acres of land with tropical gardens, then adds flamingos, and a petting zoo. You can ride through the gardens on a tram daily from 9am to 5pm and visit a small museum. Admission is $6.50 for adults, $3.25 for children 4 to 14.

An unusual stop in Fort Lauderdale's animal kingdom is **Butterfly World,** Tradewinds Park, 3600 W. Sample Rd., Coconut Creek (tel. 977-4400). Here they know just what appeals to butterflies and they see to it that the winged creatures get whatever they want. Being smart little critters, they hang around, flapping their psychedelic wings and looking ornamental. There's even a shop that sells you all the plants necessary to attract butterflies to *your* garden. Admission is $6 for adults, $4 for children 3 to 12. The flappers are on view from 9am to 5pm daily, from 1pm on Sunday.

## SPORTS

Do 55 golf courses sound like enough to keep you busy? How about 172 public tennis courts? Fleets of fishing boats? Dozens of rental sailboats, windsurfing boards, waterboggans, even hot-air balloons? Read on.

### Golf

There are 11 public courses just in Fort Lauderdale's city limits, with PGA tournament play at Inverrary, home of the annual Honda Inverrary Invitational in March. Rates vary, but public courses like the **American Golfers Club,** 3850 N. Federal Hwy. (tel. 564-8760), a 27-hole executive course near the beach, charges $18 greens fees, $16 for an electric cart. The course opens at 7:30am daily.

### Tennis

Public courts in the beach area include lighted ones at **Holiday Park** (tel. 761-5391) on Sunrise Boulevard, and **George English Park** at 1101 Bayview Dr. (tel. 566-0664). Contact the city's recreation department (tel. 761-5346) for information about all sports in the city.

### Boating

Try **Atlantic Boat Rentals** at Bahia Mar Hotel, 801 Seabreeze Ave. (tel. 467-6000) or **Bill's Sunrise Rentals,** 301 Seabreeze Ave. (tel. 467-1316) for small craft, waterskiing boats and equipment, waverunners, parasailing, even motorized water-going scooters called jet-skis. Powerboats are $45 per hour, jet-skis $50 an hour.

Rent a **sailboat** from facilities located on the beach just south of Las Olas Boulevard and at the north end of the beach about a mile north of Sunrise Boulevard, or at the Royce Resort on Galt Ocean Mile or the Marriott Harbor Beach Hotel. Rates begin at about $25 an hour.

### Bicycling and Mopeds

Bicycles built for two, one, and the timid are available at **Florida Bicycle,** 515 W. Sunrise Blvd. (tel. 763-6974), for $30 a week, and at **John's Mopeds,** 1565 N. Dixie Hwy., Pompano Beach (tel. 781-8027), for $15 a day, plus deposit.

John's Mopeds also rents mopeds for $8 an hour, $30 a day.

### Fishing

Try the ***Dragon,*** at 440 Seabreeze Ave., behind the Holiday Inn just off Las Olas Boulevard (tel. 522-FISH) for four hours of drift fishing, including equipment, for $18. There are three trips daily, at 8:30am, 1:30pm, and 7:30pm.

**Charter boats** at Bahia Mar Yacht Basin will take you after the big ones. Minimum rates are generally about $75 a person, $300 or so for six for a half-day trip and $500 for a full day, but bargain for a better deal. Call 525-7174 for information on boats and hours.

You can **fish from piers** at Dania, Lauderdale-by-the-Sea, Pompano Beach, and Hillsboro.

### Water Sports

**Scuba and Snorkeling:** At 440 Seabreeze Ave., **Divers Unlimited** (tel. 524-4862) can outfit you for less than $30 a day, but you must be certified. They're open daily from 8am to 6pm. About the same prices apply at **Lauderdale Diver,** 1134 SE 17th St. (tel. 467-2822).

A number of scuba-diving operators will take you out on diving trips, visiting both natural reefs and artificial sites like the freighter *Mercedes I* which was scuttled off Sunrise Boulevard in 1984 to create a new playground for divers.

**Surfing and Swimming:** The **Waterbrothers Surf Shop,** 1738 NE Fourth Ave. (tel. 525-4912), charges $10 a day for a board ($5 for students), and **BC Surf and Sport,** 1626 N. Federal Hwy. (tel. 564-0202), bills $10 a half day, $15 for 24 hours. Both are open daily from 10am to 7pm and have surf reports.

You can paddle around in this city's Olympic-size public pool, the **International Swimming Hall of Fame,** 1 Hall of Fame Dr. (tel. 462-6536), that's the home of major national swimming and diving competitions. It costs just $3 a day, $1.50 for students and children, and there's a small museum on the grounds chronicling the accomplishments of famous swimmers up to and including Johnny Weissmuller, Buster Crabbe, and Esther Williams.

Texas's Six Flags has opened what it likes to call the world's largest water park in the small town of Hollywood just south of Fort Lauderdale. Called **Six Flags Atlantis,** the park is located just east of I-95 at 2700 Stirling Rd. (tel. 926-1000). You won't have any trouble finding it: Just look for the submarine perched on the I-95 edge of the property. Inside you'll find swooping, snaking water slides several stories high, a wave pool that splashes you with endless breakers, an outdoor roller rink, tropical trails, a waterski show, and a lake for boating. There are plenty of shady places for picnics, plus refreshment stands and some shops. Six Flags Atlantis opened its doors in May 1983 and is quite a fun place to spend the day. Admission is $13 for adults, $10 for children 3 to 11. It opens at 11am daily, closing at 10pm or later in summer (11am to 5pm on weekends only when school is in session).

There's a long and lovely strip of beach at **Hugh Taylor Birch State Park,** 3109 E. Sunrise Blvd. (tel. 564-4521), where you can also get a look at what Fort Lauderdale was like long ago when millionaire recluse Birch redeemed his eccentricity with this donation to the city. Located at Fla. A1A and Sunrise Boulevard, the park has access to the beach through an under-the-street tunnel, a self-guided nature trail, fishing in the Intracoastal, and some beautiful picnic spots under tall pines. There are canoes and paddleboats for rent, and the park is open daily from 8am to sunset. Admission is $2 for the car and driver, $1 for each passenger.

**Waterskiing:** You can waterski without a boat at **Quiet Waters Park,** 6601 Powerline Rd. (tel. 429-0215), where a gizmo called Ski Rixen tows you around on a cable. Instruction is free and you can rent the skis for all kinds of waterskiing from slalom to trick and ski-jumping. You can even ski barefoot or on a kneeboard. You'll find the park west of I-95 on Powerline Road, between Sample Road and Hillsborough Boulevard at the Pompano/Deerfield city line. Admission to the park is $1 driver and 50¢ passengers; skiing facilities cost $11.50 an hour, $21.50 for all day, and are open from 10am to 6pm year-round.

## Skating

**Gold Coast Roller Rink,** 2604 S. Federal Hwy. (tel. 523-6783), features indoor skating and will rent you skates for 50¢. Admission is $3.50 to $5 evenings. Hours vary, but are generally 9am to midnight on Friday and Saturday, 1 to 4pm on Sunday. On Saturday night teenagers show up, so it's not a particularly good time for younger children. Other days the rink is open for private parties or by arrangement. Give them a call to see what's happening the day you want to go.

## Baseball

Baseball fans can get a look at the **New York Yankees,** who train here in spring at Yankee Stadium, 5301 NW 12th Ave. (tel. 776-1921). Tickets are $3.50 to $7.

## Pari-mutuel Sports

Watch jai-alai players toss speeding pelotas around at 150 m.p.h. at **Dania Jai-Alai Fronton,** 301 E. Dania Beach Blvd. (tel. 945-4345 or 426-4330), which is open year-round. Performance times are 7:15pm Tuesday through Saturday, and also at noon Tuesday and Saturday from November to April, Saturday only from May. Closed Sunday and Monday. General admission is $1. Summer schedules are abbreviated so it would be wise to call before setting out for the games. Minors may now attend, too.

There is harness racing at **Pompano Harness Track,** on Race Track Road (tel. 972-2000), in Pompano Beach. The track is located on West Atlantic Boulevard. You can make a lovely (and perhaps lucky) evening of it from October to April, when the park has harness races nightly, with seating in a multilevel dining room with huge walls of glass overlooking the track. Admission is $1.50 for the grandstand, $3 for clubhouse seats; dinner is moderately priced. Racing every evening, except Sunday, at 7:30pm.

For dog racing it's the **Hollywood Greyhound Dog Track,** 831 N. Federal Hwy., Hallandale (tel. 454-9400), where clubhouse admission is $1.50, 50¢ for the grandstand. It's open every night (except Sunday) and has matinees on Monday, Wednesday, and Saturday. The track is open from December 26 through April. Post times are 12:45pm and 7:45pm.

## FORT LAUDERDALE AFTER DARK

Back in the 1960s when the George Hamilton tan and the film *Where the Boys Are* put Fort Lauderdale on college maps and began the annual spring-break trek to the sea, the city's Elbo Room (at Las Olas Boulevard and Fla. A1A) acquired considerable reknown for the copious quantities of hops imbibed there. Shortly there arose competition that has now reached proportions so epidemic the city has the dubious, if unconfirmed, honor of sporting more nightspots per capita than any other city in the United States. Although there were once 3,100 cases of beer consumed monthly at the Elbo Room's competitor, the Button, there are also some slightly more high-brow activities here, including an elegant playhouse (selected by Elizabeth Taylor for the opening run of her play *Little Foxes*), plus opera and symphony. Check area newspapers or *Key* or *See* magazines for up-to-the-minute reports on what's happening.

## Cultural Events

Fort Lauderdale has long provided strong support for the arts, from a symphony orchestra to the ballet and even a children's theater.

The **Fort Lauderdale Ballet** performs at various locations and is particularly busy during the winter and Christmas holiday season when, of course, it performs the famous *Nutcracker*. You can find out when they'll be on their toes by calling them at 537-4195 or writing 508 NE 43rd St., Fort Lauderdale, FL 33334.

This city starts its budding stars out young at the **Fort Lauderdale Children's Theater,** 640 N. Andrews Ave. (tel. 763-6882), which has regular schedules of plays for children and starring children who learn their art in classes at the theater school.

South Florida has its own **symphony orchestra,** the New World Symphony, 1430 N. Federal Hwy. (tel. 561-2997), which performs on a regular winter schedule at War Memorial Auditorium in Holiday Park on Sunrise Boulevard. Tickets vary in price, averaging about $25.

**Parker Playhouse,** at 707 NE 8th St. in Holiday Park (tel. 764-0700) offers top-name performers and tickets in the $25 to $35 range. Any seat in this elegant semicircular house is a good one, and the theater is a showplace, with a seating capacity of 1,200 and long arc-shaped rows with plenty of room to find your seat without squashing yourself or someone else. Crystal chandeliers and champagne in the lobby from late November through April set the tone for appearances by such stars as Peter Ustinov, Mickey Rooney, Donald O'Connor, Shelley Winters, and Elizabeth Taylor. There are rotating art shows in the Playhouse gallery, and opening nights (Tuesday) are a study in Cadillac limousines and diamonds. There are matinees on Wednesday, Saturday, and Sunday.

Top-name opera stars like Luciano Pavarotti show up here annually, usually in January, February, or March, to perform at the **War Memorial Auditorium,** 800 NE 8th St. in Holiday Park (tel. 761-5381). Tickets vary in price according to the star, but are usually sold out well in advance.

Far out in the western reaches of the county, the **Sunrise Musical Theater,** 5555 NW 95th Ave., Sunrise (tel. 523-3309), lures top musical entertainment that has in past years included everyone from Ol' Blue Eyes to Engelbert Humperdinck, Donna Summer, comedian Don Rickles, Liza Minnelli, Joel Grey, and Santana. There's a wide range in price depending on the popularity of the star, but expect tickets to run $15 to $25 or more.

Surprisingly, a Fort Lauderdale church is one of the more prolific providers of concerts and classical music recitals. Scene of performances ranging from pianists performing Bach or Mendelssohn to choral productions by a 200-voice chancel choir or the Florida Philharmonic Orchestra is the dramatically decorated **Coral Ridge Presbyterian Church,** 5555 N. Federal Hwy. You can call them at 491-1103 to find out what will be happening and when. Tickets rarely top $8 to $10.

## Trendy Spots

Never a city to arrive late at a trend, Fort Lauderdale has quick-change nightspots—this month country and western, next month Glenn Miller. Three years ago a nightspot without a mechanical bull was bucking the tide. These days slick and woodsy decor heavy on brass and plants, loud but not label-able music, are so far "in" they're headed out the back. So don't hold us responsible if one of these chameleons has changed its hue.

As hysterically popular as **Shooter's** is these days, you practically need a shoe-horn to wedge yourself in here. You'll know why this spot is so popular when you see its chic royal-blue trim and its slick woodsy-plantsy interior, not even to mention its waterside setting beside the Intracoastal Canal. You'll find drinking and dining (accent on the former), both inside and out. Very nice spot indeed. It's at 3031 NE 32nd Ave. (tel. 566-2855), right between two other spots of considerable renown, Durty Nelly's and the Bootlegger (see "Waterside Watering Spots").

In its last incarnation, **City Limits** at 2520 S. Miami Rd., Fort Lauderdale (tel. 524-7827), was an urban cowboy's dream, complete with bull. This time around it's somewhere between disco and rock. Whatever it is when you get here, you can be sure it will have lots of decibels and plenty of action, particularly for the under-25 set. It opens at 8pm, closes at 4am.

We all know by now that comedy clubs are the hottest thing since flambé, so it should come as no surprise that Fort Lauderdale, home of trendy-before-trendy-was-trendy nightlife would be well endowed with yuppie vaudeville emporiums. Sit in the first row at one of these spots at your own risk.

**Governor's Comedy Shop,** 3001 E. Commercial Blvd. (tel. 776-5653), is part of a chain of northeast seaboard comedy nightclubs and therefore books some top names in current comedy. Yuk masters here must have film or national credits and be on the verge of leaping into the big time. Entertainment begins at 9pm Wednesday, Thursday, and Sunday. On Friday and Saturday there are shows at 8:30 and 10:45pm. Cover charges range from $5 to $8 and there's a two-drink minimum. Closed Monday and Tuesday.

A fixture in Fort Lauderdale long before comedy became the thing to do to find yourself laughing all the way to the bank, the **Comic Strip,** 1432 N. Federal Hwy. (tel. 565-8887), is as funky and funny as ever. Giggling here now for more than a decade, this too is a branch of a New York club. Eat, drink, and be merry here from 9:30pm on Sunday through Thursday, from 10pm on Friday, and at 8:30 and 11pm on Saturday. The cover charge varies from $5 to $8 and there's a two-drink minimum.

You haven't heard of the **Candy Store?** Where have you been—Outer Mongolia? This little devil of a spot put itself and Fort Lauderdale on many a map when it started a trend lovingly known as the Wet T-Shirt Contest. Droves of network came-ramen rolled in to record this important new leisure-time activity, thus keeping this place from going bust. You can see one of the competitions any Sunday, when you'll have no trouble at all finding the Candy Store: Just look for a huge crowd of goggle-eyed types hanging off the lampposts. It's in the Tradewinds Hotel at 1 N. Atlantic Blvd. (tel. 761-1888). Clue to the kind of crowd you'll find: The movie *Spring Break* was filmed here.

A young British friend of ours says she had a wonderful time at **Confetti's,** 2660 E. Commercial Blvd. (tel. 776-4080 or 776-4081), and intimated that, in-deed, she had considerably more fun than she was about to relate. Particularly spellbound by a bartender dressed all in green, Robin Hood style, this lass and many others swear by the laughs to be had at this very popular watering hole. It's cheek to cheek here (interpret that any way you like) every weekend and busy-busy every oth-er night of the week as well. Things get flying here about 9pm and keep tossing until the wee hours every night. Something weird goes on each night, from Wild Women Wednesday with no cover charge for women, wild or not, to Goose and Gander Night with freebies for goose—and since what's good for the goose is good, etc., ganders get free drinks too. Cover is $5.

Jazz fans can always find someone jammin' at **Musician's Exchange,** 729 W. Sunrise Blvd. (tel. 764-1912), which, although devoid of fancy atmosphere, is *the* southern Florida jazz center. Tickets are about $10 and performance hours and stars vary so give them a call.

Platoons of the thirsty head to the **Parrot Lounge,** 907 Sunrise Lane (tel. 563-1493), to seek a cracker and four or five brews to go with it. A hysterically popular watering spot just a block from the beach at Sunrise Boulevard, the Parrot has been squawking for many a year now and makes up in decent-and-well-run what it lacks in chic decor. There is atmosphere, however, characterized by such objets d'art as a ma-rine recon patrol canoe paddle and an autographed mugshot of Sylvester Stallone (in funky Fort Lauderdale you were expecting photos of Buckminster Fuller?). The Par-rot's an especially good choice for girls traveling without guys: They're so chivalrously friendly here they often walk lone lasses home in the wee hours. There's no admission or cover charge, drinks are reasonably priced, and hours are 11am to whenever.

**Joseph's,** 3200 E. Oakland Park Blvd. (tel. 564-7788), is a showy spot from the purple canopy over the door to the plush plum seating and cascading lights in-side. An upmarket disco here has raised dance floors, glass etchings, and swirling lights. Crowds are a little older but don't seem to lack any energy when the club's rocking from 9pm to 2am daily, later on weekends, when there is a $5 cover charge.

**Mr. Laff's,** 1135 N. Federal Hwy. (tel. 561-3440), has plenty of what the name suggests, and has since 1976, when this popular watering hole opened. Ages range widely here in this pleasant lounge rigged out in polished brass rails, wood and brick walls, lots of windows, and a skylight that lets in enough sun to keep acres of green-ery growing. Open 11:30am to 2am daily, with a band playing nearly every evening, Mr. Laff's has been cloned in the far-western reaches of the county at 2375 Universi-ty Dr. (tel. 474-5700).

**Café 66,** 2001 SE 17th St. Causeway, in the Pier Sixty-Six Hotel, (tel. 728-3500), keeps jumping to the wee hours with a band every night except Monday. An attractive spot, Café 66 attracts a wide range of ages and interests and has a $5 cover charge on occasion.

**Summers,** 219 S. Atlantic Blvd. (tel. 462-8978), is where it's at on Fort Lauderdale's famous beach strip. There's always something happening here seem-ingly day and night. What isn't going on inside is strolling past the door trying to see what's going on inside. Fun and games and rock from noon to 2 or 3am with well-known bands and singers. Tickets cost $8 to $12.

Who ever thought it would come to this, but here it is, ladies merrily boxing and wrestling and pursuing sundry other pursuits at **Pure Platinum,** 3411 N. Federal Hwy., Oakland Park (tel. 565-2996). All this goes on daily from noon to 2am, Saturday till 3am. Definitely not a spot for blushers.

**Lagniappe Cajun House,** 200 W. Broward Blvd. (tel. 467-7500), rocks to the sounds of everything from Bo Diddley to Dixieland jazz. Anchor of a beautiful little cluster of galleries and boutiques called Bon Ton Square, Lagniappe lets the good times roll from 6pm to midnight or later every night, with entertainment beginning about 9:30pm. There's a $5 to $10 cover charge for top-name entertainment, lower or no charge if you're dining in this lively restaurant.

## A Very Special Event

If you're planning a December visit to Fort Lauderdale, try to schedule it so you're here for the city's annual **Winterfest** celebration, which usually occurs about the middle of December. A week of beauty pageants, marathon runs, beach dances, parades, and Christmas-tree-lighting ceremonies is capped by the **Winterfest Boat Parade,** at which you'll discover one of the joys of visiting this always-warm city. While much of the rest of the nation shivers, you sit outside along the banks of a waterway, entertained by choral groups and ho-ho-ing Santas gliding by aboard massive yachts, trimmed in twinkling lights from gunwale to mainmast.

In Fort Lauderdale, the boat parade has become the partying apex of the year, a time when anyone who lives on or near the waterway suddenly acquires many friends. Waterway dwellers take these newfound friendships in stride, however, and the parties go on . . . and on and on.

If you don't have or can't acquire a waterside-dwelling friend in time for the parade, book a seat at one of the waterside restaurants or lounges, many of which are detailed in the restaurants and nightlife sections. Order something long and cool, then sit back and ooh and aah along with the rest as a fantasy of gleaming light-trimmed yachts glides by in a glittering trail of light and laughter. Some lounges charge a cover for the evening, and every restaurant anywhere near the Intracoastal is booked weeks, sometimes months, in advance, so act accordingly. Among the spots you might consider settling are Stan's, the Bootlegger, Durty Nelly's, Shooters, Charlie's Crab, Frankie's, Le Dome of the Four Seasons, Riverwatch at the Marriott Hotel and Marina, Yesterday's, and Benihana of Tokyo.

Budget-watchers can achieve the same goal by heading off an hour or so before the parade (first boats leave Pier Sixty-Six just after dark; times are published in local newspapers) to pull up a piece of ground alongside the waterway. Some revelers add a touch of élan to these free seats by arming themselves with a fancy picnic dinner and a bottle of champagne! Likely watching spots are on or under the several bridges connecting the beach to the mainland: at 17th Street (where you can also buy tickets and sit in bleacher seats) or at Las Olas, Sunrise, Oakland Park, and Commercial boulevards. Plan your sitting spot carefully, however, for bridges remain up until the last boat has chugged through, so you won't be able to leave until it's over if you're on the wrong side of the bridge.

Grand marshals of the parade are—who else?—Santa Claus and some other less famous celebrity. Recent GMs were Willard Scott, who broadcast his weather report from the city's beaches, and legendary comedian Bob Hope.

## Other Special Events

**Las Olas Art Festival** occurs annually at the end of March and is one of the most prestigious art shows in the state. Artists from all over the nation fill blocked-off Las Olas with every kind of artwork from handcrafted wooden ocarinas to kaleidoscopes, elegant jewelry, oil paintings, pottery, wood and metal sculpture, stained glass, the list goes colorfully on.

March is a busy month: The **New River Street Dance** gets thousands of visitors and residents dancing in the streets, and in the western half of the county, the city of Davie romps through a rootin', tootin' **Orange Blossom Festival and Rodeo.**

In April plant lovers can find a bargain on all kinds of exotic blooming things at the **Fort Lauderdale Plant Affair** in Holiday Park, while gourmands taste the offerings of a dozen or more seafood restaurants at the annual **Fort Lauderdale Seafood Festival,** which supports the efforts of the city's Historical Society.

## Waterside Watering Spots

Outdoors is where it's at, after all, and one of the tops in outdoor spots is the **Bootlegger,** at 3003 NE 32nd Ave. (tel. 563-4337), hard by the Intracoastal. This is your chance to try the one-arm crawl, with one arm clutching a martini, the other propelling you through the Bootlegger's private swimming pool. Hours are 11am to 2am daily, from noon on Sunday. Drink prices start at $2.25, with burgers and snacks available in the $3 to $5 bracket.

**Durty Nelly's,** next door at 3051 NE 32nd Ave. (tel. 564-0720), is more of the same without the pool. Drink outside in the sun or inside in the cool. Hours are 11am to 2am weekdays, on Saturday to 3am, opening at noon on Sunday. There's always a happy hour or ladies night, free hot dogs, or a twofer going here. No cover, mod sounds. Drinks run $2 to $4.

Settle into a chair on the terrace of **Coconuts,** 429 Seabreeze Ave. (tel. 467-6788), tune in to the guitar sounds emanating from the inside lounge and dining room, and you'll suddenly understand why you are vacationing in Florida. Soon some Sunday sailor will sputter up and hop out to join the fun. A pleasant spot tucked in alongside a canal just south of Las Olas Boulevard and a few strides from the ocean, Coconuts attracts a little older and quieter crowd than the more strident beach bars just a few blocks away.

Food leans toward steaks, with sirloins and filets available in several sizes and fat lobsters also on the menu. Grazing treats like zucchini, mozzarella sticks, and nachos are available, along with seafood specials like dolphin or a local catch called tilefish. Prices fall into the $11 to $20 bracket for dinner at Coconuts, which makes a nice place to play when you want to hear yourself talk. Coconuts is open from 11:30am to 2am daily, closing later on Saturday and opening at noon on Sunday.

## Lively Places

Stars of the entertainment world appear at the **Diplomat Resort,** 3515 S. Ocean Dr., Hollywood (tel. 457-8111), which has several lounges with a variety of entertainment. Prices can go sky-high for New Years' Eve and other holidays, and can be lofty for performances by top stars.

**Lagniappe Cajun House,** 200 W. Broward Blvd. (tel. 467-7500), features jazz and lively Dixieland in a lively French Quarter atmosphere and the No Problem Island Café.

**Button South,** a south-county version of the antics at the Button on Fort Lauderdale's beach, specializes in rock groups with strange names. There's entertainment nightly, a varying cover charge in the $5 bracket, and always plenty of decibels. It's at 100 Ansin Way Blvd. (tel. 454-4880).

Along what is lovingly and often all-too-accurately known as "The Strip," all the action's on foot as strollers roam Atlantic Boulevard (Fla. A1A) from Las Olas to Sunrise in search of something. Most of them find it at the **Elbo Room,** an institution in many senses of the word, **Summers on the Beach, The Button,** and the **Candy Store,** all right in a row beginning at Las Olas Boulevard and working north a couple of blocks.

**Christopher's,** at 2857 E. Oakland Park Blvd. (tel. 561-2136), attracts the three-piece-suit set at 5pm, a wild, weird, and sometimes wonderful variety of outfits later. Lots of contemporary glitz here, and some outstanding free hors d'oeuvres at happy hour. Drink prices run about $3. It's open from 11am to 2am daily, to 3am on Saturday.

Lampshade wearers and other convivial types who are convinced their future lies in generating guffaws can see if they've got what it yuks at the **Comic Strip,** 1432 N. Federal Hwy. (tel. 565-8887), sister to New York's Comic Strip. Young comics throng in here for amateur night on Monday and bomb or score in about the same proportions as professionals. It's fun! Drinks are about $3 and there's a $10 cover charge on Friday and Saturday ($7 Sunday through Thursday), and a two-drink minimum per person. Hours: 8:30pm to 2am, with shows at 9:30 nightly, and 8:30 and 11:30pm on Saturday.

## Fort Lauderdale's Favorite

There is no more popular place in the city than the fabulous **Mai-Kai**, 3599 N. Federal Hwy. (tel. 563-3272). There are Polynesian clubs here and there across the world, but there is none more spectacularly beautiful or tastefully put together than the Mai-Kai that has brought a smile and a memory to generations of families who make this their choice for special events. With a quarter of a century of experience behind it, the Mai-Kai is doing everything right, from award-winning cuisine to the tinkling waterfalls that pour into streams running through a jungle of tropical plants.

Created by Bob Thornton, a one-time collegiate visitor to the city who went on to marry lovely Mireille, the Tahitian star of his show, the Mai-Kai features ethereally beautiful Polynesian women and their burly male counterparts—and, often on Sunday, special performances by their children! All the impressive dancers perform carefully researched, authentic dances of the South Pacific. There are enough 75-r.p.m. wiggles to pique the interest, but the shows are so beautifully choreographed and written by Mireille Thornton that they can bring a shiver to your spine and perhaps even a tear to your eye.

Here you will learn why Bora-Bora is never boring-boring. Lots of wing-a-ding drink specialties here in the $5-and-up range—dare you try the Mystery Drink? Clue: Bring help, perhaps a litter. Buried in one of the loveliest tropical-jungle gardens in Florida, the Mai-Kai has several dining rooms, all of them decked out in high-backed wicker chairs, slowly swaying paddle fans, and fabrics of the islands. Dinner shows occur twice a night, usually at 7:30 and 10:30pm, and midnight Friday and Saturday although times may differ by season. A la carte entrées are in the $13 to $24 range and there's a $5- to $8-per-person cover charge.

## Discos

A classy FL favorite is **One-Up Lounge**, 3001 E. Oakland Park Blvd. (on the second floor of Yesterday's restaurant; tel. 561-4400), where a disc jockey spins the latest hits while patrons light up the dance floor. Always at the top of a trend, this lively nightclub overlooking the Intracoastal Waterway opens at 8pm and closes at 2pm. There is a $5 cover charge.

Among the newest lights in this city of nightlights is **Koz's Sports Arena**, 20 N. Federal Hwy. (tel. 467-6777). Lines snake halfway around the building on weekend evenings when all and sundry press to get in here to watch sports action on huge television screens, practice in a batting cage, or slam-dunk a few basketballs. Among the devotees are many professional players in various sports—no that's not what we meant, although that's also possible. Koz's is open from 11am to 2am daily.

**Studio 51**, 1421 E. Oakland Park Blvd. (tel. 565-5151), is hanging in there, reflective surfaces gleaming. Flash! Chrome! Mirror! Strobe! Cover charge: $7.50 on weekends! Drinks: $4! Hours: 8pm to 2am nightly except Monday and Tuesday, to 3am on Saturday. Party!

## SHOPPING

Fort Lauderdale is also a popular shopping spot that offers everything from a streetful of trendy boutiques to several huge shopping malls that are home to the poshest names in fashion, jewelry, and home furnishings, as well as several large department stores.

As far as we're concerned, to begin from the top down here means you must start on lovely **Las Olas Boulevard**, a street that has been luring wealthy boulevardiers to its treasures for generations. Whether or not you buy anything, window-shopping here is a delight, day or night.

Stretching from the ocean to Fort Lauderdale's rapidly growing downtown center, Las Olas is a study in flickering gas lamps, stately royal palms, masses of colorful flowers, tiny picturesque alleyways, and winding canals. Fascinating shops tucked away in nooks and crannies offer everything from vintage lace dresses that would have pleased your great grandmother to the trendiest of nouveau duds.

Evenings, these boutiques are trimmed in jillions of tiny white lights. Many who come to the street's sleek restaurants to dine make an evening of it with after-dinner window-shopping and perhaps a libation in front of the fireplace in the lounge at the elegant old Riverside Hotel or with the blues singers at a creole restaurant called Lagniappe.

As you will see in the restaurant section, several of the city's best restaurants are located on this lovely boulevard—Paesano, Il Giardino, Café de Paris—and now there's even a little British pub.

Among the most interesting of many interesting shops along Las Olas are: **La Belle Epoque,** a tiny antiques and vintage clothing shop one door north of the boulevard at 706 E. Las Olas Blvd. (tel. 463-0881); **Mole Hole,** 713A E. Las Olas, an eclectic gift shop with some of everything; the **Chemist Shop,** a drugstore at 817 E. Las Olas where you can buy perfumes and upscale trinkets you can't find anywhere else; **Aamartin's Furs,** at 713 E. Las Olas, a drooling place for those who never met a mink they didn't love; **Maus and Hoffman,** at 800 E. Las Olas, purveyors of Scotch plaids and tweedy things; **Polly Flinders,** at 1521 E. Las Olas, specializing in cut-rate prices on adorable smocked dresses for little girls; and **Hush!** for discount high fashion.

There are many, many more—and we're sure to hear from all the ones we've left out—including a wicker furniture shop, several antique stores, and a bevy of art galleries specializing in everything from art of Native Americans to old masters and contemporary sculptures.

There's a couple of specialty tailor shops, and even a shoe store that's so popular with winter residents the shop features a mail-in shoe repair service! Just send them your favorite floppers and they'll fix 'em up and send them back ready for another 20 years of dedicated service. It's called **Scottie's** and it's at 1102 E. Las Olas.

You bargain-hunters may luck into a couple of treasures on Las Olas at a little empire operated by the ladies of the First Presbyterian Church. These quite entrepreneurial ladies painted several church-owned houses a bright pink, named them, aptly enough, Pink House, and filled them with secondhand goodies and items made in church craft classes. Although they're no longer pink, you can still find everything there from brand-new household appliances for $10 or so, to oil paintings, brocade gowns, books, cunning hand-crocheted toy clowns and pin cushions. You'll find **Pink House** at 1302 E. Las Olas (tel. 462-7734).

If you're a shopping center fan, you can do no better than massive **Galleria,** 2500 E. Sunrise Blvd., just a few blocks from the ocean. Stores include such look-at-my-label names as Neiman-Marcus, Lord & Taylor, Jordan Marsh, Burdine's, and Saks. Boutiques include the likes of Bally, Laura Ashley, Ralph Lauren, Sharper Image, Williams-Sonoma, Brooks Brothers, well you've got the picture. In addition to fancy jewelers, a candy store and a glittering shop filled with thousands of constantly polished crystal knickknacks including a huge horse's head that may be the perfect gift for a godfather friend, there are also many moderately priced shops and a raft of restaurants.

Smaller shopping centers are scattered throughout the county and include **Broward Mall,** way out west at 8000 W. Broward Blvd.; the recently enlarged **Pompano Fashion Square** north of Fort Lauderdale at 2001 N. Federal Hwy. in Pompano; and a cluster of discount shops in a warehouse district along NW 19th Street west of Fort Lauderdale in a small community called Lauderdale Lakes.

Antiques abound in nearby Dania, a village located just south of Fort

Lauderdale's airport. So many antique sellers have set up shop there, in fact, that enthusiasts call the town's main street (US 1) **Antique Row.** Among the larger of those shops—and technically not in Dania but a mile or so north in Fort Lauderdale at 2075 S. Federal Hwy. (US 1)—is **Jan's of London,** a shop specializing in brass-trimmed campaign furniture as well as antiques.

## A VISIT TO THE "SWEET" LAND OF BLACK GOLD

Mile after mile of tall green stalks rustling in the breeze, in the air the sweet smell of—sugar!

Just 70 miles northwest of Fort Lauderdale is Clewiston, Florida's sugar capital and home of the largest sugar company in the nation. For miles around this city you'll see 300,000 acres of green cane stalks, which are reaped from October to May to produce 7,000 tons of cane and 1½ million pounds of raw sugar, about half the nation's total sugar consumption.

Here, too, is the Florida home of the U.S. Sugar Corp., which runs about everything in this sugar land and has made one lovely contribution to the area, the Clewiston Inn (more on that later).

From Fort Lauderdale, Miami, or any of the cities along the east coast as far north as Lake Worth, you can travel through fascinating central Florida's farmlands and sugar country on a roundabout trip that skirts **Lake Okeechobee,** the second-largest lake in the nation. Get there on US 27, which cuts straight through the heart of fishing, cattle, and farming country. (A word about US 27, however: It is a busy two-lane road where *very* alert driving is required.) You can also take Florida's Sunshine State Parkway north to the Lake Worth exit, turn west to just north of Loxahatchee, and go through the town of Loxahatchee. Either way you arrive at the edge of the lake upon whose existence most of southern Florida and the vast Everglades depends.

Southwest of Fort Lauderdale on US 27 is **Everglades Holiday Park,** 21940 Griffin Rd. (tel. 434-8111), where you can rent boats for a trip into the Everglades or ride atop a whizzing airboat on a $12, ranger-guided tour of the Glades. (See "Airboat Rides," in the section on Fort Lauderdale sights, for details.) Along US 27 you'll see some of the huge horned and hump-backed Brahma cattle Florida imported long ago from India when standard American-bred cattle perished from heat and insect pests. When the Brahma strain was bred into the cattle, the industry flourished and Florida is now among the top five cattle-producing states in the nation.

Massive Lake Okeechobee, the second-largest expanse of fresh water in the U.S., covers 730 square miles and nearly 500,000 acres. It has three large islands—Kreamer, Torry, and Ritta—and one way or another is a major part of the natural underground pipeline that keeps all of South Florida watered. Remnant of a prehistoric sea, **Lake Okeechobee** is the center of a powerful agro-industrial empire that produces fish, vegetables, sugar, and cattle.

This here is "bice" country, folks—that's bass to the rest of us. Bass fishing is king sport up this way, such a rite of passage that you'll see the big fellows, fittingly called largemouth bass, hanging proudly on elegant walls, offered on menus, touted by guides, and bragged upon at every corner. A Calo Nitka Fishing (that's big bass in Seminole) Competition begins in January and winds up in March with (what else?) a fish fry and a beauty queen.

Mile for mile, there are few more diversely interesting sections of Florida than the immense agricultural area that surrounds Lake Okeechobee. Beginning at South Bay and circling the lake clockwise you pass through **Clewiston,** a 16,000-person town that claims to be the richest per capita city in America, and there's every likelihood that's true (or at least it was when sugar prices were high). U.S. Sugar Corp. runs this town, importing 8,000 Jamaican laborers every winter to cut the cane with machetes.

Next up around the lake is **Moore Haven,** a cow town where big Brahmas easily outnumber the 1,300 folks who live here. A 450-year-old cypress tree called Lone

Cypress was once a hitching post for swamp boats, but changes in the lake have left it high and dry a mile inland.

About 10 miles along you'll come to a spot with a memorable name: **Fisheating Creek.** If you want to do what that name suggests, turn off on Fla. 721A, a rough road called "The Loop," that leads you to **Hideaway Restaurant,** open from 5:30am to 10pm and dishing out the delicacies of these parts: alligator, catfish, frogs' legs, and turtle, along with a few less challenging options.

This is Seminole country now and always has been. You're welcome to drive through huge **Brighton Reservation** but you won't see much native living—the Seminoles live in just plain houses, no rustic chickees or tents here. Much less commercial than the branches of their tribes in Dania and Miami, these Seminoles live close to the earth and still participate in some of the oldest tribal ritual events. If you're lucky you may see some women in ornate tribal dress, but just seeing these miles of Florida outback dotted with groves of cabbage palm may be luck enough for you.

At the northern tip of the lake is **Okeechobee City,** once a wild and woolly town named after a fiery-haired schoolteacher purported to have a personality that matched her locks. A grim Christmas Day battle between Gen. Zachary Taylor, who was to go on to become president of the U.S., and the Seminoles was won by the Seminoles, but their victory was a sad case of winning the battle but losing the war for their rights to their homeland. A monument to the battle, said to be ranked right up there with Tippecanoe and Little Big Horn as the most important tribal battles in the nation's history, is on US 441, south of town on the east side of the lake.

You can see the lake's best at **Port Mayaca,** where you can turn right of US 441 and walk on the locks.

In **Pahokee,** 13 miles south, the **Pahokee State Recreation Area** stretches for a mile alongside the lake and has a marina, tent camping sites, and a towering observation post.

At **Belle Glade,** where tons of vegetables are shipped out to winter tables across the nation, you will have completed your circuit of the lake. A migrant labor settlement and recently a high per capita count of AIDS victims here has brought much negative publicity to a city that deserves better. Next door to the city's chamber of commerce you can see a memorial to the 2,200 victims of the 1928 hurricane that sent the lake roaring over its banks and tearing across the land. Built by a Hungarian, Ferenc Varga, the statue shows a family running for their lives, the mother hanging desperately onto her baby as the storm tosses houses like toy blocks and sweeps their residents away to their death.

As you circle the lake on US 27, you will see not water but high levees, built following that disastrous 1928 hurricane. You'll see several lovely parks where you can picnic or rent boats for a little journey out onto this shallow lake that's rarely more than 15 feet deep. You can also drive up onto the levee at marked entrances and park alongside branches of the lake for fishing or picnicking.

Generations ago, early pioneers hacked through the jungles here to discover heavy muckland below, the "black gold" in which they were able to raise prize-winning vegetables in winter. Now 30 varieties of vegetables are grown in the rich soil and shipped from here to winter tables. Huge farmsteads around Belle Glade and Pahokee welcome visitors to the packing houses, and in early April Belle Glade has a Black Gold Jubilee barbecue feast to celebrate the harvest.

If you turn north onto Fla. 78 at its junction with US 27, you can visit **Brighton Seminole Indian Reservation,** which 15 years ago was an isolated village with only dirt paths rarely used by Seminoles who lived out their lives on this reservation. They still live much as they did centuries ago, clinging closer to their ancient ways than many other tribes. Technically the Seminoles are still at war with the U.S.—when Osceola was asked to sign away his tribe's lands, he answered by pinning the treaty to a table with his long knife.

Here, too, is **Indian Prairie,** called the flattest place on earth. Acre after acre, tens of thousands of them, stretch for miles dotted only by the occasional ranch house.

All along the sides of the great lake are small fishing camps that can arrange boats and guides for expeditions on the lake. Bass fishing is successful year round and you'll catch crappies from November to March, bream in summer months.

If you're a trivia collector, here's one more thing to look for as you tour this strange and fascinating area: **cabbage palms.** Clewiston produces most of the palms used in Florida churches on Palm Sunday, and the *fresh* hearts of palm served in some Florida restaurants.

This here, y'all, is the heart of South Florida cracker country, and round these parts you're likely to meet a Glades cracker boy who's worth $10 million or thereabouts, but you'll never guess his net worth from the cut of his jeans—and he'll never tell you either. This is the land of the good ol' boy, who, as they say, ain't half bad!

If you decide to stay here, head straight for the soaring white pillars of the **Clewiston Inn** (P.O. Box 1297), on US 27, Clewiston, FL 33440 (tel. 813/983-8151). Tall arched windows match an imposing double-doored entrance crowned by a coach lamp, and in the reception area you're greeted by beamed ceilings, polished cypress paneling, and a fireplace around which wing chairs and couches are gathered in cozy clusters. Rooms here don't quite match the majesty of the lobby, but they're clean, neat, and some have a king-size bed. Doves coo in a quiet garden nearby. A dining room here seems to shift management and ideas fairly regularly, but you'll always find straightforward down-home cooking, and always very moderate prices in the under-$10 range for a full-course dinner. Rates year-round at the inn are $60 to $65 double; suites and larger family rooms are available, too. The Clewiston Inn's reasonably priced restaurant is open for all three meals and closes about 9pm daily.

If you'd like to put some South in your mouth, don't miss a trip to **Old South Bar-B-Q Ranch,** on US 27, Clewiston (tel. 813/983-6390), where you'll be greeted by life-size plaster cowboys shooting it out at the OK Corral and a white plaster horse staring down from an upper-story manger. Inside, every inch of Old South that doesn't have a table on it is packed with antique tools and Old West kitsch collections. A super-spicy sauce is the number one draw here, and you can even take a bottle of it home with you. There's also pit-barbecued chicken and spareribs, pork and beef sandwiches, thick shakes, and rib-sticking fare (in the $5 to $10 range). Open from 11am to 9pm daily.

# INDIAN RIVER COUNTRY

One hundred miles long and trimmed with sandy barrier islands that separate it from the Atlantic, this vast sapphire lagoon sparkles in the sunshine. Along its banks grow citrus that is the pride of Florida—Indian River tangelos, mandarin and navel oranges, pink and white grapefruit, tangerines.

Courageous, adventurous settlers came to these lands only a century or so ago, but along the banks of this glittering river little seems to have changed in all those years. Tiny boats still bob at anchor, rustic piers jut into the river, and an occasional sailboat streams by. Along the banks of the waterway you see the architecture of early Florida: Spanish tiles crown a roof; timbered houses with wide verandas glow white in the sunshine.

These are quiet communities, small towns, tranquil places where what doesn't get done today will surely be finished tomorrow . . . or soon. In this somnolent atmosphere it's not hard to imagine long-gone days when lights twinkled in simple pioneer cabins set amid hundreds of acres of the million-dollar pineapple crop that once grew here. It's easy to visualize two-masted schooners racing across these rippling waters, bringing clothing, groceries, and medicines to riverside homes, and announcing their arrival with the deep bellow of a conch-shell horn.

In towns like Vero Beach, Fort Pierce, Jensen Beach, Sebastian, Jupiter, and Juno you won't find the glittering nightlife or the glamorous hotels of the rest of the Gold Coast, but you will see silvery mists rising off sapphire waters, an ocean sometimes flat and silver gray, sometimes booming and roaring, foaming and crashing on golden sand. Best of all, you'll find people whose welcome is as warm as their sunshine, whose love of this land runs deep.

Even the booming days of space mania didn't change these sand-fringed communities. Here, despite the tumultuous influx of launch-watchers, you'll find little of the frenetic alteration that characterizes their southern Florida neighbors. That's to the credit of these small towns that have managed, in booming, bursting Florida, to retain the charm, the pervading peace, the lulling drowsiness that made them the desirable place you'll see today—and with any luck, tomorrow.

## GETTING THERE

American, Continental, Delta, Northwest, Pan Am, TWA, United, Wardair, and USAir fly into Palm Beach International Airport, and from there **Palm Beach Airport Limo Service** (tel. 407/684-9900) will take you to towns as far north as Vero Beach for $120.

Closest airport to the region is the **Melbourne Airport,** which is served by American, Continental, Delta, USAir, and United Airlines.

Many travelers headed for the serenity of the Indian River area fly into Orlando, which is served by every major domestic airline and many international air carriers as well. In recent years many transportation companies have begun providing shuttle service between **Orlando International** and other resort areas in Central Florida. One of those operating to the Melbourne–Fort Pierce–Vero Beach area (generally known as Brevard County) is **Suncoast Shuttle** (tel. 407/676-4557, or toll-free 800/762-5466, 800/226-4557 in Florida), which will get you to and from the Orlando airport to Vero, Melbourne, Cocoa, and all those other beaches for $12 to $40. **Cocoa Beach Shuttle** (tel. 800/231-9606) has similar prices and goes to the same destinations. If you're headed for Central Florida's beach resorts, you need to plan in advance since the shuttles operate on changing schedules and require reservations.

**Greyhound/Trailways buses** (tel. toll free 800/237-8211) serve the area, as does **Amtrak** (tel. toll free 800/USA-RAIL), which stops in West Palm Beach.

## GETTING AROUND

You'll probably need a car to explore this area since public transportation is minimal or absent. Avis, Budget, Hertz, and National **rental-car companies** have offices in Stuart, Fort Pierce, and Vero Beach, and a number of other rental-car companies operate in Palm Beach and Orlando.

**Orange Blossom Coach Lines** (tel. 407/783-0561) has service between Stuart, Fort Pierce, Vero Beach, Melbourne, Indiatlantic, Cocoa, and Cocoa Beach.

---

# 1. Orientation

---

Fla. A1A runs sporadically down the barrier islands from north of Vero Beach to St. Lucie, where it crosses to the mainland. It returns to the beach at Fort Pierce, to continue down wooded Hutchinson Island to Stuart, where it returns once again to the mainland, running along the coastline to Jupiter, where it joins US 1 to Palm Beach.

Meanwhile US 1 parallels the river, running north and south beside it from Vero Beach south.

Two enchanting side trips are on County Road 707, also called the Beach Road, which meanders through mile after mile of towering Australian pines and jungly subtropical growth through some of the most exclusive real estate in Florida. It's one of the loveliest drives you'll find anywhere in the state, an avenue beneath spreading banyans. To reach a pretty beach at Hobe Sound, go straight ahead when County Road 707 turns west (if you're traveling south, turn north when the road bends to the south).

You can pick up this same scenic road east of Stuart or at Fort Pierce and travel north or south on it along the banks of the Indian River past some elegant old mansions carefully restored by history lovers. Spot this road on your map by searching out the villages of Eldred, Walton, and Ancona.

## USEFUL INFORMATION

The **Vero Beach Chamber of Commerce** is at 1216 21st St. (P.O. Box 2947), Vero Beach, FL 32960 (tel. 407/567-3491) . . . The **St. Lucie County Chamber**

**of Commerce** is at 2200 Virginia Ave., Fort Pierce, FL 34982 (tel. 407/461-2700). . . . The friendly people at the **Stuart-Martin County Chamber of Commerce** are on duty at 1650 S. Kanner Hwy., Stuart, FL 34994 (tel. 407/287-1088) . . . For **police or medical emergencies,** call 911.

## 2. Where to Stay

You won't find hordes of glittering hotels in these small towns, but there are attractive, friendly spots with a ready welcome and lots of enthusiasm for their countryside. We've selected a few in several coastal towns.

### VERO BEACH
Beachside hotels may cost a little more, but in this quiet seaside city built right on the sand they're worth the difference.

The **Driftwood Inn Resort,** 3150 Ocean Dr., Vero Beach, FL 32960 (tel. 407/231-0550), is hands down the most interesting resort in the city, and one of the most unusual hideaways in the state. Decades ago Waldo Sexton, a man fascinated with the sea, put together this resort that's built right over the sands. He filled it with everything nautical he could find—diving bells, buoys, driftwood, etc. Heaven forbid that anyone should ever try to take an inventory at this eclectic spot, where you can stay in rustic rooms with perhaps the most beautiful view of the sea on the east coast. To look at Driftwood Inn you'd think it was unlikely to remain standing another week, but it's been there for ages and ages, so don't take any bets on its longevity. As for its popularity, ask any Floridian on the east coast for his top three getaway places on the beach and the Driftwood is sure to be one of them. Beautifully old and equally rustic balconies on some of the oceanfront rooms are often a meeting spot for Floridians who sometimes take over the whole motel.

In recent years the inn has added some efficiencies and motel rooms in two wings that don't overlook the sea, and has revamped many of its quarters. Rooms here are worth the price, especially the front rooms with those weird and wonderful balconies overlooking the sea and a sunken wreck just offshore. The inn also has a small, pretty restaurant, Waldo's, and a pool. Rates are $89 to $160 from January 21 through Easter, $59 to $110 in other months.

On Sunday, the **Holiday Inn Oceanside,** 3384 Ocean Dr., Vero Beach, FL 32960 (tel. 407/231-2300, or toll free 800/465-4329), is the most popular place in town between 11am and 2pm, when visitors and residents alike pour into the oceanside Windswept Restaurant for a sumptuous Sunday brunch. Located right on the beach, the Holiday Inn has 104 spacious rooms, some with king-size beds, 12 with kitchens, plus four efficiencies, a coin laundry, heated pool, and a wading pond for the children. Rates range from $72 to $105 from February to May, about $10 to $12 lower in summer.

### FORT PIERCE
**Holiday Inn Oceanfront,** 2600 N. A1A, Fort Pierce, FL 34949 (tel. 407/465-6000, or toll free 800/465-4329), once again manages to grab off the top beachside location. It's an attractive recently remodeled oceanfront hotel with a pool, wading pool, tennis court, dining room, and cocktail lounge. Rates year-round are $55 to $85.

If you know anything about sailing signal flags, you'll soon discover that the flags at the **Dockside Inn,** 1152 Seaway Dr., Fort Pierce, FL 34949 (tel. 407/461-4824), spell R-E-L-A-X. Even if you don't read the language of the sea you'll soon get the message at the Dockside, where friendly Nick and Evelyn Guardalabene run an informal, easy-going ship, which is indeed dockside, with a long pier you can use for fishing or docking a boat. Fishing's the major sport around here, and signs on the Dockside's wall tell you about the kinds of fish you'll most likely catch at dockside or on local charter trips. Although not on the beach, the motel is on the waters of Fort Pierce Inlet. Two blocks away are miles of Atlantic beach sand where you can shell, snorkel, and scuba-dive. You might even find a gold doubloon as other lucky sea searchers have done here.

Lots of wood trim gives the Dockside a contemporary look, and it's a popular place for young families who relax poolside while the kids keep busy splashing or fishing. Rooms are furnished in homey basic beach, with wall-to-wall carpeting and sturdy furniture. Rates from mid-December to mid-April peak at $48 to $64 for a motel room, studio or one-bedroom apartment. In summer, those rates are $38 to $58, and even cheaper by the week.

## PORT ST. LUCIE

About 10 miles west of the ocean and 7 miles north of Stuart in the village of Port St. Lucie you'll find another lush golfing and tennis resort—and the state's first Club Med, officially called **Club Med Village Hotel Sandpiper,** 3500 Morningside Blvd., Port St. Lucie, FL 34952 (tel. 407/335-4400, or toll free 800/CLUB-MED).

Occupying an attractive site along the St. Lucie River, this Club Med opened in the spring of 1987 at a resort formerly called Sandpiper Bay. No fewer than 45 holes of golf are the focus of this resort, which will now be catering to those who adore the Club Med all-inclusive pricing concept: All the club's multitudes of activities, from golf to boating to all your meals, served with French wine, are included in the price you pay. You never carry money here: Just pop-it beads you buy to spend on drinks.

In case you've been living on a desert island and haven't yet heard, Club Med is a French corporation best known perhaps for its singles orientation, although that has been changing, in tune to the beat of the yuppie generation, to include families. There's now even a Baby Club for tiny youngsters.

Club Meds are everywhere these days, Martinique and Nassau, Tahiti and probably Timbuktu, but this newest property at Sandpiper Bay is only the second club in the continental U.S. Club Med spent months on a massive $10-million renovation of this property, which was quite attractive to start with, so expect to find simple but attractively decorated rooms in one of six clusters of three-story pink buildings. Each room has two beds, a separate dressing area, and private terrace or patio.

Set down on more than 1,000 acres, the club has 45 holes of golf, 19 tennis courts, a sailing school, a mini-club for children, a fitness center, an arts-and-crafts workshop, and enough other activities to keep you going all night and all day.

Rates are $130 to $160 a night per person, including room, all meals, sports, instruction, activities—everything but golf, which is $42 for 18 holes including cart.

## HUTCHINSON ISLAND

A prime-time resort is sprawling **Indian River Plantation,** 555 NE Ocean Blvd., Hutchinson Island, FL 34996 (tel. 407/225-3700, or toll free 800/444-1432 or 800/444-3389), a magnificent condominium resort four miles north of Stuart on Fla. A1A. Miles of rolling golf courses line the entrance to this tranquil resort. Scattered among ponds and winding lagoons are clusters of wooded villas. Posh condominiums are tucked away among the greens. On the ocean, a pastel 200-room hotel welcomes you with big beautiful rooms decorated in contemporary hues, balconies overlooking the sea, and big apartments that accommodate four or six. Some of the attractive rooms have king-size beds and all have big closets, comfortable chairs, and lots of extra touches designed to make you feel special. A friendly staff adds to that. There are three heated pools, charter boats, 13 tennis courts at the hotel scattered about the resort, rental boats from canoes to sailboats, fishing guides, miles and miles of deserted unspoiled beach, an 18-hole executive golf course, bicycling, a marina, waterskiing, and other water sports.

When you hunger and thirst, head for one of five restaurants including the Porch, a woodsy spot filled with plants, and the elegant Inlet restaurant, where you dine on excellent beef and seafood dishes in the $15 to $20 price range. For the children there are special events, games, and an activities department to plan their day.

No doubt about it, Indian River Plantation is a lovely place for those who like getaway vacations far (but not too far) from crowds. Rates for oceanfront suites apartments are $250 to $350 for a one-bedroom or two-bedroom hotel suite in peak season ($150 to $225 from May to mid-June). Hotel rooms are $90 to $175 year round.

## JENSEN BEACH

**River's Edge,** 2625 NE Indian River Dr., Jensen Beach, FL 34957 (tel. 407/ 334-4759), overlooks the river and has a nice rustic look; brown wood trims a two-story building. Simple but clean and attractive rooms are on lovely grounds, and there's that gorgeous strip of wide river to gaze upon in idle hours. It's one of the few motels in the area that's actually on the river's edge (not across the road from the water), and has a pool. Rates are $38 to $42 from May to December, $60 in winter —there's a three-day minimum stay.

## JUPITER

**Hilton Jupiter Beach,** Indiantown Road and Fla. A1A, Jupiter, FL 33477 (tel. 407/746-2511, or toll free 800/821-8791, 800/432-1420 in Florida), is one of the star resorts of this star-studded Indian River Gold Coast coastline. These days it's more starstruck than ever, following a multi-million-dollar, top-to-toe renovation. Rooms now feature pretty cotton prints in blues, greens, corals, and yellows, handsome cornice moldings atop print curtains, and lots of typically Floridian furniture from raffia to rattan and wickers.

The Jupiter Hilton likes to say it's 20 minutes—and 20 years—from Palm Beach, and that description of this easygoing, seaside resort seems pretty accurate to us. Here you can doff the Guccis and stroll barefoot across the dunes. You can dine at the ocean-view Sinclair's Grill where fresh fish, seafood, and meat are prepared on wood-burning convection grills, whole fish and poultry cooked on French rôtisseries. You can sample the chef's Keys-inspired cuisine, things like conch chowder and black-bean soup, fresh breads and pastries, and yummy sauces prepared with herbs grown right on the grounds.

The Sand Bar poolside beckons after a long day of windsurfing, sailing, or romping about the tennis courts. If you're here in late June or July you'll see marine biologists releasing baby turtles raised under the watchful eye of scientists who operate a carefully guarded hatchery here. Best of all, the Jupiter Theater is just across the street.

In winter months, double rooms at the Hilton are $140 to $250. From May to December, double rates fall to $90 to $145.

**READER'S TIP:** "In summer the **Hilton Jupiter Beach** has some money-saving packages that include a room for two or three days plus tickets to the former Burt Reynolds Jupiter Theater. When I stopped by the Hilton and asked for a price list, I discovered I could have gotten a room there—one not facing the ocean—for just a few dollars more than I paid at another hotel in the area that wasn't on the beach. Just ask for prices on rooms that don't face the beach" (Jerry Schultz, Boynton Beach, Fla.).

## CAMPING

There are parks and campgrounds scattered throughout the area, but **Jonathan Dickinson State Park,** 16450 SE Federal Hwy., Hobe Sound, FL 33455 (tel. 407/

546-2771), is the largest and prettiest, covering more than 10,280 acres of dense pine forests. Named after the courageous leader of a shipwrecked group, the park is a beautiful place that spreads out along US 1 over miles and miles of rolling dunes that give you an idea how this coastline must have looked when those first pioneers arrived. As a state park, it charges only $1 admission per person, $17 basic fee for campsites. It's often very crowded in summer, so camping reservations are a must; call to book space. You can rent a cottage here too (bring your own linens), for $50 a night, $275 a week. Call 407/746-1466 for cottage reservations. There's swimming, boating, fishing, picnicking, and cruises on the Loxahatchee River—or rent a canoe for $5.50 an hour and paddle your own cruise.

Farther north, **Sebastian Inlet State Recreation Area** is on a barrier island with a lagoon, coastal hammock, and mangroves tucked away behind the beach and dunes. You can camp, picnic, swim, birdwatch, fish, scuba dive, and surf on three miles of sandy beaches for $15 to $17 a day. It's about 20 miles north of Vero Beach on US A1A.

---

# 3. Where to Dine

Floridians drive for miles to have dinner at Vero Beach's Ocean Grill, and at that city's P. V. Martin's you dine among the sea oats on a long strip of deserted beach. We've picked a few favorites in cities along this coastline and grouped them by location. Remember that the prices we've cited are for entrées, but this usually includes one or two vegetables, salad, and perhaps coffee as well.

## VERO BEACH

Sea oats bend pliantly in the sea breezes and waves lap the shore around you at **P. V. Martin's,** 5150 N. Fla. A1A, south of Vero Beach (tel. 465-7300 or 569-0700), an enchanting wood-trimmed restaurant sitting alone on a long, long strip of unpopulated beach. Contemporary furnishings and banks of windows overlooking the sea are softened by hanging greenery and a warm, cozy atmosphere engendered at least in part by friendly, helpful servers. From the raw bar, try snow crab claws, clams casino, or a seafood platter. Follow that with crisp salads and excellent regional seafood concoctions or steaks and beef, for prices in the $10 to $20 range. Additional offerings are honey-wheat bread and rice pilaf. Open from 11am to 3:30pm and 5pm to midnight daily and for Sunday brunch.

People (and we admit to being among them) think nothing of driving two or three hours for dinner at **Ocean Grill,** at 1050 Sexton Plaza, Fla. 60 at the ocean (tel. 231-5409), a dining institution on this beach for generations. Start with something cool at the bar, where you gaze through a wall of windows at a sunken wreck just offshore and watch the waves roll endlessly in. Ask for a table in the back room overlooking the ocean and you'll dine in a rustic atmosphere, softened by the glow of candlelight. Try fresh seafood (coquilles St-Jacques is a top favorite here) or excellent steaks, all served with crisp salads, fresh hot breads, and a smile. Prices at Ocean Grill are in the $11 to $20 range, and the restaurant is open from 5 to 10pm Monday through Saturday, on Sunday from 4 to 9:30pm.

You can't beat **Houlihan's,** 398 21st St. (tel. 569-1522), for great munchies. In summer under the cool breeze of paddle fans the restaurant gets hot on cold salad platters, a crispy cool way to beat the heat. On Saturday night the specialty is lobster tails, but you'll also find lots of prime rib, grouper, steak fajitas for dinner, fresh fruits, vegetables, and coffee ground fresh daily. Breads, soups, and desserts are all made right here each day, too. Prices are in the $10 range, and the restaurant's open from 11am to 1am daily.

**Monte's,** 1517 S. Ocean Dr. (tel. 231-6612), cooks up more than 80 entrées to feed those who never met a strand of spaghetti they didn't love. Italian flavors predominate here, but there are a few steaks and chops on the menu to tempt those who aren't pleased by baked ziti, rigatoni bolognese, fettuccine Alfredo, veal francese, and the like. Monte's is open from 5 to 10pm daily, and prices are in the $8 to $26 range.

**The Menu,** 1571 S. Ocean Dr. (tel. 231-4614), is a very, very popular place in this city by the sea. With the ocean just a breath away, it figures that seafood is the specialty of the house, and you'll find many unusual selections here, including cobia and pompano. Those who don't favor finny fare will be happy here too, however: Much of the menu at the Menu is devoted to New York strip steaks, pork chops, ham steak, roast leg of lamb, and chicken—all of it in a reasonable $10 to $15 price range. Hours are 5 to 10pm daily.

**Forty-One,** 41 Royal Palm Blvd. (tel. 562-1141), is one of the most beautiful dining rooms in the region, a quiet, elegant spot of shining crystal, impeccable linens, and glowing candlelight. Prices are on the high side for Vero Beach, which has quite a number of restaurants in lower price brackets, but this restaurant's elegance and contemporary simplicity are worth every dollar. Forty-One is open weekdays from 11:30am to 2:30pm and 6 to 10pm daily. Continental cuisine predominates, and although beef, chicken, and veal preparations are numerous, marvelously herbed and sauced seafood is a specialty. You'll pay $15 to $24 for entrées, which also include salad and vegetable.

**Wright's Steakhouse,** at 8th Street and US 1 South (tel. 562-9832), is quite a popular local steak house. On the menu are filet mignon, New York strip, T-bone, and porterhouse, even a sirloin steak for two. You can team any of those with seafood as well. Prices are $13 to $15 for steaks, including salad and steak fries. Wright's is open from 5 to 10pm Tuesday through Sunday. Wright's also sometimes closes one other day a week, so a call first is wise.

## FORT PIERCE

A massive fireplace and pecky cedar paneling set the tone for the **Ocean Village Inn,** 2400 S. Ocean Dr. in the Ocean Village Resort (tel. 461-8822), where every table has a smashing view of the ocean rolling into this quiet strip of island sand. French touches pepper the continental cuisine, for which you'll pay $10 to $18, and the restaurant is open for lunch from 11:30am to 2:30pm daily and from 5 to 10pm for dinner daily. Closed Mondays May to October.

**Hilltop House,** 4000 N. US 1 (tel. 465-2125), is perched up on what Floridians like to call a hill and features quite a lovely view over the Fort Pierce Inlet. Hilltop House wins converts with its fresh vegetables and pays such close attention to detail that they even bone their own meat. A really top spot—literally and figuratively—along this central east coast, Hilltop House charges just $10 for every dinner on the menu, and is open Monday through Saturday from 11am to 2:30pm and 4 to 10pm for dinner, from noon to 11pm Sunday.

## STUART

The familiar blue-tiled roof of **Benihana of Tokyo** pops up here in Stuart at 3602 SE Ocean Blvd. (tel. 286-0740). Plop your shoes on a rack and step into the lounge for an unshod cool one, Japanese style. Later, dine at long tables where a talented Japanese cook performs magic with shrimp and steak, and some pretty fancy fingerwork with the huge salt and pepper shakers they toss nonchalantly into the air as they cook. Benihana has been phenomenally successful in Florida (and everywhere else), so you can count on excellent Japanese preparation of foods that seem only slightly exotic to American tastes. Figure about $20 to $25 for dinner. Benihana is sizzling from 5 to 10pm for dinner nightly, from 1 to 10pm Sunday.

## JUPITER/HUTCHINSON ISLAND

At **Indian River Plantation** (see our hotel recommendations), 555 NE Ocean Blvd. (tel. 225-3700), you dine amid lots of pretty greenery or in an elegant dining room with black-tie service. At the **Porch,** go casual for lunch, and feast on fresh seafood. Evenings, dress up a bit and head for **Scalawag's.** Start with escargots and work your way through a rack of lamb. Plan on a long walk through the grounds later. Entrées are in the $13 to $24 range, and Scalawag's is open from 5 to 10pm Monday through Saturday; the Porch from 7:30am to 9:30pm, with a Sunday brunch from 10am to 2pm.

Rage of the hour up this way is a sleek spot called **Banana Max,** 100 N. Federal Hwy., Jupiter (tel. 744-6600 or 744-3301). There's always something going on at this architectural oddity all turned out in curving lines, arches, and pink, pink, and more pink. Inside you'll find everything's up-to-date in this Jupiter haven, from contemporary furnishings to the jungly video room where something's happening until the wee hours every night (or should that be day?). You can munch your way through the menu on tastes of this and that, or go full course with a variety of steaks, seafood, and American/continental creations in the $12 to $17 range. Banana Max unpeels at 5pm daily, closing at 2am weekdays, 3am on Friday and Saturday. On Sunday they sleep late, opening at 7pm and rocking until 2am.

**READER'S RESTAURANT SELECTION—JUPITER:** "Harpoon Louie's, 1065 Fla. A1A, Jupiter (tel. 744-1300), is a really nice place to go for cocktails or for dinner. There's a deck that goes right out to the water and you can eat outside or inside. They specialize in seafood and steaks. Prices are about $8 to $25 at dinner, $4 to $11 at lunch" (Jerry Schultz, Boynton Beach, Fla.). [*Author's Note:* Harpoon Louie's is open 7am to midnight daily and has become very, very popular so you are likely to have a short wait for a table at favorite dining hours and on weekends. Entrance to Harpoon Louie's is just off US 1 at the first intersection south of the bridge. The restaurant is directly across from the lighthouse on Jupiter Inlet.]

## JENSEN BEACH

Look for the Tiki gods in Jensen and you'll be at **Chuck & Harold's Outrigger Island Grill** restaurant, at 1405 NE Indian River Dr. (tel. 220-3000), where you're greeted by an elaborate Polynesian longhouse facade complete with thatched roof and ornate straw work. A tiny fountain gurgles into a small lagoon at the entrance, and multitudes of pink, red, rose, fuchsia, and yellow flowers bloom among the greenery. Inside is more of the same very showy decor, with high-backed wicker chairs, Tiki gods, and lots of South Seas touches. Set picturesquely on the riverfront, this spot was once famous as Frances Langford's, named after a famous pop singer of the 1940s who lured crowds of her friends here in days gone by. You won't be consigned to moo goo gai pan or the like here. Instead you'll find a wide range of steaks and seafood prepared in ways familiar to Americans, although enough exotic specialties like shrimp with Outrigger sauce emerge from the kitchen to please more adventurous diners. The Outrigger is open from 11:30am to 9pm, later on weekends. Prices range from $9 to $19.

# 4. Nightlife

We did mention that this is a quiet region of the state, didn't we? Well, believe it and don't expect ring-a-ding.

Top of the line in evening entertainment is the **Jupiter Theater,** 1001 Indiantown Rd., Jupiter (tel. 305/746-5566), which presents excellent plays all year round, sometimes with star performers the likes of Farrah Fawcett, Dom DeLuise, Sally Field, and well, just lots of former owner Burt Reynolds' friends who traipse on down for a little R&R and put on some smashing performances while they're at it. You can count on a good time at the theater, and a good dinner (or brunch) too. Check local newspapers to see what's playing. For matinee performances (Wednesday and Saturday) luncheon is served at noon with curtain at 2pm.

For evening performances (Tuesday through Sunday) dinner is served at 6pm (7pm Friday and 5pm Sunday) with curtain two hours later. Prices range from $37 to $54. The theater's quite near the Hilton Jupiter Beach.

For general quiet entertainment in Vero Beach, try the Holiday Inn's **Windswept Lounge,** 2900 Ocean Dr. (tel. 569-2727), with backgammon boards, a pubby atmosphere, and guitar music from 9pm Monday through Saturday; or **Houlihan's,** at 398 21st St. (tel. 569-1522), a favorite socializing spot, open daily, entertainment nightly except Monday to 1am.

In Fort Pierce, **Player's Club** in the Holiday Inn Oceanfront, 2600 Fla. A1A (tel. 465-6000), is a hot spot that's recently been decorated and features a split-level lounge overlooking the dance floor and a disc jockey for entertainment. It opens at 8pm every day but Sunday.

**Village South Restaurant and VIP Lounge,** 2900 Ocean Dr. in Vero Beach (tel. 231-6727), has a pretty, old-worldly atmosphere livened up by the crowds who drop in here for happy hour sipping and stay on long after that for dinner and music. Happy hour here is popular because, so rumor has it, the size of the drinks increases as the price decreases.

**Marvin Gardens**—yes, it's a Monopoly theme—is often a madhouse, but it's particularly crazy when the lounge features its happy hour free buffet loaded with roast beef, spareribs, duck, vegetables. Crowds fill the interior of this woodsy spot first, then the overflow gets pushed out onto a huge outdoor deck. Join them daily from 11:30am to 1am at 3030 N. US 1, Vero Beach (tel. 567-3939). Entertainment nightly.

**Melbourne Civic Theater,** 625 Harvey Ogden Dr., Melbourne (tel. 723-1668), has regular performances throughout the year, children's plays in summer, as does the **Riverside Theater,** in Civic Arts Center, Belchland Boulevard in Vero Beach (tel. 231-6990).

**Ocean Village Inn,** 2400 S. Ocean Dr. (Fla. A1A), Hutchinson Island (tel. 461-8822), attracts high-society tourists and the local upper crust, who roll in here at happy hour to enjoy sensational views over the Atlantic. Many stay on long after night has blackened the view.

---

# 5. Seeing the Sights

Cruise the Indian River and imagine yourself a pioneer struggling to raise pineapples on its shores, or prowl among Seminole artifacts in a historical museum.

**St. Lucie County Historical Museum,** at 414 Seaway Dr. in Fort Pierce (tel. 464-6635), displays Seminole artifacts as part of an interesting study of the area's tribal heritage (the fort was an outpost during the Seminole Wars in the 1800s). Admission is free and it's open from 10am to 4pm Wednesday through Saturday.

**Hutchinson Island** is a thing to see all by itself. Miles and miles of untenanted jungle will give you an idea how these barrier islands looked to the pirates and pioneers who settled here.

On Hutchinson Island, at 301 MacArthur Blvd., is **Gilbert's Bar House of Refuge** (tel. 225-1875). Built in 1875, it was once a haven for shipwrecked sailors. Out of six similar dwellings that stood along this once-deserted coastline, it is the only one remaining. It is believed to have been named after a notorious pirate. It's open from 1 to 4:15pm Tuesday through Sunday; closed holidays. Admission is $1 for adults and 50¢ for children.

One mile north, **Elliott Museum,** 825 NE Ocean Blvd., at Stuart Beach (tel. 225-1961), houses an amazing collection of antique automobiles, including a 1953 Cunningham, a 1907 Maxwell, a Stanley Steamer, a Stutz Bearcat, a 1922 Rolls-Royce Pall Mall Phantom, and many others, plus an American collection ranging from a Seminole chickee home to a collection of shells and a group of Salem, Mass., shops brought here for display. Open from 1 to 4pm daily, the museum charges $2.50 for adults and 50¢ for children 6 to 13.

For sailing tours in these lovely waterways see what we've said about cruises in Chapter VI.

In June, Jensen Beach has a **"Turtle Watch" week,** when you can see the giant reptiles lumber ashore, dig a hole in the sand with their huge flippers, and lay their eggs. You can watch, but don't disturb the turtles or their nests, which are guarded by the state. Later in summer you can see the baby turtles making their way to the ocean as they hatch and find their sea legs.

# 6. Sports

Among several golf courses in the area are the **Indian Hills Golf and Country Club,** 1600 S. 3rd St. in Fort Pierce (tel. 465-8110), and **Dodger Pines Golf Club,** 4600 26th St. in Vero Beach (tel. 569-4400). Both have 18 holes and are public or semiprivate courses. Greens fees are $20 to $28.

Tennis players will find eight courts at **Lawnwood Tennis Complex and Recreation Center,** at Virginia Avenue and 13th Street in Fort Pierce and 12 courts scattered about St. Lucie County. The Lawnwood courts (tel. 468-1521) are free days and $1 an hour at night. **Memorial Island,** on Mockingbird Drive (tel. 231-4787), has 10 courts and costs $3 per hour per person.

There's jai-alai at **Fort Pierce Jai-Alai,** 1750 S. Kings Hwy., one mile north of Exit 56 on the Florida Turnpike (tel. 464-7500, or toll free 800/432-6147), from January to the end of July, with games at 7pm on Monday, Wednesday, Friday, and Saturday, plus matinees at noon on Monday, Wednesday, and Saturday. Admission is from $1.

You can see the **Los Angeles Dodgers** play in Vero Beach during their winter training camp from February to April here at Dodger Town, 4001 26th St. (tel. 569-4900). Tickets are $4 to $7.

This is one of the state's best **fishing** regions both in the ocean and in rivers throughout the area. Stuart, in fact, likes to call itself the "Sailfish Capital of the World." There's a four-day tournament in December during which anglers try to catch the sail-finned beauties with light tackle. To prove they really do bring in the big ones, the **Stuart Sailfish Club** record is a 477-pound blue marlin, among many others that didn't get away! Get information on sailfishing in the area from the club at P.O. Box 2005, Stuart, FL 34995 (tel. 407/286-9373).

A number of **fishing boats** are tied up at marinas in Stuart Marina, 400 NW Alice Ave. (tel. 692-4000). Try *Mustache Man* (tel. 283-8864), *Gannet* (tel. 283-6767), or *Great Escape* (tel. 286-6289). In Jupiter, try the *Barbi Doll* (tel. 747-6619), the *Blue Moon* (tel. 746-7064), or the *Shamrock* (tel. 747-1940).

**Charter boats** charge about $400 a day, $300 a half day, for four to six people.

# ORLANDO AND CENTRAL FLORIDA

**W**ho could forget little curly-haired Annette Funicello, black plastic mouse ears firmly in place, belting out M-I-C, K-E-Y, M-O-U-S-E?

Let us be the first to tell you that no one in Orlando forgets it. Not for a minute do they forget that Mickey is the mouse who roared his way through central Florida turning boondock to boomtown faster than you can say M-I-C-K-E-Y.

This dear little creature with the black plastic ears and the dragging tail is the mouse that brought millions here, who turned cow pasture into city and some of the meek into millionaires. "I have a little shrine in my bedroom," says one now-prosperous hotelier. "Every morning I get up, pull open the little drapes on the shrine, and kiss Mickey's feet."

Mickey is everywhere here. He's the phone on the desk of a sophisticated hotel executive, the base of many a lamp, center of nearly every T-shirt in town, the icon of a city gambling its future on Mickey's black nose.

Not everyone, however, shares this slavish adoration of the black-eared figment of Walt Disney's fertile imagination. Legion is the competition for the attention (and let's face it, the dollars) of tourists who flood through the Disney gates, sometimes at the rate of 80,000 a *day*. So much competition has arisen in fact that Orlando promoters, who once said you could see it all in three days, now suggest you're likely to need a week or more!

Prepare, in a world, for delighted exhaustion.

Walt Disney World alone is now so huge, there is no way to see it in a day. Depending on your interests—and your stamina—you'll need a day for the park's Magic Kingdom, a day for EPCOT Center, and a day for Disney-MGM Studios, the newest attraction. And that itinerary doesn't include such Disney diversions as Typhoon Lagoon, a new water-thrill park complete with its own typhoon legend and lagoon splashed by six-foot waves, or Pleasure Island, an after-dark park with seven different kinds of nightclubs, including one you can attend on roller skates!

Competing attractions just keep getting bigger and bigger and better and better, too. Cypress Gardens has a flashy new ice show. You'll certainly need a day at Sea World to see new Baby Shamu and the rest of the killer whale family—Kandu and Shamu, the world's heftiest ballet star. He's four tons of fun performing a graceful pirouette on his enormous tail and even planting a gentle (if somewhat damp) kiss on your waiting cheek during his daily shows at Sea World, Orlando's water wonderland. You'll want to wander along the shimmering waters of serene Cypress Gardens where the perfume of roses permeates the air. You'll want to roll across acre after acre of golden and orange citrus nestled in undulating waves of shining emerald leaves that ebb and flow across miles of silver sand dotted with gleaming sapphire lakes.

You'll need time to explore the byways and backroads in the cowboy town of Kissimmee (you pronounce it "Kih-*sim*-ee"). Once the "good hunting grounds" of the Calusa Indians, Kissimmee later became home to a passel of cowpunchers who roamed these sandy ranges, then rode right up to the bar to drink without dismounting. They still ride these ranges, herd humpbacked Brahma bulls, and show off their skills in one of the state's biggest rodeos.

In Orlando's suburbs you'll find enchanting villages like quaint Mount Dora, built on the edges of a limestone bluff and looking more like New England than New England. You can visit a settlement where Floridians have their holiday greetings postmarked—Christmas, Florida! And don't miss the small city of Winter Park, one of the state's loveliest villages, a serene retreat so perfectly primped and painted it's called "Little Europe." It is also the home of the world's largest collection of priceless Tiffany glass. If you love horses, you'll adore the horsey village of Ocala, birthplace of racing champions.

It's all part of central Florida, the land of grapefruit and Goofy, fast-paced fantasy and serene sandy flatlands, lush emerald forests, glowing golden blossoms, and glittering blue lakes. It's a land that loves children and the child in us all, that welcomes you with a grin, cares for you with casual sophistication, and sends even the most jaded away wide-eyed in wonderment—a magic kingdom indeed.

---

# 1. Orientation

---

## GETTING THERE

**Airlines** flying into Orlando include American, Bahamasair, British Airways, Continental, Delta, Ecuatoriana, Icelandair, Midway, KLM, Northwest, Pan Am, Trans-Brasil, TWA, USAir, and United.

**Greyhound/Trailways** buses (tel. toll free 800/237-8211) have service from all over the state and nation. Greyhound stops here at 300 W. Amelia St. (tel. 843-0344).

**American International Sightseeing** and a number of other tour companies have tour packages from wherever you're staying in Florida.

**Amtrak** (tel. toll free 800/USA-RAIL) has a regular schedule of train service to the area—Kissimmee is the official Walt Disney World stop. Amtrak's Auto-Train is back on track again, offering you the convenience of a car in Florida without any of the inconvenience of driving it there. Operated by Amtrak, Auto-Train begins at Lorton, Virginia, and ends at Sanford, Florida, about 23 miles from Orlando. You drive your car aboard in Lorton (which is about a four-hour drive from New York, about two from Philadelphia), and then settle into a coach seat or bedroom, and the next morning at 9am you roll into the station at Sanford. Cost of this simple way to avoid about 850 miles of driving is $70 to $140 per adult plus $115 to $249 for the car ($149 extra per couple for a bedroom compartment). Auto-Train leaves either Lorton or Sanford at 4:30pm, arriving at its destination at 9am the next morning. Daily departures from Lorton and from Sanford in the busy winter season, less frequently in summer. There are off-season special rates; call the toll-free number for exact details.

## GETTING AROUND

Every major **rental-car agency** has offices in Orlando, and dozens of smaller rental-car companies operate here as well. National is the official Walt Disney World rental-car agency, and Alamo offers inexpensive rates throughout Florida and lets you drop the car off anywhere in the state without extra charges.

## From Airport to Hotel

Orlando has grown from a small town to a huge, sprawling community that now extends, megalopolis-style, from points west of the Disney World complex all the way to Kennedy Space Center near Cocoa Beach. Just as Orlando has grown like Jack's famous beanstalk, so has the Orlando International Airport, which was once just a sleepy little runway with a couple of baggage terminals. Today there's nothing quiet about the airport, which is booming, literally and figuratively, as it grows and grows and grows, welcoming more and more airlines, many of them international carriers.

Confusion is kept to manageable levels, however, through an interesting two-sided, multi-level layout that's easily negotiated if you keep your eyes on the signs. To make life reasonably easy, the airport has located its ground transportation operations at or near the baggage pick-up area, so you are only steps away from airport-escape.

Several **rental-car companies**—National, Budget, Dollar, Superior, Avis, and Hertz—have rental desks right there at the baggage retrieval area and many other rental-car companies will pick you up one level down and shuttle you off to their nearby facilities.

In the Orlando area it's a long way from anywhere to anywhere else, so be prepared to pay some pretty stiff **taxi** bills if you're planning to find your way around by cab. Among the taxis operating from the airport to local hotels are **Yellow Cab** (tel. 422-4455 in Orlando, 846-2222 in Kissimmee) and **Town and Country Taxi** (tel. 827-6350). Taxi rates are $2.25 at the drop, $1.30 a mile. It will cost you $20 to $30 for a ride from the airport to most area hotels, which sounds expensive but looks less steep if there are several of you headed in the same direction.

If you're headed to other points in Central Florida—Vero Beach, Melbourne, Cocoa Beach, Daytona, etc.—there are more than 100 shuttle operations waiting to serve you. Airport information desks can help you find one that's going where you are and we have detailed companies operating shuttles to Daytona and to the Vero Beach–Melbourne–Cocoa Beach area in chapters focusing on those regions.

If you don't want to look there, here's the short story: Daytona's shuttle operation is called **Daytona-Orlando Transportation System (DOTS)** and can be reached at 800/331-1965; Cocoa Beach, Melbourne, Vero Beach, and other Indian River destinations have several shuttle operations including **Cocoa Beach Shuttle** reachable at 800/231-9606 and **Suncoast Shuttle** at 407/676-4557, or toll-free 800/762-5466 in Florida. Fares vary depending on how far you're going, but one-way rates range from about $12 to Cocoa Beach to $40 to Vero Beach.

If you're headed to hotels in the Orlando area, **Airport Limousine Service,**

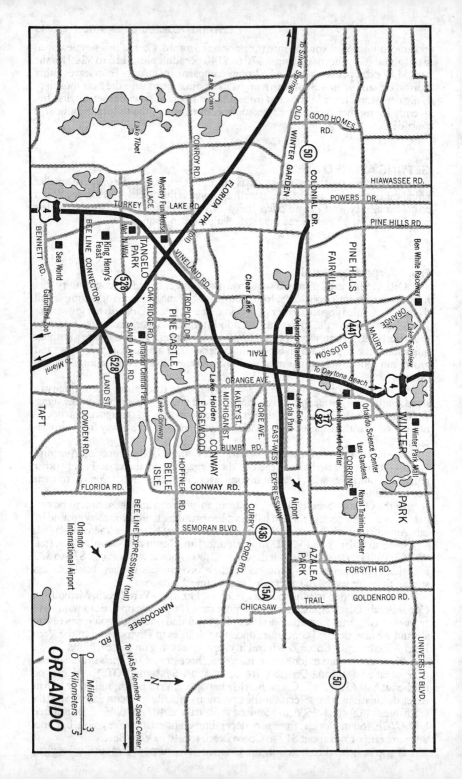

320 W. Gore St. (tel. 423-5566) operates airport limousine service to area hotels and has a ticket counter at the baggage-claim area of the **Orlando International Airport.** You'll find the limousines (actually 11-passenger vans) outside the terminal building on the second floor. Prices range from about $12 to $18 for a one-way ride to hotels, depending on how far you're going. Children's fares are about $3 lower price and you can save several dollars by buying a round-trip ticket at the airport.

Some hotels have **free shuttle service** from the airport. You can even call many of them free on telephones you'll find near the baggage-claim area.

If you'd like to arrive in style, **Carey Limos,** 1523 Pine St. (tel. 855-0442), has a booking booth at the luggage-pickup area too and will bring a Cadillac limousine around for you. Rates are about $4 higher than taxi fares and run from about $60 to $90 for most destinations. If there are enough of you traveling together, you might even save money.

## Travel Around the Area

Distances are great in the sprawling central Florida flatlands, so don't expect to drop into Sea World then walk over to Disney—it's miles just from Disney's first entrance sign to the parking lot! If you're planning to sample some of the area's great dining and lively nightlife, you'd be wise to rent a car since taxi fares over the distances here can be enormous, and public transportation isn't good after park closing hours.

To get to the attractions, however, you can rely on a variety of shuttle systems and tour buses that operate in the area.

**Rabbit Bus** (tel. 291-2424) rolls the road between International Drive and Walt Disney World, and has trips to Sea World, Lake Buena Vista shopping center, and the huge new Florida Mall. Buses pick you up along International Drive, and take you to any of those attractions for $7 round trip. They also go to Cypress Gardens, Kennedy Space Center, and Busch Gardens for $20 to $30 including admissions, about half that for children.

Another bus company operating in the area is **Mears Transportation Group** (tel. 423-5566), which has buses on the roll all along both the eastern and western sections of US 192 to Walt Disney World. They pick up at large hotels along the way every hour or so and sometimes more frequently. If you call them, they'll arrange for you to meet them, or vice versa, at a spot near your hotel.

Mears also picks up at hotels on International Drive for trips to Disney World and Sea World and has tours to Cypress Gardens, Kennedy Space Center, Wet 'N Wild, and other area attractions. Fares from hotels to Disney World and Sea World fall in the $5 to $7 range, while tours to attractions farther away, Kennedy Space Center, or Cypress Gardens, vary in price from $20 to $30.

In Lake Buena Vista, home of eight large hotels, **shuttlebuses** operate on an every-15-minute schedule. They pick up passengers at all hotels and take them to the entrance to the Magic Kingdom and EPCOT. Buses are free to hotel guests who simply display a pass issued by their hotel. Flags painted on the sides of the buses identify where they're going. Buses operate from 8am to 2am, so you can take in the nightlife at Walt Disney World and in the WDW Shopping Village.

**Gray Line** (tel. 422-0744) operates much of what moves on wheels in Orlando. The line's big bruisers ply between attractions and International Drive area hotels. You can ride to Sea World or Walt Disney World for $7 one-way for adults or children. Gray Line also operates trips to other attractions throughout central Florida (Kennedy Space Center, Busch Gardens), for varying prices beginning at about $20 to $30. **American International Sightseeing,** Tradeport Road and Express Street (tel. 859-2250), is another tour company that has trips to, from, and around central Florida.

If you're visiting Orlando in summer and want to reserve a motor home, make reservations four to six months in advance. **Holiday RV Rental,** 5001 Sand Lake Rd.,

Orlando, FL 32809 (tel. 407/351-3096, or toll free 800/351-8888, 800/351-6666 in Florida), has all sizes of rec vehicles for rent, for prices beginning at $550 to $800 a week.

## GETTING YOUR BEARINGS

Here are a few clues to finding your way around brash and booming Orlando. The main east-west artery is **I-4,** which runs from Tampa to Daytona through Orlando. You'll notice you're often driving north-south on I-4, but just keep in mind the Tampa–Daytona orientation and you'll be all right. Exits from this huge expressway take you to Walt Disney World, Sea World, Church Street Station, downtown Orlando, International Drive, Lake Buena Vista, Altamonte Springs, and Winter Park, among others.

A toll road called the **Beeline** is a fast east-west route that intersects with I-4, crosses other major highways like County Road 436, the Orange Blossom Trail, and the Florida Turnpike, and scoots eastward to Cape Canaveral. It's the quickest way to the Worlds from the airport.

A third east-wester is the **East-West Expressway,** north of the Beeline, which zips scenically across Orlando and can be reached from I-4.

From north to south the major roadways include **County Road 436,** a beltline around Orlando's east side from the Beeline, past the East-West Expressway and Colonial Drive, then bending west to cross US 17/92 and some outlying suburbs. The **Orange Blossom Trail** (also called US 441) is a north-south road with plenty of motels and restaurants—and traffic. **Orange Avenue** parallels the Orange Blossom Trail, but is farther east and goes by downtown landmarks, as does **Colonial Drive** (County Road 50).

**US 192** is the main east-west route past Walt Disney World, and stretches from Kissimmee, past many motels, to **US 27.**

## USEFUL INFORMATION

For **police or medical emergency,** dial 911 . . . For **minor medical problems,** the Family Treatment Center, 6001 Vineland Rd., one block west of Kirkman Road (tel. 351-6682), is open 8am to 8pm daily and accepts MasterCard and VISA for payment . . . For a **medical referral service,** call the Central Florida Medical Service (tel. 648-9234). Some doctors listed will even make "house" calls at your hotel or motel . . . To find out what kind of **weather** is coming, call 851-7510 in Orlando . . . To find a **baby-sitter,** check with your hotel's Guest Services desk . . . **Pet emergencies** can be handled at Veterinary Emergency Clinic, 882 Jackson Ave., Winter Park (tel. 644-4449) . . . **Eckerd's Drugs,** 908 Lee Rd. (tel. 644-6908), is open 24 hours . . . Call **Western Union** toll free at 800/325-6000. . . . Your films can be developed overnight at **Champagne Color Camera,** 1917 N. Orange Ave. (tel. 894-3362) . . . Get out-of-town newspapers at **Orange Avenue News,** 59 N. Orange Ave. (tel. 422-0954) . . . **Gooding's** is a **24-hour grocery.**

## TOURIST INFORMATION

The **Orlando/Orange County Convention and Visitors Bureau,** 8445 International Dr., Orlando, FL 32819 (tel. 407/363-5871), will help you with everything. . . . The **Kissimmee Chamber of Commerce,** 320 E. Monument Ave., Kissimmee, FL 32741 (tel. 407/847-3174), and the **Kissimmee/St. Cloud Convention and Visitor's Bureau,** on US 192 East, Kissimmee, FL 32741 (tel. 407/847-5000, or toll free 800/327-9159, 800/432-9199 in Florida), are fiercely loyal to their small town, and staffers know every millimeter of it . . . For questions about **Walt Disney World,** call the Magic Kingdom at 407/824-4321, **EPCOT** at

407/827-7414 . . . If you don't mind admitting your age, you can save a bundle of money in **Orlando's Senior Season,** from September to mid-December, when dozens of attractions and hotels offer discounts up to 50% to anyone 55 and up. The visitor center can give you exact details on Senior Season.

Orlando publishes a handy *Visitors Guide* that includes information on attractions, hotels, and restaurants in the region. It's free and can be obtained from **Orlando Convention and Visitors Bureau,** 8445 International Dr., Orlando, FL 32819 (tel. 407/363-5871).

---

# 2. Where to Stay

Hotels and motels in Orlando are clustered in several general areas: along US 192 to Kissimmee; on International Drive in an area sometimes called Florida Center; downtown; and near the airport. There are eight major resort hotels on Disney property in an area called Lake Buena Vista, and five fabulous resorts right inside the Magic Kingdom. We've divided hotels up geographically, beginning with those closest to the Kingdom, and fanning out to the airport.

## IN WALT DISNEY WORLD

Closest to the park's many diversions are four hotels and a golf/villa resort located practically at the gate to Main Street, U.S.A.—the Polynesian Resort, the Caribbean Beach Resort, the Contemporary Resort, the Grand Floridian Beach Resort, and Disney Vacation Villas, all owned by Walt Disney World. Next come eight independently owned resorts on Disney property but a little farther from the Kingdom in Lake Buena Vista.

## The Hotels

If you can afford it (or can't but are in the mood for a big splurge), Disney's 855-room **Polynesian Resort,** Walt Disney World, FL 32830 (P.O. Box 10,000) (tel. 407/824-2000), is a fabulous place to lei your head. Step over the thatched threshold here and you're transported to the South Seas, where you stay in two-story "longhouses" set amid jungle so tropical it's a wonder there isn't a volcano around somewhere. South Seas luxury in your room translates to beautiful tropical colors, king-size beds, plush carpets, big closets, and dressing rooms. Outside are two pools with lifeguards, a sand beach, water sports, a playground, sauna, beauty and barber shops, and boutiques. For dining there's a massive buffet filled with exotic treats and served in the Papeete Bay Verandah or South Seas Dining Room. At night Polynesian revues wiggle and flame in Luau Cove. Rates, year-round, are $190 to $275.

When you whiz up to the **Contemporary Resort** in the silent shuuush of the monorail and see this towering glass-and-chrome mirage, you'll think you've landed on the moon. Glass, glass, everywhere, sharp geometric patterns and miles of straight-up space are just part of the gasp-ery at this 1,053-room hotel. In your room you'll find Tomorrowland luxury too: two wash basins, extra-large beds, lots and lots of space, and hues as contemporary as a moon walk. Outside are two pools, a beach, health club and sauna, recreation room; there's also a 15th-floor lounge with top entertainment, and music for dancing every night, several excellent dining rooms, huge buffet breakfast, and lunches. The mailing address is Box 10,000, Walt Disney World, FL 32830 (tel. 407/824-1000). Rates, year round, are $180 to $270, higher for suites.

Golf fans should putt straightaway to the **Disney Inn** or **Fairways Villas,** built right next to the greens of two 18-hole courses so you won't exhaust yourself getting from coffee cup to golf cup. There's tennis here too, plus dining, lounges, shops, a health club, and contemporary decor in very attractive, spacious accommodations. More sports? Of course: boating, waterskiing, bicycles, and a heated pool. Rates are $175 to $185 year round.

One of the best-kept secrets at Walt Disney World—although we don't suppose *they* think of it that way—are the villas. Tucked away beside golf courses in shady stands of tall pines, the **Vacation Villas, Fairways Villas,** and **Club Lake Villas** are among the most intriguing places to stay on Disney property. All are apartment villas with kitchen facilities, big roomy places ideal for families. Everyone can spread out and the youngsters can run themselves into exhaustion in the beautiful wooded areas in which the villas are located. Rates are $150 to $295 year round.

Vacation Villas have cathedral ceilings and one or two bedrooms large enough to accommodate four to six people. Club Lake Villas don't have full kitchens but do have refrigerators and wet bars plus two double beds, set off slightly from a living room. Fairways Villas are handsome, woodsy two-bedroom units rimming the golf course. Six can tuck away beneath the high ceilings here.

Treehouse, anyone? Right here in the **Treehouse Villas** village are complete houses, each on its own large plot under the pines. Most of the living space is on the second floor, built up high among the top branches of nearby trees, hence the treehouse appellation. It's a lovely getaway spot that shares a pool with nearby Lake Buena Vista Golf and Tennis Club, where there's also a serene restaurant. These two-bedroom treehouses are very quiet secluded spots far from the thundering herds and might make a good choice for families looking for a little relaxation with their sightseeing. Rates are $270 to $295 year-round.

In 1988 and 1989 Walt Disney World opened two new hotels—the Grand Floridian Beach Resort and the Caribbean Beach Resort, the first new ones to be built right on Disney property in many years.

**Grand Floridian Beach Resort,** Box 10,000, Walt Disney World, Lake Buena Vista, FL 32830 (tel. 407/824-8000), is a massive hotel with no less than 900 rooms. Its theme and style harks back to days of yore in Florida when minimalism was nowhere in sight and architectural frills were part of the frivolity. Sprawled across 40 acres alongside the Seven Seas Lagoon between the Magic Kingdom and the Polynesian Resort, the Grand Floridian easily incurs visions of the Rockefellers; Florida's own favorite son, Thomas Edison, whose Fort Myers winter home echoes the design of this huge hotel; and even Teddy Roosevelt, who made sure he found time to meet his Florida voters each winter.

While those who developed Florida would be not at all surprised to see the Grand Floridian, they would surely be shocked to see a zipping monorail stopping at the door. Inside this eyeful of a hotel you will find soaring ceilings, wicker rockers, whirring ceiling fans, and a veritable forest of Victorian woodwork—indeed there are 60 miles of wooden scrollwork here!

Despite its antique look, you'll find all the required modernities from fancy suites with bars to cozy hideaway seating areas where a concierge conjures up Continental breakfasts and evening cocktails. You move about in an open-cage elevator and wander in the depths of a palm forest, the Victorian tree of choice. Five stories above the atrium lobby are ceilings inset with stained-glass domes, glittering chandeliers, and ornate metal scrolls. Rooms in the main hotel and the four- and five-story lodge buildings are decked out in soft pastels, furnished with armoires, light woods, marble-topped sinks with antique fittings, queen-size beds, and a day bed.

If you hunger or thirst or have a shopping attack, those whims can be satisfied at Victoria & Albert, where you dine in Victorian elegance, or the Gasparilla Grill and Games, where you top your own burger. Flagler's purveys Floridian foods and, outside, along what WDW likes to call the "beach," Narcoossee Nick's stocks oysters, clams, shrimp, and other seafood treats in a seaside atmosphere.

Recreational activities are myriad and include all kinds of watersports from rental boats to a swimming pool and windsurfing boards. Rates at this really quite lovely recent Disney addition are $215 to $355 for rooms in the main hotel, with the rate depending on season and type of accommodation. Suites are also available at steeper prices. Highest rates apply in December, from February through mid-April, and June through mid-August.

The second complex, the **Caribbean Beach Resort,** Box 10,000, 900 Cayman Way, Lake Buena Vista, FL 32830 (tel. 407/824-8000), an even more massive hotel sporting no less than 2,112 rooms, opened in 1989. This spot acquired notoriety not for its physical size but for the size of its rates—it is the first moderately priced hotel ever built by the Disney corporation.

Composed of gingerbread pastel village clusters of two-story buildings spotlighting the style of Trinidad, Martinique, Barbados, Aruba, and Jamaica, the resort is as colorful as a neon rainbow, but it strives to evoke the same unhurried "soon-come, mon," atmosphere that reigns in the Caribbean.

Trails and roadways winding through the "villages" connect the many arms of this hotel and connect all of them to the Walt Disney World transportation system, although the monorail does not come right to the door here—you must take a bus to reach it. Six counter-service restaurants offer bakery treats, barbecued food, and native Caribbean fare as well as the requisite hamburgers and hot dogs.

Built around a 40-acre lake, the resort thus is able to offer you yet another Disney "beach" and all the watersports you can splash and sail.

Rooms accommodate four with two double beds, although some have king-size beds. Rates are $74 to $99 year round, depending on whether you'd like to view a parking lot or the hotel's gardens or pool.

## Reservations

You can book space in any of these very busy hotels by calling 407/824-8000. You'll get the quickest response after 5pm, when things slow down a bit.

You can also write to any of the hotels at this address: Walt Disney World, Central Reservations Office, P.O. Box 10,000, Lake Buena Vista, FL 32830. For adventurous types there's a reservation desk on Main Street, U.S.A., in the Magic Kingdom, but that's a big risk since these hotels are almost always completely booked weeks in advance.

One last option here: a complete house! Called **Grand Vista Suites,** these are two- and three-bedroom houses complete with maid service, daily newspapers at the door, refrigerators stocked with staples, and lovely furnishings. They will set you back $650 to $750 a day, but for a large—and prosperous—family, they are a lovely stopping spot.

## Camping

You can't get much better surroundings for camping than Disney's **Fort Wilderness Resort** (tel. 407/824-8000), a 600-acre resort that's the most popular camping site in the state (translate: Book ahead). A huge wooded area has room for 825 not-very-rough-its with full hookups, a grill, water, and a disposal system. If roughing it in that style is a little too rough for you, rent a Fleetwood trailer that sleeps four or six and is fully equipped for $155 to $165 per night. Fort Wilderness is a fun place with campfire sing-alongs and a Pioneer Hall, where you dine on barbecue and corn on the cob and are entertained by cancan dancers and a foot-stompin' dinner show, at $30 for adults, $16 to $24 for children, depending on age. At two trading posts you can buy all the things somebody forgot to bring. Later watch Disney movies or go on Marshmallow Marsh canoe trips ($6 for adults, $5 for children) that sail you off to a marshmallow roast. There's horseback riding for $12, and full campsites are $35 to $46 a day.

## AT LAKE BUENA VISTA

Exit from I-4 at Lake Buena Vista (County Road 535) and you're transported to a luxurious world of manicured lawns, towering exquisite hotels, and none of the tawdry flash that characterizes some of the other sections of the city. No day-glo here, not even huge signs—just tasteful, subtle "announcements" at the front of the property. That alone gives you a clue to the luxury you will find—and pay for—here, to the tune of $100+ a night.

**Walt Disney Travel Co.** (tel. 407/828-3232) has dozens of tempting and money-saving packages that include accommodations at Disney resorts and hotels in Lake Buena Vista. Write to them at P.O. Box 22094, Lake Buena Vista, FL 32830, and they'll be happy to send you information on what they have to offer.

First hotel you'll see as you enter these beautifully landscaped grounds is the **Viscount,** 2000 Hotel Plaza Blvd. (P.O. Box 22205), Lake Buena Vista, FL 32830 (tel. 407/828-2424, or toll free 800/255-3050, 800/423-1022 in Florida), a favorite with families and the home of that chubby charmer, dear old Sleepy Bear. Parents can tuck in the kiddies then whiz up to the 18th floor Club Calypso to relax while watching fireworks explode over the Magic Kingdom. Rooms at the Viscount are plusher than at some other of this chain's hotels, with two queen-size beds in every room, pretty decor, and all the services and extras to make for a comfortable, pampered stay. There's a pool and game room, do-it-yourself sundaes at Chez Donut, a restaurant, bike rentals, new playground and lounge. Rooms are $109 to $159 year round, for up to four people.

Next comes the **Grosvenor Resort,** 1850 Hotel Plaza Blvd. (P.O. Box 22202), Lake Buena Vista, FL 32830 (tel. 407/828-4444, or toll free 800/624-4109, or 800/528-1234), which moved in to do a top-to-bottom rehab of the former Americana Dutch Resort. Gone now are the Dutch touches, but the hotel's many amenities remain, including a couple of restaurants and lounges, tennis and racquetball courts, a pool, game area, and playground. Now you'll find the hotel's huge lobby decked out in dramatically soft hues reminiscent of Victorian-era colors. Ceiling fans whir, and a lobby bar called Crickets offers a respite from Disney-ing. Those who seek not even a moment's respite from the Mouse can find him in many guises from T-shirts to sunglasses at the hotel's Disney-packed shop, where a yen for resort clothes can be fulfilled.

Sumptuous quality has always been a trademark of this hotel and that remains true. Rooms offer twin double beds and some have king-size sleepers. All are handsomely decorated in subtly restful shades. An unusual feature of this hotel is videocassette players in every room and a substantial library of films with which to end or begin the day. Refrigerated minibars can be found in every room too. Unusually large bathrooms are amply supplied with all the amenities you'd expect in a large and elegantly chic hotel like this one.

Those who don't want the fantasy to end even at the end of the day can sidle in for dinner at Baskerville's, which sports—are you ready?—a Sherlock Holmes Museum. Right in the middle of the dining room is a glass-enclosed re-creation of Sherlock's parlor right down to his tobacco and correspondence. Makes for an interesting diversion from the Mouse-mania that rules this part of the world. Nearby is—what else?—Moriarty's Pub, where dart players imbibe among memorabilia of that fiendish Holmes enemy. Rates at the resort, which also has two outdoor pools, a hot tub, horseshoe playground, shuffleboard, and lighted tennis, handball, and racquetball courts, are $99 to $155, depending on season and view.

Across the street, the 376-room **Hotel Royal Plaza,** 1905 Hotel Plaza Blvd., Lake Buena Vista, FL 32830 (tel. 407/828-2828, or toll free 800/248-7890), is a study in contemporary elegance that touches on but doesn't dwell on Spanish atmosphere. The 396 thoroughly modern rooms in a 17-story tower or in two-story wings are decorated in earthy, contemporary colors and have the best of everything: separate dressing rooms, big closets, private balconies. Amenities include three restaurants, a beauty salon, heated swimming pool, sauna, whirlpool, putting green, shuffleboard, and four lighted tennis courts you can play on for free.

Listen, if it's good enough for Burt Reynolds and Barbara Mandrell, surely. . . . Both those stars were guests here and the resort has named two of its suites after them. Rates range from $115 to $170 year round for double rooms. If you want to sleep where Barb or Burt slept, or in similar suites, you'll pay $375 to $750, and up.

At the **Howard Johnson Resort,** 1805 Hotel Plaza Blvd. (P.O. Box 22204), Lake Buena Vista, FL 32830 (tel. 407/828-8888, or toll free 800/223-9930), you'll find a hotel that's been so successful it's added a new wing, and now offers 323 rooms. You'll also find all the consideration and gracious service you've come to expect from this chain that's been catering to tired travelers for many years. Like all the properties in Lake Buena Vista, Howard Johnson is posh and plush, with a cheerful, bright 14-story atrium lobby and attractive accommodations. Rates are $95 to $165 double, year round; higher rates for suites.

Yet another hotel chain seeking a piece of Mouseland is **Hilton at Walt Disney World Village,** at 1751 Hotel Plaza Blvd., Lake Buena Vista, FL 32830 (tel. 407/827-4000, or toll free 800/782-4414). So how did Hilton decide to face the competition of the masses of hoteliers here? Simple, electronically. Get in the elevator here, press the button for the third floor, and shortly a disembodied voice says, "Third floor, going up." This sort of state-of-the-art digital/push button/computerized electronic wizardry turns up everywhere in the hotel, from a digital telephone system that uses the touch of a single key to adjust heating or air conditioning, control the television, and call hotel service personnel, to lights that turn on and off by themselves when people enter or leave the room. Elevators are controlled by microcomputers that talk to you and guest rooms unlock with tamperproof magnetic cards. Spacious hotel rooms in this 10-story building are done up in pretty contemporary pastels with attractive furnishings and big windows.

If you're traveling with the youngsters and would like to do without them for a few hours, a special Youth Hotel here offers accommodations for children 3 to 12 years old, complete with video room, snackbar, and play area, with meals and scheduled recreation provided.

Complimentary transportation to both Walt Disney World parks is provided by this Disney property hotel, which also has two restaurants: American Vineyards, all dolled up in brass and featuring American regional cuisine; and a lively informal family spot called County Fair, which offers buffets and an old-fashioned family-style dinner. There are also two tennis courts, two lounges with entertainment, a swimming pool and spray pool for the youngsters, and a health club.

An 813-room hotel, Hilton at Walt Disney World charges $130 to $235 double year round, higher for suites.

Last on this posh block is the **Buena Vista Palace,** an $85-million creation at 1900 Buena Vista Dr., Lake Buena Vista, FL 32830 (tel. 407/827-2727, or toll free 800/327-2990, 800/432-2920 in Florida). Buena Vista Palace takes a little medieval flavor and whips it up with lots of contemporary comforts to create a 27-story lakeside hotel with 841 rooms. You'll find a handsome Australian theme in the resort's beefy Outback Restaurant and 80 different kinds of beer! A tall central atrium soars several stories to a stained-glass roof, and in the lobby a plush bar is decorated in glowing burgundy shades. There's an interesting architectural innovation here that may confuse you at first but will delight you later: You enter on an upper level of the hotel where a serene, unhurried atmosphere prevails because all the really busy stuff—reservations, car rentals, swimming pool, exits, and the like—is going on down at ground level. Way upstairs you can dine and imbibe in a rooftop aerie, Arthur's 27, where the view of EPCOT, the Magic Kingdom, and half of central Florida is awesome. Rates are $125 to $255 year round, higher for suites.

At all these hotels, transportation to Walt Disney World is free and some money-saving packages are available.

Hyatt Hotels hit Orlando with a bang—make that a splash—when the hotel opened its fabulously showy hotel in Lake Buena Vista, just west of the Walt Disney World Hotel Village Area. You'll see its stepped-pyramid building rising out of the woodlands as you whiz by on I-4. To get to the **Hyatt Regency Grand Cypress Hotel,** 1 Grand Cypress Blvd., Orlando, FL 32819 (tel. 407/239-1234, or toll free

800/233-1234), take County Road 535 (Lake Buena Vista) exit from I-4 and head west to the second traffic light, where you'll turn left (a sign directs you). Just a short distance down that road is the entrance to this hotel, which was just the first project in a massive development here.

First, of course, came the hotel, which is now a major showplace in Orlando, no contest. Chief among its showy attributes is a quite incredible swimming pool featuring everything from a tall waterfall crashing into the pool to a suspension bridge swaying over it. You swim around and into rock grottoes, splash in streams and waterfalls, slide down a slippery waterslide set into rocks, and imbibe at a watery grotto bar. As for the hotel itself, well . . . whew! An 11-story atrium soars skyward and a fortune's worth of Asian artworks are scattered casually about hotel and grounds. Streams trickle through the lobby and ivy streams down from high overhead.

Rooms are lovely, no question about it. In a special 11th-floor Regency Club, where rates are $340, rooms are outfitted with a love seat and chair tucked into a sitting area fronted by glass doors through which the pool's dozen cascading waterfalls are visible. King-size beds are trimmed in light woods and headboards have inset fabric designed to match the bedspreads. Suites rent for $600 to $1,400. Other rooms in the hotel are a bit smaller, but by no means small. They range in price from $180 to $250 double and are also decorated in the most contemporary of furnishings in pale pastels, mauves, salmon, pink, light woods, handsome framed paintings. Tropical touches include wicker furniture, ceiling fans, and shutters.

When you've explored all the nooks and crannies of that spectacular swimming pool, you can visit the huge equestrian center or tennis-racquetball club, sail, windsurf, jog, play croquet, canoe, or paddleboat about a 21-acre lake, or sun on 1,000 feet of white sand beach. You can stroll a nature preserve, duff about on a nine-hole pitch-and-putt course, or do some serious driving on an 18-hole Jack Nicklaus signature golf course restricted to registered guests. If you need still more, find it in the health club where shiny new exercise equipment, a sauna, Jacuzzi, massage studio, and jogging clinics await. Send the small ones off to a video arcade or an outdoor playground.

Five restaurants offer an intriguing variety of places to dine. In the Cascade restaurant, Hyatt's two-level version of a coffee shop, a dramatic bronze mermaid keeps cool beneath a 35-foot waterfall. A pianist entertains here—even at breakfast! Atop the swimming pool's rocks and waterfalls, a woodsy restaurant called Hemingway's pays tribute to Key West's favorite son. Prices for steaks and seafood are in the $18 to $26 range for entrees. La Coquina, Hyatt's most elegant and most expensive restaurant, is a two-story triumph overlooking the lake. Here a harpist plays as you dine on French and continental entrees in the $19 to $29 range. Figure about $90 a couple for an elegant dinner. For casual evenings, nip into the White Horse Saloon, an urban cowboy's heaven where a slab of roast prime rib awaits. Prices in this western-themed restaurant, which serves only prime rib or free-range chicken, range from $25 for a 14-ounce cut of beef to $45 for a whopping two-pounder. Cocktail lounge enthusiasts can visit Trellises, the lovely lobby bar tucked among streams and ferns; the Hurricane Bar in Hemingway's, where a strolling musician provides evening entertainment and bartenders create a combustible daiquiri called the Papa Doble; the White Horse Saloon, a showy center trimmed with etched glass, brass, and an engraved tin ceiling; or floating Papillon Bar.

If you like large, you'll love **Marriott's Orlando World Center,** 8701 World Center Dr., Orlando, FL 32821 (tel. 407/239-4200, or toll free 800/228-9290), with 1,503 rooms the largest hotel in the state! You need a map to find your way around the lobby here, but once you do you'll find yourself strolling tranquilly amid flashy surroundings filled with plants and objets d'art. Views from a lobby balcony out over the extensive grounds are impressive, as is everything else about this massive hotel. There's every facility you can think of here and then some: an 18-hole golf course, 12 lighted tennis courts, 4 swimming pools, 4 hydrotherapy spas, and—get this—10 (!) restaurants and lounges.

Waterfalls tinkle through the multilevel lobby where palms tower over you and light filters through a glass roof high overhead—marble, brass, etched glass, a world unto itself. Rates at the Marriott are $150 to $229 year round; suites available at higher rates. Discounts, family rates, weekend rates, and Disney package plans are available in most seasons, although probably not in peak winter season.

Just outside the village, but still in the Lake Buena Vista area, is the **Vistana Resort,** 13800 Vistana Dr. (P.O. Box 22051), Lake Buena Vista, FL 32830 (tel. 407/239-3100, or toll free 800/327-9152, 800/432-9197 in Florida), which pops up out of the pastureland like a fantasy kingdom of its own. Plunked down in the quietest of settings, on County Road 535 at the Lake Buena Vista exit south, Vistana is a comfortable lagoon-laced tennis-oriented condominium resort. A massive complex of gloriously contemporary villas and town houses, each with two big bedrooms and two baths, Vistana has fully equipped kitchens, living and dining rooms, balconies or terraces, VCRs, washers and dryers, and maid service. There are huge pools and whirlpools, a general store, Tiki Bar, fitness center, snackshop, jogging trail, scheduled activities, and enough tennis courts for Wimbledon. Tennis is free, and the resort offers tennis instruction and clinics. Rates range from $175 to $275 for a two-bedroom villa for six to eight people.

A money-saver just outside the village (but only a few hundred yards away) is **Days Inn Lake Buena Vista Village,** 12490 Apopka-Vineland Rd. on County Road 535, Lake Buena Vista, FL 32830 (tel. 407/239-4646, or toll free 800/325-2525). Off by itself under a stand of rustling pines, World Inn has 245 rooms including 12 efficiencies, and refrigerators in every room. There is a coin laundry plus two pools, a large playground, and movies. Rooms are spacious and bright, with tropical colors and lots of glass. World Inn has a pretty, casual restaurant for family dining and a cocktail lounge with entertainment, plus free transportation to the Magic Kingdom, EPCOT, and Lake Buena Vista Village Shopping Center. Rates range from $75 to $95, year round.

## ON US 192

Welcome to a buyer's market! Not for 10 years have the prices in Orlando been so advantageous for the traveler—or so bargainable! This new budgeteer's paradise is the result of a recent building boom that added more than 40,000 hotel rooms at flashpaper speed—and has thousands more on the drawing boards!

This stunning proliferation of hotel quarters has led to a price war the likes of which you are not likely to find anywhere else in Florida. It's even gotten to the point that small hotel operators are bargaining down their own prices on the telephone when you call them for reservations. Some are even advertising "Make us an offer."

Even as you read, some new Orlando hotel is planning a ribbon-cutting ceremony to celebrate its opening day. Hundreds of new hotel rooms are planned or under construction.

To describe every one of the newcomers would take a book of its own, so suffice to say that if you drive into the area and begin looking for a spot to settle, begin looking on US 192. Small motels, and some not so small, have sprung up along this wide highway that is sometimes called the "Highway to the Worlds." Those "worlds" refer primarily to Walt Disney World, the entrance to which is reached from this highway, but also to Sea World, just a splash away.

Those newcomer motels, which seem to have sprung up like proverbial mushrooms, are all pretty stock material, both in ambience and in price. You'll find basic cement-block structures with clean but unprepossesing quarters: two chairs, a table, usually two double beds (usually with flowered spreads), a dresser, often a small dressing area, and a bathroom.

Owners and operators of these often-family-run motels are as exotic as their motels are not: Some are Chinese, many are Indian, some are Latin Americans, and of course many are Americans.

Price? About $30 to $50, year round; sometimes less.

While they're nothing to write home about, these motels do offer a decent, if nonchic, place to put your head each evening when you weave in exhausted from a long day at one or more of Orlando's many attractions. They have the added benefit of proximity to Walt Disney World, which is not likely to be more than a 10- or 15-minute drive away.

Starting with the Hyatt Orlando Hotel, the most expensive, and working down to the money-savers, here are our choices.

After you've seen the **Hyatt Orlando Hotel,** 6375 W. Irlo Bronson Memorial Hwy. (at I-4 and US 192 East), Kissimmee, FL 32741 (tel. 407/396-1234, or toll free 800/233-1234), you may not bother with Walt Disney World. What a place this is! Every building is painted a different color (which is helpful when you're trying to find your room in this maze of 960 others). There are four swimming pools and four kiddie pools, tennis courts, a shopping mall complete with package store, game room with electronic games, and a tot lot for the toddlers. To describe the rooms here is easy: beautiful. And big, very big, decorated in subtle earthy shades with giant dressing areas and baths and all those little touches Hyatt so thoughtfully adds: French-milled soap, shampoo, shower caps, shoe shiners, even a creme rinse.

For dining, there's a buffet restaurant with a changing theme that has ranged from Mexican to Italian to oom-pah-pah (prices about $12 for a huge buffet) and a fine Limey Jim's Restaurant, where you dine on five- or six-course Italian meals, ending with a half dozen or so specialty coffees laced with imported liqueurs. You'll pay $30 to $50 for this impressive repast, and to stay here you'll spend $119 to $129 for a double room, with suites ranging up from there. And when all other amusements pale, you can take a helicopter ride aboard a whirlybird parked on the front lawn.

Among the newest hotels in the area is **Quality Suites Main Gate East,** 5876 W. Irlo Bronson Memorial Hwy., Kissimmee, FL 32741 (tel. 407/396-8040, or toll free 800/848-4148). Here all accommodations are one- or two-bedroom suites that can accommodate six to ten exhausted attraction attendees. Each has a living/dining area, kitchens equipped with everything right down to a microwave oven and a dishwasher, and remote-control cable televisions with in-room movies. Fashionably serene decor makes for a tranquil retreat here, and you're treated each morning to complimentary Continental breakfast and each evening to a complimentary cocktail reception. Shuttle service to the parks is available at this resort located just two miles from Walt Disney World. Rates are $76 to $109 in fall and spring, $135 to $170 in peak summer and winter seasons.

The **Sheraton Lakeside Inn,** 7711 US 192 West, Kissimmee, FL 32741 (tel. 407/828-8250, or toll free 800/325-3535), just west of I-4, is quite close to Disney and has 652 high-quality rooms, a seafood saloon, lounge, deli, two heated pools and two tot pools, a boat dock, paddleboats, mini-golf, tennis courts, and poolside gazebos. Two people pay $83 to $115 year round. Children under 17 stay free.

The nearby **Comfort Inn-Main Gate,** 7571 W. Irlo Bronson Memorial Hwy. (US 192 West), Kissimmee, FL 32741 (tel. 407/396-7500, or toll free 800/218-0064, 800/218-0087 in Florida), is a pretty place on a strip of highway packed with fast-food restaurants, shops, and chain hotels. Located just one mile from Walt Disney World, the hotel has 282 spacious rooms, each with two double beds, decorated in cheerful prints. There's a shuttle service to Walt Disney World, color television, free local phone service, a pool, game room, boutique, laundry facilities, and a cozy restaurant open for breakfast and dinner (prices in the $3 range for big breakfasts; under $10 for steak, seafood, and Italian dinner favorites). Rates are $36 to $94 all year.

You know Florida and its superlatives. Well, how about the world's largest Days Inn Lodge? Yes, indeed, the **Days Inn/Days Suites** right here in Kissimmee, at 5820 W. Irlo Bronson Memorial Hwy., Kissimmee, FL 32741 (tel. 407/396-7900 for suites, 407/396-7969 for rooms, or toll free 800/325-2525 or 800/327-9126, 800/432-9103 in Florida), on US 192 east of I-4, where every suite has 700 square feet of living space, patios or balconies, and a kitchen complete with dishwasher! There are three swimming pools, a playground, and three barbecues. It is less than three miles from the Kingdom. Two people pay $69 to $118 year round and children under 18 are free.

**Larson's Lodge-Kissimmee,** 2009 W. Vine St., Kissimmee, FL 32741 (tel. 407/846-2713, or toll free 800/624-5905), seems to attract nice people and you won't find many nicer than the friendly Larson family who own and operate this very attractive resort. There's a game room, boutique, heated pool, sundeck, and a little picket fence around the children's play area. Three-story wings house the resort's 120 pretty rooms, each with two double beds, a sitting area, and picture windows. Right next door is the Black Angus Steakhouse, where you can dine for less than $15. A room or efficiency is $39 to $70 year round (children under 18 free).

This same family also runs **Larson's Lodge-Main Gate,** 6075 W. Irlo Bronson Memorial Hwy., Kissimmee, FL 32741 (tel. 407/396-6100, or toll free 800/327-9074), just a couple of miles from Disney World's main gate, hence the name. Here you'll find the same quality of accommodations in the same $39 to $55 price range, and for dining the reasonable prices of Shoney's Restaurant, a popular chain restaurant.

Dark-wood railings add a trim touch to **Rodeway Inn-Eastgate,** 5245 W. Irlo Bronson Memorial Hwy., Kissimmee, FL 32741 (tel. 407/841-8541, or toll free 800/423-3864 or 800/992-2302 in Florida), a two-story motel with spacious rooms overlooking a pool and patio. In the Riviera Lounge is nightly entertainment, and the inn's dining room features an impressive buffet. There's a playground for the children and a coin laundry to keep them clean after a day on the playground. Rates are $35 to $65 year-round.

Tennis is the focal point at **Orlando Vacation Resort,** South US 27, a mile north of US 192, Clermont, FL 32711 (P.O. Box 2527, Orlando, FL 32802; tel. 407/656-8181, or toll free 800/874-9064). You'll find lots of lighted tennis courts plus 225 very attractive quarters with lots of space and bright colors. There's a cute little Misty Harbor restaurant front and center with several different themes in several dining rooms. Excellent food emerges from the kitchen, with fresh bread every day and prices in the $10 to $15 range. A room for two at this vacation resort, which also supplies free shuttle rides to Walt Disney World, is $45 to $55, year round. Children under 17 are free.

Back on the east side of I-4 on US 192, the **Colonial Motor Lodge,** 1815 W. Vine St., Kissimmee, FL 32741 (tel. 407/847-6121, or toll free 800/325-4348 or 800/432-3052 in Florida), has 40 apartments with quite basic furnishings, but rooms clean, neat, and big enough for a family. There are two swimming pools and a game room. Motel units with two double beds go for $36 to $50, and you'll pay $54 to $60 for apartments. There's no charge for children under 12.

**King's Motel,** 4836 W. Irlo Bronson Memorial Hwy., Kissimmee, FL 32741 (tel. 407/396-4762, or toll free 800/327-9071, 800/432-9928 in Florida, 800/874-6715 in Canada), is a pretty spot that shares a little lake with an adjoining motel, the Lakeview. You can swim and row around in a boat the motel will lend you, or roam among the lovely shady pine trees scattered about the grounds. Rooms are basic with double beds, and tiled foyers, and there's a pool overlooking the lake. Rates here range from $50 to $60 year round. There is no charge for children under 17.

**Kissimmee Oaks Hotel Inn,** 4311 W. Vine St., Kissimmee, FL 32741 (tel. 407/396-4213, or toll free 800/327-9155) is a rustic resort with, nevertheless, nice new rooms. Set way back off the road, the inn has colorful accommodations with wide picture windows overlooking the grounds where giant old trees shade a lovely pool. Rooms at the inn are $36 to $85, year round; children under 18 stay free.

**Sunrise Motel,** 801 W. Vine St., Kissimmee, FL 32741 (tel. 407/846-3224), has small, simply furnished rooms, but for the money you probably can't beat this shuttered motel decorated inside in bright hues. Light paneling adds a serene note and perky flowered bedspreads are nice touches. If you've got a couple of hungry young mouths to feed, there's a Burger King across the street and a McDonald's next door. Sunrise is about 15 minutes from Disney and charges $25 to $45.

**East Gate Motor Inn** and Restaurant is another money-saver on US 192, at 900 E. Vine St., Kissimmee, FL 32741 (tel. 407/846-4600). Its brick facade pops up in the middle of a farm, although the motel itself is just off the highway. Rooms are basic but serviceable, and there's a small pool. Rates, changing seasonally, are $19 to $55.

**Embassy Motel,** 4880 W. Irlo Bronson Memorial Hwy., Kissimmee, FL 32741 (tel. 407/396-1144, or toll free 800/432-0153 in Florida, 800/325-4872 elsewhere), is a two-story spot with big glass windows across the front of every room and a swimming pool off to one side. It's located four miles east of Walt Disney World and has rooms with a dressing area and color TVs. Not far from the building is a small but pretty lake. Prices here are $25 to $70 year round.

On the same lake you'll find **Park Inn International,** 4960 W. Irlo Bronson Memorial Hwy. (US 192), Kissimmee, FL 32741 (tel. 407/396-1376, or toll free 800/327-0072, 800/432-0276 in Florida). Arches add a touch of the Mediterranean to the two-story buildings here, and sparkling Lake Cecile in the back is a good place to send the kids exploring while you grab a few minutes' peace. There's a small swimming pool in the middle of the resort too. Rooms are equipped with compact stove/sink units so you can whip up the occasional lunch for yourself. Nearby, a small shopping area features plenty of souvenirs and a family-style restaurant. Rates are $39 to $59, year round.

**Econo Lodge Main Gate East,** 6051 W. Irlo Bronson Memorial Hwy. (US 192W), Kissimmee, FL 32741 (tel. 407/396-1748, or toll free 800/446-6900), has the basic but comfortable quarters this chain has been offering for quite a number of years, in a building with just the faintest touch of Swiss chalet. They're running quite a large operation here, with a game room, laundry room, gift shop, playground, in-room VCRs, and swimming pool. Rates are $42 to $70, year round for rooms or efficiencies.

**Holiday Inn-Kissimmee,** 2145 E. Irlo Bronson Memorial Hwy. (US 192), Kissimmee, FL 32743 (tel. 407/846-4646, or toll free 800/465-4329), and **TraveLodge Kissimmee Flags,** 2407 W. Irlo Bronson Memorial Hwy. (US 192), Kissimmee, FL 32741 (tel. 305/933-2400, or toll free 800/352-4752, 800/432-4554 in Florida), are both represented along this highway. Each offers clean, comfortable quarters just like those you'd find in those chains' representatives anywhere in the nation. Rates are $49 to $75 at either property.

**Buena Vista Motel,** 5200 W. Irlo Bronson Memorial Hwy. (US 192), Kissimmee, FL 32741 (tel. 407/396-2100), has an alluring spanking-clean look about its blue and white buildings. That same simple but attractive atmosphere continues inside the rooms, which are basic but well kept and serviceable. There's a pretty swimming pool here too. Rates are $30 to $50, year round.

**Central Motel,** 4698 W. Irlo Bronson Memorial Hwy. (US 192), Kissimmee, FL 32741 (tel. 407/396-2333), is yet another new spot with Chinese-red doors and with a swimming pool at the rear of the building. Brick-trimmed doors welcome you to standard motel rooms with orange-and-brown floral-print decor. Rates here are $25 to $50, year round.

If you like Mediterranean architecture, you'll find hints of it at **Casa Rosa Inn,** 4600 W. Irlo Bronson Memorial Hwy. (US 192), Kissimmee, FL 32741 (tel. 407/396-2020), painted in a delicate pink hue. Surroundings are especially attractive here: The motel's set in a small wooded area. Rates are $32 including a Continental breakfast, rising in high season to $52.

**Sun Motel,** 5020 W. Irlo Bronson Memorial Hwy. (US 192), Kissimmee, FL 32741 (tel. 407/396-2673), is another of the multitude of tiny family-owned motels that have risen here in the last two years. Rates are $30 to $58.

To give you some more options in the busiest months, here are the names of a few of the many small places offering basic accommodations, usually a swimming pool, and best of all that proximity to Walt Disney World and all the other playgrounds here: **Chalet Motel,** 4741 W. Irlo Bronson Memorial Hwy. (US 192), Kissimmee, FL 32741 (tel. 407/396-1677); **Maple Leaf Motel,** 4647 W. Irlo Bronson Memorial Hwy. (US 192), Kissimmee, FL 32741 (tel. 407/396-0300); and the lakeside **The Key,** 4810 W. Irlo Bronson Memorial Hwy. (US 192), Kissimmee, FL 32741 (tel. 407/396-6200), all with prices as low as $17, rising to $70 double, year round.

Still more motels along US 192 (Irlo Bronson Memorial Hwy.) that are neat, clean, and fall in the $30 to $60 price range year round—

**The Palm,** 4519 W. Irlo Bronson Memorial Hwy., Kissimmee, FL 32741 (tel. 407/396-0744), is a pleasant spot with stone siding, a pool, attractive rooms, and free coffee in the lobby.

**Enterprise Motel,** 4121 W. Irlo Bronson Memorial Hwy., Kissimmee, FL 32741 (tel. 407/933-1383), is a bright, cheerful spot with queen-size beds in the rooms, HBO television service, and a swimming pool at the rear of the building (nice, less traffic noise).

**Spacecoast Motel,** 4125 W. Irlo Bronson Memorial Hwy., Kissimmee, FL 32741 (tel. 407/933-5732, or toll free 800/654-8342, 800/247-1879 in Florida), has some rooms with whirlpools, remote-control color TVs with free Home Box Office service, and king- and queen-size beds, plus efficiencies and suites. It's 3½ miles to Walt Disney World and EPCOT Center.

**Hawaiian Village Inn,** 4559 W. Irlo Bronson Memorial Hwy., Kissimmee, FL 32741 (tel. 407/396-1212, or toll free 800/821-9503, 800/342-0137 in Florida), has 114 cheerful rooms with two extra-long double beds in each, and some with kitchenettes. There's a swimming pool off on one side of the building, a small and simple restaurant, and a lounge with big-screen television. Package rates here can save you money too.

**Radisson Inn–Maingate,** 7501 W. Irlo Bronson Memorial Hwy. (US 192), Kissimmee, FL 32741 (tel. 407/396-1400, or toll free 800/333-3333), is an attractive choice for those who want to be close to Walt Disney World. Located just a few minutes' drive from the main gate to WDW, Radisson Inn is sleekly modern from its colorful woven wall hangings to its plant-bedecked restaurant and bar. That modernity continues in the guest rooms, which are decorated in soft pastels and come complete with lots of little extra amenities. Tucked into the middle of the several wings of this hotel is a swimming pool and whirlpool; outside is a jogging trail, and two tennis courts. A deli-style café offers take-out service. Rates range from $79 to $99 double, including breakfast buffet, with children under 18 free.

## FLORIDA CENTER/INTERNATIONAL DRIVE

Florida Center is a name applied to a section of Orlando surrounding International Drive. It is home to many motels and fast-food chain restaurants. To get here, leave I-4 at the International Drive–Sand Lake Road exit and head east on Sand Lake Road (also known as County Road 528A).

It was only to be expected that Sea World would not sit idly by and let Walt Disney World have all those hotels on its property. That's why you will now find a new **Stouffer Orlando,** 6677 Sea Harbor Dr., (an extension of International Dr.) Orlando, FL 32821 (tel. 407/351-5555, or toll free 800/HOTELS1), right across the street from Sea World.

On the outside this towering International Drive-area hostelry presents a rather bland white facade sparked only by a bright-blue tile roof. But on the inside, whoooeee! Built in quadrangle style, the hotel's four wings surround an atrium bigger than a couple of football fields. Birds chatter in an aviary, fish swim in the waters surrounding a multilevel cocktail lounge, and visitors stroll past buildings designed to look like a small village. Describing this skylight-topped hotel is not an easy task.

For openers, the "lobby," which is really an inner courtyard delineated by the four wings of the hotel, looks like no lobby you've ever seen. Instead cupola-topped buildings in soft greens and blues are an aviary, a gazebo-like dining center, and that cocktail lounge. A couple of leaping marble dolphins beside the entrance to the lounge keep Sea World firmly in mind, as does that aviary.

Three other restaurants reside here, one a subtly decorated, black-lacquered Chinese restaurant, another a handsome and high-priced gourmet dining room (figure $25 to $40 a person for dinner), and the third, a rather grandiose coffee shop that becomes a steak-and-seafood dining room at night.

The best rooms, to us, are those on the north and south sides of the buildings. They have pretty french doors leading to flowerbox-trimmed balconies overlooking the magnificence of the lobby below, while the others, although just as handsomely decorated, overlook Sea World on one side, the outskirts of Orlando on the other. They have not missed anything in these rooms: remote-control TV, comfortable armchairs, lovely pastel decor, marble-clad double-sink bathrooms with a huge white clam shell full of everything from shampoo to a little bag of potpourri. Quite a place indeed! Rates at Stouffer at Sea World are $169 to $229 year round. Suites range from $338 to $1,000.

Newest entrant in the hotel sweepstakes going on along booming International Drive is the **Peabody Orlando,** 9801 International Dr., Orlando, FL 32819 (tel. 407/352-4000, or toll free 800/732-2639 except Florida), which has what only one other in the world can boast: a duck parade! On the stroke of 11am every day, out strut the Peabody's legendary ducks. After a ride down on the elevator from their home up-top somewhere, they march in free-form, puffed-breast splendor across to the lobby fountain, quacking everyone up as they go. A tradition that began at this hotel's sister property in Memphis many years ago, the ducks are a small but significant part of this handsome and elegant hotel.

There is, in fact, much about this hotel that is *rara avis*. First, it's elegant and contemporary, often contradictory terms in this part of the state. Second, rooms are spacious and beautifully decorated in tranquil contemporary shades. Third, there's a pool, athletic club, and four lighted tennis courts. Fourth, it's close to Walt Disney World and Sea World, and has easy access to both of those. Fifth . . . well, this could go on forever, and after the ducks everything else is just icing anyway. Rates at this standout on International Drive are $145 to $225, with higher prices buying you more space and concierge amenities. Suites range from $325 to $1,200.

The first hotel you'll see east of I-4 is the **Orlando Marriott Inn,** 8001 International Dr., Orlando, FL 32809 (tel. 407/351-2420, or toll free 800/228-9290). So sprawling is this resort you'll almost need a map to find your way around. This glamorous resort has all the amenities of a huge hotel but looks more like a posh neighborhood. Little lakes and fountains swirl about, tiny lagoons trickle under bridges, and paths lined with palms wind through clusters of two-story villas. The glamor doesn't stop outside either. Big picture windows overlook these enchanting grounds, and inside, some rooms have big puffy couches and chairs covered in subtle earthy colors, matching drapes, and deep carpets. There are oversize beds, and some units with kitchenettes in the 1,078 rooms scattered over 43 acres. Naturally there's more: tennis courts, three pools with sundecks and wooded platforms for scenic sitting, a kiddie pool, game room and play area, a shopping mall, and the elegant Grove Restaurant with plush banquettes featuring a menu in the $20 price range for seafood and sizzling steaks, and nightly entertainment at a dancing spot called Illusions. If you fly into Orlando, they offer free airport transportation. Rates at the resort are $110 to $130 double year round. Rooms with kitchens are $20 more, and children under 13 are free.

The **Hilton Inn Florida Center,** 7400 International Dr., Orlando, FL 32819 (tel. 407/351-4600, or toll free 800/327-1363, 800/332-4600 in Florida), occupies the entrance to the north end of International Drive and has a monster of a pool, covered by a roof. If you want sun, there's a second pool outside. A 400-room hostelry that includes 20 suites, the resort also features a tropical garden. Hilton Inn has spent quite a lot of money refurbishing this hotel over the years, and now it has a bright, contemporary look and a delightfully tropical feeling. There's patio dining outside under that slick roof and a woodsy inside dining room with prices in the $10 to $15 range. Lots of families find their way here since children are free at the resort. There's also complimentary airport transportation. Peak rates are $54 to $104 all year.

**Delta Court of Flags Hotel,** 5715 Major Blvd., Orlando, FL 32809 (tel. 407/351-3340, or toll free 800/877-1133), sprawls over acres of ground on the west side of I-4 so it's a quick trip from here to most of the area's attractions. We can't think what you could want that you can't find here: electronic game room, a deli, two saunas, two lighted tennis courts, three heated swimming pools, lounges, a wading pool for children, and a handsome restaurant with continental cuisine in the $15 to $20 range. Roomy accommodations are decorated in cheery colors and have all the amenities, including private balconies. All you need to do is learn how to find your way around these 820 rooms. Two people pay $125 to $150.

One of the newest hotels you can visit in central Florida is the **Sheraton World Resort,** at 10100 International Dr., Orlando, FL 32821 (tel. 407/352-1100, or toll free 800/325-3535, 800/327-0363, in Florida 800/341-4292), right next door to Sea World. Completed in late 1980, this 807-room hotel is thoroughly modern, from contemporary prints to arched wicker headboards and brick-floored lobby, where the sun shines through a skylight onto bright banners. You can sip tropical creations beside a huge pool, or dine in the Brasserie at the hotel's deli. The Sheraton charges $89 to $113 double, and children under 18 stay free. You couldn't be much closer to Sea World than this attractive hotel.

Right across the street from **Las Palmas Inn,** 6233 International Dr., Orlando, FL 32809 (tel. 407/351-3900, or toll free 800/327-2114, or 800/833-8389), is Orlando's watery fun spot, Wet 'N Wild, so if you're a water lover this might be a good place to settle. Las Palmas has an intriguing Spanish ambience with lots of dark wood and a red tile roof. The spacious rooms here are kept up-to-date with handsome wall coverings and subtle prints. You can cool off at the pool bar while the kids romp in the playground, or join them in the game room or inexpensive Palms Restaurant. Las Palmas charges $60 to $85 year round; higher for suites.

You can't possibly miss **Star Quality Resort,** formerly High Q, at 5905 International Dr., Orlando, FL 32809 (tel. 407/351-2100, or toll free 800/327-1366, in Florida 800/247-3737)—just look for the tall tower with the huge Q on top. Rising out of the ground like a circular beanstalk, this Quality Inn is a 21-story landmark with views all over Orlando. Besides the 300 spacious, tastefully decorated and recently renovated rooms with double beds and dressing areas, there are two heated pools, saunas, a game room, barber and beauty salons, a lounge with entertainment, and a restaurant. Rates are $44 to $74, depending on the season.

**Davis Brothers Motor Lodge,** 6603 International Dr., Orlando, FL 32809 (tel. 407/351-2900, or toll free 800/841-9480), is part of a chain that also operates very inexpensive cafeterias, so you can sleep and eat inexpensively all in one spot. Nice rooms with plenty of space and a bright decor is a watchword of the Davises. You'll find a pool for adults and a separate shallow splashing spot for the kids. You can bring Fido here too. Meals in the cafeteria are buffet style, in the $5 range. Year-round rates for doubles are $37 to $90.

The **Gateway Inn,** 7050 Kirkman Rd., Orlando, FL 32819 (tel. 407/351-2000, or toll free 800/327-3808, 800/432-1179 in Florida, 800/621-3394 in Canada), is an attractive family resort made even more attractive by the presence of the inexpensive Sweden House Smörgåsbord where you can easily feed those hungry mouths at dinner buffets for $5 to $10. You'll find bright floral prints in rooms that surround a big central courtyard where a gleaming pool is the center of attention. For the kids there's a playground with swings, and for everyone there are miniature golf and games. If a little escapism is in order, try the inn's cocktail lounge. Transportation to all the area's major attractions is complimentary. Rates at Gateway range from $44 to $88 double, year round.

The Gateway Inn also operates another hotel, the **Comfort Inn,** at 8421 S. Orange Blossom Trail, Orlando, FL 32809 (tel. 407/855-6060, or toll free 800/327-9742), a little farther from Walt Disney World, where the accommodations are similar and the prices run $30 to $48 double year round.

There's more red, white, and blue than even the flag can boast at **1776 Resort Inn,** 5858 International Dr., Orlando, FL 32809 (tel. 407/351-4410, or toll free 800/327-2115). In the heart of Florida Center, the Orlando Flags sprawls around central grounds and a large pool. Paths wind through the grounds and past rooms that feature wide glass windows overlooking the trees and shrubbery. Bright tropical decor is a feature of the spacious rooms here, and outside there's a whirling ride for the kids, a 24-hour restaurant, a shady poolside lounge for parents. Year-round prices are $38 to $58, and there's no charge for children under 18 sharing a room with their parents.

The **Days Inn Universal Studios East,** 5827 Caravan Court, Orlando, FL 32819 (from I-4, take the County Road 435 North exit; tel. 407/351-3800, or toll free 800/327-2111), has a dollarwise Denny's Restaurant, big and little pools at the Caravan, and large rooms decorated in contemporary hues. Double rooms are $50 to $100 year round; suites higher. Children under 17 are free.

If you'd rather swim than almost anything else, the only place in town for you is the **Radisson Inn & Justus Aquatic Center,** 8444 International Dr., Orlando, FL 32819 (tel. 407/345-0505, or toll free 800/752-0003). Designed to lure swim competitions, this new hotel has an Olympic-size swimming pool topped by a hydraulic roof that opens or closes for the weather, high-diving boards, marked lanes, electronic timing equipment, underwater observation rooms, and seating for 3,000 of your friends to come to watch you swim. There's a complete fitness center and health club here, with simply every kind of workout equipment and class you can imagine, up to and including racquetball and handball courts. Opened in 1985, the Radisson cost $25 million and its facilities are touted as the pool to upstage Fort Lauderdale's acclaimed Swimming Hall of Fame. Even swimmers must sleep, however, and here they can do that in large, lovely rooms outfitted in muted contemporary colors, often peach and gray tones. There's a restaurant and cafeteria at the hotel, which charges $79 to $99 double, year round.

Among the moderately priced hotels on hotel-lined International Drive, the **Comfort Inn,** 5825 International Dr. (at the corner of Kirkman Road), Orlando, FL 32819 (tel. 407/351-4100, or toll free 800/327-1366, 800/247-3737 in Florida), is a pleasant choice. Beige stucco with Mediterranean touches to its architecture, this Quality Inn–operated motel is a two-story building with small, faux balconies topped by red barrel tiles. In the center of this rather large complex is a swimming pool, and at one end of the property, Denny's Restaurant offers 24-hour service. Rooms are of medium size with two double beds, cheerful color schemes, and comfortable armchairs. Rates are $38 to $78, year round, and there's no charge for children under 17 sharing a room.

One of the larger, more elaborate Econo Lodges in the country is here in Orlando: the **Econo Lodge International Drive,** 8738 International Dr., Orlando, FL 32819 (tel. 407/345-8195, or toll free 800/654-7160, 800/321-2429 in Florida). In fact it calls itself the world's largest Econo Lodge, and with 670 rooms in several four-story buildings, that's hard to dispute. Wood trim on the exterior lends the place a faintly Tudor air. Set among a stand of pines, Econo Lodge offers medium-size rooms attractively decorated with floral spreads. Few fancy amenities here, although there are VCRs in rooms now, and no fancy prices: Rates are $46 to $75 year round, $20 higher if you want a room with a whirlpool in it or a family king suite with a sitting room.

**Quality Inn Plaza,** 9000 International Dr., Orlando, FL 32819 (tel. 407/345-

8585, or toll free 800/228-5151), has 340 very attractive rooms in several buildings trimmed in burgundy and tinted windows. The lobby is draped in hanging vines and leads to the pool that forms the center of this huge complex. Located practically next door to Orlando's new convention center, it makes a reasonably priced stopping spot for business travelers. Rates are $29 to $49, depending on season.

Before Walt Disney World's Magic Kingdom made its appearance here, one of Orlando's best-known attractions was its many deep-blue, spring-fed lakes. These days, travelers whizzing through on major highways or racing from one attraction to another rarely see those sparkling lakes, which are often hidden away on backroads. There is, however, a hotel that has forsaken the world of glitzy lobbies and fake rocks to focus on the natural beauty of one of the region's largest lakes. Called the **Sonesta Village Hotel on Sand Lake,** 10000 Turkey Lake Rd., Orlando, FL 32819 (tel. 407/352-8051, or toll free 800/343-7170), this resort is different in another way: It has no hotel rooms! Instead, the Sonesta Village offers 370 two-story villas strung out in a long, winding cluster of townhouse-like structures, each with its own living room, small kitchen, dining room, and bath downstairs, and large bedrooms and a second bathroom upstairs. Tall glass doors frame green lawns rolling down to the lake. Light wood and wicker furnishings are outfitted in soothing contemporary colors—rose, beige, aqua. All villas feature two double beds in each bedroom and a convertible sofa in the living room, televisions in each room.

Circling around the edge of one of the area's largest lakes, this new 97-acre resort gives visitors a closeup look at a natural spring lake that has maintained much of its wilderness character. As you sit on a private terrace overlooking green lawns that slope gently to the shore, a snowy egret stalks by in search of lunch. While it seems as far as Mars from the hustle of Orlando's other hotel enclaves, the Sonesta Village only sounds remote. Actually it's right in the middle of things, about 10 minutes from Orlando International Airport and the same distance from Walt Disney World. Sea World is just across I-4, about a mile away.

Built at a cost of $100 million, the Sonesta Village has a formal restaurant, a casual café, and a lounge with entertainment. Activists can whiz off in sail or paddleboats, splash in the pool or whirlpool spas, play on lighted tennis courts, park the kids at a playground, stroll a wooden boardwalk that stretches out into the lake. Particularly convenient for families, the resort offers a daily supervised children's activities program and babysitting.

Year-round rates at the resort are $125 to $180 for one-bedroom villas that sleep up to six, and $180 to $270 for two-bedroom villas that sleep up to eight.

If you'd like to spread out in a woodsy, scenic setting beside another lake, settle into **Residence Inn by Marriott,** 4786 US 192, Orlando, FL 32749 (tel. 407/396-2056, or toll free 800/331-3131). All the rooms at this Residence Inn, as at all these properties, are suites with separate bedroom and sitting room, and sometimes even larger bilevel penthouse quarters. Very attractively decorated in contemporary, earthy colors and textures, the inn is in the Kissimmee area close to Walt Disney World, Sea World, and the region's other major attractions. Accommodations are in three-story buildings and some have king-size beds and wood-burning fireplaces. Out front Lake Cecile laps at the shoreline. Rates at the inn include a weekly manager's cocktail party and are $89 to $134 double a day for a one- or two-bedroom suite, lower if you're staying a week or more. There's also a second **Residence Inn by Marriott** here at 7610 Canada Ave., Orlando, FL 32819 (tel. 407/345-0117, or toll free 800/331-3131), near International Drive. Studio rooms rent for $89 and up, bilevel penthouse suites cost $129. Weekly and weekend specials available.

## DOWNTOWN

Downtown Orlando is a pretty place that surrounds sparkling Lake Eola where a fountain shoots skyward and ducks paddle. To get there, take I-4 to the US 17/92 exit and head north to Washington Street.

You'll find the **Harley Hotel** at 151 E. Washington St., Orlando, FL 32801 (tel. 407/841-3220, or toll free 800/321-2323), and wait till you see what Harley has done with the old Kahler Plaza Hotel! Once a dowdy downtowner, that old hotel is now a stunning, glittering place where candles glow, chandeliers sparkle, deep colors shine like jewels. Harley has wrought a miracle, and all Orlando is proud of this addition to its hotel ranks. Hotel rooms are decorated in gentle glowing colors and modern prints, comfortable easy chairs, pretty wall prints, and shaded brass swingout bed lamps. In the roomy baths there are shaving and cosmetic mirrors. Harley has one of the city's most entrancing restaurants: Café on the Park, where leaded glass trims bands of windows with a smashing view of Lake Eola and a peach and gray decor prevails. If you get the idea we like it here, you get the idea. Rates are $70 to $105 double, all year. Suites are higher.

Harley also owns another hotel in the area at the edge of downtown, the **Colonial Plaza Inn,** 2801 E. Colonial Dr., Orlando, FL 32803 (tel. 407/894-2741, or toll free 800/321-2323), where there's an extra touch in four of the rooms that you'll find in few other spots in the world—a private swimming pool! In 221 other rooms you'll be sans pool, but you'll still have basic accommodations, and you can always nip downstairs and soak in a Jacuzzi. Double-room rates here run $68 to $88, and $99 to $149 for pool suites.

Howard Johnson is, well, Howard Johnson, and by this time you have a pretty good idea what to expect at this reliable chain. We just have to mention one in Orlando though, because here you're not just a number but a real live person with a face and personality and everything. That's because Mac Finnane, who operates this **Howard Johnson,** at 2014 W. Colonial Dr., Orlando, FL 32804 (tel. 407/841-8600, or toll free 800/654-2000), tries so hard to know and please you that he manages to make his resort something different. A midtown hotel about 20 minutes from Walt Disney World, Finnane's HoJo's has newly remodeled rooms for which he charges $58 to $66 in peak summer and winter seasons, $48 to $52 at other times. An added bonus: Real country cooking comes from the restaurant here, along with some can't-refuse homemade bakery treats. Get there on I-4 to exit 41, Colonial Drive (Fla. 50 West). Don't confuse Mac's hideaway with the high-rise HoJo's at I-4; his is 1½ miles west of I-4.

Compared to most Orlando hotels, the **Davis Park,** 221 E. Colonial Dr., Orlando, FL 32801 (tel. 407/425-9065), is a small place with just 75 units in an enclave the owners like to call "a village atmosphere in the heart of Orlando." There is a touch of village about the place too, a homey air if you will. Paneled rooms have big dressing areas, wall-to-wall carpets, and bright colors; outside, there's a pretty pool. Davis's brick-and-wood restaurant has a coziness too, and low prices. A few rooms have cooking facilities, and double rates at this hotel, about 20 minutes from Walt Disney World, are $39.50 to $49.50, about $3 cheaper for singles.

**Best Western Orlando Inn West,** 3330 W. Colonial Dr., Orlando, FL 32801 (tel. 407/299-6710, or toll free 800/528-1234), prides itself on being newer than Walt Disney World, and now it's newer still! Frequent remodeling keeps this resort attractive with spacious rooms surrounding a winding swimming pool and a lovely landscaped garden area. Rooms have two double beds and some have couches, so you can really settle in for a relaxed holiday. King-size-bed fanciers will find some rooms with those big recliners too, and there are even rooms for nonsmokers. Denny's Restaurant, a 24-hour spot, offers meals in the $10 range or less, and the West Side Lounge has a large-screen TV where weary parents can sneak off for a couple of pleasant hours away from the darlings. Two people pay $42 to $80.

## AT THE AIRPORT

Orlando's fancy international airport is far enough off the beaten path that you can usually find rooms in this area when other hotels closer to Walt Disney World are filled.

One of our favorites is the **Gold Key Inn,** 7100 S. Orange Blossom Trail, Orlando, FL 32809 (tel. 407/855-0050, or toll free 800/432-0974 in Florida), where you can tell at a glance you've found a very special place. Massive beams streak across the lobby ceiling and a brick fireplace is flanked by comfortable couches perched on floral carpets. In your room you'll find pretty floral prints, comfortable armchairs, writing tables, lots of space, reproductions of old English prints, and pretty tiled baths. Outside, landscaped tropical gardens surround a heated pool and there's a putting green and tennis courts. Shuttlebuses stop here to take you to attractions. Rates year round are $56 to $62.

The Gold Key's Piccadilly Restaurant is its fame, and has won rafts of awards for its homemade soups and marvelously creamy concoctions, perfectly seared steaks, pink prime rib, excellent seafood served in an atmosphere glowing with stained-glass windows, floral prints, heavy wood beams, and a cozy country air. Gold Key's a treasure of a place, and as close as you're likely to come in Orlando to a gracious country inn.

Across the street is a **TraveLodge,** 7101 S. Orange Blossom Trail, Orlando, FL 32809 (tel. 407/851-4300, or toll free 800/255-3050), with attractive, large rooms in tropical colors and rates of $50 to $65, year round.

## WINTER PARK

This dazzlingly beautiful small town is just north of Orlando. You can get there by exiting I-4 at Colonial Drive East, turning north at Mills Drive, and east again on Orange Avenue. Here in this "Little Europe" of central Florida, where everything seems to glow like precious gems, are two small hotels that to our mind are, well, pearls among pearls.

Look up as you stroll Winter Park's main avenue, Park Avenue, and you'll see red geraniums spilling from tiny window boxes and white wicker furniture sitting perkily on a small balcony. That's the **Park Plaza Hotel,** at 307 Park Ave. S., Winter Park, FL 32789 (tel. 407/647-1072), a glamorous little spot that's been around a long time but has been redecorated to a fare-thee-well and is now a fascinating study in antique decor and modern comfort. Beautiful doesn't begin to cover it. How do you explain such things as an Italian tiled foyer, brick trim, whirring paddle fans, a lobby straight (and genuinely) out of turn-of-the-century times? A big, big room we love has brass beds and a sitting room, deep plush carpets, pretty pastels, and wing chairs. And when you're feeling really dramatic you can fling open the French doors and waft onto the balcony overlooking shady Park Avenue, lean decoratively on the railing, and gaze out over this beautiful old city musing on the days when everyone used to live this way all the time. For this old-world elegance you'll pay $65 to $125 for rooms or suites with balconies overlooking a lovely little courtyard or the park, where else can you be this dramatic for $100?

Such a charming village seems naturally to produce other beautiful things, and the **Langford Hotel,** 300 E. New England Ave., Winter Park, FL 32780 (tel. 407/644-3400), is certainly one of those. A family-owned hotel that's been around since 1955, the Langford has let no moss gather on the rolling stone of its success. Gigantic pines tower overhead, deep jungles of plants surround, and in the tropical garden there's a gurgling little waterfall that glitters at night by the light of Japanese lanterns, another at the hotel's Oriental spa. As for rooms, well, one has antique French chairs, a crystal chandelier, striped silk chaise, a patterned carpet, beveled mirrors, little corner bibelot shelves, and Austrian drapes at the glass entrance to a private balcony. Another is covered wall to wall in straw matting and filled with African touches like zebra-striped furniture and tall mahogany carvings. In the Bamboo Room, a long menu is filled with tantalizing beef and seafood dishes, and in the lounge and piano bar music for listening and dancing. In this glamorous setting you'll pay $65 to $85 a day, year round, for rooms decorated in an airy, South Pacific motif.

## IN SURROUNDING TOWNS

Roads are so good and easy to navigate in central Florida that you can easily stay outside Orlando and drive in for attraction-hopping, so we've outlined a few outlying hotels we think you'll like.

Clermont is a pretty town away in rolling citrus country, and near it you'll find the **Ramada Inn West Gate,** on US 192 and 27, 8000 W. Irlo W. Bronson Memorial Hwy. (P.O. Box 1386), Kissimmee, FL 32742 (tel. 813/424-2621, or toll free 800/782-1283, or 800/282-2124 in Florida, 800/322-2575 elsewhere), five miles west of the Walt Disney World gate, with 200 spacious and tastefully decorated rooms overlooking expansive grounds and an Olympic-size swimming pool. There's a game room and playground, lounge, and dining room with moderately priced offerings. Two people pay $50 to $80.

**Ramada Inn-Altamonte Springs,** 151 N. Douglas Ave. (off I-4 at Fla. 436), Altamonte Springs, FL 32714 (tel. 407/869-9000), is in the nearby town of Altamonte Springs but it's a bit of a distance from Disney, about a 30-minute drive. Here, however, one has the advantage of being a lulling distance from the crowds and near several top restaurants and a huge shopping mall. If you think you'd like to stay up this way, this resort is the place to settle. Recent renovations have made the attractive, spacious rooms even prettier, and for playtime there's a heated pool. The inn's restaurant, Wildflower, is a favorite lunch and dinner spot for local residents who retreat here for some top culinary treats and some flashily prepared flambé desserts. Prices are in the $10 to $15 range. Rates at the inn are $54 to $76, year round.

A top budget-wise motel in the Orlando area is **Susse Travelodge,** at I-4 and US 27 in Davenport, FL 33837 (tel. 813/424-2521, or toll free 800/258-1980), which charges just $40 to $60 for two to four people. Rooms are recently remodeled and have the basic amenities of phone, TV, bath, shower, heated swimming pool, ice machine, coin laundry, and free parking. This one's well located for Cypress Gardens, and it's not more than 10 minutes from Walt Disney World.

Tucked away in the small town of Howey-in-the-Hills, northwest of Orlando, is the family-owned and operated **Mission Inn Golf and Tennis Resort,** Fla. 19 and Fla. 48 (P.O. Box 441), Howey-in-the-Hills, FL 34737 (tel. 904/324-3101, toll free 800/874-9053, in Florida 800/342-4495), a Spanish-theme inn with 141 spacious rooms and 19 exquisite suites with panoramic views of the countryside or of an 18-hole golf course on the hotel grounds. Mission Inn has the charm of a private estate and all the amenities of a big-city resort: golf course, pro shop, golf carts and lessons, tennis courts, heated pool, games, and fishing in well-stocked lakes on the inn's grounds. Boating and waterskiing are available at the resort's marina, and the inn is about 30 miles from Walt Disney World and five miles east of the Florida Turnpike on Fla. 19. Limousine service from Orlando International Airport can be arranged with 48 hours' notice. Rates are $75 to $335 year round, depending on size and season.

If you like resorts and you like golf, **Grenelefe Golf and Tennis Resort,** 3200 Fla. 546, Haines City, Grenelefe, FL 33844 (tel. 813/422-7511, or toll free 800/237-9459, 800/282-7875 in Florida), is an alluring alternative to Orlando hotels. Another of the state's magnificent condominium resorts, Grenelefe is snuggled away on 950 acres of emerald-green grounds shaded by towering pines and giant live oaks. Since they're condominiums, the 850 villa apartments are all individually decorated and have contemporary touches like lots of glass, flowers, wide dressing areas, big walk-in closets, kitchens with everything from built-in processing centers to zip-lock bags, high sloping ceilings, and always private balconies for a dramatic view of trees and paths (perhaps even a quail scooting home to the family). For fun there are 54 holes of golf (18 of which were rated number one in the state by a golfing magazine), four swimming pools, spa and sauna, tennis courts, plus several shining restaurants and informal lounges. If you're touring, Grenelefe is just a 30-minute drive from Orlando's doings and 15 minutes from beautiful Cypress Gardens. Two people pay

$75 to $325 depending on room size and season, and children under 18 are free. There's airport pickup too, for $25 a person.

Finally, if you'd like the ultimate tan, **Cypress Cove Nudist Resort,** about 11 miles south of Kissimmee on County Road 531 at 4425 S. Pleasant Hill Rd., Kissimmee, FL 32741 (tel. 407/933-5870), is one of the state's largest nudist resorts. We can't say we've seen everything here, but there is a lake, plus tennis courts, paddleboats, a campground, restaurant, and rental units. Admission is $25 per couple, and you can rent a room or apartment for $40 to $85.

## FOR ROMANTICS WHO WANT MORE THAN THE MOUSE

We're talking here about Mount Dora, a town we have always known and loved as a little bit of New England but, like most Florida fans, had only driven through occasionally to renew our acquaintance with the high ridge on which it is built and the town's delightful shady-lane seclusion.

When we rolled by again recently, what to our wondering eyes should appear but a buttercup-yellow mirage, a renewed and renewing **Lakeside Inn,** 110 S. Alexander St. (P.O. Box 1390), Mount Dora, FL 32757 (tel. 904/383-4101, or toll free 800/556-5016), raising its gabled head over four green acres that roll down to the diamond-tipped waters of the lake.

An oasis in Mickey-mania Mouseland, Mount Dora looks like a Vermont village that lost its way and turned tropical. Here at the turn of the century came adventurous Yankees bent on getting a close look at the weird tropical wilderness most northern-state dwellers thought might be just a tall story. To house those early visitors, some canny developer built a 10-room inn called Alexander House, where guests spent their days fishing for bass and catfish or hunting for poisonous snakes.

Boating was just coming into its own in those days, so Alexander House, by now called Lakeside Inn, served as a base for Mount Dora's annual regatta, which was to become the granddaddy of all Florida's many regattas. As travel increased in this Gatsby era, the inn expanded. In 1930 it welcomed an exiting Pres. Calvin Coolidge, who spent the winter here that year.

Although the Lakeside Inn managed to keep operating for 101 years, in 1984 it failed to open for the first winter ever, a death knell if ever there was one. But saviors arrived in the nick of time just as developers were fighting to tear the inn down and build a condominium.

Now you can settle into a rocking chair on the porch and leave all those cares behind you as you gaze out over the green lawns and two buildings that flank them, creating a backdrop courtyard that is often the ethereally lovely setting for weddings.

Inside, wood floors have been polished to a sienna glow and small groupings of camelback couches and wing chairs welcome you to quiet talks by the fireplace. Tall windows, lots of them bay or gables, offer an unceasing view over the central swimming pool and the rippling lake beyond.

Rooms are togged out in delicate Laura Ashley prints and walk-in closets hark back to the days when winter tourists came here for the winter instead of the week. In the two other buildings on the grounds, rooms are decorated in similar style, many of them in jewel tones with reproduction furnishings. One in particular, a second-floor aerie overlooking the lake, is a stunner.

Early evenings, visitors gather in the forest-green lounge where the chef will produce a tray of delectable canapés on request. Later the action moves to the dining room, where a huge circlet of bay windows creates a dramatic setting for candlelight dinners. Outside, a giant camphor tree rustles in the breeze.

Hotel boosters are justifiably proud of their product and happy to relate details of its renovation to antique buffs, restoration fans, and anyone else who will listen. They have every right to be proud of this creation that has renewed a lovely and historic property—and Florida has few enough of those. Now brides are once again wafting across the lawns. The crack of croquet mallets once again echoes across the lake. And tea will be served promptly at 4pm, madame.

The Lakeside Inn charges $75 to $100 double, year round, higher for suites.

## BED-AND-BREAKFAST

**A & A Bed and Breakfast of Florida, Inc.,** P.O. Box 1316, Winter Park, FL 32970 (tel. 407/628-3233), is operated by Brunhilde Fehner, who includes in her roster a colonial home with a pool shaped like the state of Florida! Rates range from $40 to $65 and all accommodations come with private baths.

## YOUTH HOSTELS

Orlando is still new to the hostel game but is working on it. There is at the moment a motel that is offering hostel prices to members of the American Youth Hostel organization. It's the **TraveLodge,** 409 N. Magnolia St., Orlando, FL 32801 (tel. 407/423-1671), and rates are $13.

Young women travelers can find hostel quarters at the **Young Women's Community Club,** 107 E. Hillcrest St., Orlando, FL 32801 (tel. 407/425-2502), which accepts women from 16 through 37 who are members of the American Youth Hostel organization. Rates are $10, and there's a swimming pool at this 10-bed facility.

If you want to become a member of the AYH, contact American Youth Hostels, National Offices, P.O. Box 37613, Washington, DC 20013 (tel. 202/783-6161), or call the Florida state headquarters at 407/649-8761.

## CAMPING

There are quite a number of campgrounds in the Orlando area, offering everything from basic campsites to elaborate grounds. Walt Disney World also has its own campground called Fort Wilderness (see more on that in our discussion of accommodations in Disney World).

**Orange Grove Campground,** 2425 Old Vineland Rd., Kissimmee, FL 32741 (tel. 407/396-6655), occupies a former citrus grove so you're guaranteed plenty of shade—and an occasional orange for breakfast! A family-run campground, the park is close to Disney World and couldn't be more convenient for shopping—it's right behind Factory Outlet Mall. In business here as long as Walt Disney World, and that's more than two decades now, the campground has 200 spaces plus tent sites and will rent recreational vehicles. There's a pool, laundry, store, and recreation room. Rates are $17 to $20 for a partial or full hookup, lower for a tent site.

You can't miss **Yogi Bear's Jellystone Park Campground**—the bear's face is on billboards all over town. There are three of these parks in the area, but the closest to Walt Disney World is a pretty, wooded 600-site campground just four miles west of the park on US 192, at 8555 W. Spacecoast Pkwy., Kissimmee, FL 32741 (tel. 407/351-4394, or toll free 800/558-2954). You'll find a lake here, a mini-golf course, boating and fishing, a grocery store, restaurant, and gift shop, not to mention all kinds of special events. Rates of $21 to $22 include water, electricity, and sewage hookup. Tent sites also are available for $17.

The second of Yogi's hangouts is a 500-site campground just off I-4, 10 miles east of Walt Disney World at 9200 Turkey Lake Rd., Orlando, FL 32801 (tel. 407/351-4394, or toll free 800/558-2954, 800/327-7115 in Florida). The third is about 30 miles away in Apopka on US 1 (P.O. Box 2000), Apopka, FL 32704 (tel. 407/889-3048, or toll free 800/558-2953). Rates and facilities are similar at all three campgrounds.

**Port O' Call Campground,** 5175 US 192, Kissimmee, FL 32741 (tel. 305/396-0110, or toll free 800/327-9120, 800/432-0766 in Florida), is a massive place with a long list of facilities ranging from fishing and shuffleboard to a game room, movies, bike and paddleboat rentals, weekend entertainment, and a fancy tropical rock-bedecked swimming pool. It's about five miles east of the gates to Walt Disney World and charges $24 for two adults. There's no charge for children under 12, but additional adults pay $2. Prices include water, electricity, and the rest of those camping necessities.

---

# 3. Where to Dine

---

If there's one way to describe a central Floridian, it's shrewd. These "good ol' boys" know how to turn a dollar, and do so with alacrity and aplomb. It follows naturally that when they eyed passles of excited wee ones steaming through the turnstiles of local attractions, they raced to provide for the masses.

Wee ones' taste being what it is, central Florida became hog heaven for fast-food freaks more quickly than you can say hamburger. But as the World turned desert to Disney, it spurred the creation of architecturally impressive and gastronomically top-notch restaurants designed to appeal to the fantasy-saturated cerebrums of weary parents in search of a little comic relief. Many of these are in Winter Park, which has become the gastronomic capital of central Florida. Since the offerings are many, we've divided them up by the kind of cuisine offered.

Remember that unless otherwise specified, the prices we've cited are for entrées, which usually include salad, one or two vegetables, and perhaps coffee as well.

## THE TOP FUN RESTAURANT

Round a bend in Lake Buena Vista village and there rises before you like a ghostly return of another era, the **Empress Lilly** (tel. 828-3900), a fairyland of tiny white lights and a dazzling white triple-decker Mississippi riverboat. Home to no fewer than three restaurants, the *Empress* is, of course, another of Disney's sterling creations, with gleaming brass, etched glass, polished mahogany, a massive staircase between floors, Victorian furniture, lots of Dixieland entertainment, and romantic walks on decks overlooking the twinkle of the Magic Kingdom.

Seek out the glamorous **Empress Room,** site of upper-deck and upper-crust dining in Louis XIV elegance. Intimate banquettes, the charming maître d', Leon, harpist entertainment, the cozy plushness of a forest-green lounge—that's the Empress Room. Entrée prices go as high as $25 to $30 for dishes like oyster-stuffed veal chops or frenched lamb chops, but average about $20 to $30, and if you splurge you're likely to spend $50 to $65 a person for a sumptuous feast. A 20% service charge is added to all bills as well. Open from 5:30 to 10pm daily by reservation only. Jackets required.

Disney doesn't do things in small doses, so that (of course!) is not all. Aft, you'll find the **Steerman's Quarters,** where you dine on excellent beef concoctions in the $15 to $25 bracket in a pubby decor with wainscoting and flower-sprigged wallpaper. Don't miss the cheesecake. Open from noon to 2pm and 5:30 to 10pm daily. Disney character breakfasts are also available here at 8:45 and 10am; call for reservations.

Yes, there's still more: the **Fisherman's Deck,** where the specialty is seafood; the room, bilevel; the decor, blue velvet and gold; the ambience, dim and sophisticated; the check, $6 to $9 at lunch, $17 to $49 at dinner; the hours, noon to 3pm and 5:30 to 10pm daily. Disney character breakfasts are also available here; call for details and reservations.

And still more: the **Baton Rouge Lounge,** where banjos twang, guitarists strum, and there's a whoop-it-up good time going to 1am.

## AMERICAN/CONTINENTAL

**Park Plaza Gardens,** 319 Park Ave. S., Winter Park (tel. 645-2475), has an elegant garden atmosphere with pink linen tablecloths and formal silver place settings, etched- and smoked-glass mirrors, a greenhouse alcove, and glass roof (we could go on and on). As for the menu, it includes seafood bisque, exotic shrimp in curry sauce, flounder meunière, wienerschnitzel, baked Alaska. A very tranquil atmosphere in which to contemplate your good fortune, Park Plaza Gardens is open from 11:30am to 3pm and 6 to 10pm (later on weekends), 11am to 3pm for Sunday brunch. You'll pay about $20 to $25 for dinner entrées at this serene setting next door to quaint Park Plaza Hotel.

The **Piccadilly Restaurant** in the Gold Key Inn, 7100 S. Orange Blossom Trail (tel. 855-0050), is one of the outstanding restaurants in Orlando, an award-winner in both cuisine and decor. A pretty pub atmosphere prevails, with pewter plates, lots of wood, a yellow glow from candles, and fresh flowers. Prices are in the $10 to $17 range for entrées like roast beef with Yorkshire pudding, rack of lamb, and poached snapper. Piccadilly is open from 6 to 10:30pm daily for dinner, from 7am for other meals.

Among the newest restaurant-nightspots in town is **Park Avenue Grill,** 358 Park Ave. N., Winter Park (tel. 647-4556). An upstairs-downstairs retreat right in the middle of this beautiful boulevard, Park Avenue Grill is all decked out in bay windows, a burgundy-and-white decor, tiled bars, brass rails, and enough plants to start a nursery. There's even a garden dining room. You'll find great seafood, plus prime rib and steaks in both upstairs and downstairs dining rooms, and attractive cocktail lounges in both locales as well. Prices are in the $12 to $17 range for dinner entrees, and the restaurant is open from 11am to 11pm daily and for brunch on Sunday.

**Limey Jim's Restaurant,** in the Orlando Hyatt Hotel, at I-4 and US 192 East (tel. 239-4100), is a handsome dining room with excellent cuisine. Your check will probably be in the $20 to $30 range, but you'll dine well and atmospherically.

At **Café on the Park,** in the Harley Hotel, 151 E. Washington St., Orlando (tel. 841-3220), you'll find a place with decor as inviting as the food that's prepared in the kitchen. What's more, the view out over glittering Lake Eola, with its spouting fountain, is terrific too. A bevy of mirrors here reflect delicate shades of peach, fresh flowers, shining tableware, and many a smiling face chowing down on the likes of prime rib, scampi, shellfish, and filet mignon. Because it's part of a hotel, the dining room is open all day long, with a luncheon buffet weekdays from 11am to 2pm, and dinner from 6 to 10:30pm daily ($13 to $19 range). On Sunday there is a highlight that shouldn't be missed: The Sunday brunch stretches for a mile or so, beginning with champagne and working through enough food to keep you going for a week or so. It's $16 for adults, $8.50 for children, and you can gorge from 11am to 3pm.

Florida's lovely old architecture fell faster than a toothpick castle when development began here, so when some part of Central Florida's diminishing heritage is saved, it's a joy to behold. Such is **Historic Townsend Plantation,** 604 E. Main St., Apopka (tel. 880-1313).

Once the Eldridge-McBride House, this 4,000-square-foot wonder was salvaged by the Townsend family and has been cutting rather a wide swath across Orlando's dining scene recently. Nestled in beside a small lake, the sprawling mansion is a Victorian delight, painted and primped with a wide front veranda gazing out over rolling lawns and down to a pristine white fence.

It's fitting that good home cooking should predominate here, so this is the place to head when you've a yen for such rib-sticking favorites as southern fried chicken with honey pecan sauce, pan-fried green tomatoes, deep-fried pickles, bourbon-marinated steak, beef pot pie, all of it accompanied by salad, hot breads, fresh vegetables, and potatoes. Prices are in the $10 to $15 range for complete dinners. High tea—with scones, double cream, strawberry preserves, berry tarts, cookies, tea sandwiches—and, oh, yes, tea—is served from 3 to 5pm Monday through Saturday. For other meals, including a groaning lunch buffet table, the restaurant is open daily from 11:30am to 2pm, and 5 to 10pm, closing an hour later on weekends, and at 9pm Sunday after brunch and dinner.

All aboard for fantasyland, restaurant-style. We're off to the **Bubble Room,** 1351 S. Orlando Ave., Maitland, FL 32571 (tel. 628-3331). A clone of a similarly bubbly operation on Captiva Island, Orlando's Bubble Room is abuzz with toy trains running merrily around a diverting restaurant that will keep your eyes busy while your tummy's absorbing aged prime beef, fresh seafood, pork, poultry, and desserts that give a new meaning to sin. Bubble bursts from 11:30am to 2:30pm for lunch weekdays. Dinner hours are 5:30 to 10:00pm Monday through Thursday, closing an hour later on Friday and Saturday, and open Sunday from 11:30am to 10:00pm. Prices are in the $17 to $25 range for dinners.

   **Pebbles,** 2110 W. Fla. 434, Longwood (tel. 774-7111), has made quite a ripple in the Orlando dining stream with such innovative options as linguine with duck sauce, creative salads topped with paper-thin Chinese noodles, and other unusual combinations of herbs and fresh ingredients. A handsome dining spot that's become quite popular, Pebbles' New American cuisine is available from 11am to midnight daily, and prices are in the $10 to $17 range.

## CHINESE

   If you know your *wors* from your *woks,* you're a candidate for **Ming Garden Chinese Cuisine,** 5432 International Dr. (tel. 352-8044), or **Ming Court Restaurant,** 9188 International Dr. (tel. 351-9988), Orlando. Ming Garden has a seafood wor bar, with lobster, crab, shrimp, and scallops, Chinese vegetables, and the like, plus a wide variety of Chinese cooking from Szechuan to Hunan, Cantonese, Mandarin, and Shanghai. Rosewood furnishings and Oriental lanterns make for cozy dining at the Garden, while at Ming Court the atmosphere is created by a limpid reflecting pool, garden, and objets d'art designed to re-create the refinements of the Ming Court. Entrees are served family-style so everyone can get in on the taste testing of selections from the grill or the wok. There's a dim sum appetizer bar, exotic drinks, entertainment and dancing in the lounge, and, last, perhaps least, shark's fin soup. Prices are in the $12 to $18 range, and Court is in session from 5pm to midnight daily. Ming Garden is open 11am to 3pm and 5 to 11pm daily.

   John Rutherford, one of Orlando's best-known promoters, would never be caught far from a good restaurant. We so rely on his proven good taste for tastes that we give one of his recommendations, **Forbidden City,** 948 N. Mills Ave. (tel. 894-5005). While we haven't tried this one yet, John, who's in the running for underground gourmet of the year (at least), loves this spot which began life as a gas station! Despite the restaurant's humble past, its present is going very well, thanks to a talented chef who specializes in what some are calling "nouvelle chinoise" cuisine. Such scrumptious options as sesame chicken and orange beef are beautifully presented and perfectly cooked, and a particular favorite here is a taco-like creation incorporating Boston lettuce, chicken, and pine nuts. And MSG is forbidden at this city. Entrées are in the $8 to $10 range. Hours are from 11:30 to 2pm weekdays and 5 to 9:30pm daily except Sunday.

   **Jin Ho,** 400 S. Orlando Ave., Winter Park (tel. 740-5088), became so popular that it branched out to Altamonte Springs on Maitland Avenue (tel. 339-0790). If there are two of you, try Seven Stars Around the Moon ($20), a mélange of lobster, pork, and chicken sautéed with snowpea pods, mushrooms, baby corn, water chestnuts, bamboo shoots, and bok choy surrounded by seven butterfly shrimp. A simple, casual place with plenty of seafood and a sizzling wor bar with seafood and Chinese vegetables served over crisp rice, Jin Ho features prices in the $5 to $10 range for a meal. It's open from 11am to 10:30pm daily, from noon on Saturday and Sunday.

## FRENCH

   Genuine Tiffany windows from the McKean collection of Tiffany treasures glow at **La Belle Verrière,** 142 Park Ave. S., Winter Park (tel. 645-3377), and you will too, after a lunch or dinner in this lovely garden setting. Masses of plants and flowers play counterpoint to brick and wood, candles glow, flowers grace every table, and the menu includes vichyssoise or escargots bourguignons, chateaubriand, roast duck or rack of lamb, crème caramel, dusky chocolate mousse, and fresh oranges topped with honey and rum. Figure about $15 to $25 for dinner entrées, served from 6 to 10pm (lunch from 11:30am to 2:30pm). Closed Sunday.

Talented Swiss chef George Vogelbacher has earned many an award for **Le Cordon Bleu,** 537 W. Fairbanks Ave., Winter Park (tel. 647-7575). Well-deserved awards they are too, for this is a simply decorated but sophisticated restaurant famous for leisurely dining on sinful pastries and breads baked right here, filet de boeuf royal (baked in a puff pastry with capers and lemon), pompano with white wine sauce, and herbed filets. You'll pay about $15 to $25 for dinner entrées, and Le Cordon Bleu is open Monday through Friday for lunch from 11:30am to 2:30pm, and from 6 to 11pm for dinner daily.

A very curvaceous Winter Park friend swears she keeps her perfect proportions by dining at **Maison des Crêpes,** 348 Park Ave. N., Winter Park (tel. 647-4469). It's simple, she says: You just down a couple of these paper-thin delicacies stuffed with incredibly rich and creamy fillings, perhaps toss off a crisp cold salad of spinach, mushrooms, and avocado, then don't eat anything else for a day or two. Heaven knows it's worked for her, and even if it's not the ultimate Scarsdale diet, it's certainly a marvelously tasty way to blimpdom. Dinner prices at this cute café are $10 to $25. Maison des Crêpes is open from 11:30am to 3pm Monday through Saturday and 5:30 to 10pm Tuesday through Saturday; closed Sunday and Monday for dinner; first two weeks in July for vacation.

When an Orlando newspaper recently surveyed its readers on restaurants, **Maison et Jardin,** at 430 S. Wymore Rd., Altamonte Springs (tel. 862-4410), swept the boards not only as the best restaurant in the area but also as the favorite French spot, the restaurant with the best service, the most romantic, and the one with the most atmosphere! We hardly need say more (but, of course, will).

French for "home and garden," Maison et Jardin is exactly that, a gracious old home high atop a gentle slope of land and garden in a grove of tall trees. Ornate chandeliers glow, great walls of glass overlook the perfectly manicured lawns where a fountain burbles, and from the kitchen come innovative treats like wild rice bisque, mushrooms Thermidor, zucchini and hearts of palm salad, veal Strasbourg, pheasant Souvaroff. On the first Sunday of the month a New Orleans jazz band plays for a brunch that on any Sunday is something to behold. Recent renovations—$100,000 worth—have made this lovely restaurant even lovelier, with more Venetian crystal chandeliers, Rosenthal china, and hand-blown crystal. Winner of numerous awards, Maison et Jardin, which is lovingly called the Mason Jar by un-Frenchified Orlandoites, charges prices that will bring dinner to $38 to $40 each, but it's really worth it in elegance and excellence. Luncheon is served Monday through Friday from 11:30am to 2pm; Sunday brunch from 11am to 2pm for $13 to $20; and dinner is served from 6:30 to 10:30pm daily. Closed Sunday in summer. Jackets are required for dinner, and reservations are very, very wise.

**Arthur's 27,** in the Buena Vista Palace Hotel, Lake Buena Vista (tel. 827-3450), flies high above Walt Disney World's resort city with a view that just won't quit, past Cinderella's Castle's towers and EPCOT Center's golfball dome, across miles and miles of central Florida. Perched up on the 27th floor of the hotel, Arthur's has élan, elegance, and expensive-but-worth-it tabs, all of which combine to make this a memorable place for a very special dinner. Here you feast formally on seven courses that stretch over more than two hours of highly professional service. Culinary treats change constantly but are always nouvelle French flavors and the height of Orlando haute. You pay for this orchestrated evening to the tune of $70 to $90 per person. Dinner is from 6pm to midnight daily and reservations are mandatory.

# GREEK

Epicurus was the original epicurean after all, so it's fitting that Greek Jimmy Hansis should have named his **Epicurean Restaurant,** 7900 E. Colonial Dr., Orlando (tel. 277-2881), after that famous forebear. In a taverna atmosphere (the walls are lined with an outstanding collection of wines and a bouzouki twangs softly in the background), dine on giant Greek salads, moussaka, dolmades, kalamarakia, and pastitsio, lamb, baklava, and thick Greek coffee for dinner prices in the $10 to $25 range. Among his latest additions for adventurous diners are shark, wild boar, and alligator tail. He's open from 5 to 10pm weekdays, later on weekends; closed Sunday.

## ITALIAN

Former opera singer Joseph del Vento has found a new stage for his talents/and named it after an old one, **La Scala,** 205 Lorraine Dr. at Douglas Road, Altamonte Springs (tel. 862-3257). He comes to it well prepared, with a long background not only of arias but of arte della cucina. You reap the rewards of del Vento's many years in the kitchen with such dishes as veal sautéed with peas, prosciutto, and artichokes, or red snapper with parsley, garlic, white wine, oregano, and lemon. Fresh pastas, steaks, seafood, and veal dishes round out the menu, on which prices range from about $12 to $20. La Scala is open from 11:30am to 2:30pm weekdays and 5:30 to 10pm daily except Sunday, with later closings on weekends.

Orlo Vista, just west of Orlando, is not a town one races to visit, but if you love a good Italian dinner you'll hie over there to **Gus' Villa Rosa,** 5923 Old Winter Garden Rd. (take I-4 to County Road 435 and drive north; tel. 299-1950), and pounce on excellent pastas, potpourri of seafood, steak, and veal dishes that have won Gus Stamatin a place in the hearts of Orlando's Italiano worshippers. Stamatin has a long list of culinary credentials and has finally achieved every chef's dream, his own restaurant. Prices are in the $10 to $15 range. Try the shrimp Onassis with feta cheese. Villa Rosa, a casual place, is open 4:30 to 11pm daily for dinner, closed on Sunday.

**Villa Nova,** 839 N. Orlando Ave., Winter Park (tel. 644-2060), is a most handsome restaurant that's been operating here for more than 30 years. Now run by the skilled operators of Winter Park's very successful Park Plaza Gardens, Villa Nova features that northern Italian cuisine so favored by gourmets. You'll find such delicacies as carpaccio—paper-thin slices of raw filet in a piquant sauce—and escargots in red wine and puff pastry, mussels poached in white wine, fine steaks, fresh pastas, bucatini piccata, and a long list of veal and seafood favorites. Outstanding cooking here is complemented by one of the region's most attractive, formal dining rooms.

A recent addition to the restaurant is Baby Nova, a more casual dining spot that retains its Italian accents but features lighter fare and exotic pizzas with innovative topping choices. Dubbed "new wave Italian," Baby Nova is a lively, informal, and colorful spot lined in tile and marble. Evenings, there's high-energy entertainment in an adjoining lounge called Cheek to Cheek. Villa Nova's prices are in the $12 to $17 range for dinner, and hours are 6 to 11pm daily, from 11am in Baby Nova, where prices top out at about $12.

## JAPANESE

By now all the world, surely, has heard of **Benihana of Tokyo,** a most successful chain of upscale Japanese restaurants started by a quite colorful Japanese entrepreneur. Whether you have or haven't heard of this popular dining spot, now is your chance to try it. You sit at tables for eight at which the center of attention is the hand-is-quicker-than-the-eye talents of skilled Japanese chefs who chop, whack, flip, slice, sauté, and amaze. Dinner begins with the traditional little bowl of broth, moves through shrimp appetizers, and on to a selection of beef or seafood selections, each prepared right in front of you and served by a kimono-clad lass. It all makes for gustatorial and prestidigitorial evenings that have made this restaurant both famous and successful. Here in Orlando, Benihana is in the Hilton Hotel, 1751 Hotel Plaza Blvd., Lake Buena Vista (tel. 827-4865), and hours are 5 to 11pm daily.

One of the top Japanese restaurants in town is **Ran-Getsu** of Tokyo, a $3-million creation in Plaza International at 8400 International Dr. (tel. 345-0044). Here you dine in a Japanese garden setting, albeit a very *large* garden seating 325, complete with koi pond. Ran-Getsu likes to say its sushi bar may be the largest in Florida, and who could dispute it? Certainly it's in the running. Add to that kushiyaki options featuring grilled tidbits of beef, fish, chicken, and vegetables, and you can graze your way to nirvana. Chefs came from Tokyo to create all this, so authenticity is also on the menu. Prices are in $10 to $18 bracket, lower if you sushi and kushiyaki. Ran-Getsu is open from 5 to 11:30pm daily.

## MEXICAN

Colorfully dressed señoritas, a Mexican tile dining patio, *ole!* It's **El Torito,** at 275 W. County Road 436 in Village Shoppes, Altamonte Springs (tel. 869-5061), where after a margarita or two, a quesadilla, a tostada, perhaps some camarones flores wrapped in bacon and served with grilled pineapple and Mexican corn, and *caramba,* you're south of the border. Prices are often well under $10 and the restaurant's open from 11am to 10pm daily, an hour later on weekends.

**Chi-Chi's,** 655 Maguire Blvd., Orlando (tel. 894-0655), is decorated in a contemporary style. A chain operation that's made a name for itself here and in many another locale, Chi-Chi's delivers healthy margaritas, whopping tacos and tostadas, and wild creations of all kinds. Plenty of choices here, where you'll probably pay well under $10 for chow (we're not counting your margaritas, but you'd better), available from 11am to 10pm weekdays, later on weekends.

**Las Palomas,** 3552 E. Colonial Dr., Orlando (tel. 894-2610), is thoroughly Mexican from the handsome arched architecture to hand-painted tiles, fountains, and wrought-iron balconies. Excellent traditional Mexican dishes pour from the kitchen of this chic, upscale Mejicano spot open Tuesday through Friday for lunch from 11am to 3:30pm, and daily for dinner from 5 to 10pm, with prices in the $10 to $15 range, less for many selections. A mariachi band turns up here occasionally, too, usually on Thursday.

## SEAFOOD

Lots of people swear that **Gary's Duck Inn,** at 3974 S. Orange Blossom Trail, Orlando (tel. 843-0270), has the best seafood in all central Florida, and Gary has plenty of awards to back up their confidence. The inn promises that if you stop here once, you'll be back, and they've proven the truth of that with an operation that's been going strong since 1945. Try the fried butterflied shrimp here, where your check will be in the $9 to $17 range at dinner. Open from 11:30am to 10pm Sunday through Thursday; until 11pm Friday and 5 to 11pm Saturday.

There's nothing better than fresh, simply prepared seafood—unless it's fresh, simply prepared, *cheap* seafood. That brings us neatly around to **Shells,** 852 Lee Rd., Winter Park (tel. 628-3968). A restaurant chain that turned up so rapidly it seems to have been washed ashore in Florida, Shells has met with a wave of popular approval that often translates to waiting lines. Small wonder, for the seafood here is good, simply prepared, and definitely priced to please those among us whose wallets are slimmer than our gustatory demands. Here you down a dozen oysters for less than $2, glutton out on Dungeness crab, lobster, or stone crabs, or try any of more than a dozen seafood selections for well under $10. Key lime pie is our dessert recommendation, although strawberries and whipped cream are a temptation. Hours are 5 to 10pm daily, closing an hour later on weekends.

**Straub's,** 5101 E. Colonial Dr., Orlando (tel. 273-9330), is a popular spot—three times nominated as the best local seafood house by readers of a local magazine. Straub's has a quite extensive menu, specializing in, among other things, shrimp prepared in several different styles, including scampi and tempura and broiled over mesquite wood. In keeping with the rage for Cajun cookery, Straub's now offers blackened tuna and will prepare other kinds of fish in a similar style. Prices are in the $11 to $20 range, and the restaurant is open daily from 4 to 10pm, closing an hour later on weekends.

**Red Lobster,** 4010 W. Vine St., Kissimmee (tel. 846-3513), is a favorite in Orlando and turns out lots of what its name implies, plus other seafood and even a few landsmen dinners for moderate prices in the $10 to $15 range. It's open daily from 11am to 10pm, later on weekends. There's now an oyster bar and lounge here.

For more of the same atmosphere with a little different seafood focus, try **Lee and Ric's Oyster Bar and Seafood House,** 5621 Old Winter Garden Rd., Orlando (tel. 293-3587). The center of attention here is oysters on the half shell, raw or steamed. Trenchermen can order oysters by the bucket and nonfans can choose rock shrimp by the dozen, smoked mullet (definitely an acquired taste), snapper, flounder, snow crab, or scallops, all washed down with pitchers of beer. Opening hour here is noon daily; closing, 10 to 11pm. Your tab will be in the $10 to $15 range per person.

Wear your jeans and an expendable shirt, not to mention an expandable belt, when you try the **Chesapeake Crab House,** 9495 S. US 17/92, Maitland (tel. 831-0442), a small spot much frequented by local residents who delight in the informal atmosphere, the huge piles of crabs you hammer into shreds, and the big pitchers of beer. If you're looking for atmosphere, look elsewhere. But if you'd like to latch onto a hammer and pound away at some delectable blue crabs, head for the Chesapeake. Prices are in the $5 to $10 range (plus a $9 all-you-can-eat blue crab special). Doors open at 5:30pm, close at 10pm Monday through Saturday; closed Sunday.

**Charlie's Lobster House,** 2415 Aloma Ave., Winter Park (tel. 677-7352), turned up a few years ago and has held out long enough to be considered a mainstay here. Operated by experienced restauranteurs who created Park Avenue's Beef & Bottle, the restaurant is a jazzy fish house focusing on crab specialties but offering all kinds of fresh seafood served in a snappy setting here or dispensed to take-out buyers through a drive-in window. You can see what you're buying close up at a counter display, then march right on to the raw bar and dining room to try some of it out. Things get cooking here at 11am daily, closing at 9:30pm weekdays, at 10pm on weekends. Prices are in the $10 to $15 range for dinner selections.

**Bakerstreet Seafood Grill,** 743 Lee Rd., Orlando (tel. 644-8811), brought mesquite, the trendiest of trendy cooking substances, here to what was once a culinary wasteland. A wide range of sea treasures make an appearance here, from the ubiquitous but always-popular shrimp to grouper, dolphin, red snapper, whatever's fresh off the boats. Next door a lounge and restaurant dish up ribs, sandwiches, burgers, and the like. Bakerstreet warms up the coals at 5:30pm daily, closing at 11pm, while the lounge and restaurant next door are open from 11:30am to 2am daily. You can get in on the trend for prices in the $10 to $15 range for dinner.

## STEAKS

**Freddie's Steak House,** on US 17/92 in Fern Park (tel. 834-3373), obviously isn't adorned with a pretentious name, and inside you won't find much in the way of gilt or gewgaws, but you will certainly find superlative service, thoughtful extra touches, and great steaks and seafood—so who needs more? A frequent award winner, Freddie's begins with a brimming relish tray, a crock of Cheddar cheese, several good breads, and then moves on to seafood and those excellent steaks. You'll waddle out thankful for another "great American favorites" dinner for $12 to $17. Doors are open from 5:30pm to 2am, and there's a regular round of excellent entertainment in the lounge.

Australia comes to life down under, literally, at **Outback,** an elegant woodsy, plantsy spot "down under" the Buena Vista Palace Hotel, 1900 Buena Vista Dr., Lake Buena Vista (tel. 827-2727). Thick steaks and giant lobsters are the fare here, and they can be so large as to be downright unfair fare. A few English selections like Yorkshire pudding, steak-and-kidney pie, and bubble and squeak are slated to be added to the menu as a salute to an innovative chef-exchange program with London's fabled Savoy Hotel. Still, for our money it would be sacrilege not to take advantage of the steak-sizzling efforts here. Outback prices are in the $16 to $25 range for dinner entrées, and hours are 6 to 11pm daily. English ales? Of course, and enough other national brews to total something like 72 different kinds of beer on the list here.

Think you can work your way through 2½ pounds of T-bone? Whip over to **La Cantina,** 4721 E. Colonial Dr., Orlando (tel. 894-4491), some Wednesday and stoke up on a monster steak plus vegetable, salad, bread, and spaghetti for $20 or so. La Cantina's been pouring out those steaks for almost 50 years now, and has recently added a pretty new dining room with fireplace, fountain, and sunken conversation pit. The beef is aged and cut right here, and in their spare time the owners keep the sauce on for manicotti, ravioli, and veal. Prices are in the $10 to $17 range, and the restaurant's open from 5 to 11pm Tuesday through Saturday.

**Charley's Steak House,** 6107 S. Orange Blossom Trail, Orlando (tel. 851-7130), prides itself on the care and feeding of the multitudes who never met a steak they didn't love. Aged beef is cooked over a natural wood-burning fire here using a method the restaurant says was inspired by Seminole cookery. Seafood fans will find Australian lobster tails—big ones—on the menu, a fresh-catch item daily, langostinos. Charley's is also one of the few places in town you can find pork chops. A big salad bar is included with dinner entrées, which range in price from $10 to $19. Cocktails as well as beer and wine are available from 5 to 10pm daily, an hour later on weekends.

**Chris's House of Beef,** 801 John Young Pkwy., Orlando (tel. 295-1931), is a solid steakhouse that has been beefing up the lives of steak enthusiasts for three decades now—and in a quick-turnover town like Orlando that's a very long time. Top-quality prime rib, healthy slabs of sirloin, and tender filets pour from the kitchen portals here. You can select your own cut at a display and prove your own culinary creativity at an oft-praised salad bar. You'll pay $15 to $21 for dinner entrées here, where steaks sizzle from 11:30am to 11pm daily, closing at 10pm on Sunday. Also on Sunday there's a champagne brunch from 11am to 2:30pm; price is $11.

**Barney's Steak & Seafood,** 1615 E. Colonial Dr., Orlando (tel. 896-6864), gets rave reviews for its top-notch steaks and prime rib and seafood creations, and more top marks for a gigantic salad bar with more than 30 offerings to satisfy the rabbit in you. Many, many Orlandoites swear by Barney's, which has been serving top-quality beef long enough to win a dedicated following. Try it and you'll join the throngs. Open from 11:30am to 2:30pm on weekdays and 5 to 11pm daily. Prices are in the $11 to $21 range.

If there's one thing you are not likely to find at **Bob Ruby's Great Steaks,** in the Interior Decor Center, 999 Douglas Ave., Altamonte Springs (tel. 682-RUBY), it's humility. But why be humble when you're great? At least that's the way they figure it at this bigger-than-life spot that boasts of 450-degree platters and Texas-style, Texas-size steaks.

A comparative newcomer to the local restaurant scene, Ruby's cost $1.5 million to put together, as you will see when you get an eyeful of brass, a grand Steinway, private telephones in dining booths, and a stock exchange ticker over the bar. Prime beef is the order of the day here and the french fries are *première classe* and served with jalapeño catsup. T-bone, prime rib, ribeye, sirloin, and filets are the big draw, but there are seafood and lobster options as well. Prices are à la carte, although they include the restaurant's homemade sourdough bread and fall in the $18 to $25 range for entrées. Ruby's glitters from 11:30am to 10pm daily, from 5 to 11pm Saturday; closed Sunday.

---

**READER'S RECOMMENDATION:** "May I suggest the inclusion of **B.T. Bones,** a restaurant in Kissimmee, where we had the best, and, incidentally, the cheapest, steaks we have ever eaten?" (Susan Davies, Droitwich, Worcester, England). [*Authors' Note:* B.T. Bones, 3425 W. Vine St., Kissimmee (tel. 846-2324) has been recommended by several readers who laud it for moderate prices in the $10 to $15 range for dinner and for good steaks. Hours are 11am to midnight daily, opening at noon on Saturday and at 4pm on Sunday.]

## LIGHT MEALS

Pecan waffles, creamy homemade ice cream, fresh oranges, grapes, apples, and cantaloupe heaped over sherbet, a gasp-able banana split, giant Black Forest layer cake—have we got your attention? You'll find all this and much more at the tiny **East India Ice Cream Co.,** 327 Park Ave. S., Winter Park (tel. 628-2305), where you tread on brick walkways and dine outside in a jungle of greenery or inside in the paddle-fanned coolness of an interior jungle. Prices for most things don't top $5, and East India Ice Cream Co. is open Monday through Thursday from 8am to 11pm, on Friday and Saturday to 1am (from 10am to midnight on Sunday).

There's always some ringy-dingy fun going on at **TGI Friday's,** 6426 Carrier Dr. at International Drive, Orlando (tel. 345-8822), which has enough menu pages to create a small telephone book. There's simply no kind of grazing goody they don't serve from tacos to pasta to Reuben sandwiches, burgers, and more than 400 drink selections. Service is often as weirdly diverting as it is efficient, making this a spot much loved by the happy-hour set and popular with families as well. Friday's celebrates that week wind-down-day every day from 11am to 2am.

Who cares what they serve here, one just shouldn't miss an opportunity to try a restaurant called **Le Peep.** At last count there were two of them in Orlando, one at 4666 Kirkman Rd. (tel. 291-4580), which is reasonably near attractions, and one at 250 S. Orange Ave., in the Sun Bank Building (tel. 849-0428). Here they serve— what else?—LeBreakfast, LeBrunch, and LeLunch, featuring some interesting egg skillet dishes, pancakes, salads, soups, and what they like to call "knife and fork sandwiches" for prices in the $3 to $5 range for most selections. Hours are 6:30am to 2:30pm weekdays, opening at 7am and closing at 7:30pm Saturday and Sunday.

**JoAnn's Chili Bordello,** 1710 Edgewater Dr., between Princeton and Ivanhoe streets, Orlando (tel. 425-9865), is just too good a name to resist. If you love chili, you'll adore this crazy place where the wallpaper is red flock, the carpet is red plush, and all is offset by chandeliers and fancy drapes, à la bordello style—at least we suppose it's bordello style. Waitresses dressed in French corsets and black high heels add their bit to X-rated chilis, each of which is named after a famous, er, lady. Chilis are also rated PG and R, for those who like it hot but not quite so hot. For dessert? Cheesecake, of course. Prices range from $4 to $7, and hours are 11am to 9pm daily. Need you ask? Never on Sunday or Saturday.

## BUDGET AND FAMILY SPOTS

It's not every day you get to dine in a country store, and **Mack Meiner's Country Store,** at 921 N. Mills Ave., Orlando (tel. 896-5902), is certainly that. Oilcloth and kitchen chairs, old ads and movie posters, a player piano and sheet music make this a fun spot to tie the feedbag on the family. Most prices are in the $5 to $10 range, and barbecue's a specialty, although there are also chili, soups, and heavenly hash pie. It's open from 11:30am to 9:15pm, closed on Sunday.

When you see a line outside **Ronnie's,** 2702 E. Colonial Dr. in the Colonial Plaza Shopping Center, Orlando (tel. 894-2943), as you generally do for Sunday breakfast, you've got to figure somebody's doing something right inside. Indeed they are: a long, long menu, tables laden with bowls of kosher dills and sauerkraut, cheesecake light as a cloud and rated best in the city, pastries that are raw guilt, not to mention prices in the $5 to $10 range for most anything, less for some choices. It's open from 7am to 11pm weekdays, to 1am on weekends. You may even see jazz stars—Maynard Ferguson and George Shearing (who loves matzoh-ball soup) have been guests here.

**Morrison's Cafeterias** always produce creditable buffets at very creditable prices of $7 or less. In Orlando, there are cafeterias at 7440 International Dr. (tel.

351-0051) and at 1840 E. Colonial Dr. (tel. 896-2091), and there are three others, one in Winter Park, one on East Fla. 50 in Orlando, and one in Altamonte Springs. Open daily 7:30am to 9pm.

**International Buffet** is another top budget choice, with gigantic buffet spreads for lunch and dinner at a grand total of $6 for adults, about $2 to $4 for children! In Orlando, it's at 4442 Curry Ford Rd. at Conway (tel. 282-6929), and is open from 11am to 8pm daily.

**TGI Friday's,** at 227 County Road 436 West in Altamonte Springs (tel. 869-8085), is always a good choice for inexpensive food, and with so much of it to choose from, it will take you ages just to read the several-page menu. It's a fun place with lots of weird decor and waiters who cavort about, and TGI Friday's prices are in the under $10 bracket. Hours are 11:30am to 2am daily. Very good Sunday brunch here from 10:30am to 2:30pm.

**Holiday House,** 2037 Lee Rd., Orlando (tel. 293-4930), also has restaurants in Winter Park, Mount Dora, Deland, for a total of 13 locations including another in Orlando that's closer to Disney, at 1522 S. Orange Ave. (tel. 425-1521). They feed you well and efficiently here in a nice atmosphere on a dinner buffet that's just $6, and lunch is even cheaper—$5. The restaurants are open from 11am to 2:30pm and 4 to 8pm daily.

**Davis Brothers Motor Lodge,** at 6603 International Dr., Orlando (tel. 351-2900), has a fancy smörgåsbord, all you can eat for $5.75 at breakfast, about $4 for lunch, and under $6 for dinner.

**Baker's Square,** 345 W. Fairbanks in Winter Park (tel. 645-5767), has good and reasonably priced food in a quiet contemporary atmosphere for about $5. Choose from a long list that ranges from steaks to fantail shrimp. Open Sunday through Thursday from 7am to 11pm, on Friday and Saturday to midnight.

In the Midwest, where they breed **Steak and Shakes** about the way they breed soybeans, some gourmets/gourmands of our acquaintance swear by the glories of this chain. Here in Florida you can find them only north of a line passing more or less from Tampa through Orlando to Daytona, a source of much grief to those of us who have gloried in Chili Mac's culinary heights. For those of you who know whereof we speak, there's a Steak and Shake at 2820 E. Colonial Dr., Orlando (tel. 896-0827), with burger prices about $2, and five others scattered around town. They're open 24 hours a day.

**Fudrucker's,** 160 E. Altamonte Dr. in Altamonte Springs (tel. 831-1444), is housed in a one-time automotive center gone uptown. Now a very trendy spot, Fudrucker's gets our vote for name alone. Beside that name, it also has hamburgers, sandwiches, salads, and the like for prices in the $5 to $10 range for most goodies. Hours are 11am to 10pm daily, closing an hour later on Saturday and Sunday.

If you're staying out on International Drive, you'll find **Darryl's 1883 Restaurant and Tavern,** 8282 International Dr. (tel. 351-1883), a pleasant place to while away a couple of hours. All weathered wood, etched glass, and the like, the restaurant has something for absolutely every tastebud ranging from pasta to salads to Mexican, burgers, steaks, sandwiches, seafood, ribs—you name it, they've got it somewhere. Prices are quite reasonable, falling easily in the $5 to $7 bracket for many menu selections, $8 to $10 for full dinners. Hours are 11am to 2am daily.

Tops among the choices in these parts is **Numero Uno,** 2499 S. Orange Ave., Orlando (tel. 841-3840), where the menu tops out with paella for $12 but most selections are $5 to $6. Hours are 11am to 9:30pm daily except Wednesday.

Every bit as good is **El Bohio Café,** 5756 Dahlia Dr., Orlando (tel. 282-1723), a favorite of many locals who flock here for boliche, ropa vieja, and the like for prices in the $5 to $6 range. Hours are 11am to 9pm daily.

Two others with the same price range and similar offerings: **Medina's Café,** 2405 E. Washington St., Orlando (tel. 894-2206), open from 11am to 10pm daily except Sunday; and **La Lechonera Restaurant,** 2420 Curry Ford Rd., Orlando (tel. 894-6711), open from 11am to 9pm daily.

**Olive Garden,** 7653 International Dr., Orlando (tel. 351-1082), has moderate prices in the $10 to $12 range for complete dinners, and children's portions are available at half price with soft drink and milk refills free. Dinners are accompanied by a basketful of garlic bread sticks, a bowl of tossed salad, and a vegetable. A winner in the chain-restaurant sweepstakes, Olive Garden has been cloned many times in the Orlando area and at last count had eight restaurants scattered over the region. Hours are 11am to 10:30pm daily, closing at 11pm weekends.

**READER'S RECOMMENDATION: "The Ponderosa Restaurant,** at 6362 International Dr., Orlando (tel. 352-9343), was an excellent choice for a low-cost family restaurant. By just ordering the buffet/salad bar (for about $6), an individual has an excellent selection of fresh vegetables, salad items, hot buffet items like spaghetti, macaroni, fish, meatballs, cooked vegetables, choice of two soups, rolls, and a selection of desserts, including fresh fruits. There are also free refills on beverages and one can return to the buffet repeatedly. The Ponderosa is located on an easy-to-find road . . . the quality of the food is good and the fresh selections make for healthy eating" (Carolyn Ayers, New Hyde Park, N.Y.). [*Author's Note:* Ponderosa, which has many other restaurants in the Orlando area, is open daily from 7am to 11pm with buffets at all meals for $4 to $6.]

## A SPECIAL PLACE

A restaurant called **Al E. Gator's** obviously doesn't fit into just any category, so we're putting it in this special one by itself. It is Sea World's best sit-down restaurant, where you can try—are you ready?—a piece of alligator tail. Don't fret. Alligators have been so carefully protected in Florida that they're no longer an endangered species, so Sea World can sell the meat and never fear the forest ranger. That, of course, is not all they offer at Al E. Gator's—far from it. There are sandwiches and full meals, salads and desserts, plenty of choices from cracked conch to crab quiche, and other exotic specialties like mango muffins and swamp cabbage (in fancy places outside the Everglades that's called hearts of palm). Open daily during park hours, Al E. Gator's is at Sea World, 7001 Sea World Blvd. (tel. 351-0966). Prices range from $10 to $15 for full meals.

## ANOTHER SPECIAL PLACE

**The Mercado Festival Center,** a $20-million creation that sprang up in the center of International Drive, is both a shopping and dining center. Here you stroll on brick walkways lined with pretty landscaping while performers from belly dancers to jugglers, mimes, and magicians entertain. Gift and craft shops merge with pushcart vendors and restaurants to make this an intriguing oasis on bustling International Drive.

Certainly you'll never go hungry here. **Mardi Gras** (see "Nightlife") serves Cajun food before a high-stepping revue. **Charlie's Lobster House** (tel. 352-6929) features fresh Florida and imported seafoods. **Paulo's Café Restaurant** (tel. 352-7614) combines Italian and French specialties. **Royal Orleans** (tel. 352-8200), a cozy, intimate spot, specializes in créole and Cajun cooking. The Mercado, at 9801 International Dr. (tel. 345-9337), is open from 10am to 10pm daily, and there's no admission.

# 4. Meeting the Mouse

What a magical, mystical, laughable, lovable place the cartoonist carved out of 27,000 acres of central Florida wilderness! No matter how immune you think you are to the pursuits of childhood, when you see the pristine loveliness of this place in which even flowers seem to grow to specification, you will be enchanted. Lights twinkle, rooftops soar in gingerbready splendor, and your childhood castles in the air glitter right in front of you.

As you wander through the hundreds of things to see and do at Walt Disney's magical fiefdom, the child that lives on in even the most jaded of us begins to giggle and goggle, romp and ride, hopelessly lost in an explosion of fantasy created by the hand of a genius.

It's no wonder this giant theme park is the world's most famous diversion. Disney was determined to keep reality from intruding on your fantasy journey into your imagination. Stray castoffs and gucky wrappers barely touch the ground before they're swept away by an army of cleaners, many of them dressed in costumes to make them less noticeable. No doubt about it, this is the cleanest park in the nation, so clean in fact, that trash collected at 17 points throughout the Magic Kingdom is placed into underground, vacuum-sealed pneumatic tubes that whisk it away at 60 mph to a central compactor.

You'll never see Mickey and Minnie dragging their tails from place to place in this huge park. That duo and all Disney's other characters appear and reappear like magic, dressing and traveling in a vast network of underground tunnels, color-keyed so they don't get lost.

When you've bid your final late-night adieu to the park, another army of workers begins its shift. All night long a midnight maintenance crew is hard at work, plucking swan feathers from the lake and replacing thousands of tiny lightbulbs.

Elephants trumpet and spray, history talks, tiny people sing and dance, ghosts waft eerily around in never-failing computer-operated magic that is equally magical in its reliability.

All the efforts of workers and computers pay off, creating here a never-never land that never lets up in its appeal to your imagination. You fly with Peter Pan, sing along with dancing bears, play with pirates, and go on safari, knowing that however "real" tomorrow may be, today is pure fantasy.

Oh, go on, give in to it!

## PRACTICAL INFORMATION

If you drive to the park, it's a good idea to get there early, say 8:30am, since the crowds increase with the hour. We've been there *very* early and have yet to be first. Parking is $3, and you pay at an entrance so busy it looks like a toll booth on a major expressway.

Once you're at the entrance to the park (signs on I-4 will direct you there), follow the signs to the parking lots for either the **Magic Kingdom,** Disney's fascinating **Experimental Prototype Community of Tomorrow (EPCOT) Center,** or the newest addition, **Disney-MGM Studios.** From those parking lots, trams run constantly to the ticket booths at the entrances to all three attractions.

Be sure to write down or otherwise remember the name of your parking lot (in Magic Kingdom they're named for the Seven Dwarfs and other characters, and in EPCOT Center they have names like Communications, etc.) and the number of your parking line. On busy days there can be 80,000 people in the park—and that's a lot of silver station wagons!

Those trams whisk you off to the **Ticket and Transportation Center, (TTC),** where you buy tickets for either or both of the parks. There's a special parking lot for handicapped visitors too, and wheelchairs can be rented for $4 a day at the stroller shop just inside the entrance to the Magic Kingdom or EPCOT Center. If you have any special problems, **Guest Relations** (tel. 824-4500) is there to help you with friendly smiles and some quick thinking. **Information** is also available at 824-4321.

A little general orientation here: Monday through Wednesday, strangely enough, are the busiest days at the park, and the summer months and Christmas are the busiest seasons. Restaurants are jammed between 11am and 1pm and 5 to 7pm, so you might consider early or late meals in busy seasons.

Before we get to the delights of Disney, heed this one little warning for which you will be speechlessly grateful later: Please understand that you can walk the soles off your shoes trying to see everything in this massive park and burn your unsuspecting skin to a crisp in the Florida sunshine while you're at it. So *wear comfortable shoes and clothes, and make sure you have something to cover your skin and your eyes,* like shirts and sunglasses. No matter how cloudy or how weak the sun is, in Florida it burns—fast.

Once you've bought your tickets (hang on, we're coming to the prices), go directly to City Hall in the Magic Kingdom, MGM's Oscar's Super Service, or Earth Station in EPCOT Center, and ask for a map. Look over the list of things you want to see, then plot out a more-or-less organized course through the park. You don't have to stick to it, of course, but it will help you keep from wandering aimlessly around trying to figure out where you are and what you should do next.

Summers and holidays, the park stays open to midnight. At and after dinner hours, the lines seem to diminish and from 10pm to midnight you can often visit more attractions than you could all day.

## The Magic Kingdom, Disney-MGM Studios, and EPCOT Center Prices and Hours

Now's the time you're going to have to consider how much time you are going to spend at Walt Disney World. Now that the World contains the Magic Kingdom, Disney-MGM Studios, and EPCOT Center, there is a great deal to see. If you have only one day to spend here, you're going to have to choose among them. It's very difficult, if not impossible, to visit all in one day. In fact to make a leisurely visit to all is likely to take you three days or more. Add two days to that if you'd like to spend some time at the park's sports, shopping, and special attractions like Typhoon Lagoon, River Country, and Discovery Island.

Okay, here's what Walt Disney World costs: a one-day World Pass entitling you to visit Disney's new MGM Studios, the Magic Kingdom, or EPCOT Center (but not all three) is $32.86 for adults, and $26.50 for children (ages 3 through 9); under 3 free.

There are no two- or three-day World Passes available, but a four-day passport permitting admission to the Magic Kingdom, Disney's new MGM Studios, and EPCOT Center (All-Three-Parks Passport) is $106 for adults, and $84.80 for children. Finally, there is a five-day World Pass for $128.02 and $100.70.

Tickets may be bought with cash, traveler's checks, American Express, MasterCard, VISA, or a personal check with proper identification. Credit cards can also be used at hotels, shops, and most restaurants in the parks.

You can order multiday passports by calling 407/824-8000, or by writing Walt Disney World Co., Admissions Department, P.O. Box 10,000, Lake Buena Vista, FL 32830. Allow 15 working days for processing your request. There's a $2 postage-and-handling charge per order.

If you leave the Magic Kingdom, MGM Studios, or EPCOT Center and plan to return the same day, have your hand stamped at the exit.

If you're staying at one of the hotels owned by Walt Disney World, you can get a few dollars off on tickets. Inquire when making your reservation.

## A Little Orientation

Time for a little semantics lesson. Walt Disney World refers to the entire Disney complex, which now includes the Magic Kingdom, Disney-MGM Studios, EPCOT Center, River Country, Typhoon Lagoon, Discovery Island, six hotel complexes, and the Walt Disney World Shopping Village and Hotel Plaza. We mention this only so you don't expect to see EPCOT Center by going to the Magic Kingdom. Those two attractions are three miles apart and each occupies acres and acres of ground!

Disney's second creation was **EPCOT, The Experimental Prototype Community of Tomorrow,** which opened in October 1982, just 10 years after the Magic

Kingdom. Here in EPCOT Center, Disney takes a little more serious look at the world but still offers plenty of fun with everything from life-size dinosaurs to a 3-D movie.

EPCOT Center itself is divided into two sections separated from each other by a large lake. One side of the lake harbors the Future World exhibits provided by major corporations, and on the other side you'll find World Showcase, where nations of the world show off their cultures and products.

For a detailed look at all the magic of Walt Disney World, read our in-depth Orlando book, *Frommer's Guide to Orlando*.

## Pets, Kids, Pix

A couple more notes on protocol and then we're off. Despite the Kingdom's love for Pluto and Mickey, Dumbo and Donald, you'll have to leave Fido in the Kennel Club next door to the Transportation and Ticket Center (and pay $4 for some loving care and feeding that may spoil him for weeks). There's also a kennel at Fort Wilderness Campground, and at EPCOT Center.

Be forewarned, too, that the tiny Mickey Mouse your toddler has seen in comic books bears only surface resemblance to the park's towering Mickey, whose huge head is set on a tall strong body. This giant mouse is not always as thrilling to a two-foot person who's looking up at a monster as he is to adults. Children are often terrified at the sight of the huge cartoon characters and set up a wail that can be heard to Kansas if they are confronted too suddenly with a giant hand. So introduce little ones slowly to the World's characters so both they and you will enjoy the introduction.

If you'd like to take pictures in the park and don't have a camera, Kodak will lend you one. The company's booth is at the south end of Main Street, U.S.A., and you can borrow a camera free for your visit if you'll leave them a refundable deposit.

There's a similar deal available at the Camera Center in EPCOT Center—it's just to your right as you face the entrance to Spaceship Earth. There's also a shop at Journey into Imagination.

## Dining

As for dining at Disney, you need never fear starvation. There's food, food, and more food, from street vendors to dozens of restaurants. A few outstanding ones are **King Stefan's Banquet Hall** in Cinderella's Castle, the **Liberty Tree Tavern** in Liberty Square, and **Aunt Polly's** on Tom Sawyer's Island in Frontierland, where you can munch while sitting on a porch overlooking the water. Moderate prices prevail in the Kingdom, with lunch prices in the $5 to $7 range, and dinner under $20. You can't beat this culinary choice at Disney: frozen bananas covered in chocolate. Terrific.

For more elegant dining, Contemporary Resort Hotel's **Top of the World** (tel. 824-3611) has a Sunday brunch from 9am to 2pm at $23 for adults, $10 to $18 for children, depending on age. You can have dinner here any night at $42.50 for adults and $19.50 for children 3 to 11. Dinner is followed by a Broadway show with song-and-dance entertainment at 6:45 and 9:15pm.

At **Polynesian Resort** (tel. 824-2000) there's a daily Disney characters breakfast buffet at $10 for adults ($6 for children 3 to 11), and similar spreads at lunch. In the evening, the hotel presents a luau buffet and fabulous Polynesian entertainment at 6:45 and 9:30pm, at $29 for adults, $15 to $23 for children, depending on age.

You must have a jacket at the Contemporary Hotel, gentlemen, and no jeans no matter whose name is on the pocket (no rules like that at the Polynesian). Reservations are required at both hotels for their evening entertainment. Call 824-8000.

In EPCOT Center, the choices are fascinating and may be fattening as well. EPCOT's World Showcase, which features pavilions representing 11 nations, has full-scale and fancy restaurants "in" France, the U.K., Japan, Mexico, Norway, Italy, Germany, China, and Canada, plus other less-elaborate food purveyors.

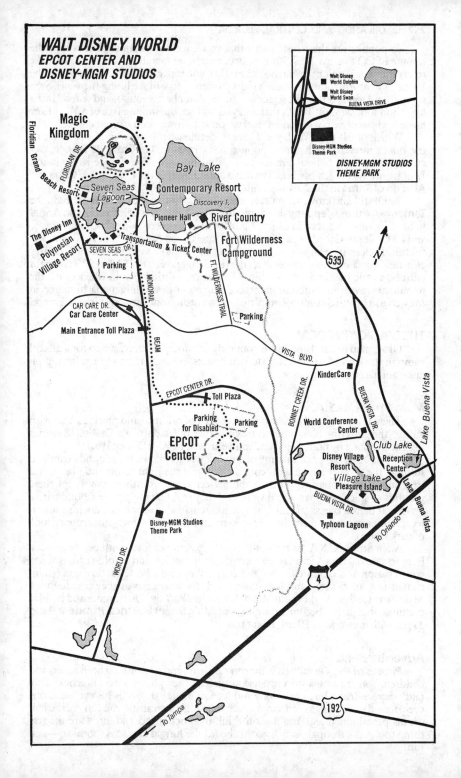

So popular are these restaurants that you must make dinner reservations the minute EPCOT opens. By 9:30am most of the restaurants are fully booked. To make reservations, go straight to Earth Station when you arrive and walk over to one of the WorldKey Information Service television screens you will see lining the walls. Step right up and touch one of the screens—go on, don't be nervous—and you will see a knife and fork symbol. Touch that and you will see the smiling face of a WorldKey hostess who will help you make a reservation at the restaurant of your choice.

Which one is that? Well, *you'll* have to decide what kind of food you'd like to try, but be forewarned that most popular restaurants are **Les Chefs de France**, created by three very famous French chefs, Paul Bocuse, Roger Verge, and Gaston Lenôtre, in the French pavilion; the **Rose and Crown** in the U.K.; and **L'Originale Alfredo di Roma** in the Italy pavilion.

You'll still find crowds, however, at the **Biergarten** in the German pavilion, the **Tempura Kiku** and **Teppanyaki Dining Room** in Japan, the **Cantina de San Angel** in Mexico, **Nine Dragons** in China, **Marrakesh** in Morocco, **Akershaus** in Norway, and **Le Cellier** in Canada's pavilion. Take whatever you can get. They're all wonderful fun. Each in its own way whisks you out of Orlando and into another country effortlessly and skillfully. Prices at all the restaurants are in the $12 to $20 range for entrees, a little higher for some things in France, a little lower in Mexico. All the restaurants have some entertainment too, ranging from strolling mariachi singers in Mexico to a beret-ed combo, complete with accordion and striped shirts, in France.

## THE MAGIC KINGDOM

Okay, map in hand and pulse pounding in anticipation, off we go for a gleeful romp in the land of mysterious haunted houses, runaway railroad cars, leering pirates, and fat, frolicking bears . . .

### Main Street, U.S.A.

There it is at the end of a two-block stretch of primped and precious Victorian village: the glittering blue-turreted magnificence of **Cinderella's Castle,** 18 stories high and topped by fluttering flags. You've arrived in Walt Disney World!

All through the park an army of smiling workers keeps the grounds trim and shining, the flowers growing on command in just the right colors and places, and trees just high enough to produce the perfect shade. Another army keeps these grounds so spick and span you'll wonder if they're following people around with a broom. If there's one single thing you'll find remarkable about the park it's the perfect cleanliness here—from the sidewalks to the shining all-American scrubbed look of park workers.

Main Street, U.S.A., is turn-of-the-century America filled with penny arcades, horseless carriages, a Victorian restaurant, silent movies, and an old-fashioned ice-cream parlor. You can ride the horse-drawn trolley or the horseless carriages (all included in your tickets), and later cavort with the characters as they parade down Main Street at 3pm in the **Main Street Character Parade.** On summer and holiday evenings, that parade becomes the glittering **Main Street Electrical Parade** at 9 and 11pm with fireworks at 10pm. Don't miss it!

### Adventureland

**Pirates of the Caribbean** is the top ride here, and a favorite of both adults and children. You sail away into a mysterious grotto, then plunge into a raucous pirate raid where a drunk buccaneer lolls and leers, a mangy dog rolls his eyes, and one eye-patched devil hangs menacingly over you and is so realistic you can see the hair on his pantalooned leg! You'll soon think the **Enchanted Tiki Birds** are the real thing too. A sail through leafy lagoons aboard the **Jungle Cruise** is soothing—and fun!

## Mickey's Birthdayland

This comparatively new "land" celebrates the Mouse's—are you ready?—60th! Ssssh, there's a big surprise party on the horizon. You'll get to help Minnie plan the whole thing, but don't, for goodness sake, let the lip slip when you stop by Mickey's house for a look at the famous Mouse's bedroom, living room, study, and kitchen.

Later, you're invited over to Minnie's house, where the surprise birthday party is being cooked up—big birthday cake and all. Then, it's on to the gala event, where a surprised Mickey shows up, looking, we might add, not a day over 21, but then mice never do look their age, do they? You'll get to wish him a happy birthday in person, shake his paw, if you like, and blow out all those candles.

## Frontierland

Brass rails line the saloon, Indians raid the wooden fort, a hilarious gang of singing bears laughs it up at **Country Bear Jamboree,** and across the river, **Tom Sawyer Island** has Injun Joe's Cave, the Magnetic Mystery Mine, and a log raft ride over to Fort Sam Clemens. Don't miss the country bears (one grown man told us he's already seen them nine times and can't wait for his tenth visit!). **Big Thunder Mountain Railroad,** newest of the park's attractions, takes you on an exciting journey aboard a runaway train. It's great fun—just watch out for that last bend.

## Liberty Square

Animated, life-size figures of our nation's leaders rise and talk to you in the **Hall of Presidents.** They gesture a little, and look so real you're tempted to step up and offer them a vote. It's a masterful display of wax creativity and Disney ingenuity. At the **Haunted House** you'll shriek with the rest of us cowards as the walls rise (or is it the floors that drop?) and ghosts exchange civilized chatter at a haunting dinner party. There's a delightful river cruise on a sternwheeler, and a high-stepping revue here too.

## Fantasyland

Ms. White and her troop of odd little men, plus Dumbo, Mickey, and the gang perform and you can fly through the night keeping a sharp eye on the leader at **Peter Pan's Flight. Small World** is just that, a globe-circling trip accompanied by tiny singing dolls in native costumes. **Twenty Thousand Leagues Under the Sea** takes you into the depths à la Jules Verne.

## Tomorrowland

**Space Mountain** is Disney's very own heart-stopper roller coaster, and **Mission to Mars** is fun. Delta Airlines has a fascinating film exhibit, Dream Flight, in a Circle Vision 360° Theater with a circular screen.

## River Country

Disney re-created the ol' swimmin' hole here just west of Pioneer Hall in Fort Wilderness, then added some typical Disney delights: three twisting, turning water-flume slides, rafts, and innertubes on which you ride down winding rapids and under waterfalls, ropes you swing on into the water, a pool 160 feet long, picnic areas, beach, and nature trail. Admission is $12.46 for adults, $9.81 for children 3 through 9. Open March to December.

## Discovery Island

You can cruise across a lake to an island lined with paths that wind through colorful perfumed foliage, flowers, and trees; watch the activities of 500 birds of more than 60 species in an aviary; see rare Galápagos tortoises and bald eagles. Admission is $7.95 for adults, $4.24 for children under 13.

That's it, and believe us, that's a day or three worth of fun and laughter, fantasyland at its best, thanks to a talented cartoonist who shared his forest of characters and stole all our hearts.

On your way back to your car, you can keep the magic going just a few minutes more by sailing to the parking lot aboard a free ferryboat that leaves from just in front of the monorail stop and cruises you back to the ticket center, where you board a tram, tired but full of memories of a kingdom that's magic indeed.

## EPCOT CENTER

Drift down from Dumbo's ear now and give a listen to the sound of the future. Here in EPCOT Center, Disney has put together a look at what you can expect from tomorrow; a glance at the past to show you how far we've come just to get to *today;* and a glimpse into the ways others live in this world we all inhabit together.

All rolled together it's called **Future World,** produced by some of the nation's leading corporations, and **World Showcase,** where 11 nations give you a glimpse into their "world."

In both these Worlds you'll find all kinds of special entertainment, from brass bands to huge walking "dolls" representing their countries, and a magnificent evening show on the lagoon in the center of it all. Performers from many nations also appear on a special stage in front of the U.S. pavilion.

Because EPCOT Center is so new—and so many people want to know what it's all about—we'll take a look now at this very special place in the World.

### Future World

Here you will find a stirring look at how our nation gets its energy at Exxon's **Universe of Energy.** You'll also get an amusing, even an exciting, look at the dawn of mankind when huge dinosaurs and terrifying pterodactyls roamed the earth and skies. Don't miss this one—you can even smell the primeval, sulfurous swamps and see the steaming upheaval of the earth. It's a kick.

Kodak's **Journey into Imagination** is a strong favorite with EPCOT crowds, and no wonder. First you go on a fanciful ride with a character named Dreamfinder, who hangs around with a little purple dragon character called Figment. With that duo you go on a chortling trip through your imagination—and goodness knows what you'll find *there!*

Here you can also see a thriller of a 3-D movie complete with Michael Jackson! Don't miss the creative playground of the future either, or you won't know what to do when the whole world is creating sound with light. Stop by, you'll see what we mean.

Not ones to be left far behind, General Motors' **World of Motion** takes you on a trip—what else?—through the history of man's search for mobility. Audio Animatronics, the life-size characters that move, blink their eyes, play ukeleles, cackle, and lay eggs, are particularly good in GM's offering. There are also some futuristic automobiles, trucks, and motorcycles on display, as well as GM's latest products.

At **Spaceship Earth** you explore man's age-old questions: Who are we? Where do we come from? Here, too, AudioAnimatronics are wonderful. They alone will show you how far we've come with our playthings.

Another big hit with the crowd is **The Land.** Presented by Kraft, The Land gives you a look into the future of food production. Here on Disney's "Land" grow cucumbers that add inches even as you watch—up to 12 inches a day! Here in an experimental greenhouse, experts from all over the world are working together to produce plants that grow in a simulated spacecraft environment, alongside other crops so each nourishes the other, in giant rotating drums, on space-saving plastic A-frames, and in nothing but air. It's downright amazing. You can eat some of the products produced there in the Good Turn Restaurant, a revolving dining spot which gives you a little preview of what you'll see on your ride through this land.

**Horizons** gives you a look at the life a family will be living in the next century: Kids going on a field trip to a seaweed farm; robots, operated by voice commands, harvesting crops; and workers harvesting crystals. You travel to the future aboard a moving "spaceship."

Jump aboard the miniaturizer and get yourself shrunk so you can join the rest of us on a journey through the human body at EPCOT's most recent addition, a Metropolitan Life exhibit called **Wonders of Life.** Here the biggest attraction is a wild, bumpy, jumpy, roly-poly Body Wars ride which you take locked in a gray chamber. On you bounce through the bloodstream, heart, lungs, and brain of a kid who's just gotten a splinter stuck in his finger. Doesn't sound like much of an injury, but you'll be surprised what happens on this wild ride that combines computerized synchrony, flight simulator engineering, and the talents of special-effects experts. One cautionary note: This is an umpity-bumpity ride that can bring on motion sickness in some people, although most of that is caused by sight rather than action motion. If you're already on this ride and feel queasy, you're likely to recover quickly just by looking away from the screen, for that is where much of the "movement" *really* is occurring. Later you can stroll through a wide variety of exhibits aimed at showing you the way to a healthy body, healthy mind. You can also witness the conception and birth of a baby accomplished with a cartoon approach that makes it quite vanilla.

All aboard the Hydrolator, it's off to **Seabase Alpha,** where you can discuss world events with a manta ray or a couple of dolphins. A recent addition to EPCOT's Future World, **The Living Seas** is a huge aquarium that is home to more than 6,000 undersea creatures living out their watery days in 6,000,000 gallons of saltwater. Here you ride through an acrylic tunnel to see who's hanging around this manmade coral reef, then you learn a little about mineral treasures that are buried beneath the waters and about our human efforts to talk to the animals, specifically the dolphins. Games, hands-on exhibits, and animated displays are all part of the fun brought to you by United Technologies Corp., which also has produced a slick film you watch on 35 video screens. Later you can watch your lunch swimming around in front of you as you dine at the glass-lined Coral Reef Restaurant built alongside this watery attraction.

## World Showcase

Here nine nations have spread out their wares and their smiles alongside a sparkling blue lake. Each has built its pavilion around its best-known architectural landmark—the Eiffel Tower, the Palace of the Doges, the Aztec pyramid.

When you step into one of these countries, you are immersed in the culture. Not only does each country look the way that country really looks, but all the employees come straight from their homelands and have charming accents. Ze French are veeery French, monsieur, and the British are veddy, veddy British. You'll love it.

You can get around on foot or on antique double-decker buses that stop in front of some of the countries. There can be a great deal of walking and standing because there are many things to see, so be prepared to hoof it. It's 1.2 miles around the lake, which you can also cross by boat. You'll see the boat dock at the end of the walkway that leads from Future World to the lake.

For a look at the restaurants in World Showcase, turn back a few pages.

Here's a brief look at each of the pavilions, starting with Mexico and moving clockwise around the lagoon:

Look to your left as you face the lake and you'll see a great stepped pyramid rising out of the flatlands. That's **Mexico,** and inside the pyramid you'll find candles glittering and an eerie blue glow creating a romantic mood in the midst of an adobe village. A jaguar snarls in the distance as you look over the piñatas and Mexican wedding dresses, the huarachis and guayaberas. A boat ride takes you on the River of Time through Mexico's past and present.

EPCOT's newest national tribute salutes **Norway.** Here you board a Viking ship in search of Valhalla and sail off up a fjord and over a cascading waterway into the land of trolls and gnomes. When you touch down again in reality, you'll find yourself in modern Oslo. A cobblestone plaza at the $35-million showcase between Mexico and China features a replica of the 14th-century castle Akershus in Oslo harbor. Surrounding architecture was inspired by the Norwegian cities of Bergen, Ålesund, and Setesdal. Shops in the plaza sell Norwegian handcrafts, baked goodies, art, carvings, and something they know lots about in Norway: woolens.

Don't skip the film in the **China** pavilion—it's one of the best-loved productions in EPCOT Center, and rightfully so. Projected on a 360° screen that wraps all around you, the film takes you to the famed Forbidden City, to the Harbin Ice Festival where ice-carving enthusiasts create bigger-than-life fantasies in ice, and to places in China that have never before been filmed by Westerners. It's spectacular! If they ever put an airline ticket machine in here, all the world will be booked on flights to China. Yes, it's that fascinating.

Oom-pah-pah, plenty of suds and pretzels, pretty frauleins, and some intriguing crafts are just part of the lure of the **Germany** pavilion. There's an especially amusing show here at dinner, complete with slap dancing and those incredible long alpine horns. Fun.

An amusing street theater and an excellent restaurant are two of the lures that will bring you to **Italy** and keep you there, stuffing yourself on laughter and linguine. You'll see gondolas floating in the lagoon out front and get a chance to buy some glittering Venetian glass and soft Italian leathers.

Ben Franklin and Mark Twain take a look at U.S. history with an assist from Chief Joseph, Susan B. Anthony, and Frederick Douglass at the **American Adventure.** All this takes place in an elegant theater. This production has the distinction of being the first Disney AudioAnimatronic creation in which one of the characters actually walks—it's Benjamin Franklin, and he walks up the stairs for a visit with Thomas Jefferson.

**Japan** invites you to enter through a massive torii gate. On the way you pass a dramatic pagoda trimmed with royal-blue roof tiles that glitter in the sun and tiny bells that dangle off the eaves. A priceless suit of samurai armor is displayed here, and there are some intriguing treasures in the Mitsukoshi department store. Japan has two very good restaurants and a lovely lounge that has the best view of EPCOT in EPCOT.

Visions of veiled ladies and ghostly spooky caftans disappearing around a corner. Clandestine whispers. Humphrey Bogart in *Casablanca.* It all comes to life at EPCOT's **Morocco** pavilion, which itself came to life in 1984 but seems, like Morocco, to have been here since the beginning of time. Here you're welcomed by a gaggle of clapping, singing, fez-topped musicians who pound on drums and strum away at stringed instruments in the shadow of a replica of the 12th-century Koutoubia Minaret.

Disney artists are a magical lot, and here they've managed to re-create the labyrinthian splendor of Morocco. A strikingly beautiful palace courtyard looks just like Spain's famed Giralda. In the small museum here you can examine some of the amazingly intricate artwork of the Moroccans. You even get a special invitation to a re-creation of a Moroccan wedding, at which the bride in an elaborately embroidered wedding gown and slippers sits high atop a pile of pillows.

Artisans were brought from Morocco to build this pavilion with its intricate tilework and carved timbers. So realistic is the mélange of streets, gates, and minarets they created that one workman is said to have looked down the street and pointed out the house in which he was born! Some of those artisans remained, and you can watch them here today weaving beautiful Moroccan carpets, pounding brass into trays and pitchers, tooling leather. That and many, many other kinds of treasures—sheepskins, gold-trimmed caftans, ceramics, woodwork, silver, and baskets (leather hats for about $8 are a favorite buy)—are sold in this mélange of bazaar shops.

Morocco sports a dining spot called Marrakesh. A study in candlelight, ornately carved plaster, tiles, carpets, costumed waiters, and a belly dancer, Marrakesh is one of the loveliest of EPCOT's restaurants. For $12 to $17 you feast on a dinner of such Moroccan specialties as couscous (a bowl of semolina topped with vegetables, beef, lamb, and chicken) or saffron-flavored harira soup. Revel in the flavors of apricots, cinnamon, almonds, honey, prunes, delicately blended with chicken, beef, or lamb, and finish it all with glasses of hot mint tea.

If you can't get reservations under the Eiffel Tower in **France** at Les Chefs de France Restaurant, toddle on over to the Pâtisserie, where the aroma alone is caloric. Croissants, tartins, gâteaux, yum. France also has a delightful movie that skims you over the countryside and into the City of Light. Some delightful shops too—take a look at the tapestry cushion covers in the Plume et Pallette. Terrific.

Things are so British at the Rose & Crown Pub in the **United Kingdom** that even the British are overwhelmed. Most people figure to hit here when exhaustion sets in so they can spend a little resting time with a cold "pint-a"—they'll even warm it up on special warmers so the beer will be the same temperature as it is in London! Tea, crumpets, and cashmeres are on sale here, and entertainment sometimes includes the Pearly Band, a group of Cockney singers and dancers in pearl-button-covered costumes.

**Canada** is justifiably proud of its *O Canada* film, another of those stirring 360° productions. This one takes you to the Calgary Stampede, downhill on skis, and to the top of Toronto's most famous landmark, the C.N. Tower. You'll hear music of a lumberjack band, visit an abandoned gold-mine tunnel, and . . . whoops, watch out for the waterfall!

Here's a little-known helper for you: All the treasures you buy—and you'll see dozens of things you want—can be sent out to the entrance where you can pick them up at **Package Pickup.** When you buy something, just ask the salesperson to send it over to Package Pickup, keep your receipt, and you'll find your treasures waiting for you when you leave. It beats carrying dozens of little packages with you everywhere you go.

## DISNEY-MGM STUDIOS

In 1989 this massive attraction introduced its third park, this one aimed at movie buffs who can go behind the scenes here to see how celluloid dreams are made.

Spread out across more than 100 acres of Disney's enormous 25,000-acre tract in Central Florida, this new attraction-within-an-attraction includes a visit to a motion-picture and television studio, a wild ride through Hollywood-created fire and flood, a chance to see how good you'd be as a television star playing in some of the screen's sit-com hits, and a ride through **The Great Movie Ride,** where an AudioAnimatronic Tarzan swings merrily through his jungle living room and slimy stuff from the "Alien" nuzzles your cheek.

Get ready to stroll Hollywood Boulevard—perhaps you'll be discovered! Along this famed boulevard you can dine in art deco–design restaurants, ogle handprints of the stars at Grauman's Chinese Theater, and buy in shops that hark back to the halcyon Hollywood days of the '30s and '40s.

At the **SuperStar Television Theater** you can face the camera, making a splitscreen appearance in your favorite sit-com, while less-adventuresome guests watch your performance on a monitor. Electronic wizardry merges live action with film clips from classic shows.

You want to see a car chase and a 14-story high dive? Well, step right into an **Indiana Jones** playground to get a look at fearless stunt workers as they leap from burning buildings, wreck cars, and generally go out of their way to make trouble.

Those of you who specialize in odd noises can rumble and grumble at the **Monster Sound Show,** where you'll be invited to compete against actual sound-effects technicians.

In the "real" Hollywood there are plenty of dining spots for conspicuous consumers, so Disney keeps that tradition alive here at Hollywood and Vine, Florida. You can see and be seen in the **Hollywood Brown Derby Restaurant,** in an art deco –era cafeteria, and in several different kinds of fast-food haunts.

Disney World always gives you ample opportunity to spend, spend, spend, and that is nonetheless true here at the Disney-MGM Studios. There are shops everywhere. In them you will find plenty of what you find everywhere else in Mouseland, plus all the movie memorabilia you can hoard, everything from movie scripts to vintage costumes actually worn by the stars, movie magazines, trade papers, soundtracks, videotapes, posters, even a vintage Sears store! Shades of *Variety.*

Those who want to see beneath the surface of the film world should head straight for the **Backstage Studio Tour tram,** which drives you around the filmmaking facilities, through a suburban village in which the houses are only facades, down a city street lined with backless "skyscrapers," and past a two-faced church!

Then its onward for a trip behind the scenes to wardrobe, scenery, backlot streets, and finally to Catastrophe Canyon, where your tram is caught in a massive Hollywood-created downpour. Having withstood the deluge, you then find yourself in the midst of an earthquake. Your tram rocks and rumbles as an oil well explodes and fires erupt, then just in the nick of time an artificial waterfall comes to your rescue.

Midway through the two-hour tour you get a brief break at a refreshment pavilion and shop in which you can have your picture taken in any of many zany costumes and listen to some strange sound effects.

During the final hour of the tour you go behind the scenes to hear how soundtracks are created and watch seamstresses stitch away at the world's largest costume collection—more than 2.5 million garments!

Here masterminds of imagination create weird scenery and Disney's famous animators draw up a storm to create the storyboards and characters that make those zany Disney cartoon characters come alive—"Now where is that wabbit?"

## TYPHOON LAGOON

In 1989 WDW opened yet another new attraction, this one called Typhoon Lagoon, a 56-acre water adventure park. Disney World always creates a "legend" to go with its attractions, and here the story has something to do with a huge typhoon that has landed you on a remote island beach.

As is the case with most remote island beaches, there's nothing to do here— nothing but . . . body surf a four-foot wave that dumps you unceremoniously onto a white sand beach, snorkel among tropical fish in a saltwater pool, whiz down massive waterslides, and float in an innertube through a tropical rain forest. Well, you get the picture, er, seascape.

**Mount Mayday** looms over Typhoon Lagoon and is crowned by *Miss Tilly,* a ramshackle fishing boat reportedly tossed by a storm to its final resting place atop this 95-foot "volcano" creation (**Typhoon Mountain**) that erupts merrily every half hour. Thaaaaat's Disney, folks.

Br'er Rabbit and the boys welcome you aboard a log boat for a trip through canyons and caverns, up and down a very strange world indeed. As you travel through this most unusual "mountain," you plunge down five watery drops, including one that plummets 18 feet, then zips right back up again, and another that drops 52 feet in two seconds!

Attractively landscaped with a beguiling tropical atmosphere, Typhoon Lagoon makes for a pleasant place to while away a day. This beach will cost you, however. Typhoon Lagoon is not included in any Passports. A one-day admission ticket is $19.35 for adults, $15.37 for children 3 to 9; a two-day pass is $31.80 for adults and $25.44 for children 3 to 9.

---

## 5. E.T. and a Kongfrontation

Grrrrrrrrrrrrh. Aaaaaaaaaaaaaaaahhh! No! No! Agggh!

What's going on here? Nothing, darlings, that's just the sound of Orlando on a roll.

That is, in fact, just the sound of Orlando ripping into the last decade of the century with all the vigor and enthusiasm that converted this once-hicktown from a cluster of unsophisticated rubes to a bevy of savvy fantasy sellers.

It is, in fact, the sound of Universal Studios, a massive city-within-a-city, a wildly amusing theme park, and a deadly serious money-maker out to set the world on film.

Now, Universal is not new to this fantasy business. They've been creating celluloid dreamworlds for more than 75 years and running a live entertainment spectacle visited by 60 million of the awe-struck for 25 years.

Step right up to the gate of **Universal Studios Florida** (1000 Universal Studios Plaza, at the junction of I-4 and the Florida Turnpike) and a whole new kind of fun begins. Here you'll quail at the sight of a roaring King Kong, fall in love with that AWOL astronaut E.T., and feel your knees buckle as the earth quakes.

Spread out over more than 400 acres, Universal's Central Florida Studios cost more than $500 million, and that's a lot of entertainment!

In business for 75 years, Universal Studios by now knows plenty about fantasy and how to make it happen. For openers they employed mega-movie creator Steven Spielberg as creative consultant. To that they added attractions based on adorably ugly E.T., terrifying King Kong, box office boffo *Back to the Future,* toothy *Jaws,* squeaky *Ghostbusters,* and a terrifying earthquake.

Here you'll see a star—and be a star! You'll see how moviemakers do the impossible and you can even do it yourself. You'll go behind the scenes to see how years of cinema thrills and chills were created and relive some of the movie moments you've most loved.

A fabulous city, dotted with lagoons and beaches, this new universe is a massive study in fancy and fantasy.

A real working film studio, on duty 24 hours a day, Universal is making movies even as you play in this giant park. Who knows when your favorite star will stroll right up to you?

Set streets you'll stroll include: **Metro**—featuring everything from Little Italy to Central Park and Coney Island; **San Francisco Bay**—starring Ghirardelli Square, Fisherman's Wharf, the Embarcadero, even a BART subway station; a **New England Village**—complete with Amity Village, a New England street, and Amity Harbor; **Hollywood**—starring Sunset Boulevard, Hollywood Boulevard, Beverly Hills, Rodeo Drive, and the Garden of Allah; **World Expo**—showing off a World's Fair site, Exposition Park, and Dr. Brown's Science Center; and **specialized sets** ranging from Angkor Wat to Psycho Hill and Bates Motel.

Hot adventures abound. Cartoonists Bill Hanna and Joe Barbera, who brought us **Yogi Bear, Huckleberry Hound,** and **the Flintstones,** among others, now bring you a "slam-bang, high-speed chase that'll take you inside the cartoon, put you in the thick of the action and leave you stretched, squashed, smashed, bashed, crashed, crushed and open-mouthed with awe and amazement." When you've recovered, they'll teach you something about how animation gets animated and you'll get a chance to try it yourself.

Then it's on to a meeting with a major monk! He'll huff. He'll puff. He'll roar.

You'll scream a lot. **Kong** is 30 feet tall, 13,000 pounds of howling terror "ready to take things into his own hands. Crushing everything in his path. Swatting planes like flies. Rampaging! Daring you to face his colossal fury. And when you do, he'll blast you with his banana breath, then twist you, turn you, and hurl your tram on the most terrifying trip you've ever taken!"

Shiver.

Rest up after that one with a trip to **E.T.**'s house. After all, he visited yours. Here you hop aboard your Star Bike and pedal across the moon. "Through the purple perfume fog. To a planet where flowers shower you with songs. And Cloud Bearers, Water Sprites, Jumpums and tickly Moot Moots shower you with love." Only you and E.T. can save the planet, and when you do he'll thank you for it with that sweet little glow of his heart light.

Awwwww.

Enough of that sweet stuff, let's have some 8.3 terror as the earth quakes beneath your feet at the park's shivery-scary **Earthquake.** "It's a heart-pounding, palm-sweating, mind-boggling, train-wrecking 8.3 Earthquake that'll rip the ground out from under you. Bring the world down around you. And swallow you alive in the fire and flood of the most terrifying, natural disaster ever. So awesome you'll wish it was only a movie."

Eeeeeeek!

So you're starting to love this terror stuff? Then bring your teeny-weeny yellow polka-dot bikini, but don't go near the water. Whoops, you did it. You're in there with . . . aaaaaaaa!!! No, no, it's . . . Jaws! "The Great White is back and this time you're in the water with him! Right up to your neck in a part every actor would die for. Nothing can stop him! Nothing stands in the way of nature's most perfect predator as he relentlessly pursues his prey. And you'd better pray for a miracle."

Shriek!

Let's ease up a bit here and buckle up for a ride **Back to the Future** with Doc Brown. "Climbing, diving, banking and blasting you back to the dinosaurs at the Dawn of Time. Rocketing you to Venice for a brush with Da Vinci. Whooshing you right through Niagara Falls. Literally hanging you up on the brink of disaster and teetering on the edge, then taking you over, plunging you down, down, down in the steepest drop imaginable." A sight, sound, and total sensory combination of seven-story-high OmniMax surround screens, space-age flight simulators, and live, cinemagic special effects. . . .

Wheee!

Is that . . . Is that . . . ? No, no, it's the Green Gobbler and the Terror Dogs. "A ghastly gathering of the ghoulish stars of one of the highest grossing films ever made! It's a brought-to-life attack by the dearly departed. An over, under, around, and see-through blitz of banshees, demons, spirits, and specters ready to slime at any time. But when the **Ghostbusters** fight back, look out! The Neutrana beams cross, the ectoplasmic energy explodes, the Stay Puft Marshmallow Man blows his top and everybody gets creamed!"

Ergggg!

Bzzzzzz . . . it's The Fly. And Frankenstein. And the Phantom of the Opera. Naw, it's all make-up and you'll learn how it's done at the park's **Phantom of the Opera Horror Make-Up Show** under the tutelage of masters of make-up.

Uggggghly.

Whodunnit? You dunnit, working with Angela Lansbury at the **"Murder She Wrote" Post Production Theater.** Here you become executive producer and do all the work from picking the star to getting it in on budget and on time.

Hmmmm.

Well, that's just a sample—there's also an **Animal Actors Stage,** starring everyone from Lassie to a huge alligator; a **Screen Test Adventure Studio,** where you'll be videotaped starring in a famous movie or one you plan yourself; **Nickelodeon,** the kid stuff that's been sweeping the nation. . . .

Fun goes on and on and on here at this new attraction, and at least some of the fun changes every day as this giant studio goes about its filming business as it entertains you.

There's no question about it—even Scrooge would love this place. Universal (tel. 363-8000) is open daily from 9am to 11pm, with hours varying in summer, on holidays, and for special events. Admission is $30.74 for adults, $24.38 for children 3 to 11; under 3, free.

## SEA WORLD OF FLORIDA

Racing right along nipping at Mickey's tail is Sea World, 7007 Sea World Dr. at the I-4 Sea World exit (tel. 351-3600), the largest marine-life theme park in the world—to see it all will take six to eight hours! Fifteen different shows are topped by star **Shamu,** the immense 4,500-pound killer whale who doesn't look to me like he'd kill anything larger than a shrimp. Shamu rides his trainer lovingly around on his back, kisses pretty girls and children, and is a somewhat hefty danseuse who performs a delicate ballet, but with no toe shoes. Dolphins, sea lions, and otters cavort on command here, and there's a talented ski team that at last check were telling—on waterskis—the story of a pirate band.

Sea World has built a huge home—Shamu Stadium—for its precious performer and all his look-alike killer whale brothers and sisters. Those big bruisers are bred here and some perform in this special stadium, which features 5,000,000 gallons of water and a performing pool 35 feet deep. Shamu's home is the largest single-species research and display facility in the world, Sea World claims, and who can dispute it? Just seeing these massive creatures is worth the visit, but seeing one of them merrily racing about with a proportionately teensy human being on its back is downright mindboggling. You'll love it.

A spine-chilling attraction at this massive park is the **Shark Encounter,** which features those fearsome denizens of the deep swimming happily (we hope) around in a tank made of enormously thick clear acrylic. You ride right among *Jaws* stars aboard a People-Mover that glides you through the tunnel while those toothy little fellows swim all around you. There are dolphins to play with, a fascinating coral reef to examine, a Caribbean tidal pool, plumed birds roaming free, a 400-foot skytower. Eight theme restaurants at the park are always open when the park is, from 9am to 7pm, to 10pm in summer and on holidays. Admission is $25.40 for adults, $21.15 for children 3 to 9 (under 3, free). A week-long pass is available—$28.95 for adults, $24.95 for children. Parking and kennels are free too.

In recent years this massive water-theme park has been thinking pink, well, black-and-white-and-pink, in honor of a mama killer whale who produced a new baby whose birth was filmed to produce quite a showy arrival for little Baby Shamu. You can see the new baby performing right alongside Mama in quite a touching little debut.

Snow is something you see precious little of in Florida—for which many are devoutly thankful. But here at Sea World, you can get a warm look at the snowy world of the South Pole on a visit to the **Penguin Encounter.** Here hundreds of formally clad little waddlers gaze quizzically at that weird bunch of folks in shorts and halters gathered outside their snowy world. There's nary a shiver in sight inside where, in fact, those odd little coots seem to be wondering why anyone would want to build a sand castle when they could have a nice roll in the snow.

To add to its snowy scenery, Sea World added a show called **Snow Fliers,** which features a high-flying troop of free-style stunt skiers zipping and zagging around Florida's only ski slope.

**Window to the Sea,** another comparatively new addition to the park, is a multimedia presentation that takes you behind the scenes at Sea World and to the bottom of the ocean, where a mini-submarine reports to you on the health and welfare of things down under.

It takes 5 to 7 hours to see this sea.

**READER'S SEA WORLD RECOMMENDATION:** "I would recommend taking the behind-the-scenes tour. Not only is it interesting (we got to see manatees, which aren't on view to the general public), but you get reserved seats at the Shamu show at the end of your tour. I also recommend getting to Sea World first thing in the morning. It takes a long time to see it all. Look up feeding times of various animals . . . it is an absolute thrill to feed a seal or sea lion or dolphin, and feeding times are limited. At the end of the day, the Polynesian Luau [see our Nightlife recommendations for more on this] is great fun . . . you should call ahead of time . . . when it's over you can catch the last show, perhaps, but at least see the fireworks and go look at your favorite animal display again" (Neil Loeb, Atlanta, Ga.). [*Authors' Note:* You must make reservations in advance for the behind-the-scenes tour, which costs $5.95 for adults, $4.95 for children, and is available from 9am to 3pm. It's a 90-minute tour, part on foot and part on short bus rides.]

## WET 'N WILD

Orlando's answer to the beach is Wet 'N Wild, at 6200 International Dr., off I-4, via exit Fla. 435 South (tel. 351-3200). Every kind of watery fun is available here, from bumper to speedboats, a surf pool where constant four-foot waves are produced by a machine. There are white-water slideways and a kamikaze slide that sends you whooshing down into a pool from a platform six stories up in the air! You can try a tiny pool with squirty games for toddlers, a Corkscrew Flume that spirals you through a figure-eight and tunnel, even a Bonzai Boggan water roller coaster that races at 30 m.p.h. into a pool. You can picnic by the lake or stoke up at the snackbars. Admission is $17.95 for adults, $15.95 for children 3 to 13, free to others. It's open daily mid-February to November from 10am to 6pm.

## MYSTERY FUN HOUSE

Get lost in the mirror maze, try to figure out the topsy-turvy room, walk the magic floor here in the weird Mystery Fun House, at 5767 Major Boulevard off I-4 at Fla. 435 North (tel. 351-3355). The price is $6.95 adults or children. Hours are 10am to 11pm daily.

## REPTILE WORLD

Some people do really strange things for a living, and one of them is the person who milks the cobra and other precious vipers at Reptile World **Serpentarium,** 5705 E. Irlo Bronson Memorial Hwy., St. Cloud (tel. 892-6905). You can see that and more than 60 varieties of reptiles, from lizards to crocodiles, Tuesday through Sunday from 9am to 5:30pm (venom extractions are at 11am, and 2 and 5pm). Admission is $3.75 for adults, $2.75 for children 6 to 17, $1.75 for children 3 to 5.

## GATORLAND

If you know someone you'd like to feed to an alligator, you can get in a little practice with some dead fish or chicken at Gatorland, on US 441, 14501 S. Orange Blossom Trail, just north of Kissimmee (tel. 855-5496). They've recently trained those toothsome creatures to leap into the air, a feat quite uncommon for these ground-loving creatures. Have your picture taken with a boa constrictor and ride a train through all the creatures' homes from 8am to 7pm, later in summer. Admission is $6.95 for adults, $4.95 for children 3 to 11.

## RIVERSHIP GRAND ROMANCE

When the fantasylands overcome you, one way to escape to something different is to sail off on the *Grand Romance,* which cruises the waterways of the historic St. Johns River on brunch, lunch, dinner, and two-day cruises. There's entertainment on board this brand-new triple-decked ship too, but just standing out on the deck and watching the world float by is entertainment enough.

Operated by American River Cruises, the 135-foot sidewheeler is a detailed replica of the steamers that sailed the St. Johns River at the turn of the century. It's luxurious and elegant with Tiffany-style lamps, teak trim, jewel-toned carpeting, and gleaming brass. You can dance on the craft's large floor or watch the activity from a seat on the mezzanine deck's grand balcony. Viewfinders will make their way to the River Rascal's Panoramic Lounge for a sweeping view of this little-known river.

As did her predecessor, the *Rivership Romance,* the *Grand Romance* will also sail on two-day trips from Sanford to Jacksonville with an overnight stop in Palatka, where guests stay in a riverfront hotel. Lunch cruises depart daily at 11am, dinner-dance trips at 7:30pm. Adult fares are $26 to $35 for luncheon cruises, $35 to $45 for dinner-dance sailings, and $223 per person for the two-day cruises to Jacksonville. Children 3 to 12 pay half fare on day cruises. You'll find the ship at the Monroe Harbor Marina, 433 N. Palmetto Ave. in Sanford (tel. 407/321-5091, toll free 800/423-7401, or US/Canada 800/225-7999). Reservations are required.

Aviation buffs should fly on over to **Flying Tigers Warbird Air Museum,** 231 N. Airport Rd. (Hoagland Boulevard), Kissimmee (tel. 933-1942), where you will see workers carefully renovating World War II aircraft. Many varieties of planes are in various stages of restoration here including a B-24 Liberator, two of the B-25 Mitchells featured in the 30-seconds-over-Tokyo raid, a TBM Avenger, and some antique aircraft including a DeHavilland Tiger Moth. Most of the planes can fly, but those that can't make for an interesting look at what gets us off the ground. Hours are 9am to 5pm daily, and admission is $5 for adults, $4 for children under 12.

## XANADU

Excuse us, we must just ring Robutler for a towel so we can pop into the spa. If this is what life in the 21st century is going to be like, let's all hope we make it. At Xanadu, US 192 and Fla. 535 (tel. 396-1992), they are convinced that they know just how we all will be living in days to come. It looks good to us! You can see if it looks good to you by stopping in at this Styrofoam mushroom of a house that sprouts in all fantasy, just down the road from, of all things, Medieval Times. Talk about time warps.

At Xanadu, which is certainly 21st century in materials, design, and architecture, you'll find a really intriguing look into the future of home construction. Circular rooms flow into each other. There's an indoor pool, a waterfall-spa in the master bedroom, a solar sauna, a greenhouse, sunken conversation pit, electronic hearth, projection television, a "house brain," security center, computer-voice command center, a central vacuum system, electronic exercise equipment, and best of all, a robot butler who never frosts you with a chilly "Really, madam." Make way, Jeeves.

You can't miss Xanadu—just look for the weirdest sight on US 192 heading east from I-4. It's open daily from 10am to 10pm (be there 45 minutes before closing time to make the tour), and admission is $4.95 for adults, free for children under 10.

## A FEW OFFBEAT ATTRACTIONS

If you still think steaks come from a steak factory, roam over to Kissimmee's weekly **cattle auction,** where you'll see real cowboys roping the main attraction of tonight's dinner. Steaks-on-the-hoof are auctioned off to cattle barons who look more like punchers than princes at this boots-and-jeans event every Wednesday— early (say, 8am)—at the city's Livestock Market, just north of US 17/92 and US 441, at 150 E. Donegan Ave. (tel. 847-3521). When the shouting's over (about noon), you can lunch at the Auction House while cowboys chase your dinner around outside. There's no admission charge.

Those plastic containers you use to grow green fuzzy things in your refrigerator are people too, you know. What's more they have a history, and you can find out all about it at **Tupperware's International Headquarters,** on US 441 and US 17/92, just south of Orlando (tel. 847-3111), which maintains a museum of food containers and tells you how they're made and what to make of them. It's open from 9am to 4pm Monday to Friday, free.

At Clermont, about 25 minutes west of Orlando on US 27, you can zoom to the top of **Florida Citrus Tower** (tel. 904/394-8585), the highest observation point in the state, and gaze out over 2,000 square miles of rolling hills and sparkling emerald citrus trees laden with orange and gold fruit. It's quite a sight, and later you can visit a glassblower's workshop, a citrus packing plant, and a candy kitchen, as well as send oranges home to frozen friends. Open daily from 8am to 6pm, the tower charges $5 for adults, $3 for students 10 to 15; younger children are free.

If you love uniforms, you shouldn't miss Friday at the **Orlando Naval Training Center,** off Corinne Drive, north of Fla. 50, also called Colonial Boulevard (tel. 646-4474), when the gobs graduate complete with 50-state salute, navy band, Bluejacket chorus, and drill team. Festivities begin at 9:45am and are free. Enter at General Reese Road.

Watch oranges go in one side while gumdrops and other dentist's delights come out the other at the **Citrus Candy Factory,** on US 27 in Dundee (tel. 439-1698). It's open from 8am to 6pm daily, later in summer, and free.

See top harness horses train from 8am to noon daily except Sunday from October through April at **Ben White Raceway,** at US 441 and 1905 Lee Rd. (tel. 293-8721); free.

**Orlando Science Center,** Loch Haven Park, 810 E. Rollins St. at US 17/92, Orlando (tel. 896-7151), amuses with an intriguing assortment of hands-on science exhibits and a planetarium. Hours at the center are 9am to 5pm weekdays (to 9pm on Friday), noon to 9pm on Saturday, and noon to 5pm on Sunday. Admission is $4 for adults, $3 for children 4 through 18. On weekends the center presents cosmic rock concerts, otherwise known as laser light shows, at 9, 10 and 11pm. Admission is $4.

Somehow we just knew it would happen. Right. Elvis Presley (!) has joined the fantasy world of Orlando attractions. Yessirree, step right up to the **Elvis Presley Museum,** 7200 International Dr., in Dowdy Plaza (tel. 345-9427). Here lives Elvis's bed, Elvis's Harley Davidson, Elvis's concert belts, Elvis's wardrobe, furniture, paintings, jewelry, glasses, gun collection, karate ghi, and oh-golly-gosh, Elvis's very own racing jumpsuit. (There's yet another Elvis Museum in Kissimmee, on US 192, 1.5 miles east of I-4, where several of Elvis's cars are displayed.) Admission is $4 for adults, $3 for children 7 to 10. Hours are 9am to 10pm daily.

If you revel in getting a look at star things, stop by another **Elvis Museum,** Old Town Shopping Center, 5770 W. Irlo Bronson Memorial Hwy., Kissimmee (tel. 396-8594 or 827-6153), where you can see still more of Elvis's stuff. You'll find this spot 1.5 miles east of I-4 on US 192 in the Old Town shopping complex. Admission is $4 for adults, $3 for children 7 to 10, and the hours here are 10am to 10pm daily.

**Central Florida Zoological Park,** US 17/92 at I-4 exit 52, at Lake Monroe in Sanford (tel. 323-4450), is home to more than 200 wild and exotic animals that occupy some pretty acreage. 'Gators, crocs, lions, and tigers stare back at you here, and the zoo also has pony rides, a children's zoo, animal-feeding demonstrations on weekends, and an elevated nature trail through a swamp. Hours are 9am to 5pm daily, and admission is $5 for adults, $2 for children 3 to 12. Take exit 52 from I-4 to find the zoo.

**READER'S RECOMMENDATIONS:** "**Walt Disney World** is flawless and the place one should go if a person could only make one trip in a lifetime. **Sea World** is certainly worth the time and the Shark Encounter is very impressive . . . the dolphin and stingray petting pools are super. Everyone should avail themselves of the guided tour there or anywhere else for that matter as they are always informative, get you behind the scenes. **Medieval Times,** a comparatively new Orlando attraction, features dinner and a jousting tournament—I'm enraptured

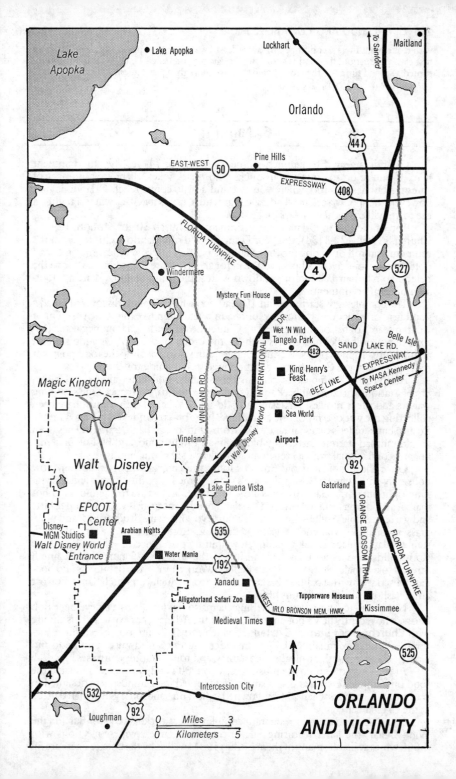

with that era but I was skeptical . . . to say the least I was more than pleasantly surprised. It's a first-class production, the food is good, the show is beyond belief. I enjoyed it so much I returned a second time and the second night felt like more than just a guest. I felt like a friend" (Carol Brown, Las Vegas, Nev.).

---

## 6. Nightlife

Orlando's geared to families, so there's plenty of wholesome entertainment here. If you're up to your ears in ducks who quack jokes, there are a number of parent-getaway spots too, where you can find a little comic relief. Orlando is not, however, the spot to seek razzle-dazzle nightclubs, nor is it a place where a night on the town will cost you two days on the job.

Top of the line in Orlando entertainment is **Church Street Station,** 129 W. Church St. (tel. 422-2434), the Walt Disney World of Orlando nightlife. From the moment you roll onto downtown Orlando's Church Street and hear the first nasal notes of a steam-driven calliope, you're in for an adventure. Here you can rise to the heights in a hot-air balloon or get down with some funky singing, dancing, foot-stomping entertainment.

The complex got started about 10 years ago when Orlando discovered it had a good grip on today and tomorrow, but hadn't yet begun to exploit the past. Out it went in search of history and turned up Church Street Station, a long-neglected railroad depot on brick-lined streets right in the center of some of Orlando's oldest architecture. Topped by a silver cupola, the aging station became the focal point for redevelopment and Church Street Station was the crowning touch.

A rip-roarin' complex of saloons, restaurants, and entertainment, Church Street Station whizzes you back to days of banjos and bar-top cancan girls, singing waiters and silent movies, Dixieland and do-si-do. What a laugh it must have been collecting the wacky array of bric-a-brac here: huge brass chandeliers salvaged from a Boston bank, teller's cages vintage 1870 from a Pittsburgh bank, train benches from an old railroad station, cast-iron tables from an English pub, and best of all, a mahogany confessional from a French monastery as a telephone booth.

Once the dilapidated old Strand Hotel, the entertainment emporium now houses five fun centers: Rosie O'Grady's Good Time Emporium, a razzle-dazzle saloon right out of the Gay '90s (or is it the Roaring '20s?) with a belt-'em-out red-hot mama, a crooning minstrel singer, Dixieland band, cancan girls with swishing skirts and garters; Apple Annie's Courtyard, a purveyor of kebabs, fruit drinks, and bluegrass music; Lili Marlene's Aviator's Pub and Restaurant, a quieter spot with stained-glass transoms, oak paneling, a walnut fireplace once the possession of the Rothschilds, and French-flavored cuisine in the $15 to $25 range; and Church Street's token male, Phineas Phogg's Balloon Works, purveyors of burgers and boogie, a disco spot with a balloon-basket balcony from which you watch dancers cavort amid flashing strobes and puffs of fog.

Never one to quit when everything seems to be done, Rosie's developer Bob Snow, who recently flew a hot-air balloon over the Atlantic, has expanded his empire with **Church Street Station Exchange,** which turns 87,000 square feet into a Victorian marketplace inhabited by Commander Ragtime's Midway of Fun Food and Games, complete with carnival, video games, and roller-skating waitresses.

At the Orchid Garden the music focuses on '50's and '60's rock 'n roll and the food on flaming desserts and specialty coffees served in an atmosphere designed to transport you to days when chiffon-gowned ladies and handsome gentlemen danced at the Crystal Palace.

You'll also find another restaurant complex here, **Cracker's Oyster Bar** and the **Wine Cellar,** the latter featuring one of the state's largest wine collections with 4,000 wines available, many of them by the glass as well as by the bottle. There are 50 imported beers on tap here at Cracker's and a wide variety of Creole cookery plus oysters, shrimp, clams, and other raw-bar treats. Entrées are in the $10 to $15 range, and hours are 11am to midnight at this one.

Finally, if you like a rootin', tootin' good time, there's no better place to look than the **Cheyenne Saloon and Opera House.** So authentic is this good-time emporium that even an appearance by Wyatt Earp wouldn't turn heads. Brass and etched glass, hand-turned wood, authentic costumes, all executed by the same skillful hands that put together the phenomenally successful Church Street Station. What are you waiting for? Get out your jeans and red bandanna, your boots and silver buckle, and get on over there, pardner. There's a bellying-up spot at the bar with your name on it. Everything's open from 11am to 2am.

**Church Street Station** is the number one, not-to-be-missed star in Orlando's nightlife firmament. Cover charge from 5pm is $14.95, which admits you to all the shows and entertainment going on here—and for $10 more you can get a pass good for a year. If you are just interested in dining at Lili Marlene's or Cracker's, you can do so without paying the cover charge. You can even book a champagne hot-air balloon flight here for $140 per person.

In 1989, Walt Disney World opened **Pleasure Island** (tel. 934-7781), a cluster of six nightclubs, six restaurants, a slew of movie theaters, and a dozen shops. Here the legend has something to do with being tossed up on—you guessed it—a pleasure island.

One does not come here to hear legends, however, one comes here to *make* them.

A play place of note, Pleasure Island begins at the glittering *Empress Lilly* double-decker paddlewheeler, which has three restaurants. Add to those the Portobello Yacht Club Restaurant, where northern Italian flavors and a to-die-for chocolate fantasy await, the Fireworks Factory, where barbecue reigns, and Merriweathers Food Market, an upscale counter-service spot. Prices are in the $10 to $20 range, less at Merriweather's, more in the Empress Room on the *Empress Lilly.*

Dining is probably not the reason you come here, however. Dancing is—in every kind of environment from a zappy, flashy disco to a club in which you ease back into the '30s. Nightclub opportunities are many and varied. Contemporary dance music—that's a euphemism for disco—rocks at **Mannequin's Dance Palace.** **Zephyr Rockin' Rollerdrome** plays 50's and 60's rock 'n roll in a beach party theme: shades of Sh-boom, Sh-boom. At the **Neon Armadillo,** feet tap to country and western tunes; at **Videopolis,** banks of video screens bend the mind to match the progressive, alternative music that provides backdrop here; and for yuks, the crowds head for the **Comedy Warehouse.** Most Disney-ish diversion of the lot is the **Adventurer's Club,** a re-creation of a 1930's nightclub featuring themed entertainment of that era.

Every night is New Year's Eve at Pleasure Island. At the stroke of varying witching hours, every nightclub has its own New Year's Eve celebration. Meanwhile, outside fireworks boom, bands and deejays play on the streets, and dancers cavort on rooftops.

Boppers over 21 can go to all the clubs; those between 18 and 21 cannot be served alcohol, but can cavort at the Neon Armadillo, Videopolis, the Adventurer's Club, and the Comedy Warehouse. Youngsters under 18 can go to all these spots but only when accompanied by a parent.

Shops on the island open at 10am, clubs open at 7pm and close at 2am. A ticket allowing admission to all five clubs is $9.95 for any age. Those who want to try one of the restaurants can do so without paying the cover charge. Drink prices range from $2.50 to $4.50. To find out what special events are going on, call 934-7182.

Among the more amusing things to do on Pleasure Island is put your mug on a mag! First, you run down your list of fantasy lives, choose the magazine cover you'd most like to grace, don yourself in one of the wigs and wild costumes they stock here by the hundreds, then step right into the photographer's haven and watch the birdie. When the snapping's over, you'll find your photograph on the cover of anything from *New Woman* to *Field and Stream, Modern Bride, Ski, Rock,* and, for the paperdoll set, *Barbie Magazine*—what else?

Island shops are stocked with all the usual Disney World memorabilia as well as some interesting fashion items, but the unsurpassed trinkets of choice are narrow plastic bands that fit around an ankle or a neck and glow happily in the dark in riveting shades of magenta, lime, or lavender.

Bands, deejays, records, singers, and occasionally stars, populate these clubs, which wind around in a maze of lanes that really are on a small island. A single ticket covers admission to all the clubs here. There is a separate admission charge to the movie theaters—$2.95 for matinees, $5.95 for nighttime shows. There is no admission if you're headed here for dining alone. You pay only if your toes are tapping and you're taking them dancing.

A similar nighttime attraction, this one to be called the **Disney Boardwalk,** is slated to appear in 1991 near the site of two new hotels, the Swan and the Dolphin, now rising near the entrance to Walt Disney World.

If you're convinced that all a man needs is a good hoss and a plate of beans, you will find many who agree at **Fort Liberty,** 5260 W. Irlo Bronson Memorial Hwy., Kissimmee (tel. 351-5151, or toll free 800/641-5151; 800/521-5152 in Florida). Don those high-heeled boots and red bandannas and git on over here where Orlando Entertains, creators of King Henry's Feast and Mardi Gras, entertains yet again with a gaggle of cowboys and Indians who whoop it up every night in an old fort.

Sprawling over 11 acres, Fort Liberty does actually offer you more than horses and beans: You're served ranch stew and biscuits, corn-on-the-cob, baked beans, barbecued pork, Southern fried chicken, unlimited wine, beer, and other accoutrements. You can get into the act here—there's plenty of audience participation—or you can just lean back on your haunches and watch Buffalo Bill's traveling medicine show shoot'em up. Price of this rowdy-dow evening is $25.95 for adults, $17.95 for children 3 through 11.

Veiled ladies and magic stallions, carpets that fly and horses that seem to, it's all part of midnight at the Orlando oasis in a spot called **Arabian Nights,** 6225 W. Irlo Bronson Memorial Hwy., Kissimmee (tel. 239-9223, or toll free 800/553-6116, 800/396-7400 in Florida). Mecca for equine enthusiasts, Arabian Nights will charm you right down to the bells on your toes with its production, which focuses on a princess and her genie, off on a magic carpet trip to find her the perfect horse.

Along the way she—and you—meet those fabulously beautiful, high-stepping, airs-above-the-ground Lippizan stallions, plus purebred, worth-a-fortune Arabian steeds, fancy-stepping Percherons and Andalusians, speedy quarter horses, big-footed Clydesdales, even a 30-inch-high miniature pony who will certainly steal your heart. There are people riding all these lovely creatures, but who looks at people when you can gaze upon a Lippizan?

To get a look at what the horsey set is all about, trot on over here for an evening that includes a dinner of French onion soup, chicken, ribs, beer, wine or soft drinks, and the show. Admission for show and dinner is $25.94 for adults, $16.95 for children 3 through 11, and showtime is 7:30pm usually but may vary. Some evenings there may be two shows, so give them a call first to see what's happening.

Some of us go to Germany and some of us settle for the Orlando version of Oktoberfest, which occurs nightly at the **Bavarian Bierhaus,** 7340 Republic Dr., Orlando (tel. 351-0191). Here they roll out the barrels—and barrels and barrels—to keep German good spirits rollicking, literally and figuratively. Add to that wienerschnitzel, spaetzle dumplings, strudel, fat pretzels, curlicue radishes, and you've got a memorable evening. Dinners are in the $7 to $12 range, and this biergarten is open every night but Monday from 5pm until the last yodeler weaves out the door.

Shoobee, doobee, doo, it's time to shake, rattle, and roll your way over to **Little Darlin's Rock 'n' Roll Palace,** 5770 W. Irlo Bronson Memorial Hwy. (tel. 396-

6499), where they're rocking around the clock in poodle skirts and saddle shoes. Here you step through a huge jukebox and drop about 25 years as you twist along to the sounds of the Shirelles, the Platters, Little Anthony, Fabian, and all the legends of the R&R era, many of whom make personal appearances here. Hours are noon to 2am daily, and admission is $8.50 for adults or for children.

Britain's lusty King Henry VIII and his bevy of beauteous brides are the focus of one of Orlando's nighttime fantasy spots, an evening of fun, feast, and general frolic known hereabouts as **King Henry's Feast,** 8984 International Dr., Orlando (tel. 351-5151, or toll free outside Florida 800/776-3501). Enter the fortified royal court and find yourself dropping back a few centuries to days of yore, when that overstuffed monarch presided over many a zany evening.

Here in Orlando the fun begins with a sip of mead, that fermented honey-based drink that kept heads rolling back in Henry's day. From there, it's on to a five-course banquet accompanied by limitless quantities of beer, wine, and soft drinks. Lift a flagon with Henry as you work your way through a feast that begins with soup and proceeds through freshly baked brown bread, salad, a palate cleanser of rainbow sherbet, chicken and ribs with sauces, vegetables, potatoes, and a finale of chocolate mousse.

As you dine, court jesters clown around, a magician shows you some fancy digital work, singers warble up a madrigal storm, and dancers in traditional court dress of the period perform for the sovereign and his royal hangers-on.

Reigning over it all is portly but powerful Henry, king of all he surveys. Possessor of a powerful voice and a solidly dramatic presence, Henry will, in seconds, have you believing yours may be the next head to roll! He's quite wonderful, as are all the cast members, particularly Henry's handsome sidekick.

All this takes place in what surely is one of Orlando's strangest sights: a moated fortification that rises up in the midst of sleek hotels like a medieval hallucination. Created by a British company of considerable imagination, King Henry's Feast is a $3.5-million creation of English stone, brick, timber, and fancy roofing tiles, topped by a 60-foot tower. Its equally imposing interior includes seating at long tables served by wine-wielding wenches. There's not a bad seat in the house and the show is quite tastefully done, great fun for children, who are worked right into the action on stage.

You can dine with royalty for $25.95 for adults, $17.95 for children 3 to 11. You'll find Henry chomping and stomping usually at 6 and 8:30pm daily, and usually at 8pm on Sunday. Show times frequently vary and this evening entertainment is often sold out, so reservations are nearly mandatory.

Those same clever Britishers who created Henry and crowd went right on up the street and opened **Mardi Gras,** 8445 International Dr. (tel. 351-5151, or toll free 800/776-3501). Designed to cash in on the nation's current fascination with all things Louisienne, this new nightspot is tucked away in a shopping complex called Mercado Festival Center, which has other nighttime amusements as well.

At Mardi Gras the fun begins at 6 or 9pm nightly (at 8pm on Sunday). You're greeted with a frosty mint julep to get things going. Then you move on to gumbo, pasta salad, blackened chicken or Cajun-barbecued fish, spicy red beans and jambalaya, cornbread muffins, and long-grained rice cooked with a Cajun smoked-pork sausage called andouille. Topper is a praline parfait.

A jazz orchestra entertains during dinner. Then as the house lights dim, out romp leggy, bespangled dancers who whiz you off on a fantasy trip to carnivals around the world from an evening in Paris to Carnaval in the Caribbean. You spend some time at the circus and meet cancan girls. Admission to this glittery production is $17.95 for adults for dinner, show, and a drink; and $19.95 for children 3 to 11.

These days, Orlando's seeming-boundless fascination with fantasy seems to be taking medieval form. At **Medieval Times,** 4510 W. Irlo Bronson Memorial Hwy., Kissimmee (tel. 396-1518) you can, as they say, thrill to the sounds of yesteryear as knights on horseback race by defending someone's honor. Medieval tournaments, complete with jousting and good-guys/bad-guys swordplay amuses you as you dine on chicken, ribs, pastry, light potables. An interesting $2-million addition to the park is a medieval village called Raimonburg, which comes complete with artisans demonstrating the talents of that era from glassblowing to weaving, enamel crafting, and blacksmithery. You can get yourself locked up in a village jail, sample medieval fare, and get a look at the latest in sadistic crafts at the torture chamber. Hours at the Village are 10am to the end of the last performance each evening (about 10pm), and admission to the Village is $5 for adults, $3 for children 3 through 12. A family entertainment, the dinner-and-show event begins at 6 or 8:30pm (the castle opens at 6pm), takes about two hours, and costs $26 for adults and $18 for children 3 through 12.

In the Magic Kingdom, the Contemporary Hotel hosts a constant round of entertainment at its **Top of the World Restaurant** (tel. 824-3611) and there's always a band for dancing. **Polynesian Resort Hotel** (tel. 824-2000) is a fantasyland of lights and lagoons that's practically entertainment in itself, but the hotel also has Polynesian luaus every night outdoors at the Luau Cove. Island dancing and music transport you to the land of grass skirts and wiggles at $29 for adults, $15 to $23 for children depending on age. Luaus are at 6:45 and 9:30pm.

**Empress Lilly**'s banjo-strumming lounge has nightly entertainment, and there's no cover or minimum. Over in the village at **Lake Buena Vista,** the lounge is one of the area's top spots for jazz, with the vibes emanating from about 8pm nightly. All the hotels in Lake Buena Vista (see our hotel recommendations) also have nightly entertainment. In summer and at Christmas, when the Magic Kingdom blazes with fireworks, there's no better place to watch than from the **Top of the Lodge** at TraveLodge.

There is also the new fun-and-games showplace at Walt Disney World Village. Called **Pleasure Island,** this new evening entertainment area opened in 1989 on six acres near the Shopping Village on Buena Vista Lagoon and features six nightclubs, including one in which the backdrop is provided by a group of friendly ghosts and one at which you dance on roller skates! Admission prices range from $6 for a one-club pass to $14.95 for a five-club entrance pass; special rates for children. Call 934-7781 for reservations.

**Sea World** also has a Polynesian Luau and show that's fun for the whole family: fire dancers, lovely Polynesians who swivel at 75 r.p.m., and a bountiful luau buffet. It's at 6:45pm, and all-inclusive admission is $24.95 for adults, $9.95 to $17.45 for children depending on age. Call 345-5195 for reservations.

Elsewhere around town, the **Langford Hotel,** at Interlachen and East New England avenues in Winter Park (tel. 644-3400), has outstanding musical entertainment sometimes with a small cover charge and jackets are required.

**Limey Jim's** at the Orlando Hyatt, I-4 and US 192 (tel. 293-4100), is another good spot for entertainment, as is **Piccadilly Pub** in the Gold Key Inn, 7100 S. Orange Blossom Trail (tel. 855-0050).

In Winter Park, a favorite gathering spot is **Shooter's,** 4315 N. Orange Blossom Trail (tel. 298-2855). This is a trendy, waterfront spot where you can see and be seen, imbibe, and listen to a lively band that plays nightly. Hours are noon to the a.m. No cover.

If you have a pressing desire to meet some of the kids of the Kingdom on their off-duty hours, begin your search at the **Giraffe Lounge** at the Hotel Royal Plaza in Lake Buena Vista (tel. 828-2828), where they congregate. Top-40 music is on tap daily here.

If you're looking for a yuppie, look at **Murphy's Vine Street Emporium,** 4736 W. Irlo Bronson Memorial Hwy., Kissimmee (tel. 396-7469 or 239-7171). A massive building seating 600, this dining and dancing and imbibing spot offers lots of flash and sizzle with live entertainment most nights. Cover charge in the emporium, which is the dance center—steak and seafood is served in Murphy's Lobster House next door—is $2 to $4.

**Crawdaddy's** rocks in several Florida locations, but here in Orlando its in the Star Quality Resort, 5905 International Dr. (tel. 351-2100). Entertainment is lively and there's plenty of food and drink at this spot, which is open daily to the wee hours, with happy hour from 4 to 7pm nightly.

Ninety-nine bottles of beer on the wall, 99 bottles of beer, tum-de-dum-dum. You can tune up to that old tune at the **Laughing Kookaburra,** where there are indeed 99 varieties of beer from which to choose. There also are showbands, dancing, nightly special cocktails, and plenty of laughs. An upmarket watering hole, the Kookaburra begins chattering at 5pm, when there's an extensive complimentary happy-hour buffet simmering, and remains kooky until 3am daily. It's in the Buena Vista Palace Hotel, 1900 Buena Vista Dr., in Walt Disney World Village (tel. 827-2727).

**J.J. Whispers,** 5100 Adamson St., Orlando (tel. 629-4779), has become quite a hot spot in recent years. Several nightclubs under one roof, this rocking spot is unmarked, but you'll find it—just look for a million or so cars! The disco is called City Lights and is open Tuesday through Sunday. Whispers Show Room features a band for dancing the same days, and several smaller rooms are for those who want to hear themselves along with the music. Hours are 8pm to 2am, and the cover charge is $3 to $5.

**Townsend's Fish House and Tavern,** 35 W. Michigan St., Orlando (tel. 422-5560), has lots of woodsy-plantsy atmosphere, marble bars, and miles of brass and copper trim. There's live entertainment here most nights, a wine bar, and plenty of burgers, fried veggies, and of course, fish. There's no cover charge and hours are 11:30am to 2pm weekdays and 5:30 to 10:30pm daily for lunch and dinner, much later in the tavern.

**Freddie's,** the popular steak house on US 17/92 in Fern Park (tel. 339-3256) (see the Orlando restaurant recommendations), can be counted on to present a songster on weekends and often other days of the week as well.

Not far from Walt Disney World, **Hollywood Nites,** formerly The Worst Bar in the Delta Court of Flags Hotel, 5715 Major Blvd., Orlando (tel. 351-3340), seems to be far from that description to the crowds who flock here. Of course, worst does have a variety of interpretations. No doubt all of them are a topic of discussion at this decibelistic spot that has some kind of party gimmick going every night of the year, and a rock 'n' roll band plays nightly except Sunday and Monday. Any night, however, you will find things rocking here among Hollywood memorabilia to 2am.

**Sullivan's Trailway Lounge** is one of the few stayers on the Orlando nightlife scene. It's been around since the early 1970s. Often jammed, Sullivan's features such stars as Mel Tillis and Moe Bandy if they're here, but most of the time it's top touring and local bands onstage at 1108 S. Orange Blossom Trail (tel. 843-2934). There's a $2 to $3 cover charge.

The **Civic Theatre of Central Florida,** 1010 Princeton St., Orlando (tel. 896-7365), has been lighting up the night with amateur and semiprofessional actors for 60 years now. A community theater, the group now takes to the boards at Loch Haven Park, where the theater has been located for 10 of its 60 years. Curtain time for each of the theater's six plays from January to June is 8pm Wednesday through Saturday, with a 2pm matinee on Sunday. Individual tickets range from $9 to $11 depending on the type of production. Season packages are available, as are student discounts.

Orlando art and cultural activities have increased greatly in recent years. The **Florida Symphony Orchestra** (tel. 896-0331) presents concerts in winter, and **Rollins College** (tel. 646-2233) has a concert series. Tickets are $5 to $10. And now you can attend opera performances by the **Orlando Opera Company** (tel. 896-7575) from November to May for $17.50 to $45.

A **Bach Festival** (tel. 646-2110) takes place in Winter Park during the last week of February.

Orlando's **Ballet Royal** (tel. 647-2717) performs several times a year, including the *Nutcracker* at Christmas. Another dance group, **Dance Unlimited** (tel. 671-2155), has an annual February concert and a spring art festival at Leu Gardens, while **Dance Company of the Academy of Dance and Theatrical Arts** (tel. 645-3847) has both a senior and a children's company performing in spring and in June.

Those dance, opera, and symphonic events normally take place at the **Bob Carr Performing Arts Center,** a 2,500-seat auditorium at 401 Livingston St. (tel. 849-2020, or for tickets 839-3900). Broadway road shows come here to the Carr also.

Add to that the **Annie Russell Theatre** at Rollins College, a fascinating theater in the grand baroque style. A regular series of seven productions runs here from October through May. Learn what is when by calling them at 646-2501.

To find out everything that's happening in the arts in central Florida, pick up a copy of **Center Stage,** a monthly magazine with a centerfold calendar of events. You can reach them at 629-0252 or call a ticket service at 407/839-3900.

---

# 7. Sports

---

If you have any time left after roaming the fascinating attractions here, use it—and some energy—on a round of sports activities.

## GOLF AND TENNIS

Among the loveliest courses in Orlando are those right at Walt Disney World. There are three courses here, the **Magnolia,** the **Palm,** and a course at the **Lake Buena Vista Club.** All three started life as desert sands but have been miraculously converted into tree-lined, water-dotted, hilly areas, interesting enough to challenge golfers on the PGA Tour route, which visits here each year. If you're a golfing fan, you'll find them challenging but not terrifying. All are par-72 courses up to 7,000 yards. Greens fees are $55 for guests of Walt Disney World Resorts, including carts. If you really want to save money, plan your outing for the hours after 3pm, when a lower twilight rate goes into effect for all golfers, resort guests or not. Starter's telephone number is 824-2270. If you've got a young Jack Nicklaus with you, try the **Wee Links,** a course especially designed for young golfers: two feet equal a yard. The cost is $10 for golfers under 17. Adults can play here too, for $13.

Many hotels in Orlando have money-saving arrangements with golf courses, so check before you head off on your own.

Other courses in the area include: **Buenaventura Lakes Country Club,** 301 Buenaventura Blvd., Kissimmee (tel. 348-7611), a par-30 course with $10 greens fees; and **Cypress Creek Country Club,** 5353 Vineland Rd., Orlando (tel. 351-2187), a par-72 course that charges $20 to $40 greens fees including cart.

There are six free asphalt tennis courts at **Oak Street Park,** Palm and Oak streets, Orlando (tel. 847-2388), open from dawn to 10pm.

## BOATING

Drive your own airboat through the backwaters of Kissimmee or rent canoes or electric boats from **U-Drive Airboat Rentals,** 4266 W. Irlo Bronson Memorial Hwy., Kissimmee, six miles east on US 192 (tel. 847-3672). Fees begin at $16 an hour for airboats, $4.50 for canoes or paddleboats, $13 for electric boats. **Walt Disney World Village** at Lake Buena Vista has a variety of boats too.

Rent a houseboat with galley, baths, and air conditioning, and tour the crystal springs of St. Johns River, from **Go Vacations** (tel. 904/736-9422). They're at 2280 Hontoon Rd. in Deland, and the boats are $1,295 to $1,595 a week depending on season.

**Dee's Ski Center,** Rte. 1, Box 595 on North Lake Juliana, in Auburndale (tel. 813/984-1160), has waterskiing instructions for $40 per lesson. Inquire about daily rates. Sailboards are available for $15 per hour and jet-skis for $20 the half hour.

To get there, take I-4 exit 21 (County Road 559) one mile south toward Auburndale, then turn right on Lundy Road.

**Ski Holidays** likes to call itself the largest waterskiing instructional group in the world, and who can prove otherwise? Skiing takes place at Lake Bryan, a clear, 350-acre spring-fed lake just minutes from the Disney hotel complex. Services range from instructional programs for first-timers to advanced training on a competition slalom course. Boat, driver, skis—the works—all for $75 per hour for as many skiers as you wish. Jet-ski rentals go for $30 a half hour or you can thrill to a parasail flight at $35 per flight, which includes a full training course.

You can write to the company for a brochure at P.O. Box 22007, Lake Buena Vista, FL 32830 (tel. 407/239-4444). To get to the skiing area, take I-4 to the Lake Buena Vista exit, turn south on County Road 535 toward Kissimmee (away from Walt Disney World), and about 200 yards south you'll see a sign directing you to the school and the lake.

## PARI-MUTUEL SPORTS

Greyhounds chase but never catch the electronic bunny at **Seminole Greyhound Park,** 2000 Seminole Blvd., US 17/92 in Casselberry (tel. 699-4510), and **Sanford-Orlando Kennel Club,** Dog Track Road (tel. 831-1600). Seminole is open May to September; Sanford, from late December to early May; and there's racing nightly at 7:30pm (except Sunday), with matinees on Monday, Wednesday, and Saturday at 1pm. Admission is $1.

Jai-alai is always a thriller, and you can see it at **Florida Jai-Alai Fronton,** 211 S. US 17/92, in Fern Park (tel. 331-9191), from October through February. Admission is $1. There are noon matinees on Monday, Wednesday, and Saturday.

## BASEBALL AND BASKETBALL

From mid-February to early April the **Minnesota Twins** train at Orlando's Tinker Field, at 287 Tampa Ave. and Church Street (tel. 872-7593). Tickets are $3 to $5. From April to September the **Orlando SunRays** play professional baseball here. Tickets are $1.50 to $3.50.

Newest residents of Kissimmee are the **Houston Astros** baseball team, who now turn up here for spring training. A 6,000-seat stadium adjacent to the Kissimmee-St. Cloud Convention and Visitors Bureau, on US 192 and US 441, is their playground. Contact them at 305/847-5000.

Orlando now has a basketball team called, what else, the **Orlando Magic.** Their first season began in the fall of 1989 at a new arena built for them at 600 W. Amelia St. (tel. 649-3200). Tickets vary in price but begin at about $4.

## FAMILY FUN

If you'd like to get in a little mini-golf or a couple of rounds on bumper cars, bumper boats, water slides, or go-carts, stop in at **Fun 'N Wheels Family Fun Park,** 6739 Sand Lake Rd. (tel. 351-5651), corner of International Drive and Sand Lake Road, Orlando, or US 192 at Osceola Square Mall (tel. 239-8038). It's open from 4 to 11pm weekdays; weekends from 10am to midnight. Rides are $1.75 each.

Ice skating in Florida? Why not? Try it at **Orlando Ice Skating Palace,** Parkwood Shopping Plaza, 3123 W. Colonial Dr., Orlando (tel. 299-5440). Rates are $4.45 for children and $4.95 for adults ($1 more on weekends); skate rental is $1.50. Whirl around from 7:30 to 10:30pm (to 1am on Saturday) Wednesday through Sunday, on Saturday at 12:30 and 4pm, and on Sunday at 2pm.

## HIKING

You can, of course, hike anywhere in Florida, but up here in central Florida is the headquarters of the **Florida Trail Association,** which can guide you to hiking trails throughout the state. There actually is a long hiking trail you can walk that takes you through the whole state. Fittingly enough, it's called the Florida Trail, 950 miles of hiking from Big Cypress Swamp in southwestern Florida along the eastern shores of Lake Okeechobee through the central highlands and Ocala National Forest and west along the state's Panhandle. The Florida Trail Association maintains the route and sponsors special events on it throughout the year, including canoe and bicycle tours, half-day hikes, and fishing trips. Organization membership is $23.

For information on their activities and maps of the route, contact the association at P.O. Box 13708, Gainesville, FL 32604 (tel. 904/378-8823).

---

# 8. Shopping

---

Orlando is a souvenir hunter's heaven, but there are now many crafts and specialty shops in the area too, plus several big shopping malls.

**Lake Buena Vista** has 27 lovely boutiques filled with treasures, and in downtown Orlando the **Orange Quarter,** at Orange Avenue and Washington Street, is tiny but pretty, and growing fast.

Factory outlets are popular here, and you can find **Dansk** contemporary china and teak products at 7000 International Dr.; **China & Glass Outlet** at moderate prices, at 62 W. Colonial Dr.; **Polly Flinders** hand-smocked dresses for little girls in Casselberry Square.

A freak-out for discount-store fanatics is **Fitz and Floyd Factory Outlet,** at the end of International Drive at Oak Ridge Road intersection (follow signs on International Drive from the Sand Lake Road exit on I-4). You'll find 70 cut-rate shops open seven days a week. They're jammed with housewares, perfumes, gifts, entertainment items, shoes, clothes—you name it, it's all here at prices 25% to 75% below retail cost.

In Winter Park, charming **Park Avenue** is one of the state's poshest shopping streets, ranking right up there with Worth Avenue in Palm Beach for beauty and buys. At one interesting shop here, Ted Dobbs, a heraldist, will research your name, and his wife, Pat, will use her calligraphic skill to inscribe your family motto on a crest—he's worked on one for the Reagan–Davis heraldry (you do remember Ronnie and Mrs. Ronnie?), and earned an invitation to the inauguration with it.

You say you'd rather make a deal than buy by the price tag? Then head right out to **Flea World,** a 104-acre flea market/mall between Orlando and Sanford. Opened in 1982, this combination of junk and junque recently spent $2 million on an expansion program designed to create still more space for Turkish bedspreads, $3 haircuts, macramé plant hangers, antique furniture, old clothes, new clothes, and general treasures, and has doubled its size.

You'll find both indoor and outdoor marketing at this very large bargain-up-a-storm playground, which features covered and paved walkways easy for elderly and handicapped treasure hunters. You'll also find restaurants here in air-conditioned buildings, even a lawyer's office and pawn shop. It's open on Friday, Saturday, and Sunday from 8am to 5pm, and admission and parking are free. Entertainment too. To get there from the Kissimmee area, take I-4 to Lake Mary Boulevard, exit 50 (about a 40-minute drive, 20 minutes from the downtown Orlando area), turn right to US 17/92 and south to Flea World. Or take US 17/92 directly from downtown Kissimmee.

**Altamonte Park Plaza,** 995 Fla. 434, Altamonte Springs, has a number of specialty shops, some discount, some not, all of them occupying an attractive indoor marketplace with a bit of a European-market air about it. Hours are 10am to 9pm daily, closing at 6pm on Saturday and Sunday and opening at noon on Sunday. To get there, take the Longwood exit from I-4.

Add to that another shopping center, **The Marketplace,** 7600 Dr. Phillips Blvd. (tel. 351-7000), just north of Sand Lake Road and west of I-4 (take exit 29 from I-4 and turn right at the stoplight), where some creative souls have opened a pretty little woodsy shopping center with Victorian overtones. Makes an interesting, casual place to stroll as well as to shop. You'll find a pub and restaurant here, childrens' and women's fashion shops, an antiques store, and assorted other boutiques. It's open daily from 10am to 9pm.

## 9. Side Trips Around Central Florida

You can have a real adventure exploring the highways and byways of central Florida, where you'll find everything from orange groves to Derby winners.

### CYPRESS GARDENS AND LAKE WALES

Head south from Orlando on US 17 (or branch off I-4 onto US 27, picking up US 17 in Haines City) and stretched out before you, behind you, and on all sides are stubby green trees. Nesting in their shining emerald leaves are the bright gold and orange orbs of Florida's most important crop, none other than citrus, the state's most prolific product. Most of it's grown right here on these slopes, which produce more than 12 million boxes of fruit each year.

### The Sights

Stop off for a look at one of the state's most elegant attractions, **Cypress Gardens,** west of US 27 on Fla. 540 at Cypress Gardens Boulevard in Winter Haven, Box 1, Cypress Gardens, FL 33884 (tel. 813/324-2111), once called by *Life* magazine "a photographer's paradise." It's a stunningly beautiful cypress swamp turned into acre upon acre of exotic flowers, with an antebellum town, where southern belles in hooped skirts make themselves part of the scenery, a Critter Encounter filled with tame pettable animals, a domed gazebo that's been the site of television shows and weddings. Wander around absorbing the hushed air of this huge tropical forest with paths that wind through ginger plants and coffee trees, ancient cypresses centuries old, and deep, hauntingly silent lagoons. But don't miss the Gardens' frequent waterskiing shows with award-winning skiers who perform precision ski tricks (like barefoot skiing and kite flying on skis) the way we all walk to the grocery. Their grand finale is a four-tiered pyramid of skiers balanced on each other's shoulders!

Cypress Gardens has a raft of restaurants and boutiques full of treasures, and for photographers there's a special section in the stands where shutter settings are marked and the skiers ski right into your picture.

Cypress Gardens has another photographer's delight, **Kodak's Island in the Sky,** a revolving platform that lifts riders slowly into the sky so they can photograph these lovely gardens from the air.

Shows here include performances by alligators and birds, plus a production, **Classical Ice,** a themed ice skating revue with lasers and dancing fountains.

Cypress Gardens is open from 9am to 6pm, with shows at varying times, and admission is $18.50 for adults, $12 for children 3 through 9 (others free).

After you've toured Cypress Gardens and **Winter Haven** (which describes what this city is for the Boston Red Sox, who train here in spring), head back to US 27 and south to **Lake Wales,** a small central Florida city built on the sloping sides of a sparkling lake fringed with citrus groves.

There are few more tranquil places in the state than stately **Bok Tower,** off US 27A, Lake Wales (tel. 813/676-1408). Rising 295 feet, this Georgian Gothic tower is set in the stillness of Mountain Lake Sanctuary atop Iron Mountain, once a sacred Indian site, and the highest point in peninsular Florida. Donated to the nation by Dutch immigrant publisher Edward Bok, the 205-foot pink-and-gray marble octagonal tower houses inside it a 57-bell carillon whose gentle notes ring out each half hour, with a 45-minute recital at 3pm each day by resident carillonneur Milford Myhre. Admission is $2, children under 12 free.

While you're here, don't miss **Spook Hill,** one of the state's wackiest sites—and it's absolutely free. Look for signs directing you there: It's off US 17 at North Avenue and 5th Street. Now, drive your car up to the designated spot, put it in neutral, remove your foot from the brake, and watch the car move slowly backward . . . *uphill!* Nobody's telling why it works that way, but there are lots of local yarns about a Native American chief protecting his people, a pirate, an alligator. Ask, maybe you can add another.

Here in Lake Wales, from mid-February to mid-April, you can see the **Black Hills Passion Play,** Passion Play Road (P.O. Box 71), Lake Wales, FL 33859 (tel. 813/676-1495), a dramatic re-creation of the final week of Christ's life portrayed by professional actors. There are Wednesday matinees at 3pm and evening performances each Tuesday, Thursday, and Saturday at 7:30pm (6pm on Sunday), and on Good Friday evening. Tickets are $6 to $12 (half price for children). The natural outdoor amphitheater in which it's performed is nestled in a citrus grove and is a sight worth seeing even if you don't make the play, now in its 38th year.

Two **unusual sports** here are hang gliding on exciting updrafts created by warm air and high elevations, and wild boar hunting, which can be done all year long with written permission from the landowner on whose property you're hunting. No license is required.

## Staying Over

In Lake Wales, where to stay and where to eat are one place: delightful and delicious, weird and wacky, funky, funny **Chalet Suzanne Country Inn and Restaurant,** on US 27 and 17A, four miles north of Lake Wales (P.O. Drawer AC, Lake Wales, FL 33859-90037, tel. 813/676-6011). A whimsical spot nestled into a 70-acre orange grove, Chalet Suzanne has won prestigious dining awards galore, and its famous gourmet canned soups went to the moon with the astronauts—no wonder it's so famous. First, the dining room is a tasteful marvel of Limoges, English and German porcelain and Italian pottery, no two dishes alike on a table (no two chairs are alike either). Rooms are a fascinating mélange of Spanish ironwork, Moorish mosaics, Turkish treasures, and Cuban tiles. Eclectic it is, intriguing it is, and skillfully done it definitely is.

Second, this small resort falls just short of incredible. Every one of the 30 guest rooms is different, each with its own name. The blue room has deep carpeting and pale-blue touches on chairs and windows. Other rooms are orchid or have brass beds, antiques like a ceramic washbowl on a stand, and one even has a bathtub made entirely of Moorish tiles. Glowing color schemes blend it all together, and there are all the modern appurtenances like color TVs, phones, and a pool.

All of this is the work of the late Bertha Hinshaw, a pillar of determination who refused to buckle in the face of an isolated outpost in Lake Wales and the Depression. Instead, she packed up her two children and tacked up signs on every byway, developed recipes that would become the rage of Florida's gastronomes, and set about creating an empire. She succeeded. Boarders came for her excellent dinners and went out to bring still more people to her door. Finally, free to indulge a passion for travel, Ms. Hinshaw visited the corners of the earth and brought back all the treasures she could find—and she was quite a finder! Her son and daughter-in-law have continued and expanded the business until now there's no place like it in Florida: Peaked clock towers pop up in unexpected places, a red British telephone booth is tucked away in a corner, there's an antique store and lots of ornate wrought iron and brick, patterned tiles, and stone urns.

You won't see anything like it anywhere else, and certainly not anyplace charging room rates of just $95 to $185 double, year round. We can't resist telling you there's a honeymoon suite where the new couple can breakfast on a little glass-enclosed terrace overlooking the dining room—but unseen to other guests—and order their breakfast delivered on a dumb waiter that sends it right up from the kitchen.

Now to the restaurant (one of Florida's most famous), which changes its menu frequently but always has broiled grapefruit and the resort's famous romaine soup. Entrées might include chicken Suzanne, shrimp curry with an array of condiments, lobster Newburg, grilled lamb chops, or lump crabmeat in herb butter. Prix-fixe meals, including several courses and hot crusty potato rolls, are pegged at $25 to $36 for lunch, $49 to $68 for dinners. There's a service charge of 18% added to the tab. Children's menus are about $12 to $15, and the restaurant's open daily for breakfast 8 to 10am, from noon to 4pm for lunch, and 6 to 9:30pm; closed Monday from May to December. You can even arrive on a private airstrip owned and operated by the Hinshaw family.

Two other nice spots in the Winter Haven area are **Lake Ida Beach Resort Motel,** 2524 North US 17, Winter Haven, FL 33881 (tel. 813/293-0942), on the shores of a lovely lake. A cluster of two-bedroom cottages, efficiencies, and motel rooms on a quiet lake, the resort has a small tiled pool, laundry, beach, pier, games, barbecue, and rowboats for fishing in the lake. Rates for two from April to December are $96 for a four-night stay. Winter rates are $34 to $46 double.

In nearby Auburndale, the **Lena Motel,** at 1802 US 92, Auburndale, FL 33823 (tel. 813/967-1558), is a tiny, moderately priced place on well-maintained grounds surrounding a small pool and patio. Right on the edge of a tranquil lake, the motel has some rooms with cooking facilities. Rates are $25 to $40 a day for motel rooms or efficiencies.

## DEBARY

Few are those who wander up to DeBary these days, but once upon a time this was the center of a very lively development begun by an Austrian count! See, Florida really does have everything.

That count's estate, **DeBary Hall,** considered by Florida's restorationists to be one of Florida's five most important historic structures, is here in DeBary. A very large house, DeBary Hall lives up to its name—it has central hallways running the entire length of both floors. Every room in the house opens onto a hallway, onto the next room, and onto a porch. DeBary Hall is exciting from several standpoints. First, it's huge and beautiful and was the property of a vintner who is said to have introduced champagne to America, or vice versa. Second, major restoration of the hall was scheduled to begin in May 1987 to turn the house into a living museum. So if you're visiting here soon, you may see restoration in process or the very shiny results of that restoration. In the meantime the hall is occupied by the Council on Aging, which uses it for a variety of senior programs.

A very welcoming Martha Hummiston is among the workers on hand when the house is open, Monday through Friday from 9am to 1pm. They will be happy to show you through this enormous home made of cypress wood shipped here from Georgia but call them first. There is no admission charge. You will find the house at 210 Sunrise Blvd., DeBary (tel. 407/668-5286). To get there from I-4, take the DeBary exit to Dirksen Boulevard and Dirksen to Mansion Road. You'll see signs directing you from there. Similar directional signs appear on US 17/92, a main road through DeBary.

## OCALA

Mile after mile of pristine white fences and emerald grass, the gleam of a chestnut flank curried to shimmering perfection, white blaze streaking down the aristocratic nose of a proud stallion, offspring of champions—that's Ocala, center of the state's racehorse country and home of turf champions like Kentucky Derby winners Needles and Carry Back, and the 1978 Triple Crown champion, Affirmed.

An hour's drive from Orlando (take the Florida Turnpike to Wildwood, then north on I-75 for 15 miles) will bring you here, where equine blood lines are discussed with far more fervor than any current events, and an impending foal is likely to outrank a human baby. Grassy knolls, limestone water, and rolling hills much like

Kentucky's famed blue grass region help shape these champions that are bred on 150 farms in the Ocala area.

If you'd like a nose-to-nose *tête-à-tête* with this prizewinning equine talent, you can stop in at any of about a dozen farms here. Farther north, about 30 miles west of Gainesville, on County Road 307 just off Fla. 26, is **Castleton Farms** (tel. 904/463-2686). This is the second-largest standard breeding farm in the world, raising foals, both trotters and pacers, for harness racing. The **Ocala/Marion County Chamber of Commerce,** at 110 E. Silver Springs Blvd., Ocala, FL 32670 (tel. 904/629-8051), has maps outlining thoroughbred farm locations and the times they are open to visitors. They can also tell you about greyhound breeding farms in the area too.

Here in Ocala in 1835 an Indian agent told the Seminole tribe it would be shipped off to the West. When they refused to go, the agent cut off gun sales, infuriating Chief Osceola who helped plan an ambush in which Maj. Francis Dade and 100 of his men were massacred on Christmas Eve near Bushnell as they rode to join the battle against the Seminoles. Osceola killed the agent too, and shortly war was in the wind. The Creeks, the Seminoles' ancestors, discovered the beauty of **Hot Springs** on the Suwanee River, about eight miles west of Trenton, centuries ago, and artifacts and fossils from those early eras can still be found here. It's also a pretty place to camp or picnic. Take Fla. 26 to Fla. 232 about four miles, and turn left on Fla. 344 to the 200-acre park. For camping information, call 904/463-9975 or 904/463-6422.

One mile east of Ocala on Fla. 40 at **Silver Springs,** you can float down cool tranquil springs in a glass-bottom boat, watch "mermaids" frolic with the fish and even hand-feed those fish yourself, or pet a real-life Bambi. Silver Springs has been ferrying two million wide-eyed visitors around in its glass-bottom boats each year for generations, and no matter how many times you see these crystal waters, it's fun to return. Admission is $14.95 for adults, $9.95 for children 3 to 12. The park is open from 9am to 5pm daily and can be seen in four to five hours. Along the banks of the Silver River, giraffes, zebra, camels, and exotic wildlife roam free. In 1978 **Wild Waters,** a splashy, water theme park opened at Fla. 40 in Silver Springs (tel. 904/236-2043, or toll free 800/342-0297 in Florida). Admission to it is $9.95 for adults, $8.55 for children 3 to 11, and the park's open from 10am to 8pm from late March to the fall, closing in mid-September. You save $2 with a combination ticket.

Umatilla is the entrance to the **Ocala National Forest,** the world's largest stand of sand pine plus a 366,000-acre wilderness of timberland that will show you how all of Florida once looked. Fla. 19, called the "Backwoods Trail," is the scenic drive. You can rent canoes here at Juniper Springs Run and Alexander Springs or ride the *Rainbow Queen* paddleboat down the Oklawaha River. For camping reservations in the national park, call 904/625-3147. It's 48 miles east of Ocala.

University students are given credit for having dreamed up the sport of **tubing,** which involves floating down a stream on an innertube. Tubing down the seven-mile-long Ichtucknee Spring on huge tubes five feet in diameter has become such a popular sport that officials had to limit the number of tubers to 3,000 a day! You can rent the tubes at nearby gas stations and a shuttlebus brings you back to the starting point, since floating upstream's a real talent. Call 497-2150 when you're making tubing plans.

Jai-alai, a racquetball-like game that originated in Spain's Basque country, is played here at **Ocala Jai-Alai** (Box 548, Orange Lake, FL 32681), Fla. 318 (tel. 904/591-2345, 376-9044 in Gainesville), from January through March and May through December. Games begin at 6:45pm daily except Sunday and Tuesday, with 11am matinees on Wednesday and Saturday. Grandstand admission is $1. You'll find the fronton two miles east of I-75 on Fla. 318, a half mile east of US 441. There's betting on the games, which you can watch from the fronton's Carom Clubhouse Restaurant.

Car buffs have an option here: **Don Garlits' Museum of Drag Racing,** 13700

SW 16th Ave., Ocala (tel. 904/245-8661). Don Garlits, a native of Florida, won 120 national titles and 17 world championships. His cars and other memorabilia of the memorable sport of drag racing are displayed in this museum, which charges $6 adults and $3 children 3 through 12. Hours are 9am to 5:30pm daily. It's at exit 67 (Belleview) off I-75.

## NEW SMYRNA

Okay, we grant you there's not a lot of reason to go to New Smyrna if you don't count some beautiful unspoiled beaches with neighborhoods to match. This section of Florida is on the grow but it's still pretty sleepy, which is what makes it a delightful side trip if you're traveling in central Florida.

Another very good reason to come over this way is to revel in a new hotel here, although hotel seems far too common a word to describe a charming riverside inn called the **Riverview Hotel,** 103 Flagler Ave., New Smyrna Beach, FL 32069 (tel. 904/428-5858). Built by the same talented folks who restored and re-created the delightful Park Plaza Hotel in Winter Park, the Riverview is more of the same: beautiful woods, an old-world feeling, airy wicker furniture, a few four-poster beds, paddle fans, tropical without any of the false pastel tropical that has turned Florida's hotel roster into a sea-green wilderness.

A ferryman used to shuttle folks across the river here and his house grew eventually into a hotel, later abandoned and lately renewed. Now snappily dressed in yellow clapboard trimmed in cream and topped with a tin roof, Riverview is circled by invitingly canopied porches that make a perfect perch for a quiet afternoon. Inside, the cool is maintained by paddle fans and plants, upscaled with French doors and books.

Urban sailors pull up at the dock and nip into the trilevel dining room to keep an eye on the water through big picture windows. Evenings, tiny white lights twinkle and all is well with the world, wherever it is. Rates at the Riverview are $70 to $100 double, depending on view and including newspaper, fresh fruit daily, and Continental breakfast served in your room or on your balcony; $150 for a honeymoon suite including champagne, four-poster, and a fruit basket.

## CASSADEGA

Here's a spooky one for you. In 1875 spiritualist George Colby, with the help of three spiritual guides, founded a town and psychic center and donated 35 acres to the Spiritualist church. Today in this small village east of I-4 about 20 miles north of Orlando, you'll see small signs outside many homes announcing the presence therein of a medium. These mediums claim not to permit charlatans in their midst, and all the mediums here (and there are many) are registered by the National Spiritualist Association of Churches. Whether or not you're interested in contacting Aunt Sarah, you'll find Cassadega a lovely old Florida town where, well, who knows what might happen?

## SEBRING

If there's no sound more fulfilling to you than a well-tuned engine roaring along at about 150 m.p.h., don't miss a trip to Sebring, about 86 miles south of Orlando on US 17 just off US 98. Each March the city is mecca for machine idolizers who trek here for the **Automobile Hall of Fame Week,** highlight of which is the 12 hours of **Sebring International Grand Prix of Endurance** for sports cars. Be forewarned that there is indeed some endurance involved in attending this event, which takes place around a dusty track crowded with fans out to enjoy a day of carburetors and Coors. Every motel in the area is packed for the event too, so don't just drop in.

If you'd like to stay here in lovely surroundings amid many lakes and orange groves, head for **Holiday Inn of Sebring,** Sebring, FL 33870 (tel. 813/385-4500, or toll free 800/HOLIDAY), on US 27 about five miles north of Sebring and five miles south of Avon Park. It's a pretty and stylish place with 146 guest rooms, restaurant, newly remodeled dance lounge, fitness room, game room, and swimming pool. Tennis and golf are nearby. Rates for two, year round, are $52 to $100.

Less expensive accommodations in the area include the 42-room **Sunset Beach Motel,** 2221 SE Lakeview Dr. (on US 27 and 98), Sebring, FL 33870 (tel. 813/385-6129), a lovely lakefront motel with a private beach. Rates are $30 to $50, year round.

Ambitious developers are hard at work trying to restore a massive old 1916 Sebring hotel called the **Kenilworth Lodge and Motor Inn,** 836 SE Lakeview Dr., Sebring, FL 33870 (tel. 813/385-0111, or toll free 800/423-5939). You can't possibly miss this huge twin-towered building as you drive through Sebring, and if you're looking for old-world elegance at quite low prices, you'll certainly want to look for it.

Villas and efficiencies, both of which have kitchens, are the most popular accommodations at this fabulous old hotel built by Sebring's founder as a sunny southern home for the super-rich. For one of those accommodations you pay $40 to $55 from December to mid-April, $10 less in summer. Rooms here are just $33 in summer, $45 in winter months, and the lodge has a small Country Vittles Restaurant open for most meals in winter, for dinner and Sunday brunch in summer. Outside there's a large swimming pool, and inside you can enjoy some lovely lake views from the hotel's lounge. Kenilworth is an hour's drive from Walt Disney World, but you'll be staying in some of the loveliest countryside in this part of the state.

## ZELLWOOD

Just outside Orlando, this small city is the winter vegetable-basket of the eastern seaboard. You can tour the miles and miles of corn, carrots, lettuce, cauliflower, and radishes, and celebrate the two-million-crate harvest at the May Sweet Corn Festival. Guided tours of the 18,000 acres of farmland are sometimes available between January and April. Call 407/886-7441 for information.

## DELAND

This is a very quiet town despite the presence of hundreds of college students who attend what may be the loveliest university in Florida, pillared and porticoed **Stetson University.** Only about 35 miles north of Orlando and not far from Daytona Beach, Deland's well worth the drive just to roam this shady, old-world campus.

While you're up here you can look in on the **De Leon Springs State Recreation Area,** off US 17, Deland (tel. 904/985-4212), where you can prowl the remains of an old Spanish sugar mill near the spring. A popular swimming hole, the spring has another unusual feature: a restaurant at which you can be sure your hotcakes are just the way you want them—you griddle your own! Every table has its own recessed griddle at **Old Spanish Sugar Mill and Restaurant,** Ponce de Leon Blvd., DeLeon Springs (tel. 904/985-5644). A waitress provides you with two handmade pitchers filled with two different batters, one made from grain stone-ground right here, fresh fruit, raw honey, unsulfured molasses, scads of different toppings including peanut butter—and off you flap, Jack. Hours are 9am to 5pm weekdays, opening at 8am on weekends. Price is $2.75 per person for all the griddle cakes you can down; lunch prices are under $5. Griddle House also sells homemade jams, jellies, and bread. You'll find the restaurant inside the recreation area, which is just off US 17/92, 35 miles from Daytona and 50 from Orlando.

Not far away, you can ride one of the few remaining privately owned ferries in Florida. You'll find it between Palatka and Astor, running from Gateway Fishing Camp on the St. Johns River. Called **Fort Gates Ferry,** the service runs daily except Tuesday from 7am to 5:30pm. On the east side of the river it runs from County Road 309 at Fruitland; on the west side from US 19 at Salt Springs campground.

Trips are $5 one way, $9 round trip, and will save you 54 miles of driving if you're headed to Ocala, Salt Springs, I-75, or St. Augustine.

## MICANOPY

Just a mile square, this small town is a sleepy spot just south of Gainesville and about a two-hour drive from Orlando. Pronounced "Micka-*no*-pea," the village sprouted from an 1821 trading post and likes to trace its history back even further to Seminole Chief Micanopy, who is said to have held court under the moss-draped oaks along the city's main street. Today history is still a very important part of life here. Micanopy has become one of Florida's top antique-hunting grounds and several artisans have settled here, opening a pottery, a cabinetmaking operation, and a stained-glass shop. All of them hold court on Cholokka Boulevard just as Chief Micanopy did—it's the town's only street!—in a cluster of handsome brick buildings listed on the National Register of Historic Places.

## GAINESVILLE

Thirty miles north of Ocala on I-75 is Gainesville, where the Gothic campus of the **University of Florida** has bred many a governor and legislator. Horticulturists who oversee Florida's massive and powerful citrus industry train here, as do veterinarians who treat the state's huge herds of cattle. For all that erudition, the university's probably best known as the chemistry department that developed famous "Gator-Ade," a drink that first hit the thirsty gullets of the university's popular football team, the fighting Gators. Look in on the university's **Florida State Museum,** which has million-year-old fossils from Florida, including a prehistoric camel. There's a walk-through exhibit of Mayan ruins, including a replica of a Mayan palace too.

Downtown, you'll see the imposing old courthouse restored for the **Hippodrome State Theater,** starring a professional cast performing in an intimate 266-seat theater. It's at 25 SE Second Place (tel. 373-5968). Shows vary in time and price is $11 to $21.

Another newly restored entertainment spot is **Florida Theater,** 233 W. University Ave. (tel. 338-0233), where the city's Civic Ballet performs.

Just south of Gainesville is the **Marjorie Kinnan Rawlings State Historic Site.** That Pulitzer Prize–winning author lived here while she wrote *The Yearling* and two other intriguing books about Florida, *Cross Creek* and *The Big Scrub.* Her home is completely furnished just as she left it, and its isolated location beside Lake Lochloosa gives you an idea how she got the ideas for those touching Florida stories. It's on County Road 325, which you can reach from Fla. 20 East (tel. 466-3672). Admission is $1.

At the **Yearling Cross Creek Restaurant,** at Blue Gill Drive and County Road 325, in Cross Creek (tel. 904/466-3033) you will be served dinners made with recipes suggested by the author in her *Cross Creek Cookbook.* Prices are in the $10 to $15 range for dinner. The restaurant is open Tuesday through Saturday from noon to 10pm, on Sunday from noon to 8:30pm.

## Staying Over

If you'd like to stay over in Gainesville, you can stay in style at the **Gainesville Hilton,** 2900 SW 13th St., Gainesville, FL 32601 (tel. 904/377-4000, or toll-free 800/HILTONS). There are 208 pretty rooms overlooking the 250-acre Bivens Arm Lake, an airy restaurant, and Juliana's of London Discothèque. Outside, there's a pool and barbecue area. The Hilton is quite near the university and also offers courtesy transportation to and from the airport. Year-round rates are $65 to $135 for two, depending on the view and size of accommodation.

A moderately priced hotel is **University Inn,** at 1901 SW 13th St., Gainesville, FL 32601 (tel. 904/376-2222). Here you'll find a tranquil central courtyard, a big

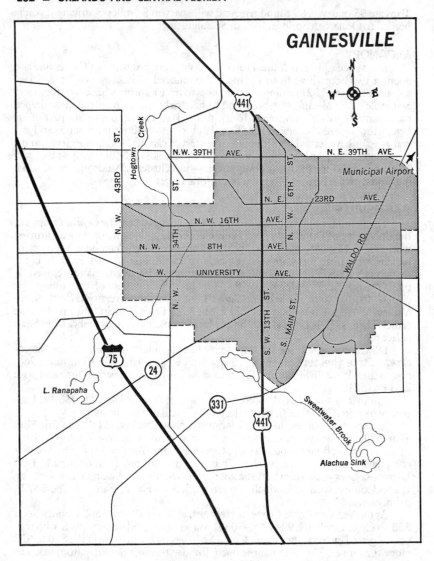

pool, a pretty lobby with a fountain in the center. Some of the spacious rooms have paneling, all are decorated in bright colors with cable color TV, HBO, and AM-FM stereo radios. There is complimentary Continental breakfast in the lobby. Rates are $28 double; additional guests are $4. Higher rates are charged during special events.

A comparatively new hostelry in town is the **University Centre Hotel,** 1535 SW Archer Rd., Gainesville, FL 32608 (tel. 904/371-3333, or toll free 800/824-5637). The University Centre has 180 spacious rooms, nine of them suites, for those living the high life. For dining there's Fiddler's restaurant and for après or pre-imbibing there's a lively lounge. Rates are $69 to $99 year round; higher for suites.

A recently built budget spot in town is **Cabot Lodge,** 3726 SW 40th Blvd. (I-75 and Archer Road), Gainesville, FL 32608 (tel. 904/375-2400, or toll free 800/331-8215). Part of an interesting group of hotels that have sprung up all over the South, this Cabot Lodge, like its sister hotels, is designed to look like a big old house, complete with screened porch and a fireplace in the living room lobby. A free Continental breakfast is a daily feature. You'll find free coffee brewing here 24 hours a day, an "honor" library with novels and newspapers, a large-screen television, free popcorn, games, and even the occasional ice-cream social. Rooms have a king-size bed and couch or two double beds, remote-control televisions, country-look furnishings, and all the amenities right down to shampoo. Rates are $50 to $60 double, year round.

A good budget choice is the **Days Stop Motel,** 4041 SW 13th St., Gainesville, FL 32601 (tel. 904/376-4423), which has just 10 small units next to a beautiful open grove of pines. Units have dressing rooms and phones, and free coffee is available every morning. Double rates are $36 to $50.

Two similar small motels are the **Sands,** at 2307 SW 13th St., Gainesville, FL 32601 (tel. 904/372-2045), which has a spiffy new wing with big picture windows; and the **Bambi Motel,** at 2119 SW 13th St., Gainesville, FL 32601 (tel. 904/376-2622). Rooms are small but so are the prices: $24 to $55 double. Bambi is close to the campus and has recently been refurbished.

---

# 10. Cape Canaveral/Kennedy Space Center

---

## SPACEPORT USA/KENNEDY SPACE CENTER

Not so long ago a trip to the moon was as much a fantasy as anything in Disney's fanciful kingdom, but these days rockets shoot skyward with ho-hum regularity at Cape Canaveral, Florida's famed moon-shot space center. Here's where the astronauts trained for their "one small step" and where in 1980 the space shuttle first took off.

Flights continue to be launched from these pads. If you'd like to be there for one, call NASA toll free at 800/432-2153 for information on launch dates and best vantage points. A limited number of passes is issued for shuttle launches. To make reservations for a launch date, call 407/452-2121 between 8am and 4pm, or write NASA Visitors Services Branch, PA-VIC, John F. Kennedy Space Center Headquarters, Kennedy Space Center, FL 32899. If you want to contact Spaceport USA for any other reason, write to them at NASA Visitors Services Branch, Kennedy Space Center Headquarters, Kennedy Space Center, FL 32899.

It's an easy day trip from Orlando to Cape Canaveral on County Road 528, the Beeline, or a pretty drive along the east coast of Florida through Indian River citrus country. From Orlando, follow the signs to the **John F. Kennedy Space Center** (*not* Cape Canaveral).

At the Kennedy Space Center and NASA launch complex now called **Spaceport USA,** begin your visit with a stop at the **Visitor Information Center** (tel. 452-2121) on Merritt Island, between the mainland and the cape about six miles east of Titusville. In the yard here are huge rockets and spacecraft. Inside, you can see a piece of moon rock and get a closeup look at Apollo capsules, rocket engines, and a lunar module. In the Gallery of Space Flight, a film details the space program's development. It's open daily (except December 25) from 8am to sunset, and is free.

Queue up then for the two-hour NASA escorted bus tours, which leave every few minutes from the Visitor Center. The tour costs $4 for adults, $1.75 for children under 12. You can take either the Blue or the Red Tour, but the Red includes the fascinating astronaut training building. Simulators reproduce conditions of an actual space flight, and lights illuminate the craft as its components are explained by the narrator.

You'll pass the 52-story Vehicle Assembly Building and the huge transporters that carry spacecraft to the launching pads, as well as get a look at a launch pad.

Kennedy Space Center has added an **IMAX Theater,** which features a 20-minute version of the film *The Dream is Alive,* depicting the launch and landing of the Space Shuttle *Columbia.* Projected on a screen five stories high and 70 feet wide, and accompanied by a sound from a six-track stereo system, it's quite an explosive production. Admission is an additional $2.75 for adults, $1.75 for children 3 to 12, for the IMAX presentation.

## A CRUISE PORT

Newest resident on this spacy block is not a rocket but a cruise ship! A couple of years ago **Premier Cruise Lines** decided they saw a potential market up this way and moved in with their newly refurbished liner, the *Royale.* Now the line sails several ships on three- and four-day cruises to Nassau and an out-island in the Bahamas. If you're headed for Walt Disney World and the thought of a few days of R&R at the beginning or end of the WDW tramp sounds wonderful to you, a travel agent can organize a package deal with hotel, transportation to the ship, and plenty of extras at quite reasonable prices.

For more on cruises from this and other ports, we'd modestly recommend another book we co-authored, *Frommer's Cruises.*

## OTHER ATTRACTIONS

NASA did not just burn up acreage with its huge blazing rockets. Most of the thousands and thousands of acres the government owns here are unspoiled wilderness, called the **Merritt Island National Wildlife Refuge,** a haven for deer and small animals, alligators, many species of birds that remain here year round, as well as migratory waterfowl, plus many endangered species. The refuge is open from 8am to two hours before sunset daily except Christmas and launch days.

Another attraction in the Cocoa area is **Canaveral National Seashore,** which begins just east of Titusville and runs north to Turtle Mound, a total of 67,000 acres of waterfront wilderness that's home to 300 species of birds and animals, some of which are on the endangered list. Administered by the National Park Service, the seashore is a serene place to roam among the sand dunes and listen to the breezes rustle through sea oats.

A 50-foot-high mound of seashells here was discarded six centuries ago by Native Americans who lived on these shores. It's called **Turtle Mound,** and can still be seen in the park on a nature trail that crosses the mound.

An entrance to Merritt Island National Wildlife Refuge is near here too, and you can take a self-guided tour through **Black Point Wildlife Drive,** which you enter via County Road 402 just off US 1 in Titusville.

## STAYING OVER

If you're staying over in the area, try the **Crossway Inn and Tennis Resort,** 3901 N. Atlantic Ave., Cocoa Beach, FL 32931 (tel. 407/783-2221), where you'll find a pool, two lighted tennis courts, and attractive rooms, some with refrigerators and some with full kitchens. It doesn't face the ocean (but is just 400 feet away from the sea) and charges $40 to $65, year round. Children under 12 stay free, and there's a game room, barbecue, and basketball court for the kids.

A moderately priced choice is **Surf Studio Beach Apartments,** 1801 S. Atlantic Ave., Cocoa Beach, FL 32931 (tel. 407/783-7100), which is right on the ocean and has just 11 units. You can select from motel rooms, efficiencies, and one-bedroom apartments for $30 to $80, year round.

**Days Inn,** 5600 N. Atlantic Ave., Cocoa Beach, FL 32931 (tel. 407/783-7621) is right on Cocoa Beach, which makes it perfect for surfing and swimming fans. An attractive spot stretched between the road and the ocean, the resort has free Continental breakfast at the pool each morning, shuffleboard, volleyball, croquet, a video-game room, and a laundry. Efficiency apartments have microwaves and dishwashers in addition to the usual kitchen equipment. Double rates are $57 to $70, year round.

**Rodeway Inn,** 3655 Cheney Hwy., Titusville, FL 32780 (tel. 407/269-7110, or toll free 800/228-2000), is three miles from Kennedy Space Center and has newly remodeled rooms, either king-size or double bed, for $39 to $65, year round. There's a swimming pool at the resort and rooms for nonsmokers.

Hilton Hotels saw the potential up this way and in 1986 opened the **Cocoa Beach Hilton,** 1550 N. Atlantic Ave., Cocoa Beach, FL 32931 (tel. 407/799-0003, or toll free 800/445-8667). A 300-room oceanfront hotel, the new Hilton is a sleek spot offering the typically Hilton hospitality and plush accommodations. You can sink into the accoutrements of a concierge floor where the morning paper appears magically outside your door or settle into the hotel's coolly sophisticated decor and spacious rooms, many of them overlooking the surf. By day you can work out in the hotel's health club, lift a couple at the pool bar, tan on the sundeck. By night you can retire to the slick depths of a dark lounge where musicians entertain or dine in style at a handsome dining room. Rates at the Hilton are $85 to $145, year round.

An outstanding restaurant in Cocoa—and in the state—is **Bernard's Surf,** at 2 S. Atlantic Ave. (tel. 783-2401). It may take you a while to read the menu, however —there are 40 appetizers and more than 100 entrées. Topping the weirdies list are such things as whale meat and fishballs, bear meat, fried silkworms, and chocolate-covered ants, but move right along past those to more usual kitchen treats. Here you'll find brimming platters of crab, shrimp, and super-fresh Florida seafood right off the owner's fleet. A combination of shrimp, crab, and mushrooms is a delicate dish, but then there are many good choices on the long list. Crisp, flaky breads are a specialty too. Prices are in the $12 to $20 range for entrées, and the restaurant is open from 11am to 11pm daily (except Sunday, when doors open at 5 and close at 10:45pm).

**Coconuts on the Beach,** 2 Minuteman Causeway (tel. 784-1422), about says it all in its name. Opened in 1986, this oceanfront restaurant spent $250,000 barely a year later to make the place even spiffier. Surf and turf fare is the order of the day here, where the views go on forever but the prices don't: You'll pay $10 to $15 or less for dinner. Coconuts cracks its doors at 11:30am daily, closing at 2am.

**Black Tulip,** 225 Brevard Ave. (tel. 631-1133), is an elegant spot amid the casual atmosphere that prevails in this region. Carpeting underfoot and intimate lighting is backdrop for continental specialties ranging from sizzling steaks to seafood, veal, and chicken options in the $11 to $15 price range for dinner entrées. Black Tulip opens its petals daily except Sunday and Monday from 11am to 3pm and 6 to 10pm.

Across the street in a courtyard at 222 Brevard Ave. is **Pasta Garden** (tel. 639-8343), a more casual restaurant under the same management. This one specializes in Italian fare, however, producing several good veal selections, and some seafood with Italian touches, plus plenty of what the name suggests. Dinner entrée prices at Pasta Garden fall in the $6 to $10 range. Pasta Garden is open from 11am to 9pm Tuesday through Saturday; closed Sunday and Monday.

Who could resist a spot with a name like **Strawberry Mansion,** 1218 E. New Haven Ave., Melbourne (tel. 724-8627)? Don't try. Strawberry Mansion has earned a spot in the heart and tummy of many a Melbourne resident and visitor, and they owe it all to an excellent kitchen that produces some of the region's best steaks and very good seafood. Best of all, the prices are as reasonable as the food is good: You'll pay about $8 to $15 for dinner here. Strawberry Mansion is open from 5 to 10pm daily.

If you're in search of a surfboard up this way, call **Ron-Jon,** 4151 N. Atlantic, Cocoa Beach (tel. 799-8820). Rental rates are $2 an hour, $8 a day.

# DAYTONA

**D**aytona humbly calls itself the "World's Most Famous Beach." There's every indication they're not far wrong. Certainly tourists have been sunning, sleeping, frolicking, and driving on these silvery sands for years. Driving? Yes, driving! As mere strips of sand these beaches have plenty of Florida competition, but as a racecourse . . . well, only in Daytona. It's been that way for nearly 100 years since Henry Flagler built his railroad and anyone who was anyone got on it and headed south.

R. E. Olds (you've heard perhaps of Oldsmobiles?) and Henry Ford, who had just started tinkering with "flivvers," were among the first sun-seeking snowbirds. They wintered at the towering old Ormond Hotel, where guests settled into rockers on the long verandas and watched those newfangled motor machines roll in and out of the garage up the street.

Something about cars arouses competitive urges. Here in Daytona those urges led Olds and Alexander Winton to the sands of Ormond Beach where they lined up cars that "rocked and popped and belched puffs of black smoke." Like modern teenagers, the two peeled off on one of the nation's first drag races, and tore straight down 23 miles of beach, nose to nose, clocking the magnificent speed of 57 miles an hour.

By 1904 a Daytona event called the Winter Speed Carnival was drawing entries from all over the world, most of them wealthy sportsmen and society financiers. Three years later Fred Marriott wrapped a mile of piano wire around the boiler of his Stanley Steamer to keep it from blowing up and raced through the timing course at a spectacular 197 m.p.h., only to crash just as spectacularly into the pounding surf. He emerged uninjured, but the accident gave rise to claims that the Stanley brothers were so upset by the spill they quit racing their cars. People still claim the Steamer's top speed is unknown because it never was tested.

Many men who were to become famous for their skill with machinery first put that skill to the test on the sands of Daytona. Glen Curtis, later to be known as the father of naval aviation for his pioneering work on flying boats and ship landing craft, once rode a motorcycle so fast here that Alexander Graham Bell asked Curtis to help him build airplanes. Daytona's favorite son, however, is all-time champion Capt. Malcolm Campbell, a millionaire English sportsman. In 1928 Campbell brought to Daytona a car powered by an aircraft engine. For days he waited for the tides to smooth out the beach, then ramrodded his flying pile of metal first to a record 206.96 m.p.h., in later years to 245 m.p.h., 253 m.p.h., 272 m.p.h., and 276 m.p.h. All that speed may not seem important, but it was—the Bluebird and Rolls-Royce engines Campbell had sped over the sands of Daytona went on to fame in a fleet of Hurricane and Spitfire fighters that beat back Hitler's Luftwaffe and halted German plans to invade Britain in World War II.

Worldwide depression smacked Daytona a mean blow, but the speedy sands were back in business again by the 1950s with a new beach racecourse, daring drivers, and a pack of cheering fans who eventually created National Stock Car Auto Racing (NASCAR), and today's famed Daytona 500.

No longer do the racing machines take to the beaches, but *you* still can—just follow the signs and drive between the bikinis—thousands of collegiate ones in spring.

Beach speed is now limited to 10 m.p.h., but that certainly doesn't mean there's no racing in Daytona. Not by a long shot. Daytona's love for speed lives on. Each year in February the Daytona International Speedway is packed with race followers who come here for two weeks of trackside reverence and revelry known as speed weeks. In July the Firecracker 400 and the Paul Revere 250 are major events on racing calendars.

Once again Daytona's sands are a playground for surfers who compete here each October, for toddlers busily carting sand buckets to the sea, for vacationing college students, and for you, the traveler, to stroll, to sun, to build castles and dreams.

# 1. Orientation

Daytona Beach is surrounded by water, with the Halifax River cutting right through the middle of the city and the Atlantic Ocean playing big brother on the east side. There are actually four towns on the beach: **Ormond Beach** on the north, then farther south **Daytona Beach** and **Daytona Beach Shores**, finally **New Smyrna Beach,** separated from the others by Ponce de Leon Inlet at the tip of Daytona Beach Shores. On the west side of the river is **Holly Hill** and downtown **Daytona.**

**Fla. A1A** runs along the beach from north to south and US 1 runs inland along the west side of the river. I-95 is still farther west, and I-4 joins **US 92** (also known as **Volusia Avenue)** to connect Orlando and Daytona Beach.

## GETTING THERE
American, Continental, Delta, and United Express fly into **Daytona National Airport,** and **Amtrak** disembarks passengers at nearby Deland or Palatka, about a 30-minute drive away. **Greyhound/Trailways** buses also serve the area.

Many people combine a visit to Orlando with a trip to Daytona—a few days at Orlando's attractions, a few days recovering on Daytona's fabulous sands. If you think you'd like to do that, you can fly into Orlando (which has much more air service than Daytona), then buzz over to the beach on the **Daytona-Orlando Transit Service (DOTS),** 1102 Mason Ave. (tel. 904/257-5411, or 800/231-1965 in Florida). If you don't have a car and don't want to rent one, that's the way to go. Fare is $20 for adults, $10 for children under 12 one way to the company's terminal, more to beach hotels.

## GETTING AROUND
**Orange Cab** (tel. 904/252-2046) has limousine service from the airport to beach hotels, for $10 to $15.

Twenty-two **rental-car companies** operate in the area, with Alamo (tel. 255-1511) leading the budget pack, and Hertz, Avis, Thrifty, National, and Dollar right behind.

Daytona's municipal transit company, **Vo Tran** (tel. 761-7700), has regular **bus routes** from 6am to 6:30pm on the beach, to the airport, and downtown at 60¢ for adults, 30¢ for children 6 to 18.

If you'd like to ride over to Walt Disney World or Cape Canaveral, **Gray Line Tours** (tel. 255-6506) has tours to many area attractions at varying times and prices starting at $15 to $20.

For taxi service, call **Yellow Cab** (tel. 252-5536) or **Daytona Economy Cab** (tel. 253-2522). Charges are about $1.80 for the first mile, and $1.20 for each succeeding mile.

All along the beach concessionaires rent mopeds and bicycles, or you can try **Moped Man** (tel. 788-4030) or **Bike Smith** (tel. 258-6550).

## USEFUL INFORMATION

For **police or medical emergencies,** call 767-2211 in Daytona Beach Shores, 253-6701 in Daytona Beach. . . . For food at any hour on weekends, try **Village Inn,** 100 S. Atlantic Ave., Ormond Beach (tel. 672-7764). . . . For quick **dry cleaning,** Romie's, at 1617 Ridgewood Ave. (tel. 767-4883), can help. . . . For a **doctor,** call the Volusia County Medical Association at 258-1611, and for a **dentist,** call 734-1355 or 253-2451. . . . **Circle K grocery stores** are open 24 hours. . . . **Weather info** at 252-5575.

## TOURIST INFORMATION

**Destination Daytona,** 126 E. Orange Ave. (P.O. Box 2775), Daytona Beach, FL 32015 (tel. 904/255-0415, or toll free 800/854-1234), has a cheerful staff ready to help out with information on accommodations or attractions, or to extricate you from problems. A free copy of the "Daytona Beach Resort Area Visitors Guide" and a calendar of events can be yours by telephoning toll free 800/854-1234 in Florida. . . . The **Ormond Beach Chamber of Commerce,** 165 W. Granada Blvd. (P.O. Box 874), Ormond Beach, FL 32074 (tel. 904/677-3454), has all the same services.

---

# 2. Where to Stay

So frequently do prices change in Daytona that reading a rate sheet is like scanning a stock market report. Business (and price) heats up here when the weather does, about February through April, drops after Easter, and rises again June through August, then drops way down in the fall. Anytime the city has a big event (like speed weeks in February, March, and July), up go the prices again, sometimes as much as $15 or $20 a day or more. Most hotels also hold out for three- or five-day minimum stays during those packed events. You can save on rooms here, as on every Florida beach, by giving up an ocean view.

## LUXURY HOTELS

The **Daytona Beach Hilton,** 2637 S. Atlantic Ave., Daytona Beach, FL 32018 (tel. 904/767-7350, or toll free 800/HILTONS or 800/525-7350), is up there with the top runners. Hilton hotels often have unusual architecture, and they've got it here in a very contemporary hotel with a saw-toothed, multilevel exterior. There are 215 luxurious rooms and suites, with lots of special touches like wing chairs, love seats, and wardrobes, hair dryers, ruffled bedskirts, refrigerators, bars, and pretty, contemporary prints. Many of the very large rooms open onto private balconies. The Hilton has two plush restaurants, two lounges with entertainment, two pools,

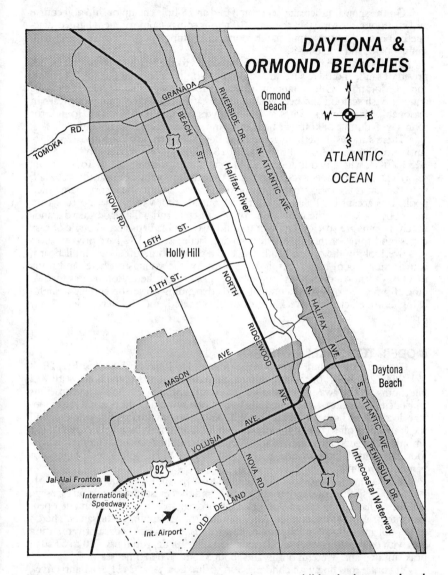

tennis courts, a putting green, sauna and exercise room, children's playground, and a game room—and of course, all that beach. Double rates here are $75 to $165, year round.

If you like golf resorts and don't mind not being right on the beachfront, we can't think of a more inviting place to stay in the Daytona area than **Indigo Lakes Resort,** 2570 Volusia Ave. (P.O. Box 10859), Daytona Beach, FL 32020 (tel. 904/258-6333, or toll free 800/874-9918, 800/874-9918 in Florida), on US 92 at I-95. Breezes rustle through tall pines and ruffle tiny blue ponds; a flock of birds soars overhead; and nestled among shade trees and gardens are attractive rooms, 212 of them, including 64 fancy suites. All are decorated in handsome clear colors, with contemporary furnishings and attractive wallpaper. Some have balconies too.

On the sprawling acreage here you'll find an 18-hole championship golf course ranked among the top 10 in the state, 10 tennis courts (some of them lighted), racquetball courts, a fitness trail, game room, and equipment for billiards, volleyball, shuffleboard, and horseshoes.

All day long the resort operates free shuttles to the beach so you won't be deprived of sand, and there's free transportation to the airport, jai alai, the speedway, and the dog track. One restaurant here provides classy cuisine with an impressive array of fresh seafood and beef while another casual stop offers you good steaks in reasonable price ranges. Rates at Indigo Lakes are $80 to $143, year round, for rooms with double or king-size beds at the inn, higher for executive suites.

There's always something going on at **Best Western Aku Tiki Inn,** 2225 S. Atlantic Ave., Daytona Beach Shores, FL 32018 (tel. 904/252-9631, or toll free 800/AKU-TIKI), where two lounges keep popping until the wee hours. To get to the resort's attractive Trader's restaurant, pass over the moon bridge near the waterfall, then dine in this exotic setting overlooking the ocean and the resort's large tiled pool. This accent on Polynesia continues outside too, where a flaring roof over the lobby looks like the prow of a Polynesian craft and a Tiki god guard stands watch. Rooms are spacious enough to hold two double beds and a couple of easy chairs, and some of them also offer cooking facilities. All 132 have private balconies overlooking the ocean. You'll also find a game room, gift shop, shuffleboard, coin laundry, pool bar, and splashing place for the youngsters here, and tours to all of Orlando's diversions can be booked right from here. Room rates for two range from a low of $40 to a high of $101, depending on season and view, slightly higher for efficiencies. Weekly rates are also offered, and children under 12 stay free.

## MODERATELY PRICED HOTELS

**Treasure Island Inn,** 2025 S. Atlantic Ave., Daytona Beach Shores, FL 32018 (tel. 904/255-8371, or toll free 800/874-7420), towers over the beach with 232 big rooms tucked away in a V-shaped building 11 stories tall. You'll find spacious efficiencies and suites, all with inviting balconies overlooking the ocean. Contemporary decor with a homey touch makes this a favorite spot with families, who can send the youngsters off to one of the two swimming pools or the game room, while less ambitious parents enjoy one of the two whirlpools, or just pull up a chair at the barefoot bar nearby. Double rates range from $49 to $116, year round, higher for penthouse rooms.

**Turtle Inn,** 3233 S. Atlantic Ave., Daytona Beach, FL 32108 (tel. 904/761-0426), has a spiffy contemporary air about it, and the cutest turtle logo you ever saw. The Turtle has just 39 spacious apartments, all decorated in bright colors and opening onto private balconies where you can watch the sea lapping at the sands. There's a big pool and units have fully equipped kitchens, queen-size beds, a private sitting area with convertible couch and Jacuzzis. To turn Turtle, you'll pay $70 to $120 in peak summer and winter months, and about $35 to $70 in other seasons.

If you're traveling with children, **Sun Viking Lodge,** at 2411 S. Atlantic Ave., Daytona Beach, FL 32018 (tel. 904/252-6252, or toll free 800/874-R469), is a place they'll love. A big hit here with the wee ones is a twisting, turning water slide that sends you splashing into a pool (and come to think of it, that sounds like fun for us so-called grownups too). At this owner-operated beach resort, there are just 91 rooms, efficiencies and suites, all set in a cozy friendly atmosphere. Tropical colors decorate rooms, and most have kitchens and will sleep six. Rooms have refrigerators and room safes too. For a double you'll pay $55 to $102, year round.

Big picture windows gaze out over the ocean at the **Daytona Sands,** 2523 S. Atlantic Ave., Daytona Beach Shores, FL 32018 (tel. 904/767-2551), a small two-story motel with just 50 rooms stretched out along the ocean. You can prowl among the sea oats here (please don't pick them), roam miles of wide beaches, and relax in modest but spacious rooms cheerful with bright colors and attractive furnishings. There's a heated pool on the grounds, and some of the rooms are efficiencies. Rates for two range from $75 to $170, year round, depending on season.

Three acres of beautiful grounds and a palm-fringed swimming pool greet you at **Plantation Island,** 187 S. Atlantic Ave., Ormond-by-the-Sea, FL 32074 (tel. 904/677-2331, or toll free 800/874-0552, 800/321-2432 in Florida). You can stay in a low-rise, two-story building overlooking a pretty pool, or in a six-story condominium overlooking the ocean and a second pool. In either place you'll find wide rooms with two double beds and comfortable chairs, kitchens, even Jacuzzis in some apartments. Vivid colors are popular here, complementing a long strip of beach and sky outside. The hotel is complete with dining room and lounge. Rates range by season from $30 to $65, higher during special events.

**Daytona Inn/Broadway,** 219 S. Atlantic Ave., (at Broadway), Daytona Beach, FL 32018 (tel. 904/252-3626, or toll free 800/874-1822, 800/251-1962 in Florida), is a contemporary spot with a bright modern lobby, tiled floors, and a Victorian-era Broadway Street Station restaurant. Set alongside the beach, the inn has lots of attractive landscaping and a big sundeck overlooking the pool. A special treat for children is a small pool centered with a spouting fountain. Rooms are big and decorated in tropical colors. Rates range from $48 to $82 year round.

A second Daytona Inn called **Seabreeze,** 1108 N. Atlantic Ave. (at Seabreeze Boulevard), Daytona Beach, FL 32014 (tel. 904/252-4363), offers similar accommodations and facilities at the same price, and has some suites that sleep up to eight.

You can't miss the **Maverick Motor Inn,** 485 S. Atlantic Ave., Daytona Beach, FL 32014 (tel. 904/672-3550)—just look for the white mustang pawing the air. That equine figure is right at the front door of this modern motel, and if you miss that, there's a horned bull's head painted out front. That western theme extends to the restaurant, and there's even a woodsy touch in the cheerful rooms of this seven-story lodge. Private balconies and lots of glass offer a nice view of the ocean, and there are some housekeeping apartments. All the rooms have refrigerators too. There's a pool for children and another for adults. Two people pay $40 to $115, year round.

**Ramada Inn Surfside,** 3125 S. Atlantic Ave., Daytona Beach, FL 32018 (tel. 904/788-1000, or toll free 800/322-1322, 800/255-3838 in Florida), rises seven stories over the sand near the tip of the peninsula on which this city lies. From a cool spot in the pool you can gaze out over this wide beach to the ocean stretching on forever. A smaller version of the same keeps the youngsters busy. Ramada keeps things trim wherever it settles, and that is no less true here where you can settle into attractively decorated rooms. Some are equipped with cooking facilities and the resort has a few suites. All rooms have color television, radio, and a private balcony overlooking the sea. A dining room and lounge stave off starvation and thirst. Rates at Ramada Surfside, which has motel rooms, efficiencies and suites in several sizes, range from $61 to $164, year round; higher for suites and during special events.

**Islander Beach Resort,** at 1601 S. Atlantic Ave., New Smyrna Beach, FL 32069 (tel. 904/427-3452, or toll free 800/USA-3452), offers kiddie pool, game and exercise rooms, cable television, volleyball, central pool (it's huge) and spa. Palm trees dot the grounds and rooms that overlook the pool and ocean are wide, roomy suites with lively colors. Rates range from $85 to $100, year round.

**Ocean Villa Motel,** 828 N. Atlantic Ave., Daytona Beach, FL 32018 (tel. 904/252-4644, or toll free 800/255-3691), is another small motel on the beach where you won't find yourself part of the masses. A two-story, 38-room motel, Ocean Villa is right on the ocean but it also has a big heated swimming pool with an aqua slide and protective windbreak. There's even a pool for the children. Wall-to-wall carpeting stretches across the rooms, and all have plenty of space and big picture windows. The friendly management will arrange for special golf privileges, and encourage you to grill outdoors on the resort's barbecue. Efficiencies and one-bedroom apartments are available for larger groups, and the resort charges $30 to $93 year round.

What a swimming pool they have at **Perry's Ocean Edge,** 2209 S. Atlantic Ave., Daytona Beach, FL 32018 (tel. 904/255-0581, or toll free 800/447-0002, 800/342-0102 in Florida). It has topped its competitors by enclosing its pool in a gorgeous solarium and heating it all with solar power. Three stories high, this solarium has a huge fern dangling from the heavy wood beams that support the translucent covering, and is filled with palms. Rooms have big picture windows so you can see the delighted splashing going on below. There's even a new addition: a solar-heated spa in the garden. Big, big rooms are beautifully decorated in splashy contemporary hues, and the mini-suites even have three double beds. Every morning you get complimentary homemade doughnuts and coffee. When you're looking for something to do, ask and they'll tell you about special golf privileges for guests. Double rates here are $38 to $115, year round, higher in suites.

## BUDGET HOTELS

**Days Inn** has three oceanside locations: 839 S. Atlantic Ave., Ormond-by-the-Sea, FL 32074 (tel. 904/677-6600); 1909 S. Atlantic Ave. (tel. 904/255-4492); and 3209 S. Atlantic Ave. (tel. 904/761-2050). You can reach all of them at the Days Inn toll-free number (tel. 800/325-2525). All charge $40 to $100 double, year round.

**Del Aire Motel,** 744 N. Atlantic Ave., Daytona Beach, FL 32014 (tel. 904/252-2563), is a family-style beachside resort with just 20 rooms, all kept sparklingly clean. Some of the attractive rooms are efficiencies, and all have a cozy, homey air about them, thanks to a friendly management intent on keeping a happy family of guests here. Located right on the beach, the motel has a tiled pool and lots of space to see the sun. Two people pay $55 to $80 in peak winter seasons, $30 to $50 in other months.

A real money-saver in the Daytona area is **Econo Lodge-Racetrack,** at 2250 Volusia Ave., Daytona Beach, FL 32014 (tel. 904/255-3661), where the rates are $30 to $55, year round. Extra persons sharing a room are $5. These very basic accommodations are not on the beach, but they're close to the speedway, jai alai, and dog track.

Lovely lawns slope down to a sparkling pool and wind among one-story buildings with Mediterranean touches at **Spindrift,** 3333 S. Atlantic Ave., Daytona Beach Shores, FL 32018 (tel. 904/767-3261). A tranquil spot right on the ocean, Spindrift has 14 units scattered about perfectly manicured grounds in simply furnished cottages, apartments, efficiencies, or motel rooms with cable television. You won't find lots of fancy amenities, but you will discover a serene spot for a vacation. Two people pay $22 to $68 year round.

## GET INN ON IT

Sad to say, Daytona lost most of its historic charm to the wrecking ball and replaced nearly all of its furbeloved Victorian architecture with the starkly serviceable but not very eye-appealing architecture of the 50s and early 60s.

One vestige of days gone by remains, however, and another inn-ovative hotel owner here has struggled to create the frothy pastel look that characterized turn-of-the-century architecture.

That whisper of the past can be seen at **The St. Regis,** 509 Seabreeze Blvd., Daytona Beach, FL 32018 (tel. 904/252-8743), which opened here 102 years ago. Now surrounded by the gritty little T-shirt and souvenir shops that have honkey-tonked Daytona, the St. Regis remains an oasis in a sea of mediocrity. Here a rainbow of colorful blossoms lines the awninged walkway. Under the spreading oak tree the village treasure stands. Wicker chairs on the porch set the tone outside, while inside a lobby full of granny-treasures from a needlepointed ottoman to an antique lamp lures you back into a less frenetic century. There are just 17 rooms here, all of them top to toe in antiques and lace, frills, and ruffles. Guests get the royal treatment from flowers to champagne and chocolates, and that's not even to mention the very good cooking that goes on in the kitchen. Rates are $85 to $95 double, including breakfast.

We have heard many glowing reports about **Captain's Quarters Inn,** 3711 S. Atlantic Ave., Daytona Beach Shores, FL 32119 (tel. 904/767-3119). CQ bills itself as a bed-and-breakfast, but you needn't take breakfast if you'd rather do it yourself or go elsewhere. Built by pert and tenacious Becky Sue Morgan, the hotel rose on the grounds of a smaller motel she operated until she put together the capital and talked officials into zoning laws that would allow her to build this new inn.

Five stories tall, Captain's Quarters has 25 units, all suites with living room, kitchen, and separate bedroom. A queen-size sleep couch in the living room converts to a bed for families. Right on the sand in Daytona Beach Shores, this attractive motel has French doors opening onto balconies where you can settle into a rocker and contemplate the wavelets lapping at your stretch of sandy shore. Suites are outfitted with tall-poster beds, comfortable oak furnishings with an antique look about them, and a kitchen equipped with dishwasher and coffee maker. Outside there's the requisite swimming pool and plenty of beach. There's even a country crafts gift shop here.

Pretty lacy touches are everywhere, setting this cozy spot apart from the masses of standard motels that line the beach here. When you step into the lace-curtained lobby you're greeted with a glass of wine or orange juice, and every morning the local newspaper appears at your door. If you opt for breakfast for two—complete with fresh bread, served in the inn's antiquey coffee shop or in your room—rates range from $75 to $95, depending on season. If you don't want breakfast, rates are $10 lower. Money-saving monthly rates are also available, and you should expect rates to be higher during race weeks and holidays when there may be a seven-night minimum.

## ROCK-BOTTOM RATES

**Daytona Beach Youth Hostel,** 140 S. Atlantic Ave., Daytona Beach, FL 32018 (tel. 904/258-6937), has a number of rooms with three beds, color television, shared bath, and shower for $12 for hostel members, $20 for nonmembers, plus a $5 key deposit, refunded if you return the key. Accommodations are no-frills, with a kitchen downstairs and pool and Ping-Pong tables available. Open 24 hours, the hostel has no curfew. Motel rooms with two double beds are available elsewhere in the complex and the rate for those is $45 to $109 double.

## CAMPING

**Tomoka State Park,** 2099 N. Beach St., also called Old Dixie Highway, at the northern border of Ormond Beach, FL 32074 (tel. 904/677-3931), is a shady spot to bed down if you're camping. Campsite rates are $20 a night for four people, $22 with electric hookup. Reservations are taken only by telephone—no letters—up to 60 days prior to arrival.

---

# 3. Where to Dine

---

Daytona has many moderately priced restaurants along the beach, and a wide selection of dining spots in the city's top resorts. We've selected some of the best in the area and grouped them roughly by price category (prices cited are for entrées, but that usually includes salad, one or two vegetables, and sometimes coffee as well).

## THE TOP RESTAURANTS

French food fanciers usually also find their way to **La Crêpe en Haut,** 142 E. Granada Blvd., Ormond Beach (on Fla. 40) in Fountain Square, next door to the Birthplace of Speed Museum (tel. 673-1999). Naturally, crêpes are on the menu here, supplemented by lobster ravioli, veal in several delectable preparations, creations in a flaky pastry shell, steak in a mustard-brandy sauce, and tournedos Rossini. You'll pay about $25 to $35 for dinners. Chic La Crêpe is open Tuesday through Friday for lunch from 11am to 2pm, and 5:30 to 10pm Tuesday through Sunday for dinner; closed Monday.

If you like an intimate romantic atmosphere, you'll like **King's Cellar,** 1258 N. Atlantic Ave. (tel. 255-3014), where you dine in the handsome dining room of an old mansion built in the 1800s. Excellent steaks and seafood have some Italian touches, and there's always some pasta around for carbohydrate lovers. Entrées generally fall in the $10 to $15 range, although the menu begins lower, and there's a special menu for children. Open from 5 to 10pm Monday through Saturday, from 5 to 9pm on Sunday; closed Tuesday.

## MODERATE

Waitresses dress in gingham and you slip right back into days of over-the-hill-to-granny's at **Marko's Heritage Inn,** 5420 S. Ridgewood Ave., on US 1 in Port Orange (tel. 767-3809). You'll see them making the bread and cinnamon rolls as you enter, then sit down to some old-fashioned food at old-fashioned prices (in the $10 to $20 range): sirloin, shrimp, crab, fresh fish, seafood chowder ladled from a tureen, and crisp salads with extravagantly rich house dressings. Shades of Mason jars and strawberry hullers! Marko's is open from 4:30 to 10pm Monday through Saturday, with a big Sunday dinner served from 11:30am to 9pm.

**Julian's,** at 88 S. Atlantic Ave. (tel. 677-6767), is one of the city's most popular spots, and deservedly so. They produce outstanding beef and seafood dishes here, but prime rib's the specialty. Pleasant, intimate, woodsy surroundings complete the package at Julian's, where you can dine on entrées in the $10 to $15 range for full-course dinners. Open from 4 to 11pm daily, the restaurant also has cocktails and entertainment.

Friendly, efficient service and a cheery atmosphere are keynotes at **Kay's Coach House,** 724 Main St. (tel. 253-1944), and prime rib is one of the most ordered specialties on the long, long menu at this pleasant spot near the beach. After dinner you can slip into the cocktail lounge for a finale. Prices at Kay's run about $10 to $15 for most dinner entrées, with some as low as $5. Open from 11am to 9pm, daily except Monday.

It seems miles away from the rollicking rip-roaring sands of Daytona, but it's really only a few miles to **Chastain's Inlet Harbor** (tel. 767-4502), in the quiet village of Ponce de Leon Inlet, home to the area's fishing clan. Nearby is the lighthouse, which you can tour after dining in an up-on-stilts setting overlooking the waters where shrimp fishermen chug off into the sunset and pelicans swoop down on their dinner. Simple cooking and simple setting here, and plenty of seafood from oysters and scallops to crab, flounder, snapper. You can even have fish for weekend breakfast (with grits, naturally), and at any meal you'll have to consumee lots to run up a bill higher than about $12 to $15. Open from noon (4pm Monday) to 9pm weekdays, to 10pm on weekends.

A newcomer that has been receiving some attention is **Steve's Venice,** 2616 S. Atlantic Ave., Daytona Beach Shores (tel. 761-2444). Northern Italian cooking, the most delicate and creamy of Italy's preparations, is served in a pleasant atmosphere with matching service. Prices for dinner are in the $10 to $15 range, and hours are 5 to 10pm weekdays, an hour later on weekends.

Decidedly not a newcomer, **Riccardo's,** 610 Glenview Blvd. (telL 253-3035), has been around for 18 years now, and for a good and simple reason: good food. Fresh pastas are whipped up each day and the same can be said for crusty breads, cheesecake, and desserts. A family operation keeps things humming here and even cuts their own prime veal out back in the kitchen. Dinner prices are in the $10 to $20 bracket, and hours are 5 to 10pm daily.

**Gene's Steak House,** 3674 Volusia Ave., on US 92 (tel. 255-2059), eight miles west of Fla. A1A near the racetrack, is a beef-lover's paradise with seven kinds of steaks on the menu, all of them served in a handsome, intimate atmosphere. You'll pay about $17 for steaks here, and hours are 5 to 10pm daily except Monday.

Seafood spots are everywhere of course, but top accolades go to **Red Snapper,** 2058 S. Atlantic Ave. (tel. 252-0212), which sells tons of that popular light, white fish each year for prices in the $12 to $20 range. Hours are 5 to 11pm daily.

## OUT OF TOWN AND INTERESTING

One of our recommended scenic drives runs from Daytona Beach to St. Augustine via Fla. A1A. Along the way, beside a quiet strip of sand just south of Ormond Beach and near the Bulow Plantation ruins, you'll see a tall stone house looming significantly over the neighborhood. In it you'll find **Topaz Café,** 1224 S. Oceanshore Blvd., Flagler Beach (tel. 439-3275), a tiny café with ambience and good food. A gem by any name, Topaz has a frequently changing menu that focuses on carefully selected regional seafood: pompano, for instance, served with a choice of several sauces. Other selections may include filet mignon with any of several sauces, chicken in interesting preparations including rolled in Romano cheese, and St. Augustine crab. Open for lunch from 11:45am to 3pm on Friday only, and dinner from 6:30 to 9:30pm Tuesday through Saturday, the café offers dinner prices in the $11 to $20 range.

## BUDGET BETS

The **Chart House** turns out seafood like Sante Fe shrimp, beef like teriyaki and kebabs, and many another goodie. It's in a nice location too, hard by the yacht harbor at 1100 Marina Point (tel. 255-9022). Entrées at this attractive spot are in the $12 to $17 range, and the Chart House is open daily from 5 to 10pm (an hour later on weekends).

Anchor Inn, a mainstay of this coastline for many, many years, is back again in different form. Now called the **Anchorage Inn,** 607 W. Dunlawton Ave., Port Orange (tel. 756-8102), the big restaurant that stands in the shade of a massive old oak "has been completely remodeled and is now the prettiest building in Daytona Beach," reports its owner. We haven't seen this one yet, but that kind of enthusiasm bodes well for this new owner who spent many years as general manager of another very popular seafood restaurant. Anchorage serves lots of seafood—"for $8, all the fresh fish you can eat," he promises—some steaks and chicken, all in a snappy new setting for prices in the $12 to $17 range. Anchorage is open from 11:30am to 10pm daily, later in the lounge. To get to the restaurant, follow Fla. A1A from Daytona Beach to its junction with US 1 and go straight from there to the restaurant. If you still can't find it, inquire at Port Orange Shopping Center—everyone will be watching this one.

When you're looking for a light lunch or dinner, try the homemade quiches and broiled hamburgers at **Bennigan's,** 890 S. Atlantic Ave. (tel. 673-3691), part of the successful chain operation that always produces pleasant greenery-filled atmospheres and inexpensive dining. Prices are in the $5 to $10 range for most things. The restaurant's open from 11am to 2am.

**Duff's Smörgåsbord,** in the Outlet Mall, 2400 S. Ridgewood Rd., South Daytona Beach (tel. 788-0828), is once again the place to head for an all-you-can-eat money-saver smörgåsbord table with meats, vegetables, salads, and desserts for under $7. The atmosphere is simple but always clean and bright, and the restaurant is open from 11am to 3pm and 4 to 8pm daily, from 11am to 8pm Sunday.

**Piccadilly Cafeteria,** in the Volusia Mall, 1700 Volusia Ave. (tel. 258-5373), features more than 100 times every day at its long, long cafeteria line where you'll pay $5 or less for most meals. Open daily from 11am to 8:30pm.

Try **New York Pizza,** 220 Broadway (tel. 257-3244), which creates hundreds of the New York variety for hungry customers every day from 11am to 3am. Free delivery. Prices: $4 to $10.

One would hardly expect to find a Hungarian dining spot in Daytona, which seems to have more junk-food spots per capita than any other town in Florida, but there it is—**Hungarian Village,** 424 S. Ridgewood (tel. 253-5712). Hugo and Anna Marie Tischler have been cooking up strüdel, lamb, pork, duck, goulash, and the like for ages. Devotees pour in here to dine in an attractive dining room that introduces you to that little-known land from which Anna Marie hails. Open every day except Sunday and Monday from 5 to 10pm, with prices from $7 to $12.

A seafood favorite is **Down the Hatch,** 4984 Front St., at Timmons Fishing Camp (tel. 761-4831) on Ponce Inlet, south of Daytona. Down the Hatch has its own fleet of ships to bring in the bacon (well, the whiting, tile fish, grouper, and snapper), and does such a sterling job of it that they offer fish specials for $6—with coleslaw and french fries! Nice setting too. Hours are noon to 10pm daily, and the average dinner price is $6 to $10.

**Norwood Seafood,** 400 2nd St. just off Fla. 44 on the beach, New Smyrna (tel. 428-4621), has been around since the 1940s and is bigger and better than ever now. Its woodsy maze of multilevels has been remodeled and expanded, and crowds are pouring into this seafood restaurant, which doles out soft-shell crabs, seafood gumbo, and oyster stew, along with lots of other snack and finger foods. Prices are in the $8 to $18 range, and hours are 11am to 9pm daily; Sunday brunch from 10am to 2pm.

---

# 4. Daytona After Dark

---

The after-dark scene is pretty quiet in Daytona. There are a number of lounges and plenty of activity for the younger set, but none of the showy nightclub life available in some of the state's larger cities.

## CULTURAL ACTIVITIES

Despite its excess of youthful exuberance during the collegiate spring-break session from late February through Easter, and its apparent welcome for gangs of motorcycle enthusiasts, the city does have a cultural life.

From June through August, an orchestra and performers stage light opera and Broadway hits in a repertory activity called **Seaside Music Theatre.** Warbling takes place at Daytona Beach Community College, 1200 Volusia Ave. (tel. 252-6200). In winter, this repertory operation moves to a local hotel, usually the Treasure Island Inn, 2025 S. Atlantic Ave., Daytona Beach Shores, remaining there from January through April, when some dramas are added to the group's list of musicals. Tickets are $11 to $16 in summer, about $20 during the winter months when dinner is included in the price. The mailing address is P.O. Box 1310, Daytona Beach, FL 32015.

**Central Florida Cultural Endeavors,** 901 6th St. (tel. 252-1511), brings in groups like the London Symphony and the Vienna Boys Choir for performances at Peabody Auditorium, 100 Auditorium St., or Daytona Beach Community College, 1200 Volusia Ave. Tickets cost $10 to $35. Their mailing address is P.O. Box 1310, Daytona Beach, FL 32015.

From December through April, concert artists of note appear at Peabody Auditorium, 100 Auditorium St. (tel. 677-0670).

Daytona Beach's **Civic Ballet,** P.O. Box 6335, Daytona Beach, FL 32022 (tel. 252-0401, ext. 260), shows off talented dancers in several performances throughout the year with *The Nutcracker* at Christmas, of course. Most performances are given in the Peabody Auditorium and tickets costs $8 to $15.

For symphony music, it's the **Daytona Beach Symphony Society,** P.O. Box

3241, Daytona Beach, FL 32018 (tel. 252-2423), which arranges performances by the Florida Symphony and presents other musical productions at Peabody Auditorium.

## DECIBELISTIC ENTERTAINMENT

Home to thundering herds of vacationing college students each spring, and party-minded folks in every season, Daytona has plenty of places to play.

The **Clarendon Plaza Hotel,** 600 N. Atlantic Ave. (tel. 255-4471), houses three different nightclubs so you can be sure there's a lively crowd there any night. Choose from Penrod's (see below) with rock-video music and two dance floors; the Plantation Club, with kinetic-light live-band shows and all the disco you can dance until the wee hours (designer jeans are better here); or 701, a bar with a big dance floor and recorded music. The cover charge varies, but it's usually about $5.

There's a show nightly except Monday at **Hawaiian Inn,** 2301 S. Atlantic Ave., Daytona Beach Shores (tel. 255-5411). At the **Best Western Aku Tiki,** 2225 S. Atlantic Ave. (tel. 252-9631), where you'd expect to see a Polynesian show, there's country music from 9pm to 2am.

**Finky's,** 640 N. Grandview (tel. 255-5059), is a cavernous revelry spot that seats a thousand merrymakers. Cover charge for deejay, bands, and special-drink nights is $5 to $8.

Rock 'n' roll is the scene at **P.J.'s,** 400 Broadway (tel. 258-5222). P.J.'s is collegiate heaven and has lots of specials and special events for spring breakers. Cover charges vary widely and often.

Lounges in many of the hotels along the beach offer quiet listening music on weekends, and sometimes nightly in the summer months.

**Penrod's Plantation Club,** 600 N. Atlantic Ave. (tel. 255-4471), is the creation of bar-entrepreneur Jack Penrod, whose lively clubs are the center of nightlife attention in several Florida cities. You can count on this spot for wet T-shirts, teeny bikinis, and plenty of suds and sounds. Open from 9am to 3am, Penrod's sometimes has a $2 to $5 cover charge.

**Top of the Boardwalk,** 400 N. Atlantic Ave., in the Holiday Inn-Boardwalk (tel. 255-0251), offers a somewhat more subdued atmosphere and beautiful ocean views from the 12th floor. A popular attitude-adjustment spot in the early evening, this lounge keeps the music going with a deejay later in the evening. There's no cover charge.

**Razzles,** 611 Seabreeze Blvd. (tel. 257-6236), sets out to razzle and dazzle with room for 500 rockers, two dance floors, a deejay, and something rockin' to the weee hours. Cover charge is $3 to $8, and all-you-can drink nights are popular. Hours are 8pm to 3am daily.

Who cares where the original place is when you can see and be seen at **The Other Place,** 642 S. Atlantic Ave. in Ormond Beach (tel. 672-2461). A very large dance floor is the lure at this spot, which has a $2 to $3 cover charge on some evenings, laser videos, rock 'n' roll, and is open to those 18 or older, as many in that age bracket have discovered. Hours are 8pm to 3am daily.

**Mac's Famous Bar,** 2000 S. Atlantic Ave. (tel. 252-9239), focuses on comedy Wednesday through Sunday, but often has a blues singer as well. Smaller than some of the massive spots this city frequents, Mac's is well loved for its casual atmosphere and hearty sandwiches. Hours are 11am to 2am and the cover is $6 for comedy shows.

**Checker's Café,** 219 S. Atlantic Ave. in the Daytona Inn-Broadway (tel. 252-3626), occupies an enviable spot right in the middle of the beach. That location guarantees activity at all hours as beach enthusiasts stop in here for a little sun-relief. Evenings there's a deejay or live music, and here the crowd usually excludes teenyboppers. There's no cover and hours are 7am to 3am daily.

**Ocean Deck,** 1275 S. Ocean Ave. (tel. 253-5224), often rocks with the sounds of reggae music, an island rhythm that sounds just about perfect in this seaside spot that has successfully combined sea with seafood and spirits. Teeny bikinis can often be seen here in this casual lounge, which has entertainment daily except Monday and is open from 11am to 3am; no cover charge.

More? **Hole Lounge,** at 301 S. Atlantic Ave. (tel. 255-6421), is big on '50s music, twist remembrances, and hula-hoop contests. At the city's **Ocean Pier,** Main Street at the ocean (tel. 253-1212), there are rock bands and the city's biggest dance floor, plus four bars, a real caboose, and lots of inexpensive drinks.

Just about everything in the city is open to 3am.

# 5. Seeing the Sights

Speed, speed, and more speed are the focus of Daytona sight-seeing, where the beach is a sight-seeing highway.

## A WORD ABOUT THE BEACH

Twenty-three miles long and 500 feet wide, Daytona's hard-packed sparkling sand is one of the tourist delights of the Sunshine State, not only for sunning but for *driving.* You can take your car right onto the sand at Ormond Beach and drive along the water's edge south to Ponce de Leon Inlet.

No matter how shallow the water looks, *don't drive in it* or you're likely to end up waiting for the tow truck. Just stick to the main strip where everyone else is driving, and don't go faster than 10 m.p.h. You can park anywhere on the beach, but take our chastened word for it that they did not put up those signs warning motorists off soft, unsafe areas for nothing.

On a wide boardwalk at the ocean, near the fishing pier and just north of Main Street, you'll find an **amusement park** that will delight the youngsters and maybe the not-so-youngsters too. There's a sight-seeing tower and sky ride open day and night in summer months, and a bandshell in **Oceanfront Park** at the north end of the promenade. The park is open from 1 to 11:30pm daily in summer, and the bandshell has concerts regularly.

At Ponce de Leon Inlet and Lighthouse you can discover some interesting facts about Florida's lighthouse system and get a look at the lighthouse (open from 1 to 8pm in the summer months, shorter hours in fall and winter).

## WHAT TO SEE

If you're here in the all-important **speed weeks** in February, you'll see cars, cars, and more cars, qualifying races, and finally the big **Daytona 500 Stock Car Race** in mid-February. A **Motorcycle Classic** roars around the track during the first week of March, and the city celebrates the Fourth of July with a summer speed week that culminates in the **Pepis 400** on the first Saturday in July. Tickets for speedway events start at $20 and go to $65. You can get them by contacting **Daytona International Speedway,** P.O. Box 2801, Daytona, FL 32115 (tel. 904/253-6711).

If you're not visiting here in those jam-packed, rip-roaring weeks, you might like to see where all the hoopla occurs. Bus tours (tel. 254-6767) of the massive racing facility go on daily from 9am to 5pm for $1 for all over 12 years old.

In Ormond Beach, the **Birthplace of Speed Museum,** 160 E. Granada Blvd. (tel. 672-5657), traces the history of beach races here and also houses a replica of a 1906 Stanley Steamer thought to have raced 190 m.p.h. so many years ago, and lots of other antique cars and interesting automotive memorabilia. It's open from noon to 4pm Monday through Saturday, and admission is $2 (children under 9, free).

Rumor does have a way of spreading wildly in Florida, and rumor has it that when John D. Rockefeller spent his winters in Ormond Beach, he one day heard a hotel clerk figuring someone's bill and demanded to know why his own tab was higher. "Why, Mr. Rockefeller," the clerk replied, "we thought you have so much money you wouldn't mind if we charged you more." Not only did he mind, but the next year he moved out—lock, stock, and millions. To add insult to injury (or vice versa), he built a huge home right across the street. So many windows did the house have that Rockefeller called it the **Casements,** and spent many a winter there. After he died, the beautiful old two-story home fell into disrepair, but was recently rescued by the city, which now operates it as a cultural center. You can tour it free, daily except Sunday from 10am to 2:30pm. Casements is at 25 Riverside Dr. (tel. 673-4701).

In Bunnell, 22 miles north of Daytona Beach (take Old Dixie Highway past Tomoka State Park), you can see the crumbling foundations of a great sugar plantation mansion, **Bulow Villa,** at Bulow Plantation State Historic Site. Parts of a sugar mill made of coquina rock are still standing, and there are several wheels and the plantation's old springhouse. Admission is free.

Legend has it that somewhere in Bulow Creek, a 13-mile-long stream that begins just south of Bunnell, a cache of gold is buried!

Daytona's **Museum of Arts and Sciences,** 1040 Museum Blvd., off Nova Road (tel. 255-0285), has a collection of Cuban art and sculpture generally regarded as one of the best of its kind in the world. Star of the museum's science collection is a giant sloth, whose remains were found in a shell pit three miles away. This Pleistocene mammal weighed about five tons and loomed 20 feet over everything else in sight. This specimen is regarded as the best preserved of its type in the nation. Hours here are 9am to 4pm Tuesday through Friday, on Saturday from noon to 5pm. Planetarium shows are on Wednesday, Friday, and Saturday, laser rock concerts Friday and Saturday. Admission is $2 for adults, 50¢ for children.

You can get a look at the waters here aboard the **Dixie Queen River Cruise,** 841 Ballough Rd. (tel. 255-1997), which offers sight-seeing, brunch, lunch, and dinner cruises, and a trip to St. Augustine for varying prices. Days and hours for these cruises vary by season, so give them a call to see when they're doing what. To give you an idea what it will cost: Brunch cruises are $21.95 for adults, and dinner cruises are $25.45; children under 12 are half price.

Teaching a horse to adopt and maintain a high-stepping pace and keep it long and fast enough to win a race requires plenty of love and patience, two qualities you can see at work at **Spring Garden Ranch,** 900 Spring Garden Ranch Rd. in DeLeon Springs. You'll find this ranch, which specializes in the care and training of harness racehorses, about eight miles off US 17 in Deland. You can watch some of the 600 sleek beauties in training at an observation window in a small restaurant or right down at trackside here at Florida's largest harness training track. Although the facility is open year round, most of the activity is from September to June from 6am to 2pm daily. There's no admission, but it might be wise to check with them first at 904/985-5654; 985-0526 for the restaurant.

## SPECIAL EVENTS

Each Thanksgiving the region gives thanks for the automobile at the annual **Birthplace of Speed Antique Car Meet.** Astors, Goulds, and Fords who raced their horseless carriages on the hard-packed sand are saluted at the event, which includes reenactments of early meets, a costume contest, and an antique car exhibit and competition. Evenings, crowds line the boulevards of Ormond Beach to watch the Gaslight Parade of cars and costumed drivers. Antique car buffs wheel and deal at an antique car flea market, and beach springs test oldtimey chuggers.

# 6. Sports

With its very pleasant climate year round and miles of water and beach, you can always find something to keep your muscles in shape in Daytona.

## GOLF AND TENNIS

All the city's 12 golf courses are within 25 minutes of the beach, and most hotels will arrange your starting times for you. Some also have special greens fees for their guests, so be sure to ask.

**Daytona Beach Golf and Country Club** (tel. 255-4517) is the city's largest, with 36 holes. There are par-three courses at **Holly Hill, Fair Green Golf Course,** and **New Smyrna Beach.**

Public **tennis courts** are at eight locations in the city, including **Seabreeze Courts,** 1101 N. Atlantic Ave. (tel. 258-9198). The city's recreation department (tel. 253-9222) can help you find the courts nearest you.

**Handball** and **racquetball** enthusiasts can bang around at **Omega 40,** 1 S. Kings Rd., Ormond Beach (tel. 672-4044), where lighted indoor courts await. Hours vary by season, and the fee for full use of all the club's facilities is $10.50 per person daily, less if you belong to an affiliated club. Omega 40 has a pool, sauna, Nautilus weights, and all the get-fit accoutrements.

## WATER SPORTS

Big rollers whiz in all along this coastline, especially in the fall and spring. If you'd like to test your balance on a board, rent one at **Daytona Beach Surf Shops,** 520 Seabreeze Blvd. (tel. 253-3366), one of the nation's oldest surf shops. Rates are $3 an hour, $10 for all day.

Jet-skis are available at the **Halifax River** at the end of the Seabreeze Bridge (tel. 252-0972), and for motorboats try **Pelican Island Marina,** 3226 Riverview Lane (tel. 761-5884), which also has ski boats. **Atlantic Scuba Academy,** at 20 N. Atlantic Ave. (tel. 253-7558), can give you the word on diving trips.

*Reef Raider* will take you out deep-sea fishing all day or on half-day trips with bait and tackle furnished for $20 a half-day. It's docked at Ponce Inlet, turn west off Atlantic Avenue at Inlet Harbor Road (tel. 767-6000). The **Inlet Harbor booking office,** 122 Inlet Harbor Rd. (tel. 767-3266) can also help you find a charter fishing expedition, and there are three piers in the area for inexpensive angling. Day sea trips cost about $350 to $500 for six.

Parasailing fans can take to the skies courtesy of **Power Chute,** on Halifax Drive in Port Orange. To get there, follow Fla. A1A to Dunlawton West, then turn right on Halifax. Rides are about $20.

**Pontoon boats** and **jet-skis** can be rented by the half hour at **J&J Jet Skis,** 841 Ballough Rd. (tel. 255-1917) from March through October, 10am to 6pm daily. Prices vary according to the size of the waterborne equipment.

**Charter boat** fishing fleets can be found at **Critter Fleet,** 4950 S. Peninsula Dr., Ponce de Leon Inlet (tel. 767-7676), and **Sea Love Marina,** 4894 Front St., Ponce de Leon Inlet (tel. 767-3406). Rates are around $40 per person, but vary widely by season, number of people, and length of the trip you want to take. For private fishing parties charter boat rates generally fall in the $450 to $600-a-day range, but it's perfectly acceptable to bargain for a better price.

If a fish dinner isn't worth quite that much to you, try fishing off one of the region's three piers: the **Ocean Pier,** in the heart of Daytona Beach, where trout and flounder are often the catch of the day; **Ormond Pier,** north of Ormond Beach, a popular place to drop a line in hopes of hooking sea bass and tarpon; or **Sunglow Pier,** south of Port Orange, where king and Spanish mackerel are king. Pier fees are about $1 per person.

## RUNNING

The Daytona Beach Parks and Recreation Department sponsors an Easter Beach Run each year on two four-mile courses along the hard-packed sands. Nearly 2,000 runners from ages 8 to 80 participate.

## PARI-MUTUEL SPORTS

The **Daytona Beach Kennel Club,** on US 92 just off I-4 and I-95, and next door to the Speedway (tel. 252-6484), has races every day but Sunday. Post time is 7:45pm, and there are matinees at 1pm on Monday, Wednesday, and Saturday. Admission is $1.

The jai-alai season runs from February to mid-August at **Daytona Beach Jai-Alai,** on US 92 (tel. 255-0222). Admission is $1 to $3 and the games start at 7:15pm, with matinees at noon Tuesday, Thursday, and Saturday.

# X

# FLORIDA'S CROWN

## 1. JACKSONVILLE
## 2. ST. AUGUSTINE

**N**owhere else in Florida will you be closer to the state's—and the nation's—roots than in this region called the Crown. Historically, it is indeed Florida's corona, for here the state was born. Here was thrown the pebble that stirred a ripple, then a tidal wave, of tourism that was to alter the future of Florida forever.

Miami was nothing but a swamp when Jacksonville first welcomed winter-weary visitors to its shores. And Jacksonville in turn was little more than primeval forest when its neighbor St. Augustine was born and burgeoned into a bustling colony.

Here in these cities you can find the past all Americans share, a past tied to all this hemisphere and to Europe as well. Here, too, you'll find a part of the state like no other. Its sands are packed as hard as concrete; its life-style is as soft and slow as its southern drawls. Mists rise off wide rivers and pines replace palms. Giant live oaks stretch massive branches over streams once sailed by steamer passengers headed for healing—if somewhat odoriferous—sulfur springs upstream in Green Cove.

To this place came first the French, then the Spanish, then the English, then rowdy Revolutionaries called Americans. They horse-traded the territory among them for 300 years after the French started the cannons booming in Jacksonville in 1562 with a little colony of upstart Huguenots. Today Jacksonville is a bustling, booming banking and insurance capital where only two French words are common —mortgage and champagne.

Fortunes sought here today have plenty of precedent—some of Florida's most famous fortune hunters have gravitated to the Crown. Pirates Jean Lafitte, Black-beard, and Sir Francis Drake sacked cities that now honor those rogues with an oceanside highway known as the Buccaneer Trail. Slave trader Zephaniah Kingsley built an enormous plantation here from profits on African lives, then named as its doyenne his African princess wife. American spy John McIntosh, tired of serving a sluggish bureaucracy, tossed together a ragtag force and warred on Spain in hopes of making Florida an independent nation—and himself president.

There have been great glossy days in Jacksonville and St. Augustine, days when yards of silk rustled and frothed across the halls of great plantation houses, when champagne bubbled and money flowed. There have also been grim days, when fires burned, cannons thundered, and men died to wrest these lands from each other. Great galleons filled with yellow gold have sailed past these shores (if they could get by the wreckers), and massive sailing ships loaded with the black gold of slavery have slithered into Fernandina to unload their shackled cargo.

Waves of trouble and joy, of victors and vanquished, have washed over the land leaving behind massive fortresses and tiny frame houses, gold doubloons and lacy wedding gowns, ragged fragments of the past that welcome you to a land no longer royal but always regal, a land that has bequeathed to all the nation the legacy of lineage.

## GETTING THERE

American, Continental, Delta, Midway, PanAm, TWA, United, and USAir fly into **Jacksonville International Airport.** The airport is on the city's south side.

**Amtrak** trains stop in Jacksonville at 3570 Clifford Lane and in nearby Palatka, which is the nearest Amtrak stop for St. Augustine (about 35 miles southwest).

**Greyhound Trailways,** at 10 Pearl St. (tel. 356-5521), connect the cities to the state and nation.

## GETTING AROUND

Hertz and Avis **rental-car companies** are supplemented by Ajax, Econo, General, Ford, Budget, and Airport Thrifty. **Value** (tel. 757-1710) is a budget leader here.

### Jacksonville

**Airport limousines** in this city are all operated by independent van operators who just show up at the airport. You can ride with one of them by just stepping outside the door and joining other passengers who are headed to various points throughout the city. Vans drop their passengers off at any destination in the region, so you may get a city tour while you're at it, like it or not. Fares are about $8 to downtown Jacksonville, about $30 to $35 to the beach.

You can go in comfort on **AAA Limo,** 15353 Duval Rd. (tel. 751-4800), which operates plush vans and is under contract to several major resorts in the region. They do, however, take individual passengers, charging $35 to $40 for one person, $15 for additional passengers.

**Taxis** charge a flat rate of $30 to Jacksonville Beach for up to five passengers, $15 to downtown hotels. Mileage fees are $1.10 a mile. Because distances are great in this sprawling city, taxi rides can get quite expensive. Call **Checker Cab** (tel. 764-2472), or **Yellow Cab** (tel. 354-5511) for cab service.

**Jacksonville City Bus Transit** system travels downtown and to the beaches. They'll be happy to give you route information at 630-3100. Bus fares are about 60¢ and the service runs from dawn to dusk.

### St. Augustine

In downtown St. Augustine there is no public bus service. You can get around easily on **sight-seeing trams** or in taxis that charge by zone. Downtown destinations are $3 to $5, beach rides about $5. **Ancient City Cab Co.** (tel. 824-8161) will also pick you up at Jacksonville Airport or elsewhere in that city for $49, one way.

---

# 1. Jacksonville

---

Towering skyscrapers erupt in a blaze of smoky-gray reflections. Silvery masses of metal streak across a deep-blue river. Jacksonville, antique river city, welcomer of conquerers for four centuries, once a bustling port and now Florida's banking and insurance center, is on the grow again.

Change is everywhere these days: new hotels, refurbished old hotels, and everywhere a surge of enthusiasm as this lovely old city strides toward yet another renaissance. Now the nation's largest city, with 840 incorporated square miles, Jacksonville has been growing in spurts like this for generations.

Through it all Jacksonville keeps its Old South flavor, thanks to a long and proud history that can be traced back even further than St. Augustine's to 1564, when French Huguenots settled at Fort Caroline. Spanish soldiers, intent on making the water safe for their gold galleons, made short work of the colony, however, so Jacksonville has about given up trying to win an "oldest city" place in Florida history books.

It certainly hasn't given up trying to lure tourists here, and by now it ought to know how. Jacksonville has been hosting chilled Yankees since the 1800s, when steamers began bringing them from New York. Once here, they settled into Jacksonville's guesthouses, or journeyed inland to spas and cool crystal springs. Long was the list of the famous who came here, including author Harriet Beecher Stowe.

You can still see the past vividly in **Mayport,** where white shrimp boats rock gently at anchor, their colorful nets swinging in the breezes, much as they have done for generations. You can see it more dramatically yet in **Fernandina Beach,** where you'll marvel at Victorian Gothic houses trimmed in lacy gingerbread and ringed by wide verandas once swept by hoop-skirted ball gowns. You can see it in the Palace Saloon, said to be the oldest watering spot in Florida, perhaps visited by pirates Jean and Pierre Lafitte, who once were lured by the action in this city President Monroe dubbed "a festering fleshpot."

As you ramble along the crumbling walls of massive Fort Clinch, roam among the gingerbread-trimmed homes, and gaze at the towering lighthouse that's been warning ships off the rocks since 1839, you'll hear the echoes of rapid-fire Spanish, clipped British tones, soft French twangs—the ghostly voices of those who fought over these strips of land for centuries, deeding it finally to the world's travelers.

Serenity and Old South drawls aren't the whole story here, however. Beneath the surface runs the fighting blood of buccaneers and pioneers who carved up this land. You'll discover that spirit in early November and late December when the entire town reverts to its rough-and-tumble roots for the traditional Florida-Georgia football clash at the Gator Bowl. Everything's high during those zany weekends, from hotel rates to most of the citizenry, who turn out in droves to cheer on the state team with the same fervor their ancestors used to remove what threatened them.

A rough-and-ready land, it has always been, beneath the plantations and pinstriped suits, a city of plots and pirates, a place to discover the strong roots on which this flowering peninsula blooms.

## ORIENTATION

Fla. A1A runs from Mayport (where you take a ferry across the river for $1) south along Atlantic Beach, Neptune, Jacksonville, and Ponte Vedra beaches. Part of the A1A strip is called the **Buccaneer Trail.**

In town, the Main Street bridge crosses the St. Johns into the main section of downtown Jacksonville. The city's Visitor and Convention Bureau is west of Main Street at Monroe and Pearl streets. Hotels are on the south side of the river, off I-95 at Gulf Life Drive.

One of the most important things to know is that with its 840-mile boundary this city is *huge,* which is why you have such a difference in airport limousine fares to the city and to the beaches.

If you're staying downtown and not planning much sight-seeing, you can get along with buses and taxis, but if you're planning to see the beaches and historic sights, you'll need a car—or a suitcase full of money.

## USEFUL INFORMATION

For **police or medical emergencies,** call 911 or 633-4111. . . . For a **24-hour drugstore,** try Eckerd's, at 4397 Roosevelt Blvd. (tel. 389-0314). . . . **Venetia Six-**

**ty Minute Cleaners** has dry cleaning service at 5627 Roosevelt Blvd. (tel. 389-7263). . . . For **non-emergency medical needs,** call the Duval County Medical Society at 335-6561. . . . For **dental problems,** call the county dental information and referral service at 356-6642. . . . If you're a midnight muncher, head for Denny's, which has **24-hour restaurants** in the city, including one at 6 Ellis Trail in Baymeadows (tel. 731-7437). . . . **weather info** at 757-3311.

## TOURIST INFORMATION

The **Jacksonville Chamber of Commerce** will be happy to help you out with all kinds of information. There are offices at 3 Independent Dr., Jacksonville, FL 32201 (tel. 904/353-0300), and 413 Pablo Ave. (P.O. Box 50427) (tel. 904/249-3868). . . . You can also get information at the **Jacksonville Visitor and Convention Bureau,** at 6 E. Bay St., Jacksonville, FL 32202 (tel. 904/353-9736). . . . The **Amelia Island–Fernandina Beach Chamber of Commerce** will help you find your way around that small town. It's at 102 Centre St., Fernandina Beach, FL 32034 (tel. 904/261-3248).

## HOTELS IN JACKSONVILLE

At this end of the state beach, hotel rooms are most expensive in summer months, although downtown hotels have year-round prices.

### Downtown

**Sheraton–St. Johns,** 1515 Prudential Dr., Jacksonville, FL 32207 (tel. 904/396-5100, or toll free 800/325-3535), is the showplace of Jacksonville. A five-story focal point for riverfront redevelopment, the Sheraton's sparkling blue roof shines as brightly as its famous neighbor, the St. Johns River. Overlooking this waterway, which was the final destination for 19th-century Yankee travelers, the hotel was completed in 1980 so it's quite contemporary. Sheraton's 350 big and beautiful rooms occupy 16 scenic areas at the waterfront, many overlooking the water or lovely grounds where tiny fountains bubble and waterfalls flow. You'll find old touches here, from a wall mural in the lobby depicting life in early 19th-century Jacksonville to the very contemporary accommodations. For dining, the Admiralty Restaurant offers outstanding continental cuisine in the atmosphere of an Atlantic steamship crossing. They've created one very lovely place at Sheraton–St. Johns, with tennis courts, swimming pool, and shopping village. Rates are $112 to $120 double, with suites from $165; big weekend reductions.

Another glittering newcomer to the region is the **Omni Jacksonville Hotel,** 245 W. Water St., Jacksonville, FL 32202 (tel. 904/355-6664, or toll free 800/THE-OMNI). Centered around a four-story atrium adorned by palms and greenery, Omni sports 345 rooms near the city's new convention center. Outside, there are sundecks and a swimming pool, while interiors are sparked by handsome marbles, soft pastels, imposing columns, skylights, and beautiful furnishings, all merging into the classy atmosphere for which Omni has gained justifiable fame. Rates run $140 to $160 year round.

Another riverside hotel is the **Jacksonville Hotel,** at 565 S. Main St., Jacksonville, FL 32207 (tel. 904/398-3561), a 296-room hostelry with spacious, frequently refurbished rooms, all lined with plush carpeting and trimmed with glass doors leading to private balconies that overlook the river and the hotel's big pool. Fanny's Row'n Club Lounge has a sporty atmosphere and lots of oars for decor. The Greenery coffee shop offers a contemporary atmosphere with lots of what its name suggests, and a tranquil view of the river. At this former Hilton, two people pay $74 to $114, year round.

A transformed hotel in the region is the former Thunderbird, now **Holiday Inn Conference Center–East,** 5865 Arlington Expressway, Jacksonville, FL 32211 (tel. 904/724-3410, or toll free 800/874-3000, in Florida 800/342-2357). Outside this sprawling resort you'll find attractively landscaped grounds, tennis courts, a pool, jogging trail, and Jacuzzi. Inside, the '60s come back to life at the Bar and Soda Shoppe crowned by a 1956 pink Thunderbird. Rooms, which have been redone and now come in soft contemporary colors, are $66 to $76, year round.

**Holiday Inn–West,** 555 Commonwealth St., Jacksonville, FL 32207 (tel. 904/781-6000, or toll free 800/HOLIDAY), is on the west side of town but not far from the city's business and financial district. Once again Holiday Inn produces bright and spacious rooms with contemporary touches, dining facilities, a pool, all the usual amenities. A double room is $55 to $60, and singles are $52 to $55.

## Hotels at Jacksonville Beach

Most Jacksonville vacationers seek a quiet spot in the sunshine of Jacksonville's 30 miles of beaches. Here's a look at the selection.

Sheraton not only has a huge new hotel in the city but it also operates the **Sheraton Jacksonville Beach Resort Inn,** at 11th Avenue South at the ocean, 1031 S. 1st St., Jacksonville Beach, FL 32250 (tel. 904/249-7231, or toll free 800/321-2037, 800/621-6738 in Florida), an eight-story hotel with 154 rooms and lovely little balconies overlooking the sea. Sheraton has king-size beds or two double beds in all its rooms, wall-to-wall carpeting, and breathtaking views. When you want some exercise, there are two tennis courts and a sparkling tiled pool. Golf arrangements are available. For dining, huge glass windows in the contemporary dining room offer a panoramic view of the Atlantic as you feast on sizzling steaks, thick slabs of prime roast beef, or seafood acquired from the pier down the way. Dinners are in the $10 to $17 range. Double rates at the Sheraton are $64 to $95, year round.

They may call it Sea Turtle Inn but there's nothing slow about the service or the effort this high-rise hotel puts out to make you happy. Located right on the beach, **Sea Turtle Inn,** at 1 Ocean Blvd., Jacksonville Beach, FL 32233 (tel. 904/249-7402, or toll free 800/831-6600), has pretty, bright rooms with lots of space and shining views of the ocean from private balconies. In the Sea Turtle Restaurant seafood is king, and on Friday you can consume copious quantities of sea treasures at a bountiful buffet. There's a pool and a game room. Rates are $80 to $105 year round.

**Holiday Inn–Oceanfront,** at 1617 N. 1st St., Jacksonville Beach, FL 32250 (tel. 904/249-9071, or toll free 800/HOLIDAY), has 150 rooms, all of them overlooking the ocean and the resort's pool, which is right on the sand. A rooftop nightclub has a razzle-dazzle lighting system and plenty of entertainment that draws throngs of locals as well as visitors. Rooms are large and airy, and decorated in the tropical colors favored by this chain—they have a wall of glass, and balconies too, so you can get a tan without leaving your room. Two people pay $60 to $98, year round.

**Eastwinds Motel,** at 1505 S. 1st St., Jacksonville Beach, FL 32250 (tel. 904/249-3858), is a cozy oceanfront motel with a pretty patio and pool. Guests gather for cookouts on the motel's grills when they're not cooking in their own small efficiencies here. Deluxe suites are also available, and the spacious rooms are decorated in bright colors. It's close to tennis and golf courses, too. Rates range from $29 to $86 year round.

**Friendship Inn Gold Coast,** 731 1st St., North Jacksonville Beach, FL 32250 (tel. 904/249-5006), is indeed a friendly place with just 31 spacious rooms, all with balconies overlooking the ocean or the heated pool in the yard. Some efficiencies and apartments are also available in this cheery place trimmed in bright orange. Double rooms at the inn are $40 to $65.

A comparatively new hotel on this beach, **Seaside Suite Motel,** 222 14th Ave. North, Jacksonville Beach, FL 32250 (tel. 904/241-7000), is first to get with the trend to all-suite accommodations. You can spread out here in pleasant two-room suites with separate living-dining area and efficiency kitchens with all the accoutrements up to and including microwave ovens. Located just a short block from

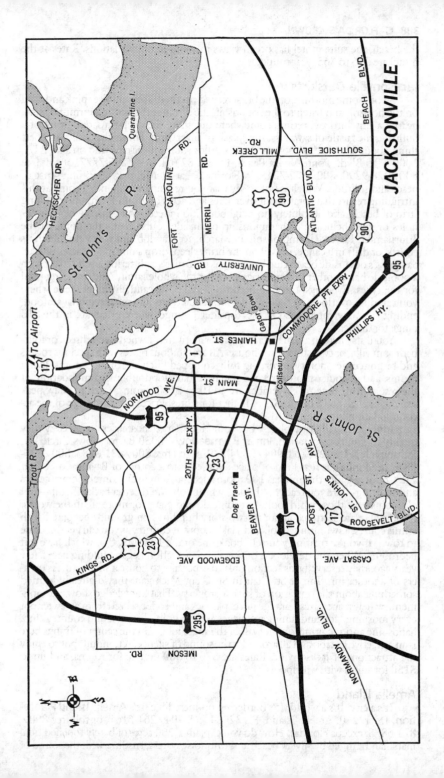

the beach, the suite-motel has ocean views in some accommodations. Rates at the motel are $46 to $65, year round.

## Jacksonville Outskirts

Sit out some morning on the big screened porches as the sun rises pink and gold on the horizon and listen to the sounds: in the distance the gentle murmur of surf, nearby a tiny bird twittering, somewhere out there the deep-throated gronk of a bullfrog, the rustle of sawgrass, the splash of silvery fish. For us that's the very best thing about **Marriott at Sawgrass,** 19 miles south of Jacksonville on Fla. A1A, 1000 TPC Blvd., Ponte Vedra Beach, FL 32082 (tel. 904/285-7777, or toll free 800/228-9290, 800/872-7248, in Florida), that silence, that pervading sense of peace and solitude. Which is not to say that you're going to fall into a coma at this intriguing resort that sprawls out over acres and acres of ground, with its own long strip of beach, and absolutely no neighbors. No indeed, you can play here on 99 holes of golf including a championship oceanside course that's the home of the Tournament Players Championship in March. You can lob and volley on 13 tennis courts, or drift in a canoe, set sail on the briny deep, drop a line in 350 acres of lake. Sawgrass's oceanside beach club has an oasis pool that's a glittering adult retreat with a poolside bar, another Olympic-size pool for the whole family, and a wading pool for the tykes. Evenings, the club becomes a flickering candlelit night scene where you can dine overlooking the sea on continental treats and great regional seafood, ending your day entertained in the Topsider Lounge, where prices are in the $15 range for dinner.

You'll stay here in a beachfront studio or a privately owned two-, three-, or four-bedroom villa, or two-story town house. All are fabulous places with spacious rooms and bright contemporary decor, big fully equipped kitchens, dining rooms, living rooms, and of course those screened porches. Rates for double accommodations at the resort from June to November are $110 to $150. From March to May, peak season, rates rise to $145 to $165, higher for suites. Prices rise as the size of the accommodation increases.

Inns are usually tiny places, but sometimes larger hostelries are so cozy they qualify for inn consideration. **Inn at Baymeadows,** 8050 Baymeadows Circle W., Jacksonville, FL 32256 (tel. 904/739-0739, or toll free 800/831-8183, 800/826-8889 in Florida), is *that* kind of place. Nestled into a corner of Baymeadows Golf and Country Club, this inn has 100 rooms decorated in lively contemporary colors and sporting—are you ready?—Jacuzzi whirlpools. We'd better back off a bit—not *all* rooms have those whirlpools, but some do and plans for more are in the works. Rooms here are scattered about in two-story buildings on grounds peppered with tennis courts, a swimming pool, and a lake, about as country as you can get this close to town. If you're treating yourself, book one of the 12 suites, 8 of which have loft bedrooms. When the developers of this Bayview section began building here a few years ago, they reserved this section of land especially to house a small inn. As owners of another inn, Inn at St. Clair in St. Clair, Michigan, they'd already learned something about the operation of such a property. That knowledge shows: complimentary newspaper, fresh orange juice, pastries and coffee served from a pewter pot every morning, golf and dining privileges at the adjoining course and country club, handsome antique prints on the wall of the small lobby. In the center of things here is an attractive gazebo and all around is the sound of silence. A tranquil spot to enjoy the attractions of Jacksonville. Rates are $70 to $80 double for rooms, and up to $150 for suites with whirlpools.

## Amelia Island

It's a city. It's a world. It's bordering-on-incredible. It's **Amelia Island Plantation,** Dept. 240, Amelia Island, FL 32034 (tel. 904/261-6161, or toll free 800/874-6878, except Florida). How do you explain 1,250 acres of barely touched tidal marshland, ringed by silvery beach and turquoise waters, rustling with the sound of breezes ruffling through the pines and tugging at tall white sea oats? Glorious? Glamorous? All of that, perhaps more. Nestled around a 45-hole Pete Dye golf course, the resort's stark contemporary lines stand out like sentinels guarding this strip of coastline. At sandside is a pool nestled into a dune, and wooden walkways lead to mile after mile of sand bordered by a forest and the Atlantic. You can ride a stalwart steed through the surf here, play on 26 tennis courts, play those 45 holes of golf, loll on the beach or at poolside, dine, dance, and make merry in elegant restaurants or a disco. You can wander aimlessly on nature preserves, explore a Native American burial mound 1,000 years old, bicycle, fish, and shop. For dinner, don a jacket or a cocktail dress and venture out to the Amelia Island Inn, which houses 24 spacious guest suites as well as a picturesque dining room overlooking the ocean. Dine on seafood straight from the waters in front of you at prices in the $15 to $25 range in the Verandah Café. You can choose from hotel rooms, or select a condominium villa with one, two, or three bedrooms (some even have four) overlooking the ocean, clustered about the fairways, or gazing down on a lagoon or lake. All the villa clusters have a pool (or two or three). Need we say that these are big, big apartments all individually decorated by owners with private balconies and spectacular views? Need we add that this is a very glamorous resort? Double rates for hotel rooms at the resort run from $128 to $195 year round, higher for larger digs.

A lovely inn on Amelia Island called the **Bailey House,** 28 S. 7th St. (P.O. Box 805), Fernandina Beach, FL 32034 (tel. 904/261-5390), was built in 1895. It is a peak-roofed turreted house located downtown in an area now part of the island's restoration district. Owners Diane and Tom Hay have filled the inn with antiques, claw-footed bathtubs, paddle fans, and Victoriana, and are offering bed-and-breakfast (all rooms have private baths) for $65 to $95, year round.

Restoration has taken Florida by storm in recent years. Some very good evidence of that can be seen at **Seaside Inn,** 1998 S. Fletcher Ave., Fernandina Beach, FL 32084 (tel. 904/261-0954). Here a dedicated couple set about the rebirth of a shuttered Seaside Inn and created this handsome three-story brick delight that perches alongside the sea like a string-bean sentinel. Atmosphere is set by ceiling fans and enhanced by intricate quilts and puffy comforters. Downstairs is Sliders, a seafood restaurant that mimics one this couple once owned and is a reference to a Louisiana idiom for oysters. Double rates, year round, at the 10-room Seaside Inn are $65 to $75.

If you consider yourself an adventurer and have an interest in historic Florida, here's a dwelling spot that is likely to fascinate you. First, a little history. Seems the Carnegie family once settled into this part of the country, operating the Palace Saloon, residing in a summer mansion, and hobnobbing with friends on Georgia's Cumberland and Jekyll islands. A great-grandson of Andrew Carnegie has retained the family manse, called **Greyfield Inn,** and now operates this nine-bedroom mansion as an inn. To get there, you board a supply launch that chugs over every day except Wednesday. Once there, you'll find yourself on an offshore island inhabited only by campers, day-trippers, wild horses, and a handful of Thomas Carnegie's descendants. Rooms have double or twin beds and share the inn's bathrooms (a library suite is the only room with private bath). Prices are a bit on the high side, but what is an adventure worth anyway? You pay $15 round trip for the boat ride ($8 on the Park Service boat) and $180 to $200 double per person a night, including all meals, plus 21% for tax and gratuities. Where else can you dine on Carnegie china and sleep in Carnegie beds? Who knows? Perhaps some of their success will rub off! Inn operators can also fix you up with a bicycle or a horse to ride, and a naturalist can provide tours and explanations of local flora and fauna. You can contact the inn's reservations center in Fernandina Beach at the Chandlery, Centre and 2nd streets, (mailing address: P.O. Drawer B) Fernandina Beach, FL 32034 (tel. 904/261-6408).

Gary and Emily Grable operate the **1735 House,** named for the year in which James Oglethorpe claimed Amelia Island for England. The inn has six—even rooms in an old lighthouse—room-suites furnished in antiques. Each air-conditioned unit has a private bedroom, a captain's bunk bed area, kitchenette, king-size bed, and a living room, furnished in wicker or rattan. Some have facilities for preparing snacks as well. Breakfast baskets filled with fresh fruit, juice, strawberry muffins, coffee, fresh baked goods, and the morning paper are delivered to your room each morning. Facilities for golf, tennis, swimming, fishing, and boating are nearby, and the Grables will pick you up at the Fernandina Beach airport. Rates are $75 to $85 double, and weekly family packages are available. The 1735 House is at 584 S. Fletcher (Fla. A1A), Amelia Island, FL 32034 (tel. 904/261-5878).

Gary and Emily Grable also operate a property management service that rents more than 100 privately owned condominiums and beach homes. Called **Amelia Island Lodging Systems,** the booking operation is at 584 S. Fletcher St., Amelia Island, FL 32034 (tel. 904/261-4148).

## JACKSONVILLE RESTAURANTS

You'll find great seafood here and a wide range of moderately priced restaurants. Remember that the prices we've listed, unless otherwise noted, are for entrées, but that usually includes a salad, one or two vegetables, and sometimes coffee as well.

### Top of the Line

For a good steak and some excellent seafood in handsome surroundings, try the **1878 Steak House,** 12 N. 2nd St. in Fernandina Beach (tel. 261-4049). Sizzling sirloins and shrimp won't cost you more than $10 to $15, and you'll eat them in an old-house atmosphere—steaks upstairs, seafood down, with homemade cheesecake both places. Steaks are sold by the ounce—figure $1.85 per ounce. Open 11:30am to 2pm and 5 to 10pm daily, closing at 9pm on Sunday.

You never know what you're going to find up this way. One of the things you will find is a very nice little restaurant—with one of the nation's top wine lists! Yes, indeed. **Surf Motel and Restaurant,** 3199 Fletcher Ave., Fernandina Beach (tel. 261-5711), a couple of years ago was cited by a wine magazine as having one of America's top-100 wine lists. While you're selecting from the eight-page list, you might as well look at the menu, which is just fine too. The Surf Restaurant creates some very good seafood dishes and offers landlubber treats like steaks, chicken, and pork chops. Prices are in the $10 to $25 range for dinner, but you can also stop in here for breakfast or lunch. Hours are 7am to 9:30pm daily, closing 30 minutes earlier on Sunday and 30 minutes later on Saturday.

**Brett's,** at 820 Ash St., Fernandina Beach (tel. 261-2660), now occupies a historic brick building that was once the telephone exchange here. Low lighting, plants, and handsome surroundings—not even to mention very good cooking with the emphasis on steaks and seafood—make Brett's a very popular place on summer evenings. You'll pay $10 to $15 for entrées, and hours are 11am to 2pm Tuesday through Friday and 5 to 11pm Tuesday through Sunday, closed Monday.

Two other stops to stoke up on the region's top-flight seafood are pubby **Snug Harbor,** 201 Alachua St., Amelia Island (tel. 261-8031), and the **Crab Trap,** 31 N. 2nd St. (tel. 261-4749). Both are open daily from 4 to 10pm and offer prices in the $10 to $15 range or less for platters of deviled crab patties, rock shrimp, boiled crabs, roasted oysters, shrimp creole, etc.

Who could resist a restaurant with a name like **Slightly Off Centre,** which is slightly off Centre Street at South 2nd Street on Amelia Island (tel. 277-2100)? A priced-right deli ($5 or so for many things) here has fresh breads and tempting pastries, sandwiches, and Cajun cuisine from 8am to 5pm daily except Sunday.

An outstanding place for beef is the **Tree Steak House,** 924 Arlington Rd. (tel. 725-0066), where dinner and salad bar prices are in the $10 to $15 range. It's open from 5:30 to 10:30pm daily (to 9:30pm on Sunday).

**Ragtime Tavern & Seafood,** 207 Atlantic Blvd. in Atlantic Beach (tel. 241-7877), is a ringy-dingy spot that's always good for a crowd and a laugh. Fresh seafood is the main lure, but equally important as a secondary temptation are New Orleans flavors that can be found here in such incarnations as beignets, chicory coffee, blackened specialties, po' boys, and Sunday jazz sessions at brunch. Dinner entrée prices are in the $10 to $15 range, and ragtime plays from 11am to 10:30pm, closing a little later on weekends.

## Budget Bets

**Patti's,** 7300 Beach Blvd. (tel. 725-1662), here for 40 years, is an oft-mentioned Italian restaurant in the Jacksonville Beach area, and it's certainly a great spot for a rib-sticking pasta freak-out that won't cost you a bundle. In fact your check will likely be around $12. It's open from 5 to 10pm weekdays, to 11pm on weekends.

For gourmet Japanese cuisine it's **leyasu of Tokyo,** at 23 W. Duval (tel. 353-0163), where there are more bean sprouts than you ever grew in a Mason jar, and wonderfully fresh vegetables prepared by experts who serve you in the usual understated delicacy of Japanese decor. Prices are in the $10 to $15 range, and the restaurant's open from 11am to 2pm weekdays and 5:30 to 9pm Monday through Thursday, later on weekends.

**Bono's Barbecue,** at 4907 Beach Blvd. (tel. 398-4248), is *the* place for barbecue, with two other locations at South Lane Avenue and Norwood Avenue. Bono's is open daily: from 11am to 10pm weekdays, later on weekends.

**Beach Road Chicken Dinner,** 4132 Atlantic Blvd. (tel. 398-7980), is the home of southern fried chicken—terrific and lots of it for $5 or less. Beach Road Chicken is open from 5 to 10:15pm Tuesday through Saturday, noon to 10pm on Sunday; closed Monday. Fried shrimp here too.

Morrison's and Piccadilly Cafeteria here, as everywhere, are sure bets for very inexpensive meals. **Piccadilly Cafeteria,** at 40 Regency Square (tel. 725-5777), is open daily from 11am to 8:30pm and features an under-$5 special daily. **Morrison's Cafeteria** has six restaurants in the area. The one at 3428 Beach Blvd. (tel. 398-1092) is an all-you-can-eat buffet open from 11am to 8pm; the others are in the Gateway Shopping Center, Orange Park Mall, Regency Square, Independent Square, and at 4415 Roosevelt Blvd. Most meals are under $5 at these cafeterias.

## NIGHTLIFE

The after-dark scene centers around this city's large hotels, including those recommended above. The Sheraton's spiffy lounge always draws crowds.

Other night action rendezvous are **Boombay Bicycle Club,** at 8909 Bay Meadow Rd. (tel. 737-9555), especially on Friday nights; **Bennigan's,** at 9245 Atlantic Blvd., and several other locations (tel. 724-0991), where you party in an atmosphere of wood, greenery, and etched glass. For bluegrass, jazz, or folk music, **Applejacks,** 1402 San Marco Blvd. (tel. 398-4242); it's closed Sunday and sometimes has a $3 to $10 cover charge. Another perennial winner is **Banana's,** 9278 Arlington Expressway (tel. 724-9566).

The **Alhambra Dinner Theater,** 12000 Beach Blvd. (tel. 641-1212), has year-round plays and musicals preceded by a buffet; tickets for both are $23 to $29. It's open from 6pm Tuesday through Sunday.

The **Jacksonville Symphony** (tel. 354-5547) performs on the beach in outdoor concerts at the Flags Pavilion in summer and at the Civic Auditorium in Jacksonville in winter. Check local newspapers to see where they'll be and when.

**Theatre Jacksonville,** at 2032 San Marco Blvd. (tel. 396-4425), bills itself as "the oldest continuously producing theater in the U.S." and has almost 70 seasons to prove it. Ticket prices and hours vary.

## WHAT TO SEE AND DO

Talk of the town for years now is **Riverwalk,** a 20-foot-wide boardwalk alongside the St. Johns River. There's always something going on here, from a New Year's

Eve show to international food festivals, a weekly Friday-night River Rally party that's become a mainstay of single social life, and a fall seafood festival.

Add to that **Jacksonville Landing,** a $42-million waterfront festival marketplace with 120 retail shops, dining spots, and entertainment pavilions.

Get a sailor's-eye view of the riverfront activity aboard **Annabel Lee,** 1884 Southampton Rd. (tel. 396-2333), a sternwheel paddleboat that sails from here on a varying schedule for $25 a person with dinner.

At Green Cove Springs, 25 miles south of Jacksonville on US 17, you'll find one of Florida's first resorts, a spa where turn-of-the-century travelers "took the waters" at sulfur springs. You can enjoy those same waters today (although we're not guaranteeing miracle rejuvenations) at **Green Cove Spring Park,** home of the mineral springs that also feed the municipal swimming pool in summer. Learn more about the spa's history at Clay County Hospital Museum in the former county courthouse at Gratio Place and Walnut Street (tel. 904/284-9644).

**Amelia Island** was named in 1735 by Gov. James Oglethorpe of Georgia in honor of Princess Amelia, the beautiful young sister of England's King George II. To get quickly to Amelia Island, take I-95 north to the A1A exit at Yulee, and follow A1A east to the island. For a scenic adventure, drive north on A1A through Jacksonville Beach and follow the signs to Mayport Ferry. Mayport is a colorful fishing village where you'll find car ferries ($1.50 per car, 10¢ for pedestrians) that leave every half hour from 6:20am to 10pm and deposit you across the St. Johns River at Fort George Island, where you continue north to Amelia Island on A1A. Amelia Island has flown eight flags and been home to the Spanish, the French, the English, and finally to combinations thereof known as Americans. **Fernandina Beach,** the island's main village, can trace its history back four centuries. Roam through the 30-block historic district that's listed in the National Register of Historic Places, and stroll streets that end only because an ocean gets in the way. You'll see some intriguing old architecture, called "Steamboat Gothic" and Queen Anne, every bit as lovely as in Key West and Savannah. Two miles wide and 13 miles long, Amelia Island was the birthplace of the state's shrimping industry. The colorful fleet still sways at anchor in Fernandina Beach and during the early May celebration of shrimping the fishermen will welcome you on board for a close look at their craft.

Look for the men in soldier uniforms at **Fort Clinch** (tel. 261-4212), in Fort Clinch State Park. Stroll through the kitchen, barracks, and supplies store, still full of uniforms and lye soap, dried beans and hardtack. To these men the year is still 1864, so don't be surprised if they ask you if you've heard a rumor that the Yanks have burned Atlanta. Admission to the park is $1.50 to $2.50 per vehicle and 50¢ to $1 per passenger (Florida residents pay the lower price); admission to Fort Clinch is $1 per person. Fort Clinch State Park is open from 8am to sunset daily; the fort itself is open from 9am to 5pm daily.

In Fernandina Beach whisky still pours at the **Palace Saloon,** 117 Centre St. (tel. 261-9068), said to be the oldest bar in Florida, a 1903 creation that sports a pair of maidens holding up the ceiling.

Here too is one end of the **Buccaneer Trail,** a whimsically named section of Fla. A1A that winds southward to **Fort George Island.** On Fort George Island lived another of Florida's colorful characters, Zephaniah Kingsley, who built an empire in slave trading and occupied what is now the oldest standing plantation house in Florida, built in 1817. Zephaniah was either quite a liberal or rich enough to make rules, not follow them—he married a black African princess. You can still see the plantation's slave cabins made of "tabby" rock, a mixture of oyster shell, sand, and cement. They are the best-preserved slave dwellings in the nation. Tours of the main house and cabins (on County Road 105, follow the signs from the ferry dock; tel. 251-3331) are at 9 and 11am and 1 and 4pm daily; admission is $1 for everyone over 6.

To see how brewmasters create the final bubbly product, visit the **Anheuser-Busch Brewery** (take I-95 north to the Busch Drive exit; tel. 751-8118), open from 9am to 5pm Monday through Saturday, with guided tours from 10am to 5pm May through October, 9am to 4pm other months. You can sample the product in the hospitality room; both tour and product are free.

For history and architecture buffs, the **Jacksonville National Bank,** at the corner of Forsyth and Laura streets, makes an interesting foray. Built in 1902, its beautiful marble interior has been restored to expose the original vaulted ceiling and 42-foot skylight. This was the first all-marble building in the state, and viewing is free.

Another interesting building is the **Riverside Baptist Church,** at Park and King streets, designed by famed Florida architect Addison Mizner. It's a combination of Spanish, Byzantine, and Romanesque architecture.

The **Jacksonville Zoo,** 8605 Zoo Rd., a half mile east of I-95 off Heckscher Dr. (tel. 757-4462), is a popular place where the youngsters can get a close look at 700 species of animals, ride rides, and view animals from an elevated observation deck. Open from 9am to 5pm daily, the zoo charges $3 for adults, $1.50 for children 4 to 12.

**Jacksonville Museum of Arts and Sciences,** 1025 Gulf Life Dr. (tel. 396-7061), has a 28-foot dinosaur and other science and anthropological exhibits. It's next to another pretty sight, **Friendship Fountain,** which sprays 17,000 gallons of water a minute 120 feet into the air and is beautifully lighted at night from 6 to 10pm. The museum is open from 10am to 5pm, to 10pm Friday and Saturday, and from noon on Sunday. Adults are charged $3; children, 4 to 12, $2.

Jacksonville Beaches Area Historical Society is quite active in restoration and historic projects. One of their latest creations is a living-history program at **Old House Museum,** Pablo Park, Beach Boulevard, Jacksonville Beach (tel. 246-0093). Here a costumed museum guide portraying the house's former owner, Mrs. Herschel Smith, delivers a chatty monologue about the life and times of her family in the 1900s. Built in 1900, the yellow house contains furnishings of the early years of the century from an ice box to a coal stove and a coil-spring bed. Maybe things *weren't* better in the good old days! Old House and 1900 Railroad Memorabilia Museum are open on Wednesday from 10am to 4pm and on Sunday from 1 to 4pm. Admission is $1 for adults, free to children.

**Fort Caroline National Memorial** is the site of the first clash between European powers—France and Spain—fighting for control of territory and continuing a religious war between the Protestant French Huguenots and the Catholic Spaniards. One of the first settlements in the nation, the French Huguenot fort was constructed 56 years before the Pilgrims' arrival. It was the first lasting colony of French Protestants in the nation and it endured for 15 months before the settlers were massacred by the Spanish in a slaughter that gave rise to the name Matanzas (slaughters) Bay near St. Augustine. Here began 200 years of conflict. You can see a replica of the fort and some typical objects of that era at the memorial, 12713 Fort Caroline Rd. (tel. 641-7155). Open daily from 9am to 5pm (free).

Two art galleries in the area are the **Jacksonville Art Museum,** at 4160 Boulevard Center Dr. (tel. 398-8336), and the **Cummer Gallery of Art,** at 829 Riverside Ave. (tel. 356-6857). The Jacksonville Art Museum has a collection of Asian porcelain and both changing and permanent exhibits. The Cummer Gallery, surrounded by beautiful formal gardens, has 11 exhibits of European and American works of art. A special feature of the museum is the 700-piece Wark Collection of early Meissen porcelain. Both are free. The Jacksonville Art Museum is open from 10am to 4pm on Tuesday, Wednesday, and Friday, to 10pm on Thursday, and from 1 to 5pm on Saturday and Sunday; closed Monday. Hours at the Cummer Gallery are 10am to 4pm Tuesday through Friday, noon to 5pm on Saturday, and 2 to 5pm on Sunday.

Now this next suggestion isn't exactly Walt Disney World, but up this way it's a long-awaited facility that's been garnering oohs and aahs. Called the **Prime Osborn Convention Center,** this old, landmark meeting place in town incorporates the city's antique Union Train Terminal and is the nation's only depot-meeting spot. There are often art exhibits here—a display of Pharaoh Ramses II's priceless treasures were the first objets d'art to be displayed. You'll find the Prime Osborn Convention Center at 1000 Water St. (tel. 798-3000).

Harriet Beecher Stowe, author of *Uncle Tom's Cabin,* moved to the picturesque town of **Mandarin** (Mandarin Road branches right from San Jose Boulevard heading south) after her publishing success. You can see her house and lots of other trim old homes in this lovely riverside village. The Stowe family homesite and orange grove is at 12447 Mandarin Rd. After Mrs. Stowe and her family moved in back in the late 1800s, her homesite and orange grove became such a popular tourist site she spent much of her time trying to figure out ways to shield the home from the eyes of some curious visitors who carried things just a little too far—they stole clothes from her clothesline. Mrs. Stowe wrote some observations on the life she saw around here in Florida in a book called *Palmetto Leaves.*

## SPORTS

Jacksonville's 65,000-seat **Gator Bowl** (tel. 633-3900) is the scene of hilarity and horseplay during the annual Florida-Georgia game pitting the two state universities. It's usually the first weekend in November, and the postseason Gator Bowl game is the last week in December. There's soccer here too.

There's greyhound racing at **Jacksonville Kennel Club,** 1440 N. McDuff (tel. 388-2623), **Orange Park Kennel Club,** US 17 at I-295 in Orange Park (tel. 264-9575), and **St. Johns Greyhound Park,** 18 miles south on US 1 in Bayard (tel. 268-5555), which share dates all year round. Admission is $1.

Golf clubs welcoming visitors include the **Dunes** (tel. 641-8444), **Jacksonville Beach Golf Club** (tel. 249-8600), and **Fort George Island Golf Club** (tel. 251-3132). Fees are $10 to $15.

Jacksonville has a number of municipal **tennis courts** scattered about the city. For information on which location is nearest you, contact the city recreation department (tel. 633-2540). **Boone Park,** at 3700 Park St., has 12 courts, some lighted. You can also play golf and tennis at **Amelia Island Plantation** and **Marriott at Sawgrass** (see our hotel recommendations).

From little bream to mighty tarpon, this is top **fishing** country. Charter and party boats leave Mayport and Jacksonville Beach each morning for trips on the St. Johns River and in the ocean.

**Sea Horse Stables,** Fla. A1A on Fernandina Beach (tel. 261-4878), rents horses for surf rides. Prices are $18 to $25 for a five-mile ride.

## PARKS

**Little Talbot Island** is a 2,500-acre park surrounded by the waters of the Atlantic Ocean, Fort George River, and Nassau Sound. You can camp, picnic, swim, fish, boat, and skin- and scuba-dive here, and stroll on a long pier out over the ocean. The park's on the Buccaneer Trail just south of Amelia Island.

**Mike Roess Gold Head Park** (tel. 904/473-4701) is a scenic ravine about 45 miles south of Jacksonville. Take Fla. 21 to 16 miles south of its intersection with Fla. 16. Three lakes dot the park, and beside a stream flowing through it are the remains of an old dam and mill. You can walk a nature trail through the ravine, camp, picnic, swim, fish, dive, and paddle a canoe or pedal a bike.

---

# 2. St. Augustine

---

Nowhere else in the state can you travel from century to century as easily as you can in this antique community that was 55 years old when the Pilgrims landed at Plymouth Rock. And nowhere else do you feel the small triumphs of the centuries melding so effortlessly into a 20th-century city. St. Augustine has merged past and present in shady narrow lanes dappled with sunlight, in massive old homes filled with families whose joys and sorrows are little changed from those of armored Spanish conquistadors or homespun-clad pioneers struggling to wrest survival from this demanding land.

You will, of course, also see the neon intrusions of this tourist-conscious age, but just beyond the plastic trappings of the 20th century you'll find haunting echoes of the past in a tiny two-room cottage where a simple soldier's family lived and loved under the spreading branches of a tall live oak. You'll find the past in the primped and polished magnificence of a reconstructed house where tea was served from a shining silver service in rooms of gilt and velvet. You'll find it in the foot-thick walls of the Oldest House, the awesome magnificence of the towering Castillo de San Marco, and in the touching simplicity of the red cypress schoolhouse.

Roam sleepy streets where bees buzz in small rose gardens secreted behind high courtyard walls. Gaze up at the massive walls of the Castillo de San Marco, where frightened townspeople once huddled in terror as a would-be conqueror set the city aflame. Stroll through velvety darkness and hear the echoes of cannons, of clanking 16th-century armor, clinking 19th-century champagne glasses, the echoes of the past here in the nation's first city.

## SOME HISTORIC BACKGROUND

St. Augustine's hero is Ponce de León, once governor of Puerto Rico. He sailed here with Columbus in 1493, then returned with an expedition of his own in 1513. Legend has it that rumor of a magical spring, a fountain of youth, brought de León here, but there are some who suggest he searched not for youth but for another valuable—gold. Whatever his quest, he landed in Easter season, Spain's "Pascua Florida," and named the land he found La Florida, claiming it, of course, for Spain.

Two years later Capt. Gen. Pedro Menéndez de Áviles arrived to establish the first permanent European settlement in the nation. A few years earlier some French Huguenots had settled at Fort Caroline, but when the Spaniards showed up and a battle ensued, the French colony was destroyed. That battle ended near what is now Marineland, where the French soldiers who escaped from their wrecked ship were summarily dispatched by Menéndez, giving name to the bay here, Matanzas, the Spanish word for slaughter.

Spain's decision to set up Menéndez de Áviles in Florida had less to do with colonization than with a desire to protect Spain's gold-filled galleons, the frequent prey of pirates who discovered a way to mine gold on the high seas. Annoyed by the Spanish roadblock on their road to fortune, pirates twice attacked St. Augustine. Those attacks spurred construction of massive Castillo de San Marco, one of the most impressive Spanish fortifications in this hemisphere.

Ever anxious to expand its empire, Britain frequently tested the strength of this massive masonry fort without success. Spain finally lost Florida, not by war but by treaty—Florida was the ransom Spain paid to England for the return of Havana in 1763.

Britain managed to hold onto the colony for 20 years. Large plantations were begun, the city became a commercial seaport, and northern Tory loyalists took refuge here. Spain, which sided with the U.S. revolutionaries in their fight against England, even planned an attack on the city during this period, a strange quirk of fate indeed.

In the diplomatic poker game that followed the Revolutionary War, Britain ceded Florida back to Spain. This time around the Spanish let everyone who had settled in the city stay, and let others join them—not a wise move. A restless ragtag mob of Floridians strained against the Spanish, once even attacking the Castillo, until finally in 1821 Spain made the best of a bad bargain and ceded Florida to the United States. Along the way Seminole uprisings erupted and the Castillo once again held prisoners, this time the courageous Seminole warrior Osceola and his cohorts.

In the late 1800s empire-builder Henry Flagler extended his railroad to the city.

Life in St. Augustine began to revolve around the fabulous resorts he built, the Ponce de Leon and Alcazar hotels. Winter visitors streamed in from cold northern climes by steamer and train. They came to spend the entire winter here, often accompanied by servants. Spend it they did too, in lavish fashion, dancing under the stars atop the old fort, parading in carriages down Avenida Menendez, applauding concerts in lavish hotel parlors.

So popular was the city that Flagler elected to extend his empire southward and St. Augustinians today claim their city gave birth to Miami.

## ORIENTATION

St. Augustine is quite a small town with a permanent population of just 15,000, so you'll find it easy to get around. If you're driving, remember that streets are narrow and parking is always a problem. The nation's oldest city is located on US 1 and Fla. A1A. From I-95, take exits to Fla. 16, County Road 207, or US 1.

Avenida Menendez runs alongside the bay. Cathedral Place and King Street run through the center of town and are one-way streets, Cathedral heading west, King going east.

US 1 is also called Ponce de Leon Boulevard, and Avenida Menendez becomes San Marco Avenue as it leaves town on the north side.

To get to St. Augustine Beach, cross the Lion Bridge at Avenida Menendez and King Street and follow Fla. A1A to the beaches.

## USEFUL INFORMATION

For **police or medical emergencies,** call 911 or 825-1070, 829-2226 in St. Augustine, 471-3600 on St. Augustine Beach. . . . For **doctor or dentist referrals,** check with the chamber of commerce, which is used to handling those problems (tel. 829-5681), or go to the emergency room of Flagler Hospital, 400 Health Park Blvd. (tel. 824-8411). . . . There's a pharmacist on duty to 9pm at **Eckerd's Drugstore** in the K-Mart Shopping Center (tel. 824-6167). . . . **Winn Dixie grocery store,** 1010 S. Ponce de Leon Blvd. (tel. 829-5509), is open to 10pm. . . . You can find gasoline and service help at Cochar Chevron, on County Road 207 at I-95 (tel. 824-9244), night or day. . . . For 24-hour film processing, try **Camera Center,** 14 Avenida Menendez (tel. 829-2468).

## TOURIST INFORMATION

Friendly folks at the **St. Augustine Visitor Information Center,** 10 Castillo Dr., St. Augustine, FL 32085 (tel. 904/824-3334), have been taking care of lost, confused, or otherwise befuddled tourists for decades and will be happy to help you with anything from a dentist to a hotel room. . . . The **St. Augustine Chamber of Commerce,** 52 Castillo Dr. (P.O. Drawer O), St. Augustine, FL 32085 (tel. 904/829-5681), can also help you with information on this fascinating city. . . . If you're here in June or October you can see Grand Illumination ceremonies, when the city honors its British heritage with a full-dress British uniform torchlight parade through the city.

## HOTELS

For us there's no better way to immerse in the fascinating history of this very old community than to plunk down in the middle of it, stroll the slumbering streets, peeking into the back lawns of centuries-old houses and peering at restoration projects still under way. Best of all, if you stay in the old city you can see it at its glowing mystical best—after the throngs of day-trippers and cursory lookers have retreated.

On the north edge of town, near the information center and the fort, is the **Best Western Spanish Quarter Inn,** 6 Castillo Dr., St. Augustine, FL 32084 (tel. 904/824-4457, or toll free 800/528-1234), a handsome place with lots of arches and rounded Spanish decor. A small hotel, the inn has just 40 rooms, all of them bright and cozy with lots of glass to let in the sunshine. Outside there's a nice pool, and the inn always has a coffee pot going in the office for free morning eye-openers. Rates are $49 to $55 double, all year.

Waken to the sounds of a horse-drawn carriage clopping by at **Whetstone's Bayfront Inn,** 138 Avenida Menendez, St. Augustine, FL 32084 (tel. 904/824-1681), and you'll think you've hit a time warp. Like the other hostelries along Avenida Menendez, Whetstone's is in the heart of the old section and has a pretty view of the bay tides rising and falling and boats passing under the Bridge of Lions. The large rooms are cheery, and there's a palm-fringed swimming pool in the center of the attractive grounds. Year round, two people pay $40 to $79 for a room with one or two beds.

**Monson Motor Lodge,** 32 Avenida Menendez, St. Augustine, FL 32084 (tel. 904/829-2277), is another good starting point for touring the city's historic district. Just a block away (and no more than a good musket shot) from the fort, Monson has 50 bright, spacious rooms, plus a restaurant and lounge that's handy when you come back exhausted from a day of sight-seeing. Monson charges $45 to $70, year round (higher on weekends), and children under 12 stay free. Most rooms have two double beds; some have king-size. Monson also has two suites, complete with kitchen, king-size bed, and color TV, for $85 to $100 a night.

The **Monterey Motel,** 16 Avenida Menendez, St. Augustine, FL 32084 (tel. 904/824-4482), looks out over the waters of Mantanzas Bay and is only two beautiful blocks from the main St. George Street historic reconstruction area. The recently remodeled Monterey has three especially pretty rooms, just at the front of the building on the second floor, with a big window overlooking the water. The very large rooms are furnished with Spanish touches, and have phones and cable television. There's a new, large swimming pool too. Because the motel's U-shaped, many of the rooms (especially on the second floor) have a nice view of the bay. Two people pay $34 to $58, any time of year, for one of the 59 rooms here. Free airport transfers, too.

Besides the main hotels (Holiday Inn and Howard Johnson each have two hotels in the area, as does Days Inn), one of the luxury hotels here is the **Ponce de Leon Resort** (mailing address: P.O. Box 98), 4000 N. US 1, St. Augustine, FL 32084 (tel. 904/824-2821, or toll free 800/824-2821 except in Florida), about three miles north of town. There are 200 spacious and attractively decorated rooms here, a restaurant, cocktail lounge, golf course, putting greens, and a huge cloverleaf swimming pool. Double rates are $70 to $100 all year round, and suites and condo units are also available at a higher price.

Another motel that's very convenient for sightseeing is the **Marion Motor Lodge,** 120 Avenida Menendez, St. Augustine, FL 32084 (tel. 904/829-2261). Right next door are the horse-and-buggy rides and sight-seeing trains that take you on tours, and it's just a few blocks to the restoration area. A two-story building with lots of wide windows overlooking Matanzas Bay, the lodge is decorated in bright colors, and has a pool, sundeck, and all the usual amenities, like phones and cable color TV. You'll pay $45 to $55 year round, for a double room.

The **Anastasia Inn,** Fla. A1A at Pope Road, St. Augustine Beach, FL 32084 (tel. 904/471-2575), is nestled alongside the sea at pretty Anastasia State Park. A two-story building with walls of glass in every room, this former Sheraton is trimmed in blues as bright as the Atlantic—and bright as the sparkling blue pool in the middle of the hotel's courtyard. The airy rooms have plush wall-to-wall carpeting, lively beach colors, and two double beds, and there are a few with kitchens. A tropical restaurant has a tempting salad bar, and there's a lounge with entertainment and dancing. Two people pay from $50 to $105, depending on season and view.

Another very pretty place to stay on this beautiful and sometimes almost-deserted beach is the **Oceanfront Holiday Inn,** 1061 Fla. A1A South, St. Augustine Beach, FL 32084 (tel. 904/471-2555, or toll free 800/874-6135, 800/872-6232 in Florida). Remodeled top to bottom and inside to out recently, this Holiday Inn now sports contemporary decor that blends well with the inn's beachside location.

Outside, you'll still see arched Spanish-style windows, but inside, big cushy chairs and lots of soft pastels greet you. Sister Sally's has become a local nightlife favorite and the hotel's restaurant makes a cool escape from steamy summer sands. Rooms at the inn, which has a poolside snackbar, a pretty beach gazebo, and video entertainment, are $85 to $125 year round; children are free.

A good budget selection is **La Fiesta Motor Lodge,** 3050 Fla. A1A South, St. Augustine Beach, FL 32084 (tel. 904/471-2220), about five miles south of Lion Bridge. It features Spanish decor and has 38 rooms on a 300-foot strip of beach, a coffee shop, a 60-foot pool, oceanview rooms, a playground for the kids, queen beds, in-room refrigerators, and shuffleboard. Double rates are $40 to $90 year round.

## Bed-and-Breakfast Inns

When we first wrote this book those many years ago, we included two delightful inns under hotel listings. In the intervening years, however, innkeepers have seen the light in this historic city, so there are now at least seven bed-and-breakfast inns, each a study in ruffles and lace, antiques, acres of handmade this and specially crafted that. Oh, to have the ruffle concession up this way!

Tops among the inn entries is **Victorian House,** 11 Cadiz St., St. Augustine, FL 32084 (tel. 904/824-5214). At first glance it would seem that to stand still here is to get a ruffle put on you. Daisy Morden, the personable and hard-working owner of this delightful white frame house, freely admits that she's not quite sane where antique lace and ruffles are concerned, so everywhere you look you'll find ruffled curtains, framed lace, frothy furbelows, and hand-stencilled wall trim.

Little touches are a delight here: Ruffled tablecloths trim night tables, a wide-brimmed, ribbon-trimmed straw hat lies casually atop an end table as if its owner had just stepped out, an antique doll sits atop a chest, delightful old books are tossed casually on a chair. Star of the show at Victorian House is an often-photographed room that sports a four-poster topped with an elaborate handmade lace canopy, but in every room here you'll find handmade quilts and hand-stencilled walls.

Not all the charm of this spot is inanimate: Ms. Daisy has some wonderful stories and a smile that will charm your socks off, whether or not you're wearing any. Daisy lives here, so you'll be dining at her table in the morning on a homemade granola that ought to be patented—while you're crunching ask Daisy about the guest who mistook the serving bowl for a cereal bowl. Rates at Victorian House, which has private baths in every room and high tea on Sunday, are $55 to $75 for two.

Just steps away is **Casa de Solana,** 21 Aviles St., St. Augustine, FL 32084 (tel. 904/824-3555). Another restored and renovated old home, Casa de Solana, built in 1763, has four antique-filled rooms, all of them suites and all trimmed with "haint blue" woodwork, a southern color designed to ward off evil spirits! Two working Majorcan fireplaces are a special feature of one carriage-house room, while another has a tiny balcony overlooking the garden and some rooms sport a view of Matanzas Bay and the Bridge of Lions. All have private bath and cable television. Rates are $100 and include full breakfast complete with grits and homemade banana bread, chocolates, a decanter of sherry, and use of a couple of bicycles. No children accepted here.

Most formal—and most expensive—of St. Augustine's charming inns is **Wescott House,** 146 Avenida Menendez, St. Augustine, FL 32084 (tel. 904/824-4301), a perfectly gorgeous old home filled with antiques. You're greeted here with a complimentary bottle of wine, and you'll find a snifter of brandy on a bedside table each night. Very expensively and elaborately decorated, Wescott House charges $75 to $135, including a Continental breakfast of croissants, coffee, fruit, and juice, bedtime turn-down service, chocolates on your pillows, and terry-cloth robes in the bathroom. Highest rates are on weekends.

For our dollars a wonderful way to sink instantly into this ancient atmosphere is the **Kenwood Inn,** 38 Marine St., St. Augustine, FL 32084 (tel. 904/824-2116). Two antiques buffs turned this magnificent three-story rambling old structure into a marvel of polished wood floors, ruffled curtains, brick-lined fireplaces, brass beds, beautiful vibrant colors and delicate pastels. Built in 1865 as an inn, the Kenwood now has its third set of loving renovators/owners, and they seem to be lavishing just as much attention on this lovely old business as did their predecessors.

Owners Mark and Kerrianne Constant oversee rooms furnished with antiques and reproductions, each in a different period and color scheme with coordinating linens. Guests who prefer a king-size bed may choose between the English theme of Room 2, the quiet elegance of the President's Room, or Captain Karl's maritime room, each with claw-footed tubs in the bath. The Honeymoon Room, which overlooks the pool and courtyard, has a four-poster canopy bed, while others feature themes from Shaker to country Victorian.

Every morning in the dining room you'll find complimentary coffee, freshly squeezed orange juice, and freshly baked fruit bread or pastry on the sideboard. Outside is a swimming pool, a pretty garden, and a wraparound veranda where you can sink into the antebellum atmosphere of this quiet street.

Kenwood is a handsome contribution to the nation's roster of charming country inns, as much for the friendly welcome you'll get from the Constants as for their considerable interior design skills. Rates at the Kenwood, which is just a few blocks from the nation's oldest house and within walking distance of the St. George Street restoration area, are just $55 to $75, year round.

A similar hostelry is the **St. Francis Inn,** 279 St. George St., St. Augustine, FL 32084 (tel. 904/824-6068), at the corner of St. Francis Street. A tiny 10-room inn, the St. Francis is tucked away behind a wrought-iron gate. A jungle of greenery and flowers surround a tiny pond, and a few steps away is a sparkling pool nestled in the last possible open area on this small property.

Each of the few rooms is different and modestly furnished. Most are small and have the high ceilings so common to pre-air-conditioning days. You'll find glass-paned french doors, tiny balconies overlooking a small park or the front pond, seven rooms with a fireplace, and wainscoting. There are no phones and not all rooms have televisions either, but the St. Francis (just a few doors from the Oldest House) is worth in atmosphere what you might sacrifice in chain-hotel space or amenities. Rates are just $49 to $98.

**Carriage Way,** 70 Cuna St., St. Augustine, FL 32084 (tel. 904/829-2467), dates back to about 1885 and spoils you with homemade cakes, touring bikes, and a bottle of champagne for special occasions. Handsome antique furnishings and an old-world atmosphere here too. Rates are $49 to $85 for rooms with baths.

Finally, **Casa de la Paz,** 22 Avenida Menendez, St. Augustine, FL 32084 (tel. 904/829-2915), is a big and beautiful home with leaded windows overlooking the bay. Pristine and pretty, this lovely, rambling house offers single- or double-room suites with private baths, central air conditioning and heat, a Mediterranean breakfast and a sherry-and-chocolates greeting for rates beginning at $50.

## Camping

**Bryn Mawr Ocean Resort,** Fla. A1A South, St. Augustine, FL 32084 (tel. 904/471-3353), has 250 campsites in an oceanside campground with laundry facilities, pool, tennis, basketball, horseshoe, shuffleboard, game room, and recreation hall. Rates begin at $19 to $28 in summer months, lower after Labor Day.

**North Beach CamResort,** 4125 Coastal Hwy., North Beach, St. Augustine, FL 32084 (tel. 904/824-1806), has 80 acres from ocean to Intracoastal Waterway, waterfront restaurants, and heavily wooded sites with full facilities and pool. Groceries are available here, and there's a boat ramp and fishing dock. Rates are $13 to $20 a day for full hookups for two.

**Anastasia State Recreation Area,** 5 Anastasia Park Dr., St. Augustine, FL

32084 (tel. 904/471-3033), on St. Augustine Beach, also has campgrounds, and as part of the state park system charges $22 to $27 a night for campsites for up to four people. Reservations by telephone only.

## RESTAURANTS

Despite its fame and popularlity, St. Augustine retains its small-town charm — and small-town fiscal morality. You get what you pay for here. In many restaurants you get delightful atmosphere as well. Prices we're quoting are for entrées, but usually include salad and one or two vegetables, and sometimes coffee as well.

### Top of the Line

If you love old houses, you'll adore the **Chart House,** 46 Avenida Menendez (tel. 824-1687), a beautiful old town house built in the early days of the city. This unusual house once featured bedrooms downstairs and the parlor upstairs so you could see out over the carriages to Matanzas Bay. These days there's a very comfortable contemporary dining room upstairs outfitted with paddle fans. Downstairs, you enter from a side lawn into a world of glowing old wood floors and a plant-filled lounge, which now features a seafood bar serving a variety of shrimp and oyster appetizers. Seafood is scintillating here, fresh from the docks, and cooked by chefs so talented they easily get our award for the city's best seafood. A grouper dinner we had here once has set the standards for us forever. So popular is this spot that you really must have a reservation on weekends and in the crowded summer months. Entrée prices are in the $13 to $25 range, and the Chart House is open from 5 to 10pm weekdays, later on weekends.

Another lovely old home that's become an equally lovely restaurant is **Le Pavillon,** 45 San Marco Ave. (tel. 824-6202), owned and cooked in by a gracious German-Swiss family, the Sinatsches. You can dine in this 87-year-old house on a candlelit screened front porch or inside in pretty rooms with the same romantic air about them. As for the dining, well how about wienerschnitzel, sauerbraten and spätzle, delicately smoked Bratwurst, German home fries, red cabbage, hot homemade rolls, or light crêpes with a long list of possible fillings? There's frequently entertainment in the evening, and Le Pavillon is a local favorite so reservations are wise. It's open from 11:30am to 2:30pm and 5 to 10pm daily. No entrée tops $17.

**The Columbia,** 98 St. George St. (tel. 824-3341, or toll free 800/227-1905), is "The Columbia" no matter where it is. One of Florida's top restaurants for generations, the Columbia got its start way back in 1905 in Tampa's Ybor City. Today there are three other locations, in Sarasota, Tampa Harbor Island, and St. Augustine. Columbia's successful formula has been transferred with equal success to each of its restaurants. So if you've tried the Columbia in other locations, you can try it here secure in the knowledge that you'll find all your old favorites — snapper Alicante, the Columbia's special salad, yellow rice, and even the well-loved blue margaritas. If you're a fan of bean soup, you'll love the Columbia's version — garbanzos, ham, and Spanish sausage called chorizo. If you're here in summer, try chilled gazpacho. This handsome reflection of Old Spain also excels at paella valenciana and *boliche,* a traditional Cuban favorite made from eye-round of beef and Spanish sausage.

Spanish entertainers warble at the Columbia, which is open daily from 11am to 9pm, later in the lounge. There is also often a Sunday brunch from 11am to 2:30pm ($10). Dinner prices here are in the $12 to $17 range, and worth every penny in ambience alone.

A very popular St. Augustine spot these days is **Fiddler's Green,** 50 Anahma Dr. (tel. 824-8897). You'll find it half a mile east of the Vilano Beach bridge right on the ocean. In keeping with its surroundings, Fiddler's Green looks as though it had just washed up on the beach. Inside, a juxtaposition of modern architecture, natural woods, and tropical furnishings combine to create a tastefully tropical ambience. In cool weather a blazing fire and a woodsy atmosphere make the Fiddler a cozy retreat. Seafood is the specialty here and comes prepared in many styles, but you'll also find

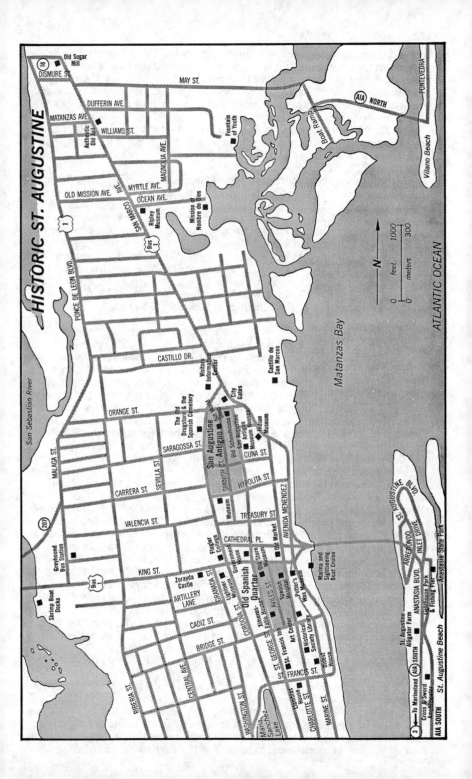

beef and chicken on this often quite innovative menu. Those who can't make up their minds can try it all with the seafood potpourri, which includes a taste of many things on the menu. Those who like it simple can try the fresh fish of the day prepared meunière, grilled, Véronique, or Dijon with a touch of mustard, cream, and tarragon. There's even one called "The Purist," featuring fresh fish dusted with paprika and broiled under an open flame.

Fiddler's Green opens at 5pm daily and goes on into the wee hours in the Sailor's Lounge, where you can sip something tropical as you watch the shrimp boats tootle home across the misty inlet. Prices for dinner at this very attractive restaurant range from $12 to $22.

A restaurant called **Raintree,** 102 San Marco Ave. (tel. 824-7211), dropped onto St. Augustine a few years ago and became an instant success. No wonder. Occupying a century-old Victorian home, with beautiful first- and second-floor balconies, the Raintree offers food as exquisitely prepared as this house was exquisitely restored. Here you get into the history of this enchanting city even as you dine on the likes of lobster Raintree, broiled with Romano and mushrooms; red snapper avocado, champagne salmon, beef Wellington or shrimp Alfredo. Steaks are sautéed with madeira or brandy and topped with béarnaise sauce. Lobster is prepared several ways here, but Florentine, featuring Romano cheese, is a specialty. Prices at the restaurant, which is open from 5 to 11pm daily for dinner, are in the $12 to $20 range. Lunch is served from 11:30am to 2:30pm and costs about $4 to $7.

## The Moderate Bracket

**Antonio's,** 798 Ponce de Leon Blvd. at the junction of US 1 (tel. 824-0971), whips up Italian magic in the kitchen. Gnocchi, macaroni, ravioli, cannelloni, and manicotti are handmade by the Digregorio family, who use only the freshest fish, the finest baby veal, and the tenderest chicken to create scaloppine marsala, chicken parmigiana, shrimp scampi. Fettuccine Alfredo is made right here, from the fettuccine to the finished product, and the cannelloni Florentine, with veal and spinach rolled in a tender piece of homemade pasta and covered with a cream sauce, is to die for. A 35-item salad bar and homemade breads round out the delights here. Prices are nice, too, with most entrées just $6 to $12. Dinner service is from 4 to 9pm daily.

**Capt. Jack's,** at 10 Marine St. (tel. 829-6846), has a nautical atmosphere from decor to menu. There really was a Captain Jack (for a change), who used to run charter boats hereabouts, but turned his talents to cookery some years back. Naturally he wasn't going to open a restaurant with a railroad theme, so today you'll see sea nostalgia around you as you dine, overlooking the city's pier on Matanzas Bay, on simply cooked seafood dishes like shrimp, the fresh catch, whole boiled shrimp in the shells. If you've had enough seafood to keep you happy for a while, try the beef-a-bob or a steak. There are children's platters too. Capt. Jack's is open from 4:30 to 9pm daily (closed Sunday) and prices are in the under $10 bracket.

It's not often you see these three words teamed up: **Salt Water Cowboys,** Dondanville Road (tel. 471-2332). But in Florida anything goes, including seaside cowboys. Despite its name, however, this waterside restaurant would have been pretty uptown for most Florida cowboys, but for today's fantasy cowpunchers this is a favorite. Bentwood twig furnishings contribute a touch of Old Florida here, but plants and some snappy architecture bring things right up-to-date. Seafood from crabs to clams and even alligator tail appear fried in a light batter, broiled, or baked, and for inland cowboys there is a variety of barbecued selections. Prices are right: You can chow down on a bucket of oysters for $5 to $7, and dinner entrées, which include salad, garlic bread, and two vegetables, fall in the $7 to $12 range. Salt Water Cowboys is open daily from 5 to 10pm.

**Captain Jim's Conch Hut Restaurant,** 57 Comares Ave. (tel. 829-8646), is perched up over the water for a pelican's-eye view of what's sailing down the coastline. On starry evenings you can dine outside under a palm-thatched roof and on any evening you can devour some first-rate seafood in a waterside setting alongside a pier. This unusual restaurant is open from 11:30am to 10pm daily, closing at 11pm on Saturday. Entrée prices are in the $10 to $13 range.

**Scarlett O'Hara's,** 70 Hypolita St. (tel. 824-6535), is one of the loveliest spots in town, and occupies a charming old renovated house at Hypolita and Cordova streets to boot. Giant old trees and lots of plants shade O'Hara's, which is off the beaten track down a quiet side street. An outdoor raw bar is a big lure here, and sandwiches and soups in the $5 range are served in an atmosphere that will transport you back to the historic days you've come here to discover. Open from 11:30am to midnight and later for nightly entertainment.

Are you ready for Capuchin monks ministering to your culinary desires, with tranquil Gregorian chants and medieval melodies in the background? We didn't think we were either, but it's amazing how fast you can adjust to these historical throwbacks as you wander down St. Augustine's St. George Street preservation area. Drop into the **Monk's Vineyard,** 56 St. George St. (tel. 824-5888), and find out for yourself what an intriguing retreat this can be from the rigors of sight-seeing. An old European look with lots of wood, wine and "monk-abilia" prevails here, and the fare runs toward excellent crêpes and quiches, salads and soups for lunch, steaks and seafood for dinner. Monk's is a most interesting hideaway and a cool shady spot with a theme miles away from conventional. Your check will be perhaps $5 for lunch, $7 to $14 for dinner, and the monks hear confessions from 11am to 9pm daily except Wednesday.

**Cap's,** 4325 Myrtle Lane, Vilano Beach (tel. 824-8794), is right on the water, and if it looks a little like famed Cap's Place in South Florida there's good reason for that. Cap's owner claims Cap Knight, after whom both these restaurants were named, as an ancestor and his portrait's right up there for all to see. What's even better to see are the fresh hearts of palm, after which you will be spoiled forever for the canned variety. Other things here will spoil you too: lots of fresh fish in several different preparations including Cajun-spicy, pastas, 'gator tail, conch, squid, you name it. Cap's is open Wednesday through Sunday from 5:30 to 8pm, from 1pm on weekends, and prices are in the $9 to $13 range for dinners.

Appetizers and sandwiches are served downstairs, seafood, prime rib, and the like upstairs at **Churchill's Attic,** 21 Avenida Menendez (tel. 824-3523). Upstairs, stained-glass and fringed lamps create pretty interiors, while views out over this historic city make for interesting exterior scenery. Churchill's is quite an attractive restaurant with an old-timey feeling and reasonable prices in the $10 to $15 range, including vegetables, fresh breads, and house salad. Hours are 11:30am to midnight daily except Sunday, when it closes at 10pm.

**Clam Shell,** 201 Yacht Club Rd., Camachee Cove Yacht Harbor, Camachee Island (tel. 829-9520), is plunked down in a marina, so water views are a given. Add to that Minorcan clam chowder, a luscious, spicy concoction that harks back to days when the region was settled by a group of Minorcan islanders. And add to that lots of fresh seafood and mounds of roast oysters plucked from these waters and you have simple but delectable dining. Clam Shell is pried open from 6am to 9pm daily, closing an hour later on weekends. Prices are in the $2 to $9 range for breakfast, $4 to $9 for lunch, and $7 to $17 for dinner.

## Budget Bets

Sooner or later everyone in town goes to the **Chimes,** 12 Avenida Menendez (tel. 829-8141), partly because it's right in the middle of things (the fort is just across the street, the restoration district a block or so away) but mostly because owner-chef James Kalivas turns out such dependable meals from sunrise to long after sunset. He makes all the pastries at this unprepossessing but very popular restaurant, and whips out waffles for breakfast, sandwiches for lunch, and steaks for dinner. He's been at it for lots of successful years, so you can be sure you'll find a high-quality and low-priced meal here: dinners under $10; breakfasts and lunches, $2 to $3. Open from 7am to 9pm daily.

Tops in trendy in St. Augustine these days is **Panama Hatties,** on Fla. A1A South across from the pier on St. Augustine Beach (tel. 471-2255). Head here to satisfy your munchies moods. Among the choices are nachos, seafood salad, burgers, sandwiches, a seafood melt, and baskets of breaded chicken breasts. A bilevel restaurant, Panama Hattie's has a lounge and package store, and an open-air, second-floor bar overlooking the sea. Prices are in the $5 to $7 range for most selections. This spot's open daily from 9am to 12:30am.

If it's just-a-little-something time, try **La Parisienne Tearoom,** 60 Hypolita St. (tel. 829-0055), where you can sin a little (not a lot, you understand) on French pastries and crunchy, flaky bakery creations, even light dinners. La Parisienne opens daily at 9am, closes at 8:30pm.

Tops for home-cookin' is **O'Steen's,** 205 Anastasia Blvd. (tel. 829-6974), where you can chow down on some of the best fried shrimp in the state, good chowder and cornbread, squash fritters, and turnip greens. Atmosphere is spartan, but O'Steen's has been a favorite up this way for generations and is well known throughout the state for its top Florida Cracker cooking. Dinner prices are in the $10 range and the restaurant is open from 11am to 8:30pm daily except Sunday.

And don't miss a morning stop at the **Denoël French Pastry Shop,** at Charlotte Street and Artillery Lane (tel. 829-3974), a cozy café that sells flaky fresh-from-the-oven pastries in a pretty bistro that's also a bakery. Closed on Tuesday, the pastry shop presents its inexpensive, mouthwatering treasures from 10am to 5pm.

## SEEING THE SIGHTS

As travel became possible for the less haughty strata of American society, St. Augustine added more and more attractions to its historic sights and today the city is filled with sometimes funky, but always fun, things to see.

Begin your visit to the city with a stop at the **Visitor Information Center,** at 10 Castillo Dr. (tel. 824-3334), where you can see an orientation movie about the city (shown twice each hour) and pick up guided-tour information and brochures to help you see it yourself. The center is open from 8am to 5:30pm daily.

A seat in a shining carriage pulled by a handsome steed is a fascinating way to clip-clop slowly through town. Call **Colee's Carriages,** 115 La Quinta Place (tel. 829-2818), from 9am to 5pm daily, to be picked up. Tours cost $9 for adults, $4 for children 5 to 11. You'll find the carriages at the Castillo entrance, 1 Castillo Dr.

To get an idea what the city has to offer, see it all aboard **Sightseeing Trains,** at 170 San Marco Ave. (tel. 829-6545). Drivers of the trams give you a lively anecdote-spiced spiel about the city as you travel through the streets. Tickets are $9 ($4 for children ages 6 to 12) and you can get off and on whenever you like. Trains run every 15 to 20 minutes, and it beats trying to drive through this city of narrow one-way streets, complicated parking, and sometimes heavy traffic. Three other tours are real money-savers: They offer packages ranging from $12 to $34 for three- to eight-hour tours including all admissions. Parking is free while on tour.

If you're sight-seeing on your own, start at the **Old City Gate,** just a short distance from the Information Center, where you'll see a replica of the original palm-log wall built in 1739 to protect the entrance to the city. A moat here was crossed by a drawbridge raised each evening, leaving night owls outside to fend for themselves. Historic St. George Street begins here, and once was called "the street to Land Gate." The Old World Shop nearby is a stop for the sight-seeing train and has tourist information and snacks.

**Castillo de San Marco,** 1 Castillo Dr., is the city's giant landmark, built in 1672 of coquina (pronounced "koh-*keen*-a"), a soft yellow stone formed from solidified masses of sand and shells. Quarried from deposits on nearby Anastasia Island, coquina (which means cockle shell in Spanish) was hauled by oxcart and floated on barges across the inlet. It took 15 years to build and so much money ($30 million) that Spain's King Philip is said to have observed dispiritedly that the fort must have been built of solid silver.

Over the years the fort has housed American Revolutionaries, Seminole leaders, Confederate and Union troops, and American deserters from the Spanish-American War. There are guided tours and firing demonstrations of historic weapons several times a day. Admission is $1 (free to children under 16 accompanied by adults). The fort is open from 9am to 5:45pm daily, later in summer.

On St. George Street across from the castillo is the city's main preservation area known as **St. Augustine's Restored Spanish Quarter,** 44 St. George St. (tel. 825-6830), entrance at 29 St. George St. Here you'll get a fascinating look at an 18th-century Spanish colonial village—actually a living museum—with authentically furnished homes and intriguing craft demonstrations by a blacksmith, leather worker, ceramicist, woodturner, printer, spinner, and weaver. You'll see a wide variety of old homes dating back several centuries. At the oldest schoolhouse, you'll see students in their seats and the schoolmaster up front directing lessons. A $3.50 ticket ($8 a family) admits you to all exhibit buildings (but not the schoolhouse); students 6 to 18 pay only $1.50. It's open from 9am to 5pm daily; closed December 25.

Don't miss the **Sanchez House** on St. George either. It's been perfectly restored, with a lovely fountain in the courtyard and shining period furniture inside, right down to antique dishes on the table. It's open from 9:30am to 5pm daily (except Thursday) and is free.

Over at 14 St. Francis St. is the **Oldest House** (tel. 824-2872), used as a residence since the early 1600s. Its Spanish coquina walls are a foot thick to keep the house warm in winter, cool in summer, and were built about 1702 after the British burned the town. The living room's on the second floor, a typical architectural style in the city. Owned and operated by the St. Augustine Historical Society, as is the adjacent museum in the Tovar House, the Oldest House is furnished with authentic antiques. Both house and museum are open from 9am to 5pm daily; admission is $5 for adults, $2.50 students, and family rate $10.

There's something naïvely charming about the **Oldest Store Museum,** 4 Artillery Lane (tel. 829-9729), which is packed wall to wall and ceiling to floor with antiques, from high-button shoes to red underwear and dill pickles. When you see the french-fry makers and apple peelers, the cherry pitters and biscuit makers, not to mention the 90% alcohol "medicines," you'll wonder if we've really progressed. It's open from 9am to 5pm Monday through Saturday, but from noon on Sunday; admission is $3 for adults, $1.50 for children 6 to 12.

As a teenager Marylyn was mortified when her father raced laughing out of the **Fountain of Youth,** but in recent years she's been wondering if she shouldn't give it a try! Those magical waters old Juan Ponce de León was searching for are supposed to flow from the stone fountain at 155 Magnolia Ave. If you don't regress immediately, you can also visit a memorial to Ponce de León, a planetarium and space globe, museum, and swan pool at $3.50 for adults and $1.50 for children 6 to 12. It's open from 9am to 5pm daily.

At San Marco and Old Mission avenues, the **Mission of Nombre de Dios and Shrine of Our Lady of La Leche** is the site of the first mission in a series of religious outposts that were to culminate finally in California's famous Mission Trail. Florida's simple log missions long ago succumbed to the ravages of time, but the mission effort is honored here. Open from 7am to dark daily; donations are encouraged.

Other stately old homes in the area are the **Ximenez-Fatio House,** 20 Aviles St. (tel. 829-3575), a historical guesthouse now maintained by the National Society of the Colonial Dames of America (open free Thursday through Monday, March to September, from 11am to 4pm); the **Dr. Peck House,** 143 St. George St. (tel. 829-5064), which was once the home of the Spanish treasurer, an important man who doled out the government's cash (open from 10am to 4pm Monday through Friday); and the **Casa del Hidalgo,** at Hypolita and St. George streets (tel. 212/759-8822), the Spanish National Tourist Office (open Monday through Friday from 10am to 4pm, free).

On King Street is a massive cluster of buildings that once was Flagler's flamboyant Ponce de Leon Hotel. Completed in 1888 after three years of construction, it remained a hotel until 1967, when it became **Flagler College.** You're welcome to wander around the grounds and look at the hotel's hexagonal dining room jutting out on the east side of the building, and peek into the main lobby where giant marble columns rise to a second-story loggia.

Flagler's other hostelry, the Alcazar Hotel, folded in the grim days of the 1930s and stayed empty until Chicago millionaire Otto C. Lightner bought it and set up his **Lightner Museum,** 75 King St. (tel. 824-2874). You'll see a 17-shop Victorian village, Tiffany glass, Napoleon's desk, and a quilt made by Abraham Lincoln's second wife. Admission is $4 for adults, $1 for children 12 to 18, and free to children under 12. The museum is open from 9am to 5pm daily.

**Zorayda Castle,** at 83 King St. (tel. 824-3097), is an odd but intriguing sight inside and out, a to-scale replica of Spain's Alhambra complete with harem quarters. If there's one thing disappointing about the real Alhambra, it's that it is so quiet and empty. That cannot be said of this look-alike. Here you get some insight into the good life accorded the Moorish kings when they were inhabiting Spain, and a glimpse of some oddities from around the world, things like a sacred cat rug said to be more than 2,000 years old and found in the casket of an Egyptian mummy. And here's a stumper: What is the secret that lies behind the door of the Tower of Princesses? We're not telling. Zorayda Castle is open from 9am to 5:30pm. Admission is $3 for adults and $1.50 for children 6 to 12; under 6, free.

Stare down Attila the Hun at **Potter's Wax Museum,** 17 King St. (tel. 829-9056), a surprisingly well done ball of wax at which you can see quite life-like figures from off-with-her-head Anne Boleyn to the signers of the Declaration of Independence in marvelous sets. Now all new from location to format, Potter's has added a multi-image theater presentation and installed a wax workshop where you can see a craftsperson making and restoring wax figures. Potter's is open from 9am to 8pm in summer, closing at 5pm in winter. Admission is $4.50 for adults, $2.50 for children 6 through 12.

In the lobby of **Government House,** 48 King St. (tel. 825-5033), the city's Preservation Board displays a large collection of Hispanic artifacts and unusual objects unearthed in continuing excavations in the region. Exhibits change monthly, and there's no charge for looking at them Monday through Friday from 8am to 5pm.

For those who would rather fight than switch, the ideal spot may be the **Gun Shop & Museum of Weapons,** 81C Kings St. (tel. 829-3727). Civil War guns, fort swivel guns, rapiers, swords, pistols, muskets, Kentucky rifles, Plains rifles, Pennsylvania rifles, and hundreds of things that go bang in the night are on display here. Admission is $2 for adults, children 50¢; hours are 10am to 6pm in winter months, closing at 8pm in summer.

**Ripley's Believe It or Not Museum,** at 19 San Marco Ave. (tel. 824-1606), should thrill trivia collectors. Its very existence is something Ripley probably should have included in his "Believe It or Nots." Admission is $5.50 adults, $3.50 for children 5 to 12. Hours are 9am to 9pm daily.

## SPECIAL EVENTS

In this lovely old city there are some wonderful moments you shouldn't miss. Among those are the **Spanish Night Watch Ceremony** on the third Saturday in June, when local historians re-create life as it was when this settlement was ruled by the Spanish. A candlelight procession, with soldiers in full-dress, parades as the town is officially locked for the night with a traditional ceremony.

In August the city celebrates its birthday **(Days in Spain Festival)** with three nights of entertainment that ranges from sword fighting to a Spanish beard contest, music, dancing, and lots of food.

December's a busy month in St. Augustine as the city celebrates the holiday season in its own inimitable style with a **Christmas Parade** of carriages, floats, costumed colonists, the works. There's also a **Regatta of Lights,** complete with elaborately decorated boats sailing up the bay and a **Grand Illumination Ceremony,** at which the city salutes its British conquerers, with a candlelight march and locking-up ceremony similar to the Spanish celebration.

Easter's a big party up this way too. You can watch the Palm Sunday **Blessing of the Fleet,** at which fishing boats and pleasure boats alike get their annual good wishes from the church at an elaborate ceremony. Here in St. Augustine the traditional Easter Parade is called **Parade de los Caballos y Coches** (Parade of Horses and Coaches), and features beautiful horses decked out in just a little more finery than their owners. Parade participants (the horses, that is) even wear Easter bonnets donated by famous women. This Easter festival comes complete with drill team, color guard, beauty queens, and an Easter Festival Royal Family and entourage of 100 costumed attendants.

If you're here in the summer months from mid-June to mid-August, don't miss **Cross and Sword,** the state's official play, performed by a cast of 70 singers, dancers, and actors, who portray the story of St. Augustine's founding and early days. It's performed outside in the St. Augustine Amphitheater, just south of the city on Fla. A1A (tel. 471-1965), at 8:30pm daily except Sunday. Tickets are $6 for adults, $4 for children under 12.

## NIGHTLIFE

Long a family vacation resort, St. Augustine is a quiet place by night but you can usually find something doing in hotel lounges at the **Ramada Beach Club** (Fla. A1A South), the **Anastasia Inn,** the **Ramada Inn Downtown,** and the **Monson Motor Lodge** (see our hotel recommendations).

The newly renovated **Monson Bayfront Dinner Theater,** in the Monson Motor Lodge, 32 Avenida Menendez (tel. 829-2277), often has shows Saturday nights and on some weekdays. Most shows are Neil Simon comedies. Cocktails are at 6:30pm, dinner at 7, and show time at 8:15pm, all for $19.

The **White Lion,** at St. George and Cuna streets across from the old fort (tel. 829-2388), is a favorite meeting spot, especially during its Lion's Roar happy hour, with entertainment nightly in an old English pub atmosphere. **Scarlett O'Hara's,** 70 Hypolita St. (tel. 824-6535), is a colorful evening meeting ground, as are **Monk's Vineyard,** 56 St. George St. (tel. 824-5888), the **Conch House Lounge,** 57 Comares Ave. (tel. 829-8646), **Pot Belly's,** 36 Granada St. (tel. 829-3101), **St. George St. Tavern,** 116 St. George St. (tel. 824-4204), and **Sister Sally's,** at the Holiday Inn, 3250 Fla. A1A (tel. 471-2555).

**Mill Top Tavern,** 19½ St. George St. (tel. 829-2329), is a very popular, breezy upstairs-downstairs watering hole right at the edge of the restoration area. Nice views and a lively atmosphere here make this a good spot to end an evening—or start one.

**Churchill's Attic,** 21 Avenida Menendez (tel. 829-3316), has musical entertainment Wednesday through Sunday.

## SPORTS

Golfers should head to **Ponce de Leon Shores Golf Course,** on US 1 North (tel. 829-5314), an 18-hole course with greens fees of $35, $11 for a golf cart. There are 20 **tennis courts** scattered around the city, and the city's recreation department (tel. 829-8807) will be happy to tell you which location is nearest you.

A favorite **canoe trip** in the area is a four-mile run on nearby Pellicer Creek. The chamber of commerce can get you paddling.

**Island Driving Range,** on St. Augustine Beach across from the Fishing Pier (tel. 824-8321), has a driving range and recreation center with an 18-hole miniature golf course, baseball pitching machines, and pool tables.

**Beach paddle tennis,** which you play with a racquet full of holes and a dead tennis ball on the hard-sand of beaches from Daytona to Jacksonville, got its start here in St. Augustine. You'll find stores for equipment around the beach.

## SHOPPING

We hardly know whether to put the **Lightner Antiques Mall** among attractions or shopping spots since it's a little of both. Part of Flagler's old Alcazar Hotel, the Antiques Mall is located in what once was the hotel's huge indoor swimming pool (look at the slope of the floor). Now antiques shops and boutiques are nestled away in the pool, which was quite a showplace—from a hallway on the second floor you could stand and watch the swimmers frolicking below, then grab a rope from rings (still in the walls), swing out over the pool, and . . . splash!

Crafts shops on **St. George Street** and at **City Gate Crafts,** at 1 St. George, have lots of intriguing handmade things from leather to silver and weavings to chocolate-chip cookies. All the craft workers in **St. Augustine's Restored Spanish Quarter** also sell their work.

Biggest shopping news here in recent years is the addition of **Fiesta Mall,** 1 King St., in what was once Potter's Wax Museum. Now filled with boutiques and dining spots, this new bazaar in St. Augustine has incorporated the old into the new so you can see a couple of old Spanish wells here and displays of artifacts unearthed in the vicinity.

We never met lace we didn't love. So we (well, at least one of us) covet every creation in **Isabela's,** 212 Charlotte St. (tel. 824-3053), a lace dream shop operated by Isabela herself. Indeed, lace lovers from all over the country call talented Isabela to ask her to whip up one of the handmade lace creations she has been designing and making since her childhood in Cuba. You can see her at work in a tiny shop on Charlotte Street between Artillery Lane and Cadiz Street. Here she stitches away on an antique sewing machine, producing some of the loveliest lace dresses, petticoats, tops, bottoms, sexy little things, and even wedding dresses, that you'll ever see. It's hard to resist buying something here, so why try? Do stop in even if it's only to talk to Isabela, whose vivacity, charm, and enthusiasm will be a highlight of your visit.

## SIDE TRIPS

Take a free ferry ride across the Matanzas Inlet, just south of St. Augustine on Fla. A1A, to **Fort Matanzas,** built by the Spanish in 1742 to seal off the southern entrance to the Intracoastal Waterway that winds past St. Augustine's doorstep. It was here, but 200 years earlier, that Pedro Menéndez de Áviles gave the shipwrecked enemy troops from French Fort Caroline a choice: Join the Spanish forces (which meant relinquishing their Huguenot Protestant religion) or die. All but about 200 died in a bloody massacre that helped limit French colonization on this continent to Canada and Louisiana. Entrance to the small fort, which is about 14 miles south of St. Augustine on A1A, is free. The 11-passenger ferry operates from 9am to 4:30pm every day.

About four miles farther south on Fla. A1A, **Marineland of Florida** (tel. 471-1111) features the hijinks of dolphins and penguins. There are dolphin shows five times a day, and 11 different exhibits explaining the wonders of the sea. Marineland is Florida's oldest marine attraction; it was built in the 1930s as an underwater movie studio and is still a delightful place that's always adding something new to its fascinating bag of tricks. Newest among those is called Wonders of the Spring, a 35,000-gallon freshwater aquarium cleverly designed to give you the feeling you're looking into one of Florida's fascinating underground springs. Believed to be the nation's largest freshwater aquarium, Wonders of the Spring has every species of Florida freshwater fish you've ever caught, and a few more besides. There's a new campground here at Marineland too, and it will certainly be the way to rough it, if you must: a swimming pool, playground, miniature golf course, cable television hookups, and dune crossover that takes you safely across the highway. Admission to the park is $12 for adults, $7 for children 3 to 11. It's open from 9am to 5pm daily.

In Palatka, about 35 miles east of St. Augustine, you can see more than 100,000 varieties of azaleas and flowering plants lying like a blanket of rainbows across the natural ravines of **Ravine State Gardens.** Deep springs beneath the limestone created these nooks and crannies, which are open daily from 8am to sundown. Admission is free, and you'll find the gardens at 1600 Twigg St. off Moseley Avenue (tel. 329-3721). To find the gardens from St. Augustine, take 207 Country Road to US 17 into Palatka. After you cross the bridge in Palatka, turn left at the fourth traffic light, where you'll see a sign directing you to these dazzling gardens.

# XI

# FLORIDA'S PANHANDLE

### 1. PENSACOLA
### 2. FORT WALTON/DESTIN
### 3. PANAMA CITY/PANAMA CITY BEACH
### 4. TALLAHASSEE

**F**loridians call it their Panhandle and a glance at a map will show you why. It's as different in geography and life-style as the old-line Southerners who live here; and it's as anachronistic, in this chrome-and-plastic age, as they can keep it.

Here in northern Florida, a charming naïveté covers canny cracker wisdom. Family is important, but hospitality is a duty, an obligation, and a very great pleasure. If you extend your hand and smile here, you'll get it all back twofold.

Soft southern drawls and antebellum mansions attest to the region's long and strong affiliation with the South, and here in the northern end of the peninsula you'll find the state's sunny—and stormy—roots.

Great pine forests cover this land, and farms spread like patchwork quilts across the rolling hills. If you think you can see more than the average number of churches here, you're right. This is a staunch section of the Bible Belt, and religion is serious business. Gospel sings draw thousands of listeners and participants. In a few places they're still arguing over the demerits of demon rum, to this day banned in a few "dry" counties.

Here, too, you'll find towns with weird and wonderful names. Some are remnants of the area's swashbuckling past and some are mysteries. There's Scratch Ankle, a bayside town once frequented by smugglers who got caught in briar thickets here and did what the name suggests. And Panacea, which is just that to landlocked Tallahasseans. And Two Egg, thought to have been named by a grocer whose first customer exchanged two eggs for a pound of flour. And Lick Skillet, whose origins nobody knows and whose chagrined residents have renamed it Lamont.

All along the coastline you'll see sand no other part of the state can claim, sand so soft it squeaks beneath your toes. Thanks to the oval shape of the grains, this strange silica cannot stick together or pack. It just floats under your toes like a bed of talcum.

Get off the superhighways here to find towns like Monticello, the state's watermelon center, a village lined end to end with antebellum plantation houses. Nearby are graves of Florida's staunchly Confederate soldiers who died in a fierce battle at Olustee—but not until they'd made Tallahassee the only southern city never captured by the Union.

Not far away at Marianna, about 60 miles northwest of Tallahassee, you can visit the state's only aboveground limestone cavern: Seminoles once watched from its depths as Gen. Andrew Jackson marched through to begin the attacks that would eradicate them.

Panhandle entertainment runs toward family activities—canoe outings on the region's crystal-clear rivers, reunions, and in election years, political parades and fish fries. If you're here for one of the last two, you'll see a Senator Fogbottom cartoon come to life, and have more fun than a duck at a june-bug social. No sleek limousines here, although you may spot the occasional Boss Hogg in a white suit. As likely as not the hopeful glad-hander will be riding triumphantly down Main Street on a tractor!

Some of the most enchanting experiences you can have in Florida are here in tiny backroad towns redolent with rustic natural beauty and populated by people whose way of life is as slow-paced and satisfying as their drawls.

If a name here sounds faintly French, it probably is. France's Marquis de Lafayette, whose aid was vital to Revolutionary Americans, began a huge plantation here, struggling to prove free Frenchmen (or any free men) could serve the South as well as slaves. His experiment died with him, but the descendants of those hardy French settlers remain and continue to prove the marquis right.

In typical northern Florida style, people here remember another Frenchman, Prince Achille Murat, nephew of Napoleon and son of the King of Naples. He is famed neither for his name nor his title, but for a quirky sense of humor much like their own: The prince served his unsuspecting guests some much admired French cuisine, then told them what local products they were consuming—sheep ears, buzzard, and alligator tail!

Last (and perhaps least) is one of the oddest entertainments around, a fish fry. The main course is mullet, a fish whose popularity, to put it gently, has not yet peaked. The main attraction, however, is a chance to see these northern Floridians having a rollicking good time. Every year 80,000 of them turn up for a mess of mullet at the annual Boggy Bayou Mullet Fry.

Like Monticello's annual watermelon seed-spittin' contest and the Wausau 'Possum Festival, this land is eccentric, fun and funny, a place where you will be welcomed warmly by folks who know and love their place in the sun, and hope you will too.

## GETTING THERE

Airlines serving Tallahassee, Pensacola, Panama City, and Fort Walton Beach include Air New Orleans, Continental, Delta, and USAir.

**Greyhound/Trailways** has service to Tallahassee, Pensacola, Fort Walton, and Panama City (tel. toll free 800/237-8211).

## GETTING AROUND

Public transportation leaves much to be desired in this section of the state, and distances are great. Besides, it's fun to drive through the backroads and byways discovering much of Florida's history as you go.

You can cut quickly from east to west between Tallahassee and Pensacola on I-10, but it's far more interesting to take off on roads like US 98 (which runs along the Gulf of Mexico), US 90 (which goes through the antebellum town of Monticello), Fla. 65 (which cuts through the huge Apalachicola National Forest), and Fla. 4 (which travels through Blackwater River Park).

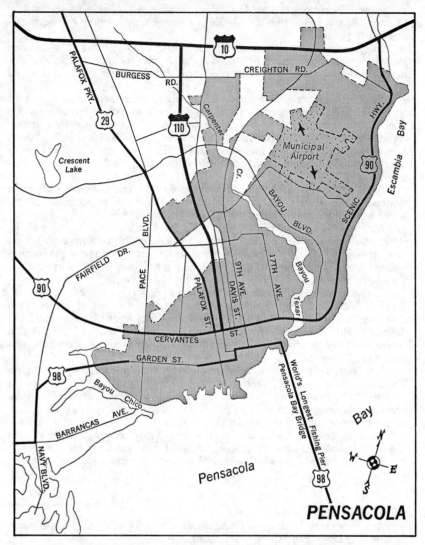

**PENSACOLA**

Major cities like Pensacola, Fort Walton Beach, Panama City, and of course Tallahassee, have **rental cars** available from major national operators like Hertz and Avis. Rates begin at about $20 to $25 a day with unlimited mileage.

## A WORD ABOUT HOTELS

In summer, droves of sun-seekers from Georgia, Alabama, and other southern states make the quick and easy run to the Panhandle's seaside cities. This march to the sea lasts from May to Labor Day, when prices are highest and hotels are filled to the brim. You need reservations in those months. In Tallahassee, hotels are very busy when the legislature is in session (it varies, but generally is between February and May), and prices rise abruptly during popular football weekends from September to December.

# 1. Pensacola

Pensacola is as different from its seaside sister cities in the Panhandle as it is from most of the rest of the state. It's had a long turbulent history during which the city has flown five different flags (if you count all the times it changed hands, it's welcomed 13 "conquerors"), so people recognize, guard, and respect "family" here, but offer that open-armed hospitality for which the South is justifiably famous.

There's the magic of history in Pensacola's quiet streets, where timber barons built ornate oak-trimmed mansions and Spanish dons courted dark-eyed and fair-haired señoritas. It's a magic that will transport you back in time to days of wasp-waisted blushing maids and lusty swaggering pirates, elegant dandies from New Orleans on prancing white horses, and candlelight plantation dinners served on hand-rubbed mahogany tables glittering under crystal chandeliers.

Yet just a few miles across a modern causeway you're firmly in the 20th century. Jet-skis roar across gulf waters and today's peripatetic sun-seekers wander hand in hand across silvery white dunes asway in sea oats that ripple like fields of Kansas wheat.

You can capture it all in Pensacola, be caught up in the ghostly swish of ball gowns rustling down jasmine-scented streets, or catch a passing sailboat to whiz away across the waters.

## GETTING AROUND

**Escambia County Transit System** (tel. 904/436-9383) operates buses that ply the streets on hourly schedules for a 50¢ fare, but don't go to the beaches.

Pensacola is a favorite spot for drive-in tourists from Georgia and Alabama, so the area is geared to four-wheeled travelers. **Renting a car** might be a good idea unless you plan to stay on the beach and skip exploring. National operations here include Thrifty, Avis, Dollar, Hertz, and National. Rates are about $20 to $25 a day, including unlimited mileage.

Taxis operating in the area include **Yellow Cab** (tel. 433-1143), **Black and White Cab** (tel. 432-4151), and **Blue and White Cab** (tel. 438-1497). Service is 90¢ a mile, about $13 to $15 from the airport to Pensacola Beach.

## ORIENTATION

**Mobile Highway** (US 10A/90) runs into downtown from the northwest. **Palafox Street** is the major north-south artery through town and **Garden Street** (which becomes **Navy Boulevard** and leads to the naval station) is the major east-west divider. To get to the beaches and Gulf Islands National Seashore Park, head south on Alcaniz Street or east on Garden Street to Gregory. Head west on Gregory and you'll see the **Pensacola Bay Bridge** (US 30/98), which goes straight to the beach.

## USEFUL INFORMATION

For **police or medical emergency,** dial 911. . . . For non-emergency help, call the **Escambia County Health Department,** 2251 N. Palafox St. (tel. 435-6500). . . . for **dental problems,** call the dental association (tel. 438-9622) or the Pensacola-Escambia Visitor Information Center (tel. 434-1234). . . . **Big B Cleaners,** at 118 E. Garden St. (tel. 433-1343), has quick dry cleaning service. . . . You can buy **groceries** around the clock at Albertson's, 5055 N. Ninth Ave. (tel. 476-7700), which also has a liquor store and pharmaceutical supplies. . . . There are **free parking spaces** just beyond Seville Quarter on Government Street, so you won't have to feed the meters if you linger at the preservation district. . . . **weather info** at 453-2188.

## TOURIST INFORMATION

**Pensacola Visitor Information Center,** 1401 E. Gregory St., Pensacola, FL 32501 (tel. 904/434-1234, or toll free 800/874-1234, 800/343-4321 in Florida), has some very nice people on duty to help you with information and maps for self-guided tours of the charming North Hill Preservation District and the naval air station. . . . The **Pensacola Chamber of Commerce** can help, too; it's at 117 W. Garden St., Pensacola, FL 32501 (tel. 904/438-4081). . . . If you're looking for a condominium rental in the area, try **Metro-Merica Rentals,** at 5900 N. Ninth Ave. (tel. 904/476-8866 or 932-9369, or toll free 800/874-9245), which lists many.

## WHERE TO STAY

If you'd like to be near the city's charming old Seville historical district and save money at the same time, there are several attractive hotels downtown. If you want to revel in the soft sand here, head for Pensacola Beach. Summer in this part of Florida is very, very busy from Memorial Day to Labor Day, when hotels are packed and charge their highest rates. Reservations are vital. We've arranged hotels by location. Downtown, by the way, is very quiet, so don't think you're going to face masses of traffic.

### Outside of Town

**Perdido Bay Club Cottages,** 10 Doug Ford Dr., Pensacola, FL 32507 (tel. 904/492-2601), was long a popular area golf resort known as Perdido Bay Resort but is in the midst of change now. Located about 16 miles west of Pensacola, the resort is a cluster of five-room brick and western cedar cottages capped with shingles surrounding a par-72 golf course. All cottages have four bedrooms and five baths plus a central kitchen, living and dining area. It's recently been sold and the golf course still calls itself the Perdido Bay Resort. That "resort" part, however, is now something of a misnomer since each of the cottages has been sold to private owners and is undergoing a major renovation. Most are now available for daily or weekly rental, along with an additional 24 town houses. There's no restaurant here at the moment, just a couple of snackbars at the golf course. Located about 16 miles west of Pensacola, the resort has a pool and tennis courts and access, of course, to the golf course. Rates fall into the $59 to $79-a-day range year round. Erwin Barger of Perdido Bay Realty (tel. 904/492-2601) can give you the latest information on this resort.

### Downtown Hotels

Latest star among Pensacola hotels is the **Pensacola Hilton,** 200 E. Gregory St., Pensacola, FL 32501 (tel. 904/433-3336, and toll-free 800/HILTONS). Here you have the best of both worlds, the antique and the brand-new, for Hilton built its glittering new high-rise hotel right behind an antique railroad station that serves as the hotel's lobby!

Whether or not you stay here, you really ought to stop by for a look. Fat over-stuffed velvet chairs and couches are perched on rose rugs edged in black. Old signs showing the way to the "Hold Luggage" counter and the ticket booth remain, as does a big old station clock, trimmed in brass, copper, and stained glass. Just off the lobby there's a lovely bar outfitted in forest green, peach, brass, and oak, and appropriately called Tickets. On the end of the "station" are the hotel's two restaurants, a cute little umbrella-clad coffee shop (open from 6am to 10pm) and the formal 1912 Restaurant, where you can dine on veal Orloff, steak with three kinds of mushrooms, or lobster in cream and sherry, for prices in the $12 to $20 range. Hours for the 1912 are 11am to 2pm for lunch and 6 to 10pm for dinner.

Hilton's 212 rooms are furnished in soft, contemporary colors and are equipped with all the usual Hilton amenities, from special soaps to fat, fluffy towels. The hotel offers complimentary airport limousine service, and its location just across the street from the city's new civic center makes it convenient for business travelers. Rates are $78 to $98 double, depending on the location and height of the room, and $204 for a fancy bilevel suite.

**Park Inn International,** 223 E. Garden St., Pensacola, FL 32501 (tel. 904/433-8331), is a moderately priced downtown hotel with a nice restaurant—the Lafitte Room, open daily from 11am to 2pm and 5 to 10pm, with prices in the $10 to $15 range for dinner—and frequently evening entertainment as well. Park Inn has 172 standard motel rooms, some with queen- and king-size beds, plus a heated indoor pool and a outdoor splasher. Recently renovated, they're quite clean and comfortable. Rates are low too: $44 to $59 year round—a 20% discount for Frommer's readers. There's a second Park Inn a bit out of town at 8500 Pine Forest Rd., Pensacola, FL 32506 (tel. 904/477-9150).

**Days Inn,** the former Lenox Inn, 710 N. Palafox St., Pensacola, FL 32501 (tel. 904/438-4922, or toll free 800/325-2525), is one of the prettiest motels near the downtown preservation district. Crisp white shutters trim this red-brick inn built on the side of a small rolling hill. An unusually homey atmosphere welcomes you to contemporary surroundings, from curtained lobby to the quiet recesses of the small adjoining coffee shop and downstairs lounge. Pleasant watercolors accent a striking peach and green decor in the spacious rooms, and there's a shell-shaped pool to play in. Days Inn will bring you here from the airport for free and likewise shuttle you to the historic district. Best of all, you don't have to go far for city information. Pensacola's information center is just across the street. You'll pay just $36 to $48 for double occupancy. Suites with a separate living room are just $60, and some rooms have a hideaway Murphy bed.

It's worth going to Pensacola for no other reason than to spend a couple of beautifully tranquil days at **New World Inn,** 600 S. Palafox St., Pensacola, FL 32501 (tel. 904/432-4111, or toll free 800/258-1103, except in Fla.), one of the loveliest tiny inns in Florida. There are just 14 rooms and two suites at this small hotel that's done up in bright shutters and surrounded by flowers, fountains, and lawns.

Inside, a cozy lobby circles around a beautiful central staircase that soars in very showy style up to rooms on the second floor. Every one of those rooms is a jewel, decorated in stylish antiques or antique styles, with high ceilings, perhaps a four-poster bed, lovely colors, wallpapers, and all the elegant accoutrements you can imagine. Four of the rooms features antique American furniture, four focus on Spanish decor, four on French, and four on English furnishings.

The adjacent Michael's restaurant is aglitter with crystal chandeliers, glowing wood moldings, handsome furnishings, and crisp linens. One room is called the Barcelona Room, and features a semicircular wall of glass overlooking a patio garden complete with tinkling fountain. Another, the Pensacola Room, is accented with original enlarged photographs of the city, and the Marseilles Room has mirrored walls and those sparkling chandeliers. Local seafood is featured, along with a variety of continental cuisine for prices in the $10 to $15 range. Hours are 7 to 9am, 11am to 2pm, and 6 to 9pm daily, closing an hour later on weekends.

Year-round rates at the New World Landing, located just beyond the downtown bustle and very near the bay, are $55 to $78 double, and $95 for one of two suites.

Really thrifty travelers should seek out **Motel 6,** 5829 Pensacola Blvd., Pensacola, FL 32505 (tel. 904/477-7522). This budget-conscious motel chain has 120 small, very simple rooms, a pool, and rates of just $27 to $30 double.

There's also a **Days Inn-North,** at 7051 Pensacola Blvd., Pensacola, FL 32505 (tel. 904/477-9000, or toll free 800/325-2525). Rates are $41 to $45 for two, all year round.

## Hotels on Pensacola Beach

**Holiday Inn Pensacola Beach,** at 165 Fort Pickens Rd., Pensacola Beach, FL 32561 (tel. 904/932-5361, or toll free 800/465-4329), is located just outside the entrance to the national park and is on the gulf. An eight-story hotel, this Holiday Inn has 150 rooms and all the services you could ask for: courtesy airport transportation, heated pool, game room, gift shop, tennis, handball and racquetball, rental sailboats, surfing, fishing, nighttime entertainment—even a baby-sitting service so you'll have time to enjoy the activities. A poolside bar overlooks the gulf so sunbathers can cool off and heat up at the same time. From April to September, Holiday Inn charges $86 to $106 double, dropping about $20 after November 1, and rising again in the spring.

The **Dunes,** 333 Fort Pickens Rd., Pensacola Beach, FL 32561 (tel. 904/932-3536), is a favorite spot for families, who relax together around the sparkling pool overlooking the ocean. (One toddler we saw was really relaxed: She tossed her teeny bikini off and jumped in Godiva style, chased by somewhat less relaxed parents.) You can have a room at the Dunes from mid-May to Labor Day for $70 to $105, depending on location, with the highest prices for rooms overlooking the gulf. In winter, those rates drop to $54 to $89. There's no charge for children. Some rooms have king-size beds, and all have dressing areas and plenty of space. Check for special rates and packages.

One of our favorites is the **Sandpiper Inn,** 23 Via de Luna, Pensacola Beach, FL 32561 (tel. 904/932-2516). It's a recently remodeled, contemporary motel trimmed in pale-gray wood decking, with floor-to-ceiling picture windows. The Sandpiper has just 32 nests, six of which are cottages, and four rooms have kitchenettes. Most units are gathered around a tiny central pool. Summer rates for one double bed are $46, rising to $55 for more elaborate accommodations. They can even arrange villas accommodating 10 people (!) for $110. Rooms here are small but immaculately maintained, with wall-to-wall carpeting and lots of contemporary touches.

Nestled in behind a dune on the Gulf of Mexico is a 24-room motel, the **Barbary Coast Motel,** 24 Via de Luna, Pensacola Beach, FL 32561 (tel. 904/932-2233), whose gray buildings blend so subtly into the dunes they almost look like dunes themselves. Barbary Coast has a spanking-new look, from pipe furniture to wall-to-wall carpeting, tiled foyer, and matching drapes and bedspreads in dark contemporary prints. All double rooms here have small kitchenettes and are located in a series of buildings usually shared with just a few other rooms. There are also small and larger suites accommodating four to six people in two separate bedrooms, plus a pullout couch. Prices range from $68 for a room with a king-size bed (without kitchen) to $81 for double rooms and suites. Rates drop about 40% in winter.

All rooms at **Five Flags Inn,** 299 Fort Pickens Rd. (P.O. Box 39), Pensacola Beach, FL 32561 (tel. 904/932-3586), overlook the gulf and swimming pool with giant picture windows. Rooms are smaller here, but prices are also smaller, ranging mid-April through September from $57 to $67 for two people in one or two double beds. They'll welcome your pets at Five Flags, and there's a lovely swimming pool running alongside the dunes.

On the eastern edge of Pensacola Beach, neighboring Navarre Beach has a **Holiday Inn Navarre,** 8375 Gulf Blvd., Navarre Beach, FL 32569 (tel. 904/939-2321, or toll free 800/465-4329), on US 98, an isolated beachside resort that once housed the cast of *Jaws II,* which was filmed hereabouts. There is a restful beach atmosphere amid the dunes and sea oats, with a tropical indoor pool and spa for entertainment, games for the kids, and tennis for exercise fans. All king-size rooms have a gulf view and there's a gift shop, two bars, a seafood restaurant, even a theater. Rates range from $88 to $160 from April to mid-September, dropping in other months to $59 to $140.

## Camping

**Cherokee Campground,** at 5255 Gulf Breeze Pkwy., Gulf Breeze, FL 32561 (on US 98, 10 miles east of Gulf Breeze; tel. 904/932-9905), is on Santa Rosa

Sound and rents space, with cable television hookup, in its travel park for $9 a night, $50 per week year round.

## WHERE TO DINE

Restaurants are so inexpensive in the Panhandle that there's hardly any point in putting them in price categories, so we've just listed them all together. You won't find many fancy places here, just very good cooking, some of the state's best seafood, and happy places where everyone smiles and drawls out that old "y'all come back" cliché—but here they really seem to mean it. Remember that the prices we've cited are for entrées, but these usually include salad, one or two vegetables, and sometimes even coffee.

**Michael's** (tel. 432-4311) in New World Inn, a lovely new inn in Florida, also has one of the city's most attractive restaurants. You'll find a description of the inn's handsome restaurants back a page or so.

**Dolphins on the Bay Restaurant,** 100 Pfeiffer St. (US 98) in Gulf Breeze (tel. 932-6678), occupies a lovely setting beneath some trees and overlooking Pensacola Bay. Seafood seems even more wonderful here with all that water around you. Goodness knows there's plenty of it on the menu: 10 different preparations of shrimp from creole to kebab, and all kinds of fish from triggerfish to amberjack, snapper, grouper, flounder, mullet, and even shark! Lobster, crab, oysters, and scallops are on the menu as well, which also has a few beef selections for those not infatuated with seafood. Prices for complete dinners fall in the $7 to $10 range. Dolphins is open daily March through August, closed Wednesday in other months, and hours are 11am to 9pm daily except Wednesday, later on weekends.

Catfish? You want catfish? Well, there's always one in every crowd. If you're that one, try **Catfish Country,** 916 E. Gregory St. (tel. 438-9019), which features freshwater catfish—all you can eat for $9—and dinners of oysters, shrimp, flounder, snapper, and the like for $6 to $7. Sandwiches, salads, and steaks here too, at similarly low prices. Hours are 11am to 9pm weekdays, to 10pm on weekends.

Got the midnight munchies? **Bay Window Deli,** 911 Gulf Breeze Pkwy. (tel. 932-0817), is open from 7am to 11pm and features all kinds of deli sandwiches, hoagies, salads, barbecue, cheesecake, even caviar and eggs Benedict. Prices are in the $5 range for most things.

For the most budget of budget meals, try the **Elk's Lodge Dining Room,** 200 W. La Rue St., at the corner of Spring and La Rue streets (tel. 432-5636), where the fellows of that fraternal organization prepare $1 breakfasts and $3 lunches—including entrée, three vegetables, soup, salad, coffee or tea, and cornbread!—and similarly inexpensive dinners every day. It's open to the public and even has take-out service. Hours are 6am to 9pm Tuesday through Friday, 6am to 3pm Saturday through Monday.

You'll have to look closely for the sign that points out **Hopkins' Boarding House,** at 900 N. Spring St. (tel. 438-3979), but once you find it you'll be enchanted. A pale-olive house with rocking chairs on the veranda, wrought-iron trim, lace curtains, and grandmotherly bric-a-brac, the Hopkins' place sits serenely under a mass of shady trees. It's a real boardinghouse, too—one gentleman rocked slowly in the afternoon sun and allowed as how he'd lived there "gettin' on to 30 years now." As they have for years, Hopkins family members still preside over this down-home spot. Join other diners at a long table, the likes of which gave rise to that boarding-house reach your mother warned against, or settle into a large round table in the parlor where you can gaze out over the lawn. Bowls heaped with cantaloupe, tomatoes fresh from nearby fields, carrot salad, and potato salad begin appearing about 11am Tuesday through Saturday, when the double doors open for lunch (closing at 2pm), and at 5:15pm for dinner, which continues through 7:30pm. The price is just $6.50. They're even open for heaping country breakfasts from 7 to 9:30am, but there are only noon meals on Sunday and they're closed all day Monday.

Menu collectors should like **Cap'n Jim's,** 905 E. Gregory St. (tel. 433-3562), where you can take a souvenir copy of the menu right with you for light reading—it looks just like a newspaper. Cap'n Jim and three of his family work together here, Jimbo in the kitchen, and Duke and Kathy in the dining room, with smiles and efficient service.

Cap'n Jim loves water and has a constant view of it from a wall of windows overlooking Pensacola Bay. As you watch the waters of the bay roll by, dine on fresh, simply prepared seafood: fresh oysters, red snapper, fat shrimp (barbecued or atop a mound of salad). The moderate prices begin at $6 to $17 and top out at about $22 for a seafood platter for two. If you've never tried homegrown freshwater catfish, now's the time. Open from 11am to 9:45pm daily except Sunday.

Pasta, pasta, and more pasta at **Scotto's,** 300 S. Alcaniz St. (tel. 434-1932), which adds to its creative pasta dishes with plenty of good veal, beef, and chicken selections as well. A beautiful restaurant that has risen quickly to popularity in this city, Scotto's is in a restored Gothic house and deserves its rave reviews. You'll find this one open from 5:30 to 10pm daily, and in some seasons from 11:30am to 2pm for lunch. Prices for dinner are in the $10 to $15 range or less.

At the **Marina Oyster Barn,** 505 Bayou Blvd., at the Johnson-Rooks 76 Marina (tel. 433-0511), you'll find some of the state's best shrimp tempura and freshly shucked-before-your-eyes bivalves. Your check will average $10 to $12 or less per person for sea treats at this simple rustic spot. Open Tuesday through Thursday from 11am to 9pm, an hour later on Friday and Saturday; closed Sunday and Monday.

Francisco Moreno built a tiny house for his daughter when she became a bride in 1879, and today you can lunch right in this minuscule honeymoon cottage at **Mr. P's Wine and Sandwich Shop** at 221 E. Zaragoza St. (tel. 433-0294). Daily specials of bean sprouts and shrimp tucked into pita bread, Reuben sandwiches, and the like ($3 to $5) are accompanied by a selection of domestic beer and wine. It's hard to imagine setting up housekeeping in such small quarters, but then it's also hard to imagine providing for 27 children and 127 grandchildren as did the house's builder! Hours are 11am to 2:30pm daily except Sunday.

You'll learn more about **McGuire's Irish Pub,** 600 E. Gregory St. (tel. 433-6789), in the nightlife section, but learn here that at McGuire's you can feast on such graze-ables as a caviar burger, corned beef and cabbage, oysters Rockefeller soup (!), Irish stew, a cheese board, fried apple sticks, nachos, a po' boy, a cannibal burger, or McGuire's terrible Garbage Burger with "some of everything—it's disgusting." Full dinners are a bit more serious—a trencherman's seafood platter, Seafood O'Fettuccini, beer-batter shrimp, peppercorn steak, ribs, or charbroiled redfish, among others. Dinner prices range from $11 to $16 and include salad, the pub's 18¢ Senate Bean Soup ("Same recipe as served in the U.S. Senate for 18¢. Can you believe these are the same guys who spend $237 for an 18¢ aircraft bolt?"), and Irish fries or baked potato. McGuire's rolls out the Irish welcome at 11am daily (from 4pm Sunday), closing when the last of the night owls begins to hoot.

So successful has McGuire's been over the years it has been amusing and amazing all comers that McGuire has opened another similarly chuckly spot called **Flounders,** 800 Quietwater Beach Rd. (tel. 932-2003). Founded by (who else?) Fred Flounder, this is another rollicking spot to spend some time dining, drinking, or, well, just floundering around. Figure to while away more than the average amount of time just reading Flounder's funny menu, where Mae Flounder advises "It's not the flounder in your life, it's the life in your flounder," and Alfred, Lord Flounder, utters these immortal words: "Better to have floundered and lost than never to have floundered at all."

You can put away a whole stuffed flounder here for less than $15, or have a go at oysters, scampi fettuccine, rock lobster tail, hickory-grilled swordfish steaks, or redfish served almondine, Florentine, au gratin, or blackened style. On Sunday morning, stagger on over for a bountiful brunch of strawberry pancakes or eggs Benedict from 11am to 3pm, and on any day expect to pay about $11 to $16 for dinner.

You'll be dining in handsome surroundings heavy on antiques that include the walls from a confessional booth—sadly, they do not talk—a turn-of-the-century brass chandelier from the ballroom of the Palace Hotel in Norfolk, and stained-glass windows from a New York convent. Flounder's is over on Pensacola Beach at the traffic light, and is open from noon to 2am daily, except Sunday when they open at 11am.

If you're looking for a cool, quiet spot as you tour the Seville Preservation District, drop into **Jamie's,** 435 E. Zaragoza St. (tel. 434-2911). Jamie's is not only sweet with flaky pastries, it's sweet to look at: a yellow candlelit Victorian house where a tiny dining room is set with fresh flowers and crisp linens. Colonial furnishings seat perhaps 30, and classical music hums quietly in the background. Jamie's began as a bakery about six years ago and has grown into this cozy little restaurant redolent in old-world atmosphere and brimming with homemade goodies. It's open from 11am to 2pm Tuesday through Saturday and 5:30 to 10pm Monday through Saturday. Every day there's a cold soup, avocado, for instance, and baked French onion soup with a touch of sherry. Gourmets will like the house pâté, a blend of chicken and sausage lightly touched with cognac and served with herbed toast or homemade bread. There are croissant sandwiches and a wide array of fresh crispy salads from hearts of palm to shrimp rémoulade. Lunch prices are $5 to $7; dinners, $15 to $20.

Another cozy spot for lunch in the Seville Preservation District is **E.J.'s Food Company,** at 232 E. Main St. (tel. 432-5886), which occupies the first home of the Southeastern Baptist Church. E.J.'s is a cozy spot with frilly lace curtains, checked tablecloths, paintings on the wall, paddle fans, and rib-sticking lunches from pecan-chicken-salad sandwiches to barbecued pork or an oyster basket, salad bar, and chicken tempura. There's a hearty special each day, and a bounteous salad bar offering enough food to hold you for a day or two. Prices are in the $2.50 to $5 range. E.J.'s is open from 11am to 2pm daily, and specializes in take-out orders and catering.

## CULTURAL ACTIVITIES

Pensacola loves a restoration, which is why the city's **Saenger Theater,** 118 Palafox St. (tel. 438-2787), a product of the 1920s, is so popular. Now renovated into a jewel of a theater, the 65-year-old Saenger was once a vaudeville theater and is now home to many music and dance performances throughout the year. Local newspapers like the *Pelican* or the *Pensacola News-Journal* tell you what's playing when, or you can phone. Tickets range up to $35, depending on the event.

The **Pensacola Symphony Orchestra** (tel. 435-2533) offers annual concerts and other local performances at various locations, and the **Pensacola Community Concerts Association** brings ballet, opera, and other musical entertainment to the city.

**Pensacola Museum of Art,** 407 S. Jefferson St. (tel. 432-6247), is the showcase for traveling loan exhibitions and has its own collection of art and sculpture as well. Hours are 10am to 5pm Tuesday through Friday, closing an hour earlier on Saturday; closed Sunday and Monday. Admission is free.

**Pensacola Little Theater,** 186 N. Palafox St. (tel. 432-8621), is the oldest continuing community theater in the Southeast and is now celebrating 51 years of performances by local players. Hours and days of performances vary, so give them a call to see what's on when you're here.

**University of West Florida,** on US 90A (tel. 474-2000), also takes to the boards with its University Theater, which presents at least eight plays annually, plus seminars, lectures, and discussions presented by notable theater experts.

In 1985 Pensacola opened a new **Pensacola Civic Center** to play host to a wide variety of entertainment ranging from the high-stepping Lippizaner stallions to the equally high-stepping Pointer Sisters and the rock group Kiss. You'll find the new center at 201 E. Gregory St. (tel. 433-6311). Ticket prices vary of course, according to the popularity of the performers, but are generally in the $10 to $20 range.

# NIGHTLIFE

Pensacola is, shall we say, a quiet place, and that's putting it mildly. You won't find razzle-dazzle nightlife here, the city is proud to say, but that doesn't mean you have to trot off to bed at sunset.

## Lounges and Hang-out Spots

The **Park Inn International,** 223 E. Garden St. (tel. 433-8331), often has entertainment. A couple of lively hang-out spots are **Trader Jon's Bar,** 511 S. Palafox St. (tel. 438-3600), which calls itself the official home of the U.S. Navy Blue Angels; **Quayside Inn,** 331 S. Palafox St. (tel. 433-9752); and the **Red Garter Saloon,** 500 S. Palafox St. (tel. 433-9229).

You never can tell when you're going to get a craving for a green beer, but if you do there's always one on tap at **McGuire's Irish Pub,** 600 E. Gregory St., just west of the Bay Bridge (tel. 433-6789), a local pubby spot boasting "feasting, imbibery, and debauchery," although presumably you'll have to see to the last of those three yourself. Friendly local folks and visitors flock to McGuire's, where a moose head presides over a massive stone fireplace and Irish of all nationalities have donated over 30,000 autographed dollar bills and 2,800 personalized mugs to the pub's collection. If you don't like crowds, forget McGuire's on Friday night, when most of the Panhandle seems to be gathered here for outrageously fat sandwiches and charcoal-broiled burgers in the $3 to $5 range. Soup and stews, steaks, fresh gulf seafood, enormous salads, and nightly parties make this a fun favorite that has gained acclaim in several national magazines. Open Monday through Saturday from 11am to 2am, on Sunday from 4pm to 1am.

Proving that "we all flounder to the beat of a different drum," **Flounder's,** 800 Quietwater Beach Rd. (tel. 932-2003), on Pensacola Beach, manages to set the tempo for many of Pensacola's hungry and thirsty. Get set here for such high-octane treats as a drink called "diesel fuel" served in a Mason jar. Every bit as notable as McGuire's, Flounder's is operated by the same unquenchable lot. Hours are 5pm to 2am daily, opening at noon on weekends. Closing wisdom: "To err is human, to flounder divine."

# THE SIGHTS

Towering live oaks draped in ghostly Spanish moss shade the streets of this lovely old Florida city, and once were its fortune-maker. At the turn of the century a timber boom made many a millionaire in these parts, and that same timber became walls of their elaborate homes. Most of these were on rolling hills in the **North Hill Preservation District** (bounded by LaRue, Palafox, Blount, and Reus streets), which you can tour with a map provided by the visitor information center.

Here you'll see etched glass and tall chimneys, wrap-around verandas, bay windows, turrets, shutters, and ornate gingerbread trim on typical old southern mansions that have changed hardly a whit in a century.

Pensacola and St. Augustine have a running feud over which is truly the oldest city in the nation, and Pensacola with its 16th-century foundations has an excellent claim to the title. Its shady, sleepy preservation district easily competes with St. Augustine's busier, better-known (and consequently more crowded) cluster of centuries-old structures.

Perhaps it is its very naïveté that makes Pensacola's **Seville Preservation District** so charming: Towering live oaks shade a small bayside park where children play, surrounded by the history their ancestors worked so hard to produce; bees buzz in gardens and there's a somnolent hush among the tiny shops and boutiques. Honeymoon cottages and sea captains' shore homes are now carefully restored, and shopkeepers will keep you spellbound with stories of the people who once worked and played, giggled and wept in these peak-roofed and pillared cottages.

Start your tour in **Historic Pensacola Village,** at 205 E. Zaragoza St. (tel. 444-8905), where you will learn a little about the background of buccaneers and boasters, timber lords and Spanish dons whose ancestors live here still. Then wander down Zaragoza Street past the Walton, Tivoli High, and Lavalle houses, past Julee Cottage, and take a moment to visit the **Pensacola Historical Museum,** in Old Christ Church, the oldest church in the nation. Next door is the two-story **Dorr House,** which fronts on shady Adams Street where you can fairly see statuesque ladies with hand-span waists and feathered hats sweeping grandly down the boulevard. All are part of the Historic Pensacola Village, which now encompasses 10 historic buildings including the **Museum of Commerce,** the **Museum of Industry,** the **T.T. Wentworth Jr. Museum** in Pensacola's former city hall, the **LaValle House, Dorr House, Julee Cottage, Bokley House,** and **Quina-Haw House.** There is an admission to the Wentworth Museum ($3 for adults, $2 for children 6 to 12), but no admission charge to the area, so you can peek and peer wherever you like. In shops here you'll find colorful handmade quilts and crocheted bedspreads, hand-dipped tapers, perfumed oils, elegant kitchenware, fine old clocks, 18th-century antiques, even a Christmas cottage with a holiday tree made of driftwood hung with sand dollars.

Shopkeepers of Historic Seville Square will be happy to send you a map of the area with shops and historic homes sketched and named so you can find your way around. Contact the shopkeepers at Seville Square Historical District, P.O. Box 587, Pensacola, FL 32593 (tel. 904/432-6717).

Edward Ball was one of northern Florida's most in-the-limelight millionaires all his long life. As trustee of the Dupont estate, he had billions under his control and was a most powerful northern Floridian. He is less well known for the funds he donated to many charitable organizations, particularly those dedicated to preserving Florida's wildlife. You can walk the **Edward Ball Nature Trail** at the University of West Florida at US 98A and University Parkway, where 2.5 miles of boardwalk honor the memory of this well-known Florida power broker. You'll find the trail on the northwest side of the campus in a wetlands area. It's open daily and is free. Hour-long guided tours are conducted weekdays by the Delta Tau Delta fraternity (tel. 474-2425 or 474-2000).

If you were glued to the television set for space activities at Cape Canaveral, you won't want to miss a visit to the **Pensacola Naval Aviation Museum** (tel. 452-3604) at the world's largest naval air station. Now a naval air station may not sound like much of an attraction, but here in Pensacola it's as fascinating as it is important to the local economy.

Pensacola likes to call itself the cradle of naval aviation, for it was here that the first group of aviators flew in those funny-looking bales of wood and wire that were to be called airplanes. Here in Pensacola the naval air station is home to the **Naval Aviation Museum,** which displays some of those early contraptions and even has a land-survival exhibit that gives you a look at a survival-skills course the swabby flyers have to survive.

To get there, take Palafox Street south to Garden Street, where the road becomes Navy Boulevard and goes straight to the naval air station. On display here is an awesome array of aircraft from Grumman Hellcats and Tigers to the Skylab command module. Let the kids try their hand at the controls of a jet trainer while you marvel at the daring of pilots who so fearlessly flew those flimsy early craft. Open from 9am to 5pm daily, it's free.

Perhaps the single most fascinating part of the naval air station is the **U.S.S. Lexington,** a massive aircraft carrier that opens its doors to one and all when it's in port. Still an operating carrier, the *Lexington* is open from 9am to 3pm daily on those occasions, and charges no admission for a look at the ship that is home to several thousand sailors.

A lighthouse on the station was built in 1825 and is still operating to warn ships away from tricky coastal waters. Its beam soars across 210 miles of the Gulf of Mexico.

One final note: The naval air station is the home of those daredevil acrobatic pilots, the Blue Angels. Technically part of the Navy Flight Demonstration Team, the Angels are U.S. Navy and Marine Corps aviators who perform here frequently and make regular appearances in the skies over many American cities.

## Special Events

One week a year Pensacolans drag out their history tomes and suit up as Spanish conquistadors to celebrate the five flags that have fluttered over this centuries-old village. This special week is the **Fiesta of Five Flags,** marking the settling of the city in 1559 by Don Tristan de Luna and his 1,500 followers. Their arrival is re-created by local residents who go all out with fancy costumes, street fairs, celebrities, beauty queens, even a four-masted antique sailing ship that sails into port for the celebration. The fiesta's in May.

Later in the year some of the more unusual festivals take place, including a **'coon hound championship** in June, a gourmet **gumbo cookout** in July, a number of **fishing tournaments** (one for sharks), and a **seafood festival** in September.

Each spring the city renews its ties with the Old South when it presents its **Mardi Gras–Krewe of Lafitte Parade.** This two-week spectacular in late February and early March includes a round of parades, street dances, and jazz festivals featuring residents in spectacular Mardi Gras costumes and masks. The finale is a Mardi Gras Ball.

Other special events in the city include a massive **St. Patrick's Day** party at McGuire's Irish Pub, which sponsors kite-flying contests, a bicycle race, Irish jig competitions, and even Irish skydivers!

At **Christmas** the city celebrates in the loveliest of ways: Carolers stroll the streets from Seville Square to Palafox Street, past shopkeepers dressed in Victorian costumes and shops decked out in holly and red ribbons.

Pensacola's **Perdido Key,** a long sandy strip of uninhabited scrub-pine island, is a favorite place for **crabbing expeditions.** We're not talking about the kind of crabbing so loved by Lucy of the Peanuts cartoon fame. We're talking of the kind that involves crab net and bucket. Armed with those, plus a pair of ancient tennis shoes, you wade along the shoreline and scoop up those scampering crabby little fellows. Fall is the best time for blue and speckled crabs, which can be spotted just beyond the point where the waves break on the shoreline. If you assign someone else in the group to bait a hook with shrimp and toss it into the surf, you may end up with a whole seafood buffet!

## SPORTS

You can play golf at **Carriage Hills Golf Course,** 2355 W. Michigan (tel. 944-5497), the **Osceola Golf Club,** Osceola Heights (tel. 456-2761), and **Tiger Point Golf and Country Club,** near Pensacola Beach (tel. 932-1333). Play on 18 holes is $9 to $30. Arrangements can be made through many beach hotels.

Largest of the tennis facilities in the area is **Scott Tennis Center,** at Cordova Park (tel. 432-2939), which has 18 courts and charges $2.65 for adults, about $2 for children, a day. The **Holiday Inn** on Pensacola Beach (tel. 932-5361), has four courts, and the **Pensacola Racquet Club,** 3450 Wimbledon Dr. (tel. 434-2434) in Pensacola has 10 courts available for $4.25 an hour, per person.

**Pensacourt Sports Center,** 3001 Langley Ave. (tel. 478-1400), has racquetball, handball, and tennis courts, aerobics, suntanning equipment, saunas, a weight room, a restaurant, and a nursery. Weekly charges are $35 single, $50 for couples, or $12 a day. It's open from 6am to 10pm weekdays, 8am to 5pm on Saturday, and 8am to 6pm on Sunday.

**Key Sailing Center,** 289 Pensacola Beach Rd. (tel. 932-5520), has all kinds of water-sports equipment for rent, including Hobie catamarans from 16 to 18 feet and windsurfing boards. Rental rates are $20 to $35 an hour (depending on the size of the boat), with lower long-term rates available. Windsurfing boards are $15 an hour, $30 a half day.

**Jet-skis,** those snowmobiles on waterskis, can be rented—including life jacket, instructions, and moral support—across from the Howard Johnson on Pensacola Beach for about $15 a half hour.

**Surf & Sail Boardsailing,** 11 Via de Luna, Pensacola Beach (tel. 932-SURF), has become the local surfboarders' headquarters. Boards are for rent for $12.50 an hour, $40 a day, and they'll teach you how to get them sailing for $30 for 60 minutes of instruction.

All kinds of fish live in the fresh and salt waters hereabouts, and all kinds of fishermen flock here to catch 'em. Big-game fishermen have a go at sailfish, marlin, red snapper, grouper, amberjack, and scamp.

Freshwater fans head for the Escambia and Perdido rivers or to the lakes and streams on Eglin Air Force Base for black bass, pickerel, bream, pike, and catfish.

Surf-fishing enthusiasts do what they do most anytime, but spring, particularly April, is considered the luckiest season. Pompano, one of Florida's most highly prized delicacies, can be caught in the surf along with another Florida fish called whiting.

**Driftfishing boats** working in the area include the *New Florida Girl* (tel. 904/837-6422) and *Her Majesty II* (tel. 904/837-6313). Party driftfishing boats tend to move their home base now and then, so give them a call to find out where they're moored. Fees are about $35 per person; half price for children.

Gamblers can put a few dollars on the nose of a sleek greyhound at **Pensacola Greyhound Park,** 951 Dog Track Rd. (tel. 455-8598), on US 98 west of the city, open year-round. Dog races begin at 7:45pm nightly with matinees on Friday, Saturday and Monday at 1:15pm (there's no racing on Thursday or Sunday). Admission is $1, grandstand seating costs an additional 50¢, and clubhouse admission and seating is $1.50.

## SHOPPING

Pensacola's downtown shopping district, known as **Palafox Place,** has had a rebirth in recent years and is now a study in lacy iron grillwork, pretty pastel storefronts, and intriguing boutiques.

The **Seville Historic District,** which stretches from Palafox Street to Ninth Avenue between Romana and Main streets, has dozens and dozens of adorable little shops selling everything from country calico to Christmas ornaments, dollhouse furniture, fashions for tall girls, small girls, children, and men, antiques, toys, jewelry, kitchenware, and artwork. Many shops and restaurants are in restored 18th- or 19th-century cottages and mansions, so you can combine shopping and historic touring. Shopkeepers have even banded together to form a group called Shopkeepers of Historic Seville, and will be happy to send you a handy map and list of the shops operating in the historic district. Contact them at P.O. Box 587, Pensacola, FL 32593.

**Bayou Country Store,** 823 E. Jackson St. at Ninth Avenue (tel. 432-5697), is packed with countrified treasures from baskets to lamps, salt-glazed stoneware in cobalt-blue designs, quilts, hooked and braided rugs, calico lampshades, and primitive prints. They're open from 10am to 5pm daily except Sunday.

**Quayside Thieves Market,** 712 S. Palafox St. (tel. 443-9930 or 476-3677), is a cluster of quaint specialty shops and small drinking and dining spots gathered together in a beautifully restored, century-old historic brick warehouse. China, antiques, collectibles, brass, copper, linens, old books—you name it and you're likely to find it here. Beneath your feet, by the way, is 60 acres of land created by ballast dumped from early sailing vessels, which loaded lumber after lightening their load by dumping everything from blue stone from Italy to lava from Mount Pelée here! You'll find the market on the waterfront (take I-10 to the I-110 South exit, then go to exit 1-C and turn right to Palafox, left on Palafox, and south to the waterfront). Market hours are 10am to 5pm Wednesday through Sunday.

**Cordova Mall,** 5100 N. Ninth Ave. (tel. 477-7562), offers more than 70 shops in an air-conditioned mall, and **Mariner Mall,** Fairfield Drive at Mobile Hwy. (tel. 456-7466), features many discount shops.

In Pensacola you'll also find the headquarters of a well-known mail-order company, **J. W. Renfroe Pecan Co.,** which operates at 2400 W. Fairfield Dr. (tel. 432-2083 or 438-9405, or toll free 800/874-1929). Renfroe passes out free samples of its pecans and pecan candies from 8am to 5pm Monday through Friday; 9am to 3pm Saturday.

## A SAND DUNE PARK

Pensacola's greatest pride is its **Gulf Islands National Seashore** (tel. 904/934-2621), a 150-mile stretch of offshore islands and keys strung between Gulfport, Mississippi, and Destin, Florida.

To get there, head to the beach across the Pensacola Bay Bridge and past Gulf Breeze, a small offshore island where you might stop to roam the **Naval Live Oaks Plantation.** Here in 1828 the live oak, the most typical tree of the Deep South, was placed under protective management to supply highly prized ship timbers. These majestic monsters, draped in spooky Spanish moss, tower here still, and you can hike through them.

There's a small toll across to the beach, then just follow the signs to Fort Pickens (you make a sharp right turn off Gulf Breeze Parkway onto County Road 399) and make a right when you reach Pensacola Beach.

On your left you'll see sailboats and the occasional adventurous parasailer flying through the air (you can try it yourself for about $20).

If you take the right fork in the road, you'll be driving down a sandy strip where condominiums are springing up like fungi on a spring morning. You can stay amid the white dunes and the sea oats in a condo by contacting the Pensacola Beach Chamber of Commerce. They'll send your name to apartment owners who will write to you about their accommodations.

Here on Santa Rosa Island in Pensacola you find mile after mile of sugary white sand. At the end of this lovely deserted strip of sand is Gulf Islands National Seashore, which charges $3 a carload entrance fee, and offers camping for $12 with electricity, $10 without. Six miles beyond the entrance to the park, five-sided **Fort Pickens** looms up like a pink mirage in a desert. Children will love prowling this giant fortification, which once imprisoned the fierce and courageous Apache chief, Geronimo. Outside the fort are several batteries built in the late 19th and early 20th centuries with rapid-fire rifles capable of hurling a 45-pound projectile more than five miles to sea in 25 seconds—not something to be facing at firing time!

Massive construction on Fort Pickens was begun in 1829. In those days the fort protected a naval shipyard on Pensacola Bay. Geronimo was its most famous inhabitant and the tiny cell in which he huddled in winter beside a small fire, chafing under his chains, is a touching sight still. Fort Pickens never really saw much action, but these days many a shutter snaps to record the massive guns.

If you like camping, Fort Pickens is a tranquil seaside park with lots of room for roaming and a pier for fishing. There are a number of park activities including a marine museum with changing exhibits of the area's wildlife (open from 9am to 5pm). In summer months there are daily activities including rifle-firing demonstrations, history lessons, children's activities, and tours of the fort. Scuba-diving and spearfishing are permitted, but some beaches are off-limits, and swimming is not recommended in the entrance channel to Pensacola Bay because of the strong rip current.

Fort Pickens is open daily (except Christmas) throughout the year. Hikers can take a self-guided nature trail or join groups shepherded by rangers in summer.

# 2. Fort Walton/Destin

It seems fitting somehow that this small sand-fringed city is geographically about halfway between the sleepy southern elegance of Pensacola and the frenetic fantasyland of Panama City. This is a spot neither garish nor elegant, neither expensive nor run-down cheap, a quiet miles-long strip of dunes and sugary soft sand with prices a family wallet can handle and a quiet acceptance of the impenetrability of life.

Like the foamy green sea that has washed upon these shores for millennia, people here are gentle and easy-going, full of enthusiasm for these rolling dunes and for each other. "There's something about it," one citywise but city-weary sophisticate confided. "No matter how far I go or how long I'm away, I'm always happy just to be back here where strangers don't look at you funny if you say hello to them on the street."

You can find whatever you want here, be it easy friendships or solitary walks on deserted beaches; high-rise, amenity-laden resorts or small, family-run apartments; activity-filled days or the peace of a snow-white dune where only a seagull's shriek breaks the silence.

Summer continues to be the major tourist season, and if you arrive anytime from Easter to Labor Day you'd be wise to make a reservation. Warm gulf breezes keep temperatures on a fairly even keel, although it's at least 10° cooler than southern Florida in winter. Prices as low as $300 a month for a posh condominium apartment are increasing the region's popularity as a winter resort.

There's a small amusement park here that doesn't begin to compare to the ringy-dingy-do of Panama City Beach. There are small but excellent restaurants where you'll find unfailingly fresh seafood and unfailingly friendly service. There are miles and miles of soft sand lapped by turquoise waters shallow enough for the children and deep enough for grownup swimmers.

It's a happy mélange of entertainments in a small-village atmosphere where anyone may soon be a friend. It's a quaint rusticity, neither shabby nor contrived, where you may find *your* kind of halfway house.

## GETTING AROUND

Unless you don't plan to leave the beach you might consider a **rental car,** available from Avis, Budget, Economy, Hertz, National, or Panhandle Rentals. **Avis** (tel. 651-0819) and **Hertz** (tel. 651-0612) have service desks at the airport. Rates begin at about $20 a day.

## VISITOR INFORMATION

Personable folks at the **Fort Walton Beach Chamber of Commerce,** 34 Miracle Strip Pkwy. SE (P.O. Drawer 640), Fort Walton Beach, FL 32548 (tel. 904/244-8191), will be happy to dig out information on anything and everything in the area. . . . Their counterparts at the **Destin Chamber of Commerce,** US 98 East (P.O. Box 8), Destin, FL 32541 (tel. 904/837-6241), will do likewise. . . . There's a **24-hour gas station** at the 7-Eleven, 408 Mary Esther Cut-off (tel. 244-1751). . . . For late-night cravings, head for the **Donut Hole,** in Destin on US 98 East (tel. 837-8824), open 24 hours. . . . For groceries any time of day or night, try **Delchamp's,** 904 Mary Esther Cut-off (tel. 243-5383).

## GETTING YOUR BEARINGS

Nearly all the activity in Fort Walton Beach and Destin is centered around **US 98,** which travels east-west along the beaches. Most addresses on US 98 west of Fort

Walton Beach have a W (for west) tacked on them. In Destin, most addresses are US 98E (for east). US 98 is also called **Miracle Strip Parkway.**

## HOTELS

In this area, hotels are located on US 98, which runs through the beach area of Fort Walton and Destin, or on Okaloosa Island just south of the Brooks Bridge over Santa Rosa Sound. We've divided them up by city and in descending order by price.

### Fort Walton

**Ramada Beach Resort,** US 98 (Miracle Strip Parkway), Fort Walton Beach, FL 32548 (tel. 904/243-9161, or toll free 800/447-0010), is Fort Walton's top spot, and what a showplace it is! Start with a huge swimming pool, in the center of which are towering rocks with waterfalls cascading over them and a grotto bar you can swim to. Move on to the rustic Buccaneer Lounge, where the bar is rigged with pirate ship sails, or to the Pelican's Roost, where you can feast on crab claws and frosty oysters on the half shell.

Shape up after a lobster dinner at the Lobster House Restaurant with a trip to the Healthy Habit Spa, complete with indoor heated pool, whirlpool, saunas, and steam and exercise rooms.

Rooms here have wall murals, dark carpets, and contemporary furnishings. There are suites with kitchenettes and separate bedrooms, some with Murphy beds. Outside, 800 feet of that Panhandle sand is stripped across the front of this 454-room resort. Add tennis courts, a kiddie pool, game room, and extras like a patio snackbar and bayou country barbecues by the pool, and you have the makings of a very impressive spot. For this you naturally pay top dollar, with peak summer-season rates of $70 to $110 double, dropping to $40 to $60 from September to March. Suites are higher.

The **Conquistador Inn,** 847 Venus Court, Fort Walton Beach, FL 32548 (tel. 904/244-6155), is an imposing six-story building hunkered down behind a tall white sand dune. Apartments have their own patios or balconies overlooking the dune, although you'll have to go up a couple of stories to see over it to the gulf. Motel rooms are available, but the apartments are especially nice here, with small kitchens separated from living rooms by an open kitchen bar. One- and two-bedroom apartments have large kitchens, plus spacious living and dining areas decorated in ocean shades. There's a pool and wooden walkways across the dunes. Rates in summer are $65 for a spacious apartment, $175 for larger quarters. Children under 6 stay free and you can bring your pet for a $5-a-day charge. In winter, prices drop to $27 to $67.

For a real look at Fort Walton's carefree beachside living, zip up to the fourth floor of **Carousel Motel and Apartments,** 571 Santa Rosa Blvd., Fort Walton Beach, FL 32548 (tel. 904/243-7658), and slip into the Stowaway Lounge. Plunk down in a rattan chair, order something cool, and while away the day staring out over the rippling waters of the gulf. The Carousel is a family-oriented operation with game room, boutique, two swimming pools, shuffleboard, and beachside gazebos. There are 107 handsome, recently redecorated rooms in a cluster of buildings, many with balconies overlooking the dunes. Rooms are very large and now feature soft contemporary colors. Some have couches or kitchens and snackbars. Summer rates range from $80 to $92 for a motel room, efficiency one-bedroom apartments, dropping about 50% in winter.

**Sheraton Coronado Beach Resort,** 1325 Miracle Strip Pkwy. (US 98), Fort Walton Beach, FL 32548 (tel. 904/243-8116, or toll free 800/874-8104), is brick inside and out. The spacious bedrooms with two double beds even have an entire wall of it behind the headboards. Vibrant colors brighten all that brick, and rooms are so large that the Coronado has added couches from which you can gaze through sliding glass doors at an entrancing view of the resort's extensive gardens and the gulf beyond. The Coronado has all the extras you'd expect in a 154-room resort, from wading pool and play equipment to refrigerators in rooms, kitchenettes, game room, restaurant, and lounge. Rates in peak summer season are $90 to $100 for rooms, dropping $30 to $40 in other months.

Another good value for your vacation dollar is the **Sandman Motel and Apartments,** 480 Santa Rosa Blvd., Fort Walton Beach, FL 32548 (tel. 904/243-1511, or toll-free 800/622-1511), a spick-and-span spot with full kitchens and bars, tiled baths and large closets, living room, and separate bedrooms, all right on the gulf. Outside, there's a mottled brick facade, shingled mansard roof, and a sparkling pool. Best of all are the rates—just $56 to $96 for one- or two-bedroom accommodations in summer.

If you can sacrifice beachside location, the **Greenwood Motel,** US 98E, Fort Walton Beach, FL 32548 (tel. 904/244-1141), on the Choctawhatchee Bay, makes up in tranquillity and friendly management what you might miss in sand. Rates for these paneled and attractively furnished bedrooms with a homey air about them are nice too: Just $44 a day double in summer for a bedroom, and there are one-bedroom apartments for $62 a day. Some rooms have balconies overlooking a large pool, and a few even offer views of the bay. The beach is just across the highway.

Vacation and business travelers flock to **Howard Johnson,** 314 Miracle Strip Pkwy. SW (US 98), Fort Walton Beach, FL 32548 (tel. 904/243-6162, or toll free 800/654-2000), at least partly for its proximity to Eglin Air Force Base, but especially for its pleasant waterside (but not ocean) location. In a manicured central courtyard magnolia trees blossom in spring, and tall river oaks shade a big swimming pool. Ask for a room overlooking the courtyard, and plan on waffles at the resort's Waffle House. You'll pay $49 to $59 double in summer, $40 to $45 in other seasons.

## Destin

You aren't going to have to read far before you discover that we love the **Sandestin Beach Hilton,** 5540 US 98E., Destin, FL 32541 (tel. 904/267-5000, and toll free 800/HILTONS). Hilton offers you very, very large rooms that are perfect for families: In the foyer of each room, tucked neatly away along one side, are two bunk beds the youngsters are going to love. Parents, granted a little privacy in the room beyond those bunks, are likely to feel pretty pleased with them, too. As if that's not enough, the rooms are also outfitted with big closets, a sink and dressing area outside the bathroom as well as in it, a hair dryer, shampoo, hair conditioner, lotion, even suntan oil. Are we finished raving on here? Not on your life. Set into the wall, and virtually invisible, is a refrigerator, a small hotplate adorned with a bright-blue enamel teakettle, and a tiny stainless-steel sink.

Now downstairs in the lobby, you'll pass by a lovely multilevel dining room ($12 to $17 price range for dinner) and a swimming pool both inside and outside the building! Add to that a cute little fleet of custom-designed Jeeps for you to putt about in, a 36-hole golf course, 24 indoor and outdoor tennis courts with grass, clay, and hard-top surfaces, sauna, boutiques, game room, movie theater, open-air seafood restaurant, cocktail lounge in a Tiki hut, water-sports facilities, and even a youth program to keep the youngsters occupied. What else could you possibly want?

Rates at this big hotel on the sands at Sandestin are $155 to $195 from May to September, dropping to $85 to $135 in winter.

Proof that people are discovering this long-asleep coast is the appearance of not one but two major condominium resorts: One of those is **Seascape Resort,** 100 Seascape Dr. (US 98E) (P.O. Box 970), Destin, FL 32541 (tel. 904/837-9181, or toll free 800/874-8104). Seascape, seven miles east of Destin, sprawls across acres and acres of Destin dunes at Miramar Beach. When you check in they'll give you a resort map, and you'll need it to find your way around this sprawling cluster of rustic wood-sided condominiums. There's a labyrinth of roads winding around a golf course, tennis courts, pools, lakes, playgrounds. And there's a gulfside beach and a beach club where you'll find dining, dancing, and entertainment in a handsome restaurant and attractive lounge. Explaining the resort's rate structure could take several pages, but basic prices range in peak summer season from $130 to $190 for villa apartments with kitchens, living rooms, queen-size beds, and one to three bedrooms. In other seasons, prices drop about 25%.

**Sandestin,** on US 98E, Destin, FL 32541 (tel. 904/837-2121, or toll free 800/874-2184), is a few miles farther east and a study in modernity with striking angular lines on its 164 slope-roofed condominium villa town houses. In the center of the resort are miles of manicured golf course. Sandestin is a very posh place with all the finest accoutrements of upper-crust condominium living: beamed ceilings, split-level apartments all individually and beautifully decorated, bicycles, games of all kinds, a spa, lounges and a handsome candlelit dining room, 48 acres of lakes, tennis on honest-to-Wimbledon grass courts (the only grass ones in the state), and 18 holes of golf (two holes of which were tagged "the lawn for the Taj Mahal" by *Golf Digest*). Outside on 440 acres of grounds you can watch porpoises playing on Choctawhatchee Bay or sit on the resort's gulfside beach. Rates for a wide variety of rooms, villas, and apartments are $65 to $350 double, dropping a bit in the fall and winter. Children under 15 stay free.

In the slightly less elevated financial brackets is a pretty place dubbed **Robroy Lodge and Marina,** on US 98E (P.O. Box 725), Destin, FL 32541 (tel. 904/837-6713). This standout resort in Destin comes complete with its own charter fishing boat. Set high over a gulf inlet (well, high for Florida), Robroy has perfectly manicured grounds with sweeps of grass and plants trimmed to a fare-thee-well. There's a small pool and a tiny rectangle of sand the resort calls its "sandbox for people who just *have* to have sand." Even the simplest rooms here are marvelously spacious and kept trim and shining with bright sunny colors. You can stow away here in the Staterooms, the Captain's Quarters with kitchens, or a super-spacious Admiral's Suite, with its own balcony overlooking the gulf. Prices begin at $35 for Staterooms and rise to $104 for the Admiral's Suite. In winter season prices drop as low as $35 a day for efficiencies.

Many accommodations in the Destin area are privately owned cottages, homes, or clusters of homes rented by a central agency. Prices vary, of course, according to the quality of the properties, but any of the companies will be happy to send you information on homes or cottages that will be just right for you. Among those with whom you should check if you're interested in a private house or cottage is **Gulfside Cottages,** operated by Earl Ugedahl and Harry Walley at 101 Snowdrift Rd. (US 98E), Destin, FL 32541 (tel. 904/837-2400), who have cottages with names like Skyward, Bimini, Viking, and Stilts I; rates vary widely so give them a call.

## An Amazing Sea-Site

There's been a fabulous addition to what was once deserted beachfront between Destin and Panama City. **Seaside Cottages,** County Road C-30A (P.O. Box 4717), Seaside, FL 32459 (tel. 904/231-4224, or toll-free 800/635-0296), is a new development in a new village called Seaside, which is not an easy place to find but is worth the search. (To get there, take a very close look at a map and locate County Road C-30A, which runs parallel to US 98 but right alongside the ocean from just east of Destin to Point Washington.)

Sooner or later you'll see Cape Cod looming up before your amazed eyes! Looking every bit like a pastel mirage, Rose Walk Cottages is actually a very carefully planned community of wood-sided, often oddly shaped little cottages painted in delicate pastels reminiscent of perhaps Bermuda or a Caribbean island. Although these are privately owned or for-sale homes-away-from-home dwellings, many of them are part of a central pool of cottages that can be rented by vacationers. Our favorite is a hexagonal charmer that is really just one big room decorated with paddle fans and white wicker furniture. A teensy bedroom is tucked away behind louvered doors, as is a bath and kitchen. Adorable.

You'll also find three-story towers here, with one room on each story, and two-story cottages with lofts and some of the loveliest countrified-tropical decor in the state. Although it's quite a difficult place to describe, Seaside and its Rose Walk Cottages are quite an easy place to live with—and in. And we are certainly ready to give it a try.

Seaside got underway in 1985 and is well on its way to being one of the state's most innovative—and most written-about—developments. Certainly they have done everything here to preserve the windswept-dune look of it all, to maintain ecological balance, and to create a development that proves there is the occasional artist among the state's many mundane developers. Even a little shopping center is something to be seen. Instead of a blank-faced row of stores, this "mall" is a cluster of small one-room wood-sided buildings in which sellers set up the wares in and around the doorway. Seaside's developers also plan to have outdoor theater performances here in busy summer months.

In the summer months, from March to September, there is a three-day minimum stay, with rates from $451 to $1,685 a week. You'll also find a cute little basket full of croissants, wine, and soft drinks included in the price. From September to March rates drop 15%.

If you have an interest in architecture, drive over here some day just to see what's going on. Plan to incorporate a stop at a lyrically lovely little café called **Aladdin's Paradise Café** at Seagrove Beach (tel. 231-4145). You'll find the café on County Road 30A in the infinitesimal village of Grayton Beach. Aladdin whips up themed dining "fantasies" and seafood treats like butterflied jumbo shrimp stuffed with crabmeat, wrapped in bacon, and broiled over charcoal; tenderloin filet flanked with fat shrimp; and fish right out of the seas a block away. Prices are in the $12 to $19 range for dinner, salad, and potato, served in a tropical atmosphere adorned with plenty of plants. Check to be sure they're open before you trek on out here, however. Hours are usually 5 to 10pm Tuesday through Saturday.

**Bud and Alley's** (tel. 231-5900) is part of the Seaside development, offers $15 to $17 dinners, and is open daily except Tuesday for lunch and dinner for American regional food and jazz.

With waves crashing and sea breezes blowing, one's thoughts turn often to seafood. When they do, turn to **Nick's** (mailing address: Route 1, Box 90, Freeport) at Basin Bayou, Route 20, west of Freeport (tel. 835-2222). It's a half hour's drive from Seaside and isn't a fancy spot, but it is definitely the place to head for wonderful Apalachicola oysters, good steamed crab, and crunchy fried seafood. It's open daily except Monday from 10am to 9:30pm, Sunday until 8:30pm, and prices are in the $7 to $10 range.

## Camping
**Fred Gannon State Park** is on Rocky Bayou, South of Eglin Air Force Base off Fla. 20 (tel. 904/897-3222), and has campsites for $10.65 with electricity, for $8.52 without. There's a swimming area, fishing in Puddin' Head Lake, two nature trails, and evening presentations by park rangers.

## RESTAURANTS
Back in 1931 brothers Cecil and Docie Bass turned a service station into **Staff's Restaurant,** 24 Miracle Strip Pkwy. (tel. 243-3482). Before long Model As were lined up outside (not for gasoline but for dinner!). Three generations later the Bass family is still dishing up delectables in a nautical atmosphere. Along the way this historic restaurant has housed a grocery, the first Western Union office and radio station, and has even been a hurricane shelter on occasion. Staff's staff has also played host to a host of luminaries from John Wayne to Bob Hope, Rosalyn Carter, Helen Gurley Brown, Cornelia Wallace, and Spencer Tracy, all of whom came to sample oyster stew and seafood gumbo, a creamy seafood casserole, and Staff's locally famous seafood platter. With all that history and those trend-maker drop-ins you'd

expect to pay plenty, but you won't: Menu prices start at just $8, and a brimming seafood platter for two is under $20. Our favorite, called "shrimp in shorts," is fat gulf shrimp wrapped in bacon and deep-fried. It's open from 5 to 10pm (closed Thursday).

If you like rustic, you should love the **Back Porch,** 1740 E. US 98 Hwy. (tel. 837-2022), where the tables are wood, the floor is wood, the fare is simple seafood, and the view from this second-floor porch is terrific. There is absolutely nothing even remotely approaching atmosphere here, but perhaps that in itself is atmospheric. Suffice to say that if you ask local residents where to go for seafood, this place is sure to be mentioned. Prices may have something to do with that: They rarely top $10. Hours at the Back Porch are 11am to 11pm daily.

Another new restaurant in town—well, new to us anyway—is **Louisiana Lagniappe,** Holiday Isle, in Sandpiper Cove Condominium, 775 Gulf Shore Dr. (tel. 837-0881). A big, airy restaurant with lots of tall windows, this attractive spot specializes, fittingly enough, in those Cajun flavors. You'll find crayfish and chicken gumbos on the menu, along with trout prepared several ways (including topped with crayfish and mushrooms), and lots of local seafood treats. Lagniappe is open from 6 to 10pm daily and is a bit hard to find—it's in the middle of a condominium complex, but you'll be all right if you follow the signs and don't be put off by the presence of security guards at the entrance to the condominiums. They'll be happy to show you the way to the restaurant. Prices are in the $11 to $23 range.

Leather wing chairs, plants, dim lights, and an attractive bar set the tone at **The Landing Restaurant,** 225 Miracle Strip Pkwy. SW (tel. 244-7134). You dine well and comfortably here at this steak-and-seafood haven on thick steaks, shrimp in several different preparations including a crispy shrimp tempura, snapper parmesan— all served with salad, potato, and hot breads. Prices are quite reasonable at this very large restaurant, falling easily into the $8 to $12 range. Hours at the Landing are 11am to 3pm and 5 to 9pm daily (except Saturday, when the restaurant is open only from 5 to 10pm).

You can't miss **Pandora's Steakhouse,** 1120 Santa Rosa Blvd. (tel. 244-8669) —just look for the beached yacht sitting smugly out there amid sand and parking lot in the middle of Okaloosa Island. Hop aboard for drinks in the yacht, then amble down the gangplank to the restaurant's lower level where hammered copper chandeliers glimmer on hefty wood beams. Meats are cut daily in the restaurant's kitchens and cooked over a wood-burning pit for prices in the $8 to $11 bracket, including Pandora's homemade breads. Open from 5 to 10pm daily, later in the lounge.

Everyone for miles around recommends **Scampi's,** US 98E, Destin (tel. 837-7686), and they're right! A two-story shingled building across from the beach just west of Destin, Scampi's has a long bar and lounge, dining on a mezzanine level, and more dining up on the second floor. Large as it is, it's often filled with diners who come here for a big bowl of spicy seafood gumbo or oyster chowder, a pound or so of Louisiana crayfish, a dozen or so Apalachicola oysters, or a platter of fried, grilled, or broiled seafood.

Atmosphere is casual but attractive, and prices are in the $12 to $16 range for entrée, salad, potato, and French bread. Really starving gourmands can stuff themselves with a "steambuck" for two that includes stone crab claws, shrimp, local oysters, snowcrab, Louisiana crayfish, new potatoes, corn on the cob, salad, and French bread (about $30 for two). You can even get a local specialty called scamp (no, it's not scampi, it's a fish) here occasionally. Hours are 5 to 10pm daily.

**Jamaica Joe's,** 785 Sundial Court, Okaloosa Island (tel. 244-4137), is a typically tropical kind of place with two large dining rooms overlooking the sea. High-backed wicker chairs fill every space not occupied by plants or paddle fans, and a waterfall ripples over some rocks to provide a view for those bored with the seascapes. On the menu is a wide range of seafood from charbroiled amberjack to flounder, jumbo shrimp, grouper parmesan, and plenty of oysters (less than $4 a dozen). You can have seafood steamed, fried, broiled, or combined on gargantuan platters here for prices in the $9 to $15 bracket. Hours are 5 to 10pm daily, later in the lounge.

When you're in the mood for a romantic, tranquil evening (we hope that's not a contradiction in terms) in lovely, formal surroundings, try the **Beachside Café and Bar,** 920 Gulfshore Dr., Destin (tel. 837-1272). Here you can dine with candlelight and roses, starched linens and formal service on quite a wonderful menu. Try, for instance, shrimp bisque, followed by a watercress salad. Then move on to snapper with two sauces, fettuccine Alfredo with pistachios, or angel-hair pasta with shrimp, snow peas, and ginger beurre-blanc. Traditionalists have several steak options. Dinners range in price from $18 to $30, including perfectly cooked vegetables and salad. Beachside is open daily from 5 to 10pm. An adjoining bar that opens at 4pm is a quiet but popular gathering spot too.

Sooner or later everyone in Fort Walton turns up at **Perri's Ristorante,** 300 Eglin Pkwy. NE (tel. 862-4421), the hands-down favorite Italian restaurant in town. A columned walkway and imposing double-door entrance to the brick building add the mandatory Roman touches. Inside, arched windows and plants, tile floors, and wall murals of Italian villas keep the theme going. Chef-owner Vittorio Perri has created a full menu of Italian specialties featuring some things you don't see often enough in Florida, saltimbocca alla romana and some Bolognese preparations. Hours are 5 to 10pm daily except Sunday and Monday. Perri's prices are in a moderate $8 to $14 bracket.

For a waterside location and cozy old-house atmosphere, **The Sound,** 108 US 98 West in Fort Walton (tel. 243-7772), gets our vote. Snuggled in beside the tranquil waters of Santa Rosa Sound, the restaurant has handsome views of the water and an inviting, homey air that's hard to leave. Seafood is the specialty here, too, and the Sound offers 18 different preparations of it, from fried soft-shell crabs to seafood St. Jacques. You can dine à la carte for about $7 to $20. Open from 10:30am to 10pm daily, the Sound is back off the highway on the western outskirts of Fort Walton Beach.

You could spend days trying out the several restaurants at the **Ramada Beach,** on US 98 (tel. 243-9161), where you can choose your atmosphere and your menu from seafood to southern cooking. (See our hotel recommendations for more information.)

**Liollio's on the Sound,** 14 Miracle Strip Pkwy. (tel. 243-5011), plays to a full house nightly as families throng here to dine on steaks and seafood with a Greek touch. Hosts John Georgiades and Paul Liollio created a wide variety of choices, but don't miss the whole bay snapper and super-size Greek salad. Windows overlook the Intracoastal Waterway and marina, candles blaze, and the happy chatter of tucking-in diners fills the air. Your bill will probably fall somewhere between $10 and $15. It's open from 11am to 11pm, later on weekends (from 5pm on Sunday).

If you're in a go-as-you-are mood, go as you are over to **Capt. Dave's at Destin Harbor,** on US 98 (tel. 837-6357). A family getaway spot, Capt. Dave's guarantees some of the freshest seafood anywhere, since the captain has only to reach his hand through the window to retrieve it from the fishing fleet that docks here. This was a favorite stopping spot for stars and crew working on the movie *Jaws II.* Prices for simply prepared seafood dishes are in the $11 to $15 bracket, and Capt. Dave's is open from 4:30 to 10pm daily.

**Jeremiah's,** 203 SE Brooks Blvd. (tel. 664-6666), is a newcomer that at last report was wowing 'em in this sandy strip of the Panhandle. Decked out in a bevy of intriguing antiques, leaded glass, and rusticity, Jeremiah's specializes in seafood and steaks you select yourself from a big glass case. You can—they tell us—even cook your choice yourself on the restaurant's impressive brick grill. Why you'd *want* to we can't imagine, but there's no accounting for trends, and the way we hear it, cook-it-yourself is officially a trend. Tucked away beside the water and barely visible, Jeremiah's manages to create its own little oasis of tranquillity in this often crowded part of the state. There's also a very large bar for those who like lots of space for lounging and the waterway views are diverting. Dinner rates range from $8 to $13, and the restaurant is open daily from 5 to 11pm.

Those dedicated to the pursuit of yet another good restaurant tell us they've found one in **Bay Café,** 233 SE Alcaniz Ave. (tel. 244-3550). Just a shrimp's wiggle from Jeremiah's, Bay Café is also tucked away under the Brooks Bridge. Once a bait shop, it's now surrounded by decks and beginning a new life as this chic little eatery. Very small indeed, the restaurant whisks up French favorites from tournedos in red wine sauce to an outstanding homemade salad dressing and French bread. Those with courage or trenchermen instincts can wind it up with lighter-than-air puff pastries topped with fruit and whipped cream. Prices are in the $14 to $18 range for dinner. The restaurant is open from 11am to 3pm and 5 to 11pm daily.

One more option, this one from long-time Fort Walton tasters Charlaine and Ed, who, as far as we can make out, may be the best restaurant-fed couple in the Panhandle. They've seen it all and are at this moment letting the *bon temps rouler* at a tiny restaurant called **Cajun Chef,** 1 Eglin Pkwy. (tel. 244-8326). Ethereal étouffée, crusty French bread straight out of the oven, and an unusual oyster-artichoke soup are among the highlights of this small newcomer. Flavors that are hard to resist and prices that are easy on the wallet make this a top-of-the-list try. Hours are 5 to 11pm daily.

Some morning or afternoon, or anytime for that matter (and we do mean *anytime*), head over to the **Donut Hole,** 635 US 98E, Destin (tel. 837-8824), where you'll find terrific fresh-baked doughnuts in an atmosphere that takes rustic to new heights. Pay no attention to the "modest going on decrepit" atmosphere, for the Donut Hole turns out some yummy crullers and good coffee 24 hours a day. Breakfast enthusiasts will adore this place, which whips up just about anything you could want for a.m. noshing and does it right in front of your wondering eyes: eggs Benedict, homemade breads and muffins hot from the oven, doughnuts to die for, cheese grits, pecan waffles with orange sauce. And at last, relief for those of us who would like breakfast better if it occurred later in the day: Donut Hole serves breakfast, they promise, "until the cook is plumb wore out, so come in anytime!" Presumably that cook is an energetic insomniac: You can—and should—breakfast here any time of night or day.

One of Destin's showplaces is the revolving restaurant at the **Holiday Inn,** on US 98 (tel. 837-6181). You're guaranteed a view here. As a matter of fact, you're guaranteed *all* the views possible here as you turn ever-so-slowly high above the shimmering waters of the gulf. Tinted glass shields you from glare as you dine amid tropical rattan in shades of peach and russet. Dinner entrées are $12 to $20. Open from 11am to 2pm and 5 to 10pm daily in summer, shorter hours in winter.

**Seascape** and **Sandestin** both have beautiful dining rooms overlooking those equally beautiful resorts. If you like elegant dining with surroundings to match, try these two sprawling resorts (see our hotel recommendations).

## NIGHTLIFE

This area's emphasis on family vacations means you won't find many bespangled dancers, but you'll still have plenty to do evenings in the larger hotels, all of which have nightly or weekend entertainment, particularly in summer.

Restaurants with lively lounges and entertainment include **Liollio's, Jamaica Joe's,** and **Pandora's.**

If you'd like to roam from nightspot to nightspot without traveling very far, head for the **Ramada Beach Resort,** on US 98 (tel. 243-9161), where there's entertainment in all three lounges.

Both **Sandestin** and **Seascape** in Destin have entertainment in their lounges.

One of the nicest nightclubs in the area is **Nightown,** at the corner of Palmetto and Azalea, just off US 98 (tel. 837-6448), which often features rock groups. If you're looking for something a little less frenetic, **Nightown's Other Bar** has easy-listening music.

At **Victor's,** 113 S. Eglin Pkwy., Fort Walton (tel. 243-1227), crowds gather for 35¢ drinks, $1 nights, and Beat-the-Clock evenings. Another favorite college crowd hangout is **Cash Moore's Faux Pas Lounge,** 106 Santa Rosa Blvd. (tel. 244-2274), where you'll see Cash's Rolls-Royce parked outside. He also operates **Smuggler's,** at 320 John Sims Pkwy. (tel. 729-2274).

For sheer hanging out on hot afternoons or lazy evenings, you can't beat a little hideaway with the enchanting name of **Hog's Breath Saloon,** 1239 Siebert St. (tel. 244-2199). It's a rustic (definitely) spot just northwest of the Brooks Bridge. The **Back Porch,** 1740 E. US 98 Hwy. in Destin (tel. 837-2022) is similar.

If you're of a more cultural bent, Fort Walton has a ballet association, a concert group, a symphony, a community theater, and a community chorus. They all give **concerts** at different times of the year (but mostly in winter months) and the chamber of commerce can tell you where and when they are.

Those entranced by the sight of females in various states of undress will find that going on at the **Matador Club,** Old Eastgate Road in Valparaiso (tel. 678-1812).

## THE SIGHTS

For a look at some other creatures who love the sea, look in at **Gulfarium,** on US 98E (tel. 244-5169). Penguins strut about in their Sunday best, seals entertain, porpoises perform, and shows are continuous from 10am to 4pm, to 6pm in summer. Admission is $9 for adults, $6 for children.

Bill and Yulee Lazarus, two dedicated archeologists, trailed the gas company as it installed lines in the area and recovered the artifacts left by the ancient Native Americans who lived here. You can see the results of their efforts at **Indian Temple Mound and Museum,** 139 Miracle Strip Pkwy. (tel. 243-6521). Exhibits in the museum (now owned by the city) depict 10,000 years of life in this Choctawhatchee Bay area. Hours are 11am to 4pm Monday through Saturday, opening at 9am in summer, closed on Sunday. Admission is 75¢ for adults; children under 12 are free.

You'll want to take a look at **Eglin Air Force Base,** which covers more than 700 square miles of land, into which you could fit the whole state of Rhode Island. Doolittle's Tokyo Raiders trained here for their raid against Imperial Japan, and equipment that destroyed Nazi Germany's buzz-bomb launchers was created here. The Son Tay Raiders, who tried to rescue Americans from North Vietnamese prison camps, worked here too. Bus tours of the base depart at 1:30pm three times a week in June, July, and August from the Officer's Club parking lot on the base. Call 881-6668 for information on the time of the tours.

One of the loveliest sights in the area is **Eden State Ornamental Gardens** (tel. 231-4214), the jewel of which is a perfectly restored mansion brimming with antiques. Part of the glory of Eden is its isolation, on a tiny, almost-overgrown road (turn north of US 98E at Point Washington). Time slips away on this road, and when you see delicate white columns and verandaed elegance of Eden, it's gone completely. You're back in another era, realizing suddenly why people fought so bitter a war to keep lands and life-styles like this intact. Admission is $1, and a guide takes you through the home and explains its furnishings and history, daily from 9am to 4pm May through September (closed Tuesday and Wednesday in other months). You can wander around the fabulously beautiful plantation grounds and picnic here if you like from 8am to sunset.

About an hour north of the beach is Florida's largest state forest, **Blackwater River,** where you can roam among 183,000 acres of pine, juniper, and oak, swim in spring-fed lakes and sand-bottomed streams, or hike a 20-mile trail that was once a trade route between Spanish Pensacola and the Creek nation.

Near here also are six other state parks: **Florida Caverns** at Marianna, **Torreya** at Bristol, **Ochlockonee River** near Sopchoppy, **Suwanee** near Live Oak, **O'Leon** near Lake City, and **Manatee Springs** near Chiefland. You can camp in any of them for $10 a night including electricity, $8 without. A pamphlet published by the Department of Natural Resources showing locations and facilities of state parks is available by writing the department at Office of Education and Information, Room 321, Crown Building, Tallahassee (tel. 904/488-3300).

It's always refreshing to find a place named just what it is, so we found **The Zoo,** 5801 Gulf Breeze Pkwy. in Gulf Breeze (tel. 932-2229), refreshing indeed. At the Zoo, the only animal attraction on this coastline, you can get nose-to-nose with 400 animals and trek through landscaped botanical gardens. There's a petting zoo, gift shop, and a lakeside restaurant to feed visitors, but the real fun time here is when they feed the other animals—more snorts, snuffles, growls, and gronks than you've ever heard. The Zoo also includes a wildlife rescue center where you can get a look at some of the walking wounded in the animal kingdom. Admission is $7.50 for adults, $4.50 for children 3 to 11, and the Zoo is open from 9am to 4pm daily.

## SPECIAL EVENTS

Once a year Fort Walton and Destin, and most of the rest of the Panhandle, celebrate the days when a canny character named Billy Bowlegs built himself a motley crew of Native Americans, army deserters, and bandits, and named himself King of Florida. He played force against force with such skill that he managed to fill his own treasure chests to the brim. Billy had a certain irrefutable style, and eventually had the whole coastline quaking at the sight of his flagship. Legend has it that much of Bowleg's loot is still buried beneath the sands of Miracle Strip. You can search for it, or just settle for a go at $500 buried with clues during the annual **Billy Bowlegs Festival,** in early June.

## SPORTS

There's lots of sports activity in these sunny towns.

### Golf and Tennis

You can play on 12 lighted courts or practice on four walls at the **Fort Walton Beach Municipal Tennis Center,** 45 W. Audrey Dr. (tel. 243-8789), where the clubhouse has lockers, showers, and a lounge area. Fees are $2.50 a day. Courts at **Sandestin** and **Seascape Golf and Conference Center** also are open to the public. Fees are $6 to $10 an hour. (See our hotel recommendations.)

**Fort Walton Municipal Golf Course,** off Lewis Turner Boulevard and Mooney Road (tel. 862-3314), is a par-72 course, has 18 holes with a pro shop, and there are no tee times or cart rentals required. Greens fees are $13 and carts are $10 for 18 holes, both cheaper after 4pm in summer.

**Seascape Golf and Conference Center** (tel. 837-9181) and **Sandestin,** both on US 98 in Destin, about 12 miles from Fort Walton, have 18-hole courses, tennis courts, and pro shops. Cart rental is required and fees are $35 to $48 including cart.

You can't miss **Magic Carpet Golf,** 1320 US 98E (tel. 243-0020), with its fantasyland of towering sphinx, Buddha, and assorted other characters, so you might as well play it. Garish as it is, it's fun, and where else can you get an hour or two of entertainment for less than $5? Hours are 10am to 9pm, later in summer.

There's also a tiny **amusement park,** open daily in summer with rides at about 50¢.

### Sailing and Water Sports

Sail away on a charter boat from **S & S Sailing,** at Deckhands Marine (P.O. Box 2232, Fort Walton, 32549) on US 98E (tel. 243-2022). Sloops 37 feet long take up to six persons on three-hour cruises for $120, a full day for $225. S & S also runs a sailing school and rents 20-foot, four-person sloops at $40 for two hours, $65 for six hours.

Most anything you can do in the water you can do at **PBS Watersports,** behind the Magic Carpet Golf Course at 1320 US 98E (tel. 244-2933), which offers parasailing, jet-skis, surf jets, and waterskiing.

## Fishing

It's downright thrilling to hook a sassy kingfish or watch a sleek marlin as it streaks through the water at speeds up to 60 miles an hour, the fastest fish in the sea. Prize-winning catches are practically ho-hum around here, and Destin humbly calls itself the "luckiest fishing village in the world." Certainly comedian Bob Hope and a host of other celebrities (not to mention hundreds of everyday Joe Fishermen) agree. Hope snagged a prize-winning blue marlin one year on his first fishing trip to the city, and won the city's prize for the biggest white marlin.

Destin's annual **fishing competitions** are many, but the best are the Cobia Derby in March and April, the October Fishing Rodeo, the billfish tournaments in August and September, and the bass-fishing competition in March.

You can seek the elusive devils of the deep from Okaloosa's pride, its **Island Pier** (tel. 244-1023), where you can drop a line 1,261 feet out into the gulf for $1.50, from charter boats (which charge about $250 to $300 a half day), or from party boats (which charge $25 to $35).

## Canoeing

Paddle your own canoe on cool, clear, spring-fed rivers bordered by white sandy beaches as you burble merrily along through mile after mile of hauntingly lonely northern Florida landscape. Here turtles sun themselves on river logs and white-tailed deer frisk through forests or sip at the water's edge.

Every year more and more people discover northern Florida's enchanting rivers, but there are enough to easily absorb the 75,000 who took up paddle and knapsack last year. So popular is this area with canoeists that the sleepy village of Milton likes to call itself "Canoe Capital of Florida." So diverse are the offerings of the area's rivers that everyone from beginning paddler to rapids challenger can find a river to test his mettle.

**Blackwater,** for instance, has deep, mysterious dark waters stained (but definitely not polluted) by the tannic acid of the cypress trees that line its banks. Crystal-clear water is the trademark of **Coldwater River,** where you can stare through the shallows at black bass finning along the bottom and drink from springs you'll see trickling down the banks. **Sweetwater-Juniper River** is the most challenging, beginning with the twisting, turning, narrow, speedy Sweetwater Creek, where logs and stumps hove out of the clear water and require a steady hand at the paddle and some experience in this sport. It's worth the effort, though, for you to drift through a tunnel of overhanging trees and finally reach the Juniper River, whose clay bluffs reach as high as 80 feet in some spots with slick slides for a slithering entrance into the waters.

Centuries ago Florida's native tribes roamed and splashed in these waters, and eagle-eyed searchers can sometimes find artifacts left behind by long-ago hunters or fishermen. All along the banks of these rivers you can pick wild blueberries, blackberries, and dewberries for a snack, and collect fascinating whorled pine knots and cedar driftwood that can someday grace your coffee table and remind you of warm magic days in the cool, crystal waters of northern Florida.

If you'd like to try canoeing, **Adventures Unlimited,** Rte. 6, Box 283, Milton, FL 32570 (tel. 904/623-6197), operates fascinating kayak, paddleboat and raft trips that wind through some of Florida's loveliest scenery. Four adventuring Sanborn family members guide the outings to Coldwater, Blackwater, Sweetwater-Juniper, and Perdido Rivers, and can outfit you for a canoe or tube trip for $7.50 per person to $34 for two (for two-day trips). Adventures Unlimited also owns a campground group cottage and cabins, two with fireplaces, on Coldwater River at Tomahawk Landing. Usually, there are no Sunday trips.

**Bob's Canoes,** Rte. 8, Box 34, Milton, FL 32570, is operated by Vern "Bob" Plowman, whose whole family has been in the canoe business since 1971. Marie Plowman takes reservations (tel. 904/623-5457) and escorts weekend canoe or tubing trips to Sweetwater-Juniper Creeks or Coldwater Creek. It takes about six hours, and canoes are rented for $9 a person a day, with trip rates varying. There are also tubing trips down Coldwater Creek with tubes for rent for $5. Bob's has recently built new headquarters in Coldwater where you can buy supplies, and sit in comfort while you're waiting to get started on this adventure. Sundays are often days of rest here.

---

# 3. Panama City/Panama City Beach

Panama City Beach is a Coney Island look-alike that looms up out of the sand dunes. Its streets are thronged with revelers, its roller coaster zooms and zips, carousels turn, and cotton candy is spun ingloriously onto new playsuits.

From May to September there's hardly a room to be had anywhere as southern travelers flock here to spend their time in traffic jams as long as the Panhandle, wending at turtle speed to the amusement parks. Fraternities and sororities, teenagers, and toddlers find this sheer nirvana. Adults, whose childlike inner cores have some limitations, may only find it a test of nerves.

You will find, however, lots of silky-soft Panhandle sand, and if you choose with care, there are many restful resorts where the klieg lights and cotton candy of the amusement park strip will spoil neither your tranquillity nor your dinner.

Be forewarned, however, that once the kids see Panama City, you will have nary a moment's peace until all the amusements here are covered, making for days of laughing fun and games that will certainly entertain the children.

Often irreverently dubbed the Redneck Riviera for its popularity as playground to conservative Southerners, the fluffy sands here sport prices too low to warrant any Riviera tag. Add to that a down-home flavor warm with welcoming southern hospitality and comfortable as old sneakers. Suffice to be to tell you that this is the first Florida city we've come across in which hoteliers and restaurateurs have subscribed to a code of ethics recognizing that "integrity means more than profits . . . and where honesty is the standard of sales and service."

Here on these powdery sands you join families still tied close enough to *want* to spend a vacation together. Panama City Beach also makes a convenient spot to settle while you explore this very interesting coastline on day trips just long enough to be fulfilling, just short enough to stay interesting.

There are many lovely strips of sand here where you can sneak away for some sailing, scuba diving, fishing, and comic relief. Restaurants are quite good, with wonderfully fresh seafood and very low prices. But above all there is a fun and funky atmosphere here that proves once again how many different kinds of fantasies there are to fulfill. Panama City has proven itself equal to all tests.

## GETTING THERE

Northwest Airlines and commuter carriers operated by Delta and Continental Airlines fly into Panama City. **Amtrak** (tel. 800/USA-RAIL) has a station in Dothan, Alabama, 79 miles away.

If you're driving to the city, you can get here on **US 98,** the main east-west artery and **US 231,** the main northern access road. Fla. 77 and 79 connect with **I-10.**

## GETTING YOUR BEARINGS

**US 98** leads into the city from west to east, but once it gets there becomes Business 98. Most motels and restaurants and attractions are on **US 98A,** which is sometimes also called Scenic 98. It runs beside the beach and parallel to Business 98, which goes to a small downtown section. Many small highways connect Business 98 and 98A. One is County Road 757, which goes from the western end of 98 south to Capt. Anderson's pier and to Thomas Drive (which is an extension of US 98A).

Thomas Drive is also called County Road 392, and goes to St. Andrews State Park. It's not as confusing as it sounds, but remember to check addresses carefully to see if they're on US 98A or on US 98. It will also help to know that address numbers on 98A get higher as you go west.

## GETTING AROUND

Twelve **rental-car companies** operate here, topped by Hertz, Avis, Dollar, and National. You can rent a bike from **Marriott's Bay Point Resort,** in the Bay Point Resort (tel. 234-6911), for $16 a day.

**Ugly Duckling Rent-a-Car,** 428 Thomas Dr. in Panama City Beach (tel. 904/234-6175), rents "pre-owned" cars at reasonable prices.

**Yellow Cab** (tel. 763-4691) operates in the Panama City Beach area. Rates vary by zone.

## VISITOR INFORMATION

The **Bay County Hospitality Association,** 12015 W. US 98 (P.O. Box 9514), Panama City Beach, FL 32407 (tel. 904/234-3193), is across from Miracle Strip Park and keeps a list of vacancies, so they can help you find a room in the busy season from April through the first week of September. They also publish a useful guide called *Dining Out,* which includes many menus from area restaurants. They're open from 8am to 5pm Monday through Friday . . . The **Bay County Chamber of Commerce,** 1215 W. Hwy. 98 (P.O. Box 9473), Panama City, FL 32407 (tel. 904/785-5206), can also help . . . The **Panama City Beach Convention and Visitors Bureau,** 12015 W. US 98 (P.O. Box 9473), Panama City Beach, FL 32407 (tel. 904/233-6503, or toll free 800/PC-BEACH), has brochures, maps, and a friendly staff armed with plenty of information on the area . . . For **police emergency** help, call 785-8477 in Panama City, 234-2285 in Panama City Beach . . . **Medical care on the beach** is available at the Bay Walk-In clinic, 8017 W. US 98 in Panama City Beach (tel. 234-8442), on the west side of the Hathaway Bridge . . . If you see **flags flying on the beach,** here's what they mean: A red flag warns of a dangerous undertow, a yellow flag cautions you to beware of an undertow, and a blue flag means calm seas. No flag does not necessarily mean the sea is safe, so you'd be wise to ask a lifeguard daily for a sea condition report . . . **Local publications** that keep you up-to-date on what's happening in town include *See* magazine and the *Panama City News-Herald.*

## HOTELS

You'll find one long, long row of hotels and motels stretching along the sands from the western edges of the city right down to the amusement parks and beyond. We've selected a few we found appealing and grouped them by price category, from deluxe to budget.

### The Luxury Leaders

Four floors streak skyward at **Sheraton Miracle Mile,** 9450 S. Thomas Dr., Panama City Beach, FL 32407 (tel. 904/234-6521, or toll free 800/325-3535), a contemporary resort nestled on the blue-green gulf waters. Sheraton delivers here, as it does elsewhere in the state, spacious rooms decorated in a contemporary style that matches its attractive exterior architecture. A wading pool for the children is a special feature, but they didn't forget adult swimmers—there's an attractive beachside pool surrounded by tables shaded by daisy-shaped umbrellas. Sailboat lessons are free, and an 18-hole golf course is just across the street (tennis courts are nearby). Evenings, the resort's Long John Silver lounge and garden-style restaurant are popular gathering spots. From May through August rates are $91 to $135; in other months, they drop to about half that amount. Several other hotels are associated with Sheraton in a marketing group called Miracle Mile Resort, 640 rooms in all, and all at the same telephone number.

If you're coming toward Panama City from the east and don't mind staying about 20 miles outside the city, **El Governor Motel,** on US 98 (P.O. Box 13374), Mexico Beach, Fl 32410 (tel. 904/785-8843), is a sensational find in the small enclave of Mexico Beach, and may be one of the best buys in the Panhandle. Two very contemporary two-story houses have been converted, and El Governor has furnished these with contemporary furniture, added walls of mirrors, plants, earth colors, a small snackbar, trim modern kitchens, wallpapered baths, and huge panes of tinted glass overlooking the sea. They're downright gorgeous and rent for $90 a day, year round. Other rooms here are just as beautifully decorated, with bright contemporary looks and views of the sea, and rates are $60 in summer, $50 in winter.

**Marriott's Bay Point Resort,** 100 Delwood Beach Rd., Bay Point, FL 32407 (tel. 904/234-3307, or toll free 800/874-7105), has always occupied an enviable spot right on an arcing, secluded bay of the Gulf of Mexico. Now, however, after its purchase and major renovation by Marriott Corp., it's more glamorous than ever. That chain dropped a bundle on renovation here, turning this sprawling resort into a glorious cluster of sunset coral buildings housing equally handsome hotel rooms and condominium apartments. A showy lobby guarded by massive stone creatures flows into a raised sitting area lighted by huge banks of windows with a view that goes on forever.

Outside, paths wind among tall pines and towering river oaks, past a quiet pool tucked in alongside the bay, so you see water even as you splash in it. Nature trails and a wooden pier stretch out across the sand to the seaside, making for a most tranquil retreat from the lively honky-tonk of Panama City Beach.

Youngsters join the Alligator Point Gang, a supervised children's program, and disappear for many hours, bent on their own kind of pursuits. Liberated parents can then take to the seas at Steve Colgate's Offshore Sailing School or putt about on the paddlewheel *Island Queen,* which shuttles guests off to secluded Shell Island. Major golf tournaments occupy duffers while anglers get in a shot at their favorite avocation at several fishing tournaments, including a $250,000 billfish tournament.

An excellent restaurant, serving a bountiful brunch at midday and candlelit dinners, is abetted by lounge entertainment. So complete is this sprawling resort, in fact, that you may never stray from its grounds. Rates at Marriott's Bay Point are $139 to $189 double for hotel rooms or a one-bedroom villa from May to September, somewhat lower in winter months. Higher rates for suites.

**Edgewater Beach Resort,** 11212 US 98A (P.O. Box 9850); Panama City Beach, FL 32407 (tel. 904/235-4044, or toll free 800/874-8686), has sprung up out of the sand in miraculously short time and is now one of the largest condominium resorts in the Panhandle. To give you an idea how really huge this place is, you get around here in electric carts! Rather a more interesting way to explore, however, is to stroll the grounds, acres and acres of them, roaming past a sleek swimming lagoon with waterfalls and a landscaped island in the middle of it, past a Caribbean-style clubhouse and dining lounge, a dozen lighted tennis courts, whirlpools, reflection pools, bridges, a beach club, poolside bar, and what seems like miles of palms on handsomely landscaped grounds.

Accommodations are in large private apartments, decorated individually and attractively in contemporary colors and prints. All have every kind of kitchen gadget, spacious living and dining areas, cultured marble sinks, washers and dryers, cable television, and as many bedrooms as you have people to fill them. There are buildings here, buildings there, buildings on the beach, buildings across the street and connected to it by a walkway. Around the perimeter of the property is a nine-hole golf course so you can choose from golf views, ocean views, or pool views. Rates for a one-bedroom apartment are $85 to $150 in spring and summer months, depending on location, and $60 to $95 a day in fall and winter months. Weekly rates are also available.

One of the most attractive condominium developments in Panama City Beach is **Pelican Walk,** 8815-A Thomas Dr. (P.O. Box 9456), Panama City Beach, FL

32407 (tel. 904/234-5564, or toll free 800/232-6636). Part of a group of several rentable condominiums owned or managed by Condo World, Pelican Walk is an arcing 10-story building with beautiful views over the gulf and beautiful views on the inside too. Many of the one-, two-, and three-bedroom apartments available here are decorated in soft pastels and all come complete with all the extras from cable television and HBO to well-equipped kitchens.

Resort amenities include two swimming pools, saunas, a hot tub, lighted tennis courts, indoor racquetball courts, shuffleboard courts, a two-level clubhouse, recreation area, and golf privileges at a nearby course. A stylish spot indeed, Pelican Walk has large balconies on every apartment so you can retreat to the outside to watch the sun sink dramatically over the gulf. Accommodations at the condominium are available by the night, week, or month, with rates of $100 a day in summer for a one-bedroom apartment, $65 in winter. Two-bedroom accommodations are $100 a day in winter, $165 in summer. Money-saving weekly rates are available too.

## The Moderate Range

**Georgian Terrace,** 14415 W. US 98A, Panama City Beach, FL 32413 (tel. 904/234-2144), has one of the loveliest pool areas in the city, a tiled beauty covered in translucent plastic and surrounded by plants and groupings of outdoor furniture. A family-owned motel, Georgian Terrace charges rates beginning at $69 to $79, for rooms with kitchens, mid-May to mid-September (lower in other months). Knotty-pine paneling gives those rooms a homey, rustic look sparked by bright colors on bedspreads and drapes and there are small private sunporches off all apartments.

If you read about restaurants first, then choose a place to stay near the best ones. Take a look at the **Rendezvous Inn,** 17281 W. US 98A, Panama City Beach, FL 32407 (tel. 904/234-8841), just across the street from the outstanding Boar's Head Restaurant (see our dining recommendations). Tennis fans will like it here too, as the resort has installed a tennis court for racqueteers. As for the rooms, they're very special, with white rattan furniture set off by light paneling and colors. From balconies you can view the sea since all rooms front on the gulf. For this you'll pay $70 to $99 for most accommodations in summer, $33 to $44 in winter.

You can have a party yourself at **Fiesta,** 13623 W. US 98A, Panama City Beach, FL 32407 (tel. 904/234-2179), where you'll find striking wrought-iron trim in a sunburst pattern that plays off the pink brick exterior walls and trim black doors of this large resort. All the very neat rooms overlook the ocean through a wall of glass, and many have private balconies or terraces. Wallpaper and tropical colors spark room decor, and kitchenettes are paneled in glowing woods. Outside, palms sway over the resort's tile-trimmed pool where you can watch the sailboats skim by in the gulf. Rates range from $53 to $68 for two people in high season, to $88 for larger units accommodating four or six.

**Flamingo Dome by the Sea,** 15524 W. US 98, Panama City Beach, FL 32407 (tel. 904/234-2232, or toll free 800/828-0400), stole our hearts. When you pass under the blue awnings and into its glorious courtyard, you step into another world, one in which owners Reggie and Linda Lancaster have proven what a little ingenuity can do with a basic motel. The Flamingo is built in a U-shape and atop it is a translucent canopy supported by a maze of wood trusses. Underneath, a pool is snuggled amid so much greenery you'll think you've lost your way in a jungle! Palms soar to the dome and tiny walkways wend through hundreds of banana trees, palmettos, ferns, and all manner of emerald-green tropical plants. A fabulously exotic place, Flamingo has huge walls of glass, and rooms decorated in cozy woods offset by bright spreads and drapes. This is our choice of many, many, and we'd gladly pay whatever they ask. Fortunately, they're only asking $59 to $89 in summer for beachside hotel rooms or rooms with kitchenettes; $29 to $69 in other months. Some rooms can accommodate up to six people.

Mary Savelle, a broker with **Sand Dollar Surf'n Sand Properties,** 9722 S. Thomas Dr., Panama City Beach, FL 32407 (tel. 904/235-2205, or toll free 800/

821-2042), writes to tell us that her company "manages condominiums of different sizes and prices throughout the beach area by a central reservation toll-free number." She does have a point: Many condominiums in the area are dollar-for-square-foot quite a good bargain indeed. Her company represents owners in Regency Towers, Sun Swept, the Summit, and Top of the Gulf, among many others, and even includes some town houses in its roster. In one of those you'll find everything from studio apartments to three-bedroom accommodations in condominiums or town houses. All have complete kitchens including dishwasher, cable color television, and stylish furnishings, plus all the usual amenities. You'll also find swimming pools, beaches, barbecue grills; perhaps whirlpools, hot tubs, snackbars, balconies, and even tennis courts at some properties. To get the complete scoop, get in touch with the company, which offers habitations ranging in price from $35 to $85 in winter months, $60 to $170 in peak summer season.

Rental condominium apartments are available by the thousands up here and are a good choice for families or groups of friends who want to stay friends while vacationing together. **Horizon South,** 17462 W. US 98, Panama City Beach, FL 32407 (tel. 904/234-6663), has one-, two-, and three-bedroom town house units available, some with washers and dryers and sundecks or patios, all with HBO and cable television. Just across the street from the beach, the Horizon South has two swimming pools, one heated, a Jacuzzi, a children's pool, shuffleboard, tennis, a game room, and an exercise room with sauna. An 18-hole miniature golf course for guests will keep the kids occupied for hours. Rates at the resort are $60 to $95 a day in summer, $385 to $545 a month in winter.

**Sugar Sands Motel,** 20709 US 98, Panama City Beach, FL 32407 (tel. 904/234-8802), is an attractive cluster of buildings alongside the ocean. You can stroll right out your door and onto the powdery sands, splash in the resort's pool, or roast some local seafood at the barbecue grill. Off by itself a bit west of the central beach bustle, Sugar Sands sits high on a dune overlooking much of what its name suggests. Accommodations here range from a one-bed efficiency to a two-bedroom suite, and prices run from $63 to $83 a day double. An annex across the street overlooks a small freshwater lake and offers prices in the lower end of that spectrum. From October to March prices are just $28 to $38 a day.

**Panama City Resort and Club,** 16790 W. 98A, Panama City Beach, FL 32407 (tel. 904/235-2002), is quite a contemporary spot offering spacious accommodations in a condominium development. A standout among its neighbors, this resort/condominium property is notable for its simplicity of line and color, both outside and inside where interesting contemporary wall hangings and arching mirrors prevail. Efficiency and one-bedroom apartments, attractively decorated, are available by the night (there's a two-night minimum) or by the week here year round for prices that range from $95 to $115 a day, cheaper by the week, depending on size and season.

**Tourway Inn,** 14701 W. US 98, Panama City Beach, FL 32407 (tel. 904/234-2147), is an attractive two-story oceanfront spot with rooms overlooking the gulf. Cooking facilities are tucked into many rooms of this large motel making it a good choice for families. Rooms come in six different configurations, some with king-size beds, some with two double bedrooms, and even executive suites with separate living and sleeping areas. Outside this very long building is an equally long strip of sand and a swimming pool. Rates at the inn, which has several branches in Alabama, are $75 to $80 from June to September, $54 to $63 in other months.

## Budget Choices

Another special favorite in the Sunnyside Beach area is **Wave-Crest Court,** 22209 W. US 98, at Kiska Beach, Panama City Beach, FL 32407 (tel. 904/234-2244), where you're welcomed at a little glass-ensconced kiosk reception area. Wave-Crest is an exceptionally trim brick building and inside are accommodations equally trim. About 20 miles west of Panama City, the resort has simple furniture, bright decor, and lovely glass-enclosed porches overlooking the water. Cotton bedspreads give the rooms a nice beach-tropical look, and pine-paneled kitchens are pleasant rustic additions. For everyone the view is downright gorgeous. What's just as gorgeous are the prices: $49 to $69 in summer season only (they're closed from October to March). A two-bedroom cottage on the beach is also for rent, for rates up to $82.

**Blue Dolphin,** 19823 W. US 98, Panama City Beach, FL 32407 (tel. 904/234-5895, or toll free 800/541-2583), is a comparatively small resort that easily fits the simple-but-nice category. Accommodations are clean and neat, and range from cottages to motel rooms to apartments. All are directly on the beach, and have televisions and simple but adequate and attractive furnishings. There's a pool overlooking the sea, and in a new building here you can have two-room quarters with separate bedroom with two double beds and a living room/bedroom combination with a double bed. Rates for rooms accommodating up to four are $56 to $71 from mid-May to mid-September, $39 to $49 in other months, the price determined by the size of the accommodation you're seeking.

**Nauticus Beach Motel,** 22217 W. US 98, Panama City Beach, FL 32407 (tel. 904/234-2871), is a pleasant, two-story retreat with a pool, courtyard, and cluster of accommodations on an upper level with panoramic views over the beach and the gulf. Right down on that beach are other rooms and apartments offering you a chance to step right out onto the sand. Decor is tropical and beach basic, and all rooms have cable color televisions, fully equipped kitchens, air conditioning, and all the basic amenities. An attractive oval pool dominates the center of the resort and barbecue grills are a favorite gathering place at sunset. A neat and attractive spot, the Nauticus Beach charges $54 to $90 for accommodations for four to eight in peak season from late May through early September, dropping to $30 to $50 from September through March. Add $15 to $20 to winter prices for spring stays March through May.

**Cobb's Gulfview Inn,** 21722 W. US 98A (P.O. Box 199), Sunnyside, FL 32461 (tel. 904/234-6051), is a few miles outside the city and is the only bed-and-breakfast we've been able to find here. Quite a find it is too: a delicately pretty Wedgwood-blue house with a rolling lawn trimmed with a rainbow profusion of flowers. Creamy lattice trim adds a pristine touch to the house, which sports wicker furniture and lovely sea views. It's well back from the highway, which makes this handsome beach home a lovely, quiet oasis along this very commercial strip of beachfront. Friendly Tina Cobb writes that she adds seasonal fresh fruit to the standard Continental breakfast and makes her own elderberry, wild plum, and mayhaw jams for guests. Rates are $55 double in summer including Continental breakfast, $45 to $50 in winter. Money-saving weekly rates are available too.

Dollar-for-space, you can get some very good bargains in the region by renting a house or condominium. Many of those are available along the tranquil sands of nearby Mexico Beach, where stilt-legged waterside (or water-near) cottages or condominium apartments can be rented for $300 to $600 a week in summer, the higher amount buying you, perhaps, a four-bedroom house. One real estate company handling many such rentals is **ERA Parker Realty,** US 98 at 31st Street (P.O. Box 123), Mexico Beach, FL 32410 (tel. 904/648-5777).

## Camping

**St. Andrews Recreation Area,** at the end of County Road 392 and right on the gulf, is a 1,063-acre paradise of beach, dune, pine woods, and marshes. Beautiful clear waters and white beaches are irresistible, and this is an enchanting place for camping. Admission is 50¢ and camping is $8 to $15. The park is open from 7:30am to 7:30pm, year round. You can contact the park at St. Andrews State Park Recreation Area, 4415 Thomas Dr., Panama City Beach, FL 32407 (tel. 904/234-2522).

**Long Beach Camp Inn,** 10496 W. US 98A, Panama City Beach, FL 32407 (tel.

904/234-3584), has 300 hookups right on the gulf, an Olympic-size swimming pool, camping supplies, barbecue facilities, and an attractive setting. Rates are $14 to $22 a night.

**Panama City Beach Campground,** 11826 W. US 98, Panama City Beach, FL 32407 (tel. 904/235-1643), has rental spaces for $12.50 to $17.50 a night, and **Venture Out in America** at 4345 Thomas Dr., Panama City Beach, FL 32407 (tel. 904/234-2247), has full hookups and camping space (no tents) at $20 for two.

## Houseboating

**Holiday Boat Rentals,** 6400 W. US 98 (at Holiday Lodge Marina), Panama City Beach, FL 32407 (tel. 904/234-0609), has furnished houseboats available for rent from $1,000 a week, year round. Holiday also rents smaller boats, ranging from 14-foot fishing boats to 24-foot pontoon craft for $105 a day. Jet-skis too: $20 for 30 minutes.

## RESTAURANTS

This is a relaxed and carefree beachside city where you won't find even one really formal restaurant, but there's some great seafood at some ridiculously low prices.

**Captain Anderson's,** 5511 N. Lagoon Dr. at Thomas Drive on Grand Lagoon (tel. 234-2225), heads the list. This place is not just popular, it's hysterically popular. Resign yourself that there is no way to beat the lines at Captain Anderson's, short of arriving at, say, noon, but face also that it's worth the wait. Definitely the hottest restaurant in the Panhandle, Captain Anderson's packs the place nightly, especially during the Memorial Day to Labor Day busy season when you may have to wait up to two hours for a chance at the captain's succulent oysters, delicate snapper, or overflowing seafood platter. Waiting isn't too tedious, though, if you seek air-conditioned shelter in the clipper ship look-alike lounge, or up top in the open-air deck overlooking the marina, where the state's largest party fishing fleet harbors. Nautical from bow to stern, Captain Anderson's broils, bakes, fries, and stirs up a storm for 500 at a clip, but many more than that gather nightly to dine in the maze of dining rooms on fat shrimp stuffed with crabmeat, carefully tended pompano, and scamp, an unusual grouper-family fish. Dinner prices average about $12 to $20 a person, including a Greek salad, and the gangplank is down from 4 to 10pm every day but Sunday, when the captain, presumably, goes fishing. Closed December 1 to January 15, sometimes longer.

Just across the lagoon is a restaurant complex that looms up on sedate Thomas Drive like a ghost ship. Panama City's landmark, the **Treasure Ship** is at Treasure Island Marina, 3605 S. Thomas Dr. (tel. 234-8881). There are restaurants, a couple of bars, a game room, gift shops, and all of it tucked away between the gunwales of a towering landlocked inch-for-inch galleon replica. To see the Treasure Ship is not to believe it. Dining here is probably a must for the first-time Panhandle visitor if for no other reason than to ooh and ahh at the sheer stupefying size of it all.

As for the restaurants, there's a cozy little water-level wharf Galley deli restaurant with prices that begin at about $6, peaking at $12 or so. Then there's a sprawling Treasure Ship Dining Room featuring seafood dishes in the $12 to $15 bracket. Hours are 4 to 10pm Monday through Saturday, 10am to 2pm Sunday. There are also two lounges on board, and the Captain's Quarters, all with entertainment to the wee hours.

It's worth a prowl around the decks, and perhaps a glass or two of something cold, as you watch the sun set over the mainsail and embark fearlessly on a voyage into the past, when craft such as this docked on these shores with *real* pirates aboard. Restaurant hours vary by day and by restaurant, but all dining areas are open for dinner daily, earlier on Sunday.

**Seahawk Restaurant,** 620 Thomas Dr. (tel. 234-6795), specializes in charcoal-broiled grouper, but can also stuff you with just about any kind of fresh gulf seafood you can name. On the beef menu are strip sirloin, prime rib, and rib-eye steaks, all served with the restaurant's salad bar, fresh fruit, and soup. Prices are in the $10 to $15 range for dinner. Seahawk is open from 4 to 10pm every day except Monday, and there's entertainment each night.

**Harbour House,** 3001-A W. 10th St. in the Ramada Inn (tel. 785-9053), has a loyal following that comes here to enjoy lovely waterfront views over St. Andrew Bay and to dine on a wide selection of fresh gulf seafood, prime rib, and charcoal-broiled steaks. Each day the restaurant features a luncheon buffet laden with nine salads, five meats, and five vegetables, with a finale of soft, slurpy ice cream. Hours are 6am to 10pm daily. Dinner prices are in the $10 to $15 bracket.

Yet another newcomer to the region is the **Bridge Tender,** on US 98 at the foot of Hathaway Bridge (tel. 234-2117). A handsome woodsy-plantsy restaurant, the Bridge Tender is right on the water so you can watch the fishing boats chugging by with your dinner. Steamed shellfish are a specialty of this attractive spot, which also offers entertainment Wednesday through Sunday. Prices are in the $10 to $15 range for dinner at the Bridge Tender, which opens at 4pm and keeps going until 2am.

**Boar's Head Restaurant and Tavern,** 17290 W. US 98A (tel. 234-6628), is perhaps the most impressive restaurant in the city, and also one of the farthest out-of-town eateries. A gorgeous hunk of wood and glass with imposing entrance and fireplaces, an old English look, and a trim plant-bedecked exterior, Boar's Head serves up prime rib of beef and Yorkshire pudding that is superb! The same can be said of Boar's Head seafood dishes, from Polynesian shrimp served in a pineapple boat to luscious fried Apalachicola oysters and creamy coquilles St-Jacques. Land-lubbers have plenty of beef choices here, and there's even a roast duckling in orange sauce. All are served with homemade bread and crisp salads. Cooking is quite sophisticated here, with such offerings as shellfish au gratin with angel-hair pasta; Grecian shrimp sautéed with tomatoes, capers, and feta cheese; steak tartare; escargots in mushroom caps; and baked oysters and artichoke hearts. For dessert fans: English raspberry trifle and macadamia-nut cheesecake brownie. A "must" stop for serious diners. Prices are low for this attractive atmosphere of giant beamed ceiling and stone walls: The average check is $12 to $18, as it has been for years. Open daily from 5 to 9pm, to 10pm on weekends (closed Monday in the off-season).

The restaurant at the **Marriott's Bay Point Resort,** 100 Delwood Beach Road off Thomas Drive and Magnolia (tel. 234-3307), won first place in an international food fiesta, which should give you a clue that there's some pretty sophisticated dining here. At Bay Point you'll dine by candlelight overlooking the Grand Lagoon on such choices as filet Wellington, steak, and scampi, or a succulent seafood platter. Average prices are in the $12 to $17 range, although a number of seafood specialties are just lower. Freshly baked pastries made right here in the restaurant's kitchens are a don't-miss item. It's open from 7am to 9:30pm.

From 11am to 11pm J. Michael fills his tiny **J. Michael's Restaurant,** one mile east of the Hathaway Bridge at 5101 US 98 (tel. 785-9257), with casually dressed diners out for a feast of creole cookery. Stained-glass windows spark the dining rooms, and a happy, friendly crowd chows down on brimming bowls of gumbo, red beans and rice, boiled shrimp, and the house special, shrimp J. Michael, a yummy tangy shrimp creole with all the trimmings. You walk out with a check that won't break banks: just $5 to $10 for dinner, lunch items from $1.75. On a hot day pull up a spicy bowl, a frosty foamy glass, and toast J. Michael. Everyone else does! Open daily.

Goodness knows, you should have no trouble finding **Angelo's,** 9527 W. US 98 (tel. 234-2531)—just look for a 20,000-pound steer named Big Gus. That big plaster devil announces the presence of a restaurant that's been around since 1957, a friendly family-owned spot that welcomes you to rooms full of western decor and open hickory-pit barbecue goodies focusing on beef, beef, and more beef. Reasonable prices and a casual atmosphere make this a popular family retreat at which you'll pay $10 to $17 for most any entrée on the menu, and that includes soup or salad and a baked potato with all the trimmings. You won't get a bum steer here—it's their line, we stole it. Gus beckons from 4 to 11pm daily in summer months, from 5pm daily March through May and in September, when the restaurant is closed on Sunday.

## Budget Dining

Mexico makes an appearance at **Loco's,** 2061 N. Cove Blvd. (that's on Fla. 77 across from Panama City Mall; tel. 769-LOCO). Loco's bills its fare as "Sonoran-style" Mexican, a less fiery version of the *tipico,* but dishes up plenty of the old standbys and a couple of unusual treats: fajitas, tortilla soup, and a blue margarita called a Locorita. Free goodies during the restaurant's Fiesta Hours from 3 to 7pm and 9 to 11pm Friday and Saturday, plus twofer drinks. Hours here are 11am to 10pm weekdays.

*Mas México?* **Los Antojitos,** 4809 W. US 98 (tel. 769-7081). Margaritas are made with wine here, and the Mexican feast includes guacamole salad, chimichangas, chili relleno, chilakilas, and sopapillas for openers. Finish that off with a deep-fried apple burro. Bring your own stretcher. Los Antojitos opens at 11am and closes at 10pm daily.

You won't find a lighthouse at **The Lighthouse,** 4723 Thomas Dr. (tel. 233-6475), but you will find an under $2 breakfast special that will get you going with two eggs, grits, toast, and coffee. A casual, beachside coffee shop, the Lighthouse has prices so low you can try anything on the menu and walk out with change from $5. There's an oyster bar, a salad bar, and rib-sticking lunches that include main course, three vegetables, bread, and dessert for less than $4! There's a lamp burning at the Lighthouse from 6am to 9pm weekdays and on weekends from 5am.

Cajun food is in everywhere these days, but it's always been a favorite up here where many visitors hail from Cajun country. To get a taste of why they want to savor their hometown flavors even on vacation, drop in at **Cajun Inn,** 477 Beckrich Dr. (tel. 235-9987). You'll find it tucked away just off West US 98A near the Edgewater Beach Resort at Palm Garden Court. Inside you can gorge on catfish po'boys, muffalettas, a "Big Mamou" burger with grilled onions, Cajun-spiced potato wedges, Atchafalaya fried oysters, Bayou Teche jambalaya, shrimp and crab étouffée, creole chicory café au lait and beignets. Prices never top $10 and hours are 11am to 10pm daily.

**The Cheese Barn,** 440 Grace Ave. (tel. 769-3892), serves crêpes, quiches, salads, pasta, and some unusual pies like strawberry pecan fluff, in a pleasant French Quarter atmosphere. Begun as a deli, the restaurant has expanded to a full restaurant that now whips up a great shrimp jambalaya, and exotic black-bean soup. Prices are quite reasonable, rarely topping $10, and hours are 11am to 9pm daily except Sunday, closing at 10pm on weekends, and open from 7:30am in the bakery for the Millionaire's Coffee Club!

**Po' Folks,** corner of US 98 and Balboa (tel. 784-0111), is a chain restaurant that opened a branch here to satisfy those with a taste for chitlins, grits, and very low prices. Country cookin's the fare here at Po' Folks, where prices are most often in the $5 to $7 range. Hours are 11am to 9pm daily, closing an hour later on weekends.

## THE SIGHTS

You'll find plenty to do here, from carousels to cruises.

## Amusement Parks

There's hardly any way of missing Panama City Beach's amusement parks—and who would want to? They're fun, fun, and more fun! Best of all, their short season means there's plenty of time to keep the dozens of whirling, twirling, stomach-churning thrillers and the park itself neat, clean, and well oiled.

**Miracle Strip Amusement Park,** at 12001 W. US 98A (tel. 234-5810), is not only the main center of attention here, it's become a landmark. We guarantee that nowhere else in the state will you hear someone tell you a restaurant or hotel is just past the roller coaster! There are dozens of rides here, from carousel to coasters and a special El Grande Cinema presentation that makes you feel as if you're soaring in planes, racing sports cars, and speeding on Everglades airboats while all you're really doing is standing still! Open from 5 to 11:30pm on summer weekdays, from 1pm on Saturday and Sunday. Admission is $12 for adults, $10 for children under 11, and includes all rides.

**Shipwreck Island,** 12001 W. US 98 (tel. 234-0368), has water bumper-car shows and zoom flumes, tube rides, and every manner of watery whoop-de-doo. Admission to the park, open April to September, is $12.50 for everyone age 10 and up, $10.50 younger children. Hours are 10:30am to 6pm daily.

## Other Attractions

This definitely isn't our sort of amusement, but there's no doubt that the **Snake-A-Torium,** at 9008 W. US 98 (tel. 234-3311), is a fascinating place to learn the easy way about snakes, alligators, and other such fearsome reptiles. Open from 8:30am to 7pm in summer and from 9 to 5pm after Labor Day, the Snake-A-Torium even has a snake-milking performance during which the venom used in medical treatments is extracted. Admission is $4.80 for adults, $3.80 for children 6 to 12.

**Gulf World,** 15412 W. US 98 (tel. 234-5271), has porpoises that shake hands and perform amazing leaps and twists, a sea lion carnival, and a scuba show, plus a shark channel featuring a static display of a great white shark. Admission is $10 for adults, $7 for children 5 to 12. Gulf World is open from 9am to 7pm daily in summer.

For a day of sailing, island-hopping, and general water sporting, haul aboard the Destiny Sail Charters, **Destiny,** which departs from the Treasure Ship Marina on $20 half-day cruises into the gulf. *Destiny* also sails off on sunset and moonlight cruises for $15 a person. You can reach the boat at 3605 Thomas Dr., Panama City Beach (tel. 234-SAIL).

**Shell Island** lies just off the coastline of Panama City and is just what its name implies, a shell hunter's dream trip. You must get there by boat, so the place to head is Capt. Anderson's Marina on Thomas Drive at Grand Lagoon (tel. 234-3435), where double-decker boats head for the island at 9am and 1pm daily ($6 for adults, $3 for children). Trips are available April to September. In season, you can go out on dolphin-feeding cruises to watch these sea clowns ham it up for their chow.

Now here's something you don't see every day: At the **Museum of Man in the Sea,** near the intersection of US 98 and Fla. 79, 17314 Back Beach Rd. (tel. 235-4101), you can get a look at relics of the first days of scuba diving from early wet suits, Spanish galleon treasure, and diving apparatus from the 1800s to a German armored diving suit built in 1913. You can even roam Sea Lab, a deep-water capsule in which four fellows once lived underwater for nine days back in 1964. Information on local dive sites and videos on salvage diving and a whale-saving expedition are also available at the museum, which is open from 9am to 5pm daily. Admission is $3.50 adults, $1.50 children 6 to 16.

**St. Andrews State Recreation Area,** 4415 Thomas Dr. (tel. 234-2522), at the end of County Road 392 right on the gulf, makes a lovely getaway spot for sunning, swimming, fishing, boating, picnicking, camping, or just exploring more than 1,000 acres of beaches, dunes, pinewoods, and marshes. Boats also leave from the park on trips to Shell Island. Fares are $5 for adults, $3 for children.

High dunes topped by dense stands of sea oats make for a very picturesque beachfront scene. Wild rosemary grows on the inland dunes near low swales of pine flatwoods and marshes. A highlight of the park is the remains of a "Florida cracker" turpentine still, once used by woodsmen who drew rosin called "dip" from pine trees, and cooked it to create turpentine and rosin, which was used to caulk wooden ships, create explosives, and in the production of soap and paper.

## SPECIAL EVENTS

A don't-miss up this way is the Panama City Beach **Indian Summer Seafood Festival,** now in its eighth year. Scheduled for the beginning of October each year, the seafood festival often features top-name entertainers and always features seafood prepared every way you can dream up and then some. Arts and crafts, a parade, the Florida State University Flying Circus, an air force jazz band, sky-diving, beauty pageant, and fireworks display—could there be more?

## NIGHTLIFE

Virtually every hotel and many, many restaurants have some kind of entertainment, most of it easy listening, vocalists or guitarists, especially in summer months when the town goes nonstop.

Restaurants with entertainment include the **Treasure Ship,** 3605 Thomas Dr. (tel. 234-8881), which has a lounge and dancing; the **Boar's Head,** 17290 US 98A (tel. 234-6628), which has dancing and entertainment; and **Captain Anderson's,** on Thomas Drive at Grand Lagoon (tel. 234-2225).

For country music, try the **Gold Nugget Lounge,** 3901 W. US 98 (tel. 769-0497), where the top-40 twangers and live entertainment ring out nightly except Sunday. A happy hour here begins at 4pm.

**Holiday Inn Beachside** has a Crow's Nest Lounge that's a popular spot on the fifth floor, with a panoramic view over what looks like most of the world, and stays open to 4am on weekends.

If you love western twang, twang, and gol dang, you're gonna love the **Ocean Opry.** You'll find zany high jinks and zealous dedication to good ole American country music and family fun. Take the kids to this one and join hundreds of other knee-slappin' funsters out for two hours of music and comedy that begins nightly at 8pm in the 1,000-seat **Opry House,** at 8400 W. US 98 (tel. 234-5464). Running the show here is the singing Rader family, who have rounded up a cast of 11 and perform all year long. Moonshine the clown is as close as Ocean Opry gets to anything spirited, but there are sandwiches and plenty of other refreshments. All seats are reserved, at $12 for adults, $6 for children 5 to 12. Ocean Opry's open every night during June, July, and August, less frequently in other months.

At **Miracle Mile Resort,** which includes the **Sheraton Miracle Mile Inn** (tel. 234-3484 for both), there's entertainment almost every night from about 6pm to the wee hours. Other popular spots are the **Breakers,** 12627 W. US 98 (tel. 234-2239); the Buccaneer Lounge at the **Best Western Bayside,** 211 W. Beach Dr. (tel. 763-4622); and the **Holiday Lodge Lounge,** 6400 W. US 98 (tel. 234-2114).

For a romantic evening on the high seas, board **Capt. Anderson's dinner boat** (that man is everywhere!), which spends its winters in St. Petersburg Beach, its summers here. You board at the marina at 5550 N. Lagoon Dr. (tel. 234-3435) at 6:30pm Monday through Saturday, dine on Delmonico steak, and dance to musical entertainment on board until the triple-decker steams back into the marina about 10pm. Prices are $22.50 for adults, $17 to $20 for children under 12, including tip. The Capt. Anderson dinner cruise operates Memorial Day through Labor Day and is a very popular outing, so make reservations, even weeks ahead of your cruise.

At **Spinnaker III,** 8813 Thomas Dr. (tel. 234-7882), things are popping day and night. A rustic wood-sided lounge out on the dunes, the Spinnaker offers you everything from parasailing to a steady round of musical entertainment, food, dancing, parties, beach umbrellas, bands, steaks, plenty of spirits, a house band, and regular appearances by guest musicians. It's open from 7pm to 4am daily, drinks are often half price, and there's always fun to be had here.

Panama City's hot spot of the year, perhaps years, is **Pineapple Willie's,** 9900

Beach Blvd. on the west end of Thomas Drive next to the Pier 99 Motor Inn (tel. 235-0928), a rustic beachside haven that serves fun and frolic inside, outside, any side you choose. Right on the sand, PW's dishes up New York deli chow and raw bar goodies, a 24-ounce drink, Long Island ice tea, and the roar of surf, perhaps to match the roar in your head. Whatever is going on here goes on daily from 11am until the bleary hours, and comes complete with live entertainment and dancing. If you want to meet someone who actually *lives* in Panama City Beach, this is the place to do so.

Another hot newcomer in the nightlife division is **La Vela Beach Club,** 8813 Thomas Dr. (tel. 234-FUNN). Once known as the Spinnaker II, this woodsy lounge on the dunes is bigger and livelier than ever, billing itself as a place to "party your pants off." Whatever you have in mind doing to your pants, this is the place to bring them for a steady round of zany competitions, live music, occasional free beer blitzes, male dance revues, legs contests, Monday-night football, very, very live entertainment, and a nonstop party. There's something free here almost always, and always someone looking for a good time. Hours are 11am to goodness-knows-when daily.

## SPORTS

On water or on land you'll find sports here, plenty of them, from diving to divots.

### Tennis and Golf

Tee off at **Marriott's Bay Point Resort's Lagoon Legend Course,** an 18-hole, par-72 challenger complete with what the resort likes to call "monster hazards."

Duffers can also go a few rounds at 18-hole, par-70 **Signal Hill Golf Course,** 9615 Thomas Dr. on County Road 392 adjacent to Miracle Mile (tel. 234-5051 or 234-3218); **Holiday Golf and Racquet Club,** an 18-hole course at 100 Fairway Blvd. (tel. 234-1800); or **Edgewater Beach Resort,** 11212 US 98A (tel. 235-4044). Greens fees vary widely from $5 a round for nine holes to $15 to $20 for 18 holes.

Golf on two miniature 18-hole courses at **Putt-Putt Golf Course,** one mile east of Hathaway Bridge at 47 W. US 98 (tel. 769-4642). It's open from spring through fall, and charges $2 to $3 per person.

The **Panama City Parks and Recreation Department** (tel. 872-3000) operates 19 tennis courts, 13 nature parks, and six community centers. The friendly folks there can give you details on these inexpensive (or free) places to play.

### Racquetball/Iron Pumping

Racquetball players and fitness fans should bounce off to the **Nationwide Fitness and Racquet Club,** 3216 W. County Road 390, Panama City, across from the airport (tel. 769-6184), where you'll be welcomed on indoor air-conditioned courts, open daily. The facility has locker rooms, whirlpools, saunas, exercise rooms, and a lounge. Opening hours vary from 6am to noon and closing from 7 to 10:30pm, so check to see what's happening when you're ready to huff and puff. Your first visit's free, then the fee for use of the facilities is $6 a day.

Tennis and racquetball fans can pursue their diversions at **Sports Park,** 15238 US 98A (tel. 235-1081), where tennis is $6 an hour and racquetball is $10 per person. Sports Park also has a whirlpool, sauna, Nautilus workout equipment, and aerobics classes.

### Water Sports

**Marriott's Bay Point Resort,** off Thomas Drive at Grand Lagoon (tel. 234-3307, ext. 4919), rents catamarans and windsurfing boards for $15 to $30 an hour, and offers snorkel trips, too.

**Hydrospace Dive Shop,** 3605-A Thomas Dr. (tel. 234-9463, or toll free 800/874-3488), will give you some underwater adventure on four-, six-, or eight-hour dive trips ranging from 2 to 20 miles offshore in 60 to 100 feet of water. Prices begin at $35 per person. Hydrospace will also teach you snorkeling and scuba-diving, too.

Panama City has an active reef-building project, and there are several sunken ships including a Liberty ship and the Grey Ghost. There are also many natural reefs and some 50 dive sites that offer fascinating looks at undersea life and rare shells.

You can rent a surfboard at **Lawrence Rentals,** 15000 W. US 98 (tel. 234-2432 or 233-1391), from 8am to 5pm for $3.50 an hour or $12 a day, plus jet-skis and wave runners and sailboats from May to September. More boards at **Surf Hut** (tel. 234-8529) open from 8am to 10pm, which charges $20 a day, $10 a half day. Lawrence also rents beach umbrellas.

**Jet Winds,** 12705 W. US 98A (tel. 235-0338), rents jet-skis for $35 an hour and sailboats for $40 an hour.

**Panama City Dive Center,** 4823 Thomas Dr., Panama City Beach (tel. 235-3390, or toll free 800/832-DIVE), has daily boat trips, rental equipment, group discounts, private classes, hotel packages, and the only certified training facility right on the beach. A staff of divers here can even take you diving in some of the freshwater springs that abound in this region.

## Fishing

Here as everywhere else along the sparkling coastline, fishing is the number one sport. To find a fishing trip, head for **Capt. Anderson's Pier,** 5500 N. Lagoon Dr., Panama City, and talk to some of these skilled fishermen (it's not out of line to wheel and deal a bit over the price of a trip). You'll pay about $200 to $250 a half day for up to six people, twice that for a full day, providing everything except food and drinks.

A number of deep-sea fishing boats operate as Capt. Davis/Capt. Anderson's fleet. The fleet (tel. 234-3435, or toll free 800/874-2415 in seven southern states), located at Capt. Anderson's Pier, has five 85-foot fishing boats that leave at 7am and return at 5pm. Rates for deep-sea fishing on party boats are $23 to $42 a person.

**Dan Russell City Pier,** also sometimes called the Panama City Beach Pier, at 16101 W. US 98A (tel. 234-3294), was built in 1978 and is more than 1,600 feet long, the longest pier on the Gulf Coast. Stretching out beyond the sandbars, the pier forms a T at the end so anglers can reach migratory fish as well as bottom fish. You can fish from the pier for $2 for adults, $1.50 for children under 12, or just stroll down it for a look at what's jumping for $1 per person. It's open around the clock.

## Pari-mutuel Sports

**Big Bend Jai-Alai Fronton** is near Panama City Beach on County Road 270A in Chattahoochee (tel. 442-4111), and is open on Thursday, Friday, Saturday, and Monday nights at 7pm from October to July. Matinee games are at noon on Friday and Saturday. Admission is $2 for general admission seats, $3 to $4 for box seats. To get to the fronton, take exit 24 from I-10 and you'll find it on 270A.

Wager on the fleet feet of greyhounds at the **Washington County Kennel Club dog track** on County Road 79 in nearby Ebro (tel. 535-4048). Open March through September, the track has racing nightly, except Sunday, at 7:30pm and matinees at 1pm on Saturday. Admission is $1 and there's a lounge and dining room, the **Paddock Room,** which offers dinner and a view of the greyhounds as they trot out for the post parade. Sandwiches and appetizers are also available in the Greyhound Room.

## Shelling/Dolphin Feeding/Boating

**Capt. Davis's Queen Fleet,** Capt. Anderson's Pier, 5500 N. Lagoon Dr., will take you out to an offshore island fittingly called Shell Island on a shell-gathering expedition or whiz you off to the open seas to feed the dolphins. (What we mean is, you feed the dolphins, he doesn't feed you to them.) Three-hour trips to Shell Island March through October; dolphin-feeding safaris, from 5:15 to 6:45pm daily. This fleet also operates half- or full-day deep-sea fishing expeditions and dinner/dance cruises. You can reach them at 234-3435; or toll-free in seven southern states at 800/874-2415. Shelling cruises are $7 for adults, $3.50 for children through 12.

**Gulf Charter Services,** docked at the Bridge Tender Marina, 6400 W. Hwy. 98 (tel. 235-2809), has half-day, full-day, and two-day trips into the gulf for king mackerel, sailfish, marlin, and more, always more. Other fishing boats in the area are operated by **Treasure Island Deep-Sea Fishing Charter,** 3603 Thomas Dr. (tel. 234-8944). On those, you can also sail away on a dolphin-feeding or sunset cruise.

**Half-Hitch Tackle Co.,** 2206 Thomas Dr. (tel. 234-2621), can get you angling in saltwater or fresh, and **C & G Sporting Goods,** 137 Harrison Ave. (tel. 769-2317), also can outfit you for this or most any other sport.

If you'd rather do it yourself, you can rent a houseboat at **Holiday Houseboat Rentals,** Holiday Lodge Marina, 6400 W. US 98, Panama City Beach, FL 32407 (tel. 904/234-0609). Rates for the boats, which come complete with kitchen and living and sleeping areas, begin at $250 for the first day, $125 for additional days.

For shorter trips, **Destiny Sailing Charters,** Slip 37, Treasure Island Marina (tel. 234-SAIL), offers sunset or moonlight wine-and-cheese cruises as well as daily sailing adventures.

A glass-bottom boat, known simply as **The Glass Bottom Boat,** offers dolphin-feeding trips, moonlight cruises, and trips out into St. Andrews Bay for a clear look at what's down under the crystalline waters here. Trip times vary by season, so give them a call to see what they're doing and when—night fishing is one of the company's options. A glassy look into the deep on a three-hour Sea School expedition on which you pull in some shrimp and visit Shell Island is $9 for adults, $6 for children under 12, while other trips to Shell Island and on dolphin-feeding expeditions are $7 or $10 for adults, $4 or $7 for children. You'll find the boat moored at 3605-D Thomas Dr. in Treasure Island Marina at the bow of the Treasure Ship (tel. 234-8944).

## SHOPPING

**Olde Towne Mini Mall,** 441 Grace Ave., is a cluster of shops and restaurants specializing in such countrified collectibles as wicker baskets, brass and copper kitchenware, and seashell note papers.

**Field's Plaza,** 12700 W. US 98A, across from the Holiday Inn on Panama City Beach, can get you togged out in typical tropical style with T-shirts, bikinis, sandals, boat shoes, and beach bag. Several shops operate here, purveying, as they put it, everything "from lotions to notions." Hours are 9am to 9pm daily.

At **Miss Gotrox,** 16826 W. US 98 (tel. 234-6916), it's Christmas all year round. Add to that Hummel figurines, Gorham dolls, and Black Forest trees.

Indian jewelry and clothing is the feature at **Maharaja of India,** 13514 US 98A (tel. 234-6488), which also has a wide variety of women's casual clothing and gold jewelry.

**Galleria,** 2303 Winona Dr., Panama City (tel. 769-4906), has a variety of interesting shops. You'll find it two miles north of Panama City Mall.

## DAY TRIPS FROM PANAMA CITY BEACH

Panama City Beach is currently billing itself as a likely spot to settle while you explore some of the intriguing sights of the Panhandle. We agree.

Start with **Florida Caverns,** an eerily fascinating cluster of underground caverns in which the Seminoles are said to have hidden while they watched Gen. Andrew Jackson march past in 1818 bent on a clear-up-the-Indian-troubles mission that would one day nearly annihilate the tribe. These days the caverns are the focal point of a state park spread over more than 1,000 acres. Although they are smaller than some of the world's best-known caverns, these caves still manage to cover about 10 acres, although you'll see only a small part of them unless you are a dedicated spelunker. Tours cover about a half mile of the underground wonderland.

While Florida Caverns may not be as big as Carlsbad and the like, they are every bit as beautiful, with a wide variety of dripping limestone formations ranging from typical stalagmites and stalactites to columns, rimstone, flowstone, and "draperies" that fold and flow like satin wrought in stone. One room, called the Cathedral Room or Wedding Chapel, has a wedding-cake formation and has even been the scene of several marriages. It takes 100 years to form a cubic inch of these limestone formations, so what you're seeing is many centuries old.

After a tour of the cavern with a park ranger, spend some time hiking through the park on well-marked trails that traverse some high ground—high for Florida—and wander past other less dramatic caves that were once home to Florida's Native Americans.

May through February are the best months to visit the caves (they often get a bit too wet in March and April). You'll find them open from 8am to sunset daily all year. Admission to the park is $2 for the car and driver and $1 for each passenger. Tour fee is $3 for adults, $1.50 for children 6 to 13. You'll find the caverns off County Road 167 at 2701 Caverns Rd., three miles north of Marianna and north of US 90 (tel. 904/482-3632).

**Marianna** was also the site of a fierce Civil War battle—women and children took shelter in the caves—an event that could have happened yesterday, so long-lasting is the memory of it here still. Reenactment of that 1864 battle occurs here annually in late October.

Another downright marvelous trip from Panama City Beach is a sojourn to **Vernon,** a teensy village that is home to **Cypress Springs Canoe Trails,** where a couple of relaxed, happy, woodsy types will sit you down in a canoe, hand you a paddle, show you how to make it work, and set you off on an adventurous trip down the crystal waters of Cypress Springs. Silence enfolds you as you drift down this forest-lined spring where the only sound is an occasional mysterious rustle at shoreside—it's usually a water-loving terrier whose nose is often seen bobbing up in the stream as he paddles along behind canoers.

If there was ever an up-the-lazy-river escapist paradise, this is it. You paddle along the spring, which pumps out 90 million gallons of water a day, until it pours into Holmes Creek, which meanders its way into the Choctawhatchee River. All the way along, the water is so clear you can see fish finning around, and if you're a scuba fan you can dive in the deeper parts of the spring and still have 300-foot visibility. On the shoreline Chinquapin Hill rises suddenly over the deepest part of the spring, called the spring pool, and on its six acres dogwood trees flower.

Somewhere along the way you'll find the perfect sandy clearing for a lunch stop; then it's on downstream where you'll be picked up and transported back to your starting point. You can canoe three miles or ten, either is a comparatively easy endeavor since it's all downstream.

You can paddle your own canoe . . . or one of theirs. You can also tube down the river in an oversize innertube that's a real treat on a hot summer day. We'd recommend a visit on a fall or spring day, in midweek, when you're likely to be the only ones out there. In summer lots of other folks get the same cool-off inspiration. You'll find Cypress Springs south of I-10 and three miles north of Vernon on Fla. 79 (tel. 904/535-2960). There's a sign pointing the way to the first sand road and the canoe-launching point is a mile down that road.

Harold and Linda Vickers, who found this their dream retreat—and one would be hard put to argue their wisdom in calling this tranquil spot home—can also arrange overnight camping trips, hayrides, diving, and snorkeling.

You needn't fear the depths here either: There's hardly a spot in the river that's more than two or three feet deep, and it's all so miraculously clear you can easily see the sandy bottom. Prices vary according to how much you want to do, but canoe rentals are $15 for the three-mile trip, $20 for ten miles, including canoe, life jackets or cushions, paddles, and transportation back to your starting point. Canoes will hold two adults and two children under 8 or one child 8 to 12. Tubing trips are $3 for a three-mile float and campsites with bathhouses are $7.50. Cypress Springs, which is about an hour's drive from Panama City Beach, is closed in December and January.

While you're here, plan a stop at what may be the least expensive restaurant in Florida: **Glen's Creekside Restaurant** (no phone), conveniently located right at the end of the three-mile canoe trail. Here two happy ladies dish up rib-stickin' family-style meals that will send you out groaning joyfully—and the tab will not set you back a cent over $5 and probably not more than $3. A delightful country spot, Glen's has all the earmarks of a dying breed—good home cooking at inexpensive prices—but we hope we're wrong about the dying part. Even if you're not going canoeing, this tiny eatery is worth going out of your way to find. You'll find it, by the way, on Fla. 79 about a half mile outside Vernon.

Other area day trips of interest include: **Eden State Gardens,** a short drive from Panama City Beach, where you can roam a lovely antebellum mansion (see "The Sights" section of Fort Walton/Destin); **Wakulla Springs** (see Tallahassee's side trips); and **Falling Waters State Recreation Area.** Falling Waters is a sinkhole, a smooth-walled pit 100 feet deep into which a small stream drops on its way to an underground cavern. You can get a look at the dramatic waterfall and the sink, then roam hilly terrain honeycombed with limestone sinks, one of the weirdest of Florida's geological oddities. You'll find the park off Fla. 77 in Chipley (tel. 904/638-4030). It's open from 8am to sunset and admission is $1 a car.

---

# 4. Tallahassee

---

These days one wonders why Tallahassee, which by anyone's standards is hardly more than a village, is the capital of a state in which more than half the population lives *south* of Orlando! South Florida legislators have certainly tried enough times to move the capital south, but it settled here in 1824 when Tallahassee was the mid-point between the bustling cities of St. Augustine and Pensacola, and here it has stayed, defying the forces of change.

Secretly, we think, some southern Florida legislators probably don't mind that at all, since this quiet town near the Georgia border can be a welcome relief from the crowded, busy streets of southern Florida's jam-packed tourist centers. Here in Tallahassee, life (except the legislative life) moves as slowly as the southern drawl you'll hear from its longtime residents.

History is important in this town, where many homes trace their ancestry to pre–Civil War days. Zealous efforts by preservationists have held back the let's-wreck-it forces of progress and restored many of the city's beautiful old homes and buildings. One of those, the oldest surviving building in the city, is a house called Columns. It was built by banker William Williams (who, understandably, needed a nickname, and selected "Money" as his monicker!). Today Money's house, where he and his wife raised 10 children, is the city's chamber of commerce.

There are still plenty of bankers—and others whose nicknames certainly *could* be Money—around these parts. These days, however, they're here to protect—or further—their interests at the state legislature, which turns up for two or three months each year to make laws that govern the fate of 12 million people. In the process, legislators and their followers cavort and carouse, raise money and hell, and frequently work themselves and everyone else into exhaustion. While they're here the city booms, and when they leave it slips back to the rhythmic pace it has known for centuries, seeming hardly to notice the change.

Tallahassee has had centuries to accustom itself to distractions. In the mid-1600s the Spanish marched through here and established missions along a trail similar to California's famed Mission Trail. A century later a troop of English and Native American soldiers marched in and destroyed the missions, leaving behind the name Tallahassee—it means "abandoned village."

On a walk along the city's Park Avenue you'll see houses dating back to antebellum days, and on a tour of the capital city you'll hear some fascinating tales of these lumbering old mansions. One house, so the story goes, was owned by two sisters who fell in love with the same man. He married the younger sister but the older one remained in the house, and soon the two were calling their token male "our husband." He died, perhaps predictably, at an early age, and his bedpost today adorns the front door of the home!

Calhoun Street is the setting for many of Tallahassee's oldest homes and is now a historic district where you will discover there's little new under the sun: The Bowen House was built in 1830 of New England pine that was cut, numbered, tagged, mortised, and pegged for instant construction in Tallahassee, one of the first prefab houses whose build-by-number markings can still be seen on the window shutters!

Built on rolling hillsides, Tallahassee has still another unusual feature: canopy roads where branches of towering old trees reach out across the road to touch each other and create sun-dappled tunnels. You can travel these canopy roads on the Old St. Augustine Road, which really *was* the old road to St. Augustine built on the mission trail, and other roads called the Miccousukee, Meridian, Old Bainbridge, and Centerville roads. Here you'll discover the elegant antebellum Tallahassee that lives on, sometimes overshadowed, but never eclipsed by modernity.

## GETTING AROUND

Avis and Hertz **rental-car agencies** operate here and have airport reservation offices. Other places to rent a car include American Rentals, Brogan Chevrolet-Buick, and Elkin's Ford Rent-A-Car.

Taltran is the city's **bus** company, and will be happy to give you route information if you call them at 576-5134. Fares are 75¢.

## USEFUL INFORMATION

For **police or medical emergencies,** call 911 . . . For **non-emergency medical problems,** call the Capital Medical Society at 877-9018 . . . If you need a **dentist,** call the dental information service (tel. toll free 800/282-9117) . . . Capitol Circle Wrecker (tel. 576-0178) has **24-hour wrecker service . . . Sullivan Drugs,** across from Tallahassee Memorial at 1330 Miccousukee Rd. (tel. 877-1166), and at Timberland Shops on the Square at 1415 Timberland (tel. 893-2171), is open to midnight every day . . . Albertson's, at 1925 N. Monroe St. (tel. 386-7135), can supply you with **groceries at any hour** . . . You can find out how to reach **state legislators** by looking in the center of the telephone book, where you'll find blue pages that also detail activities in the area and dole out some other useful information including seat diagrams of the Florida State University and Florida A&M University football stadiums . . . **weather info** at 576-7151.

## TOURIST INFORMATION

Folks at the **Florida Chamber of Commerce,** 136 S. Bornough St. (P.O. Box 11309), Tallahassee, FL 32302 (tel. 904/222-2831), will be happy to load you down with information on every region of the state. For facts and figures on retirement, family life, and business opportunities, ask for *The Sunshine Series*. . . . To discover plenty about just this city, its hostelries and attractions, call the **Tallahassee Chamber of Commerce,** 100 N. Duval St. (P.O. Box 1639), Tallahassee, FL 32302 (tel. 904/224-8116, or toll free 800/628-2866).

## ORIENTATION

Most of the things you'll want to see in Tallahassee are in a rather compact downtown area, reached on US 27 (also called Apalachee Parkway), which will take you right to the front of the Old Capitol Building, and the new one is just a block behind it. Tennessee Street (which is also US 90) passes Florida State University. I-10 runs north of town and the best exit is US 27. If you're coming up from Apalachicola on US 98, branch off onto US 319 at Crawfordville. US 98 joins Fla. 61 (Monroe Street), which goes right through the middle of the city. There's metered parking in a lot on Jefferson Street just off Monroe Street.

## HOTELS

In Tallahassee, hotel rates remain about the same all year long except during the big football weekends from September to December, but even then price increases aren't outrageous. During legislative sessions hotels are very busy, and unless you have a reservation *well* in advance you may find yourself staying far outside town—very far outside.

The 244-room tower at the **Tallahassee Hilton Hotel,** 101 S. Adams St., Tallahassee, FL 32303 (tel. 904/224-5000, or toll free 800/445-8667), is the crown jewel of Tallahassee's hotel scene. Needless to say, the place is jammed during legislative sessions as legislators and lobbyists vie for these attractive, contemporary rooms, which feature two double or king-size beds and all the thoughtful extras you expect from the Hilton chain. There's swimming, free indoor parking, and if you're really going first class, a Tower Program that includes everything from a 16th-floor aerie to a *Wall Street Journal* at your door. You won't be disappointed at the Hilton, where you're likely to meet senators and mayors, cattlemen, oilmen, and maybe even the governor in Hilton's Supper Club dining room or Lillie Langtry's library lounge. Even the coffee shop is a special place here, with greenery thriving in the rays under a skylight. Best of all, of course, and the reason it's often difficult to find a room here, is the Hilton's location: just a block from the state Capitol Building in the heart of downtown Tallahassee. Rates are $49 to $95 single, $64 to $110 double; children stay free.

Red Spanish ceramic roof tiles are the highlight landmark of **La Quinta Motor Inn North,** 2905 N. Monroe St., Tallahassee, FL 32303 (tel. 904/385-7172, or toll free 800/531-5900), at the US 27 exit from I-10. Set off by itself under a stand of towering pines, La Quinta carries its Spanish theme throughout, from Spanish leather lobby chairs to a tiny circular stucco fireplace and attractively decorated rooms with Spanish paintings, and a small central courtyard where guests gather to swim in the resort's pool. Rates at La Quinta are $45 to $56 double, about $5 less for singles, and extra persons are $5 each. Children under 18 stay free.

**Killearn Country Club and Inn,** 100 Tyron Circle, Tallahassee, FL 32308 (tel. 904/893-2186), is not only the city's leading golf course, it's also a beautiful contemporary woodsy resort in which individually decorated rooms have plush furnishings and wide balconies overlooking the wooded golf course. In the center of things is an Olympic-size pool bordered by the club's beamed-ceiling Oak View restaurant where you dine on beef Wellington, veal française, or steaks cut by the ounce (for about $1.25 an ounce) at prices in the $10 to $15 range. Rates at the Killearn Inn are $54 to $70 double for rooms, $65 for suites.

Spacious lawns shaded by giant live oaks dripping with Spanish moss are a highlight of the **Tallahassee Motor Hotel and Dining Room,** on US 27 at 1630 N. Monroe St., Tallahassee, FL 32303 (tel. 904/224-6183). Just across the street from a small lake, the Tallahassee Motor Hotel has 92 rooms, including a new wing that offers a lovely view of the vest-pocket lake. Rooms in the new wing are larger and newer, and cost a few dollars more than the rest of the accommodations in this long single-story motel. Rooms are attractively decorated with dark-wood paneling offset by bright colors. A room for two with two beds is $31 to $36, and four can stay here for $35 to $41. There's a swimming pool on the lawn, and the motel is set well back from the highway so you won't be bothered by motor noises.

There are two Holiday Inns in Tallahassee, but you'll have no trouble discovering why the **Holiday Inn University Center,** 316 W. Tennessee St., Tallahassee, FL 32301 (tel. 904/222-8000, or toll free 800/465-4329), is known hereabouts as the "round Holiday Inn." It is indeed round, a tower soaring 12 stories into the sky in a strategic location between the Governor's Mansion and the state Capitol Buildings. Holiday Inn's usual careful planning and thoughtful extras show up here as a Viking rooftop lounge, from every room a view over the city or countryside, and contemporary dark-wood furniture brightened by cheerful colors. Steaks and seafood are specialties in the inn's Camelot dining room, and each night there's an opulent buffet brimming with seafood and elaborate salads. You'll pay rates of $55 to $77 double, $5 less for singles (the higher price for king-size beds or the concierge floor). Prices are sometimes higher, and reservations are necessary during football weekends in the fall.

The **Holiday Inn Apalachee Parkway,** at 1302 Apalachee Pkwy. (US 27), Tallahassee, FL 32301 (tel. 904/877-3141, or toll free 800/465-4329), is a mile from the downtown area. Rooms are set around open shaded lawns, a pool, and courtyard and prices are $44 to $55 for a standard room or a king-size bed. Lots of specials discounts here.

There are lots of pretty things at the 100-room **Capitol Inn,** on US 27 at 1027 Apalachee Pkwy., Tallahassee, FL 32301 (tel. 904/877-6171), but for us the prettiest feature of all is the airy Patio Grill dining room, designed to resemble a small garden with brick floors, a white lattice-trimmed salad bar, matching wrought-iron touches, and lots of greenery rising from the floor and hanging from the ceiling. It's open from 6:30am to 10pm every day but Sunday, when it closes at noon. The Capitol Inn is up high on a hill for a nice view over Tallahassee's rolling country, and there's a pretty tiled pool on the grounds. The extra-large rooms have two double beds, deep pile carpeting, color TV, and contemporary decor, with separate dressing room and bath in olive tones sparked by cheery touches of yellow. Single rooms at the Capitol Inn are $36 to $41 and doubles run $41 to $46, year round. The inn whisks you free to and from the airport or to the Capitol Building or downtown in its own limousine.

A comparative newcomer to the city is **Leisure Inn,** 2020 Apalachee Pkwy. (US 27), Tallahassee, FL 32301 (tel. 904/877-4437), a quite handsome hotel that really does look more like an English country inn than a hotel. We'd guess it's designed to appeal to business travelers in search of a comfortable haven at a reasonable price. They can certainly find that here. A real sleeper among Tallahassee's bevy of basic-blah hostelries, the Leisure Inn sports a sunken parlor convenient for the hotel's complimentary morning coffee, fruit, juice, muffins, danish and croissants and a cozy lobby lined with Italian marble. Spacious rooms have wing chairs, a couch, king-size beds, good lighting, phones at bedside and on a desk, cable television with remote control, and quite attractively contemporary decor. Leisure Inn says it has managed to keep its rates at a very reasonable $42 double, year round, by eliminating cost-increasers like restaurants, lounges, convention space, and the like.

At the **Prince Murat Motel,** 745 N. Monroe St., Tallahassee, FL 32303 (tel. 904/224-3108), there's a lovely view of a historic mansion and its grounds. Tall pines shade the two-story Murat, where you'll find 28 bright, attractive rooms with telephones, cable television, tile baths, and broad picture windows overlooking a sweep of lawn at a neighboring historic home, the Johnson-Carter House. Two people will pay $26 (higher during football season and special events) at the Prince Murat, which, incidentally, is named for one of Napoleon's nephews, who built a plantation in the Panhandle and married a grandniece of George Washington.

Looking at beautiful **Governors Inn,** on Adams Street Commons at 209 S. Adams St., Tallahassee, FL 32301 (tel. 904/681-6855, or toll free 800/342-7717 in Florida), one is tempted to say that it's about time a governor did something right. However, no governor had anything to do with this handsome hotel—it was the brainchild of a Florida senator's son. In a town more often characterized by hotels that could be described as utilitarian or less, this inn dreamed up by the son of former Florida Sen. Lawton Chiles is a wondrous place indeed. Created from the remains of an old livery stable, the hotel opened in the summer of 1984 and instantly became Tallahassee's most popular hostelry.

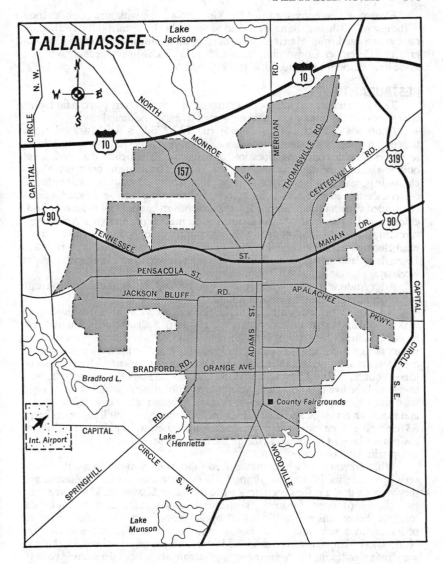

Located just a block from the old Capitol Building on a brick-lined street, Governors Inn is special from first glance to last croissant: an entrance trimmed with beveled glass and coach lamps, beams of heart-of-pine, beautiful hardwood furniture, a pine-paneled Florida Room where complimentary cocktails are served in gleaming crystal and Continental breakfast appears on silver trays. There are just 40 rooms and suites, named for past governors and filled with antiques, four-posters, perhaps a black-oak writing desk or rock-maple armoire.

Suites are sumptuous and can include a whirlpool bath, loft bedroom, working fireplace. Suite or not, you're treated to evening turn-down service, limousine service to destinations within five miles of the hotel, valet parking, daily newspapers delivered to your door, refrigerators, remote-control televisions, terry-cloth robes, shoe shines, free local calls, and discount long-distance lines.

Elegant and expensively turned out, Governors Inn is without a doubt the best of the rest in Tallahassee. Rates are $79 to $125 double for hotel rooms. The highest rates are charged from March to June; the lowest, in January, February, July, August, and December. Convertible rooms with swing-back Murphy beds are available, as are loft bedroom suites, for $139 to $200 double.

## RESTAURANTS

Thanks to the annual influx of legislators and their followers you can find some very good—and some very interesting—restaurants in the capital city.

**Andrew's 2nd Act,** 228 S. Adams St. (tel. 222-2759), is Tallahassee's class act, the city's number one restaurant in cuisine, decor, popularity, and status. While it's tops in quality, it's bottom in location, down in the "basement" of a nondescript building hard by the state Capitol Building. There's a small menu, but everything is elegantly prepared and you can dine on such delicacies as freshly shucked or baked oysters, deep-fried mozzarella cheese topped with creole sauce, a delicate seafood crêpe filled with crab and shrimp. Top that off with an entrée from a specialty beef, chicken, veal, or seafood dish. A labyrinth of dining rooms, Andrew's 2nd Act features tiny flowered tablecloths and a French country decor peppered with antiques, enameled molds, candles, and flowers. Figure $15 to $20 each for dinner served 6 to 10pm daily, later on weekends; half that for lunch (served from 11:30am to 1:30pm weekdays).

After Andrew scored his first success with his 2nd Act, he moved on to create two other restaurants in the same building.

For a quick but elegant lunch in Tallahassee, head for this same building in which you'll find **Upstairs Andrew's** (tel. 222-3446). A salad buffet is featured here from 11:30am to 2pm (prices in the $5 range) Monday to Friday, and the contemporary dining room and bar open again at cocktail hour for libations and a seafood bar. Upstairs also operates a wine bar where you can experiment with new tastes by glass or bottle. At **The Adams Street Café** here (tel. 222-3444), you can munch on bagels and the like in a very classy atmosphere redolent with attractive woods and brass and a Victorian look. Choose your delicacies from a cafeteria-style line of salad and sandwich makings, and dine in high-backed banquettes. You'll pay prices in the $3 to $5 range for a variety of soups, salads, sandwiches, and entrées from 11:30am to 2pm weekdays. On Sunday a champagne brunch is served from 10:30am to 2pm in Upstairs Andrew's.

What do you need with a smoke-filled room when you can sneak off to your very own curtained booth for dinner? That's what they do in Tallahassee, and they've been doing it for generations since the **Silver Slipper,** at 531 Scotty Lane (tel. 386-9366), opened many legislative sessions ago. Still a favorite with legislators, the Silver Slipper was destroyed by fire several years ago and moved its operation to a new restaurant tucked away on a tiny lane just north of the Northwood Mall. There the curtained booths remain private places for those in search of a clandestine tête-à-tête (or perhaps just an escape from demanding voters). If you don't care who sees you, you can dine out in the open sections of the restaurant on a variety of steaks and seafood plus some interesting specialties like quail and bacon-wrapped shrimp. Prices begin at $7, but your check is more likely to read $12 to $18 per person for dinner on the bottom line. Open from 5 to 11:30pm weekdays, to 1am on Friday and Saturday; closed Sunday.

Three Greek brothers got their start here in Tallahassee with the very successful restaurant, **Spartan Restaurant,** at 415 N. Monroe St. (tel. 224-7711). Spartan specializes in terrific seafood concoctions for which the brothers have become justifiably famous. Reasonable prices are in the $6 to $12 range. Spartan has an English Tudor look outside, and a comfortably intimate atmosphere with seafood, at those very moderate prices, again the specialty. It's open from 5 to 11pm, daily except Sunday.

Ask anyone for a good Italian restaurant in Tallahassee and they'll direct you straight to **Mom and Dad's,** 4175 Apalachee Pkwy. (tel. 877-4518), a basic red-checkered-tablecloth spot where yummy scents from the kitchen will set you salivating. Mom and Dad are the Violantes, who preside over their steaming kitchen and small restaurant with vivacity and humor, hard work, and the occasional burst of rapid Italian. Their motto is: "If you want genuine, homemade Italian food, you can fly to Italy . . . or drive to Mom and Dad's." We'd recommend the drive, and the veal and pasta offerings for which the restaurant has earned well-deserved local fame. You'll like the check too, which as likely as not will stop somewhere short of $8 to $10 a person. Hours are 6pm to midnight Tuesday through Sunday.

You will often see the *real* movers and shakers of Tallahassee at the **Golden Pheasant,** 109 E. College Ave. (tel. 222-0241)—and what we have in mind here are not legislators but their wives. A favorite lunching spot for some of the town's most powerful women (and men too, we must admit), the Golden Pheasant is just as popular evenings. No wonder. A chic and lovely spot, the Pheasant has moiré wall covering, gold-trimmed Regency furnishings, black lacquered touches, and handsome murals as backdrop to some outstanding cuisine, elegantly presented. You'll pay $14 to $24 for dinner at the Pheasant, which is open from 6 to 10pm daily except Sunday, and 11:30am to 2pm for lunch weekdays.

Lucy Ho, an elegant Chinese lady, married a University of Florida professor and set out to create her own culinary world. Create she did, and today **Ms. Lucy's Bamboo Garden,** 112-116 E. Sixth Ave. (tel. 224-9099), in Governors Square Mall, and at 2814 Apalachee Pkwy. (tel. 878-3366), are among Tallahassee's most popular restaurants. Bamboo Garden makes a wide geographical sweep of the Far East with its cuisine—Chinese at fast-food Governor's Square, Chinese on Sixth Avenue, and Chinese and Japanese at Apalachee Parkway. Bamboo Garden on Apalachee Parkway is the newer of the two full-service restaurants, and you'll usually find its proprietor there overseeing that operation (or at any of the four teahouses she runs). Bamboo Garden's dinner buffets are just $6 and the restaurant at Sixth Avenue is open from noon to 2pm weekdays and 5 to 10pm daily except Sunday. The Apalachee Parkway Bamboo Garden is open daily from 11:30am to 10pm, 5 to 10pm Friday and Saturday with average checks in the $10 to $15 range.

One of the more popular restaurants in town, **Julie's Place,** is located at La Quinta Motor Inn, 2901 N. Monroe St. (tel. 386-7181). Among lots of antiques and greenery, etched glass, and a tranquil atmosphere, you can dine on stir-fried shrimp, blackened concoctions, steaks, prime rib, crocks of onion soup, and fresh salads, or a number of specialties like French bread pizza or quiches, for prices in the $5 to $9 range. After 5pm (and all day on Sunday) there's an array of entrées in the $7 to $13 bracket. Open weekdays from 7am to 11pm, to midnight on weekends.

On cool winter days (only your very best Tallahassee friend would ever mention the word "cold"), the **Melting Pot,** 1832 N. Monroe St. (tel. 386-7440), is the perfect place for a little tête-à-tête over a bubbling fondue. But we fondue fans go there quite happily all summer long to indulge in those steaming cheese treats, beef and seafood fondue, and a finale of chocolate fondue, for prices in the $8 to $11 range. Hours are 6 to 11pm daily, closing an hour later on weekends.

A group of restaurants on the coast, not far from Tallahassee, in Panacea, or on the way to it, all advertise themselves together and offer both good food and pleasant, casual atmosphere, with prices in the $10 to $15 range for dinner. Here's who they are:

**St. Marks Restaurant,** County Road 363, St. Marks (tel. 925-6489), is a romantic, candlelit spot on the gulf. Lots of steaks make their way from kitchen to table here, abetted by plenty of fresh gulf seafood. Hours are 5 to 10pm weekdays, opening at noon on weekends.

**Angelo's,** 204 S. Monroe St., off US 98 at the bridge in Panacea (tel. 224-6216), has, of course, access to the freshest seafood, some of it caught just hours, if not minutes, before it appears here. That's why the hungry flock to this spot to gorge on broiled fish filets bathed in lemon butter, packed sandwiches, good salads, the occasional steak, soft-shell crabs, and the like. Out in front of this waterside restaurant, the occasional splash attests to all that freshness we're raving about and to the serene setting of this pleasant restaurant. You'll pay $10 to $20 for dinner here from 5 to 11pm daily except Tuesday.

Third of the group is **Spring Creek Restaurant,** Spring Creek (tel. 926-3751), another coastal restaurant designed to appeal to the beach-bound crowd. Fresh fish are featured but there are plenty of steaks on the menu too, and the finale really must be mom's world-famous chocolate-peanut-butter pie. Sunday, Monday and Tuesday there's piano entertainment, and the restaurant is open daily from noon to 10pm.

## NIGHTLIFE

Entertainers who visit Tallahassee often perform at the **Tallahassee–Leon County Civic Center,** 505 W. Pensacola St. (tel. 222-0400). Everything from basketball games to wrestling and Stevie Wonder performing on a round stage have occurred here, so to find out what's coming up, give them a call.

Things are pretty quiet at night in Tallahassee, although **hotels** like the Hilton, Holiday Inn, Capitol Inn, and Governors Inn can be counted on to produce entertainment of one sort or another.

There are often interesting things going on at the **Florida State University campus,** so check the local newspaper, the *Tallahassee Democrat,* to see what's planned.

## SEEING THE SIGHTS

History is made every day here, and preserved as well in some lovely old homes and fascinating museums.

### The Capitol

Certainly when you're here in a state that's had government by one country or another for more than 400 years, you'll want to take a look at the center from which the state's government operates. You can get an outline of the Florida cabinet system and state officials' responsibilities by writing the Office of the Clerk, House of Representatives, Capitol Building, Tallahassee, FL 32301. In the pamphlet you'll find an outline of the Capitol Building. Now you can also take a look at the state's historic old building, being restored. Florida became a state in 1845 when just 58,000 people lived in this 500-mile-long peninsula. Today almost three times that many live in Tallahassee alone, and legislators who work in this 22-story **Capitol Building** now make the laws for 12 million people, a number that's growing even as you read this —Florida is now the fastest growing state in the nation.

What you'll really want to see is one of the **legislative sessions,** which begin in April and last into June. At the west entrance to the building is a welcome station (tel. 488-6167) from which the Department of Commerce conducts guided tours from 9am to 4pm weekdays and from 11am to 4pm on Saturday, Sunday, and holidays. Florida is the Sunshine State in more ways than one: It was the first state to require that all governmental meetings be open to the public—appropriately called the Sunshine Act—so feel free to attend public meetings not only here in the capital but anywhere in the state. Florida's startlingly rapid growth, its diverse ethnic groups and vested interests make this Capitol Building a volatile place most of the time—in 1981 two of the state's legislative leaders barely avoided fisticuffs over baronial rights to power!

Budding Perry Masons can watch barristers argue before the judges of the **Florida Supreme Court,** 500 block of Duval Street (tel. 488-8845). Court's in session on the first full week of each month (except August and December) from 9:30am to about noon. A pamphlet available from the security station at the entrance will help you understand some of the legalese inside.

## Museums and Historic Sites

Mastodons and arrowheads, gold doubloons and cutlasses, are all part of Florida's dramatic history showcased at the **Museum of Florida History,** in the R. A. Gray Building, 500 S. Bronough (tel. 488-1484), open from 9am to 4:30pm Monday through Friday, on Saturday from 10am to 4:30pm, and on Sunday from noon to 4:30pm. You can sometimes find collectors' items in the museum's gift shop, and at any time you can spend fascinating hours perusing this repository of Florida history. It's free.

**Union Bank,** a few blocks east of the Museum of Florida History, has recently become a part of it, so you can now tour this columned bank built nearly 150 years ago and learn a little about the early banking in the state. Union Bank is open from 10am to 1pm Tuesday through Friday and from 1 to 4:30pm on Saturday and Sunday.

**San Luis Archaeological and Historic Site,** three miles west of downtown, is the location of an important 17th-century Spanish Mission and an Apalachee tribal Village. Excavations take place each spring when you can watch archeologists digging for clues to the past. You can also wander the San Luis site any time except Christmas and Thanksgiving days. Free guided tours are available Monday through Friday at noon; Saturday at 11am and 3pm, and Sunday at 2pm. Admission is free.

Tallahassee's **Junior Museum,** at 3945 Museum Dr. (tel. 576-1636), is a 55-acre wonderland where the small fry (and parents too) can get a look at a historic world. A one-room schoolhouse is preserved here, as is an 1880s farm, complete with farm animals and demonstrations of blacksmithing, syrup making, sheep shearing, spinning, and weaving. The plantation home of Princess Murat is preserved here too. There is also a natural habitat zoo. Open Tuesday through Saturday from 9am to 5pm and on Sunday from 12:30 to 5pm, closed Monday, the museum charges $4 for adults and $2 for children. You'll find it off County Road 371 near the municipal airport.

At **Lake Jackson Mounds Archeological Site,** 1313 Crowder Rd. (tel. 562-0042), is an 81-acre excavation area, the excavations of which indicate this area was inhabited from A.D. 1200 to 1500. Open 8am to sundown daily, and it's free.

A pretty art museum in the area is **LeMoyne Art Foundation,** 125 N. Gadsden St. (tel. 222-8800). Occupying an old home, the museum features a variety of artwork in changing shows and has a lovely garden complete with frothy gazebo. A highlight at the gallery is the annual Schubertiade, which combines classical music and the visual arts. LeMoyne is particularly pretty at Christmas when artists go all out for a holiday show. Admission is free.

You can tour the Florida **Governor's Mansion,** 700 N. Adams St. (tel. 488-4661), September to May (usually) from 10am to noon on Monday, Wednesday, and Friday. It's free.

## Nature on Display

**Alfred B. Maclay Gardens,** at 3540 Thomasville Rd. (U.S. 319; tel. 487-4556), is spread across 308 acres including 28 acres of one of the South's finest azalea and camellia collections, the prize possession and creation of philanthropist Alfred B. Maclay, whose widow gave these magnificent gardens to the state. The park is open from 8am to sundown daily; the gardens, from 9am to 5pm. Maclay Gardens and House Museum is open from January to April 30—the bloom season. Entrance fees are $3 for adults and $1.50 for children under 13. The Maclay House is closed from May 1 to December 31 but the gardens are open and the park charges $2 entrance fee for the vehicle and driver and $1 per passenger over 5 years old.

Not far away in the town of Marianna you can visit **Florida Caverns,** 2701 Caverns Rd., limestone caverns with intriguing formations and overhead lighting that reflects on water droplets creating a rainbow of sparkling colors. You can camp, swim, hike, picnic, fish, and canoe in the park, open from 8am to sunset year round.

For reservations, call 904/482-3632. Admission to the park is $1 to $2 for the vehicle and operator and 50¢ to $1 per passenger. At the caves the admission is $3 for adults and $1.50 for children 6 to 12. Camping runs $13 to $15.

A fascinating way to explore the inlets and byways in this magically beautiful part of the state is aboard a bicycle. A friendly fellow named Dave Pierce has taken over as owner and operator of **Suwanee Country Tours,** P.O. Box 247, White Springs, FL 32096 (tel. 904/397-2347), formerly called Suwannee River Bicycle Tours. Dave is featuring weekend to week-long tours across 58 to 75 miles of pretty countryside up here, and has added canoe tours on the Alapaha, Withlacochee, and Suwanee rivers to his repertoire. On either of the tours you stay overnight in small hotels or motels. New this year are cycling tours of St. Augustine, Lake Wales, Babson Park, and the Atlantic Coast from Ormond Beach to St. Augustine. Also now on Dave's "gentle adventures" list—overnight houseboat excursions on the St. Johns River. Depending on the tour and its length, prices range to $600 and include canoe, food, and lodging. Bicycles are available for rent.

## SPECIAL EVENTS

Taffeta gowns sporting the lacy cuffs and tall, stiff collars of the 16th century swish across verandas. Conquistadors stride by, armor clanging. Billowing Civil War–era hoop skirts cut wide swaths through some of the city's finest homes and flappers turn heads with well-turned ankles.

It's **Springtime Tallahassee,** equal parts Fellini film, major social event in the Florida state capital, and touchingly homespun hometown celebration. Scheduled annually in March, Springtime Tallahassee comes complete with a parade and large crafts show that fills the city's main street. A little like a mini–Mardi Gras, the festival and the parade are presided over by local hero Gen. Andrew Jackson, a controversial general and later president, said to have been disdainful of even basic social graces, and his pipe-smoking wife, Rachel. The two are elected to their coveted posts by members of the various krewes (or clubs) that preside over Springtime.

Patterned after New Orleans's famous Mardi Gras krewes, Springtime Tallahassee's several participating groups each represent one of Florida's major historical periods from the Spanish occupation of the state in the 1500s through the American Territorial era, antebellum days, the Civil War and Reconstruction periods, and finally into the 20th century.

This celebration has been going on for years since it was first dreamed up by local socialites intent on promoting their city and throwing a couple of parties in the process. It has taken some, we think, undeserved flack for its undeniable but quite forgivable elitist leanings. If you're fortunate enough to know someone who is a member of a krewe, you can have a wonderful couple of partying weeks here at this time of year. If you don't, no matter. You'll still get to see a walloping good parade —led by Andrew and Rachel seated on stomping steeds (Rachel smoking her pipe!)—beauty queens, and some fabulously beautiful costumes, many of them expensively handmade and all of them historically accurate. Tossed in on the deal is a big crafts show and sale, and many other events ranging from hot-air balloon races to breakfast in the park served by Andrew Jackson and his courtiers.

It's Hometown America at its most charming, and it's the closest you'll get in Florida to a New Orleans Mardi Gras!

## SPORTS

In a town that's about half state government and half university students, sports are more spectator than participant, although you'll find some golf and tennis, plus swimming or boating on nearby lakes.

There are few things more historical—or more hysterical—than Florida State University **football** fans, so you won't want to miss a Seminoles game if you're in town when they're playing. Everyone from doddering alumni to toddling future quarterbacks turns up for fall games when fierce competition with other Florida schools makes for many a prank. Florida A&M is known throughout the state and the nation for its high-stepping award-winning Rattlers band, which performs here at their football games. Florida State University also has a **Flying Circus** (tel. 644-4874), which performs high-flying high jinks at a special show each May.

You can roam either campus anytime too. The **Florida State University Visitor Information Center** is at 100 S. Woodward St., just off Tennessee Street, US 90 (tel. 644-3246), and has conducted tours of the campus at 3pm Monday through Friday and on Saturday at noon. **Florida A&M** has an interesting Black Archives division and a very attractive campus where visitors can get a personally guided tour from the university's public relations department (tel. 599-3414) in the main administration building. The campus is located between South Adams Street and Wahnish Way.

The city's recreation department (tel. 222-7259) will be happy to locate tennis courts for you, but two of the best are at **Jake Gaither Community Center and Golf Course,** on Bragg Drive (tel. 576-1016). Here you can play bumper pool, basketball, and tennis on lighted courts—free—and golf on a nine-hole course open every day but Christmas. Greens fees are $5 ($2.50 for high school students and senior citizens, and for twilight golf). Call for starting times at 576-1418.

The most popular **canoeing** spots are trails on the Aucilla River (about 25 miles southwest of Tallahassee), the Ochlockonee River (30 miles north and 20 miles west), the Wacissa River (at Wacissa Springs, east of the city), and the Wakulla River (about 15 miles south of town).

Bass, bream, shellcrackers, and crappies are the fish you'll catch in nearby Lakes Talquin, Jackson, Iamonia, and Miccousukee. A *Tallahassee Area Fishing Camps and Lodges Guide* is available from the Tallahassee Chamber of Commerce, P.O. Box 1639, Tallahassee, FL 32302 (tel. 904/224-8116, or toll free 800/628-2866).

From May to October you can bet on the dogs at **Jefferson County Kennel Club** in nearby Monticello (tel. 997-2561), or on the skills of jai-alai players from October to April or May at the **Big Bend Jai Alai Fronton** in nearby Quincy (tel. 442-4111). Admission to the dog track is $1. Post time is 8pm Monday through Saturday. You can dine at the Trackside dining room too. Jai-alai admission is $1.

## SIDE TRIPS
Not far from the capital are some sights worth a detour.

### A Visit to an Oyster Village
For a beautiful drive through tall pines and rolling dunes, zip off on US 98 to the sleepy fishing village of **Apalachicola.** One of Florida's last frontiers, this small town is a New England–like collage of colorful fishing boats, rambling stately old homes, some dating back to the Civil War, and sleepy streets that once surged with activity when this village was a thriving cotton port.

Here in Apalachicola lived scientist John Gorrie, who invented the one single thing that put Florida on the map and Gorrie in Washington's Hall of Fame: the principles of air conditioning and ice making! A tiny state museum here (on 6th Street, one block off US 98) is manned from 9am to 5pm daily and tells the story of Gorrie's determined efforts to find ways to keep his yellow fever patients cool.

When railroads usurped much of the cotton trade and the city port was blockaded during the Civil War, the town's importance as a port plummeted. It reached the heights again in the timber boom of the 1930s, but declined as the swamps were stripped of cypress. But Apalachicola has a way of bouncing back and today it's famous throughout the state for its **oyster beds,** which produce the succulent Apalachicola oysters you'll see on menus all over the state. Painstaking work it is, too—gulf waters cannot be dredged, so fishermen use long-handled tongs with scissor-like scoops on the end to pluck the bivalves from the bottom. About 90% of the state's oyster production is done here, and more than half of Florida's shellfish output comes from this small town.

If you're as impressionable as we are (and you are, admit it), you'll be downright dumbstruck when you arrive in the middle of Apalachicola and see a blueberry Victorian delight dominating a city block right in the middle of town. A head-turning restoration that is at once awesome and understated, the **Gibson Inn,** 57 Market St., Apalachicola, FL 32320, is a fairy-tale vision in this comparatively remote village. For years a dumpy derelict down at the heels and down on its luck, this 80-year-old hotel was slowly crumbling into the Florida dust. Then along came salvation in the form of Tallahasseans Michael and Neil Koun. They uncovered the black cypress beams, polished the wood floors, shored up the double-decker porch, painted and primped and turned it into a landborne showboat. Puffy cushions on cushy lobby chairs ache to be occupied. Four-poster beds whisper of romance. Puffy comforters, ruffled curtains, soft mauves, deep burgundy, and pale pinks, lace and enamelled metal, ceiling moldings and gold faucets, wardrobes and cabbage roses, globe lamps glowing golden—all join to destroy your last vestige of resistance. At last, a port in the storm.

In the dining room, forest green provides a soothingly dramatic backdrop for green-shaded brass lamp chandeliers, and in the lounge, days of yore are as oft-discussed as current events. Those days here included, the locals joke, times when you were issued a gun and blade at the door if you didn't bring your own!

Personable manager Jo Ann Dearing can fill you in on the intriguing history of this town and this hotel that played such an integral part in it. But perhaps you won't need her help—just give your imagination a little rein and you'll be seeing the ghosts of passengers who whiled away some interesting hours here waiting for the Lake Wimico & St. Joseph Railroad train, Florida's first, to toot in here back in 1879.

Named for Sunshine and Mary Gibson, who once owned this relic of better days, the Gibson Inn (tel. 904/653-2191) charges $60 to $80 double, $105 for a suite, $5 higher for either on weekends. Seafood—and where on earth could you get better Apalachicola oysters than here?—is a mainstay of the dining room, open daily for lunch and dinner in the $10 to $15 price range.

Other than the Gibson Inn, if you'd like to stay a while, head for **St. George Island,** a new development on an island that has welcomed pirates, the Creek tribe, and European colonists over the centuries (not to mention treasure hunters: A great pirate treasure is said to have been buried here). These days you'll find 2,000 acres of state parkland on the island and small privately owned beachfront cottages and apartments that you can rent from **Alice D. Collins Realty, Inc.,** Box 16, St. George Island, Eastpoint, FL 32328 (tel. 904/670-2758). Several of the cottages are built on stilts, some feature cathedral ceilings, and all are completely furnished. Prices range from a winter low of $175 per week to a summer high of $1,155 per week.

New star of this sandy island is a lovely inn that looks old but is brand-new in every way. Called the **St. George Inn,** P.O. Box 222, St. George Island, Eastpoint, FL 32328 (tel. 904/670-2903), this white frame structure trimmed in robin's-egg blue and wrapped in porches seems to have sprung up out of the sand, so perfectly does it fit its setting. Southern in architectural style, New England antiquey in furnishings, and laid-back in life-style, the St. George is a delight to which we are happily anticipating a return. From a rocker on the wide veranda you can look out over the sands to the sea a sandy block away. Behind the stained-glass door at the hotel's entrance lie spacious rooms decked out in puffy comforters, dark-wood furnishings, armoires that hide televisions, and paddle fans. French doors in every room lead to the wide porches that rim both floors of the inn.

You'll be greeted by owners Jack, Barbara, and Mark Vail, who found this spot and decided this was *it*. From that moment they seem to have done everything perfectly, from the comfortable lounge to the sunny restaurant decorated in cool blues and adorned with the work of local painters and potters. Wood floors shine beneath your feet. Handsome paneling keeps the Old Florida feeling going, and good-looking reproduction furnishings, including queen-size beds, offer the best of modernity in an antique setting. It's hard to imagine how they could have done this any better. Rates at the St. George Inn are $45 to $60, year round. It's wise to reserve a room here, particularly in busy summer months—there are only eight.

North of town on Fla. 65 at **Fort Gadsden** (it's about 25 miles) one of the most violent episodes in Florida's battle-strewn history took place. Built by the British as a recruitment center for Native Americans and blacks during the War of 1812, the fort was abandoned and later taken over by escaped slaves who felt they'd been left in charge by the British. Although the U.S. had no claim to the fort at that time, it felt threatened by the fort's presence and ordered it destroyed. A troop assigned to do that fired at the fort, which sheltered women and children from nearby native villages, and hit a powder magazine killing all but 30 of the 300 people inside. It was later named after James Gadsden, the famous negotiator of the Gadsden Purchase. The park's open from 8am to sunset year round. For information on camping facilities, call 904/670-8988.

A few miles north of Apalachicola on US 98 is the village of **Panacea,** where unexpectedly you'll find several good restaurants. It's surprising because this small town is way, way out in the middle of nothing at all except lovely forests, sparkling rivers, and beautiful beaches. How do they survive? Well, it doesn't hurt that throngs of Tallahassee legislators and government employees are just 38 miles away. See our Tallahassee restaurant recommendations for details.

## A DREAM OF JEANIE

Who can forget Stephen Foster's haunting melody about the beauties of Jeanie with the light-brown hair, or his melancholy lament for life "Way down upon the Swanee River"? Once a year Foster's considerable contribution to American music is remembered here in **White Springs** at the annual Jeanie Festival, when top female singers compete for title and scholarships at a competition that comes complete with attractive young women garbed in lacy hoop skirts of those long-gone (but never quite forgotten around here) days of the Old South.

White Springs, on US 41 about 10 miles northwest of Lake City, where the festival occurs in the first week of October, is a memorial to the Pittsburgh-born composer who feted the Suwannee. Foster never actually saw this crystal river lined with moss-draped live oaks, but he discovered that its shortened form, Swanee, would just fit his melody.

The second-largest river in the state, the Suwannee begins in Georgia's Okeefenokee Swamp as an inky stream, cuts through limestone banks, and turns into a jungle-lined stream where you can cruise aboard a turn-of-the-century paddlewheeler, the *Belle of the Suwannee,* on a $1 trip that hasn't changed much since this hauntingly lovely river became a playground for Yankee tourists more than 100 years ago.

Foster's Swanee song, "Old Folks at Home," is the official state song. You can hear it played on bells of the **Carillon Tower** and see rare musical instruments. The carillon and music collection are all at the **Stephen Foster State Folk Culture Center,** on US 41, three miles east of I-75 (tel. 904/397-2733). Admission to the park is $2 for the vehicle operator and $1 per passenger.

## An Ancient Spring

About 10 miles south of Tallahassee at the **Edward Ball Wakulla Springs State Park** (tel. 904/222-7279; take US 319 south to Fla. 61 and 61 to County Road 267), you can swim in a spring that's welcomed splashers for tens of thousands of years: Mastodon bones have been found in the deepest recesses of the crystal waters. At the heart of the springs more than 175,000 gallons of water a minute are filtered by limestone rock that makes the springs so clear you can't judge their depths. Along the banks of the water, you'll see sleepy alligators, shrieking bird life, and tiny forest creatures. On a glass-bottom-boat tour of this 2860-acre park you can see the fish that live here and venture out of hiding to play water games with the boat's captain.

The controversial Florida financier and kingmaker Edward Ball turned the springs into a preservation area some years back and spent much of his time here over the years. In the 1930s he built a serene old Spanish-style inn, now the **Wakulla Springs Lodge and Conference Center,** 1 Springs Dr., Wakulla Springs, FL 32305 (tel. 904/224-5950), that is today one of the state's most intriguing country inns. Floors are Tennessee marble (there's even a marble checkers set). Hefty wood ceiling beams were painstakingly painted with Florida scenes and flowers by a German artist who reportedly was a court painter for Kaiser Wilhelm. You'll see rare Spanish tiles, black granite tables, decorative arches, massive doors. In the inn's high-ceilinged rooms, dark-wood furniture and a smattering of antiques are cheerfully elegant. Downstairs there's a large dining room where you can have a full dinner of home-cooked country foods from 6:30 to 8:30pm for $8 to $15, and in winter sit by a huge fireplace where flames roar. Swim in the cool spring by day and at night sit beside it and listen to the murmur of forest creatures who live along these banks. If you'd like to see the springs, there are two different boat tours, each at $4 for adults, $2 for children. Park entry is $1 to $5.

Rates at Wakulla (which comes from a Native American word meaning "where the water flows upward like rays of heavenly light out of the shadow of the hill") are $47 to $178, year round.

## Across the Border in Thomasville, Georgia

Now this is a book on Florida so we shouldn't be doing this, but the temptation is just too great. We have to mention a side trip from Tallahassee to Thomasville, Georgia, a small enclave just 35 miles across the border. Here in just a few square miles, you can get a peek at the antebellum South that has largely disappeared from Florida—and you can stay in a plantation house so quintessentially plantation house that we swear you'll hear the ghostly swish of a crinoline some quiet evening.

Once dubbed one of the 10 most tempting rural havens in America by a national magazine, Thomasville has paved streets lined with oak and dogwood, groves of the ubiquitous yellow pine that spread across southern Georgia, and lives pretty much as it must have a century ago.

You come here not for theme parks and gewgaws but for a look at an amazingly wide variety of architectural styles ranging from **Pebble Hill Plantation House,** US319S (tel. 912/226-2344), to the furbelowed magnificence of **Lapham Patterson House,** 626 N. Dawson St. (tel. 912/225-4004). In Thomasville's cemetery is the grave of the first black graduate of West Point, and in the village is a 300-year-old oak tree, so you can see we're talking history here. Guided tours to the Lapham-Patterson House take place on the hour. Prices are $1 for adults and 50¢ for children 5 to 12. Admission to the Pebble Hill grounds is $2 for adults, $1 for children. Children are not admitted to the main house, but adults may wander through it for $5 per person.

Historic antecedents live on here in restored storefronts and in enough plantation homes to warrant a daily chamber of commerce tour of them. Add to that the visual wham of thousands of roses at the city's **Rose Test Gardens,** 1842 Smith Ave. (tel. 226-5568). It's free and open April to November. For a brochure on the village and what to see and do there, contact the **Thomasville Chamber of Commerce** at 401 S. Broad St. (P.O. Box 560), Thomasville, GA 31792 (tel. 912/226-9600). City tours are at 10am and 2pm daily, and cost $7 for adults, $3 for children 6 to 12.

Thomasville is a lovely town, well worth the 20-mile drive from Tallahassee. It's even better if you plan a stay at **Susina Plantation,** Rte. 3, Box 1010, Thomasville, GA 31792 (tel. 912/377-9644). You'll hardly believe your eyes when you roll up the drive here and see before you a veranda guarded by the massive white pillars that have surely soared over every plantation house in every film ever made about the South. An almost-cliché they may be, but gracefully beautiful and awesomely "southern" they definitely are.

Inside, the house is built like many southern plantation houses, with rooms opening off a wide central hallway, the better to keep breezes moving. Quite a lot of money was spent fixing and filling this house with beautiful antique furnishings so fetching that long-gone owners are said to prowl the halls now and again. Hand-crocheted bedspreads and eyelet-edged linens froth over high four-postered beds, blending easily with Oriental rugs, family heirlooms, and period furniture. Each of the inn's bedrooms has its own fireplace and bath, complete with claw-foot tub.

Outside, the modernities have been installed: tennis courts, stables, and a swimming pool offer places to play, while the 100 acres of the estate are an irresistible place for a stroll past a historic barn and brick kitchen, and two antique carriages.

Anne-Marie Walker does the cooking here, creating elegant candlelit dinners, freshly baked bread, and rib-sticking breakfasts and occasionally themed dinners.

No question about it, we're in love with Susina and we're in very good company—Paul Newman and Joanne Woodward were once guests here. Rates at the inn, including breakfast and dinner, are $75 per person double, $100 single. To get here, follow the Thomasville Road (US 319) or Meridian Road (County Road 155) and keep a sharp eye out for the clapboard signs that indicate the turnoff to Susina.

Special events occur here in April and December when historic homes go on display, and April is also the month for the city's popular **Rose Festival.**

# TAMPA BAY

**S**ooner or later someone would have laid claim to the lands on the shores of this huge bowl-shaped bay, but it was a fluke of history that got things going so soon in Tampa Bay: In 1527 Panfilo de Narvaez and four galleons, on an expedition to conquer, colonize, and find gold in Florida, were blown off course by a hurricane and landed on the Gulf Coast. De Narvaez went ashore to trade with the natives and in their villages found a gold ornament. He thought he'd found his treasure, but here comes the second fluke: Those gold pieces were really Spain's very own doubloons salvaged by the natives from beach shipwrecks!

It was fool's gold de Narvaez sought, for the real gold on this coast was to be found centuries later in sunshine and sand. But before that could happen, the sands of this Gulf Coast were trod by many hopefuls in search of treasure. Early on, the visitors were pirates—ex-slaves Black Caesar, José Gaspar, and Jean Lafitte—but when piracy became a somewhat perilous career, fishermen began to gather on the shores. It wasn't long before bridges and causeways connected the offshore islands to the mainland cities of Tampa and St. Petersburg.

Then some modern pirates, called promoters, moved in. They found and lost some real gold here in the boom days of the 1920s after railroad magnate Henry Plant extended his tracks south and frozen Northerners discovered the Suncoast. Soon they came in droves, to spend winters in Plant's fanciful Tampa hotel, his sprawling Belleview Biltmore, and later in the magnificence of the cotton-candy-pink Don CeSar.

F. Scott Fitzgerald came. Babe Ruth came. Teddy Roosevelt and his Rough Riders dropped in on their way to the Spanish-American War. Scots clansmen moved in to build a village called Dunedin, and brought with them bagpipes whose mournful wail you'll still hear here. Greek sponge fishermen arrived to dig in the oceans and dance to the twang of bouzoukis that still entertain bay dwellers.

These balmy water-locked lands have been salvation and selling point for generations. They've been a welcome sight for pirates and Union blockaders, Native Americans and explorers, those with giant dreams and slick schemes. Today they wait only for the sun-seeker in search of nothing more golden than sunlight and sand.

---

# 1. Orientation

---

## GETTING THERE

So rapidly has this area been growing that the number of arrivals and departures from Tampa's sleek new airport has skyrocketed in recent years. Airlines now bring thousands of international visitors from Europe on British Airways and DER Charters, and multitudes from around this hemisphere on 25 airlines, including Air Canada, American, Continental, Delta, Eastern, Midway, Northwest, Pan Am, TWA, United, and USAir.

A word here about Tampa's airport, which is generally acclaimed as one of the, if not *the,* most modern airports in the nation, so much so that it is now a tourist attraction itself. If you fly in here (and even if you don't), allow an unencumbered hour or so to zip around on people movers that move passengers from plane to terminal in 60 seconds, to ride escalators through floors hung with metal sculptures on invisible strings, and to visit the penthouse revolving restaurant and lounge. Tampa's airport is so beautifully designed that it manages to seem quiet even at its busiest, and passengers can move from automobile seat to airplane seat in less than 700 steps. In 1987 the airport became a third larger with the addition of Airspace F, which even includes a mini-mall.

On the southern end of the bay, Sarasota's small airport welcomes Continental, Delta, Northwest, Pan Am, TWA, and United.

**Greyhound/Trailways** buses also connect the cities to each other and to other parts of the state and nation. Miami to Tampa takes about six hours.

## GETTING AROUND

For limousine service from Tampa airport, call **The Limo** (tel. 822-3333), which serves all of Pinellas County (Tampa), plus St. Petersburg and the beaches, for $25. **Central Florida Limo** (tel. 276-3730) charges $10 for rides to downtown Tampa hotels.

Here, as everywhere else, taxis are expensive, the more so because distances are great. **Yellow Cab** (tel. 253-0121) charges $1.50 a mile.

Unless you plan to settle in a beach hotel and stay put right there, you'd be wise to rent a car since this is a huge area with long distances between Tampa and St. Petersburg and the Holiday Isles. All major national **car-rental companies** operate here, for prices beginning in the $70 to $90 a week range.

**Alamo** (tel. 289-4323) competes vigorously with other companies, and manages to undercut most of them, at last check offering a small car for $79 a week with unlimited mileage, and no charge if you rent the car in one city and drop it off in another. The company has an office in Sarasota (tel. 355-8896), too.

To get around these sprawling metropolises in comfort and see some of the fascinating attractions, you really *need* a car. Few travelers realize that it takes a half hour or more to drive from St. Petersburg to Tampa, from Tampa to Clearwater, from St. Petersburg to St. Petersburg Beach, and down the islands from Clearwater to Pass-a-Grille.

Unless you're content to spend your time here at or near your hotel, choose it carefully since **public transportation** operates only during daylight hours. If you are relying on local transport, the **Pinellas Suncoast Transit Authority** (tel. 530-9911) covers the county, charging 75¢ a ride. To get to the beaches you must connect with **Beach Airport Transport Service (BATS)** (tel. 367-3086). Folks at either of those transit companies will be able to tell you what bus to take where.

In Clearwater there's an addition to the transit system, the **Jolly Trolley,** a trolley look-alike on wheels that serves the city and the beaches for 25¢ a ride.

Tampa has three free trolleys called the **Free Bee,** which connect downtown free parking areas with the center of the city and other city bus routes, which you can discover by calling 251-1078.

## GETTING YOUR BEARINGS

If you're driving, it may help to know that Central Avenue divides **St. Petersburg** north-south, so TAPs (terraces, avenues, and places) run east-west, streets and ways run north-south.

The **Tampa** street plan is laid out in the quadrant system: Florida Avenue divides the city east and west, John F. Kennedy Boulevard and Frank Adamo Drive divide it north and south. The numbered avenues run east-west and the numbered streets run north-south.

To get from **Clearwater** to Tampa, take Fla. 60 (Courtney Campbell Causeway, which becomes Gulf to Bay Boulevard). Two other causeways, Howard Frankland Bridge (I-275) and Gandy Bridge (Fla. 92), cross Tampa Bay to St. Petersburg.

Other **causeways to the beach** are Belleaire (or Bay) Drive, Indian Rocks Causeway, Madeira Beach, Treasure Island, and St. Petersburg Causeways, and the Pinellas Bayway. Most are free, but one or two have small tolls.

Finally, of course, there's the famous **Sunshine Skyway** that soars majestically over Tampa Bay on its way to the Bradenton/Sarasota area.

## TOURIST INFORMATION

Every one of the Holiday Isles and St. Petersburg and Tampa has its own chamber of commerce. One way to get information on St. Petersburg, St. Petersburg Beach, Indian Rocks Beach, Largo, Dunedin, Tarpon Springs, and Safety Harbor is to contact the **Pinellas Tourist Development Council,** 4625 E. Bay Dr., Suite 109A, Clearwater, FL 34624 (tel. 813/530-6452). Personable W. F. "Bill" Sheely is director.

**St. Petersburg Chamber of Commerce** is a growing operation that is steadily building a large and helpful library of tourist materials. It's at 100 Second Ave. N., St. Petersburg, FL 33701 (tel. 813/821-4069).

In Tampa they'll be happy to help you if you call or write the **Tampa/Hillsboro Convention and Visitors Association,** 111 Madison St., Suite 110, Tampa, FL 33602 (tel. 813/223-1111, or toll free 800/44-TAMPA), where they are well stocked with visitor information. They are open weekdays from 8am to 4:45pm.

Things are changing very quickly in this rapidly growing city, so it's wise to take a look at local papers to find out what's happening when you're here. Those **newspapers** include the *Tampa Tribune,* the area's largest newspaper; the *Clearwater Sun;* and the award-winning *St. Petersburg Times,* one of the best newspapers of its size in the nation. *Tampa Bay* magazine is a slick, professional production that keeps a sardonic eye on local trends in everything from politics to happy hours.

## SPECIAL EVENTS

In February the Tampa Bay area goes slightly crazy during its annual **Gasparilla Festival.** Hundreds of otherwise staid cityfolk turn into leering peg-leg pirates-for-a-day. Actually the revelry goes on for a week, but the big day is Gasparilla Day, when pinstripe suits are exchanged for pantaloons as a full-sailed, three-masted galleon stocked with this "krewe" of pretend pirates sails into St. Petersburg harbor to relive the legend of a long-ago invasion by José Gaspar.

Twice a year, in February and October, Tampa's Spanish quarter turns out in **Ybor City** to celebrate its stately, if somewhat bellicose, past with dark-eyed señoritas in lacy mantillas and swirling skirts, strolling musicians and Latin rhythms, sidewalk feasts, and illuminated parades.

In February, fat calves and porkers who have been real pigs all year are carted, pushed, and pulled to the **Florida State Fair** at Tampa's Fairgrounds, where owners vie for blue ribbons.

St. Petersburg also vies for attention in February with its **International Food Fair** fiesta, and again in March with its **Festival of the States,** which includes a marching band competition and a two-mile-long Parade of States highlighting the wonders of the other 49.

In March the mournful wail of bagpipes fills the air at Dunedin as that city's Scottish community kicks off its annual **Highland Games.** Down the road a bit in Tarpon Springs, a Greek community celebrates **Greek Epiphany** in early January with street dances and a diving scramble for a luck-bringing gold cross.

Each November you can sample seafood at **John's Pass Seafood Festival,** while you enjoy fireworks, demonstrations, arts and crafts, and exhibits.

---

# 2. Tampa

---

In Tampa you'll see skyscrapers reaching for the clouds in shiny metallic splendor. This is a booming commercial center that's in the midst of yet another boom spiral, thanks to ever-increasing air service to the city's modern airport and a Sun Belt population boom.

Tampa is a sprawling place that encompasses several colleges and universities, MacDill Air Force Base, the fascinating antique village of Ybor City, and the area's largest attraction, Busch Gardens' Dark Continent.

Long years ago a Spanish explorer dubbed Tampa the best port he had ever seen. Today the 98-year-old city is proud of its Port of Tampa, a massive complex that sprawls over miles of ground and ships out 25 million tons of phosphate a year.

You can trace some of Florida's history from Tampa's name, although there's little agreement on just exactly what it means. Prevailing theory has it that it's a corruption of Native American word meaning a town near the bay, an area so loved by those tribes that they ran off most of the early explorers who came here from Spain in search of gold. Ponce de León didn't stay long, and neither did Hernando de Soto, who landed but fled when greeted by native arrows.

It took three centuries before change came to this wilderness. Even then you could barely call the little colony that grew up around Fort Brooke a village, let alone a city. That fort did, however, discourage some pretty unhappy Seminoles. After a couple of slumps during a Civil War blockade by Union soldiers and a yellow fever epidemic, the future arrived here in the form of railroad kingpin Henry Plant and a narrow-gauge railroad that connected Tampa to the world.

Plant and his east coast counterpart, Henry Flagler, were two rough-and-tumble types who soon were in hot competition, Plant building hotels and railroads here, Flagler moving lickety-split down east coast beaches. To go Flagler's empire one better, Plant re-created the Alhambra (at a cost of nearly $4 million) crowned by a raft of onion-shaped silver minarets topped by curving quarter moons. Intent on humbling Flagler, so the story goes, Plant sent him a telegram in 1891 inviting him to the grand opening in Tampa of what he called Florida's finest new hotel. A not-at-all-humbled Flagler shot back this succinct rejoinder: "Where's Tampa?"

Today, thanks to phosphate, Vincente Ybor's cigar factories (which moved here from Key West), the spend-iferous habits of the Rough Riders (who camped here on the way to Cuba for the Spanish-American War), the '20s land boom, shipbuilding, breweries, and finally the city's huge Busch Gardens tourist attraction, Tampa has grown into a streamlined city. No one asks "Where's Tampa?" these days.

## USEFUL INFORMATION

For **police** or other **emergencies,** dial 911 . . . The **telephone area code** throughout the Tampa Bay area is 813, but some calls between Tampa and the adjoining cities are long distance, so you might check to see if there's a local number in Tampa for outlying shops and restaurants . . . Late munchers will find **Denny's,** 1700 E. Fowler (tel. 971-9441), open 24 hours . . . For pharmaceutical needs, **Eckerd Drugs** stores are at various locations around the city (tel. 876-2485) and remain open 24 hours . . . You can get quick laundry service at **Massey Cleaners,** 3209 E. Hillsborough Ave. (tel. 238-4987) . . . There's a **24-hour gas station,** Shell, at 7756 W. Hillsborough Ave. (tel. 884-9312) . . . Find the **postal station** nearest you by checking the white pages under "U.S. Post Office," or call 228-2475. . . . For medical needs there's an **emergency walk-in clinic** at 2810 W. Buffalo St. (tel. 877-8450) . . . For the latest entertainment information call 223-1111.

## WHERE TO STAY

Most of Tampa's hotels are located near the airport, although some are downtown or out by Busch Gardens. We've divided them up by price. Since Tampa's a very busy commercial center you'll find that most prices vary little by season.

### The Luxury Leaders

**Marriott-Tampa Airport,** at Tampa International Airport, Tampa, FL 33607 (tel. 813/879-5151, or toll free 800/228-9290), is a showcase inside a showcase. Located right in the terminal, this super-soundproofed hotel offers you an ever-changing airscape, and inside things are just as dramatic: luxurious, spacious rooms, a special executives' sixth-floor lounge with complimentary cocktails and champagne, a lobby seafood bar, a revolving penthouse restaurant of considerable renown (and prices in the $15 to $20 range for dinner). Almost a city of its own, this hotel provides places to play (a cocktail lounge with backgammon boards, a pool, a disco), places to dine, and extra-special places to sleep. Certainly one of the city's prime-time properties, Marriott charges $140 to $152 double, all year; concierge level, $165; suites higher.

**Riverside Hotel-Tampa,** 200 Ashley Dr., Tampa, FL 33602 (tel. 813/223-2222, or toll free 800/288-2672), curves gently along the banks of the Hillsborough River within sight of the weird silver onion domes of Henry Plant's lurid but lovely old hotel, now the University of Tampa. Soaring high above the road, the six-story Hilton's 265 rooms have a pretty view of the meandering river as it heads for Hillsborough Bay. There's an excellent dining room called the Riverside Café and a lobby cocktail lounge with a river view. The downtown location makes it a favorite with commercial travelers, and is a good choice for those intent on downtown shopping and dining. Year-round rates are $99 to $145 double.

The **Marriott-Tampa West Shore,** 1001 N. Westshore Blvd., Tampa, FL 33607 (tel. 813/287-2555, or toll free 800/228-9290), is a 310-room, 14-story hotel on six acres of land just off I-275 about five minutes from the airport. Marriott knows plenty about building hotels, and this one has a restaurant, lounge, indoor/outdoor swimming pool, hydrotherapy pool, saunas, exercise center, game room, gift shop, complimentary transportation to and from the airport, and extra-large rooms. Rates are $118 to $135, year round ($69 to $89 on Friday and Saturday for Two-for-Breakfast); concierge level, $140 to $155; suites higher.

The **Radisson Bay Harbor Inn,** 7700 Courtney Campbell Causeway, Tampa, FL 33607 (tel. 813/889-8900, or toll free 800/333-3333, 800/282-0613 in Florida), is as far west as you can go in Tampa. It's right at the edge of the bay, and quite near the airport as well. If you anchor in this harbor, you'll find an imposing six-story, 260-room edifice in a bayside setting complete with a crescent of beach. Just across the causeway from Clearwater, the hotel, recently renovated for $4 million, has spacious rooms with private balconies overlooking the city or bay and decorated in attractive, bright color schemes. There are tennis courts, a gift shop, heated pool,

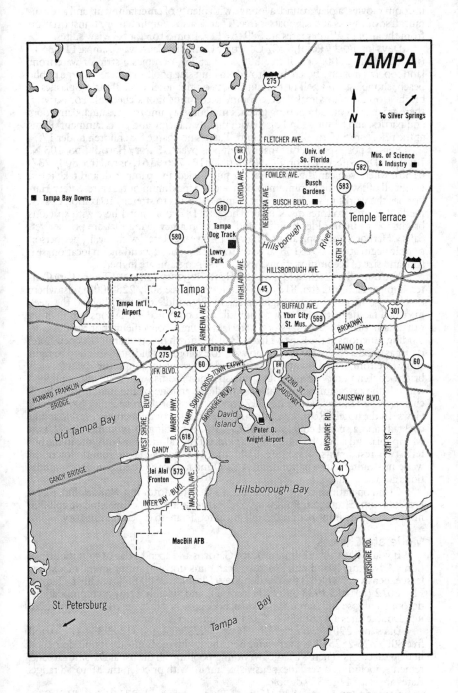

in-room movies, a playground, a lounge with plenty of entertainment, and a restaurant. Use of kayaks and sailboats is free. There's also complimentary transportation from the airport. Winter rates are $89 to $119, from $165 for bay-view suites.

**Days Inn Rocky Point,** 7627 Courtney Campbell Causeway, Tampa, FL 33607 (tel. 813/884-2000, or toll free 800/325-2525), occupies a strip of waterfront land too. It's not on a beach, but provides a king-size pool, and there's a large public beach, shopping, and golf just minutes away on the hotel's free shuttle. Splashes of bright tropical colors make these roomy accommodations cheerful. For activity, there are tennis courts, a putting green, Ping-Pong, a game room, sauna, daily tours and parties, and a lounge and disco with nightly dancing and entertainment. Rates at the resort are $55 to $75, year round. There's no charge for children under 17.

For the posh spa life, cart that avoirdupois over to **Safety Harbor Spa,** 105 N. Bayshore Dr., Safety Harbor, FL 34695 (tel. 813/726-1161, or toll free 800/237-0155), where you can dine and diet, be pummeled and pampered, and take it off, take it all off, with the minimum of pain and the maximum of pleasure. Safety Harbor has the works in spa facilities from mineral baths to stretch/relaxation classes, medical exams, golf, tennis, saunas. There's a 182-room hotel here with spacious bright rooms in an older building and others in a new wing that are prettier yet. Safety Harbor's been operating for almost 40 years. Rates, with meals, per person double begin at $121 to $165, at $165 to $222 single, depending on location, season, and size of accommodations. Spa/fitness programs are higher.

You can tell from the address of the **Hyatt Regency Tampa,** 2 Tampa City Center, Tampa, Fl 33602 (tel. 813/225-1234, or toll free 800/228-9000), just where this handsome new hotel is: right smack in the middle of town. Behind the sleek mirrored facade of the Hyatt lies a multilevel lobby filled with shops and inviting restaurants that circle a two-story waterfall. Quite a convenient spot for those attending functions at the Curtis Hixon Hall just down the street, this slick new hotel is just as good a choice for those who want to explore this old city. Slated to be right at the forefront of the downtown renaissance occurring in Tampa, the Hyatt features bright contemporary furnishings in its spacious rooms, which are also equipped with all the extra amenities that have made Hyatt one of the nation's top hotel chains. A large hotel, Hyatt has 517 rooms, many of them sporting bay or river views. In the hotel's Regency Club, you're treated to complimentary breakfasts and cocktails and a special concierge staff to do your bidding. A swimming pool, two whirlpools, and a health club help you work off the calories you consume in the hotel's two restaurants. Rates are $104 to $155 double, year round, lower on weekends. Suites with a parlor begin at $260 and fancier one-bedroom accommodations are also available.

Chain operations in the area include **La Quinta Motor Inn, Holiday Inn, Howard Johnson, Sheraton, Rodeway,** and **Ramada Inns,** all of which have toll-free numbers for rate information and fall into a moderate to expensive category.

## Moderate Choices

If you'd like to stay out near Busch Gardens and spend a day or so at the attraction's Adventure Island water park, you can bunk down in any of several nice spots, least expensive of which is the **Garden View Motel,** at 2500 E. Busch Blvd., Tampa, FL 33612 (tel. 813/933-3958). Here you'll find small but tidy accommodations decorated in rose and burgundy. A small pool is tucked into the corner of the building. Double rates are just $35 to $42 a day, summer or winter.

**Days Inn,** 2901 E. Busch Blvd., Tampa, FL 33612 (tel. 813/933-6471, or toll free 800/325-2525), has a very large hotel here with medium-size rooms decorated in tropical colors. There's a large swimming pool and all the usual Days Inn accoutrements, including a very inexpensive restaurant with prices in the $5 to $8 range. Rates are just $44 to $59 double.

**Ramada Inn North,** 820 E. Busch Blvd., Tampa, FL 33162 (tel. 813/933-4011, or toll free 800/228-2828), has a 268-unit hotel near Busch Gardens, with tennis courts and two pools for $59 to $79 double year round. **Howard Johnson's Busch Gardens,** 720 E. Fowler Ave., Tampa, FL 33162 (tel. 813/971-5150, or toll free 800/654-2000), charges $40 to $58 double.

Back in Tampa, **Tahitian Inn Motel,** 601 S. Dale Mabry Hwy., Tampa, FL 33609 (tel. 813/877-6721), is a good moderately priced inn with 79 rooms, color TV, heated pool, and a coffee shop open from 7am to 3pm daily. Prices are $44 to $54 double, for the attractive medium-size rooms here.

You'll also save at the two **Expressway Inns:** at 3693 Gandy Blvd., Tampa, FL 33611 (tel. 813/837-1971), and at 3688 Gandy Blvd., Tampa, FL 33611 (tel. 813/837-1921). Both are about four miles south of I-275 on US 92. Some of the simple but attractively furnished rooms have refrigerators (for which you'll pay a few dollars extra). Both inns have a pool and color televisions. You can bring Fido, but there's a $10 charge. Rates are $28 to $42 double, all year.

## Outside Town (But Worth the Drive)

Wesley Chapel is a tiny town that's not far from Tampa and not even an unreasonable distance from Orlando. We could tell you it's near Zephyrhills, site of the state's only officially sanctioned fox hunt, but suspecting that Zephyrhills is not yet a household word, we'll say that Wesley Chapel is about 25 minutes from Tampa International Airport. Here you'll find one of the state's newest villa resorts. **Saddlebrook,** 100 Saddlebrook Way (County Road 54), Wesley Chapel, FL 34249 (tel. 813/973-1111, or toll free 800/237-7519), a mile east of I-75. One-, two-, and three-bedroom villas at Saddlebrook are part of an $80-million condominium resort plunked down amid palms and pines 15 miles north of Tampa. All are individually and beautifully decorated, and have full kitchens, baths with terry-cloth robes for every bedroom, balconies or patios, a pool and whirlpool, restaurant, and 36 holes of golf. It's a serene spot with rolling grounds laced with tiny streams and stands of pines. In peak winter season the resort charges $140 to $165 for hotel rooms or one-bedroom apartments, and up to $240 for two-bedroom accommodations. Summer rates range from $60 to $95. Children under 12 stay free, and the resort will arrange airport pickup for $14 if you let them know 24 hours in advance.

## A Very Special Resort

**Innisbrook,** P.O. Drawer 1088, Tarpon Springs, FL 34286 (tel. 813/937-3124, or toll free 800/237-0157, 800/456-2000 in Florida), just north of Clearwater on US 19 North, is one of the state's loveliest golf and tennis resorts. Nowhere else will you find such glorious rolling acres of pineland or so many features designed to make anyone—golfer, tennis player, or none of the above—feel they're living in a wonderland. For openers, there are 1,000 acres of grounds, left for the most part in their enchanting natural state. Chipmunks chatter high in the pines, ducks swoop around the lakes, and we're betting there's not another resort in Florida with signs warning you to slow down for the peacocks! You'll find three magnificent golf courses here (two rated among the nation's top 50), 18 tennis courts, and a new tennis and racquetball center with indoor courts.

There are 1,200 suites, all located in lodges nestled among the fairways and under the pines, their wood exteriors subtly blended into the wooded surroundings. All suites are entered from center halls and have private patios or balconies. They're individually decorated, and while all are a beautiful mélange of colors and fine furniture, some are downright spectacular. They're all spacious too, and of course never far from a swimming pool since there are five on the resort. You can dine in any of three clubhouse dining rooms on huge breakfast buffets and fine continental cuisine, then spend an entertaining evening in the resort's nightclub where starspangled revues keep things hopping all year long.

We were awed when we first saw Innisbrook, and we think you will be, too. From February to May, accommodations begin with club suites at $173, higher for one- and two-bedroom suites. In summer, when rates drop about 50%, there are many money-saving golf and tennis package programs. Golf is $40 to $80 for greens fees, year round, and tennis is $16 to $20 an hour, but several package plans may save you money on those fees.

## Something New

Most elaborate of the new country inns in Florida is the **Crown Hotel,** 109 N. Seminole Ave., Inverness, FL 32650 (tel. 904/344-5555), a place that had been mentioned to us by several delighted travelers. All those raves led us to the tiny village of Inverness to see for ourselves what all the excitement was about . . . and now we know!

What a little jewel they have here! Resurrected from the run-down remains of what was once a general store, the Crown is testimony to what miracles can be wrought with $2 million. Owned by British investors who spotted the possibilities inherent in a 90-year-old building and in the growing community of Inverness, the Crown is as lacy and perky as a new Easter bonnet. There are sparkling cut-glass panels in the polished-wood doors, glowing carpets on the floors, hand-rubbed wood on the spiral staircase. In the inn's 34 rooms you'll find original wood floors polished to a fare-thee-well, shiny brass beds, ornate flounces on heavy tasseled draperies, gold bathroom fixtures, antiques and carefully chosen reproductions. Tables have polished marble tops. Doors have handsome carved moldings. Lamps have etched-glass globes and brass bases. In the lobby a 200-year-old cabinet holds an awesome collection of glittering reproductions of the British monarchy's crowns and scepters. (Ask manager Ian Young, possessor of a delightful Scots accent, to tell you what fun they had explaining those bejewelled crowns to a Customs inspector!)

Anglophiles will go all nostalgic in the Pub, an intimate, clubby spot where steak-and-kidney pie, fish and chips, and the like are on the menu each day for under $5. For evening dining don't miss the Churchill Restaurant, where sophisticated maître d'hôtel Salvatore presides over a sleek—and chic—operation. As you dine on such delicacies as lobster Evoc (Maine lobster tossed with shrimp and water chestnuts and topped with a cream sauce) or tournedos Rossini (prices in the $13 to $18 range), a pianist plays softly in the background and crystal chandeliers glitter overhead. Is tiny Inverness *ready* for all this glamour?

Outside there's a swimming pool ornamented by a lacy gazebo, and nearby are tennis courts, golfing, fishing, and boating. While you won't find bright lights and neon whoop-de-doo in Inverness, you will find a warm welcome from people who love the serenity and charm of their small village. If you want beach, the gulf is a 20-minute drive from here.

Rates at the Crown are $65 double. If you have children along, the hotel can provide you with a beautiful trundle-bedded separate room for the youngsters at a special price. Inverness is about an hour's drive north of Tampa just west of the intersection of I-75 and Fla. 44, about 30 minutes or less to Ocala, Silver Springs, Weeki Wachee Spring, and Cedar Key. You'll find the hotel right in the middle of town just half a block off Fla. 44. Just look for the antique London double-decker bus parked at the front door.

## WHERE TO DINE

You can dine on everything from paella to porterhouse in Tampa's outstanding restaurants. And remember that the prices we've cited are for entrées, but that usually includes a salad, one or two vegetables, and sometimes coffee as well.

## American/Continental

**Bern's Steak House,** 1208 S. Howard Ave. (tel. 251-2421, or toll free in Florida 800/282-1547), is without question the best-known steak house in Florida. Real fans, of which there are many, call it the best in the nation! Certainly the menu here is a study in the great American fascination with the steer. You can buy any cut of steak—filet mignon, strip sirloin, Delmonico, T-bone, porterhouse, or chateaubriand—in any thickness and any weight you can dream up. Beef is aged five to eight weeks, cut, trimmed, and weighed to order for you, then broiled over charcoal by chefs under the watchful eye of owner/chef Bern Laxer, who is in the kitchen. To get what they want in quality, they do just about everything themselves—from grinding and roasting their own coffee beans to growing their own fresh vegetables organically on their own farm. Laxer loves and collects wines, so the wine list is just slightly smaller than a telephone book and is, he claims, "the largest variety of wines ever assembled in one restaurant anywhere in the world." Few would dispute it. Bern will now even take you on a tour of the restaurant and give you a look at their new dessert room where booths are shaped like wine barrels. In there you'll be tempted by dozens of slices of sin and a huge selection of dessert wines, liqueurs, armagnacs, cognacs, brandies, aged and single-malt whiskies.

You can stake your claim on a slab of steer here—or any of dozens of other meats and seafood—for prices that begin at about $16 including French onion soup, salad, baked potato, garlic toast, and onion rings. Prices rise with your capacity to eat and to pay. Many, many people think elegant Bern's is worth every buffalo head it costs them, so reservations are mandatory anytime, but virtually impossible on weekends when this award-winning spot packs them in from flank to flank. Open from 5 to 11pm daily.

**Chuck's Steak House,** 11911 N. Dale Mabry Hwy. (tel. 962-2226), has a penchant for nature and panders to it with an aviary and aquariums scattered throughout the restaurant. With a name like that, you can figure what the specialty is, but there's also quite a selection of seafood, from shrimp teriyaki to crab, lobster tails, grouper, and swordfish mesquite-grilled, if you like. Here you get a beer passport to guide you through the dozens of different kinds of national beers from Australia's Adelaide Lager to Zaire's Nogoma—each one is described, "full-bodied" and all of that. Who would ever have believed beer would reach connoisseur heights?

Located over in the yuppieville Carrollwood section of town, this very successful restaurant is attractively decorated with modern art on the walls and colorful lamps hanging from a latticework ceiling, all of it wrapped up into several rooms that give this spot a pleasant, intimate air. Barbecued shrimp appetizers have received many an accolade. Beef, corn fed on an Iowa farm and trimmed daily here, comes in a variety of sizes and styles and is, happily, abetted by a really good salad bar, not the pale imitations that have been proliferating hereabouts.

## A Long Way for Lunch but Worth It

What's a sleek and chic dining spot like **Lunch on Limoges,** 109 S. 7th St., Dade City (tel. 904/567-5685), doing waaay up here in this small town? Who knows? Who cares? All that matters is that this very special place *is* here and is well worth the drive. Once you get here that perplexed look we can see on your face will intensify as you discover Lunch on Limoges is tucked away in what used to be the men's department of what is now a ladies fashion shop. No matter, for here will you lunch on Limoges in both the literal and figurative sense as you dine elegantly on seductive treats like pecan chicken, shrimp salad, a chicken tarragon salad rimmed with fruit or served lightly broiled on a croissant, homemade fruit muffins with fruit butter, fine soups made here daily, and desserts that make it advisable not to look too closely at the small sizes on your way out of here. Both French and New American touches appear here, thanks to owners who are quite dedicated to dining pleasures. You'll pay $7 to $10 for lunch, more depending on your indulgences. You can Lunch on Limoges daily except Sunday from 11:30am to 3pm; closed Mondays, too, in July and August. Dade City, by the way, is about 40 miles northeast of Tampa. Who cares? It's only miles.

Solid cooking, an owner who's operated other Chuck's Steak House restaurants in Conneticut where the chain got its start, and a determination to offer the best at reasonable prices have made this restaurant one of Tampa's biggest dining successes. Dinner prices here fall in the $10 to $15 range, and Chuck's is open from 11am to 2:30pm and 5 to 11pm daily, closing an hour later on weekends.

## Cuban/Spanish

Rare is the person who is not overwhelmed at the block-long magnificence of the **Columbia,** at 21st Street and Broadway (tel. 248-4961). Florida's oldest restaurant opened in 1905 and was named by a patriotic owner, grateful for the help of "Columbia the Gem of the Ocean" in freeing his native Cuba. Caesar Gonzmart, don of the third generation of the family, now oversees this must-see spot where 11 dining rooms seat 1,500 people amid Cuban tile, skylit patios, fountains, and furbelows. He also plays the violin and entertains at one of three nightly revues complete with flamenco dancers and singers. Don't fail to try the 1905 house salad—it's super in all meanings of the word. There's a four-page menu here from which we especially recommend the Spanish bean soup dotted with ham and Spanish sausage, or the chilled gazpacho resting atop a bowl of ice, picadillo Habañera prepared with capers and olives, the chicken valenciana made with tomatoes, onions, saffron, ham, wine, and asparagus. Seafood tempters include the snapper Alicante with a touch of garlic and a shrimp suprême garnish, or zarzuela de mariscos, a combination of seafoods in a light tomato sauce. Paella valenciana is worth the 35- to 45-minute wait at this enchanting spot (try a *blue* margarita while you're waiting) where dinner entree prices average $11 to $17 (topping out with lobster dishes at $25). Open from 11am to midnight daily, Sunday to 10pm, and to 2:30am in two jazz clubs, the Café and the Warehouse.

**Don Quixote,** 1536 E. Seventh Ave. (tel. 247-9454), occupies a historic site in what used to be the game room of El Centro Español in this historic city. Now it's a high-ceilinged, paddle-fanned, conscientiously maintained emporium where quantities are as large as the memories of bygone days. Even Sancho Panza would be hard-put to put away the platter-size pork chops, slabs of salted cod with a Basque touch of tomato sauce, mounds of shrimp gently glazed in wine sauce, or any of the ample treats created by the Asturian family who run Don Quixote. Prices are low, with most dinners in the $5 to $12 range. The Don is open from 11am to 2:30pm daily (except Sunday) and from 5:30 to 10pm Friday and Saturday only.

Sooner or later everyone in Tampa will turn up at **Café Pepe,** 2006 W. Kennedy Blvd. (tel. 253-6501), where the atmosphere is *español* and the Spanish food is *olé!* Huge platters of paella ($26 for two), luscious arroz con pollo, bacon-wrapped or garlic-spiced shrimp, picadillo brimming with olives and raisins, and red snapper in a special cream sauce are all made right here. Prices are the best you'll find anywhere, ringing in at an average of $10 to $15 for dinner. Dining is fun amid rapid-fire Spanish and the general clamor of al gusto dining. It's open from 11am to 11pm Monday through Friday; for dinner only on Saturday, 5 to 11pm; closed Sunday.

## Asian

For Asian cuisine in subdued surroundings, **Hanir Kwan,** 3751 W. Cypress (tel. 876-1709), gets our vote. Lovely Far Eastern ladies seat you on plump cushions and serve delectable dishes from several countries: Korean bulgogi and kimchee, Japanese sashimi, Thai or Chinese specialties, many of which are cooked right at your table. You'll pay $10 to $15 for dinner, and the restaurant's open from 11am to 11pm daily.

## Italian

**Ristorante Mama Mia,** Holiday Inn–West Stadium, 4732 N. Dale Mabry Hwy. (tel. 877-6061), bills itself as the "grandest Italian restaurant ever" and gets no dispute from the thousands of patrons who pass through these doors annually. Dine on veal and shrimp dishes, Mama Mia's delicious chicken Mama Mia, fresh breads baked right in Mama's oven. Toss back free wine and free antipasti from a huge antipasti bar, all you can consume. A bright red-and-yellow painted cart is a salad bar, and so you'll feel as Italian as possible, there's a Harry's American Bar! Dinners are $8 to $12 and Mama opens the doors from 5 to 10pm Monday through Saturday, from 1 to 9pm on Sunday.

## Seafood

In Florida someone is always out there ranking restaurants, and **Mirabella's,** at 327 N. Dale Mabry Hwy. (tel. 876-2844), frequently appears on the list of top seafood establishments. This rustic, wood-sided spot has been dishing up fresh seafood since 1952 (and catching it with its own fishing fleet since 1898). Closet sailors should adore this unabashedly nautical decor complete with trophy fish and lots of brass, not to mention offerings of oysters, clams, and good straightforward seafood preparations. Prices are in the $7 to $10 range, and Mirabella's opens Monday through Friday at 11am and closes at 10pm, on Saturday from 4pm (closed Sunday and holidays).

Just east of the International Shrine Headquarters, near the entrance to Courtney Campbell Causeway, you'll spot a hand-lettered wooden sign marking the way to **Crawdaddy's,** 2500 Rocky Point Rd. (tel. 281-0407). If there are two matching boards in this hulking mass you'll have to prove it to us. The restaurant-creation group which pulled together this amusing spot claims that in the roaring '20s Beauregard "Crawdaddy" Belvedere provided dining, entertainment, and "various distractions" for the rich who came here by yacht to, um, be distracted. You'll still find plenty of distractions at Crawdaddy's, albeit somewhat tamer than what old Beau may have devised. There's plenty to look at: long johns on the clothesline outside, hens scratching away in the pen shared with goats, the conglomeration of "antique" posters, ads, buckets, crates, sandbags, whisky barrels, and lobster traps. You can do your looking in considerable comfort in this multilevel picture-windowed maze, from upholstered wing chairs or antique Victorian couches. Adventurous diners can try alligator and more conservative munchers can go for beer-batter shrimp, lobster whisky, crunchy bass rolled in sliced almonds and corn crisps, and a variety of beef dishes in the $10 to $15 price range, including cheese or gazpacho soup, salad, baked red potatoes, and fresh breads. Open from 11am to 3pm for lunch daily, except Sunday, from 5 to 11pm daily for dinner, Crawdaddy's has entertainment nightly from 6pm to 2:30 am, plus an electronic game room.

Much of the action in Tampa these days in upscale Carrollwood where you'll find the Reebok set scampering over to **R.G.'s Restaurant North,** 3807 Northdale Blvd. (tel. 963-2356). Mainstay of the menu at this trendy indoor-outdoor spot here or 110 N. Franklin (tel. 229-5536) is fresh seafood and lots of it, in plenty of interesting preparations. You'll also find veal, good pastas, and duck on the reasonably priced menu here. What does "reasonably priced" mean? How about $10 to $18, no higher, for full dinners including vegetable, salad, the lot. R.G.'s is open from 11:30am to 2pm and 5:30 to 10pm weekdays, closing at 11pm on Saturday, at 9pm Sunday.

Here as in Orlando and Fort Lauderdale, we couldn't pass up a recommendation for **Shells,** a shekels-saving seafood house that packs 'em in every night. Atmosphere is certainly not what those crowds are looking for here—there is none, or very little. That keep-it-simple philosophy is just the way the innovative founder of this Florida chain planned it and is the same philosophy applied to the menu. You'll find simply prepared seafood here—shrimp in garlic sauce, plain stone crabs or lobster, deviled crab, with tiny new potato accompaniment—and several selections combining seafood with pasta. For finale, a couple of good but equally simple desserts—say, key lime pie or strawberries and cream. Nothing on the menu tops $10, and most selections are several dollars lower than that—a dozen oysters are less than $2. You'll find Shells branches at 202 S. Dale Mabry Hwy. (tel. 875-3467); at 11010 N. 30th St. (tel. 977-8456); and at 14380 N. Dale Mabry Hwy. (tel. 968-6686) in the Carrollwood section of town. Hours are 5 to 10pm, to 11pm on Friday and Saturday. There are also restaurant branches in St. Petersburg, New Port Richey, and Redington Beach.

## Budget Bets

Someday drive over to Plant City where, in February, you'll reel in the scent of strawberries. This strawberry capital of the world as yet has no challengers for the title. In the last days of February and the first of March, Plant City's festive **Strawberry Festival** draws crowds of red berry lovers who throng here to gorge on the massive berries on ice cream, in shortcake or topped with whipped cream, in sugar and rum, or just chomped right out in the fields.

**Morrison Cafeteria,** 717 S. Dale Mabry Hwy. (tel. 877-7119), here as everywhere offers inexpensive cafeteria dining in simple but attractive surroundings with dinners in the $5 range.

Another cafeteria chain, **Piccadilly,** has two operations in Tampa, one in West Shore Plaza, Fla. 60 at the junction with I-275, exit 21 (tel. 876-6894), and one at 2239 University Square Mall, on County Road 582 about a mile east of I-75 exit 34, not far from Busch Gardens (tel. 977-0002). Both offer prices in the $5 range and are open from 11am to 8:30pm (closed only on Christmas Day).

**Ruby Tuesday's,** Tampa Bay Center Mall, 302 W. Buffalo St. (tel. 872-9270), is an amusing spot with Victorian turn-of-the-century decor and plenty to see and do. Fare runs to grazing and basic American options, and the restaurant is open from 11am to 11pm daily, later on Saturday, but closing at 8pm on Sunday. Prices are in the $10 to $15 range. A second Ruby creates much the same atmosphere at University Mall, Fowler Street (tel. 977-2560).

## A Don't-Miss

It's a strawberry free-for-all at the festival, but any time of year it's worth the drive for some good down-home cookin' at **Branch Ranch,** on Thonotosassa Road in Plant City (tel. 752-1957). An offbeat spot 17 miles west of Tampa and about a mile north of the Branch-Forbes exit of I-4, Branch Ranch is on the outskirts of this picturesque farming village and is itself both picturesque and a working farm. You tie on the feed bag here for $8 to $15, with a relish tray, plates of preserved pickles and beets just like Grannie used to can, a basket of hot buttermilk biscuits, a jar of homemade strawberry jam. Next, out roll tin baking pans laden with summer squash, candied yams, buttered green beans cooked with country ham, chicken pot pie, entrées of chicken, beef, ham, and finally the finale—fruit cobblers, ice cream, and of course, strawberry shortcake. Branch Ranch is America's cooking heritage—all of it at once—wrapped and packaged in a barn of a building with a monstrous stone fireplace, lace curtains on the windows, and a view of passing tractors. It's open from 11:30am to 9pm Tuesday through Sunday. A reader from Madeira Beach, Florida, recommends trying Branch Ranch's excellent strawberry preserves, pickled beets, and cucumber pickles.

## NIGHTLIFE

Nightlife in Tampa is best in the area's large **hotels,** all of which have entertainment and music for dancing and listening. The Hyatt Regency and Sheraton in downtown Tampa, and the revolving restaurant and lounge at the Marriott-Tampa Airport, are good places to start, but even chain operations have lounge entertainment.

One of the best shows in town is at the **Columbia Restaurant,** at 21st Street and Broadway in Ybor City (tel. 248-4961), where you'll see flamenco dancing and hear guitar music and Latin laments. It's a fun evening with entertainment that even includes the restaurant's owner and strolling mariachis from Mexico.

If you'd just like to go out to a movie, how about an old movie or a foreign film in a theater that is itself one of the sights-to-see in Tampa. **Tampa Theater,** 711 Franklin St. (tel. 223-8981 or 223-8982), is the spot we have in mind. You can read more about it in the section on Tampa's sights. Admission is $4 adults,, $1.50 children.

You'll also often find music and dancing at **Chuck's Steak House,** 11911 N. Dale Mabry Hwy. (tel. 962-2226); there's often entertainment in the lounge too.

**Palace at Feather Sound,** 2675 Ulmerton Rd., Clearwater (tel. 572-0708), is a lively multilevel eating and imbibing spot that draws those intent on seeing and being seen as they quench hunger and thirst.

**Malio's,** 301 S. Dale Mabry Hwy., Tampa (tel. 879-3233), looks upon its operation as the Toots Shor's of Tampa. Whether or not you remember who Toots was, there is usually a laugh to be had here at this private club, which is open to visitors daily from 11am to 1:30am. There's no cover charge.

At **Comedy Corner,** 3447 W. Kennedy Blvd., Tampa (tel. 875-9129), both professional and amateur yukkers roll out the jokes. Amateur night is Tuesday, when anyone can get into the act, but the club is open every night except Monday with shows at 8:30pm, and a second show at 10:45pm Friday and Saturday. Cover charge runs $3 to $6.

**Rough Riders,** 1901 13th St., Tampa (tel. 248-2756), is an amusing dining and drinking spot that often has a band on weekends. No cover.

**Yucatan Liquor Stand,** 48811 W. Cypress St., at Westshore Blvd. (tel. 289-8445 or 289-8454), rocks, rocks, and rocks, so if what you're looking for runs along those lines, this is it for you. Open weekdays except Monday from 5pm to 1am, from 9pm on Saturday and 7pm on Sunday, this very lively spot is always packed wave to wave with funseekers. Cover charge varies from $2 to $5, and there are often ladies' nights and happy-hour buffets.

Lounges at Lani Purcell's restaurants in the Holiday Inn Tampa State Fair, I-4 and 59th St. (tel. 621-2081)—it's called the **LP Lounge** —and Holiday Inn Sabal Park Hotel, I-75 at E. Buffalo Ave. (tel. 623-6363)—this one's called **Elmo's Cabaret**—can be counted on for lively evening entertainment and dancing.

## Cultural Activities

There's been a bit of a boom in cultural activities in Tampa in recent years, so you can now find a wide range of theater, dance, and musical presentations here.

The **Tampa Ballet,** 100 W. Kennedy Blvd. (tel. 286-8635), dances October through March. The **Florida Orchestra,** 1211 N. Westshore Blvd. (tel. 286-1170 or 447-3975), entertains from September through May in Clearwater, Tampa, or St. Petersburg.

For an evening of theater, try the **Tampa Players,** performing in residence at the Tampa Bay Performing Arts Center, 1010 N. MacInnes Rd. (tel. 229-3221). Ticket prices range from $12.50 to $25. Curtain times Wednesday and Sunday are at 6pm; for all other evening performances curtain time is 7:30pm. There is also a Sunday matinee at 2pm.

There's always something happening from symphony to rock concerts at **Ruth Eckerd Hall,** in the Richard Baumgardner Center, 1111 McMullen Booth Rd., Clearwater (tel. 725-5573).

The **Tampa Bay Performing Arts Center,** 716 N. Florida Ave. (tel. 222-1010 or 221-3223), a showy spot, features a wide variety of entertainment throughout the year from ballets to rock concerts. Ticket prices vary according to the fame of the entertainers, so give them a call to see who and how much.

**Tampa Alliance of Dramatic Arts,** Village Playhouse, Village Center, 13162 N. Dale Mabry Ave., offers children's plays. Other local theater groups use this theater throughout the year as well. Prices are in the $2 to $6 range for tickets, and information is available from the Alliance at 962-7711.

Information on what is going on in the creative world hereabouts also is available from the **Arts Council of Tampa,** 1420 Tampa St. (tel. 229-2787), which helps coordinate cultural activities in the area.

## SPORTS

You'll find lots of tennis courts, golf courses, and some pari-mutuel sports scattered about the city.

### Golf and Tennis

There are public golf courses in the city at **Rocky Point Golf Club,** 5151 Memorial Hwy. (tel. 884-5141), and **Rogers Park Memorial Golf Course,** 7910 N. 30th St. (tel. 234-1911), plus courses at **Babe Zaharias Golf Course,** 11412 Forest Hills Dr. (tel. 932-8932) and many others. Greens fees are about $12 to $25 at most courses; carts, about $10.

There are **tennis courts** all over town, including 11 at **Riverfront Park,** 900 North Blvd. (tel. 251-3472). Most are free or have only a nominal charge. The city's recreation department (tel. 238-6451) will be happy to locate some near you.

### Water Sports

Most of the water sports activity in the Tampa region occurs across the causeways in Clearwater Beach, St. Petersburg Beach or any of the small islands that dot the coastline. You can, however, usually find someone renting sailboats and sometimes jet-skis or windsurfing boards on the beach at Courtney Campbell Causeway. Prices vary but generally fall in the $25 an hour range for sailboats.

### Professional Sports

The **Tampa Bay Buccaneers** (tel. 879-2827) play at Tampa Stadium, 4201 N. Dale Mabry Hwy. (tel. 876-8893), from August to December; admission is $16 to $25, but the team is hysterically popular and games are often a sell-out.

The **Tampa Bay Rowdies** soccer team (tel. 870-1122) kicks it around at Tampa Stadium too, from April through August; tickets are $5 to $7.

### Pari-mutuel Sports

You can put a few dollars on the nose of a fleet-footed greyhound at the **Tampa Greyhound Dog Track,** 8300 N. Nebraska Ave., I-275 at the Bird Street exit (tel. 932-4313), open September through early January at 7:30pm daily (except Sunday), with 12:45pm matinees on Monday, Wednesday, and Saturday. Admission is $1; clubhouse, $2.50.

**Tampa Bay Downs,** on Racetrack Road (tel. 441-9701) in the town of Oldsmar (just off County Road 584 east of US 19), brings out the silks in December with races through April at 1pm daily (except Sunday) for a $1.50 admission ($3 for the clubhouse).

See them play jai-alai at the **Tampa Jai-Alai Fronton,** 5125 S. Dale Mabry Hwy. (tel. 441-9469), January to June daily (except Sunday). Games begin at 7pm, and there are noon matinees on Monday, Wednesday, and Saturday. Admission is $1.

## SANTA CITY

If you love Christmas no matter what time of year it is, drive over to the tiny burg of Brooksville and visit **Rogers' Christmas House,** 103 Saxon Ave. (tel. 904/796-2415), where it's always December 25 (except on December 25, when it's closed). Open from 9:30am to 5pm daily, the shop shimmers with Christmas lights and has multitudes of animated displays and other kinds of shops brimming with treasures only Scrooge could resist. It's 53 miles from Lakeland, at the intersection of US 98, Fla. 50, and US 41, about 10 miles west of I-75.

Make a day of it by coming on over early and stoking up at the **Blueberry Patch,** 414 E. Liberty St., Brooksville (tel. 904/796-6005). You'll find this berry, berry good spot tucked away in an old house fittingly painted blue. A quaint stop in a quaint town, Blueberry Patch serves from early morn to early evening, and is a popular breakfast stop for those headed into the eye-boggling depths of Rogers' Christmas House, a year-round wonderland. At dinner the mainstay is seafood from bay waters. You can pick in this patch from 10am to 6pm weekdays, from 8am Saturday, and from 11:30am to 6pm on Sunday, and prices are in the $5 to $7.50 range for almost anything on the dinner menu, less for many items.

## A VISIT TO YBOR CITY

It's part of Tampa, but it seems an ocean or so away. It was here, in this antique Latin Quarter, that just over 100 years ago cigar-maker Vincente Martinez Ybor began an industry that brought this city worldwide renown—remember those famous Tampa cigars. Here, too, poet/patriot José Martí plotted and pled for support in the fight for Cuban independence.

Ybor lured the cigar-makers of Key West here in 1886 with offers they couldn't refuse and set them up in massive brick warehouses. They rolled tobacco into those famous small cylinders while a *lector* read them news, poetry, and literature as they worked. Millions of cigars emerged from these halls, and in 1893 Martí, who also composed the song "Guantanamera," appealed to workers for men, money, and machetes to help free Cuba from Spanish rule. They responded with fervor. Tampa was selected as the ideal embarkation site for an expeditionary force to Cuba, the most famous of which was Teddy Roosevelt's Rough Riders. Rough they were too: According to one story, a squad of them once rode their horses right into Las Novedades Restaurant (it's now El Goya) in a "battle" still known locally as the "Charge of the Yellow Rice Brigade."

Today the factories that housed those tobacco workers have been revamped and are home to the **Nostalgia Market,** an array of crafts and antique dealers and a small café named for Martí.

Walk the eight or so blocks of Ybor City's **Seventh Avenue** and meander through the intersecting side streets where you'll smell coffee roasting. At nearby **Navier Coffee Mill** you can buy some for $6 to $8 a pound, and find some Italian pastries to go with it at **Demmi's Italian Grocery,** a shop that's been here since the turn of the century.

In these streets you'll find 22 historical markers, plus lovely fountains and old-fashioned lamp posts. In a vest-pocket park, called Parque Amigos de José Martí, a statue of the hero memorializes the valiant Cuban effort.

Ybor City is a two-mile-square area bounded by Nebraska Avenue, 22nd Street, Columbus Drive, and East Broadway. It's filled with old grillwork and bricks, gardens and patios, and tiny cigar stores where workers still roll the smoker's delights by hand as they have for generations. Center of it all is a city block bounded by Eighth and Ninth avenues and 13th and 14th streets. Here is the three-story-high **cigar factory building** of massive oak and heart pine columns, brick and more bricks, and the same iron stairs on which Martí stood to appeal for help.

An adjoining building constructed in 1902 is the **Stemmery,** where tobacco stems and leaves parted company. Today it houses, fittingly enough, the Rough Riders Restaurant, where you can get an idea how things looked in those days: For celebrations, a bugle blares and out charge the boys in khaki campaign shirts and red kerchiefs, looking at least a little like the motley lot of cowboys, Native Americans, and outlaws Roosevelt herded off to Cuba so many years ago.

You'll certainly never starve here, for this is the center of the city's **Cuban cookery** emporiums with a dozen or so fine restaurants: Gran Café Martí has guava turnovers; El Buen Gusto features Basque caldo gallego soup; Alvarez whips out black beans and roast suckling pig; Alegria has Cuban sandwiches; Don Quixote offers super-size pork chops and salted cod with tomato and onion; and La Tropicana Café is the "home of the world-famous Cuban sandwich." Here, too, is the elegant and eclectic Columbia Restaurant, home of the blue margarita (not to mention some outstanding cuisine that you can read more about in the section on restaurants).

Take a look at **El Pasaje Hotel** on Ninth Avenue, where Winston Churchill, Frederic Remington, and Grover Cleveland stayed, and don't miss the fascinating factories, now listed on the U.S. Register of Historic Places as much, one would guess, for their exuberant staying power as for their history.

To these streets at the turn of the century came 20,000 workers, 4,000 of them employed at the Ybor factories. Cubans, Spaniards, Italians, Germans dropped roots here and set up mutual-aid societies and hospitals that are the oldest examples of cooperative social medicine in the U.S.

You can read all about it at the **Ybor City State Museum,** 1818 Ninth Ave. (tel. 247-6323), in the old Ferlita Bakery, where the immigrants' success is related in colorful exhibits. It's open from 9am to 5pm (closed noon to 1pm) Tuesday through Saturday and charges 50¢ for everyone over 6.

Twice a year, in February and November, the city turns out to celebrate its heritage with dancing and entertainment—and of course, lots of food.

You can get a map for a self-guided walking tour of the city from the **Ybor Chamber of Commerce,** at 1513 Eighth Ave., Ybor City, FL 33605 (tel. 813/248-3712).

---

# 3. St. Petersburg

---

After years of hearing stories about aged pensioners nodding off to sleep on the city's green benches, we expected to trip over canes on Main Street here. No such thing! Certainly in winter flocks of oldsters continue to make this their warm-weather bastion, but there's a decided air of the upbeat and upwardly mobile in this rapidly growing Suncoast area. There are benches still, but sorry to say they're not painted green anymore—city fathers, belabored *ad nauseum* by the "Old Folks at Home" image, painted most of them orange some years back.

It's no wonder people of every age gravitate here, for this is one of the loveliest waterfront cities in the state. Who could fail to be enchanted on a walk or drive along the bay as you see spread out before you the glittering sapphire waters of Tampa Bay on one side and emerald-green lawns, gurgling fountains, and winding walkways on the other. Sun glints off the roof of a massive Spanish mansion. Flags fly from masts of pristinely maintained sailing craft. You stroll on brick streets amid a pastel sparkle so magical it's no wonder snowbirds fly here to winter.

Refined and quiet as it may be on the mainland, if you cross the causeways to St. Petersburg Beach and its island neighbors, you enter a world of nonstop activity from the first morning beachcombing safari to the final shrieks of the a.m. discos.

St. Petersburg came by that old folks image when the American Medical Association reported that the city was a healthy place. St. Petersburg dragged out the green benches so the flood of elderly tourists could rest, and before long the city's "green bench" image was famous. These days, city promoters are working hard to change that image, perhaps in vain since the baby boom is rapidly aging! Besides, many of St. Petersburg's sprightly senior citizens are active, alert people—so active in fact that they have a softball team here that you can't join unless you're over 70!

Old it may be, and oldsters it may have, but this is undeniably a lovely city. Stroll the two miles of shoreline past much of the city's 2,000 acres of recreation area and see parks so painted, planted, and prettied you wonder if the gardeners carry rulers. Stroll among lovely old mansions renovated into even lovelier old mansions. Step back into another, more stately era, when life moved slowly and a gentleman wouldn't think of appearing in public without a tie. There's still a bit of that here in hotels, where elegant old gentlemen jump to their well-shod feet and tiny silver-haired damsels flutter and blush like new brides.

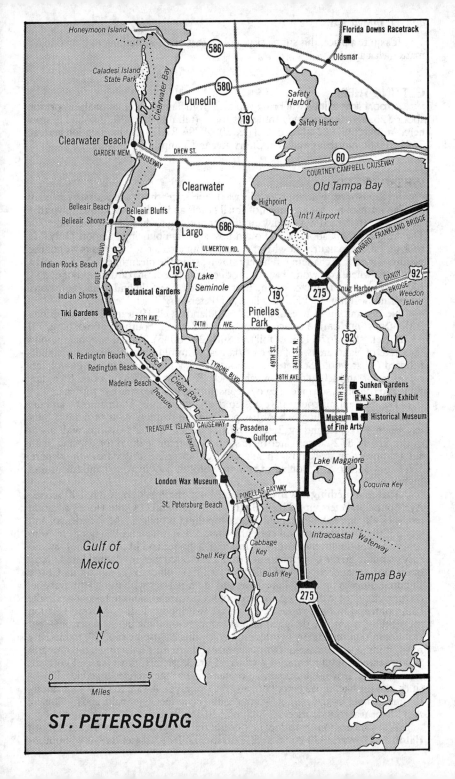

ST. PETERSBURG

It's quite a place, this sunny city, a place that offers something to everyone no matter what age.

## GETTING THERE

**Airport limousines** will bring you here from Tampa International Airport for about $25, and **Greyhound/Trailways** buses (tel. toll free 800/237-8211) stop here. **Amtrak** (tel. 822-0175, or toll free 800/USA-RAIL) also has a station here, at 3601 31st St. North, as well as in Clearwater and Tampa.

## WHERE TO STAY

St. Petersburg, which incidentally was named after the city in Russia by an early Russian immigrant, has a number of small hotels and guesthouses downtown that cling firmly to the old ways and want little or nothing to do with anyone under 70. They're quite frank about it, and often post signs announcing "Seniors Only." It took us a while to figure out what that meant, but after a few hotel visits we got the picture. Things are changing, but very slowly, so in the meantime we've selected a few hotels where you won't have to produce your Medicare card for proof of age. Most people seem to prefer staying near the beach, so you'll find many more hotel listings in the following "Holiday Isles/St. Petersburg Beach" section.

Nestled among 14 acres of tropical woodland on US 19 near the Skyway Bridge is the **Days Inn Marina Beach Resort,** 6800 34th St. South, St. Petersburg, FL 33711 (tel. 813/867-1151, or toll free 800/227-8045). Tucked away here among hundreds of plants are two of the city's largest swimming pools, tennis courts, shuffleboard (what would St. Pete be without that?), a playground, wading pool, ice-cream parlor, and 1,000 feet of private beach. The pretty, spacious rooms have glass walls and balconies so you can enjoy a constant view of the attractive gardens.

The inn's tennis courts have hosted the Virginia Slims Tournaments, and the hotel's Annapolis Sailing School has polished the nautical skills of many a Sunday sailor. Parker's Landing Restaurant is a budget-watcher's favorite, with prices in the $10 to $12 range. Later there's a not-too-frenetic disco for dancing, with entertainment on weekends. There's also free limousine service from the airport. You'll pay $45 to $85 double in summer, $69 to $99 in winter months; suites higher.

There's something new in old St. Petersburg: the **Presidential Inn,** 100 Second Ave. South, St. Petersburg, FL 33701 (tel. 813/823-7552). Quite a lovely addition to the city's regrettably small number of top-flight hostelries, the Presidential Inn was put together by two local entrepreneurs, Ted Wittner and Bill Bond, Jr., who took a look at the lovely Governors Inn in Tallahassee and liked what they saw. So they set out to go the Governors one better and created the Presidential Inn, a group of 30 rooms that occupy the fifth floor of a 12-story office tower called City Center Building. Rooms overlook Tampa Bay and are fitted out with just about every accoutrement you can dream up, from remote-control televisions to telephones in the bathroom, and in eight rooms, even private whirlpools. That downtown location means these rooms are designed primarily for the traveling business person—but that doesn't mean that any traveler can't enjoy this handsome spot. All rooms have refrigerators and one king- or two queen-size beds. At a central living room/bar area you're served complimentary Continental breakfast each morning and cocktails each evening. Downstairs, a service center can arrange secretarial service, limousines, and the like. If you fancy knowing the fancy, you'll want to know that among the guests have been singer Liza Minnelli, film reviewer Gene Shalit, and millionaire Aga Khan. Year round, prices are $85 to $130 double.

When the Hilton chain does it, it does it right, as you will see at **St. Petersburg Hilton and Towers,** 333 1st St. S., St. Petersburg, FL 33701 (tel. 813/894-5000, or toll free 800/HILTONS). Once known as the Bayfront Concourse, this hotel faltered through some lean years, but these days is faltering no more, thanks to a $23 million facelift by the Hilton chain. Now a quite handsome downtown hotel, the Hilton has served as spring training headquarters for the Mets and the Cardinals in recent memory and will greet you with just as much enthusiasm.

Located right in the heart of this quite lovely downtown, the 333-room hotel has a handsome lobby togged out in striking contemporary colors. Smashing views of the city are available on the top two levels of the hotel's towers where guests are given special treatment including a separate registration area, limited-access key security, and a hostess ready to welcome them to Continental breakfast and, later, to cocktails. Many special amenities, running the gamut from Perrier water to shoe shiners and bathrobes, are available for guests of those two floors.

Elsewhere in the hotel, rooms have two double or king-sized beds, a desk, remote-control television, radios, and all the other amenities you've come to expect from large and luxurious hotels. There's a restaurant and piano bar in the cozy lobby and a rocking Wings lounge where a biplane suspended from the ceiling serves as focal point. Rates range from $79 to $114. Suites are higher.

St. Petersburg is proud of its heritage, as well it should be, although the city has often had a difficult time salvaging the handsome old hotels that thrived during the early decades of this century. One has recently been restored, however, and is now the lovely **Heritage Hotel,** 234 3rd Ave. N. (tel. 813/822-4814). Once known as the Martha Washington Hotel, this 60-year-old property got a $3 million facelift recently but managed to retain many elements of the old property, including solid mahogany furniture in all the rooms and oak floors in the lobby. There's a restaurant and lounge, a swimming pool and whirlpool, and a very good location quite near the bay in the heart of the downtown area. A very pretty place now, the Heritage Hotel has just 71 rooms and charges $50 to $85 year round, higher for suites.

To stroll the bayfront area streets is to take a nostalgic trip down this city's memory lane of old homes and hotels, sometimes combinations of both. One of those combinations that we found appealing is the **Edgepark Apartments,** 256 1st St. North, St. Petersburg, FL 33701 (tel. 813/821-7719). A long, wide veranda trimmed in the tracery of delicate wrought iron is the perfect spot to draw up one of the wicker chairs and indulge in "jest sittin'." Pots of blooms are scattered about outside, while inside is a cavernous lobby filled with wing chairs and comfortable couches. It's a bit eclectic, but it's cozy. This is a spot that caters to senior citizens but seems prepared for the occasional well-behaved soul under 70. Furnishings in the medium-size rooms are spartanly simple but clean; there's carpeting on the floors, bright bedspreads on the beds, and efficiencies have slick kitchens. There's a television lounge downstairs and no phones or pool, but just wait until you hear the price: $170 to $200 a *month,* single, year round, 20% more for a second person!

## Bed-and-Breakfast Inns

Ron and Danie Bernard have for six years run **B & B Suncoast Accommodations,** 8690 Gulf Blvd., St. Petersburg Beach, FL 33706 (tel. 813/360-1753), and they can lead you to area residents who will be happy to welcome you into their homes for bed, private bath, and breakfast. The Bernards list a number of houses, from a Victorian home to a lakeside manse, for prices that range from $35 to $95 double in winter. They have access to hosts elsewhere in Florida too.

## WHERE TO DINE

St. Petersburg is just as schizophrenic when it comes to restaurants as it is in every other way. You'll find an elegant restaurant just around the corner from a budget spot, so we've listed a few of our choices by the cuisine they serve. (Remember that the prices we've cited are for entrées, but that usually includes salad, one or two vegetables, and sometimes coffee as well.)

## French

We haven't quite recovered yet from the shock of finding Peter Kersker's wondrously elegant **Peter's Place-Café International,** 208 Beach Dr. NE (tel. 822-8436), tucked in near the waterfront. In a region about equally divided between California contemporary and fishing village rustic, we didn't expect to find such subtle decor and all-around display of good taste, both culinary and decorative. But then, what else would you expect from such a Renaissance man as Kersker, who's first trade is the law but whose first love is good food and cooking. He could easily have plunked this lovely restaurant down in London where he now has a flat, but fortunately he didn't. So now you can enjoy a menu that changes every evening, depending at least in part on what Peter and his chefs feel like whipping up that day: artichoke hearts and escargots for starters, pâté with iced caviar, chilled dill-spiced smoked salmon, filet mignon wrapped around garlic-buttered shrimp, or something new, a couscous Maroc he discovered in his travels. Service is as smooth as the peanut-butter crème pie Chantilly, as memorable as the crème de menthe Kahlúa chocolate mousse. Feasts range in price from $25 to $35, from $5 to $10 for lunch. Open for cocktails, lunch, and dinner from 11:30am to 2pm and 6 to 10pm Tuesday through Saturday; closed Sunday and Monday and at lunch May to October. Reservations are wise.

## American/Continental

**Pepin,** 4125 4th St. N., St. Petersburg (tel. 821-3773), is popular enough to have two locations hereabouts, this St. Petersburg spot and another equally pleasant location at 19519 Gulf Blvd. in Indian Shores (tel. 596-9100). That popularity is well deserved for this restaurant, which is both consistent and content to stick to the basics—prime beef cut daily, fresh fish caught daily, simple preparations that make the most of those basics. Pork chops are the particular favorite of many diners over this way and the pompano preparation is a stand-out. Pepin's is open from 11am to 2:30pm Tuesday through Friday and from 5:30pm to 10:30pm daily except Monday, and entrée prices fall in the $12 to $17 range.

## Italian

**Lauro Ristorante,** 100 S. Ashley Dr. (tel. 221-3664), has been packing them in for years now, using as a lure some of the best Italian preparations on this coast. All the traditional favorites you've come to love can be found here—good veal, excellent pasta—refined with just the right touch of northern Italian spices and styles. What they do here they do well and in a pleasant atmosphere graced by very good service. You'll pay $12 to $21 for entrées at Lauro Ristorante, which is open from 11:30am to 2pm weekdays and daily for dinner from 6 to 11pm.

## Steaks and Seafood

People hereabouts swear by the ribs at **Spoto's,** 12999 Park Blvd. N., Seminole (tel. 393-3438), and don't mind driving out to Seminole to get them. They're known for their platter of ribs and a top-notch barbecue sauce, served in any of five dining rooms. There's entertainment and dancing nightly, and a late-night menu for insomniacs. A meal at Spoto's will set you back only about $10 to $15 or so, and the hours here are 4 to 10pm weekdays, to 11pm Saturday (from noon on Sunday) and to 1:30am in the pub.

Smoked-fish fans should head straight to **Ted Peters,** at 1350 Pasadena Ave. S. (tel. 381-7931), where chefs brown split filets over red oak in Ted's smokehouse. This is strictly a shirtsleeves and T-shirts spot, where you eat on picnic tables in summer, by a fireplace in winter. German potato salad, clam chowder, rye bread, smoked mullet or mackerel, and a frosty mug of root or real beer and you could face armies. It's open from noon to 7:30pm Wednesday through Monday, with prices in the $5 to $7 range.

St. Petersburgers and Tampans troop off like lemmings to the **Whiskey Joe's Two**, 16100 Fairchild Dr. in Boatyard Village, near the St. Pete/Clearwater airport (tel. 536-6541), for fresh fish broiled over mesquite wood. If you're off seafood for tonight, you can try some very good barbecued pork ribs, a salad bar, steaks, burgers, or chicken spiced by a smoker in the back room. Prices are in the $10 to $20 range, and the restaurant is open from 11am to 9pm daily, an hour later on weekends.

## Budget Bets

This seems to be the year we're touting **Shells**, 1190 34th St. N. (tel. 937-4270), a chain that's made big and welcome inroads into the budget dining scene throughout Florida. Still, Shells deserves praise for doling out good seafood at reasonable prices, too often a rarity in Florida. Seafood teamed with pasta is a big favorite here, but simply prepared seafoods—big baskets of unshelled shrimp, a dozen oysters, deviled crab, a variety of fish and shellfish—abound. Nothing on the menu tops $10, and most selections are several dollars cheaper than that. Oysters fans can down a dozen succulent bivalves for less than $2. Hours are 5 to 10pm, to 11pm Friday and Saturday. There are also restaurant branches in Clearwater, Redington Beach, and in nearby New Port Richey.

Another spot tucked in between stores just past the Pinellas Square Mall is the **Hickory Smoke House Bar-B-Que**, 6769 US 19, Pinellas Park (tel. 525-0948). This is a simple but significant spot with some of the town's best barbecued ribs, beef, and chicken, for prices like $6. It's open from 11am to 10pm daily.

At **Corner Feed Store**, 3291 64th Ave. N. (tel. 525-7225), you can tie on the feed bag at prices under $5. Good salads, sandwiches, sourdough bread, and soups here from 11am to 8pm weekdays, 11am to 4pm Saturday. Sunday closed.

**READERS' RESTAURANT SUGGESTIONS:** "The **Brown Derby** restaurant chain in Sarasota, St. Petersburg Beach (tel. 367-3777), etc., offers excellent value, friendly service, long hours. They're very popular so it's wise to avoid peak hours" (Ann Southmayd, Newark, Del.). [*Authors' Note:* Check the local *Yellow Pages* for locations of Brown Derby restaurants, which are usually open from 11am to 11pm or later] . . . "I discovered . . . the **Well Come In Restaurant**, 4399 Gulf Blvd., St. Petersburg Beach (tel. 360-8487) . . . about halfway between the Don Cesar Hotel and the Dolphin Shopping Center. I was looking for a budget restaurant and in the window they offer a daily luncheon special, for example, chicken and vegetable, for $4.95. My favorite was a flounder, fries, and slaw for $3.25. It is owned and operated by a husband and wife team from Chicago and has a friendly and informal atmosphere. I noticed customers from Canada, England, Germany, and a local person who said this place [is popular locally] for its specials" (John Cross, Atlanta, Ga.). [*Authors' Note:* Well Come In is open daily except Sunday from 8am to 9pm]

## NIGHTLIFE

This is not your top-of-the-line nightlife town, plain and simple. For nightlife you go across to the beaches. Still, there are a few things going on around town.

If big-band music and ballroom dancing are your style—or you'd like it to be —the enormous 2,000-seat **Coliseum**, at 535 Fourth Ave. N. (tel. 892-5202), is the place to head on Saturday and Wednesday 8 to 11pm. Admission is $5 to $10. They also fox trot up a storm at **Come Dancing Ballroom**, 5225 4th St. N. (tel. 522-3898), on Thursday at 7:30pm, and at the **Seminole School of Dance Arts**, 7182 Seminole Blvd., Seminole (tel. 392-3050), on Friday and Saturday with instruction beginning at 8pm.

For theater there's the **Dow Sherwood's Showboat Dinner Theater**, 3405 Ulmerton Rd., Clearwater (tel. 223-2545 in Tampa), which presents Broadway productions in a plush reproduction of a Mississippi riverboat. Cocktails are at 6pm, buffet dinner at 7, curtain at 8 every night but Monday and Tuesday (two hours earlier on Sunday), with matinees on Wednesday and Saturday at 11:15am. Tickets are $27 Sunday through Thursday, $28 on Friday and Saturday; matinees are $22. A ticket includes dinner, tax, and show. Reservations required.

Entertainment at the city's large **Bayfront Center,** 400 1st St. S. (tel. 893-3367), might be anything from the latest rock group to country musicians or Englebert Humperdinck, so check area papers or call the theater to see what's going on.

Downtown in Williams Park along the bayfront there's a series of free concerts by the **Florida Orchestra** with international guest artists, and the city has an opera company that presents performances during the year.

## SPORTS

You want sports? St. Petersburg gives you sports.

### Golf

There are 31 courses in Pinellas County, 15 of them public.

One of the nation's 50 best public golf courses is just three miles from St. Petersburg at **Mangrove Bay,** 875 62nd Ave. NE (tel. 893-7800), where you can tee up at $13 to $15 year around; carts are $16 for 18 holes (they're not required).

In Largo, the **Bardmoor Country Club,** 8000 Bardmoor Blvd. (tel. 392-1234), is the site of championship tournaments and has two public courses. Fees range from $10 at Indian Rocks to $18 (including a cart) at Bardmoor. Nearby **Largo Municipal Golf Course,** 12500 131st St., Largo (tel. 587-6724), has an 18-hole par-62 public course.

The **Belleview Biltmore Hotel** has a beautiful rolling course for guests and their friends at 1 Country Club Lane, Belleair (tel. 442-0229), and charges $30, including cart.

### Tennis and Shuffleboard

Courts for these two popular games are scattered about the city. The recreation department (tel. 893-7441) will be happy to tell you how to find the ones closest to you.

### Spectator Sports

St. Petersburg's Al Lang Stadium, near the Pier, hosts the **St. Louis Cardinals** (tel. 893-7940). Tickets are $5 to $10.

Drag races at **Sunshine Speedway,** 4550 Ulmerton Rd. in Clearwater (tel. 573-4598), rev up every Friday from March through November. Tickets are $8 for adults (children 2 to 12, $2). On Saturday there's stock car racing at 7:30pm.

**Indoor soccer** is played at St. Pete's Bayfront Center from January through March.

You can spectate—or participate if you're *over* 50—at Pells, Gulls, and Kings oldsters' softball games on Monday, Wednesday, and Friday at 12:45pm, and on Sunday at 1pm at **Northshore Park,** 901 North Shore Dr. NE (tel. 893-7727). **Kids 'n Kubs** (minimum age 75!) play at Al Lang Stadium.

### Sailing

**Learn how to sail** off into the sunset at Coquina Key Recreation Center, 3595 Locust St. SE (tel. 893-7738).

**Annapolis Sailing School,** which bills itself as the oldest sailing school in the nation, has been around since 1959 teaching weekend sailors how to be old salts. Thanks to a large staff, more than 120 boats, 125,000 graduates, and plenty of know-how, they say, they are able to offer you lower prices than competitors. Annapolis Sailing School now has schools in its Annapolis headquarters, here in St. Petersburg, in the Florida Keys, St. Croix, and Greenport on New York's Long Island Sound. They'll get you sailing for prices that begin at $185. You can call them toll free for information at 800/638-9192 (tel. 301/267-7205 in Maryland), or write to P.O. Box 3334, Annapolis, MD 21403. Their sailing school here is at St. Petersburg Marina Beach Resort.

## Pari-mutuel Sports

From January to May, watch the greyhounds at **Derby Lane,** St. Petersburg Kennel Club, 10490 Gandy Blvd. NE (tel. 576-1361), a very pretty track and one of the nation's oldest, open daily except Sunday from 7:30pm; matinees also on Monday, Wednesday, and Saturday. You can watch the races from an enclosed grandstand or on television in the plush restaurant. In fall the action moves to Tampa, and in spring and summer to Sarasota. Admission is $1.

---

# 4. The Holiday Isles

---

These sunny isles are every beachcomber's dream, 28 miles of soft sand and all the sun you can soak up. Their history stretches back to wild and woolly days when pirates terrorized these shores, but today the only buccaneer you'll see is a hotel.

These are the beaches for Tampa and St. Petersburg (which are not blessed with much sand of their own). So when winter tourists go home, the hometown folks move in to soak up the sun in a setting that is geographically close, but atmospherically distant.

Waters are shallow and beaches wide. There are quaint fishing villages tucked away here and there, and at the very southern tip of the islands is an artists' and writers' getaway spot with long strips of shady streets and quiet beaches. These are dazzling strips of beach that offer little of the glittering nightlife of larger cities, but all the glittering days you could want.

## WHERE TO STAY

Hotels and motels run the gamut on these islands from small family-owned and family-oriented resorts at inexpensive rates to towering hotels with every amenity. Looking at them is fun, and staying in them is more fun yet. We've arranged them geographically by island, going from Clearwater Beach on the north to Pass-a-Grille Beach on the southern tip of the chain, and in descending order by price.

## Bed and Breakfast

Here in the Suncoast area is a bed-and-breakfast network: **B & B Suncoast Accommodations of Florida,** 8690 Gulf Blvd., St. Petersburg Beach, FL 33706 (tel. 813/360-1753), operated by Danie and Ron Bernard. For information and a list of accommodations, many on or near the water in the $35 to $95 range, double, year round, write them and please enclose a self-addressed stamped envelope.

## Clearwater Beach

This island didn't get its name by chance—it really does have clear water, and pretty strips of beach with the main one right in the middle of town. On it you'll find the **Adam's Mark/Caribbean Gulf Resort,** 430 S. Gulfview Blvd., Clearwater Beach, FL 34630 (tel. 813/443-5714, or toll free 800/231-5858), which is just what its name implies, a combination of Caribbean atmosphere and gulfside location. It towers 14 stories over the sand and has 207 rooms, each with a private balcony. It's definitely a luxury resort. You'll find all kinds of services here, from babysitters to pools for the kiddies and sophisticated entertainment for weary parents. Those Caribbean touches come in with a calypso galley buffet loaded with sandwiches and fresh fruit salads, a 300-seat entertainment lounge with circular bar, and a poolside Tiki bar with steel-drum band. Spacious rooms open onto balconies overlooking the gulf, and those lovely vistas are reflected indoors where contemporary colors and furnishings prevail. Most rooms have two double beds but some offer king-size sleepers. Rates for two at the hotel are $82 to $122 in summer, $112 to $159 in the winter months.

The **Sheraton Sand Key Resort,** 1160 Gulf Blvd., Clearwater Beach, FL 33515 (tel. 813/595-1611, or toll free 800/325-3535), is on a strip of beachside land all by itself just south of Clearwater Beach on Sand Key. Here you'll find an eight-story tower capped by a Sky Lounge where musical groups provide entertainment every night. A very long tiled lobby extends across the entire first floor of the building with a lobby bar, a three-tiered dining room, and boutiques. Rooms are typically Sheraton spacious and decorated in white with muted floral-print bedspreads. They have all the usual accoutrements: color TV, phone, private balcony, even washers and dryers on each floor. Outside, there's a pretty pool and thatch-roofed picnic tables, a pool bar, and tennis courts. Rates at the Sheraton are $118 to $156 in winter months, $84 to $118 in summer.

The **Clearwater Beach Hotel,** at 500 Mandalay Ave., Clearwater Beach, FL 33515 (tel. 813/441-2425), has such a small sign you hardly know it's there. And once you start exploring these exquisite emerald-green grounds covered in vivid blooms, you hardly believe it's there! Seventy modern beach- or garden-front apartments are spread over acres of grounds, and in the main reception area you're swept back to bygone days when this white wood structure housed one of the area's first inns. It still rents those small rooms in winter, but is proud now of new, attractively furnished and spacious accommodations with sliding glass doors and beautiful views. Room 604, with its own small porch wrapped around a corner of the building, is especially nice. Jewel tones are the favorite colors here, and you'll find them everywhere from bedspreads in the paneled rooms to carpeting in the lobby. Guests gather in the hotel's dining room and chatter away at a cherrywood bar behind which reposes an art nouveau creation rescued from a Chicago watering hole. Amusing Victorian prints (one shows a swimming beauty captioned "Not the sea serpent but far more dangerous") line the walls, and in the oval sitting room is a delicately stenciled white piano. There are fresh roses on polished tables, shining brass chandeliers, high-backed cane chairs, and outside, a pool, tennis, and—shades of yesteryear—croquet. Winter rates are $125 to $190 until May 1, when they drop to $75 to $100.

There's a touch of the Greek at **Aegean Sands,** 421 Gulfview Blvd., Clearwater Beach, FL 33515 (tel. 813/447-3464, or toll free 800/331-0735)—actually more than a touch. From Greek lettering on the outside to the identification of rooms (Athena, Apollo) the resort carries out its Mediterranean connection. There are a variety of accommodations, from studio apartments (with a convertible couch and screened-off kitchen plus a separate bedroom) to hotel rooms and apartments. They're all quite spacious and nicely decorated with sturdy wood furnishings and bright tropical colors. Aegean Sands' operators now also own two other adjacent buildings—the Spyglass Motel, dominated by a huge and colorful hot-air balloon mural streaking up one side of the multistory building, and the smaller Goldenbeach Motel. All three have been recently redecorated with new carpets, drapes and kitchenettes, safes and sofa beds and are now known as the **Aegean Spyglass Resorts.** Rates throughout the complex range from $55 to $125 in peak winter months from February to April, and from $43 to $90 in other seasons.

If we were staying a few weeks in Clearwater Beach, we'd seek a room at the **Clearwater Beach Garden Apartments,** 14 Somerset St., Clearwater Beach, FL 33515 (tel. 813/442-8874), and then select their penthouse apartment on the second floor. Beyond a tiled kitchen is a carpeted living room with two convertible couches that open to queen-size beds. On the other side of glass doors is a roofed wooden balcony furnished with puffy lounges and a patio dining table. And beyond that is a view that goes on forever. The friendly folks who run this quiet spot on a beach side street, are happy to show you around their spick-and-span little enclave, which includes 14 units in four buildings and a house. There's no pool, but you can just about dive into the gulf from your apartment. In winter, rates range from $40 to $77; in summer, $35 to $63.

If you like to watch boats gliding by, head for the **Port Vue Resort,** 101 Coronado Dr., Clearwater Beach, FL 33515 (tel. 813/446-7929), which is smack dab on Clearwater's bustling marina and just a block from the beach. Tucked into a narrow space, the Port Vue looks tiny from the street but actually is four floors of spacious rooms and efficiencies with private balconies. There's a heated pool, a boat and fishing dock, a friendly management, and a very convenient location right in the middle of shops, beach, and restaurants. The prices are nice too: Motel units in winter range from $60 to $95 for rooms or efficiencies. In summer, prices drop to about $40 to $55.

Appropriately enough on-the-wing sea gulls decorate the walls at the **Beach Ambassador (Sea Gull Apartment Motel),** 674 Bayway Blvd., Clearwater Beach, FL 33515 (tel. 813/446-2688), where attractive motel rooms and efficiencies in two buildings have refrigerators and two double beds. There's a heated pool, Laundromat, and private dock, and around the corner of a second floor, a wide balcony. In peak season daily rates range from $56 to $95, about $35 to $70 in summer.

The Mediterranean roof tiles and ornate wrought-iron trim at the **New Yorker,** 332 Hamden Dr., Clearwater Beach, FL 33515 (tel. 813/446-2437), don't look much like New York, but the resort does have a touch of that city's fabled sophistication. This trim two-story cluster of apartments once won a chamber of commerce beautification award, and the interior here is just as trim as the brick-trimmed exterior. Newly renovated rooms have refrigerators and the fully equipped efficiencies have plenty of space. The New Yorker is particularly cozy at night when artful lighting reflects in the heated pool and glows in a tiny cupola atop the tiled roof. Prices here are far from New York too: just $56 to $71 double in winter, $33 to $48 in other seasons.

Three generations of the Marsh family (the fourth was born in 1980) have owned and operated the **Shoreline View Motel,** 1941 Edgewater Dr., Clearwater Beach, FL 33515 (tel. 813/446-3390). Here you'll find tastefully decorated one- and two-bedroom apartments and efficiencies, some with balconies (many overlooking the sea). Weekly rates run from $285 to $290 for efficiencies in peak season, dropping to $130 to $145 in other months.

## Belleair Beach

Technically, the **Belleview Biltmore,** 25 Belleview Blvd., Clearwater, FL 33516 (tel. 813/442-6171, or toll free 800/237-8947, in Florida 800/282-8072), isn't in Holiday Isles but in an upper-crust mainland sister of this city, Belleair. Whether or not you decide to spend the money to stay there, you ought to stop by for a look at this gorgeous old place that opened its carved doors in 1897. Another of Henry Plant's creations, the hotel is on 625 rolling acres, which include a golf course and tennis courts. It claims to be the world's largest occupied frame structure and no one's got nerve enough to dispute the claim—there's a 2½-*acre* roof! They called this "Steamboat" architecture, and inside its glowing white facade you'll find leaded-glass ceilings, stained-glass panels, fancy wood trim, glittering boutiques, and dining and dancing every night in winter months. Rooms are as spacious as they are beautifully decorated, and as lovely as the cavernous lobby, which has puffy couches and English hunt prints scattered about among tall columns. There are so many things to see and do here—golf, tennis, swimming, a fancy, new spa—we could go on forever, but that would spoil the fun of seeing it for yourself. From January to late April, the Belleview charges $175 double, with parlor suites at $190 to $290 double a day year round.

Down on Belleair Beach you'll find a strip of imposing private homes whose pastel colors are surrounded by perfectly manicured lawns and complimented by a profusion of flowers. Tucked in among them are motels you'll like as much for their elegant neighborhood as for their own amiable atmosphere.

The **Carriage House Motel,** at 3200 N. Gulf Blvd., Belleair Beach, FL 33540 (tel. 813/595-4787), is one of those two-trim contemporary buildings that look as if they would attract the carriage trade. Both buildings are decorated with handsome contemporary furniture and wall-to-wall carpeting. Maid service is weekly, with towels delivered daily, and there's a free Continental breakfast every morning in winter. Rates are $60 to $75 in summer, $75 to $95 from mid-December to May in the more expensive wing.

**Belleair Beach Resort,** 2040 Gulf Blvd., Belleair Beach, FL 33535 (tel. 813/595-1696), is a trim spot with the Gulf of Mexico on one side of this L-shaped building, a bright blue pool on the other side. In the middle are some contented guests who come here to occupy neat, simply furnished quarters just steps from the sea. Perhaps the single most outstanding feature of this two-story property is its everything-in-its-place neatness. Rates are, as they say, pretty neat too: $65 to $82 for motel rooms, efficiencies, or one-bedroom apartments in peak winter season from mid-January through April, $42 to $62 in other months.

## Indian Rocks Beach

This quiet ribbon of beach got its name from jagged red rocks at the shoreline, but its current claim to fame is a 1,041-foot fishing pier, the longest in Florida. Under it swim mackerel, kingfish, grouper, sea trout, tarpon—all just waiting for your hook.

Bob and Kay Alpaugh operate two apartment motels on this island, **Alpaugh's Gulf Beach Apartments** at 1912 Gulf Blvd., Indian Rocks Beach, FL 34635 (tel. 813/595-9421), the other a few miles away at 68 Gulf Blvd. (tel. 813/595-2589). Both occupy wide strips of beach and have homey one- and two-bedroom apartments, some fronting on the gulf, with less expensive accommodations facing the courtyards. At 1912 there are also screened cottages. At both of these trim and tidy motels rough wood exteriors fit right into the village atmosphere of the island. Neither has a pool, but there's plenty of water just steps away in the gulf. Rates are the same: $450 a week in winter, $350 to $410 in summer, and cheaper yet in fall.

## Redington Beach

Merchants moaned when they heard a new road would pass right over this area dooming them to anonymity. True capitalist spirit prevailed, however, and those moaning merchants turned disaster to delight by creating a pier and wooden walkways with a little village snuggled in between. Today it's called **John's Pass Village,** and is a favorite for tourists and locals alike, a rustic casual enclave every bit like a northern coastal fishing village (except the water's warmer). Just so you won't forget where you are, however, there's a signpost pointing the way to Greenville, Pennsylvania (1,105 miles), and to Chicago (1,157 miles from this sunny spot). In early November the annual John's Pass Seafood Festival here packs 'em in by the thousands.

The **Sails Gulf Terrace Apartment Motel,** 17004 Gulf Blvd., North Redington Beach, FL 33708 (tel. 813/391-6000), is a pristine and pretty operation centered around a sparkling swimming pool. Everything is shipshape here, from the trim dark-wood entranceways to the spacious airy rooms with crisp white bedspreads. Efficiencies and one- and two-bedroom apartments rent for $65 to $80 double from February to May, $43 to $65 in other months.

Another pretty spot is **Sandalwood,** 17100 Gulf Blvd., North Redington Beach, FL 33708 (tel. 813/397-5541), on North Redington Beach. It's a condominium motel wrapped around a pool and atrium that's beautifully lighted at night when this California-looking building sparkles. Because it's a condominium, the accommodations are especially spacious and attractive, with wall-to-wall carpeting, large closets, kitchens, tiled baths, and rates that range from $68 to $90 in winter, $40 to $59 in other months; higher for larger quarters.

You can take your choice of views at **Far Horizons Motel and Condominiums,**

17248 Gulf Blvd., North Redington Beach, FL 33706 (tel. 813/393-8791), where some rooms overlook the Gulf, while others gaze down upon a round swimming pool. That circular pool is reflected in the arches that appear throughout this property and join with roof tiles to give it a touch of Mediterranean flavor. An attractive spot with furnishings that echo those Mediterranean influences, Far Horizons has one-bedroom apartments for $60 to $70 in peak winter season from December to May, $50 to $65 in other months.

A budget selection in Redington Shores is the wildly colorful **Sinbad Motel,** 17819 Gulf Blvd., Redington Shores, FL 33708 (tel. 813/391-1585). One thing for sure: You won't have any difficulty finding its hot-pink splendor. Just look for Sinbad the Sailor Man and the tile sailing ship mural on one wall. Something about Sinbad made us giggle, but not derisively; although this spot is a crazy-quilt of color, its prices are oh-so-sensible; $25 to $35 in summer, $30 to $50 in winter. There are lots of blooming things here, and while not directly on the ocean, it's just across the road and is on the waters of Boca Ciega Bay. There's a small dock and a friendly pelican that often perches there. Rooms are simply furnished in beach basic, but are tidy and clean, and some have a nice view of the bay.

## Madeira Beach

This strip of sand was named after the pine woods (madera) the early explorers found here. You won't see much of that now, but there's still plenty of the sand and sea those courageous fellows loved.

**Sandy Shores,** 12924 Gulf Blvd., Madeira Beach, FL 33708 (tel. 813/392-1281), is an attractive five-story condominium on the beach across from John's Pass Village. All apartments here have been redecorated and have private balconies, some of which overlook the sea. Some are large enough to accommodate six to eight people, and for the space you're renting, rates are reasonable: $78 to $105 a day for a one- or two-bedroom apartment year round. Long visits get a discount too, and pets are welcome for a $30 charge.

If you're yawning after a wearying day at the beach, you can leap into the pool at **Surf Song Resort,** 12960 Gulf Blvd., Madeira Beach, FL 33708 (tel. 813/391-0284, or toll free 800/237-4816), and let the whirlpool massage whip you back into shape. Located right at John's Pass, Surf Song is a spot for independent types who don't mind doing their own housekeeping and are happy with simple but roomy accommodations with a pretty garden patio and sundeck on the beach. Rates are $515 to $700 per week in peak season (the highest rate buys a two-bedroom/two-bath spot for four). In other seasons, rates range between $340 to $600.

On the Boca Ciega Bay side of Gulf Boulevard, **Boca Kee Apartments,** at 14385 Bayshore Dr. N., Madeira Beach, FL 33708 (tel. 813/391-0721), snuggle together in an off-the-beaten-track location along the bayshore. Just three full-size apartments are operated by the Keenes, who have decorated them with cozy homelike touches from wicker chairs to ruffled kitchen curtains. Patt Keene once proudly crowed over her renovations—occasioned by water damage during a hurricane: "The apartments are even nicer now. We had another kitchen fully papered and another papered up to the chair rail. They are as sparkling as ever and were repainted after [the hurricane]. We had lovely carpeting in them before, but the insurance money upgraded even that!" Who can resist that kind of enthusiasm and obvious love of place? Keep at it, Patt.

Each apartment is different, but all have separate bedrooms and convertible couches so they can accommodate four, and in some you can even pack in guest number five. There's wall-to-wall carpeting, color TV, ceramic tile bath, the owners share their swimming pool and deck with you, and all of it's in a quiet residential area just off bustling Gulf Boulevard. Prices range from $350 to $375 a week for a waterfront apartment in peak season. Rates drop in May to $200 to $225, and there are discounts for long stays.

Another bayside money-saver is the **Skyline Motel,** 13999 Gulf Blvd., Madeira

Beach, FL 33708 (tel. 813/391-5817). Units accommodate four here, and some of the 11 efficiencies are large enough for five, and there are five one-bedroom apartments. They're not fancy either, but they're just $55 to $65 in peak season (from February to April), $35 to $40 in summer.

## Treasure Island

If there's one marvelous story that capsulizes Florida's wacky real estate boom, it's the one about Treasure Island. It seems a promoter with low readings on his sales chart had to dream up a way to sell property on this island, so he used a little Florida ingenuity and planted a rumor that treasure was buried here. His scheme didn't get too far, but the name stuck and today it's Treasure Island, where you can indeed find something of value, but it's not likely to be Spanish doubloons.

In the center of the island, the **Bilmar Beach Resort,** 10650 Gulf Blvd., Treasure Island, FL 33740 (tel. 813/360-5531), takes the honors among the higher-priced hotels. It's also one of the largest hotels in the area, although it doesn't seem so since rooms are in three separate buildings. You'll find lots to do here: miniature golf, golf nearby, two pools, 550 feet of beach, tennis courts just six blocks away, a Grog Shoppe pub with entertainment, a beach room where you'll hear Dixieland jazz, and the Grog Shoppe restaurant (prices run $6 to $19). Most rooms have balconies and refrigerators. All are spacious and decorated in modern colors. Two people pay $95 to $110 in the winter months, $75 to $90 in summer.

A little cheaper are the **Quality Inn,** at 11500 Gulf Blvd., Treasure Island, FL 33740 (tel. 813/360-5541, or toll free 800/228-5151), and the **Ramada Inn,** at 12000 Gulf Blvd., Treasure Island, FL 33740 (tel. 813/360-7051, or toll free 800/228-2828). The Quality Inn has 54 rooms, efficiencies, and one-bedroom apartments on the gulf, plus a pool, and charges $75 to $90 in winter, $35 to $50 in summer. The Ramada Inn is also on the beach, and has a pool, whirlpool, playgrounds, and 98 rooms (some with refrigerators) and 23 efficiencies. Rates for two begin at $102 to $122 in peak winter months, $59 to $88 in other months; efficiencies run about $10 additional. There's a dining room and lounge too.

**Howard Johnson** is here as well, at 11125 Gulf Blvd., Treasure Island, FL 33706 (tel. 813/360-6971, or toll free 800/654-2000), with double rates ranging from $73 to $89 in winter, $48 to $66 in summer. HoJo's restaurant is open 24 hours with prices beginning at $4.

If you're a fishing fanatic, the **Delacado,** at 7963 Bayshore Dr., Treasure Island, FL 33706 (tel. 813/360-6362), may be nirvana. Located on Boca Ciega Bay, the Delacado will send you pictures of some prize catches. There are just 14 units here, some with a view of the bay and some on the waterfront. They're basic but serviceable, comfortable, and attractive. A lighted private fishing dock juts out into the bay, suitable for a high dive on a hot day, or for mooring a 30-foot boat, if it comes to that. All apartments here have kitchens and the rates are palatable too: $40 to $55 a week in the off-season and $50 to $60 double in peak season.

On this pirate-conscious coast you'll find a resort called the **Buccaneer,** 10800 Gulf Blvd., Treasure Island, FL 33706 (tel. 813/367-1908, or toll free 800/826-2120), a cheery orange-and-white spot with ornate iron trim. Twelve of the rooms here are efficiencies; all units have color TV and daily maid service. They're medium-size and colorful, and four two-room gulf apartments are big enough for four people. Naturally, a buccaneer wouldn't be far from the water, and this buccaneer has a strip of beach right at the door. From February to May, double rooms and efficiencies are $45 to $79. In other months, prices drop to $30 to $56 double.

A pretty, money-saving place is the **Treasure Island Motel,** 10315 Gulf Blvd., Treasure Island, FL 33706 (tel. 813/367-3055 or 381-9714), which stretches from a swimming pool on Boca Ciega Bay to a private beach on the gulf. The Mediterranean tile roof and painted shutters give this small bayside motel a chipper look. You can paddle in the pool as yachts cruise by or, across Gulf Boulevard, stretch out on the pine-strewn lawn along 600 feet of private beach. Rooms are a somewhat eclectic conglomeration of furnishings, but they're clean, bright, and airy, and some have big picture windows overlooking the water. All have refrigerators and some queen- or king-size beds. In peak season you'll pay $42 to $68 a week double. In other months, rates drop to $24 to $40.

Plunk down in the living room of an apartment at the **Jefferson Motel Apartments,** 10116 Gulf Blvd., Treasure Island, FL 33706 (tel. 813/360-5826), and watch the waves lap away at the sand outside. German owners keep this spot shiny as a new pfennig, from the turf-carpeted walkways outside to the spotless kitchen, baths, and dressing areas inside. The Jefferson would be our choice for a long visit if for no other reason than the pretty view and spacious, clean, and nicely furnished quarters. There are, however, extras: horseshoes, badminton, games, a handsome heated pool and patio, gas barbecue grill, and all that beach. Best of all, you pay only $85 in high season for two people, $55 in summer, with special rates for stays of four weeks or more.

## St. Petersburg Beach

This is St. Petersburg's official beach, and it's the busiest of all the islands. One long strip of motels, restaurants, shops, and souvenirs, it's especially popular with families who crowd over here from St. Petersburg proper (about a half hour's drive away). King of the beach, and the city's pride, is the Don CeSar, an incredible pink hulk that almost saw the wrecker's ball but was saved in the 11th hour by some hard-working, history-conscious citizens. Let's start with a look at this eye-popper even though it's the southernmost hotel on the island.

It hits you like a giant mirage, this wacky mass of turreted pink cement shoving its massive bulk hard against the shoreline. This weird and wonderful cupcake of a building, pink as the icing at a christening, is none other than the **Don CeSar,** St. Petersburg Beach's flagship hotel at 3400 Gulf Blvd., St. Petersburg Beach, FL 33706 (tel. 813/360-1881 collect, or toll free 800/247-9810), the city's pride and (if a bit dumbfounded) its glory. Built in 1928 by a Florida land-boom millionaire who managed to think pink in a way nobody expected, the Don CeSar for some years after the Depression had all the value of a rose-colored elephant. During the war it housed weary airmen, and later Veterans Administration employees. In 1969 when the wrecking ball was on its way, a determined group of historians managed to find a savior who poured seven million greenbacks into these ten-inch-thick walls and re-opened the hotel in 1973. Now it's on the National Register of Historic Places so its bubble-gum facade will remain fanciful, farcical, and presumably here forever. But who cares what flamingo hue they chose for this landmark when inside are such beauties as Austrian crystal chandeliers, ornate trunks from Spain, antique light fixtures from Mexico, and beamed guest rooms with each beam cut to fit individually (there are no two rooms alike in size or decor). Everything that could be kept original here was, from the 13,900 panes of glass to that pink exterior, once so famous it was registered as Don CeSar Rouge. So well built is this bastion that after more than 50 years the Belgian concrete shows not one single crack in wall or floor.

Even if you don't stay here, this spot should be on your must-visit list for it is indeed a sight, from towering lobby to piano entertainment at afternoon cocktails, from grand staircase descending to Olympic-size pool to the candlelit elegance of the award-winning King Charles Restaurant—a glorious place since its halcyon days when it welcomed the likes of F. Scott Fitzgerald and Zelda, Lou Gehrig, Clarence Darrow, Dr. Walter Mayo, and Babe Ruth. If you stay, you can dip tired toes in an outdoor whirlpool bath while islanders strum soothing music, or rent a bike, go drift fishing, sail, or paddle your own canoe.

As the sun goes down in a burning glow of scarlet the mood changes, becoming elegant and dazzling, full of candlelight and canapés. Piano music tinkles delicately in the lobby bar as the last light of evening glitters on the sea beyond the windows of the award-winning King Charles Restaurant. Toss a few pennies into the fifth-floor fountain to ensure your return to the magic of Don CeSar. Rates are $175 to $195 in winter, higher for suites. You'll pay $115 to $145 in summer.

It's always wonderful to see what can be done with a happy combination of imagination and, let's face it, money. You can see what the two can do at **Tradewinds Beach Resort,** 5500 Gulf Blvd., St. Petersburg Beach, FL 33706 (tel. 813/367-6461, or toll free 800/237-0707, 800/282-5553 in Florida). What an amazing place this is! For openers, you can chug to your room on a motorized gondola, and when you've unpacked, wander through the resort's maze of beachfront grounds, clattering over wooden spans bridging tiny canals that curve and curl around lawns and into pools. If the lure of all that water proves too much for you, you can jump in a pedalboat and captain yourself through the waterways. Out in front a long strip of sugary sand awaits. Have a cookout on the resort's Picnic Island, dining on viands you can pick up at the resort's deli and general store. There are four swimming pools and an enclosed pool here, whirlpool on the beachfront, a sauna, sundecks, waterfalls, fountains, canoes, a health center, tennis and racquetball courts, an electronic game room, putting green, croquet court, sailboats, and windsurfers—whew!

Hotel rooms here are called efficiencies, thanks to the presence of wet bars with sink, refrigerator, coffee maker, and toaster. Quarters termed one-bedroom suites have complete kitchens with stove and other appliances. You can leave the cooking to them at a chic gourmet dining spot that features an outstanding Sunday brunch and elegant candlelight dinners in the $15 to $20 range. Or you can nip into two other more moderately priced dining spots here.

You'll know you're somewhere special the second you set foot in the lobby, where rainbow-hued parrots chirp and twitter amid trees that thrive in the sunlight that filters through a central skylight and French doors leading to a flower-bedecked courtyard. A handsomely elaborate resort, Tradewinds charges $149 to $225 in high season, higher for suites. In summer, from April through mid-December, the resort charges $82 to $150.

**Sandpiper Resort Hotel,** 6000 Gulf Blvd., St. Petersburg Beach, FL 33706 (tel. 813/360-5551, or toll free 800/237-0707), is a massive Y-shaped six-story building, and its claim to fame is a swimming pool with a roof that slides open, making this the only enclosed pool in the area. That's only the beginning, however, for there's also an outside pool, tennis courts, a game room, a general store, sailboats, and a gift shop, plus a Brown Derby beef and seafood chain restaurant, a snackbar and a pub, not to mention a gorgeous wide strip of beach and four shuffleboard courts. In high season (from mid-February through mid-April), rates are $109 to $218 for double motel rooms or one-bedroom suites, dropping in summer to $65 to $146.

It's sometimes hard to tell just when a dolphin is happy, but presumably those that occasionally frolic off the beach of the **Dolphin Beach Resort,** formerly the Happy Dolphin Inn, 4900 Gulf Blvd., St. Petersburg Beach, FL 33706 (tel. 813/360-7011, or toll free 800/237-8916), are smiling. Guests at this 21-acre resort certainly have plenty to smile about: 174 large rooms with double beds, vanity baths, color TVs, and kitchenettes; and a restaurant and lounge, serving beef and seafood, with entertainment nightly; plus a gift shop, a package liquor store, a heated swimming pool on landscaped ground, a white sand beach, and a 24-hour shopping area nearby. Room rates here are moderate, ranging from $58 to $80 in summer and $88 to $108 ($10 more for kitchens) in winter.

They come from miles around to dine and dance atop the round **St. Petersburg Beach Hilton Inn,** at 5250 Gulf Blvd., St. Petersburg Beach, FL 33706 (tel. 813/360-1811, or toll free 800/HILTONS). A favorite gathering spot for residents and visitors alike, the Top of the Hilton offers a glamorous revolving view from gulf to bay, with exotic prints in the Bali-Hi lounge, and excellent Polynesian and American delicacies in the $12 to $20 price range. This Hilton occupies its own strip of St. Petersburg Beach where you can seek solace at the poolside bar. Ride a glass elevator to the 152 spacious rooms newly decorated with contemporary furnishings in bright colors. An 11-story building, the inn has a coffee shop, that Bali-Hi revolving lounge, and a disco with nightly entertainment. Rates range from $100 to $145 in winter, $80 to $110 in summer.

The **Breckenridge Resort Hotel,** 5700 Gulf Blvd., St. Petersburg Beach, FL 33706 (tel. 813/360-1833, or toll free 800/828-3871, in Florida 800/392-5700), features a beachside swimming pool and patio surrounded by a string of Roman columns. A seven-story hotel right on the gulf, the Breckenridge has bright efficiencies, some with balconies overlooking the sea, plus tennis courts and a game room, a supper club and lounge with entertainment to the wee hours. From December to May rates range from $110 to $122, depending on location, and in other months drop to $82 to $90.

If a condominium vacation appeals to you, **Isla del Sol,** at 6355 Gulf Blvd., St. Petersburg Beach, FL 33706 (tel. 813/367-3751), is an appealing spot. Located between St. Petersburg and St. Petersburg Beach on Boca Ciega Bay, Isla del Sol has one- and two-bedroom apartments, a golf course, tennis courts, the Island House restaurant and lounge, plus card rooms and swimming rooms for each of several clusters of apartments. A large development with beautifully decorated apartments and landscaped grounds, Isla del Sol charges $525 a week from December through April, and $385 in summer for a two-bedroom/two-bath apartment. One-bedrooms are $350 a week in winter, $280 a week in summer, and there's a two-week minimum rental.

Kick off your shoes and unwind in the shade of a thatched beach hut at the **Beachcombers Resort Hotel,** 6200 Gulf Blvd., St. Petersburg Beach, FL 33706 (tel. 813/367-1902, or toll free 800/237-0707; in Florida 800/282-5553). Stroll down paths that wind through manicured lawns bordered by palms and snuggle up to something cool at the roofed beach bar. Any beachcomber should be happy here, where spacious motel rooms and efficiencies are decorated in tropical colors, with deep pile carpeting and lots of wood paneling and trim. There's also a large heated pool, a beachwear/surf shop, and windsurfer rentals, plus all the usual amenities from phones to game room to color TV and free parking. Double rates are in the $80 to $130 range in winter and $50 to $85 in summer.

**El Sirata Best Western Apartment Motel,** 5390 Gulf Blvd., St. Petersburg Beach, FL 33706 (tel. 813/367-2771), is a gulfside resort with a variety of accommodations including efficiencies, hotel rooms, and apartments, every one of them with a glassy view of the gulf. Splash in two swimming pools, play on the resort's shuffleboard courts, or relax in the lounge or TV room. There's a coin laundry to make that chore simple, and a restaurant for snacking. Rooms are clean and attractive, and there's a lovely strip of beach to roam. Rates are $75 to $130 from January to May, and $77 to $110 in other months.

There's a wide variety of accommodations at the **Alden Resort Motel,** 5900 Gulf Blvd., St. Petersburg Beach, FL 33706 (tel. 813/360-7081, or toll free in Florida 800/262-3464), almost anything you want from small apartments to a three-bedroom/three-bath suite for 12 people. Alden has several attractive buildings on the gulf: motel rooms and villas are in ground-level buildings with covered porches; most other apartments are in three- to six-story buildings facing the gulf or near one of the hotel's two swimming pools. There are two tennis courts and two Jacuzzis. Rates range from $99 to $132 for efficiency suites and one-bedroom apartments from February to May, $74 to $96 in summer, lower in fall.

**Palm Crest Resort Motel,** 3848 Gulf Blvd., St. Petersburg Beach, FL 33706 (tel. 813/360-9327), offers you a chance to get some of that famous Florida sand in your shoes on their private strip of silica. Palm Crest has a shady central garden plot, and there's a large pool right at beachside. Accommodations are available here for $52 to $64 double in winter, and $32 to $44 in summer.

Two white plaster horses and a row of stately columns welcome you to the **Col-**

onial **Gateway Inn,** 6300 Gulf Blvd., St. Petersburg Beach, FL 33706 (tel. 813/ 367-2711), where there's still another welcome surprise—a branch of the Sweden House Smörgåsbord restaurant operates here. Kiddies can splash in their own pool and romp in a special play area, while tired progenitors paddle in an Olympic-size splasher or comb the resort's 800-foot beach. Paneled walls line rooms with basic furnishings trimmed in bright tropical colors. You'll find all the amenities, right down to a Swigam pool bar, at prices ranging from $56 to $79 in summer, $66 to $104 in winter.

**Carlida Apartments and Motel,** 610 69th Ave., St. Petersburg Beach, FL 33706 (tel. 813/360-7233), likes to say it's large enough to serve you, small enough to know you. If you like to be more than a number, it's certainly possible at this small apartment motel, which features a pool and jungly tropical landscaping, including a tinkling dolphin fountain. Carlida is just a few steps from the beach, and offers accommodations including cable color TV and fully carpeted rooms. Efficiencies, rooms, and apartments with simple furnishings run $28 to $50, year round.

Another bright spot on St. Petersburg Beach is **Cadillac,** at 3828 Gulf Blvd., St. Petersburg Beach, FL 33706 (tel. 813/360-1748); it's on the gulf but it also has an annex on the bay. Rooms or apartments here range from $51 to $79 in winter, about $29 to $50 in the summer.

## Pass-a-Grille Beach

Robert Ripley, of "Believe It or Not" fame, called this village's beachside 8th Street "America's shortest and most beautiful main street." It is short indeed, and it's also beautiful, with palm-fringed beaches and aqua waters stretched out alongside it.

One of Florida's oldest vacation beaches, Pass-a-Grille got its odd name from early maps, which showed this settlement on Long Key as Passe-aux-Grilleurs, a reference to fishermen who used this point of land to cross over the island and stopped to grill their meals. A few American garbles later, and *voilà!* Pass-a-Grille.

Whatever you call it, it's a quiet little spit of land with a wide, wide beach that's usually overlooked by beach goers, who head for the livelier strips.

At the very end of the island where gulf and bay waters mingle is the last resort, **Island's End,** 1 Pass-a-Grille Way, St. Petersburg Beach, FL 33706 (tel. 813/360-5023), which gets our vote for the most scenic spot on the Suncoast. Island's End was the creation of Enid and Ken Swanson, who retired here and worked harder after retirement than they did before to get this cluster of cottages into the apple-pie order you'll see here. Now Jone and Millard Gamble, experienced innkeepers, have purchased Island's End and are carrying on the traditions established by the Swansons.

Gray weathered-wood walkways wind between four small buildings that house one-bedroom and efficiency apartments, then meander past the Gambles' own wood-and-glass aerie. There are flowers everywhere, a gazebo, covered patios, and a view that goes on to . . . perhaps Mexico? We must admit we're especially infatuated with the three-bedroom house, which sports a screened pool overlooking a sensational ocean view and homey, comfortable furniture. All the kitchens are new too, and much of the furniture is quite contemporary. The one-bedroom villas can comfortably accommodate four and rent for $425 to $520 a week in peak season, $385 to $445 in summer, a bit less in fall and spring. That house (easily big enough for six) is $120 to $135 a day, year round. When you work that out per person for six, it spells *bargain.*

## Tierra Verde

On what used to be called Cabbage Island you'll find an imposing resort called **Tierra Verde Island Yacht and Tennis Resort,** 200 Madonna Blvd., Tierra Verde, FL 33715 (tel. 813/867-8611). It's a dramatic place where you can settle in for an exhilarating visit or a loafer's holiday surrounded by the best that modern decor has to offer. Apartment accommodations here are dramatically tropical: royal-blue carpeting with matching blue-and-white spreads, white wicker furniture, a wall of glass, deep camel carpeting, and beige-and-white decor. The public rooms, too, are dramatic: wicker furniture in vivid colors, a slick piano bar. Outside is a marina, tennis, and an Olympic-size swimming pool. Dramatic indeed for Cabbage Island, and even the prices are a bit of a surprise: $80 to $125 double from December to May, $60 to $105 in other months.

## WHERE TO DINE

Some fine chefs have settled on these beaches and created restaurants recognized statewide for excellence. We've divided them up again geographically by island. The prices we've cited are for entrées.

### Clearwater Beach

From the "back to the farm" fried chicken to the relish tray and home-baked gingerbread muffins, **Heilman's Beachcomber,** at 447 Mandalay Ave. (tel. 442-4144), goes after all-American diners and lures them here in droves to this beamed-ceiling, plant-bedecked dining room. Owner-host Bob Heilman is the third generation of Heilmans to seek fame and fortune in the restaurant business since the family began back in Loraine, Ohio, in 1920. Works of local artists adorn the walls and a pianist offers quiet entertainment for dining on a wide selection of beef and seafood dishes, including Boston haddock flown in from Beantown. Of course, there's that famous fried chicken accompanied by fluffy whipped potatoes, relishes, fresh vegetables, biscuits, and gravy. Heilman's is open daily from 11:30am to midnight (from noon to 10pm on Sunday). Dinner prices are in the $10 to $21 range.

Florida restaurants either change every few years or hang on for decades—the **Pelican,** 470 Mandalay Ave. (tel. 442-3151), has managed to do both. Back in the 1930s Henry Henriquez started with a curbside fried-shrimp dispensary and hung gamely on through a 1974 fire that destroyed everything except the driftwood pelican mascot (which you'll see nesting happily on his new perch in the piano bar). The Pelican is a massive spot with red cedar beams and continues in its new avant-garde costume to lure those by now addicted to the Pelican's original stuffed shrimp mixed with lobster and crab. Grouper Grand Marnier is a good selection too, and the restaurant's bread pudding has a devoted following. Most dinner entrées are in the $10 to $17 range. The Pelican is open from 11:30am to 11pm daily, to 10pm Sunday.

Over on the mainland in Clearwater, the **Kapok Tree Restaurant,** at 923 McMullen-Booth Rd. (tel. 726-0504), is the Walt Disney World of restaurants—a fantasyland of lush formal gardens, classic statuary, bubbling fountains, and enough objets d'art replicas to make the Louvre blanch. This is simple food so you may not have the most memorable gourmet experience of a lifetime, but you'll certainly be visually overwhelmed. A massive porte cochère is supported by ten five-ton cast-stone caryatids. Palms soar skyward in a block-long glass arcade. A fat gold cherub clings to the neck of a swan atop an ornate fountain. It's definitely an experience. Average prices for an extremely wide variety of selections are in the $10 to $16 range. The Kapok Tree is open from noon to 10pm daily.

Also over on the mainland is **Siple's Garden Seat,** 1234 Druid Rd. (tel. 442-9681), which does indeed have a garden seat just like the one grandpa and grandma sat on in their courting days. However, it's not the seat but some steady good cooking that's been packing them in here for more than 60 years. A picturesque spot overlooking the Intracoastal Waterway, Siple's has a long menu ranging from 'gator meat to shrimp curry with plenty of simpler cookery in between, like scallops with fettuccine or ham with pineapple sauce. A condiment tray of relishes and sweet cherries is an unusual touch here, as are the aromatic loaves of banana bread. Dinner at this award-winning spot averages $10 to $15 a person, although there are a number of items for less. Open from 11:30am to 3pm and 5 to 9:30pm daily (closed in May).

Back on the beach, **Calico Jack's,** in the Adams Mark/Caribbean Gulf Resort Hotel, 430 S. Gulfview Blvd. (tel. 442-4442), is a popular spot for steamed clams and apple grunt served amid antiques and plants. Prices start at about $5 for dinner, and hours are 11am to 11pm daily.

If you like cool, dark interiors in a straightforward steak-and-seafood house, **Bombay Bicycle Club,** at 2721 Gulf-to-Bay Blvd. at the Clearwater Mall Shopping Center (tel. 799-1841), provides exactly that. Just over the causeway from the beach, BBC draws a youthful crowd to its nightly entertainment, and attracts diners of all ages with Mexicana, Italiano, good steaks, and seafood in the $10 to $12 range. Sneak in daily for meals, served from 11:30am to 2am. Recorded music and a record spinner provide entertainment until 2am nightly.

Yes, **Tio Pepe's,** 2930 Gulf-to-Bay Blvd. (tel. 799-3082), has Spanish food, but this is no taco parlor. Here you dine on top-quality preparations with Spanish touches that are neither foreign to the American palate nor entirely American. Add to the very good steaks, excellent shrimp, good salads, and top-flight seafood a little sangría salute. Nestled into a cozily understated setting, Tio Pepe's makes for a pleasant little dining adventure. You'll pay from $12 to $18 for dinner. Olés can be heard here from 11am to 2:30pm Tuesday through Friday, and 5 to 11pm daily except Monday, with hours on Sunday abbreviated to 4 to 10pm.

## Indian Rocks Beach

Josiane La Fosse Marin and chef Alex Aubery host what can be a spectacularly good evening at **La Cave,** 1701 N. Gulf Blvd. (tel. 595-6009). La Cave occupies what looks like a tiny house with rough wood interiors and a bistro air. Skilled French cookery draws such crowds that reservations are requested. A new fish dish, the blaff, sounds interesting, but you can't go wrong sticking to the house specialty, beef creole, or coquilles St-Jacques, or the scampi maison. It's open from 5 to 10pm, closing at 9pm Sunday, with prices in the $10 to $22 range.

## Redington Shores/Madeira Beach

If, after all the jokes about the lobster color of your skin following a day in the Florida sun, you are focused on lobster, drop into **The Lobster Pot,** 17814 Gulf Blvd., Redington Shores (tel. 391-8592). Dine in a quaint atmosphere on such choices as baked stuffed Florida black grouper or broiled deep-sea scallops. Appetizers include homemade soups and chowders, salmon, herring, clams, oysters, and a spicy seafood crêpe. Dinners are served with fresh vegetables and salad topped with a house dressing of garlic and spices. The finale is mouthwatering apple fritters, cheesecake, or Florida banana fritters. You'll pay $10 to $17 for entrées at this very popular restaurant, open from 4:30 to 10pm daily, later on weekends.

You'll need all the attentive service you get here after you've spent some time searching for **Paradise Pier,** John's Pass Village, Madeira Beach (tel. 393-1824), a teensy ramshackle spot beneath the pier at John's Pass Village. It's right up against the water under the walkways, but you have to keep a keen eye out for the sign and bend low as you enter. You can almost always find stone crab claws here, and this is the perfect rustic atmosphere to dig into those shells. Fish is straight off the boat and perfectly cooked, so go before 7pm or be prepared to take a number and wait for a place in Paradise. Prices are in the $6 to $10 range, including salad, hush puppies, and french fries. It's closed on Monday and Tuesday, open other days from 11:30am to 3pm and 5 to 9pm, to 11pm on weekends.

With a name like Ted Sonnenschein you're sure to settle in Florida sooner or later (it means sunshine). One founder of the **Wine Cellar,** at 17307 Gulf Blvd., N. Redington Beach (tel. 393-3491), Sonnenschein did just that and got at least part of his credentials at the Old Swiss House in Busch Gardens. Now chefs Karl Kumpp and Peter Schuckert prepare such favorites as choucroûte alsacienne with weisswürst, thuringer, smoked pork and sauerkraut, and Swiss cheese soup in his own popular restaurant. You can walk out of here yodeling over the cuisine and the check, which is likely to run only about $10 to $15 a person. Wine Cellar cracks a bottle daily from 4:30 to 10pm, with a lounge open to 1:30am.

**READER'S RESTAURANT RECOMMENDATION:** "We have a winter home in St. Petersburg and eat out often. I think you should consider including **Leverock's Seafood House on the Bay** of Madeira Beach in your next edition. It has the right price, delicious fresh seafood, superb location on Boca Ciega Bay just over the causeway from Madeira, and two pet pelicans Abercrombie and Fitch" (Julia Gaskill, Memphis, Tenn.). [*Author's Note:* Leverock's has long been a popular restaurant in the Tampa Bay area and is located at 565 150th Ave. at the Madeira Beach Causeway, right at the bridge (tel. 393-0459). It's open daily from 11:30am to 10pm and offers a wide variety of seafood selections, plus barbecued ribs, frogs' legs, steak, and chicken for prices in the $6 to $10 range for most options.]

## Treasure Island

Stained-glass windows, yellow light from old lamps, rich woodwork, a brick fireplace, and cozy booths—what else could it be but the **Grogg Shoppe Restaurant,** in the Bilmar Beach Resort, 10650 Gulf Blvd. (tel. 360-5531). English hunter's pie and prime ribs with Yorkshire pudding, too. Prices from $8. Open from 7am to 10pm daily.

## St. Petersburg Beach

One would hope not to emerge *gordo* (fat) from **El Gordo's,** at 7815 Blind Pass Rd. (tel. 360-5947), but one shouldn't count on it. Tacos and tamales, refried beans, tostadas, chili rellenos, guacamole—all so inexpensive *gordo* may be inevitable. What do I mean by inexpensive? How's a top price of $7.75 sound? Lots of "south of the border" atmosphere (just don't trip over the sleeping sombrero man) in two tiny dining rooms à la cantina. Open from 11am to 10pm daily, till 8pm Sunday.

Somewhere in all of us lurks the hermit-desire. In Silas Dent the desire not only lurked, it lived as did he on deserted Cabbage Key whence he rowed on occasion to the mainland to pick up some beans. Old Silas is about as close as this Suncoast can come to a folk hero, so they honored him in inimitable Florida style: with a restaurant named after him. **Silas Dent's,** at 5501 Gulf Blvd. (tel. 360-6961), looks pretty much like what Silas called home too, a haphazard collection of weathered wood and some stuff lying around outside. Inside, however, things are spiffy enough to draw crowds from miles around to dine on Shell Man's Oyster Bar and very good shellfish and seafood—even alligator. Dinners are $8 to $15, and Dent's is open from 5 to 10pm Sunday through Thursday, to 11pm on Friday and Saturday. Entertainment nightly from 9:30pm.

A must-see, if not also a must-stop, spot is the **Pelican Diner** (tel. 363-9873), one of the last of those old-time honest-to-goodness road food places, metal trailer and all, parked at 7501 Gulf Blvd. at 75th Street. An art deco delight, the Pelican serves up simple stick-to-the-ribs cuisine à la Alice's Restaurant for prices in the $5 bracket. It's open 24 hours (except 11:30am Sunday to 7am Monday)—"Never fear, someone's here."

## NIGHTLIFE

Nearly every major hotel and many smaller ones offer evening entertainment that changes regularly all year round. Some of the best and liveliest spots in town are the mirrored lounge high atop the **Hilton Inn** on St. Petersburg Beach, rooftop dining and dancing at the **Holiday Inn** and **Tradewinds Hotel,** entertainment at the **Beachcombers Resort,** and show groups at the **Caribbean Gulf** in Clearwater.

For easy listening there's a piano bar at a restaurant called **Ten Beach Drive,** at 10 Beach Dr. (tel. 823-0629), and jazz fans should head for the **Hurricane Lounge,** Ninth Avenue and Gulf Way (tel. 360-9558) on Pass-a-Grille Beach, where there's usually some serious jamming going on.

The **Breckenridge Hotel** on St. Petersburg Beach has entertainment every night, and a show on Sunday at the pool deck. There's more Hawaiian entertainment and island music at **Trader Frank's** in the Tiki Gardens attraction. San Francisco's Royal Polynesians play steel guitar music of the island in the **Wikiwiki Lounge** here.

**Palace at Feather Sound** is now an institution in local nightlife, occasionally in more ways than one. If you want to see what that means, hie on over to this zippy, multilevel spot at 2675 Ulmerton Rd., Clearwater (tel. 572-0708). There's always a lively time at this attractive club, which is open 11:30am to 2am daily except Sunday, opening at 6pm Saturday.

## SPORTS

There isn't much room for golf courses on these islands, but you'll find plenty of tennis courts and enough water sports to keep you splashing.

### Golf

Head over to the mainland where St. Petersburg has a number of fine courses, or to Clearwater where the **Clearwater Country Club,** 525 Betty Lane (tel. 443-5078), charges $15 to $35 year round, including shared cart to play the club's 18-hole course.

### Tennis

In Clearwater you can play on any of 17 courts at **McMullen Tennis Complex,** 1000 Edenville St. (tel. 462-6144), which charges about $2 an hour for day or night play. There are nine free courts at **Bayfront Municipal Courts,** 3 Pierce St. (tel. 462-6531).

On Treasure Island, there are 22 courts at the **Racquet Club,** and some are lighted. You can call for reservations at 360-6062.

**St. Petersburg Tennis Center,** 650 18th Ave. South (tel. 894-4378), has 15 Har Tru courts and a clubhouse open from 9am to dark. In Indian Shores, **Belleview Gulf Beach and Tennis Club,** at 18400 Gulf Blvd. (tel. 595-2551), has courts.

**Recreation centers** for all areas are listed under government agencies in the *Yellow Pages,* and can direct you to specific sports equipment nearby. St. Petersburg's recreation department is at 893-7441.

### Water Sports

If you want to go diving, call **Scuba Services,** 5208 34th St. S., in Madeira Beach (tel. 822-3483), which has complete equipment and instructions for both beginners and professional divers. Dive trips begin at $40.

**Windsurfing** is the latest in water sports: It combines the windpower of sailing and the tipsy-doodle of a surfboard. You can try it out at **Windsurfing Florida Suncoast** at the Beachcomber Resort on St. Petersburg Beach (tel. 360-3783). On Clearwater Beach, **West Coast Water Sports,** 464 N. Gulfview Blvd. (tel. 443-1902), can also get you windsurfing. Rates for boards are $10 to $15 an hour and lessons are available.

Sailors can get out there and sail the briny blue with the help of **Suncoast Sail Center,** Clearwater Beach Marina, 65 Causeway Blvd. (tel. 581-4662). Power- and sailboats are for rent here, with small sailboats going for $15 an hour. Small power boats run $15 to $20 an hour, $50 to $70 a half day at Beach Motorboats next door (tel. 446-5503). Sailboats can be rented behind the hotels on St. Petersburg Beach.

**Parasailing** is another wacky new water sport that uses a parachute to get you up in the air behind a powerboat. You can play at this by locating the parachuters at **Captain Mike's** behind the **Dolphin Resort Hotel,** 4900 Gulf Blvd. (tel. 360-1998) and **Colonial Gateway Inn,** 6300 Gulf Blvd., St. Petersburg Beach (tel. 367-2711). Rides are $35.

**Jet-skis** are waterskis that think they're motorcycles. Try them out at **Don Cesar Hotel**, 3400 Gulf Blvd. (tel. 360-1881).

## Fishing and Boating

If you'd like to go out on the sea but let someone else do the driving, call Capt. Memo of **Memo's Pirate Cruise**, 25 Causeway Blvd., Slip #3 (tel. 446-2587), who is always around the Clearwater Beach Marina. He shouldn't be hard to spot: He wears an eye patch, knee pants, and assorted pirate gear. For $23 to $25 ($10 for children under 12), he'll escort you and his other passengers in oho-me-bucko style on a bright red pirate ship to a deserted island for shelling, sunning, and picnics complete with free wine and beer. Memo leaves daily at 10am, and 2 and 5pm, and part of the treat is Memo himself, who has traded for pearls in Panama and cruised the Pacific.

**Suncoast Sailing Center**, at the Clearwater Beach Marina (tel. 581-4662), has two sailings daily, morning and afternoon, for $19.50 a person on a 38-foot yacht, and $22.50 for a ride on a 65-foot island schooner. The anchor is weighed at 10am, and 1:30 and 5:30pm daily.

Fishermen have lots of choices: free, a few dollars, or many dollars. If free sounds good, just look around you and you'll see **fishing piers** soaring out over the water like benedictions to Neptune. Every community has one, and the catch from these piers can be as spectacular as if you'd spent a bundle.

Izaak Walton types swear by **Big Pier 60** at Clearwater Beach (tel. 446-0060), open from 8am to midnight. **Big Indian Rocks Pier** (tel. 595-5494) at Indian Rocks Beach is open 24 hours. **Redington Long Pier** on Redington Beach (tel. 391-9398) is open night and day. Fees for the piers are $2 or $4 for adults, $1 for children, just 50¢ at Redington.

At **Fort Desoto** (tel. 866-9191) there are two free piers: Pier 2 is open 24 hours, Pier 1 from 7am to 8pm.

**Fishing boats** called party boats sail on full- and half-day expeditions for about $20 a person for an all-day trip, including tackle and bait. Among the boats operating in the area are **King's Fish Marina** (tel. 391-6111) on Madeira Beach, and *Dixie*, *Super*, and *Queen Fleet* at Clearwater Marina (tel. 446-7666). *Florida Fisherman* at **Passport Marina** in Madeira Beach (tel. 393-1947) also has overnight trips for varying prices, including berth.

For freshwater fishing, have a go at **Bass Fishing Heaven**, 8801 Seminole Blvd., which is US 19A (tel. 392-4817), in Seminole.

---

# 5. Sarasota

Silk scarves spill over a counter, an emerald glitters on black velvet, frothy soft fabrics rustle in posh shops. Streets lined with manicured lawns are cut to the inch and lined with white statues gazing benignly down on their mini-empire. That's Sarasota, glamour girl of the west coast, western Florida's answer to Palm Beach.

It's strange to think that the man who built this opulent city filled with elegant mansions and smart shops was a circus king! But there it is: This is the city of John Ringling, granddaddy of Ringling Brothers Circus, who built a home here that cost $2 million—and that was in the 1920s! Sparing nothing, he installed solid-gold bathroom fixtures and filled the manse with so many treasures you'll think you've stepped into a European palace.

However spangled and gaudy his circus, Ringling himself was an art lover and amassed one of the nation's most outstanding collections of baroque and Renaissance art, including a large Rubens collection he bought for just $150,000! When he died, the circus king gave it all, including his fortune and his magnificent estate, to the people of Florida.

Encouraged by Ringling, many artists began to settle here. In recent years the city has been home to author John D. MacDonald (Travis McGee mystery creator), MacKinlay Kantor, *Alley Oop* creator V.T. Hamlin, Syd Solomon, and Spanish artist Julion de Diego.

It's worth a trip to this charming city just to see the repertory theater productions staged in the baroque elegance of tiny jewel-box Asolo Theater, which cost $1.5 million and was brought here piece by piece from Italy. All year long you'll find players' groups performing anywhere they can find an audience. You can tour some of the nation's best-known art galleries and hear top concerts and opera in a culture-happy city that when it isn't calling itself the Palm Beach of the west coast is humbly laying claim to the title of "Cultural Capital of Florida."

## GETTING THERE

**Sarasota Airport** welcomes American, Continental, Delta, Midway, Northwest, TWA, and United.

You can also get here on **Greyhound/Trailways** buses (tel. toll free 800/237-8211); **Amtrak** trains (tel. 800/USA-RAIL) stop in St. Petersburg and Tampa.

## GETTING AROUND

There are the usual dozens of **rental-car companies,** topped by Alamo and Greyhound's budget-wise fleets, with Hertz, Avis, Budget, Dollar, and Lindo's following closely behind.

**Sarasota County Area Transit (SCAT) buses** (tel. 951-5851 for route information) travel throughout Sarasota County from dawn to dusk for 50¢, and when all else fails you can take a taxi for which you'll pay $2.80 for the first mile, $1.40 for succeeding miles. Some taxi companies in the area are **Yellow Cab** (tel. 955-3341), and **Diplomat Cab** (tel. 366-9822) which serves the airport and has executive sedans.

Limousines plying the area include **Airport Limousine** (tel. 355-9645), which serves the Tampa airport too. From Sarasota Airport, limo fees are $10 to $12; from Tampa, they're about $40.

## USEFUL INFORMATION

For **medical or police emergencies,** call the Sarasota County sheriff at 366-1811 or dial 0 (zero) for operator. . . . For non-emergency **medical or dental help,** call the county's health clinic, 2200 Ringling Blvd. (tel. 365-2020). . . . **All-Night Chevron,** at 4130 S. Tamiami Trail (tel. 921-1056), can help with car repairs and gasoline 24 hours a day. . . . **Eckerd's Drugs,** 3800 S. Tamiami Trail in the Crossroads Shopping Center (tel. 955-3328), is open until midnight. . . . **Denny's,** at 8214 S. Tamiami Trail (tel. 966-2626), is open for food service around the clock.

## TOURIST INFORMATION

You'll find some friendly faces at the **Sarasota Chamber of Commerce,** 1551 2nd St., Sarasota, FL 33577 (tel. 813/955-8187), where somebody always knows the answer to your questions. . . . **Longboat Key** has its own chamber of commerce, 510 Bay Isles Rd., Sarasota, FL 33548 (tel. 813/383-1212), as does **Siesta Key,** at 5481 Riverbluff Circle, Sarasota, FL 33578 (tel. 813/924-9696). . . . **Bradenton** also has a chamber of commerce, at 222 10th St. West, Bradenton, FL 33509 (tel. 813/748-3411). . . . Sarasota has a **Visitor and Convention Center** at 655 N. Tamiami Trail, Sarasota, FL 33577 (tel. 957-1877), which has lots of information on what to see and do in the area. . . . **Weather info** at 645-2506.

## WHERE TO STAY

When you're looking for someplace to stay in Sarasota, you have three sandy places to look and one commercial district. If sand is what you came here for (with a little sun and ocean tossed in), then you'll want to concentrate on Lido Key,

Longboat Key, or Siesta Key. If you're here to sightsee, you'll be a little closer to attractions if you select from some of the choices on US 41, but you'll have to sacrifice ocean frontage. Whichever area you choose, you'll find a variety of resorts, both small and moderately priced or large and beautiful with price tags to match. No matter where you are you'll never be more than 20 minutes or so from a beach. Let's start with the southernmost island, Siesta Key, and move north.

## Siesta Key

Old-timers hereabouts lament the growth that's turned the once-tropical jungle of Siesta Key into a popular beachfront getaway spot for both mainland residents and visitors. There's no doubt it's changed over the years. These days there are many condominiums on this quiet key, but it's still a lovely, jungly, offbeat spot where you'll find a number of small family-owned motels with moderate prices. There are beaches galore, from a large public beach with concession stands to tiny Turtle Beach, where you can picnic beside a lagoon in an atmosphere that's been touched just enough by human hands to make it comfortable.

To get to Siesta Key, take US 41 to County Road 789, which leads you directly onto the key. You'll find it easily by following the Siesta Key signs posted on US 41.

There must be something about this island that stirs creativity for this is a favorite residence of writers and artists, including Travis McGee's creator, mystery writer John MacDonald, who fled the east coast for a hideaway here.

One of the easiest ways to locate a stopping spot on Siesta Key is to seek out **Sara-sea Circle,** a few miles from the entrance to the key. Here 11 motels have gathered their wagons into a circle around a central entertainment area with shuffleboard courts, a playground, a pool, and a beach they all share. All the motels are small, moderately priced properties, perfect examples of those resorts the world calls "mom and pop" operations. They're so similar in design and direction that choosing among them can be easy: Just pick your favorite color.

Red is somebody's favorite color at red-trimmed and flower-bedecked **Tropical Shores Inn,** 6717 Sara-sea Circle, Sarasota, FL 34242 (tel. 813/349-3330). The owners are as talented with interior design as they are with landscaping—and that's talented. There are flowers everywhere here, from bright-red geraniums to orange bachelor buttons, hanging plants on porches, greenery climbing lattices. We even went beak-to-beak with a pair of nesting warblers so content they barely glanced up! Tropical Shores has a cozy little annex on the right side of Sara-sea Circle as you face the sea, where small sitting rooms and picture windows offer a view of plants and curving gravel drive, ocean and heated pool. Like most motels here, Tropical Shores particularly caters to week-or-longer visitors. You'll find motel rooms with cable television, refrigerators, and queen-size beds, plus efficiencies, and suites as well. Prices are $350 to $470 a week in winter, $250 to $330 in summer and fall.

**Sara-sea Lodge,** 6760 Sara-sea Circle, Sarasota, FL 34242 (tel. 813/349-3244), is a pretty pink-and-white motel where you'll be greeted by two fat plaster lions and a flowered central courtyard with a fountain. Motel rooms, newly redecorated, are $225 to $265 a week in summer, peaking at $330 to $385 in winter.

Another selection on Sara-sea Circle is the **Capri Motel,** 6782 Sara-sea Circle, Sarasota, FL 34242 (tel. 813/349-2626), a one-story sunshine yellow structure with a tiny courtyard. The owners offer a smiling welcome and attractively decorated beachside quarters on Crescent Beach. The Capri has clean, neat, and attractive rooms and efficiencies beginning at $50 a day in summer, $70 in winter, with lower weekly fares.

Others on this small, perfectly manicured circle are **Captiva,** 6772 Sara-sea Circle (tel. 813/349-4131); **Gulf Sun,** 6722 Midnight Pass Rd. (tel. 813/349-2442); **Water's Edge,** 6744 Sara-sea Circle (tel. 813/349-1176); **Conclare Apartments,** 6738 Sara-sea Circle (tel. 813/349-2322), run by some very nice people who grow tomatoes under their windows; **Sea Breeze,** 6748 Sara-sea Circle (tel. 813/349-0303); and **King Neptune** (see Tropical Shores, above, for address and phone).

Back on Midnight Pass Road, the main thoroughfare on the island, seek out the **Surfrider,** at 6400 Midnight Pass Rd., Sarasota, FL 34242 (tel. 813/349-2121), where you'll find 19 very spacious efficiency apartments with lovely screened porches where you can watch the sun setting over the gulf. Motel rooms, one- or two-bedroom apartments, and cottages are all available and all recently refurbished. In the middle is a hydrotherapy pool heated year round to 95°, Fahrenheit, and another cooler heated pool. For those who like having a kitchen but intend doing little or nothing with it, there's a rustic little restaurant complete with vaulted, beamed ceiling, stone fireplace, and cozy candlelit ambience, not to mention a renowned rack of lamb and other treats for prices in the $8 to $15 range (open from 5:30 to 11pm daily except Monday). Winter room rates start at $75; summer, at $59. No credit cards accepted.

## Lido Key

Since there's no bridge over Big Sarasota Pass, you'll have to go back out the way you came and head north on US 41 and around St. Armand's Circle following the signs to Lido Key. This island is quite close to the mainland (as are all these islands, actually) so it's a good place to roost if you're planning some shopping in fabulous St. Armand's Circle. It's quite a small island, but has some high-rise resorts and, at the southern tip, a park.

Here you'll come upon the **St. Armand Inn,** 700 Ben Franklin Dr., Lido Beach, FL 33577 (tel. 813/388-2161), where each of the 116 rooms has wide picture windows overlooking the gulf so you can count waves instead of sheep. There's a bit of a colonial air here, with red-brick exterior and trim white shutters. You don't have to go far from the hotel's private strip of sand for a freshwater swim—the pool is right beside the beach. Rooms are decorated in gold with dark-wood furniture, and some have kitchenettes that can become suites; some have private balconies. There's a lounge and coffee shop, sundeck, basketball, volleyball, and shuffleboard. Rates February through April are $100 to $140 double. As usual, you pay a little more for gulf-front apartments. In summer and fall, rates are $55 to $90.

There's something musical about the name **Coquina on the Beach,** 1008 Ben Franklin Dr., Lido Beach, FL 33577 (tel. 813/388-2141), and when you see the lovely flowery landscaping and balconies you'll discover still more harmony. This is a very pretty place, with floor-to-ceiling windows, spacious balconies, and a neat, trim air about it. You can choose between bedroom apartments (with king-size beds and convertible couches) and studio apartments (with living room/bedroom combinations), but all rooms have cooking facilities. There is a beachfront wing and one overlooking a small patio area, a private beach, a pool equipped with hydrotherapy jets, shuffleboard, and a Laundromat. Mornings, complimentary coffee and newspaper are available in the lobby. They'll even take in Fido if he's well behaved. Rates from the end of January are $105 to $165, dropping to $60 to $108 in other months, with discounts for long stays.

**Three Crowns,** at 1314 Ben Franklin Dr., Lido Beach, FL 33577, and its sister property **Azure Tides Resort,** 1330 Ben Franklin Dr., Lido Beach, FL 33577 (tel. 813/388-2101), between them have all kinds of accommodations to offer. Three Crowns has basic motel rooms that were recently refurbished. Or you can stay in two low-rise buildings near the tower or at Azure Tides. Between them they offer one- and two-bedroom apartments, hotel rooms, kitchenettes, and a restaurant, a well-attended outdoor beachside lounge, heated pool, a strip of beach, and a sundeck. Rates fall in the $49 to $79 double range for motel rooms year round; $99 to $225 for apartment accommodations, depending on season.

## Longboat Key

Largest of the three keys, Longboat is upper-crust Sarasota. To get there, follow the signs around St. Armand's Circle. As you leave the circle you'll pass plush Bird

Key, a conclave of elegant pastel homes in the six- (approaching seven-) figure price range.

Longboat Key's a small but very involved community that has kept building to a minimum with tight restrictions, in the process creating what may be the state's most understated shopping center. So involved are people here that the tiny local newspaper prints a list of *every* call answered by the police. Imagine doing that in New York or Miami! It makes for some lively reading though, and you'll certainly discover where the week's best parties were located.

As you drive along this key, you'll find imposing condominiums blending nicely with large resorts. Tucked in between are small, modest accommodations that seem neither overwhelmed by their neighbors nor oblivious to them. There's a certain nonconformist individualism about this key that makes it both elegant and unpretentious. It's getting rare in this state to find a barrier island unspoiled by rows of high-rises, but this is one, a wonderfully tropical island that looks just the way you'd imagine an island off the coast of Florida ought to look.

A short way up the island you'll see a small rustic sign announcing the **Colony Beach and Tennis Resort**, at 1620 Gulf of Mexico Dr., Longboat Key, FL 33548 (tel. 813/383-6464, or toll free 800/237-9443, 800/282-1138 in Florida). There are many beach resorts in Florida and increasing numbers of tennis resorts, but a beach *and* tennis resort is downright sybaritic. There are 21 courts here, scattered so strategically around the property that devotees can practically tumble out of bed onto the courts. There's a tennis pro and staff, instructors, and clinic, too.

Those who prefer to sit and wait can do so in considerable comfort in one- or two-bedroom apartments, each with living room, dining area, kitchenette, a private patio or balcony, even Murphy beds. Some beds are sleek four-posters in bleached woods.

There are shops, a gourmet restaurant (see our dining recommendations), dancing and entertainment in a lounge, and Bamboo's, a raw bar serving clams, oysters, shrimp, and stone crab claws. Snack attacks beachside can be satisfied at an oceanfront snackbar. To work it off, the Colony has a fitness and aerobic center with whirlpool, sauna, and steambath. At a water-sports center you can play on windsurfers, sailboats, and water bikes, splash in a swimming pool, fish off a pier, or bask on a quarter mile of white sand beach. Summer rates range from $225 to $270 double for a one-bedroom or two-bedroom suite with cathedral ceilings and a second-floor bedroom. In winter, rates increase to $270 to $360, and there is a $7 daily charge for children 7 to 15, $16 a day for older youngsters. All kids stay free in summer.

As you head northward on the key your eye may be caught by the long orange-and-white **Diplomat Resort**, 3155 Gulf of Mexico Dr., Longboat Key, FL 33548 (tel. 813/383-3791). An apartment resort, the Diplomat stretches out along a 500-foot strip of gulfside sand they like to call just a "sandal step away." This resort promotes its lack of restaurants, lounges, and doormen, and says that it's a spot designed for those in search of peaceful privacy. It certainly looks peaceful, with twin two-story buildings stretching from road to gulf, offering sea breezes a chance to do their cross-ventilation best. One- or two-bedroom and studio apartments are available, all with kitchens and walk-in closets, color TVs, and lovely picture windows overlooking the gulf. Prices for two range from $61 to $100 in winter, from $52 to $60 in the summer months.

If we had to choose just one place to stay on Longboat Key—and that wouldn't be easy—we couldn't resist the lure of the **Beach Castle**, 5310 Gulf of Mexico Dr., Longboat Key, FL 33548 (tel. 813/383-2639), a really lovely spot operated by the McCall family who are blessed with a flair for interior decoration. The Castle's fine location offers either gulfside or bayside views. A talented staff keeps everything sparkling, and there's a very contemporary look to the 20 apartments tucked away amid bamboo plants and fences festooned with roses. Decor runs to comfortable white rattan furniture, cool blues and greens in the spacious rooms kept neat as a pin. Moor your boat to the fishing dock, or borrow the McCalls' rowboat or a canoe and float tranquilly around Sarasota Bay, then soothe newly exercised muscles in the resort's 98°-Fahrenheit Jacuzzi or their glittering freshwater pool. All the one- and two-bedroom apartments have screened balconies, and you can choose your view, bay or gulf. There are three rate periods here, summer, winter, and fall. Prices range from $600 to $830 a week double from December to May for quarters accommodating four or five. In other months prices drop, and there are discounts for stays of four weeks or more.

If you're keeping a close watch on your wallet, **Sun 'n Sea,** at 4651 Gulf of Mexico Dr., Longboat Key, FL 33548 (tel. 813/383-5588), ought to fill the bill. Located right on the beach, Sun 'n Sea is a cluster of screened apartments, efficiencies, and one- or two-bedroom cottages scattered over lawns shaded by pines and flowering shrubs. Furnishings are quite basic: Duplex apartments accommodating four share a bathroom, but separate washbasins are tucked into the corner of each bedroom. There are compact kitchens, plenty of closet space, telephones, and color TVs, and rooms are large. Rates are just $55 to $105 in winter. Prices drop about $15 in summer and are even lower in fall.

**Buccaneer Harbor & Villa Club,** 595 Dream Island Rd. (in the 6100 block of Gulf of Mexico Drive), Longboat Key, FL 33548 (tel. 813/383-9544), is an interesting spot with a lively restaurant (see our restaurant selections) and a pleasantly tranquil atmosphere. Accommodations here are two-bedroom two-bath condominium suites with Jacuzzis in the master suite and views of the bay. Rates range from $235 to $250 a night in peak winter months, from $145 to $160 in other seasons.

## Anna Maria Island/Bradenton

The northern and most eclectic of the three islands bordering Sarasota Bay is Anna Maria Island, where you find, from north to south, Bradenton Beach, Holmes Beach, and Anna Maria Beach.

The most scenic way to reach the island is to travel north along Longboat Key crossing Longboat Pass; but you can also come here on two causeways, Cortez Road (County Road 684) and Manatee Avenue (Fla. 64), both of which extend to US 41, and to its parallel highway, US 301.

Traveling north up Longboat Key and across the path you first reach **Bradenton Beach,** a crazy-quilt spot jammed with beach cottages that line both sides of the street and tread a very narrow line between rustic and ramshackle. You'll either love this sunny, sandy strip of oceanfront, peopled by the bikini-and-sharktooth set, or you'll loathe it. It's a very busy place with lots of traffic, souvenir shops, small beer and shrimp bars, and short-order eateries.

If you opt for love and want to really absorb the atmosphere here, you can ask in any of the shops about renting private cottages in the area, or inquire at the **Anna Maria Chamber of Commerce,** 105 39th St., Holmes Beach, FL 33501 (tel. 813/778-7477), about private rentals. Or you can do this the easy way and seek out what we think are the best on the beach: Catalina Beach Resort, Via Roma, and Aquarius.

Owners Gil and Katie Pierola are Spanish and their **Catalina Beach Resort,** 1325 Gulf Dr. N., Bradenton Beach, FL 33510 (tel. 813/778-6611), reflects that heritage everywhere you turn, from its red-and-black color scheme to the ornate wood balconies and bullfight posters on the walls. Rooms are furnished with Spanish-style furniture, bedspreads are dark velvets, paintings offer views of flamenco dancers and Spanish towns. It's quite a pretty place, with medium-size rooms that are kept neat and tidy. Across the street the resort has a strip of private beach, and on the grounds there's a swimming pool, game room with bumper-pool table, a water slide, shuffleboard, laundry room, and barbecue grills. Weekly rates for two begin at $64 to $77 in winter, at $47 to $57 in summer.

Up the road a bit, **Via Roma,** at 2408 Gulf Dr. N., Bradenton Beach, FL 34217 (tel. 813/778-6691), occupies a tranquil spot along Gulf Drive and is itself a tranquil spot stretching along both sides of the beach highway. Romans loved their stat ues and so does Via Roma, which features a lawnful of whitewashed statues including, of course, Neptune with his trident. Via Roma's beachside patio area is a departure from the usual thatch-roofed chickee: It's a long, narrow gazebo supported by tall white columns. There's an attractive arched pool and formally landscaped grounds, plus a Garden annex across the road. You'll have lots of space in the rooms, and they're all decorated in attractive colors and furnishings with everything kept bright and shining. All units have kitchens now, and Via Roma features a whirlpool/hot tub as well as a heated pool. Another nice touch: Bicycles are available for guests. Motel rooms, one- and two-bedroom apartments begin at $75 from mid-December through April, at $50 in other months.

**Aquarius Motel,** 105 39th St., Holmes Beach, FL 33510 (tel. 813/778-7477), is popular with beach lovers who come here to be within steps of the shell-strewn gulf beaches. Accommodations at Aquarius include kitchens with an adjacent living room plus a separate bedroom with twin or double beds and bath. A convertible couch in the living room sleeps two more beach fans. Friendly owners can help you find your way to the best shelling and swimming spots and there's a heated pool here. Rates are $44 to $85 year round.

Holmes Beach is a serene residential area that has two lovely resorts. One of those is **Island Plantation,** at 7300 Gulf Dr., Holmes Beach, FL 33510 (tel. 813/778-1079). Tall white columns line the porch of the elegant reception area, and clusters of apartments are scattered beachside around a central courtyard. Island Plantation is a very popular place, and you'll have to reserve as far in advance as possible. Rooms have recently been refurbished and every one is different, but they all have plenty of space, bright colors, and a carefully tended look. Since there are so many kinds of accommodations available here, you would be wise to describe just what you need and ask for price quotations for weekly and monthly stays. In winter you'll pay $85 to $110 double. In summer, doubles pay $57 to $99.

Sharing the tip of Anna Maria Island is the **Blue Water Beach Club,** 6306 Gulf Dr., Holmes Beach, FL 33510 (tel. 813/778-6688), a glittering white building that arcs around a central courtyard and an extra-wide strip of beach. An English friend sometimes describes things as "neat as a bandbox," and we'd say that's the perfect description for the Blue Water Beach Club. There's a lovely bright lobby decorated in white and green, and a delightfully airy, glass-enclosed sitting-and-sipping room with white scalloped awning, hanging greenery, even a swaying birdcage. Blue Water has several different kinds of accommodations, ranging from hotel rooms to efficiencies and apartments, and they're all bright with citrus colors and sliding glass doors opening onto balconies or terraces overlooking the gulf. There's a pool shaded by banana trees in the middle of it all, and a nice friendly management. Two people pay rates ranging from $87 to $120 in high season, from $61 to $89 after April 30, less if you're staying a week or more; more for suites.

## On the Mainland

Top of the line on the mainland is the **Hyatt Sarasota,** at 1000 Boulevard of the Arts, Sarasota, FL 34236 (tel. 813/366-9000, or toll free 800/233-1234), which isn't on a beach but is certainly one of the most impressive hostelries in town. It is on the waters of a marina just across from Sarasota's Van Wezel Performing Arts Hall. Here you'll find all you'd expect from this popular chain: 297 spacious, tastefully decorated rooms, with furnishings as contemporary as the architecture. One of the city's top restaurants is here, so you can dine in the glow of candles on offerings from a creative American cuisine menu that features fine fresh seafood prepared many different ways. Down in the Boathouse you can feast in more casual surroundings in this stilt-built dining room that juts out over a lagoon. Room rates for two are $105 to $165, year round; higher on concierge levels.

Up and down Tamiami Trail you'll find large and small motels with very reasonable prices. Among the larger ones is the **Sarasota Motor Inn,** 8150 N. Tamiami

Trail, Sarasota, FL 33580 (tel. 813/355-7747), which has 158 soundproofed rooms on six acres of land crowned by a triple-arched entranceway and a flaring pagoda roof. Accommodations are spacious and nicely furnished, sparked by lively colors. Rates are $40 in winter, $30 in summer.

The **Royal Palm Motel,** 1701 N. Tamiami Trail, Sarasota, FL 33580 (tel. 813/365-1342, or toll free 800/528-1234), is also part of the Best Western chain and offers just 37 pretty rooms and efficiencies. A special feature of many rooms here are wall murals hand-painted by graduates of nearby Ringling School of Art. There's a heated pool, and the beach is just three miles away. Rates are $30 to $60.

**Best Western Golden Host,** at 4675 N. Tamiami Trail, Sarasota, FL 33580 (tel. 813/355-5141, or toll free 800/528-1234), has beamed ceilings in some rooms, dressing areas, wood paneling, and private patios or balconies in rooms that stretch across three acres of landscaped grounds. The resort is proud of its pool, ringed by palms, and also offers shuffleboard and poolside games, and a cocktail lounge with a Hawaiian flavor. Rates in winter are $38 to $78 year round.

Budget watchers should head for the mansard roof of the two-story **Econo Lodge,** 5340 N. Tamiami Trail, Sarasota, FL 33580 (tel. 813/355-8867, or toll free 800/446-6900), where a medium-size room with double bed is just $45 to $68 for two, year round. Accommodations are basic, but so is the price.

Chain motels are also well represented in Sarasota: **Days Inn, Hampton Inn, Holiday Inn, Scottish Inn;** all have toll-free 800 numbers.

**READERS' ACCOMMODATIONS SUGGESTION:** "In some places in Florida there are **homes for rent** cheaper than motels or beach cottages and apartments. **Bradenton,** for instance, is loaded with all kinds of accommodations in homes and condominiums for as little as $800 to $1,200 a month" (B. H. Sampson, Powell, Ohio). [*Authors' Note:* The city's chamber of commerce can put you in touch with people who rent homes or condominium apartments, or have B&B accommodations.]

## WHERE TO DINE

Sarasota has many fine restaurants with lots of atmosphere and quite moderate prices. We've grouped them by location so you can find one easily wherever you are. Remember that the prices we've cited are for entrées, but these usually include salad, one or two vegetables, and often coffee as well.

### Downtown and Near the Airport

**Pompano Cay,** at the Hyatt, 1000 Boulevard of the Arts (tel. 366-9000), has a very elegant setting and excellent cuisine with prices in the $10 to $17 range. That hotel's **Boathouse** is a good place for lunch and casual evening dining, too. Both are open at 11am for lunch, and the Boathouse stays open to 1am, while Pompano Cay ends lunch at 2pm and has dinner from 6 to 10pm.

To go to Sarasota without going to **Marina Jacks,** at Marina Plaza, Island Park Drive, on the Island Park Pier (tel. 365-4232), is some kind of sacrilege and the surest way to miss one of the finest views in town. There are lots of seafood dishes and a variety of salads from noon to 3pm daily, and lots more of the same for dinner from 5 to 10pm daily when prices are in the $10 to $15 range. Don't miss Marina Jacks' comfortable **Deep Six Lounge,** open from noon through late evening. Something new on Sarasota's waterfront is **Marina Jacks II,** a double-decker paddlewheeler trimmed in oak paneling and brass, serving a limited menu of dinner entrées at prices in the $10 to $18.50 range (plus a $4 boat fare for each person). Lunch and dinner cruises cast off at noon and 7:30pm daily except Monday and in September, but hours vary so check first.

You can oom-pah-pah with lots of other happy wanderers at **Old Heidelberg Castle,** 1947 3rd St., on US 301 at 3rd Street and North Washington Boulevard (tel. 366-3515), where you'll find lots of lederhosen, wienerschnitzel, sauerbraten, and the like. A great cavernous dining room, Old Heidelberg Castle puts together a rollicking evening for prices in the $9 to $16 bracket, with quite inexpensive libations at an early happy hour. Open 11am to 11pm daily except Monday.

A trim Sarasota friend of ours who looks as if she *never* eats manages, nevertheless, to pack it away at **Phillippi Creek Oyster Bar,** 5353 S. Tamiami Trail (tel. 925-4444). Although we haven't tried it yet, Marge raves about this very, very casual spot that recently upgraded its "linens" from newspapers to plain paper. Napkins remain a roll of paper towels. Here she and others toss down oysters and toss the shells into buckets, consume vast quantities of fresh-from-the-sea shrimp, and indulge in fried and broasted seafood selections in the $10 to $15 range or less for dinner. You can dine inside or outside here from 11:30am to 10:30pm.

When you're having a big mac-aroni attack, head for **Ristorante Bellini's,** 1549 Main St. (tel. 365-7380), where some good cooks produce huge veal chops extolled by many a diner plus plenty of other interesting combinations of Italian herbs married to local seafood. Antipastos here are a standout and the wine list is impressive. Prices fall in the $10 to $20 range. Bellini's is open for lunch from 11:30am to 2pm weekdays and 5 to 11pm daily for dinner.

For some of the things that have happened in this state, Florida could have invented the *Guinness Book of Records.* Certainly **Walt's Fish Market, Raw Oyster Bar, and Restaurant,** at 560 N. Washington Blvd. (tel. 365-1735), has contributed its part to that famous record: This is the site of a 1976 world-record oyster-eating event when Vernon Bass downed 684 of the little shellsters in 20.5 minutes to beat his own record of 588 in 17 minutes! Walt's has more than 40 dinners, from freshwater perch to smoked mullet, in price brackets that can go as low as $15 for two. In season, Walt's packs them in from 5pm, so arrive early to avoid feeling like an oyster yourself. Open from 11am to 10pm daily (from 4pm on Sunday), with another Walt's on Tamiami Trail.

All the tranquillity of a flower garden reigns at **Chez Sylvie,** 1849 S. Osprey Ave. (tel. 365-1921), where you are indeed greeted by a plethora of fresh flowers and enough greenery to make this a cozily romantic dining spot. Sylvie herself adds to the allure by making you welcome, and the chef does the rest with such triumphs as fish baked in a puff pastry or in paper, delicate duckling, hearty Cornish hens, light luncheon crêpes, all France's favorite flavors delivered in a charming atmosphere. There's a champagne bar here, so you might consider trying a bubbly. Entrées are in the $15 to $22 range, but a full dinner is likely to run higher. Chez Sylvie is open from 11:30am to 2pm weekdays and from 6 to 11pm daily except Sunday for dinner, although a pleasant lounge area in the restaurant remains open to 1am for dancing to piano music. You'll find the restaurant on a street that runs parallel to U.S. 41 at Hillview Avenue; it's behind Sarasota Memorial Hospital.

**Michael's on East,** 1212 East Ave. S. (tel. 366-0007), has risen rapidly to fame in this area, thanks to some most innovative cooking. On the changing menu here you're likely to find chef Michael Klauber whipping up such unusual concoctions as hazelnut gazpacho or yellowfin tuna topped with spicy tomato salsa. Just reading the menu is a taste-tester's challenge here—how much lip-smacking can you bear? In case you'd like to try some of these yourself, you can look right into the kitchen and watch how the pros are creating. Entrées fall in the $13 to $20 bracket, but your bill will go higher with the addition of all the temptations you'll meet here. Michael's is open from 11:30am to 2pm weekdays and from 5 to 11pm nightly.

## St. Armand's Key

You might have already guessed that a city peopled by artists, writers, and wealthy jet-setters is likely also to have attracted some talented restaurateurs—and you're right. Two of them are Titus Letschert and Norbert Goldner, who took this town by storm when they set up shop here years ago as **Café L'Europe,** 431 St. Armand's Circle (tel. 388-4415), and this whirlwind is still going strong. Café L'Europe wins *Holiday* awards with such palate-pleasers as bay scallops Nantua, veal piccata, mignonettes aux poivres (with black, white, and green peppercorns). The decor is enchanting, with pink bricks, arches, antique Italian tile trim, potted plants, and a mouthwatering display of delicacies at the entrance. Gastronomes come from miles around to sample food and atmosphere here, so reservations are a must. Entrée prices fall in the $15 to $25 category, although your bill will surely go higher when you see all the temptations here. Hours are 11am to 3pm daily except Sunday and 5:30 to 10:30pm daily (6 to 10pm on Sunday).

A few doors around the circle, the **Columbia Restaurant,** at 411 St. Armand's Circle (tel. 388-3987), is the Sarasota sister of the famed Ybor City Columbia. Like its renowned relative, Columbia is classical Spanish from decor to dining, which begins at 11am and continues through 11pm (from noon on Sunday). Paella is the number one specialty, followed by an excellent zarzuela de mariscos. Gulf seafoods and stone crabs are offered daily. Prices are in the $10 to $18 range for dinner.

**Charley's Crab,** 420 Harding Circle (tel. 388-3964), has taken nautical decor to tasteful new heights in dining rooms trimmed with lofty chandeliers made of delicate straw fans, white netting, and batik-looped ceiling. Try the back room for an intimate atmosphere. New offerings are displayed daily on a blackboard at the entrance and range from Canadian salmon to Boston scrod. Raw bar fans will salivate over the iced treats in the lobby. Open from 11:30am to 2pm weekdays, later in the Cafe, and 5 to 10pm daily, later in the lounge. Prices are in the $13 to $19 range.

You're guaranteed the pastry will be delectable at **Le Rendez-vous** at the French Hearth, 303 John Ringling Blvd. (tel. 388-2313), which is first a bakery, second a tearoom, and third a tiny French café. Breakfast, lunch, and dinner are served from 8:30am to 9pm daily (on Sunday from 9am to 2pm), for prices in the $8 to $14 range. Sometimes prices change in summer.

Amid all this poshness it's nice to know there's a spot you can nip in after a long day among the Guccis. **Tail o' the Pup** is the place, on St. Armand's Circle (tel. 388-2662), which is open from 11am to 9pm daily except Sunday, later in the lounge. Dine among plants and wood on everything from a $1 hot dog to $10 steaks.

## Siesta Key

You've probably seen strolling musicians, but they've got strolling magicians at **Magic Moments Restaurant,** 5831 Midnight Pass Rd. (tel. 349-9494). All the sleight-of-hand some restaurants use on tableside cookery they save here for tableside abracadabra delivered with dessert. Prestidigitational fun is the main ingredient here, supplemented by steaks and seafood served in a woodsy-plantsy atmosphere. Magic Moment's open from 5 to 10pm daily, with entertainment in the Pazzazz lounge Tuesday through Sunday. Dinner entrées run $10 to $17. Reservations requested.

Some restaurants look intriguing, and tiny **Wildflower Natural Foods Restaurant,** at 5218 Ocean Blvd. (tel. 349-1758), is one. From its carved wooden sign to its storefront entrance, Wildflower is kind of cuddly-cute. The accent is on natural foods serving seafood, pasta, and a variety of vegetable platters—everything homemade. Hours are 8am to 9pm every day. Lunch checks are likely to be under $6 and dinner will run $7 to $12.

If you love the "snug little cabin in the woods" atmosphere, you'll love the **Surfrider Restaurant,** 6400 Midnight Pass Rd. (tel. 346-1199), about which you'll find more in our hotel recommendations. It's open 5 to 10pm daily except Monday.

There's a touch of the same ambience at **The Inn Between** (isn't that a great name?), which is at 431 Beach Rd. (tel. 349-7117). Here you'll find an open-hearth fireplace, a warm woody glow, and Italian accents like fettuccine Alfredo. Plenty of beef, seafood, veal, and lamb dishes are served for prices in the $9 to $15 range. It's open from 5 to 11pm daily, except Sunday, and there's entertainment and dancing most nights.

After a long hard day at the beach, stop in at the **Old Salty Dog Pub,** 5023 Ocean Blvd. (tel. 349-0158), put some of the yellow stuff on all-beef hot dogs or sausages, roll some catsup on the home-sliced french fries, taste a little chili Chihuahua, and *voilà!* beachbum's nirvana. Open from 11am to 10pm Monday through Friday, to 11pm on Saturday, and from noon to 9pm on Sunday. Evenings, dine on grilled seafood for $5 to $10.

We'd go to the **Summerhouse,** 6101 Midnight Pass Rd., Siesta Key (tel. 349-1100), if they had nothing but the oysters topped with spinach, cheese, and Pernod, but fortunately there is more. There is, first, the setting, a beautiful one indeed with woodsy greenery everywhere and two-story windows to take advantage of it. Inside the scent of freshly baked bread is joined by the flavors of good prime rib, some interesting veal selections, good seafood, and prices in the $15 to $22 bracket for most options. A subtly chic spot, the Summerhouse also has a lounge in which a less elaborate menu predominates. Hours are 6 to 10pm daily, opening at 5pm on weekends, and from noon to 3pm for Sunday brunch.

## Longboat Key

You'll find one of the top dining rooms in the region at the Colony Resort, 1620 Gulf of Mexico Dr. (tel. 383-6464). Called the **Colony Restaurant,** this award-winner is open daily from early morn through dinner serving such delicacies as pompano amandine, shrimp in a white wine and garlic sauce, grouper topped with julienned fresh vegetables and hollandaise sauce, or a veal chop with a creamy chanterelles, mustard seed, and demi-glâcé sauce. Roast duckling with a pear sauce, chicken, lamb, and steaks, all prepared lightly but elegantly, are on the menu for prices in the $15 to $20 range for dinner entrées, à la carte. Sunday brunch here is a local tradition. Hours are 8am to 10pm.

The **Buccaneer Inn** (tel. 383-1101 or 383-4357) also has an award-winning dining room whose number-one specialty is prime ribs of beef, roasted then broiled over charcoal embers. You can look out over the nearby marina as you dine under the watchful eye of life-size pirate figures. Prices are listed in doubloons, so bring your calculators or just rely on their translations (in the $15 to $20 range). Open noon to 11pm daily.

You can settle in for all three meals at **Shenkel's,** 3454 Gulf of Mexico Dr. (tel. 383-2500), which has plenty of breakfast choices every day, stacked sandwiches at lunch, and things like chicken pot pie and Welsh surprise at dinner. Tuesday through Saturday Shenkel's serves breakfast and lunch from 9am to 2pm and dinner from 5:30 to 9pm. On Sunday breakfast only is served, from 8:30am; closed Monday.

Don't even dream of dinner without reservations at **Euphemia Haye,** 5540 Gulf of Mexico Dr. (tel. 383-3633), for this storefront restaurant seats just 65 in-the-know diners. The decor is eclectic but soothing, and back in the kitchen the chef/owners bake their own nut bread and pastries. Steak au poivre, gambreto, cappellini, and homemade pasta with pesto sauce all pour from that same kitchen, open from 6 to 10pm every day. You'll pay from $14 to $27 for dinners lauded by several major journals.

**L'Auberge du Bon Vivant,** 7003 Gulf of Mexico Dr. (tel. 383-2421), is an old house converted to an attractive country French look with copper pots, beamed ceilings, old clocks, lots of plants, and crisp white napery glistening in the glow of candles. Two couples began the Auberge, Judy and Michael Zouhar (once part of Winter Park's award-winning Le Cordon Bleu) and Madeleine and Francis Hatton. Gentlemen in the kitchen, ladies in the front, and how's this for a motto: "Love of the table is the last of the loves, but it's the consolation of all the others"? There's an impressive list of fine French offerings here for prices in the $15 range. Open from 5 to 10pm (closed on Sunday).

To dine at the **Plaza,** 525 Bay Isles Pkwy. (tel. 383-8844), is to feel that a sip of port or a touch of brandy is surely in order. As English-clubby as it is possible to get this side of the channel, Plaza is *the* spot to go when you're intent on an intimate evening surrounded by cozily impressive surroundings, fine service, and top-quality continental cooking. Discovering a place like the Plaza when all about you are crab shacks and clam shanties is like uncovering the *Atocha* in your bathtub.

Good beef, a lobster bisque that culinary memories are made of, veal, chops, seafood, and an earth-shattering dessert trolley play counterpoint to the handsome interiors, all joining for a most harmonious dining event. For this beguiling setting you'll pay entrée prices in the $18 to $26 range. Hours are 5:30 to 11pm for dinner Tuesday through Sunday, opening an hour earlier in the lounge, which also remains open later. Turn east at the only traffic light on Longboat Key to find the restaurant.

Small, but significant to seafood fans is the **Drydock,** 412 Gulf of Mexico Dr. (tel. 383-0102). This tiny place across from the golf course on Longboat Key stews up a great boathouse chowder and charbroils shrimp and other seafood and always features a daily fish special. Prices are in the $10 to $15 range and the restaurant's open daily from 11am to 8:30 or 9pm.

## On Anna Maria Island

**Pete Reynard's,** 5325 Marina Dr., Holmes Beach (tel. 778-2233), has been here since 1954 serving up good home-cooking and simple straightforward preparations of beef, seafood, baked ham, pork chops, and the like. There are three pretty dining rooms, one of which rotates so you can see the changing bayside scenery through banks of windows. You'll pay $10 to $15 for dinner, and hours are 11:30am to 9:30pm weekdays, later on weekends, to 2am in the lounge.

Way up on the tip of the island, **Fast Eddie** started out with a little marina-side eatery and drew so many fans he's expanded to an awesome two-story wood-sided California-look monster of a building overlooking a spectacular uninterrupted view of miles of gulf and beach. It's quite an apparition among the tiny beach cottages, and its prices seem an apparition too, in this day of high, high, and higher. Six people can dine here amid paddle fans and hundreds of plants on this for-six platter: six cups of gumbo, a whole barbecued smoked mullet, a pound of fried grouper, two dozen fried shrimp, a dozen smoked oysters, six crab cakes, six mounds of french fries and six of coleslaw, plus some onion ring garnishes—for $65. Shades of Diamond Jim. Fast Eddie's is at 101 S. Bay Blvd. on Anna Maria Island (tel. 778-2251), and is open from 11:30am to 9pm daily.

A special little place on Anna Maria Island is just down the street from the island's sole "attraction," the roofless, wall-less city jail. An ice-cream parlor in front at **Café Robar,** 204 Pine Ave. (tel. 778-6939 or 778-6969), conceals a tiny tiled, greenery-strewn back room that holds perhaps 20 or so diners who trek here for very skillful cooking put into practice on such delicacies as trout amandine, grouper, steaks, and king crab legs. The menu changes daily according to what's caught out in the gulf or fresh elsewhere. It's open 4:30 to 9:30pm daily for dinner. Prices are in the $12 to $20 range.

**READER'S RESTAURANT SUGGESTION:** "You should add the **Seafood Shack,** 4110 127th St. W. (just off Cortes Road), in Cortes (tel. 794-1235)—the grouper is delicious and cheaper than other area restaurants" (Michael J. Hare, Toronto, Canada). [*Author's Note:* Hours at the Seafood Shack are 11:30am to 10pm daily, closing at 9pm on Sunday, and dinner prices are in the $10 to $15 range.]

## Bradenton

The **Pewter Mug,** 108 44th Ave. E., Cortes Road, Bradenton (tel. 756-7577), has twice been selected by area magazine readers as one of the state's top six steak houses. Those who love prime rib should have a go at the two-pounder here. There are some good raw-bar offerings, plus chowders and a salad bar with gorgonzola cheese dressing. The atmosphere is California contemporary, with beamed ceiling and lots of greenery. Prices are in the $10 to $17 range, and doors open at 5pm, close at 10pm weekdays, at 11pm on weekends.

A historic spot serving lunch and dinner is **The Pier,** at the foot of 12th Street West, at Memorial Pier, Bradenton (tel. 748-8087), where you'll now find cathedral ceilings soaring over paddle fans and greenery. Memorial Pier, the site of this restaurant, has recently been restored so you're guaranteed not only historic atmosphere but a beautiful view across the water. Local seafood and prime rib are specialties here, but there's a wide range of other selections for dinner prices in the $10 to $18 range. Hours are 11:30am to 3:30pm and 4:30 to 10pm (from 11:30am to 9pm on Sunday).

## Nearby Restaurants

**Crab Trap I** and **II** are twin eateries doling out what some claim is the finest seafood on Florida's west coast. Superlatives notwithstanding, you will indeed always find fresh and simply prepared seafood here, much of it whipped into traditional form, like stuffed flounder or crab cakes. Rustic and casual, these two restaurants also include a couple of the weirder Florida offerings: gator tail and wild pig, for instance. Your dinner tab is unlikely to exceed $10. These traps spring open at 11:30am daily, close at 9:30pm but stay open a little later on weekends. Crab Trap I is at US Hwy. 19 in Palmetto, just south of the Skyway Bridge (tel. 722-6255) and Crab Trap II is at 4815 17th St. E., just off I-75 in Ellenton (tel. 729-7777).

## NIGHTLIFE

Sarasota bills itself as Florida's cultural capital, and for its size it does indeed present an awesome array of activities ranging from opera to theater, ballet, lectures, symphony, and jazz. So strong a cultural focus does the city have that in 1970 it hired Frank Lloyd Wright's Taliesin group to create the **Center for the Performing Arts,** located on prime bayfront land. The center has since become an unmistakable Sarasota landmark—it's painted a pale lavender shade and known in these parts as the "purple people seater"!

## Theater/Music

Nowhere on this side of the Atlantic will you find a theater more enchanting— or even anything like—the jewel-box **Asolo** (pronounced "Ah-so-low") **Theater Company,** 5555 N. Tamiami Trail (tel. 351-8000). A gold-and-white baroque gem built in 1798, the Asolo was once part of the castle of deposed Cypriot Queen Catherine Cornoro, who lived about 20 miles from Venice. This tiny theater has arcing tiers of white columns, gold-leafed and ornately festooned boxes, twinkling sconces, and it was the stage for stars such as Eleanora Duse. In its boxes were seated patrons like Englishman Robert Browning. In 1939 this horseshoe-shaped beauty was removed from the castle to make way for, of all things, a movie house, but an antique dealer with a keen eye stored the theater away for 20 years, and in 1949 Florida bought it and installed it in its own building on the Ringling grounds.

As the only baroque court theater in the nation, this small charmer was originally intended to go on display as an art object in itself. It was not long, however, before a fledgling group of players from Florida State University began using the theater as it was intended, performing a repertory series that became so popular the Asolo players soon became a state theater, officially known as the Asolo State Theater.

By 1986, however, theater backers had raised enough funds to move the repertory theater company into another building with larger seating capacity, but that presented a problem. How could they leave this legendarily lovely setting for some sleekly contemporary spot?

Then, lo and behold, from nowhere came the news that an ornate turn-of-the-century opera house in Dunfermline, Scotland, had been demolished, its delicate carvings, elaborate boxes, and fancy proscenium crated up and stored away until a new facility could be retained. Scotland's replacement-theater plans had fizzled, however, and Asolo's backers were able to obtain all those cartons full of elaborate plasterwork—and as part of the deal they even got the talented Scots plasterers to go with them!

In 1989 the Asolo State Theater gave its farewell performance in its old home and moved into its special new home, the Asolo Center for the Performing Arts.

Complete with elaborate carvings, this new-old theater can be found near the Ringling complex at 5555 N. Tamiami Trail (tel. 351-8000). Although the new facility has sacrificed that distinctive U-shape of the Baroque Ringling facility, it can now seat 500 playgoers with no blocked sightlines and is as cozily intimate as the former quarters—the distance from the back seat to the stage is just the same.

We first came to the Asolo to see one play, but emerged three days later, bleary-eyed but thrilled, after indulging in an orgy of play-going provided by riveting repertory players. It's nice to know that although things will change some here, they will remain the same. That means you can see these very talented performers striding the stage from mid-December through mid-August. Curtain time is 8:15pm every night except Monday, with tickets ranging in price from $13 to $25 for evening performances, from $10 to $23 for matinees, which usually take place Tuesday through Saturday at 2pm.

Meanwhile, what has long been known as the Asolo Theater will once again be part of the Ringling complex and can be visited at no extra charge when you visit the rest of this fascinating place (see more on the Ringling museums under "What to See and Do").

You can also experience the theater in action at the annual film series held here, and at poetry readings, lectures (the New York Metropolitan Museum of Art director was among the speakers in a lecture series), and musicals that are scheduled here. Information on those can be obtained by calling 355-7115.

**Sarasota Opera Association, Inc.,** 61 N. Pineapple Ave. (tel. 953-7030), presents a selection of opera and operetta productions, mostly in English, from mid-February to mid-March at varying prices.

**Players of Sarasota,** 838 N. Tamiami Trail (P.O. Box 2277, Sarasota, Fl 34230) (tel. 365-2494), present what they like to call the "most professional non-professional theater in the area" at the Players Theater, on US 41 at 9th Street across from Exhibition Hall. Performances are scheduled from September through June. Tickets are $10 to $12 for adults, $5 to $6 for students 18 and under.

September through June, and sometimes in midsummer, you can see concerts, ballet, plays, films, lectures, and a variety of current stars performing at the **Van Wezel Performing Arts Hall,** 777 N. Tamiami Trail (tel. 953-3366). Call to see what's on when you're in town.

The **Florida Studio Theater,** 1241 N. Palm Ave., Sarasota (tel. 366-9796), produces innovative and contemporary drama from January through May. Check local newspapers or the theater for current production schedules.

**Golden Apple Dinner Theater,** 25 N. Pineapple Ave. (tel. 366-5454), offers an evening out with candlelight buffet dining at 6pm and curtain at 8pm Tuesday through Sunday, from 4pm April to December. Broadway plays are performed by a local cast on a "magic carpet" stage that rolls out into the center of the audience. There are matinee lunch/shows at noon on Saturday and Sunday in winter months, with curtain at 1:30pm; tickets are $16.70. Evening ticket prices are $23 to $24 with discounts to senior citizens.

**Florida West Coast Symphony Music Center,** 709 N. Tamiami Trail (tel. 953-4252), produces a number of musical events in the region. Most take place at Sarasota's Van Wezel Performing Arts Center from December to May.

## Lounge Entertainment

There's certainly no dearth of evening high jinks in this resort community, and the entertainment changes frequently, so even if you're here for a long stay you'll find plenty to do when the sun goes down.

In Sarasota, there is good lounge entertainment in the **Hyatt Hotel** and the **Holiday Inn North,** at the **Deep Six Lounge** at **Marina Jacks** restaurant, the **Colony Beach Club** lounge, and the **Buccaneer Inn** lounge. (See our hotel and restaurant listings for details.)

On Lido Beach, the **Holiday Inn** has a roof-garden lounge and dining room with a nice view of the water and dinner dancing, which at last check tended toward big-band sounds. The **Lido Beach Inn's Pub** has long been a favorite gathering spot for residents and locals alike. The **Harley Sandcastle** also has entertainment.

On Siesta Key, there's a piano bar at **The Inn Between,** and entertainment at the **Magic Moments Restaurant.**

## Discos

At Armand Circle, the **Columbia Restaurant** has a Patio Lounge that is usually packed with dancers enjoying a red-hot combination of Latin and disco beats by per-spiring musicians who drum gamely on until 2am nightly except Sunday.

**Animal House,** 1927 Ringling Blvd. (tel. 366-3830), is an old hand at the after-dark scene and has adopted an old formula to become an instant success: lots of music, lots of people (the place holds 900), but not lots of money to get in ($2 to $10 usually). It's open daily from 3pm to 2am and features rock music.

## SPORTS

Sarasota likes to call itself the birthplace of American golf, since the game was introduced here in 1885. There are now 27 courses and dozens of tennis courts scat-tered all around the city so you shouldn't have any trouble finding something to do.

### Golf and Tennis

**Sarasota Golf Club** (tel. 371-2431) has greens fees of $28, including carts. It's about seven miles east of US 301 at 7280 Leeswynn Dr.

**Foxfire Golf Club,** 7200 Proctor Rd. (tel. 921-7757), is an 18-hole course, and the **Meadows Country Club,** at 3101 Longmeadow (tel. 378-6600), is a par-72, 18-hole course. Cart-inclusive fees are $8 to $25, lower in summer.

There are free public **tennis courts** on the beach at **Siesta Key** and six lighted municipal courts at the **Civic Center Complex** grounds just off US 41. In **Braden-ton,** there are free lighted courts at City Courts, 17th Avenue West and Wares Creek. A call to the **Sarasota recreation department** will elicit some information on loca-tion of other courts (tel. 365-2200).

### Water Sports

You can learn to sail at **O'Leary's Sarasota Sailing School,** on Island Park Bayfront (tel. 953-7505), for $12 to $25 an hour depending on the size of the boat, and rent windsurfers for $12 an hour.

Rent a boat at **Mr. CB's,** 1249 Stickney Point Rd., Siesta Key (tel. 349-4400), or **Cannons Marina,** 6040 Gulf of Mexico Dr., Longboat Key (tel. 383-1311). Rates average about $55 to $125 a day for small craft.

**Don & Mike's Boat & Ski Rental,** at Nokomia Beach (tel. 485-7345), offers boats and jet-skis, and has waterskiing lessons for $60 per hour, jet-skis for $40 an hour.

### Fishing

For deep-sea fishing, drop down to **Siesta Key Marina** or to the **Bayfront Ma-rina** near the Hyatt Hotel about 5pm or early in the morning and you'll discover everything you ever wanted to know about what they're catching and how to catch them. Charter boats take groups out fishing for about $250 to $300 for four hour fishing trips. Party-boat fishing is fun, and you can go out for a half day for $20 to $25.

### Pari-mutuel Sports

**Sarasota Kennel Club,** 5400 Bradenton Rd., between US 41 and US 301 (tel. 355-7744), sends the greyhounds after the rabbit at 8pm nightly (except Sunday) from May to September, with matinees at 1pm on Monday, Wednesday, and Satur-day. Admission is $1. In September the action moves to nearby Tampa until

January, then to St. Petersburg from January to May. The Skyline Room at the Kennel Club offers formal dining.

If you like stock car racing, you can watch them race their engines from February through November at **DeSoto Speedway,** 14 miles east of Bradenton on Fla. 64 (tel. 748-2962). The racers line up on Saturday at 5:30pm. Adults pay $8; children 6 to 12, $1. "Best hamburgers in the county," they claim.

## Baseball

Sarasota is winter home to the **Chicago White Sox,** at Payne Park just off US 301, and there's a Kansas City Minor League Complex where minor league spring training takes place. At the Gulf Coast Rookie League, newly drafted players from seven major-league teams compete.

McKecknie Field, 17th Avenue West and 9th Street in Bradenton (tel. 747-3031), is the winter home of the **Pittsburgh Pirates.** Exhibition games in February and March cost $8 to $12.

## Other Sports

On Longboat Key, you can rent a bike from **Ed's Beach Service,** 4949 Gulf of Mexico Dr. (tel. 383-4466) for $10 a day, or $35 a week. On Siesta Key in Sarasota, try **Mr. CB's,** 1249 Stickney Point Rd. (tel. 349-4400). Rates are $10 a day, $30 a week.

One last word on bicycling: Longboat Key has a 12-mile bicycle course running the length of the island, with trees for shade and a quick, cooling dip always just a few steps away.

Equestrians should head for **Myakka Valley Campground and Stable,** 7220 Myakka Valley Trail, about seven miles east of I-75 on Fla. 72 (tel. 924-8435), where you can trot five miles of wooded trails for $11 an hour, closed Tuesday and Wednesday.

## SHOPPING

If you like shopping malls, the 70 stores at **Sarasota Square Mall,** 8201 S. Tamiami Trail, should keep you busy. Siesta Key has small and casual **Siesta Village,** 5000 Ocean Blvd., with about 100 small shops and several restaurants. On Longboat Key, there's a barely visible shopping center called **Avenue of the Flowers** that's small but lovely.

On weekends, seek out bargains at the **Country Fair Flea Market** on US 301 in Palmetto, the **Roma Flea Market** at 5715 15th St. East, or the market opposite Sarasota/Bradenton Airport.

Statues from Ringling's collection ring the circle of painted, primed, and polished **St. Armand's Circle,** the area's most famous shopping district, and one so well known from coast to coast in Florida that it's almost a city in itself. There's everything here from ormolu to organdy, chocolates to cheese; you can lose weeks gazing at the treasures in these windows.

Across the bay in Sarasota, Palm Avenue is the site of **Mira Mar Plaza,** two blocks of Mediterranean architecture, wrought-iron balconies, tiny gardens, and palm-lined streets. Plunk down at the Café Prague's sidewalk tables and watch the passing parade over a lunch of wine and crêpes.

Major shopping malls in the area include **East Lake Square Mall,** East Hillsborough Avenue and 56th Street, with more than 130 stores including J.C. Penney and Montgomery Ward; **Tampa Bay Center,** at Buffalo and Himes avenues, with 152 stores in a two-level, high-tech design (anchor shops include Burdine's, Sears, and Montgomery Ward); **University Square Mall,** on Fowler Avenue west of the University of South Florida campus, where 125 retail stores surround J.C. Penney, Maas Brothers, Robinson's, and Sears; and **Westshore Plaza,** West Kennedy and Westshore boulevards, with more than 90 shops including Maas Brothers, J.C. Penney, and Robinson's.

In Clearwater, the **Clearwater Mall,** US 19 and Gulf-to-Bay Boulevard, has 150 stores including Ivey's, Gayfers and Montgomery Ward; **Countryside Mall,** US 19 and Enterprise Road, is anchored by Penney's, Maas Brothers, Robinson's, and Sears.

**Pinellas Square Mall,** US 19 South in Pinellas Park, is the budget-lover's favorite, with more than 100 stores including Montgomery Ward, J.C. Penney, and Ivey's.

**Tyrone Square Mall,** Tyrone Boulevard at 66th Street in St. Petersburg, sports more than 200 shops, including three department stores.

## SIDE TRIPS

**Oscar Sherer Recreation Area,** located two miles south of Osprey on US 41, offers 500 acres of tropical beauty with facilities for tent and trailer camping, picnic areas, nature trails, fishing, and docks. The park is open from 8am to sunset, and admission is 50¢ per person.

Even larger is **Myakka River State Park,** 13207 Fla. 72, Sarasota, FL 34241 (tel. 813/924-1027 or 365-0100), about 15 miles east of Sarasota, a serene 29,000-acre wildlife sanctuary where you can rent a bike, take an hour-long guided airboat tour ($6 for adults, $3 for children 5 to 12), or a tram tour (same prices). It's fascinating to explore these acres of Florida "prairie," and fun to picnic at tranquil wooden tables or relax under towering live oaks. There's an interpretive center that will tell you what the land's all about. You can rent canoes ($6 an hour) and campsites ($14 to $20 a night), and even roomy cabins with two double beds and a fireplace for $50 a night (you supply your own linens). It's lovely just to drive through the park. Admission is $1 to $2 for the vehicle operator and 50¢ to $1 per passenger. If you'd like to rent a campsite or stay in one of the cabins, you should reserve by telephoning 813/924-1027.

---

# 6. Tours

---

You can sit back and leave the driving—or the sailing—to them on a number of tours operating in the area.

**Gray Line Sightseeing Tours** (tel. 822-3577), will take you to the area's attractions as far afield as Walt Disney World. Walt Disney World tours cost $64 round trip and include the price of Disney admission. Other tours begin at $35.

## St. Petersburg

In St. Petersburg, the **Junior Women's Club** operates a one-hour open-air streetcar tour (winter only) along the city's waterfront at varying times. Fare is $3; for information, call 822-4982.

## Bradenton/Tampa

**Seafood Shack Showboat,** 4110 127th St., Cortez (tel. 794-3766), journeys out into the gulf every day on two-hour cruises that show you around these scenic waters. On Sunday the boat takes you farther afield for a look at the soaring stanchions of the Sunshine Skyway Bridge. Tours on this double-decker paddlewheel boat are on a varying schedule, and cost $7 to $10 for adults, $4 for children 4 to 11. When you get back, or before you go, you can nip into the Seafood Shack for a passel of shrimp or some fresh seafood that seems to have leaped right up out of the big pond in front of their door. It's open from 11:30am to 10pm daily and has dinner prices in the $10 to $15 range.

**Seascape Cruises,** based at 1080 Port Blvd., Port of Miami, Miami, FL 33132 (tel. toll free 800/432-0900), will sail you off on one-day cruises from St. Petersburg to nowhere aboard one of its big cruise ships. Once aboard, you participate in all the fun and games, swimming, dining, gambling, and general fooling around at no extra cost. One-day cruises depart at 10am and return at 8:30pm daily and cost $79 for adults, $49 for teenagers, and $15 for children under 11. If you want to rent a cabin for the day, rates run from $60. Once a month the ship sails on a four-day weekend trip to Cozumel from St. Petersburg for rates ranging from $239 to $399. Morning and late-night trips, too.

### Holiday Isles

Over in St. Petersburg Beach, the triple-decker **Capt. Anderson** sails from the Capt. Anderson Cruise Port at 3400 Pasadena Ave. S. (tel. 367-7804), on a wide variety of cruises including two-hour narrated Boca Ciega Bay cruises at 1:30pm Tuesday through Friday, dolphin-feeding, and luncheon trips. On Wednesday, Friday, and Saturday evenings, the craft boards at 6:30pm for a romantic moonlight cruise with dinner ($7 to $15) and dancing on board for $10 for adults, $2 less for children under 12. Afternoon trips are at varying times and are $5 to $12 for adults, $4 to $7 for children. The *Capt. Anderson* operates from October to mid-May. Reservations for evening cruises are wise.

---

# 7. Seeing the Sights

---

There is much to see and do around Tampa Bay, ranging from a visit to the palatial mansion of a circus king to visiting with the king of the jungle. So you can see it all with as little traveling as possible, after the superstar we've grouped the attractions by location, beginning with Tampa and moving on to St. Petersburg, the Holiday Isles, and winding up in Sarasota.

## BUSCH GARDENS

Would you want to miss a place where Tarzan and Jane stroll blithely by and a giraffe gives you the eye from on high? Certainly not, and hundreds of thousands of other bay area visitors agree, which is why Busch Gardens is the second most popular tourist attraction in the state (second only to Walt Disney World).

To go to central Florida without seeing **Busch Gardens: The Dark Continent** is to be forever plagued by other Florida travelers asking how you could have missed it. Indeed it is something to see, this massive jungle park built by the famous brewery. To get there, take I-75 or I-275 to the Busch Boulevard exit and then just follow the signs to the park (tel. 971-8282 or 988-5171). Address is 3000 E. Busch Blvd., (at 40th Street) Tampa.

Once you're there you can see all the hundreds of things there are in a variety of ways: on foot, on a monorail, or on a Skyride cable car that crosses the Dark Continent's Serengeti Plain and gives you a giraffe's eye view of giraffes.

You can also toot-toot around by a train that circles a park where animals roam free, separated by moats or other natural barriers. Out there on the plain are 500 head of big game roaming freely over a 160-acre veldt. Gazelles zip off into the distance, zebras chase each other around, and elephants amble slowly about.

Turn-of-the-century Africa is the theme, from **Marrakesh** belly dancers and snake charmers to the **Congo,** where huge Bengal tigers prowl endlessly around their domain, stopping now and then to dive in for a cool swim in their pool. There's a terrific ice-skating show and in **Timbuktu** the Dolphins of the Deep perform. In **Nairobi** night creatures prowl Nocturnal Mountain. In **Stanleyville,** named after the gentleman responsible for that "Dr. Livingstone, I presume" remark, you can see Tanzanian tribesmen practicing their ancient woodcarving art. Clydesdale horses and Koalas are new lures.

There simply is nothing more adorable than a baby anything. That's what Busch's clever designers figured when they created the **Nairobi Field Station** animal nursery. Here newborn animals that are ill, injured, or rejected by their parents are cared for by human surrogate mothers, who are quite a sight cuddling a monkey-faced "baby." This very unusual nursery was built to look like an African hospital of yore, complete with ceiling fans and a hut facade. Peek in at the babies through big viewing windows and don't miss a look at the sky-lighted playroom where the baby chimps romp. Quite amazing addition, the nursery is as sanitized as a people hospital and gets washed every day top to bottom. Even the monkeys' baby bottles are sterilized. A little aside here: More than 1,200 creatures of all species are born here at Busch each year.

A new fun thing to do here is a **photo safari** offered once a month. For that by-reservation adventure you board the back of the park's feed truck and go right out there among the animals, snapping wildly as the giraffes and gazelles prance on over for a snack.

This 300-acre park contains the largest collection of mammals, reptiles, and birds in North America—3,000 in all—and enough to do to keep you busy all day: riding the state's largest log flume ride, touring the tantalizing array of craft shops, or visiting the tigers. Some, of course, think the most fun of all is tossing back a few at the Anheuser Busch brewery, where all the beer you consume is free!

Try not to lose your head on an *African Queen* boat ride up the river to a headhunters' village, or your tummy on the Tanganyika Tidal Wave ride or the Python roller coaster, which does a complete 360° loop, and is considered one of the best roller coasters in the nation by people who rate such things. Rest up later at the cavernous Festhaus, which comes complete with oom-pah-pah.

Busch Gardens is open daily from 9am to 7:30pm. One admission of $23.95 per person (children under 2 are free) includes everything in the park except parking ($2 a car). Here, as at Walt Disney World, be sure to remember your parking lot row number. Another similarity to Disney is acreage—there's lots of it, so wear comfortable clothes and shoes (especially shoes), and remember how fast the Florida sun can burn.

Next door to the gardens, you'll find **Adventure Island,** 4500 Bougainvillea Ave. (tel. 971-7978), a 19-acre water park complete with water slides and endless surf, lots of kids' games that are also fun for I'm-a-kid-again travelers. One-day admission is $13.95 a person, with children under 2 free. After 3pm prices drop to $6.25 per person. It gets a little chilly for this kind of fun in winter, so the park is open only from March 15 to September 15, weekends only in October. Hours are 10am to 5pm, later on weekends and in summer. Children under 8 must be accompanied by an adult.

## TAMPA

One of our favorite attractions is apparently shared by the city fathers who use the minarets of the **University of Tampa** as a logo. That's fitting too, since the Tampa Bay Hotel (now the university) put Tampa on the map as a tourist destination. Henry Plant's dream hotel, the old Tampa Bay hostelry does look a bit like something someone dreamed. Atop it are bright silver minarets and around the wide verandas is Moorish gingerbread woodwork. Tampa Bay was the grandest of grand hotels when it opened in 1891. Guests arrived in private railroad cars on a spur that ended right at the hotel's lobby! If they came by water, they pulled the yachts up to a dock and walked an underground tunnel to the reception desk.

The Tampa Bay Hotel cost a staggering $3 million even in those days, and today you can see it on free tours conducted on Tuesday and Thursday at 1:30pm. You'll see the wide verandas where Teddy Roosevelt, Babe Ruth, Clara Barton, and William Jennings Bryan once rocked, and the Music Room where long windows opened onto the veranda to accommodate overflow crowds gathered for performances by Ignace Paderewski, Anna Pavlova, and Sarah Bernhardt. There are hallways so long guests used to hire rickshaws to trot them around, and a hand-carved mahogany elevator originally powered by hydraulic force, the only one of its kind in the nation. If you're exhausted, visit the basement rathskeller, under the hotel's lobby, which was used to house Spanish-American War troops and is the place the "Cuba Libre" drink was born. A small museum on the grounds houses many of Plant's priceless art objects, and is free.

To find the university, look out for those 13 silver minarets (for the 13 months of the Muslim lunar year), but if you don't see them, take the Ashley Street exit from I-275 and follow Ashley toward downtown to US 60 (West Kennedy Boulevard). Turn right across the bridge and you'll see the campus guardhouse on your left.

Free hotel tours are generally available from September through May on Tuesday and Thursday at 1:30pm; but schedules vary, so it is wise to check first. Museum tours are available daily, except Sunday and Monday, from 10am to 4pm; $2 suggested donation for adults, 50¢ for children. Tour information is available at 253-3333 or 250-6220.

The **Tampa Museum of Art,** 601 Doyle Carlton Dr. (tel. 223-8130), houses a variety of changing and permanent exhibits including the Noble Collection of Classical Antiquities, European and American paintings and sculpture, and a changing array of contemporary work. If you're traveling with children, the museum has some interesting participatory exhibits in the Lower Gallery. Guided tours are available weekdays at noon and 1pm. A great gift shop sells reproductions of artwork and lots of posters, books, jewelry, and toys. Hours are 10am to 5pm Tuesday, Thursday, Friday, and Saturday, to 9pm on Wednesday. On Sunday the museum is open from 1 to 5pm; closed Monday. Donations accepted.

The **Museum of Science and Industry,** (MOSI), at 4801 E. Fowler Ave. (tel. 985-5531), has dozens of fascinating participatory science and space exhibits, and charges a $4 admission for adults, $2 for children 5 to 15. It's open from 10am to 4:30pm daily.

A new old sight in Tampa is the **Tampa Theater,** 711 N. Franklin St. (tel. 223-8981), a 1926 rococo creation that's getting all gussied up again. You'll see painted ceilings here, a beautiful old theater organ restored to the tune of thousands of dollars, and a revamped world of flapper-era style. It's fun—and even more fun because it's still operating as a theater. Every weekend there's a film festival of old films or foreign films, films that never quite made it to Tampa theaters, and, well, just all kinds of films. You can put yourself in celluloid heaven for $4 a film. For an annual $15 membership you can see whatever they're showing over a six-month period and have a say in what that is too. Local publications like the *Tampa Tribune* or *Tampa* magazine will have information on what's playing.

Along the Hillsborough River are 105 wooded acres devoted to **Tampa's Lowry Park,** 7525 North Blvd. (tel. 935-5503), a children's delight containing a zoo ($4 adults, $2 children 4 to 12), a pet-the-deer Bambi-land, and 18 small rides (6 rides for $3 or 60¢ each). It's a pretty place at the corner of Sligh and North boulevards, and has concerts in a bandshell. Open Monday through Thursday from 10am to 6pm; Friday and Saturday until 10pm and Sunday until 8pm.

## ST. PETERSBURG

The newest celebrity resident of St. Petersburg is Salvador Dali, who, sad to say, is not here in person but is certainly here in spirit via hundreds of his paintings on display at the **Salvador Dali Museum,** 1000 3rd St. S. (tel. 823-3767). Keep a sense of humor uppermost when you visit here and you'll be rewarded with many a chuckle over Dali's whimsical paintings and sculptures, some of which make some quite amusing statements about this world of bureaucrats and bemused humankind. Don't miss the case of sculptural work that includes a replica of Dali's aphrodisiac dinner jacket, produced in 1930: It's composed of white female undergarments in place of a formal shirt beneath a black jacket covered with small plastic shot glasses filled with green liquid. A classic!

Dali, acclaimed as the founder of surrealistic art, lived in Spain and never saw this St. Petersburg tribute to his work. His paintings and sculpture ended up here when A. Reynolds Morse, a Cleveland plastics millionaire, told the *Wall Street Journal* he'd give his huge collection of Dali's works to any city that would build a museum to house it. St. Petersburg jumped to accommodate him, and built a sleek new building, all gray and white inside, to house the collection.

Open from 10am to 5pm Tuesday through Saturday and from noon to 5pm on Sunday, the museum now owns more than 1,300 pieces of Dali's work, and displays them on a rotating basis so no matter how many times you visit you'll always be seeing something new. Surrealism, by the way, is often defined as visual expression of objects in incongruous juxtapositions, fantastic arrangements, and/or hallucinatory, dream-like settings—quite a good description of this wildly mustachioed artist's controversial work. Admission is $3.50 for adults, $2.50 for students.

It doesn't sound much like a tourist attraction, but when you see St. Petersburg's **Municipal Pier,** you'll see why it is. This streak of concrete at the foot of Second Avenue has been here so long in one form or another it's become the city's symbol, landmark, and love. First constructed in 1889 by the Orange Belt Railway, it was in those days a large, ornate bathing pavilion and a toboggan slide with a horse-drawn flatcar to carry passengers from the boat docks two miles away. It's not quite that long now after several facelifts, but there's still a jitney service to carry you down the mile of concrete and shops to keep you amused. On that mile you'll see an upside-down pyramid pavilion that sits in weird splendor out over the sparkling waters of the bay, craft vendors, gift shops, a restaurant, lounge, and an observation deck, and under it is a tiny strip of sand for bathing where there was once an admission charge of 10¢! There's *no* admission here now.

A bridge isn't usually a tourist attraction either, but the **Skyway Bridge** soaring high over Tampa Bay is wondrous testimony to the skills of modern-day Caesars. This series of bridges and causeways stretches 14 miles across to Sarasota, four of them by bridge. It's a beautiful view surrounded by water and sand.

St. Petersburg is proud of its **Museum of Fine Arts,** at 255 Beach Dr. NE (tel. 896-2667), as well as it should be since this museum not only houses an outstanding collection of 17th- to 19th-century artwork, but is an arty edifice itself, with dozens of tall columns and an arched Mediterranean courtyard. It's open daily except Monday, Christmas, and New Year's Day, from 10am to 5pm (from 1pm on Sunday). At 2pm Tuesday through Sunday and 11am Tuesday through Friday there are guided tours at no charge. Admission is free, but they'd like it if you left a small donation.

If you like gardens, you can see more than 5,000 varieties of plants, bird shows and a wax museum at enchanting **Sunken Gardens,** a west coast attraction since 1903. It's at 1825 4th St. N. (tel. 896-3186), and admission is $6.95 for adults, $4 for children 3 to 11. Doors open at 9am and close at 5:30pm.

**St. Petersburg's Historical Museum,** 335 Second Ave. (tel. 894-1052), has an amazing if somewhat eclectic array of memorabilia from the city's early days, including the original city seal, which some wag sketched with mountains in the background. A 400-year-old cypress canoe is interesting, and there's a sugar bowl used by Mr. and Mrs. Tom Thumb. It's open Monday through Saturday from 10am to 5pm (from 1pm on Sunday); admission is $2 for adults, 50¢ for children under 11 years.

The **Haas Museum Village Complex,** 3511 Second Ave. S. (tel. 327-1437), is where a number of the city's old homes dating back to 1850 have been perfectly preserved and restored. It's open from 1 to 5pm Thursday through Sunday (closed in September) and admission is $2 for adults, 50¢ for children under 12.

There's a really huge collection of old homes at fascinating **Heritage Park,** 11909 125th St. N., in Largo (tel. 462-3474). You can visit a 13-room mansion from the early years of this century, a tiny (14- by 14-foot) honeymoon cottage, and a log house that's one of the oldest buildings in the country and was the birthplace of more than 50 children (not all to the same mother, we hasten to add). It's open every day but Monday from 10am to 4pm (on Sunday from 1pm). The park has tours every half hour from 10am to 4pm, but you can look on your own anytime. It's free.

**Boyd Hill Nature Center,** at 1101 Country Club Way S. (tel. 893-7236), is an intriguing place at the south end of lovely Lake Maggiore. There are six different circle trails, each an easy 15-minute walk through a microcosm of Florida fauna and flora. Admission is 75¢ for adults, 35¢ for children under 18, and there's a guided tour at 11am daily. The park is open from 9am to 5pm. You can reach it by traveling south on 9th Street to Country Club Way South; then bear right and go three blocks.

**Great Explorations,** 1120 4th St. S. (tel. 821-8885), is a charming new hands-on museum that encourages children to discover everything from geography to Chinese brush paintings. Varying exhibits add to the allure of this unusual museum, which also features a touch tunnel you feel your way through, a Bubble Trouble giant bubble and a do-it-yourself box of triangle bubbles, a fitness test, a safe you can crack if you're smart, a star you can trace while viewing the whole process through a mirror, a laser pinball game, synthesizers, a sculpture operated by sound, paintings you create with sunlight, pole puzzles and platform puzzles, and . . . well, what are we all doing here? Let's get on over there and try some of this stuff out. As much for adults as for children, Great Explorations is open from 10am to 5pm daily, opening at noon on Sunday. Admission is $4.50 for adults, $3.50 for children 2 to 17, free to younger tykes.

**READER'S SIGHTSEEING TIP:** "My family attended a performance of the **Ringling Bros. Circus** in St. Petersburg in January. Although I didn't realize it at the time, St. Petersburg is the first stop of the annual tour of the circus, and each performance is videotaped for a national television broadcast. Those who vacation in the Tampa–St. Petersburg area may take advantage of this special opportunity" (Walt Ulbricht, Kenosha, Wis.). [*Author's Note:* Mr. Ulbricht (whose very nice comments on *Frommer's Florida* were most gratefully received) and others visiting the Tampa Bay area might wander south a bit to the town of Venice to visit the winter headquarters of the circus (see the information on circus visits in Chapter XIII on Florida's Shell Coast), which does indeed begin its season with performances in a number of Florida cities.]

## HOLIDAY ISLES

One of the more unusual stops for bird lovers is the **Suncoast Seabird Sanctuary,** at 18328 Gulf Blvd., Indian Shores (tel. 391-6211), where conservationist Ralph Heath, Jr., has set up a nonprofit organization dedicated to the rescue, repair, and recuperation of wild birds. His sanctuary's been a television star several times, and is a good spot for photography since the quarry can't just up and fly away. You can even adopt your own bird with a donation. There's no admission charge, and they're open from 9am to sunset daily.

Shiver under the malevolent stare of Bluebeard and see what Cleopatra really looked like before Elizabeth Taylor at the **London Wax Museum,** 5505 Gulf Blvd., St. Petersburg Beach (tel. 360-6985). Craftspeople of Britain's famed Tussaud's Museum created these characters; everyone from Julius Caesar to Lee Harvey Oswald and—are you ready?—Rambo is here. It's open from 9am to 9pm daily (from noon on Sunday) and costs $4 for adults, $2 for children 4 to 12.

**Tiki Gardens,** 19601 Gulf Blvd., Indian Shores (tel. 595-2567), re-creates the beauty of Polynesia in 12 acres of exotic tropical blossoms, temples with peacocks, and a squawking mynah bird. There's even a Polynesian restaurant overlooking the gardens and excellent entertainment evenings. Admission to a Polynesian Trail is $2 for adults, $1 for children, all else is free. The gardens are open daily from 10am to 6pm, later in lounges and restaurants.

Perched picturesquely atop a bluff commanding a beautiful (and once useful) view of Tampa Bay is **Fort DeSoto,** a relic of Spanish-American War days complete with gun emplacements and cavernous dynamite room, neither ever used. In the shadows of this stony sentinel is an 884-acre park spread across six islands with seven miles of sparkling waterfront and three miles of silky white sand beach. You can swim and fish from piers here (free), picnic, and dress to go home in dressing rooms with showers. Toll is 65¢ and the park closes at dark.

Ponce de León anchored off these shores in 1513 to scrape the bottom of his barnacle-encrusted boat when Native Americans attacked, killing one of his men, the first white soldier to die on this continent.

**Starlite Princess,** a replica of an authentic paddlewheel riverboat, will take you out for dinner and dancing in Tampa Bay for $24.95 per person. You can also sail off on lunch and sightseeing cruises aboard the craft for $6 adults, $4 children. *Starlite Princess* docks at Hamlin's Landing, 401 2nd St. E., Indian Rocks Beach (tel. 595-1212).

Those who never met a 21 they didn't like should like this next option: a cruise aboard a ship that sails by night or day out beyond the nine-mile limit. Two ships operated by **Europa Cruise Line,** the *Europa Sun* and the *Europa Star* sail off a couple of times every day for cruises to nowhere that give you maximum time to eat, drink, and be merry, which can include sunning by the rail or bellying up to the blackjack or roulette table or one of the many slot machines. There are bingo games for those who cannot resist that divertissement. There's recreation to suit everyone. Entertainment ranges from comedy acts to singers and dancers. Meals are included in the price of the trip.

Six-hour voyages occur daily on a varying schedule, with one of the two boats usually departing at 11am, 1pm, 6pm, or 7pm. Prices vary, too, from $47 to $57 for adults and $27 for children on day cruises, the same price as adults on evening trips. You can contact the line at 150 153rd Ave., Suite 202, Madeira Beach, FL 33708 (tel. 800/688-7529), and get a look at the boats at the dock at John's Pass Village or at the Treasure Island Pier.

## SARASOTA

Humankind's ability to assimilate both the garishly gaudy and the gloriously grandiose is epitomized nowhere better than in the person of circus king John Ringling, who with one hand created the sequined world of the Big Top and with the other commanded the accumulation of a priceless art collection, which he housed in a columned Italian Renaissance architectural creation of tranquil symmetry. It remains today one of the most beautiful museums in the world.

As if that weren't enough, Ringling went on to create **Ca' d'Zan,** at 5401 Bay Shore Rd. (tel. 355-5101), a palatial bayside home for himself and his wife, Mable. It's a multi-million-dollar Venetian Gothic palazzo (hence its name, which means House of John) combining elements of the Doges Palace in Venice and the tower at the old Madison Square Garden.

One of the 10 richest men in America when he died in 1936, Ringling gave the beautiful peach art gallery and the rosy-cream stucco palazzo, his 68-acre estate, his priceless art collection, and his entire fortune to the state of Florida, which now welcomes 500,000 visitors here each year and charges them only $5, $1.75 for children 6 to 12, to tour it all. Admission includes entrance to all three parts of this complex (we're coming to the others shortly), including the Museum of Art, Ca' d'Zan, and the Circus Museum. Tours of the house are from 10am to 3pm, and the grounds are open to 6pm.

Part of what you'll see here—and even the most dedicated anti-sight-seeing souls shouldn't miss this—is the **Museum of Art,** styled after a 15th-century Italian villa, and featuring shiploads of columns, doorways, sculpture, and marble brought here from all the major cities of Italy. Galleries are laid out on three sides of a formal garden, and on the fourth side there's a raised bridge dominated by a bronze copy of Michelangelo's *David.* Atop the loggia is a balustrade adorned with 72 roof sculptures.

Some say that Mabel Ringling had the pretensions of grandeur that created the awesomely magnificent 30-room mansion that's 200 feet long and is capped by a

60-foot tower. Inside, carved and gilded furniture from the estates of the Astors and Goulds fills 30 rooms surrounding a 2½-story roofed court. There's a coffered ceiling of Florida pecky cypress framing an inner skylight of colored glass and priceless tapestries, some of which conceal a $50,000 Aeolian organ with 4,000 pipes played both electrically and manually, plus Venetian glass in every color of the rainbow. A tub in one bath is hewn from a solid block of yellow Siena marble, and there are bathroom fixtures made of gold. A bar with leaded-glass panels was once part of the Cicardi Winter Palace in St. Louis.

Convinced? There's more: a **museum of the circus** full of gilded parade wagons, calliopes, and the **Asolo Theater.** It's open from 9am to 10pm (for more about the theater, see Sarasota nightlife) and it's fabulous.

It's hard to compete with Ringling, but the **Gamble Mansion,** in Ellenton on US 301 (tel. 813/722-1017), can almost do it. This airy antebellum mansion was the home of Maj. Robert Gamble and is now a Confederate Museum. It was here that Confederate Secretary of State Judah P. Benjamin was hidden away in an upstairs room until he could escape to freedom in England where he became a successful barrister. Scarlett and Rhett would have been right at home in this shining white-columned manse that reeks of elegant, drawling days gone by. The mansion is open from 9am to 5pm Thursday through Monday. Tours are every hour, and admission is $1, under 13 is 50¢.

Ziegfeld Follies girls once preened here. Will Rogers performed here, and dancer Sally Rand waved her fans around here. Even Elvis Presley once took to the boards of what is now the **Sarasota Theater of the Arts.** Then hard times came to the old opera house building at 61 N. Pineapple Ave. (tel. 953-7030 or 366-8450). Built in the 1920s, the theater, once the hub of downtown Sarasota, became a derelict building, its handsome courtyard enclosed, its fanciful balconies shuttered. Then in 1979 the Sarasota Opera bought the old theater and talked supporters into beginning a multi-million-dollar renovation of the building.

Now a crystal chandelier, rescued from the movie set of *Gone With the Wind,* glitters in the foyer and tuxedoed opera fans once again chatter at intermission. It's worth a visit just to take a look at this historic old building, even better if you're here February through April when the Sarasota Opera Association presents four operas and performances by ballet troupes and string quartets. Opera tickets are $12.50 to $35, slightly less if you write for a subscription. In other months the building is used by organizations that sponsor lectures and other cultural activities.

It's hard to resist a music box, and it's harder yet to resist 2,000 intriguing antique music boxes ranging from calliopes to nickelodeons. Team that up with antique classic cars as they have at **Bellm's Cars and Music of Yesterday,** 5500 N. Tamiami Trail (tel. 355-6228), and the child in us all demands a visit. Some of Ringling's cars are here and they're valued at $200,000. The museum is open from 8:30am to 6pm Monday through Saturday, from 9:30am on Sunday. Adults are charged $6, children 6 to 12 years, $3.

Choo-choos and coquinas—how's that for a combination? They have them both at the **Lionel Train and Shell Museum,** 8184 N. Tamiami Trail (US 41), across from the airport (tel. 355-8184), housed in a replica of a Victorian railroad depot. Trains run automatically, although coin machines are provided so you can run them. There's even one that runs completely around the museum over 40 bridges. Hours are 9am to 5pm. Although there is an admission charge for the train displays ($2.50 adults, 50¢ children), the shell exhibit is free.

Two lovely gardens in Sarasota offer flower fans a look at jungle plants and orchids. **Sarasota Jungle Gardens,** at 3701 Bay Shore Rd., two blocks west of US 41 (tel. 355-5305), has flamingos in the flowers, leopards, parrots, alligators, and monkeys, plus bird and reptile shows, in a 10-acre jungle with winding trails. It's open from 9am to 5pm daily and charges $6 for adults, $3 for children 3 to 12 years old.

A lesser known but equally lush tropical garden is **Marie Selby Botanical Gardens,** on US 41 at 811 S. Palm Ave. (tel. 366-5730). It's a must-see for nature lovers and serious botanists, a 14-acre site that is a research center for epiphytes, bromeliads, and a glorious collection of orchids. An old Florida home on the grounds—now the Museum of Botany and the Arts—was built in 1935 by a would-be architect, who pooled the best features he'd found in a dozen or more southern mansions to create this home. It's all there—including a new boardwalk —to be toured from 10am to 5pm daily at $4 for adults, free to under-12s with an adult.

**Bishop Planetarium,** at 201 10th St. W. (Business US 41), Bradenton (tel. 746-STAR), opens its Cassegrain reflecting telescope on the first and third weekends of every month at 9pm for a free look at faraway glitter. There's a historical museum and laser rock music here too. Planetarium admission is $4 for adults, $2 for students 5 to 12 years.

Thirty miles south of Sarasota and 12 miles south of Venice, just off US 41 South, is **Warm Mineral Springs Spa,** San Servando Avenue in warm Mineral Springs (tel. 813/426-1692), where 10 million gallons of mineral-laden water flows daily—four times more water than at Baden-Baden, Vichy Hot Springs, or Aix-les-Bains. It's been a watering spot for 10,000 years: Bones discovered in underwater explorations of the hourglass-shaped sink hole are evidence of swimmers who paddled around here way back then. You can swim here now for $6 from 9am to 5pm daily.

---

# 8. Side Trips from Tampa Bay

Many small communities around the Tampa Bay area are tiny pockets of immigrant settlers who have kept their folklore intact for generations—in nearby Tarpon Springs, children's report cards are written in Greek!

It's fun exploring these small byways and backroads, where you'll discover shady streets and imposing city halls from the column-and-brick era, and meet some friendly people who'll welcome the opportunity to tell you about themselves and their communities.

Heading north from the Clearwater area you'll find the Scots community of Dunedin, then the Greek village of Tarpon Springs. Still farther north are the clear, cold waters of Weeki Wachee Springs and Homossassa Springs, and finally tiny Cedar Key, a community that's been far from the main road for decades.

From Sarasota you can make a fascinating sojourn to Florida's cattle country in Arcadia and see one of the state's biggest rodeos, or drive along the coastline to the villages of Venice and Englewood, which were once lemon plantations and are now the state's shark's teeth and circus centers.

## DUNEDIN

More than 130 years ago, two Scots created one of the first settlements on the west coast here, naming it after Scotland's Dunedin. That Scots history lives on here via the **City Bagpipe and Drum Corps** that performs at 2:30pm on the first Sunday of the month and for special occasions. They wear Elliot, Dress Stewart, and Royal Stewart tartans. In April each year they and the rest of the city turn out for revelry called the **Highland Games,** an event with everything from parades to a Military Tattoo and Retreat ceremony.

At the Kirk (church) of Dunedin you can hear one of the largest pipe organs in the South on the second Thursday and Friday of each month at 8:15pm from October through April, and for sports enthusiasts the city is the spring training ground for the **Toronto Blue Jays.**

You can spend a tranquil day here journeying by ferry to **Caladesi Island,** a 550-acre state park preserved in its natural wooded state with beautiful unspoiled beaches. Ferry trips (tel. 734-5263) cost $3.75 for adults, $2.10 for children under

12, and run from 9am to 4:30pm every hour, returning on the half hour. Don't miss that last one—it's a long swim!

There's another beach here too, with the romantic name of **Honeymoon Island Beach.** It's just a short drive from the city over a causeway.

A drive through this city on US 19A from Clearwater is a scenic route that takes you along the bay. Tall skinny palms march along beside you and rolling expanses of green lawns surround stately Old Florida homes. The former Trinity College's arches and tile roof gleam as they have for many years since this was the Fenway Resort Hotel.

Call the **Dunedin Chamber of Commerce** at 813/733-3197 for regional information, or write to them at 434 Main St., Dunedin, FL 33528.

## Food and Lodging

If you'd like to stay over in Dunedin (pronounced "Dun-*ee*-din"), you can't do better than the **Jamaica Inn,** 150 Marina Plaza, Dunedin, FL 34698 (tel. 813/733-4121), which backs up to St. Joseph's Sound and gazes out over the city's tiny marina where ferry and fishing boats are moored. Beamed ceilings, brick trim, and huge expanses of glass are architectural pluses, and bright colors give the resort a tropical look. Every room faces the water and some overlook the resort's pool from private balconies or patios.

The Jamaica Inn is also renowned in the Tampa Bay area for its fine restaurant, **Bon Appétit,** where Austrian and German chefs reign over a flower-bedecked dining room filled with silk roses and banks of blooms. Hot and cold appetizers arrive on a cart, delicate seafood, veal, and steak concoctions are outstanding, and water glasses are garnished with slivers of lemon. Prices are in the $8 to $20 range for entrées, and the restaurant is open from 8am to 10pm daily, with a massive Sunday brunch ($4.50 to $9) from 9am to 4pm. Try the German pfannkuchen (pancakes) for breakfast here.

Rates at the inn range from $45 to $72 for rooms, depending on the season, more year-round for efficiencies.

## TARPON SPRINGS

*Ya'sou* won't be Greek to you after a visit to the village of Tarpon Springs, a few miles north of Clearwater on US 19A. Here you leave Florida behind—for Greece! In this tiny village live the descendants of Greek sponge fishermen who settled here at the turn of the century and stayed here beside the sea they love although the sponge fishing declined in the 1930s when disease hit the sponge beds and synthetic sponges hit the markets.

Here you'll hear the staccato sounds of Greek as shopkeepers and fishermen gossip over a cup of thick black coffee or a sparkling glass of retsina. Try a friendly *Ya'sou* (hello or good-bye) yourself and win a glittering Greek smile. Gorge on honey-soaked baklava or musky dark olives piled atop a feta-laden Greek salad. Watch muscular young fishermen glide sensuously through the lazy movements of a Greek dance, or join a circle of dancers yourself as *Never on Sunday* comes to life in this sleepy seaside village.

Just strolling around this Hellenic haven is as much fun as any planned sightseeing tour. It's a photographer's paradise, with strings of sturdy fat sponges drying in the sun, gewgaw souvenirs, delicate hand-embroidered linens, and shrimp nets ruffling the breeze.

You can see how fishermen collect the holey little devils aboard the **St. Nicholas Boat Line** sponge boat (tel. 937-9887), which leaves every 30 minutes (just listen for the barker calling out boarding times). This boat's been sailing since 1924, and has been featured in a World's Fair and several television shows. During the $4 ($2 for children over 6) trip, a diver wearing 12-pound shoes and an 18-pound suit so he can stay on the bottom jumps overboard with a four-pronged rake and spears the bounty of the deep. Next door to the boat is **Spongeorama** (tel. 942-3771), where you can visit a free museum of sponge memorabilia, including a movie ($1.50 for adults, 25¢ for children) that will tell you how sponge is harvested and why you shouldn't use the same sponge on your nose as you'd use on your car!

If you're really interested in the industry, look for **George Billiris,** who's usually at the boat dock. He's a flashing-eyed Greek charmer whose family has worked in the sponge trade for generations. In 1981 he tried hard—but failed—to save the town's picturesque sponge exchange warehouses from destruction. Billiris spends half his year buying and selling sponges in Europe, and will keep you spellbound with the intensity of his feelings for this unusual industry.

Stop by **St. Nicholas Greek Orthodox Cathedral,** on Pinellas Avenue, an outstanding example of glittering neo-Byzantine architecture and a replica of Istanbul's St. Sophia. In its cool dim interior are Grecian marble, beautiful iconography, and glowing stained glass.

If you're here in January, don't miss the city's **Greek Epiphany** celebration, when young Greeks dive into the waters of Spring Bayou for a gold cross—and 365 lucky days! In May there's a great seafood festival, and in April there's an art show here.

The **Greater Tarpon Springs Chamber of Commerce** is at 210 S. Pinellas Ave., Suite 120, Tarpon Springs, FL 34689 (tel. 813/937-6109). Folks at the chamber can provide you with a walking tour that will take you past several of the towns lovely historic homes built around tranquil Spring Bayou by chill-fleeing northerners who discovered this spot in the late 19th century. They also can arm you with information on the things to see and do here, including visiting the largest single display of the work of painter George Inness at the Universalist Church of Tarpon Springs, Grand Boulevard and Read Street.

## Food and Lodging

If you're staying over, a good moderately priced stop is the **Scottish Inn,** 110 W. Tarpon Ave., Tarpon Springs, FL 33589 (tel. 813/937-6121), built on a slope overlooking the waters of Spring Bayou. Rooms are trim and wood paneled, and have all the usual requisites like color television. Outside there's a swimming pool in a tranquil setting. Rates are $50 in winter, about $36 to $41 in summer, for rooms or efficiencies.

A mandatory stop in the village is Louis Pappamichaloupoulos' restaurant, at 10 W. Dodecanese Blvd. (tel. 937-5101), which for obvious reasons is called **Louis Pappas' Riverside.** This family has been in the restaurant business here since 1925 when they opened tiny Riverside café. Now a new massive Pappas' welcomes even more diners through the portals and sends them out stuffed on huge Greek salads and a wide variety of seafood dishes and Greek specialties like moussaka, lamb, and pastitsio. Big windows along the water offer a picturesque view of the village's marina, and dinner prices are in the $7 to $20 range. It's open from 11:30am to 10pm daily, 11pm on weekends.

Later you'll find plenty of Tampa Bay fun-seekers at **Zorba's,** 508 W. Athens St. (tel. 934-8803), every night except Monday about 8pm. You'll think you've slipped right into a remake of *Never on Sunday* here when Anthony Quinn lookalikes take to the floor to dance in solitary splendor, saluted occasionally with a congratulatory glass of ouzo. Sometimes there's a belly dancer and there's always a singer wailing melancholy outpourings of lost love. Join a Greek circle dance where many of the laughing dancers are blonde Americans!

To get into the evening atmosphere a little more quietly, try the **Sparta** or **Athena** lounge on Dodecanese Boulevard. They're a bit more tranquil and given to evenings long on philosophical discussion.

**READER'S LODGING SELECTION:** "The Livery Stable, 100 Ring Ave., Tarpon Springs, FL 34689 (tel. 813/938-5547), charges just $25 to $30 a night in winter for two including breakfast. Very clean, friendly hosts, and a nice beach (free) is about a 10-minute drive" (Ann Southmayd, Newark, Del.).

## CEDAR KEY

An interesting day trip from the Tampa Bay area is to Cedar Key, a tiny fishing village time seems to have ignored. Once a thriving port city and a rough-and-tumble frontier town with saloons, gambling, gunfights, and general whoop-de-doo, the city slumped after depletion of the area's timber fields, an 1896 fire, and a tidal wave.

Cedar Key got its name, by the way, from the dense groves of cedar trees that once grew here and provided raw material for more than 15 pencil-manufacturing companies that once lined a three-mile strip. Eberhardt (of Eberhardt-Faber fame) once owned much of this Cedar Key forest. Its trees were the, uh (we can't resist this), root of his fortune. Cedar Key trees provided softer wood that was more easily shaped around lead. What's more, pencils made from these trees were more easily sharpened and less inclined to split. See? More than you ever wanted to know about pencils.

But alas, those pencil pushers decimated the cedar forests here and departed, leaving islanders without an industry. Undaunted, they turned to their palms for a living, but we don't mean they went begging: They made palm-frond brooms that are now heirlooms in some Florida homes. But, alas, that industry too was swept away when plastic brooms were invented.

Finally, left with little but the sea around them, those indomitable Cedar Key folks managed to turn even the Gulf of Mexico to their advantage. Most are now fishermen or cater to the tourists drawn here by wonderful seafood restaurants and small, quiet seaside motels. One of those restaurants is called **Johnson's Brown Pelican,** on Docks Street (tel. 543-5428), where you can have seafood so fresh it's practically swimming. Prices are in the $5 to $16 range, and the restaurant is open daily from 7am to 10pm.

Another enticing restaurant is called **The Heron,** Fla. 24 and 2nd Street, Cedar Key (tel. 543-5666). You dine here in an old house fitted out with turn-of-the-century accoutrements. You'll find a few steak and chicken options on the menu, but the restaurant does its best work with thick clam chowders, fat clams called quahogs, scallops, oysters, sautéed shrimp, crab bisque, and all the other kinds of fresh, fresh seafood for which the island is famous among Floridians. You'll quickly feel right at home here talking to smiling workers that include the very pleasant owner/chef Janice Coupe and her husband, Dr. George Coupe, who serves on weekends as maître d'hôtel at this attractive restaurant. Entrée prices are in the $11 to $16 range for dinner at the Heron, which is open in winter from 11:30am to 2:30pm Tuesday through Sunday and 6 to 9:30pm on Friday and Saturday. In summer the Heron is open only on Friday and Saturday for lunch and dinner, and on Sunday for brunch and lunch.

More? Sure! The **Island Hotel,** on 2nd Street (tel. 543-5111), is a rustic spot with a dining room on a screened porch, neat and pretty tables with bright linens and ferns in wine bottles. Once again seafood is the main fare, and prices fall easily in the $8 to $15 range for dinner. Hours at the Island Hotel are 6 to 10pm daily except Tuesday and Wednesday, 5 to 9pm Sunday.

To get to Cedar Key, take US 19 north to Fla. 24 west. You'll find the key about 80 miles north of Tampa, but the drive takes you through some very pretty country.

## CRYSTAL RIVER

On the shores of Crystal River, 70 miles north of Tampa on US 19, you'll find one of the oldest and longest continually occupied Native American sites in the state. Ancient tribes who lived here are believed to have roamed as far west as the Yucatán and to have built a solar observatory. To see what they found so appealing here, hop aboard a glass-bottom boat at Crystal River Springs or try a scuba-diving trip or canoeing expedition.

If you'd like to stay over, seek the pillared facade of the **Plantation Golf Resort,** on West US 44, King's Bay Road (P.O. Box 1116), Crystal River, FL 32629 (tel. 904/795-4211), an old-world resort nestled on the edge of King's Bay (take I-75 from Tampa to US 41, and then drive north to Fla. 44). Surrounded by a purple profusion of azaleas in spring and scarlet poinsettias in winter, the resort has tennis courts, two golf courses totaling 26 holes, and a pool. The rooms are large, with lots of closet space, separate dressing rooms, and bright tropical colors. Evenings, there's entertainment in the lounge, and there's a pretty restaurant, too. This is a lovely resort out in the country, all by itself in beautiful open pine lands. Rates are $70 to $95, year round, higher for villas.

## HOMOSSASSA SPRINGS

About 75 miles south of the St. Petersburg/Tampa area and half a mile west of Homossassa Springs on US 19, huge sight-seeing boats leaving from Fishbowl Drive, Homossassa Springs (tel. 904/628-2311), take visitors down a winding tropical waterway into the heart of waters known as the **Spring of Ten Thousand Fish.** You can walk underwater among thousands of finny creatures at an observatory, and watch the staffers feed the alligators and hippos at Gator Lagoon. There's a manatee rehabilitation area, where those often-injured, gentle creatures are doctored. Daily hours are 9am to 5:30pm (last tickets sold at 4pm); admission is $7.37 for adults, $4.19 for children 3 to 12 (others, free).

## WEEKI WACHEE SPRING

This spring is a little closer to the Tampa Bay area, on US 19 and Fla. 50 (tel. 904/596-2062, or toll free 800/342-0297 in Florida). Mermaids swim around the nation's only underwater theater and you can watch the nearly tame fish swoop and swerve with them. Admission to the springs, which also has bird shows, is $12.95 for adults, $7.95 for children 3 to 11. **Buccaneer Bay,** a water park, charges $6.95 for adults, $5.95 for children.

## VENICE

No place in Florida is more a circus than Venice, a small seaside village whose claim to fame is none other than the **Ringling Bros. and Barnum & Bailey Circus,** the city's most famous resident. Clowns and high-wire artists, lion tamers and trained elephants aren't keen on cold weather either, so they winter here at 1401 Ringling Dr. S. (tel. 484-9511 or 484-0496) and make forays into Florida towns for winter appearances.

Their arrival on Miami Beach generates pages of publicity each year as the elephants are trooped across a mainland bridge, toll and all. Ringling's been a winter fixture in Venice since 1959, and has its own arena where it rehearses two separate shows, the Red and the Blue. You can see the premiere of the Red or Blue Show right here for $9.50 in late December and January. At any time of year you can peek at the circus trains, while they are repaired and repainted in those flaming circus colors.

Venice is a quiet waterside town with a number of small motels lining the beach. Oddities here are fossilized sharks' teeth, which you'll find all along the shoreline. They're here because prehistoric sharks, like modern ones, shed their teeth regularly, sometimes as many as 20,000 in a 10-year period. Those on the bottom are washed up on beaches just like shells. Bones of many prehistoric creatures have been found along this 10,000-year-old coastline, and there's even said to be treasure of a somewhat less studious nature: José Gaspar's loot is rumored to be buried around here somewhere.

## Food and Lodging

If you'd like to stay in the area, try Englewood, where you'll find **Chadwick Cove Resort and Marina,** 1825 Gulf Blvd., Englewood, FL 34223 (tel. 813/474-8577). It's a new, contemporary, nautical resort with attractively decorated one-bedroom apartments with lots of glass and a striking view of the bay and gulf. Jungly landscaped grounds surround a three-story building that blends into its beachside locale. Two friendly Floridians, Ron and Joanne Fendt, run Chadwick Cove Resort and Marina, and will be happy to direct you to good seafood restaurants or likely fishing spots in the area, and may even have a shark's tooth for you. In summer and fall, you'll pay $250 a week; from January to April, rates are $400 to $450 a week.

For budget digs, **Days Inn,** at 2540 S. McCall Rd., County Road 776 East in Englewood, FL 34224 (tel. 813/474-5544), has 48 three-room suites and 36 hotel rooms near the beach. There's a large pool for swimmers, and the usual thrifty Days Inn prices range from $45 to $85 in winter, $35 to $47 in summer and fall.

In Englewood, the **Cajun Club Restaurant,** at 750 N. Indiana Ave. (tel. 474-3535), spices things up with an array of créole flavors in the $8 to $15 range. It's open from 4 to 9pm daily (noon to 8pm on Sunday), with an all-you-can-eat buffet for about $7 or $9.

## WRANGLIN' IN ARCADIA

Tucked away about 40 miles east of Sarasota is one of Florida's last remaining cowboy towns, where you'll see gun racks on pickup trucks, cowboy hats and boots, and mile after mile of rangeland stalked by long-horned, humpbacked Brahma bulls. Here in Arcadia, things are just about the way they've always been—a couple of coffee shops, a barbecue or two, and watermelons for sale at Carter's Fruit Stand. There's a handsome county courthouse with red bricks and white columns, but visitors come here for only one reason: the **Arcadia All-Florida Championship Rodeo** in July and March. It's quite an event on a huge rodeo ground with all the bronc bustin' and calf ropin' you could want. Tickets are under $10, and you can order them in advance by writing to P.O. Box 1266 in Arcadia, FL 33821, or calling 813/494-2014, or toll free 800/749-RODEO.

Get there from Sarasota by taking US 41 south to Fla. 72 West, which goes straight through town and right by the rodeo grounds. If you're staying over, the **Best Western M & M,** at 504 S. Brevard, on US 17, Arcadia, FL 33821 (tel. 813/494-4884, or toll free 800/528-1234), is a simple, attractive spot where rates are $37 to $47, in winter, a bit lower the rest of the year.

The **De Soto County Chamber of Commerce,** 16 S. Volusia Ave. (P.O. Box 149), Arcadia, FL 33821 (tel. 813/494-4033), can help you with information on the area if you're staying around a while.

# THE SHELL COAST

## 1. FORT MYERS
## 2. NAPLES
## 3. SANIBEL AND CAPTIVA ISLANDS

This is the Shell Coast, the fantasyland of your winter dreams, a cluster of sun-kissed islands for which you yearn when bitter winds whip and temperatures fall and fall . . . and fall.

It sneaks up on you, this coastline, capturing you as it has captured the famous, and the infamous, before you. More than 2,000 years before you the Calusas dipped their toes into these warm waters in search of oysters and clams, conch and periwinkles, not for shells but for their contents.

Much later, fierce José Gaspar set up camp hereabouts to conduct a terrifying but financially gratifying career in plunder and pillage. Captiva Island, they say, got its name when that legendary buccaneer stored his female captives here to maintain their trading value by keeping them safe from his lecherous pirate companions. That Isla de las Captivas is, so the story goes, today's Captiva.

Florida usually has a ghost tucked away somewhere, and Gaspar's pals are said still to roam the island of Cayo Palau in Charlotte Harbor, zealously guarding a cache buried there.

Here on the Shell Coast, today's booty has little to do with gold. White sand and pearly shells are the treasures you seek here in these slow-paced villages where conversation takes precedence over change.

Scoff as you may, cynic, but when you see these miles of talcum-white sand piled with glittering gold, pink, russet, and mauve, you too will become a shell hunter, unable to resist the lure of a tiny pink cat's paw, or a rainbowed angel's wing, or a fighting conch, the giant of the deep, its wind tunnel roaring a siren's song. You too will bend, peer, and shuffle into the "Sanibel Stoop."

## GETTING THERE

You can get to **Southwest Florida Regional Airport** on American, Continental, Delta, Northwest, TWA, United Airlines, and USAir.

To get from the Fort Myers airport to hotels in that city, call **Yellow Cab** (tel. 332-1055). Fares to beach hotels are about $25. Around-town fares are by zone, averaging $5 to $10.

To get to Naples from the Fort Myers airport, call **Airport Mini Bus** (tel. 263-3011), which will take you to your hotel door for about $24.

**Sanibel and Captiva islands** are accessible only by car or boat, and there's a $3 round-trip toll across the Sanibel bridge to the islands.

## GETTING AROUND

It is virtually impossible to get around this area without a car. You can rent one from Alamo (tel. 936-3707), a leader of the budget rental pack, and 21 other **rental-car companies,** including Avis, Hertz, National, Thrifty, Ajax, and Budget, all of which have offices in Fort Myers or in Naples.

On Sanibel Hertz (tel. 472-1468) can rent you a car.

We've included specific information on bus service routes in Naples and Fort Myers in those sections. Sanibel has no bus service.

---

# 1. Fort Myers

---

Fort Myers hardly knows what to make of it all these days. Suddenly it's booming, as twice as many planes bring twice as many travelers here, doubling the competition for a place in the sun. Just when bemused residents had grown accustomed to hearing "Fort Myers? Hmmmm. Where is that again?" in come troops of travelers and dozens of developers who know just where it is and would like a small piece of its sand to call their own.

Wherever Fort Myers is headed these days, it's traveling there fast: It's in a nip-and-tuck competition for fastest-growing city in the nation. And no wonder. It's got the prime requisites of Florida travelers—a pretty beach, comfortable resorts, good restaurants, and sometimes ridiculously low prices.

One of the state's largest retirement regions, Fort Myers is taking its rapid growth easily if a bit warily. You'll see some change under way, but you won't find alteration of the city's slow-paced mañana atmosphere or its rustic beach neighborhood. Small family-owned hostelries continue to welcome travelers who have had standing reservations here for a decade or more, and in the city's restaurants decor takes a decided second place to a good platter of seafood.

There's change in the breezes here, but this is a city peopled by those whose convictions solidified long ago, so changes are gradual and gratifying. Fort Myers's favorite son, Thomas Alva Edison, who sought solace here years ago, would hardly notice the difference.

## GETTING THERE

A number of airlines fly into Fort Myers's **Southwest Florida Regional Airport.** Among them are American, Continental, Delta, Northwest, TWA.

Nearest **Amtrak** train service is to Tampa/St. Petersburg (tel. 800/USA-RAIL), but **Greyhound/Trailways** buses (tel. 800/237-8211) also stop here.

By far the most interesting way to explore the area is by car. Distances here are great so cabs are a costly alternative even to a rental car. Rental cars operating in the region include Alamo, National, Delta, Hertz, Value, Avis, and Budget.

## GETTING AROUND

**Molly the Trolley** is a different way to travel through Fort Myers. A San Francisco–look trolley on wheels, Molly has brass handrails, a silver roof, etched glass, and red oak trim, and it's the cutest thing on four wheels. It operates from 10am to 3pm daily from the north end of Estero Island to Carl Johnson Park, and is free.

**Lee County Transit System** (tel. 939-1303) operates buses to all parts of the county, and can help you with route information. Rides are 75¢.

**Taxis** here, as everywhere, are expensive and charge by zone. Call them at 332-1055 for specific fares, but generally you'll pay $8 to $16, more from downtown to the beaches.

## GETTING YOUR BEARINGS

Fort Myers Beach is about 15 miles south of downtown Fort Myers, which centers around US 41. McGregor Boulevard, with its rows of stately royal palms, runs alongside the Caloosahatchee River and is also called County Road 867. At the Caloosahatchee River Bridge, County Road 867 becomes Fla. 80 and heads west. County Road 867 heads toward Cape Coral and intersects with County Road 865, the Fort Myers Beach road.

To reach the beach heading north on US 41, branch west at Bonita Springs on County Road 865 to Bonita Beach where 865 turns north to Estero Island, the city's beach district. To confuse matters slightly, County Road 865 is also known as Hickory Boulevard, Estero Boulevard, and San Carlos Boulevard.

To reach Sanibel and Captiva Islands from Fort Myers, take McGregor Boulevard (Fla. 867), which shoots off to the west across San Carlos Bay to the islands.

## USEFUL INFORMATION

In **emergencies,** call 911 . . . For **police help,** call 322-3456 . . . For **non-emergency medical help,** call the Lee County Medical Society at 936-1645 . . . The **Dental Health Services** (tel. 939-5646) has 24-hour emergency services, and there are branches in Cape Coral and Lehigh Acres too . . . If you get hungry at odd hours, the **Perkins** and **Denny's** have many locations open 24 hours . . . **Touch of Class Cleaners** offers same-day service at 3990 College Pkwy. SW (tel. 482-5550), and 7050 Windler Rd. (tel. 482-0565).

## TOURIST INFORMATION

The **Metropolitan Fort Myers Chamber of Commerce,** 1365 Hendry St. (P.O. Box CC), Fort Myers, FL 33902 (tel. 813/334-1133), has friendly folks who will help you out in emergencies and fill your pockets with information on the city. . . . The **Greater Fort Myers Beach Chamber of Commerce** is at 1661 Estero Blvd. (P.O. Box 6109), Fort Myers, FL 33931 (tel. 813/463-6451) . . . The **Lee County Visitor and Convention Bureau,** 2126 1st St. (P.O. Box 2445), Fort Myers, FL 33902 (tel. 800/237-6444), issues a *Lee County Visitors Guide* and a helpful list of area restaurants called *The Dining Experience.*

## HOTELS

You won't find many fancy resorts in this quiet area but you'll find lots of rustic havens at very modest prices on the beach and in the downtown area.

### Bonita Springs

**Beach and Tennis Club,** 548 Bonita Beach Rd. SW, Bonita Springs, FL 33923 (tel. 813/992-1121, or toll free 800/526-9299), is just south of Fort Myers Beach in the tiny community of Bonita Beach. A multi-storied and multi-building condominium enclave, Beach and Tennis Club has a number of apartments available for hotel use. It has all the amenities of a condominium resort, including 10 tennis courts, 2 pools and a third for children, and a beach just a few steps away. This resort is a bargain: rates are $35 to $60 year round.

**Lani Kai,** 1400 Estero Blvd., Fort Myers Beach, FL 33931 (tel. 813/463-3111, or toll free 800/237-6133), pulls out all the stops on a South Seas island atmosphere from its name (which means "haven by the sea") to its beachfront entertainment, Pupu snackbar, and Chickee Tiki sundeck bar. You can't miss this sprawling spot on Fort Myers Beach—just look for the flowers streaming up its five-story exterior and ornamenting its colorful signs. Everywhere you look here you'll find those island touches: bright floral decor, white bamboo furniture, wicker lampshades, grass mats, and Tiki gods. Lani Kai has more flowers at poolside and in the restaurant where wood paneling stretches from floor to ceiling. Hungry hordes troop in here for French and Italian preparations in the $10 bracket. From mid-December to May, rates range from $140 to $180 a day double, falling to $85 to $110 a day in summer.

A great little hideaway is a spot called the **Beach House,** 4960 Estero Blvd., Fort Myers Beach, FL 33931 (tel. 813/463-4004), where all the apartments look more like home than a home-away-from-home. The Beach House is a rambling two-story house with a third story perched atop a brick walkway to the beach. Every room is different, all 12 of them individually decorated in sometimes quite luxurious furniture. Prices range from $77 double for a non-ocean-view apartment for two to $115 for an ocean-view two-bedroom two-bath apartment on the second floor. In summer the rates begin at $40 and peak at $75 double. A nice friendly family owns Beach House, which lacks a pool but makes up for it with lots of beach and ocean.

If you dream occasionally about a little beach house, you've got it at the **Beach House Motel,** 26106 Hickory Blvd., Bonita Springs, FL 33923 (tel. 813/992-2644), on Fla. 865 at Hickory Boulevard, a cluster of beach houses up on stilts right on the gulf sands at Bonita Beach. Simply but attractively furnished, with lots of durable fabrics in bright and sunny colors and dark-wood paneling, the accommodations come in a variety of configurations, from motel rooms and efficiencies (sleeping four "in a pinch") to large one- and two-bedroom apartments with screened porches overlooking the gulf. Anglers can fish from the bridge right behind the property, walk to the pass nearby, surf-cast in the sea, or charter boats nearby. Tiny picnic tables at beachside are roofed to match their larger cottage apartments. In this very beachy spot you'll pay $50 double for hotel rooms, up to $165 for efficiencies and apartments from February to April. In other months, prices range from $40 to $145. Weekly rates are available.

## Mainland Fort Myers

Even few Floridians have explored the beauties of the meandering Caloosahatchee River, but you can get a closeup look at these blue waters at the **Tides Motel,** 2621 1st St. (Fla. 80), Fort Myers, FL 33901 (tel. 813/334-1231). Located on one of the city's famous avenues of royal palms, the Tides has 27 modest but bright efficiencies and motel rooms with two double beds or a king-sleeper, phone, and color TV. You can dine on a free Continental breakfast beside the resort's pool, or dangle your toes in the river from the edge of the motel's fishing pier. The price is right: $38 to $60 for two in winter months, $32 to $36 in summer.

**Ramada Inn on the River,** 2220 W. 1st St., Fort Myers, FL 33901 (tel. 813/332-4888, or toll free 800/228-2828), plays its river connections to the hilt, as well it should, in this attractive riverside location on the Caloosahatchee. Rooms here are clean, spacious, and comfortable, and decorated in pleasant colors, as is the rest of this restaurant. Ramada's Riverboat Restaurant and lounge are right on the river, providing a dramatic view while you dine on a giant Sunday champagne brunch or one of the restaurant's theme evenings, which range from a seafood buffet on Friday to Greek and Indian food festivals. Prices rarely top $11 for the bounteous buffets at this restaurant. Rates at this Ramada Inn are $68 to $128 double in season; lower the rest of the year. Suites available at a higher rate.

Let us qualify **Rock Lake Motel,** at 2930 Palm Beach Blvd., Fort Myers, FL 33901 (tel. 813/334-3242), by saying it's a *very* modest spot, but it is an enchanting little cluster of stone cottages plunked down around the edges of a tiny round lake. Flaming bougainvilleas pop brightly out between cottages whose small rooms are bright and clean, with windows overlooking that vest-pocket lake. They're unusual and dainty, and set far back from highway noises. If you don't mind exchanging interior luxuries like phones and carpets for exterior charms, you'll like Rock Lake (they do have television and air conditioning). Certainly you'll like the prices, which are just $34 to $38 in peak season, $20 to $25 in other seasons.

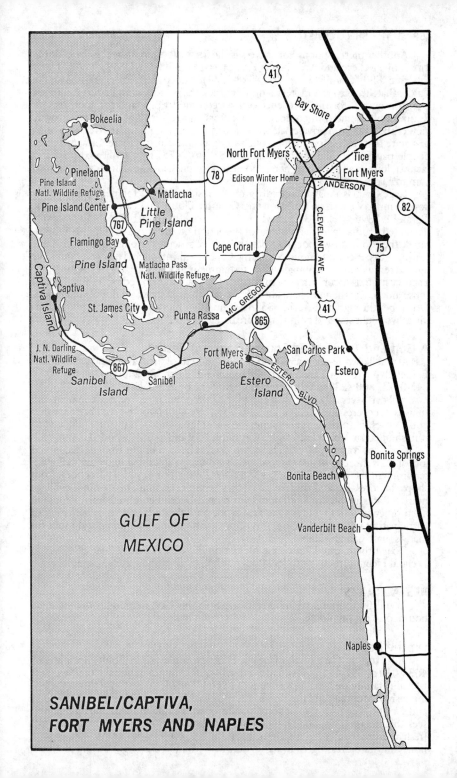

SANIBEL/CAPTIVA,
FORT MYERS AND NAPLES

Another pretty spot in Fort Myers is the **Best Western Robert E. Lee Motor Inn,** at 6611 Cleveland Ave., North Fort Myers, FL 33903 (tel. 813/997-5511, or toll free 800/274-5511 or 800/528-1234), which nuzzles right up to the Caloosahatchee River. A motel rising six stories, the Best Western Robert E. Lee has won top ratings for the excellence of its accommodations, and for good reason: Rooms are decorated in contemporary colors and furnishings, and have a lovely view of the river from private balconies. You can select a room with two double beds, or a suite that adds a convertible couch so six people can stay there. In winter, two people pay $80 to $85, and in summer, $37 to $47. There's a heated pool and Jacuzzi, lounge and pool bar here, and next door the Clock restaurant is open from 6am to 11pm.

Cape Coral is a massive, rapidly growing residential development that now has its own inn as well. **Cape Coral Inn and Country Club,** 4003 Palm Tree Blvd., Cape Coral, FL 33904 (tel. 813/542-3191, or toll free 800/648-1475), has attractively decorated rooms, many with a view of the action on the fairways. Recently redecorated, the rooms now sport soft pastels and are spacious enough for comfortable seating areas. A cozy, tranquil resort, the Cape Coral Inn offers 18 holes of golf, five lighted tennis courts, a lounge with entertainment most nights, two restaurants and a showy heated swimming pool overlooking vast acreage dotted with palms. For all those amenities, the rates here are quite reasonable: $80 to $90 double from mid-December through mid-April, $55 to $60 in other months. Golf packages, including a two-night stay and golfing fees, are bargain priced too.

## A Golf and Tennis (and Square Dancing) Resort

If you like wide-open acres, you'll find hundreds of them at **Lehigh Resort,** 225 E. Joel Blvd., Lehigh, FL 33936 (tel. 813/369-2131 or 334-2500, or toll free 800/843-0971, 800/237-2251 in Florida), an off-the-beaten-track hotel about 12 miles east of Fort Myers. Lehigh is in the midst of a popular retiree development and sprawls over acres and acres of grounds complete with two 18-hole championship golf courses. If golf's not your game, there are tennis courts, miniature golf, volleyball, shuffleboard, bicycles, a large swimming pool and a shady wooded nature trail.

Spacious rooms and villas have two double beds, a bright tropical decor, and lots of glass through which you can watch swimmers splashing in the pool. For entertainment there are three lounges and three dining rooms; you'll never be far from shops, hairdressers, and the like, since they've got everything here or in the village nearby. Rates are $89 to $170 double from mid-December to mid-April, dropping in summer to $65 to $115. One final word on Lehigh: If you enjoy watching or participating in square dancing, this resort has become a favorite do-si-do spot for many square-dancing clubs.

To get there, take I-75 to exit 23, east on Fla. 82 to County Road 884, east to Leeland Heights, then left to Joel Boulevard.

## RESTAURANTS

You'll find some intriguing restaurants in this city, ranging from a haunted house to an elegant home.

### On the Beach

**Rooftop,** in Casa Bonita Plaza at Hickory Boulevard in Bonita Springs (tel. 463-7010 or 597-4445), is where the third and fourth generations of the New York McCully family are holding forth after 11 years. The McCullys formerly ran the Flying Fish in Montauk and the Fat Flounder in East Hampton, New York. Now Terry and son Joe keep up a regular correspondence with *Gourmet* magazine readers who seek their recipes. No wonder—few are the places you'll find a salad that includes fresh mushrooms, sliced zucchini, baby shrimp, cauliflower, and tomatoes with honey-mustard dressing, or things like crayfish étouffée, crisp light shrimp tempura, swordfish marinated in soy sauce, garlic, lemon, and herbs, then charcoal broiled, or Irish whisky pie!

What's more, the setting for all these delicacies is lovely: a small waiting area with upturned kegs as tables, a bank of windows with an upper-level view of surrounding waters. As for prices, you're likely to leave having dined very luxuriously on soup, that super salad, and outstanding seafood for less than $14. It's open daily from 11:30am (no Saturday lunch) to 10pm. On Sunday there is a sumptuous brunch from 10:30am to 2pm.

Here's a short story from **Charley Brown's Restaurant,** 6225 Estero Blvd. (tel. 463-9191): "Our Gone with the Rib prime rib is so popular we run out nightly. The end." There are wood and greenery, prime rib and a big salad trolley, filet mignon, top sirloin, beef kebabs, fresh bread, homemade desserts, and prices of only $8.50 to $22.95. How's that for another short story? Open from 4:30 to 10pm Sunday through Thursday, to 10:30pm on Friday and Saturday.

You'll find **McKansas Seafood Co.,** 416 Crescent St., Fort Myers Beach (tel. 463-3838), right under the Sky Bridge at the waterfront, of course. That means watery views will entertain you while you dine at this casual spot on seafood, steak, and ribs served sizzling and fresh. Kin to Mike's Landing over at the airport (see the downtown restaurants listings), Mike's Waterfront is a popular watering hole, too. You'll pay prices in the $10 to $15 range for dinner at this rustic spot, which is open from 7am to 10pm daily Saturday and Sunday, from 11am Monday through Friday.

When your back's bright red and your knees are sore from shell searches, and you most certainly are *not* getting dressed up for dinner, head for **Top O' the Mast,** at 1028 Estero Blvd. (tel. 463-9424) down by the boardwalk, where you can crunch hot popovers and send that flaming sun right into the sea. Just outside the window, gulf waters offer up finny favors to pier fishermen, while inside these cool confines are broiled seafood platters—grouper's the house specialty—a 20-ounce cut of prime rib, fried shrimp, loaves of bread and popovers, apple butter, cheese, a relish tray—for prices in the $10 to $12 range ($23 for that big prime rib). Open daily from 11am to 11pm, to 2am in the lounge, for sipping, 5 to 10pm for dinner.

**Mucky Duck,** once known as Ye Olde Holmes House, 2500 Estero Blvd. (tel. 463-5519), not only sells spirits, it has them! Whenever old Sherlock shows up things go all mysterious, no less so at Mucky Duck, where waitresses report laughing children in the small hours and occasional weird events at other hours. But why shouldn't a poltergeist hang around? We can't think of a better spot to haunt than this excellent restaurant with its dining rooms created in a beachside home built in 1919. Over the years, many a luminary has discovered this pubby spot plunked down in the middle of Fort Myers Beach: The guest list has included Hugh Downs, authors Theodore White and Mario Puzo, baseball stars Roberto Clemente and Ted Williams, singer Perry Como, and even spooky Vincent Price. Yes, this is the same Mucky Duck that waddled to phenomenal success on Captiva Island with great views, great seafood, and a generally quacky atmosphere. Same goes here. You'll find prices in the $10 to $19 range for dinner, served from 5 to 9:30pm daily.

## Downtown

Things are looking better than ever in downtown Fort Myers these days, and nowhere better than **The Veranda,** 2122 2nd St., at Broadway (tel. 332-2065), where you dine in an antebellum atmosphere inside or out in a serene garden. Brick pavements, little umbrellaed tables, a tiny pond shaded by huge tropical trees, and a first-rate southern-flavored menu make the Veranda a top choice for luxurious dining. A historic landmark hereabouts, the restaurant occupies two turn-of-the-century houses connected by a country kitchen. Special touches like freshly ground coffee beans, homemade honey molasses bread, sweet corn muffins, and southern pepper jelly complement rich desserts and continental entrées like veal française or roast duckling royale. Prices at dinner fall in the $13 to $22 range for entrées, and after dinner there's entertainment in the lounge. Hours are 11am to 2:30pm and 5:30 to 11pm daily; later in the lounge. Closed Sunday in summer and fall.

**Shallows Seafood,** Royal Palm Square, 1400 Colonial Dr. (tel. 939-5151), is a trendy new restaurant in town. Seafood is the bill of fare here, where you dine amid paintings, handsome french doors, paddle fans, and intimate lighting. Tie into lobster, baby back ribs, lots of local seafood, a seafood platter, and 10 changing-daily specials. You'll pay $12 to $18 for dinner at this sleek dining spot open from 11:30am to 2pm weekdays (noon to 9pm Sunday) and 5 to 10pm daily.

**Mike's Landing Bistro,** Old Fort Myers Airport Terminal, Page Field Danley Drive (tel. 936-0091), is a trendy spot that serves up steaks and seafood fresh from the gulf's teeming waters. Naturally, aircraft and an up-in-the-sky theme is the principal object of decor interest here. Ask for the main dining room if you'd like to watch airplane takeoffs. You'll pay dinner prices in the $8 to $10 range, perhaps a bit higher. A lively spot, Mike's Landing is open daily from 11am to 10pm, later on weekends.

**Chart House,** 2024 W. 1st St. (tel. 332-1881), is part of a popular chain of restaurants that has been an instant success wherever it has landed. This Chart House keeps right up with its brothers and sisters, sporting interesting nautical decor, an outstanding salad bar and top-quality seafood, as well as a few selections for landlubbers. Chart House is open from 5 to 10pm weekdays, an hour later on weekends. Prices are in the $12 to $34 range.

A budget-watcher in town is **Bill Knapp's,** 13600 S. Tamiami Trail (tel. 489-3422), which serves up very reasonably priced lunches and dinners in an atmosphere redolent of Old New England. Part of a group of restaurants of the same name that moved into Florida some years ago, Bill Knapp's is a pleasant family stop as much for comfortable, casual atmosphere as for prices, which fall easily into the $5 to $10 category.

**Bennigan's,** 12984 S. Cleveland Ave. (tel. 433-1441), is part of that now-famous national chain of fun restaurants offering lots of grazing options and a slick and gleeful atmosphere in which to consume them. You'll find Bennigan's two miles south of Page Field Airport, where they roll out the welcome mat from 11am to 2am daily. Prices are in the $10 to $15 range for full meals, but you can certainly munch for less here on fried zucchini, mozzarella sticks, and the like.

**Smitty's Beef Room,** at 2240 W. 1st St. (tel. 334-4415), has occupied a secure spot in Fort Myers dining circles for more than 20 years. The focus here is prime beef, supplemented by freshly baked bread and an unusual pepper salad dressing. Brandy Alexander cream pie is a favorite for dessert. Prices are in the $10 to $15 range. Smitty's restaurant is open from 11am to 10pm weekdays, and from 11:30am to 9pm on Sunday.

A top-notch budget choice in town is a little restaurant tucked away in the **Farmer's Market,** at 2736 Edison Ave. (tel. 334-1687). Produce right off the vine comes to the market for distribution to the tables of the restaurant, where it's accorded some down-home southern cookin' touches. There's little (going on no) atmosphere here, just lots of fresh vegetables and good cooks to whip them into shape, along with some other goodies like baking-powder biscuits and cornbread. You'll pay low, low prices too, in the $3 to $6 range. The restaurant is open from 6am to 8pm daily.

A budget goody in the area is the ever-reliable **Morrison's Cafeteria,** 3057 Cleveland Ave. (tel. 334-3227). You can find inexpensive meals and a casual atmosphere here, where dinner prices rarely top $6 or $7. Hours are 11am to 8:30pm daily.

## In Punta Gorda

About 25 miles north of Fort Myers, the town of Punta Gorda has a name that sounds glamorous if you don't know what it means: Fat Point. If you think Fort

Myers is a quiet retirement village, you haven't met Punta Gorda, which until recently took quiet to new heights. These days, however, the general boom is reaching even this little fishing village, set on a point where the Peace River joins the gulf. The most recent addition to the community is a nifty new shopping and dining area called **Fishermen's Village,** in which you'll find two attractive restaurants: **Earl Nightingale's Dockside,** at 1200 W. Retta Esplanade (tel. 637-1177), and the more casual **Village Oyster Bar** (tel. 637-1212). To get to the village, turn west off US 41 on the south side of the Peace River bridge.

Earl Nightingale, you may recall, was a well-known lecturer based in Fort Lauderdale. In the restaurant to which he's lent his name, you'll find elegant dining in a two-level dining room, both levels overlooking a bank of windows through which you can watch the waters of the Peace River snaking toward the gulf. Crisp linens, candlelight, flowers, formally dressed waiters, and an elegant atmosphere prevail here, where the menu focuses on outstanding French seafood preparations and some beef and veal entrées. Could they interest you in smoked salmon garnished with cream cheese and capers, or crab and scallop cardinale topped with a sherry-laced cream sauce? You'll pay about $13 to $23 for entrées in this very pretty dining room, more if you indulge in extras. Open from 11am to 9pm daily, Nightingale's dinner service (when jackets are requested) begins at 5pm. The lounge is open from 11:30am to 9pm.

The Oyster Bar is a simple, casual place that delivers up those freshly shucked bivalves plus a wide range of seafood in a woodsy-plantsy atmosphere that goes well with the rustic shrimp-boat ambience of the dock area. Prices are under $17, and the bar's open from 11am to 8pm Sunday through Thursday, until 9pm Friday and Saturday, later in the lounge.

## NIGHTLIFE

Fort Myers does not have a population given to rip-roaring nightlife, but you can enjoy some quiet entertainment and dancing in hotels and restaurants.

**Barbara B. Mann Performing Arts Hall,** 8099 College Pkwy. SW (tel. 489-3033), is on the campus of Edison Community College in Fort Myers and boasts state-of-the-art acoustics in a 1,777-seat hall that cost nearly $7 million. Artwork created by famed Robert Rauschenberg sparks the carpeted lobby and a glass-and-oak grand staircase ascends to the mezzanine where a massive crystal chandelier scatters rainbows of light across the lobby. A very elegant hall, this performing arts center is the setting for a wide variety of concerts and performances by world-reknowned entertainers. You can find out what's going on by giving them a call.

The **Cape Coral Inn and Country Club,** at 4003 Palm Tree Blvd. (tel. 542-3191, or 800/648-1475) in Cape Coral, often has a dance band from 7:30pm to about midnight, and has two attractive dining rooms frequented by residents of this Gulf-American Corp. development.

Five nights a week, usually Tuesday through Saturday, the **Rooftop** restaurant in Bonita Springs (see our restaurant recommendation) has entertainment in its Locker Lounge. The **Ramada Inn,** 2220 W. 1st St., Fort Myers (tel. 332-1141), has dancing and entertainment in its lounge overlooking the river daily except Sunday to 2am.

There's something for just about everyone at **ABC Liquor Lounges,** 4150 S. Cleveland Ave., Fort Myers (tel. 936-1526), and 590 Tamiami Trail NE in Charlotte Harbor (tel. 995-7958). ABC lounges feature country, rock, and dance music, computerized light shows, an "earthquake" sound system, and a revolving bar with fountain. On Sunday, Monday, and Tuesday drinks are cheap; other nights, there are specials and two-for-one offerings.

At a lounge in the **Lani Kai Resort** (see our hotel recommendation) a pianist provides evening entertainment from about 9pm Monday through Saturday, and something's happening on Sunday from 1 to 6pm.

## SHOPPING

The **Royal Palm Square Shopping Center,** 1400 Colonial Blvd., between Summerlin and McGregor streets in Fort Myers, is a pleasant shopping center sporting some chic shops (Sara Fredericks is one), interesting gift shops, and a couple of restaurants.

**Bell Tower Shops,** US 41 and Daniels Road, is a Spanish-colonial-style shopping center adorned with stone fountains, courtyard, waterfalls, and streams. More than 50 stores and a few restaurants are the mainstay of this tranquil shopping center.

**Metro Outlet Mall,** 2855 Colonial Blvd., sports a Polly Flinders factory store (tel. 936-5998) carrying adorable smocked dresses for little girls at discount prices and a number of other discount outlet shops.

**READER'S SHOPPING RECOMMENDATIONS:** "During our stay on Sanibel island, we visited Fort Myers and discovered **Edison Mall** (huge and beautiful), **Metro Mall** (an outlet mall with great buys), and a **Bass (Shoe) Factory Outlet** (a huge selection and great buys)" (Sandy Hamilton, Cincinnati, Ohio).

## SPORTS

You won't have any difficulty finding a place to play in Fort Myers, which has 13 golf courses and tennis courts scattered about the city, plus all the water sports you'd expect in an oceanside city.

### Golf and Tennis

**Cape Coral Inn and Country Club,** at 4003 Palm Tree Blvd., Cape Coral (tel. 542-3191), has 18 holes open to the public (greens fees of $17 summer, $38 winter) and five Har Tru lighted courts for tennis players. **Lehigh Country Club,** 225 E. Joel Blvd. in Lehigh Acres (tel. 369-2121), has two courses, one a 6,710-yard, par-71 championship course with greens fees of $18 summer, $37 winter, and more tennis courts.

On the beach, **Bay Beach Golf Club,** at 7401 Estero Blvd. (tel. 463-2064), is open to the public seven days a week from 7:30am to dusk. In winter, rates are $13 for 18 holes, carts are $13, and fees are slightly lower in summer. Most area clubs are in the same price range.

If you've ever wanted to play the nation's most famous courses, you can go on tour here at a miniature golf course at which each hole is a replica of one of the killer holes of America's best-known golf courses. Attractively laid out, the **Best 18 Miniature Golf,** 19300 S. Tamiami Trail, on U.S. 41 six miles south of Bell Tower (tel. 267-1606), is an amusing way to while away a couple of hours. Best 18 charges $4.25 for adults, $3 for children under 10, and the course is open from 10am to 10pm.

Another miniature golf course here: **Jungle Golf,** 4038-17710 San Carlos Blvd., Fort Myers Beach (tel. 466-9797), sports jungle streams, dramatic waterfalls, and wild animals grazing in a tropical setting. Adult fees $4.50, under 12 $4.

**Bay Beach Racquet Club,** 120 Lenell Rd (tel. 463-4473), is a beachside tennis spot.

### Beaches

This coastline likes to call itself the "Lee Island Coast" nowadays and sports 50 miles of white sand beaches to prove its coast ranking. Public beaches are on Estero Island at Fort Myers Beach on **Lover's Key,** at **Carl Johnson Park,** and at **Bonita Beach.** To find Carl Johnson Park, take Estero Boulevard which runs parallel to Fort Myers Beach. About 10 miles south of Fort Myers Beach you'll find the park. There you can cross Oyster Bay to Lover's Key on a tractor-driven tram. Admission to the beach is $1 for adults, 50¢ for children. Bonita Beach is south of Carl Johnson Park, or you can get there by taking I-75 exit 18 and heading west to Bonita Beach.

For information on any of the beaches, and a pamphlet describing them and other area attractions and detailing several driving trips in the area, contact the Lee County Visitor and Convention Bureau, P.O. Box 2445, Fort Myers, FL 33902 (tel. toll free at 800/237-6444, 800/533-7433 in Florida). Ask for the self-guided driving tours brochure.

## Water Sports

Rent sailboats, catamarans, swim tubes, kayaks, aquacycles, jet-skis, speedboats, and beach umbrellas from **Island Sail and Jetski Rental,** 1010 Estero Blvd. (tel. 463-3351), behind the Sandpebble Shop on the beach. Sailboat prices start at $25 an hour and jet-skis are available.

Deep-sea fishing expeditions and charter boats leave from **Gulf Star Marina** on Fort Myers Beach (tel. 765-1500), from **City Marina** in downtown Fort Myers, or **Snug Harbor,** under the bridge at Fort Myers Beach. **Ford's Fleet** (tel. 334-2348) charges $22 a day per person for four hours of fishing in the area.

## Pari-mutuel Sports

Follow the perils of the electronic lure at **Naples Fort Myers Kennel Club,** 10601 Bonita Beach Rd. (US 41), in Bonita Springs (tel. 992-2411), which opens the second week in December and closes the third week in April, with races five or six nights a week and matinees on Monday, Wednesday, Friday, and Saturday, closed Sunday. Admission is $2 for the clubhouse, 50¢ for general admission, and the track opens at 6:30pm for night races, at 11:30am for matinees.

## THE SIGHTS

Sight-seeing in this part of the country is a little different since several companies offer cruises up nearby rivers into the interior of the state. Rivers in the area are deep blue and very calm, so you're in for a scenic, comfortable trip.

## Tours

**Showboat Everglades Jungle Cruises** chug up the calm waters of the Caloosahatchee from Fort Myers City Yacht Basin (tel. 334-7474) from December through April on any of several different cruises on three double-decker boats that also range as far as Sanibel Island, Lake Okeechobee, and the Gulf of Mexico. Cruises vary in length and price, from $7 to $139.

See what's happening on these pretty waters aboard the tri-masted schooner **Norfolk Rover,** Gulf Star Marina, Fort Myers Beach (tel. 765-SHIP). You'll find it docked under the Sky Bridge, ready and waiting to take you out sight-seeing, on bay cruises that depart daily, except Monday, at 1pm with a 6pm cruise weekends. The fare is $16 for adults, $8 for children under 15 for trips.

## Sights

Thomas Alva Edison, who shed a little light on all our lives, is quite a luminary in Fort Myers. Edison moved down in 1885, attracted by the weather, and wintered here regularly for more than 40 years. He built a 14-acre estate, and indulged his love for gardening by importing hundreds of blossoms. You can see his rambling old home where the carbon filament bulbs he created in 1910 still burn 12 hours a day, not one of them replaced! Many of the inventor's creations are displayed here too, from wax recordings to talking machines. **Edison's house** is open from 9am to 4pm Monday through Saturday, from 12:30 to 4pm on Sunday. His home is at 2350 McGregor Blvd. (tel. 334-3614) on US 41; admission is $5 for adults, $1 for students 6 to 12. Henry Ford's home next door is open, too.

**Waltzing Waters,** 18101 US 41 SE, Fort Myers (tel. 267-2533), between Naples and Fort Myers, is a fantasyland of lighted fountains rising and falling, swaying and swirling to music. Here now for over 20 years, Waltzing Waters has indoor and outdoor shows it likes to call "liquid fireworks," and that's not far off the mark. Light set to music makes a fascinating display. Waltzing Waters also operates Rainbow Golf, a putt course in a tropical setting, and a gift shop stacked with international treasures. Hours are 11am to 9pm daily. Admission is $7.50 for adults, $3.50 for students 7 to 12, which includes both indoor and outdoor performances, day and evening.

The **Lee County Nature Center,** 3450 Ortiz Ave., Fort Myers (tel. 275-3435), is a 100-acre nature center with an aviary for injured birds, a museum, and planetarium. On a boardwalk trail through pinelands you'll get a close and interesting look at Florida's exotic flora and fauna. On weekends there are tours of the center, which is open from 9am to 4pm Monday through Saturday, from 11am to 4:30pm on Sunday. Admission is $2 for adults, 50¢ for children under 12; planetarium shows are $3 for adults, $2 for children; $4.50 adults, $3.50 children for laser shows.

**Fort Myers Historical Museum,** in the ACL (Atlantic Coast Line) train depot, 2300 Peck St. at Jackson Street (tel. 332-5955), can fill you in on local history and several days a week you can see films on art, music, and poetry. Hours are 9am to 4:30pm weekdays, 1 to 5pm on Sunday, closed Saturday, and admission is $2 for adults, 50¢ for children under 12.

**Shell Factory and Fantasy Isles,** 2787 N. Tamiami Trail (tel. 995-2141), combines a billion or so shells with a storybook amusement park for the youngsters. Admission is free and rides in Fantasy Isles are 50¢ each. The Shell Factory is open daily from 9am to 5pm; Fantasy Isles is open daily the same hours but on weekends only off-season (tel. 997-4204).

## SPECIAL EVENTS

Fort Myers doesn't go in much for rip-roaring events, but has plenty of diverting moments to keep you busy and keep you coming back.

If you like to eat, a distinctly diverting event is the annual **Taste of the Town,** which usually takes place in early November. More than 50 local restaurants set up at the Lee County Alliance of the Arts building on the corner of McGregor and Colonial boulevards and dispense their proudest accomplishments. With a background of band music, the restaurateurs sell everything from soup to dessert for prices in the $1 to $2 range or less. Admission is $4, with proceeds going to the Junior League of Fort Myers.

In October that same Lee County Arts Alliance sponsors an **Art Festival,** four nights of musical entertainment on an outdoor stage. Two other Alliance activities that month are a crafts show and an antique show and sale.

Sanibel Island's **Jazz on the Green** is still tweedling along in early October and has drawn some top-name regional and national talent in recent years.

---

# 2. Naples

When you drive down Naples's main street, Fifth Avenue, you're driving down what was once a runway for aviator Charles Lindbergh, who zipped in here for vacations on nearby Sanibel Island. Lindbergh could still find a runway here, but he certainly wouldn't recognize this small town, which has grown—and is growing—as rapidly as Jack's famous beanstalk.

Naples is summer home to many Miamians and winter home to an impressive list of *Fortune* 500 types who come here to revel in its quiet, refined atmosphere, and laze in condominiums and homes whose values are fast approaching the seven-figure mark. Here you'll find some of the state's trimmest streets, and a seven-mile beach fiercely protected by strict zoning laws. Shops line the city's small downtown area and are so primped and polished you wonder if someone doesn't stroll by each morning with a bucket of whitewash. Inside these shining emporiums are an Arab's ransom in glowing jewels, designer clothes, dark chocolates, and tweed jackets perfect for cool nights in Petoskey, Michigan, where half the town spends its summers. You can find elegant treasures of all varieties on these streets (once we even saw a huge chess set, each giant piece a jungle animal!) and some attractive restaurants.

Naples is a quiet spot where nightlife ends about 10pm but tranquility goes on forever. It's a place to go to meditate on serene beaches, wander among small boutiques, a place to pause a while and consider where you're going . . . and why.

## GETTING AROUND

Taxi rates are $1.75 for the first mile, $1.25 for each additional mile. For taxi service, call **Yellow Cab** (tel. 262-1312) or **Maxi Taxi** (tel. 262-8977).

**Dolly the Trolley** clangs and dings around town 13 times a day from 9:30am to 5pm, but Dolly's a snowbird too—it only operates from December 1 to April 20, at a fare of 50¢. Call 262-4209 for exact route information.

## ORIENTATION

The **Tamiami Trail (US 41)** is the way most people come to Naples, but once the highway arrives here it becomes **Fifth Avenue** until it leaves town, when it once again is called the Tamiami Trail (which was for many years the only link between Tampa and Miami).

Several blocks around 3rd Street South are known as **Olde Naples,** and are lined with beautiful and intriguing shops that stretch from about Broad Avenue South to 14th Avenue South.

**Gulf Shore Boulevard** runs alongside the gulf in Naples and in nearby Vanderbilt Beach, but you must return from Gulf Shore to US 41 and head north for a few miles before swinging west to Gulf Shore again at Vanderbilt Beach.

## VISITOR INFORMATION

For any kind of **emergency,** dial 911 . . . The **Naples Area Chamber of Commerce** has workers who will be happy to answer your questions or help you out with problems. They're at 1700 N. Tamiami Trail, Naples, FL 33940 (tel. 813/262-6141) . . . Harvey's, in the Gulf Gate Shopping Center at 2638 Tamiami Trail (tel. 774-4737), offers **one-hour dry-cleaning service. . . .** Castel Service Center, at 1999 County Road 951 (tel. 455-1100), has **24-hour wrecker service** and diesel fuel. . . . **Clock Restaurant,** 660 9th St. N. (tel. 261-6724), is open 24 hours.

## HOTELS

Naples doesn't have many hotels, but those it does have are attractive and comfortable. We've divided them geographically so you can decide where you'd like to stay: in the downtown/Tamiami Trail area, nearby Vanderbilt Beach, or on nearby Marco Island.

### Downtown/Tamiami Trail

**Naples Beach Hotel and Golf Club,** 851 Gulf Shore Blvd. N., Naples, FL 33940 (tel. 813/261-2222, or toll free 800/237-7600, 800/282-7601 in Florida), is the showplace of Naples, a serene resort set down beside the gulf and lavished with beds of tiny yellow blossoms, hedges of hibiscus, swaying palms, and acres of green lawns. The new and spacious rooms are decorated in pale-peach contemporary prints and blond wicker furniture that echoes the resort's beachside atmosphere. You'll find large tile baths in pastel colors, big roomy closets, plush wall-to-wall carpets, and wide balconies overlooking vast expanses of emerald-green grass dotted with tiny waterfalls and crowned by an enormous pool. Wandering farther afield you come upon the resort's championship PGA golf course, where a very young Jack Nicklaus broke his first 40. For tennis fans there are Har-Tru courts, and five miles of silvery beach for beach fanatics. The Everglades Dining Room is a study in pale green and shell pink, with huge wall murals of Florida bird and Native American life. It's a place to dine by candlelight on mangrove snapper plus straightforward steaks and roasts in the $12 to $20 range and is open from 6 to 9pm. Off by itself is the hotel's Brassie's Dining Room and Lounge, where you'll enjoy entertainment that has made this spot a late-night playground of Naples.

Owned by the Watkins family since 1946, the Naples Beach Hotel has a number of package plans, especially in summer, that can save you money. Rates in winter, from mid-December to May, are $85 to $195 double, with suites and efficiencies higher. In other months, rates drop to $60 to $125. If you'd like to have meals here, they'll provide breakfast and dinner for an additional charge.

**Edgewater Beach Hotel,** 1901 Gulf Shore Blvd. N., Naples, FL 33940 (tel. 813/262-6511, or toll free 800/821-0196, 800/282-3766 in Florida), is the only all-suite hotel in Naples and is a very pretty place indeed. Small and luxurious, it rises up out of the posh Gulf Shore Boulevard neighborhood like a handsome mirage and has lost no time at all in winning top ratings. Edgewater has 124 all one- and two-bedroom suites, each with a full living room with attractive furnishings that include a sofa bed. You can watch the Gulf Coast's spectacularly colorful sunsets from a private patio or balcony, then wander in for a champagne dinner in your own dining room. Each suite has a complete kitchen with microwave oven, full refrigerator, coffee maker, and all the other appliances we couldn't live without.

If you'd rather leave the cooking to them, you can dine in the elegant roof-top Crystal Parrot, where the view of the gulf goes on all the way to Mexico, surely. On the menu there are some top seafood selections as well as plenty of landlubber choices. So well are they doing what they do here that the restaurant was named best new restaurant in the region by a local magazine.

Rates at Edgewater Beach are $165 to $395 in peak winter season, $85 to $285 in spring and summer shoulder season.

**The Tides,** 1801 Gulf Shore Blvd. N., Naples, FL 33940 (tel. 813/262-6196), is a quiet, elegant spot with its own strip of private snow-white sand. The spacious rooms have screened balconies overlooking a central courtyard where a terrace stretches down to beachside. Palms and shrubbery are scattered artfully around the property and give this handsome resort a soothing look. Rooms echo those pretty gardens, with lots of yellow and green touches and tropical rattan furniture. In winter, two people pay $65 to $105, higher for larger quarters. In the summer months (beginning about May), rates drop to $55 to $85 for hotel rooms or efficiencies.

Soothe away your worries in a hot tub at the **Best Western Buccaneer Inn,** 2329 9th St. N. (Tamiami Trail; US 41), Naples, FL 33940 (tel. 813/261-1148). Set in a shady spot near the resort's pool, the hot tub is a good spot to warm up on cool winter days or soak sedately in summer. Several two-story buildings overlook attractive lawns and two pools, so you can be sure you'll have a nice view from these spacious rooms decorated in greens and golds. All rooms have hotplates and refrigerators, so snacks are a snap. The Buccaneer has a popular restaurant where pirate flags carry out the resort's skull-and-crossbones theme. Local boats supply the Buccaneer with fresh seafood, and chefs prepare it with skill for prices in the $15 to $20 range. The Buccaneer's restaurant is open daily from 4 to 11pm. Two people pay $69 to $79 from December through mid-April for poolside rooms or suites with sitting rooms, dressing areas, and refrigerators. In summer, prices begin at $49 to $59 double.

The **Beachcomber Club,** at 290 Fifth Ave. S. at 3rd Street South, Naples, FL 33940 (tel. 813/262-8112), is an attractive downtown motel two blocks from the gulf, with screened porches where you can enjoy the tranquil atmosphere and sleek look of this small resort. It's quite near many of the town's excellent restaurants and well-stocked shops. Spacious and tastefully decorated one-bedroom apartments, efficiencies, and combinations are available, plus some larger quarters including a three-bedroom villa. Rates for two in peak season begin at $80 for motel rooms and efficiencies. In other months, prices begin at $51.

If you want to see a striking example of Florida's favorite color scheme—citrus colors—take a look at **Stoney's Courtyard Inn,** 2630 N. Tamiami Trail, Naples, FL 33940 (tel. 813/261-3870). Stoney's is a nickname for the family that owns this resort and also owns a nearby orange grove, and this may be why they so love the color of citrus. They also love tourists, and will invite you out to the groves when the fruit's ripe so you can pick your own oranges right off the trees! Back at the inn, there are even citrus colors out by the swimming pool. Stoney's is a favorite family spot you can't miss as you drive north on US 41. Two people pay $70 to $80 in the winter months (beginning in mid-January) and $40 to $50 double in summer (beginning about mid-May).

The **Fairways Motel,** at 103 Palm River Blvd., one mile east of US 41 on Fla. 846, Naples, FL 33942 (tel. 813/597-8181), is a money-saving hideaway in a golfing community called Palm River Estates, just north of downtown Naples. You couldn't find any place quieter than the Fairways, which is set down in the middle of a residential area. A friendly family runs things here, and keeps the spacious rooms spick and span. Rooms have two double beds, dressing area, and wide closets, and are decorated in golds and blues. They have sliding glass doors that open onto a tranquil central courtyard in the center of which is a sparkling Jacuzzi and pool. Prices in high season, from mid-December through mid-April, are $65 to $75 double a day. In summer, you can hardly beat the prices anywhere in the area: just $30 to $45. There's no charge for children under 12 either.

Downtown in the shady streets of Naples you'll find the **Flamingo Apartments,** 383 Sixth Ave., Naples, FL 33940 (tel. 813/261-7017). Tucked away on a serene side street, the Flamingo is a small place, just two single-story buildings facing each other across a flowery courtyard and pool where pink hibiscus bloom. The only motel room here is completely paneled, with a queen-size bed, wood wardrobe, and bright rust tones. Apartments at this interesting small resort are unusually spacious, with a wide kitchen, living room, dining room, and separate bedroom, and five have beamed cathedral ceilings. For this apartment and others like it (they sleep five) you'll pay rates as attractive as the apartments: just $57 to $84 for motel room, studio, or one- or two-bedroom apartments from mid-December to mid-April. In summer, rates begin at $30.

Despite the tranquillity and age of this pretty city, there had never been an inn here until Elise Sechrist created **Inn by the Sea,** 287 11th Ave. S., Naples, FL 33940 (tel. 813/649-4124). Here in a home built in 1937 and listed in the National Register of Historic Places, you'll find pine floors and ceilings, tin on the roof and whirring ceiling fans, shining brass headboards and white iron beds, delicately pretty floral prints. Artwork is done by local artists, and if you like a painting, you can buy it. Just 700 feet from the sea, Inn by the Sea is a charmer surrounded by coconut palms; flaming bougainvillea and white bird-of-paradise plants play counterpoint to wicker furnishings and shade a nap-intensive hammock. At a complimentary tropical Continental breakfast, fresh fruit and orange juice are abetted by homemade muffins and breads, natural cereals, and imported teas and coffees. They'll even loan you a beach cruiser bicycle and a fishing pole. "I started Inn by the Sea because I wanted to offer old-fashioned hospitality in genteel surroundings to guests who appreciate that kind of personal attention," Elise says. She has succeeded in her goal. Each of the inn's five rooms is named after nearby islands, and three of the six have private baths; second-floor quarters have shared baths. Rates at the inn range from $70 to $105 from late December to May and from $45 to $80 in other months.

**READER'S MOTEL SELECTION:** "**Naples Motor Lodge,** 250 9th St., Naples, FL 33940 (tel. 813/262-1414), is spacious and exceptionally clean. It has a convenient location and is a friendly place" (Kathleen Kemp, Madeira Beach, Fla.).

## Vanderbilt Beach

You sweep up to **The Ritz-Carlton Naples,** 280 Vanderbilt Beach Rd., Naples, FL 33941 (tel. 813/598-3300, or toll free 800/241-3333), on an oval drive and are ushered into the cool, shady recesses of a bilevel lobby by a top-hatted, uniformed doorman. Crystal chandeliers glitter, candelabras glow on a grand piano, tea is served on polished tables—elegance reigns. Tall, paned windows rise to high ceilings trimmed in elaborate moldings. Oriental carpeting lies underfoot. Huge oil paintings are subtly lighted. One of the most beautiful hotels to open in Florida in recent years, the Ritz-Carlton puts on the ritz but in subtle style, illustrating elegance without shouting about it.

A 14-story hotel with wings enclosing a tiled central courtyard where a fountain burbles, the Ritz-Carlton has its own beach, rimmed by a deep stand of palms ribboned with walkways. In your room, French doors open onto an iron-railed balcony with a view all the way to Mexico. Double or king-size beds are trimmed in dust ruffles and topped with quilted coverlets in soft shades. A refrigerator is stocked with portables; a desk, topped with fresh flowers, can double as spot for morning coffee; a terry-cloth robe hangs in a separate marble-trimmed dressing area.

Chic continues in the Grill, where paneled walls are hung with 18th- and 19th-century sporting scenes and a fire glows under a marble mantelpiece. Here you dine on the likes of venison loin chops with mint jalapeño jelly or filet of snapper with lemon butter and pine nuts. A café features a soda fountain for more casual moments and a handsomely appointed dining room has piano entertainment at dinner. Finally, for the ultimate in casual, a pavilion beach snackbar is perched high on a raised boardwalk. Afternoon tea occurs under the three-story windows of the lobby lounge where hors d'oeuvres and cocktails are served later. After dinner, there's dessert and dancing in The Club, where a band plays.

More? Of course: a heated pool, whirlpool, six lighted tennis courts, golf on a 27-hole course nearby, a fitness center, beauty salon, children's program, sailing, rental bikes, airport transport. Rates at the Ritz are $260 to $400 in peak winter season, $135 to $300 in other months; higher for suites.

Every room seems to have a dazzling view at **La Playa Beach and Racquet Inn,** on Vanderbilt Beach, 9891 Gulfshore Dr., Naples, FL 33940 (tel. 813/597-3123, or toll free 800/237-6883, in Florida 800/282-4423), but then what else would you expect in a motor inn that overlooks a waterway in one direction, the gulf in another, and has two palm-shaded pools at the front door? Gauguin is a favorite artist here, and the unusually spacious rooms are decorated in Gauguin blues or the golds with which that artist was so enamored. A wall of glass opens onto a private balcony overlooking the gulf or Vanderbilt Lagoon across the way. Downstairs at beach level is Café La Playa, where you can dine while viewing the gulf waters in a small intimate restaurant gleaming with candles and serving up shrimp tempura or lobster sautéed with peppers, onions, mushrooms, and wine, for prices in the $10 to $15 range. Sweeping in a long arc across a quiet strip of beautiful Vanderbilt Beach, La Playa is Vanderbilt's premier resort, with two heated pools and tennis courts. From mid-January to May you'll pay $100 to $295, depending on the room's size and location and the dates you select. In other months, prices begin at $75.

Beamed ceilings and paneled walls are a highlight of the spacious rooms at the **Vanderbilt Beach Motel,** 9225 Gulf Shore Dr. N., Naples, FL 33963 (tel. 813/597-3144), which stretches between the gulf and a deep-blue lagoon. The motel rooms, efficiencies, apartments, and suites have bright floral fabrics that contrast with dark-wood touches. From every unit there's a view of glittering gulf waters and the carefully tended lawns that surround the resort's pear-shaped pool. Tennis players have been allotted a place to work off steam, and there's a private boat ramp, pier, and dock. In summer, from May to mid-December, rates range from $51 to $70, $77 to $109 in winter.

## Marco Island

A few miles south of Naples off US 41 at County Road 951 is Marco Island. A University of Miami professor once dubbed Marco "Florida's Last Frontier." He termed it that just minutes before developers discovered it, and today Marco is a frontier no longer, its lonely isolation and touching loveliness fallen before the pace of progress in the form of hundreds of condominiums in every size, shape, and color. You can find out how to rent one of those by contacting the **Marco Island Chamber of Commerce** 1102 N. Collier Blvd. (P.O. Box 913), Marco Island, FL 33937 (tel. 813/394-7549).

In the midst of this mass of development is **Marriott's Marco Island Resort,** 400 S. Collier Blvd., Marco Island, FL 33937 (tel. 813/394-2511, or toll free 800/228-9290, 800/GET-HERE in Florida). This Marriott is a showplace in anybody's terms, built high over the waters with two-story windows rising from the sand capped by yet a third story of glass. Lovely vistas of garden and sea stretch out before you as you stand on the balcony of very spacious rooms decorated in deep blues and yellows. It is luxurious here, with contemporary furniture, lots of closet space, handsome wall coverings, and little extras from slick magazines to keep you up-to-date on local activities to heaps of towels and separate dressing areas.

Rates are $200 in season and range as high as $540 for suites. In summer, those rates drop to $115 to $200, higher (to $350) for one- and two-bedroom lanais or suites.

Marriott Marco Island lies beside three miles of white sand and has a fleet of Sunfish and catamarans for rent, 15 tennis courts, two pools, a par-three golf course, and a sports center for everything from volleyball to mopeds. There are four restaurants and lounges, ranging from a coffee shop to the Gulfside restaurant. Prices in the main dining room, where tableside cookery is a favorite, average $16 to $26; Sunday brunch costs $17.

To experience "our" Marco the way it used to be many years ago, have lunch or dinner at the **Old Marco Inn.** Occupying a very old island home (built in 1883), this handsome restaurant has three dining rooms bathed in the ruby-red glow of shining glassware. Overhead, crystal chandeliers glitter, and beneath them a well-trained staff serves good basic cooking, often with Austrian or German touches, things like wienerschnitzel, jaeger Madagascar. Prices are in a quite reasonable $10 to $20 range for dinner. You'll find the Inn at 100 Palm Ave. (tel. 394-3131), and it's open daily from 5:30 to 10pm, but closed for a month from about mid-August to mid-September.

A similar place, although a bit more rustic perhaps, is the **Marco Lodge,** a restaurant occupying quarters built in 1869—and for Florida that is very old indeed. These weathered gray walls have seen both little and much over the years, and today enclose quite an attractive restaurant featuring good veal and seafood in the $10 to $15 price range for dinner. Hours are 6 to midnight for dinner daily except Monday and Tuesday, with music nightly at 8pm. You'll find the restaurant at 1 Papaya St. in Goodland (tel. 394-3302), a tiny settlement just down the road from the main activity on Marco. Anyone can direct you there, and road signs also point the way. Marco Lodge has a jam session on Sunday afternoons.

**Snook Inn,** 1215 Bald Eagle Dr., Marco Island, FL 33937 (tel. 813/394-3313), is about on the opposite end of the scale from the fancy Marco Island Marriott, but it occupies quite an enviable waterside spot. Guests gather around an outdoor bar overlooking the water and dine in a rustic restaurant here in this serene setting. Accommodations are similarly simple, but kept clean and neat. There are just 15 rooms at this inn, many with small kitchens, and all the rooms were revamped in 1985 with new carpeting, drapes, and paneling added. Rates are $45 to $75, year round, with highest rates in winter, of course.

Nights the action on the island is at **O'Shea's,** 1081 Bald Eagle Dr. (tel. 394-7531). We take that back—nights *and* days the action's at this lively spot, which operates sunset, moonlight, and day cruises on a paddlewheel riverboat, has a band practically every night, and offers light dinners, full dinners, lunches, raw bar, Sunday brunch, you name it. Dinner prices fall in the $12 to $15 range at O'Shea's, which naturally specializes in seafood but has plenty of other selections as well. O'Shea's flings its Gaelic blarney around from 11:30am to the wee hours every day.

## RESTAURANTS

Miamians have long come to Naples to escape the hectic city life, then returned here later. A high-rolling crowd gets the good food it seeks at moderate prices and in quite expansive atmospheres. Dining seems to get better and better in this small town, which keeps adding new restaurants to its roster. This is such a small town that you can just roll in, park your car, and stroll through town looking at restaurants as you go. Remember that the prices we've cited are for entrées, but that these usually include salad, one or two vegetables, and sometimes coffee as well.

### French

A glamorous resident, well, two glamorous residents, of Naples are the **Chef's Garden** and **Truffles,** the former occupying the downstairs quarters at 1300 3rd St. S. (tel. 262-5500), and Truffles bustling merrily upstairs. Downstairs, a garden atmosphere prevails, with tables running alongside a wall of glass through which a tiny garden is visible. The bright contemporary design in soft shades of pink and green makes this a handsome spot to dine on Whiskey Turkey on brioche, cucumber soup, crêpes, or a jellied poached salmon at lunch, or rack of lamb or veal with morels at dinner. Upstairs, you'll be starved by the time you reach a table: To get there you have to pass a glass case containing shimmering pâtés, delicate sliced salmon, and golden cheeses. Shading the windows here are yards and yards of dramatic salmon-pink fabric echoed in peach accents on rattan chairs. In this striking decor you dine on sautéed crab cakes with avocado, caper-rimmed steak tartare, chicken piccata, elegant sandwiches of avocado, muenster, tomato, and bean sprouts on honey-wheat bread, heaping salads with Greek or Italian flavors, watercress crunchy with almonds, or unusual cold fish plates including curried mussels. Later, sensuous desserts: cappuccino white -chocolate pie, praline cheesecake. Top prices here run about $13 to $15, but many items are in the $5 to $10 range. Truffles is open Monday through Saturday from 11am to 11pm, on Sunday from 4:30 to 10:30pm with prices from $7 to $17. You'll pay about $35 to $45 for dinner at the Chef's Garden, which is open from 11am to 2:30pm for lunch, from 5:30 to 10pm for dinner Tuesday through Saturday, open Monday in winter season.

### Italian

**Farino's Casa Italiana,** at 4000 N. Tamiami Trail (tel. 262-2883), isn't much on showy decor and in fact isn't much—just one of the best Italian kitchens on the state's west coast. Valery is the fourth generation of the friendly Farino family to reign over this award-winning dining room where only a couple of wine racks and some wood paneling serve for atmosphere. But who needs fancy furbelows when from the herb-scented kitchen pour out more than 50 classical Italian dishes including zuppa di vongole, pastas, hot and cold antipasti, milk-fed veal, chicken, and seafood treats in the $11 to $16 range? Open from 5pm daily, Farino's Casa Italiana is often jammed, so reservations are a wise move.

**Paisano's Ristorante,** Village Fall Shopping Center, 5019 E. Tamiami Trail (tel. 793-4484), has been garnering rave reviews for its home-cooked northern Italian cuisine. Among the most popular selections is an aromatic garlic soup that's much more delicate than it sounds. Veal, pastas, and lots of creamy things pour from a kitchen open from 5 to 10pm daily except Monday. Prices fall easily in the $6 to $15 range for dinners.

**Villa Pescatore's** and **Plum's Café,** 8920 N. Tamiami Trail (tel. 597-8119), is another successful creation of the same fellows whose first doubleheader was the Chef's Garden and Truffles. Here they've created a moderately priced restaurant—Plum's Café—featuring lots of pastas along with other Italian and American choices. To that they've added Pescatore's, where formally clad waiters present a showy menu of innovative northern Italian culinary triumphs with the accent on seafood. Plum's casual atmosphere is open daily from 11am to 11pm weekdays, 5 to

11pm on Sunday, while Villa Pescatore's more formal ambience is presented from 5:30 to 10pm daily. Prices at Plum's fall in the $10 to $15 range while dinner entrées at Villa Pescatore are in the $17 to $24 range with à la carte choices moving the bill higher rather quickly.

## Steaks and Seafood

**St. George and the Dragon** are still battling it out at the restaurant of that name, at 936 Fifth Ave. (tel. 262-6546), where you dine in an atmosphere that's more pub than medieval, with dim lighting and some nautical touches under a vaulted ceiling. The fare is solid beef and seafood dishes (in the $10 to $26 range), an incredible conch chowder, and key lime pie. St. George packs them in, but a wait at the well-stocked bar can be a pleasant interlude, especially on weekends. Hours are 11:30am to 11pm Monday through Saturday.

**Naples Chart House** (formerly Marker 4), 1193 Eighth St. South at the end of 9th Street beside the Cove Inn (tel. 649-0033), is another top dining room in this small town. Located right at the water's edge with fascinating views of shrimp boats chugging in and out of the harbor, Naples Chart House is a high-ceiling study in heavy wood beams and walls of glass through which the setting sun glitters and gleams off crystal and crisp linens. Seafoods, beef, chicken, and veal in continental preparations are featured. Dinner averages about $13 to $35, and is served from 5 to 10pm daily, later on weekends.

**The Dock at Crayton Cove,** 12th Avenue South and Naples Bay (tel. 263-9940), is just what its name implies, a dockside restaurant plunked down beside the City Docks. Which means, of course, that there's always an interesting view of yachts and fishing boats coming and going, and some good seafood (including shark) served up in a rustic atmosphere—you read the day's menu on the blackboard. Prices are in the $4 to $12 range, and the friendly help in sailor outfits are on hand from 11:30am to midnight daily (from noon on Sunday) to make your dining ship-shape.

You'd be hard-pressed to find a pubbier spot than **Pate's Piccadilly Pub,** at 625 Fifth Ave. South (tel. 262-7521), outside Piccadilly itself. Dark wood from floor to (and including) ceiling, lots of fascinating pub signs, brass chandeliers and wall sconces, and low lighting give this restaurant that glowing golden atmosphere so familiar in British pubs. Piccadilly Pub has been winning awards for its culinary talents for years now, and is one of the most popular spots in Naples. A "Hot Brown," a slice of baked turkey topped with Cheddar cheese sauce and browned, is the pub's bestseller, and oysters Rockefeller touched with Pernod and topped in béarnaise are worth the wait you may find here in winter. Steak and seafood dishes are on the moderately priced menu, which features lunch in the $4 to $6 range, dinner from $12 to $17. Open from 11:30am to 3pm Sunday through Friday and 5 to 10pm daily, Piccadilly Pub has five dining areas and a suitable dim lounge, but the front room where sunbeams glitter through paned windows is the favorite.

## Budget Bets

**Tin City** probably ought to be listed under what to see and do since it is certainly plenty of both. An old tin warehouse with tin roof and sides, Tin City was recently converted to a fascinating shopping center in which you'll find everything from ice-cream shops to fresh doughnuts, antiques to bikinis. Here there are two restaurants well loved by local diners: **Riverwalk Fish and Ale House** (tel. 263-2734), which features lots of inexpensive seafood in the $8 to $10 bracket; and **Merriman's Wharf** (tel. 261-1811), which specializes in ribs and barbecued chow in the same range, although both have less expensive fare also. Both also have lots of wood and greenery, with the Riverwalk leaning to nautical bric-a-brac. You can eat outside on tables overlooking the wharf or inside among the oars and nets. Look up in the Wharf and you'll see an antique sleigh dangling from the ceiling; stroll through this woodsy antique atmosphere for a look at painted antique iron horses.

Tin City is at 1200 5th St. S., just off US 41 south of Naples at the intersection of 12th Street and Sixth Avenue South. Riverwalk is open from 11am to midnight Monday through Saturday (from 1pm on Sunday); the Wharf's hours are the same daily, from noon on Sunday.

**READER'S "TIN CITY" TIP:** "Most unusual item I found at Naples's **'Tin City'** was canned key lime pie filling stocked in the butcher shop. It's canned puréed key limes, perfect flavor and texture, and I've never seen it anywhere else" (Kathleen Kemp, Madeira Beach, Fla.).

## SPORTS

There are plenty of places to play in this seaside city.

Golf fans can duff at the **Naples Beach Hotel and Golf Club,** 851 Gulf Shore Blvd. North (tel. 261-2222), a par-72 course where greens fees including carts are $25 to $58, depending on season.

**Tennis courts** at the hotel are $5 an hour and there are public courts at **Cambier Park** (tel. 262-5115) in downtown Naples. The **Riviera Golf Club,** on Fla. 864, just east of US 41 South (tel. 744-1081), and **Quality Inn Golf & Country Club,** at 4100 Golden Gate Pkwy. and County Road 951 (tel. 455-1010), also have 18-hole courses open to the public. Greens fees are in the $15 to $35 range.

You can rent diving equipment at **Sealandia Scuba Center,** 625 8th St. S. (tel. 775-6646), where they can show you how to use it and arrange tours and diving trips offshore.

A most unusual craft with two carved heads astern and a thatched roof atop, *Tiki Islander,* of **Tiki Islander Tours,** 1485 Fifth Ave. S. (tel. 262-7577), goes on half-day fishing, shelling, and sight-seeing sojourns at 9 and 11am and 2 and 4pm daily for $15 to $20 for adults, $10 to $15 for children under 12. The *Tiki* is docked at Tin City, just east of Tin City on US 41.

You can rent **sailboats** at the **Naples Beach Hotel and Golf Club** for $15 to $22 an hour; it even has a few kayaks and windsurfers for those with excellent balance. Call the hotel at 261-2222.

## SEEING THE SIGHTS

You can get a wonderful look at some strange and beautiful flora and fauna at two large preservation areas here.

You are of course at the tip of the Everglades, and just 17 miles from Naples is **Big Cypress Swamp,** last refuge of the Seminoles after land-hungry white men captured their leader Osceola (under a flag of truce) and forced many of the tribe to emigrate to what is now Oklahoma. Some of the Seminoles fled into this swamp to hide, and remain here today, still able to predict hurricanes and cold winters from the activities of swamp creatures. Big Cypress joins the massive Everglades at **Collier-Seminole Park,** 6,423 acres of nature trails, camping and picnic sites, fishing, and boating facilities. It's a favorite spot for canoeing through a 13-mile loop trail at the Blackwater River and Royal Palm Hammock Creek inside the park. To get there, follow the Tamiami Trail (US 41) 16 miles east. Call 657-3771 or 394-3397 for camping information.

At **Corkscrew Swamp Sanctuary** (tel. 657-3771) you'll see the nation's largest remaining stand of virgin bald cypress and walk beneath some of the oldest trees in eastern North America. Located about 20 miles east of Naples on county road 846, the 11,000-acre park is named after a crooked creek that flows through it. From the rustic two-mile boardwalk here you can look down on huge ferns and up at rare orchids. Look carefully at the "logs"—one of them may be an alligator! Admission is $5 for adults, $2.50 for students 12 and under, and children under 6 are free.

**Everglades Wonder Gardens,** Old Business Rte. 41 in Bonita Springs (tel. 992-2591), brings the Everglades to life literally by leading you through a vast garden filled with creatures who call the Everglades their home. Certainly they're not far from their home here at Everglades Wonder Garden, which is located right at the edge of the huge marshland. Among the creatures that live here are tiny Florida deer (the smallest of the deer found in the U.S.), colorful flamingos, endangered Everglades panthers, horned owls, rattlesnakes, and alligators, of course. Admission is $5 for adults, $3 for children 5 to 15; younger children are free. Everglades Wonder Gardens are open from 9am to 5pm daily, with the last tour beginning at 4pm.

## NIGHTLIFE

**Brassie's,** at the Naples Beach Hotel, 851 Gulf Shore Blvd. N. (tel. 261-2222), is one of the top nightspots in the area, and features entertainment and dancing on weekends. The hotel's lounge is popular for dancing too.

The **Naples Dinner Theater,** 1025 Piper Blvd. N. (tel. 597-6031), is a stunning three-tiered candlelit room where you select from a buffet table that seems to extend for miles. After dinner a stage floats into view and talented performers present classic and current plays and musicals. The Naples Dinner Theater has an elegant rococo atmosphere heavy with gilt mirrors and fountains, and a ticket to an evening of dining and theater is just $29.50 to $32.50. Jackets are required and the buffets are at 5:30pm, curtain at 8:15pm Tuesday through Saturday, with $25.75 matinees at 11am on Thursday, Saturday, and Sunday.

**Tin City,** off US 41 at 12th Street and Sixth Avenue South (see our restaurant recommendations), is always lively.

## SPECIAL EVENTS

Naples whoops it up twice a year at **swamp buggy races** held on the last Sunday of February and October. Begun in 1949 to signal the start of the hunting season, this event is mud wrestling on wheels as the crazy cars with the giant wheels plunge off through mud four to six feet deep to see whose machine is king pig. They even crown a Mud Duchess. It's fun—if you stand way back. Call 813/774-2701 for information about the race, which is often shown on a national television show.

---

# 3. Sanibel and Captiva Islands

---

Cockles, conchs, and calico scallops. Tiger's eyes, ladies' ear, and kitten's paw. Sand dollars and angel wings. These are the stuff dreams are made of on Sanibel, one of the world's three top shelling beaches, and perhaps the only place in the world famous for a posture—the Sanibel Stoop, the stooped-over gait of the shell hunter!

Sanibel and Captiva are a Gauguin paradise, two islets bathed in a golden glow, fringed in powder-soft silver sands, green with misty tunnels of Australian pines. They're exotica, splashed with scarlet, lemon, and fuschia blossoms peeking from behind giant banyans and huge green sea grape leaves, flashing bright in the scarlet flight of a roseate spoonbill or the dazzle of a white heron.

Almost everyone who has seen them has been captured by the sultry tropical beauty of these islands. Include among those Anne Morrow Lindbergh, who saw reflections of her past in the shells she found here and recorded those images in *Gift from the Sea,* artist Robert Rauschenberg, journalist Roger Mudd, author Edna St. Vincent Millay, editorial cartoonist "Ding" Darling.

If you join them, you'll find yourself slipping into a lazy mañana mode, a sun-baked tropical serenity. Finally one day you'll pick up one small shell, then another and another, tuck them into a pocket and take them away where their pearly glory will forever remind you of sun-drenched days and sea-lulled nights, of breezes whispering through the pines, and a pervasive peace as eternal as a shell.

## GETTING THERE

You can get to the islands by car from Fort Myers on Fla. 867. If you're coming from the south from Naples toward Fort Myers on US 41, you'll see a small sign about four miles south of the city pointing west to Sanibel. It's easy to miss the sign, so keep a sharp eye out as you near Fort Myers. There's a $3 round-trip toll to the islands, but if you're planning several crossings you can save money with a 20-trip ticket book.

## GETTING AROUND

The **Sanibel Taxi Cab Co.** (tel. 472-4160 or 472-4169) operates 24 hours a day on Sanibel, and can arrange airport transportation from Fort Myers for $28. Taxi rates on the island are $1.30 for each mile.

**Island Moped,** at 1470 Periwinkle Way (tel. 472-5248), rents mopeds for $12 an hour, bikes for $3 an hour. They're open from 8:30am to 5:30pm daily.

**Budget Rent-A-Car** also operates on the islands. Call them at 472-0088 in Sanibel or 472-9600 on Captiva.

## USEFUL INFORMATION

The **Sanibel/Captiva Chamber of Commerce** is at the entrance to the island on Causeway Road, Sanibel, FL 33957 (tel. 813/472-1080), and can give you reams of information on everything about these islands. It's open from 9am to 8pm Monday through Saturday and 10am to 5pm on Sunday. You can use the telephone there free to find a room on the island. . . . For **emergencies,** dial 911. . . . **for medical problems,** Dr. Louis Wegryn can be reached 24 hours a day at 472-4131. . . . **Island Garage** (tel. 472-4318) has 24-hour wrecker service and is open from 8am to 5pm Monday through Saturday for repairs. . . . **Bailey's General Store,** in the Island Shopping Center (tel. 472-1516), is open from 8am to 7pm weekdays, an hour later on weekends, and until 6pm on Sunday. They have groceries, beach hats, and such, and fishing supplies, and can get your film developed . . . The **Sanibel Grog Shop** is also in the Island Shopping Center and has liquors, beer, and wine. . . . If you need **quick cleaning service,** call Prathers (tel. 472-2442). . . . There's overnight film processing at **Island Apothecary,** Palm Ridge and Tarpon Bay Roads (tel. 472-1519), where you can also find prescription service to 5:30pm daily. . . . **Western Union** (tel. 472-1516) is in Bailey's General Store too. . . . The postal **ZIP Code** for the islands is 33957.

## HOTELS

You can be certain you'll find something to suit you on Sanibel/Captiva, where accommodations range from simple rustic beach cottages to slick chain motels, one of the state's loveliest resorts, and hundreds of privately owned condominium apartments. Whatever kind of accommodations you're interested in, including condominiums, contact the **Sanibel/Captiva Chamber of Commerce** office, Causeway Road, P.O. Box 166, Sanibel, FL 33957, at the entrance to Sanibel (tel. 813/472-1080), which has a list of available accommodations. Many realtors in the area also deal in vacation condominium rentals.

Sanibel has grown so rapidly in recent years that there are now hundreds, if not thousands, of condominiums, cottages, homes, granny quarters, and any other kind of accommodation you can dream up available for rent. Many of those are listed with **Priscilla Murphy Realty,** 9706 Causeway Rd. (P.O. Box 5), Sanibel Island, FL 33957 (tel. 813/472-4113, or toll free 800/237-6008). You'll find a wide variety of prices, depending on location and size of the quarters you're seeking, but figure to pay $400 to $700 a week in summer, about double that in winter.

### The Luxury Leaders

Among the island's multitudes of condominium resorts, serene **Pointe Santo de Sanibel,** 2445 W. Gulf Dr., at Tarpon Bay Road, Sanibel, FL 33957 (tel. 813/472-9100, or toll free 800/824-5442, 800/282-7438 in Florida), is a magically quiet place far from the frenetic activity that characterizes some of the island's other accommodations. Situated on the southernmost point of Sanibel, Pointe Santo is kept immaculate and sparkling by management and owners who soon know everyone by name and seem really to care about the caliber of the resort they oversee. You can lie beside a sparkling pool overlooking the beach, wander over a footbridge to a heated Jacuzzi, or while away the hours in a wood-beamed clubhouse where a glass floor lets you follow the antics of fish swimming in the lagoon below. You can whack a few around on the tennis courts, or search for the perfect shell on miles of silver white beach. Select from spacious one-, two-, or three-bedroom elaborately decorated villas, or go whole hog in penthouse apartments with private rooftop sundecks (each is valued at more than a half a million dollars!), for prices ranging from $205 to $325 a day in peak winter season, from $105 to $205 in the summer months.

Dear old Clarence Chadwick, the man who made a fortune with his "Checkwriter" and then blew it all in an attempt to make another fortune in copra and key limes, simply wouldn't believe what's now gracing his groves. You'll have just a little trouble believing it too when you see the 330-acre **South Seas Plantation Resort and Yacht Harbour** (P.O. Box 194), Captiva Island, FL 33924 (tel. 813/472-5111, or toll free 800/237-3102, 800/282-3402 in Florida). This multi-million-dollar wonder sprang up on Captiva Island a few years ago and captured the imagination (and the wallets) of many a south Floridian. If there's something they can't provide, we have yet to discover it: There are 22 tennis courts presided over by a touring pro, 1977 Wimbledon Champ Virginia Wade, plus 18 (count 'em) swimming pools, a nine-hole oceanside golf course, a marina, 2.5 miles of private beach, a rustic Capt'n Al's Pub at harborside, Mama Rosa's for pizza, and award-winning Chadwick's Restaurant where the Friday-night seafood buffet is bounteous and the Sunday brunch could easily carry you into Tuesday.

All that and we haven't even started on where you'll stay: You can choose among seaside apartments, hundreds of them, snuggled in clusters, each around its own pool; villa efficiencies; and one-, two-, and three-bedroom cottages right on the beach, raised high over the sand on stilts. If you aren't interested in anything remotely related to a kitchen, there are rooms in Harborside Village with luxuries like double vanities. From January to June, one or two people in hotel rooms pay $150 to $190 a day; in other months $115 to $205. One- and two-bedroom accommodations begin at $160 a day in winter months, at $120 in summer. Equally attractive gulfside cottages with three bedrooms, a loft, private porches, washers and dryers, private pool and tennis court, as well as beach homes with two to four bedrooms and several baths, lofts, pool and tennis court, are also available. There is a seven-night minimum on some accommodations.

Ranging over 330 acres, South Seas Plantation has retained much of its plantation atmosphere, so you can stroll through mile after mile of wooded pine and mangrove island that hasn't changed much in many centuries, and is home to hundreds of varieties of colorful birds (occasionally you may even hear the deep-throated gronk of a bull alligator). You can learn to sail here at a branch of the prolific Offshore Sailing School, or you can let someone else do the sailing on a trip aboard the 65-foot cruiser *Fort Dearborn* (tel. 472-5111). For dining, Chadwick's is a charmingly eclectic mélange of multilevel seating areas with tropical island flavor and a mix of exotic colors. Dine here on filet mignon béarnaise or roast prime rib, shrimp in a delicate beer batter laced with sherry, or sea scallops simmered in garlic butter and white wine. Figure your check in the $20 to $30 range per person.

Finally, at King's Crown you'll dine in a former warehouse/commissary that once served plantation workers. Under the original wood beams and a massive fireplace enhanced by crystal and deep carpeting, you'll dine on raw beef dijonnais accompanied by aromatic herb and mustard sauce, lobster bisque, salads of artichokes or avocado touched with truffles, followed by soft-shell crabs sautéed with green peppercorns, fresh fish topped with coconut sauce, rack of spring lamb, roast pigeon with lime, poached lobster topped with a sauce laced with sorrel. Finish with flaming coffees and key lime pies from Chadwick's trees, which still grow here. Expect to pay in the $60-a-couple range for your splurge.

A welcome addition to Sanibel's upscale hostelries is the **Sonesta Sanibel Harbour Resort and Spa,** 15610 McGregor Blvd., Fort Myers, FL 33908 (tel. 813/466-4000, or toll free 800/343-7170). Despite its address, this handsome new hotel is right at the causeway to Sanibel, rising loftily over 80 tranquil acres there. All by itself on a peninsula of land dotted with mangroves, the hotel is quite an elegantly appointed property.

For tennis fans, it's mecca indeed—several acres are devoted to the Jimmy Connors U.S. Tennis Center, complete with 5,000-seat tournament stadium and 12 tennis courts. You can even dine in a restaurant overlooking the courts and imbibe there at a woodsy lounge. A spa and fitness center has all the required instruments of torture, an indoor exercise pool, four racquetball courts, whirlpool, saunas, and a steamroom. Outside, there's another pool.

Accommodations at the hotel are in one- and two-bedroom tower suites accommodating up to eight. Each has a complete kitchen, a living/dining area, cable television, and private balcony overlooking Sanibel. Rates are $195 to $255 in peak winter season, $125 to $175 in summer.

**Sanibel Island Hilton Inn,** 937 Gulf Dr., Sanibel Island, FL 33957 (tel. 813/472-3181, or toll free 800/237-1491, 800/282-2240 in Florida), sprawls across acres of beachfront at the eastern end of the island. Very tropical in feeling, the resort is a series of two- and three-story buildings centered around a pool and wood walkway to the ocean's edge.

Hilton always seems to come across with handsome quarters and showy public rooms, and this resort is no exception: The Brass Elephant dining room is a study in tropical drama, complete with a circular central banquette and banners flying from a ceiling rimmed in Victorian gingerbread fretwork.

Screened balconies make a nice spot for sunset-watching while inside, rooms are large and attractively furnished in soothing contemporary style. They come complete with small refrigerator and coffee maker. Suites are even more elaborate, with separate bedroom and living room, dining area, and kitchenette. Outside, lots of water-sports equipment, a pool, tennis courts, and a long, long strip of beach beckon. Rates for two begin at $125 to $205, year round; higher for kitchenettes and suites; $20 to $25 for extra persons.

## The Moderate Range

**'Tween Waters Inn,** Captiva Drive on Captiva Island, FL 33924 (tel. 813/472-5161), could hardly be more aptly named—it's snuggled in between the gulf and the waters of the Pine Island Sound, and at a narrow point on this tiny island that's snuggly indeed. Here you'll discover a helter-skelter scattering of cottages where you can settle into a super-casual, uninhibited, lazy beachcombing life. Everything's simple, from the basic white painted furniture, to uncarpeted terrazzo floors (so you don't have to concern yourself with tracking sand around), bright bedspreads with matching drapes, and even the occasional cottage with a fireplace. Don't expect anything more luxurious than maid service at this inn. It's simplicity itself, but what could be nicer than sand between your toes and days that drift by as casually carefree as the waves that lap upon the sands outside your door? Captiva's only road runs between this casual resort and the sea, but you're only steps away from the inn's private strip of beach shaded by giant sea grape trees, palms, and lacy Australian pines. A frequent guest here years ago was J. N. "Ding" Darling, a famed New York editorial cartoonist who retired to the island and created a wildlife refuge nearby that still bears his name. Rates for two are $70 to $170 in summer and $75 to $215 in winter; Christmas and October, there are lively celebrations here.

There's nary a blade of grass at the **Island Inn,** at the corner of West Gulf Drive and Island Inn Road, 3111 West Gulf Dr. (P.O. Box 659), Sanibel Island, FL 33957 (tel. 813/472-1561), just acres of sand dotted with palms and shrubbery. With all that sand around it's almost like sleeping right on the beach. Fortunately, you won't have to pull up a piece of sand since the Island Inn lures you with exceptionally attractive rooms with colorful drapes and bedspreads. Beyond those drapes are spacious balconies where you can have your morning coffee (and orange juice, of course) beneath the shade of sea grape trees. The Island Inn is a cluster of lodges, each with its own identifying name. One of them, Kimball Lodge, houses a spacious lounge, library, a second-floor sundeck, bridge tables, and (naturally) a view of the gulf. Starkey Lodge has large efficiency units with two double beds and sofa Bahama beds; Matthews Lodge features rooms with twin or two double beds, refrigerators, and efficiencies with screened balconies. Several cottages on the grounds will accommodate up to six people, and there are smaller ones for two or four. The friendly management keeps things spiffy and adds some unusual touches like an intriguing carved totem pole. In the winter months from mid-December to Easter, the inn's dining room serves all meals, two of them included in resort rates, which range from $76.50 to $143 for a double room, kitchen unit, or cottage. Summer rates (beginning about May 1 to mid-November) are $59 to $85 for rooms or cottages with or without kitchens, no meals included.

If your Florida dreams revolve around a little cottage by the sea, **Shalimar,** 2818 W. Gulf Dr. (P.O. Drawer D), Sanibel Island, FL 33957 (tel. 813/472-1353), may be for you just the paradise that name suggests. A cluster of pretty, silver-roofed cottages, this small but immaculately maintained motel is plunked right down on Sanibel's powdery sands. These cute little cottages with crisp white curtains look old worldly but provide all the modern conveniences, from complete kitchens to tile baths and comfortable, modern furnishings. Evenings, you can watch the sun set from your screened porch and days you can splash in the motel's private strip of ocean or in a heated freshwater swimming pool.

A small two-story strip of motel accommodations offers efficiencies with double beds. Both cottages and efficiencies have color television and sleep four or more. Rates for two range from $73 to $81 in summer, from $98 to $106 in winter.

Another attractive, moderately priced resort on Sanibel is the **West Wind Inn,** 3345 W. Gulf Dr., Sanibel Island, FL 33957 (tel. 813/472-1541, or toll free 800/824-0476, 800/282-2831 in Florida). A swimming pool sits serenely front and center here on large lawns that roll up to the door of the two-story wings of the building. Everything is neat and tidy here, and done up in soft, soothing colors. Many of the recently renovated rooms have kitchen areas where you can whip up something to stave off starvation, but if you hate the thought of a pot, a small restaurant and lounge comes to your rescue here. West Wind has 600 feet of beachfront, tennis courts, phones, a putting green, barbecue grills, shuffleboard, a small restaurant, and a lounge. Double rates are $125 to $140 in winter, $90 to $104 in summer, higher for two- and three-room suites.

A small stone boy staring pensively out over his domain sets the tone at **Song of the Sea,** 863 E. Gulf Dr., Sanibel Island, FL 33957 (tel. 813/472-2220), a gracious resort that likes to call itself an old-world inn. There is indeed something of the old world in this tranquil spot with rambling grounds. Mediterranean red-brick curved roof tiles lend a classic touch of old-world charm to three simple white two-story buildings set amid palms and grassy walkways. Inside, wingback chairs and oak whisper of a French country home. Despite its genteel touches, Song of the Sea is a casual, informal spot where you can soak in a modern Jacuzzi, paddle about an unusually shaped pool, roam the small well-kept grounds, or settle into a chaise and let your worries ebb with the tides. A meticulous merger of old world and new, Song of the Sea has successfully blended gentility with beachside comfort. You can choose between one-bedroom apartments in a building overlooking the beach or efficiencies in the resort's two other structures overlooking the pool. From mid-December to May, efficiencies with two double beds or one-bedroom apartments are $150 to $170. In other months, prices drop to $95 to $115.

Pale-green cottages blend perfectly into 25 acres of manicured lawns at **The Colony,** 401 E. Gulf Dr. (P.O. Box A), Sanibel Island, FL 33957 (tel. 813/472-5151), about a mile from the causeway. Cottages are scattered far apart, so they're very private hideaways indeed. If you prefer neighbors, there are two-story buildings housing sunny motel rooms decorated in a cheery green-and-orange decor and lots of windows overlooking the lawns. This seaside cluster of accommodations is back on one of the less frequented areas of the island, so you get a real feeling of getaway island living here. Still, you're not deprived of the accoutrements of civilization: There's a heated freshwater pool, cable color TV, picnic tables and grills for cookouts, rental bicycles, and best of all, 1,000 feet of shell-strewn beachfront. On a rapidly crowding island, the Colony is an unusually large property offering lots of uncluttered space with tiny walkways winding through the lawns, palms, and beautifully landscaped grounds. Rates begin at $110 from mid-December to May, at $65 in summer, a little higher for cottages. A handy map the resort will send you shows the location of cottages and rooms so you can pick the view you like best.

If the Sanibel Stoop gets to you before you've found the perfect shell, the managers of the **Gallery Motel,** 541 E. Gulf Dr., Sanibel Island, FL 33957 (tel. 813/ 472-1400), have collected some beauties you can buy. That's not reason enough to stay, but it's one of the many thoughtful extras you'll find at this tropical enclave located right on the sand at the quieter, less frenetic southeastern tip of Sanibel. Just a short walk away is the historic Sanibel lighthouse and the fishing pier on San Carlos Bay. You can choose from motel rooms, efficiencies, cottages, and apartments at the Gallery, but we're partial to the cottages, which face a central courtyard. They're especially spacious, decorated in off-white rattan furniture cushioned in bright yellow. In the living room it's fun to gather a few kindred souls at the high-stooled bar evenings and move onto small raised porches for a view of dramatic sunsets. You can't miss the Gallery as you drive along East Gulf Drive—it's painted a delicate shade of cocoa trimmed with darker shades of the same color on railings and shutters. In high season (from mid-December to mid-April), rates range from $110 to $160. At other times you'll pay $57 to $82.

Sanibel's gorgeous sand is king at most motels on the island, but at the **Jolly Roger Motel,** 3201 W. Gulf Dr., Sanibel Island, FL 33957 (tel. 813/472-1700), rooms overlook a tranquil shady strip of lawn and garden that stretches along the side of this neat and trim property. Which is not to say, of course, that the resort is without sand—it's located right on the beach. The Jolly Roger gets our vote for one of the most tranquil resorts on Sanibel for its cool, collected look and decor, and its spacious rooms set at an angle to make the most of triangular screened balconies overlooking the lawns, pool, and gulf beyond. Beachside there is a freshwater pool set up over the beach and surrounded by umbrellaed picnic tables plus a tennis court and barbecue. Some rooms have kitchens, and families can arrange for two- and three-room suites. In the winter season, beginning the middle of December, prices are $80 to $135 (7-day minimum), changing on May 1 to $60 to $85.

At the **Beachview Cottages,** 3306 W. Gulf Dr., Sanibel Island, FL 33957 (tel. 813/472-1202), you'll find cute rustic beach cottages with screened porches shaded by waving palms and rustling sea grape trees. On the beach there's a sundeck and Tiki hut; inside, cottages have fully equipped kitchens, cable TV, and simple durable furnishings much loved by families. The friendly management's around to advise on shelling, fishing, and dining at Beachview, where from mid-December to mid-April you'll pay $65 to $125 for studio efficiencies, a one-bedroom gulfside cottage, or a two-bedroom duplex accommodating four. In other months, rates range from $55 to $100.

## Budget Bets

If you'd like to enjoy all the fun and serenity of Sanibel Beach without paying beach prices, just on the Fort Myers side of the bridge to Sanibel is the best budget find you'll discover anywhere in the vicinity. Overlooking Shell Point, a retirement village, you'll find the **Shell Point Village,** Shell Point Boulevard, Fort Myers, FL 33908 (tel. 813/466-1111), built high on a rise above a huge Y-shaped swimming pool, marina, and the Caloosahatchee River. Although it's called a guesthouse (probably because it was designed primarily to house guests of the village's residents), this is no clapboard house run by a den mother. Rather, it's a modern, two-story, 39-room motel with picture windows and contemporary decor the equal of any chain-motel operation. Rooms are unusually spacious with a wall of glass overlooking the community, and feature dark-blue decor or contemporary off-white spreads with blue and rust stripes. You'll pay just $48 to $69 double from October to May, $35 in other months. There's no charge for children, but other additional guests are $5 each. If you're a senior citizen, there's a 10% discount. Meals in the glass-enclosed crystal room overlooking the village are in the $10 range. Shell Point's guesthouse is 12 miles southwest of Fort Myers, two miles north of Fla. 867 on Shell Point Boulevard, a road that heads north about two miles just east of the Sanibel bridge.

A budget-saver motel on Sanibel Island is **Kona Kai,** at 1539 Periwinkle Way, Sanibel Island, FL 33957 (tel. 813/472-1001), a lush jungly spot festooned with flowers and shaded by tall palms. Bright-pink hibiscus peek out from behind hedges and leafy bushes. Kona Kai is not on the beach and has very basic furnishings, to which the owners, LeNita and Leon Matheny, have added ceiling fans, some queen-size beds, and new carpeting. In the meantime you'll find comfortable, reasonably spacious rooms, spick and span, with lots of wood paneling and a very attractive and alluring pool set amid so much greenery it's almost like swimming in a Polynesian lagoon. Summer rates at this 12-unit South Pacific-theme beauty are $39 to $59 double daily in summer, rising to $69 to $89 in peak winter season. Kona Kai's owners now also rent one- and two-bedroom apartments about a block from the beach for rates in the same general range, some higher. Similar rates also are in effect at another affiliated property, the **Blue Heron Motel,** which is designed for beach enthusiasts as it is right across the street from a public beach (tel. 813/472-1206).

## RESTAURANTS

With so many people crammed into islands as small as Sanibel and Captiva you may have to wait a while to get into the island's restaurants in the winter season (or for that matter, in summer). It's worth the wait, however, for there are some talented cooks on the island. Because distances are so small here, we've divided the area's restaurants up by cuisine, beginning with what's almost always the most expensive, French. The prices listed, by the way, are for entrées unless otherwise noted.

### French and New American

Jean-Paul Cavanie brought a little bit of Paris with him when he opened **Jean-Paul's French Corner,** 708 Tarpon Bay Rd. (tel. 472-1493), at the Sanibel post office, 11 years back. A teensy bistro filled with fascinating bibelots (take a look at the ornate birdcage on the bar), the French Corner has a cozy, homey air about it and Edith Piaf warbling in the background. There are fresh flowers on the candlelit tables and perfumes emanating from the kitchens. Jean-Paul has a good cook, to put it mildly, who whips up a storm of escargots, filet mignon au poivre vert, and duck with fruit sauces. Fortunately prices here are nothing like Paris, with entrées topping out at $21. He's open for dinner from 6 to 10pm (closed on Sunday and May 15 to October 15).

Since 1957, **Nutmeg House,** at 2761 Gulf Dr. (tel. 472-1141), has occupied a small plot of green grass and flowers on Gulf Drive, so they must be doing something right. Dine in a tropical garden atmosphere on excellent French and Italian treats like veal Armagnac or snapper Florentine en croûte. An unusual specialty here is seafood chowder en croûte, and Nutmeg's fresh chicken and avocado salad is a special event. Expect to pay $20 to $25 for dinner, $5 to $7 more if you indulge in appetizers, soups, or special salads, which are very tempting. The Nutmeg House is open from 5:30 to 9:30pm every day but Monday, with chamber music occasionally.

**Sunshine Café,** Captiva Village Square on Captiva (tel. 472-6200), is a pleasant little bistro doing some sophisticated cooking. On the menu are such choices as smoked pork loin with tropical fruit salsa or duck with raspberry coulis with prices in the $12 to $17 range. Sunny smiles here from 11:30am to 9:30pm daily.

A few doors away, the **Greenhouse** in the same Captiva Village Square (tel. 472-6006), applies its whisks and wherewithal to some very innovative cooking, dreaming up combinations like black lobster ravioli or crabmeat agnolotti in a basil-coriander pesto or blackened tuna topped with raspberry mustard. Prices are similar to Sunshine Café. The restaurant is open from 5 to 9pm daily.

A little like the **Mad Hatter** for which it is named, this restaurant come up with the unexpected and makes it seem commonplace. How about duck quesadillas, crab cakes topped with mango and lime sauce, or sweetbread, hazelnut, and spinach ravioli with sage brown butter? Every night there are a dozen or so specials that the chef has dreamed up that day to fit whatever ingredients he has been able to locate in the local marketplace. Prices are in the $12 to $17 range for entrées. You can drop in on the Mad Hatter, 6460 Sanibel-Captiva Rd. (tel. 472-0033), daily from 5 to 10pm.

## Steaks and Seafood

For a long time we thought **Timbers Restaurant and Fish Market,** at 975 Rabbit Rd. (tel. 472-3128), was a fancy condominium sales office. When we discovered it was really an excellent steak and seafood restaurant, well, such are the joys of discovering Sanibel. At Timbers everything's fresh, fresh, and fresher, from the seafood that comes straight out of the gulf to the excellent beef, to the vegetables and salads and breads baked here. For openers, try oysters or shrimp by the half or three-quarter dozen. Scampi or sirloin is a good choice. You'll pay $10 to $20 for dinner at the Timbers, which is open daily from 4:30 to 10pm. Stop in at Twigs lounge for postprandial sipping.

There's a Tudory look about the **Iggy & Paul's Lobster House,** at the corner of Tarpon Bay Road and Periwinkle Way (tel. 472-1366), with diamond-paned glass, lots of wood and plants scattered about, and a varied menu ranging from seafood to steaks and chops in the $10 to $18 range. For children there's a special menu, and for light eaters, salad plates. The house specialty is—what else?—lobster. Don't miss the restaurant's prize-winning shell collection on the way out. Hours are 11am to 10pm daily, from 10:30 am for Sunday brunch. Maine or Florida lobsters are available at decent prices, but there's also pasta, chicken concoctions, surf-turf combos, burgers, and daily fish catches for prices in the $10 to $20 range.

**J. Todd's,** at the Ramada Inn, 1131 Middle Gulf Dr. (tel. 472-4123), prides itself on groaning-board productions designed to fill the emptiest tummies. Saturday night's buffet ought to get you through Sunday—prime rib, oysters Rockefeller, artichokes stuffed with crab, seafood Newburg, many other options, even an ice sculpture for less than $17. Todd's, quite an attractive dining room complete with linens, lots of wood, and is open from 5 to 9pm, later on weekends and has a lounge.

On Captiva, **'Tween Waters Inn** (tel. 472-5161) has two attractive dining rooms decorated with amusing sketches by cartoonist "Ding" Darling who was a favorite guest of this resort. He used to team up with manager Maggie White in pranks aimed at livening things up a bit: The duo once carefully created panther tracks in the sand opposite the inn and waited for the uproar to begin. 'Tween Waters hasn't changed much since those days, and still has a cozy little front dining room with ruffly curtains and a view across the road to the waters of the gulf. Dinners at 'Tween Waters are straightforward preparations of steaks cut to order in the inn's kitchens, shrimp, crab, scallops, and whatever unsuspecting fish was caught that day. Prices are in the $14 to $20 range for dinner, and food service is available from 8am to 11pm daily. Saturday is prime rib night; a brunch on Sunday 9am to 2pm for $12.95.

It isn't possible to resist a restaurant with a name like **Mucky Duck,** Andy Rosse Lane SW, Captiva Island (tel. 813/472-3434). Once you get there and join the other Mucky lovers, the Duck will capture you once and for all time. In a rustic atmosphere jammed with other diners chowing down on very good seafood, you're greeted by someone who recites whatever is on the fabulously good seafood menu that night. Of decor there is little to be said; of ambience, probably less; of great seafood at great prices (in the $10 to $15 range at dinner), volumes. Sooner or later everyone but absolutely everyone goes here, so if you don't trust *us*, trust the *world*. Mucky Duck is open daily (except Sunday) from 11:30am to 2:30pm and from 5:30 to 9:30pm. Don't leave without a Mucky Duck T-shirt for someone.

It would be difficult to find a crazier place than the **Bubble Room,** Captiva Road, Captiva Island (tel. 472-5558). A ramshackle three-level building, Bubble Room is built around a towering palm tree, Goofy marionettes and statues of Laurel and Hardy, and bubbles, bubbles, and more bubbles: bubbles in the stained-glass windows, bubbling Christmas ornaments, delicate glass bubbles. They're a little more serious about the food, but not much: each entrée bears some kind of Hollywood tag, like Henny Young-One (a chicken breast) and Eddie Fisherman (a grouper).

The food is quite interesting here, ranging from a big glass bubble-full of bouillabaisse to bread baked with roquefort cheese and oregano, salads of romaine, mushrooms, cucumber, pimiento, and red cabbage with buttermilk or Caesar dressing. Steaks and seafood are the mainstays, and are served with twice-baked potatoes and several vegetables. "Sweet-sixteen" desserts vary daily and are as imaginative as the prime ribs Weismuller are huge: fudge-nut brownie pie, cappuccino cheesecake, several kinds of decadent chocolate cake. You'll pay about $17 to $25 for dinner entrées here. The Bubble Room effervesces from 11am to 2pm and 5 to 10pm daily.

**McT's Shrimphouse and Tavern,** 1523 Periwinkle Way (tel. 472-3161), calls itself an "honest" place to eat on Sanibel Island, and lots of people agree. An attractive gardeny look inside is pleasant but unprepossessing, and loads of hungry islanders line up every night for simple fish preparations. McT's "McDeal" is a $8 agreement to cook whatever you provide and toss in the trimmings, or let them do the fishing and treat yourself to all the steamed shrimp or crabs you can consume. McT's has lots of oysters and shrimp, fish and chips, even a "McJawger and Chips" combo of battered and deep-fried shark. Finish off with a Sanibel mud pie and figure dinner at $10 to $15 (a few dollars more if you succumb to that pie). Open from 5 to 10pm daily, McT's is equally well known for its adjoining tavern where throngs gather nightly for jukebox music until 2am daily.

## Budget Bets

An old post office has been converted fittingly enough into the **Calamity Jane's Café,** 632 Tarpon Bay Rd. (tel. 472-6622), where you can feast on fat sandwiches, bagels, sundaes, shakes, and French-bread pizza. If someday you decide you're going to sit on the beach and never move, not once the entire day, rest easy—you won't starve: The deli will fix you a beach box packed with meats, cheeses, salads, and pickles for $10 or so, if you'll just explain your determination. Believe it, they've heard that one before. Open from 11am to 9pm daily except Sunday.

Whip up a gourmet picnic the easy way at **Si Bon,** now in Fort Myers at 5670 Trailwinds Dr. (tel. 275-6887). Escargots, quiches, classic French cooking, dessert mousses, cheesecake—now that should make ants stand up and salute! Once voted best take-out shop in the area, Si Bon is open 7am to 6pm daily but call ahead with your order.

Graze your way to oblivion at **Wil's Landing,** 1200 Periwinkle Way (tel 472-4772), where the menu begins with raw-bar treats, potato skins, nachos, onion rings, and moves onto seafood, prime beef, pasta, and salads. Prices fall in the $10 to $15 range for dinners at this attractive restaurant and lounge open from 11:30am to 2pm daily except Saturday and 4 to 9pm. You'll find entertainment and dancing here to 1am.

**Island Pizza,** 1619 Periwinkle Way (tel. 472-1581), has been a mainstay of island pizza life for years. You can eat here, take it out, or even have a pizza delivered. There's more on the menu than pizza too: spaghetti, lasagne, veal parmigiana, calzone, salads, burgers, baby back ribs, hot submarines—most everything in the under $12 price range, many under $7. Hours here are 11am to 9pm daily.

## WHAT TO SEE AND DO

You won't find any theme parks or carousels on Sanibel, an island serious about observing and appreciating nature's bounty.

One way to do that is at **Ding Darling National Wildlife Refuge** (see Parks) and another is by stopping by the **Sanibel/Captiva Conservation Foundation,** 3233 Sanibel-Captiva Rd. (tel. 472-2329). Operating from a handsome weathered old building, the island's conservationists control about 850 acres of the Sanibel's wetlands. At their headquarters you can learn a little about the ecological activity around you and learn how to find your way around the nature trails maintained by the organization.

Sanibel has a very long history of course, but much of it has disappeared in the wake of massive development that in recent years has turned it into a very busy place indeed. A quiet retreat to get a look at the past can still be found, however, tucked away on Dunlop Road. It's called the **Island Historical Museum** (tel. 472-4648), a private home that was moved here in 1982. Built of rockhard Florida pine, the museum is typical Old Florida architecture, furnished just as the early settlers would have had it. Old tintype photos, antique clothing, and other memorabilia of an age long-gone on this island make for a few poignant moments. Admission is free and the museum is open from 10am to 4pm on Thursday and Saturday, except holidays.

While you're in that historic mood, take a look at the **old lighthouse** on the eastern tip of Sanibel. It's been operating since 1884. Much of the area around the lighthouse is now a wildlife refuge. Meanwhile, the light here at one of Florida's few remaining lighthouses continues to serve as a landmark for shipping traffic in the area. You'll find the lighthouse at the east end of Periwinkle Road.

In late spring and early summer hundreds of massive loggerhead **turtles** lumber ashore here to lay their eggs. A research organization called Caretta Research tags, transplants, counts, and collects the eggs to protect them, and can tell you all about their activities so you can join them. Call them at 472-3177.

## SPECIAL EVENTS

Islanders love a party and happily welcome you to join them in several islandwide events several times a year. Among those are the **Arts and Crafts Fair,** on the first weekend in February; the **Captiva ABC Sale,** an arts-and-crafts event, in late February; the huge **Sanibel Shell Fair,** on the first weekend in March, a celebration that's now been going on for more than 50 years; and **fish fries** on July 4 and Labor Day.

## SPORTS

Shelling is the islands' major sport, but there are also some places to pursue some more common activities.

### Golf and Tennis

Golfers can putt around a par-70, 18-hole course and lob on seven tennis courts at the **Dunes Golf and Tennis Club,** 949 Sandcastle Rd. To find the courts and course, turn off Periwinkle Way at Bailey Road and left off Bailey at the Dunes sign. Call 472-2535 for lessons or golf starting times, 472-3522 for tennis court times or lessons. Or try the **Beachview Golf Club,** 110 Parview Dr. South (tel. 472-2626).

Greens fees are less than $15 to $20 at either Dunes or Beachview. The Dunes also has tennis courts, and there are public tennis courts at Sanibel Elementary School on Sanibel-Captiva Road. Many resorts have tennis facilities for guests. You'll find a racquetball court open to the public at the **Signal Inn,** 1811 Olde Middle Gulf Dr. (tel. 472-4690).

## Boating and Canoeing

Rent a powerboat and speed off into the sunset. **The Boat House,** Sanibel Marina, North Yachtsman Drive (tel. 463-8787), can get you sailing in anything from a dory to a 19-foot cruiser. They also rent a wide variety of sailboats. Boat prices range from $50 to $180 a day, excluding fuel. You'll find The Boat House half a mile east of the causeway off Periwinkle Way.

If you'd like to let someone else do the driving, book a **sunset cruise** with Capt. Mike McMillan, who sails from Jensen's Twin Palms Marina, Captiva Road (tel. 472-0071). Rates and sailings vary in price and time.

Get yourself up on a windsurfing board at **Windsurfing of Sanibel,** 1554 Periwinkle Way (tel. 472-0123), or at **South Seas Plantation** (tel. 472-5111), on Captiva Island. They'll get you flying in an hour and have all the equipment available as well. Board rentals are $25 for two hours, about $45 a day. Instructions are $20 to $30 an hour.

**Mark "Bird" Westall** (tel. 472-5218) will set off with you on three-hour expeditions to parts of Sanibel and Buck Key that few people have ever seen. One trip goes through Ding Darling National Wildlife Refuge where there are more than 250 species of birds; another trip goes to Buck Key, inhabited once by Native Americans and later by pirates. Contact Westall between 1 and 10pm to plan trips, which vary in price.

## Shelling

You'll soon be hooked, like everyone else who visits here, on a sport known as shelling. There are two types of shelling on the island, gulf shelling and bay shelling. Along the Gulf of Mexico shells are deposited along the shoreline by what is known as "floor sweeping," a combination of tide and wind that cleans the bottom of empty shells and deposits them on beaches. Shelling is especially productive after strong northwest winds and storms that deposit even more shells on the beach. City shelling restrictions—and a respect for maintenance of this unusual environment—prohibit collecting more than two live shells per species. You know a shell is live if you see the inhabitant close its trapdoor (called an operculum). If you see the tiny closed "door" over the open section of the shell, or see the creature itself, or aren't sure, leave it behind. Egg cases look like long paper leis, and should be left behind if they are not hatched and open.

For Sanibel shuffling, wear sneakers to protect your feet from broken shells and stingrays that sometimes bury themselves in the shallow sandy waters where you will be shuffling along; they'll race away and won't hurt you.

The best shelling occurs just after the peak of high tide, and every motel on the island has tide tables that will tell you just when that is. December, January, and February are the top months for shelling, but winds in March and in the fall months often turn up some beauties.

If there's a living creature in your shell or you don't know for sure that there isn't, heed this warning: Boil it out or your nose will know you didn't. Most motels on the island have tiny stoves and old pots for shell boiling. Immersing shells in a bleach and water solution kills the fishy odor and won't affect the colors. To make them really shine, add a light coat of baby oil.

A number of enterprising shell collectors have set themselves up as guides and will show you their favorite hunting grounds. The chamber of commerce can supply you with a pamphlet called *Things to Do on Sanibel and Captiva,* which provides names and numbers of seven island shell guides.

## Fishing

You can arrange fishing expeditions at any of the five marinas on Sanibel, including **Blind Pass** (tel. 472-1020), **Sanibel** (tel. 472-2723), and **Tarpon Bay** (tel. 472-1323); and on Captiva at **'Tween Waters** (tel. 472-5161), **Twin Palms** (tel. 472-1727), and **South Seas Plantation** (tel. 472-5111).

## Parks

**Ding Darling National Wildlife Refuge,** on Sanibel Island (tel. 472-1100), welcomed a million visitors last year to four miles of woodland. Alligators, otters, and manatees call this 4,800-acre preserve home, and giant sea turtles nest along its shores. A schedule of walking tours is available at the lighthouse on the island, and canoeists can rent a canoe at the trail entrance at Tarpon Bay. Admission to the refuge is free and it's open daily from 7:30am to 4pm.

You can drive through the park on a winding, five-mile drive that may take you past a rare platypus-like roseate spoonbill perched on a mud flat, or a weird anhinga (Floridians call them unhinged birds—that's how strange they look) as it dries out its big wings.

## SHOPPING

There are shops packed from the bay to the gulf, so don't think you're on some desert island. **She Sells Sea Shells,** 1938 Periwinkle Way (tel. 472-3991), is the reigning monarch of island shell shops, but has plenty of competition, including **Neptune's Treasures,** 1101 Periwinkle Way (tel. 472-3132), which will arm you with a free illustrated shell guide, and **Tuttle's Sea Horse Shell Shop,** 342 Periwinkle Way (tel. 472-0707), where a second generation of shell hounds is in command. If you could use a pair of cool drawstring beach pants, you'll find them at the **Brown Bag,** in the Periwinkle Place Shopping Center (tel. 472-1171). The **Olde House Shoppe** (tel. 472-2692) has an intriguing atmosphere in Chadwick Square. You shop for women's clothing, especially lovely cottons, in an old house.

Finally, **Three Crafty Ladies,** 1445 Periwinkle Way (tel. 472-2893), are just that.

## ISLAND HOPPING

You can see some intriguing backcountry villages by traveling to some of the nearby islands, which are home to fishermen, and in one case to a fabulous historic resort.

## Pine Island

Just north of Sanibel/Captiva is Pine Island, a barely populated conclave of infinitesimal fishing villages where people take laid-back literally. Builders have made few forays onto the island, and it remains a spot for just ambling along sandy lanes, sitting on a deserted pier, fishing, or watching the rippling sea through the windows of the ramshackle Crab Shack Restaurant, where owner Frank Passante welcomes you to the three-house village of Bokeelia with a repast of boiled shrimp and a frosty grog or two.

To get there, head north on US 41 out of Fort Myers three miles to Fla. 78. Turn left, heading west, for 15 miles. You'll pass the village of Matlacha (pronounced "Mat-la-*shay*"), and go over a little causeway where Fla. 78 dead-ends; turn north to Bokeelia or south to Pine Island's southern village of St. James City. You can find a fisherman or a boat for a chug over to Useppa, a millionaire's retreat reachable only by plane or boat.

A step back in time, Pine Island has five tiny communities: Bokeelia, St. James City, Matlacha, Pineland, and a spot known only as The Center. To find them, remember that Bokeelia is "to the right of the stop sign, St. James City is to the left"— it's that kind of place. Better yet, stop by the **Pine Island Chamber of Commerce** (tel. 813/283-0888), where a helpful lady with a lively sense of humor and perspective to go with it will help you find whatever you're looking for here.

Nautical-rustic comes to life at **Sandy Hook Crab House,** on Fla. 78, Pine Island Road, Matlacha 33909 (tel. 283-0113). Outside, spiky coral rocks guide you to an entrance outlined in bollards. Inside, antiques and assorted nautical memorabilia add to the "Gilligan's Island"-in-comfort remoteness of it all. There are some great views across the water here, and some good Maryland-style seafood cooking along the lines of soft-shell crabs, stuffed shrimp, crab imperial, roast prime rib, smoked barbecued ribs, crab cakes. You'll likely pay $10 to $15 for dinner at Sandy Hook, which is open from 4 to 9pm Tuesday through Saturday and noon to 8pm on Sunday; closed Monday.

At **Bokeelia Crab Shack,** Main Street, Bokeelia (tel. 283-2466), Gary and Regina Kricacs will welcome you into the town's old rooming house for a passel of chubby shrimp or fat local oysters. Spread out over several small rooms, the Crab Shack has spectacular views over miles of ocean and good home-cooking in the most casual of atmospheres. You'll pay well under $15 for anything on the menu here. Hours are 11am to 9pm weekdays, an hour later on weekends.

Uptown, at **Waterfront Restaurant and Marina,** 2131 Oleander St., St. James City (tel. 283-0592), you can stoke up on a seafood basket, prime rib, and the like in the island's old schoolhouse. Here, too, you'll pay prices in the $8 to $10 range for many selections. Hours are also 11am to 9pm daily.

You'll find similar offerings and similar prices and hours at **The Dock,** Winn Dixie Plaza, 9706 Stringfellow Rd., St. James City (tel. 283-0005), but **The Porthole,** 10880 Stringfellow Rd. (tel. 283-5333), stays open until 2am. Pete, by the way, has a solid local reputation for good ol' Florida cookin'. One more local mainstay is **The Lob Lolly,** on Fla. 78 (tel. 283-4567), a restaurant that has been around many years: restaurant in front, bar in back, open from 6am to 8:30pm daily except Tuesday. The price range for dinner falls easily under $15, and often under $10.

## Cabbage Key

Novelist and playwright Mary Roberts Rinehart had a cozy inn built for her back in the 1930s and today it remains an inn, now restored and operating as a restaurant and an inn with six rustic rooms. You can get there by tour boat *Tropic Star* (tel. 283-0015), Pineland Marina, on Pine Island or you can catch a boat by calling 472-7549 and sail on over here for about $15 a person. Lunch and dinner (in the $15 to $20 range) are served in a picturesque—this is what tropical hideaways were meant to look like—dining room papered with 25,000, so they say, $1 bills autographed by folks who find this an interesting way to drop a dollar. Hours: 11:30am to 3pm and 7 to 9pm daily, closing at 7pm Sunday. Guests of South Seas Plantation on Captiva also can get over here on boats that run from the marina of that resort. You can, of course, rent a boat (try Jensen's, 472-5800) and sail on over on your own wind. If you want to get in touch with Cabbage Key, which as far as we know has no other name, call 813/283-2278. Rooms here are $45 year round.

## Useppa Island

Now get this one! You pull up alongside a marina, inquire at the only lighted building around, and a friendly soul suggests you stop across the street for a drink while someone takes your luggage to the boat.

To the *what?* Hey, they mean just what they say. This new resort is on an island and the only way you'll get there is by boat! Fortunately they provide the boat, and once you settle into a beautifully decorated apartment equipped with absolutely everything you could possibly need, surrounded by an incredibly quiet strip of sand, you'll agree that this is certainly one of the most seductively luxurious resorts in the state.

**Palm Island Resort,** 7092 Placida Rd., Cape Haze, FL 33946 (tel. 813/697-

4800, or toll free 800/824-5412, in Florida 800/282-6142), is quite a substantial new development of low-rise condominium apartment buildings and private homes. No one could ask for a more tranquil place to settle than this small island just off the coast of a tiny village called Cape Haze. Getting there is quite an adventure, particularly if you arrive after dark, then set off on the five-minute putt across the dark gulf waters guided by a couple of mysterious lights twinkling through shoreside jungles.

Home here is a one- or two-bedroom villa apartment with a fully equipped laundry and kitchen, a small bar, dining room, large living room, wide expanses of glass that take full advantage of the ocean views, even a small screened porch overlooking the sea. All are decorated in handsome jewel tones, perhaps navy blue offset by lightwood furnishings and shades of peach. Winter rates at this unusual resort are $115 for a mainland Harbor Town Inn apartment, $180 to $280 for a one-, two-, or three-bedroom oceanfront island apartment. In summer, beginning April 15, and in January, rates drop to $80 on the mainland and $115 to $200 for apartments.

By day, you awaken to the sound of waves lapping at a shell-strewn beach. Shallow gulf waters and five pools beckon to swimmers, breezes rustle through the pines, a little bus scoots around to pick you up for tennis or the boat trip to the mainland for shopping, exploring, or for lunch or dinner at the island's **Rum Bay Restaurant.**

On the menu at Rum Bay (tel. 697-0566), are such treats as popcorn shrimp, sautéed or broiled swordfish; or gulf shrimp sautéed in Provençal herbs, garlic, and white wine, or wrapped in bacon and marinated in a tangy barbecue sauce. Steaks, veal, and poultry also turn up on the menu, which has quite reasonable prices in the $12 to $17 range. Hours at Rum Bay are noon to 9:30pm daily.

## Boca Grande

A millionaire's fortune does help one to discover wondrously beautiful hideaways. That's exactly what happened at two offshore west coast islands, Useppa and Boca Grande.

In the 1920s moneyed men like John Jacob Astor, Barron Collier (whose name this county now bears), Henry du Pont, and J. Pierpont Morgan happened upon the fishing haven of Boca Grande, where in spring the rich and the not-so-rich rub gunwales in pursuit of the mighty tarpon, silver king of the seas. Here they built magnificent little winter mansions that tower over the sand in awesome isolated elegance. Today's moneymakers have joined them, creating a little enclave of luxurious homes-away-from-home on the tip of this tropical island.

You can join them for a while by journeying to the stately magnificence of the **Gasparilla Inn,** on North Palm, P.O. Box 1088, Boca Grande, FL 33921 (tel. 813/964-2201), an aging grande dame, beautifully maintained, of pale limey-yellow exterior, elegant white pillars, etched glass, wood floors, sweeping verandas, and posh cottages. Today the Gasparilla Inn is almost a village in itself, albeit a small one: It has an 18-hole golf course on its own island, tennis courts, a beach club, two heated pools, even a regulation croquet court! Meals are served in a very refined style in a lofty-ceilinged dining room, and the hotel also operates a more casual seafood restaurant called the Pink Elephant, a two-story dining room a short stroll down the street. There's a grocery here, a drugstore where you can buy the Sunday *New York Times* (although it may not get there by Sunday), bike rentals, and those plush and elegant old-worldly cottages on the inn's stately grounds. To get to this quite exclusive resort—the guest list reportedly is closely screened, and once included J. P. Morgan—take US 41 north to about four miles past Port Charlotte, then turn west on County Road 771, which goes to the island.

Open only from mid-December to mid-June, the Gasparilla Inn and Cottages includes all three meals in its rates, which are $128 to $169 *per person* for a double room. The hotel can also arrange connecting rooms and adjoining private parlors for an additional charge. The Gasparilla Inn also welcomes fishing fans to its "tarpon season," which runs from mid-April to the end of June. During that time rates are

$95 *per person* double, and include breakfast and dinner. Waitresses in the inn's handsome restaurant will prepare a box lunch for an additional charge. All this is assuming you pass the scrutiny of the front desk.

Elsewhere on the island you can get into the lazy feel of the place with lunch or dinner at **Theater Restaurant,** Fourth and Park avenues (tel. 964-0806), a casual, wood-lined enclave adorned with photographs of Bogie and his famous films. Open for lunch and dinner, the two-story restaurant features Maltese grouper (get it?) topped with an orange hollandaise sauce, veal piccata Lorre with lemon and caper sauce, and shrimp Bacall or Casablanca with mango chutney, along with some less exotic treats like beef Wellington, scallops, a seafood potpourri, and bouillabaisse for dinner prices that range from $10 to $17, including salad, potato, and vegetable. At lunch, prices are in the $5 to $7 range or less. Mark's is open from 11:30am to 3pm and 5:30 to 10pm daily. Closed Sunday.

Whether or not you stay at Gasparilla Inn, Boca Grande's worth a trip for its street names alone: Where else but on a *Florida* islet would you find boulevards called Dam-If-I-Care, Dam-If-I-Know, and of course, Dam-If-I-Will?

# INDEX

## GENERAL INFORMATION

# SIGHTS AND ATTRACTIONS

## Daytona

# The Everglades

# Fort Lauderdale & Vicinity

# Fort Myers

# Fort Walton/Destin

# Indian River Country

# Jacksonville

# The Keys

# Palm Beach

# Panama City/Panama City Beach

# Pensacola

# St. Augustine

# Sanibel & Captiva Islands

# Tallahassee

# Tampa Bay Area

# Walt Disney World

# ACCOMMODATIONS

## Daytona

**Key to Abbreviations:** A = Apartments/townhouses; B = Budget; C = Condominiums; CG = Campgrounds; FC = First Class; GH = Guesthouses; H = Hostels; HB = Houseboating; L = Luxury; M = Moderately priced

# The Everglades

Captain's Table Resort, Everglades City (B-M), 110-1
Everglades Rod and Gun Lodge, Everglades City (B), 110

Flamingo Lodge, Flamingo (M), 109
Outdoor Resort and Marina, Chokoloskee Island (B), 111
Port of the Islands, Marco (B), 111

# Fort Lauderdale & Vicinity

**DEERFIELD BEACH**
Berkshire Beach Club (A), 169
Deerpath Apartment Motel (A), 169

**FORT LAUDERDALE**
Bayshore Waterfront Apartments (M/A), 167
Casa Glamaretta (M), 167
Days Inn Lauderdale Surf Hotel (L), 164
Embassy Suites (FC), 166
Five Coins Inn (M), 168
Fort Lauderdale Royce Resort (FC), 165
Ireland's Inn (FC), 165-6
Lago-Mar Hotel (FC), 164-5
Marriott Fort Lauderdale Hotel and Marina (L), 162-3
Marriott's Harbor Beach (L), 162
Pier Sixty-Six Hotel & Marina (L), 163
Quality Inn Bahia Mar Resort (L), 164
Riverside Hotel (M), 166-7
Sea Château (M), 167-8

Sheraton Bonaventure Resort and Spa (L), 164
Sheraton Yankee Trader Beach Resort (L), 163-4
Sol y Mar (H), 168
Worthington (M), 167

**HOLLYWOOD BEACH**
Diplomat Resort and Country Club (L), 169-70
Enchanted Isle Resort (F), 170
Howard Johnson Hollywood Beach Resort Inn (F), 170

**POMPANO BEACH**
Holiday Inn (M), 168-9
Howard Johnson's Motor Lodge (M), 169
Lighthouse Cove Resort (M), 169
Ocean Ranch Motel (M), 168
Palm-Aire Resort and Spa (S), 169
Sea Garden and Tennis Resort (M), 168
Sun Castle (M), 168

# Fort Myers

**BONITA SPRINGS/FORT MYERS BEACH**
Beach and Tennis Club (C), 455
Beach House (A), 456
Beach House Motel (M/A), 456
Lani Kai (B), 455-6

**LEHIGH**
Lehigh Resort (M), 458

**MAINLAND FORT MYERS**
Best Western Robert E. Lee Motor Inn (M), 458
Cape Coral Inn and Country Club (M), 458
Ramada Inn on the River (M), 456
Rock Lake Motel (B), 456
Tides Motel (B), 456

# Fort Walton/Destin

**DESTIN**
Gulfside Cottages (A), 348
Robroy Lodge and Marina (M), 348
Sandestin (A/C), 348
Sandestin Beach Hilton (L), 347
Seascape Resort (A/C), 347-8

**FORT WALTON**
Carousel Motel and Apartments (A/M), 346
Conquistador Inn (A/M), 346

Greenwood Motel (M), 347
Howard Johnson (M), 347
Ramada Beach Resort (FC), 346
Sandman Motel and Apartments (M/A), 347
Sheraton Coronado Beach Resort (M-FC), 346-7
Fred Gannon State Park (CG), 349

**SEASIDE AND VICINITY**
Seaside Cottages (A), 348-9

# Holiday Isles

**BED & BREAKFAST REFERRALS**
B & B Suncoast Accommodations of Florida, 409

**BELLEAIR BEACH**
Belleair Beach Resort (M), 412
Belleview Biltmore (L), 411
Carriage House Motel (M), 412

**CLEARWATER BEACH**
Adam's Mark/Caribbean Gulf Resort (L), 409-10

Aegean Sands (L), 410
Aegean Spyglass Resorts (M), 410
Beach Ambassador (Sea Gull Apartment Motel) (M/A), 411
Clearwater Beach Garden Apartments (A), 410-11
Clearwater Beach Hotel (L), 410
New Yorker (A), 411
Port Vue Resort (B-M), 411
Sheraton Sand Key Resort (L), 410
Shoreline View Motel (A), 411

# Indian River Country

# Jacksonville

# The Keys

# Orlando & Central Florida

# Sanibel & Captiva Islands

# Sarasota

# Tallahassee

# Tampa Bay Area

# RESTAURANTS

## Daytona

## The Everglades

## Fort Lauderdale & Vicinity

**Key to Abbreviations:** B = Budget; E = Expensive; M = Moderately priced

# Fort Myers

# Fort Walton/Destin

# Holiday Isles

# Indian River Country

# Jacksonville

# The Keys

# Key West

# Miami

# Palm Beach

# Panama City/Panama City Beach

# Pensacola

# St. Augustine

# Sarasota

# Tallahassee

# Tampa Bay Area

# AMERICAN EXPRESS CAN DELIVER CASH
## AND A REPLACEMENT CARD TO YOU WITHIN 24 HOURS,
## AS LONG AS YOU'RE IN THIS GENERAL AREA.

No matter where you are in the world, if you lose your wallet, we can get a new American Express® Card and cash in your hands usually within 24 hours.*

If you're truly in the middle of nowhere, say the African Outback, it might take a little longer. Depending upon how many wandering hippos and fallen trees our local courier must contend with.

But more often than not, you'll have a new Card and cash the next day. Something you'd expect from American Express.

So carry the American Express Card. And no matter where on earth you go, you'll never leave civilization behind.

For assistance, call your nearest American Express office, or in the U.S. call our 24-hour number 1-800-528-4800; everywhere else call collect 202-554-AMEX. Don't leave home without it.®

### MEMBERSHIP HAS ITS PRIVILEGES℠

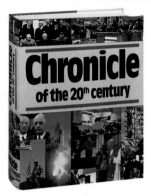
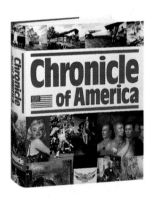

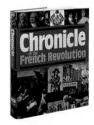